THE PAPERS OF
THOMAS JEFFERSON

BARBARA B. OBERG
GENERAL EDITOR

THE PAPERS OF
Thomas Jefferson

Volume 37
4 March to 30 June 1802

BARBARA B. OBERG, EDITOR

JAMES P. MCCLURE AND ELAINE WEBER PASCU,
SENIOR ASSOCIATE EDITORS

TOM DOWNEY AND MARTHA J. KING,
ASSOCIATE EDITORS

W. BLAND WHITLEY, ASSISTANT EDITOR

LINDA MONACO, EDITORIAL ASSISTANT

JOHN E. LITTLE, RESEARCH ASSOCIATE

PRINCETON AND OXFORD
PRINCETON UNIVERSITY PRESS
2010

DEDICATED TO THE MEMORY OF

ADOLPH S. OCHS

PUBLISHER OF THE NEW YORK TIMES

1896-1935

WHO BY THE EXAMPLE OF A RESPONSIBLE

PRESS ENLARGED AND FORTIFIED

THE JEFFERSONIAN CONCEPT

OF A FREE PRESS

SUPPORTERS

THIS EDITION was made possible by an initial grant of $200,000 from The New York Times Company to Princeton University. Contributions from many foundations and individuals have sustained the endeavor since then. Among these are the Ford Foundation, the Lyn and Norman Lear Foundation, the Lucius N. Littauer Foundation, the Charlotte Palmer Phillips Foundation, the L. J. Skaggs and Mary C. Skaggs Foundation, the John Ben Snow Memorial Trust, Time, Inc., Robert C. Baron, B. Batmanghelidj, David K. E. Bruce, and James Russell Wiggins. In recent years generous ongoing support has come from The New York Times Company Foundation, the Dyson Foundation, the Barkley Fund (through the National Trust for the Humanities), the Florence Gould Foundation, the "Cinco Hermanos Fund," the Andrew W. Mellon Foundation, the Pew Charitable Trusts, and the Packard Humanities Institute (through Founding Fathers Papers, Inc.). Benefactions from a greatly expanded roster of dedicated individuals have underwritten this volume and those still to come: Sara and James Adler, Helen and Peter Bing, Diane and John Cooke, Judy and Carl Ferenbach III, Mary-Love and William Harman, Frederick P. and Mary Buford Hitz, Governor Thomas H. Kean, Ruth and Sidney Lapidus, Lisa and Willem Mesdag, Tim and Lisa Robertson, Ann and Andrew C. Rose, Sara Lee and Axel Schupf, the Sulzberger family through the Hillandale Foundation, Richard W. Thaler, Tad and Sue Thompson, The Wendt Family Charitable Foundation, and Susan and John O. Wynne. For their vision and extraordinary efforts to provide for the future of this edition, we owe special thanks to John S. Dyson, Governor Kean, H. L. Lenfest and the Lenfest Foundation, Rebecca Rimel and the Pew Charitable Trusts, and Jack Rosenthal. In partnership with these individuals and foundations, the National Historical Publications and Records Commission and the National Endowment for the Humanities have been crucial to the editing and publication of *The Papers of Thomas Jefferson*. For their unprecedented generous support we are also indebted to the Princeton History Department and Christopher L. Eisgruber, provost of the university.

FOREWORD

ON 4 MARCH 1802, the first anniversary of his inauguration—the "day of our regeneration," as a toast by one member of a Republican Volunteers cavalry troop hailed it at a celebration in Philadelphia—Thomas Jefferson embarked upon his second year as president of the United States. On a number of occasions over the course of the next four months he expressed pleasure at the progress Republicans had made since taking office and optimism for even greater successes in the years to come. In May, as the first session of the Seventh Congress drew to a close, he observed that its accomplishments would "pretty compleatly fulfil all the desires of the people": Congress had approved most of the measures he had presented in his first Annual Message; the Judiciary Act of 1801 had been repealed and a new one passed; he had signed into law a revised naturalization act, reducing the length of residence required to qualify for citizenship from 14 to 5 years; the Military Peace Establishment Act would reorganize the army and reduce its size; internal taxes had been abolished and a schedule for the repayment of the public debt established. In short, all was "now tranquil, firm and well as it should be," as Jefferson wrote to Tadeusz Kosciuszko in April.

On 10 March, a delegation of Seneca Indians came to the nation's capital for substantive and far-reaching discussions with Jefferson and Secretary of War Henry Dearborn. The president was present for at least the first day of these formal meetings and he greeted the delegation with graciousness and respect. The visitors, Dearborn reported, took the president "by the hand." Handsome Lake, Cornplanter, and Blue Eyes delivered elegantly crafted addresses that laid out the specific concerns of their tribe regarding land titles, annuities and payments, and the heavy reliance of some Indians on their "White brothers Drink." The series of meetings, which marked Handsome Lake's debut as a spokesman in dealings with the United States government, reflected deep divisions within the Senecas and other tribes over whether to abandon accustomed ways of living and reconcile their economy and society to the prevailing cultural and social norms of the United States or to resist assimilation and revitalize their own traditions and religious beliefs.

These early March meetings anticipated one of the major concerns of this volume: relations between Indian nations and the federal and state governments. Shortly before the conference with the Senecas, Jefferson investigated a report that the governor of East Florida, a Spanish province, was preparing for an expedition against the Creeks in response to an attack on a Spanish settlement. In explaining the importance of the situation, he drew upon what he had learned as secretary of state in the Washington administration and vice president under John Adams to explain the penalties for entering Indian lands without a passport or with hostile intentions. The president made use of his abilities in behind-the-scenes diplomacy to make a "private suggestion" to Samuel Smith, chair of the committee on Indian Affairs, that because the legislation dealing with incursions onto Indian lands had just expired and an expedition against the Indians was in the offing, the committee should hasten to renew the act. Indians were "sore" at the failure of the federal government to punish offenders. Also in March, Dearborn informed Jefferson that Oneida Indians in New York wished to sell about 10,000 acres of land and that the governor of New York desired the appointment of a commissioner to attend a meeting with them about this matter. Within days, Jefferson had nominated a commissioner. In late April, the Senate ratified a treaty with the Choctaw nation, agreeing to the construction of a wagon road through their lands and providing them with farm implements and other tools. In May, an act of Congress appropriated $5,000 for running boundary lines between the Cherokees and white inhabitants of North Carolina and also for running the Choctaw line.

Although William C. C. Claiborne reported from Natchez in late April that "the Indians are entirely peaceable," Native Americans in the Mississippi Territory were not entirely happy with the United States government. That the territory was situated on a frontier that would soon be "possessed by the most turbulent spirits of the French army" in the service of a nation that was "unequivocally hostile to a republican administration" intensified the fragility of relations and centrality of the issues. It had long been clear that the fate of the Mississippi Valley was crucial to American interests, and in the spring of 1802 the problem loomed even larger, as Americans further considered the implications of the retrocession of Louisiana to France. Jefferson wrote that he took France's actions "personally" and that her decision to follow that path had created "a new epoch in our political course." To prevent France from controlling New Orleans and Louisiana to the disadvantage of the United States, he would even court England, "marry" America's fortunes to the British fleet, and augment the U.S. Navy, he found. He informed Robert Livingston, the American minister in Paris, of his intention.

Behind this immediate and critical political question, Jefferson thought, lay a growing chasm between a United States that was expanding its republican values and an increasingly dictatorial France, a nation that he could no longer understand or approve. He mused about this turn of events in his correspondence with Livingston and with longtime French friends like Pierre Samuel Du Pont de Nemours and the Comte de Volney. Jefferson tried to make sense of America's great ally, but he could neither comprehend France's "past or present state, nor foresee it's future destiny." He was honest, even blunt, in the expression of his feelings of alarm. The president appealed to Du Pont and gave the Frenchman two letters to take with him to France in April. He even hoped that Du Pont would come to Washington so that they could talk confidentially. Du Pont answered that he had no time to come in person, but would be able to understand Jefferson's letters "at half a hint, at a third of a hint." One of the letters, which he left unsealed for Du Pont to see, was a communication to Livingston, in which Jefferson remarked that whoever possessed New Orleans was the "natural and habitual enemy" of the United States. Du Pont warned against issuing threats to Napoleon, but Jefferson insisted to his friend that nothing was further from his intention. He was not menacing France, and the United States would preserve "rigorous neutrality, without the smallest partiality." The letters that Jefferson exchanged with Du Pont, Volney, and Livingston reveal in concrete detail the conflicts imbedded in his thinking about the relationship between American political and economic requirements in New Orleans and the Mississippi Territory and the nation's dealings with France, Great Britain, and Spain.

Two important legal cases came to Jefferson's desk in the spring of 1802, and they were his first encounters as president with a capital sentence. In March, he was called upon to review a court-martial proceeding against Private John Spence, an infantry soldier in the Northwest Territory, for the crime of assaulting his commanding officer. After consultation with his secretary of war, the president determined that although the defendant's guilt was not in doubt, a penalty as severe as summary execution was not justified. Spence instead was given a reprieve of 12 days in which to leave, and not return to, the Northwest Territory. Jefferson and Dearborn had found a way to spare Spence's life, but allow the sentence of death to stand.

In April, Jefferson consulted both Attorney General Levi Lincoln and John Thomson Mason, United States attorney for the District of Columbia, on the jurisdictional question of who was to sign the warrant for execution of James McGurk. The District of Columbia Circuit Court had found McGurk, an immigrant bricklayer and a resident of Washington County, guilty of beating his wife to death. Did the responsibility for ordering an execution in the District of Columbia lie with the president? Lincoln and Mason submitted detailed opinions based on their reading of Virginia and Maryland law, the United States Constitution, and the common law. Choosing not to grant a pardon, Jefferson left it to the court to order the hanging.

The president was perfectly willing to issue pardons when the circumstances of a case, for example that of "a hard working industrious man," indicated that clemency was the "proper" course of action. In part, his generous attitude on pardons was part of a pragmatic solution to the problem of a large number of small debtors incarcerated in the Washington County jail, a situation that reflected the larger issue, a "defective & oppressive" system of jails. In March, he urged Congress to adopt legislation that would provide the necessary relief to those confined in these overcrowded and unsanitary conditions. Congress in May directed the marshal of the District of Columbia to have a "good and sufficient jail" constructed and appropriated the necessary funds. Jefferson received the estimates for building materials for the facility, including 34 strong oak doors, bolts, hinges, and locks, and he drafted detailed specifications for it—two-foot-thick granite walls held together with mortar of lime, sand, and "fine sifted gravel" from the Potomac, a slate roof, and an "entablature, a regular Tuscan from Palladio."

Of science and learning, Jefferson observed that "no discovery is barren. it always serves as a step to something else." In the spring of 1802, he commented upon a number of inventions and discoveries that were communicated to him by friends or acquaintances who knew of his curiosity and wide interests. In particular, he received descriptions of systems for water purification and instructions for calculating the rising and setting of celestial bodies. Charles Willson Peale sent him sketches of the skull of a huge prehistoric bison found in Kentucky. He directed his greatest attention to describing and modifying a cipher devised by Robert Patterson. He tested it by enciphering the Lord's Prayer and part of a 1774 address from the Continental Congress, "To the People of Great Britain." He undertook this intensive work during the closing weeks of Congress at a time when the political world appeared acrimonious and frustrating to him.

Jefferson railed against the gross "lies and misrepresentations" uttered by Federalists in Congress. They had added 30 days to the length of the session and $30,000 to the cost. He begged Caesar A. Rodney of Delaware to rescue the citizens of his state from being "an embarrassment and a burthen" to the country and to run against

James A. Bayard for a seat in the House of Representatives. Jefferson also vigorously protested the "bold, direct, and false charges" that appeared in an anonymous newspaper article (written, it was later learned, by former secretary of the Treasury Oliver Wolcott) accusing him of partisanship in his appointments. To counter these accusations, Jefferson suggested to his attorney general that each head of department be asked to compile a list of the previous administration's appointments in his department to discover "whether he *found* any republican clerk." Optimistically, Jefferson reiterated his conviction that truth and reason would prevail, if they were only allowed the opportunity to defend themselves. The requirement in the new judiciary law to appoint bankruptcy commissioners in each state seemed to present increased opportunities for giving jobs to those Republicans who were their "worthy friends." In the end, however, making these appointments caused even greater division among Republicans.

Jefferson attended to purchasing books for two libraries, the nation's and his own. For the edification of members of Congress, he prepared a detailed catalogue of books to be purchased for the recently established Library of Congress. To Abraham Baldwin, the chair of the joint committee charged with obtaining books and maps, the president explained that he had chosen titles from fields of learning that belonged to "the deliberations of the members as statesmen," not to mere entertainment. In the field of history, he chose chronological works with facts and dates, not "narrations composed for agreeable reading." For his own personal collection Jefferson ordered French translations of Seneca, Lucretius, and others as he worked toward putting together a body of octavo and duodecimo editions that were of a practical size for reading.

Even in Washington, where he was occupied with matters of state, Jefferson had been keeping close watch on the renovations to Monticello. He turned to French architectural innovations to achieve more bedroom space for his family and at the same time maintain the simple, classical design of a one-story house. Even the smallest detail of the rebuilding and expansion did not escape his attention. The joists of the northwest building should be so arranged that they would be "open towards the N.W. wind to let in air" and the privies should be finished before anything else. In May, he had Antonio Giannini plant several varieties of grapes from Burgundy, Champagne, and Bordeaux in the southwest vineyard.

The Democratic majority in the House of Representatives was 2 to 1, and in the Senate 18 to 14. After another election it would be 2 to 1 in the Senate too, he predicted. Even in the case of New Hampshire,

Jefferson was encouraged by what he judged to be a victory for republicanism. In the recent elections Republicans had gained strength in the legislature and almost won the governorship, lacking "a few hundreds only" to give John Langdon a victory. Overall, the nation was "becoming one." Gratified by the new era that had come to America, he was prompted to think the time had come for someone to write a history of the country from the close of the American Revolution onward. Jefferson suggested, and Madison, he said, agreed, that Joel Barlow should return from France, settle in the nation's capital, and undertake the task. They would make sure all the public archives were open to him, and his work would be useful to Republicans in counteracting John Marshall's biography of George Washington, scheduled to appear in print in time for the next elections.

In search of "more profitable employment" for his slaves, Jefferson's son-in-law Thomas Mann Randolph embarked upon a far-reaching scheme that he thought would better the family's economic situation. Like other tobacco farmers, Randolph faced a depleted soil and declining prices for his crop. Randolph's plans, which never came to fruition, were to shift from tobacco to cotton as his staple crop and to relocate his slaves to a large plantation in the Mississippi Territory. To accomplish this goal, he would have to engage in a "little deception," allowing the slaves to believe that the Randolph family would soon be joining them in Mississippi. Convincing himself that the culture of cotton was less arduous than that of tobacco and that the climate of Mississippi was far kinder to slaves engaged in agricultural labor, Randolph also indicated that such a change would better enable him to provide economic security for his sisters and to offer his son a good education. Jefferson concurred that cotton was indeed the most profitable crop in the United States and the Mississippi Territory was well suited to it. Practically, however, he advised that overland travel was difficult and the territory dangerous.

As an alternative locale, Jefferson suggested Georgia, where the land was cheaper, the climate healthier, and the commerce not dependent on a foreign nation. In fact, mused Jefferson, he would be "delighted to own a cotton estate in Georgia, & go and pass every winter under the orange trees of that country." And always cognizant of the importance of being within reach of reliable postal service, Jefferson noted that within three years the stage would be able to travel from Richmond to Georgia in just six days, as convenient a trip as going to Bedford. With the Virginia families already settled in Georgia, all transactions would be easier. About a week later, Jefferson sent his son-in-law detailed information on varieties of cotton that could be grown in different areas of the state. He seemed so certain that Randolph would really embark upon this project, he alerted Benjamin Smith Barton that Randolph would be a good "botanising companion" for him in Georgia.

As early as March and April, Jefferson was ordering groceries, molasses, dry Lisbon wine, and cider for Monticello, hoping they would reach there in time for his arrival, "immediately after the rising of Congress." Sixteen packages of groceries were on their way. Jefferson was eager to head home, even though the break from business in Washington would be only a fortnight. He would leave two or three days after the rising of Congress; on 5 May he dashed off a letter to Robert Livingston reporting that he was "within a few minutes of setting out." He looked forward "with impatience to the moment" when he could embrace his family with all his affection. From Virginia, his son-in-law wrote him that the country was "just beginning to smile here but the earth is very bare yet from drought. Your Tufton farm is an ornament to the County—We are all well."

ACKNOWLEDGMENTS

MANY individuals have given the Editors the benefit of their aid in the preparation of this volume, and we offer them our thanks. Those who helped us use manuscript collections, answered research queries, assisted with translations, or advised in other ways are John Haldon and William C. Jordan, Princeton University; in the libraries at Princeton, Karin A. Trainer, University Librarian, and Elizabeth Z. Bennett, Colleen M. Burlingham, Stephen Ferguson, Daniel J. Linke, Deborah T. Paparone, AnnaLee Pauls, Ben Primer, Don C. Skemer, and Alan M. Stahl; Timothy Connelly of the NHPRC; James H. Hutson, Barbara Bair, and the staff at the Manuscript Division of the Library of Congress, especially Lia Apodaca, Jennifer Brathovde, Jeffrey Flannery, Joseph Jackson, Patrick Kerwin, and Bruce Kirby; Peter Drummey, Elaine Grublin, and the library staff of the Massachusetts Historical Society, especially Nancy Heywood for providing digital scans; Robert C. Ritchie, Olga Tsapina, and others at the Huntington Library; William L. Beiswanger, Anna Berkes, Robert L. Self, and Lucia C. Stanton of the Thomas Jefferson Foundation at Monticello; Nicole Bouche, Heather Riser, Regina Rush, and the staff of Special Collections at the University of Virginia Library; Eileen O'Toole and Susan A. Riggs, Swem Library, the College of William and Mary; John Deal and Brent Tarter, Library of Virginia; Dennis Northcott and the staff of the Missouri Historical Society; Martin Levitt, Roy Goodman, Charles B. Greifenstein, and Earl E. Spamer of the American Philosophical Society; the staff of the New York Public Library; the Gilder Lehrman Institute of American History and Jean W. Ashton and Edward O'Reilly of the New-York Historical Society; Charles M. Harris of the Papers of William Thornton, and our fellow editors at the Thomas Jefferson Retirement Series at Monticello, the Adams Papers at the Massachusetts Historical Society, the Papers of George Washington and the Papers of James Madison at the University of Virginia, the Papers of James Monroe at the University of Mary Washington, and the Papers of Benjamin Franklin at Yale University. For assistance with illustrations we are indebted to Alfred L. Bush of Princeton, Carolyn Gilman of the Missouri History Museum, Bonnie Coles and Barbara Moore of the Library of Congress, Dawn Bonner of the Mount Vernon Ladies' Association, Kathleen Mylen-Coulombe of the Yale University Art Gallery, Barbara C. G. Wood of the National Gallery of Art, and Ann Handler of Art Resource. Scott McClure at Yale University assisted in work on documents relating to ciphers. Stephen Perkins of dataformat.com provided essential moral and technical support for us as we transitioned into the XML preparation of these volumes. We thank Alice Calaprice for careful reading and Jan Lilly for her unparalleled mastery of what a Jefferson volume must be. We appreciate especially the support and leadership of Peter J. Dougherty, Director of Princeton University Press. Others at the Press who never fail to give these volumes the benefit of their expertise are Chuck Creesy, Daphne Ireland, Dimitri Karetnikov, Neil Litt, Elizabeth Litz, Clara Platter, Linny Schenck, and Brigitta van Rheinberg.

Beginning with Volume 24 of *The Papers of Thomas Jefferson*, Robert W. Hartle has skillfully and patiently assisted us with transcriptions and translations of French documents. His expertise has been invaluable to us, and we extend our deepest gratitude for his knowledge and dedication.

EDITORIAL METHOD AND APPARATUS

1. RENDERING THE TEXT

Julian P. Boyd eloquently set forth a comprehensive editorial policy in Volume 1 of *The Papers of Thomas Jefferson*. Adopting what he described as a "middle course" for rendering eighteenth-century handwritten materials into print, Boyd set the standards for modern historical editing. His successors, Charles T. Cullen and John Catanzariti, reaffirmed Boyd's high standards. At the same time, they made changes in textual policy and editorial apparatus as they deemed appropriate. For Boyd's policy and subsequent modifications to it, readers are encouraged to consult Vol. 1: xxix-xxxviii; Vol. 22: vii-xi; and Vol. 24: vii-viii.

The revised, more literal textual method, which appeared for the first time in Volume 30, adheres to the following guidelines: <u>Abbreviations</u> will be retained as written. Where the meaning is sufficiently unclear to require editorial intervention, the expansion will be given in the explanatory annotation. <u>Capitalization</u> will follow the usage of the writer. Because the line between uppercase and lowercase letters can be a very fine and fluctuating one, when it is impossible to make an absolute determination of the author's intention, we will adopt modern usage. Jefferson rarely began his sentences with an uppercase letter, and we conform to his usage. <u>Punctuation</u> will be retained as written and double marks of punctuation, such as a period followed by a dash, will be allowed to stand. Misspellings or so-called slips of the pen will be allowed to stand or will be recorded in a subjoined textual note.

English translations or translation summaries will be supplied for foreign-language documents. In some instances, when documents are lengthy and not especially pertinent to Jefferson's concerns or if our edition's typography cannot adequately represent the script of a language, we will provide only a summary in English. In most cases we will print in full the text in its original language and also provide a full English translation. If a contemporary translation that Jefferson made or would have used is extant, we may print it in lieu of a modern translation. Our own translations are designed to provide a basic readable English text for the modern user rather than to preserve all aspects of the original diction and language.

2. TEXTUAL DEVICES

The following devices are employed throughout the work to clarify the presentation of the text.

[...]	Text missing and not conjecturable.
[ ]	Number or part of a number missing or illegible.
[roman]	Conjectural reading for missing or illegible matter. A question mark follows when the reading is doubtful.
[*italic*]	Editorial comment inserted in the text.
<*italic*>	Matter deleted in the MS but restored in our text.

3. DESCRIPTIVE SYMBOLS

The following symbols are employed throughout the work to describe the various kinds of manuscript originals. When a series of versions is recorded, the first to be recorded is the version used for the printed text.

Dft	draft (usually a composition or rough draft; later drafts, when identifiable as such, are designated "2d Dft," &c.)
Dupl	duplicate
MS	manuscript (arbitrarily applied to most documents other than letters)
N	note, notes (memoranda, fragments, &c.)
PoC	polygraph copy
PrC	press copy
RC	recipient's copy
SC	stylograph copy
Tripl	triplicate

All manuscripts of the above types are assumed to be in the hand of the author of the document to which the descriptive symbol pertains. If not, that *fact is stated*. On the other hand, the following types of manuscripts are assumed *not* to be in the hand of the author, and exceptions will be noted:

FC	file copy (applied to all contemporary copies retained by the author or his agents)
Lb	letterbook (ordinarily used with FC and Tr to denote texts copied into bound volumes)

Tr   transcript (applied to all contemporary and later copies except file copies; period of transcription, unless clear by implication, will be given when known)

4. LOCATION SYMBOLS

The locations of documents printed in this edition from originals in private hands and from printed sources are recorded in self-explanatory form in the descriptive note following each document. The locations of documents printed from originals held by public and private institutions in the United States are recorded by means of the symbols used in the National Union Catalog in the Library of Congress; an explanation of how these symbols are formed is given in Vol. 1:xl. The symbols DLC and MHi by themselves stand for the collections of Jefferson Papers proper in these repositories; when texts are drawn from other collections held by these two institutions, the names of those collections will be added. Location symbols for documents held by institutions outside the United States are given in a subjoined list.

CSmH	The Huntington Library, San Marino, California
CtY	Yale University, New Haven, Connecticut
DLC	Library of Congress
DeGH	Hagley Museum and Library, Greenville, Delaware
DeHi	Delaware Historical Society, Wilmington
ICHi	Chicago Historical Society
InHi	Indiana Historical Society, Indianapolis
InU	Indiana University, Bloomington
MHi	Massachusetts Historical Society, Boston
MdAA	Hall of Records Commission, Annapolis, Maryland
MeB	Bowdoin College, Brunswick, Maine
MoSHi	Missouri Historical Society, St. Louis
NHi	New-York Historical Society, New York City
NN	New York Public Library
NNMus	Museum of the City of New York
NNPM	Pierpont Morgan Library, New York City
Nc-Ar	North Carolina Office of Archives & History, Raleigh
NcU	University of North Carolina, Chapel Hill
NhPoS	Strawbery Banke, Portsmouth, New Hampshire
NjP	Princeton University
OMC	Marietta College, Ohio

PHi	Historical Society of Pennsylvania, Philadelphia
PPAmP	American Philosophical Society, Philadelphia
PPCP	College of Physicians, Philadelphia
PWacD	David Library of the American Revolution, Washington Crossing, Pennsylvania
TxU	University of Texas, Austin
Vi	Library of Virginia, Richmond
ViHi	Virginia Historical Society, Richmond
ViU	University of Virginia, Charlottesville
ViW	College of William and Mary, Williamsburg, Virginia

5. NATIONAL ARCHIVES DESIGNATIONS

The National Archives, recognized by the location symbol DNA, with identifications of series (preceded by record group number) as follows:

RG 28		Records of the Post Office Department
	LPG	Letters Sent by the Postmaster General
RG 42		Records of the Office of Public Buildings and Public Parks of the National Capital
	DCLB	District of Columbia Letterbook
RG 45		Naval Records Collection of the Office of Naval Records and Library
	LSO	Letters Sent to Officers
	LSP	Letters Sent to the President
	MLS	Misc. Letters Sent
RG 46		Records of the United States Senate
	EPEN	Executive Proceedings, Executive Nominations
	EPFR	Executive Proceedings, Foreign Relations
	EPIR	Executive Proceedings, Indian Relations
	EPOR	Executive Proceedings, Other Records
	LPPM	Legislative Proceedings, President's Messages
RG 59		General Records of the Department of State
	CD	Consular Dispatches
	DD	Diplomatic Dispatches
	GPR	General Pardon Records

	LAR	Letters of Application and Recommendation
	MPTPC	Misc. Permanent and Temporary Presidential Commissions
	NL	Notes from Legations
	PTCC	Permanent and Temporary Consular Commissions
RG 75		Records of the Bureau of Indian Affairs
	LSIA	Letters Sent by the Secretary of War Relating to Indian Affairs
RG 76		Records of Boundary and Claims Commissions and Arbitrations
RG 94		Records of the Adjutant General's Office
RG 98		Records of United States Army Commands
RG 104		Records of the Mint
	DL	Domestic Letters
	GC	General Correspondence
RG 107		Records of the Office of the Secretary of War
	LRUS	Letters Received by the Secretary of War, Unregistered Series
	LSMA	Letters Sent by the Secretary of War Relating to Military Affairs
	LSP	Letters Sent to the President
	RLRMS	Register of Letters Received, Main Series
RG 233		Records of the United States House of Representatives
	PMRSL	Petitions, Memorials, Resolutions of State Legislatures
	PM	President's Messages

6. OTHER SYMBOLS AND ABBREVIATIONS

The following symbols and abbreviations are commonly employed in the annotation throughout the work.

Second Series   The topical series to be published as part of this edition, comprising those materials which are best suited to a topical rather than a chronological arrangement (see Vol. 1: xv-xvi)

TJ   Thomas Jefferson

TJ Editorial Files   Photoduplicates and other editorial materials in the office of The Papers of Thomas Jefferson, Princeton University Library

TJ Papers   Jefferson Papers (applied to a collection of manuscripts when the precise location of an undated, misdated, or
otherwise problematic document must be furnished, and always
preceded by the symbol for the institutional repository; thus
"DLC: TJ Papers, 4:628-9" represents a document in the Library of Congress, Jefferson Papers, volume 4, pages 628 and
629. Citations to volumes and folio numbers of the Jefferson
Papers at the Library of Congress refer to the collection as it was
arranged at the time the first microfilm edition was made in
1944-45. Access to the microfilm edition of the collection as it
was rearranged under the Library's Presidential Papers Pro-
gram is provided by the Index to the Thomas Jefferson Papers
[Washington, D.C., 1976])

RG   Record Group (used in designating the location of documents in the National Archives)

SJL   Jefferson's "Summary Journal of Letters" written and received for the period 11 Nov. 1783 to 25 June 1826 (in DLC: TJ
Papers). This register, kept in Jefferson's hand, has been
checked against the TJ Editorial Files. It is to be assumed that all
outgoing letters are recorded in SJL unless there is a note to the
contrary. When the date of receipt of an incoming letter is
recorded in SJL, it is incorporated in the notes. Information and
discrepancies revealed in SJL but not found in the letter itself are
also noted. Missing letters recorded in SJL are, where possible,
accounted for in the notes to documents mentioning them or in
related documents. A more detailed discussion of this register
and its use in this edition appears in Vol. 6: vii-x

SJPL   "Summary Journal of Public Letters," an incomplete list
of letters and documents written by TJ from 16 Apr. 1784 to 31
Dec. 1793, with brief summaries, in an amanuensis's hand. This
is supplemented by six pages in TJ's hand, compiled at a later
date, listing private and confidential memorandums and notes
as well as official reports and communications by and to him as
Secretary of State, 11 Oct. 1789 to 31 Dec. 1793 (in DLC: TJ
Papers, Epistolary Record, 514-59 and 209-11, respectively; see
Vol. 22: ix-x). Since nearly all documents in the amanuensis's
list are registered in SJL, while few in TJ's list are so recorded,
it is to be assumed that all references to SJPL are to the list in
TJ's hand unless there is a statement to the contrary

V   Ecu

_f_   Florin

£   Pound sterling or livre, depending upon context (in doubtful cases, a clarifying note will be given)

s   Shilling or sou (also expressed as /)

d   Penny or denier

₶   Livre Tournois

℔   Per (occasionally used for pro, pre)

7. SHORT TITLES

The following list includes short titles of works cited frequently in this edition. Since it is impossible to anticipate all the works to be cited in abbreviated form, the list is revised from volume to volume.

Abler, *Cornplanter*   Thomas S. Abler, *Cornplanter: Chief Warrior of the Allegany Senecas*, Syracuse, N.Y., 2007

Ammon, *Monroe*   Harry Ammon, *James Monroe: The Quest for National Identity*, New York, 1971

ANB   John A. Garraty and Mark C. Carnes, eds., *American National Biography*, New York and Oxford, 1999, 24 vols.

Annals   *Annals of the Congress of the United States: The Debates and Proceedings in the Congress of the United States . . . Compiled from Authentic Materials*, Washington, D.C., Gales & Seaton, 1834-56, 42 vols. All editions are undependable and pagination varies from one printing to another. The first two volumes of the set cited here have "Compiled . . . by Joseph Gales, Senior" on the title page and bear the caption "Gales & Seatons History" on verso and "of Debates in Congress" on recto pages. The remaining volumes bear the caption "History of Congress" on both recto and verso pages. Those using the first two volumes with the latter caption will need to employ the date of the debate or the indexes of debates and speakers.

APS   American Philosophical Society

ASP   *American State Papers: Documents, Legislative and Executive, of the Congress of the United States*, Washington, D.C., 1832-61, 38 vols.

Bear, *Family Letters*   Edwin M. Betts and James A. Bear, Jr., eds., *Family Letters of Thomas Jefferson*, Columbia, Mo., 1966

Bedini, *Statesman of Science*   Silvio A. Bedini, *Thomas Jefferson: Statesman of Science*, New York, 1990

Betts, *Farm Book*   Edwin M. Betts, ed., *Thomas Jefferson's Farm Book*, Princeton, 1953

Betts, *Garden Book*   Edwin M. Betts, ed., *Thomas Jefferson's Garden Book, 1766-1824*, Philadelphia, 1944

Biog. Dir. Cong.   *Biographical Directory of the United States Congress, 1774-1989*, Washington, D.C., 1989

Biographie universelle   *Biographie universelle, ancienne et moderne*, new ed., Paris, 1843-65, 45 vols.

Brigham, *American Newspapers*   Clarence S. Brigham, *History and Bibliography of American Newspapers, 1690-1820*, Worcester, Mass., 1947, 2 vols.

Bryan, *National Capital*   Wilhelmus B. Bryan, *A History of the National Capital from Its Foundation through the Period of the Adoption of the Organic Act*, New York, 1914-16, 2 vols.

Bush, *Life Portraits*   Alfred L. Bush, *The Life Portraits of Thomas Jefferson*, rev. ed., Charlottesville, 1987

Cooke, *Coxe*   Jacob E. Cooke, *Tench Coxe and the Early Republic*, Chapel Hill, 1978

Cranch, *Reports*   William Cranch, *Reports of Cases Argued and Adjudged in the Supreme Court of the United States, 1801-1815*, Washington, D.C., 1804-17, 9 vols.

Cunningham, *Process of Government*   Noble E. Cunningham, Jr., *The Process of Government under Jefferson*, Princeton, 1978

CVSP   William P. Palmer and others, eds., *Calendar of Virginia State Papers . . . Preserved in the Capitol at Richmond*, Richmond, 1875-93, 11 vols.

DAB   Allen Johnson and Dumas Malone, eds., *Dictionary of American Biography*, New York, 1928-36, 20 vols.

Dexter, *Yale*   Franklin Bowditch Dexter, *Biographical Sketches of the Graduates of Yale College with Annals of the College History*, New York, 1885-1912, 6 vols.

DHSC   Maeva Marcus and others, eds., *The Documentary History of the Supreme Court of the United States, 1789-1800*, New York, 1985-2007, 8 vols.

Dictionnaire   *Dictionnaire de biographie française*, Paris, 1933-   , 19 vols.

DNB   H. C. G. Matthew and Brian Harrison, eds., *Oxford Dictionary of National Biography, In Association with The British Academy, From the Earliest Times to the Year 2000*, Oxford, 2004, 60 vols.

DSB   Charles C. Gillispie, ed., *Dictionary of Scientific Biography*, New York, 1970-80, 16 vols.

DVB   John T. Kneebone and others, eds., *Dictionary of Virginia Biography*, Richmond, 1998-   , 3 vols.

EG   Dickinson W. Adams and Ruth W. Lester, eds., *Jefferson's Extracts from the Gospels*, Princeton, 1983, *The Papers of Thomas Jefferson*, Second Series

Evans   Charles Evans, Clifford K. Shipton, and Roger P. Bristol, comps., *American Bibliography: A Chronological Dictionary of All Books, Pamphlets and Periodical Publications Printed in the United States of America from . . . 1639 . . . to . . . 1820*, Chicago and Worcester, Mass., 1903-59, 14 vols.

Ford   Paul Leicester Ford, ed., *The Writings of Thomas Jefferson*, Letterpress Edition, New York, 1892-99, 10 vols.

Gallatin, *Papers*   Carl E. Prince and Helene E. Fineman, eds., *The Papers of Albert Gallatin*, microfilm edition in 46 reels, Philadelphia, 1969, and Supplement, Barbara B. Oberg, ed., reels 47-51, Wilmington, Del., 1985

Garner, *Black's Law Dictionary*   Bryan A. Garner, ed., *Black's Law Dictionary*, 8th ed., St. Paul, Minn., 2004

Harris, *Thornton*   C. M. Harris, ed., *Papers of William Thornton: Volume One, 1781-1802*, Charlottesville, 1995

HAW   Henry A. Washington, ed., *The Writings of Thomas Jefferson*, New York, 1853-54, 9 vols.

Heitman, *Dictionary*   Francis B. Heitman, comp., *Historical Register and Dictionary of the United States Army*, Washington, D.C., 1903, 2 vols.

Heitman, *Register*   Francis B. Heitman, *Historical Register of Officers of the Continental Army during the War of the Revolution, April, 1775, to December, 1793*, new ed., Washington, D.C., 1914

Higginbotham, *Pennsylvania Politics*   Sanford W. Higginbotham, *The Keystone in the Democratic Arch: Pennsylvania Politics 1800-1816*, Harrisburg, 1952

JEP   *Journal of the Executive Proceedings of the Senate of the United States . . . to the Termination of the Nineteenth Congress*, Washington, D.C., 1828, 3 vols.

JHR   *Journal of the House of Representatives of the United States*, Washington, D.C., 1826, 9 vols.

JS   *Journal of the Senate of the United States*, Washington, D.C., 1820-21, 5 vols.

King, *Life*   Charles R. King, ed., *The Life and Correspondence of Rufus King: Comprising His Letters, Private and Official, His Public Documents and His Speeches*, New York, 1894-1900, 6 vols.

Kline, *Burr*   Mary-Jo Kline, ed., *Political Correspondence and Public Papers of Aaron Burr*, Princeton, 1983, 2 vols.

L & B   Andrew A. Lipscomb and Albert E. Bergh, eds., *The Writings of Thomas Jefferson*, Washington, D.C., 1903-04, 20 vols.

LCB   Douglas L. Wilson, ed., *Jefferson's Literary Commonplace Book*, Princeton, 1989, *The Papers of Thomas Jefferson*, Second Series

Latrobe, *Correspondence*   John C. Van Horne and Lee W. Formwalt, eds., *The Correspondence and Miscellaneous Papers of Benjamin Henry Latrobe*, New Haven, 1984-88, 3 vols.

Leonard, *General Assembly*   Cynthia Miller Leonard, comp., *The General Assembly of Virginia, July 30, 1619-January 11, 1978: A Bicentennial Register of Members*, Richmond, 1978

List of Patents   *A List of Patents granted by the United States from April 10, 1790, to December 31, 1836*, Washington, D.C., 1872

Madison, *Papers*   William T. Hutchinson, Robert A. Rutland, J. C. A. Stagg, and others, eds., *The Papers of James Madison*, Chicago and Charlottesville, 1962- , 32 vols.
   Sec. of State Ser., 1986- , 8 vols.
   Pres. Ser., 1984- , 6 vols.
   Ret. Ser., 2009- , 1 vol.

Malone, *Jefferson*   Dumas Malone, *Jefferson and His Time*, Boston, 1948-81, 6 vols.

Mathews, *Ellicott*   Catharine Van Cortlandt Mathews, *Andrew Ellicott: His Life and Letters*, New York, 1908

MB   James A. Bear, Jr., and Lucia C. Stanton, eds., *Jefferson's Memorandum Books: Accounts, with Legal Records and Miscellany, 1767-1826*, Princeton, 1997, *The Papers of Thomas Jefferson*, Second Series

Miller, *Alexandria Artisans*   T. Michael Miller, comp., *Artisans and Merchants of Alexandria, Virginia, 1780-1820*, Bowie, Md., 1991-92, 2 vols.

Miller, *Treaties*   Hunter Miller, ed., *Treaties and Other International Acts of the United States of America*, Washington, D.C., 1931-48, 8 vols.

NDBW   Dudley W. Knox, ed., *Naval Documents Related to the United States Wars with the Barbary Powers*, Washington, D.C., 1939-44, 6 vols. and *Register of Officer Personnel and Ships' Data, 1801-1807*, Washington, D.C., 1945

NDQW   Dudley W. Knox, ed., *Naval Documents Related to the Quasi-War between the United States and France, Naval Operations*, Washington, D.C., 1935-38, 7 vols. (cited by years)

Notes, ed. Peden   *Thomas Jefferson, Notes on the State of Virginia*, ed. William Peden, Chapel Hill, 1955

OED   J. A. Simpson and E. S. C. Weiner, eds., *The Oxford English Dictionary*, Oxford, 1989, 20 vols.

Papenfuse, *Maryland Legislature*   Edward C. Papenfuse, Alan F. Day, David W. Jordan, and Gregory A. Stiverson, eds., *A Biographical Dictionary of the Maryland Legislature, 1635-1789*, Baltimore, 1979-85, 2 vols.

Parry, *Consolidated Treaty Series*   Clive Parry, ed., *The Consolidated Treaty Series*, Dobbs Ferry, N.Y., 1969-81, 231 vols.

Pasley,   Jeffrey L. Pasley, *"The Tyranny of Printers": Newspaper Politics in the Early American Republic*, Charlottesville, 2001

Peale, *Papers*   Lillian B. Miller and others, eds., *The Selected Papers of Charles Willson Peale and His Family*, New Haven, 1983-2000, 5 vols. in 6

PMHB   *Pennsylvania Magazine of History and Biography*, 1877-

Prince, *Federalists*   Carl E. Prince, *The Federalists and the Origins of the U.S. Civil Service*, New York, 1977

Prince, *New Jersey's Jeffersonian Republicans*   Carl E. Prince, *New Jersey's Jeffersonian Republicans: The Genesis of an Early Party Machine, 1789-1817*, Chapel Hill, 1967

PW   Wilbur S. Howell, ed., *Jefferson's Parliamentary Writings*, Princeton, 1988, *The Papers of Thomas Jefferson*, Second Series

RCHS   *Records of the Columbia Historical Society*, 1895-1989

Robinson, *Philadelphia Directory for 1802*   James Robinson, *The Philadelphia Directory, City and County Register, for 1802*, Philadelphia, 1801

Rowe, *McKean*   G. S. Rowe, Thomas McKean, *The Shaping of an American Republicanism*, Boulder, Colo., 1978

RS   J. Jefferson Looney and others, eds., *The Papers of Thomas Jefferson: Retirement Series*, Princeton, 2004-   , 6 vols.

Saricks, *Du Pont*   Ambrose Saricks, *Pierre Samuel Du Pont de Nemours*, Lawrence, Kans., 1965

S.C. Biographical Directory, House of Representatives   J. S. R. Faunt, Walter B. Edgar, N. Louise Bailey, and others, eds., *Biographical Directory of the South Carolina House of Representatives*, Columbia, S.C., 1974-92, 5 vols.

Seale, *The President's House*   William Seale, *The President's House*, Washington, D.C., 1986, 2 vols.

Shaw-Shoemaker   Ralph R. Shaw and Richard H. Shoemaker, comps., *American Bibliography: A Preliminary Checklist for 1801-1819*, New York, 1958-63, 22 vols.

Smith, *St. Clair Papers*   William Henry Smith, ed., *The St. Clair Papers, The Life and Public Services of Arthur St. Clair*, Cincinnati, 1882, 2 vols.

Sowerby   E. Millicent Sowerby, comp., *Catalogue of the Library of Thomas Jefferson*, Washington, D.C., 1952-59, 5 vols.

Stafford, *Baltimore Directory*   Cornelius William Stafford, *The Baltimore Directory, for 1802*, Baltimore, 1802

Stafford, *Philadelphia Directory*   Cornelius William Stafford, *The Philadelphia Directory*, Philadelphia, 1797-1801 (cited by year)

Stanton, *Free Some Day*   Lucia Stanton, *Free Some Day: The African-American Families of Monticello*, Charlottesville, 2000

Stein, *Worlds*   Susan R. Stein, *The Worlds of Thomas Jefferson at Monticello*, New York, 1993

Stets, *Postmasters*   Robert J. Stets, *Postmasters & Postoffices of the United States 1782-1811*, Lake Oswego, Ore., 1994

Sturtevant, *Handbook*   William C. Sturtevant, gen. ed., *Handbook of North American Indians*, Washington, D.C., 1978- , 14 vols.

Syrett, *Hamilton*   Harold C. Syrett and others, eds., *The Papers of Alexander Hamilton*, New York, 1961-87, 27 vols.

Tansill, *Caribbean Diplomacy*   Charles C. Tansill, *The United States and Santo Domingo, 1798-1873: A Chapter in Caribbean Diplomacy*, Baltimore, 1938; repr. Gloucester, Mass., 1967

Terr. Papers   Clarence E. Carter and John Porter Bloom, eds., *The Territorial Papers of the United States*, Washington, D.C., 1934-75, 28 vols.

TJR   Thomas Jefferson Randolph, ed., *Memoir, Correspondence, and Miscellanies, from the Papers of Thomas Jefferson*, Charlottesville, 1829, 4 vols.

Tulard, *Dictionnaire Napoléon*   Jean Tulard, *Dictionnaire Napoléon*, Paris, 1987

U.S. Statutes at Large   Richard Peters, ed., *The Public Statutes at Large of the United States . . . 1789 to March 3, 1845*, Boston, 1855-56, 8 vols.

VMHB   *Virginia Magazine of History and Biography*, 1893-

Wallace, *Death and Rebirth*   Anthony F. C. Wallace, *The Death and Rebirth of the Seneca*, New York, 1969

Washington, *Papers* W. W. Abbot, Dorothy Twohig, Philander D. Chase, Theodore J. Crackel, and others, eds., *The Papers of George Washington*, Charlottesville, 1983- , 53 vols.

 Col. Ser., 1983-95, 10 vols.

 Pres. Ser., 1987- , 15 vols.

 Ret. Ser., 1998-99, 4 vols.

 Rev. War Ser., 1985- , 18 vols.

WMQ *William and Mary Quarterly*, 1892-

Woods, *Albemarle* Edgar Woods, *Albemarle County in Virginia*, Charlottesville, 1901

CONTENTS

1802

CONTENTS

CONTENTS

CONTENTS

CONTENTS

CONTENTS

CONTENTS

CONTENTS

CONTENTS

CONTENTS

CONTENTS

[xli]

CONTENTS

CONTENTS

CONTENTS

CONTENTS

APPENDICES

ILLUSTRATIONS

Following page 318

COMMEMORATIVE MEDAL

In the spring of 1802, Jefferson sent his daughters copies of a medallion designed by John Reich to commemorate American Independence and Jefferson's inauguration as president. Henry Voigt, a Philadelphia watchmaker and chief coiner of the Mint who was, like Reich, an immigrant, oversaw the creation of the medal. The medallions that Jefferson obtained for his family were struck in silver and cost $4.25 each. The piece was also available in an alloy called white metal. The example illustrated here depicts the less costly version, which sold for $1.25. The medal is $1\frac{3}{4}$ inches in diameter. William Duane offered both varieties for sale in Philadelphia, and the medal sold "the more readily," Jefferson reported to his daughter Martha in April, because the popular prints that depicted his likeness were "such miserable caracatures." Martha, nevertheless, "found fault" with the medal's portrait of her father, for Reich had based the profile on Jean Antoine Houdon's bust, and Houdon, Martha believed, had made her father look old (Philadelphia *Aurora*, 18 Feb. 1802; Vol. 34:71-5, 167-8, 353-4; Vol. 36:239-40, 386; TJ to Mary Jefferson Eppes, 29 Mch., and to Martha Jefferson Randolph, 3 Apr.; Martha Jefferson Randolph to TJ, 16 Apr.).

Courtesy of Department of Rare Books and Special Collections, Princeton University Library.

JOHN TRUMBULL

Jefferson and John Trumbull were connected through the latter's works of art: Jefferson was a central figure in Trumbull's famous painting of *The Declaration of Independence*, and the artist made portraits of Jefferson and many of his friends and contemporaries. The two men also had a long personal relationship. In 1788 and 1789, when Trumbull was in London studying with Benjamin West and Jefferson was in Paris, the artist functioned as the statesman's personal agent in the British capital, purchasing items for him and carrying out various "commissions." Trumbull had experience with such miscellaneous assignments, for as a volunteer in the Revolutionary War, he had been an aide-de-camp to George Washington and an adjutant general under Horatio Gates. When Jefferson encountered difficulty finding passage directly from France to the United States in the fall of 1789, it was Trumbull who arranged for him to travel by way of Britain, saw to it that the ship would hold over in port a few days to give Jefferson a chance to embark, and wrote William Pitt to ask that the American diplomat's baggage, which could be expected to "contain articles highly dutied, and perhaps contraband in this Kingdom," be transferred "without being search'd or open'd." It was through Trumbull's arrangements, also, that Jefferson had met Maria Cosway in 1786. Anticipating that William Short might give up his position as his private secretary, Jefferson asked Trumbull, in the spring of 1789, to take the job if Short left. "I think it will not take a moment of your time from your present pursuit," he advised. That opportunity failed to develop when Jefferson, on his return to the United States for what he had thought would be a leave of absence, became secretary of state and did not return to France. In 1794, Trumbull became John Jay's secretary in London during Jay's negotiations with the British. Two years later, Trumbull was selected to become the fifth member of the joint British-American commission that would, under Article 7 of Jay's treaty, arbitrate some claims of American citizens against the British government. In that capacity, Trumbull wrote to Jefferson from London on 10 Mch. 1802 regarding the president's appointment of George W. Erving to a dual position as the commission's assessor and the agent for American claims (ANB; Vol. 10:xxvii-xxviii, xxix, 454n; Vol. 11:181, 598; Vol. 13:241, 280-1; Vol. 14:364-5; Vol. 15:38-9, 143-4, 151-2, 163-4, 176-9, 199-200, 467-9, 471, 515-18).

This painting of Trumbull is an undated self-portrait. Although it was once thought to date from 1812 or after, more recent scholarship suggests that Trumbull painted it in London in the period 1802-4, intending it to be the partner of a portrait he made of his wife, Sarah Hope Harvey Trumbull, whom he married in 1800. He painted other portraits during his time as claims commissioner, including likenesses of Christopher Gore, who was also on the claims commission, and of Rufus King and his wife, Mary Alsop King. In his self-portrait, Trumbull's palette and brushes are visible, but he has a large sheet of paper unfolded before him, perhaps hinting at other aspects of his career, and his hand rests on the handle of a sword. The painting is in oil on canvas, 30 inches by 25 inches (Helen A. Cooper, *John Trumbull: The Hand and Spirit of a Painter* [New Haven, 1982], 159-61; Irma B. Jaffe, *John Trumbull: Patriot-Artist of the American Revolution* [Boston, 1975], 209, 227, 229, 312; Theodore Sizer, *The Works of Colonel John Trumbull, Artist of the American Revolution*, rev. ed. [New Haven, 1967], 72, fig. 66; ANB).

Courtesy of Yale University Art Gallery, Gift of Marshall H. Clyde, Jr.

MARTHA WASHINGTON

With "sorrow unfeigned," Thomas Law penned a brief letter to Jefferson on 23 May 1802 to report the death of Martha Washington. Jefferson, who had paid Mrs. Washington a visit at Mount Vernon in January 1801, wrote a polite response to Law on 31 May, declaring an "affectionate & respectful attachment" to George Washington's widow. She was 71 years old at the time of her death. Law was related to her by marriage (Vol. 32:391-2).

James Peale created this miniature portrait in 1796, using the finest brushes to apply watercolor paints to an ivory oval that is slightly more than $1\frac{1}{2}$ inches tall and $1\frac{1}{4}$ inches wide. Peale was born in 1749. He sometimes worked as a framemaker and studio assistant for his older brother, Charles Willson Peale, who trained him as an artist. The brothers' works are in some cases indistinguishable. Both painted miniatures on ivory, although only James made the genre a particular specialty. Late in life, when his eyesight was no longer acute enough to produce the delicate portraits, he devoted most of his attention to still-life paintings in oil (ANB; Charles Coleman Sellers, "Portraits and Miniatures by Charles Willson Peale," APS, *Transactions*, new ser., 42, pt. 1 [1952], 8, 15, 19).

Courtesy of the Mount Vernon Ladies' Association.

ILLUSTRATIONS

CIPHER EXERCISE

To familiarize himself with the cipher system that Robert Patterson described to him in December 1801, Jefferson used the cipher to encode and decode the Lord's Prayer. The page shown here is Jefferson's rough draft of that exercise, written on a scrap piece of paper approximately eight inches tall and five inches wide. The four steps or "operations" into which he divided the process of encipherment and decipherment are visible on the page. In the first "operation," which was the transcription of the prayer's text into a table (at the top of the page), Jefferson departed from Patterson's instructions, writing the text horizontally rather than vertically—an innovation that Patterson readily accepted. The curvilinear markings in the second operation, in the middle of the page, were a means of setting off random letters that were introduced as part of the cipher process. What Jefferson called here the third operation, the designation of the numerical key for the cipher, is the narrow table in the upper left corner of the page. The fourth operation, the decipherment, is the table at the foot of the page, which Jefferson did not complete. He made a neater version, not shown here, of the Lord's Prayer encipherment, using a different key and confining the process to the three operations that involved transformation of the text. That refined version of the exercise, copied by Meriwether Lewis with some variation of the random letters, became the sample that Jefferson included with a detailed explication of Patterson's cipher he sent to Robert R. Livingston in Paris in April 1802 (TJ to Patterson, 22 Mch.; Patterson to TJ, 12 Apr.; Method of Using Robert Patterson's Cipher, printed at 18 Apr.).

Courtesy of the Tracy W. McGregor Library of American History, Special Collections, University of Virginia Library.

ARMY COMMISSION

The Military Peace Establishment Act, which Jefferson signed into law on 16 Mch. 1802, reduced the United States Army in size and restructured it according to a plan developed by Henry Dearborn a few months earlier. The new system cut in half the number of regiments of artillerists (from two to one) and infantry (from four regiments to two). Many of those officers who were retained in the army needed fresh commissions to reflect their new regimental assignments. The document illustrated here is one of those commissions, dated 15 Apr. 1802. It names Meriwether Lewis, the president's secretary, a captain of the 1st infantry regiment. The printed certificate is $18\frac{1}{2}$ by $15\frac{1}{2}$ inches in size. A clerk filled in the blanks and affixed a red wax seal to the document's upper corner. Both Jefferson and Dearborn signed the commission (Carolyn Gilman, *Lewis and Clark: Across the Divide* [Washington, D.C., 2003], 71, 357-8; Vol. 36:42-8; TJ to the Senate, 25, 31 Mch. 1802).

Courtesy of private owners.

WILLIAM THORNTON
ANNA MARIA BRODEAU THORNTON

This pair of portraits by Gilbert Stuart is similar in style and composition to other sets of paintings the artist made of married couples, including Carlos Martínez de Irujo and his American wife, Sally McKean Irujo (illustrated

ILLUSTRATIONS

in Vol. 35), and James Madison and Dolley Payne Madison. The portraits of Anna Maria and William Thornton are in oil on canvas, each painting just under 29 by 25 inches in size. During the period covered by this volume, the Thorntons were long-standing members of Washington's social and political society. William Thornton—born in the West Indies, educated as a physician in England and Scotland, and a self-taught architect—designed the Capitol building and was a member of the board of commissioners of the District of Columbia from 1794 until an act of Congress abolished the commission in the spring of 1802. Thornton then became the supervisor of the patent office and continued to live in Washington. The Thorntons resided two blocks from the President's House and were Jefferson's guests for dinner on multiple occasions (see Vol. 34:103, and 23 Apr. in this volume). The couple had married in Philadelphia in 1790, when Anna Maria Brodeau, whose mother at one time operated a boarding school for young ladies in that city, was 15 years old and William Thornton was 31. These portraits, which Stuart painted in 1804, are in the Andrew W. Mellon Collection of the National Gallery of Art (Carrie Rebora Barratt and Ellen G. Miles, *Gilbert Stuart* [New York, 2004], 258-60; Harris, *Thornton*, xliv, 122; ANB; District of Columbia Commissioners to TJ, 1 June 1802).

Courtesy of the Board of Trustees, National Gallery of Art, Washington.

COMMEMORATIVE MEDAL (REVERSE)

As Henry Voigt described the "Allegorical representations" on the reverse side of the Reich medal to Jefferson in December 1801, the goddess Minerva "is made to represent Liberty"—shown by the liberty cap atop her staff—"as well as Wisdom." She places the Declaration of Independence onto a rock labeled "Constitution." American prosperity and power are symbolized by a cornucopia and military equipment. The eagle, with a laurel wreath in its beak, represents the United States, and the slogan reads, "Under his Wing is Protection" (Vol. 36:240).

Courtesy of Department of Rare Books and Special Collections, Princeton University Library.

Volume 37

4 March to 30 June 1802

JEFFERSON CHRONOLOGY

1743 · 1826

1743	Born at Shadwell, 13 Apr. (New Style).
1760	Entered the College of William and Mary.
1762	"quitted college."
1762-1767	Self-education and preparation for law.
1769-1774	Albemarle delegate to House of Burgesses.
1772	Married Martha Wayles Skelton, 1 Jan.
1775-1776	In Continental Congress.
1776	Drafted Declaration of Independence.
1776-1779	In Virginia House of Delegates.
1779	Submitted Bill for Establishing Religious Freedom.
1779-1781	Governor of Virginia.
1782	His wife died, 6 Sep.
1783-1784	In Continental Congress.
1784-1789	In France as Minister Plenipotentiary to negotiate commercial treaties and as Minister Plenipotentiary resident at Versailles.
1790-1793	Secretary of State of the United States.
1797-1801	Vice President of the United States.
1801-1809	President of the United States.
1814-1826	Established the University of Virginia.
1826	Died at Monticello, 4 July.

VOLUME 37

4 March to 30 June 1802

8 Mch.	Judiciary Act of 1801 repealed.
10-17 Mch.	Meets with Seneca Indian delegation, led by Handsome Lake and Cornplanter.
16 Mch.	Military Peace Establishment Act passed, reorganizing the army and creating a military academy at West Point, New York.
27 Mch.	Definitive treaty of peace signed between France and Great Britain at Amiens, France.
29 Mch.	Forwards commemorative medals by John Reich to Mary Jefferson Eppes.
6 Apr.	Internal taxes repealed.
9 Apr.	Contributes $100 toward rebuilding Nassau Hall at the College of New Jersey at Princeton.
18 Apr.	Sends Robert R. Livingston method for using Robert Patterson's cipher.
29 Apr.	New judiciary law enacted, authorizing the president to appoint commissioners of bankruptcy.
3 May	First session of the Seventh Congress ends.
5 May	Leaves Washington for Monticello, arriving on 8 May.
6 May	Toussaint-Louverture surrenders to French forces of General Victoire Emmanuel Leclerc.
27 May	Leaves Monticello for Washington, arriving on 30 May.
1 June	Appoints Robert Brent mayor of Washington, D.C.
3 June	Proposes transportation of "insurgent negroes" to Sierra Leone.
20 June	Receives list of delinquent collectors from Treasury Department.
23 June	James Madison sends Arthur St. Clair the president's admonition of his conduct as governor of the Northwest Territory.

THE PAPERS OF
THOMAS JEFFERSON

·《 ▬▬▬▬ 》·

From William C. C. Claiborne

DEAR SIR,   Near Natchez, March 4th 1802

My appointment to this Government, (& if I am not greatly deceived, my conduct since my arrival,) has been pleasing to a great majority of the Citizens:—But from a variety of causes, some difficulties
will attend me, in the progress of my administration.—Already my
Predecessor has evidenced a disposition, to rekindle the flame of
party, & his most zealous partisans, although few in number, are
equally active in their mischievous machinations;—but I pray you to
be assured, Sir, that Justice & decision shall characterize my public
Conduct, and that nothing shall divert me, from the political course,
you were pleased to prescribe me.—

The Judges of this Territory, are violent men, greatly under the
control of their passions, and fixed in their hatred to the Second Grade
of Government, and to Republican principles;—the Secretary is not
so open in his opposition, but in sentiments & wishes, he is no less inimical;—a decided majority however, of the People, are attached to
the representative System, which at present exists, and I shall cordially unite with *theirs, my efforts* in *its* support;—but to aid me, in
such endeavours, I feel greatly the want of a Secretary, capable of
some exertion of mind, and a character in whom I could confide.—

Colonel Steele is remarked for his attachment to the policy, formerly observed in this Territory;—his office is made the place of ren-
dezvous, for the opponents *to the* Second Grade of Government, &
these Gentlemen are exclusively in his confidence;—for some Weeks
after my arrival, I attributed the Secretary's apparent apathy, concerning the affairs of this Territory, to his *then low* state of health, but
this opinion is now changed, and I see in his conduct, daily proofs of
his determined ill-will to my administration.

It is with great regret, that I express myself thus freely of a public
officer, but I am compelled to do so, from the strongest considerations
of duty—

[3]

Previous to my departure from Tennessee, I addressed to Colonel Steele, a very polite Letter, advising him of my appointment, and assuring him of my desire to possess his confidence and friendship, and ever since my arrival, I have uniformly paid him the most respectful attention; but on his part, he has been far from manifesting a corresponding disposition.—

In the discharge of my Official duties, the connection between the Secretary and myself, is necessarily intimate;—I *am* compelled to confide much to him, and on many occasions to solicit his aid in the dispatch of public business. *Thus* circumstanced, I must confess, that my present situation with Colo. Steele, is painful in the extreme, and I humbly supplicate you, to relieve me therefrom.—

If my much esteemed President, should honor me, with a continuance of his confidence, and it should be the will of the Honorable Senate, to confirm my present appointment, every exertion in my power, shall be used, to promote the happiness of this portion of the American Citizens;—but in forwarding this first wish of my Heart, I should derive great aid from a Secretary well disposed to the Second Grade of Government;—to Republican principles generally, and a man of information & firmness.—

Before I conclude, I pray you, to excuse the liberty I have taken, in addressing to you this Letter;—I again repeat, that I am compelled to do so from the strongest considerations of duty to the Government, and to myself.—

With best wishes for a continuance of your happiness, in private and public life!—

I have the honor very respectfully to be, Dear Sir, your affectionate friend and most obt. Hble. Servt.

WILLIAM C. C. CLAIBORNE

RC (DLC); in a clerk's hand, signed by Claiborne; at foot of text: "The President of the U. States"; endorsed by TJ as received 27 Apr. and so recorded in SJL.

JUDGES OF THIS TERRITORY: Daniel Tilton and Peter Bryan Bruin were appointed judges of the Mississippi Territory in 1798. Seth Lewis was appointed chief justice of the territory in 1800, replacing William McGuire (Dunbar Rowland, *Courts, Judges, and Lawyers of Mississippi, 1798-1935* [Jackson, 1935], 11-13, 16-18; JEP, 1:272, 354; Vol. 30:280-1).

Claiborne's VERY POLITE LETTER to John Steele was dated 5 Aug. 1801. It informed the secretary of Claiborne's appointment as territorial governor, but added that he would not be able to leave Tennessee for Natchez until at least the end of September. In the interim, Claiborne was pleased that Steele would continue to serve as acting governor, stating that "in your Official fidelity and integrity, I place entire confidence." He also asked Steele to engage suitable lodgings for him in Natchez and looked forward to Steele's "official co-operation, and friendly council" (*Terr. Papers*, 5:244-5).

Shortly after Claiborne wrote TJ the letter above, he also corresponded with Thomas T. Davis. TJ saw the letter and made an extract of it. In the communication with Davis dated 6 Mch., Claiborne was critical of territorial secretary John Steele. The governor repeated his allegations that a significant Federalist opposition remained in Mississippi, including the territorial judges, the secretary, and "old Winthrop." Claiborne deemed Steele to be "among the greatest enemies I have in this Territory" and attributed his behavior to a thwarted expectation of being appointed governor of Mississippi. He "never will forgive me for the disappointment," wrote Claiborne. He also informed Davis of his request that TJ not reappoint Steele as secretary when his term of office expired on 7 May, noting "I sincerely hope my request will be granted" (Tr in DLC; with extract in Meriwether Lewis's hand; at head of text, in TJ's hand: "Extract of a letter from Govr. Claiborne to Thomas T. Davis dated Natchez Mar. 6. 1802").

From Nicolas Gouin Dufief

à Philadelphie. Le 4. Mars. 1802. au milieu des rejouissances & des

Monsieur,   acclamations d'une multitude de Citoyens

Aussitôt la reception de votre lettre j'ai mis à part pour vous la chimie de *Chaptal* en 3. V.: 8o. Je me suis ensuite occupé à chercher l'édition de *l'Odyssée* que vous souhaitez. Il paroit que c'est un ouvrage rare du moins à Philada. puisque plusieurs jours d'une recherche active se sont écoulés sans pouvoir en découvrir un seul exemplaire—si, une tres belle Edon. du même ouvrage par les *Foulis*, en 2 Vs. In folio, pouvoit vous convenir au defaut de l'autre[1] faites-le moi savoir. Le prix en sera de huit dollars—cet ouvrage fesoit partie de la Collection des classiques du *Dr Franklin*

Je publierai sous peu de jours Le catalogue des livres que j'ai reçus tout recemment de *France*: il vous sera envoyé dès qu'il paroitra

J'ai l'honneur d'etre, Monsieur, avec tous les sentimens Qui vous sont dus à tant de titres Votre trés devoué serviteur

N. G. Dufief

E D I T O R S' T R A N S L A T I O N

Philadelphia. 4 March 1802.
in the midst of the rejoicing and the cheers

Sir,   of a multitude of citizens

Immediately upon receipt of your letter, I put aside for you Chaptal's Chemistry in 3 vols. octavo. I then set about looking for the edition of *The Odyssey* that you desire. It seems that it is a rare work, at least in Philadelphia, since several days of active research have gone by without being able to discover a single copy. If a very fine edition of the same work by the *Foulis*, in two vols., in folio, could suit you in place of the other, let me know. Its price will be eight dollars. This work was part of the classics collection of *Dr. Franklin*.

I shall publish within a few days the catalogue of the books that I received recently from France; it will be sent to you as soon as it comes out.

I have the honor to be, Sir, with all the sentiments that are your due for so many reasons, your very devoted servant   N. G. DUFIEF

RC (DLC); endorsed by TJ as received 8 Mch. 1802 and so recorded in SJL.

ACCLAMATIONS D'UNE MULTITUDE: on 4 Mch., the Philadelphia Militia Legion commanded by John Shee paraded through the city's streets to mark the anniversary of TJ's inauguration. According to the *Aurora*, the legion's companies dispersed after the parade "to enjoy themselves in that social manner, and partake of those pleasures which the exertions of republicans in combating a host of internal foes, abetted by external influence, so well entitle them to." The city's Tammany Society held a Native-American-themed event in their "great wigwam." Led by their "chiefs," the members then divided into 13 "tribes," representing the original states, and marched to the State House (Independence Hall), where they viewed the militia parade and "joined the procession." The Republican Volunteers, a cavalry troop commanded by Congressman William Jones, convened at the Swan on Race Street. They toasted, among other things: the president; the anniversary of the "day of our regeneration"; the "repeal of the midnight judiciary—May we soon be relieved from those who would never have reached the bench, if they had been of good behavior"; a repeal of internal taxes; and a "revision of the naturalization law." Democratic Republicans also celebrated the day in Boston (*Aurora*, 4, 5, 6 Mch.; *Philadelphia Gazette*, 4 Mch.; Boston *Mercury and New-England Palladium*, 5 Mch.).

VOTRE LETTRE: TJ to Dufief, 19 Feb.

The work by Jean Antoine CHAPTAL was *Élémens de Chymie*. Dufief obtained the three-volume third edition, published in Paris in 1796, for TJ (Sowerby, No. 831).

ÉDITION DE L'ODYSSÉE: TJ wanted the Foulis duodecimo edition of Homer's *Odyssey* in Greek and Latin. He already owned a copy of the two-volume folio edition in Greek by the same publisher that Dufief offered him from Franklin's library (Sowerby, Nos. 4267, 4270; Vol. 10:165, 201, 417; TJ to Dufief, 19 Feb.).

From Anonymous

SIR   [before 5 Mch. 1802]

Our Country by Your Assistance is happily delivered from King Craft and Priestcraft but it Labours under Lawyers Craft. I mean by Lawyers Craft, their making long Speeches to display their Abilities, and to try to pervert Justice. by this means 2 days are taken up in trying a cause of a trifling Assault, &c. by this means, tryals are put off when witnesses Come and wait att Great Expence, & 2. 3. or 400 Persons are kept from their Occupations, trials put off for 7 Years, to the great Injury, of this country and we believe if more Courts were multiply'd Lawyers would be multiply'd in Proportion. we See no hope of redress Unless from You. as Jurors we wish to Serve our Country but are tired by waiting 5 Days and doing So little buisness.

we hope you will [prese]nt Some Plan that the Buisness in our Courts of Justice may be Expedited

I believe this is the Common Language of all this Country & we wish to Lay this before you in hope of Redress. we hope you will Accept this Plain address from Your Friends and pay Such attention to it as appears to you it requires[1]

RC (DLC); undated; torn; addressed: "For His Excellency Thomas Jefferson President of the United States of America att the City of Washinton"; franked; postmarked Philadelphia; endorsed by TJ as received 5 Mch. and "Anon. postmark Phila. dilatoriness of courts" and so recorded in SJL.

In 1802, WITNESSES and JURORS in the courts of the United States received $1.25 for each day they attended in court, plus traveling expenses at the rate of five cents per mile (U.S. Statutes at Large, 1:626).

[1] MS: "requris."

To Henry Dearborn

TH: JEFFERSON TO
GENERAL DEARBORNE.   [5 Mch. 1802]

I have been looking into the case which is the subject of Majr. Foreman's letter from St. Mary's, stating that the Govr. of E. Florida proposes to enlist souldiers within our territory for an expedition against the Creeks. the statute of June 14. 1797. is only against naval enterprizes. but that of Mar. 3. 1799 regulating intercourse with the Indians, comes perfectly up to this case in sections 3. 4. 6. by which to go on the Indian lands without a passport is punishable by fine of 50. D. & 3. months imprisonment, to go on them *with an hostile intention*, or to commit on them a robbery, larceny, trespass or other crime by fine of 100. D. & 12. months imprisonment, and to murder an Indian is punisheable by death. besides this if it be known that any person proposes to go on such an expedition, a justice of peace may prevent it by arresting him & committing him to jail until he gives security against a breach of the peace. as to taking an oath of allegiance to Spain, the law will consider that as merely a cover for the crime meditated, a mere fraud, which will have no other effect than to prove a more deliberate premeditation of the crime. this case will be clearly within the positions of the Attorney General's opinion in Henfield's case, May 30. 93.

The law regulating intercourse with the Indians expired the day before yesterday. but it will doubtless be revived. I think therefore we shall be safe in making a communication to Majr. Foreman on the hypothesis of it's being in force.   TH: JEFFERSON

RC (NjP); undated. PrC (DLC). Recorded in SJL as a letter of 5 Mch. to the War Department, with notation: "enlisting souldiers by Spands."

MAJR. FOREMAN'S LETTER FROM ST. MARY'S: TJ mistook the name of Major Constant Freeman, a U.S. artillery officer in command of Fort Johnson, South Carolina. On 19 Feb., Freeman sent the War Department a copy of a letter from Captain Richard Scott Blackburn at Fort Washington on the Saint Marys River. That river separated Georgia from Spain's province of East FLORIDA and formed the southern boundary of the United States as specified by the Pinckney Treaty of 1795. Blackburn reported that the governor of East Florida had called out the province's militia in response to an attack by Indians on a Spanish settlement. Blackburn also related a hearsay report that the governor intended to enlist men in Georgia for an EXPEDITION AGAINST THE CREEKS. The governor of East Florida was Enrique White, a native of Ireland who had entered the Spanish army as a cadet and advanced to the rank of brigadier general. "It will be only necessary to swallow an Oath for the term of the Expedition," he reportedly said of the prospective recruitment in Georgia. From January to March 1802, William A. Bowles and his Native American allies laid siege to St. Marks in an ultimately unsuccessful effort to recapture that fort. Spanish authorities also held Bowles responsible for various attacks by Indians along the Florida frontiers. On 22 Mch., Carlos Martínez de Irujo wrote to Madison insisting that the United States take action. Stating that Bowles had his base of operations in U.S. territory, Irujo cited Article 5 of the Pinckney Treaty, which obliged the United States and Spain "expressly to restrain by force all hostilities on the part of the Indian Nations living within their boundaries" (Freeman to Henry Burbeck, 19 Feb. 1802, enclosing copy of Blackburn to Freeman, 11 Feb., in DNA: RG 107, LRUS; Dearborn to Mahlon Ford and others, 11 June 1801, in same, LSMA; Miller, *Treaties*, 2:319-20, 322; Madison,

Papers, Sec. of State Ser., 3:63-4; J. Leitch Wright, Jr., *William Augustus Bowles: Director General of the Creek Nation* [Athens, Ga., 1967], 152-3; William S. Coker and Thomas D. Watson, *Indian Traders of the Southeastern Spanish Borderlands: Panton, Leslie & Company and John Forbes & Company, 1783-1847* [Pensacola, Fla., 1986], 237-8; David Hart White, *Vicente Folch, Governor in Spanish Florida, 1787-1811* [Washington, D.C., 1981], 59-60; Eileen A. Sullivan, "Irish Military Men Serving Spain in North America in the 18th and 19th Centuries," *The Irish Sword: The Journal of the Military History Society of Ireland*, 21 [1999], 387-8; Heitman, *Dictionary*, 1:222, 262, 435; Vol. 33:175).

The 14 June 1797 STATUTE was "An Act to prevent citizens of the United States from Privateering against nations in amity with, or against citizens of the United States" (U.S. Statutes at Large, 1:520).

Gideon HENFIELD'S CASE was an issue for the Washington administration when TJ was secretary of state. Henfield, a mariner originally from Massachusetts, enlisted for service on the *Citoyen Genet*, which sailed from Charleston, South Carolina, as a French privateer authorized by Edmond Charles Genet. Washington's Proclamation of Neutrality prohibited Americans from serving any of the nations that were at war, and when Henfield arrived in Philadelphia as the master of a captured prize, the cabinet unanimously agreed to prosecute him as a test case. There was no statute covering that provision of the proclamation, but in an opinion of 30 May 1793 requested by TJ, Attorney General Edmund Randolph argued that the seaman could be prosecuted because according to treaties between the United States and several of France's enemies, American citizens could not fight against those countries. Treaties "are the Supreme law of the land," Randolph stated. He said that Henfield could also be indicted under common law "because his conduct comes within the description of disturbing the Peace of the United States." The prosecution of Henfield—whom a jury acquitted—contributed to the rift between the U.S. government and Genet

(Vol. 26:40-1, 130-1, 145-6, 159-61, 198, 702).

From Henry Dearborn

SIR,

War Department
5h March 1802.

Governor Clinton by his letter of the 20th. ultimo, requests that a Commissioner on the part of the United States might be appointed to attend a Treaty with the Oneida Indians for the purchase of about ten thousand acres of land, which that Nation is desireous of selling, and which has heretofore been leased out to white people.

The six Nations have also expressed a wish to dispose of a narrow strip of land, which they consider as useless to them, bordering on Niagara river, and a small tract near the former Cayuga settlement.

Accept, Sir, the assurances of my high respect and consideration.

H. DEARBORN

RC (DNA: RG 46, EPEN, 7th Cong., 1st sess.); in a clerk's hand, signed by Dearborn; addressed to "The President of the United States" from the War Department; endorsed by TJ as received 5 Mch.; endorsed by a Senate clerk as received 10 Mch. FC (Lb in DNA: RG 107, LSP). Enclosed in TJ to the Senate, 9 Mch. (see ASP, *Indian Affairs*, 1:663).

According to the War Department's register of correspondence, the LETTER that George Clinton wrote at Albany on 20 Feb. pertained "to the appointment of Commissioners to treat with the Oneida & St. Regis Indians" (DNA: RG 107, RLRMS).

The New York legislature passed resolutions in February to advance the transaction with the ONEIDA INDIANS, and in March the state and the tribe made a "provisional agreement" sealed by a payment of $300 from the state to the Oneidas. On 4 June 1802, John Tayler represented the United States when agents for New York State confirmed the sale with a treaty whereby the Oneidas ceded title to four pieces of land. The state agreed to give the tribe, in addition to the payment

made in March, $600 plus a $300 annuity. This was one of a long series of treaties, beginning in the 1780s, by which New York acquired land from the Oneidas, much of it from a tract of 300,000 acres adjacent to Oneida Lake that had been reserved to the tribe in 1788 (*Treaty Made with the Oneida Nation, At their Village, on the 4th of June, 1802, by the Commissioners of the State of New-York, Under the Authority of the United States* [Washington, D.C., 1802], Shaw-Shoemaker, No. 3448; Sturtevant, *Handbook*, 15:450, 483-4).

For the NARROW STRIP OF LAND on the NIAGARA RIVER, see Vol. 36:633, 634n.

FORMER CAYUGA SETTLEMENT: after the American Revolution, many members of the Cayuga tribe moved to Canada. Some of those who remained in New York lived with other tribes. By a treaty of 1789, the Cayugas retained a 100-square-mile tract at Cayuga Lake, but in 1795 the state of New York purchased all but three square miles of that reservation. The Oneida and Cayuga tribes were members of the Six Nations confederacy (Sturtevant, *Handbook*, 15:435, 444, 450, 502).

Memorandum from Albert Gallatin, with Jefferson's Reply

[on or after 5 Mch. 1802]

This recommendation appears unexceptionable—Mr Macon says that there is no one in that part of the country on whom greater reliance may be placed than Mr. Spaight. Mr Stone who lives nearer to, though not in the district, is absent   A. G.

[*Reply by TJ*:]

not one of the recommendations say a word about mr Cheney's politics, an omission which, in applications to this administration, I have observed to be almost invariably a proof of federalism. we must enquire into this circumstance.   Th:J.

[*Comment by Gallatin*:]

Mr Stone is not acquainted there. There is no other applicant.

MS (DNA: RG 59, LAR, 2:0158-9); undated, but see below; on a scrap of paper, with TJ's reply and Gallatin's comment on verso.

Richard Dobbs SPAIGHT, the former North Carolina governor and Republican congressman, wrote Gallatin from New Bern on 14 Feb., recommending Benjamin Cheney as a proper person to fill the vacancy caused by the death of John Easton, who had served as surveyor of the port of Beaufort, North Carolina, in the New Bern district, since 1790. Cheney was already serving as an inspector of the port discharging the duties "to the Satisfaction of those under whom he has acted." Several years earlier, he had "done the business for Colonel Easton." On the same day, Spaight also wrote North Carolina Senator Jesse Franklin, requesting that he solicit "the Cabinet" in favor of his friend Cheney, who was "a Man of an unexceptionable character, a good & attentive officer, and one Generally respected in the County in Which he lives." Franklin was asked to show Spaight's letter to David STONE, the other Senator from North Carolina, and to inform Congressman Nathaniel Macon of his wishes. On 5 Mch., Franklin sent Spaight's letter on to Gallatin, noting "I presume you are acquainted with Colo Spaight, whose rec-

ommendation I think intitled to great respect" (RCs in DNA: RG 59, LAR, all endorsed by TJ; JEP, 1:37, 39; *Biog. Dir. Cong.*).

On 15 Feb., Francis Hawks, collector at the district of New Bern, wrote Gallatin that he had appointed Cheney to fill the vacancy until the president could appoint a successor. Hawks described Cheney as a person "of integrity and diligence and fully Capable of the business" who was "worthy of the Presidents confidence," having served for many years as an "officer in the Revenue Service" (RC in DNA: RG 59, LAR, endorsed by TJ; ASP, *Miscellaneous*, 1:276, 287). Cheney himself wrote the Treasury secretary on 15 Feb., acknowledging his "Temporary appointment" and offering himself as a candidate for the office; recommendations were being sent on his behalf, which he hoped Gallatin would show the president (RC in DNA: RG 59, LAR; endorsed by TJ: "Cheney Benj. to mr Gallatin. to be Surveyor of the port & Collector of the district } of Beaufort N.C."; TJ then canceled "& Collector of the district"). On 16 Feb., John Daves, the former collector at New Bern, wrote John Steele, the U.S. comptroller, recommending Cheney. Finally, North Carolina congressman John Stanly wrote Gallatin on 3 Mch., asking him to tell the president that his long acquaintance with Cheney gave him confidence in his "Integrity & Ability" and worthiness for the appointment. No appointment to that office would be more acceptable to the citizens of the district (both RCs in same, endorsed by TJ; *Biog. Dir. Cong.*).

NO OTHER APPLICANT: on 15 Mch., Stanly again wrote Gallatin and enclosed a letter, dated 17 Feb., addressed to the Treasury secretary from 15 merchants at Beaufort recommending Brian Hellen. The merchants reported that age and in-

firmities had for several years rendered Easton unable to attend to his duties and he had chosen Hellen "to act as a Deputy in his behalf." They described Hellen as "a plain honest man" with a "ready turn for business," and Stanly testified that Hellen possessed "Integrity & ability" (RC and enclosure in DNA: RG 59, LAR; endorsed by TJ). TJ submitted Cheney's nomination to the Senate on 27 Apr. (see TJ to the Senate, at that date).

From John Hughes

SIR   Columbia State S.C March 5 AD 1802

I wrote you formerly my Opinion, of there being a propriety, of attending to ameliorate, the condition of prisoners of War, & of the certainty of a War with England, & the propriety of declairing the War in particular against its Goverment, and treating English prisoners of War, as was done, at the commencement of the Revolution, allowing the Sailors their Wages, and Ventures, out of the Prise taken—

I conceive that a vigilant attention should be kept on those, who are, or may be employed, by the british Govermt. on the footing of Citizenship, even such a man as Nicholas Madgett might have a protection—Justice intitles the sincere foreignor to favour, but, should guard against the Impostor, whose admition is banefull to the publick wellfare; and who mostly intangle their employers in Deception (justifying the old addage of) honesty is best policy—The Purport of this, is chiefly to inform you, of a discovery made in the year 1785, on an Emminence near the East End of Jamaica, in a clear Morn, with a common Tellescope of Dollands, viewing the Sun, as he emerged from the Ocean, I discovered 3 Globes, or Sattelites, near the Sun, I long suspected that such, was the Cause of the Dark Spots, seen on that Planet; from the Distance of these Globes I think the Number is 7—repeated observations convinces me of this Visual truth. I shewed it to Friend, now no more—having seen no publication of the subject, I now submit it to your consideration to assertain the Truth—

An early aversion to methodic Systems, and various impediments obstructing my persuits, have deterred me from Scientific Activity, my Days are hastning to a period, observation with you, may publish what may for some Time, otherwise perish, with an obscure individual—who is with Esteem yours   JOHN HUGHES

RC (DLC); at foot of text: "Thos Jefferson. President of the U.S. of America"; endorsed by TJ as received 26 Mch. and so recorded in SJL.

I WROTE YOU FORMERLY: Hughes to TJ, 10 Jan. 1802.

In 1798 and 1799, northern newspapers reported that a former British spy named NICHOLAS MADGETT had emigrated to the United States and was residing in Philadelphia. By 1799, he had moved to South Carolina, where he was engaged in viticulture near Columbia (New York *Time Piece*, 2 July 1798; *Aurora*, 15 Mch., 1 May 1799; Richard Hayes, *Biographical Dictionary of Irishmen in France* [Dublin, 1949], 196-7; Madgett to TJ, 10 Sep. 1805). A letter from Madgett to TJ dated 9 Apr. 1799 from Columbia, received 20 June, and TJ's reply of 26 June 1799 are recorded in SJL, but have not been found.

TELLESCOPE OF DOLLANDS: makers of optical and scientific instruments, the Dollond family of London was renowned for its high-quality telescopes (DNB; Vol. 25:352; Vol. 34:272).

To Samuel Smith

DEAR SIR   Washington Mar. 5. 1802.

This is meant merely as a private suggestion to hasten the proceedings of the committee on Indian affairs of which you are chairman. the act regulating intercourse with the Indians expired the day before yesterday. in the mean time we are told the Govr. of E. Florida is preparing to enlist men in Georgia for an expedition against the Creeks. should the interval between the expiration & renewal of the act protect from punishment such citizens as shall join in attacking the Creeks, these people will not be easily made to comprehend this legal nicety. the shorter therefore the interval is, the less time will be uncovered by the law, & the less chance of offenders escaping by the accident. the Indians are so sore on our not punishing offenders against them, that I am anxious to guard against it. on this ground you will be so good as to pardon my suggesting your attention to the speedy revival of this act. health and affectionate salutations

TH: JEFFERSON

PrC (DLC); at foot of text: "Genl. S. Smith."

On 7 Jan., after Smith presented a memorial of the Society of Friends' Baltimore yearly meeting about Indian affairs, the House of Representatives made him, Roger Griswold, Thomas T. Davis, William Hoge, and John Randolph a COMMITTEE to consider the subject. The ACT REGULATING INTERCOURSE WITH THE INDIANS was that of 3 Mch. 1799 (JHR, 4:34; Vol. 36:278-9; TJ to the Senate and the House of Representatives, 27 Jan.).

To Henry Voigt

Sir Washington Mar. 5. 1802.

I recieved my watch by Doctr. Logan, sealed up as you had delivered her. but on winding up the striking part in his presence, it clattered away until it run down, and so does as often as it is tried. I have therefore got the favor of mr Duane to take her back to you. he will be in Philadelphia some days, so that if you put her to rights immediately you may have time to see that she continues right.

I have desired mr John Barnes of this place, who acts for me in all money matters to order paiment to you in Philadelphia of 16. Dollars for the 4. medals, and of your bill for the repairs of the watch, the amount of which you will be so good as to state to mr Barnes's correspondent who will call on you. Accept my best wishes.

Th: Jefferson

PrC (MHi); at foot of text: "Mr. Henry Voigt"; endorsed by TJ in ink on verso.

For previous correspondence regarding TJ's watch and medals, see Vol. 36:239-40, 386, 565-6.

From Simon Chaudron and John James Barralet

Monsieur Philaie. 6 mars 1802

Nous vous prions d'accueillir favorablement Lhommage de L'Apothéose de Washington, que nous prenons la liberté de vous offrir.

Si c'est le patrimoine des arts que le privilège de célébrer les grands hommes, cest aussi le privilège des grands hommes, que de reçevoir les offrandes des arts

nous Sommes avec un profond Respect Monsieur Vos trés humbles & trés obeissants serviteurs Chaudron & Baralet

EDITORS' TRANSLATION

Sir Phila. 6 Mch. 1802

We beg you to receive favorably the tribute of the "Apotheosis of Washington," which we take the liberty of presenting to you.

If the heritage of the arts is the privilege of celebrating great men, it is also the privilege of great men to receive the offerings of the arts.

We are with deep respect your very humble and very obedient servants

Chaudron & Baralet

RC (MHi); in Chaudron's hand and signed by him; endorsed by TJ as received 19 Mch. from Philadelphia and so recorded in SJL.

L'APOTHÉOSE DE WASHINGTON: in 1800, Chaudron and Barralet opened subscriptions to publish an engraving of Barralet's "Apotheosis of Washington." Soon after TJ's inauguration, Barralet asked permission to place the new president's name "at the head of the Subscription list" at no charge. There is no record of a response by TJ, who had purchased a drawing of Volney by Barralet. In February 1802, Chaudron began to take out newspaper advertisements to inform subscribers that they could pick up the "Apotheosis," which was 24 inches tall and 19 inches wide, at his watch and jewelry shop in Philadelphia (*Philadelphia Gazette & Daily Advertiser*, 8 Feb. 1802; *Aurora*, 8 Feb.; Vol. 32:320n, 420; Vol. 33:316).

From Thomas Mann Randolph

DEAR SIR,   Edgehill March 6. 1802

I communicate to you early a plan I have formed for the more profitable employment of my Slaves, lest coming to you by report you might suppose the removal was meant to extend to my family allso. I have conceived a design of procuring land in the Mississippi territory & removing all my Slaves thither to establish a large Cotton plantation which I shall conduct by well selected agents from Virginia with my own personal inspection at least once in two years, while my health will permitt. The hope of executing this scheme the approaching Autumn has made me divulge it now that the Slaves may have their minds prepared: it is absolutely necessary even to suffer them to believe that the whole family may come after two crops have been made with which view the children are encouraged to talk of it and the neighbours permitted to believe that emigration is our design. Yourself and Martha only know the whole scheme & to no other will it ever be divulged. It is with reluctance we permitt this little deception but we must, for the scheme absolutely hangs upon it: my slaves are willing to accompany me any where but they know well I should be little with them while the family is at a distance & they set much value upon my presence: besides their attachment to Martha would make their departure very heavy unless they had a belief that she was to follow at some time. I need not trouble you with a statement of the reasons which have induced me to determine on this step as they are certainly all obvious to you. You know that our lands yield a good & sure interest now by rent: that the preservation of them is more certain under a tenant well restricted than under an Overseer who will either reject all restraint or use it as an excuse for making no profit. You know the risk of loss from large slave establishments after the

West India manner at this day in Virginia, and the little hope of profit from the culture of Tobacco now; with the certainty of immense gain from that of Cotton. You know that the oeconomic husbandry now necessarily introducing here from the multiplicity of objects it embraces; animals of various kinds, grapes grains, roots, manures, various & complicated instruments, geometric methods; cannot be successfully pursued by means of Slaves (who tho admirable for labor are little worth for Care & judgement,) unless upon a very small scale and when the person feeling the first interest joins in the daily business of the farm. You know that a climate without winter suits the constitution of Negroes and have heard that the Culture of Cotton is the least laborious of any ever practiced, never occasioning great fatigue & leaving abundant time for the raising provisions of every kind & all works for the Comfort of the laborers. Mere calculation, however alluring the result, could never have influenced me against my feelings: instead of suffering those to be blunted by dreams of Wealth I have encouraged my fancy to irritate & quicken them yet they join with cool reasoning to determine me on this step: they urge me strongly to remove these persons, whose happiness fortune has thrown upon my will, to a mild climate & gentle labor, with all their connexions I do or can in any way command rather than to keep them at extreme hard labor & great exposure[1] here or to trust them to the mercy of Strangers, wholly without power, or very little & only at times within my control. The same feelings will induce me to accompany them in their journey and impell me to visit them often enough to ensure their ease & comfort.—The first affections of my heart will be tortured by the disposal of my person this plan for a time commands but the greatness of the end will give me patience: the prospect it affords of puting within my power the means of executing the first wishes I have; to endow two sisters and to be prepared to give my Son the most complete education by attending institutions of learning and traveling abroad. Preparatory to the step I mean to take I have been leasing lands in Henrico & Bedford & albemarle upon safe agreements as to their preservation. My rents, including a small portion pay'le. in kind, allready come very near 1200$. yet my slaves work to greater advantage this year than they have ever done being employed upon chosen spots. I am detained by the scheme of disposing by lottery of part of my property in N'o. Milton which will be executed at our District Court in april: not so advantageously I fear as I expected for the Rivanna has not been navigable at all since you left Albemarle. That done I shall set out immediately for the Natchez through Tenessee. I shall not remain there for any consideration later than the middle of July. If I can procure land I shall move all my Slaves out except a few chosen domestics on the 1st. day of November next.—We are in good health all. The children all declared at once they could not leave Grandpapa when asked if they would go to the Mississippi.—You will oblige me greatly by any information you have or can get which may be of service to me in my scheme.

with most affectionate & constant attachment yr. &c

TH: M. RANDOLPH

RC (MHi); endorsed by TJ as received 10 Mch. and so recorded in SJL.

[1] Preceding two words and ampersand interlined.

From Abishai Thomas

Saturday March 6th [1802]

For the information of the President A. Thomas, in the absence of the Secretary of the Navy, has the honor to enclose to him a Letter receiv'd this morning from Com. Truxton, containing the pleasing intelligence that the Beef & Pork ordered for the Chesapeake about the safety of which some apprehensions were entertained has safely arrived.

RC (DLC); partially dated; addressed: "President United States"; endorsed by TJ as received from the Navy Department on 6 Mch. and so recorded in SJL. Enclosure not found.

On 5 Mch., Thomas had written Commodore Thomas Truxtun (TRUXTON) to acknowledge receipt of Truxtun's letter of 20 Feb. and to express surprise that the beef and pork ordered for the frigate CHESAPEAKE at Norfolk had not yet arrived, especially since several agents had informed the department that shipments of those provisions were made some time ago. Thomas also informed Truxtun that the secretary of the navy, Robert Smith, was in Baltimore and was expected to return to Washington "on Monday next." If the supplies had not arrived by then, Thomas presumed that Smith would direct the agent at Norfolk, William Pennock, to make up the deficiency (FC in Lb in DNA: RG 45, LSO).

From Elizabeth House Trist

Birdwood 6th. March 1802

The inclosed letter for Mr. Hawkins, I beg the favor of you to direct and forward. tis to be sure a liberty that few wou'd take with the President but I cannot forget or lose in that exalted Station My friend Mr. Jefferson my excuse for troubleing you, is the insecurity of conveyence to that quarter since I have been in this Country I have written twice which I have reason to think were never received nor have I even recd. one but *thro you*, when in Phila'd our communications were thro the Department of War but the remoteness of my situation deprived me of that expedient. nor can I willingly forego one of my greatest gratifications the occasional testimonials of being remember by those I love and esteem

I am sorry that your letter to My Son has been made publick thro my inadvertence as it has occasion'd him Mortification he observed to me that it was rather unfortunate that the character of an uncautious communication so contrary to his real disposition shou'd attach itself to him more particularly with regard to a subject which will be made a handle of by the Aristocratic facton if they get hold of, as they leave no Stone unturn'd however small to wreak their vengeance upon a Man whom they consider as having Thwarted their views Sir—As matters stand it wou'd have been better I confess not to have mention'd it. but with submission to my Sons better judgement I can not be persuaded that a circumstance like this were there was no injury meditated against Mr. Steel cou'd effect you or injure you in the opinion of any one so that my mind is tranquil on that score I wish my tongue may never betray me into greater evils—Ere I conclude I must recall to your remembrance my swarthy freind Easton for six months he has been suspended on the tenter hooks of expectation buoyed up with the hope of obtaining the Consular appointment which his friends have already solicited for him he seems almost in despair his letter by the last post excited my Sympathy in so great a degree as to make me miserable, a man possessing noble and generous sentiment under the pressure of adversity with a halpless family to support has a claim at least to my commiseration He is apprehensive that some one has prejudiced you against him, he has been inform'd that Mr Madison was not his friend but from what cause he knew not unless it is his Politicks. which he says are litterally his own and never gave offence to any Soul even when party Spirit was at the highest his liberallity never allowd him to condemn any man for thinking differently from him self. the delay of his application or rather answer to it, considerably added to his embarrasments the loss of time together with the expence will be seriously felt what ever may be the Issue Tis said that Mr Isnardi gaind his appointment by teazing and the most Officious perseverence—I have long been of opinion that a Man diffident of him self has little chance of being notice'd unless his talants are transcendently conspicuous or his friends of importance in the Political world—I have often regreted my want of talant as well as repugnance to solicitation in behalf of my friends, if

I cou'd Serve a worthy character why shou'd pride or diffidence repulse the best emotions of my heart—In this instance I supposed Mr E cou'd not want friends to recall him to your remembrance or shou'd I believe have been more troublesome to you however painful, for I am convinced you have sufficient to attend to without being teazed by my uninteresting scrbble permit me my Good Sir to reiterate my wishes for Mr Eastons promotion and if not practicable to relieve him from a state of suspence and be assured of my most sincere Respect Gratitude and Friendship   E TRIST

RC (NcU: Nicholas P. Trist Papers); addressed: "The President of the U. States Washington"; franked; endorsed by TJ as received 10 Mch. and so recorded in SJL. Enclosure not identified.

YOUR LETTER TO MY SON: in a letter to Hore Browse Trist of 17 Jan. 1802, TJ mistakenly reported the death of John Steele and invited the young Trist to consider accepting the office of secretary of the Mississippi Territory in Steele's place (Vol. 36:389).

On 5 Nov. 1801, Elizabeth Trist wrote TJ a letter introducing David EASTON, whom she had previously recommended for a CONSULAR APPOINTMENT (NcU: Nicholas P. Trist Papers; Vol. 35:82, 500). On 15 May 1802, TJ issued a commission for Easton to be U.S. commercial agent at Martinico (FC in Lb in DNA: RG 59, PTCC).

From John Archer

SIR,   City of Washington March 7th 1802

Should there be any Vacancy by Death, Resignation or otherwise of any of the Secretaries to any of the Legations to Europe, I would beg leave to mention to your Consideration Dr: John Archer Jun. He is a young Man about 25 Years of Age, whom I do recommend as a Man of Sobriety, Integrity and Industry

I am with the greatest Respect Your very Hble Servt

JOHN ARCHER

RC (DNA: RG 59, LAR); endorsed by TJ as a letter of 7 Mch. and "Dr. John Archer junr. to be Secretary legn" and so recorded in SJL but as a letter of 6 Mch. received 7 Mch.

John Archer (1741-1810) of Harford County, Maryland, graduated from the College of New Jersey in 1760 and in 1768 received from the College of Philadelphia the first medical diploma issued in America. He served as a major in the Continental Army during the Revolutionary War and was elected a Republican congressman from Maryland for the Seventh, Eighth, and Ninth Congresses. Four of his ten children, including his son John, became doctors (*Biog. Dir. Cong.*; Papenfuse, *Maryland Legislature*, 1:107-8).

From Abraham Baldwin

ABR BALDWIN TO THE PRESIDENT
OF THE UNITED STATES   March 7th 1802

It is most probable W Hobby is the author of the piece, he lives at that place and is supposed to write much for the Herald. In my former letter on that subject, I suggested there might be some foundation for such remarks, that I considered the question clearly confined to the three, of these, two had been reputed ancient whigs but modern tories, the other a uniform modern whig but not entirely free from imputation on the other head.

RC (DLC); endorsed by TJ as received 8 Mch. and so recorded in SJL but as a letter of 8 Mch.

William J. HOBBY was a leading Federalist in upcountry Georgia and reputed to be the unofficial editor of the *Augusta Herald*. Gideon Granger had removed him as postmaster at Augusta in January 1802 (George R. Lamplugh, *Politics on the Periphery, Factions and Parties in Georgia, 1783-1806* [Newark, Del., 1986], 151, 169-70; Vol. 34:594-5).

THE PIECE: on 27 Feb. 1802, the *Washington Federalist* reprinted an anonymous letter to the president that first appeared in the *Augusta Herald* on 10 Feb. Signed "A Citizen," the letter criticized TJ for the inconsistency of his removal and appointment policies, specifically citing his choice of William Stephens as U.S. district judge for Georgia. The author pointed out that Stephens had accepted British protection during the Revolutionary War and had appeared in the state's postwar confiscation and amercement lists. "Do you mean sir, to begin your career with such men," asked the author. "Can you expect no cordial cooperation, but from men of this character, have you lost all confidence in the American Revolutionary citizens?" When former Tories like Stephens are appointed in place of Revolutionary War veterans, "what are the citizens of America to expect from such an administration?" (Lamplugh, *Politics on the Periphery*, 170, 179).

MY FORMER LETTER ON THAT SUBJECT: Baldwin to TJ, 1 May 1801, in which Baldwin had recommended Stephens, George Walton, and Matthew McAllister as suitable candidates for judicial appointments in Georgia.

To William C. C. Claiborne

DEAR SIR   Washington Mar. 7. 1802.

I ask the favor of you to deliver the inclosed letters to the President of the Council & Speaker of the H. of Representatives of the Missisipi territory. they contain answers to the resolutions they were pleased to forward to me. I am gratified by their testimony to the world that I have done right in refusing to continue Governor Sargeant. as to his statement of the conversation between him and myself, the advantage is entirely on his side, because I cannot enter into controversy with an individual. it is certainly very different from what I should have given as the sum of what passed between us. certainly he has[1] made me tell him falsehoods which were useless & without an object. the world must judge between us. the error into which I ran was not the saying any thing untrue to him, but the avoiding to speak truths which would have hurt his feelings, which I wished to spare. for this tenderness I have my reward. Accept assurances of my high esteem & consideration.   TH: JEFFERSON

PrC (DLC); at foot of text: "Governor Claiborne." Enclosures: TJ to the Mississippi Territory General Assembly, 2 Mch. 1802.

Winthrop Sargent's STATEMENT OF THE CONVERSATION between himself and TJ of 1 June 1801 appeared in his pamphlet, *Political Intolerance, or The Violence of Party Spirit.* In it, Sargent avowed that TJ had assured him that, in his view, nothing dishonorable had been attached to Sargent's character, and that he would have "ample opportunity to make his representations" regarding his conduct as governor of Mississippi before an appointment to that office would be made. However, TJ had already appointed Claiborne to the governor's office on 25 May (Winthrop Sargent, *Political Intolerance, or The Violence of Party Spirit; Exemplified in a Recent Removal from Office: With a Comment upon Executive Conduct, and an Ample Refutation of Calumny; in a Sketch of the Services and Sacrifices, of a Dismissed Officer* by "One of the American People" [Boston, 1801], 31-2; Vol. 33:671, 675; Vol. 35:501-2).

[1] TJ here canceled "put into my mouth."

To Anne Cary Randolph, Thomas Jefferson Randolph, and Ellen Wayles Randolph

MY DEAR CHILDREN   Washington Mar. 7. 1802.

I am very happy to find that two of you can write. I shall now expect that whenever it is inconvenient for your papa & mama to write, one of you will write on a piece of paper these words 'all is well' and send it for me to the post office. I am happy too that miss Ellen can now read so readily. if she will make haste and read through all the books I have given her, and will let me know when she is through them, I will go and carry her some more. I shall now see whether she wishes to see me as much as she says. I wish to see you all: and the more I perceive that you are all advancing in your learning and improving in good dispositions the more I shall love you, & the more every body will love you. it is a charming thing to be loved by every body: and the way to obtain it is, never to quarrel or be angry with any body, never to tell a story, do all the kind things you can to your companions, give them every thing rather than to yourself, pity &

help every thing you see in distress and learn your books and improve your minds. this will make every body fond of you, and desirous of shewing it to you: go on then my dear children, and, when we meet at Monticello, let me see who has improved most. I kiss this paper for each of you; it will therefore deliver the kisses to yourselves, and two over, which one of you must deliver to your Mama for me; and present my affectionate attachment to your papa. to yourselves love and Adieux.   TH: JEFFERSON

PrC (MHi); at foot of text: "Anne Th. Jefferson Eleanor," connected by TJ with a brace with "Jefferson" written at the point; in ink TJ later canceled "Jefferson" and wrote "Randolph"; endorsed by TJ in ink on verso.

TWO OF YOU CAN WRITE: TJ received his first letters from Anne Cary and Thomas Jefferson Randolph on 3 Mch. They are printed at 26 Feb. TJ's first letter from his granddaughter Ellen, written with the help of her mother, is printed at 10 Nov. 1801 (Vol. 35:589; Vol. 36:743-4; Martha Jefferson Randolph to TJ, 16 Apr. 1802).

From Joseph H. Nicholson

SIR   March 8. 1802

I beg Leave to enclose you a Petition from John D: Thompson of Cecil County, who it appears has been indicted for not returning the Enumeration of the Inhabitants of that County within the Time limited by Law, and wishes to have the Prosecution dismissed. I know nothing of the Merits of his Case, but send you a Letter from Mr. David, a Member of the Executive Council of Maryland, who I am well acquainted with, and who I am persuaded would not state any thing as a fact which he did not know to be true.

It has been said that the Census of Cecil County was badly taken; and this perhaps may be the Fact; but it is, certainly, a Fact which could not be ascertained without going into a second Enumeration, and is not the Offence for which he has been indicted. I do[...] whether any Injury has arisen from the Delay, [...] respectfully, to offer an Opinion that the Relief asked for might be granted without Impropriety; more particularly as I believe the Party to be a very poor Man—

I have the Honor to be Sir, with high Consideration Yr. Ob: Hble Servt   JOSEPH H. NICHOLSON

RC (DNA: RG 59, GPR); torn; endorsed by TJ as received 8 Mch. from Washington and so recorded in SJL; also endorsed by TJ: "Thompson John D." and "to lie till trial." Enclosure: Petition of John D. Thompson, 5 Mch. 1802, responding to his indictment in Maryland district court for delinquent submission of Cecil County census returns and requesting a nolle prosequi, explaining that his family's sickness prevented him from making the return to the Maryland marshal before 15 July 1801 (RC in same; in a clerk's hand, signed and dated by Thompson; at head of text: "Thomas Jefferson President of the United States"; attested by Samuel Briscoe, justice of the peace for Cecil County, and certified by John Baxter, clerk, on 5 Mch.); and accompanied by a statement of attending physician John King that Thompson was confined to his house and unable to attend to business from 3 Oct. to 5 Nov. 1800 and for ten days in Feb. 1801 (MS in same; in a clerk's hand, signed by King; attested and certified on 5 Mch.). Other enclosure not found.

From James Walter

ESTEEMED FRIEND,   Philada. 3 mo 8th. 1802

Not having any personal acquaintance with thee, it is with extreme reluctance I thus address the Man whose eminent abilities has raised him to be head of the American Republic—

But having lately purchased a tract of Land in Randolph County Virginia on which as I am inform'd is an elegant scite for a town, which I propose laying out the ensuing summer—I so far request thy patronage as to be permitted to call it "Jefferson," conscious at the same time that posterity will duly appreciate the merits of a Washington and a Jefferson without the feeble aid of Cities and towns to commemorate their illustrious names—

Being one of the descendants of Penn I am unused to the Courtly style of sycophants, and which (if I am not deceiv'd in thy Character) is more dissonant in thy ear than unadorned truth—Accept this as an apology—

With every sentiment of respect I am thy well wisher

JAS. WALTER

If thee should condescend to favour me with an answer, please direct to No. 41 Almond St.

RC (MoSHi: Jefferson Papers); above postscript: "To Thomas Jefferson President of the U.S."; endorsed by TJ as a letter of 3 Mch. received 12 Mch. and so recorded in SJL.

A James Walter, schoolmaster and teacher, lived on Second Street in Philadelphia. In 1801, James Browne, merchant, resided at 41 Almond Street (Stafford, *Philadelphia Directory, for 1801*, 157, 168; Robinson, *Philadelphia Directory for 1803*, 263).

Memorandum from Albert Gallatin on Nominations

[9 Mch. 1802]

Edward Croft of S. Carolina Commissioner of the first division in the State of South Carolina for executing the Act entitled an Act to provide for the valuation of lands & dwelling houses & the enumeration of slaves within the United States

Nathaniel Folsom of New Hampshire—Naval officer for the district of Portsmouth

Andrew Lyle of New Jersey—Surveyor for the port of New Brunswick in the district of Perth Amboy—vice Anthony Walton White resigned—

A. G.

Note—Have the appointments[1] of Benjamin Forsyth as Master & of Thomas Allen as Mate of the Revenue Cutter taken place?

MS (DLC); undated; entirely in Gallatin's hand; endorsed by TJ as received from the Treasury Department on 9 Mch. and "Nominations" and so recorded in SJL.

For the appointment of EDWARD CROFT, see Vol. 36:625-6. For Woodbury Langdon's recommendation of NATHANIEL FOLSOM, see Vol. 35:601.

On 8 Mch., John Condit sent Gallatin a letter noting that he and his New Jersey colleagues in the House of Representatives were recommending ANDREW LYLE as surveyor of the customs at New Brunswick. Condit enclosed a letter he had received from Phineas Manning, who described Lyle as a firm Republican and man of business who was serving his second term as sheriff of Middlesex County, having won election the first time "by A handsome Majority" against a Federalist "when the Remainder of the ticket faild by a large Majority" (RC in DNA: RG 59, LAR; endorsed by TJ: "Lyle Andrew. N.J. to be Surveyor of the customs at Brunswick N.J."). TJ received the resignation of ANTHONY WALTON WHITE during the summer of 1801 (Vol. 35:84, 86n).

[1] Word interlined in place of "nominations."

To the Senate

GENTLEMEN OF THE SENATE

The Governor of New York has desired that in addition to the negociations with certain Indians already authorised under the superintendance of John Taylor, further negociations should be held with the Oneidas and other members of the confederacy of the 6. nations for the purchase of lands in, & for, the state of New York, which they are willing to sell, as explained in the letter from the Secretary at War herewith sent. I have therefore thought it better to name a Commissioner[1] to superintend the negociations specified, with the six nations generally, or with any of them.

I do accordingly nominate John Taylor of New York to be[2] Commissioner for the US. to hold a convention or conventions between the state of New York and the confederacy of the six nations of Indians, or any of the nations composing it.

This nomination, if advised & consented to by the Senate, will comprehend and supercede that of Feb. 1. of the same John Taylor, so far as it respected the Seneca Indians.   TH: JEFFERSON
Mar. 9. 1802.

RC (DNA: RG 46, EPEN, 7th Cong., 1st sess.); endorsed by Senate clerks. PrC (DLC). Recorded in SJL with notation "Taylor to hold convention betw. N.Y. & 6. nations." Enclosure: Henry Dearborn to TJ, 5 Mch.

COMMISSIONER: Meriwether Lewis delivered this message to the Senate on 10 Mch. The Senate approved the nomination the following day (JEP, 1:408, 409).

For the earlier appointment of John Tayler to represent the U.S. at negotiations with the Seneca and St. Regis Indians, see Henry Dearborn to TJ, 8 Jan. 1802, and TJ to the Senate, 1 Feb. 1802.

[1] Preceding two words interlined in place of "an Agent."
[2] Preceding two words written over an erased word, "agent."

From Robert Smith

SIR,   Navy department. 9 March 1802.

I have the honor to request your signature to the enclosed warrants for —

Daniel Eldridge   Sailing Master.
James Watson   Boatswain.
Robert Myers   Carpenter.

With much respect yr mo: ob: servt.   RT SMITH

RC (DLC); in a clerk's hand, signed by Smith; at foot of text: "the President"; endorsed by TJ as received from the Navy Department on 10 Mch. and "Nominations" and so recorded in SJL. FC (Lb in DNA: RG 45, LSP).

DANIEL ELDRIDGE, JAMES WATSON, and ROBERT MYERS were all assigned to the frigate *Chesapeake* (NDBW, *Register*, 17-18, 39, 58).

From Samuel Smith

SIR/   Tuesday [9 Mch. 1802]

I do myself the Honor to return you Mr. Coxe's Opinions—there are some Ideas, that I think useful which I have Communicated to Mr. Randolph as Chairman of the Ways & Means.—I have the honor be
    your friend & servt.   S. SMITH

RC (DLC); partially dated; address clipped: "The Preside"; endorsed by TJ as a letter of 9 Mch. Enclosures: see below.

COXE'S OPINIONS: although they were marked private, TJ may have shared Tench Coxe's letters dated 22 Feb. and 1 Mch. with Smith. Coxe advocated the establishment of commercial relations with China and a reduction in U.S. dependance on trade with Great Britain. He sought a system based on reciprocity, a principle supported by Smith, who also advocated reducing taxes on trade to increase commerce and foster prosperity. A revision of tax policy, however, would require cooperation with John RANDOLPH, chair of the Committee of Ways and Means (Frank A. Cassell, *Merchant Congressman in the Young Republic: Samuel Smith of Maryland, 1752-1839* [Madison, Wis., 1971], 113-14; Cooke, *Coxe*, 401-3). For the tension that existed between Smith, who chaired the Committee on Commerce and Manufactures, and Randolph, see Cassell, *Merchant Congressman*, 113-16.

From Tench Coxe

SIR   [before 10 Mch. 1802]

The recent events in the Island of St. Domingo, if confirmed, will evince the importance to *consumption* and *revenue* of the plan of promoting the sugar, coffee, and cocoa cultivation in China, and other yet independent asiatic states particularly the first. My best documents show that St. Domingo in 1790—yielded

of white & brown sugar above   140. millions of pound [wt.]
of coffee   77   do.
of cotton   7   do.
of cocoa—much, uncertain—Molasses 3 to 4,000,000 Gs.
of indigo   0.750,000 lbs

If the noble sugar estates in the plain of the Cape are destroyed & elsewhere, provisions burnt in the towns, the negroes and army, no intercourse with them who alone raise the produce, the old planters cut off, a french army eating up every thing that can be raised for them, this great resource of ours must be cut off. It[1] restoration, if the accounts are true, must be a work of no short time. The fate of Martinico is not certain: That of Guadaloupe probably unfavorable. The

Corsicans, the Charibs, & the Jamaica Mountain Negroes long embarrassed the french and english. It is in every view our interest to propagate the cultivation of Sugar, coffee, cocoa, ginger, pimento & molasses, in Asia. We want those articles, and we ought to endeavour by them covertly to lead from the cultivation of cotton, indigo & rice—as also tobacco.

The same ideas which have been thrown out in regard to China might be considered in reference to a guarded Communication of the same Nature with Turkish Government, whose southern territories are capable of producing sugars, coffee &ca. in great quantities. There we must expect European Jealousy and intrigue to incommode us. The Turks could injure us much in rice, indigo, cotton & tobacco, wherefore we had better take their silken manufactures, sugars, coffee, cocoa, ginger, pimento, and ivories, or set them on producing such as they do not and can produce. There are various practicable means of intercourse. Correspondence between chief Magistrate and chief Magistrate, between Minister & Minister, & between consuls and commercial officers, and permanent or occasional envoys—Œconomy might often be well consulted by correspondence. The mercantile part of foreign intercourse is chiefly by correspondence, and the political part admits of it. It is novel for governments to correspond, but it is respectfully submitted whether the novelty is not worthy of consideration. The Chinese case probably would force the adoption of that mode, as they are so jealous of foreign eyes. Were the Emperor of China, or of the Turks to transmit to this Government a number of cases of genuine, plain, well ordered specimens of the various foreign merchandizes in their markets and used and consumed by their people, it would be a curious and interesting exhibition. But were they to add true, clear, and perfect information on those and other necessary commercial subjects, it would be considered as polite, friendly and useful. We have no E. India Company or Turkey Company to do these things. Our government must be the powerful friend of trade and derive the eulogies and honors, which that class of men, who carry on trade confer upon their benefactors. The feelings & interests of the planters would also be affected by procuring sure and new wants for the productions and new and cheap supplies.

It is not without apprehension that the trouble of perusing such communications as these has been given but the motives and the prospect of utility have been relied on as excuses or palliatives—

Two more ideas will be respectfully hazarded. The Bahamas are among our worst privateering enemies in war—So are the Bermudas—Cotton is a principal article of produce in the former, which raised near 1,200.000 lbs. ten years ago. This is 300,000 Dollars at 25 cents. Bermuda is supposed to raise some cotton. It is of some consequence among our inducements to raise Cotton, that those Islands contain the most noxious privateersmen, not to say ps. that gall the fair American commerce. It is our interest that their prosperity as colonies should decline—

The other idea relates to the true state of things in the Island & colony of Cape Breton. It is conceived that providence has given to the people of these States the vast bodies of fossil fuel on & near it for their use. Treaty, war, or other circumstances must give us, one day, the Isld. of Cape Breton—The crumbling of empires has occurred— It is respectfully suggested, on this paper only, that it may be worth while to have a visit paid to such a place—an agent—a respectable and intelligent traveller making the tour of the Northern British colonies could make the requisite observations—This is a very long reflected Idea—I have the honor to be Sir, your respectful & mo. obedt. st.

RC (DNA: RG 59, LAR); undated; addressed: "Mr Jefferson" and "Private"; endorsed by TJ as received from Tench Coxe on 10 Mch. and so recorded in SJL.

FRENCH ARMY EATING UP EVERY THING: the French expeditionary force sent to reassert control over Saint-Domingue reached the island in late January 1802 (see Charles Pinckney to TJ, 6 Oct. 1801). For TJ's views on how the French forces in Saint-Domingue would impact U.S. trade with the island, see TJ to John Wayles Eppes, 1 Jan. 1802.

[1] Thus in MS.

From "A Lover of his Country"

SIR   Petersburg Va. March 10th. 1802

Excuse the Boldness of a Youth, who dares to write to the Chief Magistrate of his Country in the manner in which every *Lover of America* ought. Excuse me when I tell you I never had a *good* Opinion of You before I saw your inaugural Speech, then I entertained the most *sanguine* expectations, I should by *your* Means see this Country rise higher in Distinction & see you honoured, revered and beloved by all people; but alas! how are my Hopes blasted? the federal Republicans are exasperated at some part of your Behaviour, in the first place for turning all the Officers out of Place and appointing new Ones, a thing which *you yourself blamed* in Mr. Adams, secondly by giving One Man more than one lucrative Office, *for Instance the Collector of New Haven Port*, which you likewise *censured* in Mr. Adams, and numberless other Things which hurt the Feelings of every good Man and degrades the Character of America   All these Harms I could have supported without murmuring, had not the *Constitution* which was framed by our forefathers, and which was acknowledged by all Nations to be one of the best in the Known World; I say had not that *Constitution* been destroyed by a herd of *Fiends*, (a Title which is almost to good for the *Wretches*) who have nothing in View but *their own private* Interest and the *total* Abolition of our *Liberty*.   I endeavour to banish Fear, but I do fear, that, Alas! other Nations seeing *our own* Countrymen destroying our *Liberty*, will join with them and utterly abolish the *small Spark* of Religion & Liberty, which is still remaining.

By the God that made us, by every thing that is holy I beseech You, to endeavour to put a Stop to these proceedings, consider that people who have some Regard for Religion, Liberty and good Order, cannot and will not be content with Proceedings—every Step of which seems to *confirm* our Belief that We are soon to be Slaves, and despised by all. Once more I say, pity the Weakness of a *Youth* of fifteen, do not take what I have said as an Insult, but as the weak endeavours of a person, who has the *Interest* of his Country at Heart.

I suppose you will not do it, but I beseech you, intreat You to let All know by Letter or let the public know what is your opinion with Regard to the State of the United States of America.

With Respect yr. obt. Sert. &c.   A Lover of his Country

NB. If you do write to Me direct your Le[tter] to A.B. Petersburg Virginia

RC (DLC); torn; addressed: "Thomas Jefferson Esqr. President of the U. States City of Washington"; franked; post-marked 13 Mch.; endorsed by TJ as received 19 Mch. and "removals &c" and so recorded in SJL.

For TJ's removal of Elizur Goodrich and appointment of Samuel Bishop as COLLECTOR OF NEW HAVEN PORT, see Vol. 34:381-4, 554-8.

Conference with Handsome Lake, Cornplanter, and Blue Eyes

EDITORIAL NOTE

When Israel Chapin, the U.S. agent to the Iroquois nations, informed the War Department in January 1802 that a delegation of Seneca Indians would be setting off on a visit to Washington, he identified Cornplanter as the head of the group. Similarly, when newspapers, which took little notice of the deputation, mentioned its passage through Pittsburgh, they described the group as consisting of "Cornplanter, with several other Indians." Cornplanter had visited the seat of government before, traveling to New York City during the Confederation period and to Philadelphia during George Washington's presidency. He had also been an active ally of the United States, going to the Ohio country at the request of Washington's secretary of war, Henry Knox, in an unsuccessful attempt to persuade the Shawnees and other western tribes to lay down their arms. In 1791, Knox described Cornplanter as "our friend" (Chapin to secretary of war, 17 Jan. 1802, recorded in DNA: RG 107, RLRMS; New York *Spectator*, 17 Mch.; Catskill, N.Y., *Western Constellation*, 29 Mch.; ANB; Vol. 20:122, 125-7; Vol. 23:242).

Yet, as the documents printed below make clear, it was not Cornplanter but his older half-brother, Handsome Lake, who took the lead role in the Seneca delegation's meetings with Jefferson and Henry Dearborn in Washington in March 1802. Although Handsome Lake was a league chief—a member of the council of the Six Nations confederacy—and had attended treaty negotiations in New York State, he did not have a relationship with the U.S. government as his better-known brother did. Within Seneca society, however, Handsome Lake had begun to assume an influential role, one founded on revelatory visions he experienced during trancelike episodes in 1799 and 1800. A council of the Seneca nation in June 1801 named him "High Priest, and principal Sachem in all things Civil and Religious" (Wallace, *Death and Rebirth*, 260; ANB).

[29]

With his revelations, he offered his tribe the prospect of a renaissance. The Senecas, like many other American Indian tribes, experienced great changes during the second half of the eighteenth century. The military strength and diplomatic influence inherent to the earlier Iroquois league were largely gone after the American Revolution. By the opening of the nineteenth century, the Senecas had given up millions of acres of land, a portion of the tribe had moved to Canada, and most of those who remained in the United States lived on a scattering of reservations in western New York and northwestern Pennsylvania. They had yet to reconcile their altered society and economy with the cultural and other pressures presented by the new United States. Handsome Lake's revelations aimed at the retention and revitalization of some traditional ways and beliefs, but also contended with newer challenges such as alcoholism. He promoted temperance and the adoption of the agricultural economy, farming utensils, and technological changes that Quaker missionaries and the United States government advocated, but his visions reaffirmed Seneca religious observances rather than embracing Christianity. With time, what became known as the Code of Handsome Lake was adopted by many Senecas, spread to other Native American groups, and became the foundation of an enduring devotional practice known as the Longhouse religion (Wallace, *Death and Rebirth*, 111, 149-50, 303-18; Sturtevant, *Handbook*, 15:319, 442-8, 452-4, 496; Vol. 35:695-6).

Yet in the early years of the nineteenth century, the Senecas, like other Indian nations, were divided over such issues as what relationship to have with the United States, whether to retain or abandon accustomed ways of life, and how best to respond to changing circumstances. Cornplanter and Handsome Lake were members of the Allegany Seneca, a group that lived on reservation lands on the upper Allegheny River below the Pennsylvania-New York boundary. The two brothers had different fathers but the same mother, a woman named Gahhononeh, and through her, they belonged to a clan that was prominent in the leadership of the Allegany Seneca. When Handsome Lake experienced his first vision in 1799, Cornplanter took on the role of explaining the revelations and promoting his brother's revitalization movement. Their nephew Red Jacket, another charismatic leader, lived on the Buffalo Creek reservation in New York State. Red Jacket was the principal speaker of the Senecas' central council and had his own opinions about cooperation with the United States. Initially he resisted assimilation, but in November 1801, he asked the U.S. government for assistance in the adoption of agricultural technology and proposed to sell a strip of land along the Niagara River. A few months earlier, Handsome Lake had opened or widened a political rift by opposing the sale of that land. He also charged Red Jacket with witchcraft, accusing him of making a member of Cornplanter's family ill. In November, when Red Jacket announced that the Senecas were "determined in all our Villages to take to husbandry," he asked the government for four "pair of cattle" for the Buffalo Creek reservation, two pairs for the Tonawanda reservation, and "some" for the Allegany and Cattaraugus Creek reservations. It was in that political context, with the Allegany and Buffalo Creek groups in contention, that Handsome Lake and Cornplanter journeyed to Washington in 1802 (Wallace, *Death and*

Rebirth, 204-5, 242, 247, 248, 259-60, 265, 285, 289-91; Granville Ganter, ed., *The Collected Speeches of Sagoyewatha, or Red Jacket* [Syracuse, N.Y., 2006], xxxiv, 110-11, 116; ANB, s.v. "Cornplanter" and "Red Jacket"; Vol. 36:632-5).

An unknown number of Senecas made the trip with them. One who was certainly part of the group was a man called Blue Eyes (Document VI). Handsome Lake mentioned two younger men, his nephew Charles O'Bail and a chief called Strong, but they were not necessarily present (Document I). More than one translator accompanied the party, perhaps Jasper Parrish and Horatio Jones, both of whom had been captured and adopted by Indians while young. On several occasions they translated for the Senecas, who gave each of them a plot of land. Parrish had also accompanied a group of Tuscaroras to the capital early in 1801. Chapin, the agent, wanted to be present during the conference. He did not travel with the Senecas, so if he did attend the meetings he may have gone to Washington directly from his residence at Canandaigua, New York, which was not near the towns of the Allegany Seneca (Saccoreesa to acting secretary of war, 11 Feb. 1801, Dearborn to John Wilkins, Jr., 17 Mch. 1802, and safe-conduct pass, 17 Mch., in DNA: RG 75, LSIA; Chapin to secretary of war, 17 Jan. 1802, DNA: RG 107, RLRMS; Ganter, *Collected Speeches of Sagoyewatha*, 51, 59, 61, 68, 77, 86, 115, 119, 284, 286; Abler, *Cornplanter*, 125).

The Senecas first met with Jefferson and Dearborn on 10 Mch., and it would have been clear from the outset that Handsome Lake, not Cornplanter, was the group's leader on this visit. Meetings with visiting American Indian delegations customarily began with an address by a spokesman, laying out issues of concern (Vol. 34:505-6; Conference with Little Turtle, 4 Jan. 1802; Conference with Black Hoof, 5 Feb. 1802). On this occasion it was Handsome Lake who gave the opening talk and then dominated the Senecas' side of the conference, although Cornplanter and Blue Eyes did make relatively brief addresses during the course of the talks. According to the War Department's record of the conference, Handsome Lake made that opening speech "to the President of the United States." In his reply three days later, Dearborn confirmed that Jefferson had been present on the 10th. The visitors had, Dearborn remarked, taken the president "by the hand" at that first meeting (Documents I and II).

There is no evidence, however, that Jefferson attended the subsequent meetings with the Seneca delegation. When the groups led by Little Turtle and Black Hoof came to Washington in January and February, respectively, the president heard the opening address and was likely present when Dearborn replied for the administration. On each of those occasions, Jefferson prepared a brief direct address to the delegation as an introduction to Dearborn's detailed response. Jefferson did not follow that procedure with Handsome Lake, perhaps to avoid taking sides in an internal political contest among the Senecas. In his address on 10 Mch., Handsome Lake, claiming divine authority through revelation, promoted a cooperative relationship with the United States but condemned the chiefs at Buffalo Creek—meaning, without naming him, Red Jacket (Document I). Yet not long before, Jefferson and Dearborn had responded to the address made by Red Jacket in November, in which the chief committed the Senecas to assimilation, decried the bane of liquor, and brought up specific issues concerning annuities and land. Dearborn had also taken steps to furnish the Senecas with livestock, agricultural technology, and spinning wheels (Vol. 36:632-5). The response to Red Jacket, in the form of a written address sent to the tribe, was in Dearborn's name, not the president's. Now in March, Jefferson may have decided that for him to participate in the reply to the Seneca delegation, as he had done with the other recent Indian deputations, might show favor to the Allegany Senecas and confuse or undermine the relationship with the chiefs at Buffalo Creek who had addressed the government on the tribe's behalf. Dearborn did tell the visitors that the president wanted the Senecas to listen to Handsome Lake and "be governed by his precepts" (Document vii).

In a few months, the government's course of action regarding the split within the Senecas' leadership became clearer. The War Department received information in the spring of 1802 that Red Jacket and two other "principal Chiefs of the Seneca Nation" at Buffalo Creek had committed "a glaring outrage on the laws of the U. States" by breaking into a storehouse to take British goods that had been impounded under the revenue laws. By late August, Jefferson was convinced that Israel Chapin, who by then was no longer the agent to the Iroquois tribes, had been a Federalist partisan who influenced Red Jacket against the administration. When Handsome Lake sent an address to Washington in the fall, Jefferson responded with a long, warm letter in which he stated: "Go on then brother in the great reformation you have undertaken." The president affirmed to Handsome Lake that "in all your enterprises for the good of your people, you may count with confidence on the aid and protection of the United States, and on the sincerity & zeal with which I am myself animated in the furthering of this humane work" (Dearborn to Callender Irvine, 14 June, and to Chapin, same date, in DNA: RG 75, LSIA; TJ to Gallatin, 27 Aug. 1802; TJ to Handsome Lake, 3 Nov. 1802).

On 17 Mch., the final day of the conference, Dearborn signed a pass giving the visitors the protection and aid of the U.S. government as they returned home. Handsome Lake and his companions traveled to Washington and back home by way of Pittsburgh, probably using the Allegheny River for part of the journey. Dearborn gave them $150 for their expenses and instructed Quartermaster General John Wilkins, who was at Pittsburgh, to give them shirts and tools as well as provisions for the last part of the trip. Dearborn handed those instructions to Cornplanter to deliver, probably because Wilkins had entrusted Cornplanter with a letter for the War Department as the Senecas headed to Washington in February. Dearborn made out the pass, however, not for Cornplanter but for Handsome Lake, "with his Interpreters and associates" (Dearborn to John Wilkins, Jr., 17 Mch., and safeconduct pass, 17 Mch., in DNA: RG 75, LSIA; Document vii).

I. Address of Handsome Lake

BROTHER, [10 Mch. 1802]

I thank the Great Spirit above that I have a very bright day to talk with the Great Chief of our White Brothers—It is the Great Spirit's doings he has appointed me for that purpose—The Great Spirit looks down upon us—

The Great Spirit has appointed four Angels and appointed me the fifth, to direct our people on earth—I thank the Great Spirit that the Great Chief of my White brothers is well & Hearty—

This is the third year since the Great Spirit appointed me to guide my people and give them knowledge, good from bad. He directed me to begin with my own people first, and that is the reason why I have been so long in coming to my White Brothers—

I am very much troubled to find that my brothers, and my White Brothers, have gone astray—My brothers are lost because they make too much use of my White brothers Drink but I hope that this the last, and that they will not make use of any more. It is the reason why we do not love like Brothers. I have now come forward to make us love one another again, with your assistance—

Our White Brothers are lost for taking all our Land from us—but the great Spirit has told me to come and tell them of it. If we only step out of our doors, and look round we can see all the little land we have left—and that little we hope, and wish, our White Brothers will give us a writing on paper for it, so that we can hold it fast. If we do not settle all our business that we are now on, the Great Spirit will send a great Sickness among us all—but, if we can settle all our business, health & happiness will come and the seed of the People, and the Fruit will come forward—

Our Lands are decaying because we do not think on the Great Spirit, but we are now going to renew our minds & think on the Great Being who made us all—that when we put our seeds in the Earth they may grow and increase like the leaves on our Trees—

The four Angels appointed with me to direct the People on earth, tell me that if any man whoever he may be will look on the Great Being above us all, and do his will on Earth, when his days are out, and the Angels find he is a good man, they will grant him more Days to live in this world, and if he lives a good man, doing no evil in those days the Angels will grant him more Days—but when those days are out the Great being will take him to himself—

The like of this was never known before—These four Angels empowered me to relieve any man of any sickness whatever it may be, if he be a good man, who looks up to the Great Spirit above—but if he be a bad man and does not look up to the Great being, I cannot relieve him, and he cannot be helped if he be fond of Liquor—

Dear Brother, the Lord has considered your people as well as ours, provided we can settle all our business—He will take care of us first, and you after, if you will take notice of the voice of the Angels—

The four Angels desired me to pick out two young men of my people, that I knew to be sober Good young men to take care of all our public business—they are Charles OBeal—& Strong—

Here is my Brother Captain Cornplanter he is cried down by the Sachems of Buffalo Creek which you very well know but it is not my wish, for I very well know that he has done his endeavour for the benefit of our Nation—He is a sober man, and endeavours to make all our young[1] men sober and good—The Sachems at Buffalo Creek are all drunken men & dislike him—

I who am now talking to you, would wish you to know that half of my Spirit is here on Earth yet, and the other half is with the Great Spirit above—and I wish you to consider my business and my Nation well, that we may continue friends and Brothers—And when that takes place I will be thankful to the Great Chief of my White Brothers—and to the Great Spirit above us all—We will be good friends here and when we will meet with the great Being above we shall have bright and happier Days—

Dear Brother, that is all I have got to say because I know you have got the word of the Great Spirit among you—

FC (Lb in DNA: RG 75, LSIA); in a clerk's hand; date supplied (see Document II); at head of text: "Conyatauyou, or the Handsome Lake, to the President of the United States"; in margin at head of text: "Conference held with the Seneca Deputation."

Handsome Lake (1735?-1815) was a confederation or "league" chief of the Senecas, a hereditary position that made him one of eight men who represented the Senecas in councils of the Six Nations confederation. The name by which he is known, which is spelled "Conyatauyou" in the War Department record of the March 1802 conference and which translates into English as Handsome Lake, was not his given name. It was the title associated with his position as a confederation chief, which he assumed sometime in the 1790s. Earlier, he had been a warrior, participating in battles against the British, the Cherokees, and American settlements from the 1760s to the 1780s. From the 1770s on, he attended important negotiations between the Senecas and the United States and the talks at Big Tree in 1797, where the Senecas conveyed a large quantity of land to Robert Morris. After receiving his revelations in 1799 and 1800, Handsome Lake spent the remainder of his life articulating his prophecies and seeking to consolidate support for his views on revitalization (ANB; Wallace, *Death and Rebirth*, 116, 121, 129, 131, 133, 134, 135, 137, 139, 145-6, 181, 358n; Sturtevant, *Handbook*, 15:425, 428, 429).

In Handsome Lake's visions, ANGELS in the form of Native American men with painted faces and wearing ceremonial garb spoke to him as messengers of the Creator and guided him on spiritual journeys (Wallace, *Death and Rebirth*, 241, 242, 243, 248).

THIS IS THE THIRD YEAR: Handsome Lake began having his revelatory visions in June 1799 (same, 239-42).

CHARLES OBEAL: Charles O'Bail was Cornplanter's son and Handsome Lake's nephew. Charles and his older half-brother Henry—who could read and write, knew some English, and had lived in Philadelphia and New York for a few years—often acted as assistants to their father and uncle. The chief STRONG (also called Captain Strong) was a relative also, a member of the same clan as Handsome Lake and Cornplanter (same, 188, 285, 291, 295; Abler, *Cornplanter*, 155, 162-3, 165, 202).

The SACHEMS OF BUFFALO CREEK included Red Jacket and another political foe of Handsome Lake, Farmer's Brother (Abler, *Cornplanter*, 147).

[1] MS: "yound."

II. Henry Dearborn's Reply

BROTHERS,

Your Father and good Friend the President of the United States has taken into consideration all that you communicated to him when you took him by the hand three days agoe, and he has authorised me to give you the following answer

Brothers,

The President is pleased with seeing you all in so good health after so long a journey and he rejoices in his heart[1] to find that one of your own people has been employed to make you sober good and happy and is so well disposed to give you good council and to set before you such usefull examples—

Brothers,

If you and all the red people follow the advices of your friend and teacher the Handsome Lake, and in future be sober honest industrious, and good, there can be no doubt but the Great Spirit will take care of you and make you all happy—

Brothers,

The Great Council of the sixteen fires, and the President of the United States all wish to live with the red people like brothers, to have no more wars, or disputes, and to pursue such measures as shall most effectually contribute to their lasting comfort—For this purpose the great council of the sixteen fires are now considering the propriety of prohibiting the use of Spiritous liquors amonge all their red Brethren within the United States. This measure if carried into effect will be pleasing in the sight of the Great Being, who delights in the happiness of his common family—

Brothers,

Your Father the President will at all times be your friend, and he will protect you and all his red children from bad people who would do you any injury and he will give you a writing on paper to assure you that what Lands you hold cannot be taken from you by any persons except by your own consent and agreement—

Brothers,

The Handsome Lake has told us that the four Angels have desired him to pick out two sober good young men to take care of your business, and that he has chosen Charles OBeal and Strong for that purpose—

Brothers,

The President is willing that his red children should chuse their own agents for transacting their business, and if Charles OBeal and Strong are the men who your people generally can best confide in, he has no objection to their being appointed but it would be improper for the President to interfere in your National appointments—

Given under my hand and the Seal of the War Office this 13th: March 1802

H. DEARBORN
S of W

FC (Lb in DNA: RG 75, LSIA); in a clerk's hand; at head of text: "To Conyatauyou or Handsome Lake with his brethren and asssociates of the Seneca and Onondago Nations of Indians now at the Seat of Government of the United States."

ONE OF YOUR OWN PEOPLE: Handsome Lake, who was "employed"—that is, set to the task—by the spirits in his visions.

GREAT COUNCIL OF THE SIXTEEN FIRES: Congress.

[1] MS: "heat."

III. Address of Handsome Lake

BROTHER,   [15 Mch. 1802]

I thank the Lord for a clear sky and bright day to hear the answer of our good Father, The President of the United States—

Brother,

The four Angels have directed that all the lands which have been

reserved for the use of your red children, should be secured to them for their comfort so long as the sun shall shine, and this they desire may be done, by giving them separate deeds for each tract to which they are entitled, which when received will be placed for preservation in the hands of good sober young men of their Nation
Brother,

In consequence of a treaty held with your red children the Seneca's, in the year 1797, they sold to certain Agents of the United States, or to private adventerurs, all their lands, excepting a certain reservation on Cataragus Creek, which was afterwards surveyed by Mr. Ellicott, the lines run and bounds set by him and a Deed executed to them. This Deed has been lost, and your red children look to the justice of their Father the President for a renewal of it—
Brother,

Your red children state to their father the President, that they are entitled to another tract of land on the Allegany, containing forty two square miles. This has also been surveyed by Mr Ellicott, but no deed has been given to secure them in the possession of it. Your red children entertain fears that for want of some written instrument, when the transaction by which this reservation was meant to be secured, shall be forgotten, they may be dispossessed of their land—

FC (Lb in DNA: RG 75, LSIA); in a clerk's hand; date supplied from notation at foot of Document VI; at head of text: "Conyatauyou, or Handsome Lake."

In the transaction between the Senecas and Robert Morris at Big Tree (Geneseo) IN THE YEAR 1797, the nation gave up rights to most of the land it claimed west of the Genesee River. A RESERVATION at Cattaraugus Creek, which flowed into Lake Erie, was one of the tracts that the Senecas retained. Joseph ELLICOTT, Andrew Ellicott's brother, was affiliated with the Holland Land Company, which had bought Morris's rights to the purchase. Among the places reserved to the Senecas by the agreement of September 1797 was a 42-square-mile TRACT OF LAND on the upper Allegheny River on the New York State side of the boundary with Pennsylvania (ASP, *Indian Affairs*, 1:627; Catharine Van Cortlandt Mathews, *Andrew Ellicott: His Life and Letters*, [New York, 1908], 207; Granville Ganter, ed., *The Collected Speeches of Sagoyewatha, or Red Jacket* [Syracuse, N.Y., 2006], xxxiv; Vol. 32:549; Vol. 35:695-6).

[37]

IV. Address of Cornplanter

BROTHER,   [15 Mch. 1802]

Strongly impressed with the sentiment that the Great Spirit is displeased with his red children for the little attention which they have paid to the preservation of their lands And having received reiterated assurances from the Government of the United States, that every injury on representation should be redressed, I beg leave to state to our good father the President, that Mr Morris in purchasing the lands of your red children on the Allegany secured to them by contract certain reservations, and promised with the consent of his father, to give a deed of ten miles square for the exclusive use, benefit, and comfort of myself, of which a written memorandom was made and delivered to Captain Chapin, but nothing has since been done on the subject. No Deed has been given of the reservation, nor any security for the possession of the ten Miles square. It is hoped this matter may be enquired into—

FC (Lb in DNA: RG 75, LSIA); in a clerk's hand; date supplied from notation at foot of Document VI; at head of text: "Captain Cornplanter."

Cornplanter (1740?-1836) or Gyantwakia was also known as John O'Bail from the name of his father, John Abeel, a Dutch trader from Albany. Siding with the British during the American Revolution, Cornplanter fought against Continental forces and attacked American frontier settlements. After the war, he dropped his resistance to the United States and was present at the succession of treaties that left the Senecas with a fraction of the territory they had possessed earlier. Beginning in 1791, he lived on a grant of land he had received on the Allegheny River in Pennsylvania. Although Cornplanter was initially the energetic advocate of Handsome Lake's rev-

elations, within a few years the half-brothers came to disagree. Later, Cornplanter successfully resisted attempts to tax his land, and had a revelatory vision of his own that led him to refute his earlier service for the United States (ANB; Abler, *Cornplanter*, 72-4, 79-84, 133-4, 165).

Thomas MORRIS handled the negotiations at Big Tree in 1797 on behalf of HIS FATHER, Robert Morris. The Morrises, who used gifts of money to induce Seneca leaders to go along with the deal, gave particular attention to influencing Cornplanter beforehand. When Red Jacket attempted to break off the talks at Big Tree late in the negotiation, Cornplanter played a key role in persuading Seneca leaders to support the land sale (Wallace, *Death and Rebirth*, 180-3; Vol. 20:126-7; Memorandum on the Seneca Annuity, at 19 Nov. 1801).

V. Address of Handsome Lake

BROTHER,   [15 Mch. 1802]

The Great Spirit looks down on me this day, and expects that I shall take measures to secure all the reservations to which your red children are entitled. My anxiety on this subject is encreased by a knowledge I have of the will of the Great Spirit above us all. He expects if from me, and faithfulness to him and to my red brethren compel me to be importunate in urging a completion of this very desirable object—
Brother,

If all our business can be finished, the remainder of our days will be devoted to agricultural and such other pursuits as are calculated to render life comfortable to ourselves, and pleasing in the sight of the Great Spirit—

FC (Lb in DNA: RG 75, LSIA); in a clerk's hand; date supplied from notation at foot of Document VI; at head of text: "Conyatauyou, or Handsome Lake."

VI. Address of Blue Eyes

BROTHER,   [15 Mch. 1802]

I thank the Lord that the day has arrived when we can settle all our business, and I thank you for the friendly manner in which it has been conducted thus far—
Brother,

I wish to communicate to you that our whole Nation great and small were much pleased that we were willing to come forward to our father the President, and to consult measures for the greater security and comfort of the Nation. Your red children particularly wished us to attend the man of our Nation deputed by the four Angels to transact our business, to lighten his burthens, and to witness the manner in which the business was executed. Your red children have perfect confidence in Handsome Lake, are willing to bend an ear to his instructions, and yield obedience to his precepts. To him they have entrusted all their concerns, to be governed by his direction, wisdom and integrity—

FC (Lb in DNA: RG 75, LSIA); in a clerk's hand; date supplied; at head of text: "The Blue Eyed Chief, specially Deputed"; at foot of text: "The foregoing speeches were delivered by, Conyatauyou or Handsome Lake, Captain Cornplanter, and The Blue eyed Chief, on the 15th. of March 1802."

Blue Eyes was an Allegany Seneca (Wallace, *Death and Rebirth*, 288, 330).

VII. Henry Dearborn's Reply to Handsome Lake, Cornplanter, and Blue Eyes

To Conyatauyou, or Handsome Lake a Seneca Chief.

Brother,

Your good father the President of the United States having seen your talk of yesterday directs me to assure you, that his ears are ever open to the just complaints of his red children and his heart ever disposed to afford them releif—

Brother,

It is much regretted by your father the President that the Deeds securing to you the lands which have been reserved for the use of his red Children, when purchases have been made from them, should have been made from them, should have been lost, and he has instructed me to relieve your apprehensions on that subject by furnishing you with a written Instrument which is to be considered as a General Guarantee of all the lands within the United States to which you are entitled by reservation or otherwise with his solemn assurances that they shall not be taken from you but by and with your consent. This paper I now on behalf of the Government of the United States present you—

Brother,

Having expressed to you the sentiments of your good friend and Father the President, I will add my own best wishes for the progressive improvements of my red brethren and that the Great Spirit may always prosper their endeavours[1] after still higher and greater attainments—

Brother,

When you shall be prepared to set out for your own Country, I will cause you to be furnished with money to make you comfortable on the path, and will desire the Governments Agent at Fort Pitt to give each of you a new shirt one Ax a small Hoe and provisions to carry you home, where I wish you may arrive in safety and find your wives and children in health and comfort—

To Captain Cornplanter

Brother,

Your Good friend the President instructs me to assure you that the reports which have reached his ears that you were no longer entitled to his confidence and friendship is totally disregarded by him. He still believes you the friend of his red children and of the white people, and he hopes soon to hear that you are restored to your former rank and influence in your own nation.

Your father the President directs me to say that an enquiry shall be made in relation to the ten miles square of land on the Allegany, which you claim on the promise of Mr. Morris, and every thing done on the part of the Government that may be proper to induce Mr. Morris to comply with his stipulation—

To the Blue Eyed Chief

Brother,

Your Father the President has seen your talk and is pleased with the sentiments it contains. He advises you with the solicitude of a parent, to open your ears to the council of the Handsome Lake, to listen to his advice and to be governed by his precepts. To cultivate a spirit of peace and harmony among yourselves and your white brethren and to labour assiduously to ameliorate your condition by the introduction of agraculture and the domestic Arts—You will then become respectable among your neighbours, and receive the approbation of the Great Spirit—

Given under my hand and the Seal of the War Office this 17th: Day of March 1802.   H. DEARBORN
                                         S. of W.

FC (Lb in DNA: RG 75, LSIA); in a clerk's hand; "L.S." within facsimile seal alongside closing.

TALK OF YESTERDAY: that is, 15 Mch. WRITTEN INSTRUMENT: Document VIII.

Dearborn gave the deputation $150 in MONEY for their traveling expenses. John Wilkins, Jr., the quartermaster general, was at FORT PITT and had assisted the travelers on their way to Washington. Dearborn asked Wilkins to give each of the Senecas and each of the interpreters a SHIRT, a light ax, a hoe, and provisions (Dearborn to Wilkins, 17 Mch. 1802, in DNA: RG 75, LSIA).

[1] MS: "edeavours."

VIII. Confirmation of Title to the Seneca and Onondaga Indians

To all to whome
these presents shall come,
Greeting.

Whereas it has been represented by some of the Chief-men of the Seneca and Onondago Nations of Indians that they are entitled to certain reserved Tracts of lands lying on the Cartaragus Creek, and on or near the Allegany, and which has been surveyed, laid off, and the lines regularly run, and distinctly understood; but that they are not in possession of Deeds, securing to them the peaceable and undisturbed occupancy thereof: As well therefore to remove all apprehensions[1] from the minds of the Chief men and others of the Seneca and Onondago Nations, as to secure to them the possession of said lands it is hereby Announced and Declared by the authority aforesaid and on behalf of the Government of the said United States that all Lands, claimed by and secured to said Seneca and Onondago nations of Indians, by Treaty Convention or Deed of conveyance or reservation, lying and being within the limits of the said United States, shall be and remain the property of the said Seneca and Onondaga nations of Indians, forever; unless they shall voluntarily relinquish or dispose of the same. And all persons, citizens of the United States, are hereby strictly forbidden to disturbe said Indian Nations in their quiet possession of said Lands—

Given under my hand, and the Seal of the War Office of the United States this 17th: Day of March 1802—   H. Dearborn
                                                             Secy. of War

FC (Lb in DNA: RG 75, LSIA); in a clerk's hand; at head of text: "By authority of the President of the U. States"; in margin at head of text: "Deed given to the Seneca Nation of Indians"; "L.S." within facsimile seal alongside closing.

[1] MS: "apprehensons."

From John Dickinson

Wilmington the 10th of the
3d. Month 1802

My dear Friend,

This Letter will be delivered by Archibald Alexander, prothonotary of this County, a Man of sense and sound Principles.

He is deputed, as I understand, by the Inhabitants of the antient Town of New Castle, to make some application to Government, concerning Improvements of the Port there and the Advancement of commercial Interests.

He believes, that I am honoured by a share of thy Friendship, and has therefore desired this Introduction; and I hope, that I do not take too great a Liberty by complying with his Request.

With every respectful Recollection, I am thy truely affectionate Friend,

John Dickinson

RC (DLC); endorsed by TJ as received 19 Mch. and so recorded in SJL. Dft (PHi).

ARCHIBALD ALEXANDER, a physician in the Revolutionary War, president of the Patriotic Society of New Castle, and a founder of the Medical Society of Delaware, represented New Castle County in the Delaware assembly in 1795 and in the state senate in 1791, 1793, 1796, 1798, and 1800. In 1795, he ran for governor of his state and two years later made an unsuccessful bid for the United States Congress, each time losing to a Federalist. He was appointed prothonotary for New Castle County in 1801 and served until 1805 (Henry C. Conrad, *History of the State of Delaware*, 3 vols. [Wilmington, 1908], 1:264, 272, 297; W. H. Duncan, "The Founders of the Medical Society of Delaware: Doctor Archibald Alexander," *Delaware Medical Journal*, 79 [2007], 407-9; Liam Riordan, *Many Identities, One Nation: The Revolution and Its Legacy in the Mid-Atlantic* [Philadelphia, 2007], 124-5).

APPLICATION TO GOVERNMENT: two memorials signed by citizens of the state of Delaware were presented to the House of Representatives on 17 Mch. The first requested that New Castle be established as a port of entry for the convenience of the citizens of both Pennsylvania and Delaware; the second asked that Congress appropriate money "for defraying the expense of erecting piers in the river Delaware, in or near the harbor of New Castle." Both were referred to the Committee of Commerce and Manufactures (JHR, 4:140). In early April, Congress appropriated $30,000 for the erection and repair of public piers on the Delaware River (see Memorandum on Delaware River Piers, at 26 June).

From Christopher Ellery

March 10th. 1802—

C. Ellery begs permission to state to the President the contents of two letters, received by him, recommending Robert Champlin Gardiner, of the State of Rhode Island, for the place of Consul for the U. States at Gothenburg—One of these letters is from Lieut. Gov. Potter of R. Island—the other from John Gardiner esquire of R. Island, father of Robert, formerly a member of congress—   Gov. Potter asks, as a favor, my "solicitations with our worthy President" in behalf of Mr. Gardiner, and for information sends to me the enclosed letter— He mentions that Col. Gardiner, the father, is a firm friend to the present administration—And declares that he should be happy in the appointment of his son, provided a Consul is to be named for the place of Mr. Gardiner's residence, Gothenburg—   Col. Gardiner says that his son has resided four years at Gothenburg and is master of the language of that country & of the french, as well as versed in the trade of the Baltic—   Messrs Foster, Stanton & Tillinghast can give more complete information on this subject—For my own part, I should be pleased by a compliance with the wishes of these gentlemen, if consistent with the public good—C. Ellery tenders his highest respects to the President—

RC (DNA: RG 59, LAR); at foot of text: "President of the U. States"; endorsed by TJ as received 10 Mch. and so recorded in SJL with notation "Gardiner to be Consul"; also endorsed by TJ: "Robert Champlin Gardiner to be Consul at Gothenburg." Enclosure not found.

TJ's nomination of ROBERT CHAMPLIN GARDINER as consul at GOTHENBURG, Sweden, was presented to the Senate on 27 Apr. and approved two days later (JEP, 1:422-3). Gardiner's commission was dated 3 May (FC in Lb in DNA: RG 59, PTCC).

Samuel J. POTTER served as lieutenant governor of Rhode Island from 1790 until 1803, when he was elected to the United States Senate (Biog. Dir. Cong.).

JOHN GARDINER of South Kingstown represented Rhode Island in the last Confederation Congress in 1789 (Biog. Dir. Cong.; Vol. 15:218).

MESSRS FOSTER, STANTON & TILLINGHAST: Senator Theodore Foster and Representatives Joseph Stanton and Thomas Tillinghast of Rhode Island.

On 11 Mch., Joseph Stanton sent TJ another letter supporting Gardiner's candidacy, which likewise cited recommendations received from Samuel J. Potter and John Gardiner. "I know not the young Gentleman," Stanton admitted, but suggested to TJ that his colleagues in the Rhode Island delegation "may Give more Correct information" and deferred the nomination to TJ's "Superior Judgment and Uniform adherence to the public Interest" (RC in DNA: RG 59, LAR; at head of text: "President Jefferson"; endorsed by TJ as received 11 Mch. and "Gardner to be Consul at Gothenburg" and so recorded in SJL).

From Andrew Ellicott

DEAR SIR   Lancaster March 10th. 1802

It would be to me a singular pleasure to serve my country under your administration in any capacity which would afford a decent living for myself and family, provided it did not impose the necessity of fixing my permanent residence out of the Atlantic States, to which I am confident my family would not willingly consent.—

My own desire has been for many years past to reside at the City of Washington, and had my ideas of the manner of executing the office of Surveyor General been consistent with existing laws, my wishes might now have been realised; but I should nevertheless have supposed it my duty, to attend to the determination of every necessary geographical point within the United States: But in that extensive territorial country claimed by the public, it would be impossible to attend to, and superintend the work in detail, even by a residence in any part of it:—It has never been practicable in either of the States.— The plan which I have proposed will at some future day be adopted if the confederation should continue; because the multiplication of charts, plans, and surveys will be such, that they can only be arranged, and kept in order by a person, or persons to whom they are submitted for that purpose. Had this have been the case, (and which I early proposed,) the valuable charts that were burned in the War Office would probably have been perserved.—

I have just finished for Mr. de Lambre one of the Secretaries of the National Institute, (and at[1] his particular request,) a very long astronomical paper principally intended to correct the theory of the fourth satellite of Jupiter.—As I want to give certainty to the conveyance I would propose, (if not improper,) to have it forwarded with the public dispatches to our Minister at Paris.—

We have been extremely hurried in the Land Office ever since the meeting of our Legislature, and the Board of Property in which I have to preside has been sitting more than two months, which with the duties of Office occupies so much of my time, that I can scarcely find leisure to sleep: But this press of business will end when the Legislature rises.—I intend then to put up a small Observatory, and make a course of observations upon the refraction of the rays of light near the horizon.—

To your enquiry respecting the Almanac, I can only answer that I have no copy of it.—It was the commencement of a work which at that time I expected would have been continued;—it produced the thanks of President Washington and there ended.—

In a few days I will send you my method of calculating the rising and setting of the Sun or Stars,—it is very little more troublesome than opening an Almanac: But the method by equal altitudes is infinitely the best, and may be taken with the artificial, or reflected horizon more accurately than at sea,—the manner is particularly detailed in my printed work which you have Pages 46, 47, and 48.—

The moon will set eclipsed on the morning of the 19th. of this month, it will begin at the City of Washington at about 4.^{h} 41' A.M apparent time. I wish it could be properly observed at the City of Washington, as it would be of some importance in fixing the longitude.—

I have the honour to be with great respect and esteem your Hbl. Servt.   ANDW; ELLICOTT.

RC (DLC); addressed: "Thomas Jefferson President of the United States. City of Washington"; franked and postmarked; endorsed by TJ as received 14 Mch. and so recorded in SJL. PrC (DLC: Ellicott Papers).

TO SERVE MY COUNTRY: TJ had offered Ellicott the position of surveyor general. Since the primary functions of that office involved the sale of land in the Northwest Territory, Ellicott's insistence that he should have his PERMANENT RESIDENCE at Washington was proving to be an impediment (Vol. 36:448, 535, 579-81, 629-30).

War Department records BURNED in a fire in November 1800 (Vol. 32:435-6n).

MR. DE LAMBRE: Ellicott may have enclosed, for forwarding by TJ, a letter dated 10 Mch. to Jean Baptiste Delambre. As Ellicott informed TJ on 14 Feb., he and Delambre had begun to exchange letters on astronomical subjects. Robert R. Livingston had offered to act as the "channel" of that correspondence (Catharine Van Cortlandt Mathews, *Andrew Ellicott: His Life and Letters*, [New York, 1908], 207; John C. Greene, *American Science in the Age of Jefferson* [Ames, Iowa, 1984], 139-40, 433n).

As secretary of the Pennsylvania LAND OFFICE, Ellicott presided over the BOARD OF PROPERTY (Vol. 35:423-4; Vol. 36:535).

ENQUIRY RESPECTING THE ALMA-

NAC: see TJ to Ellicott, 24 Feb. After Ellicott sent a copy of his printed almanac to the president in November 1793, George Washington had Tobias Lear, who was then his secretary, write Ellicott a brief letter of THANKS and acknowledgment (Washington, *Papers, Pres. Ser.*, 11:443n; Lear to Ellicott, 3 Dec. 1792, Lb in DLC: Washington Papers).

Ellicott did not send the instructions for CALCULATING THE RISING AND SETTING of celestial bodies until 11 May. PRINTED WORK WHICH YOU HAVE: Ellicott had sent TJ, in installments through the spring of 1801, pages of "Astronomical, and Thermometrical Observations" from his survey of the southern boundary of the United States. In a description of the apparatus used on the survey, Ellicott described and illustrated a special cup that used water or another liquid to create an artificial horizon for taking observations, called equal altitudes, of the sun or stars to determine local time. The page numbers mentioned by Ellicott above refer to the "Observations" as separately paginated, which is how he sent them to TJ in batches and how they appear in the appendix to Ellicott's *Journal*, published in 1803. The "Observations" were also included in the fifth volume of the American Philosophical Society's *Transactions*, which was published in 1802, but with different pagination (Andrew Ellicott, *The Journal of Andrew Ellicott, Late Com-*

missioner on Behalf of the United States [Philadelphia, 1803], appendix, 46-8, plate following 52; APS, Transactions, 5 [1802], 206-8, plate following 212; Vol. 32:224; Vol. 33:371, 372n, 580; Vol. 34:120, 248; Vol. 36:485-6).

¹ MS: "it."

From George Jefferson

DEAR SIR   Richmond 10th March 1802

Mr. Taylor has to day made me a further payment of 130.$ on account of Littlebury Mosby's bond to Mr. Short; this he says will be the exact balance which was due on it, provided Mr. M. is correct in saying that he paid Colo. Skipwith 100$ on account of it—but which Colo. S: does not recollect.

So soon as this point is ascertained Mr. T. has promised me a copy of the settlement, which I will immediately forward to Mr. Barnes.

I am Dear Sir Your Very humble servt.   GEO. JEFFERSON

RC (MHi); at foot of text: "Thos. Jefferson esqr."; endorsed by TJ as received 14 Mch. and so recorded in SJL.

FURTHER PAYMENT: for the preceding payment, see George Jefferson to TJ, 8 Feb. 1802.

From Charles Le Brun

MONSIEUR!   New-york, le 10. mars 1802.

Cette lettre, que je prends la liberté de vous adresser; est Ecrite Sous les auspices de Cette bienveillance & de Cette bonté qui vous Caractérisent: C'est Sur Cette verité, que je fonde l'espoir de la voir acceuillir favorablement. j'aurais peut-être, un autre titre à faire Valoir: Celui d'Etre l'ami particulier de vôtre Illustre ami le Général Kosciuszko, dont j'ai eu l'honneur de vous remettre moi même Sa lettre de recommandation & vôtre portrait qu'elle accompagnait: Sous Ce double avantage, je me plais donc à Croire, Monsieur Le président, que vous me rendrez le Service que les Circonstances où je me trouve m'autorisent à vous demander.

Mon intention est de partir dans 18 ou 20. jours dans mon navire pour Curaçao, où je vais établir ma maison de Commerce; ainsique vous le Verrez par la Circulaire que j'ai l'honneur de joindre ici. comme les relations commerciales de Cette Ile avec la Côte ferme, Sont très grandes; & qu'il importe beaucoup à mes Intérêts d'y Etre particulierement recommandé, je vous aurai donc, Monsieur, la reconnaissance la plus grande, de vouloir bien demander pour moy, une ou deux lettres de recommandation pour Monsr. le Gouverneur de la *Gueras*, & Celui de *Caracas*; à Monsieur le Chevalier de Yrujo, Ambassadeur près de vous, de Sa Majesté Catholique. *Vous Seul*, monsieur Le président, pouvez me rendre Cet important Service: demandé par vous, Son plaisir Sera de S'empresser à vous les donner.

Ce bienfait, monsieur le président, que vous me rendrez, le Souvenir en Sera eternel; & dans mon Cœur Sera placé à Coté de ma Gratitude.

J'ai l'honneur d'Etre avec le plus profond respect, Monsieur, Vôtre très humble & Très obeissant Serviteur. Charles Brun

EDITORS' TRANSLATION

Sir! New York, 10 Mch. 1802

This letter that I take the liberty of addressing to you is written under the auspices of that benevolence and kindness that characterize you. It is upon that truth that I base the hope of seeing you accept it favorably. I would perhaps have another basis to draw upon: that of being the special friend of your illustrious friend General Kosciuszko, from whom I had the honor of delivering to you myself his letter of introduction and your portrait which accompanied it. From this double advantage I am pleased to believe, Mister President, that you will render me the service that my present circumstances authorize me to request of you.

I intend to leave in 18 or 20 days in my ship for Curaçao, where I am going to establish my commercial business, as you will see from the circular that I have the honor of enclosing herewith. Since commercial relations between this island and the mainland are very strong, and since it is very important for my interests to be especially recommended there, I shall be greatly indebted to you to request one or two letters of recommendation to the governor of *Gueras* and also the governor of *Caracas* from the Chevalier de Irujo, the ambassador accredited to you by His Catholic Majesty. *You alone*, Mister President, can render me this important service: at your request, it will be his pleasure to hasten to provide them.

This favor, Mister President, which you will do for me will be an eternal memory, and in my heart will be placed alongside my gratitude.

I have the honor to be, with the deepest respect, Sir, your very humble and very obedient Servant. Charles Brun

RC (DLC); at foot of first page: "Monsr. Ths. Gerfferson, presidt. des Etats unis"; below signature: "at Mesrs. Daniel Ludlow & Co. Merchts. New-york"; endorsed by TJ as received from Charles "Brune" on 11 Mch. and so recorded in SJL; see below for another endorsement by TJ. Enclosure: Circular letter in Spanish, dated Curaçao, 1 Jan. 1802, announcing the establishment of Le Brun's commercial house in that colony; citing his experience of 15 years in commerce in Europe, the Gulf of Mexico, and the Antilles, as well as his knowledge of the cultivation and promotion of the products of the colonies, he offers his services; his firm engages in commission sales and purchases, can equip long voyages, and can provide management of affairs, collection of overdue bills, and litigation, uniting commercial experience with caution, zeal, exactitude, and facility (RC in DLC; printed form signed by Le Brun as "Charles Brun," with dateline, heading, and portion of salutation in his hand; at head of text in Le Brun's hand: "Sñor. Dn. Ths. Gefferson presidente, de Los Estados unidos de America").

Charles Le Brun (1754 or 1755-1844) did not remain in Curaçao, but at some point returned to the United States. In Philadelphia in 1811, Mathew Carey published an instructional book Le Brun had written for children, *Le Directeur des enfans, depuis l'âge de cinq ans jusq'à douze.* According to the title page of that work, Le Brun was already a published author and translator. The next year, Carey published Le Brun's edition of *Les aventures de Télémaque, fils d'Ulysse,* a widely read work by François de Salignac de La Mothe-Fénelon that first appeared in 1700 (Philadelphia, 1812). Le Brun's *Télémaque* came out in multiple editions in the years following its initial appearance. Le Brun also translated Alexander Pope's poem, *Essay on Man,* into French with annotation. Although Le Brun published that work himself in Philadelphia in 1823—with Pope's English verse on the left-hand page facing the translation in French prose on the right-hand page— it bears a dedication to Napoleon Bonaparte dated 15 Aug. 1812. Le Brun translated into Spanish a 1798 work by Bertrand Barère, *La liberté des mers, ou, le gouvernement anglais dévoilé* ("the liberty of the seas, or, the English government revealed"). That translation, first published in Philadelphia in 1820 as *La libertad de los mares, ó, El gobierno inglés descubierto,* went through several subsequent editions. Le Brun sent a copy to TJ in 1821. He also wrote other works in Spanish. Although he signed the letter above, and the enclosed circular, as Charles Brun, his name appeared as Charles Le Brun on the title pages of his books, and that is the form of the name he used until his death. On the title page of

his translation of Pope's *Essay* in 1823, he identified himself as a U.S. citizen and an interpreter for the Pennsylvania government as well as an author. He resided in Philadelphia at the time of his death (Philadelphia *North American and Daily Advertiser,* 9 Sep. 1844; [Alexander Pope], *Essay on Man, Translated from the English by Charles Le Brun / Essai sur l'homme, traduit de l'Anglais par Charles Le Brun* [Philadelphia, 1823]; Charles Le Brun, *Vida de Fernando Septimo, rey de España* [Philadelphia, 1826]; Charles Le Brun, *Retratos políticos de la revolucion de España* [Philadelphia, 1826]; Charles Le Brun, *Los placeres del tocador* [Philadelphia, 1829]; Vol. 30:83n; Vol. 32:503n; Le Brun to TJ, 31 Dec. 1821, in MoSHi: Jefferson Papers, with TJ's copy of his reply of 13 Jan. 1822 on verso).

When Le Brun wrote to TJ again years later, he mentioned the letter of introduction that Tadeusz KOSCIUSZKO had given him (Le Brun to TJ, 31 Dec. 1821). Le Brun likely called on TJ on 9 Jan. 1802, the day that TJ received John Vaughan's letter of 29 Dec. along with, presumably, the "specimens of Coins & Medals" from Joseph Priestley that Vaughan asked Le Brun to take to TJ. In his letter to TJ, Vaughan said that "Mr Brun" was Kosciuszko's friend and came "strongly recommended." Kosciuszko's own recommendation for Le Brun has not been found and apparently was not recorded in SJL. On 9 Jan., TJ did receive a letter from Kosciuszko. Le Brun presumably carried that communication, but it was a duplicate version of the Polish exile's letter of 15 Sep. 1799, which dealt primarily with Kosciuszko's business affairs and made no mention of Le Brun (RC in Kahanowicz Collection, Polish Museum of America, Chicago, 1970, endorsed by TJ, recorded in SJL with notation "qu. year"; Vol. 31:184).

The PORTRAIT of TJ may have been one of the colored aquatint engravings that Michel Sokolnicki made in Europe from a drawing by Kosciuszko. TJ, who had a copy of the engraving at Monticello, left one in the President's House in Washington after he completed his second term as president (Vol. 30:xlii; RS, 1:668; 2:39, 106).

GUERAS: probably La Guaira, a fortified harbor on the north coast of South America that was the primary port for CARACAS and the surrounding region (Donna Keyse Rudolph and G. A. Rudolph, *Historical Dictionary of Venezuela*, 2d ed. [Lanham, Md., 1996], 318-19).

TJ inadvertently endorsed Le Brun's letter: "to be Naval officer for the port of Newport district of [R.I.]." Judging from the entries in SJL, TJ meant that notation for another letter he received on 11 Mch., one from William Crooke at Newport, 28 Feb. 1802, that has not been found.

From Charles McLaughlin

SIR,   George Town March 10th. 1802.
I received by the Baltimore Stage a Couple of Fresh[1] Cod Fish, which my Brother writes me were alive at 4 O.Clock this morning— and as I find Fish of every kind to be Scarce here at this time, I take the liberty to send One by the bearer hereof, which you will please to Accept from
Sir, your Obt. Servt.   CHS. MCLAUGHLIN

RC (MHi); endorsed by TJ as received 10 Mch. and so recorded in SJL.

Charles McLaughlin (d. 1807) owned the Union Tavern in Georgetown and shared a contract with William Evans to carry mail between Baltimore and Washington. In December 1801, and for several years thereafter, TJ paid McLaughlin for a subscription to the Georgetown dancing assembly, held at the Union Tavern (RCHS, 50 [1952], 19, 23, 37; *Wash-*

ington Federalist, 17 Mch. 1802; MB, 2:1011n, 1059, 1088, 1153; Vol. 33:415n).

BROTHER: probably Andrew McLaughlin, a Baltimore stage driver, whose "mail stage office" address was next door to Evans's inn (*The New Baltimore Directory, and Annual Register, for 1800 and 1801* [Baltimore, 1801], 39, 67; Stafford, *Baltimore Directory, for 1802*, 73; Vol. 33:39n).

[1] MS: "Frish."

To John Minor

DEAR SIR   Washington Mar. 10. 1802.
Mr. Short being incidentally interested in the suit of the US. v. mr Edmund Randolph, I had written the inclosed letter to mr Wickham, which with the documents accompanying the same, sufficiently explain the nature & extent of mr Short's interest. mr Wickham being engaged for mr Randolph, returned me the papers, and I now take the liberty of forwarding them to you with a request that you will be so good as to appear for mr Short, and take care that he be not thrown on mr Randolph for his money instead of the government of the US. you will see that both mr Pickering & mr Wolcott have explicitly acknoleged that the US. are in their opinion liable to mr

Short: but [...] mr Randolph to succeed in establishing [that credit] for himself against the US. it would make a serious obstacle to their allowing it to mr Short. I inclose you an order on Messrs. Gibson & Jefferson for your fee, and pray you to accept assurances of my great esteem & respect.   TH: JEFFERSON

PrC (DLC: William Short Papers); blurred; at foot of text: "Colo. John Minor"; endorsed by TJ in ink on verso. Enclosures: (1) TJ to John Wickham, 29 Jan. 1802, with enclosures. (2) Order on Gibson & Jefferson, not found.

John Minor (1761-1821), a prominent attorney of Fredericksburg, Virginia, had studied law under George Wythe, TJ's old law mentor. Minor himself, as was not uncommon, also instructed aspiring lawyers. He was a friend of James Monroe. TJ included Minor on the list of people to whom he intended, in the spring of 1800, to send copies of the new *Appendix to the Notes on Virginia Relative to the Murder of Logan's Family*. In April 1801, Minor wrote TJ a brief letter of introduc-

tion for John F. Gaullier of Fredericksburg. Minor, who earlier in his life had been known as John Minor, Jr., became a general in the War of 1812 (Madison, *Papers*, 14:228n; VMHB, 10 [1902-1903], 204, 311-12, 436-7; Ammon, *Monroe*, 346; Vol. 30:329; Vol. 31:553; Vol. 34:109n).

For TJ's efforts to find a lawyer to look out for William Short's interests in the government's suit against EDMUND RANDOLPH, see TJ to John Wickham, 29 Jan. 1802, TJ to George Hay, 14 Feb., and Hay to TJ, 19 Feb. For Short's claim for unpaid diplomatic salary and the suit, which was over Randolph's accounts from his service as secretary of state, see Short to TJ, 18 Dec. 1801, and Albert Gallatin to TJ, 9 Jan. 1802.

To the Senate

GENTLEMEN OF THE SENATE

I now submit for the ratification of the Senate a treaty entered into by the Commissioners of the US. with the Choctaw nation of Indians: and I transmit therewith so much of the instructions to the Commissioners as related to the Choctaws; with the minutes of their proceedings, and the letter accompanying them.

TH: JEFFERSON
March 10. 1802.

RC (DNA: RG 46, EPIR, 7th Cong., 1st sess.); endorsed by Senate clerks. PrC (DLC). Enclosures: (1) Treaty of "Friendship, Limits, and Accommodation" between the United States and the Choctaw nation, signed at Fort Adams on the Mississippi River, 17 Dec. 1801, by James Wilkinson, Benjamin Hawkins, Andrew Pickens, commissioners, and "a number of Indians"; the Choctaws agreeing to the construction of a wagon road through their lands, to connect the

northernmost settlements of Mississippi Territory and the lands of the Chickasaws; both parties confirming that "the old line of demarcation" agreed to by the Choctaws and officers of the British government, running parallel to the Mississippi River with the Yazoo River as the limit on the north and the 31st degree of north latitude the limit on the south, should be the boundary between the Choctaw nation and Mississippi Territory, with the United States agreeing to remove any of its settlements that might fall on the Choctaws' side of the line; the commissioners agreeing also to "give and deliver to the Mingos, chiefs and warriors" of the Choctaws, in consideration of their consent to the treaty, $2,000 in goods plus three sets of blacksmith's tools (printed copy in DNA: RG 46, EPIR; printed by order of the Senate; endorsed by a Senate clerk). (2) Extract of Henry Dearborn's instructions to the commissioners, 24 June 1801, concerning negotiations with the Choctaws (Tr in same; in hand of, and attested by, Joshua Wingate, Jr.; endorsed by Senate clerks). (3) Minutes of a conference between the commissioners and the "Principal Chiefs of the Choctaw Nation of Indians," Fort Adams, 12-18 Dec. 1801 (MS in same; attested by Alexander Macomb, Jr., as secretary to the commissioners; endorsed by Senate clerks). (4) Wilkinson, Hawkins, and Pickens to Dearborn, 18 Dec. 1801, reporting on their talks with the Choctaws, a "humble, friendly, tranquil, pacific people" who "opposed but few obstacles to our views"; noting that they chose not to press the Choctaws for permission to have houses of entertainment along the wagon road; the commissioners also calling attention to the problem of settlements on the Mobile, Tombigbee, and Alabama rivers and noting that the Choctaws, recognizing the necessity of changing their way of life, have asked for farm implements, other tools, and instruction in their use (MS in same; in a clerk's hand, signed by Wilkinson, Hawkins, and Pickens; endorsed by a Senate clerk). Message and enclosures printed in ASP, *Indian Affairs*, 1:658-63.

Sixteen Choctaws signed the TREATY. The Senate received the message and documents from Meriwether Lewis, and heard the treaty read, on 10 Mch. The accompanying papers were read on the 15th, at which time the Senate also had the treaty read a second time "as in committee." After postponing consideration of the matter two days later, the Senate unanimously agreed to the ratification on 29 Apr. In a proclamation dated 4 May, TJ issued the text of the treaty and declared: "Now, therefore, to the end that the said treaty may be observed and performed with good faith on the part of the United States, I have caused the premises to be made public, and I do hereby enjoin and require all persons bearing office, civil or military, within the United States, and all others, citizens or inhabitants thereof, or being within the same, faithfully to observe and fulfil the said treaty, and every clause and article thereof" (*National Intelligencer*, 10 May 1802; *Gazette of the United States*, 13 May; JEP, 1:408, 409, 410, 424).

To the Senate

GENTLEMEN OF THE SENATE

I nominate Benjamin Forsyth, 1st Lieutt. of the late St. Mary's galley, to be Master of the same as now fitted out for a Revenue cutter; Capt Howell of the galley having resigned.

Thomas Allen, late 2d. Lieutt. to be Mate of the same revenue cutter.

David Brydie Mitchell of Georgia to be attorney of the district of Georgia in the place of Woodruff.

Benjamin Wall of Georgia to be Marshal of Georgia in the place of Ambrose Gordon.

William P. Gardner of Pensylvania to be Consul at Demarara in the place of N. Rousselet, not recieved.

Andrew Lyle of New Jersey to be Surveyor[1] for the port of New
   Brunswick in the district of Perth Amboy, in the place of Anthony
   Walton White resigned.
Edward Croft of S. Carolina to be Commissioner of the first division
   in the State of S. Carolina for executing the act entitled an act
   to provide for the valuation of lands & dwelling houses & the enumeration of slaves within the US. in place of Edward Darrell
   deceased.
Nathaniel Folsome of New Hampshire to be Naval officer for the district of Portsmouth in New Hampshire in the place of Edwd. St.
   Loe Livermore.   TH: JEFFERSON
                                                        Mar. 10. 1802.

RC (DNA: RG 46, EPEN, 7th Cong.,
1st sess.); endorsed by Senate clerks. PrC
(DLC); with date added by TJ in ink.
Recorded in SJL with notation "nominations."

Meriwether Lewis delivered TJ's message to the Senate on 10 Mch. On the
same day, Georgia senators Abraham
Baldwin and James Jackson and Representative John Milledge informed Gallatin that BENJAMIN FORSYTH, "of the
Thomas Jefferson Revenue Cutter," had
died. They recommended that Captain
Henry Putnam take command of the vessel, noting his "purely republican" principles and assurances from "respectable
Characters" that his appointment would
"give satisfaction." They requested that
Thomas Allen be continued as mate (RC
in DNA: RG 59, LAR, endorsed by TJ:
"Putnam Henry. to be Master of Revenue
cutter lre of Jackson Baldwin Milledge";
Biog. Dir. Cong.). On 11 Mch., Lewis
delivered another message to the Senate
from the president. TJ wrote: "Since
my nomination yesterday of Benjamin
Forsyth to be master of a Revenue cutter,
I learn that he is lately dead, and therefore
now nominate Henry Putnam of Georgia
to be Master of the Revenue cutter late
the St. Mary's galley" (RC in DNA: RG
46, EPEN, 7th Cong., 1st sess., endorsed
by Senate clerks; PrC in DLC).
   Captain John HOWELL was offered the
command of the galley at St. Mary's in
early 1799, but he did not accept the appointment (NDQW, Dec. 1800-Dec. 1801,
363).

In his lists of appointments and removals, TJ commented that George
WOODRUFF and AMBROSE GORDON were
removed for "high federalism" as part of
his effort to appoint Republicans "as a
protection to republican suitors in courts
entirely federal & going all lengths in
party spirit." The permanent commissions for Mitchell and Wall are dated 26
Jan. 1802; TJ's lists record their appointments at 20 Apr. (commissions in Lb in
DNA: RG 59, MPTPC; Vol. 33:672,
679).
   For the appointment of WILLIAM P.
GARDNER, see Gardner to TJ, 20 Nov.
1801. His commission as consul at Dem-
erara and Essequibo is dated 11 Mch.
(commission in Lb in DNA: RG 59,
PTCC).
   Edward St. Loe LIVERMORE was serving as naval officer at Portsmouth when
Adams nominated him as U.S. attorney
for the district of New Hampshire on 18
Feb. 1801. He was confirmed by the Senate but did not receive a commission, and
TJ removed him from both positions
(JEP, 1:381, 383, 402, 409; Vol. 33:15,
219-20, 672, 676, 679; Vol. 34:129,
131n).
   On 11 Mch., the Senate approved TJ's
nominations as submitted above, except
for Forsyth, who was superseded by Putnam, and Folsom, whose was postponed.
The next day the Senate consented to the
appointments of Folsom and Putnam
(JEP, 1:408-10).

[1] TJ here canceled "of the customs at."

Sentence in the Court-Martial of John Spence

I. HENRY DEARBORN'S PRELIMINARY DRAFT [10 MCH. 1802]

II. HENRY DEARBORN'S SECOND DRAFT,
WITH JEFFERSON'S REVISIONS [20 APR. 1802]

EDITORIAL NOTE

Among the myriad duties that devolved on Jefferson as president of the United States was the periodic review of general courts-martial proceedings. According to federal law, such proceedings were to be forwarded to the president in times of peace if the court-martial involved a sentence of death, the dismissal of a commissioned officer, or any case involving a general officer. Once informed of the sentence, the president was authorized "to direct the same to be carried into execution, or otherwise, as he shall judge proper." In July 1801, a United States Army court-martial at Detroit found Private John Spence, a soldier in the First Regiment of Infantry, guilty of assaulting his commanding officer at Fort Wayne the previous May. According to section two, article five of the articles of war, a soldier found guilty of such conduct "shall suffer death, or such other punishment, as shall, according to the nature of his offence, be inflicted upon him by the sentence of a court martial." Citing the articles, the court-martial deemed Spence's crime a capital offense and sentenced him to death. The court then forwarded a copy of its proceedings to the secretary of war, Henry Dearborn, to be laid before the president as directed by law. After receiving the proceedings, Dearborn wrote on 19 Oct. 1801 to the court's presiding officer, Major Thomas Hunt, and informed him that an error was present in the recitation of the sentence, which cited an incorrect section and article of the articles of war as validation for the death penalty. The error, wrote Dearborn, "makes it impossible for the President to act on the case," and he ordered Hunt to examine the court's records and to take proper measures to rectify the mistake. Dearborn also took the opportunity to inquire about Spence's character and the circumstances of his case. "In a case affecting the life of a man," the secretary observed, "every useful information acquires great importance." Dearborn requested any additional documentation regarding Spence that "ought to have weight in the mind of the President, who is constituted by law the final arbiter of his destiny." He also asked the court to consider "a milder sentence than Death, and one which would be equally conducive to the good of the service" (U.S. Statutes at Large, 1:485; *The Rules and Articles of War, For the Government of the Troops of the United States. Extracted from the Journals of Congress, For the Year 1776* [Baltimore, 1794], 5; Dearborn to Thomas Hunt, 19 Oct. 1801, FC in Lb in DNA: RG 107, LSMA).

Spence's court-martial was Jefferson's first encounter as president with a capital sentence. The two documents printed below suggest that Jefferson

and Dearborn came to a decision only after a careful and deliberate examination of the case and its surrounding circumstances. Spence's guilt apparently was never in doubt, but neither the president nor the secretary appears
to have believed that the summary execution of the defendant was justified.
In Document I, received by Jefferson on 10 Mch. 1802, Dearborn drafted an
alternate sentence for Spence, granting the prisoner a reprieve of three days
(reduced from one month), during which time he would be permitted "to
pass into any foreign County." The basic outline of this alternative was
retained in Document II, but with emendations by Jefferson and alterations
to the details of the sentence. The length of the reprieve was extended from
three to twelve days, while the limits of Spence's exile were reduced from
"within the Jurisdiction of the United States," as stated in Document I, to
merely the Northwest and Indiana Territories in Document II. The sentence, therefore, spared Spence's life (at least temporarily) without actually
overturning the death sentence decreed by the court-martial. The subsequent activities and whereabouts of Spence are unknown.

I. Henry Dearborn's Preliminary Draft

[10 Mch. 1802]

   Having examined the proceedings of the Genl. Court Martial of
which Majr. Thos. Hunt was President, holden at Detroit in the
Month of July last past, in the trial of John Spence a private soldier
in Capt. John Whislers Company of the first Regiment of Infantry in
the service of the United States, charged with seditious conduct at
Fort Wayne on the third day of May in the year 1801, by assaulting
the immediate Commanding officer of that Garrison (Capt. Whisler)
and snaping at his person a pistol loaded with two balls;—secondly
for offering violence against said Capt. Whisler when attempting to
disarm him, by collaring the Capt. tareing his shirt, and calling him
a damnd cowardly rascal, and frequently said that he was sorry he
had not succeeded in taking the Capts life.—On which trial the said
Court found the prisoner John Spence guilty of the charges exhibited
against him, being a direct violation of the fifth Article of the second
section of the Rules and Articles of war, and did sentence him the
said John Spence to be shot to death.
   I hereby approve the foregoing sentence of the said Court.
   but
   reprieve the said John Spence from execution for the term of[1] three
days, reckoning from the day on which the Commanding Officer of

the Post at Detroit shall receive this. which reprieve, shall by these presence be considered as extended from the expiration of the aforesaid term of three days, until the said John Spence shall be found within the Jurisdiction of the United States, and no longer. immediately on receit of this, the Commanding officer at Detroit will release the said John Spence from confinement, (after reading the foregoing sentence together with the conditions of his reprieve to him, and informing him that) he is at liberty to pass into any foreign Country,[2]

Dft (DLC); undated; in Henry Dearborn's hand; endorsed by TJ as received from the War Department on 10 Mch. and "Spence's case" and so recorded in SJL.

[1] Dearborn here canceled "one month."
[2] Dearborn here canceled "which."

II. Henry Dearborn's Second Draft, with Jefferson's Revisions

[20 Apr. 1802]

having examined the proceedings of a Genl. Court Martial, of which Majr. Thos. Hunt was President, holden at Detroit on the eighteenth day of July last, for the trial of John Spence a private soldier in Captain John Whistlers Company, of the first Regiment of Infantry in the service of the United States, charged with seditious conduct at Fort Wayne on the third day of May 1801, by assailing the immediate commanding officer of that garrison, (Capt. Whistler) and snaping at his person a pistol loaded with two balls, secondly, for offering violence against said Captain Whistler when attempting to disarm him, by collaring *him* the *sd* Captain, tearing his shirt, and *using abusive language* and *expressing* frequently *regret* that he had not succeeded in taking the *life of the said* Captains[1] the said Court having[2] pronounced the following sentences, viz. the Court after taking into consideration the testimonies, adduced and after the most dispassionate consideration and mature deliberation thereon, find the prisoner John Spence Guilty of the charges exhibited against him, being a direct violation of the fifth Article of the second Section of the rules and Articles of War, do sentence him *the sd* John Spence to be shot to death.

I do approve the forgoing Sentence.[3]

[56]

but

I hereby reprieve the said John Spence from execution for the term of twelve days, after the forgoing sentence *and the approbation of it* shall be published at Detroit in Garrisons orders, and from the expiration of the said twelve days until he, the said John Spence shall be found within the Territory North west of the Ohio or within the Indiana Territory.

Given under my hand at Washington this 21st. day of April 1802.

TH: JEFFERSON

Dft (DLC); undated; in Dearborn's hand, signed by TJ; with emendations interlined by TJ supplied in italics; endorsed by TJ as received from the War Department on 20 Apr. and "Spence's case" and so recorded in SJL with notation "Spence's sentence."

[1] From "shirt" to this point, Dearborn originally wrote "and calling him a damned cowardly rascal, and frequently said that he was sorry that he had not succeeded in taking the Captains life" before TJ altered the text to read as above.

[2] MS: "having having."

[3] Dearborn originally wrote "I do hereby approve the forgoing Sentence of the Court" before TJ altered the text to read as above.

From John Trumbull

SIR   London March 10th: 1802.

Communications are preparing by the Board of Commissioners acting under the 7th. article of the Treaty between the U.S. of America & Great Britain, to Mr King the American Minister here;—and by the American Comrs. to Mr Madison the Secry. of State, explaining the doings of the Board, in respect to the appointment of Mr. G. W. Erving to the double Office of Agent for American Claims, & Assessor to the Board.

Since I have had the honor to hold the Office of 5th. Commissioner, I have cautiously abstained from holding any correspondence with the government of either Nation, on subjects relating to the Business of the Commission, lest in so doing I should seem to depart from that strict impartiality which the nature of my situation renders my first Duty; the present occasion however seems to justify a departure from that rule, and you will permit me to offer some explanations which appear to be proper for me to give, & which could not possibly have been known to, or probably contemplated by the Secretary of State, at the time these appointments took place.

When the Board of Commissioners entered upon its duties, it soon became conscious of a material want of commercial information;—the Members named by both Nations were all educated to the Law, & of course did not possess that mercantile knowledge, a necessity of which became evident at every step of its progress; and my former habits of Life, qualified me as little, for investigations which required not merely a general knowledge of mercantile transactions, but an accurate & practical acquaintance with the particular customs, & detail of the trade between the U.S. & the West Indies, in an especial manner.

The Board therefore determined, after mature deliberation, to adopt the practise of Admiralty Courts and to name two Merchants (one from each nation) as Assessors, whose duty it should be, (when the Board had determined that compensation was due in any case,) to examine the Accounts referred to them in such case by the Board, and to make up what should appear to them, to be a just account of the Amount of Loss, & report the same to the Board;—Claimants or their Agents were directed to attend the Merchants with their Accounts and Vouchers, & to give such further explanations as by them might be required:—And in order to gain all possible certainty of Equity & Correctness, it was further determined, that every Report of the Merchants, before it was acted upon by the Board, should be referred to the Agent of the opposite Party, in order that He might examine, & state in writing his objections to, the same.

When Mr Erving's credentials were presented to the Board, One of the British Commissioners observed the incompatibility of the two Offices of Agent & Assessor, and the impossibility of uniting them in one Person, without not only departing from the Orders of the Board, but violating the rules of just and equitable proceeding, inasmuch as its Effect would be to render the Claimant or his Agent, the Judge in his own Cause;—& added that should the Board conceive it proper to receive Mr. Erving in both Characters, (which He did not expect) it certainly would become the indispensable duty of the Agent of the British Government, to object in the strongest manner to the first report which should be referred to him, in which it should appear that Mr. Erving had assisted.   This argument I believe had its just weight with every member of the Commission;—to me I confess it appeared to be unanswerable; I felt, that should the occasion arise, it would be my duty to acknowledge the full extent of its force, and to act accordingly:—and I therefore cordially

& pointedly joined in recommending to Mr. Erving the Step which He has taken, and which I think does honor to his Judgment & his Moderation.

Permit me Sir! personally to repeat the assurance which as a Member of the Board, I have already given officially, (and in which I am sure that every Member as well British as American heartily joined) that on this occasion, I have felt a sincere regret in doing what may be supposed to bear the most distant appearance of disrespect to the American Government:—a sense of Duty, and an earnest desire to guard against whatever might become a ground of future misunderstanding & embarrassment in this delicate Business, have alone influenced my conduct.

May I beg your indulgence while I add a few words on the subject of Mr: Cabot—I do not remember ever to have seen him, until we met in London, on this business, nor have I since had other connexion with him, than of an official nature;—but in the course of his Official attendance on the Board, He has displayed such accurate knowledge of the Business entrusted to him, united with indefatigable industry; such suavity of manners, united with decent firmness;—& has in the course of several years experience acquired such facility order & dispatch, that I do not think it possible to replace him without manifest disadvantage; for even if other Men of equal knowledge may be found, yet no talents can supply the place of his experience; and the delay which would necessarily arise from putting the business into new hands would alone be an evil of no inconsiderable magnitude: But I am at liberty to say further, (what is no common advantage) that Mr. Cabot possesses the confidence of both parties:—And as the emolument which the Board has offered him, may not be sufficient to induce him to leave his numerous Family & his Business in America, I must beg leave to express my earnest hope that the Government of the United States will think fit to make such addition thereto as shall prevail upon him to resume his Services.

In speaking thus favorably of Mr. Cabot, I beg to assure you that I am not influenced by friendship or undue partiality, but by a full persuasion, grounded on knowledge, that his Assistance will essentially promote the equitable, satisfactory, & speedy termination of this very delicate Business.

Permit me to indulge the Hope that I still retain in your good opinion that place which I flatter myself I formerly had the Honor to hold, & which I should deeply regret to lose by any circumstance or

Action:—and to assure you of the grateful Respect & Esteem with which I have the Honor to be
Sir Your much obliged and faithfull Servant

JNO: TRUMBULL

RC (CtY); at foot of text: "Thomas Jefferson Esqe. President of the United States of America"; endorsed by TJ as received 30 May and so recorded in SJL. FC (DLC: John Trumbull letterbook); in Trumbull's hand.

Under Article 7 of the Jay Treaty, a BOARD OF COMMISSIONERS was to settle claims by Americans for "irregular or illegal" captures of merchant vessels by the Royal Navy or under British authority. Such claims related particularly to a period from 1793 to 1794 when British orders in council required the seizure of neutral vessels that were taking provisions to French colonies in the West Indies, or carrying the products of those islands to France, and the seizures were not brought before established admiralty courts. The panel, which met in London, consisted of two commissioners for Britain, two for the United States, and a fifth member selected by the others. In 1796, the commissioners for Britain and the U.S. used a drawing by lot to choose Trumbull, who had been John Jay's secretary during the negotiation of the treaty, as the fifth commissioner. Three years later, following the breakdown of the other bilateral commission established under the Jay Treaty, which by the provisions of Article 6 dealt with claims of British creditors against Americans for pre-Revolutionary War debts, the British government ordered its representatives on the seizures commission to halt their work. With the suspension of the commission's work, the American assessor, Samuel Cabot, whose task was to determine the amount of compensation for claims, obtained leave to return to the United States. In the second half of 1801, progress on negotiation of a settlement of the debt claims under Article 6

opened the way for a revival of the seizures commission. TJ appointed George W. Erving to be both the agent—representing American claimants and the United States before the commission—and the assessor. As TJ later informed Trumbull, giving Erving the dual appointment was deliberate, for reasons of economy and to avoid a multiplication of offices, and TJ believed that in such cases the integrity and character of the office-holder would prevent any conflict between the two functions. Cabot, moreover, had held both positions for a time. The commissioners, however, argued that Erving lacked Cabot's familiarity with commerce and the West Indies trade, and they wanted Cabot kept on as assessor. Erving resigned from that position, and TJ appointed Cabot to be assessor once again (Miller, *Treaties*, 2:252-3; John Bassett Moore, ed., *International Adjudications, Modern Series, Volume IV: Compensation for Losses and Damages Caused by the Violation of Neutral Rights, and by the Failure to Perform Neutral Duties* [New York, 1931], 71-3, 74-81, 102-3, 109; Madison, *Papers, Sec. of State Ser.*, 2:8n, 65, 186, 380, 383-5; Joseph M. Fewster, "The Jay Treaty and British Ship Seizures: The Martinique Cases," WMQ, 3d ser., 45 [1988], 426-52; ANB; TJ to Trumbull, 14 July 1802).

AMERICAN COMRS. TO MR MADISON: the U.S. commissioners, Christopher Gore and William Pinkney, wrote Madison on 17 Feb. to ask for Cabot's continuation as assessor. The British members of the commission in 1802 were Maurice Swabey and John Anstey (Madison, *Papers, Sec. of State Ser.*, 2:473-4; Moore, *International Adjudications . . . Volume IV*, 64; Vol. 34:324-6).

To Joseph Yznardi, Sr.

DEAR SIR   Washington Mar. 10. 1802.

The pipe of dry Pacharetti, pipe & two half pipes of Sherry, which you were so kind as to send me last, arrived here safe, and I now inclose you for the same a check of the branch bank of the US. of this place for 590.72 D amount thereof as stated in your letter, payable at the bank of the US. at Philadelphia. the wines are not yet sufficiently settled to be bottled. after their qualities shall be tried it is probable I shall trouble you for more of the dry kind, having of the sweet wines as much probably as will be used in my time. Accept my respectful salutations and best wishes for your health & a pleasant voyage.

                                              TH: JEFFERSON

PrC (DLC); at foot of text: "Mr. Joseph Yznardi"; endorsed by TJ in ink on verso. Enclosure not found.

In his financial memoranda under 10 Mch., TJ recorded the CHECK made out to Yznardi for $590.72 "to pay his bill of wines" (MB, 2:1068). TJ also noted the amount in SJL. YOUR LETTER: Yznardi to TJ, 12 Feb. 1802.

From John Wayles Eppes

DEAR SIR,   Bermuda-Hundred March. 11. 1802.

Your letter of the 3d. reached us last Evening—The one enclosing a letter to Mr. Anderson was not received until after my leaving Richmond.

I have not as yet been able to fix on a Horse that will perfectly answer as a Match for Castor—There is one in Petersburg whose form figure and colour would do well but I fear he wants height. I will take an opportunity of comparing him with my horse which will enable me to form a correct opinion—If he does not answer I know of no chance until the May Races at Petersburg at which place there will be a collection of all the fine horses of the State— I shall be at Petersburg in a few days & write to you immediately afterwards.

Our little son continues in good health—Maria was mistaken as to his teething as there is no appearance as yet—We look forward with much pleasure to the time when we shall have an opportunity of presenting him to you. The perils he has passed through render him doubly dear to us & the happiness we experience in his daily acquisition of strength size and ideas is not at present dampt by the dread of losing him—Maria is in good health & promises to write to you very shortly—Accept our affectionate wishes.

Yours sincerely

JNO. W. EPPES

RC (ViU: Edgehill-Randolph Papers); at foot of text: "Th Jefferson"; endorsed by TJ as received 17 Mch. and so recorded in SJL.

LETTER TO MR. ANDERSON: see TJ to Matthew Anderson, 31 Jan. It may have been enclosed in TJ to Eppes of the same date, recorded in SJL but not found.

MAY RACES AT PETERSBURG: probably the one-mile long Newmarket course in Prince George County. Races were held there regularly the first Tuesday in May and the second Tuesday in October (Edward A. Wyatt, IV, "Newmarket of the Virginia Turf," WMQ, 2d ser., 17 [1937], 481-95).

From Pierre Charles L'Enfant

SIR   City of washington march 12th 1802.

Under the apprehension of Impropriety in the liberty I took of adressing you, in november ultmo., but remaining Ignorant whether resting as I Deed requested leave to rest on you for settlement of the business the subject of two[1] repeated memorials to Congress be agreable to you:—the difficulties which this uncertainty set me under with regard to the Committee of claims to whom my memorials stand refered since the begining of this Congress (I having consequent to the wish Imparted to you and to the dependance I place in your goodness, beged the chairman of that Committee would delay their proceeding upon) forces on me the necessity to renew the sollicitation to you.

from dispositions testified by my last address I promised to myself that such settlement as I feel entitled to wait from government, might have been effected in some other ways than through a Committee of claim, which (besides, that, I fear from their having once already reported against the memorial) truely to my mind made it a disgracefull reflection that a recompense merited should be made necessary to claim.

of this however, sir, your Judgement best will determine, and I only advert to the Circumstance to Speak of my Embarrassment on the subject and how seeing the session of Congress fast approaching to its close now add disquietude to the apprehension of having mistaken in the manner of late request to you . . . . well persuaded nevertheless but you will excuse where the Intention was purely to prove my respect and esteem of your natural disposition:—encouraged by this hope I have here recalled to your mind all matters before stated—

and beg you to believe that the request which I made to you appeared to me proper because more flatering to my ambition to obtain my prayer through your favour

with great respect I have the honor to be sir—your Excellency most obedient and humble servant.   P. CHARLES L'ENFANT

P.S. having per statement inclosed in the late address, adverted upon speculative abusive usage of my plans of the City of washington, as a further Convictive of the great loss these have caused to me—(however as yet I can not have answer to Enquiry made in london, to state positively the amount of sale of plan there) what I have recently gained of Information on the subject authorise me to pledge myself able in some time, if it were rendered necessary, to produce manifest but the best Copies from my originals and from documents obtained as I have represented, was printed at london—by subscribtion at *three guineas the set of two² maps* which has in first Instance produced to the concerned *£20000 sterling* besides the proceed from severals secondary Editions

a transaction which having been facilitated by measure here when at the same time I was reduced to a state worst than begary—and on other part the Commissionaires map, by saling here for 25 cents the copies has opperated a depreciation of the merite and value of my work. this is a matter I think proper to mention here as being made a particular point of the claim before the Committee—and which I hope your Justice will take in Considerations with those other matters as have forced upon me the necessity to pray for Indemnification and to renew here the sollicitation of your favour to an obtainment of the proper.

with respct.   P. CH LENFT.

RC (DLC); elipsis in original; above postscript: "His Excellency Thomas Jefferson President of the United States"; endorsed by TJ as received 13 Mch. Enclosure: "Supplementary explanation" to L'Enfant's memorial to Congress on the subject of his "Concerns in the Entreprise of the City of washington," this memorial having been rejected by Congress in December 1800 and renewed by L'Enfant in February 1801, he was now reducing his representations to two "plain facts"; first, that the "Suppression" of his name from the first published plan of the city injured his reputation as its proposer; second, that wrong was done to his "fortune" when discussions with the District of Co-

lumbia commissioners and George Washington persuaded him that "Copy right" was not important, and L'Enfant therefore proceeded without a written contract; reflecting on his refusal of the commissioners' offer of 500 guineas as inadequate; exonerating the commissioners for "overlooking" L'Enfant's lack of copyright by showing that Washington, not the commissioners, directed the map's publication; stating that he retained in his possession the drawing that he carried with him to Philadelphia to be engraved; observing the growth of Georgetown to the west and north, with "upward of *300 houses*," most of which could have been erected instead "east of rock creek on the heigh City ground" to promote development along Massachusetts and Connecticut Avenues toward "the Center of the City (north and west of the Capitol)"; criticizing current efforts to reduce ground level to match the bases of the Capitol and the President's House, which were in themselves "deffective Structures, a compound as they are of different designs hobbingly patched together," in imitation of the architecture of Jean-François de Neufforge and Inigo Jones; accusing the commissioners of taking the sketches that L'Enfant left in Washington and using them to have secretly prepared in Europe a "neat handsome mape of the city" that was advertised recently in a London magazine; and concluding his statement with a calculation of his potential loss, estimated at $95,500, as stated in his memorial to Congress (MS in DLC; undated; in L'Enfant's hand and signed by him).

In a letter dated 3 NOVEMBER 1801, L'Enfant informed TJ of his MEMORIALS to Congress of December 1800 and February 1801. L'Enfant claimed compensation for his service in planning the city of Washington in 1791 and 1792.

[1] MS: "tow."
[2] MS: "tow."

Account with Zachariah Poulson, Jr.

HIS EXCELLENCY THE PRESIDENT
OF THE UNITED STATES,   Philadelphia, *March 12th*. 1802.
   To Zachariah Poulson, junr.   Dr.
For the American Daily Advertiser, from the *first* day of } $11.25
   October, 1800, to the last day of December 1801,   }

MS (MHi); printed form, with blanks filled by an unidentified hand reproduced in italics; endorsed by TJ: "Newspapers."

Zachariah Poulson, Jr. (1761-1844), succeeded David C. Claypoole as publisher of the first daily newspaper in the United States, which he continued in Philadelphia as *Poulson's American Daily Advertiser* from 1800 until 1839. He was a founder of the Philadelphia Society for Alleviating the Miseries of Public Prisons, one of the managers of the Pennsylvania Hospital, and served as librarian and director of the Library Company of Philadelphia (Brigham, *American Newspapers*, 2:947; MB, 1:426; Henry Simpson, *The Lives of Eminent Philadelphians, Now Deceased* [Philadelphia, 1859], 805-7; DAB).

To Thomas Mann Randolph

DEAR SIR   Washington Mar. 12. 1802.
   I recieved two days ago your favor of the 6th. and am very glad you made to me a full communication of your intentions, as I feel no resources within myself or without which could have supported me under the idea of separation which popular report might have brought to me. how far the enterprize may be adviseable, I am not qualified to judge; nor am I able to give you much information on the

subject. had we not unfortunately lost mr Hunter, the Missisipi representative who died yesterday, I expected to have got minute information. I know that cotton is the most profitable production of the
US. and that the Missisipi territory is well adapted to it. it is said
a labourer there will make 300. D. worth a year. we know their ex-
ports the last year (of all articles, but the chief of which was cotton)
amounted to 700,000. D. which is 200. D. for every laborer, their
whole population being but 8000. souls. the distance from Charlottesville by land to the Natchez is about 1400. miles, of which 600.
miles is through the Indian country & uninhabited. the Missisipi territory extends about 100. miles on the river, & 20. miles back from it:
and such is the soreness of the Indians, as to the alienation of their
lands, that I think there is little prospect of obtaining any more for a
great number of years; never indeed till they become agricultural,
and find they have more than they can cultivate. every thing has been
tried with the Chickasaws, the most friendly nation to us, and not
even the space to set a house of entertainment on the road can be obtained from them on any conditions. the Choctaws who surround the
Missipi territory, can bring 8000. warriors into the field: the probability is that our settlement could not bring 800. white men, to meet
them, & would leave 800. black men in their fields uncontrouled; and
it is 600. miles from any settled country of the US. it is moreover a
frontier, and Louisiana (includg. N. Orleans) shortly to be possessed
by the most turbulent spirits of the French army, whom Bonaparte
has provided that country to get rid of, and who will soon have the
Indians entirely at their beck. under these circumstances I have long
considered this little helpless speck of a settlement, thrown off at such
a distance from support and in the very teeth of powerful nations, as
in the most tremendous situation which can be imagined. Kentucky
would be their speediest support, because, tho 1000. miles off, yet
they would descend by water: but not till the blow would be struck.
should you prefer it, you can pass through Kentucky to Louisville,
500. miles by land from Charlottesville and thence go on by water
1100. miles to the Natchez. I am told it is unsafe for strangers to go
into that climate till the fall: that even in April, the season you propose to go those not accustomed to it are apt to be taken sick. we have
information that we lose 400. boatmen & seamen every year on that
river by disease. if the French get possession of N. Orleans & their
present government continues, which is unequivocally hostile to a republican administration of this, I shall consider the commerce of the
Missipi as held by a most precarious tenure.   Attending to the
importance of this enterprize on your future affairs, and believing as

I do that something of the kind is practicable & adviseable, I should think it prudent to take a comparative view of the circumstances under which other places offer themselves with a view to the same rich culture. Georgia certainly presents itself under some very advantageous aspects. the latitude is the same. the culture at least as productive; lands proper for it cheaper & indefinite in quantity; the climate healthier; the country strong, growing stronger and never to be in danger; it's commerce not dependant on the will of any foreign nation; the cotton worth more there than at N. Orleans, on account of the bad navigation of the gulph: from Charlottesville to Savannah not more than 600. miles through a thick settled country, and a stage to be immediately set up by the public for carrying the mail from Petersburg to Georgia in 10. or perhaps 8. days. the run too from Richmond round by sea quite trifling and peculiarly convenient for carrying your slaves; a country almost made up of Virginians, where you will find numbers of trustworthy friends, and where your resources in Virginia may be as well commanded as if they were on the spot, and those which the success of your enterprize may create in Georgia be as negociable at Richmond as at Savanna. you may visit your possessions in Georgia spring & fall with greater ease & much less danger to your health than you could the Missisipi territory once in half a dozen years. in fact I should be delighted to own a cotton estate in Georgia, & go and pass every winter[1] under the orange trees of that country. within 3. years from this time the stages will pass from Richmond to Georgia in 6. days; as we mean to endeavor to make all the principal mails travel 100. miles the 24. hours. I wish you to give this alternative a fair & unprejudiced consideration in comparison with that of the Missisipi territory, &, on account of the risk of health of a spring journey to the latter, to consider whether your spring journey had not better be to Georgia, where if your expectations are disappointed you can then visit the Missi. early enough in the fall to order from thence by post the removal of your slaves (proper arrangemts being made at home for that previous to your departure) and meet them on the way & conduct them to the territory quite in time to begin the crop of the ensuing year. but I am very much of opinion you will find in Georgia every advantage existing in the Missipi territory, and many important ones which do not exist there. I am not sure I should not be willing to join myself in the Southern enterprize as to such of my negroes as could be persuaded to it, as I could replace families[2] with Craven by the purchase of men alone equivalent for his purposes.—I recieved last night the inclosed pamphlet, which as it relates to the subject on which you had asked my information, I forward it to you. I shall hope that during your absence Martha & the family will come & stay here. my tenderest love to her and kisses to the dear children. affection and respect to yourself.   TH: JEFFERSON

P.S. within 3. years we can go to Georgia with as little inconvenience as we now can to Bedford, & the resources there are now as commandable as those of Bedford.

P.S. Mar. 13. since writing the preceding, I have conversed with mr Baldwin & Genl. Jackson of Georgia. they say that a labourer tends 5. acres of cotton a year: that a little below Augusta, Cotton lands are from $1\frac{1}{2}$ to 6, 8, or 10. D. the acre. that on the seacoast & in the sea-islands they are sometimes as high as 20. D. but the country there is unhealthy, whereas when you approach Augusta, it becomes hilly & healthy. they say that Sibbald's lands are really pine barrens, not to be meddled with, because they produce nothing; they are called Turkey lands, because they are so sandy you may track a turkey in them. but that there is a vast extent of pine lands with a mixture of other growth that are excellent for cotton, & cheap because of their immense quantity & the novelty of the demand for them. they say that 500. D. a hand is talked of by many: but they consider 300. D. as what may be calculated on. they affirm that there is not a single circumstance in which Georgia has not the advantage of the Missisipi. they suppose the difference of produce to be as 5. to 3. that the Missisipi territory is not the true cotton soil. it is too rich & loamy, tho' it produces it in a profitable quantity. I shall see mr Milledge who lives at Augusta, and will be able to give me more particular information which I will forward by the next post.

RC (DLC); at foot of first page: "T M Randolph"; endorsed by Randolph. PrC (MHi); endorsed by TJ in ink on verso. Enclosure: probably George Sibbald, *Notes and Observations, on the Pine Lands of Georgia, Shewing the Advantages They Possess, Particularly in the Culture of Cotton. Addressed to Persons Emigrating, and Those Disposed to Encourage Migration to This State* (Augusta, Ga., [1801]).

REPLACE FAMILIES WITH CRAVEN: for TJ's indenture with John H. Craven for the lease of fields and slaves at Monticello and Tufton, see Vol. 32:163-6.

George SIBBALD'S LANDS consisted of 500,000 acres of Georgia pine lands in the Georgia Asylum Land Company. A share in the company sold for $100 and entitled the person to 200 acres. In 1801, the Georgia legislature suspended Sibbald's payment of taxes on the company's land until 1805. Sibbald planned to travel outside of the state to encourage emigration to Georgia and settlement on his land (printed certificate for a share in the Georgia Asylum Land Company, signed by Sibbald, undated, in DLC: Broadside Collection; Sibbald, *Notes and Observations, on the Pine Lands of Georgia*, 7, postscript).

[1] TJ here canceled "on it" and interlined the remainder of the sentence.

[2] Word interlined in place of "them."

From Benjamin Rush

DEAR SIR,   Philadelphia March 12. 1802

Having just finished the labors of the Winter in the University, and hospital, I sit down with great pleasure to acknowledge your favor of Decemr last. One part of it commands my first Attention, and that is your communication of a discovery of a *flaw* in your Constitution from which you anticipate a certain, but easy passage out of life. Permit me my dear and long respected friend to request you to inform me of the Seat, and Nature of that flaw. Perhaps it is in the power of medicine to heal it, or to protract its fatal effects to a very distant day. Should my reading, or experience be insufficient for that purpose, I will lay the history of your Case before the most intelligent members of our profession in Philada: (without mentioning your name)[1] and transmit to you our united Opinions and Advice. The result of all that has passed, or shall pass between us Upon this subject, shall descend with me to the grave.

Accept of my thanks for your friendly hint to Mr Smith to attend to the interests of my son while he was an officer in the Navy. He feels with myself his Obligations to your Goodness, and regrets that the limited prospects of providing for sickness and Age while in that situation, rendered it necessary for him to quit the Service of his Country. He is still Attatched to the Sea, and expects to sail shortly probably to an East India port.

I am happy in being Able to inform you that the vaccine Inoculation is generally adopted in our city, & that its Success has hitherto equalled the best wishes of its most sanguine and zealous friends.

For several years past I have been engaged in investigating the causes, Seats, and remedies of madness, & Other diseases of the mind. Before I commit the results of my inquiries and Observations to the press, I wish to read every thing that has been published upon those Subjects. LeTude's history of the Bastile, and of a Lunatic hospital in which he was confined Under pretence of madness, I have heard contains many curious facts upon that disease. In my inquiries for this curious book I was informed that you had a copy of it. Could you favour me with the reading of it, you would add greatly to my Obligations to you. It shall be returned in a week or ten days After I receive it.

What means Alas! the renewal of the horrors of War in the West Indies?—Does our Globe, like a diseased body, stand in need of a perpetual issue of blood?—I tremble for its Consequences every where and particularly in our Country. Can nothing be done by concession, and partial emancipation to avert the Storm from the Southern states?—But I must quit a Subject upon which I am unable to suggest any thing new, or useful, and which I am sure has long commanded all the resources of your Understanding, and feelings of your heart.

With great respect, and Affection beleive me to be your sincere Old friend
BENJN: RUSH

RC (DLC); endorsed by TJ as received 17 Mch and so recorded in SJL.

YOUR FAVOR OF DECEMR LAST: TJ to Rush, 20 Dec. 1801.

In December, Rush's son, John Rush, who was a lieutenant in the U.S. NAVY, received orders to report to the schooner *Enterprize* for duty with the Mediterranean Squadron. John had abandoned the study of medicine in 1798 to join the navy as a surgeon, and received his commission as an officer the next year. His career was affected by emotional and mental problems; he did not go to the Mediterranean, but instead resigned his commission in January 1802. Later in the year, he resumed his training as a physician (George W. Corner, ed., *The Autobiography of Benjamin Rush: His "Travels Through Life" together with his* Commonplace Book *for 1789-1813* [Princeton,

1948], 261, 369-71; L. H. Butterfield, ed., *Letters of Benjamin Rush*, 2 vols. [Princeton, 1951], 2:813, 814n, 815, 842; Robert Smith to TJ, 29 Dec. 1801).

LETUDE'S HISTORY: Henri Masers de Latude spent over 30 years in the Bastille and other places of confinement in France. Several versions of his recollections appeared in print. TJ had known Latude in Paris and may have owned more than one edition of the memoirs, including one that Latude asked Elbridge Gerry to convey to TJ in 1798. The book that Rush wanted to borrow was likely the *Histoire d'une détention de trente-neuf ans, dans les prisons d'état* (Amsterdam, 1787). Latude reportedly disavowed that publication, which has also been attributed to another person (Sowerby, No. 219; Vol. 10:453; Vol. 30:578).

[1] Phrase in parentheses interlined.

From Benjamin Smith Barton

DEAR SIR,   Philadelphia, March 13th, 1802.
I am informed, that a Marine Hospital is about to be established, at the expence of the government of the United-States, in the city of New-Orleans. Should this be the case, permit to observe, that I think Mr. Oliver H. Spencer, a young man who has just completed his studies in our University, would be a very proper person to serve in the capacity of a physician to the institution. Mr. Spencer served, for some time, as a surgeon in the army of the United-States. He has spent two winters in Philadelphia, in attendance on the medical lectures, and acquired and deserved the character of a man of talents, very correct knowledge, and fair and amiable character. He has already formed the resolution of settling at N. Orleans, for which place he is to sail, in a day or two.—

In consequence of the very declining state of my health, I have formed the resolution of spending a part of the ensuing spring and summer in the country of the Cheerake-Indians. As I am obliged to leave the city, I am anxious to derive as much advantage as I can, from my absence. My objects; next to my health, in the Cheerake-country, will be the collecting of specimens of the Indian languages, materials for the natural history of the country, &c. It has occurred to me, that these latter objects might be very essentially advanced, could I be properly introduced to some of the more influencial agents in the country. I shall esteem myself under a very particular obligation to you, Sir, if you can conveniently furnish me with a letter, or with letters, to any of the respectable characters to whom I allude, mentioning to them the particular objects of my journey.

I have the honor to subscribe myself, Dear Sir, with the highest respect,[1] Your very humble and obedient servant, &c.

B. S. BARTON

RC (DNA: RG 59, LAR); addressed: "To The President of the United-States"; endorsed by TJ as received 20 Mch. and "Oliver H. Spencer to be Surgeon of Marine hosp. N.O." and so recorded in SJL. Probably enclosed in William Jones to TJ, 19 Mch., not found (recorded in SJL as received 20 Mch., with notation "Spencer to be Surgeon Marne. hosp. N.O.").

Barton's letter printed above was enclosed in one of 15 Mch. from Joseph Strong of Philadelphia to Congressman William Jones. Strong said that he had personal acquaintance with OLIVER H. SPENCER, whose "talents & acquirements plead eloquently in his favor." Strong had been told that American merchants in New Orleans were "much pleased" with Spencer's decision to move there. Spencer, who combined "acknowledged abilities" as a doctor with "admirable humanity of heart," had sailed for New Orleans on the 15th. The UNIVERSITY of Pennsylvania awarded him an M.D. degree in 1803 (RC in DNA: RG 59, LAR; W. J. Maxwell, comp., *General Alumni Catalogue of the University of Pennsylvania: 1917* [Philadelphia, 1917], 566).

[1] Preceding four words interlined.

From David Fergusson

RESPECTED SIR,   Baltimore 13th. March 1802.

This afternoon, for this Mail I beg the leave and pleasure, of handing You, the inclosed, No. 1. on Auctions—& in a few days hence—a No. 2.—on the plan, of order for Blacks.—

Respectfully,—Your very Obedt. Servt.   DAVID FERGUSSON

RC (DLC); endorsed by TJ as received 14 Mch. and so recorded in SJL. Enclosure: Essay on "Public Auctions," dated 13 Mch., and signed "Seven Friends," declaring that fraudulent practices marred the collection of taxes on public sales at auction; to "annihilate, and permanently suppress, this egregious, iniquitous, long standing, and growing evil," he proposes that "a Licence be had, for every Sale, that to Cost 250 Cents—his Oath to be taken for the amount of Sales, and that returned, which will answer as a Check upon his quarterly returns and payment, & prevent fraud"; with these changes, Fergusson predicts, an income "four times that of the Post office" (MS in DLC; in Fergusson's hand; at foot of text: "For the President of the United States, of America").

Congress passed a tax on property sold at AUCTIONS in June 1794 and in 1800, the government received $51,650.41 in revenues from sales at auction. It was one of the internal taxes repealed in April 1802 (U.S. Statutes at Large, 1:397-400; 2:148; ASP, *Finance*, 1:714; Vol. 36:600, 602n).

This is Fergusson's last correspondence with TJ recorded in SJL. For earlier proposals signed "Seven Friends," see Fergusson to TJ, 10 Aug. and 22 Sep. 1801.

From Thomas Mann Randolph

DEAR SIR,   Edgehill March 13. 1802.

Our family is as it was; happy & well: the children grow daily & improve in mind proportionally I hope: they do not appear to be naturally deficient and their Mother's diligence constancy & wit surely never were surpassed.

with true attachment   TH: M. RANDOLPH

RC (ViU); endorsed by TJ as received 17 Mch. and so recorded in SJL.

From Robert Smith

SIR   Navy department 13th March 1802

I have the honor to request your Signature to the Warrant herewith enclosed for Samuel Johnson as a Gunner in the Navy, he is now acting on board the Adams, & is well recommended by Capn. Preble.

With great respect, I have the honor to be Sir Your mo. obt Sert.

RT. SMITH

RC (DLC); in a clerk's hand, signed by Smith; at foot of text: "The President"; endorsed by TJ as received from the Navy Department on 13 Mch. and "a gunner." FC (Lb in DNA: RG 45, LSP). Enclosure not found.

To Pierre Charles L'Enfant

SIR   Washington Mar. 14. 1802.

Your letter of the 12th. is at hand. immediately on the reciept of the former one I referred it to the board of Commissioners, the authority constituted by law for originating whatever proceedings respecting this city[1] have been confided by the legislature to the Executive. their opinion, which I approved, was that they could only renew to you the offer formerly made with the approbation of General Washington, and they undertook to do this. for any thing else, the powers of the legislature are alone competent, and therefore your application to them was the only measure by which it could be obtained. Accept my respects & best wishes.   TH: JEFFERSON

RC (DLC: Digges-L'Enfant-Morgan Papers); addressed: "Majr. L'Enfant Georgetown in Maryland"; franked and postmarked. PrC (DLC).

FORMER ONE: L'Enfant to TJ, 3 Nov. 1801. THEIR OPINION: see District of Columbia Commissioners to TJ, 10 Dec. 1801.

[1] Preceding three words interlined.

From John Thomson Mason

DEAR SIR   George Town 14th March 1802

I last night reached home from Montgomery Court with the Gout in my foot so bad as to confine me to my room. The Judiciary Bill having finally passed, I now feel anxious to see something doing with the Territorial Bill, but I cannot discover from the papers that Congress are even thinking of it. Mr Peyton is with me and feels equally anxious on that subject. If Constitutionally practicable we are both of us converts to the plan of restricting the limits of the Seat of Goverment and confining it to the City of Washington. We have agreed this week to endeavour among the members to bring the question on in some shape or other, but if agreeable to you, we are very desirous to see you first, and converse with you on the subject. I cannot probably get out before Tuesday morning, on that day, at any time you will appoint, or on any other subsequent day that may be more agreable to you, we will do ourselves the honor of waiting upon you, if it is agreeable to you to receive a visit on that subject

with high respect & esteem I have the Honor to be your obedt Servt   J. T. MASON

RC (DLC); endorsed by TJ as received 14 Mch. and so recorded in SJL.

JUDICIARY BILL HAVING FINALLY PASSED: on 8 Mch., TJ signed the legislation that repealed the Judiciary Act of 1801 (U.S. Statutes at Large, 2:132). So many objections were raised against the TERRITORIAL BILL, designed to establish a system of local authority in the District of Columbia, that on 29 Mch. the House of Representatives passed a resolution to postpone consideration of the legislation until the next session of Congress (JHR, 4:166; Annals, 11:1095-6). For TJ's draft of the bill and its history, see Bill to Establish a Government for the Territory of Columbia, [before 7 Dec. 1801]. Congress, however, continued to receive memorials calling for the establishment of a "system of government or police" in the CITY OF WASHINGTON, which would be "responsible to the inhabitants thereof, by free and frequent elections." During the final days of the session, several laws were passed for the governance of the District of Columbia, including an act to incorporate the city of Washington (petitions from inhabitants of the City of Washington, in the District of Columbia, to the Senate and the House of Representatives, 26, 29, 30 Mch., 1 Apr. in DNA: RG 233, PMRSL, 7th Cong., 1st sess.; JHR, 4:160, 164, 166, 171; U.S. Statutes at Large, 2:175-8, 193-7).

TUESDAY MORNING: that is, 16 Mch. According to SJL, TJ wrote Mason on that day, but the letter has not been found.

From James Monroe

DEAR SIR   Richmond March 14. 1802.

I found your favor of the 28th. ulto.[1] communicating an extract of a letter from Dupont De Nemours relative to the claim of the artist Houdon to be paid the sum which he lost by the depreciation of the assignats in the last instalment which he recd. for the statue of Genl. Washington. I postponed an answer untill I had taken the advice of council by which I am authorised to inform you that whatever sum you state to be due shall be paid on yr. certificate of the same. I send you a letter of yours to Govr. Brooke, one of Houdon to the Govr. of Virga. and a copy of one from the banker Grand to Houdon certified by the latter, which shew that the contract was in specie, that the assignats were accepted by him with the approbation of Mr. Morris on the principle and in the expectation that they shod. be scaled. I hope and presume that Mr. Morris will be able to establish the facts not known to you, necessary to adjust the account, to your satisfaction, so that we may be enabled to pay the artist what is justly his due. We do not think ourselves authorised to purchase the bust of Franklin, without the sanction of the legislature. We are persuaded its sanction might be had at the next session, tho' are not authorised to commence a treaty or make any stipulation relative to it.[2]

The repeal of the Judiciary law of the last session forms an interesting epoch in our affrs. We shall soon see whether the party which created it are disposed and able to convulse the country on pretext of the repeal. I shod. not be surprised [to see?] the court of appls. advancing with a bold stride to effect the object. But I trust its efforts will be fruitless. Sincerely I am yr. friend & servt

JAS. MONROE

RC (DLC); torn; endorsed by TJ as received [19] Mch. and so recorded in SJL. FC (Vi: Executive Letterbook); in a clerk's hand. Enclosures: (1) TJ to Robert Brooke, 20 Mch. 1796 (Vol. 29:37-8). (2) Jean Antoine Houdon to Brooke, Paris, 8 Sep. 1796, stating that on 8 July 1785 he agreed with TJ, who was acting for the state of Virginia, on terms for the execution of a marble statue of George Washington for 25,000 livres to be paid in three installments; that "at the end of 1792," the final payment was offered in the form of 9,000 livres in paper assignats, which from the loss of value were worth only 5,625 livres in silver, leaving a balance due of 3,375 livres; he wrote to Gouverneur Morris, who was then the U.S. minister to France, and Houdon now encloses the answer that Ferdinand Grand made for Morris; William Short, Morris, and Monroe all wrote to the state government about this matter but received no answer (RC in DLC; at head of text: "His excellency the Governor of the State of Virginia"; en-

dorsed; see Vol. 8:284n). (3) Extract of Grand to Houdon, 28 Sep. 1792, stating that Morris finds Houdon's claim to be just, but cannot dispense Congress's funds without authorization; Morris will seek authorization, but meanwhile advises Houdon to accept the payment on a justified receipt, in which opinion Grand concurs (Tr in DLC; in Houdon's hand, in French; at head of text: "Copie de la Lettre de Mr Grand à Mr. houdon Sculpteur en datte du 28. 9bre. 1792"; enclosed in Enclosure No. 2).

In 1790, the French government decreed that ASSIGNATS, notes that had been issued against confiscated properties, would be legal tender (John H. Stewart, *A Documentary Survey of the French Revolution* [New York, 1951], 159-62).

[1] Interlined here in Lb: "lately on my return from Albemarle."
[2] Text in Lb ends here.

From Susannah Santoran

SIR   George Town March 14th 1802
I took the liberty to send you a valintine by poste the 14th of feby 1802 and I have ben waiting for a answer but receiv none which I have taken the opertunity to informe you where to Send the presant, as you know not where I lived and I hope that you will not take it as a miss for my making so free with your honours name[1] as I am but a poor Girl but honest and has nothing to Suport me but my hands which I hope youre honour will not be a gain gaving me a presant by Post or any way that you think proper   I remain your humble Serven

MISS SUSANNAH SANTORAN
at the Corner of high and Bridg Street with Miss MacDougal

RC (MHi); endorsed by TJ as received   [1] MS: "mane."
17 Mch. and so recorded in SJL.

From William Barnwell

HONOURED SIR   Philadelphia March 15th 1802

It was with a considerable degree of pleasure that I learned lately, you were benevolently endeavouring to turn the Legislative attention towards the situation of the Citizens of the United States in the Town of New-Orleans. altho not much inclined to prefer warm, to temperate Climates, yet in case there are any regulations formed for that Port, I would be very happy to offer my services as a volunteer in that employ. under your auspices Sir I would willingly undertake it at any time, even without Legislative aid; for from having been habituated to such situations and their diseas there is much hope of my being the more capable of opposing their ravages. Please to excuse my presumption in thus addressing your Excellency, and believe me to be

Honoured Sir Yours most sincerely   WM. BARNWELL

RC (DNA: RG 59, LAR); endorsed by TJ as received 19 Mch. and "to be Physician of hospital at N. Orleans" and so recorded in SJL.

For TJ's effort TO TURN THE LEGISLATIVE ATTENTION toward establishing a marine hospital at New Orleans, see TJ to the Senate and the House of Representatives, 24 Feb. 1802.

HABITUATED TO SUCH SITUATIONS: Barnwell specialized in the study and treatment of tropical diseases (see Barnwell to TJ, 26 Jan. 1802).

From William Barton

SIR,   Lancaster, March 15th. 1802.—

Wishing to send two copies of my book to France, I conceived it would be proper to transmit them through the hands of Mr. Pichon, the French Resident here: Yet, not having the honor of any acquaintance with that Gentleman—and it being very uncertain whether the bearer of this (Mr. Peter Shindel, my next-door Neighbour,) will have an opportunity of calling on him,—I pray, Sir, that you will do me the honor of presenting them to Mr. Pichon; with a tender of my Respects, and a request that he would be pleased to forward the books, agreeably to the tenor of the enclosed Letter. This I have left unsealed, for your perusal; in order that, if it should not meet your approbation, it may not be forwarded.—

I have the Honor to be, With the highest Respect And greatest personal Consideration, Sir, Your mo. obedt. servt.

W. BARTON

RC (MHi); at foot of text: "The President"; endorsed by TJ as received 20 Mch. and so recorded in SJL. Enclosure not found.

BOOK: Barton's recently published *Dissertation on the Freedom of Navigation and Maritime Commerce*, which he had dedicated to TJ (Vol. 35:609-10; Vol. 36:610-11).

From Elizabeth Chester

City of Baltimore March the 15th. 1801 [i.e. 1802]
The Memorial of Elizabeth Chester
Most humbly Sheweth

That Your Memorialist's Husband Samuel Chester formerly a Recruiting Officer last American War, during which time he had Enlisted 7,500 Men for the service of the United States and learned them their Exercise, and he has been Dead about 5 Months left me destitute of house or home, as he had nothing himself and Your Memorialist has been Advised to apply to Your Excellency for a little relief as She has one Daughter whom She has bound to the Milliner and Mantua making business, and has two Dollars a Week to pay for her Board which is more than I can do at present without some Assistance, She will be free in a Short time and may be able to Support me in my Old Days by her Trade.

Therefore Your Memorialist Craves some help from Your Excellency, and She will ever pray

ELIZABETH CHESTER

any Commands directed to the post office Baltimore shall be duly attended to—

RC (DLC); at head of text: "To his Excellency Thomas Jefferson Esqr. President of the United States"; endorsed by TJ as received 17 Mch. 1802 and so recorded in SJL.

Captain Samuel Chester, a private in the Maryland Line during the Revolutionary War, submitted a petition to Congress in December 1796 seeking compensation for his services as a recruiting sergeant in Baltimore County. The committee of claims rejected his request and, as of the time of his death on 3 Dec. 1801, he had not received a pension for wartime service (Harry Wright Newman, *Maryland Revolutionary Records* [Baltimore, 1967], 88; JHR, 2:612, 651; *Federal Gazette & Baltimore Daily Advertiser*, 4 Dec. 1801).

From Anthony S. Gadbury

DEAR SIR   Alexandria March 15th 1802

Nothing but the present disagreeable necessity, compels me to trouble you with this letter, not Knowing who so well to apply to; I have been traveling to the western Country, & the Northward, and have got this far on my way home. (Goochland Cty.) and am under the necessity of saying, I am without money or friends in this place, having the misfortune to have one hundred dollars stolen out of my saddle bags in Chillocothe. I have parted with the last article I can (my Watch) and have got to this place, where I have been for fourteen days, during which time I have wrote several letters home, but can receive no answer, probably owing to the death of my Brother, which I have some reason to fear has taken place since my departure, having directed a sacrafice of my property to be made rather than not remit me money, and unfortunately for me I have none of my land warrants or certificates, having left them in the hands of an agent to get surveyed and deeded in the western Country; I have therefore taken the liberty of soliciting you to lend me fifty dollars, which I promise upon honour shall be refunded in three weeks from this time. If any doubts should arise with respect to my complying with the above promise, perhaps the inclosed letter, from a gentleman of respectability to me since my departure; may in a measure serve to remove it,

Your compliance with my solicitation will relieve one who is in distress and who will be under everlasting obligations to you

I am Sir (tho a stranger) yr. Hbl St—   A. S. GADBURY

P.S. please to let me hear from you by return of mail with the inclosed letter.—   A.S.G.

RC (MHi); endorsed by TJ as received 16 Mch. and so recorded in SJL. Enclosure: Thomas F. Bates to Anthony S. Gadbury, dated Belmont, Virginia, 7 Dec. 1801, stating that he brought up Gadbury's furniture as directed, but has not heard from him since his departure; Bates has nothing of substance to communicate, not even on politics, which now seem "happily buried in oblivion"; only "the uncommon drought" and the news of peace in Europe are now to be heard; perhaps Gadbury's journey "to some of the principal Cities" and contact with "the first Mercantile characters" might enable him to send news; if not, then "a simple journal of occurrences on road, will be pleasing" (RC in MHi; addressed: "Mr. Anthony S. Gadbury" with "Philadelphia" canceled and "Chilicotha N.W. Teritory" interlined in a different hand; postmarked Richmond 7 Dec. and Philadelphia 17 Dec.).

Anthony S. Gadbury was appointed postmaster at Goochland Court House in April 1801, but resigned the office the following September. By late January 1802, Gadbury was reported as having "absconded." Back home by April 1802, he sought to counter reports circulating that he had left Goochland "with an intention to defraud certain creditors, and was never expected to return." Gadbury denied the charge and called on his creditors to meet with him on 6 May to arrange a settlement. He thereafter planned to leave the place within six months, "and when I once more absent myself, I never shall return, I candidly believe" (Stets, *Postmasters*, 258; Joseph Habersham to Gadbury, 3 Sep. 1801, FC in Lb in DNA: RG 28, LPG; Richmond *Virginia Argus*, 14 April 1802; Vol. 32:287n).

From Caesar A. Rodney

HONORED & DEAR SIR,   Wilmington March 15th. 1802.

My friend Dr. A. Alexander of the town of New Castle will deliver you this letter. He has long & faithfully served us in our State legislature & has never even during the storm veered a single point from the steady cause of Republicanism. He has also been once our candidate for Governor & twice for Representative to congress. You will receive from him satisfactory information of the State of the public opinion here, & an accurate account of the late scene thro' which we have passed.

The *Opposition* must henceforth acknowledge your cool philosophic firmness & confess that your conduct exhibits the "*justum et tenacem, propositi virum.*"

Rest assured that their rude language & intemperate threats will recoil on themselves. If there were a latent spark of firmness in the constitution temper or frame of any representative in congress some of the declamatory harangues must have excited it, into action. In that way they have excited themselves. But "there is no terror in their threats," let them marshall themselves under the judges when they please we are prepared to meet them.

My health has been much impaired again this winter. Exercise is my support & our month of confinement almost destroys me. I hope your valuable & important life is prolonged free from every complaint or infirmity. With great personal regard & esteem believe me Dr. Sir

Yours Most Sincerely   C. A. RODNEY

RC (DLC); first set of closing quotes supplied; endorsed by TJ as received 25 Mch. and so recorded in SJL.

JUSTUM ET TENACEM PROPOSITI VIRUM: "a man upright and firm of purpose" (Horace, *Odes*, 3.3.1).

THERE IS NO TERROR IN THEIR THREATS: "There is no terror, Cassius, in your threats," Shakespeare, *Julius Caesar*, 4.3.

To George Jefferson

DEAR SIR   Washington Mar. 16. 1802.

Your's of the 10th. is recieved, and I have desired mr Barnes to credit mr Short 130. D. as recieved from you, and to place them to my account: so I must desire you to debit mr Barnes & credit me the same sum, to save the risk of actual remittance. it will serve to cover my current calls with you.—I must get the favor of you to send a hogshead of molasses for me to Monticello before the season gets too warm. I hope by this time the cyder has been forwarded to you from Norfolk, and gone on, as the season for bottling is passing. we are sending hence, and also ordering from Philadelphia, some groceries, to be addressed to you & forwarded to Monticello without delay, as I shall be there for two or three weeks immediately after the rising of Congress, which I judge will be within a month from this time. accept my affectionate salutation.   TH: JEFFERSON

PrC (MHi); at foot of text: "Mr. George Jefferson"; endorsed by TJ in ink on verso.

To Robert R. Livingston

DEAR SIR   Washington Mar. 16. 1802.

Your favor of Dec. 26. was recieved the 5th. inst. and one of a later date to the Secretary of state has been communicated to me. the present is intended as a commentary on my letter to you of Aug. 28. when I wrote that letter I did not harbour a doubt that the disposition on that side the water was as cordial, as I knew our's to be. I thought it important that the agents between us should be such as both parties would be willing to open themselves to freely. I ought to have expressed in that letter the distinction between the two characters therein named, which really existed in my mind: of one of them I[1] thought nothing good. as to the other (whom you mention to be the real one contemplated) I considered him well disposed to this country, but not towards it's political principles. I had confidence in him to a certain extent; but that confidence had limits. I thought a slight hint of this might have had some effect on the choice of an agent. but the dispositions now understood to exist there, impose of themselves limits to the openness of our communications, and bring us within the extent of that reposed in the agent under consideration. consequently it is adequate to all the purposes for which it will be used. I wish you therefore not only to suggest nothing against his mission, but on the contrary, to impress him that it will be agreeable and even desirable, which is the truth. for I firmly believe him well disposed to preserve amity between that country and this. tho' clouds may occasionally obscure the horison between us, yet there is a fund of friendship & attachment between the mass of the two nations which will always in time dispel those nebulosities. the present administration of this country have these feelings of their constituents, and will be true to them. we shall act steadily on the desire of cementing our interests & affections; and of this you cannot go too far in assuring them. in every event we will recieve with satisfaction any missionary they chuse to send. not being very sure of the channel of conveyance for this letter, I have explained the former one so that you will understand it; and reserve myself on other subjects to some future occasion. accept assurances of my high esteem & consideration.   TH: JEFFERSON

RC (NNMus); addressed: "Robert R. Livingston Min. Pleny. of the US. of America at Paris"; endorsed by Livingston. PrC (DLC).

ONE OF A LATER DATE TO THE SECRETARY OF STATE: in a letter to Madison on 31 Dec., Livingston said among other things that the French government was republican neither in form nor in practice. Noting that the French showed "high favor" to monarchical governments, Livingston reported that Bonaparte, who had "severely" criticized TJ's inaugural address, considered TJ to be a Jacobin and was extremely displeased with the National Institute's decision to elect him to membership. The first consul's government, according to Livingston, would have preferred William Vans Murray as the American minister. Livingston informed Madison that he was willing to give up the position if his doing so would benefit the public good (Madison, *Papers, Sec. of State Ser.*, 2:359).

In his letter to Livingston of 28 Aug.

1801, TJ expressed concerns about the possibility that the French government would send Antoine René Charles Mathurin de La Forest or Louis Guillaume Otto as minister to the United States. Livingston had learned from Talleyrand, and reported to Madison in a letter of 10 Dec., that Otto was the ONE CONTEMPLATED for the appointment. In a letter of 26 Feb. 1802, not yet received in the United States when TJ wrote the letter printed above, Livingston asked Madison for "particular" instructions regarding Otto. Livingston reported that Otto "stands very high here. He will be charged with instructions to make a commercial treaty with us." Late in 1802, the French government announced that Otto would not be going to the United States (same, 2:304, 493; 3:26, 29n, 290; 4:277, 279n).

[1] TJ first wrote "in one of them I had" before altering the passage to read as above.

From Joseph Yznardi, Sr.

Philadelphia, 16 Mch. 1802. Acknowledging with gratitude the $590 payment for wines, he offers to obtain more wine from Spain whenever TJ may desire. As he prepares to embark for Cadiz on the *Patapsco*, his bailsman in the lawsuit instigated by Joseph Israel wishes to be released from that obligation. Israel, lacking evidence to support his suit, is dragging out the case by seeking to obtain evidence from Spain. Yznardi believes that Alexander J. Dallas would change his mind about the case if it were referred to him again. Convinced that Israel would end the suit, as John M. Pintard dropped his case, if the government will undertake his defense, Yznardi is writing to the secretary of state and asks the president to consider his lamentable situation as the victim of a lawsuit for actions he performed in an official capacity. If he did not have to leave to rejoin his family, he would supplicate himself before TJ with tears, yet surely he has said enough to touch a heart as humane as TJ's. He is certain that God will reward TJ, who is Yznardi's sole protector in the United States, for the favors he has granted.

RC (DNA: RG 59, CD); 2 p.; in Spanish; at foot of text: "Exmo. Sr. Dn. Thomas Jefferson"; endorsed by TJ as received 19 Mch. and so recorded in SJL; also endorsed by TJ: "referrd to secy. of State Th:J."; endorsed for the State Department.

From John Thomson Mason

Dear Sir   George Town 17th March 1802

It is with real diffidence that I shall enter upon the duties of Atty Genl of the US should future events induce you to wish it. Highly sensible of the Honor you did me in proposing it I explained to you the true grounds of my fears upon the subject. I shall industriously endeavour to remove them, in these endeavours I indulge myself with the hope of your friendly advice and assistance

With sentiments of high respect and real esteem I am D Sir Your obedt. Servt.   John T. Mason

RC (DNA: RG 59, LAR); endorsed by TJ as received 19 Mch. and so recorded in SJL; also endorsed by TJ: "A. Gl."

From John Minor

Dear Sir   Fredericksburg. March 17th 1802

When your Letter of the 10th Instant reached this place I was in Richmond attending the court of Chancery. it was sent forward, but did not get to Richmond untill I had left that place: the consequence of which has been that I did not Receive it untill to Day; let this my dear Sir, be my apology for an apparent neglect.

I will give entire attention to Mr Shorts Interest in the Case you mention

I am with sentiments of highest Respect & Esteem Dear Sir yr. obligd Hble Serv. JOHN MINOR

RC (DLC: William Short Papers); endorsed by TJ as received 20 Mch. and so recorded in SJL.

From Thomas Paine

DEAR SIR   Paris March 17. 1802

I wrote to you while Mr Dawson was here that I would wait the arrival of the Frigate that was to bring Mr Livingston, and return by it to America, in preference to the Maryland which you offered me; but the frigate being ordered to the Mediterranean prevented me that opportunity. As it is now Peace, though the definitive Treaty is not yet signed, I shall sett off by the first opportunity from Havre or Dieppe after the Equinoxial Gales are over.

Your Discourse to Congress has drawn a great deal of attention both here and in England, and has been printed in a Pamphlet in both Contries; that in France with a french French translation annext. I sent some Copies to a very intimate and old acquaintance of mine and also an acquaintance of Mr Monroe, Sir Robert Smyth, and I transcribe you an extract from his Answer by which you will see the opinion the Patriots form of it on this side the Water.

"With respect to Mr Jefferson's speech it is a Master-piece of simple and unaffected Eloquence,[1] and of clear honest political statement. There is no State Paper, except the celebrated one of Count Bernstorff of Denmark upon the french revolution, to be compared to it. It confirms the opinion I always had of Mr Jefferson; and I always Lamented that my return to England in 1787, to attend Parliament, prevented my Cultivating his acquaintance. I had then an excellent Opportunity from my residing at Challiot and sometimes visiting Dr. Franklin who lived at Passy very near me; and Mr Jefferson took the beautiful Villa at the Barriere where I once saw him in Company with Mr Humphries, Mr Smith and some other American Gentlemen.—It is certainly a Curious Phænomenon to hear the Executive Magistrate complain of having too much power and too much revenue. The Tories in England say the king has neither Revenue nor Power enough to govern with effect, although the Management of the public revenue, the prerogative of the Crown, and the influence he has over Parliament render him all Powerfull."

I have introduced an acquaintance between Mr Livingston and Sir

R. which is become very agreeable to both, as they are Men of the same habits and the same principles.

The Negociation at Amiens still hangs in the Wind. What the impediments are I do not know. But viewing the Matter in Mass, I can find no disposition to believe that the Negociation will be broken off, and hostilities renewed. There appears to me no object to justify such a Measure in the opinion of thinking Men in either Country, especially after the first difficulties are gotten over, that of signing the Preliminaries. I suppose the embarrassment, if there is any, may be guessed at, by supposing a truce between two Armies in which one complains that the other has altered his position during the truce.

I see that the dispute with Tripoly still remains unsetteled. I will throw out an Idea upon this subject. There are but few places in Europe where Ministers from America can be of much use. But I think if one could be sent, and well received at Constantinople it would be of Considerable advantage towards the security of our Commerce in the Mediterranean. The Porte has, on account of its religion, considerable influence over the Barbary States, and those States would, I think, be much checked in their avidity and insolence for war with us, if we were on a good standing at Constantinople.

A Daughter of Sir Robert Smyth is married to an intimate friend of mine, Mr Este, a young Man of promising Abilities, great industry, and considerable acquired property. Sir Robert has brought him forward by establishing a banking house at Paris under the firm of Sir R. Smyth and Company, and I see the business done at it will be great. I recollect that Mr Le Grand, an acquaintance of Doctor Franklin, was Banker for the United States during the American War. He is since dead, and the concerns for the United States have since that been done at Amsterdam; But as you have now no Minister there, you may find it convenient to remove it again to Paris, in which case you cannot place it, or some part of it better than in the house I am speaking of, but I will talk more about this when I have the happiness of seeing you which I hope will be soon after your receipt of this letter. I continue in excellent health, which I know your friendship will be glad to hear of.

Wishing you and America every happiness I remain Your former fellow Labourer and much obliged fellow Citizen

THOMAS PAINE

RC (DLC); at foot of text: "Thomas Jefferson President of the United States"; endorsed by TJ as received 1 June and so recorded in SJL.

WROTE TO YOU: writing to TJ on 9 June 1801, Paine presumed that he would be able to travel to the United States aboard whatever vessel took Robert R. LIVINGSTON to France (Vol. 34:281).

TJ's 8 Dec. 1801 message to CONGRESS appeared in FRENCH TRANSLATION as the *Discourse of Thomas Jefferson, President of the United-States, for the Opening of the Session. Discours de Thomas Jefferson, Président des États-Unis, pour l'ouverture de la derniere session du Congrès (Traduction Littérale)* (Paris, 1802), which had English and French texts of the message on facing pages.

Paine was a close friend of SIR ROBERT SMYTH, an English banker, baronet, and former member of Parliament who resided in Paris during the French Revolution. Smyth sympathized with the revolution, and when French revolutionary authorities, suspicious of British citizens, wanted to imprison him and expel his family, Paine interceded with a declaration that Smyth "likes neither the Government nor the climate" of England. Smyth did return to Britain for a time, but was in the process of reestablishing his banking business in Paris when he died suddenly in April 1802 (John Keane, *Tom Paine: A Political Life* [London, 1995], 421, 604n; Jack Fruchtman, Jr., *Thomas Paine: Apostle of Freedom* [New York, 1994], 283, 300, 321, 350, 372; J. G. Alger, "The British Colony in Paris, 1792-93," *English Historical Review*, 13 [1898], 674, 676-7, 679, 690-1; Vol. 32:190).

Between 1773 and 1780, and from 1784 until his death in 1797, Count Andreas Peter BERNSTORFF was foreign minister of Denmark and head of the German Chancellery. Schooled in Enlightenment thought, Bernstorff promulgated social and political reforms in Denmark but loyally supported the monarchy. Devoted to neutrality and the avoidance of war, he brought Denmark into the 1780 league of armed neutrality. In 1789, he predicted that the French Revolution would bring civil war, and two years later he declared that it would result, ironically, in despotism and a loss of individual rights. In the 1790s, he kept his country out of the coalitions against revolutionary France and wrote memorials opposing British encroachments on neutral rights. Bernstorff and TJ had some official contact when TJ was in Europe in the 1780s (Lawrence J. Baack, *Christian Bernstorff and Prussia: Diplomacy and Reform Conservatism, 1818-1832* [New Brunswick, N.J., 1980], 1-5; H. Arnold Barton, *Scandinavia in the Revolutionary Era, 1760-1815* [Minneapolis, 1986], 94-5, 172-3, 178-9, 213-15; Alastair H. Thomas and Stewart P. Oakley, *Historical Dictionary of Denmark* [Lanham, Md., 1998], 56-7; Syrett, *Hamilton*, 19:504n; Vol. 7:631, 633; Vol. 12:525-6; Vol. 13:135, 257-9, 294, 299).

William Stephens SMITH, the son-in-law of John and Abigail Adams, was in Paris in 1787 (DAB; Vol. 11:334).

Negotiators led by Lord Cornwallis for the British side and Joseph Bonaparte for the French had been meeting at AMIENS, France, since December. Envoys from Spain and the Batavian Republic also participated in the talks. Governance of Malta proved to be the most difficult issue to resolve, but in mid-March the parties reached agreement on that and other issues. They signed the treaty of peace on 27 Mch. (John D. Grainger, *The Amiens Truce: Britain and Bonaparte, 1801-1803* [Rochester, N.Y., 2004], 52-76).

MR LE GRAND: Ferdinand Grand, who died in 1794 (Vol. 29:354n).

[1] Paine first wrote, and then canceled, "Eloquence," then interlined and canceled "Elegance," before settling on "Eloquence."

From John Beckley

Washington, 18th: March 1802.

Permit me to lay before you the enclosed Certificate. The restoration of the Judiciary System, to that state in which it stood before the Act, lately repealed, was passed, necessarily occasions the State of pennsylvania to become again, an entire judicial district, and, of consequence, that the Office of one of the present Marshalls, must be discontinued.

Mr: Smith, reasonably supposes, that in addition to the fact, that nineteeen twentieths of the business of pennsylvania accrues in the Eastern district, this Certificate of his good conduct and character from men of opposite politics, will not be unavailing in the mind of the Chief magistrate, on the Question, which of the two present Marshalls shall be continued.

At his request, and on his behalf, I therefore present it, and am, with every sentiment of respect and esteem, Sir,

Your obedt: Servant,   JOHN BECKLEY

RC (DNA: RG 59, LAR); endorsed by TJ as received 19 Mch. and "John Smith to be marshal Pensva" and so recorded in SJL. Enclosure: perhaps a recommendation sent to Smith, at his request, dated 1 Mch. 1802, signed by 24 members of the Philadelphia bar, including Federalists William Rawle, James Milnor, William Lewis, Edward Tilghman, and Jonathan W. Condy and Republicans John L. Leib, Moses Levy, and Mahlon Dickerson, noting that although at the time of his appointment some entertained unfavorable opinions of him, they now agree that, as far as their knowledge extends, Smith "has been impartial vigilent and firm; and free from any cause of censure, or reproach" (RC in same; John H. Martin, *Martin's Bench and Bar of Philadelphia* [Philadelphia, 1883], 258-317; Richard G. Miller, *Philadelphia—The Federalist City: A Study of Urban Politics, 1789-1801* [Port Washington, N.Y., 1976], 68, 80, 132, 155n, 178n; Andrew Shankman, *Crucible of American Democracy: The Struggle to Fuse Egalitarianism & Capitalism in Jeffersonian Pennsylvania* [Lawrence, Kans., 2004], 162; Vol. 33:543;Vol. 34:74n; Josias Wilson King to TJ, 21 Jan. 1802).

When John SMITH successfully applied in March 1801 to be marshal of the eastern district of Pennsylvania, Beckley had submitted a certificate in his support. Early in his administration, TJ appointed Presley Carr Lane as marshal for the western district, but it was Smith who retained the office after the state became a single judicial district (JEP, 1:432, 440; Vol. 33:219, 246-8, 674).

On 30 Mch., Pennsylvania congressmen Robert Brown, Isaac Van Horne, and John Stewart wrote TJ expressing their support for Smith. They noted that he had "faithfully discharged the duties of his Office" and hoped he would continue in office "when the law creating two districts shall cease to exist" (RC in DNA: RG 59, LAR; in an unidentified hand, signed by Brown, Van Horne, and Stewart; at foot of text: "The President of the United States"; endorsed by TJ as received 31 Mch. and "Smith John. to be Marshl. of Pensva." and so recorded in SJL).

TJ viewed three other certificates or recommendations for Smith. On 27 Mch., Richard Peters certified that the marshal "has given perfect Satisfaction to me (in every Respect) in all Things which have fallen under my Observation." William Griffith, judge of the Third Circuit Court, wrote on 30 Mch. that all Smith's "official proceedings and conduct which have fallen under my notice on the bench have appeared to evince—integrity—industry—and impartiality, and all the qualifications most requisite in that office." On 6 Apr., William Tilghman acknowledged in a letter to Smith that he endorsed the testimony given by the Philadelphia bar on Smith's behalf and wished to add his opinion that the marshal's conduct was "attentive, upright, & entirely satisfactory" (all in same; last two endorsed by TJ as recommending Smith for Pennsylvania marshal).

To Benjamin Rush

TH: JEFFERSON TO DR. RUSH   Mar. 18. 1802.

I recieved last night your friendly letter of the 12th. which shall be answered the first practicable moment. in the mean time I send you Latude which I happen to have here. affectionate salutations.

RC (Swann Auction Catalogue, sale 2058, New York, 2005); address clipped: "Doctr. Benjamin [Rush]"; franked and postmarked.

To James Dinsmore

DEAR SIR   Washington Mar. 19. 1802.

This is merely to correct an error in my last. I mentioned that the brick pilasters should have their Capitals 3. courses of brick high & with 3. projections. but as the Capital should be in height only half the diameter, & that is of a brick and a half, say 13. I. the height of the capital must be of 2. courses only, each course projecting $1.\frac{1}{4}$ I. so as to make the upper one 2. bricks square.

As I suppose mr Lilly is digging the North-West offices, & Ice house I will now give further directions respecting them. the eves[1] of those offices is to be of course exactly on the level of those on the South East side of the hill. but as the North-West building is chiefly for coach houses, the floor must be sunk 9. feet deep below the bottom of the plate to let a coach go under it. then the ice house is to be dug 16. feet deeper than that. the ice house is then to be walled, circular, to a height of 4. feet above the office floors, leaving a door $3\frac{1}{2}$ feet wide on the N.W. side of it. on that height it is to be joisted with 2. I. plank, 9. I. wide & laid edge up & 9. I. clear apart from one another, running across the building, or N.W. & S.E.[2] then to be covered with inch plank. by this means it will depend on the roof of the offices for shelter from rain, and there will be a space of about 2. or 3. f. (I do not remember exactly) between it's covering and the joists of the offices. thus.

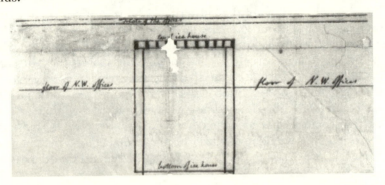

this arrangement of the joists is intended to leave them open towards the N.W. wind to let in air, which may be excluded by small shutters whenever it shall be thought better to close them. the openings are left only 9. I. square that a person may not get in at them.

Accept my best wishes.   TH: JEFFERSON

RC (DLC); addressed: "Mr. James Dinsmore Monticello near Milton"; franked and postmarked.

TJ's LAST letter to Dinsmore, recorded in SJL at 14 Mch., has not been found.

[1] Word interlined in place of "plats."
[2] Passage from "running" to this point interlined in place of "this arrangement is intended."

From George Jefferson

DEAR SIR   Richmond 19th. March 1802

I have duly received your favor of the 16th. and have in compliance therewith given you credit by Mr. Barnes for the 130:$ received of Mosby for Mr. Short.

The cyder has not yet arrived from Norfolk; which however, as yet, is of no consequence, as it could not have been forwarded, in consequence of the low water.

There have not I believe been a dozen boats down from Milton in 5 or 6. months.

I am Dear Your Very humble servt.   GEO. JEFFERSON

RC (MHi); at foot of text: "Thos. Jefferson esqr."; endorsed by TJ as received 24 Mch. and so recorded in SJL.

From Philip Myer

Sir,   Washington City March 19th 1802

The humble *petition* of the subscriber I hope will not be thought improper—I am A poor *unfortunate* Man *imprisoned* & overcome by the Iron hand of A man of fortune—It may be said i'me not imprisoned by him but may truely date all my present misfortunes through him. The person of whome i'me speaking is A residenter of Georgetown his name is John Threlkeld, he has injured me by taken the most unwarantabl liberties with my wife, he first tried all that art and seduction could invent to seduce her from *morality*, & the mariage bed; finding that would not answer his *unmanly* ends—I blush to say it, he brought in force to his aid to accomplish an end that depravity itselfe must shrink at—

One eving knowing my absince from my family, he came to my dwelling, & renewed his former conduct towards my wife with A brutality unprecedented amongst Civilized society, in this *unprotected* state he commited acts that would be unnecesary & indelicate for me to repeat—After my return I applied to the Law for redress, sory am I to say poverty was too powerful opponent against me—I *applied* to A Lawyer but with no affect for I'd no money to fee him to prosecute the cause—Not content with commiting his outrages on my wife, he sought every means in his power to prevent my futer peace, He went to Fredricksburg, & Baltimore for the purpose of urgeing my Creditors to means which would have never ben complied with but from the most vile misrepresintations he made use of, to destroy my reputation, those he could not bring over, he purchased for the intire intention of ruinig me intoto, by throwing me in Prison—In consequence of which I was arested & am now suffering the most rigorous confinement—Bail I could have procured but for the *powerful* preponderance of his influence by the means of his riches—In short every infamous subterfuge he stooped to, to destroy me & my unhappy family—

My wife, & three small children are now exsperiencing all the *misery* that *poverty* & it's attendants can entail or stamp on it's unfortunate votaries—Situated as I am, I cannot receive that Justice which the Laws hath pointed out to every individual—The condition i'me in is A scene of the most poignat distress—Laying in Jail my wife & family perishing by the harshe hand of hunger except what the inhospitable service Charity bestowes—

I hope & trust you'll excuse, & pardon this liberty which i've taken, it arises from several reasons, first, & principal one is; at present you'r not only the illustrious President of the U States, but the supreme Magistrate of this Territory as such i'me sure of not meeting with A repulse but in every respect the reverse—Seconly I address you, from *you'r* long hailed[1] Justice, magnanimity & Virtue—& lastly you'r benevolence & philantropic generosity was never refused to the hand of suffering distress & inocence—

If you should think proper to receive any further Information on this disagreeable & unhappy business, my Wife who's the bearer of this will give it You—If you will please to interfeer so far as Justice is wanting it's all that the unfortunate Writer wishes to receive from you—That this may meet you'r approbation is the fond prayer of respected Sir the forlorn   PHILIP MYER

NB an answer by the bearer of this is humbly solicited by P M

RC (DLC); addressed: "The President of the United States Washington City"; endorsed by TJ as received 19 Mch. and so recorded in SJL.

A former mayor of Georgetown, JOHN THRELKELD exchanged plant cuttings with TJ during the later years of his pres-idency. John Adams had named him a justice of the peace for the District of Columbia, but TJ did not appoint him. In 1807, TJ did name him a justice of the peace for Washington County (JEP, 2:56, 59; RS, 1:40; Vol. 36:314).

[1] MS: "haied."

To James Walter

SIR   Washington Mar. 19. 1802.

Your favor of the 8th. inst. was recieved on the 12th. I am duly sensible of the mark of respect to me which you are pleased to testify by the name you propose to give to the town you are about to establish. it is the more grateful to me as it comes from a person, uninfluenced by personal acquaintance, and who has been able to judge me by my actions, unblinded by the mists of unprincipled slander under which public prints endeavor to cover me from the view of my constituents. with respect to the name proposed I have only to observe that it has been already given by an act of the Virginia legislature to a small town laid out on James river, the situation of which however does not seem to promise success to it's establishment.   Accept my best wishes and assurances of respect & consideration.

RC (MoSHi: Jefferson Papers); at foot of text: "Mr James Walter"; endorsed by TJ in ink on verso.

SMALL TOWN: Jefferson, located 35 miles above Richmond and situated on the south bank of the James River in Powhatan County, was founded by Samuel Hyde Saunders and officially established by an act of the Virginia

General Assembly in December 1794 (Agnes Evans Gish, "'A place of considerable trade for its size' Jefferson: A James River Canal Town," *Virginia Cavalcade*, 50 [2001], 88-95; *Acts Passed at a General Assembly of the Commonwealth of Virginia, Begun and Held at the Capitol, in the City of Richmond, on Tuesday, the Eleventh Day of November, One Thousand Seven Hundred and Ninety-Four* [Richmond, 1795; Evans, No. 29796], 25). As of January 1801, the Virginia General Assembly had already established a Jefferson County, a Jeffersonville in Tazewell County, and a Jeffersonton in Culpeper County (*Acts Passed at a General Assembly of the Commonwealth of Virginia* [Richmond, 1801; Shaw-Shoemaker, No. 1584], 17, 18; J. E. Worcester, *A Gazetteer of the United States Abstracted from the Universal Gazetteer of the Author; with Enlargement of the Principal Articles* [Andover, Mass., 1818; Shaw-Shoemaker, No. 46867]).

To Joseph Yznardi, Sr.

DEAR SIR   Washington Mar. 19.

On the 10th. inst. I wrote to you inclosing a check on the bank of the US. for D. 590.72 the amount of the bill for the last wines you were so good as to send me. not knowing whether you were in Baltimore or Philadelphia, the letter laid by me two days for enquiry, and I then inclosed it to Genl. Smith, asking him to superscribe on it the proper place. I mention this because mr Barnes informs me that by a letter of your's on the 12th. you had not recieved mine of the 10th. this I know because it went out of my hand only on the 12th. I hope however you have now recieved it, and shall be happy to hear whether you have or not, as I know not to what place it was sent. Accept assurances of my esteem and consideration.

                                            TH: JEFFERSON

PrC (DLC); at foot of text: "Joseph Yznardi esq."; endorsed by TJ in ink on verso.

TJ's communication to Samuel SMITH dated on or about 12 Mch. has not been found and is not recorded in SJL.

LETTER OF YOUR'S: in a brief letter to John Barnes, written at Philadelphia on 12 Mch. and forwarded by Barnes to TJ, Yznardi noted that he was "in the eve of leaving this Country" and said that he would "be much obliged if you could forward me as soon as posibly the amount of the last wines sent to the President if he has given you any orders for it as my Son Patrick has told me" (RC in DLC; in Patrick Yznardi's hand; at head of text: "Mr. John Barnes"; addressed by Barnes: "The President—UStates"; endorsed by TJ as received 19 Mch. and so recorded in SJL).

From David Austin

Respected Sir.   Washington March 20th 1802.

The smallest attention to the principles of decorum would have forbid any farther instrusion upon your moments after the very polite note with which you was pleased to honor me; was I not still persuaded of being capable of rendering essential services to the United States, abroad.

From London, the cords of the National dulcimer might be so toutched as to vibrate in favor of our interests in the Mediterranean & elsewhere. The Barbary powers hope through Great Britain to master your armament against them. Their overtures, to this effect must be resisted. The quietus of the Barbary Coast must be served at Constantinople. The attention of the revolutionary storm needs to be kept on eastward; & not suffered to react upon the western board. We shall again be endangered, if we cannot give an eastern direction to the returning flame. From London the different powers affected by the Barbary depredation might be toutched; & if the Convention of powers at Amiens is not disolved, the A. Minister might stipulate on certain conditions for a reciprocity of privilige with them in all commercial relations.

I perceive, Sir, that as soon as the West India convulsions are disposed of, the Eye of the French administration will be upon this quarter. It is the returning[1] fire: It is the *reacting flame*. The common expectation of general felicity hath received a check in Europe, by reason of a power & principles not favorable to the interests & prospects of the first revolution.

I will not detain your moments but pray you Sir to believe, that with heartfelt satisfaction I should enter upon the theatre of foreign exertion; & doubt not should be able to allay present evils, & to arrest those to which we may be, thro' tardiness exposed.—It is a trial to me; that in my public illustrations of the operations of Providence, I cannot bring the standing & administration of the present moment *into a cooperation with Heaven's majestic design.*—Open to me the door, in such way as you please, Sir, & if I do not in ten days, do more to quiet National tumult, & to put the Ship United States, at her ease, than all the pulpits, presses & post-Offices, yet have done, I will hold my self liable to surrender the trust, at a moments warning.—

With high sentiments of esteem subscribe   DAVID AUSTIN

RC (DNA: RG 59, LAR); addressed: "His Ex'y Thomas Jefferson Esqr. President U: States Washington"; endorsed by TJ as received 26 Mch. and so recorded in SJL; also endorsed by TJ: "to be Ambassador."

VERY POLITE NOTE: TJ to Austin, 21   [1] MS: "returing."
Jan. 1802, in which TJ requested that
Austin cease writing to him.

From Tench Coxe

SIR   Philada. Mar. 20. 1802.

In the course of some recent attempts to improve the public mind
with our capacities and progress upon the subject of cotton, several
ideas, which did not appear fit for present publication, occurd. It appeared of importance that they should be placed before the government however, to be treated according to their discretion. I concluded
to make a little historical note upon the cotton business with some remarks & to introduce the ideas I mean into that note. I have the honor
now to communicate it—

There seems to be no doubt that the combination of water machinery with cotton planting will awaken several extensive and populous
countries to the capacity to produce it, which they possess in common
with us. Wherefore it seems highly expedient to consider in a confidential way, within the government, the best means of promoting the
cultivation, manufacture and exportation of it, as a branch of our
affairs, before other countries shall attempt to take it up. The possession of the Business will enable us to retain it longer and in a greater
degree than would otherwise be the case.

I find from a recurrence to the Mercantile books of my apprenticeship, that cotton of the crop of 1775 was slight from St Croix at $16\frac{1}{2}$
d. in that money for the Danish pound. This is about $13\frac{1}{2}$ cents for
the pound avoirds., at which it was deemed a good object for the
small planters.

The effect upon the white population of the Southern states is one
of vast importance, which it is prudent to wrap up whenever it is refered to in public. Here, I take the liberty to say that the militia, the
naturalization rule, the cotton business, and every other topic, which
can be made to subserve *the great end of checking, counterbalancing,
and diffusing the blacks*, should be wisely, humanely, and promptly
resorted to. By the time the convulsions in the west Indies shall be
terminated we may be in safer condition. Should any turn of affairs
put Cuba into the Situation of St. Domingo & Guadaloupe, we are to
remember that it is but 30 or 40 leagues from our continent, and the
freight is possible by barges to hardy, enterprizing and enthusiastic
men, who might be disposed to introduce mischief among the black

& red S—s in our Southern ports— The Spanish Government may revolutionize; the blacks daily encreased by importations may rise; and, in the event of a crush of the french force in St. Domingo, the blacks might excite an insurrection in Cuba. These things, with possible events in Florida, & Louisiana, ought to inspire us with prudence & forethought tho not with fear.

I have the honor to be, sir, your respectful h. Servant

TENCH COXE

RC (DNA: RG 59, LAR); addressed: "The President of the United States" and "Private"; endorsed by TJ. Recorded in SJL as received 24 Mch.

Coxe's latest essay on the SUBJECT OF COTTON, signed "Franklin," appeared in the Philadelphia *Aurora* on 20 Mch. Coxe predicted that probably 25 million pounds of cotton would be grown in the United States in 1802 and he encouraged the country's manufacture of cotton goods. He found cotton to be "a peculiarly hopeful raw material" for the U.S. because it could be "worked by labor saving machines, and by foreign artists migrating hither." According to Coxe, it was "transcendantly important" to raise and manufacture cotton in the "*proper grand division* of our country," that is, the

South, where that crop would "detain, encrease and condense free population there," and "occasion the diffusion of the other kind." For other articles by "Franklin" supporting the growth and manufacture of cotton, see the 11, 19, and 22 Feb. and 1 Mch. issues of the *Aurora*.

In October 1801, revolutionaries in GUADALOUPE overthrew Governor Lacrosse and deported him to Denmark. On 3 Dec., French authorities proclaimed the colony to be in revolt and declared that no vessel was to enter or leave the island without prior permission. On 1 Feb. 1802, the *National Intelligencer* reported that a French frigate had stopped an American vessel bound for there and ordered it away, declaring that Guadaloupe was closed to all shipping (Madison, *Papers, Sec. of State Ser.*, 2:364, 433-4).

From William R. Davie

SIR   Halifax No. Carolina, March 20th. 1802

I have the honor to acknowledge your letter of the 28th Ulto, covering that of Mr. DuPont and Mr. Barbe-Marbois respecting the business of General LaFayette: The friends of this unfortunate Patriot will feel themselves indebted to your Excellency for your polite attention to this subject; it is certainly important, if any measure should be attempted in his behalf, that the proposition should be made on a practicable and admissible principle; the mode, you have been so good as to recommend, is the only one I suppose that could be adopted to serve him, consistent with the constructions of our constitution, and the laws of France, which do not permit a citizen to receive a pension from any foreign nation, and this mode will certainly be the most honorable and therefore the most agreeable to the General.

After giving this business some consideration, I have thought however that it would not be prudent to bring it before Congress during the present session, this time appears to me, the most unfavorable that could be chosen for that purpose; the differences which have prevailed and the exertion which have been made in Congress have wrought up party spirit to the highest pitch of irritation, and one could scarcely expect amidst the conflict of angry and unfriendly passions and the animosity of party rage, a coincidence of just feeling and generous sentiment on any subject.

I have the honor to be with the highest respect—your Excellencys mo. obt. W. R. DAVIE

RC (DLC); at foot of text: "Thomas Jefferson Esqr. President of the U States"; endorsed by TJ. Recorded in SJL as received 5 Apr.

From Nicolas Gouin Dufief

MONSIEUR 20 de Mars. 1802

Vous trouverez ci inclus quelques exemplaires du catalogue que je viens de publier—Je me propose de faire venir de France une collection des nouveautés les plus intéressantes dans tous les genres—

Si vous avez des ordres à me donner à ce Sujet, soyez assuré qu'ils seront exécutés avec toute la diligence & le soin possible. En vous adressant à moi à present vous seriez Servi probablement en septembre prochain. Vous receverez le Chaptal à la premiere occasion qui se presentera pour Washington—

Recevez avec votre bonté ordinaire les assurances de mon profond respect & de mon dévouement N. G. DUFIEF

EDITORS' TRANSLATION

SIR, 20 Mch. 1802

You will find included herein a few copies of the catalogue that I have just published. I propose to order from France a collection of the most interesting novelties of all kinds.

If you have any orders to give me about this, be assured that they will be executed with all the diligence and care possible. By addressing me at present, you would probably be served by next September. You will receive the Chaptal by the first opportunity that arises for sending to Washington.

Accept with your usual kindness the assurances of my deep respect and my devotion N. G. DUFIEF

RC (DLC); at foot of text: "Le President des Etats Unis"; endorsed by TJ as received 22 Mch. and so recorded in SJL.

From Anthony S. Gadbury

DEAR SIR   Alexandria 20 Mar. 1801 [i.e. 1802]

I wrote you some days ago, informing you, I was in a disagreeable situation, for want of money in a strange place. I now have the pleasure to say I am releived by the arival of the mail the following evening.

please to inclose the inclosd letter directed to Richmond, Va.

Yrs Respectfully   A. S. GADBURY

RC (MHi); endorsed by TJ as a letter of 20 Mch. 1802 received 23 Mch. and so recorded in SJL.

I WROTE YOU SOME DAYS AGO: Gadbury to TJ, 15 Mch. 1802.

THE INCLOSD LETTER: Thomas F. Bates to Gadbury, 7 Dec. 1801, which Gadbury enclosed in his letter to TJ of 15 Mch.

To Thomas Mann Randolph

DEAR SIR   Washington Mar. 20.

Your's of the 13th. is recieved. I promised in my last I would make enquiry of mr Milledge of Augusta in Savanna on the subject of cotton, because he is a great cultivator of it, in fact the introducer of it there, very accurate & judicious. he says the blackseed cotton is cultivated in the country below Augusta, the green seed above. the former sells for 40. cents when the latter is at 20. cents: but you can cultivate twice as much of the green seed, say 8. acres to a hand, because you can use the plough, which cannot be done with the black seed. he cultivates the black at Augusta, and makes 600. ℔ & upwards to the hand. yet he has no doubt it is better on the whole to cultivate the green. the country begins about 30. miles below Augusta to be hilly & healthy, and the whole of the state above that is proper for the green seed cotton. pine lands mixed with oak & hickory bushes with a clayey bottom is good: but that without clay is absolute barrens, which is the case with Sibbald's. the lands proper for cotton between the Savanna and Ogechee from Augusta upwards sells from 4. to 6. Dollars. at the latter price it may be bought with a tolerable dwelling house & improvements. in tending the green seed you have abundant time to tend corn, of which these lands yield 4. 5. 6. barrels to the acre. he supposes a man should have 20. acres for every labourer, and that there should not be more than from 18. to 25. labourers on one plantation. he thinks the culture of the cotton requires nicer management & skill than tobacco does; the green less than the black. the black opens it's pods & loses it's cotton all at once, the green may stay in the bole through the winter to be gathered at leisure. it is frequently not gathered till March. he thinks the best counties taking all circumstances into consideration are those from Augusta to Louisville the seat of government[1] & rather above those towns. a good negro labourer, young will sell for from 550. to 600. D. Ned Rutledge's whole stock young & old averaged lately 480. D. he believes the country from Augusta and Louisville to be as healthy as any in the universe. very good for stock. from Charlottesville to Augusta is probably about 480. miles going by Prince Edwd. Charlotte C. H. Halifax C. H. crossing[2] Dan & Stanton, then by Hillsboro', Montgomery C. H. and Anson C. H. in N.C. Cambden & Columbia in S.C. to Augusta. Mr. Milledge says he will take Edgehill in his route back and stay a day with you, and give you all the information in his power. he will set out on the rising of Congress. you will find him an excellent and valuable man. he lives a little way out of Augusta, where he has almost a garden of Eden, of which mrs Milledge is the conductor, she being a great Arborist & florist. he will probably insist on your making it your home when you go, and for advice you cannot be in better hands. he says as soon as it is known you are there to buy lands you will be surrounded by people of every shade of design who have lands to sell, and against whom caution will be necessary. I will state below, another route from Charlotte C. H. passing through the country higher up. the distance perhaps a little more.[3]

I am in hopes my cyder is arrived by this time at Monticello & bottled. it is probable I shall be with you within 10. days or a fortnight after Congress rises. my stay there will be very short. tender love to my dear Martha. health and affectionate attachment to yourself.

TH: JEFFERSON

From Charlotte C. H.	
to Cole's ferry on Staunton	15.
Dix's ferry on Dan.	55.
Guilford C. H.	50
Long's ferry on Yadkin	50
Salisbury	5
Charlotte	50
Walker's	45
Herndon's on Enerie river	40
Creswell's on Saluda	40
Cambridge or Ninety six	7.
Augusta	50
	407.

RC (DLC); endorsed by Randolph.
PrC (MHi); endorsed by TJ in ink on
verso.

MY LAST: TJ to Thomas Mann Randolph, 12 Mch.

C. H.: Courthouse.

[1] Preceding four words interlined.
[2] Word interlined.
[3] TJ here partially erased "tender affect" indicating he had first intended to
end the letter at this point.

From Thomas Mann Randolph

DEAR SIR   Edgehill March 20. 1802

I expected with impatience and received with great pleasure the information & opinion your last favor contained respecting my scheme
of removing my slaves to a cotton climate. The importance of it to the
future wellfare of my family and to the comfortable existence of such
a number of human creatures as I am loaded with the care of, keeps
me in constant anxious thought on the subject. In my first reflection
on the plan Georgia occurred: the geographie & political situation of
it were strong inducements to give it a preference; the climate allso
invited but I had understood that the cotton districts of it were unproductive of I. Corn and that scarcity allways prevailed on the great
cotton plantations. I feared that profit to the Master & plenty to the
Slaves could not both be easily obtained in a midling soil, as very extensive fields must be cultivated annually in Indian corn and must be
manured & shifted too to preserve them and insure abundance of that
which I knew to be more necessary even than mild treatment moderate labor or a warm climate to Virginia Negroes. The rich loam of
the Mississippi insured that abundance allmost without labor for it
bears many annual crops of I. Corn without exhaustion; in which
case the openness & cleanness of the field renders culture nothing allmost. I am afraid the best pine land of Georgia would not yield more
corn than our old fields & that it would tire soon & require to be
farmed by crops which tend to render very laborious the future tillage
of Indian Corn. It would be long & severe to our negroes to get accustomed to the substitutes for Corn bread which I understand are
used in Georgia.—I did not know till you informed me that the
Mississippi lands were less productive in Cotton than those of Georgia and I had erred in supposing New Orleans to be the best market
for Cotton: these mistakes caused my determination being convinced
allready my people would be less taken off in raising provision. It
will be wise to make my first journey to Georgia where perhaps I
may meet with a tract of Cotton land at a low price with some

river-swamp-land adjoining which is capable of being reclaimed from the tide with Mud banks at no great expence: such land I know from experience to be the most productive of Indian Corn of any whatever, and to bear it annually without exhaustion. Such a situation in Georgia would be infinitely preferable to the Mississippi with the French for neighbors notwithstanding the wealth of N. Orleans. For if αὐτοκρατορικῶς πολιτευτέον again in France after its immense sacrifices and when there is leisure & quiet for arranging & confirming the conquests of Liberty by the establishment of a genuine free polity, my affections will abandon the nation as my sympathy does now their aims in the war of St. Domingo.

With most sincere attachment yr. &c   Th: M. Randolph

P.S. In the quantity of land Sibbald holds there might be a body of the better pine land with some tide marsh: perhaps if his scheme of a company fail he might suffer it to be picked for a better price than he has hitherto asked: but this price could not be paid by me unless on a credit of several years during which I would willingly pay him interest annually in Savannah or Richmond. I shall not set out till I have heard often from you & learnt your wishes with respect to Martha & the children in my absence: I will carry them to Washington when it may best suit you.

RC (MHi); endorsed by TJ as received 24 Mch. and so recorded in SJL.

your last favor: TJ to Thomas Mann Randolph, 12 Mch. 1802.

αὐτοκρατορικῶς πολιτευτέον: loosely translated, the phrase reads "For if 'there be despotic government' again in France."

To Elizabeth House Trist

Dear Madam   Washington Mar. 20. 1802.

Your letter of the 6th. instant has been duly recieved. I know of no inconvenience which will arise from a knowledge of our intentions to have made mr Trist the successor of mr Steele in the supposed event of his death: an event still considered as more than probable, tho from the nature of his disease he may wear for some time. I confess I would rather the appointment should not take place till mr Trist becomes a Missisipian; because the nominating him as a Virginian adds pabulum for the slanders of our opponents. if you knew the embarrasments which the irksome duty of appointment produces you would not wonder that mr Easton has recieved nothing. altho' his bankruptcy is a circumstance of commiseration which we feel as much as others, yet it is a strong objection to a consular appointment; because the merchants expect that in appointing trustees for their offices, we shall select responsible people, and they trust them on our faith. between two candidates equally worthy otherwise therefore, the one who is responsible is always preferred to him who is insolvent. still in some cases where we are satisfied of the principles of the applicant and no solvent competitor offers of equal pretensions in other respects, appointments have been made of those who have been unfortunate. I believe that in the case of mr Easton, a vacancy which is now existing can be assigned to him, and will be in a short time. mr Iznardi has had no new appointment. he was made Consul of the US. in the beginning of Genl. Washington's administration. mr Adams by one of his midnight nominations would have superseded him: but it fell through with all of that batch.—your letter to mr Hawkins is taken care of. the H. of Repr. will the day after tomorrow pass the bill repealing the internal taxes. I think they will rise by the middle of April, immediately after which I shall have the pleasure of seeing you in Albemarle, tho for a very short time. mrs Trist is still obstinately well. of this I presume mr Trist will inform you, as also that Dr. Bache is here waiting her leisure. I find you have infected mr Randolph with Missisipianism. what says Martha to this? & what must I say to it? of this we may talk hereafter. in the meantime accept assurances of my sincere and affectionate esteem & respect.

Th: Jefferson

PrC (DLC); at foot of text: "Mrs. Trist"; endorsed by TJ in ink on verso.

For Elizabeth Trist's earlier recommendation of David EASTON for an appointment, see Trist to TJ, 13 Aug. 1801.

ONE OF HIS MIDNIGHT NOMINATIONS: Henry Preble (Vol. 32:162; Vol. 35:494).

YOUR LETTER TO MR HAWKINS: not identified, but for Elizabeth Trist's and TJ's mutual interest in Indian commissioner Benjamin Hawkins, see Vol. 34:490.

The BILL REPEALING THE INTERNAL TAXES passed in the House of Representatives on 22 Mch. and the first session of the Seventh Congress adjourned on 3 May (JHR, 4:153-4, 240; see Tench Coxe to TJ, 17 Feb. 1802).

To Robert Bailey

Mar. 21. 1802.

Th: Jefferson asks the favor of mr Bailey to accept of some small articles of cloathing for his family, on the score of antient acquaintance. Would it be within the scope of mr Bailey's plan of gardening for the common market, to make a provision of endive for the ensuing winter, so as to be able to furnish Th:J. with a sallad of endive every day through the winter till the spring sallading should commence, for which Th:J. would send once a week, and preserve the week's provision here by setting them in earth, to be drawn from day to day fresh, in which way he presumes they would continue good: for which mr Bailey's market price would be weekly sent to him? he makes the enquiry now because it might possibly be requisite for him to plan his gardening accordingly for some time beforehand. he offers mr Bailey his best wishes for himself, mrs Bailey & family.

PrC (MHi); endorsed by TJ in ink on verso.

ANTIENT ACQUAINTANCE: Bailey, a market gardener in Washington, had lived at Monticello with his family for three years in the 1790s as TJ's gardener (MB, 2:913; Vol. 28:257n).

According to his financial memoranda, TJ on 19 Mch. 1802 directed John Barnes "to furnish certain clothing for Bailey in charity" to the value of $11.80 (MB, 2:1069).

From James Monroe

DEAR SIR   Richmond March 21. 1802

When lately in Albemarle I found the complition of a chmney in my house delayd by the want of abt. 350. bricks, which were not to be had in the neighbourhood. As the number is too small to burn a kiln on purpose to obtain them and as it may possibly be in my power to replace them sometime hereafter when you may have occasion, if convenient, I will thank you for as many. sincerely I am your friend & servant   JAS. MONROE

RC (DLC); endorsed by TJ as received 26 Mch. and so recorded in SJL.

To Gouverneur Morris

DEAR SIR   Washington Mar. 21. 1802.

The inclosed papers will so fully explain to you their object that I need add nothing more than ask the favor of you to state to me whatever you may recollect relative to the paiment made to Houdon in assignats, which may enable us to ascertain & pay what remains still justly due to him on account of the statue of Genl. Washington.   Accept assurances of my respect and attachment.   TH: JEFFERSON

RC (NjP); addressed: "The honble Gouverneur Morris"; endorsed by Morris. Enclosures: some or all of the enclosures listed at James Monroe to TJ, 14 Mch.; perhaps also that letter and TJ to Monroe, 28 Feb.

From Gouverneur Morris

DEAR SIR   Washington 21 March 1802

I receive this Instant your Favor of this Date. Were I at Home, I might perhaps find some Memorandum respecting the Transaction which it alludes to. Certainly I should find the Letters I have received, and Copies of those I may have written on the Subject. By the Copy Mr houdon has transmitted, of a Note from Mr Grand, it is evident that *he* at least must have misunderstood me. Hudon frequently mentioned the matter to me. I as frequently told him it was a Business in which I had no Concern nor Authority. When he seemed to be surpriz'd at this, considering the Agency you had in it, I told him that you had not, on that Occasion, acted as Minister of the United States, but meerly in Consequence of an Application to you by the State of Virginia; and to oblige that State. That, of Course, I did not succeed to your Authority *in that Behalf.* That I had, however, no Doubt but the State would honorably perform the Engagements you had taken. That the Government of the United States had indeed directed me to cause effective Payment to be made to sundry Officers formerly in the American Service, without Regard to the nominal Sum in Assignats. That I had given Mr Grand Directions consonant to the Orders I had received, but that I had no Right to give Orders respecting the Funds of the State of Virginia; nor to take Engagements for that State. I remember well that Grand wanted to cover himself under a Direction from me, which I refused to give. He was desirous of paying over the Money, And I beleive that (after having refus'd officially to take any Step whatever in the Business) I told him that, as an Individual, it was my private Opinion Mr Houdon would do better to receive the Money; and reserve, in the Receipt he should give, a Right to apply at a future Day to the State for the Difference of Value.

You will observe that the Grands were in a delicate Situation. If they held the Money of Virginia, they might thereby make themselves eventually liable for the Depreciation. If they tendered it to Houdon, he could not (but at the hazard of his Life) refuse to receive it. But he might have complain'd of hard Usage; and they thought it not consistent that, while the United States were paying in solid Coin, the State of Virginia should offer depreciated Paper. This Situation naturally induced them to state what I had said to them as strongly as it would bear

I presume that Mr Houdon has now carried his Demand, for Loss of Value, full as high as the Facts will permit. I should, therefore, suppose it advisable to scrutinize the Dates, and examine the Grounds on which the Value is taken at the *proper Date*. If Value was lost while he deliberated about the Propriety of receiving the Money which lay in Readiness for him, the State may, in Strictness, insist that he shall bear that Loss. They may perhaps think it more consistent with their Dignity not to descend into these Minutiæ, and that may for aught I know be the more correct Proceedure

I have the Honor to be with perfect Respect Dear Sir your obedient Servant
                                                    GOUVR MORRIS

RC (DLC); at foot of text: "His Excellency Thomas Jefferson Esqr. President of the United States"; endorsed by TJ as received 21 Mch. and so recorded in SJL.

COPY MR HOUDON HAS TRANSMITTED: Enclosure No. 3 listed at James Monroe to TJ, 14 Mch.

Description of a Wheel Cipher

[before 22 Mch. 1802?]

Project of a cypher.[1]

Turn a cylinder of white wood of about 2. Inches diameter, & 6. or 8. I. long. bore through it's center a hole sufficient to recieve an iron spindle or axis of $\frac{1}{8}$ or $\frac{1}{4}$ I. diam. divide the periphery into 26. equal parts (for the 26. letters of the alphabet) and, with a sharp point, draw parallel lines through all the points of division, from one end to the other of the cylinder, & trace those lines with ink to make them plain. then cut the cylinder crosswise into pieces of about $\frac{1}{6}$ of an inch thick.[2] they will resemble back-gammon men, with plane sides. number each of them, as they are cut off, on one side, that they may be arrangeable in any order you please.[3] on the periphery of each, and between the black lines, put all the letters of the alphabet, not in their established order, but jumbled, & without order, so that no two shall be alike. now string them in their numerical order on an iron axis, one end of which has a head, and the other a nut and screw; the use of which is to hold them firm in any given position when you chuse it. they are now ready for use, your correspondent having[4] a similar cylinder, similarly arranged.

Suppose I have to cypher this phrase.[5] 'your favor of the 22d. is recieved.'

I turn the 1st. wheel till the letter y. presents itself.

I turn the 2d. & place it's   o. by the side of the y. of the 1st. wheel.

I turn the 3d. & place it's   u. by the side of the o. of the 2d.

       4th.   r. by the side of the u of the 3d.

       5th.   f. by the side of the r. of the 4th.

       6th.   a. by the side of the f of the 5th.

and so on till I have got all the words of the phrase arranged in one line. fix them with the screw. you will observe that the cylinder then presents 25. other lines of letters, not in any regular series, but jumbled, & without order or meaning. copy any one of them in the letter to your correspondent. when he recieves it, he takes his cylinder and arranges the wheels so as to present[6] the same jumbled letters in the same order in one line. he then fixes them with his screw, and[7] examines the other 25. lines, and finds one of them presenting him these[8] letters 'yourfavorofthe22isrecieved.' which he writes down. as the others will be jumbled & have no meaning, he cannot mistake the true one intended. so proceed with every other portion[9] of the letter. numbers had better be represented by letters with dots over them;[10] as for instance by the 6. vowels & 4 liquids. because if the periphery were divided into 36. instead of 26. lines for the numerical, as well as alphabetical characters, it would increase the trouble of finding the letters on the wheels.[11]

When the cylinder of wheels is fixed, with the jumbled alphabets on their peripheries, by only changing the order of the wheels in the cylinder, an immense variety of different cyphers may be produced for different correspondents. for whatever be the number of wheels, if you take all the natural numbers from unit to that inclusive, & multiply them successively into one another, their product will be the number of different combinations of which the wheels are susceptible, and consequently of the different cyphers they may form for different correspondents, entirely unintelligible to each other.* for though every one possesses the cylinder, and with the alphabets similarly arranged on the wheels, yet if the order be interverted, but one line, similar through the whole cylinder, can be produced on any two of them.

---

*2. letters can form only 2. different series, viz.[12] a.b. and b.a.   say 1 x 2 = 2

add a 3d. letter. then it may be inserted in each of these two series[13] as the 1st. 2d. or 3d. letter of the series. to wit

c. a. b.	c. b. a.
a. c. b.	b. c. a.
a. b. c.	b. a. c.

consequently there will be 6 series = 2 x 3 or 1 x 2 x 3.

add a 4th. letter. as we have seen that 3. letters will make 6. different series, then the 4th. may be inserted in each of these 6. series, either as the 1st. 2d. 3d. or 4th letter of the series. consequently there will be 24. series, = 6 x 4 =1 x 2 x 3 x 4[14] x 5 x 6

dcab.	cdab.	cadb	cabd
dacb	adcb	acdb	acbd
dabc	adbc	abdc	abcd
dcba	cdba	cbda	cbad
dbca	bdca	bcda	bcad
dbac	bdac	badc	bacd[15]

add a 5th. letter. as 4. give 24 series, the 5th. may be inserted in each of these as the 1st. 2d. 3d. 4th. or 5th. letter of the series. consequently there will be 120 = 24 x 5 = 1 x 2 x 3 x 4 x 5.

add a 6th. letter. as 5. give 120. series, the 6th. may be inserted in each of these as the 1st. 2d. 3d. 4th. 5th. or 6th. letter of the series. consequently there will be 720. = 120 x 6 = 1 x 2 x 3 x 4 x 5 x 6.

and so on to any number.

Suppose the cylinder be 6. I. long (which probably will be a convenient length, as it may be spanned between the middle finger & the thumb of the left hand, while in use) it will contain 36. wheels, & the sum of it's combinations will be 1 x 2 x 3 x 4 x 5 x 6 x 7 x 8 x 9 x 10 x 11 x 12 x 13 x 14 x 15 x 16 x 17 x 18 x 19 x 20 x 21 x 22 x 23 x 24 x 25 x 26 x 27 x 28 x 29 x 30 x 31 x 32 x 33 x 34 x 35 x 36.[16] = (4648 &c— to 42 places!! —)[17] a number of which 41.5705351 is the Logarithm of which the number is 372 with 39 cyphers[18] (zeros) added to it.

MS (DLC: TJ Papers, 128:22138); undated; in TJ's hand, with notations by Robert Patterson and TJ (see note 17 below). PrC (DLC: TJ Papers, 232:41576). Dft (DLC: TJ Papers, 232:41575); entirely in TJ's hand; torn.

PROJECT OF A CYPHER: a passing reference to "my wheel cypher" in TJ's letter to Robert Patterson on 22 Mch. 1802 is apparently the only time he mentioned the cryptographic device in his correspondence. Silvio Bedini speculated that TJ devised the wheel cipher in the period from 1792 to 1793. That supposition was based on an assumption that TJ had some interest in ciphers when he was secretary of state and on his purchase, in April 1792, of an undescribed set of punches from a type founder. Bedini surmised that those were letter punches, and that TJ wanted them for stamping the letters of the alphabet into the edges of the disks of the wheel cipher. If that set of punches comprised an alphabet, however, TJ's purchase of nine more punches from the same source later that year is difficult to explain. He spent $26.20 on the two groups of punches, and it seems most likely that he invested in those tools for some personal use, such as stamping bookbindings. It may be more probable that TJ wrote the description of the wheel cipher device not in 1792 or 1793 but between 1797 and 1800. Patterson's notation on the document printed above shows that TJ consulted him about the concept of the device, and the absence of any reference to it in their correspondence implies that they discussed it in person. During TJ's term as vice president of the United States, he resided in Philadelphia when Congress was in session and he had considerable interaction with Patterson. They were both officers of the American Philosophical Society, they conferred about astronomy, and in March 1798, Patterson provided TJ with detailed advice on the moldboard plow design, loaning him a book on mathematics. TJ also had time and inclination during his vice presidency to devote attention to scientific and technical subjects. Moreover, his passing reference to the wheel cipher in the 22 Mch. 1802 letter to Patterson provides no explanation, which implies that it may have been a subject of relatively recent vintage that would be fresh in Patterson's mind. That letter, TJ's correspondence with Patterson in April, and the attention he devoted to an explanation of Patterson's cipher for enclosure to

Robert R. Livingston on 18 Apr. demonstrate his deep engagement with the problem of finding a new ciphering system. He implied to Patterson in the letter of 22 Mch. that the wheel cipher was prominent in his consideration until Patterson's cipher, described in the mathematician's letter of 19 Dec. 1801 that TJ received on 25 Dec., displaced it. It is possible that TJ wrote up the description of the wheel apparatus during the search for a new coding system in 1801-2, although if that were the case, it is not clear when or by what means Patterson could have seen TJ's description of the device. Although it is difficult to establish the date of the document printed above, it is unlikely that TJ wrote it after 22 Mch. 1802, since Patterson's cipher had displaced the wheel cipher in TJ's consideration by that date (Bedini, *Statesman of Science*, 233, 236-8, 493; David Kahn, *The Codebreakers: The Story of Secret Writing*, rev. ed., [New York, 1996], 192-3; MB, 2:868, 881; Vol. 30:160, 161n, 207n, 224, 230-1, 234-5; Vol. 31:56, 57n, 295n; Vol. 32:298).

In the inaugural volume of this series, editor Julian P. Boyd cited an assessment by the cryptanalyst William F. Friedman to name TJ's "invention of a cryptographic device"—the wheel cipher—and the drafting of the Declaration of Independence as indications of the range and power of TJ's intelligence. The two creations were, Boyd wrote, "evidences of an elevated and even inspired intellect," demonstrating that TJ "possessed many of the qualities of a genius" (Vol. 1:viii-ix; for Friedman, see ANB). We cannot be certain, however, if TJ's description of the cipher device was entirely the product of his own mind or drew on other sources. The concept of using wheels on a SPINDLE to create a cipher machine may have come from locks that opened when cylinders were aligned to spell a secret word. The *Encyclopédie Méthodique* described such mechanisms. Cipher devices using disks on an axle have been developed at different times and places, sometimes with no evident chain of transmission of the idea. In the mid-nineteenth century, Charles Babbage referred to a cylindrical cipher device similar in some respects to the one described by TJ. An apparatus developed by a French military cryptographer in the 1890s inspired the creation of similar devices for the armies and navies of other countries, including the United States. TJ's description of a wheel cipher was apparently unnoticed by cryptographers until it was discovered in his papers in the 1920s (Louis Kruh, "The Genesis of the Jefferson/Bazeries Cipher Device," *Cryptologia*, 5 [1981], 193-208; Bedini, *Statesman of Science*, 236-7; William F. Friedman, "Edgar Allan Poe, Cryptographer," *American Literature*, 8 [1936], 279).

4 LIQUIDS: the letters *l*, *r*, *m*, and *n* (OED).

SUPPOSE THE CYLINDER BE 6. I. LONG: the inexactness of the dimensions that TJ gave for the components of the device, his supposition that six inches "probably will be a convenient length" for the assembled apparatus, and his rumination about how numerals "had better be represented" indicate that the description above was a conceptual plan, not an explanation of an already-constructed prototype. TJ called the document a "project," a word often used, in his day and earlier, to refer to a proposal or conceptual design (OED). In diplomacy, "project" or its French form, *projet*, was the term used for a draft treaty that served as a starting point for negotiation (see, for example, ASP, *Foreign Relations*, 2:421, and Vol. 29:613-25, 629-30n). TJ appears not to have taken the notion of a wheel cipher device beyond the explanatory "project" printed above. The Editors have found no evidence that he built one of the devices himself or had one made, and he apparently abandoned the design after deciding that Patterson's cipher, as he told its creator in the letter of 22 Mch. 1802, would be "so much more convenient in practice." He seems never to have gone back to the wheel cipher idea. In the twentieth century, examples of the device were made following TJ's description, although those models did not incorporate 36 wheels in a six-inch span as posited by TJ in the last section of the document above (Bedini, *Statesman of Science*, figs. 21, 22).

At some unknown time, TJ created a table consisting of a grid of 30 numbered vertical columns, each of which contains a different scrambled sequence of the 26 letters of the alphabet. He did not date or endorse the table. It could relate to his plans for the wheel cipher, with each column perhaps representing the sequence of letters for one wheel, or to another cipher system (MS in DLC: TJ Papers, 128:22137, entirely in TJ's hand; Ralph E. Weber, *United States Diplomatic Codes and Ciphers, 1775-1938* [Chicago, 1979], 178-9, 191n, 612).

[1] In Dft this heading is "The wheel cypher."

[2] Word interlined in Dft in place of "diameter."

[3] In Dft, TJ first wrote "in the same order" before altering the phrase to read as above.

[4] Here in Dft, TJ canceled "an exact duplicate of them."

[5] In Dft, TJ first wrote "cypher these words" before altering the text to read as above.

[6] Word interlined in Dft in place of "<*make*> place."

[7] Preceding six words interlined in Dft.

[8] TJ here canceled "words." Dft: "words."

[9] Word interlined in Dft in place of "phrase."

[10] Remainder of sentence, through "4 liquids," interlined in Dft.

[11] Here in Dft, TJ wrote and canceled a paragraph: "the cypher may be varied for any number of correspondents by varying the arrangement of the wheels. every two of those who possess a set of them may have an arrangement private to themselves, and which cannot be understood by the others." He then wrote, as a new paragraph, a sentence that has been lost to damage except the final word, "wheel."

[12] Preceding three words interlined in place of "combinations [. . .]."

[13] Word interlined in Dft in place of "arrangements."

[14] Formula ends here in Dft.

[15] In Dft, TJ wrote out sequences of letters beginning with all combinations of three letters, and, after canceling some

series of sequences and abbreviating some others, projected the results for all combinations of five letters. In Dft those columns of letter sequences all follow the paragraph that ends "any two of them" and precede the paragraph that begins "2. letters can form."

[16] Text ends here in Dft and PrC.
[17] The equal sign and parenthetical passage are in Patterson's hand. The notation that follows, beginning "a number," is in TJ's hand.
[18] MS: "cyhers."

To Robert Patterson

DEAR SIR   Washington Mar. 22. 1802.

I recieved your favor by mr Engles. the place desired for him is not given by commission from me, but is a mere appointment by letter from the Secretary at war, and consequently rests solely with him, without my interposition. nevertheless I sent him your letter, and afterwards stated to him the weight of your testimony. you have no conception of the number of applicants for this office. the Secretary at war is making out a calendar of them, and consulting the members of Congress & others on their respective qualifications. the chance therefore of any single one is moderate.—I have thoroughly considered your cypher, and find[1] it so much more convenient in practice than my wheel cypher, that I am proposing it to the Secretary of state for use in his office. I vary it in a slight circumstance only. I write the lines in the original draught horizontally & not vertically, placing the letters of the different lines very exactly under each other. I do this for the convenience of the principal whose time is to be economised, tho' it increases the labor of a copying clerk. the copying clerk transcribes the vertical lines horizontally. the clerk of our correspondent restores them to their horizontal position ready for the reading of his principal.

There is no such thing as a meridian or any other means of keeping our clocks & watches right at this place. I have had recourse to the rising & setting of the sun, the only way of taking equal altitudes without an instrument: but these are not equal unless the eastern & western horizons are equal which is rarely the case. I have imagined the most convenient instrument I could get would be a good Hadley's quadrant (as called, tho' it be a sextant) and to set my clock by equal altitudes of the sun. I would prefer it also because I should be willing to possess this instrument, having at home a fine theodolite & Planetarium by Ramsden. I see in Jones's catalogue (London) he states the Hadley's quadrants with nonius & ivory arch from 2. to 3. guineas. one of the best of these I think would suit me. I am not at all used to this instrument, but I think they are sometimes made with a common stand (3. footed folding together as for the Surveyor's compass) to be used with the stand or without it. this would be preferable. I must ask the favor of you to chuse a good one for me, and direct the person to have it well packed and ready to deliver to such person as mr Barnes shall direct to call & pay for it. I would trouble you to select for me at the same time 2. good Farenheit thermometers. those you chose for me before suited perfectly. I must throw myself on your goodness for an apology for the trouble I give you, and assure you of my friendly esteem & respect. TH: JEFFERSON

PrC (DLC); in ink at foot of first page: "Patterson Rob."; endorsed by TJ in ink on verso.

YOUR FAVOR BY MR ENGLES: on 12 Mch., Patterson wrote TJ a letter that has not been found. According to TJ's notation in SJL, the communication, which he received on the 14th, recommended Silas Engles as the public storekeeper at Philadelphia. A letter from Engles to TJ, dated 2 June 1808 and received from Frederick, Maryland, on 5 July of that year, is recorded in SJL but has not been found. In May 1801, Patterson and Andrew Ellicott had recommended George Ingels for the storekeeper's job, which involved the management of military stores at the Schuylkill Arsenal. Ingels received the appointment by mid-April 1802 (Ingels to War Department, 16 Apr. 1802, in DNA: RG 107, RLRMS; Vol. 34:69).

YOUR CYPHER: see Patterson to TJ, 19 Dec. 1801.

The method of EQUAL ALTITUDES would allow TJ to regulate his clock by the sun, using observations of the sun's position before and after noon to find the exact time the sun reached its zenith (Richard S. Preston, "The Accuracy of the Astronomical Observations of Lewis and Clark," APS, *Proceedings*, 144 [2000], 171-2). A Hadley's reflecting QUADRANT, also known as an octant, was an instrument for measuring the altitudes of celestial bodies in degrees above the horizon. A THEODOLITE measured the angle between two points and was commonly used for triangulation by surveyors and mapmakers. In 1778, TJ acquired a

theodolite made by Jesse Ramsden, a well-known English maker of optical and scientific apparatus. TJ, who visited Ramsden's shop in London in 1786, also owned instruments made by Ramsden's brother-in-law, Peter Dollond. The term PLANETARIUM was used for models that showed the positions and orbits of the planets around the sun, such as mechanical orreries. Among the items in TJ's household in France in 1793 was "une machine qui est la boule du monde" ("a machine that is the ball of the world"). TJ bought an orrery from the Jones firm, but it was shipped directly to Virginia from London and was never among his possessions in France. Perhaps the "boule du monde" packed up in Paris was a planetarium by Ramsden (Bedini, *Statesman of Science*, 78, 151, 342, fig. 11; Maurice Daumas, *Scientific Instruments of the Seventeenth and Eighteenth Centuries*, trans. Mary Holbrook [New York, 1972], 116, 174, 179, 181, 186, 234, illus. 104; Stein, *Worlds*, 351, 356-7; Robert Bud, Deborah Jean Warner, and others, eds., *Instruments of Science: An Historical Encyclopedia* [New York, 1998], 429-30, 465-7, 613; Gloria Clifton, *Directory of British Scientific Instrument Makers 1550-1851* [London, 1995], 227-8; MB, 1:456, 614; Vol. 14:411-12; Vol. 24:726-7, 790; Vol. 25:341, 485; Vol. 26:20; Vol. 27:64; Vol. 34:272).

JONES'S CATALOGUE: William and Samuel Jones, who had taken over their father's instrument-making business in London in the early 1790s, published annual catalogues of their wares. A NONIUS was a device on an octant or sextant that showed units of arc smaller than the divisions on the instrument's main scale. IVORY was sometimes used for the scale, which was curved to fit an arc-shaped piece of the octant or sextant. The Joneses' catalogues listed Hadley's quadrants of mahogany, "with ivory arch and nonius" and fitted for "double observation"—to find the angle between two celestial bodies—for £2.2.0. The price for a Hadley's quadrant made of ebony wood, fitted with the "best" optics and a scale engraved on brass by a machine called a dividing engine, was £3 (*A Catalogue of Optical, Mathematical, and Philosophical Instruments, Made and Sold by W. and S. Jones* [London, 1799], 6; same [London, 1800?], 4; Bud and Warner, *Instruments of Science*, 420, 532; Thomas Dick, *The Practical Astronomer* [New York, 1846], 353-4; John FitzMaurice Mills, *Encyclopedia of Antique Scientific Instruments* [New York, 1983], 164; Daumas, *Scientific Instruments*, 181, 194-204, illus. 110, 113; OED, s.v. "nonius"; Vol. 25:342-3n).

[1] Word interlined in place of "consider."

From Stephen Sayre

SIR   Philadelphia 22d Mar: 1802

I have lately wrote to the Secretary of State, requesting him to favour me with a reply, so far, as to releive me from doubt & anxiety; whether I may, or may not depend on the justice, or friendship of administration—I require no reasons, or apology—let him but inform me, that he can find others more deserving, & better qualified for any office in his department, & I shall then know what steps to take—and tho I shall feel the ingratitude, & injustice of my country in silent mortification, you will find me, to bear it with a dignity worthy a better fate—

I have, in a former letter, stated to him my very unfortunate situation; being at the mercy of a creditor, for upwards of £400. Sterling, expended while in actual, and I may say, profitable service of my country—I mean for my country—the agent is unwilling; but must execute his orders, requiring him, to demand payment of me, whether Congress may, or may not, enable me to do it—I expect him every hour from New York, to put his orders in full force.

I therefore ask it, as a boon, to be inform'd, whether I may depend on the patronage of the Government, to prevent my ruin. I could make arrangements, if aided to pay by instalments out of my yearly income—for I am habituated to frugality.

I trust you will not be offended, when I thus press upon your humanity, to consider my critical situation, my past conduct, my immence losses, & unexampled sufferings—Will you condescend to read my last note to Mr Madison consult with him, & order him to write, decidedly—

Do you Sir, require proofs of my losses? Can it be a matter of doubt in your mind, whether my persecution in England was of great magnitude? Have my enemies succeeded in perverting facts so far as to make it questionable, whether those losses arose from private mismanagement, or were consequent on the irresistable tyranny of the British Government—so far as the people of England could express their opinions of that event, they condemned their own government, in my justification.

I have had the satisfaction, within these few days, to find many of that nation do not forget the national injuries done me there—for, in consequence of proposals to establish another bank, in this city, they voluntarily offer'd me all their support, & interest to make me the president of it—it is doubtful whether a charter will be granted—and if it is, I do not mean to degrade my friends by its acceptance, under the situation I am now in—from what I can judge, those democratic characters, who have taken the lead, in this project, are resolved to have a bank with, or without one—if I was assured of support from the administration, so that I might get time to settle this demand, the subscribers would, unanimously, vote me into the presidency—in that case, I would, by choice relinquish any offer you please to make me, because the business of a bank is familiar to me, & because I like this city as a place of residence.

Let me be offer'd the government of the western territory, and you would see Congress disposed to pay my demands—and I appeal to your understanding—as to the ground of my demands—The Secretary of State Reports they ought to be paid—a Committee of the House, have confirm'd that Report: & Congress, on the 9th of feb: 1799, voted payment—48. agt. 21—
If I was in any shape brought into the sunshine of executive favour, the rays of light would shed their influence on the fairness of my claims.

—kept in the back ground, & under increasing weight of forgetfulness, and the aversion, that seems natural to all men, to pay old debts my hopes are feeble indeed—It is my intention to abandon the pursuit, unless, protected by the good will of administration. Be kind enough Sir, not to impute it to vanity, or ambition, when I look to any thing so elevated as a government.

It is little more than illustrious exile—Can you find any other man, better qualified, by experience of the world, by social habits, by unalterable principles, leading to peace, harmony, & conciliation, who would thank you for the privilege of ruling over the uncultivated regions of the west? Permit me to assure you, that if an accession of wealthy Europeans can be deem'd beneficial to a new state, I know many, who would be induced, to purchase, & send their sons to settle in it—

If you do me the honor of reading my last letter to Mr Madison, you will, find many conjectures, as to what could have been the cause, hetherto, of my being so long kept in suspence, as to your will & intentions towards me—if I could discover the cause, I am confident, I could remove it—has your Secretary a list of characters ready to fill the succession, who are immaculate, & exalted above the reach of abuse? You know, well, that you do not deserve it—yet not a man in the history of nations has ever had so much of it!

As to myself—I wish for nothing so much as to be compel'd into the propriety of proving my character, unspotted.

To bring my case before the public without a necessity, would do me injury—nor can I do you so much injustice as to suppose you can be deter'd from serving those who have, by zeal, & activity, openly opposed the enemies of our country,—to neglect such men would be to desert the principles you are known to love—

—you may pity the returning prodigal—but must not forget that thy other son deserves all thou cans't give him—

I am most respectfully, Yours &c &c   STEPHEN SAYRE

RC (DNA: RG 59, LAR); endorsed by TJ as received 25 Mch. and "to be Governor of the N.W. territory" and so recorded in SJL.

WROTE TO THE SECRETARY OF STATE: Sayre to James Madison, 10 Mch. 1802 (Madison, *Papers, Sec. of State Ser.*, 3:21-2).
In his FORMER LETTER to Madison of

16 May 1801, Sayre reported his outstanding debt of more than £400 to a mercantile house at Bordeaux and their AGENT Mr. Lynch (Madison, *Papers, Sec. of State Ser.*, 1:186-7).

For the responses of Congress and its Committee of Claims to Sayre's DEMANDS for compensation, see Sayre to TJ, 7 Feb. 1802.

From William Vallance

Philada., 22nd March, 1802.

The Petition of William Vallance, Respectfully sheweth.

That having been in the Service of the United States, on board a Cutter in the Service of the States aforesaid, as first Mate for the space of Twenty Months, the greater part of the Time under the Command of Captn. Isaac Roach and the latter part under Captn. George Price. Had my Sentiments been uniform with Those to whom I was subordinate, no doubt I might have continued longer;

but to my inexpressable satisfaction, that cause of Fear no more exists, and am therefore induced to make a Tender of my services, and solicit the command of the Revenue Cutter now building at this Port. My pretentions, Sir, rest on my ability and proficiency in that line and the recommendatory proof, which I hope, to your satisfaction, I shall be able to furnish: By serving a regular Time, I have obtained a sufficient knowledge of the Bay and River Delaware, as to entitle me to hold a first rate Branch as Pilot, and for many years have been Master of Vessels in the Mercantile Line, but at present out of employ. Should you therefore be pleased to give me the Appointed and Command of the Cutter aforesaid, be assured, Sir, that nothing on my part shall be wanting to render my Station satisfactory to You and usefull to my Country, And in gratefull remembrance by,

Sir, Your most Obedient, and very Humble Servt.

WILLIAM VALLANCE

RC (NHi: Gallatin Papers); in an unknown hand, signed by Vallance; at head of text: "To Thomas Jefferson Esqr., President of the United States"; endorsed by TJ as received 26 Mch. and so recorded in SJL with notation "T"; also endorsed by TJ: "to command revenue cutter."

The revenue CUTTER *General Greene* entered service in 1797 under the command of Isaac Roach. The following year, the vessel was placed under command of

George Price and taken into service by the United States Navy. It returned to the cutter service in 1799 and was sold in 1802 (NDQW, Dec. 1800-Dec. 1801, 367; Philadelphia *Finlay's American Naval and Commercial Register*, 15 Aug. 1798; *Gazette of the United States*, 31 Mch. 1798).

TJ gave command of the REVENUE CUTTER NOW BUILDING at Philadelphia to Richard Howard (TJ to Gallatin, 10 June 1802).

To Caspar Wistar

DEAR SIR   Washington Mar. 22. 1802.

What I am now to write about will be in perfect confidence between ourselves. the legislature is likely to establish a marine hospital at New Orleans, where we lose about 400. boatmen & seamen annually by sickness. I think it probable that we shall have a run on us, of recommendations of young men, just from their lectures, unsettled, and without experience, to[1] obtain the superintendance of a hospital where we have more suffering citizens than in any other place, & suffering from peculiarities of climate. I consider the nomination to such a place as a sacred charge, and having little confidence in unexperienced physicians, I would greatly prefer those who have established a reputation by practice. I have however as yet but a single application from a Physician of any age & experience; that is a Doctr. Barnwell of Philadelphia who wishes to go to New Orleans. the object of this letter is to ask your information of his character medical & moral, and that you will be so good as to write it to me *candidly, unreservedly, and fully*, assured that it shall be confined to myself alone, to aid my judgment in selecting a superintendant. I have seen a work of Doctr. Barnwell's, which tho' liable to some criticisms as a work of literature, shews that he is not without information & discernment. but you can estimate him from experience, the best of all tests. health & affectionate salutations.   TH: JEFFERSON

PrC (DLC); at foot of text: "Doctr. Wistar."

APPLICATION: William Barnwell to TJ, 15 Mch.

A WORK OF DOCTR. BARNWELL'S:

Physical Investigations & Deductions, From Medical and Surgical Facts, published in Philadelphia in 1802; see Barnwell to TJ, 26 Jan. 1802.

[1] TJ here canceled "take."

To Nicolas Gouin Dufief

SIR   Washington Mar. 23. 1802

I recieved yesterday your letter of the 20th. and catalogue. I remark on it a work Jaques le fataliste par Diderot. if it be really by Diderot I shall be glad to recieve it with Chaptal, as also the Systeme de la Nature par Mirabeau, unless you should know that there exists an edition in petit form. in which case I would rather await your return from France, when you could perhaps bring me the petit format edition. Accept my best wishes   TH: JEFFERSON

I ask the favor of mr Dufief to bring me from France the following books.

Le Philosophie d'Epicure par Gassendi, which Lavocat (Dictionnaire) says was published in 3. vols, but does not say of what size, nor whether in French, or in Latin. I would prefer them in French rather than in Latin and of small size rather than large.

Moralistes Anciennes. I have this work as far down as 1794. when it was resumed, & the Apothegmes of the Lacedemonians were published, which I have. I wish the sequel. he there promises the Morals of Plutarch, Aristotle, Epicurus & Tacitus. I would wish them stitched only that I may have them bound uniform with the other volumes.

Oeuvres d'Helvetius, *in petit format*. I have them in 8 vo. but wish the petit format edition.

In the Parallele de l'Architecture antique et Moderne par Errard et Chambray edited by Jombert, which I possess in 8 vo. he speaks of this as only the 4th. volume of his Bibliotheque portative d'architecture, and promises a 5th. volume containing les elemens d'Architecture, painture, & sculpture, and a 6th. under the title of le Manual des artistes. I should be glad to possess the whole work compleat.

Anatomie comparative de Cuvier (I am not sure this is the title) it is in 2. vols. 8 vo. but I shall be glad to recieve whatever else he has published in the anatomical line.

Geoponica Bassi. Gr. Lat. 2. v. 8 vo. Niclas. Lipsiae. 1781.

PrC (DLC); at foot of text: "Mr. Dufief"; endorsed by TJ in ink on verso.

In addition to his nonfiction works, Denis DIDEROT, the compiler of the great *Encyclopédie*, wrote plays and novels. In *Jacques le fataliste et son maître*, a satire that was only published after the author's death in 1784, Diderot, an admirer of Laurence Sterne's *Tristram Shandy*, addressed the reader directly and played with conventions of plot and structure (Wesley D. Camp and Agnes G. Raymond, *Jack the Fatalist and His Master: A New Translation from the French of Denis Diderot* [New York, 1984], ix-xii, 183-6; Denis Diderot, *Jacques the Fatalist and His Master*, trans. J. Robert Loy [New York, 1959], vii-xxiii).

SYSTEME DE LA NATURE: when Baron d'Holbach published his *Systême de la Nature. Ou Des Loix du Monde Physique & du Monde Moral*, a critique of religion, in 1770, he did so under the pretense that it was the work of Jean Baptiste de Mirabaud. TJ later acquired an English translation published in Philadelphia in 1808 (*Dictionnaire*, 17:1265-6; *Biographie universelle*, 28:354-5; Sowerby, No. 1260).

In the seventeenth century, Pierre GASSENDI, a French astronomer and philosopher of science, devoted considerable attention to the study of the materialism of Epicurus and published *Philosophiae Epicuri syntagma*. TJ mentioned that work and indicated his admiration for the moral doctrines of Epicurus in a letter to William Short, 31 Oct. 1819 (DSB, 5:284-90; Sowerby, No. 4914).

LAVOCAT (DICTIONNAIRE): the *Dictionnaire historique et bibliographique portatif* of Jean Baptiste Ladvocat. TJ purchased multiple editions of it in 1789, one of which was probably for Madison. TJ cited Ladvocat's work in 1795 as a source of information about particular books, and in 1800 he included it on a reading list for Joseph C. Cabell (Sowerby, No. 146; Vol. 16:495; Vol. 28:358; Vol. 32:177). See also Notes on the Doctrine of Epicurus, Vol. 31:284-5

MORALISTES ANCIENNES: TJ associated the *Collection des moralistes anciens* with Pierre Charles Lévesque, who was a contributor to the series of volumes published under that title by Pierre Didot beginning in 1782. Works by Lévesque on the *Apophthegmes des Lacédémoniens*, the *Pensées morales* of PLUTARCH, and aphorisms of the Greek philosophers were among the volumes in the *Collection*. In 1788, TJ bestowed a book from the series on a young Catherine Church, writing on the flyleaf that she would enjoy "this collection of the Antient Moralists" when she was older, "when the giver will no longer exist but in the memory of a very few." TJ ordered a 14-volume edition in "petit format" from Paris in 1795 and recommended the series to Cabell in 1800 as an 18-volume collection in that size (*Biographie universelle*, 24:400; Vol. 14:28; Vol. 28:358; Vol. 32:179).

BIBLIOTHEQUE PORTATIVE D'ARCHITECTURE: Charles Antoine Jombert did project six volumes of his *Bibliothèque portative d'architecture*, but only four volumes were published (in Paris, 1764-66). The fourth volume of the set was the *Par-*

allèle de l'architecture antique et de la moderne of Charles Errard and Roland Fréart de Chambray, which first appeared in 1650. Errard and Fréart de Chambray also collaborated on a translation of Andrea Palladio's work from Italian to French, which Jombert made the second volume of his *Bibliothèque* (Sowerby, Nos. 4215, 4216; *Dictionnaire*, 12:1402; 14:1135-6; 18:763).

A year earlier, TJ had seen a copy of the *Leçons d'Anatomie Comparée* of Georges CUVIER that Thomas Peters Smith had sent from Europe for the American Philosophical Society. TJ declared the two volumes to be a "capital" and "precious" achievement, informing Benjamin Rush that it was "probably the greatest work in

that line that has ever appeared." To Bishop James Madison he wrote that "nothing like it as to extent of plan or accuracy of performance has ever yet appeared in the world." TJ did not acquire Cuvier's work until 1805 (Sowerby, No. 999; Vol. 33:437, 438n, 511, 512n; Vol. 34:68).

TJ described the GEOPONICA as a work on "the state of Agriculture in Greece in the time of Constantine Porphyrogeneta." It drew on works of Cassianus Bassus. TJ had tried to get the book in 1795, but had not managed to obtain it as late as December 1809. GR. LAT.: that is, in Greek and Latin (Sowerby, No. 690; RS, 2:81-2, 83n; Vol. 28:358).

From Gideon Granger

Mar. 23. [1802]

G Granger presents his Compliments to the President and informs him that Marbell Camden was the *last Postmaster* at Milton—his resignation was lately received. G Granger does not recollect the name of the Gentleman proposed for that office and prays the President to be kind enough to send the name by Bearer.

RC (DLC); partially dated.

MARBELL CAMDEN assumed the office of postmaster at Milton in April 1801 (Stets, *Postmasters*, 264).

On 17 Mch., the postmaster general wrote TJ: "G. Granger presents his compliments to the President and informs

him he has this moment received the Resignation of the Postmaster at Milton near Monticello. he will call Tomorrow morning to take the Name of a suitable Candidate for that Office" (RC in DLC; in a clerk's hand; endorsed by TJ as received 17 Mch. and so recorded in SJL).

From the Navy Department

[on or before 23 Mch. 1802]

Mr. Humphreys by Contract of 27th Septr 1800, was allowed 2000 Dolls ⅌ annm & all his reasonable expences paid, in consideration of his services—

RC (DLC); undated; in a clerk's hand; address clipped: "Preside[. . .]"; endorsed by TJ as received from the

Navy Department on 23 Mch. and "Humphreys to go to recieve ship timber" and so recorded in SJL.

In 1800, the United States Navy appointed Samuel HUMPHREYS of Philadelphia inspector to examine the timber procured in Georgia and South Carolina for the frames of six 74-gun ships. Robert Smith sought to rehire Humphreys in October 1801, but postponed dispatching him to Georgia when it was found that too little timber had been gathered to justify sending an inspector at that time. Smith again directed him to proceed to Georgia in March 1802, but the two men disagreed over the terms of Humphreys's service, especially his date of hire. In June 1802, Smith approved Humphreys's claim of $809.29 for services rendered from 25 Oct. 1801 to 1 Apr. 1802. Later in that same month, Humphreys was again appointed inspector, with a salary of $166.66 per month from the time of his departure from Philadelphia as well as all reasonable expenses (NDQW, Jan.-May 1800, 140-2; Smith to Humphreys, 21 Oct. 1801, 23, 30 Mch., 23 Apr., and 10, 17 June 1802, all FCs in Lb in DNA: RG 45, MLS).

From Delaware Democratic Republicans

SIR.   [on or after 24 Mch. 1802]

In compliance with the wishes of our Republican Brethren of Kent County in the State of Delaware as enjoined on us by the preceeding Resolves—We Humbly submit to your consideration the following reasons upon the subject of said resolves.

Being decidedly of opinion that Allen Mc.Lane esquire deserves not to be continued Collector of the Port of Wilmington in the State of Delaware;—we have been in expectation of hearing of his removal, but being disappointed, we are induced to believe you are persuaded that the Republicans of Delaware wish his continuance in Office. To remove which impression is the object of this Address.

We presume not, Sir, to put our Judgment in competition with yours, and would not wish to dictate to the supreme executive of the united States the conduct he should persue. But we think it our duty to inform you, that we conceive the present and past conduct of Allen Mc.Lane Esquire highly improper and undeserving of confidence from a Republican President. Could we but bring ourselves to believe that a person who has been a uniform supporter of the past dangerous and extravagant Administration—who by the Violence of his Conduct has rendered himself extremely obnoxious to the republicans of Delaware—so much so—that they had rather see any other Federalist in the State enjoying that lucrative office than himself, ought not to be favored by a President whom he has invariably endeavored to villify and abuse, we might perhaps think he should be continued—(note "Christian Federalist") especially if no Republican in the State could be found capable of filling that office. He has now been five years in the enjoyment of that office, and if he is not now to be removed, we presume, he is to Hold his office like the Judges during "good Behaviour." We cannot think it right that such officers should be continued forever in office, and we Humbly conceive that offices of Profit should circulate among the People, especially in a Republican Government, as ours is.

There is nothing, Sir, we have so much at Heart as the Interest & welfare of the Republican cause. We could wish none but firm republican Friends to be the objects of Presidential favor. Persons who have weathered the storm of Federal Persecution, and have been invariably supporters of the Republican cause, should, we think, be promoted to Offices of profit, and be rewarded for their fidelity and attachment.—At the same time we would not wish to be understood to censure your attempt to conciliate. On the contrary we applaud it. But the Federalists have no idea of conciliation. They are evidently determined on the destruction of Republicanism, and notwithstanding the disposition you have evinced to conciliate by your permitting a large majority of them to remain in office, their abuse of your Administration has been equally as great as if you had displaced every man of them. Having enjoyed a complete monopoly of Offices under President Adams, nothing will satisfy them but the same monopoly under your Administration.

We believe not a single Federalist in this state has been removed from office;—and shall Federalists always Bask in the sunshine of Presidential favor? Shall nothing satisfy them but a perpetual enjoyment of every Office of Profit in the State? And shall no change of sentiment in the People, shall no change of Public Men, produce a change of measures, or operate to the advantage of the republicans. While Jefferson is President they certainly cannot be neglected.

Be assured, Sir, that we are perfectly disinterested in our present Address—not having any particular person in view to fill said Office.

It only remains for us to express our most ardent wishes that your Administration may be prosperous and Happy. To these may the wise disposer of events be Pleased to add length of Days and every of Heavens choicest blessings.

Resolved. That said Address be signed by the Chairman and Secretary, and sent to David Hall Esquire Governor of this State, together with a Copy of the Proceedings—To be forwarded to the President of the United States.

Signed by Order of said Meeting.
ABRAHAM PIERCE Chairman.
J. HAMM. Secretary.

[117]

RC (DLC); in John Hamm's hand, signed by Hamm and Pierce; resolutions and proceedings at 24 Mch. 1802 meeting attached above inside address; at head of text: "To Thomas Jefferson. President of the United States"; endorsed by TJ as a letter of 24 Mch. received 5 June and so recorded in SJL with notation "to remove Mc.lane." Enclosed in David Hall to TJ, 31 May 1802.

In 1796, Abraham Pierce represented Kent County in the Delaware House of Representatives. Dr. John Hamm, who had studied medicine in Philadelphia with Benjamin Rush, moved to Ohio later in the decade, where he became prominent in state politics. In December 1813, Madison appointed him U.S. marshall of the Ohio district. In 1830, President Jackson appointed Hamm to a diplomatic post in Chile, where he concluded the first treaty between the U.S. and that country (*Journal of the House of Representatives of the State of Delaware, at a Session Commenced at Dover, on Tuesday, the Fifth Day of January, in the Year of Our Lord* *One Thousand Seven Hundred and Ninety-Six* [Wilmington, Del., 1796], 5; *Delaware History*, 4 [1950], 71; Donald J. Ratcliffe, *Party Spirit in a Frontier Republic: Democratic Politics in Ohio, 1793-1821* [Columbus, 1998], 156, 162; JEP, 2:445-6).

PRECEEDING RESOLVES: a "large and respectable" meeting of Democratic Republicans at the house of Daniel Cooke in Dover, Delaware passed three resolutions unanimously on 24 Mch. The first stated: "That it is the Opinion of this Meeting that Allen Mc.Lane Esquire should no longer be continued Collector of the Port of Wilmington in the State of Delaware"; the second: "That a Committee of Five be appointed to prepare and Draft an Address to the President of the United States on the subject of removing said Allen Mc.Lane esquire from Office"; and the third: "That Major Abraham Pierce, Risdon Bishop, John C. Brush, Doctr. Wm. McKee and Doctr. John Hamm be the afd. Committee" (resolutions written above inside address of letter printed above).

From Sarah McKean Irujo

Thursday March 24th. 1802.

Madame d'Irujo presents her respectful compliments to Mr Jefferson, & has the honor to send him by the bearer, two dozen bottles of sweet Paxarete wine, which the Chevalier has spoken of, to Mr Jefferson.

Madame d'—. would have had the pleasure to have sent it sooner, but being disturb'd in comeing from Philadelphia; waited till it became sufficiently fine to be presented.

RC (DLC); at foot of text: "Mr Jefferson"; endorsed by TJ as received 25 Mch.

Sarah (Sally) McKean Irujo (1777-1841) was the daughter of Pennsylvania politician Thomas McKean and his second wife, Sarah Armitage McKean. In June 1796, Sally met the recently arrived Spanish minister plenipotentiary to the United States, Carlos Martínez de Irujo. Writing to his daughter Maria in 1797, TJ said of "Miss Mckain" that she "sings better than any body I have heard in America, and is otherwise well accomplished" (Vol. 29:314). Sally and Irujo married in Philadelphia in April 1798. After the wedding, Harrison Gray Otis reported to his wife that the Spanish diplomat had "finished & executed his treaty with Miss McKean in the Romish Chapel—The ceremony was performed with due Castilian and diplomatic Gravity, after which the parties went into the country where it is probable, they threw off their *Robes of Office*, & cemented the new alliance" (quoted in Carrie Rebora Barratt and Ellen G. Miles, *Gilbert Stuart* [New York, 2004], 246). The couple's first child, a boy, died in infancy. A daughter, Narcisa Maria Luisa, was born in 1800. The family moved to Washington in 1802, after the reversal of Irujo's recall to Spain, and in December of that year she gave birth to a son they named Carlos Fernando. When King Carlos IV made Irujo the first marqués of Casa-Irujo in December 1802, Sally became a marquesa (marchioness). By 1804, TJ's administration became frustrated with Irujo and asked the Spanish to remove him as minister. The Irujos left the United States in 1808, and Sally resided in Spain for the rest of her life. As indicated by Otis's comment about the wedding quoted above, she had converted to the Catholic faith to marry Irujo. Her son's application for membership in the Order of Carlos III, a Spanish religious order, contained assertions that Sally and her parents had all been baptized as Roman Catholics in childhood and that Thomas McKean and Sarah Armitage were married in St. Augustine's, a Catholic church in Philadelphia. The family was not Catholic, however. Their active Presbyterianism was well known and formed a prominent part of Thomas McKean's personal and political identity. William Cobbett made much of that issue during the 1799 Pennsylvania gubernatorial election, questioning the sincerity of Sally McKean's conversion and branding her father a hypocrite for allowing her to renounce the faith of her childhood to marry a Spanish grandee (Roberdeau Buchanan, *Genealogy of the McKean Family of Pennsylvania* [Lancaster, Pa., 1890], 21, 112, 123-4, 133-8, 187-9; Eric Beerman, "Spanish Envoy to the United States [1796-1809]: Marques de Casa Irujo and his Philadelphia Wife Sally McKean," *The Americas*, 37 [1981], 448, 449, 451, 452, 453; Rowe, *McKean*, 300, 309, 474n; Kenneth W. Keller, "Rural Politics and the Collapse of Pennsylvania Federalism," APS, *Transactions*, 72 [1982], 30, 32-4, 50; William Cobbett, *Porcupine's Works; Containing Various Writings and Selections, Exhibiting a Faithful Picture of the United States of America*, 12 vols. [London, 1801], 9:314-15; 11:22-3; William B. Miller, "Presbyterian Signers of the Declaration of Independence," *Journal of the Presbyterian Historical Society*, 36 [1958], 167-9; Philadelphia *North American*, 6 Apr. 1841; Barratt and Miles, *Gilbert Stuart*, 247; Madison, *Papers, Sec. of State Ser.*, 8:223-4; ANB, s.v. "McKean, Thomas"; Vol. 35:392-3).

To Levi Lincoln

TH:J. TO THE ATTORNEY GENL.   Mar. 24. 1802.

I had no conception there were persons enough to support a paper whose stomachs could bear such aliment as the inclosed papers contain. they are far beyond even the Washington Federalist. to punish however is impracticable until the body of the people, from whom juries are to be taken, get their minds to rights; and even then I doubt it's expediency. while a full range is proper for actions by[1] individuals, either private or public, for slanders affecting them, I would wish much to see the experiment tried of getting along without public prosecutions for *libels*. I believe we can do it.[2] patience and well-doing, instead of punishment, if it can be found sufficiently efficacious, would be a happy change in the instruments of government. health & affectionate salutations.

RC (MHi: Levi Lincoln Papers); date
torn, supplied from PrC. PrC (DLC).
Enclosures not found.

¹ TJ here canceled "private."
² TJ here canceled "in the mean time."

To the Senate

GENTLEMEN OF THE SENATE

The act fixing the military peace establishment of the US. rendering it necessary that the officers retained in service should, in most cases be transferred into regiments different from those to which their commissions attach them, new commissions are deemed necessary for them, as well as for those entitled to promotion, and for the Ensigns newly nominated. the inclosed report from the Secretary at war exhibits the transfers, promotions, and new appointments proposed in conformity with the law: and I accordingly nominate the several persons named in the report, for commissions, according to it's tenor.

TH: JEFFERSON
March. 25. 1802.

RC (DNA: RG 46, EPEN, 7th Cong., 1st sess.); endorsed by Senate clerks as "Message of the President nominating Henry Burbeck and others to military appointments." PrC (DLC). Recorded in SJL with notation "Military nominations. general list." Enclosure: List of nominations for officers' commissions, with columns for name, present rank and unit, and rank "under the new organization"; arranged by regiment according to the new organization and by rank within each regiment, beginning with Henry Burbeck, lieutenant colonel of the first regiment of artillerists and engineers, proposed as colonel of the new regiment of artillerists; the list including officers of one regiment of artillerists and two regiments of infantry; also four engineers headed by Jonathan Williams as major, two surgeons, nineteen surgeon's mates, five candidates for commissions as ensigns in the infantry, Lieutenant Colonel Thomas H. Cushing as adjutant and inspector of the army, and Caleb Swan as paymaster of the army (MS in DNA: RG 46, EPEN; in Joshua Wingate's hand, signed by Dearborn; at head of text: "The following persons are proposed to the consideration of the President of the United States, for nomination to the several appointments annexed to their names respectively"; one emendation by TJ, expanding a reference to the existing "1 Reg: of Artillery" to include "and Engineers"; notations by a Senate clerk alongside names of Jesse Lull, Cornelius Lyman, and Zebulon M. Pike, for which see below).

Prior to the approval of the MILITARY PEACE ESTABLISHMENT act on 16 Mch., the army consisted of two regiments of artillerists and engineers, four regiments of infantry, and two troops of dismounted cavalry. Under the new act, which followed a plan that Dearborn gave to TJ in December, there would be only one regiment of artillerists and two regiments of infantry. The statute also authorized the president to establish a corps of engineers, which was to have initially seven officers and ten cadets. The corps, to be stationed at West Point, "shall constitute a military academy." Beginning on 18 Mch., Dearborn issued a series of orders to Thomas H. Cushing to start the reduction of the number of personnel and the reorganization of the regiments. Dearborn also ordered the closure of the quartermaster's department and the suspension of recruitments for the army (U.S. Statutes at Large, 2:132-7; Dearborn to Cushing, 18-22, 25 Mch., and to John Wilkins, Jr., 18 Mch., in DNA: RG 107, LSMA; Henry Dearborn's Plan for Reorganizing the Army, [7 Dec. 1801]).

APPOINTMENTS PROPOSED: Meriwether Lewis delivered this message on 25 Mch. The Senate took it up in executive session on the 26th and that day approved all but four of the nominations. The officers who did not gain immediate approval were Jesse Lull, a lieutenant of the 1st regiment of artillerists and engineers, nominated as lieutenant of the new regiment of artillerists; Cornelius Lyman, a captain of the 2d regiment of infantry, nominated for the same rank in the new 1st regiment of infantry; Zebulon Pike, major of the 3d infantry regiment, nominated for the same rank in the new 1st regiment; and Zebulon Montgomery Pike, first lieutenant of the 2d infantry regiment, nominated as first lieutenant of the new 1st regiment. The Senate referred those nominations to a committee consisting of Joseph Anderson, Stevens Thomson Mason, and Jonathan Dayton. On 31 Mch., Anderson reported that "from the information obtained respecting the rank" and "characters" of the officers, the committee recommended that "it would be expedient for the Senate to consent and advise to their appointment." The following day the Senate approved the appointments of the two Pikes, but postponed the other two. On 2 Apr., the senators postponed Lyman's nomination and rejected Lull's (JEP, 1:410-15, 416).

From Robert Smith

Navy dept: 25 March 1802.

The young Gentleman to whom the enclosed letter is addressed, has been recommended by Mr. Page, for reinstatement in the navy. If you have no objection the enclosed letter shall be forwarded.

R.S.

FC (Lb in DNA: RG 45, LSP); at head of text: "The President." Enclosure: Smith to Hugh Wallace Wormeley, 25 Mch. 1802, informing Wormeley that he has been reinstated as a midshipman in the navy and directing him to join the frigate *Chesapeake* at Norfolk (FC in Lb in DNA: RG 45, LSO).

YOUNG GENTLEMAN: Hugh Wallace Wormeley was a midshipman on the sloop *Maryland* during the Quasi-War with France. Discharged under the Peace Establishment Act, he was reinstated on 25 Mch. 1802 despite poor health. He served as a midshipman until 1805, then as a lieutenant in the Marine Corps until 1806. He was recommended to TJ for a consular post in the Barbary states in 1806, but did not receive an appointment (NDBW, *Register*, 61, 66; James F. Hopkins and others, eds., *The Papers of Henry Clay*, 11 vols. [Lexington, Ky., 1959-92], 10:626; Joseph Lewis, Jr., to TJ, 11 Feb. 1806).

MR. PAGE: probably Mann Page, who had previously recommended navy candidates to TJ (Robert Smith to TJ, 20 Feb. 1802).

From George Washington McElroy

SIR   Philada. 26 Mar: 1802

Being informed that your Excellency has been pleased to grant my solicited commission of Consul for the Canary Islands, and that your Excellency Condescended personally to have my petition complyed with in a manner which I do not merit, nor could have expected; beg leave to offer you the homage of my warmest acknowledgements and assurances of my great respect.

My Father who is now fast approaching the silent grave, and must soon pay the debt of nature, demands me to assure your excellency that the firm attachment wch. he has always entertained for you, goes with him unimpaired.

I have the honor to be your Excellencys Obliged Obdt. huml Sevt.

GEO: WASHN. McELROY.

RC (DNA: RG 59, LAR); at foot of text: "His Excellency Thomas Jefferson Esquire Prest. of the U.S"; endorsed by TJ as received 29 Mch. and so recorded in SJL.

MY SOLICITED COMMISSION: see McElroy to TJ, 14 Jan. 1802.

From Samuel Bishop

                              Collectors Office New Haven District
SIR   March 27 1802

Having received a Commission as Collector of this district during the pleasure of the President, I possess my faculties sufficiently[1] to feel grateful for the confidence reposed and for the conclusive manner in which my appointment was vindicated: — & I retain my hand writing sufficiently to express this gratitude.

Being recovered from a long season of sickniss I shall endeavour to perform personally some official acts and to cause the rest to be done to acceptance—

At my advanced age it is a source of great satisfaction that I have lived to see our National government administered by men who respect the principles of our revolution and who will apply them faithfully to the condition of our country

I have the Honor to subscribe my self with perfect respect your Humble servant—   SAML. BISHOP

RC (DLC); at head of text: "To the President of the united States"; endorsed by TJ as a letter of 22 Mch. received 5 Apr. and so recorded in SJL.

Samuel Bishop (1723?-1803), mayor of New Haven, chief judge of the county probate court, justice of the peace, and town clerk, was appointed by TJ as collector of the port on 23 May 1801 but did not receive his permanent commission until approved by the Senate in January 1802. His recess appointment and the removal of Elizur Goodrich were the subjects of an impassioned remonstrance by the merchants of New Haven in June 1801 that prompted TJ to offer an explanation of his policy on removals and appointments. Bishop, almost eighty years old, died in early August 1803. His son, Abraham Bishop, succeeded him in office (JEP, 1:402, 453; New Haven *Visitor*, 9 Aug. 1803; Vol. 33:671; Vol. 34:301, 381-4, 554-8).

[1] MS: "suffciently."

From Henry Dearborn

SIR,

War Department
27. March 1802.

I have the honor to enclose you an estimate of expenditures for the Army of the United States, for the year 1802, conformably to the Act of the 16th inst: The several items which compose the aggregate sums in this estimate, where they are not specified, will be found on a recurrence to an annual estimate made by this department, under date of the 28. of Oct. 1801.

I have also subjoined a supplementary estimate exhibiting the sums which will be required to carry the Act above alluded to, into complete operation.

With high consideration & respect, I have the honor to be, Sir, Yr. Obt. Servant

H. DEARBORN

RC (DNA: RG 46, LPPM, 7th Cong., 1st sess.); in a clerk's hand, signed by Dearborn; at foot of text: "The President of the United States"; endorsed by a Senate clerk. FC (Lb in DNA: RG 107, LSP). Enclosure: "Estimate of Expenditures for the Army of the United States for the year 1802, conformably to the Act of Congress passed on the 16th. instant, entitled an 'Act fixing the Military Peace establishment of the United States,'" 27 Mch. 1802; listing total expenditures of $948,762.08, including $292,272 for pay of all ranks, $201,027.40 for subsistence (1,435,910 rations), $93,000 for military pensions, $71,750 for the Indian Department, $70,500 for building and completing fortifications and barracks, $66,766.88 for arsenals, magazines, and armories, $66,630 for clothing, $48,000 for expenditures "of what was heretofore denominated the 'Quarter Masters Department,'" and lesser amounts for contingent expenses of the War Department, the medical department, forage, bounties and premiums, and the corps of engineers; second section of document, with heading "In addition to the foregoing estimate, the following sums will be necessary, to meet the expenditures which will arise in consequence of discharging the Officers, non Commissioned Officers, and privates, who are supernumerary by the Act of the 16th. instant, entitled an 'Act fixing the military peace establishment of the United States,' and for carrying the same into complete operation," lists expenses of pay, subsistence, clothing, forage, medical department, quartermaster's department, bounties and premiums, allowances for officers and soldiers to be discharged, and contingencies, totaling $158,500 (MS in DNA: RG 46, LPPM; in a clerk's hand, signed by Dearborn). Enclosed in TJ to the Senate and the House of Representatives, 30 Mch.

From John Page

MY DEAR SIR   Rosewell March 27th. 1802

On the night of the 17th. I received your Favor of the 20th. Ultimo & 9th. instant, & hastened to thank you for the strong proofs it conveyed to me of your Friendship, for I sat down that moment, & began to make my Acknowledgments in the best manner I could; thanking you for your candid Statement, & particularly for your permission to take time for considering your offer, with all the probable Consequences of my acceptance of it—In my haste, I have found, that, I improperly ran on beyond the limits of such a Letter as ought to be an answer to yours; as you can have no Leisure for reading long Letters, & as it must be more agreable to you to receive my final Determination expressed in a few Words, than a long statement of the Considerations which may lead me to wish for time to decide on the interesting proposition you have made; & I have therefore, after losing a Post, found it better to lose another, than to trouble you with that Letter. I have been thus long in my introduction to this, because I owe you an Apology for the delay of my Acknowledgement of the receipt of your Letter; & I owe to myself, some explanation to you of the delay which has attended *this*: for as much as I rely on your candour & Friendship, I am sorry that I have not sooner thanked you for your offer of the Post of Collector of the Customs at Petersburg. Believe me I sincerely & heartily thank you, & were not the Emoluments of the Office as yet uncertain, & (as there is no Bank in the place) the risk & Responsibility added to the labours of it, too great compared with the probable Compensation after the proposed Reduction mentioned by Mr. Gallatin, I would have immediately accepted it &[1] only asked for time to ascertain the Expence of procuring comfortable Accommodations there for my Family, & should however have entreated you, to remove me as soon as in your Power, to some place of less risk & Responsibility. I confess the unhealthiness of the Place would be also an Object of my Enquiry. But to make such Enquiries as might be desireable without endangering a Discovery of my Secret must be a Work of Time. I therefore at present can only say, that I can not refuse your offer; nor

[124]

accept it, till after more mature Consideration, which I hope will not require more time than the nature of the case will afford; as the Vacancy which it is proposed that I shall fill has not yet happened, & depends on your direction. If it be necessary that it should speedily take place; or receiving note of that necessity, I will instantly return my final Resolution.

In the mean time, I am & indeed always shall be, with the highest Esteem most sincerely yours   JOHN PAGE

RC (DLC); endorsed by TJ as received 1 Apr. and so recorded in SJL.

TJ's FAVOR of 20 Feb. and its 9 Mch. postscript made Page a tentative offer of the collectorship at PETERSBURG currently held by Federalist William Heth,

but also cautioned that Congress was considering a reduction of the office's emoluments.

[1] Preceding three words and ampersand interlined.

From Nicholas Reib

SIR!   Philada. March 27th. 1802.

I had the Pleasure to receive your Letter dated the 27th. of February in Answer to my last for which I deem myself obligated to you. by which I observe that it is not in the Power of you to promote any Settlement in regard to my Claims to the U.S. but refer me to the Legislature. I mentioned to you in my former Letter that an act had been passed Solely for me Ascertaining that I should receive payment for Months pay, Bounty and Board the back ration was struck out. The Accountant of the war office writes on the bak of my Account that I had been paid by Mr. Pierce the General Pay Master. In Consequence of which I have made an affidavet (which I hereby Inclose) Certifying that I never received a Cent from said Pierce, and if am right, the said Pierce died before my Act was passed. The Accountant also observes on the back of the Account the report of the Committee of Claims (which now lies before Congress) signed by myself and others this Petition in Connection with other Artificers was given in after my own Petition was offered, but not yet decided upon therefore the said Report has nothing to do with my Individual Account. I hope your Excellency will Excuse my Audaciousness in troubling you with my affairs I being Informed by People personally acquinted with you that know your Disposition to be Inclined to show Justice to them that it belongs which is also Confirmed by your Inaugeration Speech on the 4th of March 1801.

I therefore rest Assured that you will Endeavour to Enforce the aforesaid act passed for me in the year 1792.

I have the honour to be Sir: your most obedient Hble. Servt.

NICHOLAS REIB

P.S.

To make it more evident to you; I would wish yet to mention that Mr. Rins a Citizien of this City went with me to Mr. Ran[dolph] late Secretary of State for to be settled;[1] upon which he gave us an order on the War office, but in Vain. Afterward David Langeneker went with me to Rob. G. Harper Esqr. Concerning the Settlement & he immediately sent in the Clerk's office for the Bill Books of 1792. When the Clerk directly brought two Books, one of the Senate the other of the house of Representatives, Mr. Harper examining them told us that an Act had been passed purpoisly for Ns. Rieb, and gave me another order on the War office which was also discountenanced. Consequently I have still a proper Right to demand such Moneys as are due me.

Yours as above.

RC (DLC); frayed at margin; at head of text: "His Excellency Thomas Jefferson President of the U.S."; endorsed by TJ as received 3 Mch. but recorded in SJL as received 3 Apr. Enclosure not found.

YOUR LETTER DATED THE 27TH. OF FEBRUARY: that is, TJ to Reib of 24 Feb., which is summarized at TJ to Gallatin, with Gallatin's reply, printed at 23 Feb. 1802.

MY LAST: Reib to TJ, 17 Feb. 1802.

[1] MS: "settled Settled."

From Daniel Carroll

SIR/   Washington March 28th 1802

Since you did me the honor the other day to mention the subject of the Canal from the falls of Poto. to the Eastern branch, I have thought much on the subject, & satisfied you will excuse the liberty I am now takeing, have determined to address you a few lines—I see innumerable difficulties attending the plan you propose, one which you mentioned, the want of funds, The ground where you propose introducing the Canal into the City to wit, Pensa. avenue I do suppose, must be about thirty feet, above the levels of water street in Geo Town, & woud continue to that height, or nearly untill you woud come to the south of the Presidents house, Should this be correct or nearly so, I apprehend to remove such a body of earth, to so great a depth, woud be attended with an expence that woud not be encountered—I am allso satisfied to take the canal along tiber creek & introduce it into the eastern branch by new Jersey avenue, woud cost considerably less, than takeing through Geo Town, independant of the high ground on Pensa. avenue—With high respect I am

Sir Your Mo Obt Servt   DANL CARROLL of Dudn.

RC (DLC); at head of text: "The President of the United States"; endorsed by TJ as received 29 Mch. and so recorded in SJL.

In February 1802, the Potomac Canal Company opened to traffic its canal at Great Falls, Virginia, six miles from the company's canal at Little Falls above Georgetown. Meanwhile, a projected waterway between the Potomac River and the Eastern Branch, shown on the first published map of the city, remained unbuilt for lack of funds. While TJ was secretary of state, he had communicated with the District of Columbia commissioners about plans for the city canal and as early as 1792, he was aware of a proposal to extend the Little Falls canal into the city. In 1796, Carroll took part in a brief private effort to raise money to build the city canal (Robert J. Kapsch, *The Potomac Canal: George Washington and the Waterway West* [Morgantown, W.Va.,

2007], 33, 107-8; ASP, *Miscellaneous*, 1:258-9; Bryan, *National Capital*, 1:190-1, 288-9; Vol. 23:195, 224-5, 237, 239, 400).

A petition from inhabitants of "Washington and district of Columbia" to the Senate and House of Representatives, signed by Carroll and dated 19 Jan. 1802, asked Congress to pass an act to incorporate a company to build a canal between the Potomac River and the Eastern Branch "along the Tiber Creek, through the low grounds at the foot of the Capitol hill" (DNA: RG 233, PMRSL, 7th. Cong., 1st. sess.). On 9 Feb., the House committee to whom the petition was referred issued a report, and on 24 Mch. a bill based on the report was read before the House. On 1 May 1802, the House passed an act to incorporate the Washington Canal Company and named Carroll as a company manager (JHR, 4:54, 89, 157; U.S. Statutes at Large, 2:175-8).

To Thomas Mann Randolph

DEAR SIR   Washington Mar. 28. 1802.

Yours of the 20th. has been duly recieved. my former letters will have informed you that the lands offered by Sibbald are real pine barrens & will not bring corn at all; but that the pine lands mixed with oak and a clay foundation bring good crops[1] of corn & wheat. in a conversation which Capt Lewis had with mr Milledge the latter observed that after getting to the hilly country, some distance below Augusta, and thence Westward the Cotton soil is to be had every where, but that tho' he deemed it healthy as soon as you reach the hills, yet the farther up the country the healthier. I inclose you a note of Capt Lewis's as to a tract of land of Blackburn's for sale, in the neighborhood of the Harvies & Meriwethers. it is about 20. miles above Petersburg, which is 50. miles above Augusta. Petersburg is at the confluence of Savanna & Broad rivers, with good navigation to it at present, a very considerable and most thriving town, likely to be the principal commercial town in the state, after Savannah. we propose to open a road from Kentucky & East Tennissee to the head waters of the Savanna, which will give to those states their shortest outlet to the Atlantic, and it is thought will turn all that portion of their commerce, which will bear the land portages, to Savanna instead of New Orleans; and be the route of return for all our boatmen who go to New Orleans, as being quicker than the return up the Missisipi. this channel of communication the Western country calls for as of immense importance to them. just above Petersburg the navigation of Broad river has obstructions easy to be removed & then is navigable a good way up. the lands on that river very fine. perhaps you could get Stewart or Coulter to procure from Blackburn his terms, with a *right* in you to accept or refuse after seeing the lands. there is a good carriage road the whole way. you had better go in my chair which will be idle at Monticello. Congress expects to rise the 2d Monday (12th.) of April; and I have no doubt will rise within a week after that, when you may expect to see mr Milledge. I shall be immediately after him. there will be no occasion for your adding so much to your journey as by coming here. Martha & the family can either come on with me, or if more convenient, I can come on after a very short stay at Monticello, and send back a coachee to meet them at mr Strode's, Capt. Lewis going in it to take care of them. but all this may be settled[2] when we meet. to make you perfectly secure in all accidents as to money, perhaps mr Milledge can indicate merchants who will give money there for draughts on me payable either at the treasury here or in Philadelphia. the H. of R. has passed the bill repealing the internal taxes. they must pass a supplementary judiciary law, and some other laws which, tho' of minor consequence, are indispensable.   my tenderest love to my ever dear Martha, and the children, & affectionate attachment to yourself.   TH: JEFFERSON

P.S. I have omitted to mention that letters are recieved from Governor Claiborne shewing great uneasiness at the situation of that territory, and requesting a block house to be built and 800. stand of arms to be deposited in the center of it's population, which we have ordered. their H. of R. passed a bill prohibiting *male* slaves from being carried into the territory, which was rejected by the council. a circumstance of further consideration stated to me by some of the Western members, is that a traveller passing through the 600. miles of uninhabited country if he is taken sick, dies almost infallibly; for the want of provisions prevents his lying by in the woods, and travelling is almost always fatal to a sick person. this was one of the reasons which made us urge the Indians to let us establish houses on the road. but their jealousy denied it.

RC (DLC); addressed: "Thomas Mann Randolph Edgehill near Milton"; franked; postmarked 27 Mch.; endorsed by Randolph as received 1 Apr. PrC (MHi); endorsed by TJ in ink on verso. Enclosure not found.

FORMER LETTERS: see TJ to Thomas Mann Randolph of 12 and 20 Mch.

Meriwether LEWIS spent time in Georgia after his mother, Lucy Meriwether Lewis, married John Marks and moved from Virginia to the Broad River valley in 1784 or 1785 (ANB; Vol. 33:51-2n). LAND OF BLACKBURN'S FOR SALE: probably Samuel Blackburn, who moved from Staunton, Virginia, to Georgia after he married Ann Mathews, the daughter of George Mathews, in 1785. Mathews served as governor of Georgia from 1787 to 1788 and 1793 to 1796. Blackburn served in the Georgia state senate from 1791 to 1795 and supported passage of the infamous Yazoo land bill. Blackburn returned to Virginia in 1796 and became a successful attorney, practicing law in Bath and Augusta counties. A Federalist, he intermittently represented Bath County in the House of Delegates between 1799 and 1826. Blackburn owned land in Wilkes County, Georgia, where Albemarle County members of the Harvie and Meriwether families had moved in the mid-1780s. In 1790, Wilkes was subdivided into four counties, one being Elbert County, extending from the mouth of the Broad River, and including PETERSBURG, which experienced a period of prosperity and growth in the 1790s and during the first decade of the nineteenth century. In 1804, Jedidiah Morse described it as a "very flourishing post town" being "in a pleasant and healthful situation, on the point of land formed by the confluence of Broad with Savannah River" (DVB, 1:518-19; Ellis Merton Coulter, Old Petersburg and the Broad River Valley of Georgia: Their Rise and Decline [Athens, Ga., 1965], 8-10, 13-16;

Jedidiah Morse, The American Gazetteer, 2d ed. [Boston, 1804]; Woods, Albemarle, 386-7).

COULTER: that is, John Coalter, attorney at Staunton (Vol. 31:192n).

On 20 Dec., Governor William C. C. CLAIBORNE informed the secretary of state that citizens of Mississippi Territory were not armed and could not obtain suitable arms. The governor noted that it would greatly add to the security of the "exposed Frontier" if the president would send to Natchez about 400 muskets, as many rifles, and directions to sell them at a price that would reimburse the United States the original cost. When General James Wilkinson visited Natchez in late January, Claiborne solicited him "to erect a small Block-House, central to the population of the District as a place of deposit, for such spare Arms as may now be lodged at Fort Adams." On 29 Jan., the same day the governor presented his request, Wilkinson agreed to "the Establishment of a small party" that would be central to the population, and to the deposit of 250 to 300 arms, subject to the order of the governor. Claiborne forwarded his correspondence with Wilkinson to Madison on 5 Feb., requesting the executive to endorse the arrangement. Claiborne noted that while peace prevailed at the present time, "surrounded as it is, by numerous Indian Tribes, and with a population of Negroes, nearly equal to the number of Whites, the continuance of that Peace is certainly precarious." Claiborne advised that the spare arms at Fort Adams be located so that the militia could defend itself in time of danger. On 10 Mch., Dearborn informed Claiborne that the president had directed 500 rifles to be forwarded from Philadelphia to the territory and "three Hundred Muskets to be delivered at Fort Adams, on your receipting for them." The rifles and muskets were to be sold, under Claiborne's direction, to the militia on reasonable terms but for a price high enough to prevent purchase for speculation. On 8 Apr., Dearborn informed Claiborne that the president had approved reasonable expenditures and the use of troops from Fort Adams to build a block house for the arms. This led to the establishment of Fort Dearborn, six miles east of Natchez (Dunbar Rowland, ed., *Official Letter Books of W. C. C. Claiborne, 1801-1816*, 6 vols. [Jackson, Miss., 1917], 1:27-31, 40-4, 104, 110-12).

On 23 Jan., Claiborne informed Madison that a law "to prohibit the importation into the Territory, of Male Slaves, above the age of Sixteen," passed the House of Representatives, but was RE-JECTED BY THE COUNCIL. "This kind of population," Claiborne continued, "is becoming alarming, and will in all probability, (sooner or later) prove a source of much distress" (same, 1:38-9).

[1] Remainder of sentence interlined.
[2] Remainder of sentence interlined in place of "at our convenience."

From Leonora Sansay

Sunday [28 Mch. 1802]

An american Lady who is on the point of sailing for Port au prince presumes to solicit of Mr Jefferson a letter of Protection for that place. she is highly sensible of the greatness of the honour she solicits, but is also convinc'd that the name of Mr. Jefferson alone will preserve her from every inconvenience—

Lov'd by the subjects he makes happy, honour'd by admiring nations crown'd with political & literary glory—he stands foremost in the rank of eminent men, his name extends to the utmost borders of the globe & he shines with Distinguish'd superiority the wonder of the universe—Would Mr Jefferson accord Mrs. Sansay the honour of an interview at 12 or any other hour of this day she will more fully explain her motives for making the request, & esteem as the greatest happiness of her life the honour of having been admitted to the presence of Mr Jefferson

RC (MHi); partially dated; endorsed by TJ: "Sansay mrs." Recorded in SJL as a letter of 28 Mch. received the same day.

Leonora Sansay (1781-?) may have been the daughter of Philadelphia innkeeper William Hassall. As early as 1797 she was introduced to Aaron Burr, with whom she developed an intimate relationship that continued even after her marriage in 1800 to Louis Sansay, a French-born merchant grocer residing in New York. In March 1802, Madame Sansay traveled to Washington to visit the vice president, who mediated in the couple's troubled marriage and helped her obtain several letters of introduction for an upcoming trip to the West Indies. Although she accompanied her husband on a journey to reclaim his Saint-Domingue coffee plantation, she remained in contact with Burr, sending him semi-autobiographical accounts of the island flirtations of a woman referred to as "Clara." Leonora Sansay later returned to the United States, settling in 1807 in Philadelphia, where she made artificial flowers and wrote two novels (Kline, *Burr*, 2:702-4; Nancy Isenberg, *Fallen Founder: The Life of Aaron Burr* [New

York, 2007], 240-1, 479; Phillip S. Lapsansky, "Afro-Americana: Rediscovering Leonora Sansay," *Annual Report of the Library Company of Philadelphia for the Year 1992* [Philadelphia, 1993], 29-46; *Secret History; or, The Horrors of St. Domingo, in a Series of Letters, Written by a Lady at Cape François, to Colonel Burr* [Philadelphia, 1808; Shaw-Shoemaker, No. 15201]).

LETTER OF PROTECTION: a letter or certificate, attesting to American citizenship, and guaranteeing protection, exemption, or immunity for the holder (OED).

To Watson & Higginbotham

MESSRS. WATSON & HIGGINBOTHAM   Washington Mar. 28. 1802.

The postmaster general has applied to me to recommend a postmaster for Milton to succeed mr Camden who has resigned. being not sufficiently acquainted with the characters there who might be proper and willing to accept the office, I take the liberty of solliciting you to recommend one, whom you shall consider as fit for the office and who shall consent to accept of it. it is interesting to us all not to let the post office there fall for want of a postmaster. accept assurances of my esteem & best wishes.   TH: JEFFERSON

PrC (DLC); endorsed by TJ in ink on verso.

For the proposed partnership of John Watson and David Higginbotham, both merchants at Milton, see Vol. 35:28. Watson had served as postmaster at Milton from March 1798 to March 1799. Watson & Higginbotham's reply of 2 Apr., recorded in SJL as received on the 6th, has not been found, but on 6 Apr., Richard Anderson was appointed postmaster at Milton TO SUCCEED Marbell CAMDEN (Stets, *Postmasters*, 264).

From Abraham Baldwin

ABR BALDWIN TO THE PRESIDENT
OF THE UNITED STATES   Monday 29th March 1802

Mr Mansfield informed me several weeks ago that he should avail himself of your obliging offer by forwarding to your address a box containing fifteen copies of his Mathematical work. The delay is so much longer than I expected, that there is reason to apprehend they will not reach us. I shall write him on the subject tomorrow

RC (MHi); addressed: "The President of the United States"; endorsed by TJ as received 30 Mch. and so recorded in SJL.

Baldwin and Jared MANSFIELD were both natives of Connecticut and lived in New Haven as young men. Baldwin, four years older, was a tutor at Yale College during part of Mansfield's time there as a student in the 1770s. Mansfield published

his *Essays, Mathematical and Physical:* Shaw-Shoemaker, No. 866; Dexter, *Yale,* *Containing New Theories and Illus-* 3:432, 691-2).
trations of Some Very Important and TJ probably conveyed his OFFER to *Difficult Subjects of the Sciences* in New help distribute the book in a conversation Haven in 1801 (Sowerby, No. 3733; with Baldwin rather than by letter.

To Benjamin Smith Barton

DEAR SIR   Washington Mar. 29. 1802.

Your favor of the 13th. came to hand on the 20th. instant only. I now inclose you, from the Secretary at war, a letter to Colo. Meigs our agent with the Cherokees, and one to yourself which may answer with those of any other nation you may chuse to visit. should you visit the Creeks, you will find them assembled in May and June[1] and with them General Wilkinson, General Pickens and mr Hawkins engaged in a treaty with them. you will find these letters entirely equivalent to any which could have been written by myself. I have been obliged to adopt a rule of giving myself no letters of introduction or recommendation. it will readily occur to you to what an extent these applications would have been pushed as[2] most of those who go abroad for curiosity or mercantile speculations would have found some channel for obtaining them, and they might with some young adventurers be used for improper purposes. I am in hopes we shall have the pleasure of seeing you here on your passage. you can go in the stages as far as Petersburg in Virginia, where I think you have a brother living. should you go on a higher road, Monticello will be in your way, where I shall be about the first of May. about the middle of that month I expect mr Randolph will set out for Augusta in Georgia, whom you would find a good botanising companion. I really envy you your journey; but I am a prisoner of state. I shall be glad to hear from you in every part of your journey. accept assurances of my esteem & my best wishes.   TH: JEFFERSON

RC (PHi); addressed: "Doctr. Benjamin S. Barton Philadelphia"; franked and postmarked; endorsed by Barton as received 1 Apr. PrC (DLC). Enclosures not found.

Barton's BROTHER, Richard Peters Barton, lived about seven miles from Winchester, Virginia (W. L. McAtee, ed., "Journal of Benjamin Smith Barton on a Visit to Virginia, 1802," *Castanea: The Journal of the Southern Appalachian Botanical Club*, 3 [1938], 89-90; Francis W. Pennell, "Benjamin Smith Barton as Naturalist," APS, *Proceedings*, 86 [1942], 109n; *New-York Spectator*, 3 Feb. 1821).

[1] Preceding two words interlined.
[2] TJ here canceled "few."

From DeWitt Clinton

SIR   29 March 1802

Genl. Stevens a Citizen of the State of New York intending to make an application to you on business in which he is interested and which he informs me will come before you officially, I take the liberty at his request of informing you that his standing in New York is respectable, and his character fair: Any justice to which he is entitled will I am certain be dispensed—More he ought not to expect and I am persuaded does not.

I have the honor to be With the most respectful attachment Your most obedt servt.   DEWITT CLINTON

RC (MHi); endorsed by TJ as received 30 Mch. and so recorded in SJL with notation "Stevens."

New York City merchant Ebenezer STEVENS owned the American-built ship *Bellona*, which Captain Thomas Watson, without realizing the ship had been "employed in illicit commerce," had purchased for him in the West Indies after Stevens's vessel was shipwrecked. Upon arriving from St. Croix with sugar and rum, the ship, in quarantine, was seized by New York revenue officers, condemned, and sold by order of the U.S. district court at New York for the violations committed by the former owners. On 1 Mch. 1802, DeWitt Clinton presented a petition to the Senate on Stevens's behalf seeking special legislative relief for the

losses he had incurred. Clinton headed the committee assigned to consider the case and report to the Senate, but on 19 Apr. the committee was dismissed without having made a report. Stevens's petition had earlier been considered by the House Committee of Commerce and Manufactures, which had recommended on 12 Feb. against granting the petition (New York *Commercial Advertiser*, 2 Sep. 1801; JS, 3:186-7, 215; JHR, 4:52, 95-6). On 21 Sep. 1801, the Treasury secretary had advised Stevens that he could not endorse the "principle that the sale, abroad, of a vessel, which had incurred a forfeiture, should release her from the penalty" (Gallatin, *Papers*, 5:772). For an earlier representation in Stevens's behalf, see Horatio Gates to TJ, 13 Feb. 1802.

To Mary Jefferson Eppes

Washington Mar. 29. 1802.

I wrote, my ever dear Maria, to mr Eppes & yourself on the 3d. inst. since which I have recieved mr Eppes's letter of the 11th. informing me all were well. I hope you continue so. a letter of the 20th. from mr Randolph informed me all were well at Edgehill. mr Randolph, allured by the immensely profitable culture of cotton, had come to a resolution to go to the Missisipi territory and there purchase lands & establish all his negroes in that culture. the distance 1500. miles of which 600. are through an uninhabited country, the weakness of that settlement, not more than 800 men, with a population of blacks equal to their own, and surrounded by 8000. Choctaw warriors, and the soil and commercial position moreover not equal to Georgia for the same culture, has at length balanced his determination in favor of Georgia, distant only about 470. or 480. miles from Edgehill. the plan is now arranged as follows. Congress will rise from the 13th. to the 20th. of April. I shall be at Monticello within a week or 10. days after they rise. mr Randolph then goes to Georgia to make a purchase of lands, and Martha & the family come back with me and stay till his return, which probably will not be till the latter part of July when I shall be going on to Monticello for the months of Aug. & Sep. I cannot help hoping that while your sister is here you will take a run, if it be but for a short time to come & see us. I have enquired further into the best rout for you, and it is certainly by Portroyal, & to cross over from Boyd's hole, or somewhere near it to Nangemy.[1] you by this means save 30. miles, and have the whole of the way the finest road imaginable, whereas that from Fredericksburg by Dumfries & Alexandria is the worst in the world.—will mr Eppes not have the curiosity to go up to his plantation in Albemarle the 1st. or 2d. week of May? there we could settle every thing, and he will hear more of the Georgia expedition. I inclose you two medals, one for yourself, the other with my best affections for mrs Eppes. they are taken from Houdon's bust. present me affectionately to mr Eppes and be assured of my tenderest love.   Th: Jefferson

RC (ViU); addressed: "Mrs. Maria Eppes." PrC (MHi); endorsed by TJ in ink on verso.

TWO MEDALS: John Reich's silver medallions commemorating TJ's inauguration, which Henry Voigt had supplied (Philadelphia *Aurora*, 18 Feb. 1802; Noble E. Cunningham, Jr., *The Image of Thomas Jefferson in the Public Eye, Portraits for the People, 1801-1809* [Charlottesville, 1981], 71-3; Vol. 36:239-40, 386, 565-6).

In an invoice dated Washington, 24 June 1802, Isaac Cooper noted that on 16 Mch. he framed six medals for TJ at a cost of $3 each, for a total of $18. TJ paid the amount in full on 20 July (MS in MHi; in Cooper's hand and signed by him; endorsed by TJ: "Cooper Isaac. 18."). In 1803, Cooper conducted a business on Pennsylvania Avenue where he did carving and gilding and sold "all kinds of looking glass and picture frames." TJ made his next recorded purchase from Cooper in 1804 (*National Intelligencer*, 22 Apr. 1803; MB, 2:1131).

[1] Canceled: "from this."

From James Madison

Department of State March 29th. 1802.

The Secretary of State, to whom has been referred by the President of the United States a Resolution of the House of Representatives of the 23d Inst., requesting the President to communicate to that House such information as he may have received relative to the Copper mines on the South side of Lake Superior, in pursuance of a Resolution of the 16th. April 1800, authorising the appointment of an Agent for that purpose, begs leave to lay before him the Copy of a letter of the 24th. September 1800, from the late Secretary of State to Richard Cooper Esqr., of Cooper's Town in the State of New York, appointing him an Agent, in pursuance of the last mentioned Resolution—and the Copy of one from the Attorney General of the United States, of the 30th. March 1801, at that time acting as Secretary of State, to the said Richard Cooper, signifying to him that as the Resolution in question contemplated an execution of the work and a report thereof, in time for the consideration of Congress at its next Session, and this [had] not been done, it was thought necessary to suspend the further prosecution of it, and that he was accordingly to do so. The Secretary also begs leave to lay before the President copies of sundry other letters on this subject, which, together with those mentioned above, serve to give a view—of the whole transaction, so far as this Department has had an agency in it, tho' they do not afford the particular information required by the Resolution referred to the Secretary of State, by the President.—All which is respectfully submitted.   JAMES MADISON

RC (DNA: RG 233, PM, 7th Cong., 1st sess.); torn; in a clerk's hand, signed by Madison; endorsed by a House clerk. Enclosures: (1) John Marshall to Richard Cooper, 24 Sep. 1800, informing Cooper of his appointment as agent to collect information on the copper mines on Lake Superior and to proceed upon his mission "as expeditiously as possible"; Cooper may draw on the State Department for $1,000 and his drafts "will be honored." (2) Levi Lincoln to Cooper, 30 Mch. 1801, stating that Cooper's appointment specified that his mission and report were to be completed "in time for the consideration of Congress in their last Session"; new circumstances have rendered Cooper's agency "less necessary" and therefore "the President wishes to suspend the further prosecution of the business for the present"; Cooper is to report any arrangements made and expenses incurred, and is accountable to repay money advanced by the government. (3) Cooper to Lincoln, 25 April 1801, explaining that he accepted the appointment with the stipulation that he not commence his voyage until the spring of 1801, and that President John Adams apparently thought the act extended beyond the last session of Congress; Cooper cannot make a final report on his arrangements until he hears from one of his hands; the stores and boat he purchased with his own funds have proceeded as far as Canajoharie, New York, and will be kept in good order until he receives further instructions; Cooper assumes his men will "expect a compensation equivalent to their loss and inconvenience in the derangement of their affairs." (4) James Madison to Cooper, 13 May 1801, expresses regret over any inconvenience that Cooper's preparations may have incurred, but reiterates that the resolution of 16 April 1800 clearly stated that the expedition was to have been completed before the end of the last session of Congress; the government may still reimburse Cooper's expenditures, but Cooper is advised to reduce his claims to "as narrow a compass as possible"; Cooper may sell the boat and stores, then furnish Madison with a statement of account and all unsatisfied claims. (5) Cooper to Madison, 31 May 1801, stating that Madison does not understand his agency "in its true light"; Cooper did not receive word of his appointment until October 1800, which directed him to proceed "as soon as convenient"; the harshness of northern winters made it impracticable to depart until spring; once he received word of his appointment, Cooper "did not loose a day" and proceeded to acquire a mineralogist, tools, Indian presents, a boat, stores, and utensils for the undertaking; he departed "at the first opening of the Spring," but stopped when ordered to do so and acted at all times "within my orders"; he asks that his men be compensated and that the boat and equipment be sold as the government's; any money remaining over Cooper's "just demands" will be returned; Cooper adds that he is reliably informed that the Lake Superior copper mines "are invaluable to the United States." (6) Madison to Cooper, 6 Nov. 1801, directing Cooper to sell his boat and stores and to prepare a new account, in which any charges "must have relation to

the state of the business on the day of your receiving Mr. Lincoln's letter of the 30th. March last." (7) Cooper to Madison, 30 Nov. 1801, expressing regret that the boat and stores were not sold when the expedition was stopped, "as it would probably have been a considerable saving, but now must be a considerable loss to Government"; all charges in his account took place within the time allowed, therefore the amount of sale will be credited to the government and leave only the remaining balance due to Cooper. (8) Cooper to Madison, 13 Mch. 1802, informing him that most of the articles have been sold and that he hopes to make a final settlement with the government in a few weeks (all Trs in same). Enclosed in TJ to the House of Representatives, 31 Mch.

The RESOLUTION OF THE HOUSE OF REPRESENTATIVES of 23 Mch. 1802 is printed in JHR, 4:155. The RESOLUTION OF THE 16TH. APRIL 1800 directed the president to appoint an agent to collect information on the copper mines on the south side of Lake Superior and to ascertain whether the Indian title to said lands may be acquired by the United States. The agent was to report his findings to the president, who was to lay the information before Congress "at their next session" (U.S. Statutes at Large, 2:87; Vol. 31:548-9n).

RICHARD COOPER was the eldest son of William Cooper, the founder of Cooperstown and a former Federalist congressman. He was appointed by John Adams at his father's request (Alan Taylor, *William Cooper's Town: Power and Persuasion on the Frontier of the Early American Republic* [New York, 1995], 18, 279, 282).

To the Senate

GENTLEMEN OF THE SENATE.

The Commissioners who were appointed to carry into execution the VIth. article of the treaty of Amity, Commerce and Navigation, between the US. and his Britannic majesty, having differed in opinion as to the objects of that article, and discontinued their proceedings, the Executive of the US. took early measures, by instructions to our Minister at the British court, to negociate explanations of that article. this mode of resolving the difficulty however proved unacceptable to the British government, which chose rather to avoid all further discussion and expence under that article, by fixing at a given sum the amount for which the US. should be held responsible under it. mr King was consequently authorised to meet this proposition; and a settlement in this way has been effected by a Convention entered into with the British government, and now communicated for your advice and consent, together with the instructions and correspondence relating to it. the greater part of these papers being originals, the return of them is requested at the convenience of the Senate.   TH: JEFFERSON

Mar. 29. 1802.

RC (DNA: RG 46, EPFR, 7th Cong., 1st sess.); endorsed by Senate clerks. PrC (DLC). Recorded in SJL with notation "British convention." Enclosures: (1) Convention between the United States and Great Britain, 8 Jan. 1802, signed by Lord Hawkesbury and Rufus King; the two nations agreeing that in lieu of the provisions of Article 6 of the treaty concluded by them in 1794, the United States should pay the sum of £600,000 sterling, to be remitted at Washington in three equal, annual installments, the first payment to be made a year after the exchange of ratifications of the convention; the payments to be made in U.S. dollars at the rate of $4.44 per pound sterling; the parties also affirming that the fourth article of the 1783 treaty of peace between them, which said that there should be no lawful impediment to the collection of legitimate debts by creditors from either nation, was still binding "so far as respects its future operation"; it being agreed also that the commissioners appointed under Article 7 of the 1794 treaty should resume their proceedings, and that any sums awarded by them should be remitted in three equal, annual payments beginning one year after the exchange of ratifications of the convention (Miller, *Treaties*, 2:488-91; ASP, *Foreign Relations*, 2:382-3); appears as the final item in Meriwether Lewis's "List of papers" accompanying the message of 29 Mch. (see below). (2) King to the secretary of state, 22 Apr.

1800 (King, *Life*, 3:222-6; ASP, *Foreign Relations*, 2:394-5). (3) King to same, 13 Dec. 1800 (King, *Life*, 3:345-6; ASP, *Foreign Relations*, 2:399-400). (4) King to same, 17 Jan. 1801 (King, *Life*, 3:369-70; extract, ASP, *Foreign Relations*, 2:401). (5) King to same, 7 Mch. 1801 (Madison, *Papers, Sec. of State Ser.*, 1:7-8, with decipherment; King, *Life*, 3:398-9; extract, ASP, *Foreign Relations*, 2:401). (6) King to same, 20 Apr. 1801, mistakenly entered on the "List of papers" as 21 Apr.; with correspondence between King and British negotiator John Anstey (Madison, *Papers, Sec. of State Ser.*, 1:105-6; ASP, *Foreign Relations*, 2:401-18). (7) King to same, 21 Apr. 1801, with letters of King to Hawkesbury; the "List of papers" mistakenly identifies the annexed documents as correspondence between King and Lord Grenville (King, *Life*, 3:434-6; summary in Madison, *Papers, Sec. of State Ser.*, 1:109; extract with additional documents, ASP, *Foreign Relations*, 2:418-19). (8) King to same, 24 Aug. 1801 (King, *Life*, 3:502-4; ASP, *Foreign Relations*, 2:420; summary, Madison, *Papers, Sec. of State Ser.*, 2:65). (9) King to same, 4 Oct. 1801, with, as described in the "List of papers," "a note of conferences &ca. with Lord Hawkesbury and others concerning the convention relative to the 6th. article of the treaty of 1794; also copies of sundry letters from Mr. King to Lord Hawkesbury" (King, *Life*, 3:520-1; summary in Madison, *Papers*,

Sec. of State Ser., 2:158-9; letter with additional documents, ASP, *Foreign Relations*, 2:420-4). (10) King to same, 20 Oct. 1801, continuing his report of the negotiations, described in the "List of papers" as "a note of conferences &ca. with Lord Hawkesbury and others concerning the Convention relative to the 6th. article of the treaty of 1794" (King, *Life*, 3:527). (11) King to same, 9 Jan. 1802, announcing the completion of the convention; accompanied, according to the "List of papers," by a copy of Lord Hawkesbury's commission to negotiate a convention (Madison, *Papers, Sec. of State Ser.*, 2:380-1; King, *Life*, 4:47-8; ASP, *Foreign Relations*, 2:424). (12) King to same, 11 Jan. 1802; accompanied, according to the "List of papers," by a communication from King to Lord Eldon, the lord chancellor, of 22 Nov. 1801, and "Mr. King's *Memoir* on the subject of his negociations with the British Ministry" (Madison, *Papers, Sec. of State Ser.*, 2:383-5; King, *Life*, 4:48-51; letter with additional documents, ASP, *Foreign Relations*, 2:424-6).

In June 1801, TJ and the cabinet agreed to allow Rufus King to continue his negotiation for a lump-sum settlement of British creditors' claims against American citizens that had been filed according to the provisions of ARTICLE 6 of the Jay Treaty; see Notes on Resolution of American Debts to British Creditors, Vol. 34:323-7.

NOW COMMUNICATED FOR YOUR ADVICE AND CONSENT: Meriwether Lewis delivered the message and papers on 29 Mch. The Senate took the matter up on 3 Apr., a Saturday, and returned to the issue the following week. On the 6th, the Senate asked TJ for information about the amount of the claims (see TJ to the Senate, 8 Apr.). The Senate again considered the convention on 8, 12, and 15 Apr., requesting information from TJ on the 12th about claims under Article 7 of the Jay Treaty (see Madison to TJ, 16 Apr.).

BEING ORIGINALS: TJ evidently had Lewis draw up a list of the documents that accompanied the message. That record, titled "A List of papers, forwarded by the President of the UStates to the Senate on the of 1802, relative to, and containing the negociations of Mr. King with the British Court," identifies the eleven dispatches from King, some of them with additional documents "annexed," that TJ sent to the Senate, along with the text of the convention, on 29 Mch. (MS in DLC: TJ Papers, 121:20978; entirely in Lewis's hand, arranged in columns for dispatch number, date, and "Nature of Document"). The papers that were subsequently filed with this message in the Senate's records and printed with it in the *American State Papers* constitute a later, larger compilation of copies and extracts of documents that spans from February 1799 to April 1802 (DNA: RG 46, EPFR, 7th Cong., 1st sess.; ASP, *Foreign Relations*, 2:383-428). That compilation includes several documents that were not among the papers that TJ sent to the Senate on 29 Mch.

To the Senate and the House of Representatives

GENTLEMEN OF THE SENATE AND
OF THE HOUSE OF REPRESENTATIVES.

The Secretary of state, charged with the civil affairs of the several territories of the United States, has recieved from the Marshal of Columbia a statement of the condition, unavoidably distressing, of the persons committed to his custody on civil or criminal process, and the urgency for some legislative provisions for their relief. there are other important cases wherein the laws of the adjoining states, under which the territory is placed, tho' adapted to the purposes of those states, are insufficient for those of the territory, from the dissimilar, or defective organisation of it's authorities. the letter & statement of the marshal, and the disquieting state of the territory generally, are now submitted to the wisdom & consideration of the legislature.

TH: JEFFERSON
Mar. 29. 1802.

RC (DNA: RG 233, PM, 7th Cong., 1st sess.); endorsed by House clerks. PrC (DLC). RC (DNA: RG 46, LPPM, 7th Cong., 1st sess.); in Meriwether Lewis's hand, signed and dated by TJ; endorsed by a Senate clerk. Recorded in SJL with notation "state of prison in Columbia." Enclosures: (1) Daniel Carroll Brent to James Madison, undated, asking that Congress consider the "defective & oppressive" system of jails and warrant executions in the District of Columbia; Congress currently has no authority to erect jails; the laws of Maryland authorize state levy courts to raise $400 to repair jails, but not to construct new ones; no jail existed in Washington County when Brent took office as marshal; he rented a small house for the purpose, but it is insecure, overcrowded, and unsanitary, with debtors residing with the jailor in an adjoining house; "This consideration renders it absolutely necessary that immediate measures should be adopted respecting a Jail," Brent declares, and even if Congress acts immediately, "the summer will pass over nearly" before any action can be taken on the matter; the Alexandria jail is no better, and has been presented as a "publick nuisance" by a grand jury; in Washington, there are 14 criminals and runaways and 23 debtors currently under confinement, and Brent fears that more will soon be added from a variety of sources: from criminal prosecutions where executions are out against persons prosecuted but unable to pay their fines and fees, from criminal writs where the person arrested cannot provide bail, from civil actions where principals give up their bail, from an expectation of pending executions against persons unable to pay their debts, and from warrant executions issued by magistrates for sums

of less than $20; Brent deems the warrant system in Washington County to be "a fruitfull and Melancholy source of Commitment" and "extremely oppressive on the lower Class of Citizens"; several persons currently imprisoned for debt have been confined for 60 days for small sums and "then come out under the Insolvent Laws of Maryland"; in Brent's opinion, a better system would not imprison debtors for sums of less than $20; he closes by asking the secretary of state to lay the subject before the president for his consideration (RC in DNA: RG 46, LPPM, in a clerk's hand, signed by Brent; Tr in RG 233, PM, in Meriwether Lewis's hand, endorsed by a House clerk as "No. 2"). (2) A list of 21 debtors in the Washington County jail and the cause of their confinement, 16 of which are for debts of less than $20 (MS in DNA: RG 46, LPPM, in an unidentified hand; Tr in DNA: RG 233, PM, in Lewis's hand, endorsed by a House clerk as "No. 3"; Tr in DLC, in Lewis's hand). (3) A list of 14 criminals in the Washington County jail and the causes of their confinement, which include suspicion of murder, fines and fees, breaking jail, and the theft of horses, goods, slaves, and wood. The list also includes three runaway slaves and one suspected runaway (MS in DNA: RG 46, LPPM, in a clerk's hand; Tr in DNA: RG 233, PM, in Lewis's hand; Tr in DLC, in Lewis's hand). (4) "Dimensions of Jail in Washington County," recording that 22 debtors are housed in two lower level rooms measuring 10 feet by 14 feet and 8 feet by 9 feet, respectively, while 14 criminals and runaways are kept in two upstairs rooms measuring 9 feet by 12 feet and 5 feet by 7 feet, respectively (MS in DNA: RG 46, LPPM, in an unidentified hand; Tr in DNA: RG 233,

PM, in Lewis's hand, at head of text: "Dimentions of Jail in Washington City"; Tr in DLC, in Lewis's hand, at head of text: "Dimentions of Jail in Washington City," endorsed by TJ on verso: "Columbia marshal of Prisoners").

LEGISLATIVE PROVISIONS FOR THEIR RELIEF: on 3 May 1802, Congress passed "An act additional to, and amendatory of, an act, intituled 'An act concerning the District of Columbia.'" Section 4 of the act stated that no *capias ad satisfaciendum* would thereafter be issued in cases where judgments, exclusive of costs, did not exceed $20. Section 10 directed the marshal of the District of Columbia to have a "good and sufficient jail" built in Washington and authorized an appropriation of $8,000 for the purpose (U.S. Statutes at Large, 2:193-5).

About this time, TJ compiled a list of several debtors confined in the Washington County jail, apparently using Brent's list of debtors as his source (see Enclosure No. 2, above). TJ's list included Charles Neal and 14 others arranged by the amount of their debt, from the smallest (Neal's of $1.68) to the largest

(Rezin Shiply's of $26.01). TJ then used horizontal lines to subdivide the list by those who owed $10 or less (9 persons total), those who owed between $10 and $20 (5 persons total), and those who owed more than $20 (1 person). Adding the individual fines, TJ recorded that the 15 debtors owed a total of $151.13, with those having debts of $10 or less owing $47.62, those with debts of between $10 to $20 owing $77.50, and the person with a debt of greater than $20 owing $26.01. Of those debtors owing $10 or less, TJ identified six of them as "out," presumably meaning that they had been released from confinement (MS in ViW; entirely in TJ's hand). Another list, in an unidentified hand, and comprised of seven names from Brent's list, appears to include only persons still confined for debt in the Washington County jail, consisting of names not identified on TJ's list as being "out." Following each name is a description of the individual's character and the condition of his family, most of which are described as being in "want" or "distress" (MS in ViW; endorsed by TJ: "Prisoners").

From Robert Smith

SIR: Nav Dep 29 Mar 1802

The enclosed Warrant is for a young Gentleman recommended by Col Burr.

If you approve his Appointment be pleased to give the enclosed Warrant your Signature

I have the honor to be, with the greatest respect Sir, your mo obt St.   RT SMITH

RC (DLC); in a clerk's hand, signed by Smith; at foot of text: "President U:States."; endorsed by TJ as received from the Navy Department on 29 Mch. and so recorded in SJL with notation "a midshipman." FC (Lb in DNA: RG 45, LSP). Enclosure not found.

The ENCLOSED WARRANT appointed Richard Blackledge Jones of Pennsylvania a midshipman in the navy. Aaron

Burr had forwarded his name to Smith at the behest of Charles Biddle, who had recommended Jones to Captain Alexander Murray of the frigate *Constellation*. Jones joined Murray's crew in 1802 and remained in the navy until 1808. He was appointed the United States consul to Tripoli in 1812 (NDBW, *Register*, 29; Kline, *Burr*, 2:663-4, 687, 694; JEP, 2:277; Madison, *Papers, Pres. Ser.*, 4:329-30).

From Daniel Carroll Brent

Sir/   March 30th. 1802

In answer to your enquiry of yesterday, whether a debtor can be Confined in Jail by the Marshal for his fees, I send you herewith Mr. Masons Statement of the law which shews, that he can, except where the Debtor is released under the Insolvent law—I have, in no instance however detained a man in Jail for his fees only—
The Costs upon a debt of one dollar is as follows.

Cost of warrant & Execution that is the fees to the Magistrate & Constable is }	$0.70½
Marshal's fees Viz. Poundage	0.12¾
Serving the Casa	2.00
	$2.83¼

If the Debtor when taken into custody has not the sum Sufficient to discharge the Execution & Costs, & the officer carries him to Jail, (& he is liable for the Debt if he does not) and if the debtor remains in Jail only one day a further expence, as follows, is incured

Commitment	50 Cents
Releasment	50
1 days Confinement	20
	$1.20

So that the costs alone upon a Debt of one dollar may amount to $4.03 Cents & ¼, besides for every day the Debtor is in Jail he is chargeable with twenty Cents ℔ day—
Since Christmass 161 warrant Executions have been put into my hands, the average of debt not more than Six dollars—of these, 115, are Casas. the remaining 46, fi.fas.—a few of these Executions have been Superceded—It is in the power of the debtor at any time within two Months after the rendition of the[1] Judgement, altho execution shall have issued, to go before any Justice of the peace, together with Security, such as the Justice shall approve of, & Confess Judgment for the debt, and costs of suit adjudged, with stay of execution for six months, a Certificate under the hands of the Justice before whom the Confession of Judgment is made is a sufficient supersedeas to the Marshal to forbear serving execution upon the body[2] or goods of the person so obtaining such Certificate; but if the party be taken in execution before any certificate be produced, such certificate being afterwards obtained & produced shall be a sufficient supercedeas to the Marshal to release such person out of prison, upon that execution, the party paying or giving security to such Marshal for his fees due for that imprisonment—The magistrate before whom the Confession is

made makes return thereof to the Clerk of the County, & generally as soon as the time limited in the Confession of Judgment expires, execution is taken out against the principal & his Securities—upon executions of this Kind costs upon a Debt. of 6 Dollars may amount to $12.1½ as followes.

Cost of Warrant & Judgment	$0.70½
Clerk's fees	1.26
Marshals fees Viz poundage	.45
Serving Execution on three persons ⎫	
if all taken $2 each ⎬	6.00
if confined to Jail	
Commitment & releasment of 3 persons	3.00
1 days imprisonment of 3 persons	
20 cents each	0.60
	12.01½

Any Debtor who is in Jail for Debt and does not owe more than £200 Sterling can upon giving up all his property and remaining fifty-two days in Jail can come out under the Insolvent Law of Maryland—in which case the Debtor cannot be Confined for his fees, nor is any person liable to the officer for them—I have gone into this detail with a hope of giving you an idea of the warrant Execution System in the County of Washington tho' a recurrence to the law it self can only give you a Correct one—In the County of Alexandria, no Commitments are made for Sums less than twenty Dollars and there no appeal lyes from the Judgment of the Justice—The executions for small sums under twenty Dollars are served by the Constables & the Marshal has nothing to do with them—I think the same system might with ease be adopted here, & which is certainly less oppressive to the lower Class of people.

I have omitted to mention that in this County appeals by from the Judgment of a Single Magistrate for all sums, above twenty shillings or one hundred pounds of Tobacco—& that the Cost, upon such appeals may amount to as much as on suits in ordinary Cases

With sentiments of the highest respect I am Sir yr Obt. Sert.

Daniel C. Brent

RC (DLC); in an unidentified hand, with closing and signature in Brent's hand; endorsed by TJ as received 30 Mch. and so recorded in SJL. Enclosure: Statement by John Thomson Mason, 29 Mch. 1802, on the existing law regarding the discharge of persons imprisoned for debt, explaining that if committed to jail upon a *capias ad satisfaciendum*, the prisoner cannot demand discharge upon payment of his debt and costs, but must also pay the marshal poundage fees upon said debt and costs as well as fees due by law for his imprisonment before he can demand his release; in Maryland, whose laws in the matter apply to Washington,

D.C., Mason states that "there is no difference in this respect between a Ca. Sa. issued on a Warrant Judgment and a Ca. Sa. issued on a Judgment of a Court of Record." In a postscript, however, Mason notes that if a debtor is released under the insolvent act, "it discharges him from the sheriffs demands as well as others" (MS in DLC; in Mason's hand and signed by him).

Maryland enacted an INSOLVENT LAW in 1774, which allowed debtors owing less than £200 Sterling to be discharged from prison upon an assignment of all their property, except bedding and clothing, to their creditors. The legislature revised the act several times in the ensuing years, before repealing it in 1817 (Peter J. Cole-

man, *Debtors and Creditors in America: Insolvency, Imprisonment for Debt, and Bankruptcy, 1607-1900* [Madison, Wis., 1974], 164-5, 171-2).

CASAS: that is, ca. sa., an abbreviation of *capias ad satisfaciendum*, "A postjudgment writ commanding the sheriff to imprison the defendant until the judgment is satisfied" (Garner, *Black's Law Dictionary*, 221).

FI.FAS.: that is, fi. fa., an abbreviation of *fieri facias*, "A writ of execution that directs a marshal or sheriff to seize and sell a defendant's property to satisfy a money judgment" (same, 659).

[1] MS: "of the of the."
[2] MS: "body body."

From Aaron Burr

DR: SIR   Washingn. 30 Mar. 1802

General Stevens had command of the artillery in the Northern army during the late War and was distinguished for his bravery, his punctuality & his knowledge of his profession. His reputation & deportment in Civil life have corresponded with the expectations which might have been formed from his Military Conduct—Since the war he has resided in N york, has born various offices which he has executed with zeal and fidelity—It is with pleasure that, at his request, I bear this testimony in his favor

With entire respect I have the Honor to be Your Ob H St.

A; BURR

RC (DLC); at foot of text: "The Prest. of the U.S."; endorsed by TJ as received 30 Mch. and so recorded in SJL with notation "Stevens."

VARIOUS OFFICES: as the War Department's agent for fortifications in the city of New York in 1798, Ebenezer Stevens provided Burr with the facts, figures, and plans he required to convince the state assembly to appropriate funds for the fortification of the harbor and city of New York (Kline, *Burr*, 1:347-50, 352-4; 2:704; Nancy Isenberg, *Fallen Founder: The Life of Aaron Burr* [New York, 2007], 168-9).

From Henry Dearborn

SIR   War Department 30th, of March 1802

From a conference with a Committee of the Senate, it is proposed to make the following alterations in the list of Officers by you nominated, for the Military establishment, which is submitted for your consideration,

Captain Richard H. Greaton of the 2nd. rgt.[1] to be withdrawn

Captain John Whistler of the 1st to be introduced—

Captain Campbell Smith of the 4th. to be withdrawn

Captain Aaron Gregg of the 3rd. rgt. to be introduced

Lieut. Thomas Blackburn to be withdrawn

Lieut. John Hains of the 4th. regt. to be introduced

Alexander A Peters Surgions mate at Fort Johnson North Carolina—

Thomas I Vandike Surgions Mate for Southwest Point in Tennessee

H. DEARBORN

RC (DLC); at head of text: "To the President of the United States"; assignments of regiments interlined by Meriwether Lewis (see note below); endorsed by TJ as received from the War Department on 30 Mch. and "Nominations" and so recorded in SJL; also endorsed by Lewis with names and regiments of Whistler, Gregg, and Haines.

Joseph Anderson, Stevens Thomson Mason, and Jonathan Dayton were the COMMITTEE OF THE SENATE reviewing the nominations of army officers (see TJ to the Senate, 25 Mch.). The committee reported to the Senate in executive session on 31 Mch., after the Senate received TJ's message of that day transmitting the changes suggested by Dearborn in the letter above (JEP, 1:415-16).

VANDIKE: the Tennessee congressional delegation and David Campbell had recommended Thomas J. Vandyke for the position at Southwest Point (Campbell to TJ, 12 Feb. 1802).

[1] Preceding four words interlined by Lewis, who also interlined the designations of regiments for Whistler, Smith, Gregg, and Haines.

From William Eustis

SIR,   Washington March 30th. 1802.

General Stevens of New York has pending with the government a business of great moment, and wishes to be known to you in his true character, which is that of an upright & respectable citizen, who passed the revolutionary war with great reputation as a commander in the artillery. He is also a native of Massachusetts which may plead an apology for this representation from,

Sir, Your most respectful humble servant.

WILLIAM EUSTIS

RC (DLC); at foot of text: "The President of the United States."; endorsed by TJ as received 30 Mch. and so recorded in SJL.

BUSINESS OF GREAT MOMENT: see DeWitt Clinton to TJ, 29 Mch.

On 30 Mch., Senator Joseph Anderson also recommended Ebenezer Stevens to the president. He wrote: "In the Course of the Revolutionary War—I was acquainted with General Stevens then Lt. Colonel Stephens of the Artillery, his Character was that of an active, Judicious attentive and intelligent officer—and as a man it was equally respectable" (RC in MHi; endorsed by TJ as received 30 Mch. and so recorded in SJL with notation "Stevens").

From Richard Fenwick

SIR, [on or before 30 Mch. 1802]

Nothing except imperious necssity could actuate my intrudeing mysilfe to you'r notice—Knowing that from the high and honourable office you so meritoriously & independlantly fill you'r time must be spent in the discharge of the duties attatched to it—Knowing also you'r love of philantrophy and you'r desire to milliorate the distresses of mankind in general i'me induced to solicit the extention of you'r friendly humanity towards me—From casualities insidental to human nature i'me unfortunately the residenter of A prison, and the Father of A large helpless family—Portray to yourself A person in imprisonment A wife & six small children to exist with barely the means of doing it, it's A situation that A moments reflection must pronounce Wretched in the extreme—Fifteen days have I been imprisoned & thirty five more have I to remaine, when I shall be exonerated from confinement by the Statute for the relief of insolvent debtors—Under those considerations I humbly request you'r interference in behalfe of me in A transaction I was unintentionly & unmeaningly implicated with—Tranciently passing by the door of A Mr. Sawyer, himselfe & wife where in the act of brutally belabouring one & other. I steped in to seperate them, &c—Some time since the wife presented me, the present court have thought proper to fine me which fine & the costs accrueing from the presentment i'me not able to discharge,—from that, as it being an action where the State is prosecutor I cannot be emancipated from Jail, by the act of Insolvency when the time arives for that purpose—Therefor I hope & trust you'll be pleased to take my Condition into consideration & to exert you'r benevolent humanity in my behalfe so that it may be no impediment to my being again restored to *Liberty* & my unhappy Family—My wife whoes the bearer of this will give you any particulars you may please to desire on this truely disagreeable & unpleasant business, relying on you'r Known excellence of heart & understanding I request you'r forgiveness for this trouble & innovation—

With wishing you every blessing that this transitory life affords I'me the unfortunate— RICHD FENWICK

RC (DLC); undated; at head of text: "Thomas Jefferson Esqr. President of the United States"; endorsed by TJ as received 30 Mch. and so recorded in SJL.

Richard Fenwick was included on Daniel C. Brent's list of debtors in the Washington County jail that TJ forwarded to Congress on 29 Mch., with a message of that date. According to Brent's list, Fenwick was confined for a debt of $7 and "also for want of bail" (MS in DNA: RG 46, LPPM). His name also appears on the list of seven prisoners confined for debt that is described at TJ's 29 Mch. message. Of Fenwick, the author of the list stated that "if relieved from his present debt would be put in again. has a large family to suport who are in distress" (MS in ViW).

To Robert Gourlay

SIR   Washington Mar. 30. 1802.

In a letter to mr Jennings of July 21. 1801. I acknoleged the reciept of his of Feb. 21. and your's of Feb. 22. and of the authenticated copies of the will, and I prayed him to ask you to consider that as an answer to your letter, as I must now request you to communicate this for his satisfaction my occupations obliging me to these abridgments of private duty. mr Philip L. Grymes, uncle of mr Randolph's legatees, is lately appointed their guardian. a worthier or more responsible person could not have been appointed. I have therefore this day sent to him the parchment copy of mrs Randolph's will, and to Windham Grymes the copy authenticated in paper. I have informed them of the paiment of the bill on Govan for £100. by my correspondents in Richmond to mr Edmund Randolph, and that not having drawn on you for the £200. as permitted by your letter, that was now at mr Grymes's disposition. as he is become the legal, so is he the safest depository of whatever you may have to remit for the children. mr Randolph, tho' having the kindest dispositions in their favor, is under such difficulties that he would doubtless rather avoid any agency in their pecuniary interests. these being now put into safe hands, and with one who has much more time to attend to the duties of a guardian, than is at my command, I hope I have done the best for the wishes of my deceased friend, which was in my power. I pray you to accept for yourself and mr Jennings, assurances of my respect and consideration. TH: JEFFERSON

PrC (DLC); at foot of text: "Robert Gourlay esq. No. 54. Spring garden Cockspur street. at the Virginia coffee-house Cornhill. London"; endorsed by TJ in ink on verso.

THEIR GUARDIAN: TJ had declined the offer of guardianship of Ariana Jenings Randolph's grandchildren (Vol. 33:39-40).

The copy of Ariana RANDOLPH'S WILL has not been found (Vol. 33:40n).

BILL ON GOVAN FOR £100: on 6 May 1801, TJ forwarded a bill from James Govan of Powhite for the purchase of mourning clothes for the Randolph legatees (Vol. 34:44).

To Charles Wyndham Grymes

DEAR SIR   Washington Mar. 30. 1802.

Mr. P. L. Grymes having informed me that he was appointed guardian to yourself and sisters, I have this day inclosed to him a Notarial copy in parchment of your grandmother's will, of which yourself & sisters are the principal legatees. having recieved also a duplicate authenticated in paper, I inclose you that, with a letter from mr Jennings explanatory of the testatrice's intentions. in my correspondence with mrs Randolph I always made it a condition of my acting for her, that mr Grymes paying up one moiety of what she should be entitled to, should be released from all responsibility for the other; and that mr Randolph should not be distressed for the moiety for which he was responsible. she came fully into these sentiments, and sent me an express authority to release mr Grymes from a moiety, which I did. the bill remitted me by mr Gourlay for £100. sterl I inclosed to Messrs. Gibson & Jefferson at the time, to collect & pay to the order of mr Randolph, which they did. the draught for £200. sterl. I did not make, & have informed mr Grymes it is at his disposal. accept my best wishes for your health & success in life, and assurances of my esteem & attachment.   TH: JEFFERSON

PrC (MHi); at foot of text: "Mr. Windham Grymes"; endorsed by TJ in ink on verso. Enclosure: Edmund Jenings to TJ, 21 Feb. 1801 (not found, but see Vol. 33:40n and Vol. 34:611). Other enclosure not found.

To Philip Ludwell Grymes

DEAR SIR   Washington Mar. 30. 1802.

Your favor of Feb. 25. has been duly recieved. my object in wishing to know when a guardian should be appointed to the orphans of the late mr Grymes your brother, was that I might know to whom it would be my duty to transmit an authentic copy of mrs Randolph's will of which I was the depository. those orphans being the principal legatees, their guardian is the proper person to recieve this paper. I also send you a copy of a letter from mr Jennings, and another from mr Gourlay the executor, explanatory of the intentions of mrs Randolph. the bill on Govan for £100. sterl. for the immediate use of the children, I remitted to Messrs. Gibson & Jefferson to collect and pay as mr Edmund Randolph should direct. I think they informed me they paid the money to him. the draught on the executor for £200. I did not make; consequently it remains at your disposal. I shall immediately write to mr Gourlay informing him that I have turned over the papers to you. Accept assurances of my esteem and respect.

TH: JEFFERSON

RC (Vi: photostat); at foot of text: "Philip L. Grymes esq"; endorsed. PrC (MHi); endorsed by TJ in ink on verso. Enclosures: (1) see enclosure described at letter above. (2) Robert Gourlay to TJ, 22 Feb. 1801. Other enclosure not found.

Grymes's FAVOR OF 25 Feb., recorded in SJL as received from Brandon on 5 Mch. 1802, has not been found.

From Samuel Osgood

SIR.   New York March 30th. 1802

Permit me, Sir, to render you my sincere Thanks for the honor you did me in appointing me to the Office of Supervisor of the internal Revenue for the District of New York. — Being assured that the whole Office is soon to be abolished, and as I have been informed thro' Mr. Dewitt Clinton that you entertain a favourable Opinion of my Integrity; I beg Leave to inform you that it will give me great Pleasure to be continued in some Office under your Gift & Patronage.

The Naval Officer of this City I do not know at all. But I beleive I may say without fear of Contradiction that he has no revolutionary or republican Merit: His Abilities to execute the Duties of the Office I have never heard questioned.

If there should happen to be any Vacancy in that Office, the conferring it on me will greatly encrease the Obligations which you have been pleased already to lay me under. —

I have the honor to be, with Sentiments of the highest Respect, Your most obedient Servant   SAMUEL OSGOOD

RC (DLC); at foot of text: "Thomas Jefferson Esquire President of the United States"; endorsed by TJ as received 6 Apr. and so recorded in SJL.

Osgood was allied with the Clintonians in New York. For his appointment as SUPERVISOR OF THE INTERNAL REVENUE, see Vol. 33:331n.

Osgood replaced Richard Rogers as NAVAL OFFICER of New York City in May 1803 (Vol. 33:673; Vol. 34:126-7).

To Edward Savage

SIR   Washington Mar. 30. 1802.

Your's of the 1st. instant has been duly recieved. I was not aware of the difficulty of placing the prints on their frames, which you inform me of. the prints being at my house in Virginia, where I could not have a proper case made for them, I believe it will be better on the whole to have the frames made here, as I shall, at the rising of Congress, make a trip of a few days to Monticello, and can bring the prints safely to this place. if therefore the frames be not already in hand, I will take the liberty of countermanding the order, and of ordering them here. but if in hand, you must be so good as to forward them when done to this place. Accept my best wishes & salutations.

TH: JEFFERSON

PrC (DLC); at foot of text: "Mr. Edward Savage"; endorsed by TJ in ink on verso.

To the Senate and the House of Representatives

GENTLEMEN OF THE SENATE AND
OF THE HOUSE OF REPRESENTATIVES

The Secretary at War has prepared an estimate of expenditures for the army of the US. during the year 1802. conformably to the act fixing the military peace establishment; which estimate, with his letter accompanying and explaining it, I now transmit to both houses of Congress.

TH: JEFFERSON
Mar. 30. 1802.

RC (DNA: RG 233, PM, 7th Cong., 1st sess.). PrC (DLC). RC (DNA: RG 46, LPPM, 7th Cong., 1st sess.); endorsed by a Senate clerk. Recorded in SJL with notation "Army estimates." Enclosures: Dearborn to TJ, 27 Mch., and enclosure.

Meriwether Lewis delivered the message and ESTIMATE to the House and the Senate on 30 Mch. The House referred the papers to the Committee of Ways and Means. The Senate ordered the message and estimate to lie on the table for consideration (JHR, 4:168; JS, 3:200).

From Robert Smith

Sir/   Nav Dep 30 Mar 1802

The young gentleman for whom the enclosed is intended, has been recommended by Colo New for reinstatement in the Navy.

With your approbation the enclosed letter shall be forwarded.

I have the honor to be with the greatest respect Sir, your mo obt

Rt Smith

RC (DLC); in a clerk's hand, signed by Smith; at foot of text: "Prest. UStates"; endorsed by TJ as received from the Navy Department on 30 Mch. and so recorded in SJL. FC (Lb in DNA: RG 45, LSP). Enclosure: Smith to George Dabney, dated 30 Mch. 1802 and sent to the care of Anthony New, informing Dabney that he has been reinstated as a midshipman in the navy and is immediately to join the frigate *Chesapeake* at Norfolk (FC in Lb in DNA: RG 45, LSO).

YOUNG GENTLEMAN: George Dabney served as a midshipman on the *Chesapeake* during the Quasi-War before being discharged under the Peace Establishment Act. Shortly after his reinstatement, however, he received a medical furlough and did not return to active service until 1804. He resigned from the navy the following year (NDBW, *Register*, 14; Smith to Dabney, 5 Aug. 1802, FC in Lb in DNA: RG 45, LSO).

To the House of Representatives

Gentlemen of the
House of Representatives.

According to the desire expressed in your resolution of the 23d. instant, I now transmit a report of the Secretary of State, with the letters it refers to, shewing the proceedings which have taken place under the resolution of Congress of the 16th. of April 1800. the term prescribed for the execution of the resolution having elapsed before the person appointed had set[1] out on the service, I did not deem it justifiable to commence a course of expenditure after the expiration of the resolution authorising it. the correspondence which has taken place, having regard to dates, will place this subject properly under the view of the House of Representatives.   Th: Jefferson
Mar. 31. 1802.

RC (DNA: RG 233, PM, 7th Cong., 1st sess.). PrC (DLC). Recorded in SJL with notation "mines und. resoln Congr Apr. 16. 1800." Enclosures: see Madison to TJ, 29 Mch. 1802.

TJ's message and its enclosures were presented to the House of Representatives on 31 Mch. and ordered to lie on the table (JHR, 4:169).

[1] MS: "sat."

From John Thomson Mason,
with Jefferson's Reply

31st Mar 1802

I am requested by the wife of[1] Frederick Long to State his Case with a view to submit it to the President. at this length of time I cannot state the evidence with particularity, I can only speak generally. He was indicted upon two Counts, the one for stealing sundry articles, the other for receiving stolen goods knowing them to have been stolen. The evidence was, that he as a Cartman had assisted to move doctor Bullus, some of the articles committed to his charge, and among others a spring Lancett, of the value of five Dollars, was missing, and some time after, on searching Longs house, for other things, supposed to have been stolen, this Lancett was found in his possession. A number of Marines Cloathing had been missing from their encampment, and by the Marines were said to be stolen from them, many articles of this kind were found in his house, but this being about the time that a great number of Marines had been discharged, and it appearing that those discharged, sold, gave away, and in some instances threw away their blankets, and cloathing, the Jury acquitted Long upon the second Count in the Indictmt., and upon the first Count found him guilty of stealing the Lancett, and perhaps some few articles of cloathing which a Marine, then in service, swore had been stolen from him. The Court were I believe satisfied with the verdict, I thought it a good verdict, at all events I thought Long had no reason to complain of it. He was whipped, and is now confined for the costs of the prosecution, & perhaps for some small fine imposed upon him. He is a poor man, unable to pay those Costs, and a hard working industrious man, I wish I could say more for him. I am informed, and believe it to be true, that he is very sick with the Meazles in Jail, which is a dreadful place, that he has three or four small Children, all very sick with the same complaint, and who are suffering very much for the necessaries of life. I do most willingly release him from my fee, I have no doubt the other officers will do the same

J. T. Mason DA for the US

[*Reply by TJ:*]
Under all the circumstances of this case I think it is proper that a pardon issue to the prisoner.　　　　　Th: Jefferson
April 3. 1802.

RC (DNA: RG 59, GPR); with TJ's reply on verso.

TJ signed a pardon on 3 Apr. releasing FREDERICK LONG from the remainder of his sentence, citing Long's inability to pay his fine and his suffering in prison "under a disease that may, if not removed, prove fatal to him" (FC in Lb in same).

ASSISTED TO MOVE DOCTOR BULLUS: after dissolving a partnership in May 1801, John Bullus moved to a store of his own "east of the six Buildings" where he sold a large assortment of drugs and medicines (*Washington Federalist*, 3 June, 10 July 1801).

[1] Preceding three words interlined.

From John Minor of North Carolina

DEAR SIR/

Granville County No: Carolinia
March the 31st day 5802 or 1802

as it has been my misfortune as yet not to obtain any Pay due a brother of mine for his services in the Continental army; and who after being taken as prisoner at the sorender of Charles Town South Carolinia: returnd to this State volentered himself with General Butler; and in an action with the torys at Lynlys mill Lost his life— I administrator for the decd; to Major Thaus ajent for the state of south Carolinia made application on the 25th day February 1794 he informd me I should send my petition to Congress: and about the 3 of October next after I did so; and I know not what become of it, whether lodgd in the office or what My friend Mecon a member to Congress informs me I am now Bard by whats Cald the statute; and if I gitt it; there must be a special act passt which he rather thought would not be done But my Confidence in your goodness and Relying on your Justice and the goodness and Justice of Every member in Congress that I cannot forbare persevering to send another petition with a Coppy of letters of administration with Mr. Grays Certificate who acted as pay master at the time my Brother was in service; now I pray your Tenderness with Justice towards me and I hope Congress will the same; as my brother was a brave Sergeant of the second Continental Regiment of South Carolina tho lost his life in the militia of this state & he in fact a prisoner of war at the very time; Tax run high this year and now about to collect the direct Tax with State County & parash Tax which will not be less then 14 or 15 dollars for me and know not how I am to raise it; how Ever I speak this by way of information—I leave the matter in hand with your goodness & if I gitt it will be by some provition made by your Self & Congress which will be an Encouragement to my five sons in the next war I Ever pray &c. & Remain your friend & hble Servt

JOHN MINOR

RC (DLC); at foot of text: "To the wright honourable President of the united States of america"; endorsed by TJ as received 27 Apr. and so recorded in SJL with notation "W."

Minor had been petitioning Congress on behalf of his deceased BROTHER, Reuben Minor, since 1794, seeking "the pay and other emoluments due" for his services during the American Revolution. On 27 Apr. 1802, Minor presented another petition to the House of Representatives, "praying the liquidation and settlement" of his brother's claim, which was read and ordered to lie on the table (JHR, 2:244, 343, 628; 4:224).

General John BUTLER led North Carolina militia against a much larger Loyalist force at the battle of Lindley's Mill on

13 Sep. 1781. The battle was the bloodiest of the war in North Carolina, and resulted in the defeat of Butler's troops (William S. Powell, ed., *Encyclopedia of North Carolina* [Chapel Hill, 2006], 678-9; William S. Powell, ed., *Dictionary of North Carolina Biography*, 6 vols. [Chapel Hill, 1979-96], 1:290-1).

During the 1790s, Simeon Theus (THAUS) served as South Carolina's agent in the settlement of claims between the federal government and the states. TJ appointed Theus collector at Charleston in 1806 (Syrett, *Hamilton*, 14:295; JEP, 2:16).

MY FRIEND MECON: Nathaniel Macon.

MR. GRAYS CERTIFICATE: probably Henry Gray, who served as paymaster of the Second South Carolina regiment during the war (Heitman, *Register*, 257).

To James Monroe

DEAR SIR   Washington Mar. 31. 1802.

Your's of the 21st. is duly recieved. Chisolm is now engaged in running up for me 20. brick pilasters to my offices, which take about 4000. bricks, and I remember it was very doubtful whether we had that number. but if there be as many over it as you need, they are at your service, and I will give orders accordingly by the next post. I expect to be there myself within 10. days after the rising of Congress, and to remain a fortnight. perhaps one of your plantation visits may be so timed as to fall in with mine, say the 1st. week in May. I have not written to you on the resolutions of the assembly respecting slaves, because it does not press, and the[1] issue of the affairs of St. Domingo may influence the question. I would rather too refer it till we can have a conversation and concur in the tract to be pursued.   I have recieved a statement from Gouverneur Morris on the case of Houdon. it gives us little insight into it. I have papers at Monticello which I think will throw some light on the subject. I suspend answering your letter therefore respecting him until I shall have visited Monticello. the British convention is before the Senate. it commutes the VIth. article for 600,000. £ sterl. payable in 3. annual instalments. it will meet opposition there, & in the other house, when an appropriation is asked. it would be very ill judged not to close, for it would revive their claim of twenty odd millions of dollars awarded by the commissioners, which they would hold as a rod forever over our heads, to operate on our seaport towns, and even on Congress at will. it is now settled by our predecessors. if the bargain be hard, it is their work. that it is not more hard has been the effect of our measures. if this be given up it can never be settled but by war. affectionate and respectful salutations to mrs Monroe and yourself.

Th: Jefferson

RC (NN); addressed: "Governor Monroe Richmond"; franked and postmarked; endorsed by Monroe. PrC (DLC); endorsed by TJ in ink on verso.

Mason and plasterer Hugh Chisholm (CHISOLM) and other craftsmen worked on the service wings at Monticello in 1801 and 1802 (MB, 2:950, 1050, 1067, 1072n,

1079, 1080n; William Howard Adams, *Jefferson's Monticello* [New York, 1983], 68, 75; Vol. 29:548, 550)

RESOLUTIONS OF THE ASSEMBLY: see Monroe to TJ, 13 Feb. 1802.

For the communication from GOUVERNEUR MORRIS, see 21 Mch.

[1] TJ here canceled "events."

To Francis Peyton

Dear Sir   Washington Mar. 31. 1802.

The commission of the peace for the county of Alexandria stands thus. George Gilpin, Wm. Fitzhugh, Francis Peyton, Richd. Conway, Elisha Cullen Dick[1] Cha. Alexander, George Taylor Jonah Thompson, Abraham Faw, John Herbert, Alexr Smith, Cuthbert Powell, Peter Wise junr. Jacob Houghman & Thomas Darne. as these commissions expire with the end of the present session of Congress,[2] I have given in their names to the Senate for permanent appointment. but it occurring that some of them may have resigned or refused to qualify in which case it would be necessary to withdraw their names & substitute others before the Senate, I take the liberty of troubling you to satisfy yourself if any & who have resigned or not qualified, and in that case to recommend to me others in their place. if among those who have not qualified there be any whom it would be desireable to continue, perhaps you could know of them whether they will qualify if appointed. but if they are as well out as in, then let us avail ourselves of the opportunity of putting in such good republican characters as you will be so kind as to recommend to me. as I am desirous to send in the new nominations to the Senate by Monday at farthest, I must press on your goodness to give me the necessary information by that day. Accept my best wishes & salutations.   Th: Jefferson

RC (NN); addressed: "Francis Peyton esquire Alexandria"; franked and postmarked. PrC (ViW); endorsed by TJ in ink on verso.

For the COMMISSION of the justices of the PEACE for Alexandria, see Vol 36:312-17. While the Senate confirmed TJ's other interim appointments on 26 Jan.,

they did not consent to the PERMANENT APPOINTMENT of the justices of the peace for Washington and Alexandria Counties until 27 Apr. (JEP, 1:405, 423).

[1] TJ interlined "Elisha Cullen Dick."
[2] TJ here canceled "it is become necessary for me to give in."

To the Senate

GENTLEMEN OF THE SENATE

Since nominating to the Senate on the 25th. instant the officers who are to be transferred or promoted under the act fixing the military peace establishment of the US. I have recieved information which renders it proper that I should revoke the nominations then made of Richard Greaton and Campbell Smith captains, and of Thomas Blackburne Lieutenant. And I now nominate

John Whistler heretofore captain in the 1st. regiment of infantry to be a captain in the 1st. regiment instead of Greaton:

Aaron Gregg heretofore a captain in the 3rd. regiment of infantry to be a captain in the 2nd. regiment instead of Smith: and

John Haines, heretofore 1st. Lieutenant in the 4th. regiment of infantry to be a 1st. Lieutenant in the 2nd. regiment instead of Blackburne.

Captain Smith's nomination is revoked at his own earnest request; and those of the other two for causes, which, had they been known in time, would have prevented their nomination.

I also nominate Alexander A. Peters to be Surgeon's mate at Fort Johnson in North Carolina: and

Thomas J. Vandyke to be Surgeon's mate at South West point in Tennessee instead of Al. A. Peters who had been nominated for South West Point.   TH: JEFFERSON

Mar. 31. 1802.

RC (DNA: RG 46, EPEN, 7th Cong., 1st sess.); with blanks for number of Whistler's proposed regiment and for numbers of Gregg's and Haines's current and proposed regiments filled by Meriwether Lewis, who also interlined "1st." in front of Haines's current and proposed rank; endorsed by a Senate clerk. PrC (DLC); with blank for number of Whistler's proposed regiment unfilled; blanks for numbers of Gregg's and Haines's current and proposed regiments filled by TJ in ink; TJ also interlined in ink "1st" in front of Haines's current and proposed rank. Recorded in SJL with notation "nominations military."

[155]

Meriwether Lewis delivered this message on 31 Mch. The Senate had already approved, five days earlier, the majority of the military NOMINATIONS included in TJ's message of the 25th. On 1 Apr., the Senate revoked its previous consent to the nominations of Greaton, Smith, and Blackburn, approved the substitutions, and agreed to the appointments of Peters and Vandyke (JEP, 1:415-16).

To Simon Chaudron and John James Barralet

Washington Apr. 1. 1802.

Th: Jefferson presents his compliments to Messrs. Chaudron and Baralet and acknoleges the reciept of their letter of Mar. 6. and of the print of the Apotheosis of Genl. Washington which seems worthy of it's subject. he is as sensible of the friendly offer made of this print as he could be were he at liberty to accept it *gratuitously* as proposed: but a rule of not permitting himself to recieve presents while in public office, obliges him to ask of Messrs. Chaudron & Barralet to fill up the measure of their kind intentions by permitting him to pay for it, on which condition alone it is in his power to retain it. he prays them therefore to forward a note of it's amount to mr Thomas Claxton near the Capitol Washington, who is charged with business of this kind here, and who will remit to them the amount. he prays them to accept his best wishes & salutations.

PrC (DLC).

To Nicolas Gouin Dufief

SIR   Washington April. 1. 1802

Since writing my letter of the 23d. I observe in your catalogue Oeuvres de Seneque translation de la Grange 6. vol. 8vo. which I shall be glad to recieve with the books before written for. Accept my best wishes.   TH: JEFFERSON

PrC (DLC); at foot of text: "M. Dufief."; endorsed by TJ in ink on verso.

OEUVRES DE SENEQUE: TJ already owned a Latin edition of the works of the philosopher Seneca. A French translation by N. de La Grange, *Oeuvres de Séneque* *le philosophe*, was first published in the 1770s. A six-volume edition appeared in Paris in 1795 (J. C. F. Hoefer, *Nouvelle biographie générale depuis les temps les plus reculés jusqu'a nos jours*, 46 vols. [Paris, 1855-66], 28:847-8; Sowerby, No. 1324).

To Albert Gallatin

Dear Sir   Washington Apr. 1. 1802.

I have read and considered your report on the operations of the
Sinking fund and entirely approve of it, as the best plan on which we
can set out. I think it an object of great importance, to be kept in
view, and to be undertaken at a fit season, to simplify our system of
finance, and bring it within the comprehension of every member of
Congress. Hamilton set out on a different plan. in order that he might
have the entire government of his machine, he determined so to com-
plicate it as that neither the President or Congress should be able to
understand it, or to controul him. he succeeded in doing this, not
only beyond their reach, but so that he at length could not unravel it
himself. he gave to the debt, in the first instance, in funding it, the
most artificial and mysterious form he could devise. he then moulded
up his appropriations of a number of scraps & remnants many of
which were nothing at all, and applied them to different objects in re-
version and remainder until the whole system was involved in impenetrable fog, and while he was giving himself the airs of providing
for the paiment of the debt, he left himself free to add to it continually as he did in fact[1] instead of paying it. I like your idea of kneading
all his little scraps & fragments into one batch, and adding to it a
complementary sum, which, while it forms it into a single mass from
which every thing is to be paid, will enable us, should a breach of appropriation ever be charged on us, to prove that the sum appropriated, & more, has been applied to it's specific object. but there is a
point beyond this on which I should wish to keep my eye, and to
which I should aim to approach by every tack which previous
arrangements force on us. that is, to form into one consolidated mass
all the monies recieved into the treasury, and to marshal the several
expenditures, giving them a preference of paiment according to the
order in which they should be arranged. as for example 1. the interest of the public debt. 2. such portions of principal as are exigible. 3.
the expences of government. 4. such other portions of principal, as,
tho' not exigible, we are still free to pay when we please. the last object might be made to take up the residuum of money remaining in
the treasury at the end of every year after the three first objects were
complied with, and would be the barometer thereby to test the economy of the administration. it would furnish a simple measure by
which every one could mete their merit, and by which every one
could decide when taxes were deficient or superabundant. if to this
can be added a simplification of the form of accounts in the treasury

department, and in the organisation of it's officers, so as to bring every thing to a single center, we might hope to see the finances of the Union as clear and intelligible as a merchant's books, so that every member of Congress, and every man of any mind in the Union[2] should be able to comprehend them, to investigate abuses, and consequently to controul them. our predecessors have endeavored by intricacies of system, and shuffling the investigator over from one officer to another, to cover every thing from detection. I hope we shall go in the contrary direction and that by your honest and judicious reformations we may be able, within the limits of our time to bring things back to that simple & intelligible system on which they should have been organised at first.—I have suggested only a single alteration in the report, which is merely verbal & of no consequence.—we shall now get rid of the Commissioner of the internal revenue, & Superintendant of stamps. it remains to amalgamate the Comptroller & Auditor into one, and reduce the register to a clerk of accounts, and then the organisation will consist, as it should at first, of a keeper of money, a keeper of the accounts, & the head of the department. this constellation of great men in the treasury department was of a piece with the rest of Hamilton's plans. he took his own stand as a Lieutenant General, surrounded by his Major Generals, and stationing his brigadiers & Colonels[3] under the name of Supervisors, Inspectors &c. in the different states. let us deserve well of our country by making their interests the end of all our plans, and not our own pomp, patronage and irresponsibility. I have hazarded these hasty & crude ideas, which occurred on contemplating your report. they may be the subject of future conversation and correction. accept my affectionate salutations.

TH: JEFFERSON

RC (NHi: Gallatin Papers); addressed: "The Secretary of the Treasury"; endorsed. PrC (DLC); in ink at foot of first page: "Albt. Gallatin."

Gallatin presented his REPORT ON THE OPERATIONS OF THE SINKING FUND in a lengthy letter of 31 Mch. to John Randolph, chairman of the Committee of Ways and Means. As in his report submitted to Congress on 21 Dec., the Treasury secretary recommended that an annual appropriation of $7,300,000 be applied to the payment of principal and interest on the public debt. Noting that large installments of the Dutch debt, which had to be discharged abroad, were coming due, Gallatin also recommended that the commissioners of the sinking fund be given authority to employ a special agent in Holland to transact the business "in the most advantageous manner." Randolph annexed Gallatin's letter to the report on the public debt, which the committee presented to the House on 9 Apr. Randolph noted that economy would be achieved by making a specific appropriation to the sinking fund, "instead of leaving to it only such surplus as the Government might not choose to employ on any other object." Only in that way could the debt "ever be extinguished." The committee presented a bill providing for redeeming the whole of the public debt.

The legislation, as approved on 29 Apr., called for the annual appropriation of $7,300,000 and provided measures to more effectually secure the payment of the Dutch debt, including the power, with the approbation of the president, to employ an agent in Europe, with a compensation not to exceed $3,000 per year (ASP, *Finance*, 1:746-50; JHR, 4:190-1; U.S. Statutes at Large, 2:167-70; Gallatin to TJ, [13 Dec. 1801]).

[1] Preceding five words interlined.
[2] Preceding three words interlined.
[3] Word and ampersand interlined.

To Peter Legaux

Washington Apr. 1. 1802.

Th: Jefferson presents his compliments to mr Legaux, and acknoleges the reciept of his letter of Mar. 1. and of the bundle of vine plants which are this moment come to hand. for these he prays mr Legaux to accept his thanks. they will be immediately forwarded to Monticello, but as they will be a month getting there, he is afraid the season may be a little ahead of them. they shall however be well taken care of. he tenders to mr Legaux his friendly salutations.

RC (NjP: Andre De Coppet Collection).

Legaux's LETTER, dated 1 Mch. 1802 and received on the 19th, is recorded in SJL but has not been found. He wrote from Spring Mill, his estate on the Schuylkill River (Vol. 30:42n).

BUNDLE OF VINE PLANTS: Legaux sent TJ 30 vines of grape varieties from the Burgundy and Champagne regions of France and 30 from Bordeaux. Ten additional plants were of what Legaux called the Cape of Good Hope grape, which has subsequently been identified as the Alexander grape of American origin. On 11 May, TJ paid Antonio Giannini $1 for planting the vines in the southwest vineyard at Monticello. Legaux had offered vines to TJ in March 1801, but due to the lateness of the season TJ asked him to wait until 1802 to send them (Betts, *Garden Book*, 277; MB, 2:1072; RS, 4:524, 525n; Vol. 33:430-1).

From Wilson Cary Nicholas

DEAR SIR   [1 Apr. 1802]

I take the liberty to inform you that I have heard some uneasiness expressed at the arrangement of the officers made by the Secy. of War, under the law of this session. It is said that all the field officers are taken from the Eastern States. I am told they stand thus Artillery. Burbeck Col. Freeman Lt. Col. Jackson Majr. Porter ditto, Williams Massachusetts, McRea Virginia, Infantry, Hamtramck Col. N. York, Butler Col. Pennsylvania, Hunt Lt. Col. Mass. Cushing Lt. Col. ditto,   Majr. Connecticut Pike Majr. N. Jersey. It is likewise said that the Lt. Col's who wished to remain in the service shou'd have been retained instead of persons being promoted to that rank. I have myself formed no opinion upon this subject. I merely mean to present it to you for your own consideration, for this I can have no motive but an anxious wish that what is done by you shou'd give general satisfaction.

I am Dear Sir with the greatest respect your humble Servt.

W. C. NICHOLAS

RC (DLC); undated; endorsed by TJ as received 1 Apr. and so recorded in SJL.

LAW OF THIS SESSION: for the military peace establishment act passed on 16 Mch., see TJ to the Senate, 25 Mch.

A native of Massachusetts, Jonathan WILLIAMS settled in Philadelphia and was listed as being from Pennsylvania when appointed major of the Second Regiment of Artillerists and Engineers in 1801 (JEP, 1:378; Vol. 28:596n).

MAJR. CONNECTICUT: Decius Wadsworth (JEP, 1:411; Syrett, *Hamilton*, 26:164n).

From Robert Smith

SIR, [1 Apr. 1802]

The enclosed I have received this morning. There are some incorrect statements in it with respect to me as well as yourself. His suggestions, in his opinion, ought to be regarded as Laws.

I have prepared the dispatches for Capt Morris and have herewith sent them for your approbation—

Respectfully
RT SMITH

RC (DLC); undated; endorsed by TJ as received from the Navy Department on 1 Apr. 1802 and "Truxton's resignation" and so recorded in SJL. Enclosures: probably Smith to Richard Valentine Morris, 1 Apr. 1802, directing him to proceed from Norfolk to the Mediterranean with the frigate *Chesapeake*, where he is to join with the frigates *Adams* and *Constellation* and the schooner *Enterprize* to relieve the current Mediterranean squadron under the command of Richard Dale; authorizing Morris to draw funds from Mackenzie & Glennie of London or Debutts & Purviance of Leghorn, and to acquire supplies from John Gavino at Gibraltar or from any other Mediterranean port (NDBW, 2:99-100). Other enclosure not found, but see below.

ENCLOSED I HAVE RECEIVED THIS MORNING: the remaining enclosure to Smith's letter apparently related to the recent, and acrimonious, resignation of Thomas Truxtun from the U.S. Navy. He received command of the *Chesapeake* as well as overall command of the second Mediterranean squadron in January 1802, but resigned in March after learning that he would not be granted a flag captain as had been given to the commander of the first squadron. In a private letter to Aaron Burr of 22 Mch., Truxtun expressed his belief that his appointment "was by no means congenial to the wishes of the President" and that "it was never intended that I should proceed on the command in question, if it could be decently avoided and at the same time the appearance kept up" (NDBW, 2:19, 26, 76, 83, 94; Vol. 34:140n).

Following Truxtun's resignation, Richard Valentine MORRIS was ordered to take charge of the *Chesapeake* and was given command of the second Mediterranean squadron (NDBW, 2:82).

From Tench Coxe

SIR   [before 2 Apr. 1802]

I am informed that Congress are to rise in the beginning of April, and that the internal Revenues will be repealed before this can depart. The few republicans among my family connections, and others among our political friends concur in the hope that something permanent will be done for me before the Senate shall rise. Mr. Gallatin I am sure will testify that I have never shewn any coldness, unkindness or opposition to him on account of the loss of my Treasury standing. Genl. Muhlenberg, I am sure will bear witness that I have manifested the most perfect good humor and respect towards him in my present Situation. Nor have I abated in public evidences of my zeal for the public interests, of my coincidence in measures operating a new privation of office, or abstinence from dissentions with our political friends even when I had every thing but evidence of hostility. During seven years of suffering and exertion I cannot look back to any thing which I have omitted, to engage the confidence of the republican interest, and unhappily I have succeeded so far as to excite the envious machinations of a few persons, who have had a dangerous influence on our public councils. At this moment the conduct produced by such persons holds in the deepest jeopardy the reelection of a particular important Republican Magistrate. You have seen, in a paper *pen'd by one of those* persons, the signed declaration that the prevention of one of your measures was to be considered as a meritorious promotion of our Countrys interests! I could enlarge most impressively upon this subject. If councils so hostile to your peace—safety—and honor as a chief Magistrate are to operate in the general and state government—if secret accusations which cannot be reached in order to be faced, are to interfere with acts of simple justice towards republicans wounded in the awful struggles since the Presidency of Washington be assured, Sir, evils of no light or common kind must follow.

The customs of Philada. cannot be well filled without one in three being a man of commercial knowledge in all its details, and conversant in the political relations of our foreign trade. I submit whether any man unites a claim from anti republican injuries to him & from commercial & political preparation for the Situation beyond myself. If there is any one then let him take it with my sincere good wishes. If not then, Sir, I submit my claims. If the Senate rises a second time without some permanent provision for me, and the distributions of office at Washington & Philadelphia continue in various lines—if persons not acquainted with trade are exchanged here for commercial federalists to my exclusion, allow me to say that the world must consider Me as disgraced. If two vacancies are to be made I will cheerfully accept the worst—If only one I submit my wounds in the past service my preparation for the future. Before the present Supervisor can wind up the whole of his District he will in my opinion be elected Governor of Pennsylvania. *It is an affair in which I shall not at all interpose*, and I express the opinion in the *most perfect* confidence, but my present opinion is that extraordinary circumstances can alone prevent his failure, or give a new success to the present Governor. It will never cease to be a matter of regret to me that changes so extraordinary should occur; but *confidences unhappily reposed* have combined with other circumstances to induce the most serious danger of the event I allude to—   I go, in perfect confidence a step further—There can be no other interpretation given to recent facts,[1] than a like course being meditated as to yourself or in respect to Mr. Madison, whom vast Numbers would turn to were you to decline or die. These things it is my solemn duty to express, but in the most sacred confidence.[2]

In regard to the secret attacks upon myself, *I wish to face them*. If I cannot have the opportunity then they ought not to operate against me. Mr. Mc.Kean, tho led to neglect me in the Secretaryship, has said the strongest things of the integrity and utility of my conduct in office under him, and after an acquaintance that commenced[3] in the year 1775 before I was of age. He assured me that on your election he had instantly received eleven applications for my late office. Such was the general expectation of my restoration. Be assured, Sir, I am deeply pained to write to you so often. But I dread the effects of the Senates rising without some decent permanent provision, which I may cheerfully and affectionately say to the world well satisfies any pretensions I would wish to advance. I will not act with you any part of address or artifice, and therefore I will say that necessity for income would compel me accept the temporary & precarious[4] fragments of the internal Revenue Service, if that alone were to be given to me, but I trust Sir that I shall be saved from the mortification and injuries of seeing one office of the customs given to a person unprepared as a merchant or mercantile politician. If one only is to be vacated, I hope my pretensions to it will be considered. If two, I am in the same moderate state of contentment to receive the second. If the single office should be vacated, and confer'd on me, the benefit of my present office will devolve upon the Supervisor. It is now in perfect order. If the two offices are to be vacated, and the second confered on me, I will cheerfully execute on any terms however low[5] the business of closing the revenue service of the district. I shall be content with any thing which will defray the mere expences, for I wish only to derive from my services a decent permanent income equal to the expences of my family. It will not be forgotten that the office I held is at 3000 Dlrs. ℔ annum, was given me with the *unanimous* consent of the Senate, and that since I was deprived of it, the total salary has been 13000 Dollars—Few in the Revolution of 1776 suffered as much, Sir, as I have done to prevent *the defeat of that revolution in 1797 and since*—Few, I trust, rendered according to their talents and opportunities more numerous and effectual services—

I have the honor to assure you that my anxious solicitudes for the Success of your administration have encreased with the occasions that appear from circumstances within & without.   T. C.

Permit to add to this letter, Sir, already too long a few particulars which I am sure you would wish to know and remember. Soon after the removal of the Government from New York to Philada. I expressed an opinion before a number of members of Congress at my own table, that the Secy of State was the officer on whom the law should devolve the Governmt. in the event of the death &c. of the President and V. Prest. I found myself called on next day by Mr. J. of the Senate & an earnest expostulation took place. Mr. Hamilton considered it as a preference of a person whom he called his Enemy. The consequence was an irremovable unfriendliness and indeed hostility for the last ten years. I found a like displeasure in two Gentlemen of the S. who discovered from some table of mine, shewn naturally by you, that I had contributed to the stock of information on which your report in favor of their own fisheries was founded.—You remember the deportment of Mr. H. upon the subject of the Sea letters, which I undertook, without an idea of compensation and completely arranged so as to meet your entire approbation & that of Genl. W. You may judge of the temper & deportment to me—The like temper & deportment was manifested on the occasion of the Report upon our foreign commercial relations, for it was impossible to conceal from jealous eyes the preparation of papers extracted often from Treasury sources.

These & all other similar matters were adverted to in the trying ex-
postulations to which I was subjected for not adhering to a line of
conduct grounded, as I conceived upon geographical American party,
and personal prejudices, the whole produced, as I believe, by enmity
to the principles adopted in the Revolution of 1776—Republican
principles. These things cut me off from all chances of preferment, if
they could be prevented—My decent & fair investigations of the
principles of an eminent candidate in 1796, devoted me to sacrifice—
A few Months worked my immolation. In 1798 the publication of
those papers (The American Merchant) by which in private I had
affected the minds of many in the extraordinary Session of 1797,
brought on menaces of exile & destruction, which I will prove to you,
Sir, by several persons. In this course of firm and constant exertion
have I been, till I saw the republican cause made safe by the Success
our State election crowned by your own—Permit to ask whether a
mere indemnity in some decent form & at some early day is not
worthy of the prudent and honorable consideration of the friends of
Republican government. It is the certainty that you would be impressed with such pretensions, which has brought forth those machinations of rival & jealous spirits against me with which you have been
assailed.

RC (DNA: RG 59, LAR); undated; at
head of text: "private"; endorsed by TJ.
Recorded in SJL as received 2 Apr.

For the passage of the act to repeal IN-
TERNAL REVENUES, see Coxe to TJ, 17
Feb. 1802.

HE WILL IN MY OPINION BE ELECTED
GOVERNOR: Peter Muhlenberg was considered a serious contender in Pennsylvania's 1802 gubernatorial election, either
as the Republican nominee in place of
Governor Thomas McKean or as an opposition candidate with Federalist support. In July 1802, TJ appointed Muhlenberg to the highly remunerative
position of collector of customs at Philadelphia, effectively removing him from
the race and thus assuring McKean's reelection. At the same time, TJ appointed
Coxe to the position vacated by Muhlenberg, supervisor of the revenue for the
district of Pennsylvania (Higginbotham,
Pennsylvania Politics, 41-2; *Gazette of the
United States*, 5 Aug. 1802; Vol. 33:670).
MY LATE OFFICE: McKean appointed

Coxe secretary of the Pennsylvania Land
Office, although Coxe had expected to become secretary of the commonwealth
after McKean's election in 1799 (Cooke,
Coxe, 361-3). EXPECTATION OF MY
RESTORATION: on 23 Dec. 1797, President Adams dismissed Coxe as commissioner of the revenue, presumably for his
open criticism of Adams during the election of 1796 (Vol. 29:595).

MR. J. OF THE SENATE: William
Samuel Johnson, a Connecticut native
who supported Hamilton's policies,
served as president of Columbia College
from 1787 to 1800 and as a New York
senator from March 1789 to March 1791
(ANB; *Biog. Dir. Cong.*; Vol. 19:167n).
Massachusetts senators Tristram Dalton
and Caleb Strong were probably the TWO
GENTLEMEN who recognized that Coxe
had supplied TJ with information from
the Treasury Department for the secretary of state's 1791 report on the FISH-
ERIES. For the extensive data supplied by
Coxe, see Vol. 19:158-9, 161, 167-9, 175-
99.

Assigned by Hamilton to oversee "security of Navigation," Coxe, while commissioner of the revenue, also distributed the SEA LETTERS (Vol. 34:381n). PAPERS EXTRACTED OFTEN FROM TREASURY SOURCES: Coxe supplied TJ with studies of American trade and extensive official and unofficial information from the Treasury Department for the report on commerce, which TJ submitted to Congress in December 1793 (Vol. 27:533).

TJ described Coxe's articles on "Neutral Spoliations," which appeared in the *Philadelphia Gazette* in February 1798 under the signature of an AMERICAN MERCHANT, as "excellent pieces" (Vol. 30:124-5).

[1] Preceding four words interlined.
[2] Sentence interlined.
[3] MS: "commence."
[4] Preceding two words and ampersand interlined.
[5] Preceding two words interlined.

From Pierre Samuel Du Pont de Nemours

MONSIEUR LE PRÉSIDENT,   New York. 2 Avril 1802.

Je vous prie d'approuver que je mette sous votre enveloppe un Mémoire assez étendu que Je suis chargé de communiquer à Mr. Bushrood Washington, et qui interesse notre Ami la Fayette.

J'ai déja pris la liberté de vous adresser la Lettre que le Ministre Barbé-Marbois a écrite au Général Davies, auquel je ne savais aucun autre moyen de la faire parvenir.

Vous aurez sans doute eu la bonté de la lire, comme je vous en priais.—Et à sa situation.

Vos Plénipotentiaires avaient donné à ses amis l'esperance que le Congrès trouverait digne des Etats unis de secourir le guerrier habile et intrepide, le Négociateur honorable et intelligent, l'homme pur et vertueux qui les a secourus.

Ils avaient été jusqu'à penser qu'on pourrait lui donner,

20,000 Dollars	pour payer ce qu'il doit à des Citoyens des Etats unis;
20,000	en Bestiaux de belles races et bons instrumens aratoires pour monter sa ferme;
<u>20,000</u>	en Actions de la Banque des Etats unis.
60,000	

Y a-t-il sur cela quelques demarches de faites?

Si elles ne le sont pas, qui les fera?

Si on les fait, auront elles du succès?

Voila ce que je demande à votre amitié.

Les appuyer par vous et vos amis, c'est ce qu'il est inutile de vous demander. Vous y êtes assez porté de vous même.

La Session s'avance.—Il me semble qu'il n'y a pas un moment à perdre pour ceux qui ont cet honorable dessein.

Salut, respect, inviolable et profond attachement

Du Pont (de Nemours)

MISTER PRESIDENT,   New York. 2 Apr. 1802

I beg you to approve my having put in your envelope a rather lengthy memorandum that I have been commissioned to communicate to Mr. Bushrod Washington, which interests our friend Lafayette.

I have already taken the liberty of addressing to you the letter that Minister Barbé de Marbois wrote to General Davie, to whom I had no other way of sending it.

You doubtlessly had the kindness to read it as I begged you to. And your friendship for Lafayette must have made you take a lively interest in his situation.

Your plenipotentiary ministers had given his friends hope that Congress would find it worthy of the United States to give aid to the skillful and fearless warrior, the honorable and intelligent negotiator, the pure and virtuous man who assisted them.

They went so far as to think that he might be given:

20,000 dollars	to pay what he owes to citizens of the United States;
20,000	in thoroughbred livestock and good plowing instruments to set up his farm;
20,000	in shares of the Bank of the United States.
60,000	

Have any steps been taken about that?

If they have not been, who will take them?

If they are taken, will they have some success?

That is what I request of your friendship.

To support them, you and your friends, that is what is unnecessary to ask of you. You are quite inclined to it yourself.

The session is advancing. It seems to me that there is not a moment to lose for those who have in mind this honorable plan.

Greetings, respect, unchangeable and deep affection

Du Pont (de Nemours)

RC (DLC); at head of text: "A Son Excellence Thomas Jefferson Président des Etats unis"; endorsed by TJ as received 5 Apr. and so recorded in SJL. Enclosure not found.

J'AI DÉJA PRIS LA LIBERTÉ: Du Pont to TJ, 21 Feb. 1802. For Du Pont's request that TJ forward correspondence from François Barbé de MARBOIS to William R. Davie, see TJ to Davie, 28 Feb., and Davie's reply of 20 Mch.

LE CONGRÈS: in an act of 3 Mch. 1803 concerning military land warrants, Congress authorized warrants to Lafayette for 11,520 acres. Acts of March 1804 and March 1805 authorized him to take up the land in Orleans Territory (U.S. Statutes at Large, 2:236, 306, 329).

From George Jefferson

DEAR SIR   Richmond 2d. April 1802
I now inclose your account made up to the first of this month, by which there appears to be a balance due us of 45/8.

The Hhd of Molasses you will observe from the account, was forwarded some days ago. The Cyder has since arrived, but we have not yet met with an opportunity of sending it up—but which shall be done by the very first that offers, together with the Corks. The bottles I am sorry to inform you cannot be procured in this place. it is unlucky that I did not sooner make this enquiry, that you might have ordered them from Philadelphia. I thought it unnecessary however to send them before the Cyder, and did not suppose it possible that such an article could not at any time be bought.

Mr. Macon expects to spare you about 8 or 9 dozen of hams. he thinks it better that they should be smoaked a little more, and then they will be forwarded.

Yr. very humble servt.   GEO. JEFFERSON

RC (MHi); at foot of text: "Thos. Jefferson esqr."; endorsed by TJ as received 6 Apr. and so recorded in SJL. Enclosure not found.

To Tadeusz Kosciuszko

DEAR GENERAL   Washington Apr. 2. 1802.
It is but lately that I have recieved your letter of the 25th. Frimaire (Dec. 15.) wishing to know whether some officers of your country could expect to be employed in this country. to prevent a suspense injurious to them I hasten to inform you that we are now actually engaged in reducing our military establishment one third, and discharging one third of our officers. we keep in service no more than men enough to garrison the small posts dispersed at great distances on our frontiers, which garrisons will generally consist of a captain's company only, and in no case of more than two or three, in not one of a sufficient number to require a field officer; and that no circumstance whatever can bring these garrisons together, because it would be an abandonment of their forts. thus circumstanced you will percieve the entire impossibility of providing for the persons you recommend. I wish it had been in my power to give you a more favorable answer; but next to the fulfilling your wishes, the most grateful thing I can do is to give a faithful answer. the session of the first congress, convened

since republicanism has recovered it's ascendancy, is now drawing to a close. they will pretty compleatly fulfil all the desires of the people. they have reduced the army & navy to what is barely necessary. they are disarming Executive patronage & preponderance by putting down one half the offices of the US. which are no longer necessary: these economies have enabled them to suppress all the internal taxes, and still to make such provision for the paiment of their public debt as to discharge that in 18. years: they have lopped off a parasite limb planted by their predecessors on their judiciary body for party purposes: they are opening the doors of hospitality to the fugitives from the oppressions of other countries: and we have suppressed all those public forms & ceremonies which tended to familiarize the public eye to the harbingers of another form of government. the people are nearly all united, their quondam leaders infuriated with the sense of their impotence; they will soon be seen or heard only in the newspapers, which serve as chimnies to carry off noxious vapours & smoke, and all is now tranquil, firm and well as it should be. I add no signature because unnecessary for you. God bless you and preserve you still for a season of usefulness to your country.

PrC (DLC); at foot of text: "General Kosciuszko." Enclosed in TJ to Pierre Samuel Du Pont de Nemours, 25 Apr.

For Kosciuszko's LETTER of 25 FRIMAIRE, see 16 Dec. 1801. TJ incorrectly converted the French date to 15 Dec.

THEY ARE OPENING THE DOORS OF HOSPITALITY: on 10 Mch. the House of Representatives passed a bill "for revising and amending the acts concerning naturalization." The Senate received the bill from the House on 11 Mch. and referred it to a committee the next day (JHR, 4:129-30; JS, 3:191).

From Edward Livingston

SIR   New York Apl. 2d. 1802

The enclosed paper is I believe the only one printed here which contains the proceedings of the House of Commons on the provisional removal of the countervailing duties and the late arrangement respecting the sixth article—

I have thought it might be agreeable to you Sir to receive the earliest intelligence on these interesting subjects and have therefore taken the liberty to send you the paper which I pray you to receive with the assurance of my highest Respect.   EDW LIVINGSTON

RC (DLC); endorsed by TJ as received 5 Apr. and so recorded in SJL. Enclosure: see below.

On 2 Apr., at least two New York City newspapers printed PROCEEDINGS OF THE HOUSE OF COMMONS of 17-19 Feb.

concerning a bill to put into effect the convention recently concluded between Britain and the United States. In a footnote to the published version of his annual message in December, TJ had raised the issue of COUNTERVAILING DUTIES, additional charges that Britain imposed on goods imported in American ships. Reports that Congress was contemplating the removal of U.S. duties that favored American shipping prompted a suggestion in the Commons that the British prepare to suspend the countervailing duties upon receipt of information that the Americans had in fact removed their extra impost charges. Leave was granted for the introduction of a bill in Parliament to carry out that proposal. The New York newspapers had recently published, from the *National Intelligencer*, a summation of the contents of the convention concerning the SIXTH ARTICLE of the Jay Treaty. Newspapers in the city did not publish the text of the convention until 9-10 Apr. (New York *Commercial Advertiser*, 31 Mch., 2, 9 Apr.; *New-York Gazette and General Advertiser*, 1, 2 Apr.; New York *American Citizen and General Advertiser*, 10 Apr.; Editorial Note and Document III, Annual Message to Congress, 8 Dec. 1801).

To John Page

DEAR SIR   Washington Apr. 2. 1802.

Yours of Mar. 27. was recieved last night; and the object of the present is to assure you that you may take your own time for making enquiries and deliberating for a final decision on the proposition made you in my former letter: only let your enquiries be so conducted as not to permit the object to be suspected in the least. I am afraid it might not be prudent to take into calculation the chance of removal to any other office, unless some one were to become vacant in the state, on account of the over-proportion which Virginia has at present in the general offices of the federal government, tho' but one of these (mr Madison) has been put in by me. any room given for an imputation of partiality in me of this kind would expose me to peculiar reproach, besides increasing the clamour artificially raised against Virginia. as soon as any alteration is made by the legislature in the emoluments of the office proposed to you, I will communicate it to you. in the mean time it may be calculated with probability at what mr Gallatin has supposed. present my respectful compliments to mrs Page and accept yourself assurances of my constant and sincere friendship.   TH: JEFFERSON

PrC (DLC); at foot of text: "John Page esq."; endorsed by TJ in ink on verso. MY FORMER LETTER: TJ to Page, 20 Feb. 1802.

From Francis Peyton

DEAR SIR, Alexandria 2d. April 1802.

William Fitzhugh, Richard Conway, and Thomas Darne, have declined qualifying as justices of the peace for this county, in the place of those gentlemen I would propose, George Slacum, Presly Gunnell, and John Dundas, as characters best qualified in my opinion to succeed them, the two former are republicans, the latter a federalist, but who having long served the corporation as a magistrate would be considered a popular appointment,

I am with great respect Yr. Obt. Servt. F. PEYTON

RC (DLC); endorsed by TJ. Recorded in SJL as received 3 Apr.

CHARACTERS BEST QUALIFIED: when Peyton served as mayor of Alexandria from 1799 to 1800, Alexandria merchant George Slacum and John Dundas also served in the town government, Slacum as a member of the common council, Dundas as an alderman (Miller, *Alexandria Artisans*, 1:xxvii; 2:126). For an ear-lier recommendation of Presly Gunnell to be justice of the peace, see Vol. 34:303-4. Dundas's service to the CORPORATION included two terms as mayor during the late 1790s. Peyton and his three candidates were among the fifteen named in the commission for justices of the peace for the County of Alexandria in the District of Columbia issued on 27 Apr. (FC of commission in Lb in DNA: RG 59, MPTPC; Miller, *Alexandria Artisans*, 1:xxvi).

To DeWitt Clinton

Th: Jefferson requests the favor of Mr. Clinton's company to dinner and chess on Tuesday next at half after three, or at whatever later hour the house may rise.
Saturday Apl. 3. 1802.

The favor of an answer is asked.

RC (Philip D. Sang, Chicago, 1960); in Meriwether Lewis's hand.

From Pierre Samuel Du Pont de Nemours

MONSIEUR LE PRÉSIDENT, New York 3 avril 1802

J'ai oublié dans ma lettre d'hier de vous exposer ce que le service des Etats unis a couté à notre cher La Fayette.

J'ai sous les yeux une note du Citoyen *Morisot* Avocat au Parlement qui dirigeait ses affaires d'interêt.—Cette note constate que depuis 1777 jusqu'en 1783 il a vendu pour *Sept cent trente trois mille francs*, ou environ *cent quarante mille dollars* de ses terres, et qu'il a en outre employé aux dépenses relatives au même service tant en Amerique qu'en Europe *cent mille écus*, pris sur son revenu.

Ainsi c'est environ *un million* de francs ou *deux cent mille dollars* dont son Zêle a fait hommage à la Liberté des Etats unis.

Il ne lui reste à present que *quinze cent dollars* de revenu avec lequel il lui est impossible de payer *vingt mille dollars* de dettes dont il est encore chargé.

Telle est la position de notre honorable ami

Salut et respect. Du Pont (de Nemours)

E D I T O R S ' T R A N S L A T I O N

Mister President, New York 3 Apr. 1802

I forgot in my letter of yesterday to show you what his service to the United States has cost our dear Lafayette.

I have under my eyes a note of Citizen *Morizot*, counsel to the Parlement, who managed his affairs in this matter. This note proves that from 1777 to 1783, his lands were sold for *seven hundred thirty-three thousand francs* or about *one hundred and forty thousand dollars*, and that further he spent on expenditures relative to his own service in America as well as in Europe *one hundred thousand ecus* above his revenue.

Thus there are about *one million* francs or *two hundred thousand dollars* which from his zeal he has given in service to the liberty of the United States.

There remains to him at present no more than *fifteen hundred dollars* of revenue, with which it is impossible to pay *twenty thousand dollars* of debts with which he is burdened.

Such is the situation of our honorable friend.

Greetings and respect. Du Pont (de Nemours)

RC (DLC); at head of text: "A Son Excellence Thomas Jefferson President des Etats unis"; endorsed by TJ as received 7 Apr. and so recorded in SJL.

citoyen morisot: Jacques Philippe Grattepain-Morizot was Lafayette's business agent in France (Jason Lane, *General and Madame de Lafayette: Partners in Liberty's Cause in the American and French Revolutions* [Lanham, Md.,

2003], 58, 74; Olivier Bernier, *Lafayette: Hero of Two Worlds* [New York, 1983], 149).

vingt mille dollars de dettes: by an arrangement made by James Monroe, Lafayette used his grant of land from Congress as collateral for a loan from the Baring firm in London that allowed him to pay off his outstanding debts (Harlow Giles Unger, *Lafayette* [Hoboken, N.J., 2002], 334).

From George Jefferson

DEAR SIR   Richmond 3d. Apl. 1802

I yesterday forwarded the Cyder and Corks, together with some things written for by Mr. Randolph, at the request of your manager—by a boat belonging to one of the Faris's.

I observe in Mr. R's list that the same number of Corks are mentioned as in yours; and as I expect they are intended for the same purpose, & bottles are not included in his—I hope they find that none will be required.

I am Dear Sir Your Very humble servt.   GEO. JEFFERSON

RC (MHi); at foot of text: "Thos. Jefferson esqr."; endorsed by TJ as received 7 Apr. and so recorded in SJL.

YOUR MANAGER: Gabriel Lilly (MB, 2:1021; TJ to Thomas Mann Randolph, 9 Jan. 1802). ONE OF THE FARIS'S: at various times in the late 1790s TJ paid John, Ezekiah, George, and William Faris for transporting nailrod, groceries, and other goods (MB, 2:928-31, 939, 945, 967, 989, 1001, 1008; Vol. 31:148).

From Ezra L'Hommedieu

SIR   Albany April 3rd. 1802—

I have the honor of transmitting to you herewith certain Resolutions of the Society for the Promotion of Agriculture Arts & Manufactures, which you will please to lay before the Society over which You preside & request their concurrence in the proposed measure— You will oblige our Society by causing the result thereof to be communicated to the Secretary at this City—

I am with great respect Your most obet servt

EZRA L'HOMMEDIEU
Vice Presdt. and President pro Tem:

RC (PPAmP); in an unidentified hand, signed by L'Hommedieu; at foot of text: "To Thomas Jefferson LLD. President of the American Philosophical Society and the Members of the same." Recorded in SJL as received 12 Apr. with notation "sent to A.P.S." Enclosure: two printed resolutions from the Society for the Promotion of Agriculture, Arts and Manufactures of the state of New York, Albany, dated 24 and 31 Mch. 1802, respectively, the first noting that the objects of the various societies in the U.S. for the promotion of the arts and sciences would be encouraged "were a general medium of connection and communication established between them" and, therefore, resolving "That the President be requested to write circular letters to all such Societies in the United States, inviting them to appoint Delegates annually, to convene, in a general meeting, at the Seat of Congress, and to continue their meetings, by periodical adjournments, during the times that Congress shall be in session—Which Delegates, when so met, shall choose their President, and form rules for the government of their proceedings, and make the improvement of Agriculture, and the diffusion of all such knowledge as may tend to that general end, their primary object"; the second resolution calling for all members of both Houses of Congress, being members of the society, to serve as exofficio delegates to meet with others "from the Societies in the different States at the Seat of Congress" (broadside in same; both resolutions signed by Benjamin DeWitt, secretary, as extracts from the society's minutes; addressed: "To the American Philosophical Society at Philadelphia"; endorsed for the APS as read 16 Apr. Enclosed in Samuel L. Mitchill to TJ, 12 Apr. 1802; TJ to Caspar Wistar, 13 Apr. 1802.

Born at Southold, Long Island, New York, Ezra L'Hommedieu (1734-1811) graduated from Yale College in 1754 and studied law, eventually establishing successful practices in Southold and New York City. An early protestor against oppressive British policies in America, he served as a delegate to the Continental Congress from 1779 to 1783 and kept Governor George Clinton informed on the progress of the war. L'Hommedieu served in the New York state assembly from 1777 to 1783 and in the state senate from 1784 to 1792 and 1794 to 1809. A proponent of higher education, he served many years as a regent of the state university. L'Hommedieu was a charter member of the New York Society for the Promotion of Agriculture, Arts and Manufactures, incorporated by the state in 1793, and contributed essays to the society's

publication. TJ was elected a member of the society in 1800 (ANB; *Sixteenth Session of the Laws of the State of New York* [New York, 1793], 86-7; *Transactions of the Society, for the Promotion of Agriculture, Arts and Manufactures, Instituted in the State of New-York*, 2d ed., 1 [1801], 57-71, 133-43, 231-45, 312-13, 328-9, 335-9, 364-6; Vol. 32:8, 10-11n).

In January 1801, fellow member of the American Philosophical Society Isaac Briggs introduced TJ to the idea of organizing in each state an agricultural society that would appoint delegates to meet annually in Washington. The following month, TJ appealed to another member of the APS and president of the New York agriculture society, Robert R. Livingston, to encourage existing state agriculture societies to select members "to meet in a central society." Members who were congressmen would be good choices, as they could occasionally hold meetings in Washington on the business of the societies. At the 16 Apr. 1802 meeting of the APS, the RESOLUTIONS from New York were read and referred to a committee, which was continued on 7 May (APS, *Proceedings*, 22, pt. 3 [1884], 323; Vol. 32:501-3, 596-7; Vol. 33:199-200; TJ to Caspar Wistar, 13 Apr.; Isaac Briggs to TJ, 26 Apr. 1802). For the establishment of the American Board of Agriculture in 1803, see Vol. 32:503n.

SECRETARY AT THIS CITY: the New York society had two secretaries—Benjamin DeWitt at Albany and Samuel L. Mitchill (New York *American Citizen and General Advertiser*, 26 Feb. 1802).

To the Mississippi Territory House of Representatives

GENTLEMEN

I recieve with great pleasure the address of your honourable house of the 20th of January, and thank you for the sentiments of affection, of approbation, and of confidence which it expresses.

The interesting portion of our country which you occupy, is worthy the fostering care of the general government. impressed with a full sense of the duties I owe to your situation, I shall not fail to fulfill them with solicitude and fidelity.

With local advantages so distinguished, a fertile soil, genial climate, and precious productions, the day cannot be distant when strong in population, & rich in resources, you will, by the addition of your wealth and strength, amply retribute to your sister-states, the care and protection under which you will have been nurtured. nor shall we doubt your assistance in fortifying in our minds a strict adherence to the constitution, and to those republican principles which the patriots and heroes of '76. established and consecrated.

I pray you to be assured of my fervent wishes for your safety and prosperity, and to accept the homage of my high respect and consideration.   TH: JEFFERSON
                                                     April 3. 1802.

PrC (DLC); at head of text: "To the House of Representatives of the Missisipi territory."

TJ forwarded the above address under a brief cover letter to William C. C. Claiborne, which was also dated 3 Apr. In it,

TJ wrote: "The house of representatives of the Missisipi territory having sent through your hands the address they were pleased to present to me, permit me to ask permission to pass the answer through the same channel" (PrC in DLC; at foot of text: "Governr. Claiborne").

From Samuel Quarrier

SIR   Washington City April 3d 1802
    Imperious necessity actuates me once again to address you, it's I assure you both foreign from my feelings, & inclination to importune or trouble you on any business, more particular[1] the present—it's A liberty in me that causes many unpleasant sinsations, exclusive of those I feale from the reception of my last letter to you, disagreeable as it is my unfortunate condition is still more so, In consequence of A long imprisonment, in the wretched prison of this place, i'me at lenth emancipated on this theater[2] of action, in A Situation truley deplorable, greatly impaird in health, no prospect before me, but that which lacerates the faith already galled,[3] by passed misfortunes, and liable to be much more so (even if A situation where to offer to my accepance) by the unrelenting callousness of callumny—other causes, intirely moneyless, and sorry am I to add friendless, cruelly distressing as all this is, I was informed yesterday, that in consiquence of A fall, my Father had been confined to his bed for four weeks passed, that he was in A very weak & low state from the accident, which had broke one or two of his ribs, and otherways much injured him—On

the information I felt the most poignant regret at the misfortune, and an aditional one at my helpless condition, in not being able to repair with all possible speede to aleviate & to assist all that A fond & affectionate son could the sufferings of his Father—Its true his conduct towards me has been extreemly harsh, harsh as it has been, or may be, I can never loose sight of his being my Father, and to respect and love him, as such. Under those considerations which I've here given, & more if they would answer any good purpose, I could give I'me induced to aske the further extention of you'r benevolent Friendship towards me in furnishing me with the means to repair to the sick chamber of my Father, & to leave A place where my happyness is in A great part forever buried—The pecuniarie service i've already recieved from you is greatfully acknowledged by me—Relying on you'r known generosity & universal philantrophy, I hope & trust you'll aleviate the miserable situation of one who's experienced for his some of the severest shocks of misfortune & who's fully resolved to avoid the rocks & shoals he's unfortunately s[...] on—

With the most profound respect & esteeme Your's &c

SAML. W QUARRIER

NB You'll receive this from the hand of you'r worthy Secretary Capn. Lewis who will informe me of you'r pleasure—

RC (DLC); frayed at margin; at head of text: "Thomas Jefferson Esqr. President of the United States"; endorsed by TJ as received 3 Apr. and so recorded in SJL.

Quarrier's LAST LETTER to TJ was dated 13 Feb. 1802, seeking his release from the debtor's prison in Washington.

Previous correspondence with the president requested appointments and loans of money (Vol. 35:83, 84n, 496; Vol. 36:497-9).

MY FATHER: Alexander Quarrier.

[1] MS: "pariculair."
[2] MS: "thater."
[3] MS: "gallded."

To Martha Jefferson Randolph

MY DEAR MARTHA   Washington Apr. 3. 1802.

I recieved Anne's letter by the last post, in which she forgot to mention the health of the family, but I presume it good. I inclose you a medal executed by an artist lately from Europe and who appears to be equal to any in the world. it is taken from Houdon's bust, for he never saw me. it sells the more readily as the prints which have been offered the public are such miserable caracatures. Congress will probably rise within three weeks and I shall be on in a week or ten days afterwards. my last to mr Randolph explained my expectations as to your motions during his journey. I wrote lately to Maria, encouraging her to pay us a flying visit at least while you are here, and proposing to mr Eppes so to time his next plantation visit in Albemarle as to meet me there in the beginning of May. my last information from the Hundred stated them all well, little Francis particularly healthy. Anne writes me that Ellen will be through all her books before I come. she may count therefore on my bringing her a new supply.—I have desired Lilly to make the usual provision of necessaries for me at Monticello, and if he should be at a loss for the particulars to consult with you. my orders as to the garden were to sow & plant as usual, and to furnish you with the proceeds. order them therefore freely: you know they will do nothing if you leave it to their delicacy. I am looking forward with impatience to the moment when I can embrace you in all my affection and the dear children. it already occupies much of my thoughts as the time approaches. present me affectionately to mr Randolph, and be assured yourself of my tenderest love.

Th: Jefferson

RC (NNPM); at foot of text: "Mrs. Randolph." PrC (MHi); endorsed by TJ in ink on verso. Enclosure: for the medal, see TJ to Mary Jefferson Eppes, 29 Mch. 1802.

LAST POST: the letter from Anne Cary Randolph to TJ, of 27 Mch., recorded in SJL as received from Edgehill on the 31st, has not been found. MY LAST TO MR RANDOLPH: see TJ to Thomas Mann Randolph, 28 Mch.

I WROTE LATELY TO MARIA: TJ to Mary Jefferson Eppes, 29 Mch. For TJ's LAST INFORMATION FROM Bermuda HUNDRED, see John Wayles Eppes to TJ, 11 Mch.

To the Senate

GENTLEMEN OF THE SENATE

According to the request expressed in your resolution of yesterday I now transmit to the Senate the proceedings of the Court martial lately held for the trial of Capt Cornelius Lyman, asking the favor of their return, at the convenience of the Senate, as they are the originals.

Th: Jefferson
April 3. 1802.

PrC (DLC). Recorded in SJL with notation "court martial v. Lyman." Enclosures not found, but see below.

The Senate RESOLUTION of 2 Apr. requesting the proceedings of the court-martial against CORNELIUS LYMAN was sent to TJ by Samuel A. Otis, the secretary of the Senate (RC in DLC, endorsed by TJ with the notation "proceedings agt. Lyman"; Dft in DNA: RG 46, EPOR). Lyman was a captain in the Second Regiment of Infantry. On 26 Sep. 1801, at Presque Isle, Pennsylvania, a court-martial was convened against him on charges of conduct unbecoming an officer and neglect of duty. The court found Lyman guilty and ordered him dismissed from the service. On 4 Nov., the War Department sent TJ a communication regarding the court martial, which is recorded in SJL as received the same day but has not been found. Two days later, on 6 Nov., TJ ordered that the court's sentence not be carried out, deeming the evidence against Lyman to be of a "contradictory aspect considering that in cases rendered doubtful by opposing testimony, it would be hard to credit that which accuses, rather than that which excul-

pates" (FC in Lb in DNA: RG 94, James Wilkinson Order Book; FC in Lb in DNA: RG 98, Orderly Books of the Adjutant at Fort Adams; Vol. 35:756). On 25 Mch. 1802, TJ nominated Lyman for appointment as captain in the First Regiment of Infantry, but the Senate postponed its decision on the nomination and requested the proceedings of the court-martial. Portions of the proceedings were read on 3 and 7 Apr., and the Senate finally consented to Lyman's nomination on 12 Apr. by a vote of 17 to 5 (JEP, 1:412, 416-17, 419-20; TJ to the Senate, 25 Mch. 1802).

From William Short

DEAR SIR   Paris April 3. 1802

I take up my pen not as heretofore to trouble you about myself or my affairs, but merely to inclose you for greater caution a copy of the list of seeds of which I sent you the original in my last of Jany. 23. It is at the request of M. de Liancourt who desires to obtain them for the Society of Agriculture. I mentioned to you the reasons for which he was anxious that I should obtain of you to put this commission into the hands of some agent who might be relied on—As I then also offered the excuses of M. de Liancourt & mine for giving you this trouble I will not repeat them here—but I will mention again that I will be answerable for the expences attending this commission. It is desired that such of these seeds as can be procured at present should be sent immediately, or as well as I remember, should be recieved by the month of Jany. I have not before me at present the letter of M. de Liancourt respecting this.—As I trust my former letter will be recieved safe, this will be useless—I send it only for greater caution; & at the request of M. de L.—It has been by accident that this copy of the list was not sent sooner.—

I some time ago put into the hands of Mr Livingston one year of the *Connaissance des tems* to be forwarded to you; & he has since told me that it was sent by an American who was going to Baltimore. I count therefore on your recieving it.

My former letters have mentioned to you the extraordinary silence of Mr Barnes.[1] I have as yet no letter from him since the few lines of March, & no account since that of Jany. 1801. The not even acknowleging letters which he recieves from me is so contrary to all kind of mercantile usage, that it is quite out of my power to account for it. I ask the favor of you to get from him his acct. which he does not send me, & to insist on his laying out the cash for me immediately & successively as he recieves it, & to fix on the kind of funds to be purchased.

I could add nothing to what I have already repeated, perhaps too often, respecting my affairs—the most pressing that of E.R. I last wrote about in mine of Dec. 18. I had hoped it might have been settled independently of the suit with E.R. There has been already a great delay, & loss consequently as to me, in this affair where I was certainly passive, & where I can not think that I ought to suffer.— With sentiments of the most perfect respect & attachment I have the honor to be Dear Sir, your most obedient & humble servant

W: SHORT

The last letter which I have had the pleasure of recieving from you was that of Oct. 3. by Mr Livingston—Since its reciept I have written under the dates of Dec. 18. & Jany. 23.—I take it for granted you will have recd. that which I wrote Oct. 18. by Mr. Victor Dupont, as we have learned here his arrival at N. York in the beginning of Feby.

RC (PHi); endorsed by TJ as received 13 June and so recorded in SJL. Enclosure not found.

In his letter to TJ of 18 Dec. 1801, Short mentioned the letter John BARNES had written to him in MARCH of that year and Barnes's account of sums he had received in Short's behalf through January 1801.

E.R.: Edmund Randolph.

[1] MS: "Banes."

To Albert Gallatin

TH: J. TO THE SECRETARY OF THE TREASURY   Apr. 4. 1802.
Nicholas Reib is upon me again. I presume the report of the committee of Feb. 11. 96. herein inclosed, & the resolution of Congress therein referred to of Dec. 19. 1782. shew the true ground of his claim, and the rule of settlement, and that his account shews what he has recieved. will mr Gallatin be so good as to have these papers looked at by the proper officer, and the objection or obstacle to paiment stated that I may return him an answer once for all, with his papers.

RC (DLC); on verso of address sheet from the Navy Department; addressed by TJ: "The Secretary of the Treasury" in place of "The President of the United States," in a clerk's hand; with directions in Gallatin's hand written at a right angle to addresses: "Mr Gallatin requests Mr Nourse to give the explanations necessary to enable the President to get rid of this man. This paper & Reib's letter not to go out of Mr Nourse's hands—A.G." Not recorded in SJL. Enclosures: for the 19 Dec. 1782 resolution of Congress, see Reib to TJ, 17 Feb. 1802. Other enclosure not found, but see below.

UPON ME AGAIN: see Reib to TJ, 27 Mch. REPORT OF THE COMMITTEE: on 11 May 1796, the Committee of Claims in the House of Representatives presented a report on the 19 Feb. petition of Nicholas and Peter Reib, Andrew Bearsticker, and other artificers from Colonel Benjamin Flower's artillery regiment (JHR, 2:447-8, 550).

To John Bartram, Jr.

DEAR SIR   Washington Apr. 5. 1802.

I am desired on the part of the Agricultural society of Paris to put the inclosed list of seeds, which they want, into the hands of some person who can be relied on to furnish them genuine and fresh. I ask this favor of you. they would wish to recieve them in autumn, or as early in the next winter as possible. as soon therefore as the season has admitted the whole to be saved, or as many as can be got, I will thank you to have them packed in a secure box, and to drop me a line by post at this place[1] informing me they are ready, and sending me your bill. I will immediately have that paid, and direct a person to call on you & recieve the box. I will thank you to let me know whether you recieve this letter, and can undertake to execute it. Accept my best wishes.   TH: JEFFERSON

PrC (DLC); at foot of text: "John Bartram"; endorsed by TJ in ink on verso. Enclosure not found.

William Short had forwarded the request and the LIST OF SEEDS in his letter of 23 Jan., which TJ received on 4 Apr.

[1] Preceding three words interlined.

From Sebastian Bauman

                                   Post office new york
SIR,   March [i.e. Apr.] 5. 1802

I have the Honor to inform you that the letter for London which you sent me under Cover, came in time for the British Mail, which will be closed here on Wednesday the 7 inst., and go in the British Packet Lady Arabella for Falmouth.

I have the Honor to be with great Respect, Sir, your most ob. & very humble Servant,   S. BAUMAN

RC (MHi); at foot of text: "The Honr-
bl. Thomas Jefferson President of the
United States"; endorsed by TJ as a letter
of "Mar. [for Apr.]," received 8 Apr. and
so recorded in SJL.

LETTER FOR LONDON: probably TJ to
Robert Gourlay, 30 Mch.

From Philippe de Létombe

Paris, 15 germinal an 10.
(5 avril 1802. v. St.)

MONSIEUR LE PRÉSIDENT,

J'ai reçu, le 1er aoust dernier, la lettre infiniment obligeante dont
vous avez daigné m'honorer, de Washington, le 27 Juillet précédent.
Mon passage de Newyork à Lorient m'a été, en conséquence, on ne
peut plus agréable et je suis pénétré de reconnoissance des attentions
dont m'ont comblé et me comblent encore Monsieur Livingston et sa
famille.

Arrivé à Paris, j'y ai présenté au Gouvernement votre temoignage
tant honorable pour moi. J'en ai été parfaitement bien accueilli. On y
sait apprécier, Monsieur le Président, le haut prix d'une recommandation de votre part.

Vos extrêmes bontés n'ont pas eu moins d'influence sur ma reception par mes parens et mes amis.

Je vous supplie, Monsieur le Président, de me les continuer et de
vouloir bien agréér mon hommage des sentimens de dévouement,
d'admiration, de respect que vous doivent les bons citoyens de tous
les Paÿs.

LÉTOMBE

E D I T O R S'   T R A N S L A T I O N

Paris, 15 Germinal Year 10.
(5 Apr. 1802, old style)

MISTER PRESIDENT,

I received, the first of August last, the infinitely kind letter with which
you condescended to honor me from Washington the preceding 27 July.
Consequently, my passage from New York to L'Orient could not have been
more agreeable, and I am filled with gratitude for the attentions with which
Mr. Livingston and his family overwhelmed me and still continue to over-
whelm me.

Once arrived in Paris, I presented to the government your testimonial, so
honorable for me. Because of that, I was perfectly well received. They know
how to appreciate there, Mister President, the great worth of a recommendation from you.

Your exceptional kindnesses had no less influence on my reception by my
family and my friends.

I beg you, Mister President, to continue the kindnesses to me and to be willing to accept my tribute of the feelings of devotion, admiration, and respect that the good citizens of all countries owe you.   LÉTOMBE

RC (DLC); TJ, misreading Létombe's date, endorsed the letter as one of 1 Apr. received 11 June, and so recorded it in SJL.

To the Senate

GENTLEMEN OF THE SENATE

Since my message of January 6th. to the Senate I have recieved information that Thomas Sim Lee therein named as a justice of the peace for the county of Washington had resigned that office; and that Benjamin Stoddart and William Hammond Dorsey therein also named as justices for the same county had declined qualifying. this renders it necessary to withdraw their nominations for reappointment, which I hereby do, and I nominate in their stead Anthony Reintzell, John Oakley and Isaac Pierce to be justices of the peace for the said county.

In the same message of Jan. 6 the name of John Laird was inserted by mistake, instead of that of Benjamin More, who (and not John Laird) had been commissioned & qualified as a justice of the peace. I therefore beg leave to correct the error by restoring to it's place the name of Benjamin More, and nominating him to be a justice of the peace for the said county, & by withdrawing that of *John Laird*.

I learn also from the county of Alexandria that William Fitzhugh, Richard Conway and Thomas Darne named in the said message as justices for that county, have declined qualifying. I therefore withdraw their nominations, and I nominate in their stead George Slacum, Presly Gunnell and John Dundas to be justices of the peace for the said county of Alexandria.   TH: JEFFERSON

Apr. 5. 1802.

RC (DNA: RG 46, EPEN, 7th Cong., 1st sess.); endorsed by a Senate clerk. PrC (DLC). Recorded in SJL with notation "nomination justices Columbia."

Meriwether Lewis delivered this message to the Senate on 5 Apr. It was read and ordered to "lie for consideration" (JEP, 1:417-18). For the confirmation of the justices of the peace for both counties, see TJ to Francis Peyton, 31 Mch.

MY MESSAGE: see TJ to the Senate: In-terim Appointments, 6 Jan. 1802. In February, TJ wrote the secretary of the Senate that he had received INFORMATION regarding the justices for Washington County (Vol. 36:546). John Mason had earlier recommended ISAAC PIERCE as a candidate for justice of the peace (Vol. 34:303-4).

For TJ's mistake of inserting Laird's name INSTEAD OF THAT OF BENJAMIN MORE, see Jacob Wagner to TJ, 6 Feb. and TJ to Otis, 8 Feb. 1802.

From Henry Dearborn

SIR,   War Department 6th. April 1802.

Lieut: Jesse Lull having been rejected by the Senate, I take the liberty of proposing Peter Talman Capt: in the 1st. Regiment of Artillerists & Engineers, to be the first Lieut: in the Regiment of Artillery. I also take the liberty of proposing Henry Irwin of Pennsylvania, to be an Ensign in the 1st. Regt. of Infantry.

Accept, Sir, the assurances of my high respect

H. DEARBORN

RC (DLC); in a clerk's hand, signed by Dearborn; at foot of text: "The President of the United States"; endorsed by TJ as received from the War Department on 6 Apr. and "Nominations" and so recorded in SJL. FC (Lb in DNA: RG 107, LSP).

On 7 Apr., TJ sent the following message to the Senate: "I nominate Peter Talman to be a first Lieutenant in the regiment of artillery. he was first lieutenant in the 1st regiment of Artillerists and Engineers, not long since promoted to be a captain in the same regiment, and now willing to return to his former station. I also nominate Henry Irwin of Pensylvania to be an ensign in the first regiment of infantry" (RC in DNA: RG 46, EPEN, 7th Cong., 1st sess.; PrC in DLC). Peter Tallman (TALMAN) received his first

commission in the army as a lieutenant of artillerists and engineers in 1795, and became a captain in December 1800. The Senate approved Tallman's appointment immediately after receiving the nomination but took no action regarding IRWIN. Dearborn recommended Irwin (or Irvine), who was presumed to be a Republican, again in October 1802. TJ appointed Irwin an ensign of infantry along with four others pending Senate approval, but Irwin apparently declined the appointment and never became an officer in the army (Heitman, *Dictionary*, 1:944; JEP, 1:418; Dearborn to Peyton Gay and others, 12 Oct. 1802, Dearborn to Thomas H. Cushing, 12 Oct., in DNA: RG 107, LSMA; Dearborn to TJ, 8 Oct. 1802).

From Nicolas Gouin Dufief

MONSIEUR,   6 d'avril. 1802

Mr Duane s'est chargé de vous remettre tous les ouvrages que vous m'avez demandés À l'égard de ceux que vous désirez faire venir de France Je les ai particulierement recommandés à mon Libraire, mon voyage projetée ne pouvant avoir lieu, par une Suite de Circonstances dont le detail ne Sauroit vous interesser—

Jacques le Fataliste est attribué à Diderot par tous ceux qui sont familiarisés avec sa touche originale, quoiqui'il ne reponde pas tout à fait a ce qu'on devoit attendre d'un aussi grand máitre. Cet ouvrage & la Religieuse du même auteur furent presentés au Gouvernement français par *le Prince Henry de Prusse* qui en étoit depositaire

Je suis avec une profonde estime Monsieur, Votre très devoué Serviteur. N. G. DUFIEF

EDITORS' TRANSLATION

SIR, 6 Apr. 1802

Mr. Duane has taken it upon himself to turn over to you all the works you requested of me. With respect to those that you wish to order from France, I have especially ordered them from my bookseller, my planned voyage not being possible to take place due to a series of circumstances, the details of which could not interest you.

Jacques the Fatalist is attributed to Diderot by all those who have become familiar with his original manner, although it does not quite measure up to what one should expect from so great a master. This work and *La Religieuse* (*The Nun*) by the same author were presented to the French government by Prince Henry of Prussia, who was their authorized guardian.

I am with deep esteem, Sir, your very devoted servant,

N. G. DUFIEF

RC (DLC); at foot of text: "Le président des Etats Unis"; endorsed by TJ as received 9 Apr. and so recorded in SJL. Enclosure: Invoice, Dufief to TJ, 6 Apr. 1802, showing $3 for d'Holbach's *Systême de la Nature* in six volumes; $1.50 for Diderot's *Jacques le fataliste* in three volumes; $5 for Chaptal's *Élémens de Chymie* in three volumes (see Dufief to TJ, 4 Mch. 1802); and $14 for the six-volume *Oeuvres de Séneque* translated by La Grange; TJ added $2.25 to the total of $23.50 and drew a new total of $25.75 (MS in CSmH, in Dufief's hand, with addition by TJ and Dufief's acknowledgment of receipt in full; see TJ to Dufief, 10 Apr.).

LA RELIGIEUSE: Denis Diderot's fictional memoir and letters of a woman forced to take religious vows against her will received little attention when it was first published in serial form in the early 1780s. The work drew more notice when it appeared as a book in 1796. Numerous editions followed, including an English translation published in London in 1797 (Denis Diderot, *The Nun*, trans. Russell Goulbourne [Oxford, 2005], xii-xiv, xxxiv-xxxv).

To William Branch Giles

TH:J. TO MR GILES [6 Apr. 1802]

I inclose you an extract of a letter from mr Brown to mr Lincoln under whom, acting as Secretary of state, and Genl. Smith acting voluntarily for the department of Secretary of the Navy, but without appointment or reward, the latter part of what respected the Berceau was conducted. the other letter of Brown's which I mentioned relates merely to the details of the repairs.

The question whether the Berceau was to be delivered up under the treaty was of Executive cognisance entirely & without appeal. so was the question as to the condition in which she should be delivered: and it is as much an invasion of it's independance for a co-ordinate branch to call for the reasons of the decision, as it would be to call on the Supreme court[1] for it's reasons on any judiciary decision.   if an appropriation were asked, the legislature would have a right to ask reasons. but in this case they had confided an appropriation (for Naval contingencies) to the discretion of the Executive. under this appropriation our predecessors *bought* the vessel (for there was no order of Congress authorizing them to buy) and began her repairs; we compleated them. I will not say that a very gross abuse of discretion in a past appropriation[2] would not furnish ground to the legislature to take notice of it. in what form is not now necessary to decide. but so far from a gross abuse, the decision in this case was correct, honorable, and advantageous to the nation.   I cannot see to what legitimate object any resolution of the house on the subject can lead: and if one is passed on ground not legitimate, our duty will be to resist it. these gentlemen wish to abuse the liberality of the Majority by harrassing the Executive with malicious enquiries, and sowing tares among their enemies. so far they ought not to be indulged. they wish also to create occasions for evacuation of their ill humor. they have no doubt had the evacuation. but after indulging them with that, to give them any sanction by a vote of the house yielding to their demands, is to give colour to all the calumnies they have before uttered against the Executive. be so good as to return me the inclosed paper when you shall have made your uses of it.

RC (NN); date supplied from PrC; addressed: "Mr. Giles"; endorsed by Giles. PrC (DLC); at foot of text in ink: "Apr. 6. 1802." Recorded in SJL under 6 Apr. Enclosure: Extract from Samuel Brown to Levi Lincoln, [4 Aug. 1801], stating that the *Berceau* was captured on 12 Oct. 1800, arrived at Boston on 14 Nov., libeled and condemned on 17 Nov., sold by the order of the district court and purchased by the United States on 15 Jan. 1801; stating also that Brown "presumed it was the meaning" of his instructions from the secretary of the navy that the vessel should be restored to the condition it was in immediately prior to the battle in which it was captured; and that the vessel had to be fitted with new masts, spars, cordage, sails, carpentry, and ironwork estimated to be worth "on an average" 30 percent more than the fittings that were on the ship before it was damaged and captured (Tr in DLC, described at Vol. 35:88n, enclosed in Lincoln to TJ, 14 Aug. 1801; enclosed in TJ to the House of Representatives, 15 Apr. 1802, Enclosure No. 29).

For the repair of the corvette BERCEAU and the return of the vessel to the French government in 1801, see Vol. 34:547-9, 596-7, 662-7, 668n; Vol. 35:88, 146, 147n.

OTHER LETTER OF BROWN'S: probably Samuel Brown to the secretary of the navy, 31 Oct. 1801 (TJ to the House of Representatives, 15 Apr., Enclosure No. 31), or perhaps Brown to Lincoln, 16 Oct. 1801 (see Lincoln to TJ, 24 Oct. 1801, Enclosure No. 2).

In January 1802, TJ sent the House of Representatives an estimate of expenses for implementing the Convention of 1800. The estimate, prepared under Madison's direction, totaled $350,000 and excluded the expense of repairing the *Berceau*, which cost $32,839.54 according to the statement submitted to the House. On 3 Apr., a bill that appropriated $318,000 for various anticipated claims under the convention became law (TJ to the House of Representatives, 12 Jan. 1802). In the House on 5 Apr., Roger Griswold proposed a RESOLUTION directing the secretary of state to report if the repair of the corvette had been for the purpose of readying it for use by the United States or to prepare it to be returned to France. During the course of the ensuing debate, which occupied much of two days, James A. Bayard declared in support of the resolution that if the *Berceau* "was repaired as an American vessel, the expenditure was legal; if as a French vessel, it was not legal" and the refitting was "wanton and extravagant." Giles took the lead in opposing the resolution, saying at one point that "it appeared to him the most disorganizing motion that had ever been made in that House." To Bayard's claim that the measure was simply "an inquiry into facts," Giles responded that it was "an inquiry into motive." However, Giles wanted to show that the administration had nothing to hide. He took the position that he "was not disposed to deny an atom of information that was required to en-lighten our minds" and succeeded in getting the measure amended into a request for information only. The resolution passed by unanimous vote on 6 Apr.: "That the President of the United States be requested to direct the proper officer to lay before this House copies of all papers and documents which relate to the sale, purchase, and repairs, of the corvette Berceau; and, also, a statement of the sums paid to the respective officers and men of that vessel, specifying the period for which the payments were made; together with copies of all communications between the Government of the United States and any authorized agents of the French nation relative thereto." After passing the resolution, the House named Griswold and Giles as a committee to present it to TJ. On 8 Apr., Griswold reported to the House "that the committee had, according to order, performed that service, and that the President signified to them that he would attend to the subject contained in the resolution of the House" (*Annals*, 11:1133-54; JHR, 4:180-4).

WHEN YOU SHALL HAVE MADE YOUR USES OF IT: in the debates on 6 Apr., perhaps in reference to the August letter from Brown to Lincoln, Giles said that he "held in his hand a paper" supporting his assertion that the Adams administration made the decision to restore the *Berceau* to France (*Annals*, 11:1142-3).

¹ Word interlined.
² Preceding four words interlined.

From Louis Portas

Poliez le grand en Suisse.
Canton de Vaud Le 6e. Avril 1802.

Si Votre Excellence, a la bonté de se rapeller, de moy et de m'avoir vû a Sette, lors de son retour d'un Voyage en Italie. J'espere qu'elle voudra bien pardonner, la liberté que Je prends, de luy Recommander, un honnete Laboureur nommé Raymond, natif de l'helvetie, qui v'a sétablir en Amerique avec son Epouze & ses cinq Enfants; il desire se raprocher d'une petite colonie Etablie par ses compatriotes a fierst Wineyard au Kentuky—sur la Rive de L'Ohio—J'ose prier votre Excellence, si cela se peut, de vouloir bien luy faire accorder, dans le susdit endroit, une Concession de Terres, qui le mette a même d'y deployer son industrie—comme l'acquisition dans un pays quelconque, de Braves et honnetes citoyens, est toujours une Chose desirable dans tous les pays civilisés, et que c'est sous ce point de vue, que je Considere le sieur Raymond & sa famille Je me flatte, que vous voudrés bien y trouver l'excuse, de cette interruption, & Agréer le Respectueux homage de Votre Tres humble & trs obeïssant serviteur

LOUÏS PORTAS

EDITORS' TRANSLATION

Poliez-le-Grand, Switzerland,
Canton of Vaud 6 Apr. 1802

If your excellency is kind enough to remember me and having seen me at Sète upon his return from a trip to Italy, I hope that he will be willing to forgive the liberty that I take to recommend an honest husbandman named Raymond, a native of Switzerland, who is going to settle in America with his wife and his five children; he wishes to be near a small colony established by his compatriots at First Vineyard in Kentucky, on the banks of the Ohio. I make bold to beg your excellency to be willing to grant him, in the aforementioned place, a land concession that would enable him to put his skills to work. As the acquisition, in whatever country, of good and honest citizens is always something to be desired in every civilized country, and since it is from that point of view that I envisage Monsieur Raymond and his family, I like to think that you will kindly find in that perspective the pardon for this interruption, and accept the respectful tribute of your very humble and very obedient servant,

LOUÏS PORTAS

RC (ViW); at head of text: "a Son Excellence Monsr. Jefferson, President des Etats unis de l'Amerique à Philadelphie"; endorsed by TJ as received 23 Feb. 1804 and so recorded in SJL.

M'AVOIR VÛ A SETTE: TJ passed through Sète (Cette), a port on the southern coast of France, in May 1787, as he returned to Paris through southern France after visiting Italy. He also had some correspondence with a mercantile firm there, Guiraud & Portas. Of that firm, he wrote in 1788: "I saw one of the partners when at Cette, who spoke English well, is familiar with English usages in commerce, is sensible, and has the appearance of being a good man. But I do not recollect whether the person I describe was Guirrard or Portas. The

other partner does not speak English." Nicholas Guiraud, who held a consular appointment from the United States in the 1780s, was very likely the partner who spoke English (Vol. 9:613-14; Vol. 11:446; Vol. 12:228; Vol. 13:297-8; Vol. 14:60, 62n; Vol. 15:423).

Swiss vineyard workers led by John James Dufour had settled on the Kentucky River to raise grapes at a place they called First Vineyard. In 1802, they were in the process of obtaining land to move the enterprise to Indiana Territory. Frederick Louis RAYMOND joined the group there, at their colony named New Switzerland, in 1804 (Perret Dufour, *The Swiss Settlement of Switzerland County Indiana* [Indianapolis, 1925], 16, 18, 49, 231, 307; Vol. 32:529-33; Dufour to TJ, 15 Jan. 1802).

To the Senate

GENTLEMEN OF THE SENATE

I nominate Henry Potter of North Carolina, now a judge of the 5th. Circuit court to be judge of the District court of North Carolina become vacant by the death of John Sitgreaves.

TH: JEFFERSON
April 6. 1802

RC (DNA: RG 46, EPEN, 7th Cong., 1st sess.); endorsed by a Senate clerk. PrC (DLC). Recorded in SJL with notation "nomn H. Potter judge."

Meriwether Lewis delivered this nomination for HENRY POTTER to the Senate on 6 Apr., where it was immediately read and ordered to lie for consideration. On the next day, the Senate confirmed it and TJ signed the commission. NOW A JUDGE: Potter was one of TJ's interim appointments, and the Senate confirmed him as a judge of the Fifth Circuit Court on 26 Jan., the date on his permanent commission for that judgeship. JOHN SITGREAVES had served as district court judge from the time of his appointment in December 1790 until his death on 4 Mch. 1802 (FC of commissions in Lb in DNA: RG 59, MPTPC; JEP, 1:401, 405, 418-19; Biog. Dir. Cong.; Washington, Papers, Pres. Ser., 7:95). For Nathaniel Macon's earlier recommendations of Potter, see Vol. 33:620-1 and Vol. 34:109-10, 176-7.

To Albert Gallatin

TH:J. TO MR GALLATIN   Apr. 7. 1802.

The inclosed was communicated to me by DeWitt Clinton. he did not say, tho' doubtless he meant it in confidence. but unless restrained specially to *personal* confidence, I always think myself at liberty to communicate things to the head of the department to which the subject belongs. I shall be glad to recieve the letter back to-day to be returned

RC (NHi: Gallatin Papers); written on same side as address, in an unidentified hand, "The President of the United States"; addressed on verso: "The Secretary of the Treasury"; endorsed. Not recorded in SJL. Enclosure: see below.

Clinton may have given TJ a letter, dated 13 Mch., which he had received from Samuel Osgood at New York. Osgood reported on prospects for Gallatin's proposal that the Manhattan Company take charge of remittances to Holland for the payment of the Dutch debt (RC in NHi: Gallatin Papers). Evidently Clinton allowed Gallatin to keep the letter. For the proposal, which Gallatin had made through Aaron Burr, the bank's Washington representative, see Kline, Burr, 2:680-1.

From John S. Lillie

SIR/   Boston Goal April 7th 1802

Your well known candor induses me, although I acknowledge it to be a painful task, to be under the disagreeable necessity, to solicit an appointment, under your administration.

I am a young man, and commenced Bussiness in the Mercantile line, but, in consequence of my takeing a very active and decided part [in the] *politics* of the Day; became obnoxious to the Party who stile them[selves] *Federalists*; consequently suffered very considerably in my Bussiness. In the year '99, I quitted the Mercantile employ, disposed of my property in trade, and came forward in the arduous task of Editor of the *Constitutional Telegraphe*, in which Bussiness I have sacrificed my little property, and am reduced to the disagreeable alternative of soliciting an appointment.

I am now suffering 3 Months *close imprisonment*, together with a fine of $100, for publishing a supposed Libel, on the "*Lord Chief Justice of the Common Law of England*"; which appellation, His Honor *Judge Dana*, was pleased to apply to himself.

In Septbr. 1800 Providence was pleased to bless me with a Son, which I had Baptized at the *Old South Church* with *your name*, in honor & respect for your Excellencys character; this Child is now 18 Months old, & has *this Day*, by particular request, paid a visit to the *Venerable*, & *patriotic, Samuel Adams Esqr*, formerly your Co-patriot in Congress, a character whom I am proud to rank as one of my best friends.

If, Sir, at present, or even at any future period, you should think proper to honor me with your confidence, by confering on me any office of profit & trust, under your administration, which if I know my own heart, I can say I have exerted myself to the best of my small abilities to promote, without any viewes of profit, or emolument, but merely from principle itself.

If your Excellency should want any information [respec]ting my character &c, *Doctor Eustis*, or Col. *Varnum*, [...] the former, can give you the requisite. You will excuse Sir, the freedom I take in thus addressing you, and give me leave to subscribe myself with sentiments of the highest honor, and respect, Your Excellencys Devoted, Humble Servant.   JOHN S LILLIE

RC (DNA: RG 59, LAR); torn; at head of text: "Thomas Jefferson Esqr President of the United States"; endorsed by TJ as received 26 Apr. and "for some appointment" and so recorded in SJL.

John Sweetser Lillie (1766-1842), nephew of prominent Boston merchant John Sweetser, took over as publisher of Samuel S. Parker's semi-weekly *Constitutional Telegraphe* in October 1800 and continued as its editor until March 1802, when he began a three-month imprisonment for libel. After his release, he served thirty years as a pension clerk in the U.S. loan office and was vice president of the Republican Institution and of the Massachusetts Charitable Society (Brigham, *American Newspapers*, 1:280; Nathaniel B. Shurtleff, *A Topographical and Historical Description of Boston*, 2d rev. ed. in 2 pts. [Boston, 1872], 2:619-22; *Constitutional Telegraphe*, 30 Sep. 1801; Boston *Daily Evening Transcript*, 19 Aug. 1842; Lillie to TJ, 12 Oct. 1803).

PUBLISHING A SUPPOSED LIBEL: Lillie's *Constitutional Telegraphe* for 4 Feb. 1801 referred to an unsigned piece in the *New-England Palladium* of 27 Jan. 1801 that was "fabricated" by the "illuminati Doctor, one of the pious editors, or the lord chief justice of the *common law of England*" to disparage TJ's character. Judge Francis Dana took offense, and both Lillie and John Vinal, the author of the anonymous article, were indicted and tried for libel. Only Lillie went to jail (Pasley, *Tyranny of Printers*, 141, 276-77; Boston *New-England Palladium*, 27 Jan. 1801; *Constitutional Telegraphe*, 4, 14, and 18 Feb. 1801, 24 Mch. 1802).

Lillie's SON, Thomas Jefferson Lillie, was baptized in the Old South Meeting House in Boston where SAMUEL ADAMS had been a member since June 1789 (Hamilton Andrews Hill, *History of the Old South Church [Third Church] Boston 1669-1884*, 2 vols. [Boston, 1889-90], 2:247, 285; Dedham *Columbian Minerva*, 18 Sep. 1800).

From Albert Gallatin

SIR,   Treasury Department April 8th. 1802

I have the honor to enclose a copy of an Act, in relation to the Direct Tax, passed a few days ago, and a letter of Edward Croft, lately appointed a Commissioner for the first division of South carolina.

The last section of the Act, was introduced on my particular suggestion, and with a view to the completion of the assessment in South Carolina; & I now respectfully submit to you the propriety of making the contemplated allowance to the inspectors, whenever the commissioners shall think it necessary, and to the commissioners at all events, provided, that the same shall not in any case have a retrospective effect.

I have the honor to be with great respect Sir, Your most obedt. Servt.   ALBERT GALLATIN

RC (DLC); in a clerk's hand, signed by Gallatin; at foot of text: "The President of the United States"; endorsed by TJ as received from the Treasury Department on 9 Apr. and "S. Carola Direct Tax" and so recorded in SJL. Enclosures: (1) "An Act to amend an act, intituled 'An act to lay and collect a direct tax within the United States,'" 16 Mch. 1802 (Tr not found, but see U.S. Statutes at Large, 2:138-9). (2) Edward Croft's letter has not been found, but see John Drayton to TJ, 22 Feb., for his appointment.

The LAST SECTION of the enclosed act gave the Treasury secretary, under the direction of the president, the authority to augment the compensation of the commissioner and the principal and assistant assessors, in any division where it was found necessary in order to carry the Direct Tax into effect. The assessors or INSPECTORS were allowed up to $3 per day and the commissioners $5. Under the act of 1798, the commissioners received $3 per day and the principal and assistant assessors up to $1.50 (U.S. Statutes at Large, 1:590-1; 2:138-9).

From Samuel Quarrier

RESPECTED SIR   [on or before 8 April 1802]
once again I implore & solicit the extention of you'r benevolence to the unhappy writer of this, it might be supposed that I could not be so void of Delicasy & a sence of dignity in troubleing you On A subject wherein I'd meet with such denials as those i've experienced in this truely unhappy business—let me assure you that nothing under heaven could actuate this intrusive importuning in me, but from the wretchedness of my condition, I've left nothing undon I could do to aleviate it, i've tried to get into any business I could do, but without accomplishing my intentention, I've tried to aleviate my situation as much as was in my power, for believe me Respected Sir, if it had been in any way I could avoid troubleing you I should not have ever presumed to do it, unfortunately it is not all I want of you is as much as will take me to Richmond, where I hope in god to establish an independence of Character & good conduct under the excellent auspices of my Father, & Judge With, It's my intention to profit from my past imprudent & misfortunate actions, by A steady assidious, & industrious exercise of the first business I can procure an occupation in—I feele copiously what arises from an inactive life, by recent experience not to ever permit, the like to gain A preponderanc over me again—I'me well awar that you're many applications to the same affect this is, & that by as frequent an exercise to the solicitations you receive, in bestowing you'r benevolince you'd injur yourself materially—I appeal to just heaven in regard to myselfe, that if I could avoid troubling you in any respect whatever I would not do it, it is A melancholy truth that i'me destitute of the means of existance, except upon means that may implicate me in the same dilemma I've recently emancipated from—The longer I remain in this place the more my *situation* will become distressing, if the means where in my power to leave it, how happy should I be to embrace an immediate exit—I hope & trust you will grant the extention of you'r benevolent humanity in behalfe of the miserable son of Alexr. Quarrier—he is resolved his futur conduct shall give you no cause to repent of you'r generosity, but the reverse, that through you'r means you'r restored an indiscreet son to his

Father, & friend, A man to society to be instrumental & beneficial to them, & himselfe. At the time I recieved the 25 Dolls. from you it was my intention to have left this place immediately, but from unforseen circumstances it was impossible—I'me glad to say that where the means but in my power theres nothing to impeede my leaving this without Delay—from those reasons here given & more I could give if necessary, you'r forgivness for this almost unpardonable innovation, I hope for & you'r granting me the aid that my unfortunate condition may intitle me to, with those sentiments I remain one whose situation perhaps intitles him more to the sencebility of mankind, than to the persecutions of the world, which last he's experienced with unrelenting perceverance—

With great respect & esteem   SAML QUARRIER

RC (DLC); undated; addressed: "The President of the U States"; endorsed by TJ as received 8 Apr. and so recorded in SJL.

JUDGE WITH: George Wythe.

THE 25 DOLLS. FROM YOU: on 2 Feb. 1802, TJ sent Quarrier $25 to enable him to return to his father in Richmond (Vol. 36:497-8).

To the Senate

GENTLEMEN OF THE SENATE.

In order to satisfy as far as is in my power the desire expressed in your resolution of the 6th. inst. I now transmit you a letter from John Read, agent for the US. before the board of Commissioners under the VIth. article of the treaty with Great Britain, to the Attorney General, bearing date the 25th. of April 1801. in which he gives a summary view of the proceedings of those Commissioners, and of the principles established or insisted on by a majority of them.

Supposing it might be practicable for us to settle by negociation with Great Britain the principles which ought to govern the decisions under the treaty, I caused instructions to be given to mr Read to analyse the claims before the board of Commissioners, to class them under the principles on which they respectively depended, and to state the sum depending on each principle, or the amount of each description of debt. the object of this was that we might know what principles were most important for us to contend for, and what others might be conceded without much injury. he performed this duty, and gave in such a statement during the last summer. but the chief clerk of the Secretary of state's office being absent on account of sickness, and the only person acquainted with the arrangement of the papers of the office, this particular document cannot at this time be found. having however been myself in possession of it a few days after it's reciept, I then transcribed from it, for my own use, the recapitulation of the amount of each description of debt. a copy of this transcript I shall subjoin hereto, with assurances that it is substantially correct, and with the hope that it will give a view of the subject sufficiently precise to fulfill the wishes of the Senate. to save them the delay of waiting till a copy of the Agent's letter could be made, I send the original, with the request that it may be returned at the convenience of the Senate.

TH: JEFFERSON
April 8. 1802.

British claims under the VIth. article, distinguished into Classes, including interest to different dates within the year 1798.

	£ s d sterling
for interest during the war alone	120.645–11–1¼
for paiments into the treasuries, loan offices &c.	171.795– 0–6½
on account of impediments under the instalment laws of S. Carolina	337.868– 2–0
for alledged unlawful decisions of courts	24.658– 4–3¾
by firms in part citizens of the US.	162.483–12–4¾
debts due from states, late provinces	4.839–14–0
all description of refugees except N. Carolina	753.182– 4–2¾
on account of debts discharged in depreciated paper money	205.795–15–5½
Proprietary debts	296.778–13–8
Legal impediments generally	3,560.585–10–4½
24.809.969.37 D. =	5,638.629– 8–1

RC (DNA: RG 46, EPFR, 7th Cong., 1st sess.); endorsed by Senate clerks. PrC (DLC). Recorded in SJL as a communication to the Senate with notation "amt of claims under VIth art. Brit. treaty." Enclosure not found. Printed in ASP, *Foreign Relations*, 2:427.

In executive session on 6 Apr. concerning the convention with Great Britain and TJ's message of 29 Mch., the Senate passed a RESOLUTION stating "That the President of the United States be requested to cause to be laid before the Senate, the amount and description of claims, preferred under the sixth article of the British Treaty, and which would have been chargeable to the United States, if the principles contended for, by the British commissioners, had been established as the rules of decision by which those claims should be determined" (RC in DLC, in Samuel A. Otis's hand and attested by him, endorsed by TJ: "British debts"; JEP, 1:418).

Griffith Evans, the secretary of the bilateral commission established to handle claims under Article 6 of the Jay Treaty, submitted the STATEMENT of claims by category (John Bassett Moore, ed., *Inter-*

national Adjudications, Modern Series, Volume III: Arbitration of Claims for Compensation for Losses and Damages Resulting from Lawful Impediments to the Recovery of Pre-War Debts [New York, 1931], 22, 354-5). For TJ's RECAPITULA-TION of the statement, which he copied in the postscript above, see Vol. 34:696.

From Henry Voigt

SIR   [before 9 April 1802]

When I had your watch before to rectify, although I saw a fault in it at that time, as it was in the *construction of the movement,* (not a defficiency in workmanship,) & not having sufficient experience of the operation of a movement on that construction, I thought it certainly would answer.—But since I have had it my possession this time, I have been more particular in examining, not only the accuracy of the workmanship, but the principles upon which the striking movement was made.—In this I have now made some alteration, and find the watch to go, since, very regular, and cannot see how it is possible to miss striking now, if it be regularly wound up—

There is a Clock in my possession at present made by Mr Rittenhouse. which has a chime of Bells with tunes, and an orrery, in the Arch of the Dial, of the Seven Planets, moving in their respective Orbits: but not on their Axes.—There are no Satellites.—The Planets move in regular, periodical times, but contentric.—The Sun has likewise a concentic motion only. It shews the equation of time, the Moons Nodes, & the Eliptic, on separate circles, or smaler dials on each corner of the main dial; a description of the whole would be too long; I can only say, it is an excellent piece of workmanship in every respect, and not the worse for the length of time it has been in use, and is now put in the best order. The owner wants to part with her, and thinks it would only suit the Philosophical Society or perhaps yourself, as he wishes it to go into the hands of a Person who is acquainted with Astronomy.

You will pardon me to take the liberty of mentioning to you, that an Instrument has been shewn to me for proving Gun powder invented by Mr Jos Leacock.—I have attended its performance and found it very accurate.—I think it full as good as the Howitzer, if not better—It takes only 16 grains of Powder for a proof, which is a saving of powder,—and time may be saved as four is to one.

I am Sir your Obt Huble Servt   HENRY VOIGT

PS: The other watch shall be done, as soon, and sent as posibly—
                                                              HV:

RC (MHi); undated; endorsed by TJ as received 9 Apr. and so recorded in SJL.

YOUR WATCH: see TJ to Voigt, 5 Mch. The CLOCK Voigt describes may be the magnificent tall-case clock constructed by David RITTENHOUSE in the late 1760s for Joseph Potts of Philadelphia. Standing more than nine feet in height, it was owned by Thomas Pryor from 1774 until his death in 1801. Passing through several subsequent owners, the clock is currently in the possession of Drexel University. Voigt may also be describing a similarly elaborate Rittenhouse clock that dates to the early 1780s, which is now owned by the Pennsylvania Hospital. This clock is notable for including the planet Uranus (discovered in 1781) in its orrery, which conforms with the seven planets Voigt mentions in the above letter

(William Barton, *Memoirs of the Life of David Rittenhouse* [Philadelphia, 1813], 203; Brook Hindle, *David Rittenhouse* [Princeton, 1964], 25-6; Thomas G. Morton, *The History of the Pennsylvania Hospital, 1751-1895*, rev. ed. [Philadelphia, 1897], 337-9; PMHB, 56 [July 1932], 237-8; George H. Eckardt, *Pennsylvania Clocks and Clockmakers* [New York, 1955], 141-2).

Joseph LEACOCK of Philadelphia was a former watchmaker and glass manufacturer who was appointed the city's inspector of pot and pearl ash in 1790. In 1792 and 1793, he advised TJ on potash manufacturing and also sought his charity (Vol. 24:614, 658-60, 661, 715-16; Vol. 27:510-11, 596). A letter from Leacock to TJ, dated 5 Apr., recorded in SJL as received 9 Apr. with the notation "W." has not been found.

From Henry Dearborn

SIR,   War Department 9th. April 1802.

The following gentleman are proposed to your consideration, as Candidates for military Agencies: (viz)

For the Northern Department
    Peter Gansevoort, of Albany.
For the middle Department
    William Linnard of Philadelphia.
For the Southern Department
    Abraham D.[1] Abrahams of Savannah.

I have the honor to be, Sir, with high consideration, Yr. Obt. Servant   H. DEARBORN

RC (DLC); in a clerk's hand, signed by Dearborn, with an alteration by TJ (see note below); at foot of text: "The President of the United States"; endorsed by TJ as received from the War Department on 10 Apr. and "Nominations. Peter Gansevoort &c" and so recorded in SJL. FC (Lb in DNA: RG 107, LSP).

Sometime after writing this letter, Dearborn sent an undated communica-

tion to TJ: "Sir I am now informed by Genl Jackson that Mr. Abrahams, proposed for a Military Agent in Georgia, is Abraham D. Abrahams, and not Joseph Abrahams. with due respects I am Sir Your Humbl. Servt" (RC in DLC; in a clerk's hand; signed by Dearborn; addressed: "The President of the United States"; endorsed by TJ as received from the War Department in Apr. 1802 and "Nominn. Abrahams").

The Military Peace Establishment Act provided for the creation of the MILITARY AGENCIES, which replaced the quartermaster's department. The agents were responsible for obtaining and transporting military stores, hospital supplies for the army, and goods for Indian annuities. An army officer at each post would act as assistant military agent (U.S. Statutes at Large, 2:133, 136; Dearborn to Gansevoort, to Linnard, and to Abrahams, 5 May 1802, Dearborn to assistant military agents, 6 May, in DNA: RG 107, LSMA).

TJ nominated the three candidates on 27 Apr., the Senate approved them on the 29th, and their appointments as mili-

tary agents dated from that day. PETER GANSEVOORT was an officer of New York troops during the American Revolution. In 1777, he received a resolution of thanks from Congress for his defense of Fort Schuyler. William LINNARD later served a number of years as a quartermaster officer. Abraham David ABRAHAMS was the military agent for the southern department until 1809 (JEP, 1:422-3; Heitman, *Dictionary*, 1:150, 444, 634; DAB, s.v. "Gansevoort, Peter"; TJ to the Senate, 27 Apr. 1802).

[1] First name and initial interlined by TJ in place of "Joseph."

From William Kilty, William Cranch, and John Thomson Mason

The Case of the United States against Daniel McGinnis

Daniel McGinnis having been much beat and abused by a certain James Carroll and others in the Month of July 1801 Gave information to the Grand Jury and a presentment was made by them at September Term 1801

Daniel McGinnis was recognised in the sum of fifty Dollars with John Barber and Alexander King his securities in the sum of twenty five dollars each for his appearance at the next Court to testify for the United States against James Carroll. The Recognizance was called and forfeited at December Term 1801 and a writ of Fiere Facias has issued to March Term 1802 which has been returned Nulla Bona

The Court are credibly informed that McGinnis was prevented from attending agreeably to his recognizance by his being on the water and by the badness of the Weather which detained him longer than he had expected—

And in as much as there appears to have been no neglect on his part and he has been very much injured by the beating as above stated; and in as much as he did appear at this Term and prosecute the accused to conviction and it would be an additional hardship on him to pay the forfeited recognizance being a poor labouring man.

We hereby respectfully Recommend to the President of the United

States to remit the whole of the said forfeited Recognizance to the said McGinnis and his Securities—

WILLIAM KILTY
WILLIAM CRANCH.
JOHN T. MASON Atty for the
Dist. of Columbia
April 9th 1802

RC (DNA: RG 59, GPR); in a clerk's hand, signed by Kilty, Cranch, and Mason; with TJ's opinion at foot of text: "April 11. 1802. Let a pardon issue Th: Jefferson"; endorsed by TJ as received 10 Apr. and so recorded in SJL with notation "recommend McGinnie for pardon"; also endorsed by TJ: "Mc.Ginnie's case for pardon." Enclosure: Certificate of Uriah Forrest, clerk of the circuit court of Washington County, 9 Apr. 1802, attesting to the accuracy of the facts in the case of Daniel McGinnis as stated by Kilty, Cranch, and Mason (MS in same).

TJ issued a pardon on 13 Apr., remitting the fines incurred by DANIEL MCGINNIS, JOHN BARBER, and ALEXANDER KING (FC in Lb in same). McGinnis may be the same person from whom TJ received a pardon request on 23 Jan. 1806. Signing with a mark, the petitioner was identified as "Daniell McGinnas" and described as a "free mulatto man" who was convicted and fined for assault and battery (RC in same).

THE COURT: Kilty served as the presiding judge and Cranch as an associate judge of the circuit court for the District of Columbia (Vol. 33:380, 416-17).

From Thomas Mann Randolph

DEAR SIR,   Edgehill April 9. 1802.

Your letter inclosing Captain Lewises memorandum came to me regularly: I return him thanks for the information and express my gratitude to you for the credit you offerr me with the Georgia merchants. Long sickness or a broken limb should allways be deemed possible and provided for before hand.—Martha received the medal today: the execution is fine but Ceracchi was much better worth copying than Houdon. So good an imitation of the marble would be admirable.—The Country is just begining to smile here but the earth is very bare yet from drought. Your Tufton farm is an ornament to the County.—We are all well.

yours most affectionately   TH: M. RANDOLPH

RC (MHi); endorsed by TJ as received 19 Apr. and so recorded in SJL.

YOUR LETTER: TJ to Thomas Mann Randolph, 28 Mch.

John H. Craven leased TJ's TUFTON FARM (Vol. 32:108-10).

[196]

To Nicholas Reib

SIR   Washington Apr. 9. 1802.

On the reciept of your letter of Mar. 27. I had a thorough examination of your case made. the inclosed papers will shew you the result and that the Executive having done in it every thing which the law authorises, no applications to them can be of any avail to you. I return you the papers inclosed in your letter to me. Accept my best wishes.   TH: JEFFERSON

PrC (DLC); at foot of text: "Mr. Nicholas Reib"; endorsed by TJ in ink on verso. Enclosures not found, but see below.

On 8 Apr., Albert Gallatin forwarded TJ a letter of the same date received from Joseph Nourse, the register of the Treasury, regarding Reib's claim. In his brief cover letter, Gallatin described the information provided by Nourse to be "as correct as can be obtained" (RC in DLC; undated; endorsed by TJ as a letter of 8 Apr. received from the Treasury Department on 9 Apr. and "Reib's case" and so recorded in SJL, but as received 8 Apr.). In his reply to Gallatin, Nourse stated that he could not locate a record of John Pierce's certificate to Reib either in the War Department or in the register of certificates issued. Nourse noted that the register "is exceedingly numerous" and unindexed, "so that particular Corps cannot be correctly designated." Although he had not found the certificate, Nourse nevertheless assumed, based on Reib's credit of $135, that it was in the register. If more satisfactory information was required, Nourse suggested consulting William Simmons, the accountant of the War Department, since Nourse's own inquiry to him was limited to a request for the number and amount of Pierce's certificate to Reib (RC in same; Cunningham, *Process of Government*, 121, 330).

To Nicolas Gouin Dufief

SIR   Washington Apr. 10. 1802.

I recieved yesterday your favor of the 6th. and the books forwarded by mr Duane. La Grange's translations are new to me, and I am so much pleased with that of his Seneca, that I will thank you to forward me also his Lucretius with the Latin text. has the Seneca of La Grange been ever printed with the Latin text? if it has I should be glad if you would order it from France. if not, order me another French copy unbound: to which may be added, if you please Le Systeme du Monde par La Place, 2. vols. 8vo and La Religieuse de Diderot and Le bon sens said to be by him also, both in petit format. I will immediately desire mr Barnes to have paiment made of the bill inclosed in your last with the [...] additional.[1] Accept my best wishes.   TH: JEFFERSON

PrC (DLC); blurred; at foot of text: "Mr. Dufief"; endorsed by TJ in ink on verso.

De la nature des choses, published in Paris in 1794 and reprinted in 1799, paired N. de La Grange's French translation of *De Rerum Natura* by Titus LUCRETIUS Carus with the original Latin text (Sowerby, No. 4461).

LE SYSTEME DU MONDE: *Exposition du système du monde*, a work of astronomy by Pierre Simon Laplace that was published in Paris in 1796. James Monroe brought a copy of the work from France for TJ in 1797. However, only in 1809 did Monroe get his books unpacked and inform TJ that he had the title for him (Sowerby, No. 3801; RS, 1:348).

Denis Diderot did not write a book called LE BON SENS. The work that TJ wanted was probably *Le Bons sens: ou idées naturelles opposèes aux idèes surnaturelles*, an anonymous abridgment of Baron d'Holbach's *Systême de la Nature* (Sowerby, No. 1292). Another book titled *Le Bon sens* (Paris, 1788), published pseudonymously as from the pen of a gentleman of Breton, was by the Comte de Kersaint. TJ assembled a PETIT FORMAT collection of octavo and duodecimo editions that were of a practical size for reading (Douglas L. Wilson, *Jefferson's Books* [Charlottesville, 1996], 27).

BILL INCLOSED IN YOUR LAST: on 10 Apr., TJ asked John Barnes to remit to Dufief $25.75, the amount, with TJ's addition, of the invoice enclosed in Dufief's letter of the 6th (MB, 2:1070).

[1] Preceding four words interlined.

Memorandum from Albert Gallatin

[10 Apr. 1802]

The paper "Sinking fund" is sent to show Steeles sentiments in 1799 & the project then existing to destroy the sinking fund. Steele did not understand fully the subject & is mistaken as to the application of a particular law; but it is immaterial to the general purpose —

The letters from Baltimore give me hopes that we will not be losers by A. Brown's failure —

MS (DLC); entirely in Gallatin's hand; undated; on a scrap of paper, clipped at foot of text; addressed: "[Pr]esident of the United States"; endorsed by TJ as received from the Treasury Department on 10 Apr. and so recorded in SJL with notation "project in 1799. to stop paimt. of public debt"; also endorsed by TJ: "that in 1799. there was an intention to suppress sinking fund. i.e. stop paimt of debt." Enclosure: perhaps "A Review of the Sinking Fund Since the 8th of May, 1792, by John Steele as Comptroller," 29 Sep. 1799, prepared for the secretary of the Treasury (Henry M.

Wagstaff, ed., *The Papers of John Steele*, 2 vols. [Raleigh, N.C., 1924], 2:778-84).

BROWN'S FAILURE: the Treasury Department had endorsed Baltimore merchant Aquila Brown's bills of exchange on Amsterdam for the payment of the Dutch debt. The bills, including one for 60,000 guilders, were protested for nonpayment and returned to the Treasury Department (Gallatin, *Papers*, 13:760; 15:101, 563, 570; Wagstaff, *John Steele*, 1:299; Henry Wheaton, *Reports of Cases Argued and Adjudged in the Supreme Court of the United States*, 12 vols. [Philadelphia, 1816-27], 3:172-4).

From Nathaniel Ingraham,
with John Steele's Note

Rhode Island District &c. Bristol R.I.
April 10th. 1802.

The petition of Nathaniel Ingraham of Bristol in the District afore-said, mariner,

Respectfully sheweth,

That at the February term of the District Court, for Rhode Island District, AD. 1801, an Action quitam was prosecuted against him by John West Leonard, who sued as well in behalf of the United States as of himself for the sum of   Dollars:—That said Action was continued from said term to the May term of said Court, and thence certified up to the Circuit Court, at their Novr. term AD. 1801, when a Verdict & Judgment were rendered against your Petitioner for the sum of Fourteen Thousand Dollars & costs of suit:—And that Execution hath been sued forth thereon, & your Petitioner commit-ted by virtue of said Execution to Gaol, where he is now confined a Prisoner.

Now your Petitioner would beg leave humbly to represent, that the vessel, of which he was master, and about which he was prosecuted was captured, carried into New Providence and there condemned to-gether with all her Cargo:—That all the Property he had in the world, a small quantity of necessary household furniture and wearing apparel only excepted,—was lost in that condemnation:—That he is now poor, without any thing but the Labor of his hands to depend upon, advanced in life with a large and helpless family, besides a Par-ent bowed down with old age and sickness, to support:—And, that he must necessarily remain a Prisoner, without hope, the remnant of his days, dependent on charity for the necessaries of life, & afflicted with the cries of an afflicted family involved in equal distress, without the interposition of executive mercy.—Wherefore he humbly prays the Presidt. to take his unhappy case into his wise and humane con-sideration, and to remit the aforesaid Judgment in behalf of the United States, and to direct a discharge therefrom, or to extend such other relief as in the Executive wisdom & humanity may seem meet & proper, and he as in duty bound will ever pray, &c.

NATHANIEL INGRAHAM

[*Note by John Steele*]

I have no knowledge of the prosecution, except what may be col-lected from the petition. Before the Presidents decision, it wd. be well to obtain from the court or the Dist. Attn. a report on the case. By this report, if properly made, it will be easy to determine whether the Executive ought to interpose or not. *The violations of the act to prohibit the slave trade have been very frequent in R Island, and the difficulty of convicting offenders greater than elsewhere.*   J. S.

RC (DLC); in an unidentified hand, signed by Ingraham; at head of text: "To Thomas Jefferson, President of the United States"; a certificate subjoined below signature signed by 51 officeholders, merchants, tradesmen, and mariners of Rhode Island, including Jonathan Russell, Nathaniel Phillips, Gustavus Baylies, and several members of the D'Wolf family, testifies that Ingraham's circumstances are "truly represented" in his petition and "earnestly" recommending that his prayer be granted; note in Steele's hand written perpendicular to TJ's endorsement on verso of last sheet of petition signatures; endorsed by TJ as received 22 Apr. and "Petition to be discharged from jail" and so recorded in SJL.

Nathaniel Ingraham was captain of the sloop *Fanny*, a vessel owned by Rhode Island slave trader James D'Wolf. In the summer of 1800, the *Fanny* was returning from Africa with a cargo of 70 slaves bound for Savannah when it was captured by a British privateer and taken to New Providence, where the vessel was condemned. On 31 Dec. 1800, JOHN WEST LEONARD, a special prosecutor appointed by the Treasury Department, charged D'Wolf and Ingraham in the U.S. District Court of Rhode Island with engaging in the slave trade. A jury acquitted D'Wolf after a brief trial, but a U.S. circuit court found Ingraham guilty in November 1801, fined him $14,000 ($200 for each slave), and sentenced him to two years in prison. According to the historian Jay Coughtry, Ingraham was the only Rhode Islander ever imprisoned for violating the federal slave trade laws. TJ received additional petitions from Ingraham throughout 1802 and 1803, but the president was hesitant to grant a pardon, declaring that Ingraham's situation "merits no commiseration." After permitting him to serve out his two-year prison term, TJ remitted and released Ingraham from the federal government's moiety of the $14,000 judgment against him (Jay Coughtry, *The Notorious Triangle: Rhode Island and the African Slave Trade, 1700-1807* [Philadelphia, 1981], 222-3; TJ to Christopher Ellery, 9 May 1803; David Leonard Barnes to TJ, 8 Feb. 1804; presidential remission for Nathaniel Ingraham, 21 Feb. 1804, FC in Lb in DNA: RG 59, GPR).

To George Jefferson

DEAR SIR   Washington Apr. 10. 1802.

Your favors of the 2d. and 3d. are recieved, and I will attend to the having some funds remitted to you. you will recieve shortly a quarter cask and 2. boxes of wine shipped to you by mr Sheaff of Philadelphia, some nailrod and hoop iron from Roberts & Jones, to which will perhaps be added a quarter cask from Robertson & Brown of Norfolk, all to be forwarded to Monticello, where I expect to be for a fortnight or three weeks immediately after the rising of Congress. Accept my affectionate salutations.   TH: JEFFERSON

PrC (MHi); at foot of text: "Mr. George Jefferson"; endorsed by TJ in ink on verso. Recorded in SJL with notation "1. qr. cask Sherry & 2 boxes Sauterne from Sheaff 1. qr. cask Lisbon from Robertson & Brown."

According to SJL, TJ wrote ROBERTSON & BROWN on 10 Apr., but the letter has not been found. TJ requested that a quarter cask of dry Lisbon wine be sent to Monticello (MB, 2:1070). The 17 Apr. reply of the firm, recorded in SJL as received from Norfolk on the 22nd, is also missing.

From Philip Mazzei

A JEFFERSON   Pisa, 10 Apr. 1802.

Colle lettere di Milano mi pervengano[1] sul punto che son di partenza le 2 sue dei 29 Aprile 1800 e 17 Marzo 1801. Da queste vedo, che sonosi smarrite tutte le mie dall'8 xbre 1797 al 6 xbre 1800, e che le sue pure a me dirette ànno avuta la meda. sorte. Dopo l'indicata mia del 6 xbre 800, nel mandarlene la copia, il 5 Febb. 801, aggiunsi una breve descrizione dei mali della povera Italia, dove avrà veduto che le sedi delle scienze, in vece d'esser rispettate, come Ella à supposto, sono state le più perseguitate e straziate. Le scrissi susseguentemente il 2 Luglio, alla copia della qual lettera il 30 del do. mese, aggiunsi che il Corriere portore dell'originale era stato assassinato in Provenza, e Le mandai la traduzion toscana del suo Divino Discorso pronunziato nell'assumer la Presidenza degli S.U.[2] Il 28 7bre Le scrissi pochi versi, relativamente a dei noccioli di 4 qualità di pesche che Le mandai. Il 15 9bre Le diedi avviso della cambiale di £1417.10., rimessa da Mr. Jn. Barnes of George Town agli amici Vanstaphorst per me; dissi che supponevo venirmi da Lei (benchè non me ne sia venuto avviso nè prima nè dopo); Le mandai la 2.da copia della mia del 2 Luglio, e un'esemplar d'una 2da. edizione del suo discorso corretta e non piena d'errori come la prima che non avevo potuto correggere. In varie delle dette lettere Le dissi dei fatti, tendenti a provare che bisognerebbe mettere sur un meglior piede i. Consolati nei porti d'Italia, o di averci almeno un Consol generale salariato, o piuttosto un'Incaricato d'Affari, che potesse trattar direttamente con i varii Governi. Ora Le ne inculco la necessità con più calore, a motivo di quel che ò inteso ultimamente in Livorno da persone, della cui buona fede non posso dubitare. Ci bisogna qua una persona, che non solo invigili sulla condotta dei consoli e Viceconsoli, come ancora ò già detto in 2 lettere almeno, ma che abbia una reputazione onde poter influire sulla condotta degli Americani, i quali, o per deduzione dei nostri nemici, o di persona per altre cause interessata ad indurli in errore si conducono in maniera da non dar buona idea di loro stessi, da far poco onore ai lor compatriotti, e finalmente da progiudicare al commercio degli S.U.[3]

Ella probabilmente avrà ricevuto tutte le lettere che le ò mandata posteriormente a quella del 6 xbre 1800 per bastimenti americani, con quali spero pure di ricever le sue. Potendo, fanno i viaggi diretti tra Livorno e varii porti d'America.

S'io ritorno a tempo, come spero, Le mandero quest'anno poche piante di buone pesche e d'Uve da mangiare, e procurerò d'averne maggior quantità e varietà per gli anni venturi. Quanto all'uva, le manderò barbatelle in vece di maglioli, per maggior sicurezza che si attacchino, e perchè ne abbia il frutto più presto.

Quando ero in Pollonia diedi a frutto al C. G. P. 2500 zecchini, a condizione che doveva restituirmi il capitale il 13 xbre 1794. Sul principio pagò il frutto puntualmente, e poi, oltre al non avermi reso il capitale, à trascurato di pagare il frutto a segno, che ora al mio credito è di 3090. S'io moio prima d'esser pagato, è certo che la mia povera vedova e la mia cara Orfalina non n'avranno mai un soldo. L'inc. d'A. di Russia in Genova, mio A. mi da le maggiori speranze, che l'Imper. A., se ricorro a lui, mi farà pagare anche le spese di viaggio, e il Principino Cz., mio vero Amico, che qua [...]ebbe in Parigi, è l'intimo Amico di Alessandro. Ecco il motivo che mi fa intraprendere un sì lungo e disastroso viaggio, mentre cammino verso i 72 anni, e che m'impedisce di poter soccorrere adesso la famiglia Derieux; [per] cui ò speso in altri tempi più di 300 lire st.

Mi conservi la sua tanto a me cara benevolenza, e mi creda di vero cuore Suo Aff:mo

Servo e Amico &c.

EDITORS' TRANSLATION

TO JEFFERSON   Pisa, 10 April 1802.
   I received your two letters of 29 April 1800 and 17 March 1801, respectively, among the letters which came to me from Milan as I was about to leave. I learn from these that all my letters, from 8 December 1797 to 7 December 1800, have been lost, and that your letters to me have suffered the same fate. In sending you a copy of 5 February 1801, of my previous letter of 6 December 1800, I added a brief description of the sufferings of poor Italy, wherein you will have noted that the seats of the sciences, instead of being respected as you had supposed, have been the most persecuted and tortured. Subsequently, I wrote you on 2 July, adding, to a copy of my letter of the 30th of the aforementioned month, that the messenger, bearer of the original copy, had been assassinated in Provence. At the same time I sent you the

Tuscan translation of the inspired speech you delivered on assuming the presidency of the United States. On 28 September, I wrote you a few lines about the four kinds of peach stones which I had sent you. On 15 November, I sent you word about a bill of exchange for 1417 francs, 10 sous, sent to me by Mr. John Barnes of Georgetown through our friends the Van Staphorsts. I said that I believed it came from you, although I never received any word to that effect either before or since. I sent you a second copy of my letter of 2 July, and a copy of the second edition of your speech, now corrected and no longer full of errors as it was in the first printing, which I had had no chance to correct. In several of the aforementioned letters I mentioned some facts to show the need for putting the consulates of the Italian ports on a firmer footing, or at least why we should have a salaried consul general, or better a chargé d'affaires, with power to deal directly with the various governments. Now I insist more than ever that such steps are necessary, because of what I heard recently in Leghorn from persons whose sincerity I cannot doubt. Someone is needed here not only to supervise over the conduct of the consuls and vice-consuls, as I have already stated in at least two letters, but further, to influence by the weight of his own reputation the conduct of Americans who, led astray either by our enemies, or by other persons who for selfish reasons wish to lead them into error, behave in a less than favorable manner, reflect little honor on their compatriots, and harm American commerce.

You will probably have received all the letters I have sent you since the one of 6 December 1800 by American ships. I also hope to receive yours by the same channel, since American vessels can sail directly from Leghorn to various American ports.

If I return in time, as I hope to do, this year I shall send you a few young shoots of good peach trees and some edible grapes. In the future I shall not fail to see to it that you get more and of greater variety. As for the grapes, I shall send you shoots rather than slips, not only in the hope that they may take root with greater certainty, but also in order that you may enjoy their fruit much earlier.

When I was in Poland, I entrusted to the C.G.P. 2500 *zecchini* at an interest, on the condition that he returned to me my principal by 13 December 1794. At first, he paid the interest punctually, but then he not only failed to return the initial capital (the principal), but he also omitted to pay the interest on time. As a result, he now owes me 3090 *zecchini*. If I die before being paid, it is clear that my poor widow and my dear "orphelina" will never get a dime. The chargé d'affaires in Genoa, a friend to me, gives me high hopes that the Emperor A. will have my travel expenses covered, if I appeal to him, and the young prince Cz, who [. . .] in Paris, is intimate friend to Alexander. This is the reason why I undertake such a long and dangerous journey as I approach 72 years of age and that prevents me from helping, at this moment, the Derieux, for whom in the past I have already spent more than 300 pounds. I hope you will maintain your benevolence to me, which is so dear to me, and trust that I am truly your most affectionate servant and friend etc.

Dft (Archivio Filippo Mazzei, Pisa, Italy); part of a conjoined series of Mazzei's drafts of letters to TJ, where it precedes Mazzei's letter of 17 Apr. 1802 (see Margherita Marchione and Barbara B. Oberg, eds., *Philip Mazzei:*

The Comprehensive Microform Edition of his Papers, 9 reels [Millwood, N.Y., 1981], 6:908-10). RC recorded in SJL as received from Pisa on 19 Sep. 1802, but not found.

SON DI PARTENZA: in April 1802 Mazzei departed Pisa for a six-month trip to St. Petersburg in an effort to acquire his share of a pension, which Russia began to pay on assuming debt obligations from the final partitioning of Poland (Margherita Marchione and others, eds., *Philip Mazzei: Selected Writings and Correspondence*, 3 vols. [Prato, Italy, 1983], 3:209).

LE MANDAI LA 2.DA COPIA DELLA MIA DEL 2 LUGLIO: Mazzei to TJ, 2 July 1801, not found, but see Vol. 34:692n.

Mazzei also sought to collect money with interest from a loan he made in 1792 to Count Jan (Jean) Potocki (C.G.P.), the Polish historian and writer (Howard R. Marraro, "Unpublished Mazzei Letters to Jefferson," WMQ, 3d ser., 1 [1944], 391-2; RS, 3:44n).

LA MIA POVERA VEDOVA E LA MIA CARA ORFALINA: Mazzei's second wife, Antonia Antoni Mazzei, and their daughter, Elisabetta (Vol. 32:273-9).

IL PRINCIPINO CZ.: Adam Jerzy Czartoryski, son of Prince Adam K. Czartoryski, was a close friend of Russia's new emperor, Alexander I (Marchione and others, eds., *Philip Mazzei*, 3:209).

[1] Mazzei here canceled "altempostesso, ma," meaning "at the same time, but."
[2] Canceled: "stampato alla macchia," meaning "printed clandestinely."
[3] Canceled: "La Danimarca parche abbia riconosciuto la necessità o almeno l'utilità di un console generale in questi porti, poichè nè à ultimamente creato uno che deve[...]," meaning "It looks like Denmark has acknowledged the necessity or at least the advisability of having a general consul in these ports, since it has recently created one, who is supposed to [...]."

From Deborah Stewart

SIR.   Philadelphia April 10th. 1802

While your attention is directed to so many, and such important Public objects, I feel considerable reluctance in claiming a share of it for the family of Gen: Stewart, which was known to you, and which I flatter myself you have not entirely forgotten. Permit me however with perfect reliance on your benevolence and politeness, to solicit your Patronage for the eldest son of that family; who is entering into life, with a charecter and talents that reflect honor on his Father's memory, while they promise to his Mother and several brothers and sisters that support and protection, which an unexpected change in thier fortunes, has rendered almost the only remaining source of consolation and hope. I will not encroach further on your time sir, with the feelings that arise out of this subject; but I have confided to Gen: Smith the task of presenting to you a letter from my son to me, in which his views and wishes are explained: I pray you to receive and countenance his application. It is in my power to furnish the most respectable testimonials of his worth and diligence: independant of a

Parents praise; and be assured that while you confer on me, the highest obligation, I can receive, you will awaken in his mind the warmest sentiments of gratitude. I shall be happy to be honored with an expression of your disposition on this occasion, either through Gen Smith, or in any other way that you may think proper.

I pray you to accept the assurances of my best wishes for your health and happiness, and to believe that I am your sincere frend and obdt. sev: D STEWART.

RC (DNA: RG 59, LAR); endorsed by TJ as received from Mrs. Stewart on 14 Apr. and "William Stewart her son, to be Consul at Smyrna" and so recorded in SJL.

In 1781, Blair McClenachan's daughter Deborah (1763-1823) married Walter Stewart, a native of Ireland who served in the Pennsylvania Continental Line during the Revolutionary War and retired as a brevet brigadier general. Her husband was a prominent merchant, member of the state militia, inspector of the revenue, and surveyor of customs for Philadelphia prior to his death in 1796 (PMHB, 47 [1923], 275; APS, *Transactions*, new ser., 42, pt. 1 [1952], 202, 299; *Philadelphia Minerva*, 18 June 1796).

ELDEST SON: born in 1781, William Stewart was one of eight children and a godson of George Washington. He received an appointment as the first U.S. consul at the Turkish port of Smyrna with a commission signed by TJ and dated 3 May 1802 (FC in Lb in DNA: RG 59, PTCC; JEP, 1:422, 423; PMHB, 22 [1898], 381-2).

From Caspar Wistar

DEAR SIR   Philada. Apl. 10. 1802—
I have delayed my reply to your favour of March 22d. in order to inform myself more fully respecting some of the heads of your inquiry—   My acquaintance with Dr Barnwell commenced about a year & a half since, in consequence of a communication he made to the A.P.S., which was ordered to be published, but was lost by the Printer. He has since then sometimes visited me, & conversed respecting medicine, but I have only seen his practice in a single case.

From his conversation I learn that he has made several voyages to Asia in the medical service of the British East India Company, & that he has thought & read a great deal upon the diseases of warm climates; he has also read much on medicine generally.

From his conversation I have likewise derived an opinion that his practice was successful, & that he was treated with respect by the Physicians who superintend the medical affairs of the East India Company.

As to his moral character I can say nothing from my own knowledge, & he is so much a stranger here, that but few persons know him. He was introduced to our friend Mr Patterson about the year 1792 soon after his arrival from Ireland—Mr P. has seen him frequently since then, & considers his conduct as uniformly correct & regular, & as an instance mentions that the Doctor when stationed (as Surgeon in the service of the United States) at Norfolk, happened to be in Philadelphia, upon furlough, at the time a yellow fever appeared at Norfolk, & that he instantly repaired to his Post.   Another Gentleman who had some knowledge of a case which the Doctor attended, considers him as very attentive & very successfull, but as extremely attached to his own opinions, & disposed to attend but little to those of others who differ in sentiment from him.

Having thus stated to you my opportunities of forming an opinion, I will add that my opinion is certainly very favourable, as he seems to possess three great requisites, viz Experience, Knowledge of the experience of others, and Assiduity,—his experience seems to be of that kind which will be wanted in the place under consideration, as it has been acquired by voyages to very warm parts of the Globe. Under these Circumstances I cannot but regard him as an acquisition for the place, & would certainly appoint him, (if I were to make an appointment) in preference to any one I recollect that would be willing to engage in the business. At the same time I ought to add that I feel some solicitude on the subject, as these sentiments are the result of conversations, & not of a knowledge of his practice, & as he does not appear to have acquired much knowledge of the World & therefore may not avoid those difficulties in the regulation & management of a Hospital which will arise in the way of every one, but may be avoided by management & address—This last circumstance arises from his recluse & studious habits, which probably will dispose him to devote himself to his business, & this probability is increased by the ardour which he shows in the cultivation of medical Science.

This sir is a full, candid, & unreserved, account of all that I know respecting the gentleman in question, & I assure you that your injunctions were unnecessary, for the importance of the subject must excite very strong sensations indeed in the mind of every person of reflection, & your truly paternal solicitude has produced in me such sentiments of grateful respect as would effectually do away every thing like reserve.

Impressed with these sentiments I beg leave to assure you of the warmest good wishes of your affectionate friend

CASPAR WISTAR JR

RC (DNA: RG 59, LAR); at foot of text: "His Excellency the President of the United States"; endorsed by TJ as received 12 Apr. and "Barnwell to be Director of hospital at New Orleans" and so recorded in SJL.

COMMUNICATION: William Barnwell had submitted papers to the American Philosophical Society in December 1795 on heat, air, and disease, and in August 1796 on aspects of the climate of North America and Europe. He was elected to membership in the society in January 1802 (APS, *Proceedings*, 22, pt. 3 [1884], 235, 241, 320).

To Levi Lincoln and
John Thomson Mason

Sentence of death having been passed by the Circuit court of Columbia, against a citizen[1] of Washington county, guilty of an aggravated murder, a question arises Who is to sign the warrant for execution?

By the act of Congress 1801. c. 86. the laws of Maryland, as they existed at that date, are in force in Washington county: and by the law of Maryland 1795. c. 82. the Governor of Maryland is authorised to issue a warrant of execution against any person sentenced to death by any court of that state. but the state of Maryland having now no jurisdiction over the county of Washington in Columbia, the Govr. of Maryland personally, cannot exercise this act of highest jurisdiction, the signing a warrant for the death of a Man in Columbia.[2]

The laws of Congress have given to the President of the US. the nomination of judges, justices, attornies, marshals and officers of the customs in Columbia, as elsewhere: and to the circuit courts of Columbia the power of appointing constables, inspectors, surveyors and to all other offices necessary for the district under the laws of Maryland or Virginia. but have not given either to the President or the Circuit court specially all the powers possessed by the Govr. of Maryland, nor generally executive powers which might, by description, render either equivalent to the Governor of Maryland, so as to authorise their assuming this particular function exercised by the Governor under the Maryland act of 1795.[3]

The constitution of the US. gives the President power to grant reprieves & pardons for offences against the US. but a power to pardon is not a power to punish.

The act of Congress 1790. c. 9. §. 33 says the manner of inflicting punishment of death shall be by hanging until dead, §. 14. that the courts of the US. shall have power to issue all writs necessary for the exercise of their jurisdiction; & 1792. c. 36. that all writs & processes issuing from the supreme or circuit courts shall bear test of the Chief Justice, shall be under the seal of the court & signature of the clerk, & that the forms of writs, executions, & other process, & the forms & modes of proceeding in suits, in those of common law, shall be the same as are now used in the sd courts under the 'act to regulate processes in the courts of the US.' 89. c. 21. [contind. 90. c. 13. contind. 91. c. 8. repealed 92. c. 36. §. 8. & therefore omitted in the statute book; but improperly, because the first act, tho' repealed must be recurred to for explanation of the phrase 'now[4] used under the act to regulate processes.'][5]

Had the trial & sentence in the present case taken place in Alexandria, where the Common law principle prevails that the warrant for execution must be under the hand & seal of the judge [4. Blackst. 396.] who would have signed the death warrant? who would sign such a warrant on sentence of the Circuit court of the US. in any other state?

The opinion of the Atty General is requested in this case for the government of the President.[6]   TH: JEFFERSON
                                                          April. 11. 1802.

RC (MHi: Levi Lincoln Papers); brackets in original; endorsed by Lincoln. FC (DLC); entirely in TJ's hand, being his retained copy of a memorandum sent individually to Lincoln and Mason; concluding paragraph differs from RC (see note 6 below). Recorded in SJL as "Mc.Gurk's case."

Mason was U.S. attorney for the District of COLUMBIA (Vol. 33:380). CITIZEN: James McGurk; see his petition at 19 Apr. below. ACT OF CONGRESS 1801: the "Act concerning the District of Columbia" of 27 Feb. 1801 specified that the LAWS OF MARYLAND would continue in force in the part of the district that had been ceded by that state. A Maryland law of 1795 that specified "the power of the governor in certain criminal cases" required the governor to issue a WARRANT OF EXECUTION for a death sentence. A federal statute of 3 Mch. 1801 supplementary to the act of 27 Feb. 1801 laid out the powers of the federal circuit court for the district, including the appointment of CONSTABLES and some other offices in the district's counties (U.S. Statutes at Large, 2:104-5, 115;

Laws of Maryland, Made and Passed at a Session of Assembly . . . in the Year of Our Lord One Thousand Seven Hundred and Ninety-Five [Annapolis, Md., 1796], chap. 82. ACT OF CONGRESS 1790: Section 33 of an act "for the Punishment of certain Crimes against the United States," approved 30 Apr. 1790, specified HANGING as the form of execution for federal capital offenses. Section 14 of an earlier statute, the 24 Sep. 1789 act to establish courts of the United States, gave the courts POWER TO ISSUE writs as needed "for the exercise of their respective jurisdictions." The ACT TO REGULATE PROCESSES, which was also passed in September 1789, was continued in May 1790 and February 1791. A new act "for regulating Processes in the Courts of the United States" was approved on 8 May 1792 (U.S. Statutes at Large, 1:81-2, 93-4, 112-19, 123, 191, 275-9).

4. BLACKST. 396: TJ cited the 1770 Oxford edition of William Blackstone's Commentaries on the Laws of England (see Sowerby, No. 1806).

OPINION OF THE ATTY GENERAL IS REQUESTED: it is not known if the concluding paragraph of the memorandum as Mason saw it matched the FC or was worded similarly to the memorandum that Lincoln received (see note 6 below).

[1] FC: "a citizen (Mc.Girk)."

[2] In margin of FC at the head of this paragraph, TJ wrote: "the Govr: of Maryld:?"

[3] FC continues here without a paragraph break. In margin of FC at the head of this paragraph, TJ wrote: "Presidt. or Judges as Executive?"

[4] TJ underlined this word in FC.

[5] In margin of FC at the head of this paragraph, TJ wrote: "Judiciary?"

[6] TJ wrote this sentence, his signature, and the date perpendicularly in the margin. In FC this paragraph reads: "The above grounds of doubt in the mind of the President are submitted to the Attorney Genl. mr J. T. Mason for consideration, and his opinion is requested for the government of."

From James Ogilvie

SIR,   Stevensburg Academy April 11th. 1802

I am this moment apprised that it is probable you will pass thro' Stevensburg on the 15th. Inst: On that day, my junior pupils will undergo a public examination in the forenoon, & in the afternoon, original orations will be pronounced by the senior students. Indulging a hope, that you may find it convenient to honour the Academy with your presence, I take the liberty to observe, that few circumstances could afford me higher satisfaction, than the accomplishment of this hope.

I congratulate you on the glorious termination of your arduous political campaign, & enjoy elevated pleasure in expressing the sentiments of reverential respect & cordial esteem, which the patriotism, magnanimity and wisdom that continuously mark your conduct in the execution of your difficult, delicate & momentous duties, ought to kindle in every ingenious & impartial mind—

JAMES OGILVIE

RC (DLC); endorsed by TJ as received 6 May and so recorded in SJL with notation "Culpep. Acad."; also endorsed by TJ: "Stevensbg academy."

James Ogilvie taught at Fredericksburg Academy before becoming a professor at Stevensburg Academy in Culpeper, Virginia. There he wrote the pamphlet, *Cursory Reflections on Government, Philosophy and Education*, published in Alexandria in January 1802. He resigned from Stevensburg Academy the following year to pursue juvenile instruction "on a more conspicuous and extensive theatre" (Sowerby, No. 3199; *Alexandria Advertiser*, 22 Jan. 1802; Richmond *Virginia Argus*, 22 Jan. 1803; Vol. 28:401-4).

From Pierpont Edwards

SIR, New Haven April 12th 1802

Shou'd the appointment of commissioners of bankruptcy be by law vested in the President of the United States, I have to request, that my son Henry Waggaman Edwards, of this city, may be appointed one of the commissioners for this district—He is well known to the Vice-President, and to Mr Granger—I am with the highest respect and most sincere regard

Your Obed Servt PIERPONT EDWARDS

RC (DNA: RG 59, LAR); at foot of text: "Excellency Thomas Jefferson"; endorsed by TJ as received 16 Apr. and "Henry Waggaman Edwards to be a Commissioner of bankrupts" and so recorded in SJL.

BY LAW VESTED IN THE PRESIDENT: under Section 14 of the "Act to amend the Judicial System of the United States," approved on 29 Apr., the president received the power to appoint "from time to time, as many general commissioners of bankruptcy, in each district of the United States, as he may deem necessary." The judge of the district had the power to select up to three of those appointed to act on a particular case, and they were allowed $6 per day while employed on a case (U.S. Statutes at Large, 2:156, 164).

In the House debate over this section of the judiciary bill, the Federalists maintained that the power to appoint the commissioners should remain with the district judges. The Republicans argued that the judges had abused that power by appointing improper persons and allowing "enormous emoluments." James Bayard argued that the president would have difficulty filling the appointments, noting, "The ordinary characters, fit to fill these offices, and willing to fill them, are infinitely below the knowledge of the President" (*Annals*, 11:1223-7).

In early July, TJ appointed HENRY WAGGAMAN EDWARDS and three others as general commissioners of bankruptcy for New Haven and Middlesex County, Connecticut (Appendix II, Lists 1 and 2).

From Albert Gallatin

[12 Apr. 1802]

Ogden versus Tucker

Since Mr Ogden applied for those documents, Mr Pearson, the federalist mentioned in his letter, met Tucker & with another man's assistance, assaulted & beat him. He was indicted & the *federal* Judges of the County of Burlington have fined him *one dollar*—

Mr Ogden has called several times for an answer and he must have one. Will you be good enough to look at the two drafts contained & say which is the best made? and will you also assist me in the wording of the answer? For doubtless it will be used—

Your's respectfully A. G.

An early answer will oblige me much—

RC (DLC); undated, but see TJ's note on enclosure; above postscript: "*The President*." Enclosure: Draft of Gallatin to Aaron Ogden, undated, reading as follows: "The Secretary of the Treasury presents his respects to Mr Ogden and has the honor to inform him that transcripts of documents, such as Mr Ogden has applied for, never are and cannot with propriety be furnished on the application of individuals"; with a second paragrah: "On the present occasion, the personal quarrel between the former Collector of Egg harbour & the member of the State Legislature in whose name Mr. O. made the application renders it improper that any official information on that subject should be communicated through his channel" (Dft in NHi: Gallatin Papers; in TJ's hand at foot of text: "Approved Th:J Apr. 12. 1802"; endorsed by Gallatin: "Apr 1802 Copy to Mr Ogden N.J. in Senate"). Other draft not found.

New Jersey Senator Aaron OGDEN, on behalf of William Pearson, perhaps sought documents from the Treasury Department pertaining to a complaint against Ebenezer Tucker, which led to his resignation as collector at Little Egg Harbor in 1799 (see Vol. 35:365-6). On 10 Feb., the Burlington County grand jury presented the Court of Quarter Sessions with an indictment against Pearson, a member of the state legislature. He was charged and convicted of assault and battery against Tucker. According to Tucker, William Coxe, another state representative, watched while he was beaten by Pearson. "A Friend to Justice" scoffed at the ONE DOLLAR fine, noting "what would have been the sentence of this same Court had William Pearson or William Coxe been waylaid and treated as they treated Ebenezer Tucker?" (Trenton *True American*, 2 Feb., 2 Mch., 25 May 1802; Trenton *Federalist & New-Jersey State Gazette*, 16 Feb. 1802). For Tucker's central role in other political controversies in early 1802, see Prince, *New Jersey's Jeffersonian Republicans*, 105.

From Albert Gallatin

Treasury Department 12th April 1802

The Secretary of the Treasury respectfully submits to the President of the United States the propriety of nominating a proper person to fill the office of Supervisor of the North west District. The duties have been heretofore performed by Thomas Worthington with the commission only of Inspector. But he cannot, without the commission of Supervisor, appoint collectors; and there are at present several vacancies. It was understood that he should receive the appointment of Supervisor as soon as a salary was fixed by law. This has been done by the Act to repeal the internal taxes.

RC (DNA: RG 59, LAR); at foot of text: "The President of the United States"; endorsed by TJ as received from the Treasury Department on 13 Apr. and so recorded in SJL with notation "Nominn of Worthington Supervisor of N.W. district"; also endorsed by TJ: "Nomination. Worthington."

SALARY WAS FIXED BY LAW: see Gallatin to TJ, 3 Jan. 1802.

From Levi Lincoln

Sir   Washington April 12th 1802

I have the honor of stating my ideas on the subject submitted to my consideration by your favor of yesterday. The Courts of the Columbia District, are national ones created by statute. Their powers are merely judicial, unless in particular instances particularly expressed, or necessarily implied. The mere establishment of these courts did not of course include, a particular extent of jurisdiction in reference to objects, or a given mode of procedure. Their powers are given, defined & directed by law. Their powers are different in different counties. The power in question, is not given to them expressly, nor does it necessarily attach itself to any part of their duty. It is not so with the President. The constitution vesting him with powers, the right to exercise them on some objects takes place, so soon as they are brought into existence. The moment, that a district or a state is formed with a national judiciary, a right vests in the President to exercise those powers, which he is authorized to exercise in other districts or states in the United States—No statute provision can be necessary for this purpose—

The law providing that the Courts of the U.S. shall have power to issue all writs & processes necessary for the exercise of their jurisdiction, and the one of 1792. c. 36. which enacts that all writs and processes issuing from the Supreme and circuit court, shall bear test of the chief justice, shall be under the seal of the court, and the signature of the clerk, and that the forms of writs, executions and other processes, and the forms and modes of proceeding in suits, in those of common law, shall be the same as are now used in the said Courts under the act to regulate processes in the courts of the U.S. can, in my opinion, be construed to refer only to such writs and processes as were returnable to the court, on which they could act, or to such as issued in pursuance of some order or judgment of theirs, & which were returnable to them, in their ordinary course of the administration of Justice, and not to warrants for the Execution of sentences of death on a capital offender—

The laws of Virginia and of Maryland being adopted for the district of Columbia, operate in the respective counties in the same manner as tho' they had been particularly enacted by Congress for that purpose. They must however be so constructed, as to be accommodated to the constitutional provisions of the national Government.

Separate from any custom, or law directing the matter particularly,

I think the copy of the judgment of the Court delivered to the marshall, would justify him in discharging the duty, which the law devolves upon him, by executing the sentence of the court. For the execution of most sentences, inflicting corporal punishment, if not all, those of death excepted, the officer has no other warrant. The time for executing such sentences is usually left to his discretion. In favor of life, and to give dignity & respect to man, in the execution of a criminal a more solemn form has been usually adopted, especially in this Country. In most of the States, & I beleive in all the northern ones, it has been the practice for the Executive to sign death warrants, on the convictions in the State courts. If so, and if, on general principles, and those of common law, the copy of a judgment of a court would be a sufficient warrant, as it is in virginia, for the officer to execute the sentence of death, I think it right and safe, to consider the President as vested with the power of signing the death warrants on the capital sentences of the national courts—In no view of the matter does it abridge the rights of others, in no view is it unfavorable to the prisoner. It seems to be an act necessarily incident to the power of granting reprieves & pardons for offences against the U.S. of a capital nature; otherwise a precipitate execution of a convict, under the sentence or warrant from the court, might place him out of the reach of that mercy, which his country had in reserve for him—

The Art. 2d Sec 1. of the Constitution provides that the Executive power shall be vested in the President of the U.S. The exercise of no power is more completely, & seriously executive, than the one in question. A conviction, and a sentence of death has been awarded. The President has been furnished with a copy of the judgment. It has not been carried into execution. The law requires that it should be. By the 3d Sec. of the above mentioned Art. The President is to take care that the laws be faithfully executed. The warrant to the officer, is notice that neither reprieve or pardon will intervene, and that the law must have its course. In the judgment the mode of Execution, & the place where, is pointed out. The prisoner is to be taken to the gaol, from whence he came, and from thence to the place of Execution, & there be hanged by the neck untill he be dead. The officer who is to take the criminal, back to the gaol, is the one designated by law, to execute the sentence of death, on him. The taking him back to the gaol, is a part of the sentence—All that remains is to fix the time for the complete execution of it—In common cases, this is left with the officer—In an act of the, highest importance to an individual & to society, it has usually been left with the executives of the several states, the reason of the thing, a very strong analogy, and I think, the Constitution, on convictions in the national courts, places it in the President

I have the honor to be Sir with the highest respect your most obt Sert · LEVI LINCOLN

RC (DLC); at head of text: "President of the United States"; endorsed by TJ as received 13 Apr. on "Mc.Girk's case" and so recorded in SJL.

For the 1789 law that empowered courts to issue writs NECESSARY FOR THE EXERCISE OF THEIR JURISDICTION and for the 1792 act "regulating Processes in the Courts," see TJ to Lincoln and John Thomson Mason, 11 Apr.

From John Thomson Mason

April 12th 1802

Upon examining the authorities I find it settled, at Common Law,

1. That the time and place of execution make no part of the Judgment in capital cases 4. Blac. Com. 404. 1 Hal. P.C. 368. 2 Hawk. 658

2. That the Court having power to give Judgment of death, necessarily possesses the power of awarding execution 2 Hal. P.C. 406.

3. That formerly the Judge of the Court who pronounced Sentence issued a precept under his hand and Seal ordering execution to be done, without fixing either day or place (with an exception as to two Courts) 4. Blac. Com. 403. appen. no 3. 2 Hal. P.C. 409.

4. That the law authorizes, And the practice for a long series of time has been for, the Judge to award execution by simply signing a Roll of the prisoners convicted with the Sentence pronounced against each written in the margin opposite to his name, without issuing any writ or precept 2 Hawk. 657. 2 Hal. P.C. 409. 4 Blac. Com. 403.

The Statute of the 25. Geo. 2. c. 37 makes the day of execution and the disposition of the body when executed a part of the Judgment of the Court upon a conviction for murder. But that Statute never was in force either in Virginia or Maryland. Thus at Common Law we find the practice settled as to the mode of awarding executions in Capital cases. As to the time of execution the practice tho' settled is variant in different Courts, in some the day is fixed by the Court, in others it is left discretionary with the Executive officers of the Courts. I presume upon principle it is not important which fixes the day, in either case the execution must be done in a reasonable time. That the

Courts who gave Judgment should award execution, is I presume founded on the principle (no doubt a sound one) that the power of Judging necessarily draws after it, as incident thereto, the power of inforcing the Judgment given.

From whence the idea arose of awarding a death warrant to inforce the execution of a Judgment given by a Court it is difficult to conjecture.

Had the case of McGirk happened in the County of Alexandria where the Common Law principle prevails, I presume the Authority of the above cases would have directed the mode of proceeding, except that the Court, not in their Judgment, but upon their records, would have directed the day of execution; the law of Virginia which allows the convict thirty days to live after sentence passed, if it does not make it necessary that the Court should fix the day of execution, has probably introduced the practice of doing so. Since I came to the bar such has been the practice in Virginia, I beleive no death warrant ever issued, I think none was necessary, I think none would be necessary in the County of Alexandria.

What has been the practice in the Circuit Courts of the United States under the laws of Congress I do not know as I have never attended one of those Courts. By the laws of Congress the Circuit Courts have cognizance of the Offence of Murder committed in a place under the exclusive jurisdiction of the United States, the punishment for such an offence is ascertained to be death, and the mode of inflicting the punishment of death is ascertained to be by hanging.[1] If the principle be a sound one that the right to judge carries with it the power of inforcing an execution of that Judgment, without resorting to the authority of cases adjudged as explanatory of the principles of the Common Law, it would follow as a necessary consequence that the Court which passes sentence of death, have the power, and are bound to award execution on that Judgment. Upon convictions then in a Circuit Court of the United States a death warrant will be unnecessary.

In what manner a Circuit Court ought to award execution is a subject worthy of consideration. I cannot discover that any act of Congress give directions on this subject. The 14. Sec. of the act of 1790. c. 20 Seems not I think to imbrace the case, because speaking of writs known and used at Common law, it can hardly be supposed that Congress intended to extend the provision to a case where writs had never been issued, and were in law deemed necessary. If the law then has prescribed no form of proceeding, by which the Court shall effect an object, Which it makes it their duty to effect, it follows that the

Court themselves must devise the mode of their proceeding to effect that object. If the Judges shall not think themselves justifiable in adopting the mode practiced in England of issuing a precept under their hands and Seals, the prisoner McGirk must I presume remain in prison until the meeting of the next Court

What the practice in the State of Maryland was previous to the act of 1795, I cannot from any observation of my own say, I have understood that it was always customary for the Governor to issue death warrants, I have however searched dilligently into the old laws of Maryland upon that subject, and can find no legislative provision authorizing the practice. If such was their mode of proceeding, I am at a loss to know from whence they derived it.

By the act of 1795. ch. 82 the Governor, whenever sentence of death is pronounced against any criminal by the Judgment of any Court of the State of Maryland, is obliged to issue a death warrant. And by the act of Congress passed in 1801. c. 86. The laws of Maryland as they existed at the time of the passage of that law are declared to be in force in the County of Washington. But I presume this must be taken to mean such laws of the state of Maryland as in their nature could be made to operate here, of such discription this law is not, and therefore I presume deserves no weight in the consideration of the question. The same law of Congress in the 3d Sec. gives to the Circuit Court of the District of Columbia all the powers which by Law are vested in the Circuit Courts of the United States. Whether therefore the Court setting here be considered as having in this respect Common Law powers, or the powers vested in the Circuit Courts of the United States, still it is their duty to award execution and a death warrant is not necessary.

The Chief Justice and Judge Cranch have been Maryland practitioners, and supposing that the power of directing execution vested with the Executive they have fixed no time and taken no measures to have their Judgment executed. I was, at the moment they were about to proceed to pass sentence, asked by the Court where the power of directing execution rested, impressed I suppose in the same manner that the majority of the Court were, with the recollection of the Maryland practice, I joined them in supposing it rested with the Executive, upon examining the subject I am satisfied I was wrong.

I have the Honor to be with great respect your Obedt Servt

JOHN T. MASON

RC (DLC); addressed: "The President"; endorsed by TJ as received 12 Apr. on "Mc.Girk's case" and so recorded in SJL.

4. BLAC. COM. 404: Mason cited a 1773 Oxford edition of Blackstone's *Commentaries*. The section on executions that fell on pages 403-4 of the fourth volume of that edition was on pages 396-7 in the 1770 Oxford edition cited by TJ on 11 Apr.

1 HAL. P.C. 368: Sir Matthew Hale, *Pleas of the Crown*.

2 HAWK. 658: William Hawkins, *Treatise of the Pleas of the Crown*.

APPEN. NO 3: in the edition of Blackstone's *Commentaries* that Mason consulted, one appendix presented an example of an "Entry of a Trial *instanter* in the Court of King's Bench, upon a collateral Issue; and Rule of Court for Execution thereon," which included an order for an execution (William Blackstone, *Commentaries on the Laws of England*, 5th ed., 4 vols. [Oxford, 1773], 4: appendix, v-vi).

STATUTE OF THE 25. GEO. 2. C. 37: "An Act for better preventing the horrid Crime of Murder," passed by Parliament in 1752 (*The Statutes at Large, From the Twentieth Year . . . to the Thirtieth Year of the Reign of King George the Second* [London, 1769], 440-1).

One section of the LAW OF VIRGINIA that established the state's General Court in 1777 allowed defendants to have legal counsel and required an interval of at least one calendar month between the judgment of a sentence of death and the execution of the prisoner (William Waller Hening, ed., *The Statutes at Large; Being a Collection of All the Laws of Virginia*, 13 vols. [Richmond, 1809-23], 9:417).

The April 1790 act "for the Punishment of certain Crimes" that TJ cited in his memorandum to Levi Lincoln and Mason on 11 Apr. prescribed punishment for murders committed in the EXCLUSIVE JURISDICTION of the United States (U.S. Statutes at Large, 1:113).

14. SEC. OF THE ACT OF 1790: the "Act to establish the Judicial Courts of the United States," approved 24 Sep. 1789. For that act, the 1795 law of the STATE OF MARYLAND, and the 1801 federal law "concerning the District of Columbia," see TJ to Lincoln and Mason, 11 Apr. The 1801 statute created the circuit court for the District of Columbia and gave it the powers VESTED IN THE CIRCUIT COURTS of the United States (U.S. Statutes at Large, 1:73-4; 2:105).

CHIEF JUSTICE: William Kilty.

[1] MS: "haning."

From Samuel Latham Mitchill

SIR   Capitol, April 12. 1802

Permit me to offer you the inclosed Letter which I received by yesterday's Mail from Albany. I suspect from what Mr. L'Hommedieu has written to me, that the Conversation about an Association of Agricultural Societies which I heard from you, some time ago, has given rise to that Communication. In the absence of the President of the New York Society Mr. Livingston in France, the functions of that place are performed by the Vice-President Mr. L'H. I am Sir; yours with great Respect   SAML L MITCHILL

RC (DLC); at foot of text: "To Th. Jefferson President of the United States"; endorsed by TJ as received 12 Apr. and so recorded in SJL. Enclosure: Ezra L'Hommedieu to TJ, 3 Apr. 1802.

SOME TIME AGO: see TJ to Isaac Briggs, 29 June 1802.

From James Monroe

DEAR SIR   Richmond April 12. 1802

I find among the papers in the council chamber an acct. adjusted
by you between Houdon and the Commonwealth. Perhaps you have
a copy of it at Monticello, which may be the document to which you
wish to recur before you decide on his claim. If this paper is material
it shall be sent to you, tho' to me it appears as if it cod. not be, as the
sole or principal question is, what the depreciation was on the last
payment made. I have no doubt that it is a wise policy to adjust the
difference with Engld. relative to the 6th article on the terms proposed in the project before the Senate. It is important to settle ami-
cably our affrs. with Europe so as to deprive any of the great powers
especially of the "causa billi" or pretext for war. I wod. buy up any
such latent pretention, at some sacrifice. It will give me pleasure to
meet you in Albemarle the first week in May if possible. But I fear it
will be impossible. I am forc'd to be there on the 20th. of this month
to meet any offer that may be made for my land above charlottesville
which I have advertised for sale on that day. If I attend on that day,
which it is very incumbent on me to do, it will not be in my power to
return to the council, which immediately ensues, and be back during
yr. transient visit in Albemarle. Still it may happen as I will certainly
be there if practicable.

yr. friend & servt.   JAS. MONROE

RC (DLC); endorsed by TJ as received
15 Apr. and so recorded in SJL.

ACCT. ADJUSTED BY YOU: the document that Monroe saw in the files in Richmond was a statement of account prepared by Jean Antoine Houdon on or
after 20 Oct. 1788. The statement listed
Houdon's expenses of his trip to the United States in 1785 to make the bust of
Washington. The expenditures, made
from July through December 1785, totaled 12,568 livres and 18 sous. Five payments to Houdon from 28 Nov. 1785 to 20
Oct. 1788 totaled 11,550 livres, 17 sous,
and 9 deniers, leaving a balance due to
the artist of 1,018 livres and 3 deniers.
At the foot of the statement, TJ wrote:
"M. Houdon having accompanied Dr.
Franklin to America, who was equally
employed with myself by the state of Vir-

ginia, the expences herein charged were
under his eye & authority till Houdon's
departure from America. the subsequent
articles were examined and approved by
Th: Jefferson" (MS in Vi: Executive Papers; undated and unsigned; in Houdon's
hand; at head of text: "Relevé des Mémoires Quittances et Bordereaux que Mr
houdon a Conservés relativement à ses
dépenses pour son voyage de Paris en
Amérique et son retour en cette ville Luy
et 3 Elèves pour le Servir et l'aider dans
son travail, depuis le Mois de Juillet 1785
jusqu'au trente un Decembre Même
Année" [statement of bills, receipts, and
notes that Monsieur Houdon kept relating to his expenditures for his voyage
from Paris to America and his return to
this city, for himself and three apprentices
to serve and assist him in his work, from
the month of July 1785 until 31 Dec. of

that year]; with signed declaration by TJ; endorsed by TJ: "Houdon's acct. of expences of his voyage to & from America";

endorsed with the date 20 Oct. 1788 in an unidentified hand).

From "Noname Iota"

SIR.   Baltimore April 12. 1802

I had an inclination to address you for some time, I know So much of the Manœuvres of the p. office that I judged the attempt hazardous at best—if not highly dangerous—I do at this time alter my handwriting as much as possible to make the subject intelligible.—Now, to the point. The most dangerous man belonging to the City, Washington, is J Wheaton, Sergeant. his family is in Canada, his Brother is a Captain in the B. Service at Quebec & he did come to New York, to Phila. & I suppose comes to Washinton regularly every year, in coloured cloathes. Now J Wheaton is the greatest Aristocrat, spie, informer &c of any man within the Scope of yr. Authority or power, and your Enemies among the Judges have availed themselves of their influence over the post Masters, to find out your secrets—now endeavour to intercept Wheaton's dispatches beyond the Hudson, for he will not send them by the Ordinary Carriages untill out of reach, or secure his papers or set a spie to know Whether his Brother is come down this time, & you'll find a nest pregnant with the seeds of every evil; Critical times are approaching;—The B & F fleets will be on our Coast, & in our rivers this Summer. *Chase* our Judge has been seen by the writer of this locked up in the post office Baltimore with Mr. Burrall—the post Master—You can easily devise a cypher & have letters dropt into the Suspected offices, and tried from post office to P Office and you'll be able to detect defaulters—

With due respect   NONAME IOTA

RC (DLC); endorsed by TJ as received from "Anonymous" on 13 Apr. and "about Wheaton & the post offices" and so recorded in SJL.

J WHEATON, SERGEANT: Joseph Wheaton, the sergeant at arms of the U.S. House

of Representatives (see Wheaton to TJ, 1 Feb. 1802).

Justice Samuel CHASE of the United States Supreme Court was an ardent Federalist and critic of TJ's administration (ANB). Charles BURRALL was the postmaster at Baltimore (Vol. 33:426-7).

From Robert Patterson

Sir   Philada. April 12th. 1802

I have been honored with your favour of the 22d Ult. and feel, with a lively sense, the obligation I am under for the interest you were pleased to take in behalf of my friend, though the appointment has fallen on another worthy gentleman of the same name. I am not a little flattered with the notice you have taken of my cypher—Your alteration will certainly very much facilitate the labour of the Principal, without greatly increasing that of the copyist. There is yet another alteration, relative to the *Key*, which, I conceive, would be of considerable advantage—Instead of expressing it by *figures*, which are so liable to be forgotten, it may be expressed by a single word or name, which may always be remembred, without committing it to writing. For example, suppose the key-word Montecello—the letters of this word are to be numbered according to their place in the alphabet, any letter *repeated*, being referred to a second, or third alphabet—thus the letters in the above word be numbered as follows

M   o   n   t   e   c   e   l   l   o
4,   6,   5,   7,   2,   1,   8,   3,   9,   10.

the second e, l, and o being referred to a second alphabet, and according numbered 8, 9, 10. This key-word will then signify that there are ten vertical lines in the section, which are to be transcribed, in horizontal lines in the order of the above figures viz. 4th. 6th. 5th. &c The same word may also be used to signify the number of supplementary or insignificant letters at the beginning of the respective lines, as 4 at the beginning of the first, 6, at that of the second &c Or *two* key-words may be used; the first to signify the number and order of lines in the section, and the second, the supplementary letters. When the two words do not consist of an equal number of letters, then so many of the first letters of the least word may be subjoined to the end of it, as to make their number equal—Thus *James Maddison*, as a key, would be written and numbered in this manner

J   a   m   e   s   j   a   m   M   a   d   d   i   s   o   n
3,   1,   4,   2,   5,   7,   6,   8;   4,   1,   2,   8,   3,   7,   6,   5.

There is but one wooden Sextant, that I can find, to be disposed of at present in this city. It is a very good one—with telescopes, tangent and adjusting screws, and every other appendage complete—the price 45 dollars. A stand might be made for it at no great expense. A very little practice, however, would render the use of the instrument, both in measuring vertical and horizontal angles, without a stand, as easy as with one. The Thermometers are ready, but as I have not yet seen or heard from Mr. Barnes, I must request you to send me such further directions, relative to the purchase of the sextant, and sending on the instruments, as you may think proper

An experiment which Mr. Raphael Peale lately exhibited before a number of citizens, at the Coffeehouse, has excited a good deal of attention. It is a complete depuration of even the foulest water, by causing it to pass through a filter composed of successive strata of sponge, sand, & charcoal—He succeeded with water taken from Dr. Wistar's mascerating-tub, so putrid that the smell of it could scarcely be borne by the company. He has since extended his experiment, and, as he conceives with success, to the separating of fresh water from salt— not indeed by simple filtration, but by previously mixing with the salt water a certain substance, which he says is cheap and of small bulk comparatively. I fear however, that [he may] have been deceived, in these latter experiments—but as [he is?] preparing to repeat them with true sea water, the result, which I shall take the liberty of communicating as soon as known, will determine.

I have the honour to be with the most perfect respect & esteem Sir, your most obedient servant RT. PATTERSON

RC (DLC); torn; addressed: "Thomas Jefferson President of the United States city of Washington"; franked; postmarked Philadelphia, 13 Apr.; endorsed by TJ as received 15 Apr. and so recorded in SJL.

The problem of purifying WATER, especially drinking water for ships at sea, received much attention. Raphaelle Peale learned to use sand, sponges, and charcoal as filtrates after seeing a demonstration of a device that had been patented in France. After he built and demonstrated his apparatus in Philadelphia, he wrote to his brother Rubens, who was in New York City exhibiting a mastodon skeleton. From Raphaelle's instructions, Rubens built one of the filtering devices using stacked flowerpots that held sand and charcoal, with sponges in the pots' drain holes, all enclosed in a tin casing. Rubens then put on a public demonstration in New York as his brother had in Philadelphia. Charles Willson Peale, who also experimented with water clarification, implied that carbonic acid played a role in Raphaelle's system. A French author writing in 1801 asserted that if filtration proved inadequate, one could employ "albuminous and gelatinous matter," acids, fats, lime, cream, or blood as agents to help purify water (Peale, *Papers*, v. 2, pt. 1:426, 427n, 508-9, 512-13n; M. N. Baker and Michael J. Taras, *The Quest for Pure Water*, 2d ed., 2 vols. [Denver, 1981], 1:38-40; Jean-Pierre Goubert, *The Conquest of Water: The Advent of Health in the Industrial Age*, trans. Andrew Wilson [Cambridge, 1989], 53-4).

DR. WISTAR'S MASCERATING-TUB: Raphaelle Peale exhibited his filtration device before merchants and ship captains at the City Tavern in Philadelphia. "The experiment proved to be a simple and easy mode of purifying the most offensive water, which came out perfectly pure and bright, and was tasted by all the company," reported the *Gazette of the United States*. "Dish water, water from a stagnant pool, and water from the anatomical hall were used." The latter was apparently water from a receptacle that Caspar Wistar used to soak soft tissue from bones in the preparation of anatomical samples. Wistar, who taught at the University of Pennsylvania, earned a reputation for the quality of his lectures on anatomy and his use of visual aids. He later wrote the first American textbook of anatomy (*Gazette of the United States*, 7 Apr. 1802; *Aurora*, 5 Apr.; ANB; John B. Blake, "Anatomy," in Ronald L. Num- bers, ed., *The Education of American Physicians: Historical Essays* [Berkeley, Calif., 1980], 33; OED, s.v. "maceration").

From Pierre Samuel Du Pont de Nemours

MONSIEUR LE PRÉSIDENT,   New York 13 Avril 1802.

Les circonstances politiques et commerciales, entre la Contrée à laquelle je dois la naissance et celle qui m'a donné un généreux azyle, me semblent exiger que je fasse en France un voyage, que je colorerai sous des raisons et des affaires réelles de Commerce; mais dont le principal but sera de tenter encore de servir mes deux Patries de mon très grand Zêle et de mes faibles lumieres.

Le voyage de mon Fils en 1797, ses efforts et les miens ont, avec ceux de l'estimable Docteur Logan, beaucoup contribué au rapprochement qui eut alors lieu, et dont la derniere convention a été le résultat.

Ces sortes de carrieres conviennent à mes habitudes et à mon coeur.

J'ai un vif désir avant de m'embarquer de passer un jour à Washington City, une heure avec vous. Et j'espere pouvoir le satisfaire dans le cours de la semaine prochaine.

Si la multitude d'affaires que me donnent un départ si précipité, et une absence qui sera inevitablement de plus de six mois, qui peut être d'un an, ne me laissait pas le tems de faire cette course à Vashington, daigneriez vous m'écrire un mot qui éclairât ma conduite plus que ne le peuvent mes propres pensées?

Je saurai vous entendre sans grandes explications: mais j'aimerais mieux vous parler et j'y ferai mon possible.

Salut et respect.   DU PONT (DE NEMOURS)

EDITORS' TRANSLATION

MISTER PRESIDENT,   New York, 13 Apr. 1802

The political and commercial circumstances between the country to which I owe my birth and the one that gave me a generous asylum seem to make it necessary for me to make a trip to France, which I shall disguise under the color of commercial and real business affairs, but the real purpose of which will be to try again to serve my two fatherlands with my very great zeal and feeble wisdom.

My son's voyage in 1797, his efforts and mine, along with those of the worthy Doctor Logan, contributed greatly to the rapprochement that took place then, and of which the last convention was the result.

Those kinds of careers suit my habits and my heart.

Before sailing, I have a lively desire to spend a day in Washington City, and an hour with you. I hope to be able to satisfy it during the coming week.

If the plethora of business given me by such a precipitous departure and an absence that will inevitably be longer than six months, perhaps a year, should not allow me the time to pass by Washington, would you condescend to write me a note that would enlighten my conduct better than my own thoughts can?

I will be able to understand you without great explanations, but I should prefer to speak with you and I will bend every effort to do so.

Greetings and respect.   DU PONT (DE NEMOURS)

RC (DLC); at head of text: "a Son Excellence Thomas Jefferson President des Etats unis"; endorsed by TJ as received 15 Apr. and so recorded in SJL.

VOYAGE DE MON FILS: in 1797, Victor du Pont was the French consul in Charleston, South Carolina, when his government decided to make him consul at Philadelphia and provisional consul general for the United States. When du Pont arrived in Philadelphia in the spring of 1798, John Adams refused to issue him an exequatur, but before du Pont left for France he had discussions with TJ and others that enabled him to brief Talleyrand and the Directory about American perspectives on relations between the two countries. Also in the spring of 1798, George LOGAN embarked on his controversial journey to France. Early in 1799, TJ declared that Logan's "enthusiastic enterprize" had been "fortunate" in softening French attitudes toward the United States (Georgia Robison Beale, "Bosc and the Exequator," *Prologue*, 10 [1978], 143-50; Vol. 30:380n, 386, 417, 418-19n, 631).

To John Isaac Hawkins

SIR   Washington Apr. 13. 1802.

The Forte piano which you made for me, and which I had great reason to be satisfied with on every account but one, has from a single cause become entirely useless, I mean that of not staying in tune. at first it would remain in tolerable tune for a day or two, and I hoped that when all it's parts should take the set to which they might have a tendency when new, that it would become settled & hold it's tune. but it grew worse & worse, till at length it would not stay in tune one single hour, and in that situation has continued upwards of a twelvemonth, so that it is entirely disused. I am shortly going to Monticello and had a thought, if you approved, to have it securely packed, and sent to you in Philadelphia to be cured of this defect if possible, and to be returned to me when in order. I would willingly meet the expence of the double transportation & of any operations you may find necessary for it, if you will undertake it. Colo. Cabell's answers well. I shall await your answer to this proposition.

TH: JEFFERSON

P.S. I have never permitted a single project to be tried by any person towards curing the defect, so that the instrument remains precisely as it came out of your hands.

PrC (DLC); in ink at foot of text: "Hawkins John"; endorsed by TJ in ink on verso.

John Isaac Hawkins (1772-1854), an English-born entrepreneur, inventor, and instrument maker, settled in Bordentown, New Jersey, in the 1790s and then worked mainly in Philadelphia from 1800 to 1803. Among his inventions, several of which were patented, were the collapsible violin, self-sharpening pencil, paper ruling machine, trifocal glasses, physiognotrace, and polygraph. In May 1803, before returning to England to claim an inheritance, he received a patent for the polygraph, as his "pentagraph and parallel ruler" duplicating machine was known, for which Peale received American manufactory rights. Skilled as a civil engineer, Hawkins proposed several public infrastructure projects in England, including a tunnel under the Thames River, before facing financial difficulties and re-

turning to the United States in 1848. In 1852 he published a monthly magazine in Rahway, New Jersey, *Journal of Human Nature and Human Progress*. Throughout his career, Hawkins received the admiration and sometimes financial support of TJ, for whom he designed and sold an upright fortepiano in 1800, wrote three pieces for his inauguration as president, shared a description of his claviol, and supplied a polygraph (Michael D. Friesen, " 'Mentor-General to Mankind': The Life and Work in America of John Isaac Hawkins" [M.A. thesis, Northern Illinois University, 2001]; Helen Cripe, *Thomas Jefferson and Music* [Charlottesville, 1974], 55-7, 74-5; *Aurora*, 18 Feb. 1802; Vol. 31:365; Vol. 32:xxxv; Vol. 33:xlviii; Hawkins to TJ, 16 July 1802).

For TJ's purchase, in 1800, of a Hawkins FORTE PIANO for his daughter Mary to play, see Vol. 31:365-6; Vol. 32:xxxv.

From Alexander White

SIR   Commissioners Office 13th April 1802

In consequence of what you were pleased to mention this morning I send a rough sketch of a Resolve respecting a subject which I do not feel myself competent to act on I have examined the Essays of Nicholas King while he was in the employ of the Commissioners, and acting under the auspices of Doctor Thornton, from which it appears that their Idea was to carry a Water Street 80 feet wide through the whole extent of the Potowmac and Eastern Branch, one hundred feet distant from the Channel, leaving all the space between that and the shore which in some instances I am inclined to believe is not less than one thousand feet, under water until it shall be filled up. I do not see the propriety of this, and have drawn the Resolve in such general

terms, that without deviating from it, the President may direct the Street to be laid out in any manner he may think most proper—
I shall with great pleasure facilitate your views, but unless I can get away on Saturday next it will subject me to considerable inconvenience—I am with sentiments of the highest respect

Sir Your most Ob Sevt   ALEXR WHITE

RC (DLC); at foot of text: "President of the U States"; endorsed by TJ as received 13 Apr. and so recorded in SJL.

RESOLVE RESPECTING A SUBJECT: on 8 Apr., a special committee of the House of Representatives presented a report on the disputes between the commissioners of the District of Columbia and property owners over alterations made to the plan of the city of Washington. The report closed with resolutions calling on the president to finalize the conveyance of public grounds to the United States and to have an updated plan of the city prepared and published, conforming as nearly as possible to the so-called "Appropriation Map" prepared by James Dermott in 1797 (*Annals*, 12:1304-6; JHR, 4:184;

Ralph E. Ehrenberg, "Mapping the Nation's Capital: The Surveyor's Office, 1791-1818," *Quarterly Journal of the Library of Congress*, 36 [1979], 306).

NICHOLAS KING presented a plan to the District of Columbia commissioners in March 1797, which called for the creation of a WATER STREET along the district's waterfront on the Potomac River and Eastern Branch. Illustrated with a set of 12 maps showing an enlargement and revision of the waterfront sections of Dermott's 1797 Appropriation Map, the plan was not implemented by the Adams administration (Herman R. Friis and Ralph E. Ehrenberg, "Nicholas King and His Wharfing Plans of the City of Washington, 1797," RCHS, 66-68 [1969], 34-46). See also William Thornton to TJ, 17 Apr.

ENCLOSURE

Draft of a Resolution for the City of Washington

Resolved, as the opinion of the Board that a Plan of the City of Washington on which the public appropriations, as they are described in the several Acts of the Presidents of the U States directing the conveyance thereof to the Commissioners; the squares or Parcels of ground which have been divided, or prepared for division, as building lots; and the Streets as actually laid out on the ground, shall be plainly and distinctly delineated—ought to be engraved, and published under the sanction of the President of the U. States— And that a Street round those parts of the City which bind on navigable water ought also to be designated on such plan so that the same, in such parts as are covered with water, may hereafter be made, agreeably to an established Rule—

MS (DLC); undated; in White's hand.

From Philip Wilson

Washington
the 13th: April 1802

I am the unfortunate Claimant for the Ship Mentor; so long yr: Supplicant for Compensation, of the British Government for the Destruction of that Ship; and Cargo: in time of Peace; the pursuit of *Superior Velocity*, in the Sailing of Shipping, caused me to build that Ship; I having been bred in the Mercantile line of Trade from an early period of my life, made the Stepping of Masts, and form of Vessels for Fast Sailing my Studdy. Would your Excellency permit me the honour to lay before you three Drawings of Ships: i.e. An 80 Gun Ship on two Decks; A Ship for War or Trade, of 500: tuns burthen; And what would make a beautiful Tender, or Sloop of War of 18: Guns: I doubt not—*Under your Excellencys Patronage*—they, with the *Hydrostatic Discussion* thereto belonging, might be productive of Velossity in your Navy, Superior to any in Europe, or any other part of the World. The Experiment might be readily made by building the smalles Ship of 260: tuns, tunnage, which with all the other, are finished for the Floor & Carpenters; And when built and prepared in the properest manner for Sea: If she does not sail round or faster than the fastest sailing Ship of any in the Chesapeak, Delaware, or United States (whoes Shipping for Velocity is equal to any in the World) I shall forfeit all pretence to any place or Profit for my Research & trouble.

They are constructed on the principles of a Hydrostatic Discussion and Deliniation of 47: propositions founded on simple reasoning and Demonstration; and Supported by the Natural Phylosophy of[1] Sir Isaac Newton;—With 10: or 11: general Rules for Drawing—From which a Ship of more Velocity, and other good properties, may be formed, than any that ever yet gave Chase to, or Ran from an Enemy in the most impetious Sea. I shall wait your Excellency's commands And am with the most profound respect,

Honoured Sir, Your obedient Citizen and humble Servant

PHILIP WILSON
at Mr: Roades's Inn,
near the Treasury

RC (DLC); at foot of text: "His Excellency Thomas Jefferson President of the United States &ca &ca."; endorsed by TJ as received 13 Apr. and so recorded in SJL. Enclosures not found.

A former Philadelphia merchant, Philip Wilson sent TJ several letters during the 1790s and early 1800s, most of which have not been found. His most recent letter was dated 25 Mch. 1801 from

Philadelphia, which TJ recorded in SJL as received 28 Mch. Since at least 1790, Wilson had been petitioning various government officers for aid in settling his claim against the British government for the destruction of the *Mentor*, his merchant vessel that was lost to British warships in 1783 after fighting between the U.S. and Great Britain had been suspended. More recently, Wilson had unsuccessfully sought compensation from Congress for supplies provided to Continental forces during the war (JHR, 3:732-3; 4:17; Vol. 18:347-8n; Vol. 20:637-9; Vol. 24:697; Vol. 33:690).

MR: ROADES'S INN: the hotel of William Rhodes, near the intersection of 15th and F Streets in Washington (Vol. 35:706n).

[1] MS: "of of."

To Caspar Wistar

Apr. 13. 1802. Washington

Th: Jefferson presents his friendly salutations to Doctr. Wistar and incloses him a letter from the Vice President of the Agricultural society of N.Y. on the subject of uniting all the Agricultural societies of the United States by the link of a Central society at the Seat of the Genl. government: to be communicated to the American Philosophl. society.

he has recieved Dr. Wistar's letter of the 10th. inst. & thanks him for it.

PrC (DLC); endorsed by TJ in ink on verso. Enclosure: Ezra L'Hommedieu to TJ, 3 Apr. 1802.

To Abraham Baldwin

DEAR SIR   Washington Apr. 14. 1802.

I have prepared a catalogue for the library of[1] Congress in conformity with your ideas that books of entertainment are not within the scope of it, and that books in other languages, where there are not translations of them, are to be admitted freely. I have confined the catalogue to those branches of science which belong to the deliberations of the members as statesmen, and in these have omitted those classical books, antient and modern, which gentlemen generally have in their private libraries, but which cannot properly claim a place in a collection made merely for the purposes of reference.

In History I have confined the list to the Chronological works, which give facts and dates with a minuteness not to be found in narrations composed for agreeable reading.   Under the Law of Nature & Nations I have put down every thing I know of worth possessing, because this is a branch of science often under the discussion of Congress & the books written in it not to be found in private libraries.

In law, I set down only general treatises for the purpose of reference. the discussions under this head in Congress are rarely so minute as to require or admit that Reports & special treatises should be introduced. The Parliamentary collection I have imagined should be compleat. it is only by having a law of proceeding, and by every member having the means of understanding it for himself, and appealing to it, that he can be protected against caprice & despotism in the chair. the two great Encyclopedies form a compleat supplement for the sciences omitted in the general collection, should occasion happen to arise for recurring to them. I have added a set of dictionaries in the different languages, which may be often wanting. this catalogue combined with what you may approve in those offered by others, will enable you to form your general plan, and to select from it every year to the amount of the annual fund of those most wanting. I have noted on it those which by the printed catalogue I find you already possess. in estimating, the amount of an annual selection, folios may be stated as costing 1½ guinea, quartos a guinea, 8 vos. 8/ 12 mos. 4/ in England, & in France three fourths of those prices, in neat but not splendid bindings. Accept assurances of my respect & friendly consideration.   TH: JEFFERSON

PrC (DLC); at foot of text: "Mr. Baldwin." Enclosure printed below.

The act of 26 Jan. 1802, which authorized TJ to appoint a librarian for the LIBRARY OF CONGRESS, also stipulated that the unexpended balance of the $5,000 appropriated by Congress in April 1800 for the purchase of books and maps be directed by a joint committee consisting of three senators and three congressmen. Baldwin chaired the group which was made up of fellow senators DeWitt Clinton and George Logan and congressmen Joseph H. Nicholson, James A. Bayard, and John Randolph (William Dawson Johnston, *History of the Library of Congress* [Washington, D.C., 1904], 35; E. Merton Coulter, *Abraham Baldwin: Patriot, Educator, and Founding Father* [Arlington, Va., 1987], 217; U.S. Statutes at Large, 2:56, 128-9; *Annals*, 11:196).

TJ NOTED, with check marks in the left margin of his enclosed list, the titles that corresponded to those in librarian John Beckley's PRINTED CATALOGUE. This eight-page *Catalogue of Books, Maps, and Charts, Belonging to the Library of the Two Houses of Congress*, published by William Duane in Washington in April 1802, included a numbered list of 964 volumes consisting of 222 titles arranged by folios, quartos, octavos, duodecimos, and nine maps and charts. The list provided estimates of prices for individual titles and complete sets of volumes (Shaw-Shoemaker, No. 3259; John Y. Cole, *For Congress and the Nation: A Chronological History of the Library of Congress* [Washington, D.C., 1979], 5).

TJ also received a list of 94 additional titles recommended for the Library of Congress that John Dickinson sent to George Logan, his cousin, on 20 Apr. Among the books suggested were histories, memoirs, travel writing, and works on agriculture, crop cultivation, and animal husbandry. Some of the titles already appeared in Beckley's catalogue (RC in DLC; addressed: "George Logan Senator in Congress"; franked and post- marked; endorsed by TJ: "Library Committee on the Library").

[1] Preceding three words interlined.

ENCLOSURE

List of Books for the Library of Congress

Law of Nature and Nations

√   Rutherforth's institutes of natural law. 8vo.
      Puffendorf devoirs de l'homme et du citoyen. 2.v. 12mo.
      Beller's delineation of Universal law. 4to.
√   Grotius's Laws of war with Barbeyrac's notes.
√   Puffendorf's law of nations with Barbeyrac's notes.
√   Burlamaqui sur la droit naturelle et Politique 4to.
      Wolff droit de la nature et des gens. Lat. Fr. 6.v. 12mo.
√   Vattel's law of nations.
      Vattel. Questions de droit naturel. 12mo.
      Recueil de discours par Barbeyrac. 2.v. 12mo.
      Cumberland's law of nature. 4to.
      Grotii mare liberum. 24o.
      Martens' Modern law of nations. 8vo.
      Ward's foundation & history of the law of nations 8vo.
      Zouch de judicio inter gentes, et de jure faciali.
      Bynkershoek opera. 6.v. 4to.
      Wicquefort de l'Ambassadeur. 2.v. 4to.
      Le ministre public par du Franquesnay 12mo.
      L'art de negocier par Pecquet. 12mo.
      Maniere de negocier par Callieres. 2.v. 12mo.
      Mably droit publique[1] de l'Europe. 3.v. 12mo.
      Negociations du President Jeannin. 12mo. 2.v.
      Ambassades de la Boderie en Angleterre. 5.v. 12mo.
      Negociations &c. du compte d'Estrades à Londres 9.v. 12mo.
      Lettres et negociations de J. de Witt. 5.v. 12mo.
      Histoire de la traité de Westphalie par d'Avaux. 6.v. 12mo.
      Dumont Corps universel diplomatique. 8.v. fol.
√   Jenkinson's collection of treaties. 3.v. 8vo.
√   Chalmer's collection of treaties 3.v. 8vo.
      Rymer's federa.
      [Muratori?][2]
      Hazard's state papers.
      Memoires sur les droits de France et de l'Angleterre en Amerique. 4.v. 4to.
      Robinet. Dictionnaire universel morale politique & diplomatique. 31.v. 4to.
      Code de l'humanité par Felice. 13.v. 4to.
Maritime
      Lee's treatise on captures. 8vo.

√   Molloy de jure maritime. 8vo.
    Il Consolato del Mare.
    Shardü leges navales Rhodiorum et selectae Rhodiorum
    Vinnius's commentary on the laws of Rhodes.
    Us et Coustumes de la mer par Clairac. 4to. including L. of Oleron &
        Wisby.
    Heineccii scriptores de jure maritimo. 4to.
    Schomberg on the maritime laws of Rhodes. 8vo.
    Robinson's admiralty reports. 8vo.
    several tracts on Neutral rights by Jenkinson, Schlegall, Croke & others.
    Valin

Law.
    Lord Kaim's general principles of Equity fol. 2d edition.
    Abridgment of cases in equity. 8vo.
    Fitzherbert's abridgment. fol.
    Broke's abridgment. 4to.
    Rolle's abridgment. fol.
    Bacon's abridgment. 8vo.
    Comyns's Digest. 8vo.
√   Viner's abridgment.
    Spelmanni Glossarium. fol.
√   Jacob's dict. by Ruffhead. fol.
    Cuningham's Law dict. 2.v. fol.
√   Coke's institutes. 8vo.
√   Blackstone's commentaries.
√   Wooddeson's lectures on the laws of England. 3.v. 8vo.
√   Reeve's history of the English law. 4.v. 8vo.
√   Reeves' history of the laws of shipping and[3] navigation. 8vo.
    Rastal's collection of statutes. fol.
    Pickering's collection of statutes 8vo.
    a complete collection of all the laws of every state should be made.
    Staundfort's Pleas of the crown. 4to.
    Hale's Pleas of the crown. 2.v. 8vo.
    Hawkins's Pleas of the crown 3.v. 8.vo.
√   Foster's crown law. 8vo.
√   State trials. compleat. fol.

Law Merchant
    Malyne's lex mercatoria. 2.v. fol.
√   Postlethwaite's dictionary 2.v. fol.
√   Beawe's Lex mercatoria.
√   the latest book of rates.

Foreign law.
    Calvini lexicon juridicum. fol.
    Corpus juris civilis Gothofredi. 2.v. fol. [it contains the Institutes, the
        Digests, the Codex, & Novels]
√   Domat's civil law. 2.v. fol.
    Institution du droit François par Argou. 2.v. 12mo.
    Commentaire sur l'Ordonnance de la Marine. 2.v. 12mo.
    Frederician code, and such other Summary digests of the laws of other
        countries as are known.

Parliamentary.
    Brady on government. fol.
    Petty's constitution & laws of England. 8vo.
    Sommers's rights of king and people 12mo.
    Bacon on the government of England. 4to.
    Smith's republic of England.
√   De Lolme on the constitution of England.
    Burgh's political disquisitions. 3.v. 8vo.
    Stuart's historical dissertation on the English constitution. 8vo.
    Spelman's works. fol.
    Thurloe's state papers[4]
√   Rushworth's collection 8.v. fol.
    Elsynge - Scobell [I do not recollect the particular titles[5]
    Arcana parliamentaria.
    Hollis's remains. 8vo.
    Orders of the H. of Commons. 12mo.
    Pettus's constitution of parliament. 8vo.
    Brown's privilegia Parliamentaria. 8vo.
    Petyt's antient rights of the Commons of Engld. 8vo.
    Hale's jurisdiction of parliaments. 8vo.
√   Atkyn's power of parliaments.[6]
    Selden on the judicature of parliaments. 12mo. his works
    Dewes' journal.[7]
    Ryley's placita parliamentaria. fol.
    Prynne's parliamentary writs. 4to.
    Hakewell's modus tenendi Parliamentum.
    Petyt's Jus parliamentarium. fol.
√   Lex Parliamentaria. 8vo.
√   Hatsell's Precedents of proceedings in the H. of Commons.
    Aylesbury election.
    Bohun's debates.[8]
    the Case of Ashby & White. 8vo.
√   Journals of the H. of Commons.
√   H. of Lords.
    Townshend's historical collections. fol.
√   a compleat collection of Parliamentary debates from the Parliamentary
        history in 24.v. 8vo. down to the present day.
√   Debates of the Irish Commons.
Political arithmetic, Commerce &c.
√   Petty's political arithmetic.
√   Sinclair on the British revenues. 8vo.
    Arithmetique Lineaire de Playfair. 4to.
    Wallace on the numbers of mankind. 8vo.
    Table des vivans de Susmich.
√   Anderson's history of commerce. 6.v. 8vo.
√   Smith's Wealth of nations.
√   Steuart's political economy. 2.v. 4to.
    Arbuthnot on antient coins and measures.[9]
Geography.
    Atlas portatif de Grenet et Bonne. 4to.

the Atlas'es of Delisle and Danville.
√   Jeffery's American Atlas.
    Busching's geography 6.v. 4to.
    Encyclopedia de Diderot et Dalembert. abt 30.v. fol. 35. guineas
    Encyclopedia Methodique[10]
    Dictionaries Scapula, Hederici, Ainsworth, Calepinus XI linguarum, Dictionaries of the academies of France, Spain, Crusia, Johnson's dict. and good dictionaries of all the other modern languages.
History.
    Annales Romaines par Macquer. 12mo.
    Histoire universelle de Bossuet. 2.v. 12mo.
    Essai historique et chronologique de l'Abbé Berlié. 12mo.
    Abregé chronologique de l'histoire ancienne avant J.C. par La Combe. 12mo.
    Abregé chronologique de l'histoire des Juifs. 12mo.
    Abregé chronologique de l'histoire des Empereurs Romains Richer. 2.v. 12mo.
√   Histoire ancienne de Milot. 4.v. 12mo.
√   Histoire ancienne de Rollin. 13.v. 12mo.
    Newton's chronology. 4to.
√   Blair's chronology fol.
√   Priestly's chronological & biographical charts.
√   Dictionnaire de Bayle 4.v. fol.
    Dictionnaire de Moreri. 10.v. fol.
    Collier's historical dictionary. 4.v. fol.
    Wood's Athen.[11]
    Dictionnaire historique et bibliographique par Lavocat. 4.v. 12mo.
    Dictionnaire historique par un societé de gens de lettres. 9.v. 8vo.
    Dictionnaire de diplomatique par Dom. de Vaynes 2.v. 8vo.
    The Chronologist of the war 1789-96. 12mo.
    Abregé chronologique de l'histoire universelle par Hornot. 12mo.
    Introduction a l'histoire de l'Univers de Puffendorf 4.v. 12mo.
    Tablettes chronologiques de l'histoire universelle de Fresnoy. 2.v. 8mo.
    Tableau chronologique de l'histoire de l'Europe de 476 à 1648. 8vo.
    Abregé chronologique de l'histoire d'Espagne et de Portugal. 2.v. 12mo.
    Abregé chronologique de l'hist. de France par Henault. 2.v. 12mo.
    Abregé chronologique de l'hist. & du droit public d'Allemagne par Pfeffel. 2.v. 12mo.
    Abregé chronologique de l'histoire du Nord par La Combe. 2.v. 12mo.
    Abregé chronologique de l'histoire de Pologne par l'Abbé Coyer. 2.v. 12mo.
    Abregé chronologique de l'histoire d'Angleterre par Salmon. 2.v. 12mo. Eng. if to be had.
    Historical register. 8vo.
    Annual register. 8vo.
American history. all the travels, histories, accounts &c. of America, previous to the revolution, should be obtained. it is already become all but impossible to make a collection of these things. standing orders should be lodged with our ministers in Spain, France & England, & our Consul at

Amsterdam to procure every thing within that description which can be hunted up in those countries.

London.	12mo.	15. @	.75	=	11.25	
	8vo.	84. @	1.67	=	140.	
		70. @	2.	=	140.	
	4tos.	31. @	4.	=	124.	
	fol.	48. @	7	=	336.	= 751.25
Paris.	12mo.	70. @	.75	=	52.5	
	8vo.	15. @	1.5	=	22.5	
	4to.	79. @	4	=	316.	
	folios.	57. @	7.	=	399	= 790.

MS (MoSHi: Jefferson Papers); entirely in TJ's hand, including brackets, except where indicated (see note 2); undated; check marks added by TJ (see letter above); calculation of expenditures in London and Paris at foot of document added by TJ at a later date, probably before 16 July (see TJ to William Duane, 16 July). PrC (DLC); blurred; lacks TJ's check marks; lacks calculation of expenditures.

The list was evidently approved by Baldwin and the congressional committee and returned to TJ (see TJ to John Beckley, 16 July 1802). HAZARD'S STATE PAPERS: lacks TJ's check mark, but included in Beckley's catalogue.

ROBINSON'S ADMIRALTY REPORTS: lacks TJ's check mark, but included in Beckley's catalogue.

[1] Word interlined.
[2] Entry interlined. Brackets supplied by Editors.
[3] Preceding four words interlined.
[4] Entry interlined.
[5] Entry interlined.
[6] Entry interlined.
[7] Entry interlined.
[8] Entry interlined.
[9] Entry interlined.
[10] Entry interlined.
[11] Entry interlined.

From Nicolas Gouin Dufief

MONSIEUR,   14 Avril. 1802

Vous recevrez sous peu de jours un second exemplaire de l'élégante traduction des Oeuvres de Senèque, (prix 9 dollars les 6 volumes brochés) & le Lucrèce Latin français. J'ai parcouru avec attention les catalogues des Principaux Libraires de Paris, Il n'y est fait aucune mention d'une Edition de Seneque, traduite par la Grange avec le texte original—ce qui me porte à croire qu'il n'en existe réellement point—Je ne laisserai pas de donner ordre à mon libraire de m'envoyer un exemplaire de cette edition si toutefois elle avoit été publiée— Dans ce cas Je reprendrois celle que je vous adresse. La Religieuse & le bon Sens en petits formats Seront particulierement recommandés ainsi que l'exposition du Système du monde par le profond Géomètre *La Place*. Le Bâtiment qui doit porter ma demande ne partant que dans quinze jours ou 3 Semaines Je pourrai faire exécuter les ordres qu'on m'enverra avant ce tems-là—

Je Suis avec un profond respect votre tres devoué Serviteur

N. G. DUFIEF

E D I T O R S '   T R A N S L A T I O N

SIR,   14 Apr. 1802

You will receive in a few days a second copy of the elegant translation of the works of Seneca (price nine dollars for the six paper-bound volumes) and the Latin-French Lucretius. I have attentively consulted the catalogues of the principal Parisian booksellers; there is no mention therein of an edition of Seneca translated by La Grange with the original text, which leads me to think that it does not really exist. I will not fail to order a copy of that edition from my bookseller if in fact it has been published. In that case, I shall return the one I am sending you. *La Religieuse* and *Le bon sens* in small format will be specially ordered again as well as the *Exposition du systême du monde* by the profound geometer La Place. Since the ship that will carry my request will not leave for two or three weeks, I can dispatch orders that are sent to me before then.

I am, with deep respect, your very devoted servant,   N. G. DUFIEF

RC (DLC); at foot of text: "Le Président des Etats Unis"; endorsed by TJ as received 16 Apr. and so recorded in SJL.

From Edward Stevens

SIR   Philadelphia April 14th: 1802

The Bearer, Mr: O Hebert is an english Gentleman of easy Circumstances, interested in a Patent Right for a Discovery of a Mode of applying Steam for the Cure of certain Disorders. Altho' the Discovery is not altogether new, yet I believe the Mode of Application is perfectly so. I am willing for the Good of Humanity to suppose that it possesses all the Virtue attributed to it by it's Proprietor. The Interest which you take in the Promotion of Science in general; and more especially when it tends to the immediate Good of Mankind will excite a favourable Impression as to the Subject of this Letter and will I hope plead my Apology for presenting him to you.

I am, with Sentiments of the highest Respect, Sir Your most obedt: Servt: EDWARD STEVENS

RC (MoSHi: Jefferson Papers); at foot of first page: "The President of the U. States"; endorsed by TJ as received 19 Apr. and so recorded in SJL with notation "by mr. Hebert."

Edward Stevens spent most of his early years in the West Indies, where he was a childhood friend of Alexander Hamilton on the island of St. Croix. He attended King's College in New York, studied medicine at the University of Edinburgh, then entered practice on St. Croix and later at Philadelphia. In 1799, he was appointed U.S. consul general for Saint-Domingue, serving in the post until resigning in 1801. Although he enjoyed good relations with Toussaint-Louverture during his tenure, Stevens was also harshly criticized by Jacob Mayer, the U.S. consul at Cap-Français, and others for using his office for personal gain and harboring pro-British sympathies. TJ replaced him with Tobias Lear in May 1801 (Syrett, *Hamilton*, 9:287n;

26:117n; Tansill, *Caribbean Diplomacy*, 58-64, 78, 81-2; Madison, *Papers, Sec. of State Ser.*, 1:127-9; 8:563-4; Vol. 33:447-8, 670, 675).

Physician H. O. HEBERT presented TJ with an engraving of his proposed "Air Pump Vapour Bath," as used in England to treat victims of gout, rheumatism, and other maladies. On 19 July 1802, he would write TJ that a working model of his machine was completed and "fit for immediate Operation" (*Hebert's Air Pump Vapour Bath* [Philadelphia, 1802; Shaw-Shoemaker, No. 2391]).

To Alexander White

TH: JEFFERSON TO MR WHITE.   Apr. 14. 1802

Not yet sufficiently possessed of the state of proceedings respecting the city, I am afraid of taking up an erroneous idea. I have in the inclosed draught of a resolution expressed my idea of what is wanting to be done *at this time* that you may see if I view it, according to the fact, & correct me if otherwise. it differs from yours principally in leaving out the part respecting making the public appropriations, which I think had better be passed over till the plan is made correct. my idea is that then we should examine what parts of that plan have been already fixed & made unalterable by the proclamations or other instruments executed by the preceding presidents, and if any thing remains unfixed, issue a proclamation or execute a deed, supplementary to the former instruments, and fixing irrevocably every thing not so fixed. I mean irrevocably except by the legislature. friendly salutations.

PrC (DLC); with enclosure pressed on same sheet at foot of text. Recorded in SJL with notation "correction of plan."

DIFFERS FROM YOURS: see resolution enclosed in White to TJ, 13 Apr.

ENCLOSURE

Draft of a Resolution for the City of Washington

Whereas sundry lots and fractions of lots for building have been laid out on the ground of the city of Washington which are not yet described by lines on the plan of the city, particularly within certain squares or spaces left open in the sd plan, and the water-lines on the said plan are not exactly conformable with those lines as they exist actually on the ground:

Resolved that it is expedient that the said building lots or fractions within the said squares or open spaces or elsewhere which have been laid out on the ground & not yet entered in the plan, should be exactly entered thereon[1] and that both the high & low water marks be delineated on the said plan in exact conformity with those lines as they exist on the ground[2] in order that a water street may be laid off adjacent to the high water mark: that the engraved plate with which the printed plans have been struck off, be then corrected in exact conformity with the original so amended, and a new edition of plans be issued proportioned in number from time to time to the calls for them. and that   be employed to make the said corrections in the original, by actual survey, wherever that shall be necessary, for which he shall recieve   for every perch of line which he shall survey & delineate

PrC (DLC); undated; pressed on same sheet as letter above.

[1] Word interlined.
[2] Passage from here to "high water mark" interlined.

From "Yankey Doodle"

Sir   Philadelphia April 14 1802

I have told you in my last Letter that I Soon Send you another the object of my Letter is that you Shall See how you Shall act in this Case Sir a few day's ago—an affray took place on board the Spanish brig it Contain's as follow's the mariner's having Consulted a lawyer about how they Could get Paid the Lawyer told them that must keep possesion brig until the monday following when he Should Seize the brig—and Sell her in a public vendue The Carpenter's hearing this They went and Consulted with another lawyer when the Sheriff Sent one of his men to take possesion of her in such a brutal maner that they began to drive people out of her one had not patience enough to bear this Scandalous treatment he lifted the hand spike and Struck one of the men on the head then the Sheriff Come with a five hundred men to take possesion of her they did take possesion they took the Spanish Colour broke in a thousand pieces and began huzza wich was at least one hour and then Sent the people to jail that is all I know about this uncommon proceeding—

You must put your Spectacles to read this   YANKEY DOODLE

you must Send your answer by the aurora as Soon as you can good by So as every read it

RC (DLC); endorsed by TJ as received from "Anonymous" on 18 Apr. and "rescue of Spanish brig" and so recorded in SJL, but as received 17 Apr.

The AFFRAY on the SPANISH BRIG lying at Southwark took place on 7 Apr. A writ of attachment had been served on the *Cabo de Hornos* by a sheriff's officer, who was directed to return and chain the vessel to the wharf for greater security. The seamen on board had previously libeled the brig for their wages and received a decree of condemnation against it. The sale of the vessel was to take place the same day as the sheriff's officer returned to secure the brig. Believing the officer's actions would interfere with their claim, the seamen resisted and attacked him. Informed of the assault, the sheriff and a number of constables and citizens boarded the brig and arrested 16 members of the crew (*Gazette of the United States*, 8 Apr. 1802; Madison, *Papers, Sec. of State Ser.*, 3:180-2).

To the House of Representatives

GENTLEMEN OF THE
HOUSE OF REPRESENTATIVES.

I now transmit the papers desired in your resolution of the 6th. instant. those respecting the Berceau will sufficiently explain themselves. the officer charged with her repairs, states, in his letter recieved Aug. 27. 1801. that he had been led by circumstances, which he explains, to go considerably beyond his orders.[1] in questions between nations who have no common umpire but reason, something must often be yielded of mutual opinion to enable them to meet in a common point.

The allowance which had been proposed to the officers of that vessel being represented as too small for their daily necessities, and still more so as the means of paying, before their departure, debts contracted with our citizens for subsistence, it was requested on their behalf that the daily pay of each might be the measure of their allowance. this being sollicited and reimbursement assumed by the Agent of their nation, I deemed that the indulgence would have a propitious effect in the moment of returning friendship. the sum of 870. D 83 c. was accordingly furnished them for the five months of past captivity, and a proportional allowance authorised until their embarcation.

TH: JEFFERSON
April 15. 1802.

RC (DNA: RG 233, PM, 7th Cong., 1st sess.); endorsed by clerks of the House of Representatives. PrC (DLC). Recorded in SJL with notation "Berceau." Enclosures (all Trs in DNA: RG 233, PM, 7th Cong., 1st sess., in clerks' hands): (1) Stephen Higginson & Co. to secretary of the navy, 19 Nov. 1800, extract, about landing the captured crew of the *Berceau*. (2) Same to same, 5 Dec. 1800, extract, about accommodation of the prisoners. (3) Same to same, 12 Dec. 1800, extract, about condemnation and advertised sale of the corvette by the district court, and giving a general report of its condition. (4) Secretary of the navy to Higginson & Co., 19 Dec. 1800, ordering purchase of the corvette; printed in NDQW, Dec. 1800-Dec. 1801, 39. (5) Higginson & Co. to secretary of the navy, 22 Dec. 1800, extract, reporting that the physician who treated the prisoners wishes to have his account settled and that the marshal has postponed the sale. (6) Same to same, 16 Jan. 1801, extract, reporting that on 15 Jan. their agent purchased the *Berceau* for $8,000 and its guns and maritime stores for an estimated total of $12,000. (7) Secretary of the navy to Higginson & Co., 17 Feb. 1801, ordering the transfer of prisoners to Philippe de Létombe. (8) Secretary of the navy to Létombe, 17 Feb. 1801, informing him that orders have been given to transfer to him 150 French prisoners at Boston, 25 at Providence, R.I., 100 in Connecticut, "8 Blacks" at New York, "90 do." at Frederick, Md., and 8 at Charleston, S.C.; printed in NDQW, Dec. 1800-Dec. 1801, 125. (9) Létombe to secretary of state, 10 Ventose Year 9 (1 Mch. 1801), extract, stating that the officers of the *Berceau* are in "deplorable" condition and the agents of the French government cannot act as "commissaries of prisoners"; the United States must provide the officers' subsistence, for which the government of France "is holden for the reimbursement"; see Vol. 34:668n. (10) Levi Lincoln, as acting secretary of state, to Létombe, 10 Mch. 1801, concerning details of the transfer of prisoners. (11) Secretary of the navy to Higginson & Co., 10 Mch. 1801, ordering that before they are transferred the French prisoners are to receive "cheap clothing" as necessary and each officer is to receive money equal to $2 for each week that he has had to pay for his own subsistence. (12) Same to same, 14 Mch. 1801, ordering that the French prisoners at Boston be sent to New York. (13) Louis André Pichon to secretary of state, 28 Ventose Year 9 (19 Mch. 1801), informing him that the first consul of France has issued orders for implementation of the convention between the United States and France even though the pact has not yet received final ratification; Pichon wishes to know the intentions of the United States regarding execution of the convention; see Vol. 33:349n; Vol. 34:668n; enclosing a list of decisions of the French Council of Prizes concerning 12 captured American vessels (with erasure and overwriting of one word possibly by TJ); enclosing also an extract of Pierre Alexandre Forfait, French minister of the marine and of the colonies, to agents of the French government in the colonies, 21 Vendémiaire Year 9 (12 Oct. 1800), informing them of their responsibility to begin enforcing the convention between the two countries and warning particularly against allowing privateers to interfere with the commerce of friendly and allied nations (in English; English date added by TJ); enclosing also an extract of Talleyrand, minister of foreign relations, to Pichon, 14 Nivose Year 9 (3 Jan. 1801), stating that he has ordered the Council of Prizes to postpone indefinitely any decisions relating to U.S. vessels; this decision is not intended to prevent restitutions but "to render them both more prompt & more certain"; once the convention is ratified France will issue a decree "which shall replevy for the Americans all the prizes, the restitution of which, has been engaged for" (in English; English date added by TJ). (14) Secretary of the navy to Higginson & Co., 20 Mch. 1801, stating that the *Berceau* is to be restored to France under the Convention of 1800 "with all her guns, ammunition, apparel & every thing belonging to her," and stating that "This business should be done as if no reluctance accompanied the restoration. We are now at peace with France, & we should act as if we returned to a state of amity with pleasure. Let there be no cause of complaint against the Government or it's Agents"; printed in NDQW, Dec. 1800-Dec. 1801, 150. (15) Same to same, 20 Mch. 1801, ordering that payment for subsistence of the officers of the corvette be made from their statement of account of actual expenses rather than at the rate of $2 per week. (16) Same to Samuel Brown, 1 Apr. 1801, extract, ordering him to ascertain the state the corvette "was in at the time of her Capture, as to her armament stores & provisions, & to cause her to be put in the same condition before she is delivered up to the French Government"; printed in NDQW, Dec. 1800-Dec. 1801, 171). (17) Pichon to secretary of state, 13 Germinal Year 9 (3 Apr. 1801), requesting that the United States provide for the subsistence of all the French prisoners from the various locations until they can be embarked; the expenditure should be "placed to the account of the French Republic" and Pichon will arrange for repayment; see Vol. 34:668n. (18) Secretary of the navy to Brown, 10 Apr. 1801, regarding disposition of the prisoners; printed in NDQW, Dec. 1800-Dec. 1801, 185. (19) Pichon to secretary of state, 1 Floreal Year 9 (21 Apr. 1801), asserting that French officials in the West Indies are implementing the Convention of 1800 and preparing to make restitution for prizes captured since the convention was signed; for TJ's notations in the margin of the original letter, see Vol. 34:570-1n. (20) Monsieur Bourcier at Puerto Rico, the delegate of French agents in the Windward Islands, to Létombe, 4 Floreal Year 9 (24 Apr. 1801), extract, stating that upon receipt of official word of the convention, he released all captured vessels that were not yet sold and "took measures for defending the interests of the Americans, who might have claims for restitution to establish" (dated in TJ's hand: "Apr. 29. 1801"). (21) Secretary of the navy to Brown, 4 May 1801, regarding payment to the physician who attended the French prisoners from 15 June 1799 to 1 Apr. 1801. (22) Same to same, 18 May 1801, regarding 69 French prisoners sent to New York for transportation to Boston and transfer to the custody of French officials. (23) Pichon to secretary of state, 18 June 1801, extract, acknowledging that France is responsible for $15,000 advanced by the U.S. for the aid of refugees from Saint-Domingue as well as for advances made for the subsistence of prisoners; when the United States prepares accounts for all such expenditures "I shall think myself sufficiently authorized to settle and adjust them"; summarized in Madison, *Papers, Sec. of State Ser.*, 1:327. (24) Brown to secretary of the navy, 24 June 1801, extract, reporting that the *Berceau* was returned to French custody on 22 June; the captain of the corvette has asked for silver and china for his cabin, but Brown will not furnish those items without authorization, since he doubts that they were on board at the time of the vessel's capture. (25) Secretary of the navy to Brown, 3 July 1801, extract, stating: "There is no doubt that

the *Berceau* has been sufficiently repaired & furnished: of course no more expence must be incurred on the part of the United States on her account"; requesting a statement of repairs and supplies furnished for the vessel "& the precise state & condition she was in as to her equipments of every kind, on her delivery to the officers appointed on the part of the French republic to receive her"; printed in NDQW, Dec. 1800-Dec. 1801, 266. (26) Secretary of the navy to Pichon, 8 July 1801, enclosing a statement showing that the U.S. navy agent at Boston expended $870.83, equal to 4,750 livres, for the pay of the officers of the *Berceau*; this expenditure being separate from payments made for the officers' subsistence while they were prisoners (with statement of payments in hand of and signed by Thomas Turner, accountant for the Navy Department, 9 Apr. 1802). (27) Pichon to secretary of state, 10 July 1801, extract, concerning restitutions (at head of text in TJ's hand: "July 10. 1801. Extracts of a letter from mr Pichon to the Secretary of state"); for TJ's notations in the margin of the original letter, see Vol. 34:570n. (28) Brown to secretary of the navy, 13 July 1801, extract, reporting that the French do not yet have the *Berceau* ready for sea, which prolongs the period in which the United States advances funds for subsistence of the crew (endorsed); enclosing Brown to Marc Antoine Alexis Giraud, commissary of the French government at Boston, 30 June 1801, reiterating that he is not authorized to furnish any article that was not on board the corvette "anterior to her coming into possession of the United States" and stating that all items to be furnished by the U.S. are ready to be placed on board the vessel (endorsed). (29) Brown to Lincoln, [4 Aug. 1801], extract (in Meriwether Lewis's hand; at head of text: "Extract of a letter from Samuel Brown navy Agent at Boston to Levi Lincoln esqr. without date, but recieved August 27th. 1801"); see TJ to William Branch Giles, 6 Apr. 1802. (30) Pichon to Madison, 6 Vendémiaire Year 10 (28 Sep. 1801), reporting that Rear Admiral Jean Baptiste Raymond Lacrosse, governor of Guadeloupe, has referred to the French government the cases of restitutions for prizes taken after the signing of the convention; enclosing an extract of a letter from Lacrosse to Pichon, 14 Fructidor Year 9 (1 Sep. 1801), stating that American ships are "carrying away our black cultivators"; that one ship captain has been arrested and convicted; yet regarding "general measures upon this subject," Lacrosse suggests, as "a proof of the indulgence of the French government towards the subjects of a nation with which we ought to be intimately connected," that Pichon confer with the U.S. secretary of state because Lacrosse is "convinced beforehand" that the secretary of state "will find no measures severe enough for punishing such a violation of the laws of our territory"; printed in Madison, *Papers, Sec. of State Ser.*, 2:148-9. (31) Brown to secretary of the navy, 31 Oct. 1801, providing, as instructed, an account of the repairs to the *Berceau*; stating that due to the quality of the work and materials, "there cannot be a doubt" that the vessel was returned to the French in better condition than it was in immediately before the battle in which it was captured; enclosing a summary statement that the original cost of the corvette was $13,349.44, the commission on the purchase was $266.98, and the repairs cost $32,839.54 for a total of $46,455.86; noting that the convention was signed 30 Sep. 1800, ratified by the United States with exceptions, 18 Feb. 1801, agreed to by Bonaparte, 31 July, and promulgated by the president on 21 Dec. 1801; enclosing also a detailed statement of payment by Higginson & Co. to the district court for the purchase of the vessel and items of equipment sold separately for $13,349.44; enclosing also a detailed "Abstract of the Repairs & Expenditures on the French Corvette Le Berceau" including $18,345.10 in goods from the public property and $14,210.24 in cash

payments for a total of $32,839.54. (32) List of judgments by the French Council of Prizes in cases involving American ships to 3 Brumaire Year 10 (25 Oct. 1801), from Fulwar Skipwith, possibly enclosed with this message (among enclosures to TJ to the House of Representatives, 20 Apr. 1802; printed in ASP, *Foreign Relations*, 2:438-9, as the last of the enclosures listed above); see Madison, *Papers, Sec. of State Ser.*, 2:211, and Skipwith to TJ, 30 Oct. 1801. Message and enclosures printed in ASP, *Foreign Relations*, 2:428-39.

RESOLUTION OF THE 6TH. INSTANT: see TJ to William Branch Giles, 6 Apr. The House of Representatives received this message from Meriwether Lewis on 16 Apr. After the message was read, the House appointed William Eustis, Benjamin Tallmadge, Philip R. Thompson, John Campbell, and John A. Hanna a committee to examine the documents relating to the *Berceau*. On 23 Apr., Roger Griswold proposed a resolution whereby the committee would "be instructed to inquire whether any further appropriations are necessary to cover the expense which has arisen for the purchase and repairing that vessel for the French Government, and for advancing to her officers their monthly pay." Samuel Smith moved to amend the resolution to remove the reference to the French government, but at Giles's request Smith withdrew his motion "in order to save time." Griswold's resolution then passed without discussion or a roll call. The session ended without further action by the House on the expenditures for the *Berceau* (JHR, 4:204-5, 219; *Annals*, 11:1232).

¹ TJ here canceled "this was not known here till the receipt of his letter." TJ also made the cancellation in ink on PrC.

From Bishop James Madison

Dear Sir, Wmsburg Apr. 15. 1802

I am greatly obliged to you for your Favour, by the last Post. From the Examination, which I have been able, as yet, to give the Work, it appears to contain much valuable Information; & to[1] do real Honour to the mathematical Talents of it's Author. But for your Goodness, it is probable, I should have remained a Stranger to so interesting a Work; especially as the Americans have not been, hitherto, distinguished for such abstruse Researches.

In the Evening Post of New York, of the 3d of this Month, there is a most infamous Acct. of our College; & what might be esteemed most strange in other Times, you are made the Author of all the Mischeif—& of all the Evils which the College has so widely disseminated. The Paragraph betrays a Malignity of Heart, which must excite the Detestation of every one, who is enabled to judge of the abominable Falsehoods, which it contains. I have addressed to him a short Letter, which, if he does not publish, shall appear in all our Papers.

I rejoice in the good Work of the present Session of Congress. Nothing was so essential as to clear away the Rubbish of the preceeding Administration; & I do hope it will be done effectually.— Beleive me to be, with the greatest Respect & Esteem, Dr Sir—Yr Friend & Sert. J MADISON

RC (DLC); endorsed by TJ as received 19 Apr. and so recorded in SJL.

YOUR FAVOUR: not found or recorded in SJL, but TJ probably enclosed with it a copy of Jared Mansfield's mathematical essays, which TJ had offered to help distribute; see Abraham Baldwin to TJ, 29 Mch. 1802. A MOST INFAMOUS ACCT. OF OUR COLLEGE: a duel between two students at the College of William and Mary that resulted in their expulsion. The Federalist press recounted an ensuing protest by members of the student body, vandalism to the local church and St. George Tucker's house, and Tucker's alleged resignation as professor. The cause of the MISCHEIF was given as "the blessed effects of the modern, or Jeffersonian system of religion" and the university's pursuit of "party-politics, instead of science." A later account extracted from the *Commercial Advertiser* reported that one of the expelled students, a native Virginian, had been a proponent of the "modern right of insurrection" against legitimate authority at Princeton and was expelled from that institution prior to leading the insurrection at William and Mary (*New-York Evening Post*, 3, 16 Apr. 1802; see also Steven J. Novak, *The Rights of Youth: American Colleges and Student Revolt, 1798-1815* [Cambridge, Mass., 1977], 21). ABOMINABLE FALSEHOODS: William Duane charged that the *New-York Evening Post*'s account of the episode was a "false fabrication" and that the duel had occurred three years earlier but the *Post*'s publisher Michael Burnham defended the source of the original story's veracity

(*New-York Evening Post*, 3 and 13 Apr. 1802).

A SHORT LETTER to the editor of the *New-York Evening Post*, by "An inhabitant of Williamsburg," reported errors in the paper's earlier account. The author claimed that the college maintained its regular schedule of lectures, that only five or six students were involved and only a few panes of glass were broken, and that

Tucker did not resign his professorship. The college "boasts of Mr. Jefferson, as one of her brightest ornaments; and will continue to boast, so long as virtue, and science, and pure republicanism, and the best interests of America, shall be cherished within her walls" (same, 24 Apr. 1802).

¹ MS: "to to."

From Philip Wilson

[on or before 15 Apr. 1802]

Pray your Excellency grant me in some way protection from cruel Delay and wrong; The Committee of Claims, put me off the third year, although the Auditor gave me an acknowledgement that the *Rice* and *Claret*, I supplied to Comy. General Blains Department, is entered in account in that office, as "Unsettled for."

Mr. Smith, Secretary of the Navy, does not understand my Naval Architecture, or my Discussion thereon. Through some Superintendance, I might introduce it into American Shipping of War &c.— Indeed your Excellency, I fear it will be necessary thereto ere long; as the designs of the French are not understood.—

I have not money to carry me home, nor to procure a dinner to my Wife and Children, whom I left in want: under the worst of ills: great poverty—Our Cloaths all pawned and eat up by Usance.

Pray Your Excellency grant Relief to Your Cruelly oppressed Citizen   PHILIP WILSON

RC (DLC); undated; at foot of text: "His Excellency the President of the United States &c."; endorsed by TJ as received 15 Apr. 1802 and so recorded in SJL.

On 15 Dec. 1801, Wilson submitted a petition to the House of Representatives for settlement of his claim for supplying

RICE AND CLARET to the Continental army in 1778, which was referred to the Committee of Claims. Reporting on 28 Dec., the committee recommended that Wilson's memorial "ought not be granted." The same committee rejected a similar petition from Wilson in December 1800 (JHR, 3:732-3; 4:17, 26).

From Henry Dearborn

SIR,   War Department. 16th. April 1802.

I take the liberty of proposing the following gentlemen as Ensigns in the Regiments of Infantry, in the service of the United States: (viz)

Simeon Knight	Vermont	1st. Regiment
Joseph Dorr	ditto.	1st. ditto.
George T. Ross	Pennsyla.	2d. ditto.

Accept, Sir, the assurances of my high respect   H. DEARBORN

RC (DLC); in a clerk's hand, signed by Dearborn; at foot of text: "The President of the United States"; endorsed by TJ as received from the War Department on 16 Apr. and "Nominations" and so recorded in SJL; also endorsed by TJ "Knight Simeon & others." FC (Lb in DNA: RG 107, LSP); in a clerk's hand.

Simeon KNIGHT and Joseph DORR received ensigns' commissions dated 29 Apr. George Thompson ROSS had been a lieutenant of artillerists and engineers from December 1796 until his resignation in May 1801. On 3 May 1802, he was commissioned as an ensign and second lieutenant of the 2d infantry regiment (Heitman, *Dictionary*, 1:379, 606, 846).

To Philip Ludwell Grymes

DEAR SIR   Washington Apr. 16. 1802.

Your's of the 11th. is recieved. I find that writing to mr Windham Grymes at the same time as to yourself, I have by mistake mentioned to both that I had inclosed mr Jennings's letter, whereas I had but one to inclose, and that probably went to mr W. Grymes. Mr Jennings expressing a doubt therein how a particular expression in the will might be construed by our laws, mentioned what the testatrice intended by it. I answered him that our law was the same as the English on that subject, & as the expression in the will would effect her intention in England, it would probably do the same here. Accept my assurances of respect and friendly consideration.

TH: JEFFERSON

PrC (MHi); at foot of text: "Philip L. Grymes esq."; endorsed by TJ in ink on verso.

YOUR'S OF THE 11TH.: Grymes to TJ, 11 Apr. 1802, has not been found but is recorded in SJL as received from Brandon on 15 Apr.

AT THE SAME TIME: on 30 Mch. 1802, TJ wrote to both Charles Wyndham Grymes and Philip Ludwell Grymes.

I ANSWERED HIM: TJ to Edmund Jennings, 21 July 1801.

To George Jefferson

Dear Sir   Washington Apr. 16. 1802.

By a vessel sailing this day for Norfolk mr Barnes sends 16. packages of groceries &c addressed to mr Taylor, to be sent on to you. these being for use while I shall be at Monticello I must pray you to forward them by the first boat, as they will, with good luck, only arrive in time for me. accept assurances of my affectionate esteem

Th: Jefferson

PrC (MHi); at foot of text: "Mr. George Jefferson"; endorsed by TJ in ink on verso. Recorded in SJL with notation "Groceries go off this day."

VESSEL SAILING THIS DAY: John Farrall, master of the sloop *Three Sisters*, in port at Georgetown, received 16 marked and numbered packages from John Barnes on 15 Apr. to be delivered to James Taylor, Jr., merchant at Norfolk. Farrall charged $4 for the shipment (bill of lading in CSmH; printed form, with blanks filled by a purser or clerk, signed by Farrall; endorsed by Barnes as sent to Taylor "for Richmond" on account of the president; endorsed as paid in full by same purser or clerk; endorsed by TJ: "Farral").

From George Jefferson

Dear Sir   Richmond 16th. April 1802

I have lately received, and have to day forwarded to Johnston & Richardson of Norfolk, to be by them sent on to Mr. Barnes by the first opportunity, seven dozen of Mr. Macons hams; being all that he can spare.

I am endeavouring to make up the quantity you require, and hope shortly to procure such as may be relied upon.

The two boxes & Cask of wine from Philada. arrived some days ago, and were yesterday forwarded on to Milton by Wm. Faris.

The nail rod is not yet received—nor has any of your Tobacco yet come down.

I am Dear Sir Your Very humble servt.   Geo. Jefferson

RC (MHi); at foot of text: "Thos. Jefferson esqr."; endorsed by TJ as received 19 Apr. and so recorded in SJL.

James Madison's Report on Claims under Article 7 of the Jay Treaty

The Secretary of State, to whom has been referred by the President of the United States a Resolution of the Senate passed on the 12th. day of this month, requesting the President to cause to be laid before the Senate the Amount of claims preferred under the seventh Article of the Treaty of Amity, Commerce & Navigation with Great Britain, and of the sums awarded by the Commissioners and paid by the British Government, and a statement of the principles adopted by the said Commissioners in their proceedings under the said Article; thereupon respectfully submits the following Report to the President. That agreeably to an estimate made on the 9th. of May 1798 by Samuel Cabot Esqr. at that time an Agent of the United States under the 7th. Article of the said Treaty, the claims preferred under that Article amounted to the sum of One Million two hundred and fifty thousand pounds sterling. The Document herewith submitted to the President, containing a general statement of monies received on Awards of the Commissioners will shew the sums awarded by them, and paid by the British Government under the Article in question of the said Treaty.

It does not appear from any researches which the Secretary has been able to make, that the precise principles on which the Commissioners have proceeded, can be otherwise deduced than from the awards made in the several cases which have been decided. Any statement of them in detail is presumed not to be within the intention of the Resolution.

All which is respectfully submitted

JAMES MADISON
Department of State 16th April 1802

MS (DNA: RG 46, EPFR, 7th Cong., 1st sess.); in a clerk's hand, signed by Madison; endorsed by a Senate clerk. Enclosure: Statement by George W. Erving, London, 1 Dec. 1801, of payments awarded under Article 7 of the Jay Treaty; summarizing £93,755 received by claimants through Erving's predecessors as agents for American claims, Samuel Bayard and Samuel Williams, and through private agents; showing also approximately £1,400 in "Public Advances," which Erving noted had been made in only 9 of 40 cases of payment of claims; Erving stating also that 17 cases had been dismissed by the board of commissioners, and that the amount of expenses paid by claimants was "impossible to ascertain" (MS in same; in Erving's hand and signed by him; at head of text: "Statement of Monies received by Awards of the Commissioners acting under the 7th. Article of the British Treaty"; endorsed by a Senate clerk); printed in ASP,

Foreign Relations, 2:428; for Bayard and Williams as agents for American claims, see John Bassett Moore, ed., *International Adjudications, Modern Series, Volume IV: Compensation for Losses and Damages Caused by the Violation of Neutral Rights, and by the Failure to Perform Neutral Duties* [New York, 1931], 29-30, 74. Enclosed in TJ to the Senate, 17 Apr. 1802 (see below).

The Senate passed the RESOLUTION on 12 Apr. during consideration of the convention with Great Britain for settlement of claims under Article 6 of the Jay Treaty (JEP, 1:420; TJ to the Senate, 29

Mch.). On 17 Apr., Meriwether Lewis delivered the communication printed above and its enclosure to the Senate with a brief message from TJ: "Gentlemen of the Senate I now transmit you a report of the Secretary of state with the document accompanying it on the subject of your resolution of the 12th. instant concerning the VIIth. article of the treaty between the United States and Great Britain. Th: Jefferson Apr. 17. 1802" (RC in DNA: RG 46, EPFR, 7th Cong., 1st sess., endorsed by a Senate clerk; PrC in DLC; recorded in SJL with notation "Report of Secy. state & documents VIIth. art. Brit. treaty").

From Martha Jefferson Randolph

Edgehill April 16 1802

I recieved with gratitude and pleasure inexpressible, my dearest Father, the elegant medal you sent me. it arrived safely with out a scratch even, and is I think a good likeness; but as I found fault with Houdon for making you too old I shall have the same quarrel with the medal also. you have many years to live before the likeness can be a perfect one. Mr R— desired me to tell you that as his trip to Georgia was but to take a view of the country, a few weeks sooner or later would make no material difference with him and his anxiety to conduct such a family of little children thro the difficulties of the journey would naturally induce him to pospone his as it will be attended by no great inconvenience to himself. Ellen and Cornelia have had an erruption attended with fever which has been prevalent in the neighbourhood certainly not the chicken pox but what else we cannot determine. Ellen is well and Cornelia much better. Virginia is certainly for size and health the finest child I ever had cutting her teeth with out fever, disordered bowels or other indication of her situation but the champing of her gums and the appearance of the teeth them selves. the others go on better than they did last winter. Jefferson is reading latin with his Papa but I am seriously uneasy at his not going to school, Mr Murray with whom we proposed putting him has his number complete and will not I fear take another. Anne translates with tolerable facility, and Ellen reads, not very correctly it is true, but in a way speedily to do so I hope. for which I really think we are indebted to your letter expressing your surprise at her having in so

short a time learned to read and write; she began with it her self, and by continually spelling out lines putting them together and then reading them to who ever would listen to her, she convinced me of the practicability of carrying on reading and spelling together before in the regular course of the business she[1] had got into two syllables. the writing she attempted also but the trouble was so much greater than any end to be answerd by teaching her at so[2] early a period that very reluctantly I prevailed upon her to defer that part of her education to a more distant one. so much for my hopes and fears with regard to those objects in which they center. the former preponderate upon the whole, yet my anxiety about them frequently makes me unreasonably apprehensive, unreasonably I think for surely if they turn out well with regard to morals I *ought* to be satisfied, tho I *feel* that I never can sit down quietly under the idea of their being blockheads—
adieu Dear adored Father we look forward with transport to the time at which we shall all meet at[3] monticello tho not on my side unmixed with pain when I think it will be the precursor of a return to the world from which I have been so long been secluded and for which my habits render me every way unfit, tho the pleasure of seeing you every day is a good that will render every other evil light—once more adieu the children are clamorous to be remembered to you and believe your self *first* and unrivaled in the heart of your devoted child

M. Randolph

RC (MHi); addressed: "Thomas Jefferson President of the United states Washington"; endorsed by TJ as received 19 Apr. and so recorded in SJL.

For the ELEGANT MEDAL, see TJ to Martha Jefferson Randolph, 3 Apr. MR. MURRAY: perhaps Matthew Maury, who succeeded his father James Maury as rector of Fredericksville parish and master of a school for classical studies (Woods, *Albemarle*, 268-9; Vol. 20:331; Vol. 24:573, 578).

INDEBTED TO YOUR LETTER: see TJ to Ellen Wayles Randolph, 27 Nov. 1801.

[1] MS: "he."
[2] MS: "to."
[3] MS: "a."

From Caesar A. Rodney

Wilmington April 16th. 1802.

HONORED & DEAR SIR,

I take the liberty of introducing to your acquaintance Dr. Joseph[1] McCreery, a young gentleman of very amiable character & manners, who has read or rather studied medicine under Dr. J. Tilton of this place a man proverbial for his rigid honesty & inflexible integrity. Dr. McCreery has lately passed his examination as a physician in the

University of Penna. & wishes employment in the hospital about to be established at New Orleans. His medical talents I am assured by those who are judges, justly entitle him to solicit the first place in such an institution. He will carry with him, however, ample & satisfactory recommendations on this head.

I have only to mention further, that in addition to the very many good qualities he possesses he is a disinterested Republican. With great personal & political regard I am Dr. Sir Yours very Sincerely

C. A. RODNEY

RC (DNA: RG 59, LAR); endorsed by TJ as received 21 Apr. and "Joseph Mc.Crery to hospital at N. Orleans" and so recorded in SJL with a brace connecting it with James Tilton's letter also of this date (see below).

DR. JOSEPH MCCREERY (Macrery) graduated from the school of medicine at the University of Pennsylvania in 1802. James TILTON, a fellow Wilmington alumnus of the institution, who received his medical degree in 1771, became the first president of the Medical Society of Delaware (W. J. Maxwell, comp., *General Alumni Catalogue of the University of Pennsylvania: 1917* [Philadelphia, 1917], 563, 566; Thomas C. Stellwagen, "Delaware Doctors," *Historical and Biographical Papers of the Historical Society of Delaware*, 3 [1897], No. 19:7, 14; Vol. 34:488n).

¹ "Joseph" interlined in place of "William."

From Robert Smith

SIR!   Nav Dep 16th Apl 1802

Mr Charles Ludlow for whom the accompanying nomination is intended, has been mentioned to me in terms of very high Approbation, by many respectable Nautical gentlemen—He is intended for the Adams.

I have the honor to be, with the greatest respect, Sir, your mo: ob: st: RT SMITH

RC (DLC); in a clerk's hand, signed by Smith; at foot of text: "President United States"; endorsed by TJ as received from the Navy Department on 16 Apr. and "Nominations" and so recorded in SJL. FC (Lb in DNA: RG 45, LSP). Enclosure: undated draft of message to the Senate, nominating Charles Ludlow to be a lieutenant in the navy (MS in DLC; in same clerk's hand).

CHARLES LUDLOW was a nephew of Daniel Ludlow, the navy agent at New York City. He served as a midshipman on the frigate *United States* during the Quasi-War. Aaron Burr recommended him to Samuel Smith in May 1801, stating that Ludlow was "well spoken of by the officers of Navy of whom I have enquired" (NDBW, *Register*, 32; Kline, *Burr*, 1:577-8).

On 20 Apr., Smith wrote TJ again regarding Ludlow, urging the rapid approval of his nomination. Smith informed the president that the frigate *Adams*, for which Ludlow was intended, would depart within five or six days. "Her sailing orders will be prepared this day," wrote

Smith, "& if agreeable to you, I wish to send Mr. Ludlow's Commission with them" (RC in DLC, in a clerk's hand, signed by Smith, at foot of text: "President U: States," endorsed by TJ as received from the Navy Department on 20 Apr. and "Ludlow" and so recorded in SJL; FC in Lb in DNA: RG 45, LSP).

TJ submitted Ludlow's nomination to the Senate on 21 Apr., which approved it the following day (RC in DNA: RG 46, EPEN, 7th Cong., 1st sess., endorsed by a Senate clerk; PrC in DLC; recorded in SJL with notation "nomn Ludlow military"; JEP, 1:421).

From James Tilton

SIR   Wilmington 16 April 1802.

The bearer, Doctor Joseph McCrery, who has Just passed the medical school of Philadelphia, presents himself to you, in hopes of the appointment of physician to the hospital, which is to be established at New-Orleans. Much might be said in favour of this young gentleman. I shall only observe that, in addition to the Diploma, which he will receive in May next, I can vouch for his extensive science, his good morals, his assiduous application to business, and his universal acceptance & estimation among his acquaintance. As he has attended the practice of my shop, and lived in my family, for several years past, I speak from certain knowledge of him, and think him admirably qualified for the duties he proposes to undertake.

With great respect, I have the honor to be, Sir, your most obt. Servt.   JAMES TILTON

RC (DNA: RG 59, LAR); at foot of text: "Thomas Jefferson Esqr."; endorsed by TJ as received 21 Apr. and "Joseph Mc.Crery to hospital at N. Orleans" and

so recorded in SJL with a brace connecting it with Caesar A. Rodney's letter also of this date.

From Elias Boudinot

Mint of the United States
Philadelphia 17th. April 1802

The Director of the Mint, being informed by the public News Papers, that a Bill has been brought into Congress for abolishing of the Mint, cannot, consistent with his duty, omit, respectfully to represent the Case of some of the Officers, Clerks and Workmen of the Mint, to the President.

The Salaries and Wages allowed in the Mint have not been increased since the first establishment of the Institution, notwithstanding the great rise in the prices of every necessary of life, for several years past.—They have submitted to a bare subsistence without complaint, from the Idea, that their Employment was permanent, while they behaved well, and that Peace and reduced prices of food, would give them an opportunity of making up former deficiencies—Add to this, that their constant habits in the Mint, have made it difficult for them, at once, to return to their former occupations with advantage.—If the Mint should be abolished, it will be some time before they can get again into full Employment, and of course must suffer, essentially, even as to their necessary support.—

The Director therefore submits their Case to the Consideration of Government, and does not doubt but some small provision will be made for them, in Case of their intire dismission from the public Service

In this representation it is not meant to include the Director, Assayer or Treasurer, as neither of these do depend on their Salaries for support.—All which is respectfully submitted to the President by

his obedient humble Servant   ELIAS BOUDINOT Director

RC (DLC); at head of text: "To The President of the United States"; endorsed by TJ as received 19 Apr. and so recorded in SJL. FC (DNA: RG 104, DL). Tr (DNA: RG 233, PM, 7th Cong., 1st sess.; in Meriwether Lewis's hand, with Boudinot's signature supplied by TJ; endorsed by a Senate clerk).

For the BILL in Congress proposing the abolishment of the MINT, see Henry Voigt to TJ, 11 Feb. 1802. TJ's papers contain an undated list of the OFFICERS, CLERKS AND WORKMEN of the Mint compiled by Boudinot, which includes the job title and annual salary of 24 employees. Salaries range from $2,000 for the director to the $330 received by the workmen employed in operating the press, opening ingots, and assisting the assayer (PrC in DLC: TJ Papers, 235:42187; in a clerk's hand).

DIRECTOR, ASSAYER OR TREASURER: that is, Boudinot, Joseph Richardson, and Benjamin Rush (Frank H. Stewart, *History of the First United States Mint, Its People and Its Operations* [Camden, N.J., 1924], 80, 90).

TJ forwarded Boudinot's letter to the House and Senate on 20 Apr. In a brief covering letter, TJ stated, "The object of the inclosed letter from the Director of the Mint at Philadelphia, being within legislative competence only, I transmit it to both houses of Congress" (RC in DNA: RG 233, PM, 7th Cong., 1st sess., endorsed by a House clerk; PrC in DLC; RC in DNA: RG 46, LPPM, 7th Cong., 1st sess., endorsed by a Senate clerk; recorded in SJL with notation "Mint"). The Senate ordered Boudinot's letter to lie for consideration, while the House referred it to the Committee of the Whole House, which was considering the bill for abolishing the Mint (JS, 3:215; JHR, 4:211).

On 25 June, Boudinot drafted another letter for the president on the difficulties he confronted as director of the Mint. Specifically, Boudinot complained that the collector at Philadelphia was demanding duties on a shipment of copper blanks imported from England by the Mint. Importing copper blanks saved considerably on costs, Boudinot explained, and no duties had ever been charged on previous shipments. "It seems as if every opposition was made to lessening the Expenses of this Institution," Boudinot complained. If duties must be paid, which would also require his frequent attendance at the custom house, Boudinot would be forced to revert to purchasing more expensive domestic copper. "The copper Coinage will not bear the Expence, & be worth continuing," declared Boudinot, and he hoped to receive the president's instructions on the business soon. This letter, however, was apparently never sent. It is not recorded in SJL and an endorsement on the draft states that "The letter to the President was not sent, the Copper having been admitted without payment of Duties" (Dft in DNA: RG 104, GC).

From Henry Dearborn

SIR,   War Department 17h. April 1802.

I have the honor to propose to your consideration, Jared Mansfield of Connecticut, as a Captain in the Corps of Engineers.

With sentiments of sincere respect, and high consideration, I am, Sir, Yr. Obt. Servant   H. DEARBORN

RC (DLC); in a clerk's hand, signed by Dearborn; at foot of text: "The President of the United States"; endorsed by TJ as received from the War Department on 17 Apr. and "Nominations Mansfield Jared." FC (Lb in DNA: RG 107, LSP); in a clerk's hand.

Jared MANSFIELD was the author of the *Essays, Mathematical and Physical* mentioned in Abraham Baldwin's letter to TJ of 29 Mch. and Bishop James Madison's of 15 Apr. At the time, Mansfield was teaching at a school in New Haven, Connecticut. He was commissioned a captain of engineers on 3 May (DAB; Heitman, *Dictionary*, 1:688).

To Levi Lincoln

DEAR SIR   Washington Apr. 17. 1802.

I hasten to call your attention to the resolution of the Senate of the 15th. instant now inclosed, on the subject of the lands of the US. in the state of Tennessee, at this time, because while the members of Congress are here you may be able to collect such information on the subject as to enable you to shape your course in the execution of it with more facility as well as correctness. Accept assurances of my respect & attachment.   TH: JEFFERSON

PrC (DLC); at foot of text: "Levi Lincoln esq. Atty Genl. of the US." Recorded in SJL with notation "resoln of Senate on Tennessee lands." Enclosure: see below.

On 8 Apr. the SENATE agreed to appoint a committee "to examine and report what regulations ought to be adopted" with regard to lands in Tennessee claimed by the United States. The senators from Tennessee, Joseph Anderson and William Cocke, were the only senators to vote against the motion. The committee of five included senators from Kentucky, North Carolina, Pennsylvania, and Virginia. The committee's report, submitted by John Brown, proposed a resolution asking the president "to give directions to the Attorney General to collect, digest, and report to Congress, at their next session, such documents and other information relative to the lands claimed by the United States within the state of Tennessee, under a deed of cession from the state of North Carolina, executed in December, 1789, as shall best serve to exhibit the extent of the claims reserved by the second condition expressed in said deed; and how far the said reservations have been satisfied: also, the situation and probable quantity of said lands which may be at the disposition of the United States, consistently with the conditions of the said deed of cession, and with existing treaties with the Indian tribes." Anderson and Cocke failed to get the resolution limited to lands "to which the Indian claim is extinguished, and which is not covered by legal titles under the state of North Carolina." Tennessee's senators were again the only dissenters when the resolution passed on 15 Apr. (JS, 3:206, 210, 211, 212-13).

From Philip Mazzei

CAR.MO SIG:RE E AMICO   Venezia, 17 Apr. 1802.

Avendo dovuto trattenermi in questa disgraziata Città, ò inteso un fatto, che difficilmente credo, e che mi dispiacerebbe molto se fosse vero: Spero, che la presente arriverà a Livorno in tempo da porter partire coll'istesso bastimento che porterà quelle che Le scrissi di Pisa il 10 del corrente.[1] Mi è stato domandato il perchè gli S.U. tengono un Console a Trieste, e non a Livorno, che è un porto di tanto maggiore importanza. Avendo io risposto, che vi è stato sempre, dopo che i bastim. Am. frequentano il Mediterraneo, mi è stato soggiunto, che non potevasi credere, poichè un giovane Am. stabilito in Livorno, e che certamente non è Console, à l'incombenza di provvedere a ciò che può bisognare alla Squadra che abbiamo nel Mediterraneo.[2] Se ciò fosse, bisognerebbe attribuirlo a qualche intrigo, mentre non procedesse dall'ignoranza o inavvertenza del Ministro della marina.[3]

Un [tal] procedere non ci farebbe onore; ed essendo vero, non saprei cosa pensar del Console, se non è immediatamente chiesta la sua dimissione. Il tempo mi manca per dirle altre cose, relative a questo paese affliggenti ♅ chi ama l'umanità, [ma] che secondo Lucrezio dovrebbero servir di consolazione agli Americani.

"Dulce mare magnum turbantibus equora ventis &c."
Suo Dev.mo s.o e Aff. Am.

EDITORS' TRANSLATION

DEAREST SIR AND FRIEND   Venice, 17 Apr. 1802
Having had to remain in this wretched city, I have heard something which is difficult to believe, and which would grieve me immensely if it were true. The present letter will reach Leghorn I hope in time to leave on the same boat bearing the letter I wrote you from Pisa on the 10th of the current

month. I have been asked why the United States has a consul in Triest and not in Leghorn, which is a port of so much greater importance. Having replied that there has always been one at that post, because American ships frequent the Mediterranean, it was suggested to me that such was hard to believe since a young American, established in Leghorn, and certainly not the consul, is charged with the responsibility to provide for the needs of the squadron we have in the Mediterranean. If this were so, it would have to be attributed to some intrigue, unless it were not to arise from the ignorance or thoughtlessness of the Secretary of the Navy.

Such a procedure would not do us honor, and if it were true, I would not know what to think of the consul, if his resignation were not asked for immediately. I lack the time to tell more of this country, most trying to a lover of humanity, but which, according to Lucretius, should be a source of consolation to the American people.

"Dulce mare magnum turbantibus equora ventis, etc."
Your very devoted servant, and very affectionate friend.

Dft (Archivio Filippo Mazzei, Pisa, Italy); part of a conjoined series of Mazzei's drafts of letters to TJ, where it precedes Mazzei's letter of 3 Feb. 1803 (see Margherita Marchione and Barbara B. Oberg, eds., *Philip Mazzei: The Comprehensive Microform Edition of his Papers*, 9 reels [Millwood, N.Y., 1981], 6:911-12). RC recorded in SJL as received from Venice on 19 Sep. 1802, but not found.

On 7 Feb. 1798, John Adams nominated Thomas Appleton of Massachusetts as U.S. consul at Leghorn. In a letter to Madison of 15 Jan. 1802, Appleton outlined his activities since his arrival there in 1798 and repeated his desire to be appointed naval agent. He claimed to be the only consul out of 18 at Leghorn who was not "charged with the Concerns of the Marine of their Nation" and the only U.S. consul in the Mediterranean who had "experienced this disgrace." The firm of DeButts and Purviance had been acting as U.S. agents at the port until Henry DeButts's death in early December 1801 (JEP, 1:260; NDBW, 2:28, 50-1, 100; Madison, *Papers, Sec. of State Ser.*, 2:311, 400; DNA: RG 59, CD).

DULCE MARE MAGNUM TURBANTIBUS EQUORA VENTIS: the first line from the second book of Lucretius's *De Rerum Natura* (*On the Nature of Things*), which loosely translated means, "Pleasant it is, when over a great sea the winds trouble the waters."

[1] Mazzei canceled: "Voglio aggiungere una notizia intesa qui casualmente, la quale merita d'esser verificata da chi tien le redini del governo degli S.U.," meaning "I would like to add a piece of news I heard by chance here, one that deserves to be verified by the one who holds the reins of the U.S. government."

[2] Mazzei canceled: "e che perciò credevasi che non vi fosse. Spero che non sia vero," meaning "and that, therefore, it was believed there was none. I hope this is not true."

[3] Mazzei canceled: "Untale schiaffo dato al Console non ci fa onore mentre il fatto sia come ò inteso," meaning "Such a slap in the Consul's face does not do us any honor, provided the truth of the matter is how I heard it."

To Robert Patterson

Dear Sir   Washington April 17. 1802.

Your favor of the 12th. is duly recieved. mr Barnes will write by
the present post to his friend mr Michael Roberts inclosing funds to
enable him to pay the bill for the Hadley's quadrant and thermometers, which I will pray you to direct the person from whom they are
bought to have packed properly: but first to have a stand accomodated to the quadrant: for tho' at sea the hand is the only thing which
can counteract the motion of the vessel, on land a stand is more agreeable. but it should be so accomodated as to be readily detached. I presume one of the stands found ready made in the shops, with it's ball
& socket, can be made to answer by making only the fixed socket in
addition to the other.

We are introducing your cypher into our foreign correspondences.
but it often happens that we wish only to cypher 2 or 3. lines, or one
line, or half a line, or a single word. it does not answer for this. can
you remedy it?

If mr Peale can succeed in producing fresh from *salt* water by a filtering apparatus, it will be a valuable discovery. there are parts of the
world where a want of pure water may render the separation of *im-
purities* by filtration of value, provided they are better separated, or
more cheaply, than by distillation. but besides the utility of the immediate discovery, no discovery is barren. it always serves as a step to
something else.

I shall leave this place for Monticello about a week after Congress
rises to be absent about 3. weeks. I think they will rise about the last
day of the month. Accept my best wishes and affectionate esteem.

                                                    Th: Jefferson

PrC (DLC); at foot of text: "Robert Patterson esq."; endorsed by TJ in ink on verso.

From Robert Patterson

Sir   Philada. 17th. April 1802—

I had the honour, a few days ago, of mentioning to you an interesting experiment which Mr. R. Peale had exhibited before a number
of citizens; namely, the depuration of foul or putrid water, by simple
filtration through sponge, sand, & charcoal;—that he had also succeeded in an attempt to render salt water fresh, and that he was

preparing to make the experiment with true sea-water—He has this day made that experiment; and, I am happy to announce, with complete success. I did not indeed see the experiment performed, but afterwards examined both the sea-water, and the fresh-water drawn from it. The sea-water was taken up near Amboy, and was perhaps but little different from that of any other part of the ocean; & the fresh water appeared to me as pure as our best pump or hydrant-water. In the experiment of today, Mr. Pcalc assures me that the proportion, in bulk, of the fresh water to the ingredient previously added, was as 8 to 1: and he flatters himself that, by farther trials, he will be able greatly to increase this proportion.—

The ingredient he uses (which he as yet keeps a secret) is, he declares, easily procured, or made, in all parts of the world; and that, as an article of commerce, its[1] value is greatly increased by the process.

If any thing further should occur, relative to this subject, worthy of your notice, I shall do myself the honour of communicating it.

I am, Sir, with the most perfect respect and esteem—your obedient hum. Servt.— RT. PATTERSON

RC (DLC); endorsed by TJ as received 20 Apr. and so recorded in SJL.

A FEW DAYS AGO: Patterson to TJ, 12 Apr.

[1] MS: "is."

From William Thornton

SIR   City of Washington April 17th: 1802.

When the Board of Commissioners transmitted, on the 31st. Jany: 1797, the new plan of this City to President Washington, for his Sanction, it was with a design to have a conveyance of the public Grounds, from the Trustees, but it was not considered by all the members of the Board as a compleat Map of the City: it rather contained a discription of the public appropriations and such reservations as the Board unanimously recommended: there were many others the possession of which would be highly beneficial to the Public, and these with the Calculation of their Contents, & my Idea of a water Street, and other Subjects relating to the Establishment of a more correct plan of the City I think it a duty respectfully to submit to the Consideration of the President.—

Every thing that tends to promote the Health of a City is certainly worthy of the attention of the public, but more especially of those under whose superintending Care its destinies are placed.—Public Squares and open Spaces not only become very important on account of public Institutions, but also give great opportunities of embellishment, as well by useful and ornamental Edifices & Erections, as by planting them with Trees.—They not only ornament but tend to the Salubrity of a City; and, no doubt, the public would eagerly embrace the power of reserving for future appropriation, such open Spaces as the plan of this City furnishes.—In addition to those already reserved, I should recommend the following.—

The propriety of establishing a Water Street I believe is universally admitted, because nothing tends so certainly to preserve Health as the free circulation of Air, and nothing would more effectually secure this end, than a road laid off round the water property of the City.—

The Board of Commissioners in virtue of the powers vested in them, by the Act of the Maryland Legislature, to licence the building of wharves in the City of Washington, & to regulate the materials, the manner, & the extent thereof, published, on the 20th. of June 1795, a permission, to the Proprietors of Water-lots, to wharf, and build as far out into the River Potomak and the Eastern Branch, as they think convenient & proper, not injuring or interrupting the Channels or Navigation of the said Waters; leaving a space wherever the general plan of the Streets in the City requires it, of equal breadth with those Streets; which, if made by an individual holding the adjacent property shall be subject to his separate occupation and use, until the public shall reimburse the expense of making such Street: but the power of the Commissioners derived from the State of Maryland, being limited to the assumption of the Jurisdiction over the Territory of Columbia by Congress, further Authority appears to be requisite.—Whatever regulations may however be made, they will doubtless comprise the general tenor of the preceding; for, without permission to wharf as far as the Channel, the water property will be of no service: and if this permission be granted, and the wharves made to the Channel they will extend from one hundred to two thousand feet, from the present high-water Mark, although the Tide does not rise above four feet: and in conformity to this Idea many Squares have been laid down in the published plan of the City, below the high-water mark; making, with propriety, the general Course of the Channel round the City the limit thereof.—To prevent any deception it would have been more correct if the high-water mark had been also delineated, which may hereafter be done.—Though the Distance of

wharfage above-mentioned appears very great, yet it is only calculated to the edge of the deep water, and not generally exceeding thirteen feet, under the impression that it would soon be as deep as the
Channel by the confinement of the Current.

When William Penn founded Philadelphia, he wisely designed a
Water-Street, between which & the River no Buildings of any sort
should be erected. He had even laid off public Walks with Trees near
the River to preserve the purity of the Air: but the avarice of his
Successors defeated his benevolent Intentions, and Philadelphia has
already deeply mourned, and, it is feared, will again lament this violation of the original Plan.—The extent of Ground intended by the
founder of Philada: to be kept open, might perhaps be unnecessary,
and objected to by the mercantile World, because the Intention of
keeping the Borders of the River free from every species of nuisance
and impurity may be fulfilled, without the inconveniences which
would result from placing the Warehouses so remote from the River:
yet in Bourdeaux, and many other Seaports of Europe, where Business is very extensively carried on, we hear of no murmurs arising
from the remoteness of their Warehouses from the Water; and yet
the Vessels are not permitted to approach the Key, but anchor at
a distance, and the Business is carried on by Lighters. If these Inconveniences are considered by the People as overbalanced by the security they enjoy from imported pestilential Diseases, it will be
impossible to find Objections where Vessels would be permitted to lie
along the Keys, and where the Warehouses might be placed as near
as the intermediate Room for Business would admit. To discover this
Distance I enquired of several mercantile Characters the requisite
length of Wharfage for every use, and they generally agreed on one
hundred feet. This Distance, then, I would assume as the space
generally for Wharves, and lay out a Street or Road (to be left as
the Wharves are made, in the same manner as the other Streets) of
eighty feet between the Wharf ground and the Buildings; on the
River-side of which line no permanent Building of any species should
be erected, but the Ground between the Street & the River might be
occupied by Goods Wares Merchandize &c, subject to be removed
within limited Times as the general regulations of the City may hereafter require.—Independent of the Advantage of preserving the Air
from any interruption round the Water limits of the City, most of
the Proprietors would be materially benefitted: for the general Regulations of the City expressly declare the Terminations of the Streets
and Avenues in the River to be public Property when paid for by

the public, even if made by Individuals, however contiguous & necessary to their private Property. Extensive mercantile Establishments might, in Cases where Streets or Avenues intervene, be thus cut off from necessary Accommodations: and, that such Cases of intervention do exist, may be seen in various parts of the City, & to a greater extent than could at first be imagined.—

	Square
The West end of Virginia Avenue cuts off part of the Water Property of Square No.	1
The South end of 28th. Street West cuts off part of the Water Property of Square No.	2
The S.W. end of N. Hampshe: Avenue cuts off part of the Water Property of Square No.	12
The S.W. end of Maryland Avene. cuts off the principal part of the Water front of Square No.	233
The W. end of South F Street cuts off part of the Water front of Square No.	270
The S. end of 12 Street West & the W. End of South G Street cut off the Water fronts of Squares	329 & 355
The S. End of 11th: Street West, and the W End of So. H Street cut off part of the Water fronts of	South of 355 & 390
The S. end of 10th: St: W. & the W. End of So. H. Stt: cut off the Water front of Sqr: No.	391
The S. End of 9th. St. W. & the Wt. End of So. K. St: cut off the Water front of Square	So. of 415—
The S. End of 8th: St. W. & the W End of So. L St: cut off the Water front of Sqre:	W of 471
The So. End of 7th: St. W. cuts off part of the Water front of	473
The So. End of 6th: St: W. cuts off the whole Water front of	504
The So. End of So. Capitol Street wd cut off the whole of the Water front of Square No: 667, or	E of 667
The So: End of ½ Street East cuts off part of the Water front of Sq:	S of 708
The So. End of 1st. Street East cuts off part of the Water front of Square	707
The E End of So. P Street cuts off part of the Water front of Sq: Et. of	705
The E. End of So. N St: cuts off a large portion of the Watr. front of Sq: E of	1025
The E. End of M St. So. cuts off part of the Water front of Sqe:	1080
The E. End of So. K Street cuts off the whole Water front of Sqe:	1123

In every Case above stated, besides various inferior ones, the Proprietors would, if a plan were adopted in conformity to the Sections accompanying this, have a Water-front in general equal to the front of the Squares, but in many Instances more extensive, being equal to the hypothenusal Lines which the Lots present to the River. These spaces would be occupied as private property, subject to the Regulations above mentioned, and would be no impediment to the Air of the City nor to the prospect of the River from the Streets, as every Species of Building or Erection, of a permanent nature, would be prohibited.— Besides the Advantages relating to the Health of the City and also obtaining more extensive Wharfage, there would, by this plan be a great addition to the following Squares—South of 12—Square 22—Sq: 300, with its addition of Sq: 301—Sq: 329—Sq: So. of 355—Sq: 390—Sq: 391 Sq: Wt: of 471—Sq: 472—Sq: 505—Sq: 506 Sq: So: of 506—Sq: So: of So: of 506—Sq: So. of 667—Sq: 667—Sq: 664— Sq: Et. of 664 & 662 if the former Water Street can be abolished without injury to Individuals, which would give square fronts instead of Diagonals, as at present.—Sq: 1001—Sq: E. of 1025—Sq: 1067— Sq: 1080—Sq: 1079 & Square 1117.—The last Consideration, in this Street, and not unimportant is its tendency to beautify the City, which in every part on the river side would present regularity & order instead of Collections of Nuisances and pest-houses, as in Philada: and other principal Cities & Towns on this Continent.—

I should also recommend a detailed Description of the Breadth of the Streets & Avenues, as well as the Appropriations and reservations; and, with the Consent of the Proprietors carry $\frac{1}{2}$ Street E: through, to the river, without leaving it interrupted by Square E of 708—& also carry $\frac{1}{2}$ St: West to the River, now interrupted by Squares E of 667, & E of So: of 667.—

I should propose giving a Name to the Avenue between the President's Square & Capitol—suppose Tennessee; & give names to $\frac{1}{2}$ Street East & $\frac{1}{2}$ Street West—$4\frac{1}{2}$ Street & $13\frac{1}{2}$ Street.—

A Survey I think ought to be made of the best mode of conducting the Water of the Tiber below the Capitol, letting it flow from as high a source as can well be obtained, not only to command Water in various Directions in case of Fire, but also to fill the Canal, which, by having a Lock at each end of its level, would not only save an immense labour and Expense in digging, but would tend to keep the Water-course perfectly sweet. If the Canal be sunk through its whole extent to its requisite Depth to admit Boats—viz four feet in low Water, it will be, in some places, above twenty feet from the Surface, which would render any Communication from above with the Water impracticable, or at least very inconvenient. Besides, as the Tide flows into the Canal from both ends, there would be a constant deposit at the point of Junction, which would stop its Navigation, added to which Miasmata would arise from such a quantity of stagnant Water, to the Danger of every Inhabitant on its Borders—all which would be remedied by the mode proposed, and this at a very reduced Expense.—

Lastly, when the Plan is prepared, and all the Explanations correctly made, they may be deposited a certain time for public Inspection, that all whom they concern may have an Opportunity of making their Objections, prior to the final Adoption of the Plan by the President of the United States.—

Accept Sir my highest respect & Consideration—

WILLIAM THORNTON

RC (DLC); at foot of text: "President of the United States"; endorsed by TJ as received from Thornton as "Washington Commr." on 20 Apr. and "Water street" and so recorded in SJL. Dft (DLC: William Thornton Papers).

NEW PLAN OF THIS CITY: that is, James Dermott's Appropriation Map of 1797 (Harris, *Thornton*, 1:410n).

From Tench Coxe

SIR [before 18 Apr. 1802]

The papers announce that the legislature is to rise in ten days. This critical and peculiar situation in which I am placed impels me, contrary to my intention, to address you once more before the conclusion of the Session.

It was in the Month of Decemr. 1800, that a gentleman now in Washington then recently returned from that place, informed me here, that a number of the persons who were afterwards nominated to the Senate by you, were fixed on for various offices at Washington, and that no provision was made or settled for me—It is now sixteen months since that period—the Legislature have been twice in session, and numerous appointments have been made at Washington & Phila. The gentleman who received my office on my urgent extrusion, has retained it, and will probably continue in it longer than the present collectorship of the Revenue will last, the latter office being limited to one small scene in perfect order, while the other extends over the numerous & disordered collectorships, which it must require more time to close. Both offices belong to the same system. Both must have been expected to be abolished at the same time, or nearly so. My situation be assured, Sir, has been thought extremely delicate in respect to that office, and it has occasioned much remark by friends, and foes and dispassionate and candid men concerned only for a rational execution of Government—

I have undergone considerable difficulty in justifying my acceptance of the office I now hold, and the reasons uniformly given to me are such as confirm the correctness of the reasons for which I avoided the acceptance of it from June till October. I have lost the office which I resigned at Lancaster, and after it has been filled by another Gentleman, I can have no thought of regaining it—I find myself in this expensive Town, and the present emolument of my office declining from the notice of its objects being to cease. The office itself is to terminate in a short time. The world see me yet unprovided for—*yet unrestored*[1]—*my old office held by him that extruded me*—The best Branch of it here given to another (Genl. M) and I a non commissioned officer of the system. I submit to you, Sir, whether the most negative character, extruded as I was, would not be lowered by these circumstances in the public eye—I submit, Sir, whether I have merited it—whether there is any man who has labored more, or with more effect, or with more injury to himself *to prevent a counter-revolutionary operation* from 1792 to 1801 than I.

In this state of things & under such circumstances it is supposed you are about to make one or more changes in the customs. I have recd. nothing yet from your justice or your friendship, and am a Merchant, who have joined practice in navigation, importation & exportation, to practice in superintending our commerce for two years in the Treasury, and to reading, and study in the foreign & domestic Theory & legislation of it—With what success, I submit. In all commercial countries such men are employed by good & wise rulers. On these grounds I beg you, Sir, to consider my pretensions to the *one* place in the Customs, wch. you may vacate, if only one—and to the second, if two. I beg you Sir to consider whether, Genl. M. having recd. one office from you & I assurances after his appointment to that, whether, I say, I am not entitled to any vacancy which I can fill as well as he, if there be one only vacated. If there be two, I shall express my *cheerful* disposition to take the least profitable.

I repeat, *in confidence*, that he cannot remain in it. I am satisfied the event, I mentioned will take place in Pennsa. unless he does what many republicans think no man has a right to do. At all events however the question of giving one gentlemen *two capital* appointments to the delay of claims such as you have been pleased to say mine are, is respectfully submitted. Permit me to express to you my sincere belief & apprehensions that your giving him a *second* and *commercial* appointment to my exclusion, after so long delay will do all in your power to consummate my depression and disgrace—The trivial appointment of a commr. of Bankruptcy, which Judge P. will have the power to render fruitless by running upon the three he likes, to the exclusion of the other two will neither maintain my large family, repair my substantial losses, nor restore me to public honor and confidence. The office cannot produce 1200 Dollars ℔ annum, and is a very uncomfortable & inconvenient one.

The question in regard to me remains with you, Sir. After asserting the justice of restoration to office, in ordinary cases of extrusion, the rising of the legislature without an acceptable substitute & after filling substitutes known to be acceptable, with others, will be a situation the hardship of which I cannot but most sensibly feel. I should be unjust to you, Sir, and to myself to conceal my anticipation of the pains & evils of such a situation. I perceive that I shall be unable to endure my situation without seeking relief, and that relief can only be in a seclusion from my political Connexions and relations in the Bosom of my family. The world will see that if an office in the customs does not afford an opportunity to provide for me, nothing ever can—and they will consider my disgrace as deliberate and complete. In this *trying* situation, it will be my endeavour, with the support of heaven, to maintain a temperate, virtuous and judicious conduct—May God grant that so bitter a cup as exile at the hands of my friends may pass from me. Yet such, Sir, appears to me to be the inevitable afflicting consequence of your exhibiting me on the rising of the legislature in the Situation I have mentioned. I entreat you to pardon this last effusion of a deeply wounded spirit. On serious reflexion I could not justify the omission of this final attempt to avoid the evils I deprecate—

I have the honor to be, Sir, yr. mo. respectf. servt.

TENCH COXE

RC (DNA: RG 59, LAR); at head of text: "(Private)"; endorsed by TJ as received 18 Apr. and so recorded in SJL.

GENTLEMAN WHO RECEIVED MY OFFICE: William Miller, commissioner of the revenue (Vol. 34:449n). For Coxe's

ACCEPTANCE OF THE OFFICE of revenue collector at Philadelphia, see Vol. 35:582-4. FILLED BY ANOTHER GENTLEMAN: Andrew Ellicott succeeded Coxe as secretary of the Pennsylvania Land Office (Vol. 35:424n).

GENL. M: Peter Muhlenberg, supervi-

sor of the revenue for the district of Pennsylvania. EVENT, I MENTIONED: see Coxe
to TJ, [before 2 Apr. 1802].

JUDGE P.: Richard Peters, judge of the

U.S. district court of Pennsylvania (JEP,
1:97).

[1] MS: "urestored."

To Robert R. Livingston

DEAR SIR   Washington Apr. 18. 1802.

A favorable and a confidential opportunity offering by Mr. Dupont
de Nemours, who is revisiting his native country, gives me an opportunity of sending you a cypher to be used between us, which will give
you some trouble to understand, but, once understood, is the easiest
to use, the most indecypherable, and varied by a new key with the
greatest facility of any one I have ever known. I am in hopes the
explanation inclosed will be sufficient.

Let our key of letters be   6.5.1.2.7.9.8.4.3 | 9.2.3.1.7.8.5.4.6 | 3.1.4.2.8.5.7.6.9.
& the key of lines be   9.4.7.6.1.8.5.2.3 | 2.1.8.9.6.5.7.3.4 | 7.6.9.3.1.2.4.5.8.

and lest we should happen to lose our key or be absent from it, it is so
formed as to be kept in the memory and put upon paper at pleasure;
being produced[1] by writing our names & residences at full length,
each of which containing 27. letters is divided into 3. parts of 9 letters
each;[2] each of the 9. letters is then numbered according to the place
it would hold if the 9 were arranged alphabetically. thus.

6. 5. 1. 2. 7. 9. 8. 4. 3. | 9. 2. 3. 1. 7. 8. 5. 4. 6. | 3. 1. 4. 2. 8. 5. 7. 6. 9.
r   o   b   e   r   t   r   l   i | v   i   n   g   s   t   o   n   o | f   c   l   e   r   m   o   n   t
9. 4. 7. 6. 1. 8. 5. 2. 3. | 2. 1. 8. 9. 6. 5. 7. 3. 4. | 7. 6. 9. 3. 1. 2. 4. 5. 8.
t   h   o   m   a   s   j   e   f | f   e   r   s   o   n   o   f   m | o   n   t   i   c   e   l   l   o

robertrli alphabetically arranged would be
1. 2. 3. 4. 5. 6. 7. 8. 9.
b   e   i   l   o   r   r   t

the numbers over the letters being then arranged as the letters to
which they belong stand in our names, we can always construct our
key. but why a cypher between us, when official things go naturally
to the Secretary of state, and things not political need no cypher? 1.
matters of a public nature, and proper to go on our records, should go
to the Secretary of state. 2. matters of a public nature not proper to be
placed on our records may still go to the Secretary of state, headed by
the word 'private.' but. 3. there may be matters merely personal to
ourselves, and which require the cover of a cypher more than those of
any other character. this last purpose, and others which we cannot
foresee may render it convenient & advantageous to have at hand a

mask for whatever may need it.   but writing by mr Dupont, I need use no cypher. I require from him to put this into your own & no other hand, let the delay occasioned by that be what it will.

The cession of Louisiana & the Floridas by Spain to France works most sorely on the US. on this subject the Secretary of state has written to you fully. yet I cannot forbear recurring to it personally, so deep is the impression it makes in my mind. it compleatly reverses all the political relations of the US. and will form a new epoch in our political course. of all nations of any consideration France is the one which hitherto has offered the fewest points on which we could have any conflict of right, and the most points of a communion of interests. from these causes we have ever looked to her as our *natural friend*, as one with which we never could have an occasion of difference. her growth therefore we viewed as our own, her misfortunes ours. there is on the globe one single spot, the possessor of which is our natural & habitual enemy. it is New Orleans, through which the produce of three eighths of our territory must pass to market, and from it's fertility it will ere long yield more than half of our whole produce and contain more than half our inhabitants. France placing herself in that door assumes to us the attitude of defiance. Spain might have retained it quietly for years. her pacific dispositions, her feeble state, would induce her to increase our facilities there, so that her possession of the place would be hardly felt by us, and it would not perhaps be very long before some circumstance might arise which might make the cession of it to us the price of something of more worth to her. not so can it ever be in the hands of France. the impetuosity of her temper, the energy & restlessness of her character, placed in a point of eternal friction with us, and our character, which though quiet, & loving peace & the pursuit of wealth, is high minded, despising wealth in competition with insult or injury, enterprizing & energetic as any nation on earth, these circumstances render it impossible that France and the US. can continue long friends when they meet in so irritable a position. they as well as we must be blind if they do not see this; and we must be very improvident if we do not begin to make arrangements on that hypothesis. the day that France takes possession of N. Orleans fixes the sentence which is to restrain her forever within her low water mark. it seals the union of two nations who in conjunction can maintain exclusive possession of the ocean. from that moment we must marry ourselves to the British fleet & nation. we must turn all our attentions to a maritime force, for which our resources place us on very high ground: and having formed and cemented together a power which may render reinforcement of her settlements here impossible to France, make the first cannon which shall be fired in Europe the signal for tearing up any settlement she may have made, and for holding the two continents of America in sequestration for the common purposes of the United British & American nations. this is not a state of things we seek or desire. it is one which this measure, if adopted by France, forces on us, as necessarily as any other cause, by the laws of nature, brings on it's necessary effect. it is not from a fear of France that we deprecate this measure proposed by her. for however greater her force is than ours compared in the abstract, it is nothing in comparison of ours when to be exerted on our soil. but it is from a sincere love of peace, and a firm persuasion that bound to France by the interests and the strong sympathies still existing in the minds of our citizens, and holding relative positions which ensure their continuance we are[3] secure of a long course of peace. whereas the change of friends, which will be rendered necessary if France changes that position, embarks us necessarily as a belligerent power in the first war of Europe. in that case France will have held possession of New Orleans during the interval of a peace, long or short, at the end of[4] which it will be wrested from her. will this shortlived possession have been an equivalent to her for the transfer of such a weight into the scale of her enemy? will not the amalgamation of a young, thriving, nation continue to that enemy the health & force which are at present so evidently on the decline? and will a few years possession of N. Orleans add equally to the strength of France? she may say she needs Louisiana for the supply of her West Indies. she does not need it in time of peace, and in war she could not depend on them because they would be so easily intercepted. I should suppose that all these considerations might in some proper form be brought into view of the government of France. tho' stated by us, it ought not to give offence; because we do not bring them forward as a menace, but as consequences not controulable by us, but inevitable from the course of things. we mention them not as things which we desire by any means, but as things we deprecate; and we beseech a friend to look forward and to prevent them for our common interests.

If France considers Louisiana however as indispensable for her views she might perhaps be willing to look about for arrangements which might reconcile it to our interests. if any thing could do this it would be the ceding to us the island of New Orleans and the Floridas. this would certainly in a great degree remove the causes of jarring & irritation between us, and perhaps for such a length of time as might produce other means of making the measure permanently conciliatory to our interests & friendships. it would at any rate relieve us from the necessity of taking immediate measures for countervailing such an operation by arrangements in another quarter. but still we should consider N. Orleans & the Floridas as no equivalent for the risk of a quarrel with France produced by her vicinage.[5]—I have no doubt you have urged these considerations on every proper occasion with the government where you are. they are such as must have effect if you can find the means of producing thorough reflection on them by that government. the idea here is that the troops sent to St. Domingo, were to proceed to Louisiana after finishing their work in that island. if this were the arrangement, it will give you time to return again & again to the charge. for the conquest of St. Domingo will not be a short work. it will take considerable time and wear down a great number of souldiers. every eye in the US. is now fixed on this affair of Louisiana.[6] perhaps nothing since the revolutionary war has produced more uneasy sensations through the body of the nation. notwithstanding temporary bickerings have taken place with France, she has still a strong hold on the affections of our citizens generally.—I have thought it not amiss, by way of supplement to the letters of the Secretary of state, to write you this private one to impress you with the importance we affix to this transaction. I pray you to cherish Dupont. he has the best dispositions for the continuance of friendship between the two nations, and perhaps you may be able to make a good use of him. accept assurances of my affectionate esteem & high consideration.   TH: JEFFERSON

RC (NNMus); at foot of first page: "Robert R. Livingston." PrC (DLC). Recorded in SJL with notation "cypher. Louisiana." Enclosures: Documents I and II of Method of Using Robert Patterson's Cipher, 18 Apr. Enclosed in TJ to Pierre Samuel Du Pont de Nemours, 25 Apr.

SECRETARY OF STATE HAS WRITTEN TO YOU: in a letter dated 1 May, Madison expressed the U.S. government's dissatisfaction with the slowness of France in fulfilling its obligations for payments under the Convention of 1800. Madison also said that the Louisiana situation "becomes daily more and more a source of painful apprehensions." In particular, if France gained control of the mouth of the Mississippi, "the worst events are to be apprehended. You will consequently spare no efforts that will consist with prudence and dignity, to lead the Councils of France to proper views of this subject, and to an abandonment of her present purpose." Madison instructed Livingston to learn if the cession of Louisiana included New Orleans and the Floridas "and endeavour to ascertain the price at which these, if included in the Cession, would be yielded to the United States." TJ, Madison advised, "wishes you to devote every attention to this object" (Madison, *Papers, Sec. of State Ser.*, 3:174-7).

[1] Word interlined in place of "taken from the."

[2] TJ here canceled "and numbers from 1. to 9. are arranged according to the acciden."

[3] TJ here canceled "much more."

[4] Preceding four words interlined. TJ may have first written "long or short, when it will be wrested" and then altered the passage.

[5] Sentence interlined.

[6] Word written over partially erased "St."

Method of Using Robert Patterson's Cipher

I. DESCRIPTION OF METHOD,
[18 APR. 1802]

II. SAMPLE ENCIPHERMENT:
THE LORD'S PRAYER, [18 APR. 1802]

III. SAMPLE ENCIPHERMENT:
"TO THE PEOPLE OF GREAT-BRITAIN," [N.D.]

E D I T O R I A L   N O T E

Jefferson received Robert Patterson's letter of 19 Dec. 1801, in which Patterson described the cipher that he had invented, six days after it was written. On 22 Mch. 1802, Jefferson acknowledged the letter and informed Patterson that he had "thoroughly considered" the cipher. By 18 Apr. 1802, Jefferson completed an explanation of the "Method" of using the cipher (Document I below), created a sample using the text of the Lord's Prayer (Document II), and had Meriwether Lewis copy the explanation and sample to send to Robert R. Livingston in France.

Jefferson worked up another example of the use of the cipher, this one using a portion of a 1774 address from the Continental Congress, "To the People of Great-Britain" (Document III). The document has an orderly appearance and Jefferson made a press copy of it, which may mean that he expected to use it, like the encipherment of the Lord's Prayer, as an instructional example. However, he did not have Lewis copy the exercise that was based on the 1774 address, nor did he send it to Livingston. Although Jefferson enciphered only a portion of the address, it was a much longer passage to unravel than the Lord's Prayer: the address spanned 30 letters across by 38 lines down, in contrast to the prayer's 19 letters by 15 lines. He may have decided that the longer text was impractical as an introduction to the cipher.

Jefferson's early drafts of his explanation of method and of the exercise using the Lord's Prayer have survived. He did not put dates on any stages of those documents or on the "To the People" exercise. Early on, he made certain modifications to Patterson's cipher, the most significant of which he related to Patterson in the letter of 22 Mch. In the first step of encipherment, Patterson had written the passage in vertical columns (see, in the letter of 19 Dec., his "First Draft" of a sample encipherment, Vol. 36:172). Patterson then transposed the text by shuffling the order of the horizontal lines of that transcription. Jefferson switched the vertical and horizontal axes. His initial transcription of the passage to be enciphered was in horizontal lines reading from left to right rather than columns reading top to bottom. He took care, as he described the technique in the letter of 22 Mch., to put "the letters of the different lines very exactly under each other." He then mixed the order of the vertical columns and transcribed each column as a horizontal line to create the enciphered text. That modification of the process, to transcribe the passage initially as horizontal lines of text rather than vertical columns, appears in Jefferson's drafts of the "Method" and the Lord's Prayer encipherment. That is to say, he made the decision to change the axes of the transcription at the outset of his work with Patterson's system.

He also rotated the axes of the cipher's key, although he did not have that change in mind at the beginning. Patterson wrote the key vertically, with a column of digits indicating the scrambled order of the lines and another column for the number of extra letters to be inserted at the beginning of each line (Vol. 36:171). Jefferson followed that method when he first drafted the explanation of the cipher and the Lord's Prayer example (see notes to Documents I and II). When he put the "Method" and trial encipherments into final form, however, he recognized that his rearrangement of the layout of the text in the first stage of encipherment called for a horizontal "key of lines," read from left to right, since the cipher process would involve the reordering of a series of columns running from left to right. The other part of the key gave the number of random letters that would be introduced at the beginning of each line. Patterson's directions on 19 Dec. related the number of letters to the particular line by showing the key as two columns of digits. Since Jefferson's technique arrayed the "key of lines" horizontally, he wrote his "key of letters" that way also.

Jefferson made another significant alteration to the key system, one that he did not report to Patterson in his letter of 22 Mch. Patterson had described, and used for his sample encipherment in the letter of 19 Dec., one key of lines and letters that applied to all sections of the enciphered text. Jefferson, however, designated a different key for each section. Thus in the Lord's Prayer, which in the first "operation" had 19 columns, Jefferson divided the text into three parts, two sections of 9 columns each and an additional section of 1 column, and gave each section its own key (see Document II). While Patterson's design allowed sections to be any number of lines up to nine, Jefferson, in the documents printed below, always used nine columns as the prescribed size of a full section. In the encipherment of the address "To the People of Great-Britain," he specified keys for four sections of nine columns each (the encipherment used only three lines of the fourth section—see Document III).

In his letter of 12 Apr., Patterson accepted Jefferson's idea of putting the first operation of the ciphering process on the horizontal axis. Patterson also suggested the use of a name or other word as a mnemonic aid for conveying and remembering the key. In doing so, Patterson still assumed that the same key would be used for every section of an enciphered text. Jefferson quickly absorbed the suggestion of a mnemonic aid and adapted it to work for keys to multiple sections. When he wrote to Livingston on the 18th, only three days after receiving that letter from Patterson, he explained how his own and Livingston's names and places of residence would produce keys for three sections of nine columns each. The explanation of "Method" and the sample using the Lord's Prayer had probably already been prepared by the time Jefferson received that suggestion from Patterson, since the key used in the method description and for the Lord's Prayer encipherment was not based on Jefferson's and Livingston's names. Jefferson also made no mention in the method statement of using proper nouns to develop a key.

In his draft of the explanation and his initial working up of the Lord's Prayer encipherment, Jefferson organized the process of encoding and decoding as four stages or "operations." One of those operations was the creation of the key. He subsequently eliminated that as a separate stage and put the whole process into three operations. The first step was the transcription of the text in horizontal lines, with space between letters to allow for reading down the vertical columns. The second operation was the encipherment of the passage, which Jefferson thought, in his letter to Patterson on 22 Mch., might be performed by a "copying clerk." The clerk would begin the process by using vertical lines to divide the paper of the first operation into sections of nine columns each and numbering the columns in each section. In Jefferson's sample encipherments, the first operation showed those steps already completed. To put the text into cipher, the clerk would then read down each column, taking them in the order prescribed by the key and transcribing each column as a line of text. That transcription became the text labeled in the samples as the second operation. In making it, the clerk would insert random letters at the beginning of each line in accordance with the key, and put some arbitrary letters also at the right end of most lines. (The letters added to the right end of the line did not follow a key, since they were to become evident during the decipherment; see below and Patterson's letter of 19 Dec.). In the Lord's Prayer, for example, the first line of the encipherment was, according to the key, the first column of the first operation, read downward and beginning "o h n h a," with eight arbitrary letters inserted at the beginning and no arbitrary letters added to the right end of that line. The next line of the second operation was the fifth column of the first operation, with three decoy letters on the left end and six on the right end. In this fashion the clerk would work through the entire text of the first operation. The finished transposition of the Lord's Prayer was 19 lines long, corresponding to the 19 columns of the first operation, and presented the enciphered text in the form in which it would be sent.

In his examples, Jefferson showed the first steps of the third operation, which was the decipherment by the receiver, directly on the text of the second operation. He (and Meriwether Lewis, in the copy sent to Livingston) numbered the lines of the second operation to identify their proper sequence within each section of the text. The decipherer then, as Jefferson described the process in Document I, "dashes his pen through all the insignificant letters" at the beginnings of the lines as specified by the key. In the sample exercises, Jefferson and Lewis struck through the unwanted letters at the left end of each line in the second operation; in Documents II and III below, those canceled letters are shown in italics. With the letters that were not part of the message eliminated, the clerk was to take the first letter of line 1 of the first section, then the first letter of the other lines of that section in their proper order, then the first letters of the lines of the other sections, then the second letter of each line following the same sequence, then the third letter, and so on. The resulting transcription—labeled as the third operation in the sample encipherments—would be the deciphered message. During the decipherment, the random letters at the right-hand ends of lines would "betray themselves at once," as Jefferson expressed it in Document I, "by their incoherence" (see the end of Document II for Jefferson's illustration of that process in the decipherment of the Lord's Prayer).

In the draft version of his explication of the use of the cipher, Jefferson noted that care was needed to avoid making mistakes in deciphering a passage (Document I, note 12). The two potential problems that he mentioned in his draft, omitting a letter or copying a letter twice, could arise during decipherment by the message's recipient, as he noted, but could also occur in the earlier step of the process, when the sender encrypted the text. Having omitted two letters when he first worked up the Lord's Prayer and having seen the outcome of those slips when he unlocked the passage, Jefferson would have known that errors were possible during encipherment (see descriptive note to Document II). Lewis dropped a letter from the enciphered text of the Lord's Prayer, unwittingly illustrating how difficult it could be to transcribe a jumbled sequence of letters even when no transposition was involved. Jefferson did not state a third potential problem, the misreading of a letter, which could occur during encipherment or decipherment. Lewis mistook a letter in the Lord's Prayer example, writing "w" for "u." Jefferson, in his encipherment of the 1774 address, twice wrote "p" instead of "n," and his final version of the prayer included a sequence of three incorrect letters. The latter mistake would have been noticeable in the decipherment, except Jefferson, in making up the fair copy, simply wrote out the deciphered passage as he knew it should have appeared rather than painstakingly working it out letter by letter (Document II, notes 1-2, 4; Document III, notes 1, 5).

A few scattered errors of single characters might have little effect on the meaning of a message (see Document II, descriptive note; Document III, notes 6-7). A mistake in using a key, or putting rows or columns in the wrong order during encipherment or decipherment, could be more detrimental. Jefferson may have come near to making such errors in his experiment with the address of the Continental Congress to the British people. An evident interlineation in that encipherment may indicate that he either initially overlooked a column of the text or was temporarily mistaken about the sequence of lines for one section. Whatever the cause of the stumble, he became aware of it and resolved it before he wrote out his decipherment, which follows the correct sequence of lines. Also in his work with that text, he erred several times when he made marks to set off the extra letters at the left end of each line. He fixed those misplaced marks, which may have been the result of following an incorrect key sequence, and they did not affect his decipherment. They could have had more serious consequences if he had been attempting to unpack someone else's encryption rather than his own (Document III, notes 2-3).

Although in his letter of 22 Mch. Jefferson informed Patterson that he was recommending the cipher for use in official diplomatic correspondence, it was never used for that purpose. When Jefferson sent the explanation to Livingston on 18 Apr., he expected that they would sometimes employ the cipher in their private letters. Livingston, however, was accustomed to "nomenclator" codes that substituted groups of digits for words, syllables, and letters. That system had long been in use in American diplomatic correspondence, and Jefferson used nomenclators to encode sensitive information in his own private letters in the 1790s, as late as 1800. Livingston, as secretary of foreign affairs for the Confederation Congress in the early 1780s, had been instrumental in expanding the size of the code to contain 1,700 word elements. Deeming the Patterson cipher "extreamly difficult & laborious in the practice," Livingston would not give up the nomenclator system, which he considered "equally secure & more easy in the use." Madison also continued to favor nomenclators for the State Department, furnishing one to James Monroe in 1803. Madison employed such a code himself in correspondence with Livingston and Monroe (Ralph E. Weber, *United States Diplomatic Codes and Ciphers, 1775-1938* [Chicago, 1979], 151-8; David Kahn, *The Codebreakers: The Story of Secret Writing*, rev. ed. [New York, 1996], 184-5; Madison, *Papers, Sec. of State Ser.*, 4:78-9, 80-1n, 110-11, 115, 121, 204, 205n, 277-8, 279n, 328-31, 352, 385, 386n, 411-12, 500-1, 502n, 511-15, 525-30, 532n; Vol. 28:96, 100, 355-6, 449, 451n, 510-11, 512n; Vol. 31:300, 301n; Livingston to TJ, 28 Oct. 1802).

Jefferson gave considerable thought and time to understanding Patterson's cipher and developing what amounted to a manual for its use. Despite all that attention, however, and despite his interest in finding a new cipher system, he failed to implement the Patterson cipher for diplomatic dispatches. Perhaps Jefferson came to realize that other people might find the Patterson cipher unwieldy to use, baffling, and intimidating. Not everyone could readily perceive the elegance that Jefferson and Patterson, the professor of mathematics, found in the cipher.

I. Description of
Method

[18 Apr. 1802]

Method of using Mr. Patterson's cypher.

1st. Operation.—In writing the original[1] paper which is to be cyphered, use no capitals, write the letters disjoined, equidistant, and
those of each line vertically under those of the one next above. this
will be greatly facilitated, by using common black-lines, chequered
by black-lines drawn vertically, so that you may place a letter between every two vertical black-lines. the letters on your paper will
thus be formed into vertical rows as distinct as the horizontal
lines.[2]

2d. Operation.—To cypher. divide the vertical rows of the page into
vertical columns of 9 letters or rows in breadth each, as far as the
letters or rows of the line will hold out. the last will probably be a
fractional part of a column. number the vertical rows of each column from 1 to 9. in regular order. then on the paper to be sent to
your correspondent, begin as many horizontal lines as there are
vertical rows in your original, by writing in the beginning[3] of each
of every 9 horizontal lines as many insignificant letters from one to
nine as you please; not in regular order from one to nine, but in-
terverting the order of the numbers arbitrarily. suppose[4] e.g. you
write 8. insignificant letters in the first line, 3.[5] in the 2cd. 1. in the
3rd. 6 in the 4th. &c. you will thus have the horizontal lines of your
2cd. paper formed into horizontal bands of 9 lines each, of which
this, for instance, will be the key, or key of insignificant letters as it
may be called.

8.3.1.6.9.4.7.2.5. | 2.9.1.8.4.6.3.7.5. | 3.6.9.2.8.5.7.4.1 |[6] then copy
the vertical lines of the 1st. paper, or original, horizontally, line for
line, on the 2cd.; the columns in regular succession, but the vertical lines of each arbitrarily; as suppose you copy first the 1st. vertical line of the 1st. column, the 5th. next, then the 2cd. then the 8th.
&c. according to this, which may be called the key of lines

1.5.2.8.7.9.6.3.4. | 8.3.6.1.4.7.2.5.9. | 7.3.5.8.4.1.9.2.6. | 3.2.1.
then fill up the ends of the lines with insignificant letters, so as to
make them appear of even lengths, and the whole[7] is done.[8] your
correspondent is to be furnished with the keys thus.[9]

key of letters. 8.3.1.6.9.4.7.2.5. | 2.9.1.8.4.6.3.7.5. | 3.6.9.2.8.5.7.4.1. | 2.1.3.
key of lines. 1.5.2.8.7.9.6.3.4. | 8.3.6.1.4.7.2.5.9. | 7.3.5.8.4.1.9.2.6. | 3.2.1.

3d. Operation.—To decypher. your correspondent takes the[10] cyphered paper you have sent him, and first, by the key of letters, he dashes his pen through all the insignificant letters, at the beginning[11] of every line. then he prefixes to the lines the numbers taken from the key of lines in the order in which they are arranged in the key. then he copies the 1st. line of the 1st. horizontal band, writing, on a seperate paper, the letters vertically one under another (but no exactness is necessary as in the original operation.) he proceeds next to copy line No. 2. vertically also, placing it's letters by the side of those of his first vertical line: then No. 3. and so on to No. 9. of the first horizontal band. then he copies line No. 1. of the 2cd. horizontal band, No. 2. No. 3. &c. in the regular order of the lines and bands. when he comes to the insignificant letters at the ends of the lines, they will betray themselves at once by their incoherence, and he proceeds no further. this third paper will then, in it's letters and lines, be the true counterpart of the 1st. or original.[12]—

MS (NNMus); in Meriwether Lewis's hand; undated; at head of text: "Cypher. Mr. Patterson's"; with emendations in TJ's hand (see notes below); endorsed by Livingston. MS (DLC: TJ Papers, 128:22130); entirely in TJ's hand; undated; at head of text: "Method of using mr Patterson's cypher"; endorsed: "Cypher mr Patterson's." PrC (same, 232:41574); lacks endorsement. Dft (ViU); entirely in TJ's hand; undated; on recto of Dft of Document II; at head of text: "Method of using this cypher"; endorsed: "Robert Patterson's cypher"; with significant variations as noted below. Enclosed in TJ to Robert R. Livingston, 18 Apr. 1802.

[1] Word interlined in MS in DLC.
[2] Here in MS in DLC, TJ partially erased "divide." Dft: "1st. operation. write your letter in horizontal lines, not distinguishing words, but each letter disjoined, & those of <one> each line falling vertically <over> under those of the preceding line. when done, divide the whole page into columns of not exceeding 9. letters each (counted horizontally) and number the vertical rows in each column with the figures 1. 2. 3. 4. &c."

[3] Word corrected by TJ from "begining."
[4] Word interlined by TJ.
[5] Digit apparently changed by TJ from "2" to "3," here and in MS in DLC.
[6] MS in DLC continues: "2.1.3."
[7] MS in DLC: "work."
[8] Dft: "2d. operation. transcribe the vertical lines, horizontally, not in the order of the numbers 1. 2. 3. &c. but promiscuously, and making the <horizon> lines as horizontally transcribed, overjet one another by arbitrary & different numbers of letters. then fill the deficiencies of each line at both ends, with insignificant letters which however had better be of consonants & vowels duly mixed that they may not betray themselves."

[9] Dft: "3d. operation. state the key, by arranging the numbers of each line in the order in which they have been promiscuously written, and by the side of each number place the figure <shewi> expressing how many insignificant letters there are at the beginning of the line. this key may be <safely> sent in the letter as it would not probably be understood but would be better previously lodged with your correspondent, and

changed from time to time by safe con-
veyances."

[10] Word interlined by TJ.

[11] Word corrected by TJ from "begining."

[12] Dft: "4th. operation to decypher.
first prefix to each line it's proper number from the key, and dash out or erase
the insignificant letters at each end of
every line. then copy <the 1st. letter of the
line No. 1. 2. 3. 4. &c. in their numerical
order> the horizontal line No. 1. vertically, then No. 2. by it's side, vertically also,
No. 3. the same & so on; and when all the
horizontal lines of the cyphered letter
shall be written vertically in their due
order, and one column after another, the
<letter> paper may be read horizontally.
to prevent mistakes in this last operation
it will be well to mark every letter of the
cyphered paper with a dot as you copy it,
lest you should by mistake copy the same
letter twice or not at all."

II. Sample Encipherment:
The Lord's Prayer

[18 Apr. 1802]

1st. Operation, or Original.

1	2	3	4	5	6	7	8	9	1	2	3	4	5	6	7	8	9	1
o	u	r	f	a	t	h	e	r	w	h	i	c	h	a	r	t	i	n
h	e	a	v	e	n	h	a	l	l	o	w	e	d	b	e	t	h	y
n	a	m	e	t	h	y	k	i	n	g	d	o	m	c	o	m	e	t
h	y	w	i	l	l	b	e	d	o	n	e	i	n	e	a	r	t	h
a	s	i	t	i	s	i	n	h	e	a	v	e	n	g	i	v	e	u
s	t	h	i	s	d	a	y	o	u	r	d	a	i	l	y	b	r	e
a	d	a	n	d	f	o	r	g	i	v	e	u	s	o	u	r	t	r
e	s	p	a	s	s	e	s	a	s	w	e	f	o	r	g	i	v	e
t	h	e	m	t	h	a	t	t	r	e	s	p	a	s	s	a	g	a
i	n	s	t	u	s	a	n	d	l	e	a	d	u	s	n	o	t	i
n	t	o	t	e	m	p	t	a	t	i	o	n	b	u	t	d	e	l
i	v	e	r	u	s	f	r	o	m	e	v	i	l	f	o	r	t	h
i	n	e	i	s	t	h	e	k	i	n	g	d	o	m	a	n	d	t
h	e	p	o	w	e	r	a	n	d	t	h	e	g	l	o	r	y	f
o	r	e	v	e	r	a	n	d	e	v	e	r	a	m	e	n		

key of letters.   8.3.1.6.9.4.7.2.5. | 2.9.1.8.4.6.3.7.5. | 3.
key of lines.   1.5.2.8.7.9.6.3.4. | 8.3.6.1.4.7.2.5.9. | 1.

2cd. Operation, or transcript in cypher.

1 *abountga*ohnhasaetiniiho

5 *inf*aetlisdstueusweewmirb

2 *oueay*stdshntvnersndotvxu

8 *qunkep*eakenyrstntreana

7 *wunmyoned*h¹ybiaoeaapfhra

9 *pson*rlidhogatdaokndnpr

6 *aqindna*tnhlsdfshsmsterlbm

3 *tor*amwihapesoeepeofvxpu

4 *lonvx*fveitinamttriovtslm

---

8 *tq*ttmrvbriaodr²xovsdufvnp

3 *aostvnxue*³iwdevdeesaovghe

6 *r*abceglorssufmlmxldrsbnot

1 *foanqubc*wlnoew⁴isrltmide

4 *besn*ceoieaufpdnideraediio

7 *mcednr*reoaiyugsntoaoevu

2 *pov*hognarvweeientvrrsl
5 *thabcne*hdmnnisoaubloga
9 *bnxur*ihetertvgtetdyddxm
1 *lvu*nythuereailhtfanffsbii

3rd. Operation, decyphering.
ourfatherwhichartin
heavenhallowedbethy
namethykingdomcomet
hywillbedoneinearth
asitisinheavengiveu
sthisdayourdailybre
adandforgiveusourtr
espassesasweforgive
themthattrespassaga
instusandleadusnoti
ntotemptationbutdel
iverusfromevilforth
ineisthekingdomandt
hepowerandthegloryf
oreverandeveramen.

---

sote
nfsw
dvlm[5]

MS (NNMus); in Meriwether Lewis's hand; undated; with the three operations arranged side-by-side on the page; canceled letters shown in italics; contains three errors in the second operation that were not carried over into the decipherment in the third operation (see notes 1, 2, and 4 below). MS (DLC: TJ Papers, 232:41578-9); entirely in TJ's hand; undated; with each operation on a separate page; in several instances the canceled letters at the beginnings of lines in the second operation differ from the letters Lewis used; with some cancellation and overwriting of letters to correct the decipherment in the third operation. PrC (same, 232:41583); three pages pressed on a single sheet; endorsed by TJ: "Cypher. mr Patterson's." Dft (ViU); entirely in TJ's hand; undated; on verso of

Dft of Document I, being an address cover with a partial address in an unidentified hand: "The President of"; endorsed by TJ: "Robert Patterson's cypher" and "Mr. Patterson's cypher"; consisting of four operations, the third operation being the key, in two vertical columns of numbers labeled "order of lines" and "insignificant letters"; both parts of the key differ from the key used in later versions, resulting in a different encipherment in the second operation; with first operation arranged as 23 columns (two sections of nine columns each and one section of five columns) and 12 rows, ending the text with "foreverandeve"; on second operation TJ drew snaking vertical lines to set off the random letters inserted during encipherment; last operation is incomplete, TJ arraying the decipherment again as 23 columns, completing the first three rows and the first 15 columns of the fourth through twelfth rows; TJ adding carets at two locations in the second and fourth operations and making the following notation, using the word "columns" to signify what Patterson called "sections" (see Patterson to TJ, 19 Dec. 1801): "note at these marks ^ in the 1st. and 2d. columns a letter was omitted. it's effect may be remarked in the 2d. and 3d. transcripts, at the same marks"; in the fourth operation, the two omissions of letters noted by TJ result in "forgive u our" instead of "forgive us our" and "as w forgive" instead of "as we forgive." Enclosed in TJ to Robert R. Livingston, 18 Apr. 1802.

OUR FATHER WHICH ART IN HEAVEN: for the encipherment, TJ used the form of the Lord's Prayer that appeared in the standard Anglican liturgy, the 1662 revision of the *Book of Common Prayer*. The 1752 edition of the prayer book that TJ inherited from his father, in which TJ recorded births and other family events, contained this text of the prayer (*The Book of Common-Prayer, and Administration of the Sacraments, and other Rites and Ceremonies of the Church, According to the Use of the Church of England* [London, 1662]; *The Book of Common Prayer* [Oxford, 1752]; [John Cook Wyllie], *Thomas Jefferson's Prayer Book* [Charlottesville, 1952]; S. L. Ollard, Gordon Crosse, and Maurice F. Bond, eds., *A Dictionary of English Church History*, 3d ed. rev. [London, 1948], 133-4; Vol. 28:xxxviii-xxxix).

SOTE NFSW DVLM: the three groups of letters at the foot of the document, which also appear in the MS in TJ's hand, were a demonstration of how the decipherer of a message would recognize the superfluous letters added to the right end of the lines. To unravel an enciphered message such as the one illustrated by the "2cd.

Operation" above, the decipherer would, according to TJ's instructions in Document 1, first use the cipher key to mark out the superfluous letters at the left end of each line and identify the proper sequence of lines within each section. The next step was to write down the first letter of each line, taking the lines in order as specified by the key, then the second letter of each line, the third letter of each line, and so on. TJ said that the "insignificant letters" added to the right ends of lines would reveal themselves during the decipherment. In the sample above, there are no superfluous letters on the right end of line 1 in the first section of the "2cd. Operation": the 15 uncanceled letters of that line are all part of the message. With the sixteenth letters of lines 2 through 5, however, the decipherer would find the sequence "s o t e." The seventeenth letters of those lines produce the sequence "n f s w," and the eighteenth letters make "d v l m." By that point, TJ presumed, the decipherer would know to go "no further" along each line (Document 1), having discovered the point at which the contents of the message ceased and the randomly inserted letters began.

[1] Lewis omitted a second "h" here.

[2] Lewis here followed the MS in DLC, but the next three letters should be "n r n," not "x o v," to complete the eighth column of the second section of the first operation.

[3] In MS in DLC, TJ interlined the remainder of this line in place of "hognarvweeie" (see line 2 of this section of the second operation).

[4] Lewis misread this letter in MS in DLC, where TJ wrote, correctly, "u."

[5] The three groups of letters at the foot of the document were written by Lewis, erased, and rewritten by TJ in a slightly different position.

III. Sample Encipherment:
"To the People of Great-Britain"

152879634 | 836147259 | 735841926 | 312694758   key of lines
831694725 | 291846375 | 369285741 | 825163974.   key of letters
first operation.

1	2	3	4	5	6	7	8	9	1	2	3	4	5	6	7	8	9	1	2	3	4	5	6	7	8	9	1	2	3
w	h	e	n	a	n	a	t	i	o	n	l	e	d	t	o	g	r	e	a	t	n	e	s	s	b	y	t	h	e
h	a	n	d	o	f	l	i	b	e	r	t	y	a	n	d	p	o	s	s	e	s	s	e	d	o	f	a	l	l
t	h	e	g	l	o	r	y	t	h	a	t	h	e	r	o	i	s	m	m	u	n	i	f	i	c	e	n	s	e
a	n	d	h	u	m	a	n	i	t	y	c	a	n	b	e	s	t	o	w	d	e	s	c	e	n	d	s	t	o
t	h	e	u	n	g	r	a	t	e	f	u	l	t	a	s	k	o	f	f	o	r	g	i	n	g	c	h	a	i
n	s	f	o	r	h	e	r	f	r	i	e	n	d	s	a	n	d	c	h	i	l	d	r	e	n	a	n	d	i
n	s	t	e	a	d	o	f	g	i	v	i	n	g	s	u	p	p	o	r	t	t	o	f	r	e	e	d	o	m
t	u	r	n	s	a	d	v	o	c	a	t	e	f	o	r	s	l	a	v	e	r	y	a	n	d	o	p	p	r
e	s	s	i	o	n	t	h	e	r	e	i	s	r	e	a	s	o	n	t	o	s	u	s	p	e	c	t	s	h
e	h	a	s	e	i	t	h	e	r	c	e	a	s	e	d	t	o	b	e	v	i	r	t	u	o	u	s	o	r
b	e	e	n	e	x	t	r	e	m	e	l	y	n	e	g	l	i	g	e	n	t	i	n	t	h	e	a	p	p
o	i	n	t	m	e	n	t	o	f	h	e	r	r	u	l	e	r	s	i	n	a	l	m	o	s	t	e	v	e
r	y	a	g	e	i	n	r	e	p	e	a	t	e	d	c	o	n	f	l	i	c	t	s	i	n	l	o	n	g
a	n	d	b	l	o	o	d	y	w	a	r	s	a	s	w	e	l	l	c	i	v	i	l	a	s	f	o	r	e
i	g	n	a	g	a	i	n	s	t	m	a	n	y	a	n	d	p	o	w	e	r	f	u	l	n	a	t	i	o
n	s	a	g	a	i	n	s	t	t	h	e	o	p	e	n	a	s	s	a	u	l	t	s	o	f	e	n	e	m
i	e	s	a	n	d	t	h	e	m	o	r	e	d	a	n	g	e	r	o	u	s	t	r	e	a	c	h	e	r
y	o	f	f	r	i	e	n	d	s	h	a	v	e	t	h	e	i	n	h	a	b	i	t	a	n	t	s	o	f
y	o	u	r	i	s	l	a	n	d	y	o	u	r	g	r	e	a	t	a	n	d	g	l	o	r	i	o	u	s
a	n	c	e	s	t	o	r	s	m	a	i	n	t	a	i	n	e	d	t	h	e	i	r	i	n	d	e	p	e
n	d	a	n	c	e	a	n	d	t	r	a	n	s	m	i	t	t	e	d	t	h	e	r	i	g	h	t	s	o
f	m	e	n	a	n	d	t	h	e	b	l	e	s	s	i	n	g	s	o	f	l	i	b	e	r	t	y	t	o
y	o	u	t	h	e	i	r	p	o	s	t	e	r	i	t	y	b	e	n	o	t	s	u	r	p	r	i	z	e
d	t	h	e	r	e	f	o	r	e	t	h	a	t	w	e	w	h	o	a	r	e	d	e	s	c	e	n	d	e
d	f	r	o	m	t	h	e	s	a	m	e	c	o	m	m	o	n	a	n	c	e	s	t	o	r	s	t	h	a
t	w	e	w	h	o	s	e	f	o	r	e	f	a	t	h	e	r	s	p	a	r	t	i	c	i	p	a	t	e
d	i	n	a	l	l	t	h	e	r	i	g	h	t	s	t	h	e	l	i	b	e	r	t	i	e	s	a	n	d
t	h	e	c	o	n	s	t	i	t	u	t	i	o	n	y	o	u	s	o	j	u	s	t	l	y	b	o	a	s
t	o	f	a	n	d	w	h	o	h	a	v	e	c	a	r	e	f	u	l	l	y	c	o	n	v	e	y	e	d
t	h	e	s	a	m	e	f	a	i	r	i	n	h	e	r	i	t	a	n	c	e	t	o	u	s	g	u	a	r
a	n	t	i	e	d	b	y	t	h	e	p	l	i	g	h	t	e	d	f	a	i	t	h	o	f	g	o	v	e
r	n	m	e	n	t	a	n	d	t	h	e	m	o	s	t	s	o	l	e	m	n	c	o	m	p	a	c	t	s
w	i	t	h	b	r	i	t	i	s	h	s	o	v	e	r	e	i	g	n	s	s	h	o	u	l	d	r	e	f
u	s	e	t	o	s	u	r	r	e	n	d	e	r	t	h	e	m	t	o	m	e	n	w	h	o	f	o	u	n

d t h e i r c l a | i m s o n n o p r | i n c i p l e s o | f r e
a s o n a n d w h | o p r o s e c u t | e t h e m w i t h | a d e
s i g n t h a t b | y h a v i n g o u | r l i v e s a n d | p r o
p e r t y i n t h | e i r p o w e r

2d. operation, or cyphering.

1. *itatsbar* | whtatnnteeborainiyyanfyddtdtttarwudasp
5. *ail* | aolunrasoeemelganriscahrmhlonaenboiaty | ewrho
2. *s* | hahnhssusheiyngseoondmotfwihohnnistsie | nbeclp
8. *ontwrt* | tiynarfvhhrtrdnshnarntroeehthfyntrlwtt | m
7 *jmieriynp* | alrareodtttnnoip[1]teloadifhstswebaiucdan
9 *vhro* | ibtitfgoeeeoeystednsdhprsfeioatdirahbh | yrhegno
6 *wrsterl* | nfomghdanixeioaidisteneetolndmdtrsrnhi | cp
3 *oz* | enedeftrsaenadnasfucaeuhrenefetmtehogr | swnhe
4 *uawim* | ndghuoenisntgbagafrennteowacasiehtennt | c

---

8 *am* | gpisknpsstleoedageentnywoehoeitseepuor | mursodwerhbto[2]
3 *qvenaprue*[3] | lttcueitielearaeraoialtheegtvipesdsrar | ystne
6 *m* | tnrbassoeeeudsaeatgamsiwmtsnaegsetnenw | qram
1 *nahpymwe* | oehtericrrmfpwttmsdmteoeaorthihtseioyeu[4] | x
4 *tlnr* | eyhalnnesayrtsnoevunneeacfhienlmoeoovp | nople
7. *acsset* | odoesauradglcwnnnhriiitemhtyrrhtrhocge | brrh
2. *axh* | nrayfivaeceheamhohyarbstmriuarehhnmphi | f
5. *dhyawle* | daentdgfrsnreaypdertssrtoatochiovrnsio | stjeam
9 *seylu* | rostodplooirnlpseiaetgbhnreufteoimrtu | ntrdweet

---

7 *xem* | sdienernputoialoeaoiiersocilnuomuheia | pumtaong
3 *osteno* | teudoiteovnniieuuanhtforcabjlcamsmchi | yrh
5 *woahyalen* | esisgdoyuriltifttigieisdstrscttchnpme | nas
8 *sa* | bocngnedeohsnsnfanrngrpcrieyvsfplostn | prewr
4 *giastrdl* | nsnerltrsitacvrlsbdehlteereuyeinseiev | tchl
1 *tpaoi* | esmofcoanbgsflosrntdeseoaslsuadlgtier | enotp
9 *mfirtni* | yfedcaeocuetlfaectidhtrespsbeggadfohd | erv
2 *ibop* | asmwfhrvteeilcwaohatdonap[5]piolnfenontl | omx
6 *s* | sefcirfastnmslusrtlrrbuetittoohoowlws | buebivtlals

---

3 *dstocewr* | eleoiimrhrpegeomrfseooeeaedsdresfneeo | dog
1 *nb* | tanshndptsaeootnhsoetyintaaoyuocrofap | undbont
2 *fdtam* | hlstadopsopvnrieeoupstzdhtnaeavteurdr | erbg

3d. operation, or decyphering.
whenanationledtogreatnessbythe
handofibertyandpossessedofall

theglorythatheroismmunificense
andhumanitycanbestowdescendsto
theungratefultaskofforgingchai
nsforherfriendsandchildrenandi
nsteadofgivingsupporttofreedom
turnsadvocateforslaveryandoppr
essionthereisreasontosuspectsh
ehaseitherceasedtobevirtuousor
beenextremelynegligentintheapp
ointmentofherrulersinalmosteve
ryageinrepeatedconflictsinlong
andbloodywarsaswellcivilasfore
ignagainstmanyandpowerfulnatio
nsagaip^{6}sttheopenassaultsofenem
iesandthemoredangeroustreacher
yoffriendshavetheinhabitantsof
yourislandyourgreatandglorious
ancestorsmaintainedtheirindepe
ndanceandtransmittedtherightso
fmenandtheblessingsoflibertyto
youtheirposteritybenotsurprize
dthereforethatwewhoaredescende
dfromthesamecommonap^{7}cestorstha
twewhoseforefathersparticipate
dinalltherightstheliberteisand
theconstitutionyousojustlyboas
tofandwhohavecarefullyconveyed
thesamefairinheritancetousguar
antiedbytheplightedfaithofgove
rnmentandthemostsolemncompacts
withbritishsovereignsshouldref
usetosurrenderthemtomenwhofoun
dtheirclaimsonnoprinciplesofre
asonandwhoprosecutethemwithade
signthatbyhavingourlivesandpro
pertyintheirpower:

    MS (DLC: TJ Papers, 128:22131-2);
entirely in TJ's hand; undated, but written after TJ's receipt on 25 Dec. 1801 of
Robert Patterson's letter of 19 Dec.; endorsed by TJ: "Cypher"; first operation is
on one sheet, second and third operations
are on a composite sheet made by attach-
ing two pieces of paper together; in the
first operation, TJ added the numbers at
the heads of the columns and the vertical
rules in pencil; in the second operation he
added vertical strokes to set off the arbi-

trary letters at the beginnings and ends of lines; he struck through the arbitrary letters inserted at the beginnings of lines, shown in italics; his decipherment in the third operation includes two errors introduced in the second operation (see notes 1 and 5-7 below). PrC (DLC: TJ Papers, 232:41581-2).

WHEN A NATION LED TO GREATNESS: for this trial encipherment, TJ selected a passage from the Continental Congress's address "To the people of Great-Britain," approved by the Congress on 21 Oct. 1774. TJ enciphered most of the text of the three opening paragraphs of the appeal, which began, "When a Nation, led to greatness by the hand of Liberty. . . ." He ran out of room on the page of his first operation and truncated the third paragraph by ending with "by having our lives and property in their power" (omitting the conclusion of the sentence, "they may with the greater facility enslave you"). The address was reprinted in several American cities in 1774 as part of *Extracts from the Votes and Proceedings of the American Continental Congress, Held at Philadelphia on the 5th of September 1774.* TJ owned a copy published in Williamsburg that year, which he had bound into a volume with other pamphlets of the period, including his own *Summary View of the Rights of British America.* The address was also printed in London in 1775 with the title *To the People of Great Britain.* TJ was not a member of the Continental Congress in 1774 (Worthington C. Ford and others, eds., *Journals of the Continental Congress, 1774-1789,* 34 vols. [Washington, D.C., 1904-37], 1:81-2, 129; Sowerby, 3:253-9, Nos. 3085, 3094).

[1] This letter should be "n."

[2] TJ interlined this line.

[3] In this line and at least a dozen other lines in the second operation, TJ initially misplaced the vertical strokes by which he marked off the random letters at the left end of the line. He partially erased those strokes and made new ones in the correct positions before striking through the random letters.

[4] The vertical stroke should come before, rather than after, this letter.

[5] This letter should be "n."

[6] This letter should be "n," in the word "against"; TJ introduced this error in the enciphering process (see note 1 above).

[7] This letter should be "n," in the word "ancestors" (see note 5 above).

To Anne Cary Randolph

Apr. 18. 1802.

Th: Jefferson to his very dear granddaughter Anne C. Randolph.

I send you, my dear Anne, more poems for our 1st. volume. Congress will rise about the last day of the month, and it will not be many days after that before I shall be in the midst of you. in the mean time all is well here, and I have not time to say more, except that you must kiss all the little ones for me, and deliver my affections to your papa & mama. health & tender love to you all.

PrC (CSmH); endorsed by TJ in ink on verso. Enclosures not identified.

From Bartholomew von Heer

SIR—   Philada. 19th April. 1802

I have the Honour of Informing you that in Justice to myself on or about the 14th Inst. I addressed a Petition to the Senate & House of Representatives of the U.States, praying to be placed on the pension List and which I think myself intitled to, as well as any of my Brother Officers who have served their Country as I have done through the Whole of the Revolutionary War—

Having had the Honour of being acquainted with you at Head quarters, in the Hour that tried Mens souls, and being at present aged, infirm, & weak, on Account more especially of the wounds I received in the service of the US. & notwithstanding the commutation I recd. & which I was obliged to sacrifice at a Low Rate.—I am therefore under the Necessity of asking from Congress a pention for future support—

Permit me dear Sir, to ask your interferrence in my Favour (which if with propriety, you can grant) will ever be considered as one of the most singular, marks of Friendship & Charity due to an old Soldier—

Accept of my highest regard & due consideration

BARTHW. VON HEER

P.S—My Petition I inclosed under Cover to Messrs Lieb & Genl. Heester Members from Penna—

RC (DLC); at head of text: "To Thomas Jefferson Esqr. President of the United States of America"; endorsed by TJ as received 21 Apr. and so recorded in SJL.

A former Prussian officer, Bartholomew von Heer offered his services to the United States in 1776. From 1778 until the end of the war, he commanded the Maréchaussée Corps, a troop of light dragoons that served as part of George Washington's personal guard. Heer remained in America after the war, settling in Pennsylvania, and spent much of his time seeking compensation from Congress for his wartime services. On 22 Apr. 1802, the House of Representatives received Heer's most recent petition, praying that he be placed on the list of pensioners in consideration of the wounds he received during the war, which rendered him "incapable of obtaining his livelihood by labor." The House tabled the petition. The Committee of Claims rejected a nearly identical petition from Heer in January 1800 (Washington, *Papers, Pres. Ser.*, 3:328-9; Heitman, *Register*, 561; Worthington C. Ford and others, eds., *Journals of the Continental Congress, 1774-1789*, 34 vols. [Washington, D.C., 1904-37], 28:64-5; JHR, 3:535, 561; 4:213).

From James McGurk

[on or before 19 Apr. 1802]

The Petition of James McGurk

Respectfully sheweth—

That he has Lately been tried in the Circuit Court of the Distorit of Columbia (for suposed murder) found guilty and sentenced to suffer death, which sentence no doubt will be put into Execution ere Long Unless Prevented by the interference of your Excellency, in whose benevelence only depends the excistance of the Unfortunate wretch James MGurk who will be hurried into eternity and meet that alwise Judge Unprepared—

Death is a terror to the human heart, but more so, to Such a wretch as I am—

The Charactor of the nation over which you now preside is Known for the mildness of its Laws and the humainety of those that Executes them

your Excellency Predicessor is also Known for their humainety and never Suffered a wretch to be put to death where they with safity could prevent it

Surely then I cannot be without hops of my Days being Prolonged in a Land over which a Jefferson presides—in your Excellency is the hopes of the nation over which you now preside and the hopes of the Unfortunate James McGurk,

Therefore the Almighty I trust will derect and support your Excellency in all your Proceedings and derect you to releve the distressed whenever it is in your Excellency power to do it with Safity, which may be done in the Present Case, and grant such relief as you may think proper, and your Petitioner will as in duty bound iver pray—
JAMES MCGURK

I throw my Self at your feet for mercy on my life hoping you will not See Inosent Blood Spild

RC (DNA: RG 59, GPR); in an unidentified hand, postscript and signature by McGurk; undated; at head of text: "To his Excellency Thomas Jefferson Esquire President of the United States of America"; endorsed by TJ as received 19 Apr. and "Petition for pardon" and so recorded in SJL; endorsed by a clerk.

James McGurk (d. 1802) was an immigrant bricklayer. On 10 Apr. 1802, the circuit court for the District of Columbia found him guilty of the beating death of his wife. According to evidence presented in the case, McGurk, who was prone to drunken rages, assaulted his pregnant spouse multiple times. After a series of beatings in August 1801, Mrs. McGurk gave birth prematurely to twin boys. The babies had bruises on their bodies and were either stillborn or died within minutes of their delivery. Mrs. McGurk died in January 1802, several days after another episode of severe physical abuse by her husband. She was about 22 or 23 years old. When William Cranch, the court's presiding judge, passed sentence, he reportedly said that James McGurk's "offence was much aggravated, by the deceased having been his wife, who ought rather to have received protection at his hand, than such barbarous treatment as to occasion her death." After his arrest in January, McGurk was held in a small brick building that served as the district's jail. In October 1802, an appeal for clemency in his behalf stated that the condemned man was "confined in a Room scarcly seven feet square, loaded with near 60 lb of Irons." The prisoner wrote letters to TJ that McGurk's attorney, Augustus B. Woodward, thought would be too "intrusive" to deliver until August 1802, when Woodward apparently took the letters with him on a hurried trip to Monticello to appeal for an emergency stay of execution. Woodward also carried a petition on McGurk's behalf bearing the names of more than 150 people, many of whom had Irish surnames. In letters to newspapers, prompted by an outcry against the delays in McGurk's execution, Woodward argued against the death penalty in general but also contended that the crime was not intentional murder because McGurk had not meant to cause his wife's death. McGurk made two appeals to TJ for clemency during October, writing one of them on the day of his execution. TJ did not respond to those pleas, and McGurk was hanged on 28 Oct. 1802. He was the first person to be executed under the jurisdiction of the District of Columbia. The hanging was a public event, at a gallows erected for the purpose, and some members of the crowd reportedly cut off bits of the hangman's rope afterward as talismans against toothache and headache. According to recollections published years later, some people who objected to McGurk's burial near the remains of their loved ones surreptitiously removed his coffin from its grave. His remains were found and returned to the grave, but the offended parties clandestinely disinterred the corpse a second time and reburied it in another location, where it remained (*Washington Federalist*, 14 Apr., 1, 3, 8 Sep. 1802; *National Intelligencer*, 29 Oct. 1802, 29 Nov. 1845; Cranch to Woodward, 20 Sep. 1802, in DNA: RG 59, GPR; Christian Hines, *Early Recollections of Washington City* [Washington, D.C., 1866], 31, 61-5; RCHS, 33-34 [1932], 296-7; Woodward to TJ, 16 Aug. 1802; Woodward and others to TJ, [ca. 16 Aug. 1802]; McGurk petitions, 10, [28] Oct. 1802; "Friend" to TJ, 23 Oct. 1802).

IN ALL YOUR PROCEEDINGS: legal questions pertaining to the warrant for McGurk's execution prompted TJ's queries to Levi Lincoln and John Thomson Mason on 11 Apr. TJ apparently decided that the circuit court, at its July term, should resolve the matter of authorization for carrying out the sentence. The court set the execution for 28 Aug., prompting Woodward to make his trip to Monticello, where he succeeded in getting TJ to grant a reprieve of two months. Some Federalists used the delays to argue that TJ was too lenient and claimed that he showed special favor to this criminal because McGurk had entered the office of the *Gazette of the United States* in Philadelphia one evening in 1799 carrying a sword and looking for John Ward Fenno. The individual found guilty of assault on one of Fenno's associates in that incident, however, was not James McGurk but a different person, John McGurk. There were also claims that James McGurk had been one of a gang of toughs who lurked about Washington and intimidated Burr's supporters early in 1801, before the resolution of the presidential election by the House of Representatives (*Gazette of the United States*, 9 Apr. 1799, 12 Aug. 1802; *Porcupine's Gazette*, 11 Apr. 1799; Georgetown *Olio*, 5 Aug. 1802; *Washington Federalist*, 27 Aug., 10 Sep. 1802; *National Intelligencer*, 30 Aug. 1802; *New-York Gazette and General Advertiser*, 10 Sep. 1802; Baltimore *Republican or, Anti-Democrat*, 13 Sep. 1802; Easton, Md., *Republican Star*, 23 Nov. 1802; Madison, *Papers, Sec. of State Ser.*, 3:517).

From John Page

Rosewell April 19th. 1802

Accept my dear Friend, my sincere Thanks for your Favor of the 2d. instant—& for the friendly & candid warnings which you gave me, in your former letter, respecting the dangers of the Office which you offered me. I confess that I shuddered at the thoughts of them, & should have immediately declined an acceptance of your Offer had I not thought that Delicacy required that I should take the time you offered to make up my Judgment on a view of the whole Subject; & that possibly my Son Francis, who by the persuasion of Mr. W. P. Byrd had acted as a Clerk in Col. Otway Byrds Office at Norfolk during the last four Months of his life, might wish to act with me in that Capacity till qualified to succeed me should I be able to procure the Collector's Office for him. But having sounded him, I find that if I could procure it for him even now, he would not accept it; so much had he been shocked at seeing the Risk the Collector was exposed to, & at hearing of the actual loss which he sustained before the Bank was established at Norfolk. I must therefore my dear Sir confess that I am afraid to accept your Offer.

You had mentioned Norfolk, but although there is a Bank there, & living is much cheaper there, I have been well assured[1] on account of the Vicinity of Oysters & excellent Fisheries, & a better Market, than at Petersburg, I should have been afraid to have gone even thither, on account of the unhealthiness of the Place: and this consideration operates powerfully on my Mind with respect to Petersburg. I see the force of the reasons which you assign for not offering me a post in the General Government, & I declare I had rather never have one, than that you should be censured for bestowing it on me. Indeed one Consolation I have in declining your present Offer is, that should you remove the Collector of Petersburg, you will not now be charged with doing it through partiality to a Friend, who in the public Opinion is utterly unfit for it, although you, & a few others, I have the pleasure to know, think that I am qualified for it; & that I would faithfully discharge the duties of the office should I once engage to discharge them.

I will confess to you my Friend, from whom I wish to conceal no Secret of my Heart, that after despairing of getting into any place which might tolerably suit my Disposition, & afford me the means of saving at least a part of the Produce of my Estate, whilst at the same time it would enable me to procure a better & yet cheaper Education for my Children than I could otherwise procure for them, I had flattered myself, that could I be so happy as to become the Successor of our Friend Monroe, I should compleatly obtain what had been the Object of my Wishes; and I had consented that my Friends, who had long since wished to see me in that Office, might use their influence to procure it for me. The post you offer is, it is true, a Certainty, &, probably, its tenure for life—the other an uncertainty, & possibly only for one year; for three years at the most—But three years possibly are equal to the Term of my capacity for holding any office; & the Risk, Responsibility, & immense Labor & confinement added to the painfull Circumstance of asking a number of Persons to be my Securities for the due discharge not only of *my* Duties, but for that of at least three or four Clerks, are such Considerations as induce me to prefer that Uncertainty of obtaining the Object, & its short & precarious Tenure, if obtained, to the Certainty of possessing for life the office which you have kindly offered me. Should I be disappointed, I shall have the Consolation of reflecting on the purity of my Intentions &[2] Wishes— as amongst them was that of promoting the good of my Country, by supporting the Republican Cause, & the constitutional Independence of the State Governments; & my Hope is that I should be able[3] to exhibit an Example of Economy, which I should also hope would be imitated with Advantage to our Fellow-Citizens, & to the Principles of our Government: to introduce rational Conversation on interesting Subjects, as a Substitute for drinking, & Gaming; & to revive our Philosophical Society, so as to diffuse amongst our Countrymen a Spirit of useful Enquiry in the Arts, Agriculture &c I say should I fail in my Attempt, I shall have the Consolation of reflecting, that not merely my own Convenience, but the public Good was my Object; & that having failed, I should have a better right to retire entirely from the View of all public Objects, & be solely occupied the remainder of my days in the management of my domestic Affairs. Not to intrude too much on your precious time my Friend, I will now only add that Mrs. Page unites with me in presenting to you our best Wishes & sincerest Thanks for the friendly offer you have made assuring you that we are truely sensible that you have done all for us that your Situation would permit.

I am my dear Sir most sincerely and affectionately your Friend

JOHN PAGE

RC (DLC); endorsed by TJ as received 24 Apr. and so recorded in SJL.

FRANCIS Page was the youngest surviving son of John Page and his first wife, Frances Burwell. In 1809, acting on TJ's recommendation, James Madison appointed Francis collector at Yorktown, Virginia (T. B. McCord, Jr., "John Page of Rosewell: Reason, Religion, and Republican Government from the Perspective of a Virginia Planter, 1743-1808" [Ph.D. diss., American University, 1990], ix; Madison, *Papers, Pres. Ser.*, 1:77-8).

OTWAY Byrd served as collector at NORFOLK from 1797 until his death in 1800 (JEP, 1:251; Washington, *Papers, Ret. Ser.*, 4:86).

A branch of the BANK of the United States was ESTABLISHED AT NORFOLK in 1800 (Bray Hammond, *Banks and Politics in America, From the Revolution to the Civil War* [Princeton, 1957], 127).

SUCCESSOR OF OUR FRIEND MONROE: that is, Page wished to succeed James Monroe as governor of Virginia.

[1] Preceding five words interlined.
[2] Word and ampersand interlined.
[3] Preceding eight words and ampersand interlined.

To William Short

DEAR SIR   Washington Apr. 19. 1802.

The present occasion by mr Dupont is so favorable, that tho constantly[1] immersed in business or society, without a moment's intermission, Congress being in session, I cannot omit to drop you a line; whether it will be long or short will depend on the interruptions. my last to you were of the 17th. of March and 3d. of Oct. of the last year: since which I have to acknolege the reciept of yours of Apr. 19. June 9. Oct. 18. Dec. 18. of the last year, & Jan. 23. of the present. in that of Dec. 18. was inclosed one for mr Barnes, which, as you left me a discretion on the subject, I did not deliver, because I knew he had written to you at times intermediate to the date of the one you acknoleged the receipt of. his method is to write when he has something to inform you of, and to send his letter to his friend at New York who finds an occasion for conveyance. you must not therefore be surprised at not recieving letters from him by particular persons going hence. I informed him for instance of this opportunity by mr Dupont: but he says he wrote to you by the way of New York about 6. weeks or 2. months ago, which I recollect because he shewed me the letter. he was on the point of investing all your money in hand when we recieved news of peace, say about the latter end of November. the sixes were then at and near par. I knew that peace would produce many bankruptcies, and of course bring to market all the stock held by the bankrupts. it accordingly fell and continued to fall till lately, when it was I believe down to 96. at that point it began to look up, and he instantly sent orders to purchase for you, and in the course of a few weeks he will invest about 4000. dollars for you, & then write to you. you have lost $1\frac{1}{2}$ per cent in interest, but will gain 3. or 4. per cent on the capital. I should be sorry that any thing should induce mr Barnes to withdraw his agency. I could not find a single person in America in whom, from a most intimate knowlege of him, I could repose equal confidence, for integrity, activity, punctuality. he is not a broker: he does but a little business, on commission, & never risking a cent. his whole income on this is probably not 1000. D. a year, & his whole expences not beyond 700. D. the worst is that he is 70. years old: but as active as a boy, & hardly ever had an hour's sickness. be assured that he is a precious depository for you. a little kindness too attaches him by his heart-strings. he will probably remove back to Philadelphia within the present year, where he can do your business on the spot & from his own knolege. here he is obliged to trust to correspondents which occasions delay, and sometimes loss of opportunity of seizing the favorable moment at market. I have advised him to invest your money in the 3. percents. we are appropriating a sum of 7,300,000. D. annually to the redemption of our debt, in the order of time in which it is redeemable. the whole will be redeemed in about 16. years, except the three percents, which we have no right to redeem but at par, altho' their price hitherto has been only at half par, or as far as 60. at most. two years surplus of revenue will redeem them at par, and probably it will be thought better to do that than to let them die out. tho' therefore at their present price they yield but an interest of 3. p. cent annually, yet in 16. or 17. years they will add $66\frac{2}{3}$[2] per cent at once to the capital, which I think renders them more profitable than even the eights, which from their price yield but 7. per cent. this too is about the profit on bank stock. in consequence of this view the threes have begun to rise a little, altho' the law is not yet actually past the Senate.—I wrote you formerly that the government, when it declined settling the affair of your 9000. D. till E.R.'s suit should be determined, promised me to invest 8000. D. (the balance supposed due you nearly) immediately in subscriptions to the 8. percent loan then open. I understood it to be actually done, and never doubted until enquiring lately[3] at the Secretary of state's office, the chief clerk informed me that from the excess of the subscriptions beyond the extent of the loan, not above one fourth part was effected. (I have not the exact sum in my memory). consequently you will recieve but 6. instead of about $7\frac{1}{2}$ per cent on what was not subscribed of the balance due you. E.R.'s suit is still undecided. I always took for granted the attorney of the government would take care to shew that E.R. was not responsible to you, and consequently was so to the US. who were bound to answer over to you. I discovered very accidentally about a month ago, that on an argument of the case, this had been so little impressed, that one of two judges had been of a contrary opinion. I immediately therefore employed counsel for you separately, to attend to the single point of proving your claim on the US. and consequently their claim over on E.R. and I sent him authenticated copies[4] of the documents necessary to prove it, copies of which I now inclose to you. I hope the next session of the court will put an end to it: and that I shall be able in my next to inform you it is finished. it is very desireable for me, considering my personal position, that this matter should be finally settled as agreed by the preceding administration, without any new interference on my part. however this desire must have it's limits, beyond which it shall not be permitted to delay the justice due to you.— Pendleton & Lyons have made no further payment: so that you have not lost the possession of any further sum, and the acceptance of their note by the government is an additional assumption on their part of a responsibility to you.—mr Barnes's accounts will inform you of the reciepts from the James river canal, and from Mosby. Mayo's debt is still pursuing by mr Jefferson, who has followed both up with great diligence.

We have lost one or two of your largest & best tenants from Indian camp, and got very petty ones in their place. I had a survey made of all the clearings with an intention of obliging the tenants to clear towards one another till they should meet, and thus form one large opening, which I would have endeavored to get into one or two hands. but my departure leaves it impossible to pursue the plan, and the place in a very disagreeable situation indeed. a parcel of little distinct patches of clearing in the hands of small distinct tenants. they pay their rents indeed so far; but they are not getting the farm into a desireable shape; and I have avoided giving them the leases for 5. years which I had intended if I could have retained the large tenants. I believe I should do well to engage my manager at Monticello to superintend the tenants, see that they cultivate the lands by rotation according to compact, clear in proper directions, and pay their rents, giving the collector 5. per cent on the latter, not as a thing which he would regard, but to lay him under legal responsibility. you seem to think rent is the sole measure of the value of lands here. this is far from being the case. I could sell your Indian camp tomorrow for the double of what it cost you. you have had it about 8. years. besides about 5. percent annual profit by rents you have added $12\frac{1}{2}$ per cent annually to your capital. so great an advance in value must not be expected to continue. I got those lands below what they would then have sold for to common purchasers on paiments less prompt & sure. but lands have risen in our neighborhood in a most extraordinary degree. the profit by tenants is still precarious and difficult. I have fine farms on the opposite side of the river unoccupied for the last 5. or 6. years for want of tenants.—I have not yet sent you a commission for books and wines, with which I must trouble you this summer, because as yet it has not been convenient. the office I hold is allowed a plentiful salary, but no outfit. the consequence is that my private as well as public income has been all fully employed. this has been the reason why I have not commenced the discharge of your monies in my hands. I shall be at ease by the completion of my outfit in the course of the summer, and then shall appropriate from one to two thousand dollars (the smaller sums in the beginning) quarterly which come into mr Barnes's hands as my factor here [to] the regular extinction of that debt. this being recieved at the same time with your own quarterly income, shall be regularly invested with that by him.—your box of books arrived here without any previous information, & without my being able to devise from whom or whence they came. I opened the box therefore, examined those [ly]ing on the top, and soon conjectured they were yours. I recieved afterwards your letter informing me of them. they are therefore reserved here in safety, having never [been] disturbed, except the upper layer which was dry & in good condition. they [are] not in my way at all, nor do your affairs here or in Richmond, in the hands of mr Barnes & mr Jefferson give me any embarrassing trouble. those in Albemarle cannot, because I am not there; but your interests will I believe require I should [leave?] them under some superintendance. immediately on reciept of yours of Jan. 23. I inclosed the list of plants desired by M. de Liancourt on behalf of the Agricultural society of Paris, to J. Bartram near Philadelphia, the only person I know in the US. who is likely to fulfill their intentions, desiring him to attend during the summer to the collection of the articles desired, and as soon in autumn as the seeds can all have been in readiness for gathering, to pack them, send me his bill for paiment, and I will then direct what is to be done with them. be so good as to communicate this to M. de Liancourt with the tender of my friendly esteem, and the assurance that I am glad of any opportunity of giving him proofs of it.—the Consulship at Smyrna, for which a person was recommended to you by Madame de Chastellux has been given to a mr Stewart, a native citizen, son of the late General Stewart one of our revolutionary officers.—I ought to have informed you in my last letter that mr Patricot had recieved in due time the one you inclosed to me for him. I now send his acknolegement of it, which may be satisfactory to his friends.—I will at some leisure moment prepare the sequel of our account subsequent to that rendered in my letter of April 13. 1800. but having before that turned over all your other affairs to mr Barnes, except Indian camp, so that they should not enter at all into account between us, the sequel will not have a single article in it except the reciept of rents for that tract, and some disbursements for taxes & other small matters. I pray you to make my friendly respects acceptable to our mutual friend, and to be assured yourself of my constant and sincere affection.   TH: JEFFERSON

PrC (DLC: Short Papers); faint; at foot of first page: "Mr. Short"; endorsed by TJ in ink on verso. Enclosures: (1) Copies of enclosures to TJ to John Wickham, 29 Jan. 1802. (2) Patricot to TJ, 1 Feb. 1801, not found (see Vol. 32:505n). Enclosed in TJ to Pierre Samuel Du Pont de Nemours, 25 Apr.

WE ARE APPROPRIATING: see TJ to Albert Gallatin, 1 Apr.

E.R.'S SUIT: for Short's claim for unpaid salary and its connection to the government's lawsuit against Edmund Randolph, see TJ to Wickham, 29 Jan.

Jacob Wagner was CHIEF CLERK of the State Department.

George Jefferson was assisting with the collection of John MAYO's and Littleberry Mosby's debts to Short (Vol. 34:198n).

TJ prepared a form for LEASES on Short's Indian Camp property in Albemarle County in 1800 (Vol. 31:506-7, 518).

MANAGER AT MONTICELLO: Gabriel Lilly.

The BOX OF BOOKS came into TJ's care several months before Short's belated explanation, in his letter of 18 Oct. 1801, arrived (Vol. 35:444-5, 463).

Short had forwarded the request concerning the U.S. CONSULSHIP AT SMYRNA in his letter of 18 Dec. 1801.

A letter from Short to TJ on 18 Sep. 1800 enclosed one from a member of the PATRICOT family in France to his brother, a Saint-Dominguean refugee in the United States. The Patricots had connections to the La Rochefoucauld family (Vol. 32:157, 158n, 331, 372, 474-5, 505).

[1] Word interlined.
[2] Figure interlined in ink in place of "[40]."
[3] Word interlined.
[4] Word interlined in place of "papers."

From Charles Douglas

SIR/   Alexandria. 20th. April 1802.

I return your Treatise on the Kine Pock with many thanks.—You will find it in good order.

Some few have been inoculated here with success. But we seem by no means zealous to enter into the importance of the object—And that join'd to common prejudices will impede it.

We continue to inoculate with the Variolous matter.

I am Sir Your respectful & Obedt. Servt.   CH. DOUGLAS

RC (DLC); at foot of text: "Thomas Jefferson Esqre. &c &c &c"; endorsed by TJ as received 23 Apr. and so recorded in SJL.

I RETURN YOUR TREATISE: Douglas had written to TJ in June 1801, requesting information on smallpox vaccination and a supply of vaccine matter. TJ replied that his pamphlets and prints on the subject were in the possession of Dr. Edward Gantt and that Douglas was welcome to peruse them whenever he wished (Vol. 34:467-8, 471).

From Joseph Fay

SIR   New York 20th. April 1802

At the request of Mr. Rathbone, I take the freedom to mention my acquaintance with his son, who is Esteemed a young Gentleman of respectable Character and connections, a regular bread Merchant, and promising Talents; I am informed that he is desirous of obtaining an appointment as commercial Agent to some Port in Europe. I am of opinion that he would be Capable of discharging the duties of such an office with reputation to himself, and to his Country.

I am very respectfully Your most Obedient Humble Servant

JOSEPH FAY

RC (DNA: RG 59, LAR); at head of text: "His Excellency Thomas Jefferson"; endorsed by TJ as received 23 Apr. and "Rathbone John to be Consul" and so recorded in SJL.

On 16 Apr., New York merchant John RATHBONE had written James Madison on behalf of his SON, John Rathbone, Jr., who was in France and desirous of a con-sular appointment in Europe. Enclosing an unidentified letter of recommendation, Rathbone's letter also included a list of 11 cities for which his son wished to be considered, ranked in order of interest. Rathbone closed by asking that Madison "lay this application before the President of the United States" (RC in DNA: RG 59, LAR; endorsed by TJ).

To the House of Representatives

GENTLEMEN OF THE
HOUSE OF REPRESENTATIVES

I transmit you a report from the Secretary of state with the information desired by a resolution of the house of representatives of the 8th. of January relative to certain spoliations and other proceedings therein referred to.   TH: JEFFERSON

April 20. 1802.

RC (DNA: RG 233, PM, 7th Cong., 1st sess.); endorsed by a House clerk. PrC (DLC). Recorded in SJL with notation "Rep. of Sy. of state & documents on Span. spolians." Printed with enclosures in ASP, Foreign Relations, 2:440-58.

The RESOLUTION of 8 Jan. asked the president "to cause to be laid before this House such information and documents as are in possession of the Department of State, relative to spoliations committed on the commerce of the United States, under

Spanish authority; and, also, relative to the imprisonment of the American Consul at Saint Jago de Cuba." The House appointed James A. Bayard and John Randolph to present the resolution to TJ. Just prior to adopting the measure, the House approved a resolution that requested estimates of the costs of implementing the Convention of 1800. TJ responded to the resolution about the convention, which Randolph and Bayard also conveyed to him, within a few days of its passage (JHR, 4:43; TJ to the House of Representatives, 12 Jan. 1802).

ENCLOSURE

From James Madison

Department of State, April 18th 1802

The Secretary of State respectfully reports to the President the information requested by the Resolution of the House of Representatives, of the 8th of January last relative to Spoliations committed on the Commerce of the United States, under Spanish authority; and also, relative to the imprisonment of the American Consul at Saint Jago de Cuba.

This Report has been delayed longer than was wished: but the delay has been made unavoidable by the sickness and absence of the Chief Clerk in this Department, who had partially gone through the necessary researches, and could most readily have compleated them.   JAMES MADISON

RC (DNA: RG 233, PM, 7th Cong., 1st sess.); in Daniel Brent's hand, signed by Madison ; endorsed by House clerks. Enclosures: (1) Charles Pettit to Madison, Philadelphia, 10 Oct. 1801, Pettit writing from Philadelphia as the head of an insurance company regarding American ships captured by the Spanish under the pretext of a blockade of Gibraltar (Tr in same, in a clerk's hand; see Madison, *Papers, Sec. of State Ser.*, 2:170). (2) Thomas FitzSimons to Madison, 10 Oct. (Tr in DNA: RG 233, PM, in a clerk's hand; Madison, *Papers, Sec. of State Ser.*, 2:168-9). (3) Philadelphia Chamber of Commerce memorial to TJ, 10 Oct. (Tr in DNA: RG 233, PM, in a clerk's hand; Vol. 35:425). (4) Clement Humphreys to Willing & Francis, 26 July 1801; John Gibson to Willing & Francis, Nicklin & Griffith, and Henry Nixon, 31 July; Richard Flim to Nicklin & Griffith, 3 Aug.; and Gibson to Willing & Francis, Nicklin & Griffith, and Nixon, 7 Aug.; all written at Algeciras, Spain, concerning the capture of the armed American ship *Molly*, of which Gibson was the captain, by Spanish privateers (Trs in DNA: RG 233, PM, in a clerk's hand). (5) Samuel Elam to TJ, 10 Nov. 1801 (same; Vol. 35:593-5). (6) Extracts of letters from David Humphreys to the secretary of state, 13 June, 19 Aug., 30 Sep. 1800, 13 Jan., 6 Nov. 1801, regarding captures of American vessels (Trs in DNA: RG 233, PM, in a clerk's hand; Madison, *Papers, Sec. of State Ser.*, 2:231). (7) Extracts, Josiah Blakeley to secretary of state, 1 Nov., 26 Dec. 1801, reporting that the Spanish intendant at Santiago, Cuba, ordered Blakeley's arrest and the seizure of his books and papers; Blakeley, the U.S. consul at Santiago, does not know the charges against him but suspects that they originated with a shipment that had false papers using his name; Blakeley is collecting information and hopes that the U.S. government will support his claim against the Spanish authorities for damages (Trs in DNA: RG 233, PM, in a clerk's hand; Madison, *Papers, Sec. of State Ser.*, 2:216, 342). (8) Report of American ships captured by the French and their privateers and taken into Spanish ports in Europe and Africa between October 1796 and August 1799; compiled by Moses Young, 1 Oct. 1799 (Tr in DNA: RG 233, PM, in a clerk's hand; for Young as consul at Madrid, see Madison, *Papers, Sec. of State Ser.*, 3:434; Vol.

32:162). (9) Reports of American ships captured by the Spanish and taken into Spanish ports; compiled by Young, 1 Oct. 1799 (Tr in DNA: RG 233, PM, in a clerk's hand). (10) Abstract of captures of American vessels by Spanish cruisers or other ships under Spanish authority from April 1797 to August 1801, after the treaty between the United States and Spain, for which complaints have been lodged with the U.S. government (same).

SICKNESS AND ABSENCE OF THE CHIEF CLERK: Jacob Wagner suffered from a "lingering disorder" that forced him to seek medical treatment outside Washington and prevented him from working in the State Department from the middle part of March until November 1802 (Madison, *Papers, Sec. of State Ser.*, 3:xxvii, 47-8).

From "S"

SIR   Baltimore 20 April 1802

In our former presidents administration there was days appointed by that Honourable Gentleman for fasting & Prayer and which was observed as such throughout the whole continent; It is with extreem Reluctance that I must say, that nothing Similar to this has ever occurred Since Your administration, I am at a loss Sir to know what Your objections can be to Such a Step, is it because it is a religious one, I think not, It must be then that you have forgot that Such a thing is Servicable to Society—reflect My dear Sir for only one moment, and Your own Good Sence will readily convince you of the impropriety of forgetting such an Important object of Neglect,[1] it is attended by many evil Consequences—In the first place, any person whom have not the honour of Your acquaintance, would readily Suppose that the eroneous misrepresentations which are in Circulation in regard to your Religious principals, are too well founded, this is a thing of the greatest Importance to you, therefore loose No time in Convincing the World, that this report has arrose from Naught—

Yr. friend   S

RC (DLC); at head of text: "The Honble The President of the United States"; endorsed by TJ as received from "Anon." on 22 Apr. and "fast days &c" and so recorded in SJL, but as a letter of 10 Apr.

FASTING & PRAYER: George Washington issued national days of thanksgiving during his administration. As president, John Adams issued two days of "solemn humiliation, fasting, and prayer" in 1798 and 1799. TJ expressed his opposition to national fast days in his draft reply to the

Danbury Baptist Association, 1 Jan. 1802 (Charles Ellis Dickson, "Jeremiads in the New American Republic: The Case of National Fasts in the John Adams Administration," *New England Quarterly*, 60 [1987], 188, 191; James D. Richardson, ed., *A Compilation of the Messages and Papers of the Presidents, 1789-1908*, 11 vols. [New York, 1908], 1:268-70, 284-6; Vol. 36:254-6).

[1] Preceding two words interlined.

To Volney

Your friendly letters of 5. & 6. Messidor came both to hand in due time, and soon after them I recieved the model of the pyramid, in good order, which you were so kind as to send me, and for which I pray you to accept my grateful thanks. it has corrected the idea I had preconcieved of the form of those masses, which I had not supposed to appear so flat. whenever any good work comes out giving a general view of Egypt, it's inhabitants and antiquities, not too long for one in my situation to have leisure to read, I will thank you to indicate it to me. probably you will know beforehand whether such an one is to be expected.—I am glad you were able to engage so fine a writer of English to translate your work. a better hand you could not have found. when you shall be done with the manuscript you recieved from mr Mc.lure it is desired that it may be burnt. your invocation was printed here and excited a desire for the publication. an account of the United states, whether physical or civil, cannot but be looked for with anxiety.   I shall say nothing of your country, because I do not understand either it's past or present state, nor foresee it's future destiny. those on the spot possess alone the facts on which a sound judgment can be formed. believing that forms of government have been attempted to which the national character is not adapted, I expect something will finally be settled as free as their habits of thinking & acting will admit. my only prayer is that it may cost no more human suffering. you congratulate me on my accession to the helm of this government. personally it is no cause of congratulation. but I see in it a proof of the too favorable opinion you form of me. in fact my countrymen are so much in the habits of order, and feel it so much their interest, that they will never be wanting in the support of the existing government,[1] tho' they may disapprove & mean to change it at the first return of their right of election. you saw this disposition more severely tried than it ever was, or probably ever will be again. principles & pursuits were then brought forward, the most adverse to those of the nation in it's sound state of mind, and maintained for a short period by delusion, terror, corruption & every artifice which those who held the power & resources of the nation could put into exercise: yet the people soon corrected themselves, and brought things back to their course by the regular exercise of their elective franchise. we are reducing our government to the original simplicity of it's forms, suppressing offices useless to the public and created only to increase the patronage & strength of the Executive beyond the controul of the Legislative branch of the government. we have reduced our military to small garrisons of a company or two for our posts, & our navy to what is merely necessary to act in the mediterranean. these economies have enabled us to[2] repeal all our internal taxes, reserving only those on commerce, which besides supporting the government enable us to consecrate 7,300,000. D. a year to the discharge of our public debt which it will extinguish in 17. years. our predecessors you know had added to it from 5. to 10. millions. we have restored our judiciary to what it was while justice & not federalism was it's object; our alien-law is made again what it was before nearly; the sedition law expired, and will be marked by the formal censure of the constituted authorities. the main body of our citizens are come back to one mind in all the states South of those of New England; and even of these Rhode island and Vermont have joined us, and New Hampshire has been within a very small number of votes of manifesting[3] the same in the choice of their governor. in Massachusets the progress is slower. federalism still triumphs there, and is yet more strong in Connecticut. the empire of the priesthood over those states is the cause of their slow recovery from their delusions. but they advance, because they are essentially with their fellow citizens of the other states. we have now 12. republican governors, and of the 4. others, 3 are obliged to neutralize themselves, one only (of Connecticut) acting decidedly on his old principles. the leaders of the quondam party however become more bitter as they are more impotent; they fill their newspapers with falsehoods, calumnies & audacities far beyond any thing you witnessed while here, and happily these vehicles, like the flues of our chimnies, give an innocent conveyance and discharge to smoke & vapours which might be dangerous if pent up in their bowels. we are going fairly through the experiment whether freedom of discussion, unaided by coercion, is not sufficient for the propagation & protection of truth, and for the maintenance of an administration pure and upright in it's actions and views. no one ought to feel under this experiment, more than myself. Nero wished all the necks of Rome united in one, that he might sever them at a blow. so our ex-federalists, wishing to have a single representative of all the objects of their hatred, honour me with that post, and exhibit against me such atrocities as no nation has ever before heard or endured. I shall protect them in the right of lying and calumniating, and shall go on to merit the continuance of it, by pursuing steadily my object of proving that a people, easy in their circumstances as ours are, are capable of[4] conducting themselves under a government founded not in the fears & follies of man, but on his reason, on the predominance of his social over his dissocial passions, so free as to restrain him in no moral right, and so firm as to protect him from every moral wrong, which shall leave him in short in possession of all his natural rights; nothing being more demonstrable than that he has no natural right in opposition to his social duties. this is the object now nearest to my heart. I am too old to do more than set it into motion, and leave it to those whom the virtue of our people shall hereafter call to their affairs to go on with & establish it's success. an important means of giving free course to this experiment is to keep[5] Europe and it's quarrels at a distance. on this subject we are not without some uneasiness: but I hope that wise calculations on that side the Atlantic will dissipate our inquietudes and leave our relations with them in their present state. I count greatly on the wisdom of your chief. but on this subject it is not for me to speak.—I rejoice to hear that your situation is agreeable. no one wishes a continuance of it more sincerely than I do: nor can any one with more truth assure you of his respectful & sincere affection and attachment. let me hear from you freely, all obstacles being now removed.

TH: JEFFERSON

PrC (DLC); at foot of first page: "M. Volney." Enclosed in TJ to Pierre Samuel Du Pont de Nemours, 25 Apr.

LETTERS OF 5. & 6. MESSIDOR: that is, 24 and 25 June 1801. Soon after writing those letters, Volney sent TJ a model of the Great PYRAMID (Vol. 34:437-42, 454).

The accomplished WRITER OF ENGLISH was Joel Barlow, who had undertaken to complete the translation of Volney's *Les Ruines, ou, Méditation sur les Révolutions des Empires*. TJ had translated most of the book's chapters and sent them to Volney in the care of William Maclure. TJ wanted his role in the translation kept quiet, and Volney, in his letter of 24 June, had inquired about what to do with that MANUSCRIPT after the printers were finished with it. To promote the forthcoming translated edition, Volney asked Louis André Pichon to have the book's INVOCATION distributed in the United States. The invocation appeared in American newspapers in the spring and summer of 1801 (New York *Spectator*, 13 May 1801; Vol. 33:341-2; Vol. 34:438, 440, 441-2n).

In 1803, Volney published his

ACCOUNT OF THE UNITED STATES as a *Tableau du Climat et du Sol des États-Unis d'Amérique*. In translation it was called a *View of the Climate and Soil of the United States of America* (Vol. 29:xxxviii).

ALIEN-LAW: the revised naturalization act, signed into law by TJ on 14 Apr., repealed the naturalization law of 18 June 1798, which had required a residence in the United States of 14 years before new immigrants could become citizens. The 1802 law reduced the residency requirement to five years, the term prescribed by the naturalization act of 29 Jan. 1795 (U.S. Statutes at Large, 1:414-15, 566-9; 2:153-5; Vol. 30:299, 301n).

The SEDITION ACT expired on 3 Mch. 1801. An attempt early in that year to renew the act did not succeed (U.S. Statutes at Large, 1:597; Vol. 32:419n).

YOUR CHIEF: Napoleon Bonaparte.

[1] TJ first wrote "support of their government."

[2] TJ here canceled "[reduce]."

[3] Word interlined in place of "doing."

[4] TJ here canceled "being."

[5] TJ here canceled "ourselves."

To Henry Dearborn

Th:J. to Genl. Dearborne   Apr. 21. 1802.
The guarding our arms at New London & Manchester stands on totally different ground. the former was at my request, delivered verbally to Governor Monroe about the 15th. of April 1801. certainly not a week sooner or later. the latter was in the time of the insurrection of their slaves and no more chargeable to the Union than the other expences of their militia on that occasion. I should have concieved the former as needing no appropriation, but paiable out of the contingent fund of the time, as the hire of persons to repair the arms, or the house or any thing else occasionally.[1] is it possible there could be no existing fund chargeable with the preservation of the public arms, exposed to destruction under my own eye?

RC (DLC); on verso of the cover of an unidentified letter addressed to TJ as president; addressed: "The Secretary at War"; on verso in Dearborn's hand: "make a Statement of what the whole amount of the within claim is distinguishing, the expence at Manchester, the expence at New London prior to the 15th. of April, and what was subsequent to the 15th. of April."

In June 1801, James Monroe confirmed that he and TJ had previously had a conversation about guarding U.S. arms and gunpowder at NEW LONDON, Virginia. Monroe also stated that he would have a statement submitted to the War Department for a "like expence" incurred in the protection of federal arms stored at MANCHESTER, Virginia. Concerned about the prospect of "insurgent negroes," TJ in November 1800 had urged Monroe to ask the U.S. government to protect the arms at New London (Vol. 32:248; Vol. 34:347, 614).

[1] TJ originally ended the letter here, before adding the final sentence.

To Pierre Samuel Du Pont de Nemours

Dear Sir   Washington Apr. 21. 1802
I cherish the hope of seeing you here in the course of the present week as your letter of the 13th. gives me to hope. I believe that the destinies of great countries depend on it. such is the crisis now existing. I shall say to you much which I cannot commit to paper. should I not see you, I shall forward some letters of which I will ask your care, and then express to you my Adieux and wishes for your happiness and a pleasant voyage.   Th: Jefferson

RC (DeGH); addressed: "M. Dupont de Nemours. New York"; franked and postmarked. PrC (DLC); at foot of text in ink: "Dupont de Nemours."

From Mary Jefferson Eppes

Eppington April 21st [1802]

I have written to you twice My Dear Papa by Dr Walker who was prevented the first time from setting out by the death of one of his sisters, after having seen the last sad duties paid to her he return'd to the Hundred & gave me my letter I then wrote again but it was forgot by Mr Eppes who was the only one up when the Doctor went off in the morning. I recieved your last with the medals which I think very much like you, mine will be very precious to me dear Papa during the long seperations from you to which I am doomed & which I feel more cruelly at this time than ever, My father kindly offer'd the only pair of horses he had, to enable us to go up, but more were wanting & Mr Eppes could not spare his own from the plough at this time. it gives me pleasure to know that you will have my dear Sisters society this summer, if I could how gladly would I join you during part of it but 'till the last of july the horses will be constantly in the plough. My[1] little son grows daily & is daily becoming more dear & interesting to us he indeed[2] supplies the place of all company to us when at home for there we have no neighbours. he has no teeth yet tho' I think it cannot be long before he has as his gums have appear'd to be very painful to him at times for a long time. I have not said any thing to you about the money in Mr Jeffersons hands as Mr Eppes used it while in Richmond Adieu My dear Papa I shall write again by Crity when she goes up, I hope you had no objection to her spending this winter with me, she was willing to leave home for a time after the fraca's which happen'd there & is now anxious to return adieu once more my dear Papa believe me ever yours with the warmest affection

M EPPES

P.S. Mama desires me to send her best affections to you & thanks for the medal. I have been also desired to remind you of the spectacles you promised to procure for her

RC (MHi); partially dated; endorsed by TJ as a letter of 21 Apr. 1802 received on 30 Apr. and so recorded in SJL.

YOUR LAST WITH THE MEDALS: TJ to Mary Jefferson Eppes, 29 Mch. 1802.

BY CRITY: that is, Critta Hemings, the nursemaid for Francis Wayles Eppes; see Vol. 35:579-80.

SPECTACLES: TJ was a frequent customer of the Philadelphia company McAllister & Matthews, who made and sold spectacles, canes, whips, and hardware. In May 1800, he placed three orders for glasses for family and friends. On 22 Oct. 1801, TJ paid $15.67 to McAllister & Co. for spectacles, possibly those for Elizabeth Wayles Eppes (MB, 2:1017, 1193; Vol. 36:695). TJ planned to bring the spectacles to his sister-in-law himself,

but acknowledged in July that he had had
them for at least six months while waiting
for a "direct conveyance" (see TJ to Mary
Jefferson Eppes, 1 May and 2 July 1802).

[1] Canceled: "baby."
[2] Word interlined.

From Albert Gallatin

DEAR SIR   April 21st 1802

I enclose a rough draft of articles which have been substantially
agreed on with the Commissioners on the part of Georgia. Will you
be good enough to examine them; and I will wait on you to morrow
in order to know the result of your observations & give some necessary explanations.

Respectfully your obedt. Servt.   ALBERT GALLATIN

RC (NNPM); at foot of text: "The
President of the United States"; endorsed
by TJ as received from "<Departmt.
Treasury> Gallatin Albert" on 21 Apr.
and "Georgia convention" and so recorded in SJL with Gallatin's name written
over Treasury Department. Enclosure:
perhaps Gallatin's sketch of an agreement with the Georgia commissioners
arranged as seven articles, including the
first calling for a "mutual cession & release of lands on either side of the boundary line which lines shall be Chatahochie
from the Spanish line to & thence by a
straight line to Nickajack"; the second establishing a territory from the lands ceded
to the U.S. to be organized with the priv-
ileges granted by the Northwest Ordinance, "the non slave clause excepted,"
and following the same procedures to become a state; the third article consisting
of two options: in the first the U.S. agrees
to pay Georgia $1,000,000 out of the first
proceeds of sales of land, in the second the
U.S. agrees to pay $1,500,000 "in the
same manner, provided that if they shall
lose any part of the sd. lands, by a legal
decision confirmed by the Supreme Court
of the United States," a proportionate
deduction shall be made "estimating for
that purpose the whole territory at 50 millions of acres"; the fourth article stating
that lands in Georgia for which "the indian title has not been extinguished shall be
purchased as early as they can be obtained
on reasonable terms" from the Indians

"for the use of Georgia & at the expense of
the United States," being "fully understood that no lands shall be thus obtained
except by the free consent of the Indians";
the fifth article, stating that the proceeds
from land sales, after the payment to
Georgia, shall be "applied solely for the
common use of the U. States Georgia included," with the U.S. confirming "such
title, obtained from Great Britain &
Spain, as they may think reasonable"; the
sixth article defining conditions for the
settlement of claims within the territory;
and the seventh conditioning the agreement on the nonrepeal of the U.S. law authorizing the negotiations and Georgia's
"fixing the boundary line above stated as
that of the cession" by a date to be determined (Dft in NHi; undated; entirely in
Gallatin's hand; endorsed by Gallatin:
"Sketch of agreement with Georgia
Comrs."). See Gallatin, *Papers*, 7:33.

Abraham Baldwin, James Jackson,
and John Milledge served as COMMIS-
SIONERS for the state of Georgia. All
were members of the Seventh Congress
(*Biog. Dir. Cong.*). For the appointment
of Gallatin, Madison, and Lincoln to
serve as the U.S. commissioners in the
boundary negotiations with Georgia, see
TJ to the Senate, 5 Jan. 1802. YOUR OB-
SERVATIONS: on 23 Apr., Gallatin noted
TJ's objection to the provision "that the
Indian title to all lands in Georgia should
be at the expense of U.S." (that is, the

fourth article described in the enclosure above). When Gallatin communicated the president's objections to Jackson, the congressman became "violently incensed" and threatened Georgia's withdrawal from the agreement, noting in one of four letters he wrote to Gallatin on 23 Apr. that it was a great "departure from Mr Gallatin's own proposals, made with the consent of his Colleagues." According to the Treasury secretary, TJ "seeing that the Commrs. had really verbally agreed withdrew his objection." Gallatin concluded: "I think that his objection was proper, & that we had been too hasty in agreeing to the condition" (Gallatin, *Papers*, 7:39-41). For the negotiations between 22 and 24 Apr., which led to the signing of the articles of agreement on the evening of Saturday, 24 Apr., see Jackson's letters to Gallatin, in same, 7:32, 39-44. For the articles of agreement, see TJ to the Senate and the House of Representatives, 26 Apr., described in Enclosure No. 2.

From John Isaac Hawkins

SIR   Philadelphia 21st. April 1802

Yours of the 13th. inst. was handed me by Mr. Paterson. I should have been much surprised at the weakness of the frame of the Forte Piano I made for you, had I not previously heard of the defection of two other of my instruments, in the same particular, it gives me great pleasure however that I can assure you from sufficient Experience, that I can remedy the defect intirely, & make the instrument keep in tune as well as those I have lately made, which is much longer than any other Forte Pianos whatever, for this purpose I shall be glad you will send it as soon as possible, as I expect to go to London in a few weeks, I am very sorry that my pecuniary embarrassments oblige me to add, that I must in order to prevent delay, charge you with the repairing, I suppose about 40 dollars, but I shall do it with the positive condition that you will allow me to be indebted to you the amount, to pay as soon as I am able, which will be immediately after my arrival in England whither I go, as soon as I can raise funds for my passage, to receive property which has fallen to me by the death of a relative.

I am Sir Your Obt Sevt.   JOHN I. HAWKINS

RC (DLC); addressed: "Thomas Jefferson President of the United States Washington"; franked; postmarked 22 Apr.; endorsed by TJ as received 23 Apr. and so recorded in SJL.

Hawkins was aware of the difficulty of keeping a FORTE PIANO in tune and, in 1800, had offered five lessons at a dollar a lesson to teach individuals how to tune their own instruments. In March 1802, he advertised that "particular business" was calling him to Europe and that all persons indebted to him should settle their accounts (*Claypoole's American Daily Advertiser*, 19 June 1800; *Poulson's American Daily Advertiser*, 10 Mch. 1802). TJ shipped the defective forte piano to Philadelphia for repair or exchange in June 1802, but there is no record that Hawkins sent TJ a replacement (see George Jefferson to TJ, 11 June and TJ to Hawkins, 17 June).

From Robert Smith

SIR, Ap. 21. 1802

Mr Neilson the writer of the enclosed Letter is a Gentleman of respectability in the State of Maryland. And no person Contributed more than he did to the triumph of Republicanism in that State.

Yours Respectfully RT SMITH

RC (DNA: RG 59, LAR); endorsed by TJ as received from the Navy Department on 22 Apr. and "Doctr. Raphl. Smith to be Superintt. hospitl. N. Orleans" and so recorded in SJL. Enclosure: Roger Nelson to Smith, dated Frederick, Maryland, 7 Apr. 1802, in which Nelson recommends his friend Dr. Raphael Smith to be superintendent of the marine hospital at New Orleans proposed by TJ; Nelson describes Smith as "a Young Man of finished Education" and fluent in French, Spanish, and Italian; he was educated in Rome, studied medicine at Frederick under Dr. Philip Thomas, and also attended medical lectures at Philadelphia; Smith left Maryland on 22 Mch. to establish a practice in New Orleans, and Nelson considers him to be "perfectly correct in his Habits and very attentive to business" (RC in same).

Roger Nelson (NEILSON) was an attorney and member of the Maryland legislature. He served as a Republican in Congress from 1804 to 1810 (DAB; Biog. Dir. Cong.).

From William Baker

DR SIR April 22 1802

The repeal of the late Judiciary carrying with it the potomack district, leaves me no views of advantage from my Marshalsy! The changes which have been made, and are now making by Congress, will necessarily create new offices—I know you will excuse me when I inform you that the inducements which prompted me to solicit an appointment at the commencement of your Presidentcy are now greatly increased by the heavy losses I have sustained in Fitzgeralds insolvency, and in security ship!

Thus circumstanc'd I have consulted several of my Friends in and out of the Goverment upon the elegibility of these new offices, and my competentcy to discharge the dutys—It is suggested that an Auditor will be appointed instead of accountants, and that an appointment here would be honorable and yeelding a support—It is unusual I know for medical men to understand business of this kind, but I have receiv'd a regular education in accounts and know myself capable! The office of Superintendant in the City has been recommended to me as desireable; and my Friends have stated That as I am interested in the prosperity of the City—as I have been long acquainted with the affairs of it—as I hold no lots in it to make me partial—and as I know most of the inhabitants of the district, You might consider such a person as likely to lessen your own fatigue in this additional duty assigned you by law!—However Sir you may arrange these things I am sure it will be right whether I am included or not; but I must beg leave to declare with candour and sincerity that any office which would amount to a decent support would be a blessing to my Children and myself—permit me also to say that if any information shall be necessary upon those essentials which gives "to Character its stamp" I beg leave to refer you to Robert Smith Genl Smith & Walter Bowie Esqrs with whom I have serv'd in publick life—To Gabriel Duvall and John T. Mason Esqrs who have done with me a great deal of business as lawyers, and who have known my conduct in the most trying situations of difficulty and distress—Or to my neighbours of the oldest standing.

I have a deputy marshal in Alexandria Mr Lewis Summers who will continue to act until July. However, I will not resign myself unless I can fill some Post; merely that I may[1] keep the old *Rotten Vessel* afloat 'till she *Lawfully* sinks.—I will Just add a few words—That under the contemplated constitution A Chancellor was to be appointed and I supposed the Register might do after some time; but (sincerely to my sorrow, for it will hurt the majority in Congress more than all they have done will do them good) it seems the Bill is not to pass! I am Dr Sir with the highest respect and esteem
yr most Obt Serv   WM BAKER

RC (DNA: RG 59, LAR); addressed: "Thomas Jefferson Esqr President of the United States"; endorsed by TJ as received 22 Apr. and so recorded in SJL with notation "to be auditor or Superintt. of Washn."

For Baker's recess APPOINTMENT as marshal for the district of Potomac, see Vol. 34:208; Vol. 36:318, 325, 332.

FITZGERALDS INSOLVENCY: John Fitzgerald, former mayor and collector of Alexandria as well as president of the Potomac Company, left much real estate and debt upon his death in December 1799. His executors advertised the sale of his property to raise money for security demands against him. In August 1801, the U.S. district attorney filed a bill in equity against Robert T. Hooe and the executors, claiming that Fitzgerald had died insolvent and in arrears to the government for

$57,000. An injunction to stay the sale of his property, alleging that the United States was entitled to a prior lien, was dismissed in May 1802 although claims against the estate continued in court for several years (*Alexandria Advertiser and Commercial Intelligencer*, 4 Apr. and 9 July 1801; *City of Washington Gazette*, 14 May 1818; Washington, *Papers, Pres. Ser.*, 1:187; Cranch, *Reports*, 1:318-20; 3:73-92; Vol. 35:683).

LEWIS SUMMERS, a native of Fairfax County, Virginia, became a judge and, from 1817 to 1818, represented Kanawha as a delegate in the Virginia Assembly (Leonard, *General Assembly*, 290; George W. Atkinson, *History of Kanawha County* [Charleston, W.Va., 1876], 250-1).

[1] Preceding three words interlined in place of canceled "to."

From Henry Dearborn

SIR   [22 Apr. 1802]

The claims in favour of the State of Virginia for guarding the public stores belonging the United States, at Manchester and New London, as transmited by Govr. Munro, are as follows,

viz. for guarding stores at Manchester, in
the months of Septr. & Octobr. 1800. $543.44
for Do. at New London prior to   ⎫
the 15th. of April 1801   ⎬   410.83
                                     ⎭
for Do. at New London subsequent   ⎫
to the 15th. of April   ⎬   1259. 2
                                     ⎭

H. DEARBORN

RC (DLC); undated; at foot of text: "the President of the United States"; endorsed by TJ as received from the War Department on 22 Apr. and "claim of Virginia for guards" and so recorded in SJL.

From Henry Dearborn

SIR   April 22d. 1802

Will it be proper for me to apply to the chairman of the Committee of ways & means for an appropriation of five or six thousand dollars for defraying the expences of compleeting the line between the Cherokees and North Carolina, and for runing and marking the Chocktaw line, and also for ascertaining and runing the lines of the reserved tracts in the Northwestern & Indiana Territories, or should the application be made by your self.

with respectfull consideration I am Sir Your Huml Servt

H. DEARBORN

RC (DLC); at foot of text: "the President of the United States"; endorsed by TJ as received from the War Department on 22 Apr. and "approprn for Indian lines" and so recorded in SJL.

APPROPRIATION: an act of Congress for military appropriations, approved 1 May 1802, included $5,000 for "running certain boundary lines between the Indians and white inhabitants of the United States, and for ascertaining the lines of sundry reserved tracts of land in the Indiana and Northwestern territories" (U.S. Statutes at Large, 2:183).

From Nicolas Gouin Dufief

MONSIEUR,   22. Avril. 1802

Je profite avec empressement de l'occasion de Mr Petit de Villers pour vous envoyer les deux traductions de l'elève de *Diderot*. J'aurais bien voulu y joindre l'ouvrage sur la Russie, mais je n'ai pas été Jusqu'ici heureux dans mes recherches—Si je réussis à le trouver soyez assuré de ma diligence à vous l'adresser

Voici la liste de quelques ouvrages nouveaux que je viens de recevoir

De l'Esprit des choses, ou coup-d'Œil philosophique sur la Nature des êtres & sur l'objet de leur existence; Ouvrage, dans lequel on considère l'homme comme étant le mot de toutes Les Enigmes, par le Philosophe inconnu—2 vol 8o   3.

L'Aurore Naissante, ou la Racine de la philosophie, de l'Astrologie & de la Théologie, &ca. par le même. 2 vol 8o—   3

Cours de Littérature, par la Harpe. 11 vol 8o *de hazard*   12

Agréez l'hommage de mon respect.   N. G. DUFIEF

EDITORS' TRANSLATION

SIR,   22 Apr. 1802

I hasten to take advantage of the occasion offered by Mr. Petit de Villers to send you the two translations of Diderot's *The Pupil*. I should have liked to join thereto the work on Russia, but until now, I have not been successful in my searches. If I succeed in finding it, be assured of my diligence in sending it to you.

Here is the list of some new works I have just received:

On the Spirit of Things, or, a Quick Philosophical Look at the Nature of Beings and the Object of their Existence; a Work in which Man is Considered as the Key of all Enigmas, by the Unknown Philosopher. 2 vols. in 8o   3

The Dawning of the Day, or the Root of Philosophy, Astrology, and Theology, etc., by the same. 2 vols. in 8o   3

Course of Literature, by La Harpe. 11 vols. in 8o by chance   12

Accept the offer of my respect,   N. G. DUFIEF

RC (DLC); at foot of text: "Thos Jefferson, Esqre."; endorsed by TJ as received 24 Apr. and so recorded in SJL.

TRADUCTIONS DE L'ELÈVE DE DIDEROT: it is not clear what book Dufief meant by this reference. TJ's requests for that work and the one relating to Russia have not been found.

Louis Claude de Saint-Martin used the pseudonym LE PHILOSOPHE INCONNU (the Unknown Philosopher). *De l'esprit des choses* was one of his treatises. Saint-Martin translated *L'Aurore naissante* into French, but Jakob Boehme, a Lutheran mystic, was the author of that work, which first appeared in German in 1612 (André Jacob, ed., *Encyclopédie*

[305]

philosophique universelle, 4 vols. [Paris, 1989-1998], v. 3, pt. 1:1444-5; *De l'esprit des choses*, in Louis Claude de Saint Martin, *Œuvres Majeures*, ed. Robert Amadou, 9 vols. [Hildesheim, Germany, 1975-2008], v. 5, pts. 1-2; Donald M. Borchert, ed., *Encyclopedia of Philosophy*, 2d ed., 10 vols. [Detroit, 2006], 1:624-5;

Edward Craig, ed., *Routledge Encyclopedia of Philosophy*, 10 vols. [London, 1998], 1:799-801).

Jean François de LA HARPE wrote *Lycée, ou Cours de littérature ancienne et moderne*, the first installment of which was published in Paris in 1798.

From Joseph Yznardi, Sr.

EXMO. SEÑOR   Philadelphia 22 de Abril de 1802
Muy Señor mio, y de mi Mayor Respecto
me ha sido forsozo dar Fiansa por la Suma de 12 mil $ sobre el Mal Pleyto del Capn Isrrael en el qe he Nonbrado por mi Nuebo defensor á Mr. Dalas Asegurandole qe V.E conoce mi Justicia, y qe desea se me haga y Confio en qe dos Renglones privados á Mr Dalas serán Suficientes para qe aga anular dicho Pleyto, y no dudo Mereser este favor á V.E antes de enbarcarme pues tengo Ajustado mi pasage en el Navio Equator para Cadiz
390 Gallones Contenian los Vinos qe mandé a V.E cuyos Dros de 156 $ Cunplirá el pago en Nobre á Cuyo Intento Escrivo al Gral Smith para qe a su tienpo ce entienda con Mr. Barnes
El dador de la presente es mi antiguo y particular Amigo Mr. Isaac Cushing conpañero de la Respectable Casa de Samadet, y Cushing de Marcella, en donde me aseguran, no Admiten á Mr. Catalan de consul, qe Ciento, pero si desgrasiadamte fuere Cierto, aseguro á V.E qe Mr. Cushing es digno del nonbramiento, por todos quantos Respectos sean Condusentes, al desenpeño de la dignidad del Enpleo
Suplico a V.E tenga la vondad de permitirme lo Recomiendo á V.E, y Mras Ruego á Dios gue su Vida ms. as
Exmo. Señor BLM de V.E su mas Obte. Servr

JOSEF YZNARDY

EDITORS' TRANSLATION

MOST EXCELLENT SIR   Philadelphia, 22 Apr. 1802
    Dear Sir, and with my greatest respect:
    I have been forced to pay bond in the sum of $12,000 for the wrongful lawsuit by Captain Israel in which I have named as my new lawyer Mr. Dallas, assuring him that Your Excellency knows my rights and wishes that I receive justice, and I trust that a couple of confidential lines to Mr. Dallas will be sufficient to have him get the said lawsuit dismissed. And I do not doubt

that I deserve this favor from Your Excellency before I embark, as I have arranged for my trip in the ship *Equator* heading for Cadiz.

The wines I sent to Your Excellency consisted of 390 gallons, the duties on which of $156 I will pay in November, for which reason I wrote to General Smith so that he would deal with Mr. Barnes.

The bearer of this letter is my old and special friend, Mr. Isaac Cushing, partner in the respectable house of Samadet and Cushing in Marseilles, where they have assured me that they will not accept Mr. Cathalan as consul, which I regret, but if it were unfortunately true, I assure Your Excellency that Mr. Cushing is in every respect worthy to carry out the dignity of the post.

I beg Your Excellency to have the kindness to permit me to recommend him to Your Excellency, and meanwhile I pray to God to protect your life many years.

Most Excellent Sir, your most obedient servant kisses the hand of Your Excellency.   JOSEF YZNARDY

RC (DLC); at foot of text: "Exmo. Sr. Dn. Thomas Jefferson"; endorsed by TJ as received 26 Apr. and so recorded in SJL.

The ship EQUATOR had been advertised for sale in Philadelphia during the first half of March. When Yznardi finally sailed for Cadiz in the first days of June, it was aboard a Spanish ship, the *Principe de la Paz*. Yznardi or a member of his family may have had a financial interest in that vessel, for when the ship left Philadelphia, newspapers listed the captain's name as "Iznardi" (*Philadelphia Gazette*, 1 Mch., 3 June; *Gazette of the United States*, 15 Mch.; NDBW, 2:208).

LOS VINOS: according to TJ's financial memoranda, the $156 for duties on the wines that Yznardi had sent him earlier in the year was paid on 6 May (MB, 2:1115; Yznardi to TJ, 12 Feb. 1802).

In addition to Yznardi's letter printed above, ISAAC CUSHING probably brought other recommendations to Washington, including one to TJ from Benjamin Lincoln at Boston on 14 Apr. That letter, received on the 26th, has not been found, but according to SJL it related to Cushing's bid for the consulship at Marseilles. Cushing likely also carried a letter that William Jones in Philadelphia wrote to Madison on 22 Apr., which according to its endorsement Madison handed to TJ. Jones wrote on behalf of his "particular mercantile friends" in Philadelphia and

noted that Richard Dale joined in commending Cushing's "character and merits" (RC in DNA: RG 59, LAR; endorsed by TJ in part: "Cushing Isaac to be Consul at Marseilles"; see Madison, *Papers, Sec. of State Ser.*, 3:151). In Washington on 26 Apr., William Eustis wrote a brief note to an unspecified recipient: "Dr. Eustis takes the liberty of enclosing two letters from two respectable merchants recommending Mr. Cushing for the Consulate at Marseilles—these with other evidences, adduced by Mr. Cushing, carry strong conviction of his fitness for that office." TJ endorsed Eustis's communication but did not record it in SJL, which may mean that Eustis originally sent it to Madison (RC in same; endorsed by TJ: "Cushing Isaac to be Consul at Marseilles"). The enclosures, both written at Boston, 15 Apr., were letters to Eustis from the merchants John Codman and Samuel Prince. Both writers praised Cushing, who was from Scituate, Massachusetts, and was a relative of William Cushing of the United States Supreme Court. Isaac Cushing, Prince asserted, "under many Trying Circumstances hath Evinced his Regard & Attachments to the Constitution of our Common Country on those Original Republican Principles which Actuated the patriots of '75" (RCs in same). On 28 Apr., Lucas Elmendorf wrote a letter in Washington, apparently to Madison, saying that he was not acquainted with Cushing himself but knew someone in New York who knew him and could attest that he was an American citizen and partner of "a very respectable and Creditable mercantile House" in Marseilles (RC in same; endorsed by TJ: "Cushing Isaac to be Consul at Marseilles Elmendorf to mr Madison").

To James Cheetham

SIR   Washington Apr. 23. 1802.

I shall be glad hereafter to recieve your daily paper by post, as usual, and instead of sending on the Republican Watch-tower, you will retain it, and at the end of the year send it to me in a volume bound in Blue boards.—it is proper I should know what our opponents say & do; yet really make a matter of conscience of not contributing to the support of their papers. I presume Coleman sends you his paper, as I understand the printers generally do to one another. I shall be very glad to pay you for it, & thus make my contribution go to the support of yours instead of his press. if therefore, after using it for your own purposes you will put it under cover with your american citizen to me, it shall be paid for always with yours.— I shall not frank this to avoid post office curiosity, but pray you to add the postage to your bill, which I have desired mr John Barnes of Georgetown, who is my agent in money matters, to have paid by his correspondent in New York. I believe it is mr Ludlow, but am not certain. but whoever it is, he will be desired to call on you. Accept my salutations and best wishes.   TH: JEFFERSON

PrC (DLC); at foot of text: "Mr. Cheetham"; endorsed by TJ in ink on verso.

YOUR DAILY PAPER: TJ subscribed to the New York *American Citizen* throughout his presidency. The REPUBLICAN WATCH-TOWER was Cheetham's semi-weekly newspaper. In May 1803, he charged the president $3 for the annual subscription and the next month $3 for binding the *Watch-Tower*. William COLE-MAN edited the *New-York Evening Post*, a Federalist newspaper. On 14 Apr. 1803, Cheetham charged TJ $8 for issues of the newspaper for the year beginning 22 Apr. 1802 (MB, 2:1123; statement of account with James Cheetham, 26 Apr. 1802 to 21 June 1803, MS in DLC).

ADD THE POSTAGE TO YOUR BILL: Cheetham charged the president 37 cents for postage paid on 26 Apr. (same). CORRESPONDENT IN NEW YORK: Charles Ludlow (Ludlow to TJ, 24 June 1803).

To Madame de Corny

Washington Apr. 23. 1802.

I recieved, my good friend, your letter of May 19. on the 3d. of September. such are the delays to which correspondences across the ocean are subjected. it is true as you say, that I had not written to you for some years; but equally true, my friend, that I had not recieved a letter from you within that time. the reason I presume was the same with both. such was the state of your revolutionary course, that, with you, the most innocent correspondences were unsafe. here, altho' we did not guillotine, the agitations of your country were very sensibly felt. our citizens divided into friends & enemies of your revolution, and each became jealous of the other & ready to denounce them. my former connections in France rendered plausible the imputations of a partiality to that nation inconsistent with the trusts confided to me by my own country, of which circumstance ill disposed persons made great use. during such a state of the public mind therefore, duty as well as prudence rendered it necessary for me to deny myself all correspondence with my friends there; which I did without a single exception. but the very messenger who carried our ratification of the pacification between our two countries, carried my friendly salutations to you. these considerations will I hope justify me from reproaches of silence, and leave me nothing to see in them but proofs of the continuance of your friendship. I never could obtain the least information respecting you till the return of mrs Munroe, who gave me to understand that you had been in a state of sufferance, but were then comfortably re-established. I have never seen mrs Church since her return to America. we are 350. miles apart; a distance which in this country is not easily surmounted. in our party divisions too it happened that her nearest friends were my bitterest opponents; and altho' that could not affect our mutual esteem, it tended to repress the demonstrations of it. Kitty has continued to write to me from time to time. She is to be immediately married to a mr Cruger of New York, the son of a wealthy English merchant residing there. it would surprise and delight us all to see you here, and me most of all to have recieved you at Monticello. but I knew that impossible from the effect of sea voiages on your health. you do not mistake my inclinations when you suppose they would be better satisfied at Monticello than here. my strongest predilections are for study, rural occupations, & retirement within a small but cherished society. born, as I unfortunately was, in an age of revolution, my life has been wasted on the billows of revolutionary storm. the sweet sensations & affections of domestic society have been exchanged with me for the bitter & deadly feuds of party: encircled with political enemies & spies, instead of my children & friends. time however & the decay of years is now fast advancing that season when it will be seen that I can no longer be of use, even in the eyes of those partial to me: and I shall be permitted to pass through the pains & infirmities of age in the shades of Monticello. and I assure you that, even at this price, I look forward to that retirement with anxious desire. my health & spirits have hitherto remained firm and[1] unbroken. but it is not in nature that this should continue long to one who has entered his 60th: year.   I am sorry to find by your letter that you are become so recluse. to be 4. or 5. months without descending your stairs, & that too in Paris where the public walks present so much to cheer the gloom of life, is not well calculated for your happiness. I have admired nothing in the character of your nation more than the chearfulness & love of society which they preserve to great old age. I have viewed it as a pattern which I would endeavor to follow, by resisting the inclinations which age brings on, of retiring from society, & by forcing myself to mix in it's scenes of recreation. do you so also, my friend. consider chearfulness as your physician, and seek it through the haunts of society whenever it has withdrawn from the solitude of your own room: your excellent dispositions should not be lost to those among whom you are placed. I should ask you for some account of the friends we have mutually known in Paris; but I fear it would be asking a necrology to which I would not bind your recollections. keep your mind then on more pleasing subjects, & especially on the remembrance of your friendships among which none claims a warmer place than that I constantly bear to you. accept the sincere assurance of this, with my affectionate wishes for your health & happiness.   TH: JEFFERSON

PrC (DLC); at foot of first page: "Madame de Corny." Enclosed in TJ to Pierre Samuel Du Pont de Nemours, 25 Apr.

MESSENGER: John Dawson, who in the spring of 1801 carried letters and greetings from TJ to several of his acquaintances in France (Vol. 33:270, 274, 288, 338, 341, 359, 453; Vol. 34:106-7, 143n, 281, 292, 403).

MRS CHURCH: Angelica Schuyler Church.

Catherine Church—KITTY—married Bertram Peter CRUGER, a native of the Dutch West Indies, on 25 Mch. 1802 (Cuyler Reynolds, comp., *Genealogical and Family History of Southern New York and the Hudson River Valley*, 3 vols. [New York, 1914], 3:1171).

[1] Preceding two words interlined.

From John Redman Coxe

DEAR SIR/   Philada. April 23d. 1802
     I feel that it necessary to apologise for thus encroaching on your valuable time; at the same time you will permit me to return you my most sincere thanks for your very polite attention in transmitting to me, through Mr. Jno. Vaughan, a portion of Vaccine Infection,

which has enabled me to introduce this invaluable blessing in this City, & also to extend it very considerably through this & most of the Southern States.—

Having attended particularly, since I recd. the Infection in Novr. 1801. to the progress of the disease, & from various sources derived many facts which I feel anxious to communicate to the public, in hopes of its aiding the speedy extension of so grand a discovery; I presume to request your permission to allow me to introduce in my treatise, the valuable letter which accompanied this valuable present.—Should you permit this May I ask if you have tested any of the persons whom you previously Vaccinated, with Variolous matter, & what was the result.—

I know I am encroaching greatly on your time, but hope the importance of the subject will be my excuse.—

I am Sir with the highest respect yr. obedt. Servant

JOHN REDMAN COXE

RC (DLC): at foot of text: "His Excely. Ths. Jefferson"; endorsed by TJ as received 25 Apr. and so recorded in SJL.

THE VALUABLE LETTER WHICH ACCOMPANIED THIS VALUABLE PRESENT: TJ's letter to John Vaughan of 5 Nov. 1801, which accompanied the vaccine matter that TJ forwarded for Coxe's use, included a detailed account of his vaccination experiments at Monticello, with a particular emphasis on the proper time for taking matter from persons infected with cowpox. It was reprinted, with TJ's permission, in Coxe's 1802 treatise, *Practical Observations on Vaccination: Or Inoculation for the Cow-Pock* (Sowerby, No. 953). For details on Coxe's vaccination efforts in Philadelphia, see Vol. 35:604-5, 698-9; Vol. 36:189.

From William Duane

23d April 1802

Wm. Duane's respects—No copies of the Country Aurora have ever been reserved, and only ten of the daily paper; if the Daily Aurora will be acceptable, it will be to be ordered[1] from Philadelphia, as none of 1801. are yet bound. No map of Maryland is to be had here. I have ordered two different copies from Philadelphia, which if they should not be acceptable or either of them, can be kept here for sale, they being in demand.

RC (DLC); addressed: "The President." Recorded in SJL as received 4 May.

COUNTRY AURORA: a tri-weekly edition of the *Aurora* had been printed since the 1790s. Beginning in November 1800, the edition was published under the title *Aurora, for the Country* (Brigham, *American Newspapers*, 2:892).

[1] Thus in MS.

List of Newspapers

Boston	Chronicle	3.	} Genl. Varnum
	Telegraph	3.	
Connect.	American Mercury	2½	} mr Granger
	Bee	1.	
Albany	Albany register.	3.	
N. York	American citizen		} mr Cheetham of N.Y.
	Republican Watch T.		
Phila.	Poulson	11.25	to mr Poulson Phila.
Baltim.	Alx Martin		to himself in Balt.
Washn.	Smith. Univ. gazette	} 10.	to himself
	Natl. Intelligr.		
	Duane	13.	to himself
	Literary Advertiser	2½	to mr Lyon
N.C.	Raleigh Register.	3.	to mr Macon the Speaker
Kentucky	Palladium	2.5	to mr Brown of Kentucky.

Apr. 23. 1802: desired mr Barnes to pay the above.

MS (MHi); entirely in TJ's hand; endorsed by TJ on verso: "Newspapers."

Massachusetts Republican congressman Joseph B. VARNUM had subscribed on TJ's behalf since 1797 to the semiweekly *Independent Chronicle*, a major source of Jeffersonian news in New England. TJ also subscribed for two years to the Republican semiweekly, *Constitutional Telegraphe*, published in Boston in 1802 by John S. Lillie (MB, 2:964, 976, 1017, 1035).

Gideon GRANGER subscribed on TJ's behalf in 1800, 1802, and 1804 to the Hartford, Connecticut, Republican weekly *American Mercury* published by Elisha Babcock (same, 2:1015, 1123).

ALBANY REGISTER: TJ had been a subscriber to John Barber's semiweekly Republican newspaper since at least 1800 (same, 2:1123).

For POULSON and his *American Daily Advertiser*, see TJ's account with Zachariah Poulson, 12 Mch. 1802.

Alexander MARTIN established the Baltimore *American*, a Republican daily newspaper in 1799. On 9 Apr. 1802, TJ gave an order on John Barnes for $14 for a two-year subscription dating from 24 Mch. 1801 (MB, 2:1070).

Samuel Harrison SMITH published a weekly version of the *National Intelligencer* in Washington, D.C., entitled the *Universal Gazette* (Brigham, *American Newspapers*, 1:106-7; Vol. 34:529).

William DUANE, editor of the Philadelphia *Aurora*, established in May 1802 the *Apollo*, a short-lived Washington newspaper that was intended as a daily or triweekly. It failed, presumably for lack of subscribers (Brigham, *American Newspapers*, 1:98-9; 2:891-2).

James LYON and Richard Dinmore published the *American Literary Advertiser*, a Washington-based weekly established by the Franklin Press in March 1802 (same, 1:98; Vol. 34:405).

North Carolina Congressman Nathaniel MACON carried TJ's subscription money for the *Raleigh Register,* published by Joseph Gales (MB, 2:1019).

Senator John BROWN of Kentucky subscribed for TJ to the *Palladium: A Literary and Political Weekly Repository* published at Frankfort (same, 2:1018, 1035).

From Thomas Martin

SIR   Detroit April 23rd. 1802

It is truly distressing to me to trouble you, at the same time I am bound to do it for the tender thoughts that I have for my little family. I have not been Officially informed of my being disbanded but from information think it must be the case, I am Old and getting rather infirm. I have no trade, nor am I able at this time of day to do any thing for my self or family, therefore do hope that if disbanded it will be[1] in your Power to do something for me, pray Sir look at my Situation, here in a strange Country with Mrs. Martin & five Children without Money or friends, or a home to go too. What must I do, Where must I go, or how must I live, perhaps there will be some Vacant Post, and if there should, do humbly Solicite you for it.

I am and can be Proved Was always your Sincere Friend

THO: MARTIN Majr
1st. US. Regiment

RC (DNA: RG 59, LAR); at head of text: "To the President of the United States"; endorsed by TJ as received 23 May and so recorded in SJL; also endorsed by TJ: "to some office."

Thomas Martin (d. 1819) served as an officer in the Virginia line during the American Revolution. Commissioned a lieutenant in the U.S. Army in 1790, he had risen to the rank of major by 1799. Discharged under the Military Peace Es-tablishment Act of 1802, Martin settled in Kentucky, where he sent TJ additional requests for employment in 1803 and 1804, only one of which has been found. In 1804, he was appointed military store-keeper at Newport, Kentucky (Heitman, *Dictionary*, 1:693; ASP, *Military Affairs*, 1:182; Henry Dearborn to Martin, 1 Apr. 1802, FC in Lb in DNA: RG 107, LSMA; Martin to TJ, 16 Sep. 1803).

[1] MS: "will in."

From Gouverneur Morris

[23 Apr. 1802]

Mr Morris presents respectful Compliments and is much oblig'd to Mr Jefferson for his kind Attention Mr M. will endeavor to have the Plan of a parquet executed if his Carpenters have not already gone too far in preparing Materials for one of their own Contrivance

RC (DLC); undated; endorsed by TJ as received 23 Apr. and so recorded in SJL.

Morris began building a new mansion at Morrisiana after he returned from Eu-rope in 1798. Perhaps the subject of PAR-QUET floors came up when Morris attend-ed a dinner at the President's House on 6 Apr. (Anne Cary Morris, ed., *The Diary and Letters of Gouverneur Morris*, 2 vols. [London, 1889], 2:424; DAB).

To William Thornton and Others

Friday Apl. 23. 1802.

Th: Jefferson requests the favor of Doctr. & Mrs. Thornton & Mrs. Breadeau to dine with him on Monday next, the 26th. Inst. at half after three oclock.—

The favor of an answer is asked.

RC (DLC: William Thornton Papers); in Meriwether Lewis's hand; addressed: "Doctr. Thornton." Not recorded in SJL.

William Thornton, his wife Anna Maria Thornton, and her mother Ann Brodeau were frequently invited to DINE at the President's House; see Charles T. Cullen, "Jefferson's White House Dinner Guests," *White House History*, 17 (2006), 39, and Vol. 34:103.

Memorandum from Albert Gallatin, with Jefferson's Comment

[before 24 Apr. 1802]

North Carolina recomnds

Laurence Mooney present surveyor of Winton has been absent, in Ireland, five years & his business done by deputy. *he is returned and to be continued*

Frederick B. Sawyer present surveyor at Newbiggen Creek has removed 25 miles

The above communicated by Mr. Johnson M.C. for N. Carolina who makes the enclosed recommendat[ions]   A. G.

MS (DNA: RG 59, LAR, 8:0397); undated; in Gallatin's hand, with words supplied in italics added by TJ, probably after receiving Gallatin's letter of 24 Apr. Enclosure: perhaps two recommendations on a scrap of paper in Charles Johnson's hand, the first for James L. Shannonhouse as surveyor at Newbiggin Creek "in the room of Frederick Sawyer moved from thence" and the second for Thomas N. Brickell as surveyor at Winton in the place of Laurence Moody (that is, Mooney) "many years absent in Europe" (MS in same, 1:1072-3; undated; unsigned; endorsed by Gallatin: "Surveyors North Carola. recommended by Mr Stone & Mr Johnson").

In a letter of 10 Dec. 1801, Hardy Murfree informed Charles Johnson that LAURENCE MOONEY, the surveyor at Winton, had gone to Ireland shortly after his appointment, leaving James Frasure, his deputy who lived ten miles away, in charge. Murfree recommended Thomas N. Brickell, a justice of the peace and former sheriff, for the position, noting that he lived "on the spot" (RC in DNA: RG 59, LAR; endorsed by TJ: "H. Murfree to Chas Johnson Thos. N. Brickell to be surveyor of the port of Winton, N.C. vice Laurence Moody, absent in Europe"). George Washington appointed Mooney to the surveyorship in February 1795 (JEP, 1:171).

M.C.: member of Congress.

From Mathew Carey

S<small>IR</small>,   Philada. April 24, 1802

Well knowing how much you are liable to be persecuted with the applications of the vain, the idle, and the interested, and how many important objects must necessarily occupy your mind, I hope you will believe that nothing short of the magnitude of the subject on which I presume to address you, could have forced me to trespass on you.

For a considerable time past, it has been strongly impressed on my mind, that notwithstanding the goodness of our cause, we have suffered, and are suffering very severely, by the industry, the talents, the zeal, and the abominable, though plausible, misrepresentations, of the federal Editors, throughout the union, but particularly in this city. There are four daily & two weekly papers printed here, which are hostile to the cause of republicanism. We have only one paper in our defence. That the war is waged on very unequal terms, no man in his senses can dispute or deny.

Although the disparity in point of numbers in this city has been long as great as it is at present, yet the prospect has latterly become vastly more alarming than it was formerly. The resources & energies of Mr. Duane, when not distracted by different & discordant objects of pursuit, amply atoned for the inequality of numbers. Of him it may be truly said, ipse[...] I am fully persuaded, that to him we chiefly owe our preservation from the awful & tremendous dangers which menaced us during the close of Adams's administration. And enjoying my portion of the benefits of the happy change that has taken place, I trust I shall never be found deficient in point of gratitude towards the instrument that has produced them.

But how great Soever have been the past services of the Aurora, candour obliges me to assert, and for the truth of the assertion[1] I appeal to the good sense & discernment of my fellow-citizens, that it has for a considerable time past, been deficient of the spirit & energy which formerly distinguished it. The most artful and deceptious falsehoods, published in the opposition papers, have passed for weeks without refutation or notice. And I know instances of many well meaning men, who have taken it for granted, that because those calumnies were not denied, they could not be disproved.

On this subject I should offer my sentiments with hesitation, did I not find them corroborated by every man of understanding with whom I have had any communication respecting it. And as I scorn subterfuge, & feel perfectly satisfied of the imperious necessity of the measure which I mean to suggest, I shall give you the names of a few of the persons who presently and entirely accord with me on the subject—Joseph Priestley, jun. James Reynolds, Joseph Clay, Abraham Small, John L. Leib, J. Ronaldson, J. Binney, James Thackare, & Dr. Porter. To these I might make large additions: but I suppose I have given enough to rescue me from the unjust imputation of sounding a false alarm.

But the present situation of the Aurora is so far from wonderful, that it would be miraculous were it otherwise. So limited are human powers, that perhaps there is not one man in ten thousand capable of doing justice to so many and such diversified objects as occupy Mr. Duane's attention. When one man has four or five different kinds of business to manage, some of them must, and perhaps all of them will suffer. It is no reflection on Mr. Duane, nor does it argue any distrust of his capacity or powers, to assert that he is unable to do what few of the sons of men can perform.

Deeply concerned at this state of things, I have suggested a plan for applying a remedy, which has met with the most unqualified approbation of the persons I have named, and many more. This plan is

1. To raise by subscriptions 520 Dollars yearly, to pay a suitable person a weekly salary of ten Dollars, for writing paragraphs & essays, to refute the groundless charges brot. against the republicans, & to occasionally carry the war into the enemy's quarters.

2. To furnish the chief part of his productions to the Aurora, in the first instance; but occasionally to send supplies to Boston, New York, & Baltimore.

When this idea first occurred to me, I felt as sanguine of its success as I ever was of any plan in the course of my life. I could not allow myself to apprehend any difficulty in raising the money. I was well aware of the surprizing effects to be produced by the unwearied efforts of an intelligent & able individual, undividedly directed towards the all-important object of correctly informing the public mind. The measure I conceived was one of such obvious and permanent necessity, as could not fail to carry instant conviction to every unprejudiced mind.

To my astonishment, however, as well as mortification, I found that Mr. Duane, whose paper was to be incalculably benefited by the plan, felt much disinclined towards it. His objections are of various kinds:—

1. The money cannot be raised.
2. The cause does not suffer for want of writers, & therefore
3. The measure is totally unnecessary.

4. He wd. not consent to allow any thing to be inserted in the Aurora without his approbation.

To suppose the money cannot be raised, pays a very poor compliment to the republicans. If we have not public spirit to raise 500 Dollars annually to assist in saving the commonwealth, from impending dangers, we are among the most worthless of the human race, & instead of the form of government we are blest with, we should have a despotism similar to that of the Moors or Turks. I feel perfectly satisfied, that so far from there being any difficulty in raising the small sum necessary, $5000 might be raised, for a plan sanctioned with the approbation of men of understanding & influence. In fact, to obviate totally this objection, I offered, and still offer, to be responsible, in the most unequivocal manner, for the expenses of one year, & depend upon being reimbursed, as soon as the benefit of the scheme are fully ascertained.

The second objection rests upon grounds very unfortunately void of foundation in toto. The cause actually suffers, and very severely. I shall not enter into the question whether the opposition party possess more talents than we have:—but I am egregiously deceived, indeed, if vastly more talents are not employed against us, than in our favour. There is, besides, far more energy & industry. There is but one way of ascertaining this beyond controversy; and this, by comparison of any number of papers printed on our side in Washington, Baltimore, Philadelphia, New York, or Boston, with an equal number on the federal side. This wd. evince a woeful deficiency.

To the third item, I say, that even if the cause does not suffer, still the contemplated measure wd. be highly serviceable. The press in a free country & under an elective government, is omnipotent. To the press we owe our recent miraculous escape. The press laid our enemies prostrate. The press alone can hold them in that state, or elevate them once more to that commanding station they held a few years back. And an army never was more near a complete defeat, than when reposing in full security in consequence of a triumph. It is the same in the political warfare. Unless our system is very considerably altered, I apprehend we will afford a terrible lesson on that subject.

The fourth objection against the plan is made on a ground which I have given no pretence for. I never contemplated, nor could I for a moment have conceived, that a single paragraph of two lines, was to be forced upon Mr. Duane. Were I the editor of a paper, I never wd. submit to such a degradation. And I could not wish to expose him to what I would revolt at myself. Mr. Duane should have the inspection of every essay or paragraph, & the absolute & unconditional power of rejection.

I shall conclude this long letter, with assigning the reason why I have thus trespassed on you. Should you regard the matter in the same point of light that I do, it will be an easy matter, on suggesting the plan to some of the most zealous & disinterested republicans in Congress, to raise a subscription, previous to the adjournment, adequate to the accomplishment of the end in view. Should you, however, on due reflection, regard my alarm as groundless, or the proposed remedy unequal to the removal of the evil, you will, I trust, pardon the liberty I have taken.

I am, Sir, with Sincere esteem, your obt. hble. Servt.

MATHEW CAREY

P.S. To institute a contract between the doctrines boasted by the federalists, in & out of congress, when they had the government in their hands, & those they advance at present, wd. afford ample employment for an industrious man, and produce the happiest effect.

The contents of this letter I wish communicated to Mr. Duane.

There is a suitable person, a Mr Lithgow, ready to undertake the Business.

RC (DLC); at head of text: "Thomas Jefferson, Esqr. President of the United States"; endorsed by TJ as received 27 Apr. and so recorded in SJL.

PAPERS PRINTED HERE: at least four daily Philadelphia newspapers supported the Federalist party—*Poulson's American Daily Advertiser, True American, Philadelphia Gazette & Daily Advertiser*, and *Gazette of the United States*. The important Federalist weeklies in the state were the *Lancaster Journal* and the *Pittsburgh Gazette* (Higginbotham, *Pennsylvania Politics*, 20). Other newspapers in circulation in Philadelphia in 1802 were the *Independent Whig, Philadelphia Repository and Weekly Register, Temple of Reason, Aurora General Advertiser, Neue Philadelphische Correspondenz*, and *Pennsylvania Gazette* (Brigham, *American Newspapers*, 2:869, 891-2, 911, 912-13, 921, 926-7, 933-4, 947, 950, 953-4, 955-6, 965).

John LITHGOW, possibly an emigrant from Scotland who settled in Philadelphia, was secretary of the Society of Artists and Manufacturers, author of three pamphlets, and a promoter of factory-based manufacturing in the United States. In April 1802, he took over the proprietorship of *The Temple of Reason*, a weekly newspaper established in New York that had moved to Philadelphia in 1801 (Philadelphia *Aurora*, 29 Oct. 1803; Michael Durey, "John Lithgow's Lithconia: The Making and Meaning of America's First 'Utopian Socialist' Tract," WMQ, 3d ser., 49 [1992], 675-94).

[1] Preceding six words interlined.

Commemorative Medal

John Trumbull

Martha Washington

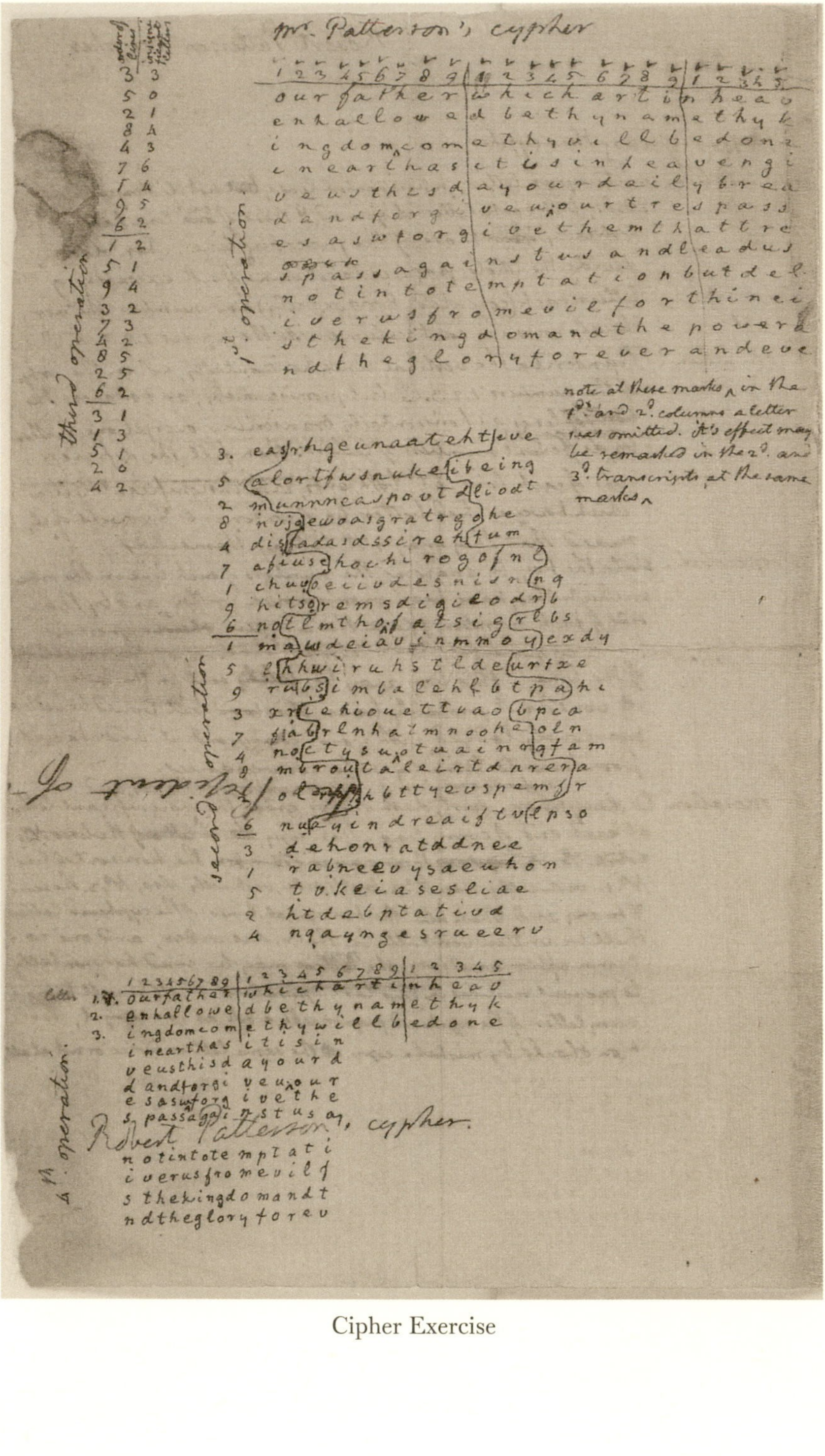

Mr. Patterson's cypher

ourfather | whichartinheav
enhallowed | bethynamethyk
ingdom‸come | thywillbedone
inearthas | itisinheavengi
veusthisd | ayourdailybrea
dandforgi | veu‸ourtrespass
esasweforgi | vethemthattre
spassagai | nstusandleadus
notintote | mptationbutdel
iverusfro | mevilforthinei
sthekingd | omandthepowera
ndthegloru | yforeverandeve

note at these marks ‸ in the 1st. and 2d. columns a letter was omitted. It's effect may be remarked in the 2d. and 3d. transcripts at the same marks ‸

1st. operation

second operation

third operation

3. easrhgeunaatehtjeve
5 alortfwsnukelibeing
2 munnncaspoutdliodt
8 nujdewoasgratrgdhe
4 disfadasdssirehtum
7 afeuschochirogofnl
1 chuyoeiiudesnisrng
9 hitsoremsdigiedrb
6 notlmthofatsigrlbs
1 mawdeiauinmmoyexdy
5 ehhwiruhstldeurtxe
9 rubsimbalehfbtpahe
3 xrlehioouettuaobpca
7 flabrlnhalmnoohedln
4 noetysuotuainogtam
8 mvroutaleirtdnrera
2 olrfhbttyeuspamfr
6 nuuindreaifsvepso
3 dehonratddnee
1 rabneeuysaeuhon
5 tukeiaseseliae
2 htdabptatiud
4 nqayngesraeerv

Robert Patterson's cypher.

4th. operation.

Letter	123456789	123456789	12345
1.	ourfather	whichartin	heav
2.	enhallowe	dbethyname	thyk
3.	ingdomcom	ethywillbe	done
	inearthas	itisin	
	veusthisd	ayourd	
	dandforgi	veu‸our	
	esasworgi	vethe	
	spassagai	nstusa	
	notintote	mptati	
	iverusfrom	evilf	
	sthekingdo	mandt	
	ndtheglory	forev	

Cipher Exercise

Army Commission

William Thornton

Anna Maria Brodeau Thornton

Commemorative Medal (Reverse)

From William C. C. Claiborne

Dear Sir,   M.T. Natchez, April 24th. 1802

On last evening, I had the honor to receive your much esteemed favor of the 7th. Ultimo, together with its enclosures;—the Letters to the President of the Council, and Speaker of the House of Representatives of the Mississippi Territory, have been carefully delivered, and were received with great pleasure by the Gentlemen, to whom they were addressed.—

The Resolutions which the Legislature adopted in relation to Mr. Sargent, (I am very certain) Speak the Sentiments of a very great Majority of the Citizens of this District, and are the only testimonials of his services in this quarter, which he has merited.—

I thank you for the Pamphlets you enclosed me;—they had not before reached me, & unless it were, *some extracts which had been published in the News Papers*, I had no certain information of their Contents:—the Author (I have understood) brought with him, to this Territory, several hundred Copies, but the distribution has been so partial, that few Citizens have yet been gratified with the perusal.—

The conversation which Mr. Sargent states to have passed between himself and the President, I saw detailed, in a Northern Paper several months since, and that it was a gross misrepresentation, is the opinion of every Citizen, whom I have heard speak upon the subject;—in these times, it seems to be the peculiar province of certain disappointed Individuals, to calumniate Public men, and to misrepresent public measures; But I am happy to find, the existence of this fact, so generally known, that the falsehoods of the day gain little currency, and tend infinitely more to accelerate, than check the progress of truth, on the Public mind.—

The proceedings of Congress (as far as I am informed thereof) have offord'd me great Satisfaction;—the repeal of the Judiciary System, I discover was warmly opposed by the Minority, and has excited in a great degree their Sensibility;—the alarm however, with respect to the *Constitution, and the Union*, will I think be confined to the Capital;[1]—the Citizens of the United States, have resumed their old habit, of thinking for themselves, & I shall be disappointed, if with the information which the debates have given upon this subject, the repealing Law should not in every point of view, be approved of; by a decided Majority of the American People.—

In this quarter, every thing wears at present, a favorable aspect;—

the Indians are entirely peaceable, our Spanish Neighbours accommodating, and this Territory increasing rapidly in population, Industry, Wealth, and in attachment to self Government.—

With assurances of my great Respect I have the honor to subscribe myself, Your faithful friend   WILLIAM C. C. CLAIBORNE

RC (DLC); in a clerk's hand, signed by Claiborne; addressed: "The President of the United States"; endorsed by TJ as received 8 May. Recorded in SJL as received 8 June.

[1] MS: "Captital."

From Pierre Samuel Du Pont de Nemours

MONSIEUR LE PRÉSIDENT,   New York 24 avril 1802.

Votre aimable Lettre ajoute à ma peine parce que je me vois dans l'impossibilité de prendre dix jours qu'il me faudrait pour la course à Washington.

Il faut que je parte avant les calmes, car il faut que j'arrive.—Un petit caillou mis à tems et à propos peut arrêter ou détourner le cours d'un torrent.

J'entendrai vos lettres à demi mot à tiers de mot.

Mon coeur, ma raison, mes principes, mon amour pour les deux pays entendent les vôtres.

Je pouvois assurer de votre inviolable et courageuse neutralité dans le cas où la guerre se renouvellerait, ou serait déja renouvellée.

Je crois pouvoir dire que vous connaissez tellement la justice et les avantages de la liberté du commerce, que pourvû qu'on prenne de sages et efficaces moyens de payement on pourra trouver dans votre Pays des fournitures abondantes.

Ne dois-je pas repousser l'idée trop répandue que tout souvenir des anciens services des Français soit éffacé de la mémoire des Americains?

On prétend que vous avez eu la pensée d'achetter la Louisiane. S'il y a quelque chose de vrai, je crois cette pensée salutaire et acceptable.

J'ai celle de conserver à votre nation la liberté du commerce de st domingue au moins pour un tems assez long.

Je verrai le chancelier Livingston. Peut-être ne lui serai-je pas entierement inutile auprès des Personnes avec lesquelles il est dans le cas de traiter, et par la connaissance que j'ai des mœurs de la nation.

J'aurais voulu savoir en partant si notre cher La Fayette peut esperer de la part des Etats unis un témoignage honorable et utile d'affection?

Et, chose bien moins importante, mais qui pourtant m'interesse, si le celebre Houdon peut esperer qu'on placera dans une salle du Capitole le superbe buste de Franklin dont je suis ici dépositaire et qu'il a besoin de vendre.

Ne regardez pas mon voyage comme une retraite. Vous voyez son motif. Je laisse en Amerique mes deux fils, leurs Femmes, mes petits enfans, toute ma fortune et toutes les espérances du repos de mes vieux jours.

Pendant mon absence, protégez mes Enfans.—L'aîné est un véritable americain, homme d'esprit négociant estimable à tous les égards.—Le second a beaucoup d'instruction particulierement tournée vers les arts utiles. Dieu lui a donné un grand courage et un cœur républicain. Sa Manufacture de Poudre à feu qui nous coutera plus de quarante mille dollars perfectionnera beaucoup cette branche d'industrie dans les Etats unis, et sera en même tems un moyen de richesse et de puissance.

Salut et respect.   Du Pont (de Nemours)

Je compte partir de Philadelphie le 5 may par le Benjamin Franklin.

Veuillez donc m'adresser a Philadelphie vos lettres.

EDITORS' TRANSLATION

Mister President,   New York 24 Apr. 1802

Your kind letter adds to my distress, because in my situation it is impossible for me to take the ten days that would be necessary for me to take a trip to Washington.

I have to depart before the calms, for I must arrive. A small pebble, placed in the right place and at the right time, can block or turn aside the course of a torrent.

I shall understand your letters at half a hint, at a third of a hint.

My heart, my reason, my principles, my love for both countries understand yours.

I could give assurance of your inviolable and courageous neutrality in case war should break out or would already have broken out.

I think I can say that you know so well the justice and the advantages of freedom of commerce, that, as long as wise and efficient means of payment are made, abundant supplies can be found in your country.

Must I not repel the all too widespread idea that all memory of French former services has been erased from Americans' memory?

It is claimed that you have thought of purchasing Louisiana. If there is some truth to it, I think it a salutary and acceptable thought.

My desire is to preserve for your nation freedom of commerce with Saint-Domingue at least for an extended period.

I shall see Chancellor Livingston. Perhaps I shall not be entirely useless to him with the persons he needs to deal with, and also through my knowledge of the nation's customs.

I should have liked to know upon my departure whether our dear Lafayette can hope for some honorable and useful token of affection from the United States?

And, something much less important, but in which I take an interest, whether the renowned Houdon can hope that the superb bust of Franklin, which I have in my possession and which he needs to sell, will be placed in some hall of the Capitol.

Do not consider my voyage as a retreat. You see its purpose. I leave in America my two sons, their wives, my grandchildren, my entire fortune, and all my hopes for rest in my declining days.

During my absence, protect my children. The elder is a true American, a man of wit, a worthy businessman in all respects. The second has a great deal of education, especially weighted toward the practical arts. God has given him great courage and a republican heart. His gunpowder factory, which will end up costing us forty thousand dollars, will bring great improvements to that branch of industry in the United States, and will be at the same time a means of wealth and power.

Hail and respect　　　　　　　　　　Du Pont (de Nemours)

I expect to leave Philadelphia the 5th of May on the Benjamin Franklin. Thus, kindly address your letters to me at Philadelphia.

RC (DLC); at head of text: "a Son Excellence Thomas Jefferson Président des Etats Unis"; endorsed by TJ as received 26 Apr. and so recorded in SJL.

votre aimable lettre: TJ to Du Pont de Nemours, 21 Apr.

l'aîné: Victor Marie du Pont. Pierre Samuel Du Pont de Nemours's second son was Éleuthère Irénée du Pont de Nemours.

Du Pont wrote another version of this letter on 24 Apr., but did not send it to TJ. The contents of that letter suggest that he wrote it first, before he received TJ's of the 21st. In the unsent letter, Du Pont included several of the topics contained in the letter printed above, using similar language but with some paragraphs in a different order. The earlier version did not include the first four paragraphs of the letter above, nor the paragraphs on Louisiana and Saint-Domingue. When he wrote the first letter, Du Pont expected to leave the United States on 10 May. He did not name the ship. He said that his inability to see TJ before his departure contributed to his sorrow at leaving what he called a beautiful and good country and a wise and honest nation ("ce beau et bon Pays, cette sage et honnête nation"). He referred to his own enthusiasm ("Zêle") in seeking good relations between the United States and France and deemed his task useful and necessary—"utile et même nécessaire" (FC in DeGH, in Du Pont de Nemours's hand, signed, at head of text: "a Son Excellence Thomas Jefferson Président des Etats unis"; Dft in same).

From Albert Gallatin

DEAR SIR   April 24th 1802

I am prevented from going to day to the office, & beg leave to refer you to the office of the Secretary of State for a precise description of the office of surveyor. & indeed of the several others[1]—I think it to be "Surveyor of the port of   in the district of   (*State*)." My only doubt is whether the words "in the district of   " be necessary.

There are to my knowledge but three vacancies connected with the Treasury Department vizt

William Nichols   Naval officer of the "port"[2] of New-port
Thomas Worthington   Supervisor of the "North West" district
Benjamin Cheney   Surveyor of the port of Beaufort in the
                                   district of New Bern North Carolina

The recommendations of *Cheney* are enclosed. It is necessary to appoint before the recess.

It is also proposed to appoint
Robert Anderson New as Collector of the port of Louisville Kentucky vice M'Connell to be removed.

For the propriety of appointing a new collector for the port of Little Egg harbour New Jersey, the President is referred to the enclosures on that subject. Observe, however, that they are transmitted by his predecessor "Tucker" who had been removed for delinquency.

The style of the two other officers of North Carolina who have not resided is I believe,[3] but it is best to obtain from Wagner the true style of each

Surveyor of the port of Winton in the district of Edenton N. Carolina

Do—of the port of Newbiggin Creek in the district of Camden N. Carolina

I believe that each of the surveyors ought also to be appointed inspector of the port. But of that also it is necessary to enquire. I beg your pardon for giving you a trouble of enquiry which I should have taken; but it is only in the office of State that records are kept of the commission & style;

Mr Stone has this moment called on me to let me know that Moody or Moony the surveyor of Winton has returned; & that it is both his & Mr Johnson's wish that he may be continued. Mr Johnson was the person who had recommended his removal.

Respectfully Your obedt. Servt.   ALBERT GALLATIN

David Duncan collector of Michillimakinack ought to have the commission of inspector, if he has not received it. Has a successor to White surveyor of New Brunswick New Jersey been appointed?

RC (DLC); endorsed by TJ as received from the Treasury Department on 24 Apr. and "Nominations" and so recorded in SJL. Enclosures: (1) Certificate signed by James White, dated Tuckerton, New Jersey, 17 Oct. 1801, stating that William Watson, collector at Little Egg Harbor who lived 50 miles away in Burlington, was frequently absent from his post, making it impossible for Richard Willets to obtain papers for the sloop *Sally* on 26 Apr., after waiting an entire day; and certifying that Watson "is now absent and has been these ten days to endeavour to set aside our republican votes and there is no Deputy left to do the business of the office" (MS in DNA: RG 59, LAR). (2) Statement by William Rose, taken under oath before Ebenezer Tucker, one of the judges of the Court of Common Pleas and for the county of Burlington, 29 Nov. 1801, declaring that Rose began serving on the revenue boat *Paterson* at Little Egg Harbor on 2 Oct. 1800, under the direction of William Watson, at the wage of $20 per month, but having received only six months of service, having received only $50 in pay (MS in same; in Tucker's hand, signed by Rose). (3) Certificate by Ebenezer Tucker, 1 Dec. 1801, stating that on 22 Aug. 1801 he observed the revenue boat *Paterson* cruising without a full crew and upon inquiry found that Collector Watson had assigned Thomas Wardle, one of the crew, to aid him with personal business (MS in same; in Tucker's hand and signed by him). For other enclosures, see below.

See TJ to the Senate, 27 Apr., for the PRECISE DESCRIPTION OF THE OFFICE. WILLIAM NICHOLS: that is, Walter Nichols, elected as a representative from Newport to the Rhode Island General Assembly for the first time in April 1801. He served as naval officer at Newport until his death in 1823 (*Newport Mercury*, 21 Apr. 1801; 4 Jan. 1823). For recommendations of BENJAMIN CHENEY, see Memorandum from Albert Gallatin, with Jefferson's Reply, printed at 5 Mch.

ROBERT ANDERSON NEW did not replace James McConnell, who was characterized by TJ as a "delinquent," until October 1802 (Vol. 33:673). See Little Egg Harbor, New Jersey, Republican Citizens to TJ, 1 Oct. 1801, for a memorial seeking a NEW COLLECTOR at that port.

TWO OTHER OFFICERS OF NORTH CAROLINA: Laurence Mooney and Frederick B. Sawyer (Memorandum from Albert Gallatin, [before 24 Apr. 1802]).

For the appointment of DAVID DUNCAN as collector, see Vol. 34:572-3. SUCCESSOR TO WHITE: in March, TJ nominated Andrew Lyle to succeed Anthony W. White (TJ to the Senate, 10 Mch. 1802).

[1] Preceding five words and ampersand interlined.

[2] Gallatin wrote "district" directly above this word. Neither "port" nor "district" was used when TJ submitted the nomination to the Senate (see TJ to the Senate, 27 Apr.).

[3] Gallatin here interlined the remainder of the passage through "style of each."

List of Candidates for Appointments

[ca. 24 Apr. 1802]

State

<Wm. Cutting of N. Y. to be a Commr. bkrptcy of N. Y.>
[Robert Champlin Gardiner of R.I. to be Consul at Gothenburg
3 Michael Mc.Clary of N.H. to be Marshal. v Bradbury Cilley expird.
Wm. Stewart Pensva. to be Consul at Smyrna.

1. John Steele late Secy. of the Missi. T. to be Secretary
2. Edwd. Harris of N.C. to be judge of the 5th. circuit v. Hen. Potter appd District judge

Treasury

<collector at the port of Erie, vice> Thos. Forster

Robt Anderson New of Kentucky collector for Louisville Kentucky vice Jas. Mc.Connel

2. Silas Crane of N.J. to be collector of Little Egg harbor N.J. v. Wm. Watson
1. Walter Nichols of R.I. to be Naval officer at Newport vice Croke
5. Thos. Worthington of N.W.T. to be Supervisor of the N.W. district

<Thos. N. Brickell of N.C. to be Surveyor of the port of Winton N.C. vice Laurence Moody absent in Europe many years.>

3. James L. Shannonhouse of N.C. to be Surveyor of the port of Newbegun creek in the district of Cambden N.C. vice Frederick Sawyer who has removed   qu. if Inspector also
4. Benjamin Cheney to be Surveyor of the port of Beaufort N.C. v.   Easton dead. qu. if Inspector also
6. David Duncan to be Inspector of the port of Michillimakinac.

<Andrew Lyle of N.J. to be Surveyor of the customs at Brunswick N.J qu if Inspector also>

9. <Richd. Howard to be captn.> } of revenue cutter.
   <Joseph Sawyer to be 1st. mate> }

War

<Abraham D. Abrahams of Georgia. to be Military Agent in Georgia>
Jared Mansfield of Connecticut. to be Captn. in corps of engineers.
Peter Gansevoort of N.Y. to be military agent for the Northern departmt
Wm. Linnard of Pensva to be do.   Middle do.
Abraham D. Abrahams to be do.   Southern do.
Simeon Knight. Vermont. to be ensign in the 1st. regimt of infantry
Joseph Dorr   do.   do.   do.
George T. Ross. Pensva.   do.   2d do.

Navy

MS (DNA: RG 59, LAR, 6:0087); entirely in TJ's hand; undated, but see below; perhaps compiled in several sittings; arranged in two columns, with entries for "State" and "Treasury" in the left column.

TJ evidently requested that the Heads of Departments send recommendations for appointments to be acted on by the Senate before the close of the session.

Dearborn sent his nominations in letters to TJ of 9, 16, and 17 Apr. The arrangement of the War Department nominations in the list above indicates that the president did not start the list until he had all of Dearborn's recommendations. Gallatin was probably the last to provide candidates. It was the subject of his letter to TJ of 24 Apr. At the end of the letter Gallatin provided information, which prompted TJ to cancel the nomination of Thomas

N. Brickell. See TJ to the Senate, 27 Apr., for the final list of nominations.

On 13 Apr., Brockholst Livingston wrote the secretary of state recommending William CUTTING, a New York City attorney who had married into the Livingston family, as a commissioner of bankruptcy. The appointment did not require Senate approval. Cutting did not receive the appointment (RC in DNA: RG 59, LAR, endorsed by TJ: "Livingston Brockhorst, to mr Madison Wm. Cutting of N.Y. to be Commr. bkrptcy"; Madison, *Papers, Sec. of State Ser.*, 3:127). MICHAEL MC.CLARY: John Langdon wrote Madison on 6 Apr. recommending McClary, who served as a state senator and adjutant general of New Hampshire, as marshal. He received the appointment and served in the position until the year of his death (RC in DNA: RG 59, LAR, endorsed by TJ: "<*mr Langdon to mr Madison*> Michael McClary to be Marshal v. Cilley expired";

Madison, *Papers, Sec. of State Ser.*, 3:106-7). Edward HARRIS served as U.S. judge for the fifth circuit during the remaining months of the court's existence. He went on to represent New Bern in the state legislature and in 1811 was elected a judge of the North Carolina Superior Court (William S. Powell, ed., *Dictionary of North Carolina Biography*, 6 vols. [Chapel Hill, 1979-96], 3:51-2; Madison, *Papers, Sec. of State Ser.*, 3:211).

For complaints against Thomas FORSTER, see Gallatin to TJ, 25 Jan. 1802. LAURENCE MOODY: that is, Laurence Mooney.

Richard HOWARD served as master and JOSEPH SAWYER as first mate of the revenue cutter on the Delaware River until Howard was dismissed for misconduct in 1805. Sawyer left the revenue cutter at the same time (Gallatin, *Papers*, 7:196; 10:480; Gallatin to TJ, 5 Mch. 1805, in DLC). Their appointments did not require Senate confirmation.

To Wilson Cary Nicholas

TH: J. TO MR. NICHOLAS   Apr. 24. 1802.

I am anxious to recieve the British convention, because the moment I do, I shall lay it before both houses with a message for appropriation. for altho' the next Congress might by possibility appropriate in time to make the first paiment, yet so great a remittance if pressed in time, might be made to great disadvantage. Great Britain too may want confidence in our ratification, if the legislature remains still free to refuse an appropriation; and, tho' in session, should actually rise without having made one. their satisfaction as well as ours, requires that no doubts or uncertainties should remain on either side: and it is moreover fair that the instrument should be tried and finally passed on, under the circumstances & considerations existing at the time, rather than on such as the events of another twelvemonth might bring into operation. I suggest these ideas to your reflection, that if approved, the advice of ratification may be expedited, and the convention laid before both houses before the appropriation time passes.

PrC (DLC).

The Senate approved RATIFICATION of the convention with Great Britain on

26 Apr. by a vote of 19 to 2, the two nay votes coming from George Logan and Thomas Sumter, Sr. (JEP, 1:415, 417, 418, 420-2).

To James Oldham

SIR   Washington Apr. 24. 1802.

I recieved your favor of the 16th. by the last post, whereby I observe you are engaged on the N. Western cornice of the house. I would much rather have the 2d. and 3d. air-closets finished before any thing else; because it will be very disagreeable working in them after even one of them begins to be in use. I shall be at Monticello within a fortnight from this time. Accept my best wishes.

TH: JEFFERSON

RC (Facsimile in Raab Autographs Catalogue, Ardmore, Pennsylvania, January 2003).

Oldham's FAVOR of 16 Apr., recorded in SJL as received from Monticello on the 19th, has not been found. TJ recorded in his financial memoranda under 16 May, "On settlement with James Oldham, to Apr. 13. 1802. when his first year ended there was due to him then 232.40 which he chuses should lie on my hands. I promised to settle interest on it as I do on Dinsmore's" (MB, 2:1072).

In his notebook for the remodeling of Monticello, TJ referred to the indoor conveniences or privies as AIR-CLOSETS. One was located adjoining his bedroom and two were off the first and second floor south stair passages. These small interior spaces consisted of skylit shafts that extended below the floor to the subcellar where each was joined by a single masonry-lined sink or conduit, probably intended for the transport of waste ("Monticello: Notebook for Remodelling, [1794-1797]," in MHi; Fiske Kimball, *Thomas Jefferson Architect* [Boston, 1916], 59, 161; William L. Beiswanger, "Monticello's Privies," Monticello Research Report, 2003, at the Thomas Jefferson Foundation, Inc.).

From Robert Patterson

SIR   Philada. April 24th. 1802

Agreeably to the directions in your favour of the 17th I am getting a stand made for the sextant, and the whole will be carefully packed up, and, by Mr. Roberts, sent on, by water, in the course of a few days.

With respect to the *cypher,* when applied to a single word or line, I would observe, that in *strict conformity* with the general system, *each letter* must, in this case, be considered as a column or *vertical line*; and, with its supplemy letters prefixed, must be transcribed into a horizontal line. Thus, if the word Louisiana were to be written in cypher, and the key

B e n j a m i n   F r a n k l i n,
2 3 7 5 1 6 4 8   2 7 1 6 4 5 3 8

it would, with its supplementary letters prefixed, and a few adjoined, stand thus,—

2 *ma* o *muo*[1]
3 *emikmio* u
7 *a* a *art*
5 *smandy* s
1 *dwyx* l *sso*
6 *ommix* i *ey*
4 *srr* i *mrs*
8 *mamreeie* n
9 *dy* a *stry*

This, it must be confessed, appears somewhat unwieldly, and the great proportion of suppy[2] to significant letters would considerably increase the labour of the copying clerks—But the remidy is easy, and that without deviating *in the least* from the general use of the cypher—it is only for the Principal to write the word or part to be cyphered in short horizontal lines, one under the other, each consisting of about 3, 4, or 5 letters, for then the copy or cypher will consist of as many lines only as the number of letters in each line of the original. For example, if we take the same word and key as before, the Principal would write it thus

    L o u
    i s i
    a n a

and the copyist thus—

    daosntt
    amrilrruia
    rliaoeem

Here the labour of the copying clerk is sufficiently diminished while that of the Principal is no way increased, and yet the difficulty or impossibility of decyphering, without the key, completely preserved

Perhaps, Sir, I ought to apologize for having troubled you with what *now* appears to have been a premature acct. of Mr. Peale's discovery—Upon enquiring of him to-day respecting the progress of his experiments, he candidly acknowledged that he had been deceived; and that in no instance had a *single drop* of fresh water been separated from salt, or pure sweet water from putrid; and that what had *appeared* to be separated by the filter was no other than what the sand & charcoal had previously imbibed; for on continuing the process he obtained nothing but the original water, clear and colourless indeed but without any alteration either in taste or smell—Obstinate Nature will not be coaxed into any deviation from her accustomed path!—

I am, Sir, with the most perfect respect & esteem Your obed. hum. Servt.   R. PATTERSON

RC (DLC); addressed: "Thomas Jefferson President of the United States city of Washington"; franked; postmarked 25 Apr.; endorsed by TJ as received 27 Apr. and so recorded in SJL.

The SEXTANT or Hadley's quadrant suffered damage during shipment to Washington, and TJ had to send a piece of the instrument back to Philadelphia for repair (TJ to Thomas Whitney, 13 June 1802; Whitney to TJ, 2 July 1802).

HAVING TROUBLED YOU: Patterson to TJ, 12 Apr.

[1] Within this encipherment, letters that Patterson wrote very faintly to set them off are printed in italics.

[2] That is, "supplementary."

To Martha Jefferson Randolph

MY DEAR MARTHA   Washington Apr. 24. 1802.

Your letter of the 16th. and mr Randolph's of the 9th. both came to hand by the last post. since that too I have seen S. Carr who tells me you do not mean to include Virginia and Anne in your visit to this place. against this I must remonstrate. every principal respecting them, and every consideration interesting to yourself, mr Randolph or myself, is in favor of their coming here. if Virginia owes a visit to Dungeoness (as S. Carr says) the winter season will be more safe & convenient for that. knowing that mr Randolph's resources must all be put to the stretch on his visit to Georgia, I insist that they be not touched by any wants which the visit of the family to this place might produce; but that all that shall be mine. as to the article of dress particularly, it can be better furnished here, and I shall intreat that it be so without limitation, as it will not be felt by me. let there be no preparation of that kind therefore but merely to come here. Congress will rise in a few days. I think I can now fix the 5th. or 6th. of May for my departure and the 8th. or 9th. for my being with you. mr & mrs Madison go about the same time: that of their return is unknown to me, but cannot be much later than mine. I think it will be for your ease & convenience to arrive here after mrs Madison's return, and consequently that this will give time for me after I get back here to send a carriage to meet you on a day to be fixed between us. some groceries, intended for use while we are at Monticello, were sent from here a week or 10. days ago. I hope they will arrive in time, and wish their arrival at Milton to be attended to.—mr Milledge will dine with me to-day, and be able perhaps to tell me on what day he will be with you. a mr Clarke, son of Genl. Clarke of Georgia, & a very sensible young man goes with him. I think they will be at Edgehill a day or two after you recieve this.   present me affectionately to mr Randolph & the family, & be assured of my tenderest love.   TH: JEFFERSON

P.S. on further enquiry I doubt if Congress will rise before the last day of the month. this will retard mr Milledge's departure, but not mine.

RC (NNPM); with postscript written in left margin; at foot of text: " Mrs. Randolph." PrC (CSmH); lacks postscript; endorsed by TJ in ink on verso.

For TJ's introduction to Elijah CLARKE, Jr., see Vol. 35:144.

To Caesar A. Rodney

DEAR SIR   Washington Apr. 24. 1802.

I have yet to acknolege your favor of Mar. 15. recd. the 25th. I had hoped that the proceedings of this session of Congress would have rallied the great body of our citizens at once to one opinion. but the inveteracy of their quondam leaders have been able by intermingling the grossest lies and misrepresentations to check the effect in some small degree until they shall be exposed. the great sources and authors of these are in Congress. besides the slanders in their speeches, such letters have been written to their constituents as I shall forbear to qualify by the proper term. I am glad to observe that you have been properly struck with these things: and that you confide in the progress of republicanism notwithstanding them. the vote for your governor shews the majority of your state was then republican, and I cannot but believe it will increase. I am told you are the person who can unite the greatest portion of the republican votes, and the only one perhaps who can procure the dismission of your present representative to that obscurity of situation where his temper & principles may be disarmed of all effect. you are then, my dear Sir, bound to do this good office to the rest of America. you owe to your state to make her useful to her friends, instead of being an embarrasment and a burthen. her long speeches & wicked workings at this session have added at least 30. days to it's length, cost us 30,000. D. and filled the union with falsehoods & misrepresentations. relieve us then, my dear Sir, from this hostile procedure, by undertaking that office which your fellow citizens will gladly confide to your truth, candour & republicanism. a man standing under such circumstances, owes himself to his country, because they can find no other in whom they can all agree to have confidence. be so good as to answer me on this point and to be assured of my affectionate esteem & respect.

TH: JEFFERSON

RC (DeHi); addressed: "Caesar A. Rodney esquire Wilmington D."; stamped and postmarked; endorsed by Rodney: "President offers pressing reason to stand a Candidate." PrC (DLC).

YOUR GOVERNOR: David Hall (see Rodney to TJ, 27 Dec. 1801).

YOUR PRESENT REPRESENTATIVE: James A. Bayard, leader of the Federalist minority in the House of Representatives. Bayard led the debate against the repeal of the Judiciary Act of 1801 that dominated the House during the last two weeks in February and continued until its passage on 3 Mch. (see TJ to Thomas Mann Randolph, 21 Feb. 1802). In his address against repeal, Bayard defended the philosophy and policies of the Federalists over the preceding 12 years and attacked the president. Cataloguing several of TJ's appointments, including Charles Pinckney, William C. C. Claiborne, James Linn, and Edward Livingston, Bayard charged "the present Executive, leaving scarcely an exception, has appointed to office, or has, by accident, indirectly gratified every man who had any distinguished means in the competition for the Presidential office, of deciding the election in his favor" (Morton Borden, *The Federalism of James A. Bayard* [New York, 1955], 96-105, 121-2; *Annals*, 11:640-1). For other attempts by the Delaware congressman to obstruct administration measures, see Vol. 36:219-20, 417n, 602n, 618-19.

Rodney accepted TJ's challenge TO DO THIS GOOD OFFICE and ran against Bayard in the congressional election of 1802 (see Vol. 32:217-18). Although Rodney was victorious, two years later Bayard accepted an appointment to the U.S. Senate. He took his seat on 15 Jan. 1805 and remained in the Senate until March 1813 (*Biog. Dir. Cong.*; js, 3:434; Borden, *Federalism of Bayard*, 143).

From Joseph Dougherty

SIR   [on or before 25 Apr. 1802]

What I have to Communicate to you is More than I Can do when face to face so I beg lave to do it in this manner so as it may be Correct. In the first place Mary is requested by Mr. Lamaire to Count the Linens belonging to the House She Dont. wish to refuse it but she is not willing to do it on the Acount she knows the number will be far short of what it should be This circumstan should not gone so far without being prohibited. as for My part I knew there was pilferers in the House. it was kept from me as Much as possible. Last sumer when Mary was sick Betsy took a 5. D Bank note out of her pocket when she thought she was asleep. At the same time Mary was a weak heard her open a box and take it out. when Mary asked her for the note she Denied with an oath Said She know nothing of it. It was kept secret from me for a Long time. Christopher being My old fellow Servant would it not been looked. on as an hard circumstance to be the first in the House to hurt his Character at this time the Room occupyd. by Christr. is all times kept locked. what is in it I Cant tell there is no one goes into it but himself

I hope Sir you will not think that I by so doing Do wish to insinuate or gain any thing by it. No far be it from me. I only wish every one to have what is their own And not that honest people should be inocently apprehended

I would before this time have let you know of this but I thought Mr. Lamaire the only on to look after Such things but He is two easy a man for Betsy & Christr. The only request I ask of you Sir is that you will not Mention my name in this matter

There is someting as yet of more Importance that I Dont wish to Let you know untill I try to investigate the truth

Your Hble Servt.   Jos. Dougherty

RC (MHi); undated; endorsed by TJ as received 25 Apr. and so recorded in SJL.

Joseph Dougherty (ca. 1774-1832) was an Irish-born staff member in John Adams's executive household who continued to serve as presidential coachman and head of stables throughout most of TJ's two terms. In September 1801, he delivered from Philadelphia a coach special-ordered for the president. After leaving presidential employ, Dougherty maintained a friendly correspondence with TJ, writing him on animal husbandry, especially on breeding merino sheep. In 1810, he requested a loan to start a Washington-based ale and porter bottling company, which proved short lived. After TJ sold his personal book collection to the Library of Congress in 1815, Dougherty offered to superintend the wagon transport of books from Monticello to Washington (Lucia Stanton, "A Well-Ordered Household: Domestic Servants in Jefferson's White House," *White House History*, 17 [2006], 6, 12, 19, 23; MB, 2:1036; RS, 1:3-4; 3:241-2; Vol. 33:426; Vol. 35:329, 757-9; Dougherty to TJ, 15 Feb. and 7 Apr. 1815).

Dougherty's wife, MARY Murphy, was a member of the domestic staff of the President's House as was BETSY Süverman, wife of presidential footman CHRISTOPHER (John Christoph) Süverman (Stanton, "A Well-Ordered Household," 9, 12; Vol. 34:489n, 566n).

To Pierre Samuel Du Pont
de Nemours

DEAR SIR   Washington Apr. 25. 1802.

The week being now closed during which you had given me a hope of seeing you here, I think it safe to inclose you my letters for Paris lest they should fail of the benefit of so desireable a conveyance. they are addressed to Kosciuzko, Volney, Madame de Corny, mr Short, and Chancellor Livingston. you will percieve the unlimited confidence I repose in your good faith and in your cordial dispositions to serve both countries, when you observe that I leave the letter for Chancellor Livingston open for your perusal. the first page respects a cypher, as do the loose sheets folded with the letter. these are interesting to him & myself only, and therefore are not for your perusal. it is the 2d. 3d. & 4th. pages which I wish you to read, to possess yourself of compleatly, and then seal the letter with wafers stuck under the flying seal that it may be seen by no body else if any accident should happen to you. I wish you to be possessed of the subject, because you may be able to impress on the government of France the inevitable consequences of their taking possession of Louisiana: and tho', as I there mention, the cession of N. Orleans & the Floridas to us[1] would be a palliative; yet I believe it would be no more; and that this measure will cost France, & perhaps not very long hence, a war which will annihilate her on the ocean, & place that element under the despotism of two nations, which I am not reconciled to the more because my own would be one of them. add to this the exclusive appropriation of both continents of America as a consequence. I wish the present order of things to continue: and with a view to this I value highly a state of friendship between France & us. you know too well how sincere I have ever been in these dispositions to doubt them. you know too how much I value peace, and how unwillingly I should see any event take place which would render war a necessary resource; and that all our movements should change their character and object. I am thus open with you because I trust that you will have it in your power to impress on that government considerations, in the scale against which the possession of Louisiana is nothing. in Europe, nothing but Europe is seen, or supposed to have any weight in the affairs of nations. but this little event, of France possessing herself of Louisiana, which is thrown in as nothing, as a mere make-weight, in the general settlement of accounts, this speck which now appears as an almost invisible point in the horizon, is the embryo of a tornado which will burst on the countries on both shores of the Atlantic and involve in it's effects their highest destinies. that it may yet be avoided is my sincere prayer, and if you can be the means of informing[2] the wisdom of Buonaparte of all it's consequences, you will have deserved well of both countries. peace & abstinence from European alliances are our objects, and so will continue while the present order of things in America remains uninterrupted. there is another service you can render. I am told that Talleyrand is personally hostile to us. this I suppose has been occasioned by the XYZ. history. but he should consider that that was the artifice of a party, willing to sacrifice him to the consolidation of their power: that this nation has done him justice by dismissing them; that those in power now, are precisely those who disbelieved that story, and saw in it nothing but an attempt to decieve our country: that we entertain towards him personally the most friendly dispositions: that as to the government of France, we know too little of the state of things there, to understand what it is, and have no inclination to meddle in their settlement. whatever government they establish, we wish to be well with it.—one more request, that you deliver the letter to Chancellor Livingston with your own hands; and moreover that you charge Made. Dupont, if any accident happens to you, that she deliver the letter with her own hands. if it passes thro' only her's & your's I shall have perfect confidence in it's safety. present her my most sincere respects, and accept yourself assurances of my constant affection, and my prayers that a genial sky and propitious gales may place you after a pleasant voyage in the midst of your friends.   TH: JEFFERSON

RC (DeGH); addressed: "M. Dupont de Nemours New York." PrC (DLC). Enclosures: (1) TJ to Tadeusz Kosciuszko, 2 Apr. (2) TJ to Volney, 20 Apr. (3) TJ to Madame de Corny, 23 Apr. (4) TJ to William Short, 19 Apr., with enclosures. (5) TJ to Robert R. Livingston, 18 Apr., with enclosures. Enclosed in TJ to Sebastian Bauman, 26 Apr.

[1] Preceding two words interlined.
[2] Word interlined in place of "making."

From Thomas McKean

DEAR SIR,   Washington April 25th. 1802.

If the Bill, altering the mode of appointing commissioners of bankrupts, shall pass into a law, I will name two more gentlemen for that office to your consideration, Messrs. Alexander James Dallas & Robert Mc;Kean—My son has had a college education, and, tho' bred a merchant, he has studied the laws relating to policies of insurance, bankrupts, bills of exchange & the law-merchant, and understands them as well as most practitioners; so that I think him qualified for the place.

The sickness of one of my horses has detained me here some days longer than I expected, but I intend to set off for Baltimore this afternoon.

Adieu, my dear Sir; may you long enjoy health and happiness. Your most obedient and very humble servant   THO M:KEAN

RC (DNA: RG 59, LAR); at foot of text: "His Excellency Thomas Jefferson"; endorsed by TJ as received 25 Apr. and "his son & Dallas to be Commrs. of bkrptcy" and so recorded in SJL.

TJ appointed ALEXANDER JAMES DALLAS a bankruptcy commissioner for Pennsylvania in June 1802 (*National Intelligencer*, 18 June 1802; Appendix II, Lists 1 and 2). McKean had earlier applied to TJ for a position for his SON (see Vol. 32:434-5).

From James Monroe

Dear Sir   Richmond april 25. 1802

I returned on friday from Albemarle without having accomplished the object of my trip by the sale of my land above Charlottesville. In my absence an alarm took place at Norfolk relative to the negroes, wh. was felt here, but which seems to have little foundation for it. Such is the state of things that it is hasardous for me, in regard to the publick opinion, to be absent from this place at any time. I shall send you the document referrd to in my last respecting the acct. of Houdon, which may perhaps supercede a reference to that you have in Albemarle. You will be so kind as return this, it being the original filed in the council chamber.   I heard with concern on my return that a bill before Congress proposes a postpon'ment of the meeting of the court of appeals, to some later period than the existing law provides for. I fear that such a measure wod. produce a bad effect. I am persuaded it wod. inspire a doubt among the people of the propriety of the late repeal, since it might be construed into a disinclination in the authors of it, to meet the court on that subject. Any measure which admitted such an inference wod. give new character & tone to the federalists, & put the republicans on the defensive. If the repeal was right we shod. not shrink from the discussion in any course which the constitution authorises, or take any step which argues a distrust of what is done or apprehension of the consequences. A postponment by law of the meeting of the court is also liable to other objections. It may be considered as an unconstitutional oppression of the Judiciary by the legislature, adopted to carry a preceding measure which was also unconstitutional. Suppose the Judges were to meet according to the former law notwithstanding the postpon'ment, and make a solemn protestation against the repeal, and this postponment, denouncing the whole proceeding as unconstitutional and the motive as impure. It might be said and truly that they had no right to meet by the law; yet as they wod. claim to meet under the constitution to remonstrate against the law as having violated the constitution, it is probable that that objection wod. not be attended to. If they attack the law, I mean the act of repeal, and are resolved to avail themselves of the occasion it furnishes, to measure their strength with the other departments of govt., I am of opinion that this postpon'ment wod. give new colouring to their pretentions, new spirits to their party, and a better prospect of success. It will perhaps not be possible to avoid the collision and the crisis growing out of it. A measure of the kind referr'd to invites it.

The best way to prevent one is to take a bold attitude and apparently invite it. The court has a right to take its part, and ought not to be deprived of any pre'existing means. I am not apprehensive of any danger from such a collision, & am inclined to think the stronger the ground taken by the court especially if it looks towards anarchy, the better the effect will be with the publick. The people will then have a simple, tho' important question before them. They will have to decide whether they will support the court, or in other words embark again[1] under the auspices of the federal party; or cling to an admn. in two of the departments of govt. which lessens their burdens & cherishes their liberty. It is even probable that such a collision may produce in many respects a beneficial effect. The mild republican course of yr. admn. has tended to put at repose the republicans & relieve from further apprehention the federalists. In such a state of things the former have little motive for exertion. Having overthrown their adversaries they think it beneath their character to pursue them further. Many from the habit of activity they had acquired, from independance of spirit, rivalry or other cause, begin to seperate from each other & even criticise the measures of reform that are proposed. But shod. the federalists rally under the judiciary, and threaten any thing serious, it is presumeable that the republicans will revive from their lethargy and resume their former tone. These ideas having occurr'd to me on this subject & I have thought proper to submit them to yr. consideration.

I am sincerely your friend & servt　　　　　　　Jas. Monroe

RC (DLC); endorsed by TJ as received 29 Apr. and so recorded in SJL.

The alarm in norfolk was sparked by reports of an alleged slave conspiracy to burn the city on the Monday after Easter. The episode was part of a broader insurrection panic that swept much of Virginia in 1802, resulting in the arrest, trial, and conviction of slaves in a number of urban and rural locales. In the Norfolk case, two slaves, Jerry (Jeremiah) and Ned, were convicted on the questionable testimony of another slave and sentenced to death. Unconvinced of their guilt, Monroe granted them a temporary reprieve and succeeded in having Ned's sentence mitigated to sale and transportation. Acquiescing to the demands of Norfolk mayor John Cowper, however,

Monroe allowed Jerry to be executed (Bertram Wyatt-Brown, *Southern Honor: Ethics and Behavior in the Old South* [New York, 1982], 426-34; Ammon, *Monroe*, 199-201; Monroe, *Writings*, 3:346-7, 350-1; cvsp, 9:263-304).

document referrd to in my last: see Monroe to TJ, 12 Apr.

The measure before congress was the proposed act "to amend the Judicial System of the United States," which had passed the Senate and gone to the House of Representatives on 9 Apr. Under the 1789 statute that established the federal judiciary, the Supreme Court had met twice each year, in February and in August. The bill under consideration in April 1802 authorized only one annual session of the court, to begin on the first Monday of February. That provision remained in the act as it became law on 29 Apr. (JHR, 4:190; *Annals*, 11:1205-11, 1213-14; U.S. Statutes at Large, 1:73; 2:156).

LATE REPEAL: the overturning in March of the 1801 Judiciary Act.

[1] Word interlined.

From David Austin

MAY IT PLEASE THE PRESIDENT.   Baltimore April 26th. 1802

Having attended the hand of national fulness as long as finances would serve, & having pressed for attention by means which decency or delicacy would scarcely warrant, I find myself set down in this City.—My thoughts are for Phila. or farther eastward: still as I am likely to pass a few days with the good people of this place I am induced once more to signify to the President that it is with regret that I leave these parts; & find myself detatched from that field of service in which I had hoped opportunity would have presented to prove the success of my theory on the subject of national harmony.

The perfect unison contemplated can scarcely be hoped for, until certain chords are toutched, which on the eastern board of the national instrument, bear but a bass tone, in the national concert.—

Though it may be a little surprizing that the order of providence should place the President of the U: States on high Episcopal ground, yet such is truly the fact. The Combined Energies of earthly & of heavenly things centre, as to the U: States, in the President's chair. Of consequence a double bow needs to be drawn from this source. As the President may understand more perfectly how to touch the cords of national policy, than those of spiritual administration, I have thought I might have aided to tone this instrument a little, so that it should lull to rest both our own nation, & by the harmony of its high example produce a sympathy of movment in relation to others; but now Alas; I can only continue to tell what it is that constitutes national harmony, but, as no man by writing or speaking can write the characters of a fine piece of Music, such as a Lady below stairs has at the moment I began to write begun to play, so I cannot enter fully into the operation until the spiritual bow is allowed to pass across the jarring & ill-toned dulcimer of our present National Instrument.—I presume the President does not prize his Spiritual elevation so highly, as to be indisposed to impart by Commission Authority to produce the same harmony in the moral, as the President designs to produce in the national world.—

Besides this Sir, I need some provision for my support. My whole time has been given to these things, & I have paid little attention to my immediate concerns, whilst I saw such an amazing field of human felicity opening before me.

If I have suffered loss I care not, so be, I can only by industry & exact attention to business once more gain my daily bread.—

I attend your call Sir; & you need not fear that the rugged pursuits of Moral investigation have so far blunted my sensibilities as a man, that I shall be insensible to a favor confered.

The Gen: Assembly of the Presbyn. Church sit soon at Phila. & other Conventions of Clergy. They expect something from me; but I am without strength, until the Presit pour a little National oil upon my head. At Evan's Hotel, & on the wings of [spl.] harmony I have the honor to wait the Prest. commds.   D. A.

RC (DLC); addressed: "Th: Jefferson Prest. United States Washington"; franked and postmarked; endorsed by TJ as received 27 Apr. and so recorded in SJL.

SOME PROVISION FOR MY SUPPORT: on 1 May 1802, TJ wrote an order on John Barnes to pay Austin $20 in charity (MS in OMC, in TJ's hand and signed by him, signed by Austin acknowledging payment, endorsed by Barnes; MB, 2:1071).

To Sebastian Bauman

SIR   Washington Apr. 26. 1802.

The inclosed letter to mr Dupont, it is very important should be put safely into his hand, as he is near his departure for France. but as he had apprised me he might have a temporary absence from New York before his departure, I have thought it safest to commit them to your particular care, to be delivered to him if now at New York, or whenever he may return there, so that he may get the packet before his departure. accept my respects & best wishes

TH: JEFFERSON

RC (CtY); at foot of text: "Mr. Bauman"; endorsed. Enclosure: TJ to Pierre Samuel Du Pont de Nemours, 25 Apr., with enclosures.

From Isaac Briggs

Sharon, near Brookeville,
RESPECTED FRIEND,   26th. of the 4th. Month 1802.

It was with a high degree of satisfaction, I observed in a letter I lately received from my friend Dr. Saml L. Mitchill of New York, the following paragraph:—"In consequence of a suggestion of the President of the United States, I had previously written to Mr. L'Homme-dieu an account of the Project of attempting to mature a National Agricultural Society. I hope these communications will have their effect and dispose the friends of Agriculture in the different States to cultivate intercourse with each other;—and eventually to mature a plan upon a scale equal to the importance of the subject in which they are engaged."

Since the receipt of Dr. Mitchill's letter the President of the Farmers' Society in this neighbourhood has received a circular communication from the Society instituted for the promotion of Agriculture, Arts, and Manufactures in New York, inviting us and other similar societies to concur with them in appointing delegates to meet at the seat of Congress during their session.

The pleasure I derive from a knowledge of these events receives no small augmentation from a recollection of the correspondence which I assumed the liberty of commencing with thee.

If I use greater freedom than becomes the extreme difference of our spheres in society, I must draw my excuse from thy own facility of access, and inviting affability, which have encouraged me to proceed; in addition to the pleasure I have always enjoyed in intercourse with men of science.

There is no doubt but our society will concur in the plan proposed by that of New York—We shall then want some members, resident in the City of Washington, delegated to meet in the National Society, on our behalf. I have already, by his permission, proposed Secretary Madison, as an Honorary member—his name will be submitted to ballot, at our next meeting, on the 8th. day of next month.

The principal object of this letter is to solicit permission to propose thy name also.—Our meetings are quarter-yearly, and a candidate cannot be elected at the meeting in which he is proposed. May I expect information on this point previously to our next meeting? The mail for Brookeville, is closed in Washington, in the evening, I believe, of the third day of each week.

What is the President's opinion of Thomas Moore's performance?—It is his *first* as an Author.

I am, with much respect, Thy friend,   ISAAC BRIGGS.

RC (DLC); addressed: "The President of the United States; Washington"; franked; postmarked 27 Apr.; endorsed by TJ as received 28 Apr. and so recorded in SJL.

John Elgar was the PRESIDENT OF THE FARMERS' SOCIETY at Sandy Spring, Maryland, in Briggs's neighborhood (Madison, *Papers, Sec. of State Ser.*, 3:474). CIRCULAR COMMUNICATION: see the enclosure described at Ezra L'Hommedieu to TJ, 3 Apr. 1802.

Briggs served as a driving force in the establishment of the NATIONAL SOCIETY. James Madison, who became an HONORARY MEMBER of the Farmers' Society at Sandy Spring on 8 May 1802, was elected president of the American Board of Agriculture at the founding meeting held in the library at the Capitol on 22 Feb. 1803. Other officers elected included Samuel L. Mitchill and George Logan, vice presidents, and Briggs, secretary. Senator Robert Wright and Congress-

man Joseph H. Nicholson served as Maryland's members of the board's committee of correspondence (*National Intelligencer*, 25 Feb. 1802; Madison, *Papers, Sec. of State Ser.*, 3:474; 4:1, 343). Meriwether Lewis, who became a member of the Farmers' Society and represented the Territory of Columbia on the board's correspondence committee, was probably TJ's unofficial representative to the American Board of Agriculture (Arlen J. Large, "The Phantom Farmer: Lewis and the American Board of Agriculture," in Robert A. Saindon, ed., *Explorations into the World of Lewis and Clark*, 3 vols. [Great Falls, Mont., 2003], 1:122-5).

THOMAS MOORE'S PERFORMANCE: *The Great Error of American Agriculture Exposed: and Hints for Improvement Suggested* (Baltimore, 1801); see Briggs to TJ, 30 Jan. 1802. Moore's treatise discussed methods of tilling the land and advocated deep rather than shallow plowing.

Statement of Account with Thomas Carpenter

Thomas Jefferson Esq.

1802.			Dr
January 29.	To Thomas Carpenter—		
	Putting new facing to an under Waistcoat		$1.50
	To 3 pr linnen drawers & 3 pr fustain Drawers		13.50
	To a pr Overhawles of Quean's rib		5.50
March	22	Making a Silk Coat & trimings	3.25
		6 Pearl Buttons	25
April	19.	New facing an under Waistcoat	1.50
		To a pr Overhawles Quean's Rib	5.50
		To a pr of Do— Nankeen	3.—
		Repairing John a Coat & a pr Pantaloons	75 ⎫
	26—	To a Livery Jackett for the Stable boy	7.50 ⎭
			$42.25

MS (ViU: Edgehill-Randolph Papers); in Carpenter's hand; addressed: "Mr Jefferson"; endorsed by TJ.

OVERHAWLES: overalls were trousers or leggings worn over other clothing while traveling or as protection against wet weather. The cloth that Carpenter used in this case was very likely a material more commonly known as queen, or queen's, cord, a ribbed cotton fabric of English origin (OED; Phyllis G. Tortora, ed., Robert S. Merkel, consulting ed., *Fairchild's Dictionary of Textiles*, 7th ed. [New York, 1996], 453; *Newburyport Herald*, 2 Nov. 1802; *New-York Gazette and General Advertiser*, 12 Nov. 1803; Salem, Mass., *Essex Register*, 22 May 1822).

JOHN Freeman, a Maryland slave whose labor TJ hired in this period, worked in the dining room of the President's House (MB, 2:1043; Vol. 33:508n).

On 21 June, TJ wrote an order on John Barnes to pay Carpenter the $42.25 for his account to 26 Apr. In his financial memoranda, TJ designated that $7.75 of the amount (apparently a mistotaling of the final two entries in Carpenter's statement) was "for servts." He noted that the remainder of the payment—which he recorded as $34.50, due to his mistake in adding the amount for the servants' clothing—was for his own clothing (MB, 2:1076).

From Charles Johnson

SIR   Washington 26th April 1802

I have just had the honour of receiving your two Notes of this date. My present very reduced situation leaves me little room to hope that I shall be able to comply with your invitation to dine with you on Wednesday: for which be pleased to accept my thanks.

W T. Muse who recommends Mr James L Shannanhouse to be Surveyor of New-begun creek, is clerk of Pasquotank County, and is a very respectable, influential, sound, active Republican, & I am convinced would not have recommended Mr Shannanhouse unless he was of similar principals. I have besides heard from others that Shannanhouse is a Republican & Sawyer not. I am sure if I doubted it, I would not have recommended him: As no one is more fully apprised of the necessity of filling all offices possible, with Republicans than I am. I am unacquainted at Beaufort, & with the characters there & in its vicinity. The Surveyor at Winton, so long absent, has lately returned, in whose room I had recommended another. As there is now no vacancy there, & the office will no longer be executed by so exceptionable a Deputy, I beg leave to withdraw my recommendation of Mr Brickle. This I had requested Mr Stone to acquaint Mr Gallatin with. As he may have omitted it, I think it necessary to repeat it to you.

I had lately a letter from Charles Holt Editor of the Bee in Connecticut, which excited my compassion in a high degree I would transmit it to you; but that I have put it into the hands of Mr Williams my Colleague to try what can be done among the Members for him, as I am unable myself to use any exertions. He complains of being cruelly treated by his still implacable enemies & persecutors & of being quite neglected by his Republican friends. Since the change in Administration, four Republican papers have been established within sixty Miles of him, which have deprived him of many subscribers, the printing for the U.S. is given to others, and what is harder, as I am informed, 'tho' he does not mention it, one half of it to a Federal paper. His Creditors seeing him thus totally neglected are falling upon him—So that this devoted Martyr! this Hero of Republicanism! Who alone dared to wave *Her* Standard in the very center, in the very head quarters of *Her* enemies; is now about to be immured in that very Prisen for debt, from whence he had been so lately liberated from persecution. Surely Sir! this is not right, if there is nothing in the private character of the Man to authorise it; to which I own I am an entire stranger, and only know him as a Republican who has suffered persecution; & who's intrepidity & zeal I have admired. You will I trust Sir excuse this freedom, which I would not venture to take; but that I consider it necessary for you to know the State of the Union, which is impossible, unless you receive information, & that you would receive it on this subject there appeared little probability. Besides it seems to me highly important that the Republican lamps should not be suffered to die away, & be extinguished, for want of a little oil to supply them, which might have been so easily, so unexceptionably applied & have had an auspicious effect even on the general cause. Even this trifling event should it happen, will afford triumph on the one hand & humiliation on the other; at least I feel it so.

I would add some further information—but am too weak, which must be my apology for the inaccuracies of this, & for failing to answer the notes by your servant. Permit me to add that I am with sentiments of the strongest attachment to, & the warmest wishes for the success & happiness of your Administration, upon which I consider the existence of Republicanism to depend, with the greatest respect Sir

Your Obed Servant   CHAS. JOHNSON

RC (DNA: RG 59, LAR); at foot of text: "Thos. Jefferson Esqr Presdt of the U.S."; endorsed by TJ as received 26 Apr. and so recorded in SJL with notation "Shannonhouse. Cheney. Holt"; also endorsed by TJ: "Shannonhouse to be Surveyor Newbegen creek. Cheny Benjamin. Holt Charles."

A native of Scotland, Charles Johnson (d. 1802) was a planter and former state senator from Chowan County, North Carolina. A former Federalist, he was elected as a Republican to the Seventh Congress in 1801, but died shortly after the close of its first session (William S. Powell, ed., *Dictionary of North Carolina Biography*, 6 vols. [Chapel Hill, 1979-96], 3:287; *Biog. Dir. Cong.*).

TJ's TWO NOTES OF THIS DATE to Johnson have not been found.

William T. MUSE recommended James L. Shannonhouse (SHANNANHOUSE) for the Newbiggin Creek surveyorship in a letter to Johnson dated 9 Oct. 1801. In it, Muse stated that he knew of no one who could fill the office "with more Credit, or that is so capable of Transacting the business as Mr S." The current surveyor, Frederick B. SAWYER, resided some 30 miles from the port and, according to Muse, had filed no returns for more than a year. Shannonhouse had agreed with Sawyer to conduct the business of the office for half his salary, but Muse alleged that Sawyer continued to draw his entire salary from the collector before Shannonhouse could collect his share. He therefore no longer considered himself bound to transact any business other than to

enter and clear vessels that arrived at the port (RC in DNA: RG 59, LAR; endorsed by TJ: "James L. Shannonhouse to be surveyor of the port of Newbegun creek vice Frederick Sawyer, who has removed").

The SURVEYOR AT WINTON was Laurence Mooney. Johnson had recommended Thomas N. Brickell (BRICKLE) as his replacement (see Memorandum from Albert Gallatin, [before 24 Apr. 1802]).

Convicted under the Sedition Act in 1800, CHARLES HOLT, editor of the New London *Bee*, served three months' imprisonment and was fined $200. TJ subscribed to Holt's paper and contributed money for the payment of his fine, but Holt received no printing contracts from the new administration. Confronted with declining sales and mounting debts in Connecticut, Holt relocated to Hudson, New York, at the invitation of Republicans wishing to establish a newspaper in the vicinity. The first issue of Holt's Hudson *Bee* appeared in August 1802, and TJ continued his subscription to the paper throughout his presidency (Pasley, *Tyranny of Printers*, 140-7; MB, 2:1123, 1173, 1206, 1242; Vol. 32:49-50n; TJ to James Monroe, 17 July 1802).

To the Senate and
the House of Representatives

GENTLEMEN OF THE SENATE AND OF THE
HOUSE OF REPRESENTATIVES

In pursuance of the act entitled 'an act supplemental to the act intituled an act for an amicable settlement of limits with the state of Georgia, and authorizing the establishment of a government in the Missisipi territory' James Madison Secretary of State, Albert Gallatin Secretary of the treasury, and Levi Lincoln Attorney General of the US. were appointed Commissioners to settle by compromise with the Commissioners appointed by the state of Georgia the claims and cession to which the said act has relation.

Articles of agreement and cession have accordingly been entered into and signed by the said Commissioners of the US. and of Georgia, which, as they leave a right to Congress to act upon them legislatively at any time within six months after their date, I have thought it my duty immediately to communicate to the legislature.

TH: JEFFERSON
April 26. 1802.

RC (DNA: RG 233, PM, 7th Cong., 1st sess.); endorsed by a House clerk. RC (DNA: RG 46, LPPM, 7th Cong., 1st sess.); endorsed by a Senate clerk and attested by Samuel A. Otis. PrC (DLC). Recorded in SJL with notation "Convention with Georgia." Enclosures: (1) James Madison, Albert Gallatin, and Levi Lincoln to TJ, 26 Apr. 1802, enclosing a copy of the agreement with the commissioners appointed by the state of Georgia in pursuance of the acts relating to the settlement of the Georgia boundary; they note that "The nature and importance of the transaction have induced the insertion of a clause, which renders it necessary that the subject should be communicated to Congress during their present session" (RC in ViW, in Gallatin's hand, signed by Madison, Gallatin, and Lincoln, at foot of text: "The President of the United States," endorsed by TJ as received 26 Apr. and so recorded in SJL; Tr in DNA: RG 233, PM, endorsed by a House clerk as "No. 2"; Tr in DNA: RG 46, LPPM, endorsed by a Senate clerk). (2) "Articles of Agreement and Cession" entered into on 24 Apr. 1802 between the commissioners of the United States and those of the state of Georgia, in which the state of Georgia cedes all claim to lands south of the state of Tennessee and west of the Chattahoochee River from the boundary between the United States and Spain, thence up said river to the mouth of the Uchee Creek, thence in a direct line to Nickajack on the Tennessee River, thence up said river to the south boundary of the state of Tennessee; in return, the United States is to pay $1,250,000 to the state of Georgia from the sale of the ceded lands, to open a land office within one year, and to confirm title to lands granted by Great Britain and Spain in the ceded territory to settlers residing within the same before 27 Oct. 1795; all of the ceded territory is to be considered "a common Fund, for the use and Benefit of the

United States, Georgia included," and to be disposed of for no other purpose; the United States is also to extinguish Indian title to Tallassee County, the forks of the Oconee and Ocmulgee Rivers, and all other lands in the state of Georgia; the ceded territory is to be admitted to the Union once it contains 60,000 free inhabitants, on the same terms as states admitted under the Northwest Ordinance of 1787, except for the article forbidding slavery; the cession and agreement is to be in full force once assented to by the Georgia legislature, provided that said assent is given within six months and that Congress shall not during the same period repeal any part of the acts authorizing the agreement and making the same binding on the United States (Tr in RG 233, PM, in a clerk's hand, including signatures of six commissioners and witnesses, Jesse Franklin, Samuel A. Otis, and John Beckley, endorsed by a House clerk as "No. 3"; Tr in DNA: RG 46, LPPM, in a clerk's hand, including signatures of six commissioners and three witnesses, endorsed by Senate clerk).

Congress passed AN ACT SUPPLEMENTAL TO THE ACT for the settlement of the limits of Georgia on 10 May 1800, Section 10 of which authorized the commissioners appointed by the United States under an act of 7 Apr. 1798 to negotiate a final settlement with the commissioners from Georgia and to receive on behalf of the United States any western lands ceded "on such terms as to them shall appear reasonable." The commissioners for the United States were also to investigate settlers' claims to the ceded lands and to lay their findings before Congress. The settlement was to be completed before 4 Mch. 1803 and any money paid to the state of Georgia was to be taken from the proceeds of the sale of the ceded lands (U.S. Statutes at Large, 1:549-50; 2:69-70). For the background on the cession of

Georgia's western land claims, as well as the state's efforts to secure land cessions from the Creek Indians, see Vol. 31:549n; Vol. 33:175-8; Vol. 34:129-30, 558-60; Vol. 35:71-3.

COMMISSIONERS APPOINTED BY THE STATE OF GEORGIA: Abraham Baldwin, James Jackson, and John Milledge.

TJ's message was read in the Senate and House of Representatives on 26 Apr. Three days later, on 29 Apr., the Senate referred it to a committee consisting of Uriah Tracy, Stevens Thomson Mason, and John Breckinridge. Reporting on 1 May, Tracy stated that due to the "very late hour of the session" and a "total want of all information and facts" on the subject, the committee could not "recommend any measure as necessary to be adopted on the subject." On 3 May, the last day of the session, the House defeated a resolution calling for the repeal of that portion of the act of Congress that authorized the commissioners of the United States to "conclusively settle by compromise" the western land claims of the state of Georgia (JS, 3:222, 227, 231; JHR, 4:222, 237).

From Robert Smith

SIR: Nav Dep 26 April 1802

Mr Jas Roach, the young gentleman for whom the enclosed Warrant is intended—has been mentioned to me in terms of approbation—

Should you approve his appointment, the enclosed will require your signature—

I have the honor to be with the greatest respect, Sir, your mo ob: st.   RT SMITH

RC (DLC); in a clerk's hand, signed by Smith; at foot of text: "President U: States"; endorsed by TJ as received from the Navy Department on 26 Apr. and "Midshipman" and so recorded in SJL. FC (DNA: RG 45, LSP). Enclosure not found.

Commissioned a midshipman on 26 Apr. 1802, James ROACH was not called into active service until 1805. Accused of neglect of duty off Cadiz in June 1805, was suspended from service and sent home (NDBW, Register, 46; 2:500-1; 6:113-14, 179, 243).

From Ebenezer Tucker

SIR   Tuckerton N.J. April 26th. 1802.

I take the liberty of enclosing an additional Proof of the inattention of the Collector of this District to the Duties of his Office, the people here of all parties are disgusted with his Conduct, they come to and go from the Office, & Cannot get their bussiness done, and the present Administration Really suffers reproach even by its friends, and enemies, by Continuing this man in Office. he has been frequently heard to Say that he expects his discharge every Post, nor is he modest enough to speak a Respectfull word of the present Administration.

but every thing that is done (he says) is truly Jacobincal, to Continue this Mr. Wm. Watson in office, who, is saying and doing every thing he Can against the Goverment. to the exclusion of Capt Silas Crane. who has been recommended to Succeed him, will tend to relax the exertions of the Republicans in the District of Little Egg harbor, & have a fatal effect on the Cause, and to remove him & appoint (Capt Crane) a native and a respectable freeholder of the district will be a very Popular thing for the Goverment. I trust the President will excuse the Liberty I have taken in Addressing myself in behalf of the People (at their request) directly to the President, as I expect Mr. Secretary Gallatan is so much Occupied with Congress that it would be improper[1] at this time to write him on the Subject. I am with Sincear regard Very Respectfully, your Very Hbl. Srvt.—   EBN: TUCKER

RC (DNA: RG 59, LAR); endorsed by TJ as received 30 Apr. and so recorded in SJL; also endorsed by TJ: "Crane to be Collector Little Egg harbor." Enclosure: probably the statement by Captain Richard Willets, 16 Apr. 1802, declaring his inability to obtain an enrollment and license for the sloop *Barny* at the collector's office at Tuckerton that day, William Watson being absent at Burlington "where he has been most part of the Winter & Spring," leaving no one in charge, thus making it difficult for Willets to accomplish "his Bussiness" (MS in same; in Tucker's hand, signed by Willets; notarized by Tucker).

Born in Burlington County, New Jersey, Ebenezer Tucker (1758-1845), a Revolutionary War veteran, served as a New Jersey congressman from 1825 to 1829 (*Biog. Dir. Cong.*). For his career, see note at Little Egg Harbor, New Jersey, Republican Citizens to TJ, 1 Oct. 1801.

For an earlier recommendation of SILAS CRANE, see same.

[1] MS: "impoper."

From Angelica Schuyler Church

New York April 27—[1802]

Depending on your indulgence Sir, I send my son, the bearer of this letter to your Excellency; to solicit your good offices, by which he may obtain redress, for extreme severity, and the most degrading humiliation: which he has suffered: his ship and cargo illegally and violently seized by the Portuguese our friends and Allies; at a moment of undisturbed peace and security, when on the Coast of Para asking there for those supplies never refused to Ship in distress.

I appeal Sir to your justice and your power as our chief magistrate and protector, and also from a persuasion that you will render me a service which will not violate your duties, when it gratifies the wishes of a Mother.

From business I naturally return to the recollection of times happily passed at the Barriere, they were enlivened by an easy agreeable friendship embellished by instruction and always remembered with satisfaction and regret.

By recent letters from france, Mrs. Cosway is studying at the Louvre; my friend Madame de Corny much depressed in her fortunes, but still brilliant by her wit and charming from her manners—

My daughter is happily married and I have no doubt but she will do for me what your daughters have done for you; yet when I am writing to you Sir, how can I believe that I may soon become a grandmother; Adieu   A CHURCH

RC (DLC); partially dated; endorsed by TJ as a letter of 27 Apr. 1802 received on 5 May and so recorded in SJL.

John B. Church, Jr., the second SON of John B. Church and Angelica Schuyler Church, sought REDRESS in the 1802 maritime insurance case of John B. Church, Jr., against Tuthill Hubbart. Young Church had insured for $20,000, the cargo of the American brigantine *Aurora*, which was seized by Portuguese warships off the coast of Brazil in June 1801. He sought exception to a clause in the policy stating that the insurers were not liable for seizure by Portuguese for illicit trade. The case came before a Massachusetts federal circuit court in April 1802. That court ruled in favor of the defendant in October 1803. The case was appealed to the U.S. Supreme Court, which, in March 1804, reversed the decision and ordered the case remanded (Syrett, *Hamilton*, 25:481; 26:867; Julius Goebel, Jr., and Joseph H. Smith, *The Law Practice of Alexander Hamilton*, 5 vols. [1964-81], 5:272-5; Cranch, *Reports*, 2:470-1).

For Maria Cosway's studies at the LOUVRE, see Maria Cosway to TJ, 25 Feb.

From Robert Leslie

SIR   Philada April 27th 1802

before I went to London, I made you a Small Clock with a Sceleton frame, which I was informed did not perform well. I tharefore Wrote to Mr Price, to return you the money you paid for it, and send the Clock to me, Some time after which, I received the Clock, and Supposed Mr Price had refunded the money. I have now finished the examination of Mr Prices Books and papers, and do not find any thing on the subject, and am therefore of opinion he has not returned you the money. if So, I will thank you to inform me when Convenient, also the amount you gave for the Clock, as I do not recolect it, and my former Shop Book ware left with Mr Price and not now to be found. I had also a large House Clock, made for you which was not compleat when I went a way, I left orders with the man[1] that made it, to attend to it till it gave satisfaction. I find in Mr Prices Books that he paid the man 14 Dollars for work done to it after I left the City but do not know wheather it was compleat or not, and will thank you to inform me

I am with respect your Humble Servt ROBERT LESLIE

RC (MHi); at head of text: "The President of the United States"; endorsed by TJ as received 30 Apr. and so recorded in SJL.

Leslie WENT TO LONDON in 1793 and did not return to the United States until 1800. The SMALL CLOCK with a skeleton frame may have been the "little balance clock" mentioned by TJ in his letter to Leslie of 12 Dec. 1793, which Leslie's assistant, Peter Spurck, "could not make go at all." "He told me so before hand," TJ explained, "so that I did not receive it" (Vol. 27:508; Vol. 32:514n).

Shortly before departing for London, Leslie formed a partnership with Philadelphia watchmaker Isaac PRICE, which lasted until Price's death from yellow fever in September 1798 (Philadelphia

Independent Gazetteer, 5 Jan. 1793; *Gazette of the United States*, 18 Sep. 1798; *Philadelphia Gazette*, 12 Apr. 1799; Vol. 26:463).

LARGE HOUSE CLOCK: that is, the Great Clock designed by TJ and made by Peter Spurck, which hangs in the entrance hall at Monticello. Spurck was forced to alter the clock considerably before it worked properly, a situation TJ believed was brought about by the "bungling manner in which he had made it." TJ's memorandum books record payments to Spurck of $15 in August 1793 "in part for clock" and of $12 in January 1794 "balce. for great clock" (Vol. 27:lii, 508, 839-40; MB, 2:900, 911).

[1] MS: "may."

To the Senate

GENTLEMEN OF THE SENATE

I nominate Edward Harris of North Carolina to be a judge of the fifth circuit, vice Henry Potter who has accepted the office of District judge.

Michael Mc.Clary of New-Hampshire to be Marshal of the district of New-Hampshire vice Bradbury Cilley whose commission is expired.

Robert Champlin Gardiner of Rhode island to be Consul at Gothenburg.

William Stewart of Pensylvania to be Consul at Smyrna.

Walter Nichols of Rhode island to be Naval officer at Newport vice Robt. Croke deceased.

Silas Crane of New Jersey to be Collector of Little Egg harbour in New Jersey, vice William Watson, superseded for non-attendance on his duties.

James L. Shannonhouse of N. Carolina to be Surveyer & Inspector of the port of Newbegun creek in N. Carolina, vice Frederic Sawyer who has removd. from thence.

Thomas Worthington of the North Western territory to be Supervisor of the North Western district.

David Duncan of the Indiana territory to be Inspector of the port of Michillimakinac.

Jared Mansfield of Connecticut to be a Captain in the corps of Engineers.

Simeon Knight of Vermont to be ensign in the 1st. regiment of infantry.

Joseph Dorr of Vermont to be ensign in the 1st. regiment of infantry.

George T. Ross of Pensylvania to be ensign in the 2d. regiment of infantry.

Peter Gansevoort of New York to be military agent for the Northern department.

William Linnard of Pensylvania to be military agent for the middle department.

Abraham D. Abrahams of Georgia to be military agent for the Southern department.

Benjamin Cheney of North Carolina to be Surveyor & Inspector of the port of Beaufort in North Carolina vice John Easton deceased.

TH: JEFFERSON
April 27. 1802.

RC (DNA: RG 46, EPEN); with check mark added in left margin by each name, probably by a Senate clerk as the nominations were approved; endorsed by a Senate clerk and attested by Samuel A. Otis. PrC (DLC). Recorded in SJL with notation "Nominations. a general list."

Meriwether Lewis on 27 Apr. delivered the nominations to the Senate, where the message was read and ordered to lie for consideration. On 29 Apr., the Senate consented to all but two of the appointments, DAVID DUNCAN and JARED MANSFIELD. These were referred to Stephen R. Bradley, Joseph Anderson, and Uriah Tracy for consideration. Upon the recommendation of the committee, the Senate consented to the appointment of Duncan on 1 May and Mansfield on 3 May (JEP, 1:422-4).

To the Senate and the House of Representatives

GENTLEMEN OF THE SENATE AND OF THE
HOUSE OF REPRESENTATIVES

The Commissioners who were appointed to carry into execution the VIth. article of the treaty of Amity, commerce & navigation between the US. and Great Britain, having differed in their construction of that article, & separated in consequence of that difference, the

President of the US. took immediate measures for obtaining conventional explanations of that article for the government of the Commissioners. finding however great difficulties opposed to a settlement in that way, he authorised our minister at the court of London to meet a proposition that the US. by the paiment of a fixed sum, should discharge themselves from their responsibility for such debts as cannot be recovered from the individual debtors. a Convention has accordingly been signed fixing the sum to be paid at six hundred thousand pounds sterling, in three equal and annual instalments, which has been ratified by me with the advice and consent of the Senate.

I now transmit copies thereof to the two houses of Congress, trusting, that in the free exercise of the authority which the constitution has given them on the subject of public expenditures, they will deem it for the public interest to appropriate the sums necessary for carrying this convention into execution.   TH: JEFFERSON

April 27. 1802.

RC (DNA: RG 233, PM, 7th Cong., 1st sess.); endorsed by a House clerk. PrC (DLC). RC (DNA: RG 46, LPPM, 7th Cong., 1st sess.); in Meriwether Lewis's hand, signed and dated by TJ; endorsed by Senate clerks. Recorded in SJL with notation: "British Convention." Enclosure: Convention between the United States and Great Britain, 8 Jan. 1802 (MS in DNA: RG 233, PM, 7th Cong., 1st sess.; in a clerk's hand; signed by Lord Hawkesbury and Rufus King, with seals).

The House of Representatives, after receiving this message and the January 1802 CONVENTION with Great Britain from Meriwether Lewis on this day, referred the matter to the Committee of Ways and Means. John Randolph, for the committee, reported a bill on 29 Apr. that the House considered and approved the same day. The Senate, which had ratified the convention on 26 Apr., apparently received only TJ's message, and not the enclosure, from Lewis on the 27th and gave it to a committee consisting of Wilson Cary Nicholas, Jonathan Dayton, and George Logan. The House's bill reached the Senate on the 30th. On 3 May, the final day of the first session of the Seventh Congress, the Senate approved the measure and TJ signed it into law. The act appropriated $2,664,000 to be paid to Britain in installments, as specified by the convention (JHR, 4:224, 227; JS, 3:223, 229, 233; U.S. Statutes at Large, 2:192; TJ to the Senate, 29 Mch.; TJ to Nicholas, 24 Apr.).

From John Archer

SIR.   City of Washington April 28th 1802

Doctr: Joseph MCreary of Wilmington State of Delaware is desirous of being appointed a Surgeon to the Hospital to be established at New-Orleans. He is recommended to me by Doctr: Geo: Monro of the State of Delaware as a Gentn. of Talents well qualified to discharge the Duties of his Profession, sober and industrious and firmly attached to the present Administration—Dr: Monro is a Gentn. of Repute in whose Recommendation I place the greatest Confidence, I therefore recommend Dr: MCreary to your Consideration for the aforesd Appointment

I am with the greatest Respect & Esteem   JOHN ARCHER

RC (DNA: RG 59, LAR); endorsed by TJ as received 28 Apr. and "Doctr. Jos. Mc.rary Wilmington to be surgeon to the hospital at N. Orleans" and so recorded in SJL.

George MONRO, a native of New Castle and a 1784 graduate of the University of Pennsylvania with a bachelor of medicine degree, was a member of the Royal Medical Society at Edinburgh, the American Philosophical Society, and the Medical Society of Delaware. He was related by blood or marriage to the first two Republican governors of Delaware (Henry C. Conrad, *History of the State of Delaware*, 3 vols. [Wilmington, Del., 1908], 3:1064-5; John A. Munroe, *Federalist Delaware, 1775-1815* [New Brunswick, N.J., 1954], 178; Philadelphia *Pennsylvania Evening Post*, 5 June 1784; Philadelphia *Pennsylvania Packet and Daily Advertiser*, 23 Apr. 1789; *Federal Gazette & Baltimore Daily Advertiser*, 6 Aug. 1796).

From John Brown
of Boone County, Kentucky

                          Boone County State of Kentucky
SIR   April 28 1802

I have the Pleasure to inform you that I have forwarded to Mr. Peale a Present to the Sosiety, of Curious Matter. It consists of Part of the skull Bone, the neck Joint on the head, the Pith of the left Horn now Twenty one Inches in Circumference, the end off & in a decay'd State. I suppose it to have been Part of the head of the Animal whose large Bones are found in so many Parts of America & in such numbers formerly at the place called Big Bone (Kentucky). It was found by Uriah Hardesty an Honest Citiz. who felled Hunting in the Bed of a creek (for some months in the Year dry) falling into the Ohio River about Six miles below the mouth of Licking river & 12 or 14 miles North of Big Bone 2 or 3 miles from the Ohio. (there has not been any other Bones discovered near the Place) I thought Proper to make Mr Peales Museum the Place of Dépot to give him an Opportunity of Placeing it on his Skileton for the present that every advantage might be had from a View of the whole together. It will their wait the Orders of the Sosiety who will hence make whatever disposition of it they may think Proper—

I shall be highly Gratified when the time shall Arrive that the

Sosiety shall think Proper to Promulgate their Oppinion on it—Be Pleased to Present with it, to the Sosiety, & for your Person Accept, the Homage of my sincere Respect, & High Consideration.

JOHN BROWN

RC (PPAmP); at head of text: "To Thomas Jefferson President of the Philosophical Sosiety of America &c. &c. &c." Recorded in SJL as received 11 June from "Brown John. Boone county. K." and "sent to A.P.S."

The John Brown who wrote the communication above was not the United States senator of that name from Frankfort, Kentucky, who was TJ's acquaintance and correspondent. When TJ received this letter, however, he thought that it was from Brown of Frankfort. In August 1802, TJ forwarded to the senator the thanks of the American Philosophical Society. Senator Brown sent the society's letter on to its proper recipient, the

"Gentn. of my name who took charge of the Bones referred to" (TJ to John Brown, 14 Aug. 1802, and Brown to TJ, 26 Nov. 1802).

Following his excavations of mastodon remains in the Hudson Valley, Charles Willson PEALE did not have a complete specimen of the animal's skull. Learning that a large SKULL BONE had been found in Kentucky and that John Brown of Boone County might be able to obtain information about it, Peale wrote to Brown in January 1802, addressing him as "Major" and directing the letter to Columbia, which was in the Northwest Territory across the Ohio River from Boone County (Peale, *Papers*, v. 2, pt. 1:392-3; C. W. Peale to TJ, 21 Jan. 1802).

From Nicolas Gouin Dufief

MONSIEUR,   April 28. 1802

Mon Libraire à Paris, me fait quelquefois la Galanterie de mêler avec les livres que je lui demande des brochures quand il les croit propres à m'interesser. Je les destine à mon tour, après les avoir parcourues, à ceux qui comme vous ont la bonté d'encourager mon établissement—Parmi celles qu'il m'a envoyé dernièrement, il S'en trouve une où j'ai lu quelque chose de fort Juste à votre Sujet—J'ai pris la liberté de vous l'adresser comme une de celles que je vous dois—

Agréez l'hommage de mon respectueux dévouement—

N. G. DUFIEF

EDITORS' TRANSLATION

SIR,   28 Apr. 1802

My bookseller in Paris sometimes pays me the compliment of interspersing the books I order from him with pamphlets he thinks suitable to interest me. After having leafed through them, I pass them on to those who, like you, are kind enough to encourage my business. Among those he sent me recently, there is one in which I read something quite true concerning you. I have taken the liberty of addressing it to you as one of the things that I owe you.

Accept the tribute of my respectful devotion. N. G. Dufief

RC (DLC); at foot of text: "Ths Jefferson, President of the United States"; endorsed by TJ as received 29 Apr. and so recorded in SJL. Enclosure not found.

From Michael Leib

Sir, Washington April 28th. 1802.

The power of appointing Commissioners of Bankruptcy being very properly delegated to you by a law, which has just passed the Legislature, I take the liberty to name to you two gentlemen, who are, in my apprehension, well calculated, both as to character and qualifications to fulfill this trust—John W. Vancleve and Samson Levy are the gentlemen to whom I allude—They are respectable practitioners of the law, independent in their circumstances, and disengaged from all mercantile or speculating connections—

I have taken the liberty of recommending men of this description, because they are not likely to expose the Executive to censure by the commission of acts of Bankruptcy themselves; because the practise has heretofore obtained of appointing Commissioners not engaged in commerce; and because I feel a persuasion, that they will be acceptable to our friends—

As I have no other object in view in this nomination, than the promotion of our common cause, the general good, I trust you will pardon the liberty I have taken in offering to you my opinions—

With sentiments of sincere respect I am, Sir, Your obedient servant M Leib

RC (DNA: RG 59, LAR); at foot of text: "The President of the United States"; endorsed by TJ as received 28 Apr. and "Levy & Vancleve to be Commrs. bkrptcy Phila." and so recorded in SJL.

In June 1802, TJ appointed JOHN W. VANCLEVE, a member of the Philadelphia bar since 1797, a general commissioner of bankruptcy for the district of Pennsylvania. Admitted to the Philadelphia bar in 1787, SAMSON LEVY was among the Republicans who signed the memorial to the Senate against repeal of the Judiciary Act of 1801. He was not appointed a bankruptcy commissioner (John H. Martin, *Martin's Bench and Bar of Philadelphia* [Philadelphia, 1883], 287, 319; Higginbotham, *Pennsylvania Politics*, 42-3; *Gazette of the United States*, 5 Feb. 1802; Appendix II, Lists 1 and 2).

From Catherine Church Cruger

April 29th. 1802—

Permit me my dear Sir to introduce my Brother to the honor of your notice—his journey has for motive Business of a very interesting nature in which he will have to sollicit your favor, & I shall not be of our family the one who will not share the obligation it will confer on him, & the pleasure of knowing that the wrongs he has suffered will find redress—

It is very long since I have heard of my friend Maria. I do not however think of her the less & hope that she & Mrs. Randolph are well & happy—Do me the favor to remember me to them & accept my dear Sir the constant assurance of my esteem & attachment

CATHARINE CRUGER

RC (MHi); endorsed by TJ as received 5 May and so recorded in SJL.

MY BROTHER: John B. Church, Jr. For the WRONGS he suffered, see Angelica Schuyler Church to TJ, 27 Apr.

From Christopher Ellery

April 29th. 1802

C. Ellery wishes to peruse, before he leaves Washington, the letters written under a feigned signature, to the President, from Newport, the last summer and respectfully solicits the loan of them—with permission to copy if he should desire it after reading—

RC (DLC); at foot of text: "President of the United States"; endorsed by TJ as received 29 Apr. and so recorded in SJL.

LETTERS WRITTEN UNDER A FEIGNED SIGNATURE: Ellery refers to the two letters TJ received from Nicholas Geffroy of 1 and 7 Aug. 1801. Ellery exposed them as forgeries and accused John Rutledge, Jr., of South Carolina as being their author. Both of the Geffroy letters to TJ were reprinted in the Newport *Rhode-Island Republican* on 18 Sep. 1802 (Vol. 35:3-6, 156-7).

To John Wayles Eppes

DEAR SIR
Washington. Apr. 29. 1802.

It is now long since I have heard from Maria or yourself. Congress will rise certainly on the 3d. and I shall leave this on the 5th. for Monticello where I shall be one fortnight, and return hither. I mention my movements that if you should be meditating a visit to your plantation about that time we may meet, and at any rate that you may know whither to direct a letter to me. no important question remains now before Congress unless they should bring on the amendment of the constitution for designating votes for President & V. President, which is hardly probable, both houses being now very thin. present my tenderest affections to my ever dear Maria, and be assured of my sincere attachment.

RC (ViU); signature clipped; addressed: "John W. Eppes at Bermuda Hundred near City point"; franked and postmarked.

AMENDMENT OF THE CONSTITUTION: in February, Eppes had forwarded to TJ several amendments to the Constitution proposed by the Virginia General Assembly, one of which was to distinguish between president and vice president in casting votes in future elections. On 12 Apr., Senator DeWitt Clinton put forward just such a resolution, including the provision that it be submitted to the states for ratification. After discussing whether it was proper to bring such a weighty matter as a constitutional amendment to a vote so near the conclusion of the session, on 1 May the House declined to postpone a vote on the proposed amendment and passed the resolution, 47 votes to 14. The 14 negative votes came from Federalists. On Monday, 3 May, the Senate supported the House proposal 15-8, just one vote short of the two-thirds required. At half past seven that evening, after a joint committee from the House of Representatives and the Senate waited upon the president, TJ "informed them he had no further business to communicate" and both houses adjourned until the first Monday in December (*Annals,* 11:259, 303-6, 1285-94, 1296; Vol. 36:490-2). For the debate on the amendment during the end of the session, see Tadahisa Kuroda, *The Origins of the Twelfth Amendment: The Electoral College in the Early Republic, 1787-1804* (Westport, Conn., 1994), 118-22.

To Heads of Departments

Th: Jefferson asks the favor of the heads of the departments to examine and consider the charges of Colo. Worthington against Govr. St. Clair with the answer of the latter and the documents in support or invalidation of the charges; & to favor him with their opinion in writing on each charge distinctly, whether 'established' or 'not established,' and whether those 'established' are sufficiently weighty to[1] render the removal of the Governor proper?[2]

TH: JEFFERSON
April 29. 1802.

PrC (DLC). Enclosures not found, but see below.

For the CHARGES by Thomas WORTHINGTON against Arthur ST. CLAIR, and St. Clair's defense of his tenure as governor of the Northwest Territory, see Charges Against Arthur St. Clair, at 30 Jan. 1802.

[1] Canceled: "to justify."
[2] TJ first wrote "render his removal proper" before altering the text to read as above.

From John Heard

SIR—   Woodbridge April 29th. 1802.

The Collector Mr Daniel Marsh of the Port of Perth Amboy and the Captain of the Revenue Cutter, was Drowned Yesterday in taking the Cutter to Amboy. it is supposed She has Sunk, as She has not been seen since. Several of my friends has called on me this day advising me to make application immediately to you for that Office, as they supposed there was not the least doubt but that I would have the preference to any of those that have applied as it is the wish of the People in general that I should have the appointment, I applyed, some time ago previous to Mr Bell appointment, I have the Honor to hold a Commission under you as Marshal, from the recommendation of the Vice President. it was his intentions to have recommended me for the Collectors Office, but was too late as Mr Marsh went to Washington unexpectedly and was appointed. I find the Marshals Office of this state is not productive I Should have wrote to Colonel Burr and the Members of Congress of this State. but I understand they have left the City of Washington. if you do me the Honor to appoint me Collector of the Port of Amboy I Shall See that my Deputy attends to the Marshals business untill you shall appoint another Marshal—

I have the Honor to be with your Most Obedt. humbe Servt.

JOHN HEARD

RC (DNA: RG 59, LAR); at foot of text: "The Honorable Thomas Jefferson Esqr."; endorsed by TJ as received 2 May and "to be Collector of the port of Perth Amboy" and so recorded in SJL.

John Heard (ca. 1754-1826), son of Nathaniel Heard of Woodbridge, New Jersey, fought in the Revolutionary War with the Fourth Continental Dragoons. Author of *The New-Jersey Trooper's Pocket Companion*, published in Newark, New Jersey, in 1800, Heard served as brigadier-general of the New Jersey cavalry (Newark, N.J., *Centinel of Freedom*, 7 Jan. 1800; Heitman, *Register*, 283; Washington, *Papers, Rev. War Ser.*, 5:152; 11:240). For a discussion of his appointment, first as U.S. marshal and then as collector of customs at Perth Amboy, see Vol. 33:183-4.

I APPLYED, SOME TIME AGO: President Adams was criticized for appointing Andrew Bell, the only candidate who was not a war veteran, instead of Heard, John Angus, or one of the other contenders (*Centinel of Freedom*, 15 Apr. 1800).

From Samuel Meredith

SIR   Philada April 29th: 1802

As the Agency which my Son in Law John Read Junr. at present holds respecting British Debts will probably soon cease, & it will be some time before he can recover his professional business which his attention to his Office obliged him to give up, Should a Vacancy happen in the Commissionship of Bankruptcy for this state, permit me to recommend him to your Notice as a person capable of filling the Appointment, His diligence & attention in his present office I hope will be considered as strong testimonials in his favour, & should you think proper to confer the appointment on him, I shall regard it as a further instance of your polite attention to me

With wishes for Your health & happiness I am Sr. Your most humble Sevt.   SAM MEREDITH

RC (DNA: RG 59, LAR); at foot of text: "The President of the United States"; endorsed by TJ as received 1 May and so recorded in SJL.

JOHN READ served as general agent for the settlement of British debt claims under the Jay Treaty from 1797 to 1809. He had married Meredith's daughter, Martha, in 1796 (DAB; Vol. 30:428n; Vol. 33:547-8).

Notes on Charges against Arthur St. Clair

[ca. 29 Apr. 1802]

1. The Ordinance,[1] in the paragraph respecting counties, speaks of laws adopted or made, which must refer both to the 1st. & 2d. stage of government; it then gives the Govr. power to lay out[2] counties from time to time, reserving a right to the legislature *thereafter* to alter them. this may mean that the Govr. is always to lay out first, & the legislature thereafter to alter, or it may mean that the Govr. is to lay out during the 1st. stage of govmt, and the legislature to do it in the second, reddendo singula singulis. the first construction renders the power reserved to[3] the legislature null, because the Govr. having a negative will not permit the other branches to act against his opn manifested in the original laying out: the 2d construction gives it full effect, & must therefore be understood to be that intended by Congress[4], who certainly meant to reserve a practicable right to the legislature, not a nugatory one, & the rather as the forming counties is an act of law making not of the

execution of a law.—the place of dispensing justice may not seem essentially legislative, at first view but to rest naturally with those who are to dispense it:[5] yet when we consider it in all it's relation's to public convenience as well as justice[6] at how early a date it was deemed a grievance in England, and fixed by law, and how universally so in these states, this gives a sure practical construction of what Congress must have intended.

2. the policy of giving a negative on laws to the Executive seems to be 1. to provide protection against the legislature for the other independant departments. 2. to protect[7] such portions of the citizens as might be oppressed by a local or partial interest happening to be predominant in the legislature at the moment. but not to set up the judgment of a single individual in cases of ordinary legislation against the collected wisdom of the nation. if these ideas be just, Govr. Sinclair is guilty on the 2d. charge.

5. the ordinance permits the whole territory N.W. of the Ohio to be divided by Congress into 3. or 5. states, and sais whenever any of the said *states* shall have 60,000 &c. it shall be recieved in Congress. the change of boundary proposed by the late act of the N.W. legislature did divide the population into two parts, so that both would have been much longer reaching 60,000. than if the boundaries remained as fixed by the ordinance. that the act dismembered that portion of territory which claimed to be a state, is certain. that Govr. Sinclair assented to it at least is certain. that he promoted it by his influence and with a view to continue himself & friends the longer in place & power is suggested by many, and will be judged of by every one accdg to the opinion entertd of his attachment to his office, or his power of preserving his mind unbiassed by that attachment or any other particular[8] views. see St. Clair's lre to Harrison printed State papers Mar. 14. 1800.

6. the censure implied in this charge seems to be not so much in the Governor's giving[9] commissions during pleasure in the judiciary line, tho' a tenure for life there is familiar, as the making the Attorney general an officer for life, a thing unprecedented, at it's being in the case of his own son. the reason assigned by the Governor that he gave him this fixed tenure because he at that time proposed himself to retire from office, & meant thus to protect his son against his successor, admits the fact charged & is far from justifying it.

7. Admitting the tenure of every commission, without any special limitation to be during the will of him who grants it, the conduct of the three justices whose commission was revoked, and that of mr

Finlay whose resignation was not accepted, is not sufficiently clear of blame, to fix the charge of arbitrarily influencing & controuling the judiciary.

8. this charge is admitted to be true, by Govr. Sinclair, in the case of his son in law made Recorder of Clermont while he lived in Hamilton. see page 20. he urges some matters in justification. several other instances are stated by Worthington & Miegs. Wills's case pa. 46.

9. this cannot be decided but on a view of the laws.

4. that one of these acts was meant as a compensation for the other is not proved. see pa. 24.43.

3. the real charge here is that the Govr. and judges selected laws from the codes of the states to give themselves fees. I was a member of Congress, & I believe of the commee which prepared the first plan for the organisation of the new states. a legislature to be composed of the Govr. & judges was a measure of necessity in the earliest stages of those territorial governments. yet we were sensible it was fundamentally wrong to subject free men to laws made by officers of the Executive. it was determined then they should not *make* laws themselves, but adopt[10] from the codes of the states, which being past by free men for their own government it was supposed would never be oppressive. but no one dreamt of their selecting laws to give themselves fees. for to what a length[11] might not this be carried by[12] entitling themselves to fees for every act which was allowed a fee in any single state. their salaries were certainly understood to be in lieu of all emoluments. yet they early began this abuse. Govr. Sinclair and his associates set the example. it was not unnoticed. but as every one had rather another should pass personal censures than himself, the first laws for this purpose were laid by myself before Congress, with the other laws, without any comment, the power of repealing being in them. partly from much business, partly from no individual member being willing to come forward as the denunciator the thing went on till the arbitrary & intolerable temper of Govr. Sarjeant urged it[13] on the notice of Congress. on the 12th. of Feb. 95. this among other legislative practices had been disapproved by the H. of R. (report pa. 8. 9 Feb. 19. 1801) and lost in the Senate. but Feb. 19. 1801. a commee of friends to Sarjeant appointed by his friend Sedgwick, reported it an abuse, but not proceeding from criminal intentions, and therefore resolved[14] that there ought to be no further proceedings for mal admn against him; to which resoln the House disagreed by a vote of 50. against 38. tho' a federal

house; but this being late in the day of the 3d. of Mar. 1801. on which day they were to rise, nothing further could be done. but Govr. Sarjeant's time expiring soon after, his commission was not renewed for this among other reasons.

MS (DLC: TJ Papers, 124:21416); undated; entirely in TJ's hand.

REDDENDO SINGULA SINGULIS: "by rendering each to each"; that is, assigning separate things to separate persons, or separate words to separate subjects (Garner, *Black's Law Dictionary*, 1303).

LATE ACT OF THE N.W. LEGISLATURE: for the December 1801 act of the territorial assembly calling for a redivision of the Northwest Territory along the Scioto River, see William Goforth to TJ, 5 Jan. 1802.

ST. CLAIR'S LRE TO HARRISON: that is, St. Clair to William Henry Harrison, 17 Feb. 1800. This letter was subsequently printed with a 1 Jan. 1800 petition from George Tevebaugh and others, from Knox County in the Northwest Territory, the latter of which was read before the House of Representatives on 14 Mch. 1800 and ordered to lie on the table. See Charges Against Arthur St. Clair, at 30 Jan. 1802, Document I, and JHR, 3:626.

MR FINLAY: for St. Clair's criticism of justice of the peace Samuel Finley, see Charges Against Arthur St. Clair, Document I.

CASE OF HIS SON IN LAW: for the appointment of Samuel Robb, St. Clair's son-in-law, see Charges Against Arthur St. Clair, Document II. WILLS'S CASE: see same, Document III.

As a MEMBER OF CONGRESS in 1784, TJ was chair of the committtee appointed to prepare THE FIRST PLAN for the temporary government of the western lands ceded by the state of Virginia. The committee's report served as the basis for the Northwest Ordinance of 1784, which directed temporary governments of any territory "to adopt the constitution and laws of any one of the original states" (Vol. 6:584-5, 614).

ARBITRARY & INTOLERABLE TEMPER OF GOVR. SARJEANT: for the Congressional investigation of Winthrop Sargent's conduct as governor of the Missis-

sippi Territory, see Vol. 34:81n. On 12 Feb. 1795, in a rebuke of Sargent's conduct as secretary and acting governor of the Northwest Territory, the House of Representatives passed a resolution disapproving several laws passed by Sargent and the judges of the territory (JHR, 2:324).

REPORT PA. 8.9 FEB. 19. 1801: TJ cites the printed 19 Feb. 1801 report of the House committee investigating Sargent, entitled *Report of the Committee Appointed to Enquire into the Official Conduct of Winthrop Sargent, Governor of the Mississippi Territory* (Washington, D.C., 1801; Shaw-Shoemaker No. 1531).

VOTE OF 50. AGAINST 38.: the recorded House vote on the 3 Mch. 1801 resolution was 38 in favor and 40 opposed (JHR, 3:844-5).

Around the same time as the above notes were written, TJ also prepared a brief list of documents relating to the charges against St. Clair. Written on a fragment of paper under the heading "Documents wanting," the list refers to evidence in the case against St. Clair that was apparently mislaid or yet to be received:

"pa 45. No. 3. Sinclair's lre to Harrison
    34. No. 4. Finlay's deposn.
        some depns. respecting Baldwin
    41. proclamns erecting 3. counties
        printed sheets of journals of
        legislature
    43. Worthington's paper No. 4.
    48. No. 5. Miegs to Worthington
    50. No. 6. 3 depns. on charge 10. viz
        Mc.Gowan's, Dunlavy's White's"
(MS in DLC: TJ Papers, 124:21415; undated; entirely in TJ's hand).

[1] TJ first wrote "Although the Ordinance" before altering the text to read as above.

[2] Preceding two words interlined in place of "establish."

[3] Preceding two words interlined in place of "of."

4 Word interlined in place of "the legislature."

5 Preceding eleven words and punctuation interlined.

6 TJ here canceled "it must be imagined."

7 TJ here canceled "certain."

8 Word interlined.

9 TJ here canceled "the justice."

10 Word interlined in place of "select."

11 TJ here canceled "of."

12 TJ here canceled "selecting."

13 Word interlined in place of "the thing."

14 Word interlined.

From Edward Savage

SIR   New York April 29—1802

I Recd your favour of the 30 of March at that time the fraimes ware all made, I Beg your forgiveness for not Answering your Letter Sooner. I put it of from Day to Day Expecting to have an oppertunity of Sending the fraimes at the Same time I wrote. the Schooner Tryal is the first oppertunity that I have meet with:

there is a Mr Anderson in the City of Washington who will be a good hand to put the prints into the Frames, I have had the frames as well Made as I Could git them Done, the glass is well Secur'd in the fraimes and a frame to Strain the prent on.

I have paid for the Large fraimes and Glass ten Dollars
Each, 4 of them   40
5 Small fraimes & Glass's at 3.50   17.50
                                                57.50
Packing Cases 1.25 Commission 5 pr Cent   4.25
                                                $61.75

if it is agreeable to you to Send me the amount of the Bill Soone, you will Oblidge me very much, as the first of May is a Day hear when Every one thinks of Settling their yearly Rent and the Scarcety of money makes Every one press for his Due.

I am Sir with Great Esteem your Obedent Sert.

EDWARD SAVAGE

RC (DLC); at foot of text: "President of U.S."; endorsed by TJ as received 2 May and so recorded in SJL. Enclosure: Bill of lading dated 29 Apr. 1802 for "2 Box's Directed to Thomas Jefferson President of the United States" by the schooner *Tryal*, Ludlam Smith, bound from New York City to Washington, D.C., with a freight charge of 12½ cents per foot (MS in same; printed form, with blanks filled by Savage; signed by Ludlam Smith).

From Samuel Smith

SIR/   Washington 29. April 1802

I do myself the honor to inclose you a letter I have recieved from J. H. Purviance. permit me to Say that I know no Gentleman who I think every way So Compleatly qualified to Succeed Mr. Sumpter or who Could be So useful to Mr. Livingston. I am sir/

with the highest Esteem your friend & servt.   S. SMITH

RC (DNA: RG 59, LAR); endorsed by TJ as received 29 Apr. and "Purviance John H. to be Secy. legn at Paris" and so recorded in SJL. Enclosure: John H. Purviance to Samuel Smith, Baltimore, 23 Apr., asking Smith to confirm the news that Thomas Sumter, Jr., soon would be leaving his post in Paris and, if so, "whether by your friendly recommendation and such other as you might have the goodness to procure for me to Mr. Livingston, I might reasonably hope for a preference" (RC in same).

SO COMPLEATLY QUALIFIED: for other expressions of confidence in the abilities of John H. Purviance, who had served as James Monroe's secretary while he was minister to France, see Vol. 35:174n, 445n, 683.

From Sebastian Bauman

SIR,   Post office new york April 30. 1802.

I have the honor to acknowlidge your letter of the 26. inst, Covering one for Mr. Duport, which I delivered in Person to his son, Mr. Duport himself I Could not see, he being unwell. any thing Sir, which may require dispatch, or of a Confidential nature you have to pase through the Post Office here which I have the honor to hold, you may I hop Sir, Confide in my punctuality, and in whatever you may Command me, for it is & always has been my Sincer desire to do whatever is Enjoined on me with the strictest honor and entegrity.

I am with great respect Sir, your most Obdt. & very humble Servt.   S. BAUMAN

RC (MHi); at foot of text: "Thomas Jefferson Esqr. President of the United states"; endorsed by TJ as received 2 May and so recorded in SJL.

From Joseph Bloomfield

RESPECTED SIR,   Trenton, New Jersey, April 30th: 1802.

I take the liberty of transmitting the enclosed. I have letters from Perth-Amboy, which mention that Daniel Marsh, late Collector of that Port, was drowned on the 27: inst.

John Heard raised a company of Dragoons, always kept a full company, and served with great credit and reputation during our revolutionary war, and is now general of the cavalry of this State.

He was defeated in his application to Mr. Adams, for the Collectors-office of the Port of Perth Amboy, when Andrew Bell, was appointed, & indeed, expected the office when Danl. Marsh was commissioned.

As Genl Heard will resign the office of Marshal, I beg leave to solicit the appointment of Collector of the Port of P. Amboy in his behalf; as I am very confident, it is universally desired by the Republicans in that district, and indeed I believe, no man would be more acceptable to the public in general.

It is unpleasent to say any thing unfavorable of any man: but I think it a duty, that in case Capt. John Angus, a Scotchman, of P Amboy, Should be recommended, by the federal characters from that quarter, to mention, that in the Summer of 1800—Angus promised me & the Republicans of Middlesex county to do all in his power at the Autumn Elections, in favor of the Republican tickets: instead of which, he joined & was a most violent partisan in the opposition, & actually exposed & give copys of a confidential letter, I had written to him from the convention, we held 30: September 1800 at Princeton, on the Subject of the Presidential and Congressional elections.—It would be indiscreet to trouble you, with further particulars, but the appointment of Angus, would grieve every Republican in this State; for the part he has lately Acted at the elections, & particularly in 1800, is as generally known as reprobated by every man of honor and principle, of all partys.

If Genl. Heard shall be appointed, I engage, if the Commission shall be transmitted under cover to me, to forward his resignation of the Marshalls office before he shall receive the Commission of Collector of the port of Perth Amboy.

If Congress shall not have adjourned before this reaches Washington, I beg leave to refer to the Representatives in Congress, from this State, as well of the character of Genl Heard as of Capt Angus, particularly to Messrs. Condit & Southard, whose residence is within the district of the port of Perth-Amboy.

[363]

I have now to apologize for the freedom I have taken, and avail my-self of this opportunity of renewing assurances of my high respect & esteem, & that I am,

most truly & sincerely, Your devoted Servant

JOSEPH BLOOMFIELD

RC (DNA: RG 59, LAR); at foot of text: "The President of the United States"; endorsed by TJ as received [2] May and "Heard to be collector of the port of Perth Amboy" and so recorded in SJL. Enclosure: John Heard to Bloomfield, Woodbridge, New Jersey, 29 Apr., informing the governor that the body of Daniel Marsh "was found on Long Island and brought to Elizabeth town this morning" and requesting that

Bloomfield immediately write the president recommending him for the office of collector at Perth Amboy (same).

Bloomfield chaired the CONVENTION which met in PRINCETON in September 1800. He signed an address on 30 Sep., encouraging the people of New Jersey to support TJ, the author of the Declaration of Independence, as president (Newark, N.J., *Centinel of Freedom*, 14 Oct. 1800).

To John Redman Coxe

SIR   Washington April 30. 1802.

I have duly recieved your favor of the 23d. and am happy to learn that you mean to favor the public with an account of the vaccine inoculation from your own experience, which I am persuaded will be highly useful. I think it an important object in such a work to bring the practice of the inoculation to the level of common capacities: for to give to this discovery the whole of it's value, we should enable the great mass of the people to practise it in their own families & without an expence, which they cannot meet. to do this I concieve but a single point essential, which is to enable them to be sure that the matter is in a proper state; and I question if unexperienced people can be guided in this by any thing but the date, or distance of time from the inoculation at which the matter is *always* good. but is there such a point of time? I thought from my trials there was; but more extensive observations are necessary to ascertain that, and what the true point of time is. mr Vaughan had asked me to permit my letter to him to be published. my objection to it was that I am not a medical man, that it would be exhibiting myself before the public in a science where I might be exposed to just criticism, and that the observations of the medical gentlemen themselves would soon furnish what was better. if however the letter can be useful as a matter of testimony, or can attract the notice or confidence of those to whom my political course may have happened to make me known, and thereby engage their belief in a discovery of so much value to themselves and mankind in general, I shall not oppose it's being put to that use. I will only ask that if there be any incorrectness of expression in it, open to obvious criticism, you will be so good as to rectify it. Accept assurances of my esteem and respect. Th: Jefferson

RC (PPCP: Gilbert Collection); addressed: "Doctr. John Redman Coxe Philadelphia"; franked and postmarked. PrC (DLC).

John VAUGHAN twice asked TJ for permission to have his LETTER of 5 Nov.

1801 published. TJ declined, however, fearing that in so doing he "would be entering an Arena on which I am not qualified to exhibit before the public" (Vaughan to TJ, 19, 20 Nov. 1801; TJ to Vaughan, 24 Nov. 1801).

To Pierre Samuel Du Pont de Nemours

DEAR SIR   Washington Apr. 30. 1802.

Your's of the 24th. has been recieved; and the most important object of it anticipated by mine of the 25th. the rest of it I will now answer mot à mot. you may give assurance of our religious & rigorous neutrality, without the smallest partiality to the one or the other nation, should the war be rekindled. you may say that our supplies will be free and abundant to both parties, they paying for them to the satisfaction of the merchants. the vexations & spoliations on our commerce in the W. Indies, and the capricious conduct of the government of France previous to the summer of 1798. has effaced much of the sentiments of gratitude entertained here towards them: with some entirely; but with the great portion of our people there is still a sensible affection for that nation.—Louisiana we do not want. the island of New Orleans & Florida are desireable for the sake of peace; but it must be a very moderate sum of money indeed which we could give for them. we are poor, in debt & anxious to get out of debt, and a great portion of those who would be assessed for the price, would feel no interest in the purchase; in which case it is against our principles to call on them for money. the Floridas are a mere slip of barren sand, not above 20. or 30. miles wide in most places & 500. miles long.[1]— the commerce of St. Domingo is very interesting to us, and very necessary to the prosperity of that colony. but it is also most essential that it be carried on according to rules rigorously observed and not liable to be violated by the arbitrary and ignorant conduct of officers there. nothing was ever worse judged than their late conduct there. Villaret-Joyeuse was properly sensible of this, and explained it with so much moderation and good sense as produced a disposition to acquiesce in it. Le-Clerc is a good souldier, but used to carry every thing by force he appears[2] neither to respect nor to consider the character of the nation with whom he seems to disregard a collision. he listens without judgment to the tales of those who wish to make mischief between us, and acts inconsiderately in consequence of it.— with respect to La Fayette you know my heart is with him: but my situation disarms me from every degree of activity in his favor. Congress, by the constitution, can *give* nothing. that power remains wholly with the separate states. Congress can only indemnify; to do which they cover themselves under the authority given them by the constitution of *paying the debts of the US.* it will readily occur to you too that his claims would not be recieved by the present persons in power, two thirds of whom were too young to be witnesses of the services of Fayette, with the same partiality and enthusiasm as they would have been by those who were witnesses & fellow labourers with him. you know how sacredly we regard our civil authority, & especially that of the legislature. his endeavor to march his army to Paris to controul the legislature of that country made a deep & unfavourable impression on many here, who have never known the circumstances inducing that attempt, nor been able, from a personal knowlege of the purity of his views, to satisfy themselves they must have been such as to justify him.[3]—I wrote to the Governor of Virginia proposing to him to engage the state to take Franklin's bust, but it cannot be done but with consent of the legislature of the state, which will not meet till December. he will then propose it. I wrote also on the subject of the balance still due to Houdon for the Statue of Genl. Washington. he has authorised me to settle that myself, and will immediately pay any sum I award on it. I cannot do it but by recurring to papers which are at Monticello. I set out for that place on the 6th. of the coming month (next Thursday) shall return here by the last day of the same month, and will then immediately settle it and have the money paid to any person you will be so good as to indicate in a line to be left for me before you go. I shall always be happy to be useful to your sons for their own merits as well as yours. present to Made. Dupont the assurances of my high esteem & respect, and accept yourself those of my affectionate attachment: and once more Adieu.

TH: JEFFERSON

RC (DeGH); addressed: "M. Dupont de Nemours."

MOT À MOT: word for word.

Admiral Louis Thomas VILLARET de JOYEUSE had written to TJ on 16 Feb. 1802 about the arrival of the French expeditionary force in Saint-Domingue.

ENDEAVOR TO MARCH HIS ARMY TO PARIS: as the Jacobins gained power in the summer of 1792, Lafayette, who was a general in the French army, sent an address to the Legislative Assembly and appeared before that body in uniform to insist on the suppression of the radicals and adherence to the existing constitution. When the assembly did not respond to his demands and he failed in an attempt to mobilize national guardsmen against the radicals, Lafayette left Paris to get his army, which was stationed on the border with Belgium. During his absence from the capital the Jacobins denounced him, took custody of the royal family, and decreed the suspension of the monarchy. Lafayette, unable to make his soldiers obey his orders to march on Paris, crossed into Belgium, where the Austrian army captured him before he could reach neutral territory (Harlow Giles Unger, *Lafayette* [Hoboken, N.J., 2002], 281-7; John H. Stewart, *A Documentary Survey of the French Revolution* [New York, 1951], 298-9, 306-7; Vol. 24:138, 139n, 275-6, 335, 503; Vol. 32:428).

WROTE TO THE GOVERNOR OF VIRGINIA: TJ's letter to James Monroe of 28 Feb. 1802 mentioned the two works of sculpture by Jean Antoine HOUDON.

[1] Preceding sentence interlined.
[2] Word interlined in place of "seems."
[3] Someone, perhaps Du Pont de Nemours, drew a brace in the margin to mark the section of the letter relating to Lafayette.

From Pierre Samuel Du Pont de Nemours

MONSIEUR LE PRÉSIDENT   New York 30 Avril 1802.

J'ai recu votre lettre et vos dépêches.—J'ai lu celle dont vous m'avez permis de prendre connaissance.—Je les remettrai avec fidelité, et j'en appuierai le contenu de tout mon faible pouvoir.

Je conçois toute l'importance de leur sujet. C'est le but principal de mon voyage.—une guerre qui me priverait du doux azyle de l'Amerique, à moins que je ne me déterminasse à une abdication entiere de ma Patrie natale serait personnellement pour moi le plus grand des malheurs.

Mais puisqu'on réussit d'autant mieux qu'on est plus éclairé, qu'on a des instructions plus étendues, qu'on a plus de moyens de varier, d'appuyer ses insinuations et ses discours, permettez-moi de vous faire quelques observations, permettez-moi même de vous opposer quelquefois le langage de ceux avec lesquels j'aurai à traiter; car pour arriver à une conciliation, il faut avoir prévu et pesé tout ce qui sera dit de part et d'autre.

Le fonds de votre raisonnement est celui ci.—"La Louisiane ne pourra être à la France que jusqu'à la premiere guerre.—À cette premiere guerre, l'interêt de la posseder nous fera prendre une part offensive dans les hostilités.—Et les Anglais empêchant par leur marine d'y apporter des secours, notre position géographique, la Puissance militaire que nous y pourrons employer surpasseront nécessairement la résistance dont une métropole éloignée et inférieure en marine pourra fournir les moyens."

Un militaire pourra comprendre aisément que le poids *d'une colonne* qui va depuis le district de maine jusqu'au mississipi doit en effet percer le *front de bandiere*, tel qu'il pût être, qu'on établirait sur les rives de ce fleuve.

Mais un jeune militaire, dont les ministres ne peuvent conserver leurs places qu'en encensant perpétuellement l'orgueil militaire, sera beaucoup plus offensé que touché de cette raison. — Et s'il n'y a qu'elle en avant, nous pouvons regarder la négociation comme manquée.

Voici comme on lui parlera pour soutenir par des raisons politiques *l'irritation* qu'aura excitée la menace, plus ou moins enveloppée de protestations, de le déposséder malgré lui.

"Les Etats unis" lui dira-t-on "et même leur Président, trahissent une ambition de conquête que vous devez réprimer. — La Louisiane entre les mains de l'Espagne ne les inquietait point, parcequ'ils ne regardent pas l'Espagne comme une Puissance; et qu'ils ne voyaient dans cette colonie du Mississipi qu'une auberge pour se reposer, et un magasin nécessaire à l'armée par laquelle ils comptent un jour faire la conquête du mexique. — Mais c'est précisement pour conserver le mexique avec plus de sureté que l'Espagne vous a cedé cette colonie. — Elle a voulu que la puissance des deux Etats contint dans de justes bornes cet esprit d'invasion que les Etats unis ne peuvent et ne veulent plus dissimuler. — Vous manqueriez à votre Allié, si vous cédiez le poste avancé qu'il vous confie."

Que votre nation en général, Monsieur le Président, et surtout que les ambitieux de votre nation pensent à la conquête du mexique, cela n'est pas douteux. — Il y aura beaucoup à gagner pour les généraux, pour les officiers, et même pour les soldats. L'armée sera recrutée très aisement.

Mais il y aurait beaucoup à perdre pour les Etats unis, et surtout pour un Philosophe ami de l'humanité et véritable ami de sa Patrie comme leur Président Jefferson.

L'armée conquerante sera corrompue à tout jamais. — Ceux de ses guerriers qui reviendront dans l'intérieur y rapporteront tous les crimes et tous les vices.

Ceux qui resteront dans le Pays vaincu en formeront pour les Etats unis un voisin redoutable, avec lequel il faudra être dans un etat de guerre permanent.

Si le Général victorieux y fonde une monarchie, elle ne sera certainement pas alliée de votre République.

Si vous pouvez y fonder une République, vous tenterez en vain de la conféderer avec vous.—déja vous voyez combien il faut de sagesse, de prudence et de circonspection pour maintenir la confédération entre vos seize Etats.—que serait-ce avec une République nouvelle presque aussi puissante à elle seule qu'ils le sont tous ensemble, beaucoup plus riche, et dont le centre du Pouvoir serait à une aussi grande distance du centre de votre confédération.

Le mexique entre les mains des Espagnols ne peut vous nuire en rien; et par des inventions de Commerce faciles à concevoir peut vous servir beaucoup.—le mexique animé par une révolution, et porté à la hauteur de votre civilisation par vos citoyens qui s'y domicilieraient, qui pour lui quitteraient votre territoire et cesseraient de l'améliorer, serait ce qu'on pourrait imaginer de plus funeste à votre paix, à votre liberté, à votre prospérité.—Il vous nuirait comme votre rival de puissance. Il vous nuirait bien plus encore comme séduisant perpétuellement et vous enlevant sans cesse votre population.

Il ne suffit pas que vous, Président, n'ayez point cette pensée, il faut persuader à la France et à l'Espagne que vous ne l'avez pas; et il faut la déraciner chez votre nation, en lui montrant dans quelle suite de malheurs l'entrainerait cette tentation fatale.

Il est donc nécessaire de vous renfermer avec la plus grande[1] sévérité dans le motif d'assurer un débouché certain aux produits de vos Etats de la cumberland, de la Wabash, des deux rives de l'ohio et de la rive gauche du mississipi lui même.

Mais on dira que cette liberté du commerce que cette sureté des débouchés peuvent vous être garantis par un Traité avec la France aussi bien que par un Traité avec l'Espagne;—que ce Traité maintenu par l'interêt réciproque serait un gage d'amitié durable au lieu d'être une source de querelles entre les deux nations;—et qu'enfin, s'il était violé de la part des Français, vous retrouveriez toujours, mais avec plus de dignité et de justice, les ressources de la Puissance territoriale contre une colonie faible et isolée que vos amis les Anglais empêcheraient d'être secourue.

On demandera pourquoi cette grande inquiétude contre les Français, qui sont très disposés à vous laisser les Ports du mississipi ouverts sous de faibles droits de douane ou d'entrepôt qu'un traité de commerce pourrait régler, tandis que les anglais plus jaloux, plus hautains, ne paraissent point vous inquiéter ni vous déplaire au Canada, quoiqu'ils vous refusent par le St Laurent un débouché qui serait presque aussi naturel que celui du mississipi, un debouché que deux canaux, l'un à niagara, l'autre partant de la monongahela et qui ne couteraient pas deux millions de dollars pourraient rendre de la plus grande importance pour vos Etats de l'ouest nés et à naitre.

On dira que ces sentimens si pacifiques à l'egard des Anglais, si hostiles et dejà s'exprimant en menaces à l'égard des Français rentrant en possession d'un de leurs anciens patrimoines, dont une partie et la plus belle partie nous a déja été cédée par l'Espagne et ne vous sera point contestée par eux, montre en faveur de l'angleterre une partialité dont la nation et le gouvernement français doivent être choqués et aussi inquiets que vous le paraissez vous même.

On dira, et certainement en ce point on aura raison, que si les Anglais vous flattent, sur l'appas d'une alliance passagere pour dépouiller l'Espagne, de vous laisser devenir la seconde Puissance maritime, ils vous trompent; que votre confiance en eux vous trompe.—Les anglais détestent et détesteront toujours les secondes et même les troisiemes Puissances maritimes.—Ils vous le feraient durement sentir, si vous arriviez à cet honneur plus dispendieux qu'utile. Les persécutions qu'ils vous feraient essayer rendraient alors votre Alliance à la France, et tout le sang versé dans l'intervalle serait perdu.

Il n'y a que la France qui désire que vous soyiez une Puissance maritime. Il n'y a que les Anglais qui le craignent.

Toutes ces choses posées, on soutiendra que vous n'avez besoin de la nouvelle orléans et des embouchures du mississipi que pour le libre et perpétuel débit des productions de vos Etats de l'ouest et qu'un traité de commerce suffit pour vous les assurer parfaitement et sur vos propres vaisseaux.—A cela que répondre?

Cependant vous aimez mieux un Traité qui vous cede la propriété, qu'un Traité qui vous garantirait l'usage. Et je ne nie pas, d'abord que cela ne puisse vous être meilleur, et ensuite que cela ne soit pour la France que d'une importance mediocre.

Mais il faudra commencer par convenir d'un point: Savoir, que les Etats Unis n'eleveront jamais aucun nouveau désir sur la rive droite du Fleuve; que son usage sera égal et commun entre les deux nations; et que le milieu de son cours sera la limite entre les deux etats.—car il est vraiment de l'interêt des trois Peuples, et de celui du monde, que la Puissance de la France et de l'Espagne concourent à repousser la tentation que les Etats unis pourraient avoir un jour de conquerir le mexique.

Ce point arrêté, on voudra connaitre quel est votre moyen de persuasion pour obtenir l'arrangement que vous désirez.—celui de dire: *cédez nous ce Pays, sans quoi nous le prendrons*, n'est pas du tout persuasif.—*Nous le défendrons* est la premiere réponse qui se présente à tout homme.—*Nous vous préviendrons* pourrait être tacitement la seconde dans la politique ordinaire.—Et tous les malheurs que nous voulons empêcher auraient lieu.

Vous voulez la cession d'un territoire que la France possede légitimement.—si vous disiez: *cédez-nous ce qui nous convient de la Louisiane, cédez-nous les Florides*[2] *et nous determinerons les Anglais à vous rendre le canada,* si vous disiez au moins, *nous prenons l'engagement à la premiere guerre de contribuer à vous remettre en possession du Canada,* ce seraient des propositions quelconques, ce serait parler.—et j'oserais vous garantir que la France vous donnerait par son canada toute la liberté du commerce, tous les débouchés que les Anglais vous refusent.

Mais peut-être le premier point est-il au dessus de votre crédit sur l'angleterre.—Peut-être encore ne voudriez vous pas prendre l'engagement formel du second, quoique vous sembliez déja prêts à vous unir avec les Anglais contre nous au sujet de la Louisiane.

Où donc est votre moyen d'acquérir, et de persuader à la France une cession amiable de la propriété?

Hélas! Monsieur le Président, la liberté des conventions, le goût naturel de tous les Peuples, de tous les individus pour les richesses, et la pauvreté dont toutes les grandes Puissances sont sans cela attaquées, à laquelle il n'y a que les Puissances du second ordre qui échappent, ne vous laissent qu'un moyen quand vous n'avez point d'échange de même nature à offrir.—c'est l'acquisition, c'est le payement en argent.

Calculez ce que vous a couté le très faible armement que vous avez fait il y a trois ans.—Voyez ce que vous couterait la guerre la plus heureuse avec la France et l'Espagne.—et abonnez vous pour une partie . . . pour moitié je suppose.—Les deux nations auront fait un bon marché. vous aurez la Louisiane et vraisemblablement les Florides[3] pour la moindre dépense possible; et cette conquête n'en sera ni envenimée par les haines, ni souillée par le sang humain.

la France vous demandera le plus qu'elle pourra. Vous offrirez le moins que vous pourrez. Mais offrez assez pour la déterminer s'il se peut avant la prise de possession, car l'interêt du gouvernement, celui des Prefets et celui des compagnies de commerce deviendraient des obstacles puissans.—Ces Traités doivent être faits vite:[4] plus longtemps on y marchande et plus on fait un mauvais marché. le plus mauvais de tous serait la rupture.

Daignez m'ecrire à new york à ce sujet. J'ai la certitude de ne pas partir avant le dix de may, et je puis rester quelques jours de plus Selon le vent et les affaires.—si j'avais été forcé de partir avant d'avoir recu votre lettre, mon Fils vous la renverrait et vous chargeriez le chancelier Livingston de m'expliquer votre pensée.

comptez sur mon Zêle inalterable, sur mon attachement inviolable, sur ma reconnaissance pour votre amitié[5] sur mon tendre et profond respect.　　　　　　　　　　　　　　　Du Pont (de Nemours)

Mister President　　　　　　　　　　　　　New York, 30 Apr. 1802

I received your letter and dispatches. I read the one you allowed me to look at. I will deliver them faithfully, and will argue for their content with all my feeble power.

I understand all the importance of their subject. It is the main purpose of my trip. A war that would deprive me of the sweet shelter of America, unless I totally renounced my homeland, would be the greatest of misfortunes for me personally.

Yet, since one succeeds all the more when one is enlightened with broad information and is more able to vary one's discourse and suggestions and give evidence for them, allow me to make a few observations. Allow me even to counter with the language of those I will have to deal with, for in order to arrive at a conciliation, it is necessary to foresee and weigh everything that will be said on both sides.

The core of your reasoning is this: "Louisiana will only remain French until the first war. In that first war, our interest in possessing it will force us to go on the offensive. And since the English navy will avert any assistance to Louisiana, our geographical position and the military power at our disposal will necessarily overcome any resistance that could be offered by a remote mother country with inferior naval power."

A military officer will easily understand that the weight *of a column* that extends from the district of Maine to the Mississippi will indeed break through whatever *line of attack* might be positioned along the banks of that river.

Yet, a young officer, whose ministers cannot keep their positions without constantly extolling military pride, will be much more offended than convinced by that line of reasoning. And if it is the only one presented to him, the negotiations will fail.

Here is what people will say to him to prolong, through political reasoning, the *irritation* that will be caused by the threat, however veiled, to dispossess him against his will.

"The United States," they will say, "and even its president, reveal an ambition for conquest that you must stop. The country did not worry when Louisiana was in Spanish hands because it does not consider Spain to be a major power; it viewed this Mississippi colony merely as a way station and a necessary armory for the army with which it someday expects to conquer Mexico. But Spain ceded that colony to you precisely to secure its hold over

Mexico. Spain wanted the power of two countries to contain within reasonable limits the spirit of conquest which the United States no longer can nor wishes to hide. You would fail your ally if you gave up the front line she entrusted to you."

Mister President, there is no doubt that your nation as a whole, and especially your most ambitious citizens, think about conquering Mexico. There would be much to gain for the generals, the officers, and even the soldiers. It would be very easy to recruit an army.

But there would be much to lose for the United States, and especially for a *philosophe* like their President Jefferson who loves mankind and is a true friend of his country.

The conquering army will be corrupted forever. The soldiers who return will bring home every crime and vice.

Those who will stay in the conquered land will constitute a formidable neighbor with whom the United States will need to be in a permanent state of war.

If the victorious general establishes a monarchy there, it will certainly not be an ally of your republic.

If you can found a republic there, you will try in vain to make alliances with it. You already see how much wisdom, prudence, and circumspection it takes to maintain the confederation among your sixteen states. How much more difficult it would be with a new republic, much wealthier and almost as powerful by itself as all your states together, and whose center would be so far away from the center of your confederation.

As long as Mexico remains in Spanish hands, it will not be able to harm you. Indeed, it can be of great service to you through commercial arrangements that are easy to imagine. If Mexico were stirred up by a revolution and developed to the level of your civilization by your citizens living there (who left your territory and stopped improving it), this would be the greatest imaginable disaster for your peace, freedom, and prosperity. Mexico would then be your harmful rival for power. It would even do harm by perpetually attracting your population to emigrate.

It is not enough that you, as president, do not have this intention. You must persuade France and Spain that you do not have it, and you must root it out of your citizens' minds by showing them the series of misfortunes which that fatal temptation would provoke.

It is therefore necessary to limit yourself to a goal of providing guaranteed markets for the products of your states on the Cumberland, the Wabash, the two banks of the Ohio, and the left bank of the Mississippi.

People will say, of course, that this free trade and these guaranteed markets can be ensured by a treaty with France, and another with Spain; that such a treaty, maintained by reciprocal interests, would be a token of durable friendship rather than a source of quarrel between the two nations; and that, ultimately, if the French broke it, you could always use the resources of territorial power (but with more dignity and justice) against a weak, isolated colony, which your English friends would not allow to be helped.

People will ask why you should be so worried about the French who are most willing to keep the Mississippi ports open, with modest fees for storage and customs which could be set by a trade treaty, whereas the more arrogant and jealous English do not seem to worry or displease you in Canada, even though they deny you an outlet through the Saint Lawrence, which would be almost as natural as through the Mississippi. Two canals, one at Niagara, the other beginning at the Monongahela River, at a cost of less than two million dollars, could be of the greatest importance for your western states, present and future.

People will say that such conciliatory feelings toward the English, who are so hostile to the French and have already threatened those who recover their former possessions, a part of which, indeed the finest part, have already been ceded by Spain (a fact they will not dispute), shows a bias in favor of England that must shock the French nation and government, and worry them as much as it seems to worry you.

People will say, and certainly on this point they will be right, that if the English charm you with the lure of a temporary alliance to despoil Spain and let you become the second maritime power, they are deceiving you; that you are deluded by your trust in them. The English hate and will always hate the number two and even the number three naval power. They would let you know it harshly if you reached this honor which would be more costly than useful. The attacks they would make you endure would prompt you to renew your alliance with France, and all the blood that had been shed in the meantime would be rendered useless.

Only France wants you to become a maritime power. Only the English fear it.

Considering all these things, people will argue that you need only New Orleans and the openings of the Mississippi for the free and permanent delivery of products from your Western states, and that a trade treaty would suffice to guarantee this on your own ships. Who could argue with this?

Nevertheless, you would rather have a treaty that cedes ownership than a treaty that guarantees usage. And I do not deny, first, that it would be better for you, and second that it is not terribly important for France.

But you would have to begin by agreeing on one point: namely, that the United States would never claim the right bank of the Mississippi; that the use of the river would be equally shared by the two nations; and that the middle of the river would mark the border between the two states. For it really is in the interest of three countries as well as the world that France and Spain unite to repel the temptation the United States might some day have to conquer Mexico.

Once this point is settled, one would ask what means of persuasion you would use to obtain the arrangement you want. The one that says "surrender this country to us; otherwise we will take it by force" is not at all persuasive. "We shall defend it" is the inevitable first reaction. In ordinary politics, the second would be, tacitly, "we shall forestall your action." All the misfortunes we would like to ward off would then occur.

You would like the transfer of a territory France legitimately owns. If you said, "Hand over to us what we need in Louisiana, give us the Floridas, and we will persuade the English to return Canada to you"; if you said, at least, "We pledge to help you regain Canada when the first war takes place," these are proposals we could talk about. And I daresay France would grant you, in her Canada, all the free trade and all the markets the English refuse you.

But perhaps my first point overestimates the credit you have in England. As for the second, you might not want to make a formal pledge, although you seemed decided to join the English against us about Louisiana.

How then do you intend to acquire Louisiana and persuade France to surrender its ownership in an amicable way?

Alas, Mister President, contractual freedom and a natural taste for wealth in all nations and all individuals (poverty strikes all great powers and only second-rate powers escape it) leave you with only one alternative, since you have no land to trade: it is financed purchase.

Calculate the cost of the inadequate armament you acquired three years ago; see what the most auspicious war with France and Spain would cost you, and be prepared to spend only a fraction of this, say half of this sum. It would be a good deal for both nations: you would have Louisiana and, most likely, the Floridas for the lowest possible cost, and the conquest would neither be embittered by hatred nor sullied by human blood.

France will ask the highest price she can. You will offer the least you can. But offer enough to convince her before taking possession; for the interest of the government, the prefects, and the trading companies would become powerful obstacles. Such treaties must be done quickly: the longer you bargain, the worse the outcome. Worst of all would be a failure.

Please write to me in New York about this. I will certainly not leave before the tenth of May, and I may stay a few days longer, depending on the winds and business. Were I compelled to leave before receiving your letter, my son would send it back to you and you could charge Chancellor Livingston with explaining your thoughts.

You can count on my unfailing zeal, my inviolable faithfulness, my gratitude for your friendship, and my affectionate and profound respect.

Du Pont (de Nemours)

RC (DLC); at head of text: "a Son Excellence Thomas Jefferson Président des Etats Unis"; ellipses in original; endorsed by TJ, who misread the date, as a letter of 20 Apr. "probably for 30," received 3 May and so recorded in SJL.

votre lettre et vos dépêches: TJ to Du Pont, 25 Apr., with enclosures. The enclosure that TJ left unsealed for Du Pont to read—celle dont vous m'avez permis de prendre connais-sance—was TJ to Robert R. Livingston, 18 Apr.

un jeune militaire: Napoleon Bonaparte was the unnamed "young officer" whose opinions Du Pont attempted to anticipate.

[1] Preceding three words interlined.
[2] Preceding four words interlined.
[3] Preceding four words interlined.
[4] Remainder of paragraph interlined.
[5] Preceding six words interlined.

Memorandum from Christopher Ellery and Joseph Stanton, Jr.

Persons worthy to be appointed Commissioners of Bankrupts in the State of Rhode Island &c—

Constant Taber		
Samuel Vernon		of Newport, County of Newport
Thomas Peckham		
Paul M Mumford		

John Waite	South Kingston	
James Sheldon	Richmond	
William Taylor	So. Kingston	
Thomas Rumreill	North Kingston	County of Washington
Amos Cross	Westerly	
Thomas Cole	No. Kingston	
George Thomas	No. Kingston	

James D. Wolf	Bristol	
Charles Collins jun.	Warren	County of Bristol
Gustavus Baylies	Bristol	

Benjamin Tillinghast	East Greenwich	County of Kent

The subscribers have the honor to recommend to the President of the United States the gentlemen whose names are above written as Commissioners of Bankrupts—

CHRIST. ELLERY
JOS: STANTON

April 30th. 1802

MS (DNA: RG 59, LAR); in Ellery's hand, signed by Ellery and Stanton; at foot of text: "President of the U States"; endorsed by TJ: "Rhode isld. Commrs. of bkrptcy"; TJ drew a diagonal line through the candidates for the counties of Washington, Bristol, and Kent and added in pencil in the left margin: "no appmt necessary in these places no courts held there"; TJ also added in pencil at foot of text: "mr Foster is to furnish names for Providce."

Joseph Stanton, Jr. (1739-1807) repre-sented Rhode Island in Congress as a senator from 1790 to 1793 and as a representative from 1801 to 1807 (*Biog. Dir. Cong.*).

CONSTANT TABER, SAMUEL VERNON, THOMAS PECKHAM, and PAUL M. MUMFORD all received appointments as commissioners of bankruptcy for Rhode Island in June 1802 (Newport *Rhode-Island Republican*, 26 June 1802). For the recommendations by Theodore Foster for commissioners at Providence, see Arthur Fenner and Theodore Foster to TJ, 15 June 1802.

From Albert Gallatin

DEAR SIR   April 30th 1802

I feel extremely anxious to take my family to New York—Both my children are sick; change of air is essential in their disorder; and change of situation is not less so to Mrs. G. at present.

I called this morning, but you were absent, in order to obtain your consent for my absence on that occasion as early after the adjournment of Congress as you think it may take place without injury to the public service. I know but two laws within my department which will require attention & some new organisation. The most important is that concerning hospitals; on that subject I may give such immediate temporary directions as may be necessary and as will procure us the information wanted to organise a well digested system. The other relates to the surveying of the lands within the Vincennes grant on Wabash, which requires your co-operation only because you are to appoint a person to direct the surveying, instead of the surveyor general doing it. The thing cannot be done until the outer lines shall have been ascertained & I understand that that part of the business is left with the War department. What relates to mine may be postponed till after your & my return. I only wish you to wait till that time before you appoint the person who is to direct the laying off the land. As to the measures which relate to the sinking fund & Dutch debt, I will make my journey serviceable by acquiring the necessary information on the probability of obtaining bills &a.

I will send within two days an opinion on the subject of St. Clair; but every document substantiating the charges is missing.

I understand that a law has passed making new districts, for which new officers may be necessary. I will send you the information I can collect to morrow. The New Jersey members have been applied for in relation to the Commissioners of Bankruptcy. From Philadelphia & New York I will bring information on my return.

With sincere respect and attachment Your obedt. Servt.

ALBERT GALLATIN

RC (DLC); addressed: "The President of the United States"; endorsed by TJ as received from the Treasury Department on 30 Apr. and so recorded in SJL.

The act regarding marine HOSPITALS, which TJ signed on 3 May, gave the president the power to distribute from a general fund the monies collected for the relief of sick and disabled seamen and to establish marine hospitals at Boston and New Orleans (see TJ to the Senate and the House of Representatives, 24 Feb.). PERSON TO DIRECT THE SURVEYING: according to the law, the president was to appoint a person or persons to survey the lands around Vincennes (U.S. Statutes at Large, 2:179-80)

NEW JERSEY MEMBERS: the five congressmen—John Condit, Ebenezer Elmer, William Helms, James Mott, and Henry Southard—were all Republicans (*Biog. Dir. Cong.*; William Helms to TJ, 30 Apr.).

I WILL SEND YOU THE INFORMATION: see Memorandum from Gallatin, printed at 1 May.

From Albert Gallatin

Treasury Department April 30th. 1802

In pursuance of the President's request, the Secretary of the Treasury, submits the following opinion on the subject of the Charges exhibited against Governor St. Clair, observing however, that every Document in support of the Charges is missing, and that the territorial laws would assist in forming a more correct view of an important part of the subject. The Charges & references to documents on one part, the Governor's defense and the documents presented by him on the other part, are all the papers which the Secretary has seen.

1st. Charge—"Erecting Counties & fixing Seats of Justice by proclamation."

The fact is admitted but defended on the ground of right derived from the Ordinance. In my opinion, the fair & only rational construction of that Instrument limits the Governors power of erecting Counties to the first stage of Government. Yet, the expressions are not sufficiently precise to preclude doubt, or at least argument, in favor of the contrary opinion. But that right, if granted to the Governor in the Second Stage of the Government, is so extraordinary & contrary to the intent & Spirit of the Instrument, that it should be construed strictly; and the locating of the Seats of Justice being a legislative power, no where expressly given to the Governor, ought not to have been exercised by implication, as derived from the at best doubtful authority, of erecting Counties.

2d. Charge—"Putting his negative on useful & necessary laws."

This is a discretionary power. That it was abused is not sufficiently established. The negative put on the Tavern & Marriage laws, may make an exception, but falls more properly within the scope of the two following charges—

3d. Charge—"Taking illegal fees—"

This appears fully established by the defence, though the document No. 2, which consisted of a letter from the Governor to the Prothonotary of Ross County, directing the collection of fees, and of the amount of the fees accordingly collected & paid over to the Governor, be missing. The fees for Marriage & Ferry licenses were taken without even the color of a law. The law authorizing the fees for Tavern licences is said to have been adopted from the Pennsylvania code; the laws of Pennsylvania direct the payment of a certain sum for each Tavern license, but it is payable to the Treasury of the State: the fees under the pretended territorial law, are for the use of the Governor. The law is not adopted from any State code; it is *made* & therefore null *ab initio*: and the fees collected under it are illegal.

4th. Charge—"Negativing the laws annulling those fees and approving the law giving him 500 dollars as a compensation for the same.—"

The facts, that the territorial legislature passed at the same time laws annulling the fees, and a provision giving to the Governor 500 dollars; and that the Governor rejected the first & approved the last, keeping the fees & accepting the gift are established; but it is not proven, that there was any connection between those several laws, nor that the 500 dollars were meant as an equivalent for the fees.

5th. Charge—"Attempting the division of the Territory and the alteration of the Constitutional boundaries of the intended States—"

Fully established by the admission of the Governor, by his letter to Mr. Harrison, and by his sanction of the territorial law of last session.

6th. Charge—"Granting to his Son a Commission, as Attorney General, during good behaviour, whilst all his other commissions were revokable at will—"

Admitted; the motive assigned by the Governor, the fear that his son might be displaced by the Governors supposed Successor

7th. Charge—"Improper interference with Judiciary proceedings—"

The document in the case of Judge Finley is missing. The conduct of the Governor in the case of the Justices of Adams County, appears to have been proper & their attempt to remove the seat of Justice an usurpation.

8th. Charge—"Appointing to Offices, persons residing out of the County—"

Except in the case of Mr. Robb, the persons thus appointed appear to have removed to the proper County on receiving the appointment. But the charge seems established in the case of Mr. Robb, son in law of the Governor, who holds the Office of Judge in the County of Hamilton where he still resides, and that of Recorder of Deeds for the County of Clermont, which he exercises by deputy.

9th. Charge—"Neglecting the Organisation of the Militia—"

The documents in support of this charge have not been seen by the Secretary—

10th. Charge—"Hostility to a republican form of Government."

The document said to substantiate that charge is missing. Some loose conversation on the subject is admitted by the Governor.

Of the preceding charges the 3d. 5th. 6th. & 8th. are the only ones which appear established. The two last, although the Acts evince improper partiality for his family, do not seem to afford, alone, sufficient grounds for removal. Either of the two others, the taking illegal fees, or attempting to dismember the Territory or State, is, in the Secretarys opinion, sufficiently weighty to justify the appointment of a Successor: the first obviously so; the last, though not morally, yet politically still more reprehensible. As an Administrator of that Government and the Organ of the general Government in the Territory, it was his duty to keep it entire according to the existing provisions established by those from whom he derived and in whose name he exercised his authority; instead of which he seems to have been the prime mover of Acts tending to foment internal dissentions and to defeat the Ordinance of 1787, an Ordinance which was grounded on a compact between the United States & Virginia, and is the Charter of the people of the Territory. The boundaries therein established could not until the admission of the state in the Union, when it will be embraced by the provisions of the Constitution, be alter'd without the consent *of the people of the Territory*, of Congress & of Virginia. Any Act of the territorial legislature on the subject was an Assumption of power not belonging to them & ought to have been discountenanced & negatived by the Governor.

But although a removal is justifiable on those grounds, the propriety of that measure under present circumstances, appears doubtful. Congress having provided for the admission of the new State in the Union, the Age, infirmities & past services of the Governor, may be a sufficient reason why the mortification of a removal should be spared, if by the Assent of the territorial Convention, his Office shall of course expire with the Colonial form of Government, Should, however, by the dissent of the Convention, the present form of Government continue any longer, those reasons could not have any weight. In the present situation of things, the difficulty of appointing a proper Successor affords an additional reason for continuing the Governor until the result is ascertained. It would be extremely difficult to find a proper Character out of the Territory, who would, under present circumstances, consent to remove there for that purpose; nor does it seem eligible, when the Colony is merging into an independent State, that the Supreme Executive should seem to believe, that it is necessary to seek for a man fit to govern, out of the Territory. And yet, although there are doubtless, there, many Individuals perfectly qualified, the information of the President is very limited on that subject; and the Characters most conspicuous from Office or other circumstances, either are amongst the Accusers of Governor St. Clair, or intimately connected with them, or would not exchange their present situation, for that of a temporary Governor.

Respectfully submitted by   ALBERT GALLATIN

RC (DLC); in a clerk's hand, signed by Gallatin; at foot of text: "The President of the United States"; endorsed by TJ: "St. Clair's case. mr Gallatins opinn."

THE PRESIDENT'S REQUEST: TJ to Heads of Departments, 29 Apr.

St. Clair appointed Edward Tiffin PROTHONOTARY OF ROSS COUNTY on 1 Sep. 1798. A brother-in-law and political ally of Thomas Worthington, Tiffin became a leading Republican and vocal critic of St. Clair's administration (*Terr. Papers*, 3:512; ANB).

AB INITIO: from the beginning (Garner, *Black's Law Dictionary*, 5).

CASE OF THE JUSTICES OF ADAMS COUNTY: for the dispute over the location of the seat of Adams County, see Charges Against Arthur St. Clair, at 30 Jan. 1802, Document III. For St. Clair's alleged HOSTILITY TO A REPUBLICAN FORM OF GOVERNMENT, see same.

ADMISSION OF THE NEW STATE: Congress passed the Enabling Act on 30 April 1802, which authorized the inhabitants of the eastern division of the Northwest Territory to create a constitution and a state government (U.S. Statutes at Large, 2:173-5).

From William Helms

SIR   Washington 30th April 1802

By the Judiciary Law just passed the two houses of Congress, the appointment of Commissioners of Bankrupcy is with the President of the United States, permit me to mention the name of John W. Van Cleive Esquire as a person whose Appointment would be satisfactory, This gentleman is originaly from Jersey where I was well acquainted with him, and know his principles to be good, and his integrity unimpeachable—

With due respect Your Obedt. Servant   W. HELMS

RC (DNA: RG 59, LAR); at foot of text: "The President of the U.S."; endorsed by TJ as received 30 Apr. and "Van Cleive John W. to be a Commr. of loan" and so recorded in SJL but as "Commr. bkrpt."

Born in Sussex County, New Jersey, William Helms (d. 1813), a Revolutionary War veteran, served in the New Jersey General Assembly in 1791 and 1792. He was one of five Jeffersonian Republicans elected to Congress from New Jersey in 1800 and served in the House of Representatives from 1801 to 1811. He then moved to Hamilton County, Ohio (*Biog. Dir. Cong.*; Prince, *New Jersey's Jeffersonian Republicans*, 63-5).

New Jersey congressman John Condit also recommended Vancleve, as recorded on an undated scrap of paper, probably by Meriwether Lewis: "John Van Cleave who is recommended for some appointment is thought to be by Dr. Condit a proper Character" (MS in DNA: RG 59, LAR, 7:0194; *Biog. Dir. Cong.*).

From William Jones and Joseph Clay

SIR   Philada. 30 April 1802

As the Judiciary bill now pending before the Legislature invests the Executive with the power of nominating the commissioners of Bankruptcy, we are invited to address you on this subject by motives of justice to an individual, and a knowledge of your disposition to appoint men in all respects worthy of the public confidence.

We therefore beg leave to represent that Mr Thomas Cumpston one of the present commissioners for this district is a gentleman universally and highly esteemed for the rectitude of his conduct and general good character.

We believe Sir, that in the exercise of his functions as a Commissioner he has been faithful and impartial—is well qualified for the office; and that his reappointment would give very general satisfaction.

We are Sir, with the highest regard Yours very respectfully

WM JONES
JOSEPH CLAY

RC (DNA: RG 59, LAR); in Jones's hand, signed by Jones and Clay; at foot of text: "The President of the U States"; endorsed by TJ as received 4 May and "Thomas Cumpston to be Commr. bkrptcy" and so recorded in SJL.

THOMAS CUMPSTON was appointed a commissioner of bankruptcy for Pennsylvania in June 1802 (TJ to Albert Gallatin, 10 June 1802).

To Levi Lincoln

[on or after 30 Apr. 1802]

The Attorney general will be pleased to carry into execution the inclosed resolution of the Senate of Apr. 30. respecting the claims of John Cleves Symmes.   TH: JEFFERSON

PrC (DLC); undated. Enclosure not found, but see below.

A 30 Apr. RESOLUTION OF THE SENATE requested that the president direct the attorney general to examine the 1788 contract between the United States and JOHN CLEVES SYMMES for a grant of land in the Northwest Territory. Lincoln was to report his findings at the next session of the Senate, together with his opinion as to whether Symmes "has any claims, and what, upon the United States, in virtue of the said contract, or any other contract, or law predicated upon the same." Symmes sought a patent for additional lands in the Northwest Territory that he claimed were still due to him under the 1788 contract. In his report to the Senate, presented on 28 Jan. 1803, Lincoln concluded that Symmes "appears to have no claims on the government, founded on a legal right, or on a particular equity growing out of a fair and reasonable construction of his contract" (JS, 3:228-9, 257; Beverley W. Bond, Jr., ed., *The Correspondence of John Cleves Symmes, Founder of the Miami Purchase* [New York, 1926], 20-1; Levi Lincoln, *Report of the Attorney General, on the Contract with John C. Symmes: In Pursuance of the Resolution of the Senate, of 30th April Last* [Washington, D.C., 1803], 23).

From Thomas McKean

DEAR SIR,   Baltimore April 30th. 1802.

As the power of appointing Commissioners of Bankrupts is at last vested in the President of the United States, I am induced by duty & affection to name Doctor George Buchanan for your consideration as a Gentleman qualified for one of them in the district of Maryland.

Altho' he has the degree of Doctor of Physic, and the practise of Physic has been his only profession, yet he has for several years acted as a Justice of the peace for this city and is still in that character and I will venture to say that his talents and character are at least upon a par with most of those, who have hitherto been appointed Commissioners of Bankruptcy in this State, and his affection to the constitution and present administration of the U.S. is far beyond that of any of them.

I foresee, that you will have many bitter enemies in your power by this law, and be enabled to shew attention to some of your worthy friends, which affords me a very considerable satisfaction.

Accept, dear Sir, of a tender of the best services and most sincere attachment of Your Excellency's, Most obedient And most respectful

THOS M:KEAN

RC (DNA: RG 59, LAR); at foot of text: "His Excellency Thos. Jefferson Esq."; endorsed by TJ as received 1 May and so recorded in SJL.

Dr. GEORGE BUCHANAN received his medical degree from the University of Pennsylvania in 1789 and set up practice in Baltimore. In June 1789, he married Letitia McKean, Governor McKean's daughter. Buchanan advised TJ on a treatment for headaches in 1790. He did not receive the appointment (Washington, *Papers, Pres. Ser.*, 5:5n; Rowe, *McKean*, 266; Vol. 16:487; Appendix II, Lists 1 and 2).

To John Milledge

April 30. 1802

Th: Jefferson presents his compliments to mr Milledge and incloses him an itinerary from hence to mr Randolph's, with a strong recommendation to him to let no man's persuasion induce him to vary the route in any part, Th:J. after near 30. years travelling and trying every road, having by little and little learned this particular route, which he believes no other person is acquainted with, and having found it from his own experience to be the shortest that exists, and far the best.

RC (ViU). Not recorded in SJL.

John Milledge (1757-1818) was a distinguished Revolutionary War veteran and political leader from Georgia, who served as attorney general and a state legislator before his election to Congress in 1792. Resigning his seat in the House of Representatives in May 1802, he was elected governor of Georgia the following November. He returned to Congress in 1806, filling the U.S. Senate seat vacated by the death of James Jackson. While in Congress, Milledge was a reliable Republican who provided TJ with advice on appointments and Indian affairs in Georgia. He retired from public life in 1809 and dedicated himself to his highly successful planting endeavors. TJ held Milledge's planting abilities in high esteem and the two men corresponded on agricultural subjects both during and after TJ's administration (ANB, *Biog. Dir. Cong.*; RS, 1:596-7, 666-7; 3:636-7; 4:39-40).

ENCLOSURE

Itinerary from Georgetown Ferry to Edgehill

from George town ferry to

(1.)	Thomas's (blacksmith)	6.	miles
	Oxroad	$2\frac{1}{2}$	
	Richd Fitzhugh's	4	
	Lane's on Centerville road	11	
(2.)	Songster's	$4\frac{1}{2}$	
	Bull run	5.	
*	Brown's tavern	5.	tolerable
(3)	Slaterun church.	$5\frac{1}{2}$	
(4)*	Elkrun church.	$14\frac{1}{4}$	pretty good house
	Norman's bridge	9.	
*	Herring's	4	private entertt. clean & tolerably well
*	Stevensburg	5	will do.
	Somerville's mill	8.	
	Downey's ford	3	
*	Orange court house	9	good house
*	Gordon's	10	good house
*	Bentivoglio	8	miserable place
	mr Randolph's	10	
		114.	

*taverns

[384]

Observations.

from George town ferry turn down the road half a mile towards Alexandria, till you come to an old house on the right, just below which you will see an obscure road turn up a gullied hill side, which you are to take. it is impossible to give directions as to right and left thro' the route; the way must be enquired from one stage to another. observe that the general course of the road is South West.

(1.) here you go directly across the Alexandria road (unless you wish to feed or refresh) in which case you go a quarter or half a mile up to Colo. Wren's tavern, a good one, and return back to the same place. from Thomas's, crossing the road you go by mr Minor's. after entering the Oxroad, you leave it and go through the plantations of 3. or 4. mr Fitzhugh's, a good road, but very zig zag: insomuch that if ever you come to a fork of a road[1] leave always the direct one, &[2] take that which changes your course, which is frequently done at right angles. but you will be in plantations all the time and can get directions. the road, tho' private, is free to every body.

(2.) at Songster's, enquire the new road & ford across Bull run, which are better than the old, and shorter.

(3) just before you come to Slate run church you enter a large road at as acute an angle as a V and seem to turn almost back in turning down the road. about half a mile below the church, you leave the great road taking one which passes thro' a gate on the road side.

(4) at Elkrun church get very particular directions for the road to Norman's bridge or ford, because it is very difficult. the difficulty proceeds from your crossing several large roads running up and down the country, and when you enter one of these, you have to turn up or down it half a mile or a mile to find a road leading across from it, somewhat in this manner.

indeed you will have seen a good deal of this from Slate run church to Elkrun church, where good enquiries and attention is requisite. If you could go to Wren's tavern the overnight (which is but 7. miles from George town)[3] the stages would be

1st. day breakfast at Brown's
lodge at Elkrun   } 42 miles

2d. day breakfast at Stevensburg
lodge at Orange court house } 38.

3d. day. breakfast at Gordon's
dine at mr Randolph's   } 28.

otherwise the stages will be difficult, there being no taverns but those I have noted.

MS (ViU); entirely in TJ's hand.

Richard FITZHUGH's plantation was formerly part of the vast Ravensworth tract in Fairfax County that had belonged to Henry Fitzhugh, who divided the land among his five sons and their uncle. Richard LANE's ordinary was situated on the western boundary of the tract (MB, 2:1071-2; Vol. 35:568-9).

NORMAN'S BRIDGE crossed the Rappahannock River between Culpeper and

Fauquier Counties. In previous and subsequent travel accounts, TJ refers to this site as Norman's ford (MB, 2:834, 1232; Vol. 29:530; Vol. 31:244; Vol. 35:568; TJ to James Madison, 9 May 1802; TJ to Henry Dearborn, 26 Aug. 1805).

BENTIVOGLIO tavern was built by Francis Walker and located on the Turkey Sag road in Albemarle County

(Alfred J. Morrison, *The Beginnings of Public Education in Virginia, 1776-1860* [Richmond, 1917], 157-8).

[1] TJ here canceled "take."
[2] TJ here canceled "turn off."
[3] Closing parenthesis supplied by Editors.

From Caesar A. Rodney

Wilmington
HONORED & DEAR SIR, April 30. 1802. Friday Morning

The Court in Sussex County adjourning much earlier than usual, furnished me with an opportunity of returning home, previous to the sittings in Kent County; or I should not have had the pleasure of receiving your affectionate & flattering *letter* of the 24. inst:, for these two weeks to come, which would have been to me matter of serious regret. On my arrival last night I found *it* on my table & embrace the earliest opportunity of a reply.

I have viewed with sensations more easily conceived than expressed the many wanton attacks which have been made on the wholesome measures of administration. The unmanly[1] calumnies on the Chief Magistrate are mere vapours which a sun beam of his reputation must disperse or a single ray of his character dispel. It really seems as if truth was forgotten by the Opposition & their scriblers & a regard for it, it appears to me, they consider criminal. They stop at no falsehood however bare, & no slander however malicious interposes any obstacle. I have felt myself compelled at moments when health & business would admit to take up the pen, but our paper has been occupied with the debates so much as not to afford room for any thing more than a paragraph now & then upon prominent points. I have in store a pretty lengthy address to your late Marshall of Virginia on the subject of his attack.

Hitherto I have declined all the pressing solicitations of my fellow citizens on the subject of standing a poll as Representative to Congress. During my late circuit I have been most earnestly & anxiously solicited by a great number some of whom I was rather surprized at, from their former opinions. You know my situation in life, but what sacrifices ought not to be made at the public shrine. To support you, & your administration I am ready to risk my health, to sustain any professional loss or to hazzard my existence. Under the impressions

you suggest in such friendly terms I shall comply with your wishes &
I do trust error has not made any progress here & if I can judge correctly Republican zeal has not abated since the last election. The
struggle however will be an arduous one, but if aught[2] can effect the
object I trust no honorable means will be spared.

My health is improving by attending to a little farm I have lately
purchas'd on the hill to the Westward of Wilmington within a mile
of the town. I hope in the course of this summer to restore it perfectly.
Governor Hall & myself talk of paying you a visit in June & perhaps
our District attorney G. Read will join us.

Should my health continue impaired, if elected, tho' I may not be
able to go thro' the labours of a draughts-man I trust I shall be able
to raise my feeble voice in the house. at all events in my opinion the
highest honor which can be enjoyed by a virtuous mind, is the reflection of having allowed no personal consideration, to stand between it
& the firm independent & manly discharge of public duty.

Beleive me my Dear Sir, to be with great personal regard & political esteem, in haste Yours most Sincerely   C. A. RODNEY

RC (DLC); endorsed by TJ as received
2 May.

OUR PAPER: Wilmington *Mirror of
the Times, & General Advertiser*. LATE
MARSHALL OF VIRGINIA: David Meade
Randolph.

The stone mansion on Rodney's LIT-
TLE FARM was called "Cool Spring"
(ANB).

[1] MS: "umanly."
[2] MS: "ought."

Query from Albert Gallatin, with Jefferson's Reply

[April 1802]

Is it worth while to institute an enquiry?
Banning is a very weak man.   A.G.

[*Reply by TJ*:]
I think he should be called on to shew that no inconvenience is produced by his non-residence, or be compelled to move to the port, or
lose his office.   TH:J

MS (NHi: Gallatin Papers); undated,
but see below; on a scrap of paper, with
an undated query from John Randolph
to Gallatin written on the other side:
"Will you look at the enclosed bill & say

whether it is right? particularly the last
clause. yrs. J.R. jr."

Gallatin forwarded a number of documents to TJ with his query regarding

Robert BANNING, who had served as collector at Oxford, Maryland, since 1795. Jacob Gibson, a prominent resident of Talbot County, wrote Gallatin on 2 Apr., regarding numerous complaints from Talbot and Dorchester counties that the federal officer did not reside at the port, causing "frequent Delays to Vessels." Gibson enclosed vouchers and "Petitions from most of the water men" in the district to justify the Treasury secretary's interference. He recommended John Willis, who resided in Oxford, as a proper person to replace Banning (RC in NHi: Gallatin Papers, endorsed by Gallatin on address sheet: "Talbot, Ct. Md. Ap. 1802 Jacob Gibson & others to remove Banning"; JEP, 1:171). Gibson may have enclosed two undated petitions addressed to the House of Representatives and the Senate, both in the same hand, with little variation in wording, the one signed predominately by residents of Talbot County, the other by residents of Dorchester County. As "watermen and owners of Vessels," they wanted Congress to compel the collector to reside at Oxford. They also spoke against the cutter at the port being kept at U.S. expense, "She being of No use to the Publick." Gallatin may also have forwarded an undated certificate signed by Thomas Pamphilon and John Cockey, residents of Oxford, testifying that vessels were delayed for hours because no one was there to conduct business, leading masters and owners of vessels to plead to have a resident of the port appointed. They closed by noting: "mr. Banning Says Sooner than he will move to oxford with the office they may Take it away from him and be damnd." Richard Barnaby and Mordecai Cockey signed a certificate dated 3 Apr. in which they testified that the cutter belonging to the port of Oxford was of no use to the government because it was primarily used as a pleasure boat. Gallatin may also have sent TJ a letter Joseph H. Nicholson received from Thomas Coward, dated 3 Apr. 1802. Coward complained that Banning refused to use the revenue cutter to board the schooner *Nancy*, suspected of carrying a "Cargo of Negroes," some entitled to freedom. Coward had served as a security for the purchase of the schooner when he thought it would run as a packet between Easton and Baltimore. He feared he would never see the vessel again and blamed Banning for his loss (all in NHi: Gallatin Papers; see Gallatin, *Papers*, 9:303-5). More serious charges were brought against Banning in 1803. The final decision to replace him with Willis was made in February 1804 (JEP, 1:464; Gallatin, *Papers*, 8:177-8; Gallatin to TJ, 20, 21 Feb. 1804).

To Abraham Baldwin

DEAR SIR   Washington. May 1. 1802.

A mr Putnam of Georgia was lately appointed to the command of a revenue cutter on the recommendation of yourself, Genl. Jackson & mr Milledge; and I trust on good grounds. the Washington Federalist however of Apr. 30. charges him with having been tried and convicted of having stolen a gold watch. a charge so specific brought forward in the public papers, I have always supposed sufficient to make it the duty of the Executive to enquire into it. it becomes necessary therefore for mr Putnam to justify himself if innocent: and as we do not hold courts of enquiry, the only way would be by bringing the question before a jury by way of action against the three editors Caldwell, Kirkland & Rind. may I ask from your friendship to ap-prize mr Putnam that we shall expect to hear from him on this subject? Accept assurances of my high consideration & esteem.

TH: JEFFERSON

PrC (DLC); at foot of text: "Mr. Baldwin."; endorsed by TJ in ink on verso.

For the RECOMMENDATION, see note to TJ to the Senate, 10 Mch. CHARGE SO SPECIFIC: the accusation against Henry Putnam was included in the extract of a letter from Savannah printed in the *Washington Federalist*. THREE EDITORS: according to the masthead, the newspaper was edited by William A. Rind "& Co." Elias B. Caldwell, clerk of the U.S. Supreme Court, was referred to as an editor of the newspaper in 1804. Putnam resigned his position in early 1804 (Brigham, *American Newspapers*, 1:95-6; Pasley, *Tyranny of Printers*, 240-1; DHSC, v. 1, pt. 1:163-5, 168n; *Washington Federalist*, 30 Apr. 1802; Gallatin, *Papers*, 9:343; Gallatin to TJ, 16 Feb. 1804).

To Mary Jefferson Eppes

MY DEAR MARIA   Washington May 1. 1802.

I recieved yesterday your's of April 21. bringing me the welcome news that you are all well. I wrote 2. or 3. days ago to mr Eppes to inform him that Congress would rise the day after tomorrow, that on the 6th. I should set out for Monticello where I should stay a fortnight, & had some hopes of meeting him there. it is even possible that Congress may rise to-day, which makes me so full of business that I have barely time to repeat to you the above information. I deem this necessary because I directed the other[1] letter to City point, whereas I find you are at Eppington. I send by Dr. Logan to the care of mr Jefferson Richmond[2] some books for you, which I imagine you will find means of getting from thence. mrs Eppes's spectacles I will carry with me to Monticello. Doctr. Walker was here, but did not call on me or I should have sent them to her by him. the want of horses shall not prevent your paying us a visit, long or short, while your sister is here, as I can hire a good coachee here to go for you to the Hundred, on any day that shall be agreed on. your sister will come in the same way. present my affections to mr Eppes father & son, mrs Eppes & family, and accept my constant & tenderest love.

TH: JEFFERSON

RC (ViU); addressed: "Mrs. Maria Eppes at Eppington near Colesville"; franked.

I WROTE 2. OR 3. DAYS AGO: TJ to John Wayles Eppes, 29 Apr.

SOME BOOKS FOR YOU: see Mary Jefferson Eppes to TJ, 21 June 1802.

[1] Word interlined.
[2] Word interlined.

To Albert Gallatin

DEAR SIR   Washington May 1. 1802

Decide according to your own & mrs Gallatin's inclinations on the time and extent of your absence from hence. I sincerely sympathize with you on the circumstances which produce the necessity. I leave this myself on Thursday, and shall stay at home one fortnight. mr Madison goes about the 11th. as I learn and will return a little after me. I wish to write finally to mr Page on the subject of the Petersburg collection. can you now say to what it has been reduced, so that I may inform him? have you thought of an Additional auditor, & does not the law give us a fortunate occasion of enlisting Clay in our service? I must have a conference with you on the subject of defending ourselves regularly in the newspapers, on the case of Steele of Missisipi &c but I shall probably be at the Capitol a good part of to-day, if not to-night, if that will facilitate the rising of Congress to-day. accept assurances of my cordial esteem & respect   TH: JEFFERSON

RC (NHi: Gallatin Papers); addressed: "The Secretary of the Treasury"; endorsed by Gallatin on address sheet: "oath of allegiance." PrC (DLC); endorsed by TJ in ink on verso.

SYMPATHIZE WITH YOU: all of the Gallatin children had been "sick with the measles & hooping cough." Catherine Gallatin, born the previous August, died on 24 Apr. (Gallatin, *Papers*, 7:75; Vol. 35:170n). TJ wrote John PAGE about the collectorship on 7 May.

In March 1802, Gallatin proposed to eliminate the offices of the accountants in the war and navy departments and replace them with a second AUDITOR of the Treasury. A bill was introduced in the House of Representatives on 2 Apr. 1802

to carry out the Treasury secretary's recommendations, but on 30 Apr. further action on the measure was postponed until the next session of Congress. A second auditor in the Treasury Department was not appointed until 1817. In August 1801, Gallatin and TJ had considered possible positions for Joseph CLAY, a Philadelphia Republican who served as a clerk at the Bank of North America (Cunningham, *Process of Government*, 106-7; JHR, 4:229; Charles Lanman, *Biographical Annals of the Civil Government of the United States, During its First Century* [Washington, D.C., 1876], 509; Vol. 35:23, 100-1, 102n, 107, 118, 125). For Gallatin's evaluation of Clay for a Treasury position, see Gallatin to TJ, 19 Oct. 1802.

Memorandum from Albert Gallatin

                                         [ca. 1 May 1802]

District   East River (taken from Yorktown Virga.) includes Matthews County—a collector & surveyor to reside there 200 dollars each

port delivy Bennet's creek (Edenton) ceases as port of delivery and Tombstone on Salmon Creek institd. with a surveyor *do.*   Slades Creek (Washington N.C.) port of delivery surveyor to reside there 150 drs.

District   Marietta. N.W. Territory—Collector 150 dollars

New District on Mississip: at pleasure of President, one other port of entry & delivery—collector customs &a.

MS (NHi: Gallatin Papers); entirely in Gallatin's hand; undated, but see below.

Gallatin's first leter to the president of 30 Apr. promised information on appointments required for the revenue districts established by Congress. For the act establishing the districts, see U.S. Statutes at Large, 2:181-2. See Notes on the Establishment of New Revenue Districts, 1 May, for TJ's own summary of the legislation.

To James Jackson

DEAR SIR   Washington May 1. 1802.

You will probably have seen in the Washington federalist of April 30. mr Mitchell appointed Atty of Georgia on your recommendation, denoted a man of most infamous character. this is merely calling of hard names which I never notice. but the editors pretend that they are possessed of a fact which is too bad for publication. whether the fact be of such a nature as to make it the duty of the Executive to have it investigated, they do not enable us to judge, and yet say enough to leave us under blame if no enquiry be made. will you be so good as to consider whether it is best to expect that mr Mitchell shall himself call for and properly notice the fact, so as to justify the nomination, or what else might be better done. Accept assurances of my high esteem & respect   TH: JEFFERSON

PrC (DLC); at foot of text: "General Jackson"; endorsed by TJ in ink on verso.

For Jackson's RECOMMENDATION of David Brydie Mitchell, see Vol. 34:592, 594n. The *Washington Federalist* of 30 Apr. included an "Extract of a Letter from a gentleman in Savannah, to his friend in this place," in which the writer charged that the citizens of Savannah were outraged by the appointment of Mitchell in place of George Woodruff, "a most respectable citizen." TOO BAD FOR PUBLICATION: the editors interrupted the extract, inserting, "Here follows an instance of his conduct so immoral and debauched, that it is impossible to describe it in words sufficiently chaste for the public eye."

From James Jackson

Sir,   Washington, May 1st, 1802.

I have been honored with your letter of this morning, respecting the attack on Mr Mitchells character, in the Washington Federalist of yesterday.

I had understood, that the extract was sent to Mr Governeur Morris, who had it inserted—I this morning questioned Mr Morris if this was the case, who denied it—To call on the Editors of that calumnious paper, without recourse to violent measures would be nugatory—and violence would do no service to the republican cause, nor would it meet your approbation

As candour ought to prevail in every communication with the Chief Magistrate of the Nation—I inform you that I think I can guess, at the charge levelled at Mr Mitchell.

If I am not mistaken, it is founded on a rumour, which has slept for Years past, and probably never would have been revived but for the envy excited by his present appointment—it was this—On Mr Mitchells marriage, the best part of twenty Years since, his Wifes sister went & resided with them: it was asserted, that she had a child, or was with child, whilst under his roof.—a child she certainly had—his enemies imputed the Child to him—this however has never been proved by the Oath of the Lady, who has since been married, nor in any other way—Young Men were about the house, and his Friends imputed the Act to one of them—the subsequent conduct of Mrs Mitchell, who is an amiable Woman, justified this—so great an outrage it must be supposed, would have driven her from his house; and in fact his enemies attempted a breach between them, but in vain— She has constantly resided with him from that time to the present, and I believe that they possess as much affection for each other, and live as happily together, as most married persons in the Union, I make this assertion from my intimacy with the Family—She has had four, if not five, Children by him since the rumour

Since that period also, Mr Mitchell has successively filled the Offices of Attorney General, and Judge of the Superior Court of Georgia, with honor to himself and reputation to the State—the latter of which he resigned, to return to the bar not long since, to the regret of the Government and the Citizens at large, who considered him as one of the best Judges, that ever sat on the bench of that State—his practice as a Lawyer became instantly extensive. He has also been frequently elected a Member of the Legislature for Chatham County—in which Savannah is situated, and is at this time

the Senator representing the commercial capital of the State, and is
also its Mayor; and I have understood was unanimously elected—Mr
Mitchell after filling the different inferior grades of Militia appointments, was as late as last March, unanimously, as my information
goes, elected Colonel of the Chatham regiment of Militia of which
Regiment the first, and best disciplined, in the State, the Militia
of Savannah compose one Battallion, and which battallion Colo
Mitchell commanded for several Years past—In short, at the bar,
on the bench, in the Legislature, City Council, or the Field, Colo
Mitchell has commanded the respect and affections of a vast majority
of his Fellow Citizens.

His private character is as unimpeachable as his publick—and except the rumour before alluded to I never heard a blemish imputed to
it—In his private walks of life he is generally respected, and beloved;
and that his principles are purely republican, the very attack on him
is the highest proof

I flatter myself that you will do me the justice to believe, that had
Mr Mitchell been the infamous character represented, that I never
should have recommended him to your notice for an appointment
under your administration

Should this letter not prove satisfactory, and you should deem it
necessary—an enquiry can be made in Georgia, where I am convinced Colonel Mitchells appointment will be supported by nine
tenths of all the people of that State.

Whilst on this subject I beg leave to add, that the charge against
Captain Putnam, is an entire novel thing to me which I never before
saw or heard of

I have the honor to be with profound respect Sir—Yr most Obedt
Servt   JAS JACKSON

RC (DLC); at foot of text: "The President of the United States"; endorsed by
TJ as received 3 May and "Mitchell's
case" and so recorded in SJL.

MITCHELLS MARRIAGE: David Brydie
Mitchell married Jane Mills in 1792, ten
years after emigrating from Scotland to
claim an inheritance in Savannah, where
he studied law and was admitted to the
bar. Noted as a vehement Jeffersonian
REPUBLICAN, Mitchell's political advocacy reportedly led to a duel later in 1802, in
which he killed William Hunter. The

Federalists defended Hunter, who had recently resigned as navy agent at Savannah, claiming he was "ignominiously removed from office" after having served
under the previous administration, although Hunter was not appointed until
June 1801. Mitchell was elected to his
first of three terms as governor of Georgia
in 1809 (James F. Cook, *The Governors of
Georgia, 1754-2004*, 3d ed. [Macon, Ga.,
2005], 83-5; New York *Commercial Advertiser*, 8 July 1802; *New-York Evening
Post*, 4 Sep. 1802; NDQW, Dec. 1800-
Dec. 1801, 374).

To Robert Leslie

Sir   Washington May 1 1802.

I recieved last night your's of Apr. 27. I do not believe I ever paid for the skeleton clock, as I never recieved it. it would not have entirely escaped my memory if I had, so that I am pretty certain you have nothing to refund. with respect to the house clock, I had occasion to employ the man who made it after you went away, to rectify her more than once. but as I employed him myself, I always paid himself, so that if he took paiment moreover from mr Price, it was a double paiment. I could ascertain these facts by going over my books, which at this time is not in my power, but will do at leisure if necessary. my idea is strong that there is nothing between us either way. accept my best wishes & respect.   Th: Jefferson

PrC (MHi); at foot of text: "Mr. Robert Leslie"; endorsed by TJ in ink on verso.

Notes on the Establishment of New Revenue Districts

[ca. 1 May 1802]

Agenda under the law making new ports
after June 30 the District of East river (Virga) established
> the proper place for the port of entry & delivery to be designated by Presidt
>> Collector & Surveyor of the customs to reside thereat to be appd by Pres.
> Bennet's cr. N.C. put down as a port of delivery
> port of delivery establd. at the Tombstone on Salmon creek
>> Surveyor of the customs to be appointed to reside there
> a port of delivy establd. at Parmly's at the mouth of Slade's cr. N.C.
>> Surveyor of customs to be appd to reside there
immedly. establd. the district of Marietta
> Collector of the customs to be appd to reside at Marietta
when Pres. thinks proper may estab. a port of entry & delivy on Missi. to reside where he shall designate.

Collector of customs to be appd
Surveyor or Surveyors to be appd to reside at such
places as he may designate as ports of delivery only

MS (DLC: TJ Papers, 128:22143); entirely in TJ's hand; undated, but see below.

Although Gallatin promised to send TJ information on the new revenue districts established by Congress, TJ took his own notes on the legislation, perhaps as he signed the act on 1 May. On or after 30 June, TJ was to provide a collector and surveyor for the DISTRICT OF EAST RIVER, formed out of the district of Yorktown, in Virginia; a surveyor at TOMBSTONE, established as a port of delivery in place of Bennet's Creek, in the district of Edenton, in North Carolina; and a surveyor at SLADE'S Creek, established as a port of delivery in the district of Washington, in North Carolina, "on a certain tract of land, intended and designated for a town, whereon William Parmley resides." The act called for the immediate establishment of the DISTRICT OF MARIETTA on the Ohio River in the Northwest Territory and the appointment of a collector of customs to reside and keep an office at the town of Marietta, "the sole port of entry and delivery for the said district." ON MISSI.: Congress also gave the president the right to establish a second port of entry with a collector and ports of delivery with surveyors on the Mississippi River (U.S. Statutes at Large, 2:181; Gallatin to TJ, 30 Apr. [first letter]).

From David Stone

Saturday 1st May 1802

The enclosed note from Mr. Stanley contains a recommendation of Mr Selden Jasper as Surveyor at Slade's Creek. No other person at this place has any knowledge of Mr Jasper or any one else in that quarter

DAVID STONE

RC (DNA: RG 59, LAR); addressed: "The President of the United States." Enclosure: John Stanly to Stone, undated, suggesting that Selden Jasper would discharge the duties of surveyor at Slade's Creek, North Carolina, "with Ability and Integrity"; Stanly has no authority to nominate Jasper or to accept for him if appointed, "but the necessity of a present appointment will be met" (same, endorsed by TJ: "Jasper, Selden to be Surveyor of the customs at the port of Slade's creek N.C. appmt to be made July 1. 1802. recommendn by mr Stanly," also endorsed by TJ: "James Clarke to be Surveyor at the tomb-stone port N. Carolina. recommdd. by mr Stone"; see Albert Gallatin to TJ, 1 July and TJ to Gallatin, 2 July 1802).

A Federalist from New Bern, John Stanly (STANLEY) served in the House of Representatives from 1801 to 1803 and from 1809 to 1811 (*Biog. Dir. Cong.*). SELDEN JASPER represented Hyde County in the North Carolina House of Commons in 1798. He did not receive the Slade's Creek surveyorship, since TJ considered Stanly's recommendation of him to be "very suspicious." The appointment instead went to Henry Tuley (John L. Cheney, ed., *North Carolina Government, 1685-1979: A Narrative and Statistical History* [Raleigh, 1981], 238; JEP, 1:433; TJ to Gallatin, 2 July, 14 Aug. 1802).

From Thomas McLean

MOST HONORED CITIZEN   Frederick County May 2nd 1802.

Should any perticular mode or title of address to the first Magistrate of the United States exist; the unimportance of such form will sufficiently apologize for my ignorence of it.

Although a man in political eminence can always find matters of importance sufficient to exercise his utmost powers of judgment; yet, when any thing new in science, or in the application of principlis already known is presented; so far from being burdensome to a philosophic mind, that by changing for a moment the subtleties of political scrutiny for the simple truths of philosophy, the mind gains additional energy for its necessary pursuits. Whether the following is new or not I cannot at present determine: I can only say that my knowledge of it resulted from investigating the application of first principles. But before I proceed to the discription of what I judge to be new; let me first discribe an easy mode of comprehending the principles to be applied. If the Bridge-tree or that part of the frame of a merchant mill, on which the spindle is placed, was raised until the runner would not touch the bed stone, it would then require no more power to give it an hundred revolutions pr. minute than what would overcome the friction of the machinery at that speed. If this stone was taken off (which suppose to be four feet diameter) and another of equal weight, but of twenty feet diameter was put upon the same spindle; then because in both cases, there is no other resistance to the motion of the machinery than its friction; the same power which gives an hundred revolutions pr. Minute to one tun weight of four feet diameter, would give an equal number of revolutions to an equal weight of twenty feet diameter: their difference however, could be no more than what the resistance of the air might make, which must be very Small. And according to Forguson, centrifugal forces are as the square of their distance from the centre: and because the radius of a circle of four feet is two feet, and a circle of twenty feet is described by a radius of ten feet; therefore the centrifugal force would be, as the square of two to the square of ten, that is, as four to an hundred. If then, centrifugal force can be encreased, without a proportional encrease of the power necessary to produce it, that force can be applied; and this is what I judge to be new.—

Let A B be a cylinder of sheet copper or other metalic substance suppose two feet diameter and fifteen in length: let one end of this cylinder be fited perfectly tight with rivets and solder to the middle

of the tube C D which should be of such size that the apertures covered with the valves F F (which must be fitted air tight) valves F F
taken together shall be equal to the area of the cylinder A B. Let G be
an hollow axle upon which is screwed the pump H. Let the Cylinder
A B be set perfectly perpendicular upon its axis K, with its end B immersed in water. Let it be exhausted by the pump H until it stands
full of water. In this condition it is plain that it would be as easy to
communicate motion to it, as to the spindle of a merchant mill, and
that it would require no more power to give it any degree of motion
than what would overcome the friction of its centres and the resistance of the air to its motion at that speed. If the centrifugal tube C D
is made fifteen feet in length, and to revolve upon its axles K G sixty
times pr. minute, because the main radius of the centrifugal tube
would then move with a velocity of thirty one feet pr. seccond; or in
other words with the speed of water under fifteen feet head; therefore, the water contained in the tube C D propelled by centrifugal
force to its extremities will press upon the inner surface of the valves
with a force equal to fifteen feet head of water. If the velocity of this
centrifugal mchine was encreased to seventy five and an half revolutions pr. minute, then the Centrifugal force of the water in the tube C
D would open the valves F F and the water would issue with a speed
of eight feet pr. seccond: because, the speed of the main radius of the
centrifugal tube would then be eight feet pr. seccond more than the
speed of water under fifteen feet head. If the velocity of the machine
was still encreased, the pressure of the Atmosphere would supply it
with water until the issue at the valves would require more than
would be supplied by eighteen feet head, which is the remaining
pressure of the Atmosphere after raising the water fifteen feet in the
Cylinder A B. According to an [expe]riment which I made in order
to ascertain the power necessary to overcome the friction [of a] merchant mill at a certain speed, it would seem that a centrifugal machine such as I have just discribed would raise thirty times as much
water as would overcome the friction of the machinery at seventy five
revolutions pr. minute. Thus it appears in theory, which is all I can
give upon any subject; for my circumstance is such that it is not in my
power to determine by experiment. I need not discribe to you its use
if in practice it would correspond with this theory; but even then it
can be of no use to me unless some person would give me something
for my right of patent. If you can spare a moment from matters of
more importance I would fondly know your sentiments of it. I live at
the foot of the North mountain in Frederick County Virginia near the

line of Berkeley. A letter to me directed to the care of William Sommerville post master Martinburg Berkeley County, Virginia would easily find its way to me. I have been thus minute, in discribing my place of residence because I am so little known

With the highest respect for your sentiments both moral and political I am

Your most obedient And very humble Servant

THOMAS McLEAN

RC (DLC); torn at seal; endorsed by TJ as received 30 May and so recorded in SJL.

FORGUSON: McLean probably refers to James Ferguson, the self-educated Scots natural philosopher and inventor, whose writings on astronomy and mechanics sought to make their subjects comprehendable to lay readers. TJ owned copies of Ferguson's works and recommended them to others (DNB; Sowerby, Nos. 3735, 3793; RS, 1:581; Vol. 12:488; Vol. 16:543; Vol. 30:594; Vol. 32:180).

To Thomas Mann Randolph

TH:J. TO T M RANDOLPH   Washington May 2. 1802.

I forgot this was post day till the moment of the mail's being made up. I have only time therefore to say Congress rises tomorrow. mr Milledge & mr Clarke will probably set out in the evening, be at Orange courthouse on Wednesday evening & go thence to dine with you on Thursday. I shall be two or three days after them. tender love to my dear Martha & the young people & affectionate attachment to yourself. Adieu.

RC (DLC); endorsed by Randolph. PrC (CSmH); endorsed by TJ in ink on verso.

From Theodorus Bailey and Philip Van Cortlandt

SIR,   Capitol, 3d. May 1802.

We take the liberty to recommend the following Gentlemen as suitable persons to be appointed Commissioners of Bankruptcy in and for the District of New york, pursuant to the 14. Section of the late act amending the Judicial System of the United States—vizt. Pierre C. Van Wyck, of the City of New york, and Samuel Hawkins and James Tallmadge Junior, of Poughkeepsie in the County of Dutchess.—All these Gentlemen are in the practice of the Law as

Attornies and Counsellors—and we do not hesitate to vouch for the soundness of their morals and republican principles.

We have the honor to be, Sir, with great consideration and respect, your most Obedt. Servants, THEODORUS BAILEY

PH. V. CORTLANDT

RC (DNA: RG 59, LAR); in Bailey's hand, signed by Bailey and Van Cortlandt; at foot of text: "The President of the United States"; endorsed by TJ as received 3 May and "Commrs. bkrptcy" and so recorded in SJL.

Born in Dutchess County, New York, Theodorus Bailey (1758-1828) began practicing law in Poughkeepsie in 1778 and served with the New York militia during the Revolutionary War. He served as a Republican congressman for three terms and returned to the House of Representatives in late 1801 to fill the vacancy caused by Thomas Tillotson's resignation. In 1802, he also was a member of the New York State Assembly. Bailey served as a U.S. Senator from 4 Mch. 1803 to 16 Jan. 1804, when he resigned to become the postmaster at New York City, a position he held until his death (*Biog. Dir. Cong.*; Vol. 33:330-2). For consideration of the appointment of Bailey, either as supervisor of the revenue or naval officer of New York, see also Vol. 33:627-8;

Vol. 34:127-8, 158-9n, 256; Vol. 35:62-3, 332-3, 518-19.

For a previous recommendation made by Van Cortlandt, see Vol. 34:164-5.

LIBERTY TO RECOMMEND: TJ included the three lawyers endorsed by the New York congressmen on his list of recommendations, but they did not receive appointments in June, when TJ named nine New York commissioners. No appointees were from Poughkeepsie (*National Intelligencer*, 18 June 1802; Madison, *Papers, Sec. of State Ser.*, 3:321, 454-5; Appendix II, List 1).

Three names are recorded, perhaps in Van Cortlandt's hand, on an undated scrap of paper: "William P. Vanness"; "Doctr. Brown brother in law to VP"; and "Mr. Green." They are connected by a brace with the notation: "of the City of N.Y. & chreatures of VP." TJ endorsed the paper: "notice by Bailey & Van Cortlandt" (MS in DNA: RG 59, LAR, 11:370). For connections between William P. Van Ness, Timothy Green, and the vice president, see Vol. 36:81-2, 84-5, 87n, 474, 478n.

To Joel Barlow

DEAR SIR   Washington May 3. 1802

I have doubted whether to write to you, because your's of Aug. 25. recieved only Mar. 27. gives me reason to expect you are now on the ocean. however as I know that voiages so important are often delayed, I shall venture a line by mr Dupont de Nemours. the legislature rises this day. they have carried into execution steadily almost all the propositions submitted to them in my message at the opening of the session. some few are laid over for want of time. the most material is the militia, the plan of which they cannot easily modify to their general approbation. our majority in the H. of Representatives has been about 2. to 1. in the Senate 18. to 14. after another election it will be of 2. to 1. in the Senate, and it would not be for the public good to have it greater. a respectable minority is useful as Censors. the present one is not respectable; being the bitterest remains of the cup of Federalism, rendered desperate & furious by despair. a small check in the tide of republicanism in Massachusets which has shewed itself very unexpectedly at the late election, is not accounted for. every where else we are becoming one. in R. Island the late election gave us 2. to 1. thro' the whole state. Vermont is decidedly with us. it is said & believed that N. Hampsh. has got a majority of republicans now in it's legislature; and wanted a few hundreds only of turning out their federal governor. he goes assuredly the next trial. Connecticut is supposed to have gained for us about 15. or 20. percent since her last election; but the exact issue is not yet known here. nor is it certainly known how we shall stand in the H. of R. of Massach. in the Senate there we have lost ground. the candid federalists acknolege that their party can never more raise it's head. the operations of this session of Congress, when known among the people at large, will consolidate them. we shall now be so strong that we shall certainly split again; for freemen, thinking differently & speaking & acting as they think, will form into classes of sentiment. but it must be under another name. that of federalism is become so scouted that no party can rise under it. as the division into whig & tory, is founded in the nature of man, the weakly & nerveless, the rich and the corrupt, seeing more safety and accessibility in a strong executive, the healthy firm and virtuous feeling confidence in their physical & moral resources, and willing to part with only so much power as is necessary for their good government, and therefore to retain the rest in the hands of the many, the division will substantially be into whig and tory as in England *formerly.* as yet no symptoms shew themselves, nor will till after another election.　　　　I am extremely happy to learn that you are so much at your ease that you can devote the rest of your life to the information of others. the choice of a place of residence is material. I do not think you can do better than to fix here for awhile till you can become again Americanised, and understand the map of the country. this may be considered as a pleasant country residence, with a number of neat little villages scattered around within the distance of a mile & a half, and furnishing a plain & substantially good society. they have begun their buildings in about 4. or 5. different points at each of[1] which there are buildings enough to be considered as a village. the whole population is about 6000. Mr. Madison & myself have cut out a piece of work for you, which is to write the history of the US. from the close of the war downwards. we are rich ourselves in materials, and can open all the public archives to you. but your residence here is essential, because a great deal of the knolege of things is not on paper but only within ourselves, for verbal communication. John Marshal is writing the life of Genl. Washington from his papers. it is intended to come out just in time to influence the next presidential election. it is written therefore principally with a view to electioneering purposes. but it will consequently[2] be out in time to aid you with information as well as to point out the perversions of truth necessary to be rectified. think of this, & agree to it; and be assured of my high esteem and attachment.   TH: JEFFERSON

P.S. there is a most lovely seat adjoining this city, on a high hill, commanding a most extensive view of the Potomac, now for sale. a superb house gardens &c. with 30. or 40. acres of ground. it will be sold under circumstances of distress, and will probably go for the half of what it has cost. it was built by Gustavus Scott, who is dead bankrupt.

RC (NjP); at foot of first page: "Mr. Barlow"; endorsed. PrC (DLC). Enclosed in TJ to Pierre Samuel Du Pont de Nemours, 3 May.

YOUR'S OF AUG. 25: TJ had received two subsequent letters from Barlow, dated 4 and 26 Oct. 1801, before he received the one of 25 Aug. (Vol. 35:141-2, 385-6, 509-10).

SMALL CHECK IN THE TIDE OF REPUBLICANISM: on 5 Apr., Massachusetts held elections for governor and the state senate. Elbridge Gerry was the Republican candidate for governor, as he had been in 1800 and 1801, and he once again challenged Caleb Strong. As election returns came in through April, it was clear that Strong had not only won again, but had gained several thousand votes over the previous election. Republicans struggled to make a convincing case that support for Gerry had at least held even and had not declined (Boston *Constitutional Telegraphe*, 17 Mch. 1802; *Salem Gazette*, 8, 13, 26, 27 Apr.; *Newburyport Herald*, 9, 23 Apr.; New Bedford, Mass., *Columbian Courier*, 16 Apr.; Boston *Columbian Centinel*, 24 Apr.; Brookfield, Mass., *Political Repository*, 27 Apr.; George Athan Billias, *Elbridge Gerry: Founding Father and Republican Statesman* [New York, 1976], 304; Vol. 31:511n; Vol. 33:598n).

Rhode ISLAND held legislative and gu-bernatorial elections on 21 Apr. Arthur Fenner decisively won a new term as governor, and according to one newspaper report it was "ascertained beyond a doubt that there will be a greater majority of Republicans in the House of Representatives, than the last year" (Boston *Independent Chronicle*, 29 Apr.; Norwich *Connecticut Centinel*, 20 Apr.).

The annual elections in VERMONT took place in September (Walpole, N.H., *Farmer's Weekly Museum*, 31 Aug. 1802; Concord, N.H., *Courier of New Hampshire*, 23 Sep.).

N. HAMPSH.: for John Langdon's challenge to John Taylor Gilman for the New Hampshire governorship, see TJ to Langdon, 5 May. That election took place early in March (*Newburyport Herald*, 12 Mch. 1802).

According to one report, CONNECTICUT remained "firm and federal" after its elections in mid-March. Another account, also from a Federalist, said that the state, "yet unshaken," still spurned "the mazy paths of philosophers" (*New-York Evening Post*, 15 May).

Barlow did not return to the United States until 1805, and then did not take up writing the HISTORY that TJ had in mind. Barlow did write about American historical themes, but in the form of an epic poem, *The Columbiad*, which expanded upon and revised his earlier opus,

The Vision of Columbus. In 1807, when *The Columbiad* was published, Barlow purchased the SUPERB HOUSE in the District of Columbia, which he named Kalorama (James Woodress, *A Yankee's Odyssey: The Life of Joel Barlow* [Philadelphia, 1958], 247, 255-7; Stephen Blakemore, *Joel Barlow's Columbiad: A*

Bicentennial Reading [Knoxville, Tenn., 2007], 15-16; Barlow to TJ, 4 Aug. 1805).

[1] Preceding two words interlined.
[2] Word interlined in place of "therefore."

Memorandum from John Brown and John Breckinridge

John Rowan
Daniel Weisger } of Frankfort
John Inston

James Morrison
John A. Seitz } of Lexington
John Bradford

We think the above Gentn. will be proper persons to be appointed as Commrs of Bankruptcy in the State of Kentucky. May 3rd 1802.

J BROWN
JOHN BRECKINRIDGE

MS (DNA: RG 59, LAR); in Breckinridge's hand, signed by Breckinridge and Brown; endorsed by TJ as received 3 May and "Commrs. bkrptcy" and so recorded in SJL.

On 12 June, TJ appointed the six men recommended by the Kentucky senators as bankruptcy commissioners for the state (*National Intelligencer*, 11 June 1802; Appendix I; Appendix II, List 2).

From DeWitt Clinton

SIR   Washington 3 May 1802

I had the honor of mentioning to you Yesterday, the expediency of postponing the appointment of Commissioners of Bankruptcy for New York, until more accurate information can be obtained: This shall engage my early attention on my arrival at that place.

I am the more confirmed in the prudence of this plan, from information that various candidates have either applied or been recommended, who in my opinion ought not to be favored in this way—
Such as Comfort Sands and John Blagge late Bankrupts—
James Fairlie and William Cutting who hold lucrative offices under

the State Govt. And who notwithstanding their being men of fair reputations, ought not to be permitted to engross too much.—

Joseph Brown, William P. Van Ness & Timothy Greene, active engines of a faction hostile to the administration and whom emoluments of this kind will not soften but enable the more to carry on their schemes.—

I am with the most respectful attachment Your most Obedt servt

DEWITT CLINTON

RC (DNA: RG 59, LAR); at foot of text: "The Presdt. of U.S."; endorsed by TJ as received 3 May and "Commrs. of bkrptcy" and so recorded in SJL.

TJ appointed JAMES FAIRLIE, clerk of the New York Supreme Court, to serve as a bankruptcy commissioner in New York City. He was recommended by Samuel L. Mitchill and Brockholst Livingston (Syrett, *Hamilton*, 18:20n; *Longworth's American Almanac, New-York Register, and City Directory, for the Twenty-Sixth*

Year of American Independence [New York, 1801], 166; Madison, *Papers, Sec. of State Ser.*, 3:321; Appendix II, Lists 1 and 2).

Brockholst Livingston wrote Madison on 13 Apr. recommending New York attorney WILLIAM CUTTING as a commissioner. He was not appointed (RC in DNA: RG 59, LAR, endorsed by TJ: "Wm. Cutting of N.Y. to be Commr. bkrptcy"; Madison, *Papers, Sec. of State Ser.*, 3:127; *National Intelligencer*, 18 June 1802; Appendix II, List 1).

To Pierre Samuel Du Pont de Nemours

TH: J. TO MR DUPONT   Washington. May 3. 1802.
Another letter to embarras you with, and a repetition of good wishes for your health & happiness.[1] I set out on the 5th. instant for Monticello.

RC (DeGH); addressed: "Monsr. Dupont de Nemours on board the Benjamin Franklin Philadelphia." Enclosure: TJ to Joel Barlow, 3 May.

[1] TJ originally ended the letter here, before adding the final sentence.

From George Jefferson

DEAR SIR   Richmond 3d. May 1802
    I have procured from Smithfield and have forwarded to Norfolk to be sent on to Mr. Barnes as before, six Casks containing six dozen hams; which from the character given them I hope may prove as good, as perhaps even Colo. Macons.

The groceries, including a cask of wine from Norfolk, arrived a few days since; and were to day forwarded on to Milton, with 80 Bundles of nail-rod, & 8 of hoop-iron.　　　The linen I am sorry to inform you I did not send; as there is not a good piece in this pitiful City. I concluded it was better for you to wait a while than to have such as you are not accustom'd to wear.

I am Dear Sir Your Very humble servt.　　　Geo. Jefferson

RC (MHi); at foot of text: "Thos. Jefferson esqr."; endorsed by TJ as received 13 May and so recorded in SJL; also endorsed by TJ: "hams. groceries. wines. nail rod. linen."

From James Mease

Sir　　　　　　　　　　　　　　　　　　Philadelphia May 3d. 1802

It is with much diffidence that I take the liberty to recommend my father Mr. John Mease to you; for any office which you may think his talents entitle him to.—As you are entirely unacquainted with him I beg leave to state a few particulars of his history.

He is a native of Ireland, and arrived here in the year 1758.—Ten years after, he commenced with a handsome Capital, to do business for himself, and continued in trade until the war commenced. He then joined the volunteer Corps of Horse in this City, and remained in it, during the whole war. when the British took possession of this City, he fled with other patriots, leaving his house as he had inhabited it; and extensive stores filled with W: India produce. His loss amounted in goods alone to £10,000—

After the peace he again entered into trade, and continued engaged therein until about the year 1790. He then accepted of some local appointments from our City Corporation, and when the office of Commissioner of the Revenue was instituted, Mr Coxe appointed him one of his Clerks.—He continued in the office until Mr Miller succeeded Mr Coxe, when he was removed, under the specious pretext of œconomy, but a relation of Mr Miller's was soon after chosen to fill his place and he was then informed by Mr Rogers one of the Clerks, that his crime was having *voted for* the *Republican electors ticket*. The fact was as stated. He had never concealed his political sentiments, and previously to the election in 1796 he had declared his intentions in the office, to vote as he did.—These facts can be fully authenticated.—He left the office with a cheerful heart, consoling himself that a change would take place in our administration, and Thank God it has at last been effected.

My father is at present employed as one of the Admiralty Survey-ors, but as I know his talents are adapted to a discharge of the duties of a more extensive sphere, I should be very happy to see him in a sta-tion in which he could render his Country greater services than he at present is permitted to perform. He is a complete merchant, very ac-tive in both body and mind, and devoted to business. Mr Coxe will be able to give some information respecting his talents, but my friend Dr Rush will furnish it most minutely if required.

I should have taken the liberty to write to you upon the subject of my father some months since, could I have obtained his permission, but upon my expressing a wish to address you in his favour he ex-pressly forbid Me, and it was not until lately, that he would permit the Communication I at present trouble you with.

I have now only to beg pardon for the length of my epistle, and to subscribe myself with every sentiment of respect your very humble Servt   JAMES MEASE

RC (DNA: RG 59, LAR); at foot of text: "The President of the U States"; en-dorsed by TJ as received 13 May and "his father to office" and so recorded in SJL.

JOHN MEASE, a Revolutionary War veteran and Philadelphia shipping mer-chant, was one of five appointed by Tench Coxe to run the newly established office of the commissioner of the revenue in 1792.

His annual salary as a clerk was $400. Mease served as one of the ADMIRALTY SURVEYORS of the port for 30 years (Cooke, *Coxe*, 242, 246-7; Syrett, *Hamil-ton*, 13:448-9; Washington, *Papers, Pres. Ser.*, 7:537-8; George Valentine Massey, II, *The Mitchells and Days of Philadelphia with Their Kin* [New York, 1968], 113-14; ANB, s.v. "Mease, James").

To Thomas Mann Randolph

DEAR SIR   Washington May 3. 1802

This will be handed you by mr Milledge who takes the route by Edgehill on purpose to give you information on the subject of Geor-gia. mr Clarke, a son of Genl. Clarke, of that state is with him. he is a sensible young man & has been studying the law here some time under John Thompson Mason. having before mentioned these gen-tlemen in my letters, nothing more need be added. I wrote to you by yesterday's post and mentioned that I should be two or three days after these gentlemen, and consequently with you on Saturday or Sunday. health and affectionate regard to you all

TH: JEFFERSON

PrC (MHi); at foot of text: "T M Randolph"; endorsed by TJ in ink on verso. Recorded in SJL with notation "by mr Milledge."

To the Senate

GENTLEMEN OF THE SENATE

I nominate John Heard of New Jersey to be Collector of the port of Perth Amboy vice Daniel March deceased.   TH: JEFFERSON
May 3. 1802.

RC (DNA: RG 46, EPEN, 7th Cong., 1st sess.); endorsed by a Senate clerk. PrC (DLC). Recorded in SJL with notation "nomn of Heard."

Meriwether Lewis delivered TJ's message to the Senate on 3 May, the last day of the session. The Senate immediately confirmed Heard's appointment (JEP, 1:424-5).

From David Austin

RESPECTED SIR   Washington May 4th 1802.

On my returning to New England it would add greatly to the Obligations I am already under to the President, if he would favor me with a small token of his attention so far as relates to an appointment to the Office of Collector for the Port of New London in the State of Connecticutt. The place is but a very short distance from the residence of my father in Law & of Mrs Austin who is at present, with her father. The family is opulent & distinguished for their probity & punctuality. Mrs A. is a Candidate for perhaps 30,000 dolls. at her father's discease, who is a man of 80 years of age, & she is unwilling to leave the neighborhood of her parentage & patrimony. On this account my residence at any distance from her is rendered inconvenient. It would greatly accelerate the harmony of public opinion, in relation to the present state of politicks if the President could favor me with this office. Through the State of Connecticutt, & especially in the Counties contiguous to New London my family, friends & Class-mates in the professional department are thickly settled.

I trust that few things could be done which would cause a greater falling off, in relation to the opposition to Government, made in those parts, than this very act. And the President may be assured that the weight of influence, I have in those parts would prove, in comparison with the influence of the person now holding the Office as a seventy four to a batteau.

Besides, as this Gentleman has held the Office from its institution, there can be nothing repugnant to the principles of reciprocating benefits, in the change.

I would thank the Presid't for the favor; & Mr Granger will tell the

President, that no man has moved the principles of revolution, in the State of Connecticutt as I have done.

Wishing the President a prosperous Journey, by the Will of God, Subscribe with all esteem yr Obet. friend & Servt

D. AUSTIN

RC (DLC); addressed: "The President of the United States Washington"; endorsed by TJ as received 4 May and "to be Collector of New London" and so recorded in SJL.

FATHER IN LAW & OF MRS AUSTIN: Austin married Lydia Lathrop of Norwich, Connecticut, in 1783. She was the only daughter of Dr. Joshua Lathrop, a physician and successful businessman of Norwich. Austin's wife came into a substantial inheritance following the death of her father in 1807 (Dexter, *Yale*, 1:741-2; 4:91, 93).

PERSON NOW HOLDING THE OFFICE: Jedediah Huntington had served as collector at New London, Connecticut, since 1789 and continued in the office until 1815 (Prince, *Federalists*, 66-72).

To Mathew Carey

SIR   Washington May 4. 1802.

I have recieved your favor of April 24. and am duly impressed with the truths it contains. I am satisfied that truth & reason can maintain themselves, without the aid of coercion, if left free to defend themselves. but then they must defend themselves. eternal lies and sophisms on one side, and silence on the other, are too unequal. the public mind is neither well enough informed of all facts, nor strong enough, to decide rightly without the aid of developement on the side of defence as well as attack. no one paper has universal circulation. it is therefore interesting to institute others so as to fill the circulation in all parts. I have no doubt of the utility of multiplying papers of defence to a judicious extent. in my situation however[1] I cannot take a prominent part in any thing of that kind. I can only be a contributor in a just proportion, leaving to those less exposed to criticism, and whose conduct less affects the public cause to take an active part in instituting what is necessary. this consideration prevents my making the communication suggested in your letter. Accept my best wishes and respects.

TH: JEFFERSON

RC (PHi); at foot of text: "Mr. Matthew Cary"; endorsed as received 6 May. PrC (DLC); endorsed by TJ in ink on verso.

[1] Word interlined.

From Samuel Hanson

Dear Sir,   The Retreat, May 4th, 1802

My Friend, Mr. Carr, this moment informs me that you were so obliging as to make enquiry, on my account, respecting the supposed resignation of Mr. Wagner. That report was circulated in this neighbourhood—in consequence of information given to Mr. Saml. Carr by Mr. Henry Brown on Sunday last, who mentioned it as a certain fact. Mr. Brown being a Clerk in one of the offices, the authority was supposed to be good. Mr. Carr having mentioned a circumstance—the Sale of Mr. Wagner's furniture in a few days—which would seem to indicate either his resignation, or his intention of it, I take the liberty of sending up to ascertain the matter; and to request the favour of you to employ your good-offices with mr. Madison in obtaining the appointment for me.

Understanding that a knowledge of the French and Spanish Languages is necessary to the discharge of the office, I beg leave to state that I can translate the French with great facility; and that I will engage to acquire the Spanish, in the same degree, in the course of a few weeks. This promise, if I do not deceive myself, my previous acquaintance with the Latin & French Tongues will enable me to perform. I am sensible, Sir, that it will require all your indulgence to excuse the trouble which, directly and indirectly, I give you. My only apology is, the distressed situation of my family, consisting of a wife and Six helpless children.

With perfect respect and Esteem Dear Sir Yrs

S Hanson of Saml

RC (DLC); addressed: "The President of the United States By S. Hanson of Saml junr"; endorsed by TJ as received 4 May and so recorded in SJL.

On 21 June, TJ's nephew Dabney CARR, Jr., wrote to James Madison, recommending Hanson, an "acquaintance of long standing," but declined to vouch "whether he be competent to supply the place of Mr Wagner" (Madison, *Papers, Sec. of State Ser.*, 3:329).

SUPPOSED RESIGNATION OF MR. WAGNER: by late March, state department chief clerk Jacob Wagner had taken his physician's advice to move to Baltimore, where he hoped to alleviate a "lingering disorder" and to continue the duties of his office away from Washington. Both the *Gazette of the United States* and the *Philadelphia Gazette* reported on 23 Apr. that Wagner had resigned "in consequence of extreme ill health." On 30 Apr., Wagner informed Madison he needed to take a leave to recover from "the heavy oppression and gloom" under which he had been working. Madison refused to accept the resignation and observed that Wagner had brought on his ailments by too closely attending to his duties and should not "retire until his health was perfectly restored." Wagner did not return to his post until November 1802 (*Washington Federalist*, 12 May 1802; Madison, *Papers, Sec. of State Ser.*, 3:47-8, 89-90, 168).

For Hanson's DISTRESSED SITUATION after his removal as cashier of the Bank of Columbia, see Madison, *Papers, Sec. of*

State Ser., 3:200-1 and Vol. 35:42-7, 399-400.

To James Jackson

DEAR SIR   Washington May 4. 1802.

I recieved yesterday your favor of the 1st. inst. it is so essential to the public good, to the credit of the administration and of republicanism itself that the transaction of the public affairs be committed to the best men only, that when a charge is brought openly before the public against one by name whom I have appointed, I think it my duty to look into the fact and correct it if true, or have the public informed if it be false. your recommendation of mr Mitchell was sufficient to satisfy me when I saw the scandalous paragraph in the Federalist, that it was false and the offices he had held strengthened the testimony. the statement which I have seen in the Literary advertiser is sufficient to justify the appointment to the public, and therefore this matter may be considered as done. mr Putnam will of course feel the necessity of a decisive justification in his case. Accept assurances of my friendly esteem & high respect.   TH: JEFFERSON

PrC (DLC); at foot of text: "Genl Jackson."

LITERARY ADVERTISER: probably the

American Literary Advertiser. The issue with the justification of David Brydie Mitchell's appointment has not been found.

To Levi Lincoln

TH:J. TO THE ATTY GENL.   May 4. 1802.

The inclosed paper signed Claudius is so bold, direct & false in it's assertions respecting the clerks, that it ought really to be contradicted. would it not be worth while to ask of each head of department whether he *found* any republican clerk in his office & how many, and to state the fact, not naming the authority, but appealing to the notoriety of the fact. perhaps even the names as given in to Congress by the heads of departmts and printed[1] might be reprinted and a defiance to point out one of them as republican, except those newly appointed & who might be printed in Italics.—I am always clear that truth & reason can maintain their ground if free to defend themselves. but th[at] they must defend themselves. we are agreed in this necessity and that each must do his part. you are directly attacked by name in this paper, that the defence seems yours of right. health & happiness. I go tomorrow.

RC (MHi: Levi Lincoln Papers); torn at seal; addressed: "Levi Lincoln esq. Attorney Gen[eral]." Enclosure: see below.

The article SIGNED CLAUDIUS, which appeared in the *Washington Federalist* on 4 May, was taken from the *Connecticut Courant* and reprinted in many newspapers, including the *New-York Herald* on 3 Apr. Several months later, former Treasury secretary Oliver Wolcott was recognized as the author of the piece. "Claudius" charged that TJ had falsely accused the previous administration of intolerance. He cited Lincoln, in particular, as making false charges in the essays signed "A Farmer." Wolcott especially disagreed with Lincoln's assertion that in March 1801 there were about 100 clerks in the four principal government offices, all of them Federalists since no others were allowed. According to "Claudius," under the Adams administration "there never was an instance of a dismission on the ground of political opinion, or under circumstances which could afford a colour of justice for the accusation of intoler-ance" but under the present administration, "many an honest man has been ejected from office; his character questioned and his family reduced to distress, on the ground of this undefined offence." Wolcott called Lincoln, writing as "Farmer," guilty of "suppressing the truth and asserting a falsehood" (*Troy Gazette*, 15 Sep. 1802). For Lincoln's essays, see Vol. 35:305-6.

NAMES AS GIVEN IN TO CONGRESS: at the request of the House of Representatives, the department heads prepared statements naming the clerks in their respective departments and giving the compensation received by each during 1799, 1800, and 1801. Robert Smith and Henry Dearborn submitted their reports on 29 Mch., Madison on 30 Mch., and Gallatin on 8 Apr. All were printed (see Shaw-Shoemaker, Nos. 3304, 3311, 3326, 3329). For evidence supporting Lincoln's claims, see Cunningham, *Process of Government*, 174-5, 177-82, 328-32.

[1] Preceding two words interlined.

From Robert R. Livingston

DEAR SIR   Paris 4th. May 1802.

I am sorry so soon after my arrival here to trouble you with any thing that relates personally to myself, & which I fear will be not less painful to you, than it has been to me.

From Mr. Sumter's first entrance into my family I have treated him with all the attention in my power, I have (as far as he would permit me) introduced him wherever I visited myself, & have extended indulgencies to him in the management of his office, which perhaps my duty to the public would not Justify. I did not indeed ask him to lodge at my house, because, considering him as a young Gentleman of fortune, who would enter into Society, & not be perfectly at ease under the restraints of a private family, & because having my wife & Children with me, I wished to have some hours that I could pass with them unembarrassed by the presence of a Stranger; I however re-

quested him to lodge in the Vicinity & to dine with me; this arrangement appeared perfectly agreable to him & continued 'till his marriage, nor had I the smallest reason to believe that he was in any way[1]
dissatisfied 'till a few days before the date of his letter (No 1). I sent
a servant to him with my dispatches requesting him to take the servant with him, as they were pretty large, to see them delivered to
Madame Brogniaut & to know when she meant to go,[2] as I wished to
write farther, or at least not to leave the papers in her hands 'till she
was on the eve of departing. The reasons for these precautions are
obvious from the nature of the dispatches. Mr Sumter returned them
by the servant with this short answer "I won't go"—His own letter
will explain this transaction & to this I refer. He has not thought it
proper in his Second letter (No 4) to answer my questions relative to
the nature of the message that he thinks Justified this extreme disrespect. To You Sir, he may be more explicit.

Knowing how important it was to preserve harmony between persons so closely connected I determined to pass over this rude reply
without notice. I sent the dispatches to Madme. Brogniaut by Coll.
Livingston & received Mr. Sumter & his wife at dinner with my usual
attention, & transacted some business with him, in the office, without the slightest mention of what had passed. I then delivered him
the note (No 2) to copy being in answer to one (No 3) from Ct.
Cobentzel; And a letter from Govr. Monroe, in answer to one in
which he requests to get two swords, for officers to whom they were
voted by the Legislature—After retaining these, 24 hours, they were
returned with a refusal to copy them for reasons contained in his letter No 1. It was no longer possible for me to be silent.[3] I wrote him
the letter No 4, which produced the answer No. 5. and on the reex-
amination of Ct. Cobentzel's note, the farther answer No 6.—I make
no sort of comment Sir, upon any of these papers. all that I know relative to the Causes of his discontents, are contained in his letter; he
has not thought it proper to particularise them in his reply to mine. I
can only say that I have myself, as have all my family, treated him
with the utmost attention on every occasion, and particularly in some
so interesting to him, as not easily to be forgotten. We did not indeed
believe that he would remain long in France, because nothing in this
country ever appeared to please him; but we believed that when he
returned, it would be with Sentiments of friendship towards us.[4]—
You will see, Sir, how impossible it will be for me to continue to act,
with Mr. Sumter, longer than is absolutely necessary, to receive your
decision. If after reading his letters (to which alone I am content
to refer) you think his temper and talents promise advantages to his

Country from continuing him in the diplomatic line, I pray[5] that he may serve his apprentiship under some other person;[6] since it becomes necessary for me to say that I will only continue to act with him untill I am honored with your answer.[7] It is certain that if I had not had Gentlemen, who acted as private Secretaries, I should not without other aid than Mr. Sumter, have been able to perform, the duties of the office, which must always be very ill executed, by a man, who has no sources of information but his public Correspondence, or no aid but a Secretary, who splits hairs about the extent of his duties, who weighs in the nicest balance, what is public & what a private correspondence, & who treats his principal with rudeness, when he differs with him about the extent of his duties.—It may be proper to mention, that if as I venture to presume, I am upon Mr. Sumters recall to name my own Secretary; my choice will not fall upon connection of my own, 'tho it would certainly not disparage Mr. Sumter's talents or address to compare them with those of the Gentn. in my family. As this letter may be the subject of discussion, I deny myself the pleasure, of entering at present on any other subject—And pray You to believe that I am, Dear Sir, with sentiments of the highest esteem & respectful consideration,

Your Most Obt. Hum: Servt.   ROBT R LIVINGSTON

RC (DLC); in a clerk's hand, signed by Livingston; at foot of text: "The President of the United States"; endorsed by Livingston: "To the president of the United States"; endorsed by TJ as received 9 Feb. 1803 and so recorded in SJL. Dft (NHi: Robert R. Livingston Papers); dated 28 altered to 29 Apr. 1802. Enclosures: (1) Count Cobenzl to Livingston, Paris, 26 Apr., inquiring about Jean Baptiste Entrès, originally of Rothenburg, who has been a merchant in New York and whose relatives in Austria have had no news for about 20 years (Tr in DNA: RG 59, DD; in a clerk's hand, in French; probably the second dispatch of a series, with "No 2" at head of text and a similar notation by Livingston; endorsed); on 12 May 1803, Madison transmitted a copy of this letter to Edward Livingston as mayor of the city of New York (Madison, *Papers, Sec. of State Ser.*, 4:598). (2) Livingston to Cobenzl, 26 Apr., stating his suspicion that Entrès is long dead and his property dispersed; Livingston will, however, forward Cobenzl's inquiry to the mayor of New York (Tr in DLC; in a clerk's hand; endorsed by Livingston as No. 2). (3) Thomas Sumter, Jr., to Livingston, Paris, 27 Apr., explaining in response to a complaint from Livingston why he has not kept the legation office, which is in Livingston's house and to which Sumter currently holds the key, open on a regular basis; he asks that they reach agreement on the "nature and content" of his official duties, noting in particular that the collection and filing of newspapers "after they are dispersed about your house, cannot be my business"; referring to "the letter of the President, to my father, proposing the appointment" (Vol. 33:440-1), Sumter says that although the letter states that he would perform the duties of a private secretary, the president "certainly did not expect or intend, that the services of a Secretary of Legation, were to be dictated by the discretion of the Minister," as the president "could not have meant to offer me the situation of a drudge"; as for Livingston's wish that Sumter "record in a book, all your correspondence, for the use of future Legations," Sumter might agree to that practice "so far as the correspondence is official," but there is no evidence of a precedent for it among the papers of Livingston's predecessors; if Livingston were to consider "with what facility a Minister may increase & extend his correspondence, & that it is much more easy & agreable to write than to copy & recopy, you would perceive that no one man could keep pace with him, unless he submitted to be a perfect slave"; Sumter's refusal to copy letters that Livingston wrote to Monroe and to Cobenzl was to prevent "the increase to this kind of extra-official business"; Sumter says that his refusal to see to the delivery of the dispatches to Madame Brongniart was not because he considered it outside his duties "but on account of the manner in which the demand was made," declaring that "under the same circumstances, I should have acted in the same way to the President"; Sumter again asserts that TJ "could not have intended to offer me the place of a drudge"; he closes by saying "that whatever difference we may hold, in opinion, on this subject, it shall not diminish my zeal to serve the United States in my station, nor the deference which I owe to your rank and talents; nor yet, the friendship which I entertain for your & all your family" (Tr in DLC; in a clerk's hand; at head of text in Livingston's hand: "No. 1"). (4) Livingston to Sumter, 27 Apr., declaring that he has received Sumter's of this date "with equal surprise & pain"; that he had not known of Sumter's dissatisfaction until he received Sumter's "rude message" concerning the delivery of the dispatches; that the legation office needs to be open on a regular basis, and the time required of Sumter, as well as his responsibilities, must depend to some degree on circumstances as well as on Livingston's discretion; having two private secretaries to handle his personal correspondence, Livingston asks Sumter to state "what extra official business, I have ever even asked of you"; Livingston's understanding of Sumter's duties is that he will "copy all dispatches to the government & men in public characters," with "the Minister & not the secre-

tary being the sole judge of their propriety"; he will make duplicates and triplicates as necessary and see that the dispatches are delivered; he will keep an account of business transacted in the office and organize the newspapers; "A Secretary should also mingle in society particularly that of other Secretaries who are generally young men of rank; & rising into consequence, from whom much useful information may be collected beneficial to himself & of which he should enable his principal to avail himself"; the secretary should "do every act that in the opinion of the Minister the public interest may require not inconsistant with the character of a gentleman"; Sumter should have managed the upkeep of the office; Livingston himself has had to collect and organize the newspapers; regarding letterbooks, "I shall not Sir on this, or on any other occasion ask as a favor from the Secretary of Legation what I think it my duty to direct, but submitting your letter to the President, He will I presume give such orders as he thinks proper on the subject"; Livingston overlooked the "extraordinary disrespect" of Sumter's response concerning the delivery of the dispatches, "wishing to pass over what had happened as a little gust of passion"; Sumter's behavior "convinces me Sir of your wish to make a break between us"; the demands of the duties of the secretary's office have been slight, but "of this however the President who has seen my dispatches will judge"; Sumter should make his charges more specific: "Conscious of having upon every occasion treated you not only as a Gentleman for whose family I entertained the highest respect, but with peculiar delicacy & friendship arising from personal regard, I shall be anxious to learn those hidden causes of dissatisfaction, that I may unwarily have given you"; if Sumter wishes to resign, "surely Sir it will be more for your interest & honor to assign some domestic reasons for it than to seek a cause in an imaginary complt. against me"; Livingston returns to Sumter the letter from TJ, which contains nothing "to justify your construction of the duties of your office"; Livingston could in turn "shew you that the President writing on the subject of your appointment gives me the most explicit assurances that you would be ready to perform the duties of a private Secretary (which however I have never asked of you) & that he has known no instance in which a Secretary of Legation was not as perfectly pliant as a private Secretary, & that your instructions should be pointed on that subject" (Vol. 33:433; Vol. 34:62-4); if Madison did not give Sumter such explicit instructions, "yet I had hoped that the President had not neglected to give them to you verbally—whether you have followed them or not our respective letters will enable him to judge"; reciprocating Sumter's "professions of respect & personal friendship," Livingston states that the differences between them have put "such an end to that confidence which ought to subsist between a Minister & his Secretary as must separate us at no distant day"; he closes by asserting his interest in Sumter's "future pursuits & the pleasure it will afford me to learn that they are productive of honor & happiness to yourself your Country & your friends" (Tr in same; in a clerk's hand). (5) Sumter to Livingston, 30 Apr., asserting that "I am not at all frightened at your letter"; if their differences over his duties "must be decided either by your own despotic rules, or by an appeal to a higher authority," Sumter prefers "the latter, where I may expect to find Justice & delicacy mixed with discretion & legitimate power"; he regrets only "giving pain to ourselves & to Mr. Jefferson, who will doubtless be mortified" to learn that such appointments "will be always liable to be thwarted by the assumption of authority, where men in high stations conceive their power bounded in any direction, only by their own wills"; Livingston's construction of the secretary's duties puts Sumter "unconditionally at your discretion," whereas Sumter believes that he is "so much a free Agent as to Judge of & resist imposition"; Livingston regards having Sumter as secretary of legation "an imposition"; Sumter "shall make free to use the sentiments & temper which I think Justified by those which are displayed in such parts of your letter as are personal"; their correspondence will give TJ "the

details of your accusations and my defence—& you are also welcome to see all I shall write to him on this occasion"; Sumter will continue to perform his duties "with as much convenience to you as possible, without embracing the system of slavery, which you have prescribed for me"; in a postscript Sumter asks to see the note from Count Cobenzl to confirm for himself whether it is public or private in nature: "perhaps your promise to direct the enquiry to the Mayor of N York instead of the Sy. of State might have led me into the error" (Tr in same; in a clerk's hand; at head of text in Livingston's hand: "No 4"). (6) Sumter to Livingston, 1 May, a note returning with thanks the copy of Count Cobenzl's communication; Sumter had previously failed to notice the count's reference to an order from his court, but since Cobenzl did not use his own or Livingston's titles and Livingston expected to send the note to the mayor of New York rather than the United States government, Sumter still believes that "it partakes more of the character of a private letter" and that any ensuing correspondence between the mayor and Livingston "would certainly not have been official in my view of the thing"; pursuit of the Entrès matter is unlikely to produce results "unless it be to fulfil your idea of the measure of the duty of a Secretary" (Tr in same; in a clerk's hand; endorsed by Livingston and labeled by him "No 6"). (7) Sumter to Livingston, 6 May, stating that he has heard from Fulwar Skipwith about a conversation between Skipwith and Livingston concerning Livingston's "present disposition" concerning the rift between them, and "as you have given the opening, I shall willingly advance to the ground of harmony on which we stood before"; without either of them giving up his own view of the duties of the secretary of legation, "we may accommodate the thing in practice for a short time, as I shall desire my dismission by the first opportunity"; his resignation will be on the basis that "the appointment is not what I expected it to be; it need not be known that any cause of discontent had arisen between us"; he will open the legation office regularly in the afternoon and will assist other times if the business of the office requires it and he is available; he does this partly "from a respect to the feelings of Mr. Jefferson, who I have no doubt intended to give to each of us in due proportion a mark of his confidence & friendship"; perhaps this "temporary arrangement" will prove "that we can forego our private feelings & our sentiments in favor of what is due to public harmony"; he hopes that he and his wife "will remain on the same footing also with your family as heretofore" (Tr in same; in a clerk's hand, with a note by Livingston regarding underlining in the transcription; endorsed by Livingston and labeled by him "No 1"). (8) Livingston to Sumter, 6 May, stating that "I embrace with pleasure the expedient you propose" to keep the differences between them from widening or "becoming a source of uneasiness to the President or our friends"; Livingston and his family will continue to give "our sentiments of esteem" to Sumter's wife (Tr in same; in a clerk's hand; Livingston added his signature, endorsed the letter, and labeled it "No 2"). Enclosed in Livingston to TJ, 28 Oct. 1802.

'TILL HIS MARRIAGE: Thomas Sumter, Jr., married Nathalie Delage de Volude in March 1802 (S.C. Biographical Directory, House of Representatives, 4:547; Vol. 35:292n).

MADAME BROGNIAUT: Louise d'Egremont Brongniart was the mother of Louis André Pichon's wife, Émilie Brongniart Pichon. Madame Brongniart, whose husband was a prominent architect, visited her daughter in Washington, D.C., in 1802 (Louis de Launay, Une grande famille de savants: Les Brongniart [Paris, 1940], 19, 22; Tulard, Dictionnaire Napoléon, 304-5; Vol. 32:430, 431n; TJ to Livingston, 10 Oct. 1802).

COLL. LIVINGSTON: Livingston's son-in-law, Robert L. Livingston, who was married to Livingston's younger daughter, Margaret Maria. Livingston's older daughter, Elizabeth, was also married to a member of the extended family, Edward Philip Livingston. Both daughters and their husbands had accompanied Livingston and his wife, Mary Stevens

Livingston, to France (George Dangerfield, Chancellor Robert R. Livingston of New York, 1746-1813 [New York, 1960], 50, 281-2, 309, 363, 380-1, 386; Vol. 35:63-4).

CT. COBENTZEL: Count Philipp (or Jean Philippe) Cobenzl, the Austrian minister to France. His cousin, Count Ludwig (Louis) Cobenzl, was vice chancellor for foreign affairs for Austria (Tulard, Dictionnaire Napoléon, 427; Karl A. Roider, Jr., Baron Thugut and Austria's Response to the French Revolution [Princeton, 1987], 97; Karl A. Roider, Jr., "The Habsburg Foreign Ministry and Political Reform, 1801-1805," Central European History, 22 [1989], 165).

Livingston wrote to JAMES MONROE on 27 Apr. about the TWO SWORDS and other matters, including Louisiana and affairs in France. Monroe had requested Livingston's assistance in obtaining the swords in a letter of 15 Dec. 1801 (Daniel Preston, A Comprehensive Catalogue of the Correspondence and Papers of James Monroe, 2 vols. [Westport, Conn., 2001], 1:115-16, 123).

AS THIS LETTER MAY BE THE SUBJECT OF DISCUSSION: after reaching an accommodation with Sumter on 6 May (Enclosures 7 and 8 above), Livingston refrained from sending this letter to TJ. In a letter to Madison on 12 May, Livingston noted simply that Sumter had "determined to resign for reasons which I presume he will explain to the president." On 18 May, Sumter wrote to Madison requesting the president's leave to resign from "an appointment which I find different from what I expected it to be." Madison replied in August, accepting the resignation, but that communication has not been found and perhaps did not reach Sumter. In his letter to Madison on 12 May, Livingston asserted that if he were allowed to name Sumter's replacement he would "make no appointment in my own family nor any which the president shd not fully approve." In October 1802, Madison informed Livingston that the president had received Sumter's resignation and "allows you to appoint a private Secretary." That month, before he received that authorization, Livingston wrote to TJ that Sumter, who had not received a response to his resignation, still considered himself secretary of legation and had again refused to copy correspondence that he did not consider to be official in nature. That second rupture with Sumter prompted Livingston to send the above letter and its enclosures to TJ, who received them early in February 1803 (Madison, *Papers, Sec. of State Ser.*, 3:220, 228, 498, 568; 4:25, 170-3; Livingston to TJ, 28 Oct. 1802; TJ to Livingston, 3 Feb. 1803).

¹ MS: "was." Dft: "way."
² Dft: "when she proposed to sail."
³ Here in Dft Livingston canceled "but I had determined to write to him in such a style as would enable him with honor to retract."

⁴ Dft: "towards me & now <*in this I have been cruelly disappointed>*."
⁵ Dft: "beg."
⁶ Dft: "master."
⁷ Here in Dft Livingston wrote: "I am thoroughly satisfied that the endeavour to make diplomatic characters by chusing secretaries of Legation from among the young men of fortune or connection from whom they expect support at home and rendering them independant of their principal,—will I fear be found ineffectual I am sorry that my own experience shd. have evinced this truth & I shall be very unwilling to have another experiement made at my expence."

From Robert Smith

SIR!   Nav Dep 4 May 1802

Mr. John R Leaycraft of New York, & Mr. Drury M. Allen of Buckingham County, Virginia, have been strongly recommended for Midshipmen in the Navy—

I therefore do myself the honor to enclose Warrants for them, wc. require your signature, should you concur in their appointment—

I have the honor to be, most respectfully, Sir, Your ob servt.

RT SMITH

RC (DLC); in a clerk's hand, signed by Smith; at foot of text: "Prest. United States"; endorsed by TJ as received from the Navy Department on 4 May and "Midshipmen" and so recorded in SJL. FC (Lb in DNA: RG 45, LSP).

From John Strode

WORTHY SIR   Culpeper 4 May 1802

If unhappily for me I am destined to absence as you pass my humble dwelling, pray let not that make any differance with you, or those that are with you. but honor it once more I humbly intreat You with Your presence for One Night. My Little Daughter and every One at the place will be all Obedience & respect   With all due regard

I am Sir Yr. most Obdt   JOHN STRODE

RC (MHi); at foot of text: "Thomas Jefferson Esqr"; endorsed by TJ as received 6 May and so recorded in SJL.

As he often did on his trips to and from Monticello, TJ spent a NIGHT at Strode's home, recording a payment of 75 cents for "Strode's vales" on 7 May. He also recorded a payment to Strode during his return to Washington later that month (MB, 2:1072-3; Vol. 33:315, 445).

From David Austin

SIR.   New York May 5th AD 1802

At the period of my departure from Washington, in the zeal of circumstances I dropped to the President, a letter containing a statement, wh if memory serves, needs to be corrected.

The expressions convey an idea, that there is something ecclesiastical, attached to the Chair of the United States. The President will scarcly believe this to be an accurate statement; and in his own declaration, that those things must remain to such means or instruments as Providence might employ, seemed, already, correct upon the subject.—

I wish thus delicately to toutch this Article, as I am sensible the matter has appeared masked with features, not fully decyphered. The Most High is a glorious sovereign; & moves gloriously uncontrouled. He giveth not account of his designs, fully unto any: and sometimes for a testimony unto others, hath caused his servants to be brought in bands, before the rulers of the people.

With every suitable acknowt for the aid shewn, & the civilities expressed,

subscribe, with all defference,   DAVID AUSTIN

P.S. I am at this moment, about to embark for Norwich, Connecticutt.—

RC (DLC); at head of text: "Th: Jefferson P.U.S."; endorsed by TJ as received 7 June and so recorded in SJL.

A LETTER: Austin probably refers to his letter to TJ of 26 Apr.

To Pierre Samuel Du Pont
de Nemours

DEAR SIR   Washington May 5. 1802.

I am this moment setting out for Monticello, yet the reciept of your favor of Apr. 20. (for 30.) obliges me to scribble a line to explain some ideas which seem not to have impressed you exactly as they exist in my mind. nothing can be farther from my intention than that the observations I made should be considered as menaces. Men will act from their interests. I meant to suggest what might appear to be the interests of this country should France possess herself of the only outlet we shall have for half our productions; and that the persons in authority at that time might think it necessary to pursue what would be deemed their interest. it is as if I foresaw a storm tomorrow and advised my friend not to embark on the ocean to-day. my foreseeing it, does not make me the cause of it, nor can[1] my admonition be a threat, the storm not being produced by my will. it is in truth our friendship for France which renders us so uneasy at seeing her take a position which must bring us into collision. we had counted on her as a friend under all circumstances, because according to our present relations we can never have cause of dissension. but she is now to place herself in that precise point where the most frequent causes of irritation will arise.—be assured that your idea that we think of the conquest of Louisiana, is not that of a single reasonable and reflecting man in the US. that the day may come, when it would be thought of, is possible. but it is a very distant one: and at present we should consider an enlargement of our territory beyond the Missisipi to be almost as great a misfortune as a contraction of it on this side. we deprecate the step contemplated by France the more because it may hasten that day. we certainly wish the Missisipi through it's whole course to be the boundary & common property between us and whatever nation adjoins us. as to paying a price for the island of N. Orleans & the Floridas we are too poor to pay any sum which France would feel. we are in debt, and wish to pay our debts. however, there will be a considerable sum several millions[2] to be paid us by France under the late convention (we have already paid to her citizens what has been decided in their favor.) this money will be pressingly called for by the individuals to whom it is due. perhaps France in the present state of her finances might be embarrassed to make the paiment. perhaps we could undertake to pay our own citizens as the price of the cession of N. Orleans & Florida. but this is a hasty suggestion on my part, and which does not depend on my sole will. yet we could talk of it provisionally.—we are entirely sensible of the danger of putting ourselves so much in the power of England as the course hinted by me would do. it is one of the aggravations of the misfortune we should be thrown into on the change of friends. it would only be better than to have no friend. you think we should be as uneasy to obtain the free use of the St. Laurence as the Missisipi. not at all; that of the St. Laurence would not be worth a copper to us. the most direct channel for our NorthWestern commerce is down the Hudson. we would rather wish there was a dam across the St. Laurence: indeed nature makes one of ice the greater half of the year.—I must now depart, and therefore end my letter. the nature of the communications I have made to you, my friend, prove the unlimited confidence I repose in your dispositions towards this country as well as France: it is because you wish well to both, because I wish well to both, and believe the present affair highly interesting to both, that I consider you as capable, by your representations, of saving both. mr Livingston knows of my communications to you, and will freely consult with you on the subject. accept the assurances of my constant & affectionate esteem & respect.   TH: JEFFERSON

P.S. I have not[3] time to write more than three lines to mr Livingston. as I shewed you my letter to him, I pray you to shew him this to you. I shall therefore only say to him that I have asked this of you, to save me the necessity of further explanations to him which I have not now time to make. I pray you to deliver him the inclosed letter.

RC (DeGH); addressed: "M. Dupont de Nemours on board the Benjamin Franklin Philadelphia"; franked. Enclosure: TJ to Robert R. Livingston, 5 May.

YOUR FAVOR OF APR. 20. (FOR 30.): Du Pont de Nemours dated his letter 30 Apr., but without close examination the 3 might be read as a 2.

AS TO PAYING A PRICE: the fourth article of the Convention of 1800 required restoration of, or restitution for, captured property that had not been "definitively condemned" by the time of the signing of the convention, captures made before the exchange of ratifications, and anything condemned "contrary to the intent" of the convention. Congress had appropriated $318,000 to cover French claims that fell into those categories. A much more CONSIDERABLE SUM was prospectively due

from France to the United States, from seizures of American ships in the West Indies without proper condemnation by courts and because of belated action by the French Council of Prizes. France was not in a position to pay those claims, according to dispatches from Robert R. Livingston (Miller, *Treaties*, 2:459-62; Madison, *Papers, Sec. of State Ser.*, 2:142-3, 303-4, 359, 390, 422, 468n, 493, 494n; TJ to the House of Representatives, 12 Jan. 1802, and enclosures).

MUST NOW DEPART: TJ left Washington on Wednesday, 5 May, and reached Monticello on Saturday the 8th (MB, 2:1071-2).

[1] Word interlined in place of "is."
[2] Preceding two words interlined.
[3] Word interlined in place of "only."

To Albert Gallatin, Henry Dearborn, and Robert Smith

May 5. 1802.

Th: Jefferson asks the favor of the Secretary of the Treasury, Secretary at War & Secretary of the Navy to carry into execution the inclosed resolution of the H. of representatives of May 3. 1802. desiring a statement of expenditures from Jan. 1. 1797. by the Quarter Master Genl. the Navy agents, for the Contingencies of the Naval & Military establishments and the Navy contracts for timber & stores; each so far as the matter lies within their respective department.

RC (Wheaton J. Lane, Princeton, New Jersey, 1951); addressed in Meriwether Lewis's hand: "Robert Smith esquire. Secretary of the Navy"; endorsed by Smith. PrC (DLC). Enclosure: Resolution of the House of Representatives, 3 May, requesting the president to cause the proper officers to prepare statements, including a detailed account of the expenditures and "application of all public moneys," which passed through the quartermaster general's department from 1 Jan. 1797 to 31 Dec. 1801; a similar account of expenditures of the navy agents; an account of the moneys drawn out of the Treasury "for the contingencies of the Military and Naval Establishments" for the same period; and copies of contracts made by the Navy Department for the purchase of timber and stores, and the accounts of moneys paid under the contracts; all to be presented to the House during the first week of the ensuing session of Congress (JHR, 4:237).

Representatives Robert Williams, a Republican from North Carolina, and Thomas Morris, a Federalist from New York, were appointed to present the 3 May resolution to the president. TJ submitted the requested STATEMENT OF EXPENDITURES to Congress on 23 Dec. 1802 (JHR, 4:237, 257).

To John Langdon

MY DEAR FRIEND   Washington May 5. 1802.

I am this moment setting out on a short trip to Monticello, but must first congratulate you on the progress of republicanism in your state, proved by your coming so near to your competitor, and by the increased strength in the legislature. ça ira. let me at the same time ask you to recommend to me 4. persons to be commissioners of bankruptcy in Portsmouth, and if you have any other town of considerable commerce where bankruptcies will probably happen, recommend 4. others for that. it would be best to have 2. lawyers and 2 merchants in each, but 1. lawyer & 3. merchants may do. let them all be republicans. the sooner I hear from you the better. I have but a few minutes left and a thousand things to do in them. I must therefore conclude with assurances of my best affections and great respect.

TH: JEFFERSON

RC (NhPoS: John Langdon Papers); addressed: "John Langdon esquire Portsmouth N.H."; franked and postmarked. PrC (DLC).

The PROGRESS OF REPUBLICANISM in New Hampshire was exemplified by the state's recent contest for governor between Langdon and his COMPETITOR, John Taylor Gilman, the Federalist incumbent since 1794. Although Langdon was defeated, the Republican vote total increased by more than 3,500 from 1801, while Gilman's margin of victory declined from 5,649 in 1801 to just 1,624 in 1802. After unsuccessful campaigns in 1803 and 1804, Langdon finally defeated Gilman in 1805 to become New Hampshire's first Republican governor (Hosea B. Carter, comp. and ed., *The New Hampshire Manual for the General Court, With*

Complete Official Succession, 1680-1891 [Concord, 1891], 151; Lynn Warren Turner, *The Ninth State: New Hampshire's Formative Years* [Chapel Hill, 1983], 144, 187).

ÇA IRA: it'll be fine.

ASK YOU TO RECOMMEND TO ME: Langdon was among TJ's most trusted advisors on appointments in New England. Most recently, in a letter to Gallatin dated 20 Nov. 1801, Langdon had recommended Massachusetts state senator Aaron Hill, describing him as "a man of Talents Integrity, and good Republican who has borne the heat and burthen of the day" (RC in DNA: RG 59, LAR, endorsed by TJ: "Hill Aaron to office"; Vol. 34:173n; Vol. 35:601, 675n). Hill would be appointed postmaster at Boston late in TJ's administration (Stets, *Postmasters*, 145).

To Robert R. Livingston

DEAR SIR   Washington May 5. 1802.

I am within a few minutes of setting out on a short visit to Monticello, and must therefore be very short. 20 years of intimate acquaintance with M. Dupont de Nemours has given me an unlimited confidence in him. his dispositions in favor of this country as well as France are unquestionable, and his talents so well known that I presume his opinions will have great weight with the French government. I thought therefore I could not do better than to impress him with all the consequences of the measure which was the subject of my letter of Apr. 18. to you, nor impress him with a sense of the extent of my confidence in him more than by permitting him to read that letter which I did. by his answer I found he recieved false impressions of the scope of the letter. I have written[1] him therefore an explanatory one this moment, and being much hurried I have not time to copy it for you, but have desired him to communicate it to you. I must pray you therefore to excuse this abridgment of labor, which the moment has forced on me. I have got further into this matter than I meant

[421]

when I began my letter of Apr. 18. not having deliberately intended to volunteer so far into the field of the Secretary of state, who will go on with the subject hereafter as heretofore. Accept assurances of my constant friendship & respect. TH: JEFFERSON

RC (NNMus); addressed: "Robert R. Livingston M.P. of the US. Paris"; endorsed by Livingston with notation "private." PrC (DLC). Enclosed in TJ to Pierre Samuel Du Pont de Nemours, 5 May.

AN EXPLANATORY ONE: TJ's letter of this date to Du Pont de Nemours.

[1] TJ first wrote "I wrote" before altering the phrase to read as above.

To James Madison

TH:J. TO J. MADISON   May 5. 1802.

I think it is dean Swift who says that a present should[1] consist of something of little value, & which yet cannot be bought for money. I send you one strictly under both conditions. the drawing was made by Kosciusko for his own use, and the engraving also I believe. he sent me four copies, the only ones which have come to America. the others I give to my family, and ask yourself & mrs Madison to accept of the one now sent.

RC (privately owned, Philadelphia, 1999). PrC (DLC).

For an earlier paraphrase of Jonathan SWIFT by TJ, see Vol. 36:202.

For the drawing MADE BY KOSCIUSKO, see Charles Le Brun to TJ, 10 Mch.

[1] TJ first wrote "that only a present which could" before altering the passage to read as above.

From Robert Patton

Post office Philada 5th May 1802

Mr. Patton presents his compliments to the President of the United States & begs leave to inform him that, he has received his note, enclosing a letter for Mr. Dupont, which shall be delivered immediately on his arrival in this City.

RC (DLC); endorsed by TJ as received 13 May and so recorded in SJL with notation "Patten PostM Phila."

TJ's NOTE to Patton has not been found but it enclosed TJ to Pierre Samuel Du Pont de Nemours, 3 May.

To Charles Willson Peale

DEAR SIR   Washington May 5. 1802.

I am this moment setting out on a short visit to Monticello, but a thought coming into my head which may be useful to your son who is carrying the Mammoth to Europe, I take time to hint it to you. my knolege of the scene he will be on enables me to suggest what might not occur to him a stranger. when in a great city, he will find persons of every degree of wealth. to jumble these all into a room together I know from experience is very painful to the decent part of them, who would be glad to see a thing often, & would not regard paying every time but that they[1] revolt at being mixed with pickpockets, chimney sweeps &c. set three different divisions of the day therefore at three different prices, selecting for the highest when the beau-monde can most conveniently attend; the 2d. price when merchants and respectable citizens, have most leisure; & the residue for the lower descriptions. a few attending at the highest price will countervail many of the lowest and be more agreeable to themselves & to him. I hope and believe you will make a fortune by the exhibition of that one, and that when tired of shewing it you may sell it there for another fortune. no body wishes it more sincerely than I do. accept my assurances of this and of my great esteem.   TH: JEFFERSON

RC (TxU); at foot of text: "C. W. Peale esq." PrC (DLC).

CARRYING THE MAMMOTH TO EUROPE: Rembrandt Peale and his younger brother Rubens had mounted a mastodon skeleton for public display in New York and intended to take the exhibition to Europe. They arrived in London with the skeleton in September (Paul Semonin, *American Monster: How the Nation's First Prehistoric Creature Became a Symbol of National Identity* [New York, 2000], 330-3).

[1] TJ here canceled "cannot."

To John Smith

SIR   Washington May 5. 1802

I have to acknolege the reciept of your Latin grammar, by post for which I pray you to accept my thanks. my occupations will probably not permit me immediately to have the satisfaction which I have no doubt I shall derive from the perusal of it: but I am pleased with every effort to facilitate the acquisition of the Greek & Latin languages. I do not give into the modern doctrine that the time spent on those languages is time lost. they usually occupy a portion of life when the mind is not strong enough but for matters of memory. they have furnished us with the only models of rational, correct, and chaste composition: no other antient nation having left, nor any modern one (not conversant with these models) having produced, any works of that character. the luxury too of reading them in their original language is one for which I feel more thankful to those to whom I owe it than for any of the things which the world usually calls luxuries. under these impressions I see with pleasure the taste for these languages cultivated, and ascribe to you the merit you may justly claim in this work. permit me to join here my thanks for the other volume also, and to tender you my best wishes and respects.

TH: JEFFERSON

PrC (DLC); at foot of text: "Mr. John Smith. Dartmouth."

John Smith (1752-1809) was a tutor and professor of Latin, Greek, and Hebrew at Dartmouth College from 1778 until 1809. He was also librarian for 30 years, trustee, and minister of College Church in Hanover, New Hampshire. The first edition of his *Newhampshire Latin Grammar: Comprehending All the Necessary Rules in Orthography, Etymology, Syntax, and Prosody; with Explanatory and Critical Notes, and an Appendix*, was published in Boston in 1802 (*Dartmouth Gazette*, 30 Jan. 1802;

Baxter Perry Smith, *The History of Dartmouth College* [Boston, 1878], 211-17, 452-3; Sowerby, No. 4788).

THE OTHER VOLUME: Smith may have sent TJ a copy of one of his earlier published sermons, *The Duty, Advantages, and Pleasure of Public Worship, Illustrated in a Sermon Preached at the Dedication of the Meeting-House, in the Vicinity of Dartmouth College, December 13, 1795* (Hanover, N.H., 1795; Evans, No. 29528) or *A Sermon Preached in Randolph, June 3, 1801, at the Ordination of the Rev. Mr. Tilton Eastman* (Randolph, Vt., 1801; Shaw-Shoemaker, No. 1333).

From John Churchman

HONOURED PRESIDENT   Boston May 7th. 1802

I take the Liberty to send herewith a copy of an improved Variation Chart, hoping it will be received as a token of Respect, together with a Sheet of Letter Press as published in the third Edition of the Magnetic Atlas, It contains Actual observations by which the Variation has been found at Sea—

The Chart has had of late a very extensive Circulation, particularly in these Eastern States, & many experienced Navigators have given ample testimony of its usefulness—

One favour I have to ask which I suppose no one else can Grant, I hope to be pardoned for this Liberty, I have several times written to that eminent Astronomer Andrew Ellicott Esqr. hoping he would favour me with his observations of the Latitude Longitude & Variation of the compass at the following places, viz The Junction of the

Ohio & Missisipi, the Natches & New Orleans & the several places of the Line of demarkation South of Georgia the East end of it would be important. I believe its in the Parallel of 31° North I understand by the Present Secretary of State that he has also written to the said Astronomer on my behalf, without success no Doubt the Personage to whom I now address myself either as President of the United States, or of the Philosophical Society (who have manifested their Discernment in the Election of their President) may be able to procure them, if not I dont know who else to apply to, I am now about to set out on a Voyage to St. Petersbourg in Russia, & if these observations can be transmitted to me there, to the care of George Steen Esqr. at St. Petersbourg, it will give me pleasure for I am willing to acknowledge the Benefit to the Gentleman who made the observations.

Some years ago I believe John Russell Esqr. now somewhere about the City of Washington, was appointed commercial agent at St. Petersbourg, I understand he was not received because he represented a Republican Government, The commerce between that Country & America has lately increased, they say about seventy Sail of American Ships sailed to Petersbourg last Summer, I know not whether a commercial Agent will be thought necessary or not, at the present time, should the President think proper to lay any commands upon me, I will endeavour to obey them, with faithfulness, particularly in making some enquiry, & whether Such a Commercial Agent would not be likely to be acknowledged at this time.

With the greatest sentiments of Respect I hope to be permitted to make an offering of my service & esteem

JOHN CHURCHMAN—

RC (DLC); addressed: "The President of the United States"; endorsed by TJ as received 18 July and so recorded in SJL. Enclosures not found, but see below.

Churchman's VARIATION CHART, which contained two maps, and the third edition of his MAGNETIC ATLAS were both published in 1800. In 1797, TJ received an earlier edition of Churchman's book, which he passed along to the American Philosophical Society (Ben A. Smith and James W. Vining, *American Geographers, 1743-1812: A Bio-Bibliographical Guide* [Westport, Conn., 2003], 34-5; John Churchman, *The Magnetic Atlas, or Variation Charts of the Whole Terraqueous Globe*, 3d ed. [New York, 1800]; Vol. 28:364, 365n).

James Madison had written to ANDREW ELLICOTT on 18 Nov. 1801, asking him to provide Churchman with the data from the observations made when Ellicott surveyed the southern boundary of the United States. Ellicott replied to Madison six days later, saying that he would prepare the information in his "first leisure hour," even though Churchman's theories concerning magnetic variation "cannot be rendered useful, even admitting the principles to be correct" (Madison, *Papers, Sec. of State Ser.*, 2:249-50, 268-9).

ST. PETERSBOURG IN RUSSIA: Churchman began sending copies of his publications to the Russian Academy of Science in the early 1790s. Earlier, the academy's director, Princess Ekaterina Romanovna Dashkova, had put Benjamin Franklin up for membership, and Franklin returned the favor by seeing to the election of the princess as the first female member of the American Philosophical Society. In 1795, on Dashkova's initiative, Churchman became the second American elected to the Russian academy (Eufrosina Dvoichencko-Markov, "The American Philosophical Society and Early Russian-American Relations," APS, *Proceedings*, 94 [1950], 549, 554-8; Nina N. Bashkina and others, eds., *The United States and Russia: The Beginning of Relations, 1765-1815* [Washington, D.C., 1980], 267-8, 290-1; Leonard W. Labaree and others, eds., *The Papers of Benjamin Franklin*, 39 vols. to date [1959-], 34:196n).

When John Miller RUSSELL, a Boston merchant, presented a commission as United States consul at St. Petersburg in 1795, the Empress Catherine refused to accept his credentials because the United States and Russia did not have a treaty establishing direct relations (Bashkina, *United States and Russia*, 289-90, 291-2, 357; Madison, *Papers, Sec. of State Ser.*, 4:524; Vol. 32:3, 4n).

From Henry Dearborn

SIR,   War Department May 7. 1802

I this day recd. a letter from Mr. Holt storekeeper at New London, informing me there is reason to believe the Negroes in that quarter have it in contemplation to possess themselves of the Arms at that place, notwithstanding the small guard which is station'd there— considering the expence of a larger guard and a Storekeeper, and the impropriety of having our public arms kept at a place not contemplated as a permanent magazine, I am of opinion that an immediate removal of the Arms and powder now at New London to Harpers ferry is advisable, and if you approve of the measure I will send a suitable person to superintend the removal in a manner the least expensive which I presume will be by land to James River and then down the River to Richmond, and from thence by water to Georgetown and then up the River to Harpers ferry—The relative expence of transportation in the foregoing manner, or direct by land cannot be sufficiently ascertained but by enquiries at Richmond and in the vicinity of New London—

I have the honor to be with sentiments of Esteem Your Obedt. Huml Servt   H. DEARBORN

RC (DLC); at foot of text: "The President of the United States"; endorsed by TJ as received from the War Department on 13 May and so recorded in SJL with notation "arms to be removd: from New London"; also endorsed by TJ: "arms at New London Virga." FC (Lb in DNA: RG 107, LSP).

NEGROES IN THAT QUARTER HAVE IT IN CONTEMPLATION: among the Virginia locales alarmed by alleged slave insurrection plots in 1802 was Campbell County, where the New London arsenal was located (Ammon, *Monroe*, 200).

From James Madison

Dear Sir   Washington May 7. 1802

Mr. Lear arrived here the day before[1] yesterday a few minutes after your departure. He confirms the information as to the imprisonment of Capt: Rodgers & Davidson. Inclosed is a copy of le Clerc's explanation on the subject, of my letter to Pichon with his answer, and of a letter to Mr. Livingston which I shall forward to Philada. this evening, that it may overtake the despatches already in the hands of Mr. Dupont. The other information given by Mr. Lear is that the state of things in St. Domingo augurs a protracted if not a doubtful warfare, that the ports abound, and superabound with every necessary, that money has lately arrived both from France & from the Havanna, that the irritations between the French & the Americans are occasioned by faults on both sides, and that there probably is a mixture of antirepublican venom in those of the French. From a confidential communication made to him, it appears that the idea in the Army is that Republicanism is exploded, that Monarchy must be forced, and that Buonaparte is the proper successor to the cashiered dynasty; but that it is the Army &c. and not the nation that wishes this revolution.

Mr. Smith is not yet returned from Baltimore Mr. Gallatin left us this morning. Genl. Deabourn will go for a few days to Philada. on monday or tuesday.

I inclose a recommendation of A Collector for Amboy, that in case you decide in your absence, all the candidates for that vacancy may be before you.

With the most respectful attachment I remain Yours

JAMES MADISON

RC (DLC); at head of text: "private"; endorsed by TJ as received from the State Department on 13 May and "Lear. Rogers. Davidson. Le Clerc. Pichon. Livingston" and so recorded in SJL. Enclosures: (1) Extract of letter from Victoire Emmanuel Leclerc to Tobias Lear, 25 Germinal Year 10 [15 Apr. 1802], justifying his imprisonment of John Rodgers and William Davidson, accusing Rodgers of making angry remarks and spreading false reports about the French in order to promote his own speculations, while Davidson aroused Leclerc's suspicions because of the name he gave his vessel (PrC in same, in French; Madison, Pa-

pers, Sec. of State Ser., 3:195). (2) Madison to Louis André Pichon, 6 May 1802, protesting the arrest of Rodgers and Davidson and criticizing the grounds that Leclerc has claimed to justify his actions; Madison asks Pichon to "employ the weight of your interposition in accelerating the release of Capt. Rodgers and Mr. Davidson and repairing the wrongs they have suffered" (PrC in DLC, in a clerk's hand, signed by Madison; Madison, Papers, Sec. of State Ser., 3:190-1). (3) Pichon to Madison, Georgetown, 7 May 1802, assuring the secretary of state that he will write to Leclerc on the subject of the arrests and expressing confidence that the French general will quickly make any reparations due to the United States once he realizes the consequences of his actions (PrC in DLC, in French; Madison, *Papers, Sec. of State Ser.*, 3:199). (4) Madison to Robert R. Livingston, 7 May 1802, enclosing extracts of the correspondence between Tobias Lear and Leclerc on the subject of the arrests, as well as a copy of Madison's 6 May letter to Pichon; Madison believes that the French government will not hesitate to "manifest on the occasion its respect for the character and friendship" of the United States, as well as its own commerce, and speedily afford "every reparation of which the case is susceptible"; Livingston is to adopt a similar tone on the subject in order to maintain the friendly relations between France and the United States; Lear has returned from Cap-Français, reports that the French administration of Saint-Domingue is "perfectly military," and doubts that they will be able to pacify the island; the commerce of the island has suffered by French "indiscretion" as well as "misconduct" by some Americans, but the ports at present "abound with every species of necessary supplies"; Madison will forward this letter to Pierre Samuel Du Pont de Nemours, who will carry dispatches to France (PrC in DLC; Madison, *Papers, Sec. of State Ser.*, 3:196-7). (5) John Halsted to Madison, Perth Amboy, 4 May 1802, applying for the position of collector at Perth Amboy, which became vacant at the death of Daniel Marsh; enclosing a recommendation to the president, acknowledging Halsted, an alderman of the city, as a "proper person" for the office of collector, signed by 34 subscribers, including Anthony Butler and Joseph Marsh who also signed a certificate, noting that when Halsted previously served as collector of the district, he conducted the office with "utmost Propriety," keeping the books "in the most correct and fair State" (RC in DNA: RG 59, LAR, endorsed by TJ: "Halsted John to mr Madison to be Collector of Perth Amboy"; JEP, 1:10, 12).

On 10 Apr., Victoire Emmanuel Leclerc informed Tobias LEAR that he had no authority to recognize him as general commercial agent of the United States in Saint-Domingue and that he was to cease immediately carrying out the functions of the office. The French general also accused Lear of discouraging American trade with the island and of acting "to excite differences" between the United States and France. Lear vehemently denied the allegations, but consented to the revocation of his duties as commercial agent. Lear left Cap-Français on 17 Apr. and arrived at Hampton Roads two weeks later (Madison, *Papers, Sec. of State Ser.*, 3:120-1, 147; Alexandria *Times; and District of Columbia Daily Advertiser*, 5 May 1802).

John RODGERS of the sloop *Nellie*, a former captain in the U.S. Navy, and William DAVIDSON of the *St. Domingo Packet* of Philadelphia were arrested and imprisoned by French authorities at Cap-Français on or about 12 Apr. The reasons given for the arrests were unclear, with Rodgers vaguely charged with making anti-French statements while Davidson was alleged to have engaged in trade with Toussaint-Louverture and placed a figurehead of the revolutionary on the bow of his vessel. The two men were released near the end of April and ordered never to return to the island "under pain of Death" (Madison, *Papers, Sec. of State Ser.*, 3:147, 196n, 270-2; Tansill, *Caribbean Diplomacy*, 92-6; John H. Schroeder, *Commodore John Rodgers, Paragon of the Early American Navy* [Gainesville, Fla., 2006], 24-6; Vol. 33:340n; William Davidson to TJ, 10 June 1802).

[1] Preceding four words interlined.

To John Page

MY DEAR FRIEND   Monticello May 7. 1802

The operation which Congress has [performed] in the [...] the custom house officers [...] was expected. from that at Petersburg particularly they have taken only the salary of 250. D. which they have given to Richmond. consequently the emoluments will be as represented in the paper sent you, only deducting the 250. D. this I think will make it about 750. D. a year more than mr Gallatin then [expected]. on this view of the subject I cannot but again propose it to you, being unwilling you should not have the best place it will ever be in my power to dispose of in this state. I am not without hopes your son will give you his aid; or that you can find some other entirely trust-worthy. Colo. Byrd's misfortunes probably proceeded from a want of the power of self-denial: which your integrity will sufficiently guard against. I believe he was also too easy in his credits to the merchants. on that subject, a rule being laid down by you, & inflexibly persevered in, they will arrange themselves to it without difficulty, as they do in their transactions with the banks. this attention and keeping yourself the key of the strong box will effectually guard against the possibility of loss. take the subject therefore my friend once more into consideration, and let me know your final determination, keeping now as before, inviolably secret that anything is contemplated, until we make it public. be so good as to present my respects to mrs Page, and to be assured yourself of my affection[ate &] constant attachment. I am here only for a fortnight.   TH: JEFFERSON

PrC (DLC); faint; at foot of text: "John Page"; endorsed by TJ in ink on verso.

For the act passed by CONGRESS in late April regarding the compensation of officers employed in the collection of duties on imports and tonnage, see TJ to Page, 20 Feb. 1802.

From Robert Smith

SIR!   Nav Dep 8th. May 1802

I do myself the honor to enclose Warrants for

Jno. N. Canon—Boatswain &

David Loring—Gunner—

Should you approve their appointment these Warrants will require your signature—

These gentlemen have been in the frigate President, her last cruise— & are highly recommended by Commdre. Dale & Capt. Barron.

I have the honor to be, with the greatest respect Sir, your most obt servt.   Rt Smith

RC (DLC); in a clerk's hand, signed by Smith; at foot of text: "President United States"; endorsed by TJ as received from the Navy Department on 17 May and so recorded in SJL with notation "nomns gunner. boatswain"; also endorsed by TJ: "nominations." FC (Lb in DNA: RG 45, LSP).

From Isaac Story

Most respected Sire,   Marblehead May 8. 1802

In my former letter I announced my intention of resigning my ministerial function, which has since been effected—in a most amicable manner with my people.—

I feel now desirous of some honorary appointment in the civil line; for it is my earnest wish to be of public benefit;[1] so long as I exist, however easy my outward circumstances may be.—

By reading the public prints, I find, in the judiciary bill, that the power of appointing Commissioners of Bankruptcy has been transferred from the District-Judges to your Excellency, which induces me to write on the subject.

An appointment of this kind would be very grateful to my feelings, as it would carry me back to Boston, the place of my Nativity, & where the chief of my children now reside, & appear fixed.—

Should you see fit to grant this my request, of appointing me a Commissioner of Bankruptcy, it will lay an obligation upon me, as lasting as life.—

Believe me to be with the homage of most profound respect, your devoted servant,   Isaac Story

P.S. You will find my Brother's name on the list of Representatives, that voted in favor of an address being presented to you by the Legislature of Massachusetts;—& also of the other member from this Town—

N.B—No Town in all New England is so united in republican principles & in favor of President Jefferson, as the Town of Marblehead.

This appears conspicuously in the votes of Governor: Mr. Gerry had 254 votes, & Mr. Strong only 24. And had the Fishermen been at home, Mr. Gerry would have had 150 more votes—

Hence should you put a mark of distinction on one of its Inhabitants, it would have a most pleasing Effect.—

Governor Clinton, when at Boston, made the same remark–He said that Marblehead was the most republican town, he knew of

RC (DNA: RG 59, LAR); addressed: "His Excellency, Thomas Jefferson Esqr. President of the united States; Washington"; franked and postmarked; endorsed by TJ as received 17 May and so recorded in SJL with notation "to be Commr. bkrptcy"; also endorsed by TJ: "Applies to be Commr. of bkrptcy Boston."

MY FORMER LETTER: Story to TJ, 11 Jan. 1802.

For the proposed ADDRESS to TJ by the LEGISLATURE OF MASSACHUSETTS, see Benjamin Hichborn to TJ, 25 Jan. 1802 and Levi Lincoln to TJ, 13 Feb. 1802. Among the legislators favoring the address were Representatives Elisha Story and Joshua Prentiss of Marblehead (Boston *Constitutional Telegraphe*, 6 Feb. 1802; *The Massachusetts Register and United States Calendar for the Year of Our Lord 1802, and Twenty-Sixth of American Independence* [Boston, 1801], 23 4).

[1] Word written at bottom of sheet and marked for insertion here.

From John Vaughan

DEAR SIR,   Philad: May 8. 1802

Your favor enclosing D. Griffith on Longitude was recieved, & the acknowledgement for it is now enclosed—we have been attentive of late to make the acknowledgement immediate.

We are very desirous of possessing, for the Society, Copies of the two enumerations or Census, & know not how to do it but through your kindness; I would further take the liberty of enquiring whether the Insertion of them in the 6th Vol, would not be interesting & important—

I enclose an Extract of a letter from Mr Dunbar to me which is interesting—he is like yourself a warm friend to the encouragement of Science & letters, it would be fortunate for the Country, if these ideas became more prevalent—

I have sent the Vaccine Virus to Mr Dunbar, & shall send more; but in order to multiply the chances of his recieving it, it would be an agreeable circumstance if your Physician could also send him a Supply by Post.—The Vaccine Innoculation gathers strength hourly, *no* respectable practitioner opposes it.

I remain with respect Your obt Servt   JN VAUGHAN

D Sir

Since writing above, a french pamphlet has fallen into my hands, relative to purifying water—It appears, that, James Smith, in the year 6. (Three years ago), exhibited the effect of his machinery for that purpose at Brest, but before he had disclosed the secret he disappeared—without disclosing *his*[1] Secret—

The *Commission*, which had seen his Experiments, reported favorably to the Minister—who in reply, Stated that 1780—The marine had adopted a Machine invented by Bouibe, destined to purify Ship Water—after a trial had been made in a long Voyage of the Ship Diademe 1783. Bouibe communicated his Secret & it was adopted; nevertheless, it soon fell into disuse, the reason unknown—

Year 6. The Minister directs a Comparison between *Bouibe's* plan *& Smiths*—Bouibe & Smith being both absent this order remained unexecuted until the year 8—when finding one of Bouibe's machines, & collectg all the information they could relative to Smith's, particularly from Thaumur (who had assisted Smith) & who had analysed the purified waters—the minister gave above Directions. Year 8. floreal. Lescallier, Membre de l'Institut, arrived at Brest with *Barry* (ancient Commissy of Marine)—they investigate, & at last succeed, in discovering, Smith's method, & try a Variety of experiments, which all prove Satisfactory—& decidedly give the preference to Smith's method, which was adopted by the French & Spaniards.

Take a Cilinderical Wooden Vessel (dimensions annexd) let the Inside be well burnt so as to be charred—6 Inches from the bottom have a *crossbarred moveable frame*, resting on small shoulder pieces, & supported in the middle by a Strong pin, calculated to bear a Considerable weight, cover this with a thick cloth or[2] woolen Strainer, put a layer of Oak Bark (Ross taken off) ground so as to be open & Stringy, & crossed—then have a second circle on which a Double hair cloth is to stretched—then fill in gently the mixture viz half the *Bulk*[3] of charcoal, pounded, & half *the bulk* of good limestone pounded, to within a foot of the Top, then 3 or 4 Inches Sand, then a Wooden Cover full of holes, & a Straining Cloth on that, on this pour the water in ten minutes, comes out purified—When the Limestone is ground, it is to be sifted, & washed in another sieve; it is to be washed until the Water comes off clear—In washing the Charcoal, there sinks to the bottom, an insoluble Sediment which is to be mixed with the washed charcoal–It is curious, that in Varying Experiments *Salt water* was put in & *fresh* water came out; they were on the point of sending an express to the Chief Consul—but after a time the water came from it brackish & afterwards Salt—The fresh water proved to be, the moisture adhering to the Substances, when the first water passed thro', which was driven out by the Salt Water pushing on— *Thus far I have got* in the book which is published by *Barry*; Smith is Since returned, obtained a Patent & again exhibited at Brest, & obtained the approbation of Institut &c

Young Mr Peale has not been able yet to pursue his Expt.; I find this Commission, concieve this apparatus will make salt water, *less*

Salt, but *not fresh;* The application of the Sponge, sand & charcoal, appears to be Smith's, who uses no lime, The above Description was by the Commission—This method far Superior to Lowits (of which an acct. in Bordley on rural affairs new Edition) because he put 24 drops Vitriolic acid with 1½ onz Charcoal—which is expensive & wants renewing—Smith is a Scotchman, obliged to fly on acct of his political sentiments—left Brest Suddenly, in consequence of an order for *all strangers*[4] to leave the Seaports—Smith in partnership with Cuchet, has established at Paris a Manufactory, of these Machines, one the size of a Tea Urn will give 10 quarts a day, are made ornamental & fitted to Vases, Urns &c—

If any books are Sent for to France for the Library—This pamphlet of Barry's should be procured—*Michaux* has published a Valuable work on American oaks with highly finished engravings—sold here for 10 Ds. bought by Dr Barton—

Makenzies Tour has appeared, printed here—

Forsyth on Gardening & fruit Trees is also in the Press, it contains his method of restoring Wood & bark to Wounded trees.—

Bouibe's method, was a filtering Stone, in which a layer of Sand or ground Stone was placed, & a machine for raising, breaking & giving air to the Water, the water lost its[5] bad taste of Every thing, except the taste of the Cask, & was never quite clear—Method less perfect & less Convenient, altho' the *Airing machine* could be *at will* converted into a machine for raising water 40 feet, & be used as a fire Engine— Expence *600 Dolls*—required 4 men, easily deranged & not easily repair'd—Smiths machine &c for a large Vessel would not Cost more than 12 or 15 Ds:

27 Inch Diamt
High 3 feet 7 Inch[6]

Circular board full of holes to let the water pass thro', & upon this a Cloth or Woolen Strainer, loosely laid on, that it may be easily clean'd.
Sand—
Limestone pounded, & Charcoal pounded, washed & mixed, in equal quantities by bulk
Bark (oak) or Tan

Vacancy six Inches—The Cock to be fixed close to the bottom, & close to the Xbarr'd frame, air holes, that the water may be impregnated with Atmospherical air

above machine fit for the largest men of War & will give 225 pints of water in an hour

RC (DLC); addressed: "Thomas Jefferson President of the United States Washington City"; Vaughan addressed the letter before he wrote the postscript; endorsed by TJ as received 13 May and so recorded in SJL. Enclosures: (1) Acknowledgment from the American Philosophical Society of the receipt of Dennis Griffith's letter to TJ of 8 Oct. 1801 (see below); not found; see Griffith to TJ, 10 July 1802. (2) William Dunbar to Vaughan, Natchez, 21 Mch. 1802, expressing his interest in the discoveries of fossil skeletons of large animals; noting that his own region is lacking in such fossil evidence, he describes the soil and strata; he laments the lack of government support for the collection of information relating to natural science and astronomy, declaring that "it would seem that the speculations of the generality of our politicians, are confined within the narrow Circle of the Customs & Excise, while literature is left to weep in the back ground"; he hopes that this will change with TJ as president, "& that under his auspices & protection, Arts, Sciences & Literature may take a flight, which will at length carry them as far beyond those of our European brethren, as we soar above them in the enjoyment of national liberty"; Dunbar continues to make meteorological observations; he suggests that Vaughan send "some fresh Vaccine virus" to him by post, in case the batch that Vaughan sent on 10 Dec., which Dunbar has not yet received, proves "impair'd in its Virtue" from the long trip by sea (Tr in DLC; in Vaughan's hand and endorsed by him).

YOUR FAVOR: TJ's most recent letter to Vaughan, on 14 Jan. 1802, said nothing about enclosing the communication from Dennis GRIFFITH to TJ of 8 Oct. about a possible means of finding LONGITUDE (Vol. 35:411-12). If TJ wrote a separate note to Vaughan transmitting Griffith's letter to the APS, the communication has not been found and he did not record it in SJL. ACKNOWLEDGEMENT: the society received Griffith's letter at a meeting on 7 May (APS, *Proceedings*, 22, pt. 3 [1884], 323).

6TH VOL: the sixth volume of APS *Transactions* did not appear until 1809 and did not include the census reports.

The FRENCH PAMPHLET was *Manière de bonifier parfaitement, avec facilité et économie, au moyen d'un appareil simple et solide, les mauvaises eaux à bord des vaisseaux de guerre et de commerce, ainsi que dans tous les pays; mise en usage dans la marine de l'État vers la fin de l'an 8*, printed in Paris in the Year 9 (1800-1). JAMES SMITH, who was from Glasgow, had learned about using charcoal for water filters in Scotland. He demonstrated his filter at Brest for a commission of the French naval ministry—the MARINE—in 1797, and the next year obtained a French patent. Smith did not intend to keep his device a secret, but he was absent from Brest, due to an *arrêté* by the Directory requiring foreigners to leave French ports, when the ministry sought to compare his method to one created by the Sieur Bouïbe and tested by the French navy in the 1780s. Citizen THAUMUR, a pharmacist, had been a member of the earlier commission and undertook a reconstruction of Smith's system. Daniel LESCALLIER, a career naval and colonial administrator, was a nonresident associate of the National Institute of France and the author of books and pamphlets on various maritime subjects. In 1810, the French government made Lescallier the French consul general for the United States. Étienne BARRY was a former commissary general of the navy and commissioner for the colonies (*Manière de bonifier*, 1-2, 5-12, 34-6, 72-4 126-7; M. N. Baker and Michael J. Taras, *The Quest for Pure Water*, 2d ed., 2 vols. [Denver, 1981], 1:38-9; Alexis Rochon, "Memoir on the Purification of Seawater, and on Rendering it Drinkable without any Empyreumatic Taste, by Distilling it in Vacuo," *Repertory of Arts, Manufactures, and Agriculture*, 2d ser., 24 [1814], 368; *Biographie universelle*, 24:287-90; Amable Charles, Comte de Franqueville, *Le premier siècle de l'Institut de France, 25 Octobre 1795-25 Octobre 1895*, 2 vols. [Paris, 1895-96], 2:143-4; *Biographie des hommes vivants*, 5 vols. [Paris, 1816-19], 1:223).

Johann Tobias Lowitz (LOWITS), a chemist working in Russia, had performed experiments to demonstrate the utility of charcoal for deodorizing and clarifying water (Baker and Taras, *Quest for Pure Water*, 1:26-7, 38, 76n, 449-50). In the revised edition of his agricultural guide called *Essays and Notes on Husbandry and Rural Affairs*, TJ's acquaintance John Beale BORDLEY briefly described Lowitz's prescriptions for using charcoal and vitriolic acid to improve water quality (John Beale Bordley, *Essays and Notes on Husbandry and Rural Affairs*, 2d ed. [Philadelphia, 1801], 480; Vol. 31:387-8; Vol. 32:117-18).

FOR THE LIBRARY: that is, the Library of Congress. Vaughan, who was treasurer of the American Philosophical Society, had already obtained the *Manière de bonifier* for the society, along with a separate publication relating to Smith's filtration device (APS, *Proceedings*, 22, pt. 3 [1884], 320, 324).

The book by André MICHAUX on oak trees, *Histoire des chênes de l'Amerique, ou descriptions et figures de toutes les espèces et variétés de chênes de l'Amerique Septentionale*, was published in Paris in 1801. TJ later acquired the book for his library (Sowerby, No. 1084).

MAKENZIES TOUR: Alexander Mackenzie's *Voyages from Montreal, on the River St. Laurence, through the Continent of North America, to the Frozen and Pacific Oceans; In the Years 1789 and 1793: With a Preliminary Account of the Rise, Progress, and Present States of the Fur Trade of that Country*, was first published in London in 1801. John Morgan published a Philadelphia edition in 1802. TJ considered the maps of that printing to be inferior, and he bought another edition in 1803 (Sowerby, No. 4087; TJ to James Cheetham, 17 June 1803). Morgan also published the book by William FORSYTH, *A Treatise on the Culture and Management of Fruit Trees* (Philadelphia, 1802). The book was originally written for horticulturalists in Britain. Morgan's edition included an introduction and notes by William Cobbett that adapted the work for use in America. In 1809, TJ recommended Forsyth's book for the Library of Congress (Sowerby, No. 808; RS, 2:82).

[1] Vaughan underlined this word with two strokes.

[2] The diagram appears here in MS, at the top of a page. Vaughan apparently drew it there before he expected to continue this paragraph onto that page.

[3] Word underlined with two strokes.

[4] Preceding two words underlined with two strokes.

[5] MS: "it."

[6] Line written perpendicularly alongside diagram.

From "A Lover of his Country"

SIR   Petersburg Va. May 9th. 1802

Some Time in February last I wrote to You—to which I beg Reference concerning the Opinion I then entertained of You and your proceedings—Since then I have waited with Impatience for either a private or public Declaration of what You and your Tribe of foreign Outcasts really had at Heart—but that Declaration has not yet appeared—but you and your jacobinic-Democratic Tribe of Sycophants still continue to carry on Your hellish Deeds—which I pray God may not prove the Destruction of this Country—which all the powers of that warlike Nation Britain could not do—even

Tommy Jeffersons *Bosom Friend France* endeavoured to injure us—but by the prudent Conduct of your predecessor John Adams—their Designs were frustrated—even since they have set You by their midnight Machinations into the presidential chair—exasperated at your mean-low-unbecoming Behaviour—are detaining our Ship in their Harbours—contrary to the Inclination of the Seamen—these and a great many Hardships we endure are on account of your proceedings—I beseech you in the Name of God—of every thing that is sacred—and in the Name of every American to alter Your System of Conduct—do you or can you suppose that Men who have fought hard in Defence of their Liberty—and who have inculcated true federal Republicanizm into the Minds of their Children—I say can or will these Men and their Sons allow you to keep your present Tract long—No they cannot—they lay their Grievances before You—instead of lessening them—You tenfold increase them—under the cloak of Œconomy—how many Sums of the public Money has been put to Use—for which Use you can find no Law to authorise You—I do not say that You squander the public Money—but it is done by *your Sycophants*—

Not content with being made president—You are eternally upbraiding Mr. [Adams] our late Worthy President—with things that You yourself do in every point—God knows—had you followed Mr. Adams's System of Cond[uct] America would have been better off—than it is—or is likely to be during Your Administration—

I advise You for your own Sake as well as for the Sake of our Country—to reform Your Conduct like a true Repentant and let the Americans—more particularly the Virginians see they were not mistaken in the Choice of President, for Sir if you do not—I could almost venture to swear that in the Course of two Years or perhaps less Time you have not one real Friend—for those You have here and in Richmond are daily—nay hourly forsaking You—even Callender whom you always upheld has entirely forsaken Your Cause—Had I seen such a Letter as this addressed to You twelve Months ago—I should have thought the Writer insane—but Sir when You consider the many Hardships We are likely to undergo—nay are now suffering—I say if You consider that all the evils we endure originate from Your imprudence—you cannot for a moment blame Me—with either impudence or presumption In Hopes that the feeble Efforts of a Youth of fifteen—may in some Measure assist in the Reformation of the Conduct of the president of the United States—I beg leave to subscribe myself   A Lover of his Country

RC (DLC); torn; addressed: "Thomas Jefferson Esqr: City of Washington"; franked; postmarked 8 May; endorsed by TJ as a letter of 9 May received from "Anonymous" on 17 May and "abuse" and so recorded in SJL.

I WROTE TO YOU: an author signing himself "A Lover of His Country" wrote to TJ from Petersburg on 10 Mch. 1802. TJ pardoned and remitted the fine for James Thomson CALLENDER, who had been convicted under the Sedition Act in 1800. The journalist became embittered by his failure to receive an office under the Republican administration, seeking in particular the Richmond postmastership. In February 1802, he joined Henry Pace in publishing a Federalist newspaper, the Richmond *Recorder: or, Lady's and Gentleman's Miscellany*, which became the mouthpiece for attacks on the Virginia Republican elite. The Baltimore *Republican or, Anti-Democrat* of 8 May charged that Callender lacked "political honesty" and had become "almost federal" in his praise of James A. Bayard (ANB; DVB, 2:520-2; Vol. 33:46, 157-8, 216, 232, 309-10, 566; Vol. 34:186, 205n).

To James Madison

TH:J. TO J. MADISON.   Monticello May 9. 1802.

The road through Ravensworth is rendered absolutely impassable for a four wheeled carriage by a single change made lately by one of the mr Fitzhughs in his plantation. you must not therefore attempt it, but go on to Fairfax C.H. & there turn off to Songster's. Bull run is now passed at an excellent ford, and the hills by a great deal of work have been made quite good. the road between Elkrun church & Norman's ford is bad, as it generally is, but it will be better by the time you come on. all the rest is fine.

I think mr Wagner should be instructed to take decisive measures for having a sheet of the laws printed daily till done. a person direct from Kentucky, tells me a person of known credit had reached there from New Orleans which he left March 6. and affirms a French governor had arrived there, without troops, and had taken possession of the government. he was so positive that if we have nothing later from thence, I should think it possible. Adieu affectionately.

RC (DLC: Madison Papers). PrC (DLC); faint; date in dateline overwritten in ink to "May 6. 1802"; endorsed by TJ in ink on verso as "May 6." Recorded in SJL at 6 May 1802.

HAVING A SHEET OF THE LAWS PRINTED: see Daniel Brent to TJ, 21 May.

To James Monroe

My dear Sir   Monticello May 9. 1802.

I arrived here yesterday & shall stay here a fortnight only. on my return to Washington I shall have to appoint Commissioners of bankruptcy for the several states. in this I propose to appoint 4. for Richmond & Manchester, and 4. for Norfolk. do you think those of Richmond could serve for Petersburg, or had I better appoint 4. there also. I wish 2. to be lawyers & 2. merchants, tho they might[1] stand in the proportion of 3. & 1. either way where characters cannot be found in the desired proportion. I must ask you to recommend for Richmond & Manchester, & also Petersburg if necessary, observing not to recommend a single federalist, as I am determined to confine appointments to republicans until a due proportion be held by each in the public offices. in this case too the partiality of the judges would give every thing to the federal members if there were any. Could I rely on Colo. Newton at Norfolk to recommend for that place, and confide to him my purpose to appoint no federalists? if you think not, I must ask you to recommend for that place also. as to this last point I should wish your immediate advice, because if I am to apply to him I should do it with as little delay as possible. Accept my affectionate and constant esteem.   Th: Jefferson

RC (NN); addressed: "Governor Monroe Richmond"; franked; postmarked Milton, 14 May; endorsed by Monroe. PrC (DNA: RG 59, LAR); endorsed by TJ in ink on verso.

[1] TJ first wrote "that they" then altered the text to read as above.

To Thomas Sumter, Sr.

Dear Sir   Monticello May 9. 1802.

I omitted before the rising of Congress to enquire for proper characters to appoint in South Carolina as Commissioners of bankruptcy. mr Calhoun too, best acquainted in Charleston was gone; and if there, he has not the same determination which I have against appointing a single federalist until the two parties have their due proportion of office, and especially in this case where the federal partiality of the judges would give the whole business to the federal members of the commission. I would wish to name 4. in Charleston, of which it would be better that 2. should be lawyers & 2. merchants; however the proportion might be of 3. and 1. either way, where proper characters could not be found in the desired proportion. so also if there be any other commercial town sufficiently considerable to produce bankruptcies, 4. should be named for it. will you permit me to ask the favor of you to recommend to me. tho' you are not very minutely acquainted in Charleston, yet you have much better means of enquiring than I have. as I consult no other on this occasion, I will ask your information as soon as you can give it with satisfaction to yourself. I am told many bankruptcies are expected immediately in Charleston, which renders an early nomination for that place more important than for the others. I am here for a fortnight only; so your answer will find me at Washington. Accept assurances of my sincere esteem & respect. TH: JEFFERSON

PrC (MoSHi: Jefferson Papers); at foot of text: "Genl. Sumpter"; endorsed by TJ in ink on verso.

MR CALHOUN: that is, John Ewing Colhoun, who, along with Sumter, represented South Carolina in the United States Senate.

From John Barnes

SIR   George Town 10th May 1802—

May this meet you amidts the social scene of Domestic happiness!—Contrasted, with the late trying perplexeties—of disappointed Ambitious Men—are disquietudes inseperable with your preeminent station—though shielded by the most Virtuous Actions.—

I judge it, necessary to inform you, that my Note in favr of ML., was unsuccessfull at B. of C. thro. the want of B. paper to draw upon—This resource failing will oblige me to have recourse to Other Means.—

Of the Lists you left with me $1819.32. have already been discharged. beside some other viz—13.82. not there Noticed…. the $2000. Compensation recd this day. I have ℔ this Nights Mail remitted to my friend Mr Chas. L Ludlow—New York, together with $500—and Moreover requested of him to advance me (for one mo. only.) $500. with the $1000 already in his hands, is $4000—for the immediate purpose to that amt in 3 ℔Ct Stock—in the name of W.S. on a full Assurance of my reimbursing him every deficiency—and I flatter my self, in the hope of his friendly Compliance there affected, I shall be at ease—and not till then.—

for the insuing Mo—(including Mr Ludlows $500.)—your next Mos. Compensation must be Applied—while that of July, say 6th. or

8th. will meet your Notes then become payable, the remnants, whatever they may be, will be carefully reserved to sustain your weekly expenditures &c. &c. untill the begining of Augst:—on the whole—I trust and flatter my self these will meet your Approbation.—

I am most Respectfully Sir, Your Obedt. Hble Servant,

JOHN BARNES

RC (ViU: Edgehill-Randolph Papers); at foot of text: "The President UStates at Monticello"; endorsed by TJ as received 13 May and so recorded in SJL.

ML.: Meriwether Lewis. B. OF C.: Bank of Columbia. For Lewis's previous notes with the Bank of Columbia, see Vol. 36:77-8.

W.S.: William Short.

From Charles W. Goldsborough

THE PRESIDENT— Nav: dep: 10. May—1802.

The enclosed exhibits a view of the deposits made with the Treasurer of the Navy—the drafts upon him, & the balance in his hands of monies subject to the orders of the Secretary of the Navy: for the week ending 8 instant.

I have the honor to be Sir; your mo: ob: servt.

for ROB: SMITH
CH: W: GOLDSBOROUGH
Ch: Clk: Nav: dep:

FC (Lb in DNA: RG 45, LSP). Recorded in SJL as received from the Navy Department on 13 May and "Warrants." Enclosure not found.

A member of a distinguished Maryland family and a Navy Department clerk, Charles W. Goldsborough (1779-1843) became chief clerk of the department in 1802, succeeding Abishai Thomas, and served in the position until 1813. His long career in the Navy Department later included service as a clerk for the commissioners of the navy and chief of the bureau of provisions and clothing. In 1824, he published an early history of the navy entitled *The United States' Naval Chronicle* (*Appleton's Cyclopædia of American Biography*, 6 vols. [New York, 1888], 2:672-3; *Baltimore Patriot*, 18 Mch. 1813; *Daily National Intelligencer*, 26 Apr. 1815; Washington, D.C. *Daily Madisonian*, 15 Nov. 1843; Vol. 35:447n).

TREASURER OF THE NAVY: Goldsborough probably refers to the accountant of the Navy Department, Thomas Turner (ASP, *Miscellaneous*, 1:304).

To George Jefferson

DEAR SIR Monticello May [10] 1802.

I arrived here the day before yesterday on a visit of one fortnight [only and am] in hourly hope of seeing my groceries [arrive] from mr

Barnes as well as a quarter cask of wine from Robertson [and Brown] of Norfolk. I have never heard yet from Bedford [whether my tobacco is] down or not. on my departure from Washington I [desired] mr Barnes to remit you 300. dollars on my account. accept assurances of my affectionate esteem.   TH: JEFFERSON

PrC (MHi); faint; at foot of text: "Mr. George Jefferson"; endorsed by TJ in ink on verso.

From Étienne Lemaire

M'ONSIEUR   du 10 Mais 1802

Je prend la libertez l'honneur de vous Saluer pour prevenir, que Cremer est party apres a voir Engager Ses Enfeant, Et a leser Sa n'ouvel fâme vûe qu'il, ne pouvoi, pas vive Ensenble. Je Vous previens Mr. N'eyant pas d'ant Se moment personne pr., aider a Ebrame ou a Nétoÿer l'a maison Vottre Encien portiez Edward Etant Bien fachez de vous avoir quiter dant le tant, plutot par Etour deri que Refletion donc il, m'entemoigne tout les regret possible il, Sepromet, que Si Monsieur veux le Reprendre a Son, Service, qu'il, Rentreroit avecque Beâucoupe de Satisfaction Et que Mr. n'auroit lieu d'ettre Satifait de Son, Service et Son exatitude il Medit que Mr. tellor ne Se defait de lui que parcequil, est parti a la Canpâgne pr. 6. Moy—Mr. Voudera Monhoré petite reponce a Se Suget—Je fini avec tout latachement possible Je Sui Vottre tres unble tres afaitionné Serviteur

                                                    ETIENNE LEMAIRE

EDITORS' TRANSLATION

SIR   10 May 1802

I am taking the liberty and honor of greeting you to inform you that Kramer departed after having hired his children. He left his new wife since they could not live together. I also inform you, Sir, that there is no one right now to help Abraham or to clean the house. Your former porter, Edward, dismayed at having left you when he did, out of an unthinking impulse rather than reflection, expressed all possible regret and assured me that if you should wish to re-engage him on your staff, he would be very pleased to return and would give you reason to be satisfied with his service and punctuality. He tells me that Mr. Taylor is letting him go only because he left for the country for six months. Please could you send me a brief response about this? I conclude with all possible faithfulness. I am your humble and devoted servant.   ETIENNE LEMAIRE

RC (MHi); endorsed by TJ as received 13 May and so recorded in SJL.

François Étienne Lemaire (d. 1817) was the steward of the President's House from September 1801 through TJ's presidency. After saying goodbye to Lemaire in March 1809, TJ wrote that "my heart was so full that I could utter but the single word Adieu." TJ called Lemaire's conduct "so marked with good humour, industry, sobriety & economy as never to have given me one moment's dissatisfaction." Were TJ "to be again in a situation to need services of the same kind," he informed his former employee, "yours would be more acceptable to me than those of any person living." Originally from the outskirts of Paris, Lemaire was in Philadelphia by July 1792, serving as primary cook for the French minister to the United States, Jean Baptiste Ternant. Lemaire was working for William Bingham in 1801, when, as Bingham prepared to leave the United States, Carlos Martínez de Irujo brought Lemaire to TJ's attention and Philippe de Létombe helped recruit him as maître d'hôtel for the President's House. Lemaire was the highest paid member of the domestic staff, earning $30 per month. He kept the household accounts, bought groceries and provisions, and was responsible for other expenditures, including the wages of the other members of the staff. One of TJ's granddaughters surmised that Lemaire must have made "a small fortune" in his time at the President's House. She also thought that her grandfather overrated the "portly and well-mannered frenchman," although Lemaire was "a civil and a useful man and merited reward." By 1814, Lemaire was back in Philadelphia, working as a barber and identified sometimes as Stephen Lemaire. A few years later, he lost $5,000 on a bad loan to a friend. The loss did not ruin him—he was thought to have $10,000 in assets at the time of his death—but he suffered a mental breakdown and apparently drowned himself. After learning of his former steward's demise, TJ said that he would not have thought that Lemaire possessed "gloom enough to bring himself to so tragical an end" (MB, 2:1053-4n, 1054, 1056, 1242; RS, 1:55-6; list of household of Jean Baptiste Ternant, 1 July 1792, in DNA: RG 59, NL; *Poulson's American Daily Advertiser*, 8 Aug. 1814; *Kite's Philadelphia Directory for 1814* [Philadelphia, 1814]; *Robinson's Original Annual Directory for 1817* [Philadelphia, 1817], 272; Vol. 33:269; Vol. 34:544-6, 568, 685; Vol. 35:6-7, 24-5, 437; Honoré Julien to TJ, 7 Nov. 1817, and TJ to Julien, 25 Dec. 1817, both in DLC).

CREMER EST PARTY: John Kramer, a footman, had begun his employment at the President's House in May 1801. His wages were $12 per month plus a drink allowance of $2. TJ's record of Lemaire's accounts for January 1802 included $20 for "charity to J. Kramer" (MB, 2:1042, 1045, 1064; Vol. 34:489n).

POUR AIDER A EBRAME: Abraham Golden performed miscellaneous duties and was the servant to the president's secretary (MB, 2:1043n, 1057; Vol. 33:531; Vol. 35:394-5, 590).

The previous October, EDWARD Maher had abruptly left his position on the household staff. His subsequent employer may have been the Alexandria merchant George Taylor (Vol. 33:235; Vol. 35:421-2).

List of Vaccinations

1802   Vaccinations
       with the thread.

May. 10. *<John Hemings.>* failed
   John Perry
   <his apprentice.> failed
   <Henrietta.> failed

19. John Hem.
          Perry
    Henrietta.
    Virginia Rand.
          Critta's child[1]
26. Ned's Fanny
          Gill
          Israel
    Isabel's Amy
              Lovilo
    Minerva's Nanny
              Jack
    Mary's Isaiah
    mr Drake.
    Sally's Beverly
              Harriet
    Betty Brown's Bob.

MS (Roger W. Barrett, Chicago, 1947); entirely in TJ's hand; on verso of the list of inoculations of 7 Aug.-17 Sep. 1801 (Vol. 35:34-5), and on the same sheet as lists of vaccinations dated April-May 1816 and 17 Mch. 1826.

One method of preserving the cowpox vaccine for later use was by drawing a THREAD through a pustule on the skin of a person who had been successfully vaccinated; see Vol. 35:8, 120-1, 170, 174, 604, 680. The list printed above indicates that TJ succeeded in inoculating JOHN PERRY with vaccine from a thread on 10 May. Nine days later TJ probably used fluid directly from an eruption on Perry's skin to vaccinate others, including at least two people whose vaccinations from the thread on the 10th had failed, John Hemings and the woman identified only as HENRIETTA. On 26 May, TJ continued the cycle by vaccinating a dozen more people, probably from pustules of individuals he had vaccinated on the 19th. TJ and Benjamin Waterhouse had found in 1801 that fluid from pustules was most effective about eight days after inoculation (same, 34-5, 166, 198, 213, 278; Waterhouse to TJ, 29 Jan. 1802).

[1] Entry interlined.

From Joseph Dougherty

SIR   City of Washington May 11th 1802

I beg Leave to inform your Honour that last Sunday John Kramer went from here for and on the account of his new Wifes ignominious behavior.   Edward Maher is taken in his place. If he is continued Sir you may rest assured that his stay wont. be more than two or three months Moreover you know Sir that he is a verry Disagreeable Man in a family although he is a good Servant Sir My house is rented

& nearly finished the Man who rents it Advances money to finish it by my Contract I am to build a Kitchen This old Bilding at the N:W Corner of this House would answer the purpose verry well I made application to the Commissioners to purchas it. But they are not willing to take it down without your approbation

I am Sir your moste Hbl'e Serv't   Jos. Dougherty

RC (MHi); endorsed by TJ as received 17 May and so recorded in SJL.

From Andrew Ellicott

Dear Sir   Lancaster May 11th. 1802
I ask pardon for not furnishing you sooner with the method I use for calculating the rising and setting of the heavenly bodies.

In almost every one of our popular books of navigation, we find the declinations of the principal fixed stars, with that of the sun for every day in the year, and a table of logarithms, which is all that is necessary for calculating the semi-diurnal arcs.

The rule is

Add the tangent of the sun's or star's declination, and the tangent of the latitude of the place of observation together, and take 10 from the index, the remainder will be the sine of an arch, which converted into time, and added to six hours if the declination is north, or taken from six hours if the declination is south, will give the semi-diurnal arch.

Example

Suppose on the first day of May the sun's declination to be 14.° 57′, and the latitude of the place of observation to be 38.° 53″ north.[1]

Then   Tangent of the declin.   log.   9.42653
        + Tangt. latitude   log.   9.90656
                                          19.33309
        −   10.
            equal the S. of 12.° 26″ log.   9.33309

To convert degrees, minutes, and seconds into time, divide by 15, and multiply the remainder, if any, by 4 and place the product one denomination lower, that is, if the remainder is degrees, call the product minutes and so on let the above 12.° 26′ be the

Example[2]

15) 12.° 26′
    0. 48
        1.44
    0. 49.44

This 49.′ 44″ added to 6 hours will give 6.h 49.′ 44″ for the semi-diurnal arc of that day, and be the time of sun setting, and taken from 12h will leave 5.h 10.′ 16″ for the time of sun rising.—

Suppose the declination of the sun to be 23.° 28′ north, and the latitude the same as above

Then Tangent 23.° 28.′	log	9.63761	
+ Tangent 38. 53	log	9.90656	
		19.54417	
− 10		10.	
equal the sine of 20.° 30′		9.54417	then

```
15) 20°. 30′
       1. 20
           2
       1. 22
```

which added to 6.h will give 7.h 22′ for the semi-diurnal arc of that day, and be the time of sun setting, and taken from 12 will leave 4.h 38′ for the time of sun rising and when doubled will give 14.h 44′ for the length of the longest day in the City of Washington.

When the declination of the sun or star is south the sine found by the logarathims is to be deducted from 6.h to obtain the semi-diurnal arc, As for

Example

On the 1st. day of November when the sun's declination is 14.° 25′ south,—the semi-diurnal arc will be had as follows.

Sun's decli S.	14.° 25′ log. Tgt.	9.41005	
+ Latd.	38.° 53 log. Tgt.	9.90656	
		19.31661	
−		10.	
S.	11.° 58′ log. S.	9.31661	then

```
15) 11°. 58′
       0. 44
           3.52
       0. 47.52
```

which taken from 6 hours will leave 5.h 12.′ 8″ for the semi-diurnal arc, and be the time of sun setting, and the semi-diurnal arc taken from 12.h will give[3] 6.h 47.′ 52″ for the time of sun rising,—and the semi-diurnal arc doubled will give 10.h 24.′ 16″ for the length of that day.—

This method may seem tedious to those not in the habit of making such calculations but after working a few examples it will be found to take so little time as to render an Almanac unnecessary and has moreover the advantage of being made for the precise latitude of the place.—The rising of the sun or stars in the U.S. will be accelerated nearly 3 minutes from the effect of refraction, and their setting equally retarded, which when the horizon is tolerably good may be allowed for.—But when the horizon is broken by hills the correction will be very difficult, as the effect of the altitude of the hills will be combined with that of the refraction.—

A few days ago I received a letter from the ingenious Mr. William Jones of London informing me that the new Planet lately discovered by Mr. Piazzi at Palerme has been observed in England by Doctr. Maskelyne Mr. Herschel and others; but he does not inform me in what part of the heavens it is to be seen.—

I expect to get my transit instrument set up in three, or four weeks, by which I shall be able to increase the number, and value of my observations.—I have with great difficulty, and patience, placed a reticule of spider's web, (the first ever executed) in the focus of this instrument: and intend accomodating my large Telescope with a diaphram, to observe the eclipses of Jupiters satellites,—this precaution appears necessary, and is strongly recommended by de la Lande in a late work.—

The Legislature of this Commonwealth has complimented me with the use of the large reflecting Telescope, which was executed, and imported, for the purpose of observing the Transit of Venus in the year 1769,—it is much the best instrument of the kind upon this continent, and is sent to London to be put in complete repair, at public expense.— The duties of my office prevented me from doing it myself.—

Some time next month, I shall have another paper relating to the eclipses of Jupiter's satellites ready for Delambre* one of the Secretaries of the National Institute, which I shall have to request my friend Mr. Madison to forward to our Minister Mr. Livingston at Paris—

I have the honour to be with the greatest respect, and esteem, your sincere friend   ANDW; ELLICOTT

* Jerome de la Lande in speaking of this great man makes the following observation "Jean Baptiste Joseph de Lambre est n'e à Amiens le 19th. Septr. 1749 Je place ici date, parceque je le regard comme devant faire époque dans l'histoire de l'astronomie.—

RC (DLC); at foot of text: "Thomas Jefferson President of the U.S. and of the A.P.S."; with notations by TJ (notes 1-2 below); endorsed by TJ as received 31 May and so recorded in SJL. PrC (DLC: Ellicott Papers).

TJ was acquainted with WILLIAM JONES of London, the maker of precision instruments (Vol. 14:346, 411-12; TJ to Robert Patterson, 22 Mch. 1802).

The NEW PLANET was Ceres, first observed by Giuseppe PIAZZI early in 1801. Calculations of its orbit by Carl Friedrich Gauss enabled astronomers to find the object in the sky again later that year.

Nevil MASKELYNE had been astronomer royal and director of the observatory at Greenwich since 1765. In 1802, William HERSCHEL, who had discovered the planet Uranus in 1781, coined the term "asteroid" for bodies such as Ceres that orbited the sun but were neither comets nor, in Herschel's opinion, planets (DSB, 5:299-300; 6:328-9, 334; 10:591-2; DNB, s.v. "Maskelyne, Nevil").

By a joint resolution approved 6 Apr., the Pennsylvania General Assembly agreed to have the REFLECTING TELESCOPE that had been obtained to observe the 1769 TRANSIT OF VENUS put into good repair and made available for Ellicott's use (*Acts of the General Assembly of the Commonwealth of Pennsylvania: Passed at a Session, Which was Begun and Held at the Borough of Lancaster on Tuesday the First Day of December, in the Year of Our Lord One Thousand Eight Hundred and One* [Lancaster, Pa., 1802], 285).

Joseph Jérôme Le Français de Lalande's comment about his protégé and collaborator, Jean Baptiste Joseph DELAMBRE, appeared in the third edition of Lalande's text, *Astronomie* (DSB, 4:14, 17n). Translated, it says in reference to Delambre's birth at Amiens on 19 Sep. 1749 that "I put the date here because I consider it to mark an era in the history of astronomy."

[1] Here in margin TJ wrote: "lat. of Washn."

[2] Here in margin TJ wrote: "another method is, as every degree is 4.' of time, and 15' of a circle is 1'=60" of time, multiply the degrees & minutes by 4. & the result will be minutes & seconds of time. thus $12°–26' \times 4 = 49'–44''$."

[3] Word lacking in MS.

From Andrew Ellicott

DEAR SIR   Lancaster May 11th. 1802

This will be handed to you by Mr. Dinsmore, who was several years our Agent in the Cherokee nation, the duties of which he performed with singular reputation; and to his exertions in a great measure, is owing the introduction of some of the arts among that people—He has lately been appointed by the Secretary of War agent to the Chocktaws, among whom I have no doubt he will be found extremely useful, and do credit to the appointment.—He, and Col. Hawkins possess each others confidence, which is essential to the success of the business in which they are concerned.

I have the honour to be with great sincerity your friend and Hbl. Servt.   ANDW; ELLICOTT

RC (DLC); at foot of text: "Thos. Jefferson President of the U.S."; endorsed by TJ as received 31 May. PrC (DLC: Ellicott Papers).

MR. DINSMORE: Silas Dinsmoor served as the government's agent with the Cherokees from 1795 to 1799. In that period Benjamin Hawkins was the principal agent for Indian affairs south of the Ohio River. Henry Dearborn APPOINTED Dinsmoor the agent to the Choctaw nation in March 1802 (Cletus F. Fortwendel, Jr., "Silas Dinsmoor and the Cherokees: An Examination of One Agent of Change," *Journal of Cherokee Studies*, 17 [1996], 28-48; William G. McLoughlin, *Cherokee Renascence in the New Republic* [Princeton, 1986], 42-5; Dearborn to Dinsmoor, 12 Mch. 1802, in DNA: RG 75, LSIA).

From John Wayles Eppes

DEAR SIR,   Bermuda-Hundred May 11. 1802.

Your last letters the one to Maria by the way of Colesville & the other to me by City point have been received. I am sorry it is not in our power to join you at Monticello—The trip requiring four horses renders it impossible to draw them from their work at this season without a sacrifice of our crop. To keep four horses for that trip only for all others we can perform without extra horses would be a heavy charge and consume a great part of the profit of so small a farm as mine! If I could conveniently make the arrangement I would gladly leave this place and fix immediately at Pant-Ops, that Maria might always be with you when your public duties allowed of your being at[1] Monticello. I think however that one temporary establishment is enough and whenever I build I wish to settle comfortably for life— My funds not being equal to that object I have proposed to Maria to sell the Land you have given her in Bedford and to employ a part of the money in forming a comfortable establishment at Pant-Ops and either to lay out the residue of the money in Land in the neighbour-hood of Monticello or vest it in some species of property which could not be affected by any change which may take place in this State, & in case of confusion or difficulty at any future period might prove a valuable fund. Unimproved Lots in the Federal city purchased & im-proved yield I am told a handsome interest on money and would per-haps be better property than U. States paper being more permanent. The Bedford property employed in this way would yield income im-mediately & will not employed as a farm be profitable for years even if I had Negroes to work on it which is not the case. The forming a farm from the woods is a work of time & from my own experience I judge that no profit can be drawn for four years at least—The renting of Land too unless under the immediate eye of the proprietor is liable to very strong objections.

We have been at home only a few days after a trip of three weeks to Eppington—Maria has had a pain in her face again within four or five days past & is not at present very well—Our little son is in good health & has two teeth—

Accept for your health our affectionate wishes—

Yours Sincerely   JNO: W: EPPES

RC (MHi); addressed: "Thomas Jefferson President of the U. States Monticello near Milton Albemarle"; franked; postmarked City Point, 14 May; endorsed by TJ as received 24 May and so recorded in SJL.

YOUR LAST LETTERS: TJ to Mary Jefferson Eppes, 1 May 1802 and TJ to John Wayles Eppes, 29 Apr.

In October 1801, TJ proposed giving his daughters and sons-in-law land in

BEDFORD county near his Poplar Forest tract; see Vol. 35:418-20, 503-4.

¹ MS: "a."

From Gideon Granger

SIR—   Baltimore may 11. 1802
The Elections of New York State have gone agt. us for Congress. all is not right   I will write fully frm. New York   the mail is waiting
    Yours   G GRANGER

RC (DLC); endorsed by TJ as received 13 May and so recorded in SJL.

I WILL WRITE FULLY: see Granger's letter to TJ from Philadelphia on 14 May.

From James Madison

DEAR SIR   Washington May 11. 1802
    I have nothing new since my last either from Europe or the W. Indies. The elections in N. York are not yet finally known. It is suggested that the efforts of the minority have prevailed beyond the apprehensions of the majority. Cabot accepts his mission on the terms proposed to him. I have just recd. letters from Erving shewing the turn which the affair took in London, to be such as was conjectured. The compatibility of his Agency with an Assessorship was denied by the Commissioners & made the ground of rejecting him. The Controversy ended in his relinquishing his pretensions, & of course he is prepared for the ground on which we have placed him. He is evidently soured with King & the Board, but professes a superiority to all personal considerations when in the way of his public duty. I inclose a solicitation for office according to the wish of the candidate. I inclose also a letter from S. Sayre which will deserve no other attention than as it brings to view the necessity of thinking of proper persons for the service he recommends himself for. I am at a loss for proper characters myself, & I do not find that any are particularly in the view of those more capable of pointing them out. My horses are not yet arrived.
    Yrs. always most respectfully & affectionately.
                                        JAMES MADISON

Yrujo has just delivered me a long narrative of a riot in Philada. which ended in an insulting destruction of a Spanish flag in the harbour, for which he claims due reparation to the honor of his Master. He suggests that a reward be proclaimed for the apprehension of the offenders, which of itself will heal the wound, if the offenders cannot be traced. I shall consult Mr. Lincoln in the case. My first thought is that a letter be written to Govr. McKean, on the idea of its not being within federal cognizance.

RC (DLC); at head of text: "private"; endorsed by TJ as received from the State Department on 13 May and "Cabot. Erving. Sayre. Yrujo" and so recorded in SJL. Enclosure: Stephen Sayre to Madison, Philadelphia, 5 May 1802, writing to save him the expense of making a request in person, asking if he may expect an appointment in TJ's administration, and suggesting that he is the best person to settle the boundary "in upper Canada, between the United States & the British Government" (RC in DNA: RG 59, LAR; endorsed by TJ: "for Office"). For other enclosure, see below.

Madison had informed Samuel CABOT that TJ would reappoint him as assessor for the commissioners arbitrating claims under Article 7 of the treaty with Great Britain, but since George W. ERVING would be the agent for claims, Cabot's annual compensation would be $1,500 rather than the $2,500 he had received previously. Cabot, writing from Boston on 1 May, complained about the salary cut but accepted the terms (Madison, *Papers, Sec. of State Ser.*, 3:153-4, 178-9).

Erving had written Madison two lengthy letters on 6 Mch. 1802 detailing the commission's refusal to allow him to serve as assessor. He believed that the American commissioners, Christopher Gore and William Pinkney, blocked him because they were Federalists, and that Rufus KING had done nothing to stop them (same, 6-9).

SOLICITATION FOR OFFICE: perhaps John Webb's letter to Madison of 30 Apr., requesting an appointment as bankruptcy commissioner at Charleston, South Carolina. Webb enclosed a copy of a letter he had written to Senator John Ewing Colhoun two days earlier. Fearing that Colhoun had left Washington, Webb requested that Madison submit the letter and a certificate to the president. In the certificate, dated 28 Apr., Thomas Bee, Theodore Gaillard, Daniel D'Oyley, and four others testified that the Charleston merchant was competent to perform the duties of the office "in which Capacity he now acts & has acted since the operation of the Bankrupt Laws." Webb was previously appointed by Judge Bee (RC and enclosures in DNA: RG 59, LAR, endorsed by TJ: "Webb John to mr Madison to be Commr. bkrptcy Charleston S.C."; Madison, *Papers, Sec. of State Ser.*, 3:169). Uncertain if Madison had received his letter, Webb again wrote the secretary of state on 4 June and enclosed a 27 May letter from Colhoun, who noted that he would have supported Webb's application in Washington if it had arrived before he left the city. Webb also enclosed the original 28 Apr. certificate (RC and enclosures in DNA: RG 59, LAR; endorsed by TJ: "John Webb to be Commr. bkrptcy Charleston"). TJ entered Webb's name on his list of candidates for bankruptcy commissioner, but then canceled it, noting "qu. politics?" (see Appendix II, List 1).

In his LONG NARRATIVE to Madison, Carlos Martínez de Irujo protested the lowering and shredding of the Spanish brig's FLAG, an outcome of the riot that had previously been reported to TJ by a pseudonymous writer ("Yankey Doodle" to TJ, 14 Apr.). While waiting for a legal opinion from Levi Lincoln, who on 12 May concurred in Madison's view that the case did not fall under federal jurisdiction, Madison wrote Thomas McKean, requesting that the governor ensure a full investigation, and asked U.S. attorney Alexander J. Dallas to assist the Pennsylvania authorities. He also wrote Irujo, to assure him that an investigation would proceed. McKean informed Madison in August that the investigation had been concluded near the end of July. After making restitution, the guilty parties were granted a *nolle prosequi* by the state attorney general, a resolution that seems to have satisfied Irujo (Madison, *Papers, Sec. of State Ser.*, 3:180-82, 214, 216-17, 217-19, 493; Madison to TJ, [29 Aug. 1802]).

From Michael Weyer

HONOURABLE SIR   Cumberland Allegany County May 11th 1802
I Consider it a Just duety to inform you, that I Last wiek have got on the track of a valuable Silver mint, of which I have had a pice of ore in my hands, and I am by it Persuated that it is a valueable one, and that I would be Rewarted for the Discovery there of
Sir I am your very Humble Sarand.   MICHAEL WEYER

RC (DLC); at foot of text: "Most Honourable Thomas Jefferson President"; endorsed by TJ as received 23 May and so recorded in SJL.

Weyer also wrote James Madison early in his presidency (Madison, *Papers, Pres. Ser.*, 2:265).

From Pierre Samuel Du Pont de Nemours

MONSIEUR LE PRÉSIDENT,   New York 12 May 1802.
Je reçois vos lettres à tems et avec un grand plaisir. Vous ajoutez beaucoup à ma reconnaissance, rien à mon Zêle qui ne pouvait augmenter, peu à mes moyens d'exécution.

Les motifs, les raisons, les inductions, les prévoyances, vous me les donnez: je les ai dans la tête et dans le coeur. Les facilités doivent être augmentées et hôtées. Les aspects déterminans doivent être présentés promptement à une jeune Cour dans la position de celle avec laquelle vous avez à traiter.

Il est sûr que si vous prévoyez la brouillerie, la guerre, et leurs fâcheuses suites, il faut les prévenir par une sorte d'abonnement qui vous procure ce que vous désirez, et qui sera toujours une grande économie. Car la guerre la plus heureuse, indépendamment des calamités qui en sont inséparables et de l'espece de subordinnation où elle vous mettroit vis-à-vis de l'Angleterre, coutera nécessairement à votre Trésorerie le quadruple de la plus forte somme à laquelle on puisse évaluer un arrangement de convenance et de bienveillance réciproque. Elle coutera dix fois plus à votre commerce, à votre agriculture, à votre nation.

Je connais l'état de vos Finances. Je sais qu'elles sont d'une mauvaise nature qu'il vous est impossible de changer.—Mais pour vos besoins réels et pacifiques, elles sont d'un assez grand produit.

Vous pouvez payer vos dettes en moins de quinze ans.—Quand, pour acquerir la nouvelle Orléans et les Florides, et pour le faire sans guerre, vous devriez reculer cette époque de trois ou quatre années, vous auriez fait un excellent marché, même pécuniairement.

La Nouvelle Orléans sera toujours de fait la capitale des deux Louisianes; parce que c'est une ville toute bâtie, et que l'autre est à bâtir, parce qu'il y a des magasins et des quays tout construits, et parce qu'on y parle français de sorte que les Français y seront toujours rappellés. Ce sera au profit de votre nouvelle Orléans qu'ils cultiveront l'autre rive du Fleuve.

Les Florides ne valent rien à *cultiver* en *labour* ou pour des grains. Mais pour élever des moutons, des Vigognes, des chevaux, des mulets, elles peuvent être un Pays précieux. L'Arabie où sont les plus beaux chevaux du monde ressemble aux Florides par le sol et par le Climat. Et les Florides ont un grand avantage sur l'Arabie: c'est qu'elles sont couvertes des meilleurs bois de construction et ne manquent pas de Riveres pour en faciliter l'exploitation et le débit.— Un Gouvernement sage, comme le votre; qui dans ses concessions saurait prendre des mesures pour que ces bois ne fussent pas entierement détruits et pussent se régénerer tandis qu'on en coupera une partie, y trouverait pour son Peuple et pour lui la source constante d'une grande richesse.

Il y a dans tout cela matiere à calcul.—Et, puisque ce Pays vous convient, c'est l'avis de mon Zêle qu'il y faut mettre tout de suite une bonne estimation, même large et généreuse, propre, comme je vous le disais, à frapper une Cour.—En pareil cas, trop grande économie, c'est dépense; et marché manqué; devient ensuite marché onéreux.— La somme offerte et acceptée n'exclura en aucune maniere la compensation du tout ou de partie de cette même somme avec celle qui peut être due par la France à raison du Traité.

Convenir du Prix est le point capital. Arranger les formes de payement, et imputer sur ce payement les soustractions qui seraient de droit, n'est qu'une affaire subséquente qui va d'elle même.

Tout le reste de vos instructions est facile à suivre, et sera suivi très exactement.

Vous faire avoir pleine et amiable justice, procédés obligeans, bon payement pour les fournitures faites par vos citoyens à St. Domingue est un des objets sur lesquels j'ai pris mission de moi même.

Il est vraisemblable que le Général Le Clerc aura trouvé trace et preuve du Traité secret, des conventions plus ou moins explicites qui ont eu lieu entre les Ministres de votre Prédécesseur et Toussaint l'Ouverture; et qu'il y faut chercher la cause de l'usage qu'il a fait contre Mr. Lear du pouvoir stipulé par le Traité de renvoyer les consuls sans explication: pouvoir que vos Plénipotentiaires ont demandé et que la France ne voulait point établir.—L'humeur assez juste qu'il aura conçue à cet sujet, les fournitures d'armes négociées par le Général Maitland pour Toussaint, effectuées par les Etats Unis, employées contre notre armée, auront motivé la maniere dont quelques américains ont été traités.—Je ne doute point que le mécontentement sur cet article ne soit passé en France, et que je ne l'y trouve assez amer. Mais je répondrai aisément que puisque ces torts sont ceux du Gouvernement qui a précédé le vôtre, on ne peut pas vous les imputer. Vous ne reprochez point à notre Gouvernement actuel ceux du Directoire.

Conserver aux Citoyens des Etats unis le Commerce de Saint Domingue, celui de la Guadeloupe et celui de Cayenne, est un autre point qui convient entierement à ma Politique parcequ'il est à l'avantage mutuel des deux Nations, quoique très contraire aux préjugés de nos négocians et aux vues des Compagnies financieres de Paris.— Mais j'en espere le succès, parce que Bonaparte est homme de génie et d'un caractere fort au dessus des idées vulgaires.

En voici assez sur les affaires publiques.

Ce que vous me dites relativement à La Fayette me cause un vif chagrin.—Nul homme n'a une vertu plus noble et plus pure.—Comment lui reprocherait-on d'avoir été fidele à la constitution qu'il avait juré de défendre?—Cette Constitution, quoique très Républicaine, ne l'était pas, il est vrai, autant que lui et moi l'avions désirée, l'avions proposée; mais elle avait reçu notre serment.—J'ai comme lui combattu de la plume et de l'épée pour la soutenir, tant que la Nation elle même n'en a pas eu adopté une autre: et je ne me crois pas coupable.—la poignée de brigands du 10 aoust n'était pas le Peuple, n'etait pas même la centieme partie de celui de Paris.—Cette révolution s'est faite malgré la Legislature et malgré la Nation, surtout malgré les bons citoyens.

D'ailleurs, il ne s'agit pas ici de notre révolution, mais de la vôtre et de votre liberté.—ce sont celles là qui ont couté à la Fayette sept ans de sa vie et sept cent mille francs de sa fortune.

Quoique vos jeunes gens puissent n'avoir pas une idée nette, ni un chaud souvenir de ses services, il doit y en avoir plusieurs disposés à s'honorer en proposant à la Majesté des Etats Unis *d'indemniser* un Patriote éclairé, un Guerrier illustre, qui les a bien et gratuitement servis, et de lui rembourser dans son malheur environ la moitié de ce qu'il a dépensé pour eux lors de son opulence.

Vos Plénipotentiaires l'avaient fait esperer à ses amis.—Ils avaient même indiqué la forme de lui donner vingt mille dollars en bestiaux de belle race et bons instrumens aratoires pour monter sa ferme, vingt mille dollars en argent pour acquitter ses dettes les plus pressantes dont la pluspart sont à des citoyens de l'amérique,[1] et vingt mille dollars en actions de la Banque des Etats unis.

Je sais que ce n'est point à vous à *proposer* cela.—Mais rien n'empêche que vous le *suggeriez*, ou le *fassiez* habilement *suggerer* à quelque jeune membre de la Chambre des Representans amoureux de la justice, de la dignité et de la gloire américaines.

Faut-il y renoncer?—J'en serais affligé pour votre Nation plus que pour La Fayette qui n'a pas même idée de ce que ses amis tentent pour lui dans cette occasion.

Je vois que Houdon sera moins malheureux. Je vous en remercie.[2] Ne l'oubliez pas. C'est à mon Fils Victor auquel je laisse à New York les pouvoirs que Mr. Houdon m'avait donnés qu'il faudra remettre l'argent qui lui est et lui sera du.[3]

Je vous remercie pour mes enfans.—C'est dans l'Etat de Delaware, près Wilmington, sur le Brandy Wine que nous avons enfin fixé notre manufacture de Poudre à feu.—Nous y sommes très à portée de Philadelphie pour rafiner votre Salpêtre.—Une fois rafiné, vous le garderez sans déchets et, à votre premier ordre, on pourra vous en faire avec la plus grande célérité de la Poudre supérieure en force aux meilleures de l'Europe.—Mais, mon excellent Ami, ne la brulez pas contre nous.—Vendez la plustôt dans nos Colonies.

Salut et respect.   Du Pont (de Nemours)

Je ne suis point parti par le Franklin. Je pars de New York par le *Virginia Packet*.

Mister President,   New York 12 May 1802

I received your letters in time and with great pleasure. You have added much to my gratitude, nothing to my zeal, which could not be greater, and little to my plan of action.

You have provided motives, reasoning, implications, and cautions, which are now in my head and my heart. The advantages must be heightened and enhanced and the determining factors must be presented promptly to the young court with which you must deal.

Certainly, if you consider conflict, war, and their negative consequences, it is necessary to prevent them with the kind of good will that will secure what you want. This will always be more economical, for the most successful war, independent of its attendant calamities and the subordinate position in which it would place you, in relation to England, would necessarily cost your treasury four times more than the highest sum one could estimate for an arrangement based on mutual agreement and good will. The cost would be ten times more to your trade, your agriculture, and your nation.

I know the state of your finances. I know they are in a bad state, which you cannot change, but they suffice for your real and peaceful needs.

You can reimburse your debts in less than fifteen years. If you must delay this date by three or four years in order to acquire New Orleans and the Floridas without war, you will still have made an excellent deal, even financially.

New Orleans will always be the capital of the two Louisianas, since it already exists, and the other city is not yet built; it already has warehouses and docks, and they speak French, so the French will always be remembered. It will be in the interest of your New Orleans for them to develop the other bank of the river.

The Floridas are not worth anything for *tilling* or grain, but can be valuable for raising sheep, vicuñas, horses, and mules. Arabia, which has similar soil and climate, is home to the most beautiful horses in the world, and the Floridas have a great advantage over Arabia: they are covered with the best lumber for construction and with rivers to help exploit and transport it. A wise government, like yours, which would take steps in its land grants to ensure that the forests not be entirely destroyed, that they regenerate when one part is cut, would find them to be a constant source of great wealth for its people and itself.

There is room for calculation in all of this. And since this country suits you, it is my zealous opinion that you should immediately make a good appraisal, broad and generous even, in order, as I told you, to impress a court. In cases like this, too much economy turns into an expense and a lost deal. It becomes an onerous negotiation. The sum that is offered and accepted does not in any way preclude compensation of all or part of the same sum with the amount France might owe because of the treaty.

Agreeing on a price is the essential point. Arranging the forms of payment and calculating the legitimate withholdings from the payment are secondary matters that will follow automatically.

All the rest of your instructions are easy to follow and will be followed precisely.

I have taken upon myself the mission of obtaining full and amiable justice, helpful procedures, and fair payment for the arms provided to Saint-Domingue by your citizens.

It is likely that General Leclerc found evidence and proof of the secret treaty, the more or less explicit agreements that took place between your predecessor's ministers and Toussaint l'Ouverture. That would explain his use of it against Mr. Lear, since the treaty stipulated the power to expel consuls without explanation: a power your plenipotentiaries requested and France did not wish to establish. Leclerc's fairly accurate assessment of the subject, the arms General Maitland negotiated for Toussaint, furnished by the United States and used against our army, would explain the way some Americans were treated. I have no doubt that the displeasure over this affair has spread to France and that I will find bitterness there. But I will reply without hesitation that those errors were made by the previous administration. You cannot be blamed, just as you do not blame our government for the errors of the Directory.

I fully support preserving trade for United States citizens with Saint-Domingue, Guadeloupe, and Cayenne because it is in the best interest of both countries, even though it goes against the prejudices of our traders and the opinions of the financial companies in Paris. I hope to be successful, since Bonaparte is a man of genius with a character that sees well above ordinary ideas.

That is enough about public affairs.

What you say about Lafayette causes me deep chagrin. No man has a nobler or purer virtue. How could one reproach him for having been faithful to the constitution that he swore to defend? It is true that this constitution, although very republican, was not as republican as he and I wished and proposed. But we swore to it. Like him, I fought with the pen and the sword to uphold it as long as the nation itself had not adopted another one, and I do not feel guilty. The handful of brigands of August 10 was not the people, not even a hundredth of the Parisian people. This revolution was undertaken despite the legislature, despite the nation, and, especially, despite good citizens.

Besides, this is not about our revolution but about yours and your liberty. Those are the ones that cost Lafayette seven years of his life and 700,000 francs of his fortune.

Even if your young people do not have a clear idea or fond memories of his services, there must be several who are honorably inclined to appeal to the magnanimity of the United States to *indemnify* an enlightened patriot, an illustrious warrior who served them well and freely, and to reimburse him in his misfortune for about half of what he spent for them in his opulence.

Your plenipotentiaries made him think he could place hope in his friends. They even suggested a way of giving him $20,000 in fine cattle and agricultural equipment to start his farm; $20,000 in currency to reimburse his most pressing debts, most of which are to American citizens; and $20,000 in shares of the Bank of the United States.

I know it is not your role to *propose* this. But nothing prevents you from *suggesting* it, or from subtly *having* it *suggested* by some young member of the House of Representatives who is enamored of American justice, dignity, and glory.

Must we give up? I would be afflicted for your country, more than for Lafayette, who has no idea what his friends are trying to do for him in these circumstances.

I see that Houdon will be less unfortunate. Thank you. Do not forget him. I am leaving with my son Victor in New York the powers Mr. Houdon gave me to pay him the money that is and will be owed to him.

Thank you for my children. We finally established our gunpowder factory in the state of Delaware, near Wilmington, on the Brandywine. We are close to Philadelphia to refine the saltpeter. Once it is refined, it keeps without deterioration and, whenever you give the order, we can immediately make you gunpowder that is stronger than the best in Europe. But, my excellent friend, do not explode it against us. Sell it, instead, in our colonies.

Greetings and respect.   Du Pont (de Nemours)

I did not sail on the *Franklin*. I am leaving from New York on the *Virginia Packet*.

RC (DLC); at head of text: "A Son Excellence Thomas Jefferson Président des Etats unis"; endorsed by TJ as received 23 May and so recorded in SJL.

UNE JEUNE COUR DANS LA POSITION DE CELLE AVEC LAQUELLE VOUS AVEZ À TRAITER: Du Pont used the term for a royal court or monarchy, *une cour*, to refer to Bonaparte's government.

TRAITÉ SECRET: in August 1798, British General Thomas Maitland had negotiated a secret convention with Toussaint-Louverture, which secured the removal of British troops from Saint-Domingue in exchange for Toussaint's pledge not to attack Jamaica and to open the island's trade to Britain. Early the following year, Maitland traveled to Philadelphia with instructions to secure American cooperation in carrying the convention into effect. In April 1799, Maitland, British minister Robert Liston, and Secretary of State Timothy Pickering agreed to a set of regulations to govern the reestablishment of trade with Saint-Domingue, which would be established under British authority and with American assent. Maitland then sailed to Saint-Domingue, where, with the close cooperation of the American consul general, Edward Stevens, he secured Toussaint's assent to the terms of the Philadelphia agreement on 13 June 1799. Although no American signature appeared on the convention, it was understood by all parties that the United States would nevertheless be bound by its terms. Under this second secret convention, the ports of Cap-Français and Port-au-Prince were opened to American and British trade. In return, Toussaint promised to restrain privateer activity and pledged noninterference with other Caribbean colonies (especially Ja-

maica) and the southern United States. Immediately after the signing, Maitland arranged to have arms and munitions sent to Toussaint from Jamaica, an action to which Stevens consented with Pickering's approbation. In addition, American vessels began arriving to provide Toussaint's army with desperately needed provisions. Since American laws prohibited the export of arms and munitions, Pickering strongly recommended that Toussaint maintain good relations with the British to secure these materials, although French officials would later complain that weapons for Toussaint were being imported directly from the United States. The supplies Toussaint received from this renewed trade, in addition to the military assistance of the United States Navy, proved vital to his success in solidifying control of the island by 1800 ("Letters of Toussaint Louverture and of Edward Stevens, 1798-1800," *American Historical Review*, 16 [1910], 74-81; Tansill, *Caribbean Diplomacy*, 40-69, 71, 83; Gordon S. Brown, *Toussaint's Clause: The Founding Fathers and the Haitian Revolution* [Jackson, Miss., 2005], 152-61, 168, 205-6; Michael A. Palmer, *Stoddert's War: Naval Operations during the Quasi-War with France, 1798-1801* [Columbia, S.C., 1987], 157-9, 162-4; NDQW, Aug.-Dec. 1799, 157-8; Vol. 31:9-11).

CE QUE VOUS ME DITES RELATIVEMENT À LA FAYETTE: TJ to Du Pont, 30 Apr. The BRIGANDS of 10 Aug. 1792 were the radicals who rebuffed Lafayette and overthrew the monarchy (John H. Stewart, *A Documentary Survey of the French Revolution* [New York, 1951], 306-7).

SUR LE BRANDY WINE: near the end of April, Éleuthère Irénée du Pont de Nemours arranged for the purchase of a farm on Brandywine Creek four miles from Wilmington, Delaware, as a site for a gunpowder mill. Victor du Pont remained in New York, where he oversaw another family company (Saricks, *Du Pont*, 286-7, 292).

In the summer of 1801, as his sons' plans for gunpowder manufacturing took shape, Du Pont had proposed to refine saltpeter (SALPÊTRE) for the U.S. government in exchange for a portion of the finished product (Vol. 34:617-20, 650; Vol. 35:74).

JE NE SUIS POINT PARTI PAR LE

FRANKLIN: the *Benjamin Franklin* left Philadelphia about 19 May, bound for Amsterdam. Du Pont, his wife, and a grandchild sailed from New York for Le Havre aboard the brig *Virginia* on 1 June (New York *Commercial Advertiser*, 1 June; *New-York Evening Post*, 10 June; Saricks, *Du Pont*, 292-3).

[1] Du Pont possibly first wrote "des Etats unis" before revising the phrase to read as above.

[2] Du Pont here canceled "pour lui."

[3] Sentence interlined.

From Arthur Fenner

SIR.   Providence 12th May 1802

Permit me to introduce to you Coll Henry Smith the bearer of this Letter. He is a Gentleman of Respectable Character in this State, much esteemed by the Citizens of the Town of Providence in which he was Born and now resides He has expressed a wish of being made known to your Excellency.

Coll Smith can inform you of the result of our late Election—

I pray you to accept assurances of my high consideration & esteem

ARTHUR FENNER.

RC (DLC); at foot of text: "President United States"; endorsed by TJ as received 4 June and so recorded in SJL; also endorsed by TJ: "by Colo. Smith."

HENRY SMITH was a prominent Rhode Island merchant who, along with four other Providence citizens, had sent congratulations to TJ on his inauguration. As president of the state senate, Smith succeeded Arthur Fenner as governor

upon Fenner's death in office in 1805 (Robert Sobel and John Raimo, eds., *Biographical Directory of the Governors of the United States, 1789-1978*, 4 vols. [Westport, Conn., 1978], 4:1334-5; Vol. 33:187-8).

For the results of the ELECTION in April 1802 in which Fenner was reelected governor for the twelfth consecutive time, see TJ to Joel Barlow, 3 May.

From "A Sybilline Voice"

[before 13 May 1802]

tow circumstances, are frequaintly laid hold, on, And eagerly represented, as objects of complaint. One is our Ships being up, and rotting in harbour, the oather is, the defenceless state of the Nation, owing to the discontinuence, of the Military astablishment, the first seems to be look'd upon as a greavence, among many Republicans, the sourse, of the last may be easyly treased—Steady! Keep the Ground you have made—   A SYBILLINE VOICE

RC (DLC); undated; endorsed by TJ as received from "Anonymous" on 13 May and "Navy rotting. army reduced" and so recorded in SJL.

For two other undated letters TJ received from this author under the pseudonym of "The Voice of A Sybil" and "A Sybill leafe," see Vol. 35:575-6.

To John Barnes

DEAR SIR   Monticello May 14. 1802
I recieved yesterday your favor of the 10th. and am sincerely concerned at the disappointment at the bank of Columbia. this proves farther the propriety of my curtailing expences till I am within the rigorous limits of my own funds, which I will do. in the mean time I must leave to your judgment to marshall our funds for the most pressing demands, till I can be with you. mr Jefferson has sent on 7. doz. more of hams. I have been concerned to learn that his house has suffered by Hooper's failure. however, as they never buy but with ready money, & consequently owe nothing, it will only have the effect of curtailing their business a while. but it is a reason for considering the remittance to them as among the pressing ones. the post days for this place are Tuesday & Friday. letters to be put in at Washington before 6. oclock P.M. health and affectionate salutations.

TH: JEFFERSON

PrC (CSmH); at foot of text: "Mr John Barnes"; endorsed by TJ in ink on verso.

HOOPER'S FAILURE: Richmond merchant Thomas Hooper, of the firm of Hooper & Toler, had purchased TJ's tobacco in 1798. At that time, George Jefferson had assured TJ that Hooper was "a man in high credit," but added

that he was also "rather too adventurous for his capital." After his bankruptcy, Hooper later recommenced business in Boston, where he died in 1808 (Richmond *Virginia Argus*, 9 Mch., 5 June, 7 July, 23 Oct. 1802; Boston *Democrat*, 27 July 1808; Boston *Columbian Centinel*, 27 July 1808; Vol. 30:349, 358, 372-4).

To Henry Dearborn

DEAR SIR   Monticello May 14. 1802.
I recieved yesterday your favor of the 7th. and entirely approve your proposition to remove the arms from New London. I suppose it would be generally a good rule to break up all the small deposits and

carry them to the great magazines where they may be kept in order, guarded, & always ready. health & affectionate salutations.

TH: JEFFERSON

PrC (DLC); at foot of text: "Secretary at War." Recorded in SJL with notation "removal arms from N. London."

Despite TJ's approval of the plan to REMOVE THE ARMS FROM NEW LONDON, military stores remained there for many years thereafter. In a 6 June 1812 letter to Secretary of War William Eustis, TJ expressed his surprise that a quantity of stores were still housed near New London "in an old log house," where their exposed and unguarded state disconcerted both the "timid" and the "grumblers & malcontents" of the neighborhood. TJ suggested moving the supplies to Lynchburg, describing the thriving town as "the most central and convenient place for a deposit of stores" in Virginia (RS, 5:104-5).

From Gideon Granger

DEAR SIR   Philadelphia Friday. May 14. 1802.

From Letters recd. here yesterday it appears that the elections in New York are not as bad as heretofore represented. Col. Thomas is elected not Williams—Van-ness has lost his Election—*Col. Burr will be sorry for* this. It is doubted whether Mr: Elmendorf has lost his Election. It is certain the Republican Tickets for their State Legislatures have succeeded in the Counties which compose the District— and it cannot be forgotten that Col. Burr was in 1800 returned a member from Orange one of these Counties. Ambrose Spenser writes that the Republican Ticket for Senators has prevailed in the great Western district by a handsome Majority this is very Important. It shows a great Change in our favor with the true Agricultural Interests of the State. Report says That Thos: Morris has lost the Election If so I presume Olivr: Phelps my friend is elected. on the whole as advised at present it appears, that a Superior Exertion of the Renslear Interest has produced a majority in Vanness' district. That in Van Courtlands County by a Small majority they have gained State Representatives by some unknown cause. That the fate of Elmendorf is doubtfull—tho tis certain that a cause easily understood has produced an Effect.

With Esteem   GIDN GRANGER

RC (DLC); endorsed by TJ as received 23 May and so recorded in SJL.

Newspaper accounts in early May indicated that Federalists had won a substantial number of congressional seats in the late April ELECTIONS IN NEW YORK. Under the new apportionment law, the number of Representatives allotted to New York increased from 10 to 17. In the end, five Federalists won House seats in the Eighth Congress, including Gaylord

Griswold, of Herkimer County; Henry W. Livingston; Joshua Sands, of the second congressional district in New York City, who defeated John Broome; George Tibbits, of Rensselaer County, who defeated Josiah Masters; and Killian K. Van Rensselaer, of Albany County. The early newspaper accounts incorrectly reported that incumbent Congressman David THOMAS, a Republican from Washington County, had been defeated by John WILLIAMS, a former Federalist congressman. An accurate account was published in the *New-York Evening Post* on 11 May, with the previous error noted (*New-York Evening Post*, 7, 11 May; New York *Commercial Advertiser*, 7 May, 11 June; Catskill, N.Y., *Western Constellation*, 24 May; U.S. Statutes at Large, 1:253; 2:128; *Biog. Dir. Cong.*).

BURR WILL BE SORRY: in Columbia County, Livingston defeated the incumbent congressman John P. Van Ness. For Van Ness's friendship with Burr, see De-Witt Clinton's Statement on a Political Faction in New York, [before 10 Dec. 1801]. The four Federalist candidates for the New York assembly from Columbia County also won election (*New-York Evening Post*, 6 May; *Journal of the Assembly of the State of New-York: at Their Twenty-Sixth Session, Begun and Held at the City of Albany, the Twenty-Fifth Day of January, 1803* [Albany, 1803], 3).

Conrad E. ELMENDORF, a Federalist from Kingston, ran for Congress from Ulster and Greene Counties. The *New-York Evening Post* reported that he was running against Lucas Conrad Elmendorf, the Republican incumbent, but Lucas Elmendorf had declined to run for reelection. The Republican candidate John Cantine received a certificate of election after an error in Elmendorf's name, made by an election inspector, disqualified at least 120 votes, which, if counted, would have given Elmendorf the victory. Plans were made to contest Cantine's seating in the House of Representatives, but he re-

signed before the Eighth Congress convened and Josiah Hasbrouck, a Republican, was elected in his place (*New-York Evening Post*, 5 May, 14 June; Catskill, N.Y., *Western Constellation*, 24 May; New York *Commercial Advertiser*, 11 June; New York *American Citizen and General Advertiser*, 14 June; *New-York Herald*, 3, 10 July 1802; *Biog. Dir. Cong.*). COUNTIES WHICH COMPOSE THE DISTRICT: in the New York senate the middle district included Columbia, Ulster, Greene, Orange, Dutchess, Rockland, and Delaware counties (*National Intelligencer*, 7 June).

AMBROSE Spencer (SPENSER), a Connecticut native who moved to Columbia County, was DeWitt Clinton's political ally in 1802 and served as a state senator representing the middle district and as attorney general of New York (Kline, *Burr*, 1:477n; *Biog. Dir. Cong.*; *Journal of the Senate of the State of New-York: At Their Twenty-Fifth Session, Begun and Held at the City of Albany, the Twenty-Sixth Day of January, 1802* [Albany, 1802], 3; *Journal of the Assembly of the State of New-York: At Their Twenty-Fifth Session, Began and Held at the City of Albany, the Twenty-Sixth Day of January, 1802* [Albany, 1802], 67-8, 110-11, 122).

Thomas MORRIS did not run for reelection in 1802. Oliver PHELPS, a Connecticut native who lived in Canandaigua, Ontario County, won the election against two other candidates (*Biog. Dir. Cong.*; New York *Commercial Advertiser*, 11 June 1802).

VAN COURTLANDS COUNTY: Philip Van Cortlandt retained his seat as a congressman from Westchester County. An early report from the county indicated that at least half of the Federalist candidates would be elected, but Republicans won the county's four seats in the state assembly (*New-York Gazette and General Advertiser*, 4 May; *National Intelligencer*, 7 June 1802).

From John Langdon

My dear President   Portsmo. May 14h. 1802.

I was honor'd the last evening with your highly esteemed favo'r of the 5h. Inst. pray you'll accept my thanks for your kind congratulations on our late Republican struggle in this State, our success has been greater then I had a right to expect, considering the Malice and Violence of the Tory Federalists both *in* and out of Office, who have used their utmost influence, spreading their falshoods and calumnies in every direction possable, supported by the Excutive (Gilman) Interest; however I think they have over Acted their part, which will eventually ruin them. It is well known among my friends here, that I wish for no office in the State, but I think it my duty to aid the Republican cause, and support the true old fashion principals to the utmost of my power, which by the blessing of Divine Providence I shall steadily pursue—The proceedings of Congress at their late Session must and will give General satisfaction all falshoods and Calumnies to the contrary notwithstanding, the Candor and moderation of the Republican Members of both Houses has done them great honor, while on the other hand the Violence of the opposite party have disgrace'd themselves. Agreably to your request I recommend John Goddard Esq. and Mr. John McClintock Mercht. Henry S. Langdon and Charles Cutts Esq. Lawyers for Commissioners of Bankruptcy in this Town, they are gentlemen of Character and Respectability—I do not see the least Necessity, at present, of any other appointments, as Portsmouth is the only large tradig Town in the State, the Towns of Dover, Durham, Rochester, Exeter New market, are all within Twenty miles of this place, the Town of Concord about fifty miles from hence where our Legislature meets great part of their time is the most central and perhaps as proper a place for Commissioners should any more be appointed—

I am not informed whether any measures have been taken relative to our District Judge Mr. Pickering who is totally deranged quite Raveing, and the time (of Jeremiah Smith one of the Circuit Judges will soon expire, and I hope he will never have any other appointment, as he is a most violent Federalist) of course we have no Judge to grant a Commission of Bankruptcy should there be a call; there was no District Court held the last term, as Mr. Smith did not think proper to attend. your goodness will excuse me for mentioning this. Wishing you every Blessing beleive me my Dear Sir with the highest possable consideration and respect,

Your's Sincerely   JOHN LANGDON

RC (DNA: RG 59, LAR); addressed: "President of the United States Washington"; endorsed by TJ as received 30 May and so recorded in SJL with notation "Commrs. bkrpcy"; also endorsed by TJ:

"John Goddard
John Mc.Clintock } to be Commrs.
Henry S. Langdon } bkrpcy
Chas. Cutts.   } Portsmouth"

JOHN GODDARD, JOHN MCCLINTOCK, and HENRY S. LANGDON each received appointments as commissioners of bankruptcy in June 1802 (Appendix II, List 2; *National Intelligencer*, 18 June 1802).

Patriot and jurist John PICKERING had served as the U.S. district judge for New Hampshire since 1795. Already prone to erratic behavior at the time of his appointment, a condition worsened by his increasing alcoholism, Pickering suffered a complete mental breakdown by 1800. His duties were quietly assumed by the U.S. circuit court judge, JEREMIAH SMITH, but the repeal of the Judiciary Act in 1802 forced Pickering back to active service on the federal bench. His subsequent misconduct led TJ to forward complaints made by New Hampshire Republicans against the judge to the House of Representatives on 3 Feb. 1803. Impeached by the House, Pickering was convicted by the Senate in March 1804 and immediately removed from office (ANB; Lynn Warren Turner, *The Ninth State: New Hampshire's Formative Years* [Chapel Hill, 1983], 148-9, 211-14).

To Étienne Lemaire

TH: JEFFERSON TO MR LEMAIRE.   Monticello May 14. 1802.

I recieved yesterday your's of the 10th. of May: and am not sorry for the departure of Kramer; as, tho' he had several good qualities, he was awkward & ignorant. but I think it better not to take Edward. he is a very capable servant, but stands too much on etiquette. I like servants who will do every thing they are wanted to do. he is moreover so fickle that he has served all the masters in the world, never staying 6. months with the same. I think you had better apply to mr Rapin to get one who could act as porter, & at the same time take care of the Cabinet, setting room, & Oval room, leaving the Dining room and hall for John. he should be sober, diligent and good humored.[1] health & affectionate salutations.

PrC (MHi); endorsed by TJ in ink on verso.

[1] TJ here canceled "until such a one."

JOHN: John Freeman.

To James Madison

TH: J. TO J. MADISON   Monticello May 14.

I wrote you on the 9th. but whether the new post had got into motion at that time I know not. it related chiefly to the road. yesterday I recieved your's of the 7th. & 11th. it really seems doubtful whether the conduct of Le Clerc proceeds from the extravagance of his own character, or from a settled design in his government. so many things lately wear the latter appearance that one cannot be without suspicion. your letter to Livingston will give them an opportunity of developing their views. the fact respecting the insult on the Spanish flag deserves enquiry. I believe the fray began by one of the crew knocking down a peace officer, whereon the sheriff & posse took the whole crew, and had them committed, taking possession of the ship in the mean while for safe keeping. this I have collected from the newspapers & some anonymous letters sent me on the occasion. if the state government will take it up, it will be best to give it that direction.— Sayre's letter is highly impudent.—I recieved from your office some commissions to sign. such as you had signed I now return to the office. the others I have thought it would be shortest to inclose to yourself to be left at Orange C.H. affectionate esteem and respect.

RC (DLC: Madison Papers); address sheet torn; addressed: "James Madison Se[cretary of State]"; postmarked Milton; endorsed by Madison. PrC (DLC).

YOUR LETTER TO LIVINGSTON: see

Enclosure No. 4 listed at Madison to TJ, 7 May.

SAYRE'S LETTER: see enclosure listed at Madison to TJ, 11 May.

COMMISSIONS: for TJ's appointments dating to 14 May, see Vol. 33:679.

To Robert Smith

Monticello. May 14. 1802.

Th: Jefferson presents his friendly salutations to the Secretary of the navy and incloses him a letter from mr Page asking a furlough for a son of Genl. Spotswood. if it be within rule it is worth while to oblige the Genl. (tho' a true federalist) as well as mr Page

PrC (DLC). Recorded in SJL with notation "furlough for Spotswood." Enclosure: probably Mann Page to TJ, 9 May 1802, recorded in SJL as received from Mannsfield on 13 May, but not found.

SON OF GENL. SPOTSWOOD: probably George W. Spotswood, a midshipman in the navy since 1799. Smith had recently granted him permission to make a voyage to Europe (NDBW, *Register*, 52; Smith to George W. Spotswood, 11 May 1802, Lb in DNA: RG 45, LSO).

"A reall friend" to Albert Gallatin, with Jefferson's Note

Sir   Middlesex May 15 1802

It may Be considered as rude in any one to interfear in the affairs of government but those to whomes care it is submitted but however that may be you may be assured that the one that now addresses you has been for years back and is now a friend to the two Great carrectors Jefferson & Gallentin. the author of this Knows not who is responsable for appointments, but this much comes immediatly within his Knowledge, that we are all interested in the faithfull collection of the revenue and paying prompt the money when collected, and in case of a default it some times happens that the heads of departments are censurd, under a [just] belief of this the author begs leve to ask wheather it would be impropper to cause an inquiry to be made of Genl Hard, collector of Amboy Situation. the sheriff of Middlesex's docket can perhaps sho by it on this business. the appointment of Genl. Hard may be pleaseing to his friend in Trenton and the Tores and Federals of Amboy but the republicans of Middlesex is not please to see money placed in such hands,   this hint is ment friendship and it is hoped it will be taken so by mr. Gallentin,

A reall friend to the present Administration

NB. The author hopes secrecey in this matter, as he wishes not to exagerate but only give such hints that will Justifi an honest hart, which the inquirey will more then sufishently demonstrate

[*Note by TJ*:]

I recieved an anonymous letter also; it was dated Woodbridge May 19. and appears to be in the natural hand of the writer, disapproving in a friendly way of Heard's appointmt. on recurring however to Govr. Bloomfield's letter every doubt of the propriety of the appointment is removed (except that he says nothing of his circumstances) before I sent in the nomination to the Senate, I desired Capt Lewis to consult the representatives of N. Jersey. he did so, & they not only approved, but were just then preparing a similar recommendation of Heard. the anonymous informn may render vigilance proper as to Heard's accounts.   Th:J.

RC (NHi: Gallatin Papers); with undated note in TJ's hand written below postscript; addressed: "Albert Gallentine, Esqr. Secretary of the Treasury Washington."

Andrew Lyle served as sheriff of Middlesex County, New Jersey (see note to Memorandum from Albert Gallatin, printed at 9 Mch.).

anonymous letter: "A republican

of Woodbridge" to TJ, 19 May. TJ received the letter on 30 May and therefore wrote this note after that date. Gallatin probably did not forward the letter above to the president until after he returned to Washington from New York on 3 June (*National Intelligencer*, 7 June 1802).

Joseph BLOOMFIELD'S LETTER recommending the appointment of John Heard is printed at 30 Apr.

From Caesar A. Rodney

HONORED & DEAR SIR,   Wilmington May 16th. 1802.

It is of considerable importance to the cause of Republicanism, that we should be in the possession of the journals of Congress since Mr. Bayards first entrance into the house of Representatives. They will furnish a faithful record of his political transactions & exhibit a true picture of his public conduct. As the election approaches his acts will be blazoned forth in this State, with all that industry for which his supporters are so remarkable & it will be necessary for us to represent them in their proper light from authoritative documents. It is rarely to be expected that disinterested men will use the same active exertions as those who are governed generally by selfish motives or ambitious views; yet I trust Republican energy will manifest its utmost vigour in the cause of truth & virtue this season.

I have in vain endeavoured to obtain the books to which I have referred from various quarters, & this has induced me to mention the matter, to you, under an idea that you may possibly put me in the track of procuring them.

As far as I can discover the acts of the session have made many converts here, who have forsook the path of error into which they had strayed. If the gaining of our *last State election* does not produce an apathy in the political body similar to that felt in the human, after a great exertion (which I hope will not be the case)[1] the result of the *ensuing one* will be as favorable as the former. Mr. Bayard it is said contrary to his former declarations & intentions will stand a poll & I do believe the struggle will be a hard one; but altho I entertain the highest opinion of his legal knowledge & talents, I am by no means one of those who over rate his political powers. I firmly believe he has, since he directed here, contributed to increase our numbers rapidly, & that it is owing to some peices of his bad policy that we have gained a State election; such as advising Mr. Basset to grant the commission of Sheriff to the person lowest on the return &c. I suspect he has been much overated this winter at Congress. I have in vain looked for some master strokes of a politician in his conduct but can find none, & I have felt a confidence ariseing from the very circum-

stance of his taking the lead, under an impression that he is calculated to reduce a majority to a minority & to make a minority grow
every day less. We rarely find a man unite the talents of a great
lawyer with those of a great statesman. Politics are as much a science
as the law. One he has studied, the other he has not.

The points they will play upon here are readily seen

1. A Virginia Faction
2. Not giving us two Represen.
3. Not extinguishing State ballances
4. Continuing the act for augmenting the salaries &c.

These are the grounds they will seize & to all of them we shall be furnished with ready & apt answers. Our Congressional men have already commenced the work & are as closely watched. I have never
suffered my political opinions to interfere with my personal familiarity with Mr. Bayard, nor on the other hand have I ever in single instance permitted our friendly habits, to obstruct my political course.
At this crisis, at every hazzard I shall maintain the post assigned to
me & relinquish it only with my life.

With great political regard & personal esteem I remain Dr. Sir
Yours most Sincerely. C. A. RODNEY

P.S. Will you be good eneough to accept the enclosed which I beg
leave to present you.

RC (DLC); endorsed by TJ as received
23 May and so recorded in SJL. Enclosure not identified.

James A. Bayard entered INTO THE
HOUSE OF REPRESENTATIVES in 1797 as
a member of the Fifth Congress (*Biog.
Dir. Cong.*).

While governor, Richard Bassett, Bayard's father-in-law, granted the COM-
MISSION OF SHERIFF to Joseph Israel instead of Charles Anderson, the popular
choice (Elizabeth Donnan, ed., *Papers
of James A. Bayard, 1796-1815* [Washing-
ton, D.C., 1915; repr. New York, 1971], 6;
Vol. 35:427-9).

TWO REPRESEN.: for the debate on the
apportionment bill and Bayard's attempt
to increase Delaware's representation, see
Rodney to TJ, 27 Dec. 1801. STATE BAL-
LANCES: on 12 Feb., Bayard spoke in
favor of a resolution to bring in a bill to
extinguish the debt owed by individual
states to the United States. According to
the June 1793 report of the commission-

ers for settling the accounts with the
states, Delaware owed $612,428. On 16
Mch. 1802, the bill for "extinguishing
state balances" was postponed until
the next session of Congress. Bayard declared himself in favor of the bill and
voted against the postponement (*Annals*,
11:498-9, 1016-17; Washington, *Papers,
Pres. Ser.*, 13:154-5).

Before the House voted on 25 Mch. to
continue in force the 2 Mch. 1799 act for
augmenting the salaries of certain officers
of the government, Bayard called for the
compensation of members of the House of
Representatives to be reduced from $6 to
$4 a day. The Federalists argued that the
reduction would be a fair way to extend
the Republicans' call for economy in government. Republicans such as Thomas
Claiborne of Virginia argued that the
"unavoidable effect of reducing the compensation so low that men of moderate
property could not hold seats, would
be that Congress would be filled with
nabobs." Republicans noted that the high

cost of living in Washington, D.C. meant salaries had already been reduced (*Annals*, 11:1077-83; *Biog. Dir. Cong.*; U.S. Statutes at Large, 1:729-30; 2:152).

[1] Words enclosed in parentheses interlined.

From Gideon Granger

Dr Sir   New York May. 17. 1802

Owing to causes which I have not time to explain The federalists will have 6 or 7 members of Congress. They ought not to have more than four—Their Legislature will be 70 or 72 Repub: agt. 30 or 28 fedl.—Their Senate 20 repub: agt. 12 fedl. of these not more than 6 are of that certain Interest which *walks in darkness*. All is perfectly safe in this State. The passions of minority are great. Yours sincerely

GIDN GRANGER

RC (DLC); at foot of text: "The Presidt."; endorsed by TJ as received 23 May and so recorded in SJL. Enclosed in TJ to Madison, 24 May 1802.

THEIR LEGISLATURE: for a later, slightly higher count of Republicans elected to the New York Assembly, see DeWitt Clinton to TJ, 31 May.

From James Monroe

Dear Sir   Richmond May 17. 1802

I did not receive yours of the 9th. till the day before yesterday (15). I am sorry it will not be in my power to see you while at home. many considerations of a publick nature keep me here for the present, the most urgent of wh. is, the trials which are in train in several parts of the state of slaves on the charge of conspiracy & insurrection, and the applications growing out of them for pardon or transportation without our limits, of those who are condemned. Of condemned I recollect abt. 10. or 11. examples whose fate is yet to be decided on by the Executive. This business still holds an equivocal aspect in my view of it. The spirit of revolt has taken deep hold of the minds of the slaves or the symptoms wh. we see are attributable to some other cause. After all the attention wh. I have paid to the subject my mind still rests in suspense on it. It wod. have given me pleasure to confer with you on this head, that you might commence the measure wh. was deemed most expedient to forward the views of the state, respecting this interesting object of its policy. Tho indeed there is so little range for preference of places, the few which present themselves being respectively attended with so many difficulties, that nothing seems so eligible as to open the door to each for the State, that is to the W. Indies, Africa, & to some position west or so. of the Missisippi. Whether it will be practicable in either case is incertain especially the first mentioned. I am inclined to think however that the sooner it is ascertained respecting each the better. I am persuaded the day is not distant when this subject must have a definitive regulation from the councils of the country.

I will write you more fully in my next wh. will be addressd (I presume) to Washington on the subject of yours. It is doubtful whether the comrs. for Richmond & Manchester will be able to act for Petersbg also. The doubt however proceeds from my not knowing the compensation allowed them. Professional men lawyers or merchants wod. not leave this to attend there for a trifling sum. On the other hand if the sum was an object the addition of Petersbg wod. make it more so. I will give you some names in my next accomodated to either arrangment. Colo. Newton is a very worthy intelligent man with good political views, but I do not think that I wod. ask of him a nomination under any restriction. The *fact* of such a *letter* wod. probably become known in the place and might excite personal hatred to you without advancing the publick good, for altho I wod. appoint no federalist yet it may have its good effect that the avowal of that sentiment shod. be known as rarely as possible otherwise than by the act. I say I wod. appoint no federalist, by which I mean not till it wd. be done with safety, or rather advantage to the republican cause; wh. it can at no time be unless he be a republican. I will inquire who are suitable characters for such an office in Norfolk, but wod. not wish you to rely on me as I must report their pretentions are the opinion of others. very sincerely I am

yr. friend & servant   JAS. MONROE

RC (DLC); endorsed by TJ as received 21 May and so recorded in SJL.

From Joseph Rapin

VOTRE EXELENCE   de philadelphia le 17 May 1802

après la Conversation que jai eus avec Mr Le Capitaine Louis aux Sujet de la Balourdise de Jean Cremer et de lincapabilitée de Christoph, je prand la Libertée de vous proposer pour Remplacer Ces deux movais domestique   le valet de chambre qui a èté au Service de Monsieur Beingham Cinq-années de Suitte, il est tres

fidelle, attentif a Ses devoir et aime a Rester a la Maison   je n'en
Connois auqu'un qui puisent Convenir a votre Exelence aussi bien
que celui la et pour plus ample information Mr le Maire pouras vous
Satisfaire attendu quils ont Resté ensemble   Son nom est
Duval jai eus Conversation avec lui et lui ai Semplement dit que d'ap-
près les détaïl que le Capitaine Louis mavoit fait de quelques domestique de votre Maison que j etois persuadé que to ou tard vous auriez
Besoin de quelqu'un cela etoit a propos attendu qu'il me demandoit
Si je Savois quelque place qui puisent lui Convenir Je lui dis donc que
je le Recommanderois a Mr le président et que Si il fesoit affaire la,
que Ses devoir Serois, davoir Soing des habillement du president d
arranger Ses cheveux de mettre le Couvert de Soigner et nétoyer
Largenterie et vererie &c et d ouvrir la porte il me dit que Cetoit a peu
près Ses ocupation Lors qu'il etoit chez Mr Beingham alors un autre
domestique peut tres bien arranger les Lampes et Couteau et avoir
Soing de faire les feux des appartements—je L'ais interoge aussi de ce
qu'il gagnois chez Mr B—. il ma dit que Ses Gage etoit 16 dolards par
mois et que la Reforme des vetement de Son Maitre qui lui aloit tres
bien Sans les faire aranger a Sa taille je pence qu'il demandera 18
dolards pour Gage et habillem. et peutêtre quelque chose de Moin Si
Son Linge est blanchi ala Maison

depuis le depart de Mr Beingham le dit Duval C'est assosié avec un
Marchand d Estampe et autres Bagatelles L'associé C'est Marié et la
Compagnie est dissu et Duval peut en moin de douze jours etre Rendu
a washinton S'il plais a votre Exelence de L'engager   Cristoph
est chez moi le docteur lui a Commencé les Grands Remedes qu'il
espere pouront detruire la Cose qui affecte le meilleur de Ses yeux qui
na point du Catare et que dans deux Semaines le dit docteur Saura
Si la vue du Malheureu peut se Recouvrir car S'il ne peut pas voir
avec Son meïlleu oeÿl dans L'espace de deux Semaine L'opération
Seroit inutille attendu qu'après qu'il lui auroit, enlevé la Catare la
même Cause qui affecte le meilleur de Ses yeux existeroit encore dans
l autre qui est celui qu'il ne voy pas du tout   alors dans la non
Reussitte la Maison de charitée ou L hopital Seroit très necessaire
pour ce pauvre infortuné et dans L autre Cas S'il Recouvre un peut de
sa vue, avec une petite Recomandation de votre Exelence il pouroit
trouver une petite place permanette pour Garder la porte ou quelque
chose de Semblable dans quelque Burreaux de la douane ou quel
quautre Bureaux ou Maison de ville ou hopiteaux

    Jai Lhonneur d être votre Exelence votre tres attaché et Encien
Serviteur   RAPIN

EDITORS' TRANSLATION

YOUR EXCELLENCY,   Philadelphia 17 May 1802

After my conversation with Captain Lewis about John Kramer's stupid action and Christoph's incompetence, I am taking the liberty of suggesting a replacement for these two bad servants. The valet who served Mr. Bingham for five straight years is very faithful, attentive to his duties, and likes to be home. I do not know anyone who would suit your excellency as well as he would. Mr. Lemaire could provide further information since they stayed together. His name is Duval. I talked to him and told him, simply, that based on the details Captain Lewis had given me about a few of your house servants, I was convinced that you would need someone sooner or later. This came about because he was asking if I knew of any position that might be appropriate for him. I said I would recommend him to the president and that, if he were chosen, his duty would be to take care of the president's clothing, to arrange his hair, set the table, polish and care for the silver and glassware et cetera, and open the door. He says that was more or less what he did when he was at Mr. Bingham's. Another servant can very well take care of the lamps and knives and mind the fires in the rooms. I also asked him what he earned at Mr. B's. He told me his salary was $16 a month along with his master's used clothing, which fit him very well without alteration. I think he would request $18 for salary and clothing, perhaps a little less if laundry were included.

After Mr. Bingham's departure Duval partnered with a dealer of prints and other items. The partner got married and dissolved the company, so Duval could be in Washington within twelve days, if your excellency wished to hire him.

Christoph is at my house. The doctor began a major treatment that he hopes will destroy the thing that is affecting his better eye, the one without the cataract. In two weeks the doctor will know if the unfortunate man can recover his sight. If he cannot see in two weeks with his better eye, the operation would be useless, since after removing the cataract, the same cause that affects the better eye would still exist in the other one, which does not see at all. If the treatment does not succeed, this poor unfortunate will have to go to the hospital or poor house. If he partially recovers his eyesight, he might, with a recommendation from your excellency, find a simple, permanent position as a doorman or some similar position in a custom house or other office, home, or hospital.

I am honored, your excellency, to be your faithful and longtime servant.

                                                              RAPIN

RC (MHi); below signature: "No 100 Market Street philadelphia"; endorsed by TJ as received 23 May and so recorded in SJL.

LE CAPITAINE LOUIS: Meriwether Lewis was in Philadelphia during the middle part of May. He was there by the evening of the 13th, when he attended a gathering at Thomas McKean's house. During his visit to the city, Lewis saw the waterworks designed by Benjamin Latrobe, called on George Logan, and probably had his portrait made by Saint-Mémin. Lewis may have been on his return journey to Washington by 24 May. On that day he attempted to call on John Dickinson in Wilmington, Delaware, but

Dickinson was not at home (Donald Jackson, ed., *Letters of the Lewis and Clark Expedition with Related Documents, 1783-1854,* 2d ed. [Urbana, Ill., 1978], 677-9; ANB, s.v. "Latrobe, Benjamin Henry").

On 4 May, TJ had given John CHRISTOPH Süverman an order on John Barnes for $14 as advance payment of one month's wages (MB, 2:1071).

Statement of William Short's Tenements

A statement of mr Short's tenements, for mr Lilly.

Joseph Price holds a tenement from Carter for life, as is said, at 20. Dollars a year. I have never seen his lease nor do I know it's contents but from report. he has paid up to the end of 1800.

George Haden. by a survey made by mr Nicholas Lewis in 1800. of all the cleared lands in mr Short's tract, which were then occupied on rent by his tenants, (a plat of which survey is in my possession) George Haden held those in the plat marked as follows.

		acres perch.		
G.H.	No. 1.	8–45	in rye	
	2.	7–[48.]	corn	
	3.	17–120.	oats, cotton &c	in 1800.
	4.	1–20.	rest	
I.H.	5.	5–43.		
		40–46 being 40.¼ acres.		

40–46 being 40.$\frac{1}{4}$ acres.

his rent is 40. Dollars. he has paid up to the end of 1799. and £3.6 towards his rent of 1800. he owes therefore for 1800. £8.0[4] and £12. for 1801. besides tobo. his last settlement with me was 1800. Nov. 1[3].

Charles Lively holds, by the same survey, as follows.

		acres perch.		
C.L.	No. 1.	5– 100.	in corn	
	2.	6–17	in corn	in 1800.
	3.	10–60	wheat	
	4.	3–12.	oats	
		25–29. say 25. acres.		

he pays 7/ an acre for the whole. his last settlement was Nov. 4. 1800. when he paid up the rent of 1799. he has an order on me from R. Richardson for £8. in part of his rent for 1800. and he owes a balance for that year & the whole for 1801.

Richard Shackleford holds the fields marked

		acres perch.		
R.S.	No. 1.	7–49.	in oats	
	2.	6–[72].	in corn	
	3.	[85]	in tobo.	in 1800.
	4.	1–[60]	in tobo.	
	5.	[5]–	[rest]	
		24–[106]		

I have never had a settlement with him. the lands he holds were formerly Cornelius's and Terril's. he pays a dollar an acre for all but that in tobo. for which he pays one fourth of the tobo. his rent for 1800. was 22. D 75 c & $\frac{1}{4}$ of the tobo. made in No. 4. he was to have No. 3. rentfree that year for clearing it.

Robert Terril held

		acres perch.		
R.T.	No. 1.	7–56	in corn	
	2.	10–89	rest	in 1800.
	3.	13–67	wheat & corn	
	4.	7–100	top of mountn.	
		48–152		

his rent averaged 8/ an acre annually, say £19.9 a year. he settled with me Nov. 23. 1800. & gave a written acknolegement of £49.1 money due, besides one fourth of the tobo. made in 1800. the quantity not then known. I gave orders on him since, but do not know what he has paid on them.[1]

General rules to which every tenant is subject.

he is tenant only of the open land, which he is to divide into 5. equal fields having only one of them in corn, 2. in small grain, and 2. at rest, unpastured or in clover or peas, each year; and no one field is to be in corn more than once in 5. years, nor in small grain more than twice in 5. years.

he has the privilege of wood from the woodlands for fuel, fencing, building repairing, & utensils for his farm, & range for his stock, and is to leave fencing & buildings equal in value to those existing when he came on the land.

he is to clear lands only on previous consultation with the landlord; it being understood that no clearing is to be made but between distinct parts of his own farm, or between his farm & one of the other tenements in order that we may be getting the whole into one body.

he has the lands which he clears one year rent-free for clearing them; then as long as they are tended [in tobo.] he pays a fourth of the inspected tobo. charging a fourth of the carriage & warehouse charges. when put into any thing else they pay a money rent. Haden, Lively, Shackleford & Terril have tobo. rents to settle in addition to the money rents before stated.

In consideration of Lively's plantation being small, I agreed he should divide it into four shifts, 1 for corn, 1 for wheat, & 2 at rest, or in clover or peas, in rotation, until he could clear a 5th. shift.

TH: JEFFERSON
May 17. 1802.

PrC (DLC: William Short Papers); entirely in TJ's hand; faint.

¹ Here in ink, TJ heavily canceled a passage ending with "[1801 & 1802]."

A PERCH is a unit of land measurement. An acre consists of 160 perches (OED).

From "A republican of Woodbridge"

SIR.   Woodbridge May 19th 1802

Nothing could be more unexpected to the republicans in this part of the Countery than the appountment of Genl. Hard Collector of Amboy he having ben a persicuting federal, and even persicuted a brother Officer and had him expelled or suspended from the cincinaties Society for his Pollitical creed, until Mr. Adams refused him an appointment and it is not knowing what he is now. besides he was Marshel, and on the heales of that to be appointed Colector it seemes as tho after the republicans has ben striving to obtain the election of our President for such men to be appointed what they pleas to ask, while men of better Tallants, and firm republicans, is neglected is hard indede and further it cannot be suposed, that the Presidant could be Informed that Hard is intangled so that all his property is now and has ben for some time under Execution, and that he keepes himself out of the way of the Sheriff, that the Good Judgment of our Presidant it is suposed would not have incuraged such an appointment had he ben informed of his situation, and his Principles. I wish that the riter of this will be excused for this bold address, & I trust will when the Presidant is infórmd. that it is to give him Just information and an inquiring he pledges himself as a true republican, and one who has used uncommon Exertions for the cause, what is here stated will be proved true.

A REPUBLICAN OF WOODBRIDGE

RC (DNA: RG 59, LAR); at head of text: "To the President of the united States"; endorsed by TJ as received 30 May and "against Genl. Herd as Collector of Amboy" and so recorded in SJL.

ADAMS REFUSED HIM AN APPOINT-MENT: see John Heard to TJ, 29 Apr.

To Gideon Granger

Monticello. May. 20. 1802.

Th: Jefferson asks the favor of the Postmaster general to send no letters for him to this place, after he recieves this, as he will be in Washington in the course of the ensuing week.

PrC (DLC). Not recorded in SJL.

TJ arrived in WASHINGTON on Sunday, 30 May (MB, 2:1073).

To Étienne Lemaire

DEAR SIR   Monticello May 20. 1802.

I shall be in Washington towards the latter end of the next week, say about the 29th. or 30th. of the month. the more I have considered the proposition to recieve Edward again into service, the more fixed I am against it. besides the circumstances in his character which I mentioned to you, I had good reason to believe he read the papers which happened to be on my table whenever I went out of my cabinet; and it was impossible for me to lock them up every time I stepped out of the room. it was therefore a recommendation of Kramer to me that he could not read writing. I am in hopes mr Rapin will be able to send us a good one from Philadelphia. accept my best wishes.   TH: JEFFERSON

PrC (DLC); at foot of text: "Mr. Lemaire." Not recorded in SJL.

From John Barnes

SIR   George Town 21th May 1802

On the 19th. I was hond. by your favr. 14th.—had my dependence rested *wholly* on the successful event of a disct. at B of C. it would most Assuredly have been a serious misfortune—but your next Mos. Compensation will prove equally effective—as well curtail an useless expence of $21.—nor will any demand, on your a/c be. in the least suspended. by that disappointment—discounting—in many Cases— is a temptation & risque—to numberless unforeseen inconvenien- cys—neither am I sorry, (since the effect Ceases) it hath alarmed your Resolution of Curtailing your expenditures—Messrs. G & J. $300— was remitted the 6th Inst. am exceedingly Concerned at their unfor- tunate connection with Mr. Hooper—for the expected seven dozen Hams. when I am informed of their Amt. shall, if possible, be remit- ted instantly.

My advices from Mr Ludlow N York, are—that the 3 PCts. are very scarce and even a 61-62. that he is not willing to give more than 60. unless Authorized—to be again disappointed. would I fear in- crease WS. Anxiety—if not create—an unfavorable Alarm. I there- fore—at all [events] wrote him, to secure me $6000. of that stock. will Amt. to $3,680—and upwards.

—the good Genl Ks 1st. & 2d. sett of exchange for ƒ2500 guilders a 40 Cts. is $1000.—are already on their passage to Amsterdam, (the 3d sett with me)—

I called yesterday, on Mr Le Mair—they have been busily em- ployed in preparing for your expected return.

I can readily perceive—there wants some more permanent & Cor- rect regulations, Respecting the lower Class—Marriages—as well Seperations—as in the polite world, still continues—and without some Radical reform, I fear the evil will increase—Washington & Geo Town. without your aid & presence are of themselves but dull, lifeless, idle places, & without your forstering hand must continue so:—Health, a speedy & save return, await you—

I am Sir, Your mst Obed. H St.   JOHN BARNES

RC (ViU: Edgehill-Randolph Papers); blurred; at foot of text: "President UStates at Monticello"; endorsed by TJ as received 1 June and so recorded in SJL.

GENL KS 1ST. & 2D. SETT OF EX- CHANGE: the $1,000 remitted to Tadeusz Kosciuszko was for interest and divi- dends received on 45 shares of 8 percent stocks of the United States and for 20 shares of Bank of Pennsylvania stock. In a 15 May 1802 letter to Kosciuszko, Barnes enclosed a statement of his account from 23 July 1800 to 15 May 1802 and in- formed the general that a bill of exchange for ƒ2,500 guilders in favor of Van

Staphorst & Co. of Amsterdam had been remitted to him on 26 Apr. An identical payment had been made to Kosciuszko in April 1801 as well. Barnes gave copies of the 15 May letter and Kosciuszko's ac- count to TJ on 22 June 1802 (Trs in MHi; endorsed by TJ: "Kosciuzko Genl. his acct with mr Barnes to May 15. 1802."). The third set of exchange, dated 7 May 1802, was drawn on P. & C. van Eeghen of Amsterdam by I. C. Van den Heuvel of New York City (MS in same; *Longworth's American Almanac, New- York Register, and City-Directory, For the Twenty Seventh Year of American Inde- pendence* [New York, 1802], 340). For background on Barnes's handling of Kosciuszko's financial affairs, see Vol. 31:51-3, 560-1, 587n; Vol. 33:288-9; Vol. 35:50n.

From Daniel Brent

SIR,   Department of State, May 21st 1802.

I take the liberty to send you herewith a letter from Mr Dallas to the Secretary of State, just received at this Office, and the petition of David Jackson, therein referred to, together with a statement of the Jury by which he was tried, and found guilty of larceny, recommending him to the President of the United States for a pardon. I have the Honor likewise to send enclosed a recommendation in favor of Simon McIntosh Esqr., for the Office of Commissioner of Bankrupts at Charleston, South Carolina, received also since the Secretary's departure.

Mr Madison having intimated to me, that you had expressed much solicitude concerning the publication of the laws of the last Session of Congress—that it might be speedily compleated—I have thought it would be satisfactory to You to learn the present state of that work. I do myself the Honor, therefore, to inform you, that the Printing is done to Chap. 42, inclusively, making 112 pages, and bringing the work up to the first day of this month, the last law printed being approved of on that day. Mr Smith is possessed of all the remaining Copy; and he supposes it will occupy about 60 pages more. I have the Honor to be, with the highest respect,

Sir, Your very Obedt hble servant,   DANL BRENT.

RC (DLC); at foot of text: "The President of the United States"; endorsed by TJ as received from the State Department on 23 May and "David Jackson's case Mc.Intosh to be Commr. bkrpts." and so recorded in SJL. Enclosures: (1) Alexander J. Dallas to James Madison, Philadelphia, 15 May 1802, forwarding a petition for pardon to the president by David Jackson, along with a supporting recommendation from the jury at his trial; Dallas describes Jackson, a 15-year-old boy convicted of larceny on the high seas by the U.S. circuit court at Philadelphia on 14 May, as "a poor Lad, without family, or friends, in this part of the Continent"; the captain with whom Jackson sailed prosecuted him and "does not give him a good character"; but if the president sees fit to pardon Jackson, Dallas will prevail on the prison inspectors to find Jackson a master, "with whom there will be some chance of his reformation" (RC in DNA: RG 59, GPR). (2) Petition of David Jackson to TJ, undated, stating that he has been convicted of stealing two pairs of shoes worth $4 from John Case, that he is but 15 years of age and was "seduced into this transgression by the Indiscretion of youth"; Jackson is now "sincerely repentant" and has already spent almost nine months in prison in Philadelphia; if the "Infamous punishment" of the circuit court is carried out, it will condemn Jackson "to misery and detestation during the rest of his Life" (same; in an unknown hand, signed by Jackson with his mark). (3) Statement of Andrew Leinan, foreman, and 11 others, Philadelphia, 14 May 1802, members of the jury at Jackson's trial, recommending him to the mercy of the president in consideration of his "tender years and the Imprisonment he has already suffered" (same; written on verso of Jackson's petition to TJ; signed by Leinan and 11 others; endorsed by Daniel Brent). (4) William Marshall, Dominick A. Hall, Theodore Gaillard, O'Brien Smith, Paul Hamilton, and Daniel D'Oyley to James Madison, Charleston, 30 Apr. 1802, recommending Charleston attorney Simon McIntosh to be a commissioner of bankruptcy, describing him as "a gentleman of Talents and Integrity" and a "steady, undeviating Republican in the worst of Times" (RC in DNA: RG 59, LAR; endorsed by TJ).

Daniel Brent (ca. 1773-1841) had been recommended to TJ for a federal clerkship by Richard Bland Lee in 1790. Hired by the Treasury Department, Brent resigned in January 1794, but subsequently returned to government service as a State Department clerk sometime before the start of TJ's presidency. He served as acting chief clerk of the department for most of 1802 during the extended illness of Jacob Wagner. Brent was named chief clerk of the State Department in 1817 and held the position until 1833, when he was appointed U.S. consul at Paris (Syrett, *Hamilton*, 15:592, 663; Madison, *Papers, Sec. of State Ser.*, 3:xxvii, 47-8; *Daily National Intelligencer*, 14 Mch., 24 Sep. 1817; JEP, 4:344; Philadelphia *North American*, 24 Feb. 1841; Vol. 17:354-5; Vol. 33:512, 513n).

TJ issued a pardon for DAVID JACKSON on 1 June 1802 (FC in Lb in DNA: RG 59, GPR).

SIMON MCINTOSH was appointed a commissioner of bankruptcy for SOUTH CAROLINA in place of Dominick A. Hall, who declined his appointment (Appendix II, List 2).

For TJ's concern regarding the PUBLICATION OF THE LAWS OF THE LAST SESSION OF CONGRESS, see TJ to James Madison, 9 May. Samuel Harrison SMITH received most of the federal printing contracts granted during and by the Seventh Congress (Vol. 36:120-2).

From Richard Richardson

DR. SIR   Lusea Jamaica May 21th 1802

Having wrote you some time since, and not gitting an Answer Inducis Me to think It has not as yet Come to Hand, I wrote you by the way of new york, as theer is Seldom, an opertunity occuring from this littel port to any part of virginia, finding this, I Imbrace it, I am Extreamly anctious to hear from you, and More so, to see you, I Mentioned, the Situation of My affairs In this Ilant vearey fulley when I wrote you last, and I would not wish to be troublesome to you by any Means, I only wish your advice on the subject which has Been Ever given Me, for want of Money, and friends, and being an, Americhan I am afraid, I Shall Meet with a Consederrable loss In My property before I Can Recover it, peopel from americah Meet with But a bad Reception hear, if I was a Scotchman My Business would be Easily dispenced with, for the want of Money, I am Induced to follow My Business In this place, which are vearey Much against My Inclina-

tion, But necessitey is the Mother of Invention, and I am Compelled
to, for a livelyhood, for which I get a hundred and forty pounds pr.
annum a year, this Enabels Me to board and Cloath Myself, this
Climit is veary hot and unhealthy I have had two vearey sevear attacks of the fever since My arriveal hear, and have often wished Myself with you again, the peopel of this Ilant are vearey Much afraid of
the french troops In Saint domingo the govinnor has been all Round
the Ilant Examinning the troops and the Molishey the have about
seavinteen sloops of war off this Cost watching the french, grate Confusion has been hear since hostilliteys has Commenc between france
and Ingland and since the treaty has been signed grate Bankrupsy is
occuring Everey day In this Ilant among the Merchants hear, arti-
cales are vearey High hear perticular provisions such as flour Corn
Meat Beef pork salt fish, I am afraid their will be a famin In the Ilant,
if it does not Rain soon their has not been Rain Enough to wet the
ground one Inch In nine Month and Continual norths all vegitation
burnt up the feelings Brought on Me from the situation of the poor
Affrichans hear, are truly distressing they are the only thing which
oppress My Mind Most, they are alowd only one day In Every weak
for a support, and often that day turns out to be a sunday, which they
are oblege to feed themselvs all the following weak from, their Clothing are an ozenburgs frock given them once a year by their Masters
their labour is often painful to—feelings like Mine the farmers hear
have sustain a Consederrable loss from the preasant drouth In their
Crops of Shugar and Rum and from Everey appearance thy next
Crop will fall vearey far short of this, Shugars are offered for Cash at
36£ pr. Hed wtt, Rum for 4 £/1 pr. gan. flour In Exchange for Rum
or Shugar sell for £10 pr. Brl. Mess Beef In Exchange sell for £16.
pr. ditto pork In Exchange good sell for £10. pr. ditto Hearings In
Exchange sell for nine dollars pr. Barrel. the ships that Brings out
supplys for veary large Estates hear, fell veary far shart of prvisions
this year they say they Cant be had at home The farmers In genaral
have lost a grate quantitey of stock occasioned, from such a long
drouth the vessel I write you by has Come to norfolk by My directions for provision for this littel place its situation is on the north of
the Ilant twenty two Miles from Montegabay towards the west End
of the Ilant the diet of this Ilant is not wholesome to new Commers
their yams and plantains does not agree with them at first and having vearey littel fresh provisions it Requirs two or three Months to
get Seasoned to it Beef is a quarter of a dollar a pound hear at its lowest price I should be Extreamly hapy to hear from you and Mr. and,

Mistress Randal I hope you are all well I often think of you all, and your goodness towards Me, and sincarly wished Myself back In the oald stone house with you again which would have Been a treat as, a pallace to some hear, I Must Conclude with wishing you heath and happyness I dear sir Your Most obedient Humble Servent

RICHARD H RICHARDSON

Should you feel disposed to write Me you will be good Enough to direct it to the post office of Lucea Should A letter Reach this Ilant with thes directions I shall get it. Dr. Sir, yours. RD. H. RDSON

RC (MHi); at foot of text: "Mr. Jefferson"; postscript written in margin perpendicular to first page of text; endorsed by TJ as received from Port Lucy, Jamaica, on 30 June and so recorded in SJL.

HAVING WROTE YOU SOME TIME SINCE: see Richardson to TJ, 20 July 1801.

From Madame de Tessé

a Paris 1er Prairial an 10 [i.e. 21 May 1802]

L'habitude de craindre me laisse, Monsieur, L'inquietude de vous paroitre insensée ou ingrate, malheur auquel je ne puis echaper si vous n'avés pas Reçu mes hommages Lorsque vous avés eté mis a la Tete de votre Gt. et ensuite L'expression de ma plus sensible Reconnoissance Lorsque vous avés daigné vous souvenir de moi.

mr. Short vous dira que jai changé de fortune mais peu de situation. mes Gouts et mes attachemens sont Restes les mêmes, et je trouve dans ces Gouts et ces attachemens tout L interet dont la vieillesse est susceptible. une de ses plus grandes jouissances est de se Reporter en arriere dans les plus belles saisons de la vie et a ses epoques les plus honnorables. celle qui m'a permis de pretendre a votre estime ne peut etre absente de mes plus heureux souvenirs. mon interet est donc lie a ma Reconnoissance et vous Repond de la sincerite des sentimens avec lesquels j'assure de mon Respect le President des Etats unis et ne cesserai jamais de former des voeux pour le bonheur et la Gloire de monsieur Jefferson. NOAILLES TESSÉ

mon mari vous presente ses Respéctueux hommages. nous esperons que mr. Short nous fera honneur près de vous des commissions que nous lui avons donnees, pour nous Ramener vers L'extravagance de planter et de semer passé 60 ans.

Malheur a celui qui ne vit que de sa vie!

EDITORS' TRANSLATION

Paris, 1 Prairial Year 10 [21 May 1802]

My worrying nature makes me fear, Sir, that I might seem insensitive or ungrateful to you, a misfortune I cannot avoid if you did not receive my congratulations when you were named head of your government and, later, the expression of my utmost gratitude when you were kind enough to remember me.

Mr. Short will tell you that my fortune has changed but not my situation. My tastes and emotional attachments have remained the same, and these tastes and attachments give me all the pleasure old age can derive from them. One of my greatest joys is to look back on the best seasons of my life and on its most noble periods. One of my happiest memories is when I felt I merited your esteem. My self-interest is thus linked to my gratitude and echoes the sincere feeling with which I assure the president of the United States of my respect. I will never cease wishing happiness and glory to Mr. Jefferson.

NOAILLES TESSÉ

My husband will send you his respectful wishes. We hope Mr. Short will do us the honor of transmitting the things we entrusted to him, in order to bring us back to the extravagance of planting and sowing after age 60.

Woe to him who lives only for his own lifetime!

RC (MoSHi: Jefferson Papers); English date supplied; addressed: "A Monsieur Jefferson"; endorsed by TJ as received 5 Aug. 1802 and so recorded in SJL. Probably enclosed in William Short to TJ, 28 July 1802, not found, but recorded in SJL as received from Norfolk on 5 Aug. (see TJ to Short, 12 Aug. 1802).

MES HOMMAGES: TJ did not receive the congratulations that Madame de Tessé apparently wrote to him after the presidential election. He did get brief news of her from the Marquis de Lafayette. He addressed her a letter in March 1801, and received the EXPRESSION of her regard that she wrote in reply on 14 June of that year (Vol. 33:369-70; Vol. 34:336-9).

DES COMMISSIONS QUE NOUS LUI AVONS DONNEES: Madame de Tessé provided William Short with a list of seeds and plants that she wanted from the United States. Short passed the information along to TJ, who endeavored to obtain some of the items for her (TJ to Short, 2 Dec. 1802; TJ to Madame de Tessé, 30 Jan. 1803).

From Robert R. Livingston

DEAR SIR   Paris 22d May 1802

I was a few days ago honoured by your letter of the 16th. March. I called on the minister the next day & made him the communications you wished. Mr Otto is not yet returned from Great Britain & it seems still a matter of uncertainty who is to replace him or who is to come from thence to Paris Lord Wetworth not being yet appointed. A number of persons are talked of here for England among the most probable are Bertier the minister of war & Genl Marmont. As the embassies of France are upon the present systim extreamly lucrative & splendid this is much sought after.

My Letter to Mr. Madison that accompanies this will give you the present state of our affairs here if they are not such as are to be wished I can only say that nothing has been left unassayed by me to render them so. I am fearful Sir that you will find what you suppose the fund of friendship & attachment between the people of both nations a slender tie to bind them together. The people already count for nothing here in affairs of government they receive the direction of their rulers, & the harsh measures of our late administration have given all those who now hold the reins very unfavorable sentiments of us. You will easily see that it can not be the wish of the present governors to cement the union. If France takes possession of Luissania & the Florida's I see plainly that the interest of our country will compel us, however reluctantly, to form a connection with her rival as a barrier against her power & her ambition, I see too in this sentiment the triumph of our political opponents in the US. but it is not personal or party views that will restrain you from acting as the interest of our country may require & it is better to look forward to this event than to have it forced upon us. When the changes that have taken place here shall cooperate in America with the delays in the discharge of the debt due to our merchants & with the late violations of their rights. When the restrictions which France will impose upon our commerce even to the injury of their own shall be felt I think it highly probable that the sentiments of our own people will undergo a change as sudden as that which this government has experienced. I see but one line of conduct left for us to persue. It is to omit no means to[1] fortify our sea ports, and to conciliate the affections of the western people to act with such firmness as shall indicate our independance of all foreign powers & to place our militia on such a footing as to prevent any fear of the best troops in Europe.

I believe we have no danger to apprehend, yet Sir I count nothing on this head certain. The papers I have sent you relative to projects in Luissiania may make an impression which may lead to measures that we must resist. So also may the wants of the armaments in the islands concurring with the temper of leaders who have been more used to demand than to ask, & to take, than to demand.

On the subject of the defense of our ports I can not but think that Mr. Fulton's diving boat & battery are very worthy of consideration the construction is ingeneous & it appears to me that it would be extreamly difficult to devise any plan for securing a ship from the effect of his battery. It consists of a canister of powder & a lock with very long Upright triggers which will fire the powder on striking the bottom of a ship & as the action of the powder is prodigiously increased by the compression of the water it can not fail to destroy the largest ships. This discovery has excited much curiosity & some alarm in England where it has lately been mentioned in parliament the galleries having been cleared for the purpose. Humanity may shudder at such inventions & yet if they render naval attacks hazardous humanity may gain by the discovery. The existing circumstances here I fear render your situation very delicate. I am satisfied that you will find among those whose place entitles them to confidence intriguers who will charge your moderation with timidity & your exertions with rashness, & who will hope by creating a defection of our friends to triumph thro' the agency of our enemies. I have had hints of this sort but it is not from Paris that I should send American politicks to Washington.

I give you no news from here because I presume you will see my letters to the secretary of State & the papers from which you will collect all that this place affords at present. In natural improvements no expence is spared, & you will think wh. me that the removal of the houses that filled the grand square in front of the palace is not one of the least either in the beauty of the effect, or the magnitude of the expence. Yet this is already in a great measure effected.

The gardens & Royal houses are all kept in order even those at a distance & great improvements are making at[2] St. Cloud which is to be occupied by the first Consul. Every thing is done to gratify the taste of the people for pleasure, & they are satisfied to substitute that for freedom. Bread in Paris is $4\frac{1}{2}$ S: & in the country 6. I can not accuratly learn the state of the crops tho I believe they are not very promissing. The grapes in this country are entirely cut off by the frost how far it has reached I know not, but as we have found it sufficiently cold to keep fires every day for ten days past & had frost at night I think it probable that the mischief is pretty extensive. I yesterday dined with Mr Tallerand at his country seat & found the Judas tree the Laburnum the mulbery & several other tender plants very much injured so that I think it possible that the rie in blossom has also suffered if the frost has extended far south. This would be a very serious calamity. I am sorry to find more consequence attached in Europe to our party divissions than they merrit. Our country however stands very high in the general esstimation, & it costs me no little postage & time to pay for, & read the numerous letters brought me from various quarters containing inquiries relative to it, or soliciting encouragmt for emigrants. They still believe that we possess neither arts sciences or manufactures & that we are willing to purchase the dealers in them at the highest rate.

I have the honor to be dear Sir with the highest respect & esteem Your Most Obt hum: Servt   ROBT R LIVINGSTON

Mr. Paine who has just entered desires his respectful comps. He proposes to vissit you shortly.

RC (DLC); endorsed by TJ as a letter of 27 May received 5 Aug. and so recorded in SJL, with endorsement corrected to 22 May. Possibly enclosed in William Short to TJ, 28 July, not found (see note to preceding letter).

CALLED ON THE MINISTER: Talleyrand.

After Louis Guillaume OTTO negotiated the cessation of hostilities between France and Great Britain with Lord Hawkesbury in 1801, he became France's minister plenipotentiary to Britain. In the spring of 1802, the French government named Antoine François Andréossy to succeed Otto as minister to Britain and offered Otto the position of minister to the United States, which Otto declined (Jacques Henri-Robert, *Dictionnaire des diplomates de Napoléon: Histoire et dictionnaire du corps diplomatique consulaire et impérial* [Paris, 1990], 93-4, 281; Vol. 35:297n, 386n, 398n).

LORD WETWORTH: Charles Whitworth, a baron of the Irish peerage. He had been successively envoy to Poland, Russia, and Denmark. He was nominated as the British minister to France in June 1802, but he and Andréossy did not take up their respective posts until autumn (DNB; John D. Grainger, *The Amiens Truce: Britain and Bonaparte, 1801-1803* [Rochester, N.Y., 2004], 114).

Bonaparte had named one of his generals, Louis Alexandre Berthier, MINISTER OF WAR in November 1799. Auguste Frédéric Louis Viesse de MARMONT, an artillerist, was another of Bonaparte's commanders from earlier campaigns (Tulard, *Dictionnaire Napoléon*, 203, 1144).

In his letter to MADISON, dated 20 May, Livingston indicated that prospects of restitution from France for ship sei-

zures were poor. He gave a note to the French government protesting the treatment of American merchant vessels at Saint-Domingue, although he did not have instructions from Washington on the matter. Livingston also reported on a meeting with Talleyrand in which the French minister was vague about his government's plans for Louisiana. It was difficult to obtain reliable information, Livingston pointed out, because Bonaparte made all decisions on his own. France was no longer a republic, Livingston asserted, but was ruled solely by the proud and self-centered first consul, who had recently promulgated his concordat with the pope, established the Legion of Honor as an order of nobility, reestablished slavery in the colonies, and sought lifetime authorization for his powers as consul (Madison, *Papers, Sec. of State Ser.*, 3:157, 159n, 206n, 207, 219-20, 229-33; Tulard, *Dictionnaire Napoléon*, 452, 673, 1228).

PAPERS I HAVE SENT: Livingston sometimes included copies of the official French newspaper, the *Moniteur*, in his dispatches (Madison, *Papers, Sec. of State Ser.*, 3:34, 157, 159n, 365, 367n). PROJECTS IN LUISSIANIA: in his letter to TJ on 26 Dec. 1801 and in a dispatch to Madison in April, Livingston conveyed his understanding that General Jean Baptiste Bernadotte would command an expedition to take possession of Louisiana. Livingston had also speculated, in a letter to Madison in March, France might use blacks from the West Indies as troops to garrison Louisiana (same, 61, 156-7).

TJ had learned of Robert FULTON's design of a DIVING BOAT from Joel Barlow and from the inventor himself (Vol. 32:143, 144n; Vol. 35:509-10).

BATTERY: Fulton also planned arrays of explosive mines, often called torpedoes, that could be used to close an enemy's harbors (Cynthia Owen Philip, *Robert Fulton: A Biography* [New York, 1985], 99-100, 113-16, 237).

Earl Stanhope, a radical member of the House of Lords who had vociferously opposed war against revolutionary France but was less inclined to support Bonaparte's regime, initiated discussions in PARLIAMENT of Fulton's inventions relating to sea warfare. Stanhope was himself an inventor and an advocate of steam propulsion, and he developed his own plans for sea mines and a mine-sweeping boat. Fulton and the reform-minded aristocrat had exchanged ideas and criticism about various designs beginning in 1793, although the earl did not furnish the financial patronage that Fulton desired (DNB; London *Times*, 3 Sep. 1807; Philip, *Fulton*, 26-36, 54-6, 58, 154-5, 166).

The Tuileries PALACE was Bonaparte's official residence in Paris. John Trumbull described the imposing assemblage of royal apartments and public rooms, which stood near the Louvre, as "the vilest possible jumble of antique and Gothic, perfectly, utterly bad." Changes to the exterior of the large edifice after Bonaparte took up residence there included the removal of trees in the courtyard, installation of a series of ornamental busts along the facade, and demolition of some buildings in the vicinity. The first consul also initiated interior alterations that stretched over several years (Howard C. Rice, Jr., *Thomas Jefferson's Paris* [Princeton, 1976], 30; Tulard, *Dictionnaire Napoléon*, 1661-3).

ST. CLOUD WHICH IS TO BE OCCUPIED BY THE FIRST CONSUL: Saint-Cloud was on the road from Paris to Versailles, not far from Auteuil. The gardens at Saint-Cloud were a great attraction before the French Revolution, and TJ, as he mentioned in his famous "Head and Heart" letter, made an excursion there with Maria Cosway early in their acquaintance. Saint-Cloud was the site of key events of the Brumaire coup that placed France under Bonaparte's rule in 1799. Although he continued to have his primary residence at the Tuileries, Bonaparte by 1802 stayed frequently at the former royal château at Saint-Cloud (same, 1498-9; Rice, *Jefferson's Paris*, 20, 96; Vol. 10:445).

The severe FROST ruined the wine crop through much of France, particularly in the north (*Gazette of the United States*, 7 Aug. 1802; Charleston *City Gazette and Daily Advertiser*, 17 Aug. 1802).

AT HIS COUNTRY SEAT: Talleyrand hosted dinner parties at a mansion in Neuilly (David Lawday, *Napoleon's Master: A Life of Prince Talleyrand* [London, 2006], 123).

[1] Livingston here canceled "strengthen."

[2] Livingston here canceled "Versailles."

From Robert Smith

SIR!   Nav Dep 22nd May 1802

I do myself the honor to enclose you Warrants for Mr J Downes & Mr. L. Alexis, which will require your signature should you approve their appointment—also a Commission for Doct Smith—

The two first mentioned of these gentlemen have been serving in the capacity of *acting Midshipmen* for several years—They are mentioned in very handsome terms by their Commanding officers.

Doct. Smith was out in the Prest. but never recd his Commn.—

He is mentioned to me by his Commg. officers as being entitled to notice.

I have the honor to be, with the greatest respect & esteem, Sir, your mo ob St.   Rᴛ Sᴍɪᴛʜ

RC (DLC); in a clerk's hand, signed by Smith; at foot of text: "Prest: U: States"; endorsed by TJ as received from the Navy Department on 31 May and "commissions &c" and so recorded in SJL. FC (Lb in DNA: RG 45, LSP).

John ᴅᴏᴡɴᴇs and Louis ᴀʟᴇxɪs both served on the frigate *Constitution* during the Quasi-War. William C. sᴍɪᴛʜ previously served as an acting surgeon's mate on the frigate *President* in the Mediterranean. All three men received commissions dated 1 June 1802 (ɴᴅǫᴡ, Dec. 1800-Dec. 1801, 315, 326; ɴᴅʙᴡ, *Register*, 1, 16, 51).

From Jonathan Williams

Sɪʀ   Mount Pleasant near Philadelphia May 22. 1802
After having ascertained by repeated Experiments that the Coast of America, and the eminences of Land upon it can be discovered by the varied Temperature of the Sea; it became a very natural suggestion that by a judicious use of the Thermometer a correct Chart might be made, which would not only be usefull to mariners by indicating soundings, when they could not heave the Lead; but to Society at large by discovering Fishing Banks, at present perhaps unknown.— To do this effectually would require a cruising Voyage, under the direction of an able Astronomer and draftsman accustomed to make Philosophical Experiments, from the Capes of Florida to Nova Scotia, and within the Gulph Stream; But such a Voyage, for such an Object, is not within the Power of any individual: To Government it would only be a particular direction to an ordinary Cruiser, & occasion no extraordinary Expence.

Now that the President of the Philosophical Society, and The Cheif Magistrate of the Union are in one person, I may without hazard of impropriety submit this suggestion to your Opinion: The apprehension however of exposing myself, to an imputation of vanity on a subject which may in some respects be considered as personal, would probably have prevented this communication if I had not received the inclosed Letter from an experienced french mariner, who has been some time settled on the north River, but who is about returning to France. This declaration that he will apply to the french Government for a Cruizer to perform this service to Humanity, if we do not, renders it a Duty in me, at least to lay his Letter before you.—The Consideration of your many & important employments during the session, is the only reason that I did not make the communication immediately.

When I last had the honour of seeing you I mentioned a magnetic oddity. I have by repeated experiment found it to be still more odd, for the experiment will not be the same with one bar of Iron that has been some time in a vertical Position, & another that has been lying in a horizontal position during a long time. The former will retain its polarity, for some time when lying down, tho' it will not be so strong as when erect; the latter will have no polarity at all (unless in a North & South direction) when in a horizontal position; but will in an instant possess that quality if put in a vertical position. The Distance from Pole to Pole in the same Bar is very irregular, & varies from two feet to two Inches: A Bar of steel will retain its Polarity in all positions.

I have the honour to be with the greatest Deference & Respect Sir Your faithfull & obedient Servant   JONA WILLIAMS

RC (DLC); at foot of text: "Thomas Jefferson Esqr President of the American Philosophical Society"; endorsed by TJ as received 30 May and so recorded in SJL. PrC (InU: Jonathan Williams Manuscripts). Enclosure: Eugène Linet to Williams, 16 Feb. 1802; Linet has read Williams's *Thermometrical Navigation* and states that using temperature readings to aid navigation "will certainly prove of the highest importance & of more universal benefit to Navigators than any operation made use of to rectify their reckoning on the approach of land"; shipwrecks are common on the coast of North America because, in part, of navigational errors caused by currents; the coast is also along "a parallel of Longitude," and most captains are unable to calculate longitude to help them know when they are approaching land; because the water along this coast becomes shallow at a steep rate, it is possible when a ship is pushed by "a good breeze" to come up on a shore only hours after finding no bottom by the use of a sounding line; the ability to ascertain the direction of currents by water temperatures would alone make a great contribution to navigation; he recommends that a cruise be made to take observations and conduct experiments along the entire coast; since an American made the discovery of thermometrical navigation, the United States government should make that survey, but if that government should decline, Linet is confident that the first consul of France would authorize a voyage for the purpose; in closing, Linet asks if Williams's work has been translated into French, expressing an interest in undertaking the task himself (DLC).

ASCERTAINED BY REPEATED EXPERIMENTS: Williams first collected readings of water temperature under the direction of his uncle, Benjamin Franklin, on a voyage from Europe to America in 1785. Data that Williams collected on subsequent voyages confirmed Franklin's idea that the Gulf Stream was warmer than the ocean to either side of it and convinced Williams that water temperature could also help seafarers locate coasts, icebergs, and submerged banks and rocks. He submitted a paper and supplementary data to the American Philosophical Society in 1790. Seeing that report in the society's *Transactions* prompted William Strickland to make temperature readings on trips from Hull to New York in 1794 and from Philadelphia to Falmouth in 1795. Strickland passed the results of his observations along to Williams, who transmitted them to the APS for publication. Williams compiled his views and findings under the title *Thermometrical Navigation*, which he published in 1799 and sent to TJ early the following year (APS, *Transactions*, 3:82-100; 5:90-103; Louis De Vorsey, "Pioneer Charting of the Gulf Stream: The Contributions of Benjamin Franklin and Willam Gerard De Brahm," *Imago Mundi*, 28 [1976], 109-11; Vol. 31:308).

NORTH RIVER: the Hudson (Jedidiah Morse, *The American Gazetteer*, 2d ed. [Charlestown, Mass., 1804]).

From Gideon Granger

DR: SIR   Suffield May 23d. 1802

The vote for Candidates for Congress is at the ratio of 7,000 federal to 3,800 Republican in Connecticut. There are more than Sixty Republican Members in the House of Representatives. and it is certain that the friends of the Administration increase in the state. They have a hard time—Their perseverance is Wonderful—but they are not dispirited & may well be calculated on—Honle. Perpoint Edwards has returned this day from Vermt: & informs that State is Safe beyond a doubt. The federalists are very bitter—boast much—but in truth gnash their Teeth in dispair—

Your sincere friend   GIDN GRANGER

RC (DLC); at foot of text: "Thos: Jefferson Esq"; endorsed by TJ as received 30 May and so recorded in SJL.

From Thomas Law

SIR   Mt Vernon Sunday morng. 23 May 1 PM.

With sorrow unfeigned I inform you that Mrs Washington has terminated her well spent life about half an hour, after suffering with calm fortitude a fever for 17 days.—Dr. Craigk with unceasing assiduity afforded all the relief that was in the power of medicine but in vain.

The distress of all around agitates me too much, & prevents me from expressing the keen sense I entertain of the Loss of one who so nobly & amiably fulfilled every duty.

I remain With esteem & respect Yr. mt. Obt. He St.

THOS. LAW

RC (DLC); endorsed by TJ as received 30 May and so recorded in SJL.

According to newspaper accounts, the 71-year-old Martha WASHINGTON died on 22 May at Mount Vernon and was buried there three days later. At her death, she was surrounded by family members, including Law, who was married to her granddaughter Elizabeth Parke Custis Law, and was attended by Alexandria physician and close family friend James Craik (Ellen McAllister Clark, *Martha Washington: A Brief Biography* [Mount Vernon, Va., 2002], 54; Alexandria *The Times; and District of Columbia Daily Advertiser*, 24 May 1802; *Philadelphia Repository, and Weekly Register*, 29 May 1802; Washington, *Papers, Col. Ser.*, 2:168-9; Vol. 32:270n).

From Samuel Brown

SIR,   Lexington May 24th: 1802.

Since my return from Washington, I have made very particular inquiries respecting a Skull found near the Big Bone Lick, resembling those which were discovered, 70 or 80 years ago, in Siberia, & which were supposed by Naturalists, to belong to Animals of the *Ox kind*. I am happy that I can now assure you, that the information which I communicated to you, on that subject, last winter, was perfectly correct. I have conversed with several gentlemen of respectability who have seen the skull & have examined it with considerable attention. A Mr John Brown of Cincinnati, has got possession of it & passed Wilkinsonville with it, on the 7th of last month. I imagine that it is his intention to present it to the Philosphical Society at Philadelphia—Mr McClellan who was at Wilkinsonville when Mr Brown descended the River, remarks that there seemed to be a very singular disproportion between the Horn & the size of the Head. His discription of the figure of this skull corresponds so well with that given by Gmelin of those collected in Siberia, that I am pretty confident it belonged to an Animal of the same species—It, certainly, has no resemblance to the head of the Elephant, Mammoth or Megalonyx. Dr Wistar or Dr Barton, will, I trust, give to the world, a minute discription of this fragment, which I believe is the only one of the kind which has yet been discovered on our Continent. The enormous size of the Horn, will in all probability, suggest the specific name of this unknown animal—

Permit me to quote the passage in Gmelin to which I have refered—

"There have been found, in the Earth, heads of an animal *totally* different from an Elephant & I have seen a head of it at Iackutzk which had been sent from Anaderskoi-ostrog & was, according to my information, perfectly similar to that found by Portn-jagen—I myself had one which I sent to the imperial Cabinet at Petersburgh—In fine I learned that on the Banks of Nischnaja-Tunguska similar heads are not only found every where dispersed but likewise other bones which unquestionably belonged not to the Elephant, such as Shoulder bones ossa sacra, ossa innominata & leg bones which probably belonged to the same animal to which the above head ought to be attributed & which should by no means be exclused from the *Ox kind*. I have seen leg bones & hip bones of this species concerning which I have nothing particular to remark except that they appeared to be extremely short in proportion to their thickness."

Relation dun voyage a Kamshatka"

With sentiments of the most profound respect I have the honor to be Yo. Mo. Obt. SAM BROWN

P.S. Mr Edward West has gone to Washington from this place in order to procure Patents for several Mechanical inventions—The simplicity of his manners & the deficiency of his education cannot conceal from your discerning Eye his uncommon ingenuity—You are infinitely more competent to appreciate the merits of his several discoveries than I am. I shall therefore say nothing concerning them.— He is an honest & virtuous Citizen— S.B.

RC (DLC); addressed: "The President of the United States Washington"; franked; postmarked 28 May; endorsed by TJ as received 10 June and so recorded in SJL.

WHICH I COMMUNICATED TO YOU: no letter from Brown on this subject has been found or is recorded in SJL. He perhaps communicated with TJ in person, or was referring to contact that he had with Charles Willson Peale (Peale, *Papers*, v. 2, pt. 1:392; Peale to TJ, 6 June).

Natural scientist Johann Georg GMELIN was a member of a scholarly expedition that left St. Petersburg, Russia, in July 1733, and spent more than nine years collecting information and specimens in Siberia. Gmelin published a four-volume report in German, *Reise durch Sibirien*, which appeared in an abridged French edition in 1767 under the title *Voyage en Sibérie*. The expedition provided a variety of scientific and cultural information about Siberia. In a letter to TJ in 1792, James Madison quoted Gmelin's account regarding the looming effect of mountains in certain atmospheric conditions (DSB; Margery Rowell, "Linnaeus and Botanists in Eighteenth-Century Russia," *Taxon*, 29 [1980], 17-20; Robert J. Theodoratus, "Waclaw Sieroszewski and the Yakut of Siberia," *Ethnohistory*, 24 [1977], 112-13; Vol. 24:135).

RELATION DUN VOYAGE A KAMSHATKA: that is, "account of a journey to Kamchatka."

EDWARD WEST had a clock and watch shop in Lexington, Kentucky, beginning in the 1780s. He invented several devices, and in July 1802 received patents for a nail-cutting machine and for improvements in nail production, gunlocks, and steamboats. West was Brown's son-in-law (John E. Kleber, ed., *The Kentucky Encyclopedia* [Lexington, Ky., 1992], 941; *List of Patents*, 28).

From John Lambert and Others

RESPECTED SIR   Trenton New Jersey May 24th 1802

The Subscribers Representatives in the Legislative Council of New Jersey being informed, that the Office of Marshal of the United States for the District of New Jersey, has become Vacant, by the Appointment of Genl. Heard to the Office of Collector of Perth Amboy; take the liberty, to recommend to the President, *Doctor Oliver Barnet*, of the county of Hunterdon, for the Office of Marshal. We are induced to solicit this Appointment, as we know that Dr. Barnet from his Central situation, Independance in Life, Capacity and Intelligence, will be able to execute the duties with the greatest ease to himself, and satisfaction to the public.

We beg leave to add, that He has ever distinguished himself for his attachment to the Principles of the Revolution & most particularly in the late Elections, in support of the present Administration—& we think the appointment will most esentially serve the cause of Republicanism in New Jersey.

JOHN LAMBERT
DAVID MOORE
WILLIAM PARROT
CHARLES CLARK
WM. M'CULLOUGH
DAVID WELSH
THOS. LITTLE

RC (DNA: RG 59, LAR); in an unidentified hand, signed by all; at foot of text: "To the President of the United States." Probably enclosed in Joseph Bloomfield to TJ, 24 May, not found, but recorded in SJL as received from Trenton on 30 May and "Dr. Olivr Barnet to be Marsl."

A native of Lambertville, in Hunterdon County, New Jersey, John Lambert (1746-1823) began serving in the New Jersey General Assembly in 1780. A member of the Legislative Council of New Jersey from 1790 to 1804, Lambert was vice president of the 13-member council in 1802. He served as acting governor of New Jersey from 15 Nov. 1802 to 29 Oct. 1803. Lambert was one of the early Republicans in the state noted "as

friends of the farmer and working man." He represented New Jersey in the House of Representatives from 1805 to 1809 and in the Senate from 1809 to 1815 (*Votes and Proceedings of the Twenty-Seventh General Assembly of the State of New-Jersey* [Trenton, 1802], 3; *Biog. Dir. Cong.*; Walter R. Fee, *The Transition from Aristocracy to Democracy in New Jersey, 1789-1829* [Somerville, N.J., 1933], 71n).

For earlier recommendations of OLIVER BARNET as U.S. marshal of New Jersey, see Vol. 33:183-4 and Vol. 34:5-6. TJ appointed Barnet on 3 June 1802 (*National Intelligencer*, 4 June; Appendix 1). His permanent commission as "Marshal in and for the New-Jersey District" is dated 25 Jan. 1803 (commission in Lb in DNA: RG 59, MPTPC).

From Étienne Lemaire

MONSIEUR   Washinton du 24 Mais 1802

J'e prend libertez Et l'honneur D'e Repondre a vôttre dernier, datez du 20—Et Recûe, l'e 23. Mr. Je vous prie de vous tranquilizé aûsitot que J'e recûe la premier que Mr. m'a fait l'honneur de m'eCrir Je reMercié Edwar J'en, Et arettez ûne, aûttre qui a de Bonne Recomendation Ses ûne hom d'un âge—mur Et Sorbre, Et inteligent, bien prope, Mr. Je Recûe, une lettre de Mr. Rapin qui m'e marque qui ofre a Mr. le Si d'e vant, valet de Chanbre d'e Mr. Bimgham Mr. Je vous prie En grace de Croir de moy l'a Sincer, veritez, que Se n'est pas l'home qu'il vou feaut Sans vous fair de detail, de Sa Conduite il est Bien Sur prenant que Mr. Rapin ne mâe pas fait part de tel Chosse avant que de Crir vue qu'il N'e le Connoit pas Come Moi il, N'e parlle pas la l'angne du toute Sa Se n'est Rien, Sil n'e voit pas d'auttre de feaut. Je vous diré le reste apres vôttre Retour—

Je fini avecque honneur vottre tres afectionné Serviteur

E LEMAIRE

EDITORS' TRANSLATION

SIR   Washington, 24 May 1802

I am taking the honor and liberty of answering your last letter, dated the 20th and received the 23d. I want to reassure you immediately, Sir, that I received the first letter you did me the honor of writing. I let Edward go. I have hired someone who is well recommended. He is a mature and sober man, intelligent and very clean. I received a letter, Sir, from Mr. Rapin which bothers me; he offers Mr. Bingham's personal valet to you. Sir, I beg you to take my word for it that he is not the man you need. Without going into details about his conduct, it is nevertheless very surprising that Mr. Rapin did not inform me of such a thing before writing, since he does not know the valet as I do. He does not speak the language at all. That would not matter if he did not also have other defects. I will tell you the rest when you return.

I conclude with the honor of being your very affectionate servant,

E LEMAIRE

RC (MHi); endorsed by TJ. Recorded in SJL as received on 30 May.

LA PREMIER: TJ to Lemaire, 14 May.

DE BONNE RECOMENDATION: William Fitzjames was the person hired to fill John Kramer's place on the household staff (MB, 2:1074).

To James Madison

DEAR SIR   Monticello May 24. 1802.

Our postrider having mistaken his day, brought us no mail on Thursday last. yesterday I recieved a double one. in it were the inclosed letters. those from Dupont & Granger are forwarded for your perusal, and I will recieve them again when I see you at your own house. the one from Dallas to yourself on Jackson's case I recieved from mr Brent; the recommendation of the Attorney of the district, & of the jury, & the circumstances of the case seem to be a good foundation of pardon, which I would wish to have issued therefore unless you disapprove it. they do not mention when the execution is to be; but probably it would be well to lose no time lest the pardon should get too late. if your clerks have it in readiness I will sign it on my arrival in Washington which will be in six days from this time. I will be with you on Thursday or Friday at farthest, unless rain prevents, and take your commissions for Washington. I have forbidden any mail to be forwarded to me later than the one recieved yesterday. present my best respects to the ladies, and accept my affectionate salutations yourself.   TH: JEFFERSON

RC (DLC: Madison Papers); at foot of text: "The Secretary of State." PrC (DLC). Enclosures: (1) Pierre Samuel Du Pont de Nemours to TJ, 12 May 1802. (2) Gideon Granger to TJ, 14 May 1802. (3) Granger to TJ, 17 May 1802. (4) Alexander J. Dallas to Madison, 15 May 1802 (see Enclosure No. 1, listed at Daniel Brent to TJ, 21 May 1802).

From James Penn

SIR   Grove May 24th. 1802

I take the liberty of offering you my tract of land on which I live for sale—I do not know that you are inclinable to purchase, but if so the place I think will add considerably to the value of your estate here—I hold about 1400 acres binding on your line at least a mile or more, lying between the poplar forest and New London better watered than any tract of land I ever saw of its size affording between 100 & 200 acres of choice meadow ground—On it a plantation of nearly 400 acres cleared land lying uncommonly well, a fertile soil, laid out to in fields with great regularity, under good enclosures and the ground in good preservation, having for years past paid much attention to the improvement of the soil—The Dwelling house is large and convenient other buildings suitably adapted. I believe there is no tract of land of its size in this country that can be so hansomely divided for tenants as this. It may be divided into ten tenements each well watered with a proper porportion of meadow ground and lying convenient to the markets of Lynchbg. N. London & the great public road. Should Mr. Jefferson be disposed I will shew the land to any person he may direct—Should you incline to purchase & we agree on the price, the time of payment will be immaterial if within five years carrying interest

I am with the greatest respt. your Most Obt. servt.

J: PENN

RC (MHi); endorsed by TJ as received from Bedford County on 1 June and so recorded in SJL.

James Penn owned several tracts of land in Bedford County and neighboring Campbell County. TJ responded to the proposed SALE in a brief note of 9 June: "Your favor of May 24. has been recieved since my return to this place. tho' consid-erably attached to the lands I possess adjoining yours, yet I am not at present disposed to add to them by new purchases. thanking you therefore for the politeness of your offer, tho' I cannot avail myself of it, I pray you to accept my best wishes and respects" (PrC in MHi; at foot of text: "Mr. Penn"; endorsed by TJ in ink on verso).

From Charles Pinckney

DEAR SIR,   May 24: 1802 Sitio near Madrid

I will now continue the confidential communication which I received, and which I hinted at in the last Letter I wrote you; but had not time to go into as the opportunity closed upon me before I expected it—it was in substance that *the Court had been tricked by M. Urquijo into the cession of Louisiana* without being aware of *it. that it was a thing patched up between Berthier and Urquijo when he was here as Envoy Extray: to get Spain* to declare *war against Portugal & that a different paper had been given to the King to sign* from that *he had approved in the rough draught: that when the Prince of Peace was appointed to negociate with Lucien Bonaparte the treaty which was lately published at Paris the Prince attempted to dispute the fairness and* validity *of the transfer; but that the French held them to it. and added them that nothing could save their mines and South American possessions,* [but having the French as a][1] *barrier*, and that in consequence *of the cession they would guarranty them* that not withstanding *the thing had been* acquiesced *in with great reluctance and to use the term of my informant surliness, on the part of Spain* that so many restorations were to be made *her and so many difficulties thrown in the way* that to please *her and smooth them over France at last agreed that*

[494]

Etruria should be considered always *as a sort of dependency or* appendage *of Spain and held by a Branch of her family*—that there can be no doubt *Spain has very great* uneasiness *on the subject: that she knows not which to dread most France or America; but that she* infinitely *prefers the neighbourhood of America,* that in that case in the worst of events *she would have only one to contend with; but* that the chance was *if the French possessed Louisiana and became powerful there they and the Americans might one day* understand *each other and then she would have both. he further* said *that Spain looked upon her possessions in South America & the W. Indies as her's but for a time and that if the U. States went on to progress for the next twenty years as they had* done in the last *that not only Spain, but other powers would have to owe every thing to their moderation as far as respected American possessions*—*as their land* and if they chose to make an exertion *in that way their naval forces in that quarter of the* world *would be irres-is-tible*[2]—*that the European naval powers* always Jealous *of each other could never venture to share a sufficient number of ships or a sufficient force to resist with effect*—*that this added to the Americans* being *at home and with the* constant and immediate *use of every thing they wanted and the shelter* and *aid of their ports and their* unexampled and continued *progress in numbers commerce and revenue* made *them an object* very much to be attended to *by all the powers having and* valuing, *their possessions in America.* that the constant conversation, almost, *with the French Minister and others* was on this subject. *that my proposition had been sent off* immediately *to the Minister of Spain at Paris and that there in fact would the question of the Floridas be* decided. *that it was certain no* answer *would be given to me until the return of a courier or some* answer *was recieved from Paris*—This is the substance of my first information, and from a channel I implicitly rely upon *In consequence I wrote* immediately *to our Minister at Paris and gave him notice that he might use his exertions to obtain the aid and* influence *of France, if he could* persuade *them* as *I think he might that their true interest* consisted[3] in wishing *us the Floridas and the* undisturbed *possession of our share of the navigation of the Mississippi. If France* wants *them herself or if she* (to use their own words) *is preparing for* grand *events in our quarter of the world she will oppose the cession* and I think her conduct on this occasion may in some measure be consider'd as a test of *their intentions in America or at least in that neighbourhood.* I have no doubt *our Minister in Paris will inform you fully with respect to the* disposition *of France and from me you will hear every thing that* the most unremitted, but discreet industry will permit. I was sorry to find, both in France and Spain a too general opinion entertained that our uncommon rise and unexampled increase of numbers, added to our particular local situation—called for the vigilant and perhaps Jealous attention of Europe or at least of the maritime part of it. There are certainly *other strong reasons to make most of them view us with attention: they may* perhaps *consider us as I expressed myself in one of my letters to* Mr Madison *as the only ark which has in the general* deluge *floated* untouched *and as* still *containing those seeds which may one day again burst into* Life and people *a world of liberty. It is an ark which they may not* wish the same safety & success to *as we suppose. Indeed in many* conversations *I have had with the Ministers here who may be called, with respect to American questions, neutral—those who are not from maritime Countries or such as have possessions in our quarter of the world*—some of them seem to possess an anxiety to impart to me the unfriendly & jealous opinions they have heared expressed with respect to our Government & Country—for instance *the Prussian Minister who* speaks *English very well and who* having been some time *in England,* appears to have caught a fondness, for even that portion of Liberty which *the English* enjoy—he has frequently opened himself to me in praise of our Government & Laws and particularly the freedom of the Press there enjoyed. he has frequently too expressed his uneasiness for us about *the French holding Louisiana* and in almost every conversation he has with me, repeats this observation "ah Sir your Excellent and Innocent Government knows not how many Enemies it has in Europe." *There has also been here* for nearly *fourteen years as their Minister* a very able and learned *one from Saxony, who in the time of Urquijo is* said *to have governed Spain by his* influence: *This man as* a true and liberal Philosopher is of course attached to the principles of our Government—he does not hesitate to avow it— *The King of Spain having* broken *off the match* intended *between the daughter of the Elector of Saxony and the Prince of Asturias in favor of the princess of Naples the Elector and his Minister are both* displeased *so much so that this able and* ancient *Minister is* desired *to withdraw.—*

He has frequently expressed himself to me respecting the unexampled rise of our Country, and the attention she attracts from the Maritime powers, and when I have endeavoured to say, certainly there can be no reason for this Jealousy, or even particular attention—that we are a harmless innocent nation of Planters & Merchants—without armies or navies—only anxious to send you our good things, and to take yours in return: that some of our Citizens are a little fond of Money, and that we only wish to be left at peace and quietness to obtain it by fair and honorable Commerce & Agriculture—that these are our great persuits: that if there is any Ambition among us it is entirely of a literary nature, to excel as orators or writers: that there can or ought not to be the least Jealousy of us—because we have more Territory already than we know what to do with, and that as to Islands or distant Colonies, we would not accept them, if they were presented to us. When I reason in this way, they answer it is very well to say so—the Government, like the Individual who is really Ambitious and has great designs, always endeavours to conceal them until prepared to develope its plans—Do you think, says the *Saxon* to me one day, that we know nothing of United America here? is it not easy to see the reason why your public men, who are doubtless instructed to do so, hold the language you do? does not your President do the same—while he is obliged, in giving a state of the Nation to the Legislature to confess its unexampled rise, and the prospects it has: he endeavours at the same time to impress the Opinion that you are without Ambition and have no views, but to the settlement of your own Country and the increase of Men susceptible of Happiness and habituated to Economy & Industry—This is all very well and we will suppose that your President and present Rulers, and the opinions of your People are really such; yet who will answer that the same principles and opinions shall govern twenty or even ten years hence?—give a Nation strength and opulence and it will be impossible for her to be perfectly content and tranquil.—*she will have some ambitious*[4] *and restless*[5] Statesmen *spring up to disturb the peace of others and* situated *as United America is she will be very apt to consider the neighboring possessions as a part of her own* Family, *that have been too long* separated *from her, and their present owners as* strangers *who have no right to interfere in her* Family *concerns. She will be very* likely to say *to them keep to your own quarter of the Globe and leave us to ourselves. This say they the French see plainly and so does Spain and hence the cession of Louisiana, which will be peopled with troops black as well as white and is* intended *to be very strong.* Upon the whole his information went to convince me *that the French are extremely desirous of having the Floridas themselves and will of course oppose our getting them*—wishing however to be convinced, if possible, of the true state of things I wrote to the Prince of Peace that if he had consider'd the nature of the application, (a copy of which I had inclosed him) and particularly the part of it that respected the Floridas, I would have the pleasure of an interview with him whenever he would fix—in his answer he requested me to postpone it until the decision or end of their Negotiations "now depending with France"—as nothing

important could be done, until we knew their issue. From this I conjecture that France is still pursuing her negotiations with Spain respecting the Floridas & the Boundaries of Louisiana. *In consequence
I wrote again to our Minister at Paris not having recd. any* answer *to
either of my former letters to him* until the 12th Ulto, when *his communications which were in cypher went to confirm me of the truth of all
I had heard respecting the Floridas and Louisiana.* as he has no doubt
communicated to you fully the information & opinions, he has transmitted to me you will find from them that *there exists at present no
probability of our either soon receiving an* answer *respecting the Floridas or when recd. of its being such a one as we could* wish—*he seems by
his letter to me to fear that the Floridas are not now in the power of
Spain and to confirm the opinion I* always *had, that if any thing is to be
done on this subject it must be at Paris.*—For my own part I shall do
all I can, and in the way most pleasing to the Court here; and most
likely to do the best that can be now done—having brought it before
them in the way I have, I shall not endeavour, by too pressing or repeated applications to precipitate a reply on a subject, which I fear is
very embarrassing to them—on the contrary, I will let them take their
own time, and this I beleive will be the best way—I apprehend too
that they are a little sore on the subject of Money.—
The French who have been very much accustomed to *make the Country of their enemy the theatre of war and the means of supplying their
armies* cannot now do so *on the St. Domingo expedition for this large
sums of* efficient *money are necessary,* and it is said that *as Spain is
now bringing home her long accumulating treasures from South America, that serious propositions have been made to her for the loan of such
sums as are extremely* inconvenient *for her to furnish but which she
does not know how to refuse*—it is beyond a doubt that the current Expences of the French Government far exceed their present Revenues
and that Holland and Spain must furnish the means for the greatest
part of the West India Expedition, about the events of which you
must be much better informed than we are here, as the *press is so
much under the harrow both in France and Spain,* that it is impossible
ever to know the true state of things *from that.*—
I could wish very much, to be able to give some opinions on the
probability of Events in Europe; but this is a subject, now become
so intricate, that, the more I consider it, the more I am involved in
doubt—*Bonaparte's conduct in* consolidating *the Executive power of
the Italian Republic with that of the French and in the Concordat with
the pope,* and the consiquent proceedings *in the French Legislature on*

the subject of Religion makes it extremely difficult to *penetrate his further designs.*—

Almost *all the real republics which* until lately *hoped he would have* relinquished *a part of his present enormous powers and given to France something like a free Government, now begin to despair and to* suppose *that in fixing the principles and consolidating the power of the Italian Republic he has so clearly developed his own principles as to leave France little room to hope for an amelioration of her situation while he can retain his present power.*—There are others also who think that supposing Bonaparte to be out of the question, the European Nations he controuls at present, are infinitely *too corrupt to receive a Government like ours, or indeed any other* kind of System, *than that military one which is at present imposed on them*—that from their Habits, Opinions and Manners *and their total want of knowledge of the nature of a free Government and particularly from their corruption they are so accustomed to see every thing done by money or if possible other* still *worse means of favor or* influence—*that in fact they have lost their ignominy* in the peoples Eyes and it seems now to be a wonderful & almost incredible thing to them that any Governments or their Tribunals should be conducted *upon other principles or in an honorable or* uninfluenced *manner.* Many of them speaking of the *corruption and customs of Europe* and hearing *my accounts of the purity and honor of our Governmt. and tribunals* and how dreadfully *we should conceive the possibility of money* influencing *our measures or* decisions, have said they beleive'd *we were too honest for the rest of the world* and that *our Govt.* must work Miracles, *if with all the intercourse we have with other nations it should* still *be able to keep our* Citizens and officers *honest. Such are the manners of this side of the* Globe, *and* such their opinions of us; but I trust that we shall be able to shew them, that as the Governments and Laws of Countries never fail to fashion the opinions & Manners of their Citizens our own, will for ages, continue to receive their impressions from a System, which is as different from any thing I have yet seen, as Jove's, was represented to be from that of Pluto.

I am waiting with anxious impatience to know the result of the Negotiations pending between France and this Government on which, as the Prince of Peace told me, will depend a great deal and as soon as I know them, and the effect they will have here, I will inform you.—

The Credit of this Government is rising fast in its pecuniary concerns—their Vales Reales (a Kings Debt), was more than 30 p Cent Discount when I arrived here, & is now, in Cadiz at 4, & here at 8 p

Cent, & will soon be at par—they have receive'd large quantities of Specie from America and will have more than Thirty Millions of Dollars in addition by December.—

I have mentioned in my former Letters the great number of Claims I met here, and how much they have increased the Business of this Mission so much so, that I am kept constantly at work with Reclamations and the Business that flows from them.—I beleive, except the French, that I have more Business than all the rest of the Foreign Ministers put together, for the Trade to Spain has been and now is much more extensive than I had expected[6]

Since writing the above I have been informed a courier is arrived with the intelligence that it is contemplated to declare Bonaparte Consul for Life—some say for 20 Years & that Bernadotte is immediately to go out with a Squadron & Troops to Louisiana to take possession of it.—if this is true you will no doubt hear it much sooner from Mr Livingston than from hence & it will serve to confirm some of the information I have transmitted you—

I expect to return from Aranjuez in the latter End of June.—The Court will go to Barcelona in September to meet the families of Naples & Etruria, & possibly Portugal on the subject of the intermarriage; & to see & congratulate each other on the conclusion of their Dangers & difficulties.—I am hopeful this Letter will find you & your friends all well & happy & with my best Wishes & most respectful & affectionate compliments I remain With the sincerest Regard

Dear Sir Yours Truly CHARLES PINCKNEY

RC (DLC); in a clerk's hand, with dateline, final two paragraphs, closing, and signature in Pinckney's hand; written partially in an unidentified code, with interlinear decipherment in James Madison's hand reproduced in italics (see Madison, *Papers, Sec. of State Ser.*, 3:251-7); endorsed by TJ as received 19 Aug. and so recorded in SJL. Enclosed in Pinckney to Madison, 24 May (same, 248-51).

SITIO: as indicated by Pinckney in his final paragraph, the *real sitio* or royal residence was, in this case, the palace at Aranjuez, about 30 miles south of Madrid. The royal family was there in the spring of 1802, following a practice that imitated the French court by not remaining fixed in the capital city. The custom also had roots in Castillian history. King

Carlos IV and Queen María Luisa regularly made El Escorial, a large palace constructed originally as a monastery and located about 25 miles northwest of Madrid, another *real sitio* (Douglas Hilt, *The Troubled Trinity: Godoy and the Spanish Monarchs* [Tuscaloosa, Ala., 1987], 9, 85, 135, 141; Germán Bleiberg, ed., *Diccionario de Historia de España*, 2d ed., 3 vols. [1968-69], 1:1288-91; 3:671-5; Madison, *Papers, Sec. of State Ser.*, 3:251).

LAST LETTER I WROTE YOU: the last communications that TJ had received from Pinckney were from October 1801, when Pinckney was in France on his way to Spain. Since his arrival in Spain, Pinckney had written several official dispatches that reached Madison, although a portion of Pinckney's correspondence was still not getting through (Madison,

Papers, Sec. of State Ser., 3:30-2, 53-6, 65-7, 79-82, 104-6, 142-6, 234-7; Vol. 35:395-8, 534-41).

Mariano Luis de URQUIJO was the Spanish foreign minister in 1800, when Bonaparte sent Louis Alexandre BERTHIER to Spain as special envoy. At San Ildefonso on 1 Oct. 1800, Urquijo and Berthier signed the secret preliminary articles in which France agreed to establish a northern Italian kingdom, Etruria, for a son-in-law of the king of Spain, and Spain agreed to cede Louisiana to France. Manuel Godoy, the primary adviser to the Spanish crown, to whom the king had given the title PRINCE of the PEACE, and Napoleon Bonaparte's brother LUCIEN signed the treaty at Aranjuez, 21 Mch. 1801, that formalized the arrangement (Tulard, Dictionnaire Napoléon, 203; Parry, Consolidated Treaty Series, 55:375-8; 56:45-9; Vol. 32:397n; Vol. 33:295n, 406n).

LATELY PUBLISHED AT PARIS: not until January 1802 was Robert R. Livingston able to obtain a copy of the Aranjuez treaty to send to Washington. Two months earlier Rufus King had sent an unauthorized copy from London (Madison, Papers, Sec. of State Ser., 2:254, 389).

Laurent Gouvion Saint-Cyr served as the FRENCH MINISTER to Spain. His counterpart, the MINISTER OF SPAIN AT PARIS, was José Nicolás de Azara (Tulard, Dictionnaire Napoléon, 815; Teófanes Egido, Carlos IV [Madrid, 2001], 268).

QUESTION OF THE FLORIDAS: as the French and Spanish governments worked out details of the transfer of Louisiana, Florida was a point of contention. The French sought to include East and West Florida in the territory that was to come under French control. The Spanish resisted, and in the end kept the Floridas. The Spanish also wanted assurance that France would not cede Louisiana to another country, such as the United States or Great Britain, and complained that the French were not fulfilling all their obligations regarding Etruria. The negotiations continued through the summer and into the autumn of 1802, forcing Bonaparte to delay sending civil officers and a military

contingent to take control of New Orleans and Louisiana. As Pinckney stated to Madison in his dispatch of 24 May, when he tried to broach the subject of the Floridas the Spanish government told him that the matter was "of so much consequence & importance that his Majesty requires time to consider it." Pinckney decided that he had no choice but to "wait to see, with patience, what will be the result & seize every opportunity & use every proper influence to obtain a favourable conclusion to it." Pinckney also informed Madison that the Spanish appeared to be "extremely occupied" with the effects of the Amiens peace treaty on "their Armies & navy & colonial Establishments" (E. Wilson Lyon, Louisiana in French Diplomacy, 1759-1804 [Norman, Okla., 1974], 106-7, 120, 124-6; Ronald D. Smith, "Napoleon and Louisiana: Failure of the Proposed Expedition to Occupy and Defend Louisiana, 1801-1803," in Dolores Egger Labbe, ed., The Louisiana Purchase and its Aftermath, 1800-1830, vol. 3 of The Louisiana Purchase Bicentennial Series in Louisiana History [Lafayette, La., 1998], 54-5; Alexander DeConde, This Affair of Louisiana [New York, 1976], 103-5, 148; Madison, Papers, Sec. of State Ser., 3:249).

OUR MINISTER AT PARIS: Robert R. Livingston.

The PRUSSIAN MINISTER was a diplomat named Rohde (Hilt, Troubled Trinity, 69, 109). Baron Phillip de Forell had been the ambassador of SAXONY to Spain since 1791 (Miguel Ángel Puig-Samper, "Humboldt, un Prusiano en la Corte del Rey Carlos IV," Revista de Indias, 59 [1999], 330).

The Spanish monarchs agreed to marry their son Fernando, the PRINCE OF ASTURIAS, to a PRINCESS OF NAPLES and the Two Sicilies to improve relations between branches of the Bourbon royal house (Hilt, Troubled Trinity, 133-7; Carlos IV, King of Spain, to TJ, 6 July 1802).

CONTEMPLATED TO DECLARE BONAPARTE CONSUL FOR LIFE: on 11 May, forestalling an initiative to put a 10-year limit on the first consul's powers, the consuls decreed that a national plebiscite would be held on the question of giving Bonaparte life tenure as first consul

(Thierry Lentz, *Le Grand Consulat, 1799-1804* [Paris, 1999], 336-42).

¹ Preceding six words of decipherment smudged; the passage was recovered by editors of the Madison Papers from elements of the code deciphered elsewhere in the text (Madison, *Papers, Sec. of State Ser.*, 3:251, 256n).

² So in the original, Madison piecing the word together from the code.

³ Two undeciphered elements of the code appear here in MS. Apparently they have no effect on meaning.

⁴ MS: "ambition," but should probably be, as confirmed by the decipherment of "serious" later in the letter, "ambitious" (Madison, *Papers, Sec. of State Ser.*, 3:254, 257n).

⁵ MS: "resless."

⁶ Remainder of letter in Pinckney's hand.

From Abraham Hargis

SIR   May the 26th 1802

as I have often Wrote to the superintendant respecting the situation of the Light House &c at Cape Henlopen & have not been answered by him, I at last went to the City of Philadia & informd him of the business he informd me he was makeing out his returns to close the business & to be done with the department he allso informd me that the Commissioner of the Revenue was out of Office & that no such & office existed & new no other resorce than to trouble your excellency with a few lines as I conceive the situation of this place requires immediate attenshan—as the foundation of the Light House & dwelling house is giveing Way the arch of the Kitchen Chimnay oil vault roof & doar is in bad order. the wharf (at which the Oil & all the articles is landed) is going to rack—the business in this place has been badly Conducted for this 6 years past—formerly I had the supplying the Light House with articles Oil & Glass excepted for which the former superintendant paid me 48 Dols. pr year & for the constant & yearly repairs in keeping the foundation of Light House Dwelling house &c up by brushing loging &c 38 Dols. for inspecting the oil bringing it to Light House 60 Dols. all which the feds. has taken from me. the former superintent Wm. Allibone inspected this place once a year The preasent superintendant never come near to see what was wanting or to Give orders of any kind When I informd that repairs was wanting he would reply there was no money to do any thing with. so but little repairs was attended to & frequently I have been kept nine months before I could Get my sallery & was Obliged to pay intrest to my creditors which redoosed my small salery which is too small for the labour & Expence of this place—

I have kept the Light House ninteen years & it was never in such bad repair I am ashamed to see publick property in such condition—

& the federlists would fain pirsuade people that it is owing to a republican adminestration but I am able to convince them that it was
under the Fedl. administration that this took place for when a republican had the supplying & repairing they them selves kno it was kep
in good order. I mus confess I am disappointed in not seeing Republicans in office in place of those who have thus acted—Please to excuse the Liberty of this observation I am Honoured Sir your Verry
Hbl Svt to Command   ABRM HARGIS
                    Keeper of Cape Henlopen Light House

RC (NHi: Gallatin Papers); at foot of text: "To the Honbl. Thos. Jefferson President of the United States"; endorsed by TJ as received 5 June and "Cape Henlopen lighthouse" and so recorded in SJL. Enclosed in TJ to Gallatin, 6 June 1802.

Abraham Hargis (d. 1811) served as a lieutenant in the Pennsylvania line of the Continental Army, prior to becoming keeper of the Cape Henlopen lighthouse at the mouth of the Delaware Bay. He remained in that post until securing an appointment as an inspector for the port of Wilmington, Delaware, in 1806 (Heitman, *Register*, 274; Gallatin, *Papers*, 13:306).

WROTE TO THE SUPERINTENDANT:

William McPherson (ASP, *Finance*, 1:771).

Before the federal government assumed control over the Delaware Bay lighthouse, Hargis received a salary of £130 plus £13 for supplies from the state of Pennsylvania. In letters to the secretary of the Treasury in 1790, Superintendent William ALLIBONE described the conditions at the Cape Henlopen lighthouse, urged repairs, and defended Hargis's salary. President Washington, however, thought his compensation was too high. Under a new contract, Hargis reluctantly agreed to a reduced annual salary of 266.66\frac{2}{3}$ (Syrett, *Hamilton*, 6:468, 475, 479, 514, 561, 562; Washington, *Papers, Pres. Ser.*, 5:533).

Statement of William Short's Tenements

Since writing the preceding I have settled with Richard Shackleford. his lands have been tended as follows

	as. ps.	1800	1801	1802
No. 1.	7–49.	oats	rest	corn
2	6–72	corn	wheat	rest
3	85	new in tobo.	tobo.	corn
4	1–60	tobo.	corn	wheat
5	5–	rest	corn	oats & wheat

his rents, to the end of 1801. amounted to 59. D 45 c. he has furnished
13 Dollars and given me an order on mr R. Anderson his mercht. for
46. D. 45 which is accepted

John Speirs holds

		as perch	1801	1802
R.T.	No. 1.	17 56	wheat	corn & rest
	2	10–89	corn	wheat & oats
	4	7–100	tobo. & rest	tobo. & rest
William Reynolds holds			1801	1802
R.T.	No. 3.	13–67	corn & rest	wheat oats corn

Joseph Price has paid up to the end of 1801.　　Tᴴ: Jᴇғғᴇʀsᴏɴ
　　　　　　　　　　　　　　　　　　　May 26. 1802.

PrC (DLC: William Short Papers); entirely in TJ's hand, as an addendum to the statement dated 17 May.

TJ recorded the ᴏʀᴅᴇʀ ᴏɴ Richard Anderson for $46.45 on 27 May (ᴍʙ, 2:1073).

From Benjamin Smith Barton

Dᴇᴀʀ Sɪʀ,　　　　　　　　　　　Philadelphia, May 27th, 1802.
I take the liberty of introducing to your knowledge, the bearer of this, Dr. Edward D. Smith, of Charleston, S. Carolina, who is now on his return to his native place. Dr. Smith is a young man of very uncommon merit, ardently attached to science, and not less so to the interests of republicanism. These circumstances have procured for him many friends in Pennsylvania. I could not deprive myself of the pleasure of making him known to you, in his passage through Washington.—
I am happy, Sir, to inform you, that our Philosophical Society proceed with spirit. Their sixth volume will shortly be committed to the press.
I acknowledge, with many thanks, the receipt of your kind & valuable letters. They will be of most essential use to me in my journey, which I design to set out upon in two or three weeks.
　　With the greatest respect, I am, Dear Sir, Your very humble Servant, and affectionate friend, &c.　　　　B. S. Bᴀʀᴛᴏɴ.

RC (DLC); endorsed by TJ as received 1 June and so recorded in SJL.

Edward Darrell sᴍɪᴛʜ graduated from the College of New Jersey in 1795, then earned his medical degree in Philadelphia in 1800 under the tutelage of Benjamin Rush. Returning to his native Charleston, he practiced medicine and later taught chemistry at South Carolina College in Columbia (Joseph Ioor Waring, *A History of Medicine in South Carolina, 1670-1825* [Charleston, 1964], 315-16; J. Jefferson Looney and Ruth L. Woodward, *Princetonians, 1791-1794: A Biographical Dictionary* [Princeton, 1991], 311).

ʏᴏᴜʀ ᴋɪɴᴅ & ᴠᴀʟᴜᴀʙʟᴇ ʟᴇᴛᴛᴇʀs: see TJ to Barton, 29 Mch. 1802.

From Charles Willing Byrd

Secretary's Office—Cincinnati—
SIR   N.W. Territory. May the 27th 1802

As I have to discharge the united and important duties both of Governor and Secretary of the North Western Territory, I think on the fairest principles of equity that I should enjoy the honors and emoluments of the most considerable Appointment of the two. I am conscious that I stand upon delicate ground, and that a solicitation of this nature in my behalf from a third person, would be deemed more consistent with propriety. But in truth you cannot view me in the light of a common Candidate, my application being for an Office the labours and duties of which have already devolved on me. It will not be an extravagant assertion to say, that with the smallest exertions I could have procured a Petition in my favor for the Appointment of Governor with several thousand Subscribers to it; but having heard, tho' it has since been contradicted, that a Successor to Governor St. Clair in the event of his removal was already designated, I discouraged the importunities of my friends on that subject. It will readily occur to you, Sir, that when performing the duties which are attached to the Office of Governor, a considerable encrease of trouble as well as expence must unavoidably accrue, and that the pitiful salary of seven hundred and fifty dollars per annum with the title of Secretary, is not an adequate compensation.

In making this appeal to your justice I fear I have committed an intrusion upon your time and occupations, but I confide in your indulgence and flatter myself that you will pardon the trespass.

Accept Sir the assurances of consideration with which I have the honor to be respectfully yr—mo—ob—servt—

CHARLES WILLING BYRD

RC (DNA: RG 59, LAR); at foot of text: "The honble, The President of the United States"; endorsed by TJ as received 15 June and "to be govr. of N.W. territory" and so recorded in SJL.

A native of Virginia, Charles Willing Byrd (1770-1828) was appointed secretary of the Northwest Territory at the end of 1799. During his tenure, he frequently clashed with Governor Arthur St. Clair and aligned himself with the Republican leadership of the territory. During St. Clair's absence from the territory from March to July 1802, Byrd served as acting governor, making numerous appointments that aroused the governor's ire and thwarting Federalist efforts to delay implementation of the Enabling Act. Following St. Clair's removal from office in November 1802, Byrd served as interim governor until the territory became the state of Ohio in March 1803. That same month, TJ nominated Byrd to be the U.S. district judge for the new state, a position he held until his death (JEP, 1:330-1, 447; Randolph Chandler Downes, *Frontier Ohio, 1788-1803* [Columbus, 1935],

222-5, 236-7; Alfred Byron Sears, *Thomas Worthington, Father of Ohio Statehood* [Columbus, 1998], 58-9, 89, 97; *Biographical Directory of the Federal Judiciary, 1789-2000* [Lanham, Md., 2001], 412).

From William Canby

Brandywine Mills 27th 5 mo 1802

Esteemed friend Thomas Jefferson, thy Assertion, (when I attended with Dorothy Ripley, on her application for thy concurrence with her desire, to attempt the education of abt. 64 female black or colored Children of those called free)—"that thou apprehended they were not of equal capacity with the Whites," gave me concern, having long since been informed, that our friend Anthony Benezet, (some Years occupied in their Tuition), declared his sentiment, that they were of equal Capacity; & having myself been witness to instances of their good improvement, in the Scool since continued for their benefit in Philadelphia. Yet I think with concern, there is also truth in thy experience of their incapacity—for it appears to me, it is permitted by the allwise disposer of events, that Mankind departing from his righteous Law written in the inward part, which is blotted thro' want of inward attention unto obedience; being thereby only kept alive, & predominant to the subjection of Nature.—for want of this they may be so blinded, & so confederate in wrong courses, as to oppress Mankind, not only as to bodily power, but also to degrade the Natural Capacity for a long time; but this being contrary to Justice, & the Rights of Mankind; tho' it cannot I think prevent the salvation of the Soul of the oppressed, or the divine intercourse, with his own life, raised as beforesaid.—yet I think this oppression by one part of his Creation over the other will not always continue unreproved; & as it is a departure from his righteous government only, which (generally) deprives of his blessing act, or inward; & makes punishment Necessary, so the longer it is continued, & the greater the extent, the greater is the punishment, or Overturning, necessary to dispel the cloud of separation, or that which prevents the effusion of all good.

with my best wishes for thy further attainment of this most Necessary, inward, & divine Life, & Communion; without which we cannot I think, know the existance of the divine Being, & Principle, nor enjoy fully the benefit of it, but by a principle of the like kind being raised in us, seeing like must communicate with its like; I bid thee heartily farewell.   WM. CANBY

RC (DLC); endorsed by TJ as received 30 May and so recorded in SJL.

William Canby (1748-1830) was from Brandywine Village, a part of Wilmington, Delaware, noted for its many flour mills. Although his family was prominent in that business, Canby devoted his energies to the Society of Friends and became a beloved figure among Quakers in the region. In 1813, TJ responded to a letter from Canby with one of his more explicit commentaries on Christian faith, in which he praised the teachings of Jesus as perhaps the world's purest moral system, while denouncing sectarianism and advocating universalist principles. The exchange was widely reprinted in nineteenth-century newspapers (William Canby Biddle, *William Canby, of Brandywine, Delaware: His Descendants Fourth to Seventh Generation in America* [Philadelphia, 1883]; Carol Hoffecker, *Brandywine Village: The Story of a Milling Community* [Wilmington, Del., 1974]; TJ to Canby, 18 Sep. 1813, in DLC).

Earlier that month, Canby had accompanied DOROTHY RIPLEY, an English missionary, on a trip to Washington and the President's House, where they met with TJ on 5 May, with the goal of gaining TJ's approval of a plan to start a school for African American girls in the capital. In her memoir Ripley reported that TJ wished her success but also declared that "I am afraid you will find it an arduous task to undertake" and later added, "I do not think they are the same race; for their mental powers are not equal to the Indians." Ripley argued that training people under such a view would "prove only a curse to the land," a sentiment that gained the approval of Henry Dearborn and District of Columbia Commissioner William Thornton, who were also in attendance. Following a brief exchange about the President's own slaveholding, the meeting ended cordially. There is no evidence that the proposed school was ever founded (DNB; Dorothy Ripley, *The Extraordinary Conversion, and Religious Experience of Dorothy Ripley, with Her First Voyage and Travels in America* [New York, 1810], 63-6).

ANTHONY BENEZET, a Quaker reformer and abolitionist, founded a school for African Americans in Philadelphia (ANB).

To George Jefferson

DEAR SIR   Monticello May 27. 1802.

I am setting out this morning on my return to Washington. being in want of 500. lb. of bacon here for our workmen, I must ask the favor of you to procure and forward that much by the first safe boats to Gabriel Lilly my manager here and in general to answer his applications for what he may want here, without my special order, as his discretion may always be trusted. I have not heard from mr Barnes since I left Washington, but take for granted his having remitted [to you] 300. D. as desired, which shall shortly be further added to. accept my affectionate salutations.   TH: JEFFERSON

PrC (MHi); faint; at foot of text: "Mr. George Jefferson"; endorsed by TJ in ink on verso.

Étienne Lemaire's Memorandum of Items for the President's House

Mai 1802 d'u 28—
Etat D'e Ce qu'il, feaut pr. la maison D'u president
Savoir

Linge de table	6	N'aple pr. 1. table de 6. Couvert
	3	douzaine de torchon pr. Nétoÿé les vert
	2	ideme pr. la Cuisinne
	2	ideme de Serviette pr. les Chanbre de Maitre
porcilaine	1	Service de porcilainne blœux bien, a Sorti pr. 25. Couver
	1	ideme pr. le té Et Câffée pr. 30—Maitre
verrie	12	Carâffe pr. de l'eau, de 2. grandeur
	4	douzaine de goblet, a bier
	2	ideme peti pr. le ponge
	2	duzaine ideme a vin—vert a patte
faÿance	12	basin, blanc, Et l'eur Bouteille pr. les Chanbre
	12	ideme de pôt, de Chanbre
	12	ideme—a ânce pr. Metre de l'eau
	18	pôt Et bouteille de diferante grandeur pr. les chéminé
	2	douzaine de plat de diferant grandeur Et 3. d'ouzaine d'asiette Comûne
Couteaût Et fourchete	3	douzainne de Couttiaût pr. le premié Service
	3	ideme d'e fourchette
	2	grand Couteaut a d'epséz
	2	ideme de fourchete
Couteau	3	ideme de desert
	3	ideme de fourchete

EDITORS' TRANSLATION

28 May 1802
Inventory of what is needed for the President's House
Specifically:

Table Linens	6	tablecloths for 6 place settings
	3	dozen dishtowels for glassware
	2	ditto for kitchenware
	2	ditto napkins for the master chamber

Porcelain	1	matching service in blue porcelain for 25 settings
	1	ditto for coffee and tea for 30 people
Glassware	12	carafes for water of two sizes
	4	dozen beer steins
	2	dozen small punch glasses
	2	dozen stemmed wine glasses
Ceramics	12	white basins and pitchers for the bedrooms
	12	chamber pots
	12	water pitchers with handles
	18	pots and bottles of different sizes for the fireplaces
	2	dozen platters of various sizes and 3 dozen serving dishes
Knives and Forks	3	dozen knives for the first service
	3	ditto forks
	2	large carving knives
	2	large carving forks
Knife	3	(dozen) dessert knives
	3	(dozen) dessert forks

MS (MHi); entirely in Lemaire's hand; endorsed by TJ: "Mr. Lemaire's memm things wanting for mr Claxton June 1802" and "Claxton Thomas."

From Thomas Mendenhall

ESTEEMED SIR,   Wilmington May the 28th. 1802

You will readily recollect my having taken the liberty early under your Administration of offering myself as a Candidate for the Collectors office of this Port in Case a Vacancy should happen from resignation or otherwise. as every thing in that department remains in statu quo, and the final Issue of that application is to me inscrutable you will pardon this intrusion.

By a refference to that application, you will observe my pretentions to office, were founded on the result of information that might be obtained from such Characters, as I deemed to be in Your Confidence, and whose Zeal for the Public good & your repose, could not be diminished by any private Interest, or Personal considerations.— On the present occasion I have had no opportunity of Consulting my friends, as, I but Just now learnt that a Commander was yet to be appointed for the New Revenue Cutter destined to Cruize in the Delaware River & Bay; if so, it is a case in point, & for which you will have the goodness to beleive me fully Competent; as I ought from my Experience to be as good a Pilot in the Delaware, as in the Atlantic Ocean. Beleiving this officer will be respected according to his merits;

from a variety of Considerations I am induced to offer myself for that station; should this Meet your approbation, & I should be favoured with a Commission, I shall regard it with the highest satisfaction, as an invaluable assurance of the good oppinion you are pleased to entertain for me.

Accept Sir my best wishes for your wellfare & believe me with profound respect Your Obt Hl Svt   THOMAS MENDENHALL

PS. if recommendations are considerd necessary, if I could be indulged with that intimation through one of my friends J. Mason or J. Dickenson I would immediately forward such as would be satisfactory. TM.

RC (DLC); at head of text: "Thomas Jefferson Esqr. President of the U.S."; endorsed by TJ as received 30 May and so recorded in SJL; also endorsed by TJ: "to command a Cutter."

OFFERING MYSELF AS A CANDIDATE: in April 1801, Mendenhall applied to be collector at Wilmington, Delaware (Vol. 33:644-6).

From James Monroe

DEAR SIR   Richmond May 30. 1802

I annex a note of persons qualified for the office of comrs. under the bankrupt law, for the places to wh. they are affixed. It is thought it will be better to appoint comrs. at Petersbg. separately from those at this place. Of Norfolk I can say nothing as yet, but expect to be able to do it in a few days. I was requested by Colo. Lambert sometime since to give him a letter to you wh. I did to day. I informed him at the time I gave it him, that I shod. send in other names (without mentioning at whose request) observing to do justice to the pretentions of every one. He is neither Lawyer nor merchant. Sincerely I am yr. friend   JAS. MONROE

It is possible that George Hay may act; of this I know nothing but will have him sounded & write you by the next post

Richmond

William Duvall. Lawyer.	Richmd.
George W. Smith — L.	R.
Benjamin Hatcher Mercht.	Manchester
Jacob I. Cohen, late mercht.,	R. a jew & foreigr. but very worthy character—
Joseph Gallego, mercht.	R. foregnr. but also very respectable

Micajah Davis, quaker Mercht.   R. in the comn. line
Saml. Pleasants, printer   R.
James Lowndes, quaker,   R.
    Either of the five last named will supply the fourth place—
        Petersburg—
Archibald Thweatt   Lawyer
Thos. Bolling Robertson.   L
John McRae   Merch:
Thomas Burchett—   merch:

RC (DNA: RG 59, LAR); list of recommendations on separate sheet; endorsed by TJ as received 2 June and "Commrs. bkrptcy Richmd. Petsbg." and so recorded in SJL.

On 18 June, the *National Intelligencer* reported that George HAY, William DuVal (DUVALL), George W. SMITH, Benjamin HATCHER, Archibald THWEATT, Thomas Bolling ROBERTSON, John MCRAE, and Thomas BURCHETT had been appointed bankruptcy commissioners for Virginia. The appointment of Burchett, however, may have been an error. In the letterbook copies of bankruptcy commissions, the name of the final Virginia commissioner was altered to read "Robert Birchett" (list of commissions, in Lb in DNA: RG 59, MPTPC; Appendix II, List 2).

From James Monroe

DEAR SIR   Richmond May 30. 1802.
    Colo. David Lambert of this city has requested me to communicate to you his desire to be employ'd as a comr. of banruptcy, with which I readily comply. He is a respectable citizen who has held several offices of credit, among wh. is the command of the rgt. of the city which he lately voluntarily resigned; he was comr. under the act for choosing Electors of P. & V. Presidt., & has been a comr. under the bankrupt law by appointmt. of the federal court. I have understood and believe that he discharged the duties of the trusts reposed in him with propriety; some of which were under my immediate view, on the authority of which I speak. Having long known & esteemed him, at his request, I readily add his name to the list of those who are desirous of obtaining this office. I am with great respect & esteem
    yr. very humble servt.   JAS. MONROE

RC (DNA: RG 59, LAR); endorsed by TJ as received 7 June and "David Lambert to be Comr. bkrptcy Richmd." and so recorded in SJL.

From Craven Peyton

DEAR SIR   Stump Island 30th May 1802

Kee & my self have not yet bargained but make no doubt but we shall soon, if you can with convenience forward the small sum which is between us to Richmond it will Oblege me much being compeled to pay a sum there the last of this week. I calculate that James L. Henderson will be in this county by the time I return from Richmond. & the instand Any thing is done you shall hear from me.

with much Respt. yr. Mst. Obet.   C. PEYTON

RC (ViU); endorsed by TJ as received 2 June and so recorded in SJL.

KEE: possibly John R. Kerr. For Pey-

ton's efforts to acquire, on TJ's behalf, the property of JAMES L. HENDERSON and the other Henderson heirs, see Vol. 35:342-4, 454-5, 580-1; Vol. 36:11.

From Thomas Sumter, Sr.

DEAR SIR—   Stateboro 30th May. 1802

I have recieved your favr dated Monticello the 9th & Post marked Milton the 14th Inst.—and have duely considered the Same—the result of my opinion is—, that Messrs. John Blake Simeon Theus Theodore Gaillard & Dominick Hall Esqrs. are well quallified, both as Merchts. & Lawyers to discharge the duties under the appointment Contemplated. the two Gentlemen first nomd Possess extensive Knowledge in Commerl business, & also in Public Transactions, are of Very respectable Standing—Mr. Gaillard is Considered an emminent Lawyer & is Now Speaker of the House of Representatives—Mr. Hall has been heretofore made Known to you—I take the Liberty to Suggest Should any of these Gentlemen decline to act, & it were deemed not improper to Suffer an Individual to exercise discretion in making New appointments, I am Persuaded Mr. Blake would execute Such Trust with Great fidelity & fully to Satisfaction—

Permit me, Sir, to Congratulate you, on the reestablishment of Peace in Europe. Humanity dictates a wish that it may prove of Long duration, but experience Will induce us to fear, a difrent State of things Will Soon intervene—

I have Just recd Letters dated 5th. march— from my Son. the Minister & family were in health—he Speaks in Very respectful Terms of him[1]

I rather Suspect my Son will not remain Long in that Country not mearley on account of his being disposed to marry—but rather on other considerations—

The Crops through the extensive range of Country Which I Passed—are remarkably Promising—& now in this State—they are much better than any ever Seen in it—

Should any thing here after Occur, in which my attention & exertions can be rendered usefull—Shall be happy to recive your Commands—

I am Dear Sir With the highest respect, your obedt Servt

THOS. SUMTER

PS

The V. Pt. has not yet returned from his more distant Southern Tour—it is not easy to decide, Which discovers the Most Zeal, our Co[...]il assemblies, or those Convoked for religious exercises—it would Seem So much bustle, is intended to produce Somthing extra-oridnary—the Perticulars aluded to, No Doubt Will be Seen fully detailed in Print   T S

RC (DNA: RG 59, LAR); torn; endorsed by TJ as received 17 June and so recorded in SJL; also endorsed by TJ: "John Blake Simeon Theus Theodore Gaillard Dominic A. Hall } Commrs. bkrpcy Charleston"; with note by TJ, probably written at a later sitting: "Wm Moultrie Benj. Cudworth Francis Dickinson Thos. Somersall Simon Mc.Intosh John Webb."

On 22 June, commissions were prepared appointing John BLAKE, Simeon THEUS, Theodore GAILLARD, Dominick A. HALL, William Moultrie, and Benjamin Cudworth commissioners of bankruptcy for South Carolina. Blake, Theus, and Hall each declined the appointment, while Moultrie resigned his commission in April 1803 (Appendix II, List 2; Madison, *Papers, Sec. of State Ser.*, 3:392-3, 4:480).

For the deteriorating relationship be-

tween Sumter's SON, Thomas Sumter, Jr., and the American MINISTER[1] to France, Robert R. Livingston, see Livingston to TJ, 4 May.

On or about 20 Apr., Aaron Burr left Washington for a brief SOUTHERN TOUR, during which he was honored with public receptions at Raleigh, Charleston, and Savannah. Republican and Federalist critics of Burr alike speculated on ulterior motives for his visit to the southern states, although its main purpose was ostensibly to see his daughter, Theodosia, who was expecting the birth of her first child. He left Charleston on 17 June and arrived at New York City six days later, accompanied by his daughter and her newborn son, Aaron Burr Alston (Kline, *Burr*, 2:717-18, 719-20; Syrett, *Hamilton*, 26:21-2).

[1] Word written over "the Minister."

From Thomas Worthington

Sir   Chilicothe May 30th 1802

I have the pleasure to enclose to you two receipts one for the entry the other for the tax on lands therein mentioned—You will observe Sir that I have paid the tax for the present year of course there will be none due untill one year hence

I have the honour to be with the highest respect Sir Your Obt St

T. Worthington

RC (MHi); at foot of text: "The President of the United states"; endorsed by TJ as received 15 June and so recorded in SJL. Enclosures not found.

From DeWitt Clinton

Newtown near New York

Sir   31 May 1802.

I handed Mr. Gallatin a list of six names for Commissioners of Bankruptcy in New York and of three for Albany: As he may not probably know or recollect the characters of these gentlemen, I have taken the liberty to make some remarks in the enclosed paper: It is highly important that no mistake should be committed at present in appointments in the City of New York—a little faction exists there who under the garb of republicanism are doing all that malice and activity without talents or respectability can do, to injure the republican cause: Measures are persuing to develope their views—I am persuaded that *now* is the time to strike—They certainly will oppose us on the eve of every ensuing election and that is a most inexpedient period for attacking an internal enemy when we are engaged with a foreign one: but of this, I shall take the liberty to speak more at large on a future occasion

Our Elections have turned out most propitiously—We have Eleven certain out of the seventeen Members of Congress: Joshua Sands succeeded in this Way—He lives in the republican County of Kings, which can give upon an emergency from 150 to 200 Votes Majority. some of the little faction industriously circulated that his success was certain—This discouraged the republicans in Kings who did not turn out as they might have done, not thinking it worth while to act unnecessarily against a Country man: In Rensselaer County we carried the Assembly ticket and lost the Member of Congress; This was owing to holding up a person who had formerly been a violent federalist but who is now a sincere republican—In Greene & Ulster Counties We Obtained 4 out of 6 Members of assembly and failed in the member of Congress—This is also ascribable to an injudicious selection of a Candidate: So that it was certainly in our power to have pared down the federal strength to three Members—an enclosed paper contains the names & some remarks on the characters elected.—

Our Senate previous to the last Election contained 43 Members and our Assembly 108—They have been reduced, the first to 32 and the other to 100 Members.

Last Year—The Senate stood thus.

	Republicans	Federalists
	19	24
And the Assembly	82	26

And they now stand

	Republicans	Federalists
Senate—Certain—	20	12
Assembly—		
probably but not certain	76	24

Our Senators continue in office four Years—so that this change is of immense importance.

I have the honor to be With the most respectful Attachment. Your most Obedt Servt.   DeWitt Clinton

In our state Legislature we have not six Men at the utmost (I do not believe 3) in the views or interests of the little faction.—

RC (DNA: RG 59, LAR, 2:0297-9); addressed: "The President of the United States"; endorsed by TJ as received 3 June and "Commrs. of bkrptcy" and so recorded in SJL.

THREE FOR ALBANY: the names Abraham G. Lansing, Nicholas N. Quackenbush, and George Merchant "of Albany" appear on a scrap of paper (MS in DNA: RG 59, LAR, 1:1094; probably in Clinton's hand). TJ entered the names on his list of candidates for bankruptcy commissioners (see Appendix II, List 1). All three received commissions dated 10 June 1802 (list of commissions in Lb in DNA: RG 59, MPTPC).

LITTLE FACTION EXISTS: see Vol. 36:81-2, 83-8.

LOST THE MEMBER OF CONGRESS: Josiah Masters, a native of Woodbury, Connecticut, who practiced law in Rensselaer County. He won the next congressional election and served in the Ninth and Tenth Congresses (New York *Commercial Advertiser,* 11 June 1802; *Biog. Dir. Cong.*). For the victory of John Cantine, the Republican congressional candidate in GREENE & ULSTER COUNTIES, over the Federalist Conrad E. Elmendorf, see Granger to TJ, 14 May.

THEY HAVE BEEN REDUCED: a constitutional convention was held in Albany in October 1801 with the power to reduce and limit the number of senators and members of the state assembly. The number in the assembly was set at 100, never to exceed 150 members. The number of senators was fixed at 32. Eight senators were to be elected in 1802 (*Journal of the Convention of the State of New-York: Began and Held at the City of Albany, on the 13th Day of October, 1801* [Albany, 1801], 39-41).

I

Candidates for Bankruptcy Commissioners

For Commissioners of Bankruptcy in the City of New York
Mercantile Characters
John Broome—Candidate for member of Congress—former President of the Chamber of Commerce—a very respectable man—
William Edgar—a man of large property & fair character—late a member of our State Convention
Solomon Townsend—a man of property—an invariable republican and old Citizen
Law Characters
Jonathan Persee Junior—A young man of considerable promise—His appointment will give great satisfaction to all the republican bar—he ought by no means to be over-looked.
Daniel D. Tompkins—Also—a member of our State Legislature.
Nathan Sanford—Also reputable in talents—
Characters who ought not to be appointed on account of their holding lucrative offices in the State
James Fairlie, Wm. Cutting.
On account of their being incurable Members of the little faction
Thomas Smith, Timothy Greene, William P. Van Ness, Joseph Brown.

MS (DNA: RG 59, LAR, 2:0300); undated; entirely in Clinton's hand.

TJ entered Clinton's six recommendations on his list of candidates for bankruptcy commissioners (see Appendix II, List 1). All except SOLOMON TOWNSEND received commissions for the District of New York dated 10 June 1802 (list of commissions in Lb in DNA: RG 59, MPTPC). For the application of THOMAS SMITH and a recommendation sent by Congressman Lucas C. Elmendorf to Gallatin on his behalf, see Kline, *Burr*, 2:711-12.

II

Comments on the Congressional Election in New York

Republican Members of Congress

John Smith
Samuel L. Mitchill
Philip Van Cortlandt   } re-elected
David Thomas

Beriah Palmer
Andrew Mc.Cord   } members of the Old republican party—In
Isaac Bloom   whom every reliance may be placed
Frederik Sammons

John Patterson   } The two first Emigrants from Massachusetts—
Oliver Phelps   the last from Connecticut.
Erastus Root

Patterson was a Brigadier Genl. in the Massachusetts Line during the War—Root is a young lawyer who has been often in our state Legislature—Phelps is the only man that can be suspected of inclining to the views of the little faction but I feel persuaded his patriotism and intimacy with Mr Granger will keep him straight—These men have been undeviating republicans since their settlement in this State.

Federal do

Joshua Sands ⎫
Henry W. Livingston ⎬ Decent men of moderate talents

Killian K. Van Rensselaer } re-elected

George Tibbets ⎫ Emigrants from Connecticut —bitter
Gaylord Griswold ⎬ and weak—the last a lawyer—

Coendrat E. Elmendorf } a vapid Attorney—

A Question will arise whether he is elected—Our Judges on the Returns have not decided.

MS (DNA: RG 59, LAR, 2:0301); undated; entirely in Clinton's hand.

FREDERIK SAMMONS: that is, Thomas Sammons, newly elected congressman from Montgomery County, who was also a member of the New York Constitutional Convention of 1801 (*Biog. Dir. Cong.*).

For Clinton's earlier assessment of Oliver PHELPS, see Vol. 36:81-2.

From Henry Dearborn

SIR   War Department May 31. 1802.

I take the liberty of proposing for your approbation, Henry B. Brevoort, for an Ensign in the 2d. Regiment of Infantry.

I have the Honor to be with great consideration Sir, Your Mo. Ob. Servt   H. DEARBORN

RC (DLC); in a clerk's hand, signed by Dearborn; at foot of text: "The President of the United States"; endorsed by TJ as received from the War Department on 31 May and "Henry B. Brevoort to be ensign" and so recorded in SJL. FC (Lb in DNA: RG 107, LSP).

HENRY B. BREVOORT received his ensign's commission, dated to 7 May 1802,

and eventually rose to the rank of major in the United States Army. Settling in the Michigan Territory after the War of 1812, he later served as register of the land office at Detroit and as an Indian agent at Green Bay. He died at Detroit in 1858 (JEP, 1:434; 2:24, 199, 525; 3:315, 324; Columbus *Daily Ohio Statesman*, 11 Apr. 1856, 11 Feb. 1858).

From David Hall

SIR   Lewes May 31st. 1802

At the request of a number of respectable Citizens of the County of Kent in this State, I have the Honor of transmitting to you, an address soliciting the removal of Allen McLane, from the office of Collector of the Customs, for the Port of Wilmington. I know of no Character more obnoxious to the republicans of this State than Mr. McLane, no one who has taken more undue means to crush the republican Interest, and who when one of the Governors privy Council exerted all his influence to dispossess every Republican of the offices they held under this State, a removal of this man from office (if consistent with the plan you have laid down to walk by) would I am convinced be very gratifying to every Republican in the State of Delaware.

I am informed a number of applications have already been made under the supposition that a removal will take place; among the number of respectable characters, the name of Colo. Nehemiah Tilton has been mentioned, having been acquainted with the Colo. for a long time believing that his appointment would be most agreeable to a great majority of the Republicans of this State and knowing him to be well[1] qualified to fulfill the duties of that office and entertaining no doubt of his fidelity in the performance of them I have taken the Liberty of recommending him in case of a removal to fill that post.

I must take the Liberty of mentioning one more friend Mr. Abraham Hargis the Keeper of the Light House near this place, he considers himself as not well treated by the superintendant Mr. McPherson who has on repeated applications refused to give any order for the repairs of the foundation of the Light House which is very much decayed, and unless speedily attended to will be attended with great expence. He has been refused the payment of his Salary Mr. McPherson alledging he has not been supplied with money to answer such demands; this I view as a federal trick to cast a Stigma on the present administration — Mr. Hargis some years derived some pecuniary advantage from the superintendance of the purchase of oil and other supplies for the use of the Light House of this he has been deprived and the same has been bestowed on Judge Rodney this Mr. Hargis considers as an act of Injustice as he is under the necessity of performing the greater part of the Duty—

I have the honor to be Sir, Your Excellency's most obedient and very humble Servant   DAVID HALL

RC (DLC); endorsed by TJ as received 5 June and so recorded in SJL. Enclosure: Delaware Democratic Republicans to TJ, printed at 24 Mch.

Born in Lewes, Sussex County, Delaware, David Hall (1752-1817) received a classical education, studied law, and was admitted to the bar in 1773. He served in the Revolutionary War, enlisting as a private. In April 1777, he received a commission as colonel. Seriously wounded in the battle of Germantown, Hall returned to Delaware and resumed his law practice.

By 1796, he and other Delaware veterans were leading the Republican opposition in the state. Hall served as governor from 1802 to 1805. In 1813, he became a judge of the court of common pleas (Robert Sobel and John Raimo, eds., *Biographical Directory of the Governors of the United States 1789-1978*, 4 vols. [Westport, Conn., 1978], 1:214; John A. Munroe, *The Philadelawareans and Other Essays Relating to Delaware* [Newark, Del., 2004], 201, 206, 213). For Hall's victory in the contested gubernatorial election of 1801, see Vol. 35:427-9.

BESTOWED ON JUDGE RODNEY: already in May 1790, lighthouse superintendent William Allibone contracted with Philadelphia merchants to supply oil to the Cape Henlopen lighthouse. Under another contract, Daniel Rodney received $60 per year to transport oil and other necessities to the lighthouse. A Federalist, Rodney served as a judge of the Delaware court of common pleas from 1793 to 1806 (Washington, *Papers, Pres. Ser.*, 5:421-2; *Biog. Dir. Cong.*).

[1] MS: "will."

To Thomas Law

DEAR SIR   Washington May 31. 1802

I recieved yesterday evening your letter of the 23d. instant, informing me of the death of mrs Washington: and I recieved it with great & sincere concern. an acquaintance of five and twenty years, in times & circumstances of various and trying aspect, had made me a witness of her constant course in whatsoever was benevolent and virtuous in life, had marked her in my judgment as one of the most estimable of women, and had inspired me with an affectionate and respectful attachment to her. this loss is the more felt too as it renews the memory of a preceding one, of a worthy of that degree which providence, in it's wise dispensations, sees fit rarely to bestow on us, whose services in the cause of man had justly endeared him to the world, and whose name will be among the latest monuments of the age wherein he lived, which time will extinguish. my own sense of these losses enables me to sympathise sincerely in the afflictions of the family, to whom I pray you to tender assurances, & to accept them yourself, of my highest esteem & respect.   TH: JEFFERSON

PrC (DLC); at foot of text: "Mr. Law."

IN TIMES & CIRCUMSTANCES OF VARIOUS AND TRYING ASPECT: after a visit to see Martha Washington at Mount Vernon almost five months before her death, Massachusetts congressman Manasseh Cutler reported: "Her remarks were frequently pointed, and sometimes very sarcastic, on the new order of things and the present administration. She spoke of the election of Mr. Jefferson, whom she considered as one of the most detestable of mankind, as the greatest misfortune our country had ever experienced. Her unfriendly feelings toward him were naturally to be expected, from the abuse he has offered to General Washington, while living, and to his memory since his decease" (William P. Cutler and Julia P. Cutler, *Life, Journals, and Correspondence of Rev. Manasseh Cutler, LL.D.*, 2 vols. [Cincinnati, 1888; repr. Athens, Ohio, 1987], 2:56-7).

From Robert Lawson

DEAR SIR, [Richm]ond May 31st. 180[2]

I had the honor of receiving your very friendly and sympathetic Letter of the 22nd. of June last;—and moreover diriv'd essential benefit from the fifty dollars plac'd by your benevolence, in the hands of Major Duval for my use. For which be pleas'd, Sir, to accept the only Tribute in my Power to tender,—my cordial and gratefull thanks. At that time I was severely attack'd with the flux; and which, with short intervals of abatement, continued to afflict me until late in the month of November. I have not in time been out of the House, where I have been upwards of twelve months, since I came to it.

I had calculated upon my eldest Son coming in to assist [me] in returning to Kentucky but by Letters rec[eived fro]m my Family, dated [...] of last month, I [...] others of the same Avocation, engag'd in carrying on considerable buildings in Nashville in Tenesse, in the Stone mason line, which without a departure from his engagements, renders his coming in impracticable. A Person who is carefull; who well knows my unhappy state of decripitude, and who has drove a waggon from this City to Lexington in Kentucky and back;—offers to furnish two good Horses, and in a light Stage waggon to be furnish'd, to carry me out for £60

My Friends to whom the Proposition has been communicated think it not unreasonable; and well knowing my ardent desire to get back to my Children, will do all in [their] power to accomplish it. But, Sir, to raise £60. purchase [a] Stage, with a necessary Sum to defray Expences in travelling by a few, comparatively speaking, who have contributed w[ith] a liberal hand to m[...] me here for upwards of twel[ve] mon[ths]

RC (ViW); torn and frayed; incomplete. Recorded in SJL as received from Richmond on 4 June 1802.

TJ paid Lawson FIFTY DOLLARS in charity through a draft payable to William DUVAL on 20 June 1801 (Vol. 34:398-9, 410).

MY UNHAPPY STATE: Lawson, who had served in the Continental army and Virginia militia during the Revolutionary War, received 10,000 acres in the Virginia military district as bounty lands for his service. Financial difficulties and an intemperate lifestyle plagued him throughout his retirement (John H. Gwathmey, *Historical Register of Virginians in the Revolution, Soldiers, Sailors, Marines* [Richmond, 1938], 462; Lloyd DeWitt Bockstruck, *Revolutionary War Bounty Land Grants* [Baltimore, 1996], xxiii, 307; Vol. 34:360-1).

From Caesar A. Rodney

HONORED & DEAR SIR, Wilmington May 31st. 1802

This will be handed to you by Capt. Davis formerly of this port, who commanded lately the ship St. Domingo packet & who was imprisoned by the orders of Genl. Le Clerk. He goes to Washington to lay before Government his case, with a view to prevent any future transactions of the like nature. The character he bears at this place, is respectable, & I have been induced to give him this letter from the solicitation of some of our own citizens, tho' his present residence is in Philada. There are also political reasons which weigh with me on the occasion. He informs me that whilst at Baltimore he was visited by some *Federal characters* particularly *judge Chase* who told him the goverment would take no defe[nse] in the business. I have stated to him, that whatever slander or malice *prepense* may suggest to the contrary he will find the present administration purely American & that *you* will pay to the complaint of every citizen, that attention which the constitution & laws of the country enable the Chief Magistrate to bestow. He attributes the suggestions of Chase & others to their proper sources, as *he, himself,* is I am informed a Republican, but however honest he may be in that sentiment, as I know not how prudent he is you will no doubt act with that caution which you have on other occasions manifested, & which is so necessary in the high station, which thank heaven, you fill. With great esteem believe me

Dr. Sir Yours Sincerely C. A. RODNEY

RC (DLC); frayed at margin; endorsed by TJ as received 21 June and "by Capt Davidson" and so recorded in SJL.

CAPT. DAVIS: that is, William Davidson (Madison to TJ, 7 May).

From John Berry

[on or before 1 June 1802]

The Petition John Berry of Georgetown District of Columbia Respectfully Sheweth

That he has been indited and fined in two Cases as it will appear by the Annexed transcripts, and by Virtue thereof confined in the Goal of the City and County of Washington District of Columbia, Since the twenty sixth day of March Last past, is unable to pay the fine or Costs accruing thereon or any part thereof—

That he has subsisted ever since partly on what the Unfortunate Debtors confined in the Debtors Appartement of said Gaol thought Proper to spare him

That he has an aged mother that has been theis six years past and now is depending for House rent fire wood and other support from what can be spared from his hard earings—

To add to both their missfortunes about fourteen days Since he met with the Missfortune as to Break his Leg—is unable to move without help and may be considered at Present as an object of Charity,

Therefore he trusts and hopes that your Excellency will be pleased to take the Premises into your consideration and grant him relief by remiting said fines and your Petitioner will as in duty bound ever pray—

JOHN BERRY
his × mark

RC (DNA: RG 59, GPR); undated; in an unidentified hand, signed by Berry with his mark; at head of text: "To his Excellency Thomas Jefferson Esquire President of the United States of America"; endorsed by TJ as received 1 June and so recorded in SJL with notation "petn for remitmt. of fines, viz 10.01 D for trespasses"; also endorsed by TJ: "petn for pardon"; with notations by John Thomson Mason, Uriah Forrest, Dr. John Bullus, and Daniel Carroll Brent relinquishing their fees in the case, with Brent adding that "the Jailor must be consulted to know whether he will relinquish his." Enclosures: (1) Statement of Henry Dunlap, Thomas Davis, and Everard Gary, undated, citizens and residents of Washington, D.C., declaring that they have known John Berry "for some years past" and believe him to be the only source of support for his mother (MS in same; in an unknown hand, signed by Dunlap, Davis, and Gary; written on verso of Berry's petition). (2) Summary of fines and costs incurred by two indictments by the U.S. Circuit Court against Berry; the first of which was for a breach of the peace, carrying a fine 1 cent plus costs of $10 for attorney fees, $5 for marshal's fees, and "562½" for costs of the Mayor's Court; the second indictment was for a breach of the peace on Samuel Gardner with a fine of $10 plus costs of $10 for attorney fees, $4.50 for marshal's fees, and $26.25 for witnesses (MS in same; in Uriah Forrest's hand; attested by Forrest as clerk of court).

On 2 June, TJ issued a remission of Berry's fines (FC in Lb in same).

From William C. C. Claiborne

Mississippi Territory
Town of Washington June 1st. 1802

DEAR SIR,

On last evening, I received your Letter of the 3rd of April, enclosing your *Answer* to an Address, from the House of Representatives of this Territory, and *which*, I shall, with great pleasure, forward to the Speaker of that Body.—

With assurances of my highest respect;—I have the honor to subscribe myself—Your faithful friend, and most obt. Hble. Servant

WILLIAM C. C. CLAIBORNE

RC (DLC); in a clerk's hand, signed by Claiborne; at foot of text: "His Excellency, Thomas Jefferson President of the United States"; endorsed by TJ as received 11 July and so recorded in SJL.

YOUR LETTER OF THE 3RD OF APRIL: see TJ to the Mississippi Territory House of Representatives, 3 Apr. 1802.

From the District of Columbia Commissioners

SIR,   Commissioners' Office 1st June 1802

This being the expiring hour of Office, we leave the Books, plans, papers, Instruments and other articles belonging to the Commissioners' Office in the custody of Mr. Munroe, our Clerk, to be delivered to the Superintendant, when appointed by the President; except the books and Vouchers requisite to compleat the Accounts in comformity to the Act of Congress; which Accounts have been commenced and progressed in as far as our time would allow.—

We are, Sir, with Sentiments of the highest respect Yr mo. Obt. Servts

WILLIAM THORNTON
ALEXR WHITE

Mr. Dalton's indisposition has prevented his attendance for a few days.—

RC (DLC); in Thomas Munroe's hand, signed by Thornton and White; at foot of text: "President of the U.S."; endorsed by TJ as received 1 June and so recorded in SJL. FC (Lb in DNA: RG 42, DCLB).

A 1 May 1802 ACT OF CONGRESS replaced the board of commissioners in the city of Washington with a single superintendent, to be appointed by the president. The commissioners' offices were to cease on 1 June and all city records were to be delivered to the superintendent. The act also directed the commissioners to settle their accounts with the Treasury Department and pay any remaining balance against them to the superintendent (U.S. Statutes at Large, 2:175-8).

From Moses Myers

SIR   Norfolk June 1st. 1802

Permit me the Honor to Introduce Admiral Hartsinck (Commanding the Squadron of the Batavian Republic in Hampton Road, & for which I am agent) to your Civilities—The object of the Admirals Journey is to Pay You his Personal respects, & I am happy Sir to Inform you—that the Impressions on his mind are very favorable indeed as relates to our Country—which has been very flattering to me—

The Admiral will be extreemly Gratified in the honor of Your personal Acquaintance & I have taken the Liberty to assure him you wou'd be glad to see him

I have the Honor to be with much respect Sir Your very Obt. St—

Moses Myers

RC (DLC); at foot of text: "Thomas Jefferson Esqe."; endorsed by TJ as received 7 June "by Admiral Hartsink" and so recorded in SJL.

Ships of the Batavian Republic under the command of Vice Admiral Pieter HARTSINCK had transported French infantry regiments to Saint-Domingue as part of Leclerc's expeditionary force. After disembarking the troops, Hartsinck took his squadron, which included three ships of the line, a brig, and perhaps other vessels, to Chesapeake Bay. He left some of the ships at Hampton Roads while he continued up the bay to Baltimore for refitting and supplies. Hartsinck's ultimate destination was Java (Batavia) in the East Indies, a Dutch colony that had been captured by the British and was restored to the Batavian Republic as a provision of the truce between Britain and France (*Middlebury Mercury*, 24 Feb. 1802; Providence, R.I., *United States Chronicle*, 25 Feb. 1802; Savannah *Georgia Gazette*, 4 Mch. 1802; *New-York Herald*, 14 Apr. 1802; New Bedford, Mass., *Columbian Courier*, 21 May 1802; New York *Daily Advertiser*, 8 June 1802; Simon Schama, *Patriots and Liberators: Revolution in the Netherlands, 1780-1813* [New York, 1977], 450; Parry, *Consolidated Treaty Series*, 56:213, 292).

YOUR PERSONAL ACQUAINTANCE: when Hartsinck found himself in Baltimore again a few years later, he recalled paying his respects to TJ in Washington during his visit in 1802 (Hartsinck to TJ, 6 Feb. 1808, in DLC).

From Thomas Newton

Dr Sir   Norfolk June 1. 1802.

I have this day taken the liberty of introducing Admiral Hartsink of the Batavian republic to you, he intends up by water & probably this will reach you before his arival. we have had much pleasure in his Company here the good order kept with his men is pleasing to all here. I have some fine Brazil wine arived if you should want shall be glad to supply you

with great respect & wishes for yr health I am—yr obt Servt

Thos Newton

RC (DLC); endorsed by TJ as received 5 June and so recorded in SJL.

INTRODUCING ADMIRAL HARTSINK: in another letter to TJ that was also dated

Norfolk, 1 June, Newton wrote: "Dr Sir It gives me pleasure to introduce to you, Admiral Hartsinck of the Batavian republic, with whom I have hopes we shall have great connection in friendship & Commerce. we have had much pleasure here, in the Company of the Admiral and his officers, their friendly disposition & the good dicipline kept on board their vessels & the Conduct of their men on shore, is pleasing to all parties. with the greatest respect I am yr. obt Servt" (RC in DLC; endorsed by TJ as received 7 June "by Admiral Hartsink" and so recorded in SJL).

From John Page

My dear Sir   Rosewell June 1st. 1802

I am greatly obliged to you for the repetition of your kind offer, contained in your Letter from Monticello. Indeed, I am so struck with it, after what has passed between us, as to resolve to give up my Opinion to yours, & to rely entirely on your Friendship.

I lament now, that I have lost so much time in deciding on your Proposition; as my Wife's Situation will scarcely permit me to leave her for a Week, & she can not be moved till after her lying in, about the first of next Month.

After she shall be in such a Condition that I may venture to leave her to follow me, & I may apply my Mind free from Anxiety on her account, with a proper undivided Attention to the Duties of the office, you may command my Services, & rely upon my Zeal & Fidelity in office, as well as on my Friendship & Gratitude, and you may be assured that I will pay the strictest Attention to the Cautions which you have suggested, & to the Instructions which the Secretary of the Treasury may think proper to give. I would even accept the Appointment at once, & go myself to the Office before her lying in, were it not, that, in case of my Detention with her on my return to visit her at that critical & trying time, I might lose the Reputation which I wish in entering upon the Business of the Office to establish, of Assiduity, Vigilance & Punctuality. My Son Francis was as much struck by your Kindness as I was, & has consented to afford me his Assistance. He has had some Experience in Business & possesses I think in an high Degree some of the essential Qualifications in a Person who should be entrusted with any Share in the Business which I have agreed to undertake.

Your Favor from Monticello was long on its way it was marked at Milton 15th. May, & did not come readily from York. On this account I delayed my Acknowledgments till I supposed I might address them to you with certainty at Washington.

Mrs. Page unites with me in returning our thanks to you for Your Favors, & in presenting our Respects & best Wishes

I am my dear Sir your much obliged Friend & obedient Servant

JOHN PAGE

RC (DLC); endorsed by TJ as received 5 June and so recorded in SJL. Enclosed in TJ to Albert Gallatin, 6 June 1802.

LETTER FROM MONTICELLO: TJ to Page, 7 May 1802.

From Elkanah Watson

RESPECTED SIR   Albany 1st June 1802

Under the Respectable recommendations Inclosed; I feel the less diffidence in Introducing myself to your Knowledge, especially as Lieut. Govr. Van Rensselaer one of Our recent electors & my Intimate friend as well in Social, as in political Life, for a Series of years, Informs Me he has the honour of a personal acquaintence with you.

Haveing resided at Nantes in France Several of the arduous years of Our revolution (an American Merchant) I was in habits of Intimacy with Doctr. Franklin & the principal of Our leading Charecters in Europe as well as in America in the eairly Stages of Our Revolution; but I was Never So fortunate as to See you or be Known by you.

The object of this Introduction, is to Solicit the appointment of Mr. Simon Lynch a respectable Merchant at Nantes in France as American Consul at that Port, Should the appointment remain Vacant.

During the 5 years I resided at that place, I was Well acquainted with the father of Mr. Lynch who was esteemed one of the Most respectable Merchants there.

He is of Irish extraction, in consequence the English language is in a Manner the mother tongue of Mr. L— altho' born in Nantes. He has made the Tour of the United States, even into the Very Interior upon the Ohio, & the North Western territory. He has extensive personal Knowledge and correspondence with Our principal American American Merchants a'Long our Sea bord; and from my personal Knowledge of him, and his unblemished reputation (which If necessary can be amply Supported by commercial Houses in Several of Our Sea Ports) I am persuaded No person can better Supply the Vacancy—and it Will afford Me peculiar pleasure Should you See Cause from this Statement to honour him with that appointment. I will farther add that Mr. L— is a Staunch Republican in principal. The Last Consul at Nantes Mr. Dobrie—who lately died, was a Guernsey Man, & for many years filled that Station with distinguished propriety. I am aware that Gouverment have wisely adopted a prefference to American Charecters, But from the peculiar advantages of Mr. L— situation, and respectable Standing, & being also Informed, that their is No American Mercht. of Respectability established at that Port; I presume the prefference alluded to cannot in this Instance impair my hopes in favour Mr. L— I make free also to Inclose you a circular-Letter I Recieved from Mr. L— as an evidence that he is already devoted to the Interest of Our countrymen.

Our comptroler Mr. Jenkins (whose father was also one of Our State electors) Informs Me, he Was nominated by the recommendation of Chanceller Livingston for the Office I Now Solicit for my worthy friend Lynch.

With profound Respect and esteem. I have the Honor to be Sir Your He. St. ELKA. WATSON

I Should also have accompanied this Letter with a line from my next Neighbour & Intimate friend Govr. Clinton—but for his absence

RC (DNA: RG 59, LAR); at foot of text: "Thomas Jefferson Esqr: President United States"; endorsed by TJ as received 10 June and "Simon Lynch to be Consul at Nantes" and so recorded in SJL. Enclosure: Circular from Simon Lynch, dated at Nantes, 8 Jan. 1802, offering his services in presenting claims to the French Council of Prizes "to obtain justice and Satisfaction from the unwarrantable depredations committed on the American trade" (printed circular in same; signed and partially dated by Lynch; at head of text: "Mr. Elkanah Watson Albany"; with a postscript in Lynch's hand and a note by Watson explaining that a young man referred to in the postscript is his son, whom "I have placed in the House of Mr. Lynch"; endorsed by Watson). For other possible enclosures, see below.

Elkanah Watson (1758-1842) began his career as an apprentice to John and Nicholas Brown in Providence, Rhode Island. He was in Europe from 1779 to 1784. During that time he had business partnerships at Nantes, one of which was with Benjamin Franklin's nephew, Jonathan Williams. Watson settled in Albany in 1789. He owned farms, was a banker, promoted agricultural fairs, wool production, and turnpike construction, and advocated the construction of a canal from Albany to the Great Lakes (ANB).

RESPECTABLE RECOMMENDATIONS INCLOSED: although Watson's letter and the two written in its support, Jeremiah Van Rensselaer's of 3 June and Elisha Jenkins's of the 4th, all reached TJ on 10 June, TJ's record in SJL does not show that they arrived as a bundle.

In August 1802, Watson again urged the appointment of SIMON LYNCH to the position at Nantes by writing to Madison and having Van Rensselaer do so also. Madison passed those letters along to the president. TJ named William Patterson, who had Robert R. Livingston's support and had previously received a nomination as commercial agent at L'Orient, to the position at Nantes. In the spring of 1804, Patterson made Lynch his deputy (Madison, *Papers, Sec. of State Ser.*, 3:515, 520-1, 538-9, 555; 7:126-7, 531; Vol. 33:672, 677; Vol. 35:371, 664; TJ to Madison, 10 Sep. 1802).

Livingston thought well of the qualifications of Elisha JENKINS and had suggested him for the post of naval officer at New York City (Vol. 35:62).

From Francis Mentges

SIR/   Philadelphia 2 June 1802—

It is with extreme regret, that I venture to trespass upon time devoted to affairs of greater moment, to request your Attention for a few minutes to a representation which it is necessary for me to make I trust I shall be pardoned for the intrusion as my Claim is only for Justice, and for that consideration Knowing of me what you do, I am confident you will not refuse Ought I to add, as with truth I may, my present circumstances render this application Absolutely necessary—

from the Copy of a letter from Mr M'Henry, formerly Secretary of War herewith enclosed and marked A, you will see the Nature of an Appointment which I held for some years as connected with the expenditures in the Account (marked B) also enclosed, and that Gentlemans Opinion of my Conduct, permit me also to submit to your attention the following circumstances which I stated to General Dearborn in a letter dated the 19 Decr last (marked C) I do conseive from these facts, that I am entitled to a greater Commission on the monies expended by me in this Agency, than, that which is paid for common receipts & expenditures, and have accordingly claimed the allowance of 5 p. Ct. The Comptroller of the Treasury, who it may be presumed, is better acquainted than any other officer with the difference in the Nature of expenditures made by me, and those for which the usual Commission is allowed, will, I have no doubt readily admit the justice of granting me a more liberal compensation, but the present Secretary of war has denied me the ballance of Dr. 1721.58 Cts. which by a reference of my account, it will be seen that I still claim, and has directed the Accountant of his Department to close my Account without that allowance as will be seen by his Letter, D, in which he notified me that my accounts with the public are accordingly finaly closed, Against that settlement or finaly close, made, without my consent I do protest and solemnly disavow it, humbly submitting a Consideration of all the Circumstances attending my Claim and of the seperate grounds upon which it stands, to your Candour and Justice and requesting your favorable interference in my behalf—Whilst before you with a Claim upon your Justice I would also prefer one, to your Benevolence, my services to this Country have been of long continuance, they commenced in her hour of Danger you know what they were, you know too whether or not in every situation in which I was placed, I did my duty and received the Approbation of my Superiors. I was not so fortunate as to amass wealth or even a Competency in 21 years Service, it is necessary that I should still be in some employment, which would bring a pecuniary compensation and the Nature of the Services to which I have been attached for so long a time renders the public service most suitable for me, the present Secretary of War, has been pleased to promise me & my friends that he would not be unmindful of me, I beg leave also to request your favorable Attention if any thing that might with propriety be conferred upon me should offer It is not much I ask, may I request, that you will not think my relation too tedious or my Application unbecoming, I have the Honor to be with high Consideration

   Sir/Your Ob hb Servant   F MENTGES

RC (DLC); at foot of text: "The President of the United States"; endorsed by TJ as received 3 June and so recorded in SJL. Enclosures: (1) James McHenry to Samuel Dexter, Philadelphia, 9 June 1800, stating that Mentges has been serving as inspector of troops and garrisons under an appointment by Henry Knox, and that he has also been given the general agency relative to the fortifications on Mud Island, in which capacity he is responsible for procuring materials, paying workmen, and disbursing all monies; for said agency Mentges is "intitled to the usual Commissions" and McHenry believes he has carried out his duties with "Integrity and Deligence" and saved "a Considerable Sum to the public." (2) Account of Francis Mentges with the United States, closing 18 Dec. 1801, in which Mentges claims a balance due to him of $1,721.58½. (3) Mentges to Henry Dearborn, Washington, 19 Dec. 1801, acknowledging Dearborn's letter of 1 May 1801 that directed an end to his agency at Mud Island and stating that he has submitted his accounts to the accountant of the War Department for final settlement; Mentges explains the causes of the "very extraordinary expenses" incurred while executing his agency; he visited Mud Island thrice weekly to see the number of men at work, take regular accounts of the work done, and to pay the workmen every Saturday; advances were made to masons who were under contract, for which Mentges retained receipts; he bypassed Philadelphia merchants and contracted directly with nearby sawmills, saving between 40 and 50 percent on costs; he saved additional money by negotiating favorable contracts for stone, brick, lime, and sand; Mentges continually traveled to quarries and sawmills to "Keep the work going forward and all at my own Expense"; yellow fever outbreaks in 1797, 1798, and 1799 forced banks to remove to Germantown and obliged Mentges to quit the city as well, which increased his traveling expenses; Mentges trusts that these considerations shall be taken into account and can be confirmed by the comptroller of the Treasury, with whom Mentges has accounted for the largest sums expended and all of his transactions; Mentges believes he has acted with fidelity, saving the public a considerable sum, and hopes that Dearborn will therefore "agree to my final Settlement at the rate of 5 per Cent Commission on the Expenditures." (4) William Simmons to Mentges, Department of War, Accountant's Office, 10 May 1802, stating that the secretary of war, in consultation with the comptroller, has directed that Mentges be allowed additional compensation as agent of fortifications to balance his account; a statement has thereby been made and the sum of $1,913.27 passed to Mentges's credit, "which finally closes your accounts on the Books of this office" (Trs all in same).

KNOWING OF ME WHAT YOU DO: Mentges had previously written TJ on 4 Mch. 1801, summarizing his military service and seeking a new appointment (Vol. 33:161-2).

From John Beckley

DEAR SIR, Washington, 3d: June 1802.

I have been requested to add what I know of the person named in the enclosed. He was, during my residence in Richmond, an Alderman of that City for a number of years, and always maintained the Character of an active, useful, intelligent Magistrate, with strict integrity in private life.

If the appointment of Commissrs. to act in philadelphia is not concluded, I would beg leave to mention the name of Hugh Ferguson Esqre. one of the new City representatives in the State Legislature, a Merchant by profession and a Man of great worth, whom for Years I have well known. I also embrace this occasion to inform you that in respect to the name of a Mr: William Duncan, who has probably been mentioned to you, I am advised that an objection to him exists of a nature to forbid any appointment whatever, which, if Requisite, will be fully made to you, by the person who has communicated the objection to me.

With great esteem, I am, dear Sir, Your obedt: Servt:

JOHN BECKLEY.

RC (DNA: RG 59, LAR); endorsed by TJ as received 7 June and "Hugh Ferguson to be Comr. bkrptcy Phila" and so recorded in SJL. Enclosure not identified.

For an earlier application by HUGH FERGUSON that was delivered to the president by Beckley, see Ferguson to TJ, 16 May 1801. TJ entered Ferguson's name on his list of candidates for bankruptcy commissioners, but he was not selected (Appendix II, Lists 1 and 2).

WILLIAM DUNCAN, clerk of the Pennsylvania House of Representatives in 1800, served as secretary of the 1801 meeting of Democratic Republicans in Philadelphia, at which Ferguson was chosen a candidate for the Pennsylvania Assembly. An auctioneer, Duncan probably experienced financial difficulties in 1802. In May, a notice appeared that the partnership with his brother was being dissolved. Duncan requested that all accounts with the firm be settled, but assured the public that he was continuing in business at 7 South Front Street. By December 1802, Andrew Pettit, another auctioneer, occupied Duncan's store (*Poulson's American Daily Advertiser*, 10 Nov. 1800, 12 Oct. 1801, 21 May 1802; *Gazette of the United States*, 4 Dec. 1802).

To Robert Brent

DEAR SIR Washington June 3 1802

The act of Congress incorporating the city of Washington has confided to the President of the US. the appointment of the Mayor of the city. as the agency of that officer will be immediately requisite, I am desirous to avail the city of your services in it, if you will permit me to send you the commission. I will ask the favor of an answer to this proposition.

Will you also do me that of dining with me the day after tomorrow (Friday) at half after three? Accept my friendly and respectful salutations.   TH: JEFFERSON

PrC (DLC); at foot of text: "Robert Brent esq."

An ACT OF CONGRESS of 3 May 1802 provided for the incorporation of Washington, D.C. and authorized the president to select a mayor, who was required to be a U.S. citizen and a resident of the city prior to the annual appointment (U.S. Statutes at Large, 2:196).

Brent's COMMISSION as mayor was signed by TJ and Madison and dated 1 June (FC in Lb in DNA: RG 59, MPTPC).

From Robert Brent

DEAR SIR   Washington June 3d 1802.

I have had the honor of receiving your favor of this date, asking my acceptance of the appointment of Mayor under the late act of Congress for incorporating this City—

Altho I feel great defidence in the Talents I possess for exiciting that duty, in a manner which may afford general satisfaction—yet feeling it a duty to contribute my feeble aid for the public service I will venture upon its duties

I beg you Sir to accept my thanks for the honor which you are about to confer on me and for the obligeing manner in which you have been pleased to communicate it.

I will, with pleasure, accept your polite invitation to dinner on Friday next—With Sentiments of much respect & Esteem I have the honor to be Sir Your Obt Ser   ROBERT BRENT

RC (DLC); endorsed by TJ as a letter of 3 June received 2 June and so recorded in SJL.

To James Monroe

DEAR SIR   Washington June 3. 1802.

I observe that the resolution of the legislature of Virginia, of Jan. 23. in desiring us to look out for some proper place to which insurgent negroes may be sent, expresses a preference of the continent of Africa, or some of the Spanish or Portuguese settlements in S. America: in which preference, & especially as to the former I entirely

concur. on looking towards Africa for our object, the British establishment at Sierra Leone at once presents itself. you know that that
establishment was undertaken by a private company, & was first suggested by the suffering state of the blacks who were carried over to
England during the revolutionary war, and who were perishing with
want & misery in the streets of London. a number of benevolent persons subscribed for the establishment of a company who might carry
these people to the coast of Africa, & there employ them usefully for
themselves, and indemnify the company by commercial operations:
Sierra Leone was fixed on as the place; the blacks then in England
were carried thither, and a vessel or vessels sent to Nova Scotia which
carried to the same place the blacks who had gone to that country. the
settlement is consequently composed of negroes, formerly inhabitants
of the Southern states of our union. having asked a conversation on
this subject with mr Thornton, the British Chargé des affaires here,
he informs me the establishment is prosperous, and he thinks there
will be no objection on the part of the company to recieve blacks from
us, not of the character of common felons, but guilty of insurgency
only, provided they are sent as free persons, the principles of their institution admitting no slavery among them. I propose therefore, if it
meets your approbation, to write to mr King our minister in London
to propose this matter to the Sierra Leone company who are resident
in London; and if leave can be obtained to send black insurgents
there, to enquire further whether the regulations of the place would
permit us to carry or take there any mercantile objects which, by
affording some commercial profit might defray the expences of the
transportation. as soon as I can be favoured with your sentiments on
this proposition & your approbation of it, I will write to mr King that
we may have the matter finally arranged. should any mercantile operation be permitted to be combined with the transportation of these
persons, so as to lessen or to pay the expence, it might then become
eligible to make that the asylum for the other description also, to wit
the freed negroes and persons of colour. if not permitted, so distant
a colonisation of them would perhaps be thought too expensive. but
while we are ascertaining this point we may be making enquiry what
other suitable places may be found in the West Indies, or the Southern continent of America, so as to have some other resource provided,
if the one most desireable should be unattainable. in looking out
for another place we should prefer placing them with whatsoever
power is least likely to become an enemy, and to use the knolege of
these exiles in[1] predatory expeditions against us. Portugal, and Holland would be of this character. but I wish to have your sentiments on

both branches of the subject before I commit it by any actual step. Accept assurances of my affectionate and high esteem & respect.

TH: JEFFERSON

RC (Vi); addressed: "Governor Monroe Richmond"; franked; postmarked 4 June; endorsed by Monroe as "relative to the slaves"; also endorsed "copied for Assembly." PrC (DLC).

For the RESOLUTION OF THE LEGISLATURE OF VIRGINIA concerning the search for a place to which rebellious slaves could be transported, see Monroe's letter to TJ of 13 Feb. 1802. ADMITTING NO SLAVERY AMONG THEM: prominent British abolitionists including Granville Sharp and William

Wilberforce initiated the incorporation of the Sierra Leone Company in 1791. The act of Parliament that incorporated the company prohibited any connection to the slave trade or slavery "in any manner whatever" (*An Account of the Colony of Sierra Leone, from its First Establishment in 1793* [London, 1795], 5; James W. St. G. Walker, *The Black Loyalists: The Search for a Promised Land in Nova Scotia and Sierra Leone, 1783-1870* [New York, 1976], 101-2).

[1] TJ here canceled "committing."

From James Monroe

DEAR SIR   Richmond June 3. 1802.

From some distant allusion it was inferr'd that Mr. Hay wod. not act as a comr. of bankruptcy. The proposition was not directly made, so that he did not refuse; it was only inferr'd that it was not an office which he was desirous of. I have not yet been able to form a list for Norfolk, but expect soon to do it, which shall be transmitted without delay. In the interim there is no reason why you shod. not proceed if you are already sufficiently advised. Richd. Evers Lee wod. answer, as wod. Littn. W. Tazewell, if the latter wod. act, tho' presume he wod. not, as he is a notary publick wh. it is thought is worth four or five hundred pounds there.

yr. friend & servt   JAS. MONROE

RC (DNA: RG 59, LAR); endorsed by TJ as received 6 June and so recorded in SJL.

To Martha Jefferson Randolph

MY DEAR MARTHA   Washington June 3. 1802.

I arrived here on Sunday morning (May 30.) to breakfast without having experienced any accident on the road, other than being twice taken in soaking rains: but my water proof coat was a perfect protection. mr and mrs Madison arrived the day after. I find they have not yet got clear of the measles here, so that either at home or here your family will hardly escape it. it is now time for you to fix a day for my having you met at mr Strode's, and it would be well if you could do it so that a postday should intervene, & give me an opportunity of acknoleging the reciept of your letter so that you may be sure it has not miscarried. observe that the post which leaves Milton on Monday cannot carry back an answer till the Sunday following, & that which leaves Milton on Friday, returns with an answer on the Thursday following, taking a compleat week each. I will state on the 2d. leaf of this letter the stages and distances of the road & some notes. you must let me know whether you would rather that I should send horses & a carriage, or horses alone, as it will be perfectly equal to the person who furnishes me. I shall send John with them as the driver will not be acquainted with the road, and it is a difficult one to find. it is generally a good & a safe one except the last day's journey which is very hilly, and will require you to get out of the carriage in several places on the Alexandria road between Fairfax court house & Colo. Wren's which is 8. miles, and once after you pass Wren's. I am not without fear that the measles may have got into your family, and delay the pleasure of seeing you here: but I expect to hear from you by the post which arrives tomorrow morning. my affectionate attachment to mr Randolph, kisses to the children, and tenderest love to yourself.   TH: JEFFERSON

RC (NNPM); at foot of text: "Mrs. Randolph." PrC (MHi).

Itinerary from Edgehill to Washington

from Edgehill		
to Gordon's	18. miles.	A good tavern, but cold victuals on the road will be better than any thing which any of the country taverns will give you. lodge at Gordon's go
to Orange courthouse	10. miles	to breakfast. a good tavern. on leaving Orange courthouse be very attentive to the roads, as they begin to be difficult to find.
Adams's mill	7. miles.	here you enter the flat country which continues 46. miles on your road.
Downey's ford	2.	here you ford the Rapidan. the road leads along the bank 4 miles further, but in one place, a little below Downey's, it turns off at a right angle from the river to go round

a gut. at this turn, if not very attentive, you will go strait forward, as there is a strait forward road still along the bank, which soon descends it & crosses the river. if you get into this, the space on the bank is so narrow you cannot turn. you will know the turn I speak of, by the left hand road (the one you are to take) tacking up directly towards some huts, 100 yards off, on a blue clayey rising; but before getting to the huts, your road leads off to the right again to the river. no tavern from Orange courthouse till you get to

Stevensburg	11. miles.	you will have to stop here at Zimmerman's tavern (brother in law of Catlett) to feed your horses, and to feed yourselves, unless you should have brought something to eat on the road side, before arriving at Stevensburg. Zimmerman's, is an indifferent house. you will there probably see mr Ogilvie: he will certainly wish to be sent for to see mr Randolph.
mr Strode's	5. miles.	it will be better to arrive here in the evening. on stopping at his gate, you will see Herring's house about 2 or 300 yards further on[1] the road. you had better order your servants (except your nurse) horses & carriage & baggage (not absolutely wanting at night) to go straight there, where those sent from here will be waiting for you.
Bronaugh's tavn. at Elkrun church.	13. miles.	the only tavern you will pass this day. obliging people.
Slate run church.	14½ miles.	here you leave the flat country & engage in a very hilly one.
Brown's tavern	5½ miles.	here you will have to dine & lodge being the first tavern from Bronaugh's.[2] a poor house, but obliging people.
Fairfax court house	15. miles.	you can either breakfast here, or go on to
Colo. Wren's tavern	8. miles.	a very decent house and respectable people.
George town ferry	6. miles.	

PrC (MHi); endorsed by TJ in ink on verso.

[1] MS: "on on."
[2] Preceding six words interlined.

To Joseph Rapin

DEAR SIR   Washington June 3. 1802.

Your favor of May 17. came to me at Monticello a day or two only before I was setting out on my return to this place; and since my return an accumulation of business has prevented me from sooner answering it. I am very thankful to you for your attention to my want of a servant, and should without hesitation have taken the one you have recommended, but that Mr. Lemaire had engaged one during my absence who was already in place. some difficulty might have arisen from the proposition for 18. dollars a month, lest that should have furnished grounds to the other servants (to whom I give but 14. D. including drink) to expect a rise of their wages. perhaps however this might have been accomodated. I will immediately desire mr Barnes to remit something to Christopher, and sincerely wish he may recover his sight. should he not do it, I imagine Philadelphia is much more likely than this place[1] to offer some employment of which he would be capable. his wife is a very able bodied woman, and may aid him by her earnings.   I am very happy to learn from Capt. Lewis that you are yourself in so easy a situation. accept my best wishes for your prosperity and health.   TH: JEFFERSON

RC (PWacD: Feinstone Collection, on deposit PPAmP); at foot of text: "M. Rapin." PrC (MHi); endorsed by TJ in ink on verso.

REMIT SOMETHING TO CHRISTOPHER: in his financial memoranda under 4 June, TJ noted that John Christoph Süverman and his wife "are no longer in my service after this day." Four days later, TJ asked John Barnes to give Süverman $20 "in charity." Previously TJ had recorded a donation of $10 to Süverman in October 1801, and he gave him $10 in July 1802 and $30 in May 1803. TJ later described

Süverman as "a very honest man." Süverman's pay from May 1801 until his discharge was $12 per month plus a $2 drink allowance. HIS WIFE Betsy first appeared in TJ's memoranda of President's House accounts in October 1801, earning $8 in wages each month and a drink allowance of $1. Süverman lost his eyesight, and in 1810 was surviving in Washington "from hand to mouth" by selling groceries (MB, 2:1040, 1053, 1054, 1071, 1074, 1077, 1101; RS, 2:364; 3:49).

[1] Preceding three words interlined.

From Sir John Sinclair

SIR   London 29 Parliament Street 3 June 1802

I expected to have had the Honour of hearing from you before this time, on the Subject of the publication of General Washington's Letters, but I hope to have that pleasure soon. In the interim I beg to send an Engraving of the proposed Monument and a plan of the new town of Thurso, in which it is proposed to be erected.

You will also herewith recieve two copies of a paper on Longevity which may be reprinted in America, if you should approve of that Idea. I hope to recieve by your obliging assistance very satisfactory answers from America to the Questions in Appendix No. 1.

It would give me much pleasure to hear that a Board of Agriculture was established in America, and I still rely that under your auspices it will be happily effected.

I have the Honour to be with great truth & regard Your faithful and obedient Servant   JOHN SINCLAIR

RC (DLC); endorsed by TJ as received 26 Sep. and so recorded in SJL. For enclosures, see below.

For the facsimile edition of WASHINGTON'S LETTERS to Sinclair, published in London in 1800, see Sinclair to TJ, 6 June 1800 and 22 June 1801. In June 1802, Cottom & Stewart, book dealers in Alexandria, proposed to publish the letters from the London edition on a "superfine wove Paper" as soon as they obtained 500 subscribers. The Alexandria publication, which appeared in June 1803, was entitled *Letters from His Excellency George Washington, to Arthur Young, Esq. F.R.S. and Sir John Sinclair, Bart. M.P. Containing an Account of His Husbandry, with His Opinions on Various Questions in Agriculture; and Many Particulars of the Rural Economy of the United States* (see Shaw-Shoemaker, No. 5536). The editors explained that instead of publishing only the letters to Sinclair on fine paper as at first proposed, they had decided to print Washington's correspondence with Arthur Young, as well. By preferring "utility to elegance, and by deviating from their former proposal," they were able to "furnish, without any additional expence, the General's corre-

spondence with both these gentlemen" (advertisement in *Letters from His Excellency George Washington,* 4; *Bartgis's Republican Gazette,* 6 Aug. 1802; *Alexandria Expositor, and the Columbian Advertiser,* 1 June 1803).

The ENGRAVING OF THE PROPOSED MONUMENT in memory of Washington has not been found, but a London newspaper reported that the monument was about to be erected in one of the squares of Thurso (*Washington Federalist,* 4 Feb. 1802). For the plan of the town, see Vol. 31:91 and Vol. 34:414.

Sinclair's PAPER, *An Essay on Longevity,* was published in London in 1802 (see Sowerby, No. 985). Twenty questions appeared in the first appendix, including inquiries on how heredity, exercise, diet, gender, marital status, profession or "situation of life," physique, "disposition or temper," town or country living, climate, sleeping habits, and other customs impacted longevity. Sinclair also questioned: "What are the rules regarding medicine which are accounted the most useful and salutary?" and "What are the rules adopted by those who have attained great age?" (Sinclair, *Essay on Longevity,* 16-17).

From Jeremiah Van Rensselaer

SIR   Albany 3d June 1802

My perticular frend Elkanah Watson who has resided in this City about thirteen years, expressing a wish to recomend to your Notice Mr. Simon Lynch, merchant of Nantes in France as American Consul in that City—Permit me Sr. to recomend Mr. Watson to your Attention—during several years of our Revolutinary war he was at the head of a Respectable House in Nantes; from his Standing in Society, his long experience in buiseness, and his Attatchment to the principles of our Revolution; such representations as he may Make on the Subject of Mr. Lynch, I am perswaded will be found entitled to the Confidence of Goverment.

I am Respectfully sr. your Most Obt. Huml sert

JER V RENSSELAER

RC (DNA: RG 59, LAR); at foot of text: "Thomas Jefferson. Esqr. President. United States"; endorsed by TJ as received 10 June "in favr. of Watson who recommends Lynch as Consul at Nantes" and so recorded in SJL.

Jeremiah Van Rensselaer (1738-1810), the president of the Bank of Albany, had served in the U.S. House of Representatives in the First Congress and was a former member of the New York legislature. He was the state's lieutenant governor from 1801 to 1804 (*Biog. Dir. Cong.*).

From "Honesty"

SIR   [before 4 June 1802]

If you would turn your attention to men & their intrigues. you would give Sattisfaction to your best freinds. honest your self you cannot judge of the baseness of others. you are under a delusion in Suposeing by your continuing sertain men in their officises to conciliate all partys. you are only nourishing vipers who will sting you when oppertunity offers—the true republicans tho they are not willing to own you in an error—are allmost in despair at your neglect of them. you have I know a difficult part to act, one man begs you to keep him in his place, another gains the interest of a few to solicit for him, the Mr. Bittles [...] to such prevailing power, Mr. Dallas has talents that [would] be serviceable to any party, time will prove him [...] true or not, he has had no temptations to swerve as the republicans have allways suported him, his bosom freind swift *was* an ennimy to his country untill interest reversed his creed—are such to be trusted, they are not the voic of the people, give your own freinds some Imoluments—

it will make them more Influentiall, they will then be firm, philadelphans will never forget the fast day Major Macpherson called forth his soldiers & armed them against the people—

yours   HONESTY

RC (DLC); undated; torn at seal; endorsed by TJ "Anon. from Phila for removg. all federalists" and so recorded in SJL. Recorded in SJL as received 4 June.

THE MR. BITTLES: perhaps a reference to Charles Biddle, a Federalist who was appointed to a minor office by Governor McKean and served as prothonotary of the Philadelphia County Court of Common Pleas, and the Revolutionary War veteran Clement Biddle, a Philadelphia merchant to whom President Washington entrusted much of his Philadelphia business. He served as U.S. marshal for Pennsylvania from 1789 to 1793 (Rowe, *McKean*, 322; Higginbotham, *Pennsylvania Politics*, 60; Kline, *Burr*, 1:152n;

ANB; Washington, *Papers, Pres. Ser.*, 1:27; Robinson, *Philadelphia Directory for 1802*, 29; Vol. 27:108-9, 117).

District Attorney Alexander J. DALLAS had formerly served as secretary under governors Mifflin and McKean. BOSOM FREIND SWIFT: possibly attorney Charles Swift, who served as Philadelphia register and probate of wills (Rowe, *McKean*, 304-6; Robinson, *Philadelphia Directory for 1802*, 237; *Poulson's American Daily Advertiser*, 5 Feb. 1801; DHSC, v. 1, pt. 1:194n). William McPherson (MACPHERSON), naval officer at Philadelphia and militia commander of "McPherson's Blues," led the military expedition against John Fries (see Vol. 34:426-8).

From Elisha Jenkins

SIR   Albany 4 June 1802

At the request of Mr Elkanah Watson of this City, I take the liberty to address you, upon the subject of an application he is about to make to the Government, in favor of Mr Simon Lynch, who he is desirous should be appointed to fill the Consulate of Nantes,—I have no personal knowledge of Mr Lynch but I am persuaded, from a long acquaintance with Mr. Watson, who was at the head of a respectable commercial establishment at Nantes, during the 2 or 3 last years of the American war, that he would recommend no Gentleman, for that station, but one in every respect competent in point of talents, and respectable, for charactar—

With due respect and consideration I am Sir, Your Obedt. Hble Serv.   ELISHA JENKINS

RC (DNA: RG 59, LAR); at foot of text: "The President of the United States"; endorsed by TJ as received 10 June and "in favr. Watson who recommends Lynch as Consul at Nantes" and so recorded in SJL.

Elisha Jenkins (ca. 1769-1848) was comptroller of the state of New York, from 1801 to 1806. In 1783-4, his father, Thomas Jenkins, created a proprietary association of merchants and whalers from Nantucket, Providence, and other

New England ports to found the community of Hudson, New York. Elisha Jenkins engaged in a variety of business activities, including commerce, finance, shipping, and real estate, initially as a member of his father's firm in Hudson and later in Albany. He was the secretary of state of New York from 1806 to 1809 and mayor of Albany from 1816 to 1819 (Nantucket *Inquirer*, 26 May 1848; George Rogers Howell and Jonathan Tenney, *Bi-Centennial History of Albany. History of the County of Albany, N.Y., from 1609 to 1886* [New York, 1886], 662; Stephen B. Miller, *Historical Sketches of Hudson* [Hudson, N.Y., 1862], 6-8; Syrett, *Hamilton*, 15:665-6; 26:96-7, 98n; Hudson *Gazette*, 15 May 1794, 3 Mch. 1801; *Albany Register*, 20 Nov. 1797; Hudson *Bee*, 27 May 1806; *Albany Gazette*, 25 Sep. 1806).

From William Kilty

SIR   June 4th 1802

I am requested by Mr Edward Nicholls to Address to you a letter on his behalf, respecting his Qualification for the appointment of a Commissioner under the Bankrupt Law, which He tells me He is a Candidate for

Mr. Nicholls had been for some years past engaged in the Practice of the Law, in the State of Maryland, but has for some time past resided in the City of Washington and has been employed as a Clerk in Mr Gallatin's department—This station He has lately Quitted and has shewn to me Mr Gallatins reply to his letter of resignation, in Which He appears to have been satisfied with his Talents and services

An ill state of Health, and a Consequent Indisposition for Close Study have prevented Mr Nicholls from Attaining to Eminence in the Profession of the Law, but He possesses good natural Talents, and has had the Advantage of an uncommonly good Education— And his Knowledge of the Law is such as to add to his pretensions to the office in Question

I think it proper to Add that Mr Nicholls has uniformly supported the Republican interest, in the Worst of Times—And that He has a deserving and somewhat numerous family dependent on him for support, and that of Course the emoluments to arise from the appointment which He Sollicits would be to him of some importance.

I forward this letter enclosed to Mr Nicholls at his request And He will have the Honour of Waiting on you with it—I flatter myself with the Hope of his succeeding unless some one better Qualified should apply, and am

With Great respect Your Obt Sevt   WM KILTY

RC (DNA: RG 59, LAR); at foot of text: "Thos Jefferson Esqr"; endorsed by TJ as received 10 June and "Edward Nicholls to be Commr. bkrptcy" and so recorded in SJL.

Edward C. Nicholls's LETTER OF RESIGNATION to Albert Gallatin, dated 7 Apr. 1802, stated his intention to quit his Treasury clerkship by the second Tuesday in May, when the General Court for Maryland was to convene. "I shall be thankful to you," Nicholls added, "for some recommendatory document in any shape you may be pleas'd to word or convey it" (Gallatin, *Papers*, 6:943). For Nicholls's previous attempt to secure an appointment, see Nicholls to TJ, 25 Jan. 1802.

To Benjamin Dearborn

June 5 1802

Th: Jefferson presents his compliments to mr Dearborne and returns his Manuscript and his thanks for the opportunity of perusing it, which he has done with very great satisfaction. the observations of mr Dearborne suggested the following quaere in the case of the common beam as well as mr Dearborne's. let any degree of strength, or of inflexibility, for a beam be *given*: would it not be better to procure that strength by an open-work, rather than a solid beam, inasmuch as it would be lighter. thus ━◅▭▭▻━ tho mr Dearborne applies a happy correction to this evil, yet the less there is to correct the better.

PrC (DLC).

Benjamin Dearborn (1754-1838) had operated schools in Portsmouth, New Hampshire, and Boston before opening a small factory for the manufacture of his many inventions, the most prominent of which was a portable balance for weighing, which he termed the vibrating steelyard and which earned a patent in 1799. In addition to his work with mechanical objects, Dearborn published manuals on the instruction of arithmetic, grammar, and music, and a proposal for the more humane treatment of debtors (Emma Forbes Waite, "Benjamin Dearborn: Teacher, Inventor, Philanthropist," *Old-Time New England*, 52 [1951], 44-7).

Dearborn had been introduced to TJ in 1799, but it is not known when he shared a MANUSCRIPT with him. TJ was likely responding to material later published in Philadelphia in 1803 as *The Patent Balance Compared with Other Instruments for Weighing*, which proposed the adoption of Dearborn's invention by Philadelphia's public market. In Nov. 1802, TJ purchased a small steelyard from Dearborn for his personal use (MB, 2:1086; Vol. 30:617-8).

From Delaware Democratic Republicans

SIR, [5 June 1802]

We beg leave to address you on a subject which we deem momentous and important. We do not wish, Sir, to obtrude our sentiments upon you, on a measure, to the accomplishment of which the Constitution has assigned to you the entire power, and the absolute discretion. But in the confidence that the voice of the People will be indulgently heard by a republican President of the united States, we earnestly solicit from your hands the removal of Allen McLane, from the collectorship of the Port of Wilmington, in the District of Delaware. In doing this we are not influenced by motives of ill will or enmity towards that officer; but on grounds, and principles which will conduce to the public weal, and promote the views of Republicanism.

The conduct of this officer has assumed a shape the most violent and intolerant towards those of his fellow Citizens who have opposed him on points of a political nature. The influence of office in his hands, instead of promoting the happiness of those around him, has, in many instances, been perverted to purposes the most selfish and time-serving: Nay, Sir, prosecutions and convictions have been Occasioned by his agency (in cases where we believe the parties to have been innocent) which have plunged into distress, impoverished and made helpless several families. In short, the course of his political Career since the organization of the present Constitution, has been marked by a conduct almost amounting to Madness, and by a violence as dangerous to the repose of society, as it is criminal: Exhibiting a behaviour of this kind for a series of years, and likely again to re-act the scenes, to which we have, but Slightly alluded, we are deeply impressed with the policy, and necessity of his Speedy and immediate removal.

In addition to the reasons we have already given, we think our present republican administration would be strengthened in their measures and in their duration by appointing to stations of honor and profit, those who are devoted to the best interests of their Country.

If Hostility to the measures of the present rulers of our public affairs should be encouraged by suffering the authors of such conduct to enjoy posts of influence and wealth, the ardor of Republicanism will be damped, and the exertions of our friends will be parylized by disappointment.

May the almightly and supreme ruler of the Universe lengthen out

your Days, and encrease the prosperity of the nation by continuing to you the Blessings of Health and Activity—
Signed by Order of the Delegation

DANL. BLANEY. Chairman
Attest.
RISDON BISHOP Secy.

RC (DLC); in John Bird's hand, signed by Blaney and Bishop; date supplied from minutes of meeting written above inside address (see below); at head of text: "To Thomas Jefferson, President of the united States"; endorsed by TJ "Address to remove Allen Mc.lane" and so recorded in SJL. Recorded in SJL as received 10 June. Enclosed in John Bird to TJ, New Castle, 8 June 1802, stating "The Chairman of the Democratic Republican Delegation of the State of Delaware, hath charged me with the inclosed Address—, desiring at the same time, that I should forward it with all possible expedition to the President of the United States," which he does with "pleasure" and with "much respect and consideration" (RC in same; at head of text: "His Excellency Thomas Jefferson, Esquire"; recorded in SJL as received 10 June with notation "coverg Address from Dover").

Daniel Blaney, a surveyor, worked in Delaware in the 1790s and in 1797 was hired to prepare a survey of New Castle. In 1803, Benjamin H. Latrobe described him as a "good clever surveyor" and hired him to do surveys for the Chesapeake and Delaware Canal Company. Blaney moved from Port Penn to New Castle in 1804. He served as recorder of deeds for New Castle County from 1804 to 1811. Risdon Bishop had a farm near Dover and regularly took a leadership role in Democratic Republican meetings in Kent County. On 23 May 1801, he served as secretary of the meeting that met at Daniel Cooke's house in Dover to promote the successful bid of David Hall for governor (Latrobe, *Correspondence*, 1:346-50; Wilmington, *Mirror of the Times*, 6 June 1801; 9 June 1802; 25 Feb., 14, 21 Apr. 1804; Gallatin, *Papers*, 7:521).
Democratic Republicans met at Dover on 5 June 1802 to select "a suitable Char-

acter to be supported by them at the next general Election, as Representative to Congress." After agreeing unanimously on Caesar A. Rodney as the candidate, the delegation "took into consideration the removal from office of the present Collector for the Port of Wilmington in the District of Delaware" and unanimously adopted the address printed above (minutes of 5 June meeting attached to RC printed above; Wilmington *Mirror of the Times*, 9 June 1802).

ALLEN MCLANE learned of this proposal for his removal and wrote John Steele and Gallatin in his own defense. McLane discovered that several of his political enemies, including Risdon Bishop and Abraham Pierce, were among the jurors who were called for the meeting of the U.S. circuit court in Dover on 3 June but discharged when there were no cases to be heard. Republican leaders used the time between 3 June and their scheduled meeting on the 5th to gain support for an address to the president urging the collector's dismissal. Although urged by his friends to send a "Counter address to the President," McLane informed Steele that because of the recent "friendship and Justice" shown to him by the administration, he "thought it unnecessary to trouble" the president until officially informed of the charges. He argued that merchants in Wilmington and Philadelphia who knew of his attentiveness to his duties wanted him continued in office. Only Nehemiah Tilton and one other person in Wilmington opposed him, and Tilton wanted the collectorship for himself. In his letter to the Treasury secretary, McLane stressed his Revolutionary War record and his ability to garner letters and certificates of support from every state in the union. He was not an enemy of the present administration, as some had charged, but was being persecuted by office seekers (McLane to Steele, 12 June, in DLC, endorsed by TJ: "Mc.lane Allen," and enclosing an extract by an unidentified correspondent to McLane, Kent County, Delaware, 8 June, in same; McLane to Gallatin, 12 June, in same; Wilmington *Mirror of the Times*, 5 June 1802).

From Robert King, Sr.

SIR   Surveyors Office June 5th 1802—

Mr. Munroe having informed me, that you wished to have a general Statement of the business of the Surveying department; and that he apprehended misinformations had been given you, of the State of the Business in that Office; to render this clear, I must give you a detail of the general Transactions of the Office. Being detained longer in England, by the Several Inclosure Commissions, and Navigation Surveys &c. in which I was concerned I arrived here in September 1797. On my Entrance into the Surveying department, I found the Graduation of the Streets the Business then going within the Office. The laying off Lots for Buildings &c. was the Business in the Field. A great number of Assistant Surveyors, had been employ'd in Setting out the Streets, under Mr Ellicott, who committed a great number of Errors, so that lots cannot be laid out with Certainty, without remeasuring each Square. Therefore the Ranges of the Streets, ought to be examined throughout the City, and that as soon as possible, that Buildings may not prevent the rectification. The levels which were taken of the City for obtaining Sections of the Streets, refer to Flat Stones, placed at the Intersections of the Streets, many of these are altered or lost, by Plowing or forming the Streets, that a revision of the levels will be necessary and the Stones replaced which are found erroneous. All the City, North of K Street and Massachusetts Avenue, is yet to level, and Section plans of it, to lay down; and Plans of the Squares with the Lots, for facilitating the Graduations to make. The Woody parts of the City are so grown with underwood and Bushes, that the Ranges of the Streets cannot easily be found and will require clearing. Mr Dermott who was Calculator and made the Divisions of the Squares into Lots having for misconduct been removed from his Office, and his Successor having resigned, I was ordered by the Board, to make my Self acquainted with the Business of that Office. On entering this new employ I was obliged to Suspend the Graduation of the Streets, and apply my Self to the Unravelling the bewildered State, of the proprietors Accounts, and as much had been committed to memory, and most of the documents relative to the proprietors Lines, having been taken from the Office, by Mr Dermott,

who claimed them as his own, Saying that he had taken the references to the proprietors Lines in his own Time (after Office Hours)
that the Several proprietors Claims cannot Equitably be Setled without taking a great number of these references again. I believe that
there is not yet any account of the proprietors, perfectly Setled. There
have been very few new divisions made, except the points introduced
into the plan for George Walker, since my coming into the Calculators Office. Mr Dermott told me that the whole had been divided
previous to that Time leaving the Accounts to be Setled after, the
Commissioners having been so inattentive and precipitate in doing
the Business that no regular account had been kept of the division,
the Slips of paper on which they were done, frequently not being
given into the Calculators Office, or Brought to Account. I have
seen Slips of Division in their Office since the 1st of this Month, of
Squares which Stood in the Accounts of this Office as undivided,
This rendered it imposible for me, who alone had the Current Business of both the Surveyors, and Calculators Departments, to attend,
to make much progress in clearing up the Accounts where all the information was to glean out of Scattered papers and accounts. It will
require a large and Correct plan of the City whereon to lay down the
Several proprietors Lines, that the Squares cut by them, and their
proportions may appear. I think two Good Calculators will require a
year to bring out the State of the Accounts, after which One of them
may be dispenced With. The Surveyor will have full employ in the
Current Business of the Office and attending to the Graduation of the
City, taking referrences to the Lines and other duties, the Surveyor
will for many Years require a Good Assistant Surveyor as the Levels
will be to take of all the City North of K Street and Massachusetts
Avenue, A labourer also will be required to assist in Measuring and
Clearing the Ranges of Wood. There is a considerable part at the
East end of the City on which Stones have not been planted at the
Corners of the Squares, I believe if the Board had been possesed of
Sufficient Funds, it would not have been left in this State. For the two
last years I have had no Assistant in the Office, and before that
my youngest Son who was employed in Registering the Recorded
Squares could be of little Service to me, more then Supplying the
necessary information to Gentlemen applying about Business when I
was sent out by the Commissioners. He had in the Office two Dollars
pr Day but the Commissioners wishing to have this business compleated as soon as possible agreed with him that instead of working
only Office Hours he should employ his whole time at a Stated price
pr Square. After this on application made to the Board by Mr Barry

who saw that my Business was too much for any One Man to execute, the Board requiring my Attendance at the Office until the Hour of One. In the Afternoon I had to do the Field business which occur'd which generally kept me out late in the Evenings, and was very laborius, for all which extra Time I had no compensation, my agreement being for only Six Hours pr Day. The Board at his remonstrance took off from me the Duty of laying out Lots, and that Office was conferred on my Son Robert who was appointed and an Allowance fixed of 2 Dollars pr. Lot, to be paid by the proprietors. In this State are things at present in this Office. I had heretofore lived in Hopes that when Congress took the Direction that they would have fixed a Salary to the Office similar to those given to Surveyors in other places. But under the present circumstances I cannot think of engaging for less then 1000 Dollars pr Annum. I shall also Stipulate for employment for my Son Robert, otherwise I cannot engage my self without great Injury to my Family. If this cannot be agreed to, I am willing to do the current duties of the Office at the Same rate as heretofore until I can get ready for departing, or Some other person be appointed.

I am with the greatest respect Yours　　　　　　　R KING

RC (DLC); addressed: "His Excellency the President of the United States"; endorsed by TJ as received 6 June and so recorded in SJL.

Robert King, Sr. (d. 1817), originally of Yorkshire, England, began working in the Surveyor's Office of the Federal District in 1797. In England he had made navigational surveys and marked off large tracts of land for government-mandated enclosure. Three of his offspring were also in the United States, and one of his sons was the surveyor, draftsman, and artist Nicholas King. Robert King, Sr., returned to Britain in 1802 (Latrobe, *Correspondence*, 1:223-4n; Ralph E. Ehrenberg, "Mapping the Nation's Capital: The Surveyor's Office, 1791-1818," *Quarterly Journal of the Library of Congress*, 36 [1979], 304; Ralph E. Ehrenberg, "Nicholas King: First Surveyor of the City of Washington, 1803-1812," RCHS, 69-70 [1971], 31-2, 46n).

GENERAL STATEMENT OF THE BUSI-NESS: King also compiled an inventory of instruments, books, and plans that were in the Surveyor's Office as of 31 May (Ehrenberg, "Mapping the Nation's Capital," 290, 304, 317n).

From 1791 to 1793, Andrew ELLICOTT made the initial survey of what became the District of Columbia (ANB). James Reed DERMOTT worked in the surveying office from 1792 to 1798 (Vol. 33:204-5).

EXCEPT THE POINTS INTRODUCED INTO THE PLAN: at the instigation of property developer GEORGE WALKER, the district commissioners agreed to a division of some of the triangular pieces of land formed by the intersection of the city's avenues and streets (Bryan, *National Capital*, 327-8; Harris, *Thornton*, 493-5).

YOUNGEST SON: Robert King, Jr., worked in the Surveyor's Office beginning in 1798. In 1801 his job was the enumeration of houses in the district (RCHS, 69-70 [1971], 46n).

From John F. Mercer

In Council Chamber Annapolis

Sir,   June 5. 1802

Considerable time has elapsed since the Executive of this State addressed the Commissioners of the City of Washington, pressing the
payment of the Interest due on several loans made for the use of the
City and repayment of the principal sum of fifty thousand Dollars,
forfeited by a neglect to pay the Interest: your Communications on
this subject to Congress and the subsequent proceedings of that
Body are now known.

The condition of the Loan of fifty thousand Dollars imposed a
peremptory duty on the Executive to put in Suit the private Securities taken for this Sum, and although the Act of the last Session of
this Legislature has been considered as conferring in some measure a
descretionary power over all debts due to the State, yet it has by no
means rendered the duty less urgent.—The motives which have hitherto suspended this measure, have been already detailed, and you no
doubt Sir will sufficiently appreciate them.

There are however circumstances belonging to this subject which
have not been communicated and which probably may still remain
unknown to you:—The inconsiderable taxes levied by the State of
Maryland, are to be considered rather as means of internal police and
regulation than as objects of revenue.—She has relied for the support
of the State Government almost wholly on the growing interest of an
accumulated Capital, the produce of the United industry and economy of her Citizens.

of this a very considerable portion (the Funds they had formerly
invested in Bank Stock of England) you are already apprized has
been long and injuriously withheld. they have not only been deprived
of the use of their monies, but they have been subjected to considerable expences in the assertion of their right.

The property which the State holds in the Funds of the United
States constitutes that subject which has been heretofore the most
productive and on which she has chiefly relied. a very great proportion of this has been from time to time loaned by the State for the use
of the City of Washington after having contributed to its primary
establishment by a liberal donation.—Yet for more than two Years
past, the State has not received one shilling of the Interest due on
these loans.

other considerable Sums advanced to promote Public Institutions as yet remaining unproductive, you will readily imagine that the pressing application made to the Commissioners originated in motives of indispensable duty and that unless the Interest at least due on these loans to the City of Washington shall be speedily discharged, the State may be exposed to inconveniences from which her ample resources and liberal conduct should have exempted her.

Under such circumstances, this Executive confides that the law of the last Session of Congress, which commits this subject wholly to your discretion, will be carried[1] into that prompt execution which may meet the exigences of the State of Maryland, and particularly as the United States have made the transaction their own no motive, of interest or convenience, can now exist longer to defer the punctual and honorable discharge of the Interest of the debt.

In expressing this confidence, of the Executive you will permit me to remark that sentiments of high personal respect and veneration for the principles which guide your administration mingle with the expectations they have formed, and to assure you individually of the respectful consideration with which I have the honor to be Sir your most obedient humble Servant   JOHN F. MERCER

FC (MdAA: Letterbooks of Governor and Council); in a clerk's hand; at foot of text: "The President of the United States." Recorded in SJL as received from Annapolis on 11 June with notation "T."

TIME HAS ELAPSED: for the letter of 2 Feb. addressed by Mercer to the commissioners, see the enclosure described at the District of Columbia commissioners to TJ, 8 Feb. 1802. TJ sent COMMUNICATIONS on the Maryland loans to Congress in January, which led to legislation that guaranteed repayment of the loans through appropriations from the U.S. Treasury, if sufficient funds were not raised from the sale of lots (U.S. Statutes at Large, 2:175-6; TJ to the Senate and the House of Representatives, 11 Jan. 1802).

PUT IN SUIT: District of Columbia commissioners Gustavus Scott and William Thornton, with Uriah Forrest and James M. Lingan, as their sureties, secured the $50,000 loan from Maryland (Vol. 33:480-2, 508-11; Vol. 35:97-100). LAST SESSION OF THIS LEGISLATURE: for the actions of the Maryland government regarding the Federal District loans due the state, see Albert Gallatin to TJ, 10 Jan. 1802.

BANK STOCK OF ENGLAND: for the state's continuing and ultimately successful attempt to gain control of funds invested in the Bank of England before the American Revolution, see Vol. 23:589, 609n.

[1] MS: "be arried."

To Albert Gallatin

June 6. 1802.

Th:J. incloses to mr Gallatin a letter from the keeper of Cape Henlopen lighthouse which seems to call for attention: also another attack on Mc.lane. J. Page accepts the offer of the place at Petersburg, but cannot conveniently go till some weeks hence. his letter is also inclosed.

RC (NHi: Gallatin Papers). Enclosures: (1) Abraham Hargis to TJ, 26 May. (2) Delaware Democratic Republicans to TJ, [on or after 24 Mch. 1802], enclosed in David Hall to TJ, 31 May. (3) John Page to TJ, 1 June.

From Cyrus Griffin

SIR—   Wmsburg June 6th. 1802—

I take the liberty to make a request, if perfectly agreable to yourself, that in the appointment of general commissioners of Bankruptcy for Virginia, you will be so good as to include, for the Norfolk District, Henry Hiort Attorney at Law, Thomas Willock and John Dunn Merchants, & for the Petersburg District Robert Hines Attorney at Law, Edmund B. Holloway and Edwin Fort Merchants. These Gentlemen have acted from the commencement of the Bankrupt Business with entire approbation, are Men of understanding, and now well experienced in that intricate and difficult Law. I have no intimate private connexion with any of these Gentlemen; but assume this liberty merely from public consideration. The President will therefore excuse the trouble I give to him. I fervently hope that you have enjoyed the best health, since I had the pleasure of paying my respects at Washington. I should have encroached one minute more in taking leave, but found myself very unwell on the day I had the honor of dining with you: prudence told me I ought to return home with all expedition.

Be pleased to accept my sincere respects and attachment.

CYRUS GRIFFIN.

RC (DLC); endorsed by TJ as received 12 June and "Commrs. bkrptcy" and so recorded in SJL.

From Charles Willson Peale

Your obliging letter wrote at the moment you were setting out for Monticello,—I sent to my Son Rembrandt at New York, and I doubt not he will profit by your hints of different times and prices, to seperate and accomodate the Variety of Company that probably will desire a sight of the Skeleton. In order to improve and fit my Son Rubens to conduct my Museum, I have permited him to accompany his brother—further, he will be serviceable in making the Exchanges, knowing the present subjects of my Museum—as I mean to supply them with the various Animals, that I have been storing up for many years, which will give me a great advantage of exchange, for although they will be supplied with many duplicates of the variety of Birds belonging to this part of America, yet in return for them, my sons will not take duplicates, and only such specimens as are wanting to complete my Collection of foreign subjects.

The Legislature of Pennsylvania having granted me the use of a principal part of the State-House, gives an opportunity of displaying the Museum in an orderly manner, and to render it more strikingly useful than heretofore, I am writing the Classical and common Names on, or near each subject—so that a catalogue, unless a descriptive one, would be useless. Such a Museum, easy of access, must tend to make all Classes of the People, in some degree, learned in the science of Nature, without even the trouble of Study. Whether a diffused knowledge of this kind, may tend to mend their Morrals, is a question of some import.—furnishing the Idle and disapated with a great and new sourse of amusement, ought to divert them from frivolous and pernicious Entertainments—It is fully demonstrated that viewing the wonderful structure of a great number of *beings best formed for their respective stations*, elevates the mind to an Admiration and adoration of the Great Author!—I have seen folly stoped in its carier, by the sight of a few articles in this Repository—excuse me, as this is one of my Hobby Horses.

Doctr Sillman, last January, gave me the upper part of a head, which he said he would forward by the first boat in the Spring—his account of it agrees with the account of it by a Mr. John Brown (I suppose the Major) which I have lately received, dated Kentucky 28 of march 1802. he says "This will acknowledge the receipt of your letter (which came to my hand two days ago) on the Subject of Part of the Skull Bone of a large Animal, which I am in Possession of.

I set out in two or three days for the Orleans shall take it with me

agreable to my first Intentions & intend to come by sea to Philadelphia will be there as soon as Convenient—This Piece of matter consist of the uper Part of the head the Joint Joining the neck Bone
Intire with the lower Part of the Pith of the left Horn on the Skull in
Perfect shape but very much decayed the uper end off Thickest Part
of the Pith 21 Inches round a more Particular discreption would be
difficult shall leave it at present & submit to more able hands when it
arrives with you

I had intended it for your Museum as the most Proper Depot to
Satesfy the Public Eye But think it Most consistant for me to make the
Philosophical Society the Proprietors—I do not think it would come
whole across the mountains in a Waggon." The remainder comple-
mentary. I have also received a Letter from Doctr Saml. Brown dated
"Lexington May 18. 1802.

"agreeably to my promise, I renewed my enquiries respecting the
Animal with a large horn, immediately on my arrival in Kentucky
& have now no hesitation in assuring you that the information which
I communicated to you, last winter, on that subject, was perfectly correct—a Gentleman of respectable character & of some taste for Natural History had the good fortune to see the Skull on the 7th of last
month at Wilkinsonville. Mr John Brown of Columbia had it possession & intended sending it by water to Philada. It has an evident resemblance to the Head of an Ox or Bison. All accounts agree that the
horn must have been, at least 18 Inches in circumference at the base.

One Gentleman assures me that he could pass his hand through
the great feramen of the occepetal Bone but observes that the head of
the Animal appears to have been uncommonly small in proportion to
the Horns—

I am still pretty confident that this Skull is similar to those mentioned in a note under the article Elephant in Smellies Translation of
Buffons natural history—

I hope this curiosity will arrive safe and that we shall collect other
Bones of the same animal in some part of our extensive western
country."

A Young Gentleman (whom I was informed is your secretary)
assured me that the head which you obligingly offered to procure
for me, was not that which Major Brown possessed, or that given by
Doctr Sillman—

It is a pleasing circumstance that we have now so good a prospect
of knowing more of these Interesting Animals.[1]

I am fearful that this precious relick will not arrive here in time
for my Son to see it before his departure. What he expects from me

respecting it I cannot tell. At one time he said he would even take a trip to Kentucky to get a sight of it. but his anxiety to cross the Ocean in a pleasant season, withall his desire to be on the great sceine of action may also hasten him. He has taken his Passage in the Ship Juliana which sails between the 14th. & 20 Instant, and he is hurrying me to procure him letters of Recommendation from some Gentlemen of this City who promised such favours. The Success of Exhibition in New York enables him to pay the expences of crossing the Ocean with a surplus sufficient to make them welcome and easy untill they open again. It seems to be a general opinion that they will make a profitable jaunt of it. we comfort ourselves that if my Sons do not make a fortune, at least, the opportunity of improvement is important. And Rembrandt has promised me not to trust to his memory but to note down every thing worth observation. He is but little acquainted with the world, but he is a water drinker, and I hope will not be wanting in industry or Economy, And that he will return to his Country a valuable Citizen.

Want of time has prevented me from communicating to you sundry matters—on the Mammoth—on some useful discoveries—particulary that on making sea water fit for drinking—Raphaelle has been making a variety of Experiments, success seemed to attend some of them—he will persue it I hope with ardor, but painting portraits at a low price obliges him to be constant at work. Knowing your love of useful arts and Science enduces a desire in me to offer my mite. I wish you health, and am with much respect your friend   C W PEALE

RC (DLC); at foot of text: "His Excellency Thomas Jefferson Esqr President"; endorsed by TJ as received 9 June and so recorded in SJL. Dft (Lb in PPAmP: Peale-Sellers Papers).

YOUR OBLIGING LETTER: TJ to Peale, 5 May.

In March the PENNSYLVANIA assembly had granted Peale permission to house his museum in the State House (Peale to TJ, 21 Jan. 1802).

DOCTR SILLMAN: John Sellman (same).

William Smellie's TRANSLATION of the Comte de Buffon's Histoire naturelle, générale et particulière first appeared in Edinburgh in 1780 under the title Natural History, General and Particular. Smellie, a Scottish printer who compiled and edited several works relating to natural science, taught himself French in order to translate Buffon's opus (DNB).

YOUR SECRETARY: Meriwether Lewis, who had visited Philadelphia in May (Joseph Rapin to TJ, 17 May).

Owned by the firm Coit & Phillips, the ship JULIANA made regular crossings carrying freight and passengers between New York and London. Although the owners advertised a departure date of 20 June from New York, the ship did not sail for London until early in July (New-York Evening Post, 17, 20 May; New York Commercial Advertiser, 7 June; New York American Citizen and General Advertiser, 5 July 1802).

[1] Peale first wrote "this Interesting Animal" before altering the phrase to read as above. Dft: "this interresting Animal."

From Daniel Carroll Brent

SIR/   June 7th. 1802

Agreeable to your desire, I have spoken to Mr. Hatfield to furnish a plan for the Jail. This he has promised to do, which when done shall be sent into you—I transmit herewith several plans which have been handed to me & from which some useful hint may perhaps be taken—

With sentiments of the highest respect I am Sir yr Obt. Sevt.

DANIEL C. BRENT

RC (DLC); endorsed by TJ. Recorded in SJL as received 7 June. Enclosures not found.

For the architect George Hadfield's PLAN FOR THE JAIL, see Brent to TJ, 26 June.

From Henry Dearborn

War Department

SIR,   7th. June 1802

I take the liberty of proposing for your approbation John Livingston for a Cadet in the Artillery.

I am &ca.   H. D.

FC (Lb in DNA: RG 107, LSP).

Following his appointment as cadet, JOHN LIVINGSTON reported to the military academy at West Point, New York. In April 1803, he was made a second lieu-tenant in the Regiment of Artillerists and sent to Fort Nelson, near Norfolk, Virginia (Heitman, *Dictionary*, 1:636; Dearborn to Thomas H. Cushing, 8 June 1802, Dearborn to Livingston, 25 Apr. 1803, both in DNA: RG 107, LSMA).

To Robert King, Sr.

SIR   Washington June 7. 1802

Your favor of the 5th. has been duly recieved, and I thank you for the statement of business to be done in the surveyor's department of the city. you observe that you cannot continue in that office for less than 1000. D. pr. annum, nor unless your son Robert be employed. you have doubtless read the act of Congress suppressing the board of Commissioners and substituting a superintendant. in order to in-demnify the treasury of the US. for the sums that will have to pay for the city, to the state of Maryland, they have directed that after the pai-ment of the debts remaining due at the dissolution of the board, every dollar recieved either of what is due to the city or on future sales of lots, shall be paid into the treasury of the US. thus rigorously circumscribed, we are so far from feeling an authority to enlarge former allowances that on the contrary it is deemed a duty to suspend every operation which would call for money, and which is not essentially necessary to be done at this time. under these circumstances, candor obliges me to be explicit, and to say that I am not at liberty to augment the former allowance to yourself or to join your son Robert in the employment: as it is my duty to conform my wishes to the will of the legislature. I pray you to accept my respects & best wishes.

TH: JEFFERSON

PrC (DLC); at foot of text: "Mr. R. King"; endorsed by TJ in ink on verso.

From Edward C. Nicholls

City of Washington

SIR. June 7th. 1802.

My peculiar Situation will, I hope, plead my Apology to the chief Magistrate of the United States, for this personal Address.—After an Absence of some Weeks from the City, I repair'd hither this day, in full Confidence of finding at my House, Letters from Judge Kilty and Judge Sprigg, in my favor for the Office of one of the Commissioners under the Bankrupt Law.—by some Accident those Letters have miscarried, and I am reluctantly Compell'd, to make Application, for the present, in this way.—

If, in your Arrangements for the Good of the Union, I may be deem'd deserving of public Confidence, my Study shall be to continue to merit it.—

I remain very respectfulfully, yr. Obt Servant—

EDWD. NICHOLLS

RC (DNA: RG 59, LAR); endorsed by TJ as received 8 June and "to be Commr. bkrptcy" and so recorded in SJL.

LETTERS FROM JUDGE KILTY: see William Kilty to TJ, 4 June. JUDGE SPRIGG: Richard Sprigg, Jr., resigned from Congress in February 1802 to become an associate justice of the Maryland Court of Appeals (Madison, *Papers, Sec. of State Ser.*, 1:57). No letter of recommendation from Sprigg has been found or is recorded in SJL.

From Josiah Smith

Pembroke in the County of
Plymouth Massachusetts
the 7th of June 1802

HONRD & DEAR SIR

Since my Return to Massachusetts from Washington I have Conversed with a Considerable Number of Republicans in Boston Salem & other Parts of Massachusetts who are of Opinion that the officers of Government Collecting the Import Duties are the more Violent in their Opposition to the General Government & that they are More Dareing & Insolent on account of the Moderation & Lenety Shewn unto them & also by reason of the number of People Imployed by them they do affect the Elections of Massachusetts to a Considerable Degree Employing those Printers who are Continually Publishing Matters & things against the Conduct of the General Government & Influencing all whome they Imploy in all our Elections & being Informed that an attempt will be made to Remove the Collector for the Port of Plymouth in this State I would Beg Leave to Recomend Henry Warren as a Suitable Person to Fill that office a Son of your Old & Esteemed Friend General James Warren who for a Number of years Past have been Persecuted for their Political Principals a Singular Instance Lately hapened at our Late Election he had for a Considerable Number of years officiated as Clerk of our House of Representatives with applause but for his open Manly aprobation of the Measures of the Present Administration an attempt was made to Displace him & he obtained by one Vote only the Emolument which is about 1200 Dollars annually will be a releif to the Family of your Friends

I am Sir with affection & Esteem your most obedient Humble Servt

JOSIAH SMITH

RC (MoSHi: Jefferson Papers); at foot of text: "to Thomas Jefferson President of the United States"; endorsed by TJ as received 13 June and "Henry Warren to be Collector of Plymouth" and so recorded in SJL; with an undated note in Dearborn's hand on verso: "if any change is to take place in the office alluded to, Mr. Warren would undoubtedly be a suitable character to fill the office. H.D."

Born in Pembroke, Massachusetts, Josiah Smith (1738-1803) graduated from Harvard College in 1774, studied law, and became a practicing attorney. He served two years in the Massachusetts House of Representatives and four years in the Senate between 1789 and 1797, the year he became state treasurer. Elected as a Republican representative to the Seventh Congress, he did not stand for reelection. On 7 July 1802, TJ appointed Smith a bankruptcy commissioner at Newburyport (Biog. Dir. Cong.; list of commissions in Lb in DNA: RG 59, MPTPC; Appendix II, List 2).

COLLECTOR FOR THE PORT OF PLYMOUTH: William Watson, whose conduct was investigated by the Treasury Department in 1801. HENRY WARREN WAS previously recommended for the Plymouth collectorship by his father James Warren, who described the incompetence of Watson and the anti-Republican sentiments at Plymouth in a letter to TJ of 5 Sep. 1801. In the summer of 1802, TJ offered Henry Warren the collectorship at Marblehead. Several months after he declined that appointment, Warren replaced Watson at Plymouth (Vol. 34: 531-4; Vol. 35:221-3; Gallatin to TJ, 9 Aug. 1802).

On 29 May 1802, the Boston *Columbian Centinel* reported on the effort TO DISPLACE Henry Warren as clerk of the Massachusetts House of Representatives. He received 73 votes, while the other candidate, Federalist Kilborn Whitman, received 72.

From Daniel Carroll Brent

SIR/   June 8, 1800 [i.e. 1802]

I take the liberty of announcing to you the issue of the election of yesterday—The votes stand thus. of those elected

1	Danieal Carroll	204
2	Geo: Blagden	202
3	James Barry	164
4	Will: Brent	157
5.	Benjn. More	129
6	James Hoban	124
7.	Nicholas King	124
8	Saml. H Smith	121.
9	Augt. B Woodard	123
10	Will Prout	120
11	Tho Peter	115
12	Jno Hewitt	98

In haste, yrs Respy   DANIEL C. BRENT

RC (DLC); endorsed by TJ: "Washington Common council."

ELECTION OF YESTERDAY: under the 3 May 1802 act of Congress incorporating the city of Washington, the city council was to consist of 12 members elected annually on the first Monday of June. The votes were to be counted the following day in the presence of the district marshal (U.S. Statutes at Large, 2:195-7; Vol. 36:33). Results of the election were announced in the 9 June edition of the *National Intelligencer*, which identified Carroll, Blagden, More, King, Smith, and Hewitt as Republicans and added that "at least one, perhaps more of those which succeeded on the Federal ticket, are also Republican."

To George Jefferson

DEAR SIR   Washington June 8. 1802.

Mr. Craven Peyton of Albemarle, to whom I owed a balance of 131.47 D has desired me to remit it to meet a paiment he has to make in Richmond. lest he should be in Richmond or on the road, I have thought it best not to send it to Albemarle, but to lodge it with you to be delivered to himself or his written order: and I give him notice by another letter this day sent to Albemarle that he may call on you for the letter inclosing the money, or send to you for it. accept assurances of my affectionate attachment.   TH: JEFFERSON

PrC (MHi); at foot of text: "Mr: George Jefferson." Recorded in SJL with notation "Peyton's lre." Enclosure: TJ to Craven Peyton, 8 June (first letter).

To Craven Peyton

DEAR SIR   Washington June 8. 1802.

Your favor of the 2d. instant was recieved by last post, desiring a remittance of the balance of 131. D 47 c due you on our settlement of May 22. I accordingly now inclose you 140. Doll. in bank bills of the United states, as these cannot be got exactly to the fraction desired. I hope it will be recieved in time for your purpose.   sundry approaching calls for money render it absolutely necessary that in purchasing the remaining shares of the tract, we throw the paiments into another year, say to the distance of a twelvemonth if possible: not but that, where there would be danger of losing the purchase, without a shorter paiment, a shorter might be agreed to in a particular instance, but I could not do it in the whole. the shares in the present mill are not worth purchasing at all, because it will be entirely useless after the ensuing fall. accept my best wishes & respects.

                                         TH: JEFFERSON

PrC (ViU); at foot of text: "Mr. Craven Peyton"; endorsed by TJ in ink on verso. Enclosed in TJ to George Jefferson, 8 June.

OUR SETTLEMENT: TJ recorded the transactions in his financial memoranda (MB, 2:1073, 1074).

To Craven Peyton

DEAR SIR   Washington June 8. 1802.

Lest you might be gone to Richmond, as mentioned in your letter of the 2d. instant, I have thought it best to send the balance you desired, to mr George Jefferson of that place; and have accordingly inclosed 140. D. this day in a letter addressed to you, sealed, and have desired him to deliver it to yourself or to your written order; so that you can apply to him on your reciept of this.   in that letter I have mentioned the necessity of postponing to the next year any other paiments which may be hereafter agreed on.   accept assurances of my friendly attachment.   TH: JEFFERSON

RC (CtY); addressed: "Mr. Craven Peyton near Milton"; franked and postmarked. PrC (ViU); endorsed by TJ in ink on verso.

YOUR LETTER OF THE 2D. INSTANT: probably Peyton to TJ, 30 May, which TJ received on 2 June.

From Stephen Sayre

SIR   Philaa. 8th June 1802

My unfortunate situation compels me to repeat my just complaints. Seperated from my family—consequently, at double expence—you will not, I hope, be offended at my importunity

I may not have inform'd you—but have most certainly inform'd your Secretary of State—that I dare not reside in the State of New Jersey, since the last congressional election, lest a prosecution should take place there for a large sum—a debt contracted for the public service in 1777 & 1778. The lawyers in that state having denounced vengeance against me. Here I may, if compeled to the unpleasant necessity, prevent an endless confinement

Do not suppose me capable of heighting this picture of distress—I know, too well, that pleadings on the grounds of poverty are the least effectual—they have no weight with your cabinet ministers—I have some hopes they may touch your feelings—therefore make them known—

As I am now in some measure settled in this state, let me ask, if any of the Comrs of Bankruptcy are to be removed, why you should neglect an old servant of the public? At all events, let it be understood, that you wish to serve me, by being the secretary to the Commissioners, upon the change—this would be better than to be a Comr—being more profitable—I wish only to pay the debt—since Congress will

not pay me—you would never be troubled by me after that is done—
The house which lent me the money, was friendly to our cause—they
ought long since, to have been paid—

Let me ask—Why does your Secretary at War keep a fellow in
office here, who was the most active scoundrel with the Spartan
Band—he may be a judge of ham & malasses—but not of articles necessary for an army—nor have our friends here any hopes of employment, while he is in office—

I wish you could hear the murmurs of your best friends as to this
very man. But you will perhaps hate me for this plain dealing—therefore I conclude, by saying I am

respectfully yours &c   STEPN SAYRE

RC (DNA: RG 59, LAR); endorsed by   DEBT CONTRACTED FOR THE PUBLIC
TJ as received 11 June and "for office" SERVICE: see Vol. 35:416-17.
and so recorded in SJL.

From John Vaughan

SIR   Philad. 8 June. 1802

A desire to be useful, induces me to make the present Communication, consisting of hints extracted from recent European publications,
which are worthy perusing—

Sam Bentham, Esqr. recd lately a Gold medal, for discovering the
following method of preserving water sweet in Long Voyages it was
bestowed by the Socy. for the encouragemt. of Arts &c—It is detailed
in their Transactions. 1801—also in Tillochs Journal Vol. 12th. page
12.—He made Cases or Tanks of strong wood & lined them with
Tinned Copper sheets manufactured by Chas. Wyat bridge Street
London—the water having no contact with the wood—The shape of
the Cases was adopted to the hold of the ship, some made to fit close
under the platform, by which means, the quantity of water stowed, in
the same space, was considerably greater than could have stowed, in
the same space by means of Casks—He provided them for 2. Vessels
say 40 Tons to each in 16 Tanks, & 30 Tons stowed in Usual manner—The water was used as wanted, but always kept in reserve,
whilst the other water was good—In some of the Tanks the water
had remained $3\frac{1}{2}$ Years, from which 25 Galls were sent to the Society
& found as sweet, as when first put in—It was taken from a Tank
holding 700 Gs. & accompanied by the proper Certificates—

A work has lately been published in France by—*Barry*,[1] giving an
acct. of the method invented by Smith, of sweetening foul water by an

easy process—the experiments made at Brest under direction of the
ministry of the Marine, & proved very satisfactory—Smith has obtained a patent in France—the principle is as follows, the mechanical
execution I am ignorant of, but our Minister at Paris could very readily obtain information or a Model if necessary—

Blanket Doubled

haircloth Doubled
strong board full of holes
well supported

The water is put in at Top. The Blanket (or Sponge) takes off the
gross particles of Dirt & can be cleaned as often as required—The
sand takes off some of the Dirt & the charcoal destroys all the bad
smell, & the most nauseous & filthy water becomes immediately fit
for use. The holes underneath the board & round the Cask, is to
admit Atmospheric air into the water, to give it liveliness, the water
is drawn off at A.—

At Fort Miflin the following method I was told is in use—

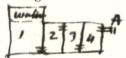

A large box, of which one part (which is to receive the water) is
higher than the rest, no 1, 2, 3, 4 are four compartments filled with
gravel or sand, growing finer as the numbers progress until it comes
out at A perfectly clear—Water rising upwards, filters better; Even
here the Blanket would be of use, to keep the sand longer clean—The
Charcoal alone can destroy the fœtid smell & is a Russian discovery—
for family use some plan like Mr Peales exhibition would answer

The Water is placed in the Top & rises thro' the sponge like a
syphon over the Outside, runs thro' the sand then thro' the Charcoal,
& is fit for use—Smith places his apparatus in an urn like a Tea Urn,

& upon very moderate terms—The french Navy has adopted the
principle, after a Variety of Experiments—An Idea prevailed at first
that salt water could be made fresh, but it appeared to be illusory on
further experiment—Distillation appears to be the only process to
obtain this end—

Bosquet[2]—has enrolled a Patent in England for preserving Vessels
from Decay, nuisance & leakage—by filling the void spaces between
the Planks, lining & timbers, with melted pitch, temper'd with Tar to
be more tenacious & mixed with Cork shavings, Charcoal Dust, Ox
hair &c rendering the Composition firm, adhesive, & almost everlasting, where the timbers are at a distance from each other, pieces of
Cork wood or strips of Boards &c may be introduced to fill up in part
& save the Composition—Ships of War in England supposed to last,
12 to 13 years, Patentee supposes after 20 ys. with his application, the
Vessel would be better than at 12. ys. with only usual precautions.—
Inside of the vessel *now* most perishable, *then* most lasting, rats ban-
ished, rot prevented; acts as so much ballast, is lighter however than
water—£400 @ 500£ stg. would fortify (by his method) a first rate
India Man—p. 249 the above taken from Monthly Magazine—April
1802. In same Number page. 213. An acct. of the Use of Mirrors in
Lighthouses by E. Walker, who refers to another paper by himself
in the Magazine of Decr. 1801 & also to another signed *Nauticus*. in
Feby. 1802. Mirrors have been much used in France, from whence no
doubt information could be procured.—Those in England commencd
1777. some acct. is given in *Hutchinsons* practical Seamanship—
Concaves of Copper silverd[3] disapproved of—Walker invented a
Concave composite glass Mirror 18 Inches in diameter, which would
appear larger than a star of the first Magnitude at 14 miles with a
lamp of 10 single threads of fine Cotton several lighthouses erected
on his principle which gave Satisfaction on acct. of their goodness &
œconomy—Our Minister at London, could procure every necessary
information, & models if requisite—The Brethren at the Trinity
house would willingly give information & none more able as the light
houses are generally under their direction—Walker lives at Lynn
Regis—I had not the book in my possession long enough or I would
have copied the whole article—

A society for promoting Naval Architecture, exists in England, 2.
Vol. of their Transactions have appear'd, the 3d is in the press—
They have also published experiments to ascertain resistance of
different shaped bodies immersd 6 feet below the surface of water,
going at the rate of 1 to 8 miles—published by J Sewell Cornhill—
I some time since sent one part, relative to preservation of ship

timber—another part contains an acct. of the effect of oil in preserving timber for vessels or in Bridges. The Work contains many Useful hints—

A Mr Millington of Barbadoes, now of London has found out a Method of preserving Potatoes several years for long Voyages—Vide Young's Annals Vol. 34 page 511—He peels the Potatos & rasps or grinds them (an apple grinder would I suppose Answer), he then puts the Mash into strong cloths & presses out the Juice (a Cyder press would answer) the Cake (which should be about the size of a Cream cheese) should then be thoroughly dried, & will keep for 3 or four years, the bulk is reduced $\frac{5}{6}$ & the weight $\frac{1}{2}$—when dressed by steam or water it resumes its original bulk nearly & are like mashed potatoes—The liquor which comes from it, being mixed with an equal quantity of water, & sufferd to remain an hour or two, gives a Sediment, which makes fine Pastry or fine Starch, & possibly might pay for the Manufactory. Experiments might immediately be made— Potatoes injured by Frost, if thus treated, become eatable—Care should be taken to leave, no dirt or decayed parts in the Potatoes.— With a sufficient provision of this article, & of portable soups made from coarse pieces, & bones broken up upon Rumfords principles, the health of our sailors might be much preserved.

The diffusion of Useful knowledge has of late been much increased, by a few periodical publications, the possession of which as to the past, & the early obtaining the future continuation is of great importance, & cannot be too strongly recommended—Viz.

Nicholson's Journal—4th series, this now continued in a new series 8vo.

Tillochs Philos: Magazine 8vo. 11 Vols are published

Repertory of arts—Twelve or 13 Vol. 8vo are published—a new series is commencing

All these publications are monthly—& contain a general acct. of the progress of science, & of the new discoveries; similar publications, amongst which the Annales de Chimie, are making in France—

The Reviews, would be useful, as giving an acct. of almost all new publications—The Monthly Review perhaps the best—of *Magazines*—The Monthly—is the best calculated to give information of what is useful in the progressive developements of useful knowledge—I have taken the liberty of adressing the above to you, that if you judge the hints or information of sufficient importance, you will put them in a proper channel to made use of—

The Kentucky head bone arrived this day, Mr Peale is making a sketch to send to you—It does not appear to belong to the Mammoth—

I remain with the greatest respect, Dear sir Your obt Serv

JN VAUGHAN

On 2d May. The Vaccine Virus had not yet succeeded with Mr Dunbar
it was in Kentucky—I have by four or five opportunities since sent further supplies & wrote to Dr Brown to forward some from Kentucky—The Practice spreads most rapidly here—in Town & Country.—

Forsyth on *Fruit & forest Trees* has this day been published reprinted here—8vo. $2\frac{50}{100}$ 13 Plates—It contains also his method of curing diseased Trees for which he received in England £4000 stg premium—

RC (DLC); at foot of text: "Thomas Jefferson Prest. of the United States"; endorsed by TJ as received 12 June and so recorded in SJL.

Samuel BENTHAM, a naval architect and Great Britain's inspector general of naval works, won a GOLD MEDAL offered by the Society for the Encouragement of Arts, Manufactures, and Commerce, a British organization, as a premium in chemistry for the best method of preserving fresh water on sea voyages. The *Philosophical Magazine*, a publication edited by Alexander Tilloch, reprinted Bentham's report of his experiment from the society's transactions. Bentham was the brother of philosopher Jeremy Bentham (*Transactions of the Society Instituted at London, for the Encouragement of Arts, Manufactures, and Commerce*, 19 [1801], 27-8, 191-6; *Philosophical Magazine*, 12 [1802], 12-14; DNB).

See Vaughan's letter of 8 May for the publication by Étienne BARRY that described the water filtration method of James SMITH.

MR PEALES EXHIBITION: Raphaelle Peale's demonstration of a water filtration apparatus in Philadelphia; see Robert Patterson to TJ, 12 Apr.

Abraham BOSQUET also designed lifesaving equipment (*Monthly Magazine*, 13

[1802], 249-50; *Naval Chronicle*, 7 [1802], 133-40).

The communications by Ezekiel WALKER to the British periodical *The Monthly Magazine* documented Walker's involvement in building reflecting lighthouse lamps. NAUTICUS disputed the originality of Walker's designs (*Monthly Magazine*, 12 [1801], 402; 13 [1802], 6-8, 212-15).

HUTCHINSONS PRACTICAL SEAMANSHIP: William Hutchinson, *A Treatise on Practical Seamanship*, first published in Liverpool in 1777.

Most lighthouses in England and Wales were under the authority of TRINITY HOUSE of Deptford Strond, an institution that began as a seamen's guild and benevolent association. The governing body of Trinity House was a group known as the elder brethren (James Taylor, "Private Property, Public Interest, and the Role of the State in Nineteenth-Century Britain: The Case of the Lighthouses," *Historical Journal*, 44 [2001], 753-4, 755; R. H. Coase, "The Lighthouse in Economics," *Journal of Law and Economics*, 17 [1974], 362-7).

A few months earlier Vaughan had called TJ's attention to the publications of the Society for the Improvement of NAVAL ARCHITECTURE. Vaughan's brothers were members of the group. The association was formed in 1791 with the goal of improving Britain's fleet for the conflict with France. The society undertook experiments for a few years, but then ceased its research due to a lack of interest in its work and a shortage of funds (S. Pollard, "Laissez-Faire and Shipbuilding," *Economic History Review*, new ser., 5 [1952], 99; Vol. 35:698-9, 722).

Langford Millington's description of his method for PRESERVING POTATOES was published by order of the Society for Bettering the Condition of the Poor. The article appeared in Arthur Young's *Annals of Agriculture, and Other Useful Arts*, 34 [1800], 511-18.

RUMFORDS PRINCIPLES: as an adviser to the elector of Bavaria during the 1780s and 1790s, Benjamin Thompson, Count Rumford, began to investigate economical means of feeding soldiers and the needy. In Britain, he urged the Royal Institution to appoint a committee to study the preparation of soups as nutrition for the poor. Drawing on his experience running workhouses in Munich, Rumford developed soup recipes that relied on carefully apportioned amounts of cheap ingredients such as barley, peas, potatoes, and stale bread, earning him an international reputation that sometimes took the form of scorn and ridicule (DNB; W. J. Sparrow, *Knight of the White Eagle: A Biography of Sir Benjamin Thompson, Count Rumford* [London, 1964], 13, 121, 188-92; *The Complete Works of Count Rumford*, 4 vols. [Boston, 1870-75], 4:401-4, 413-22, 484-9).

Since 1797, the British chemist William Nicholson had edited and published the *Journal of Natural Philosophy, Chemistry, and the Arts*, commonly referred to as NICHOLSON'S JOURNAL (DNB).

REPERTORY OF ARTS: the first volume of *The Repertory of Arts and Manufactures*, a compendium of original papers along with selections from the published transactions of various learned societies, appeared in London in 1794.

A group of French scientists affiliated with Antoine Laurent Lavoisier, including Pierre Auguste Adet, commenced the ANNALES DE CHIMIE in 1789. Publication was interrupted by the Terror but resumed in 1797, and the journal began to incorporate papers on physics as well as chemistry (Maurice Crosland, "Research Schools of Chemistry from Lavoisier to Wurtz," *British Journal for the History of Science*, 36 [2003], 333, 342, 345-8).

TJ had a long familiarity with the MONTHLY REVIEW, a British serial begun in 1749 that contained reviews of printed works in a range of subjects. During the 1780s, he tried to assemble a complete set of the *Review*'s issues and recommended the publication to others as a source of information (Sowerby, No. 4721; Vol. 6:127; Vol. 10:166; Vol. 13:177, 367, 376).

Earlier in 1802, Dr. Isaac E. Gano had begun using the cowpox VACCINE to inoculate people in Frankfort, Kentucky (New York *Spectator*, 20 Feb. 1802; Madison, *Papers*, Sec. of State Ser., 6:313).

William Forsyth's book (see Vaughan to TJ, 8 May) contained observations on diseases of FRUIT and FOREST TREES and described "a particular method of cure, made public by order of the British government."

[1] Vaughan underlined the name with three strokes.

[2] Name underlined with three strokes.

[3] Word interlined.

From Caspar Wistar

DEAR SIR,   Philada June 8. 1802.

I feel a considerable degree of embarrassment on the present occasion, but trust to your good nature for excusing the liberty I take, &

the trouble I give you—My object is to state to you that I have for a long time been acquainted with the character of Mr G. Latimer,* & have known him personally for some years, & that he has allways appeared to me to be a man of business & of great punctuality & accuracy. I believe this is the general opinion here respecting him, & particularly among the merchants—I am afraid the sentiment "ne sutor ultra crepidam" will arise in your mind, but if you will forgive me you may laugh at me—

Have you seen McKenzie's account of his journeys across the Continent & to the Northern Ocean—he had very peculiar advantages for such an enterprize, & happily availed himself of them. It is reported here that he is at New York, on his way to the North West Country, & that he has provided himself with the Vaccine Virus for the benefit of the unfortunate natives. His melancholy account of the effects of the Small Pox in that Country must add greatly to your satisfaction on account of your exertions to diffuse the benefits of that very happy discovery—

I hope to have the pleasure of transmitting to you a copy of the plate representing the bones of the fore foot of the Megatherium or Animal of Paraguay, it is in my possession and I wait only for a description, which I have heard of, but not seen—

Our impatience to see the bones of the head of the Mammoth is wound up to a high pitch—A Gentleman from the Westward, who had seen the fragment of a head, thought Mr Peales imitation of the head of the Elephant by no means like it—Of this subject I believe you know more than I am able to tell you I will therefore only beg leave to add that

With affectionate Esteem I am your Sincere friend

C. WISTAR JUNR.

---

* The Collector

RC (DLC); at foot of text: "His Excellency The President of the United States"; endorsed by TJ as received 10 June and so recorded in SJL.

The adage NE SUTOR ULTRA CREPIDAM, sometimes translated as "cobbler, stick to your last," admonishes against overstepping one's expertise. Recording the anecdote in which the proverb had its origin, Pliny the Elder gave the expression as "ne supra crepidam sutor iudicaret"—criticism by a shoemaker should not go beyond the subject of shoes (*Natural History*, xxxv, 85).

Alexander Mackenzie returned to Canada in 1802 after spending two years in Britain, where he had been knighted in recognition of his overland expeditions from Britain's Canadian provinces to the Arctic Ocean and the northern Pacific coast. A Philadelphia edition of the ACCOUNT OF HIS JOURNEYS had recently appeared (see John Vaughan to TJ, 8 May). The ADVANTAGES that impressed Wistar may have included

Mackenzie's affiliation with the North West Company, which enabled him to establish a base for his expeditions at Lake Athabasca west of Hudson Bay. Mackenzie also had access to French Canadian voyageurs and Indian interpreters and hunters to make up his traveling parties, as well as stocks of trade goods and some geographical information from Indian tribes. Between his two expeditions he went to England to learn the principles of navigation. Mackenzie had several years' experience in the fur trade and described himself as "endowed by Nature with an inquisitive mind and enterprising spirit; possessing also a constitution and frame of body equal to the most arduous undertakings" and "familiar with toilsome exertions in the prosecution of mercantile pursuits." He "not only contemplated the practicability of penetrating across the continent of America, but was confident in the qualifications" and "animated by the desire, to undertake the perilous enterprise" (DNB; W. Kaye Lamb, ed., *The Journals and Letters of Sir Alexander Mackenzie* [Cambridge, 1970], 15, 18-21, 57, 58, 163, 237).

Mackenzie's published journals included an overview of the fur trade that named several examples of the disastrous EFFECTS of smallpox on indigenous peoples in British North America. The disease "destroyed with its pestilential breath whole families and tribes" and consequently hurt the fur trade, which was Mackenzie's source of livelihood (Alexander Mackenzie, *Voyages from Montreal, on the River St. Laurence, through the Continent of North America, to the Frozen and Pacific Oceans; In the Years 1789 and 1793* [London, 1801], xiv, xvii, liii, lvii, lxxvii, lxxviii, lxxxii, cxvii; DNB).

TJ and Wistar, who had both studied the megalonyx fossils from Virginia in 1797, were interested in similarities and differences between the megalonyx and the skeleton of the MEGATHERIUM that had been excavated in South America and mounted in Madrid. Charles Willson Peale acquired illustrations of the megatherium bones from Philippe Rose Roume, a former French commissioner to Saint-Domingue who was in the United States for several months in 1801-2. Roume first obtained pictures of the fossils in Spain in 1795. Peale put the illustrations on display in his museum in Philadelphia, in the same room as the mastodon skeleton from New York State (*Philadelphia Gazette*, 10 Mch. 1802; APS, *Transactions*, 4 [1799], 526-31; Robert Hoffstetter, "Les rôles respectifs de Brú, Cuvier et Garriga dans les premières études concernant *Megatherium*," *Bulletin du Muséum National d'Histoire Naturelle*, 2d ser., 31 [1959], 538-9; Laurent Dubois, *Avengers of the New World: The Story of the Haitian Revolution* [Cambridge, Mass., 2004], 196, 226; Peale, *Papers*, v. 2, pt. 1:381-6, 440, 443n; Madison, *Papers, Sec. of State Ser.*, 2:74, 94; Vol. 29:298-9, 300n; Benjamin Smith Barton to TJ, 9 Feb. 1802).

BONES OF THE HEAD OF THE MAMMOTH: that is, the partial skull that John Brown of Boone County, Kentucky, sent to Peale; see Brown's letter to TJ of 28 Apr. and Peale's of 6 June. For the arrival of the fossil in Philadelphia, see Peale's letter of 10 June.

The mastodon skeleton that Peale exhibited in Philadelphia lacked the upper part of the skull, so Peale drew on the anatomy of the ELEPHANT to create replicas of the missing bones (Peale to TJ, 21 Jan. 1802).

To David Campbell

DEAR SIR   Washington June 9. 1802.

My ordinary duties render me very slow in answering the favors of my friends. hence this late acknolegement of yours of Feb. 7. recd.

Mar. 8.   you will doubtless have learned that Doctr. Vandyke has been continued in service.   with respect to the disposal of your son now of 12. years of age I can only say what I should do with a son of my own, if I had one to educate. I should continue him at a country school till he was master of the languages I wished him to learn. I should then send him to Wm. & Mary college for mathematics, natural philosophy, & Rhetoric. I do not mention moral philosophy because no lectures can make that plainer than the books themselves written on the subject & which ought to be put into his hands. attendance on lectures on that subject therefore is time lost. I think Wm. & Mary college the best on the continent as far as the subjects go which make an ordinary part of collegiate education. at Philadelphia alone are regular courses of lectures given in Botany, Natural history, Chemistry & Anatomy. after about 2. years therefore at Wm. & Mary, I should send a son for one year to Philadelphia, & if I[1] intended him for the law, he should first read a year or two in the country under good direction, & then go and take a course of lectures in law at Wm. & Mary college. the whole of this course would occupy from 5. to 6. years after the languages are acquired. out of this you can select the parts which come within the plan of education you propose for your son, & know my opinion of the best place where each portion of it can be acquired.—I am happy to learn that the course pursued by the administration gives content. I think the proceedings of the last session of Congress must have been satisfactory to every man not determined to be dissatisfied. accept assurances of my esteem & high respect.   TH: JEFFERSON

PrC (DLC); at foot of text: "Judge Campbell."

YOURS OF FEB. 7: Campbell's letter was dated 12 Feb. 1802.

[1] Word supplied by Editors.

From David Hall

SIR   Lewes June 9th. 1802

I have the Honer of transmitting to you, an address from the Grand & general Juries, summoned to attend the Circuit Court of the United States, lately held in the Town of Dover; agreeably to their request—I have the Honor to be

with the highest respect Your most Obt hble Servt
                                         DAVID HALL

RC (DLC); at foot of text: "His Excellency Thos. Jefferson"; endorsed by TJ as received 15 June and so recorded in SJL; also endorsed by a clerk: "Allen McLane Collector Wilmington The address respts McL's removal, because he has been in office 5 yrs. / is a federalist, / advocates a general removal of federalists." Enclosure not found, but see Delaware Democratic Republicans to TJ, 5 June 1802.

From Levi Lincoln

Washington June 9th 1802

On examining the charges against Governor St. Clair, and his defence, unaccompanyed with any documents, I some time since wrote the inclosed, & delivered those papers to the secretary of the navy. I have perused the vouchers which were put into my hands yesterday, in support of the charges, and find nothing, which changes the opinion which I had formed on reading the defence, excepting that there appears to be some legal justification for the fees for the licences to Innholders, and that his interference, to influence the conduct of a majestrate, appears much more exceptionable—This being the case you will have the goodness, to excuse my not transscribing the first draught—

I have the honor to be, Sir, most respectfully your Hum. Sevt—

LEVI LINCOLN

RC (DLC); at head of text: "President of the United States"; endorsed by TJ as received 12 June and "St. Clair's case" and so recorded in SJL.

ENCLOSURE

From Levi Lincoln

SIR   Washington May 25th 1802

In examining the charges against Govr. St. Clair and his defence, it is perceived, that an improper exercise of a confidence, or of a discretion, which had been placed in him, constitute an important part of them. This discretion can be rightfully exercised only when it aims at the ends for which it was intrusted. It is not directed by any special provisions, either in the ordinance, or in any statute—General principles, accommodated to the situation of the territory, promotive of its interest, are the laws binding on the Govr., within his sphere of action, & must direct, & limit his power, where it is not otherwise done—A violation of these principles, from party, sinister, or improper, views; or forsaking them, in multiplied instances, innocently, from imperfect, or mistaken, views, as really finds an imputation on the character of the Govr., to the purposes of deciding on his removal, as if he had violated the provisions of positive statutes. The enquiry is not, of a criminal nature, for the purposes of punishment. In such a case, the trial would be on different principles, and proof of the breach of actually existing laws, with an express, or an implied criminal intent, would be necessary—

The questions are, as to the qualifications for the office and the utility, & policy, of continuing him; and the charges are—

1st. That "He has usurped legislative powers by the erection of Counties, and location of seats of Justice, by proclamation on his own sole authority—

Obs. The Govr's. defence admits the fact. the question is, was it an usurpation of power? not, was power discretely exercised? A strict construction of the ordinance, in my opinion, gives to the Govr. the power of erecting the Counties, and of appointing the County officers—A very liberal construction of the power for erecting Counties, might imply a power of fixing the place for holding the Court: But as this, is usually considered as belonging to legislative power, and as it is not necessarily connected with the erecting of a County, or with the administration of justice in it—I am inclined to think, the ordinance gave the Govr. no authority, to locate the seats of justice. The court may be held in one County, for *that*, & for its neighbouring County—The Govr. is to lay out the County. The powers & duties of the majestrate, when, and where to meet, and the business to be transacted, are matters to be defined, and regulated by the legislature. However, as this is a matter of some perplexity of construction, I think a different one might very innocently be adopted.

2d. That "He has misused the power of negativing legislative acts, by putting his negative on laws useful and necessary for the territory—

Obs. In the exercise of these discretionary powers, he by the ordinance, is made the judge, of the utility, and the necessity of the laws, which the assembly may enact. It would be difficult to say without more knowledge than is furnished by the papers, that this power was used either wantonly or injuriously.

3 That he has refused to perform the duties of his office, but on the payment of arbitrary fees, not established by any lawfull authority.

Obs. The taking of the fees alluded to, are admitted by the defence, which denies that it was done, arbitrarily. This is a question of fact, resting on the evidence. If the charge is supported, the conduct of the Govr. must be highly censurable. It can never be excused in one placed at the head of the Govt to inforce the execution & to guard against the violation, of law. There is nothing in the papers which shows that the fees admitted to have been taken, were authorised by law. The argument in the defence seems to be, this: That a thing, which has not been previously forbidden by law, or not censured in the first instance of its existance, is to be considered as legally authorised—I see neither justification, or apology for the Govr. in this part of his conduct—

4. He has negatived acts of the legislature abolishing those fees, and passed the act giving him $500 as a compensation for that abolition, & thereby holding both the fees and the compensation—

Obs This charge by recognizing the propriety of a law for the abolishing of those fees, & a compensation of $500 therefor to the Govr. seems to involve a justification of the preceeding charge—However, if the abolishing

[569]

law, and the giving law, were understood by the parties, to be but the parts of a measure having in view a certain object, there was unfairness, in assenting to the one, & negativing the other, and the unfairness, was the greater on account of those complementory terms, used in the giving act, from which the Govr. in part, derives his defence. This understanding can be known only to the Govr. & to the makers of these laws. I have seen only the Govrs explanations. They are plausible—But it is difficult to beleive, that the legislators would have given the $500 on the idea of the fees being retained—

5 He has attempted to effect the dismemberment of the territory and to destroy the constitutional boundaries in order to prevent its advancement to the rights of Self Government, to which its numbers would intitle it.

Obs There are, and can be, no proofs of the motives which influenced to this measure, but from, the nature of the thing, and the avowal of the accused—It is not easy to find in the subject matter, those which will satisfactorily account for an attempt, in the Governor of a territory to abridge the extent of his own jurisdiction, and of course his own emoluments & importance, and thereby for a time, deprive the people of rights & priviledges which they would otherwise be intitled to—It is not in nature that this attempt should have nothing in view, but the interest & happiness of the Governed—It is more like bartering the priviledges of the people for the continuence of his own power—

6 He has granted Commissions generally during pleasure but that to the Atty Genl. to his own son during good behaviour.

Obs: This, in every view of the matter, must be considered as improper & highly censurable. Other officers, holding during pleasure, it formed an inviduous distinction. The more so, on account of the difficulty that some judicial officers had made, respecting the tenure of their commissions, and the reasoning of the Govr on that occasion against their being during good beheavour—

During pleasure, is the only proper tenure, for a ministerial officer, dependent, for his appointment on a Governor, who is made, and continues, at the will of the President, and in a temporary Govt, where changes may often become useful, some times necessary—A new Govr. ought to have the same power of selecting the officers of his Govt which his predecessor had—In a Country, where there is a general deficiency of legal information, in which are but few law characters, It must be of importance that the Atty Genl. should possess the confidence of the people, and the friendship & esteem of the Govr.—The defence contains no justification. At best, it admits the doing an actual wrong to the public[1] to secure an improper and a possible advantage, to an individual connected with himself. This conduct, & his motives, are highly censurable & as justified by himself, involving this reproach, either that the President would appoint an improper person to succeed him, or that his successor would act improperly in his office. In short, it is apparent that the Govr. meant, to make that provision for a son, which he would have thought not proper, to have made for a stranger, and to abridge the Gubernatorial power in his successor, which he had, and would have thought necessary to have, had the exercise of himself on the supposition of his continuing in his office—The proof of this, is, in the circumstances he states, & his actually removing from office justices, who differed from him in opinion on a question of law—as appears by the next charge—

7 He has endeavoured arbitrarily to influence and contravene the judicial proceedings of the judiciary and has revoked & effected the surrender of commissions of those, who refused to bend to his will—

Obs. The Govr's legal ideas respecting the competency of the excluded witnesses, were undoubtedly correct. But, that he should think it right to remove judges from their offices, because they mistook the law, is strange; And especially, in reference to a point, which, formed an exception to a general principle, and about which, altho the law is now clearly settled, the books contain various opinions—The Govr's right to remove from office is not to be exercised capriciously, his discretion should be governed by reason, & propriety. Justices may innocently imbrace, & after able investigations, erronious opinions, but if the abandonment of these opinions, at the instance of another, is the condition of their continuing in office, dependent, & degraded indeed is their situation. It seems impossible that this should be the only motive for the act complained of—

8 He has appointed persons residing out of a county to offices, the duties of which were habitually performed in them—

Obs: The instance, excused in the defence, is, the Govr's. son in law, who being a justice of the peace and of the Common Pleas in the County of Hamilton, was on the erecting of the County of Bomont, appointed recorder of deeds there, which he has discharged by deputy—The excuse is, that no person residing in the County town qualified for the office could be found to give the necessary security, nor a suitable house obtained for the purpose. It is to be remembered that the Govr. erected Counties at his own descretion. Why did he erect a new one, before population, could furnish, from within itself, men, and the accommodations, necessary for its support. The idea, of discharging the duties of such an office altogether by a deputy, and of a non resident County officer, is new, & justifiable on no principle whatsoever—

9th That he has neglected and thereby obstructed the organization of the militia for the defence of the territory by withholding the appointments of officers twelve months after a law had passed establishing the same.

Obs: This business, has generally been attended with difficulties & delay; Perhaps not greater in the territory than in many other places, where no particular blame attaches to the Commander in Chief. The reasons assigned in the defence are plausible, and if supported to me satisfactory—

10 That he avowed his hostility to the form, and the substance of a republican Govt. & his contempt of our malitia regulations.

Obs:—Judging, as I have of the other charges, from the defence, I doubt if this ought to be considered of much consequence. So much depends on the parties to the conversation, the matter, the manner, the occasion, and the design—so often imperfectly heard, or misconceived, that it is difficult to place much[2] confidence on it—

The foregoing are my impressions on examining the charges & the Govr's. defence. I have no doubt but that there has been, that departure from duty, and abuse of power, which will justify the President in a removal—There are other reasons. As a measure of justice and of right, it appears to me to be clear, the Govr., nor his friends, would have any reasonable grounds for

Complaint—As a question of policy there may be some doubt. In reference to the territory abstractedly considered, I am inclined to think it would be useful, and also in its immediate effects on them, in their connection with the United States—How it would impress the public mind, is uncertain. It would be improved by the opposition, to create new, & to strengthen its old prejudices. But these I would risque,[3] rather than the republicanism of the territory, if that is the alternative—

Most respectfully yours   LEVI LINCOLN

RC (DLC); at head of text: "President of the United States."

COUNTY OF BOMONT: that is, Clermont County (Charges Against Arthur St. Clair, at 30 Jan. 1802, Document II).

[1] Lincoln here interlined the preceding three words in place of "to prevent a possible."
[2] Lincoln here canceled "intire."
[3] MS: "rique."

To Thomas McLean

SIR   Washington June 9. 1802.

Your favor of May 2. was not recieved till a few days ago. however strong my preference of subjects of the nature of that of your letter yet the business of my present station requiring the whole of my time and attention, forbids me to give any portion of either from it's duties. I have been obliged therefore to forbid myself to enter into philosophical speculations. should you propose to secure to yourself by a patent the benefit of the ideas contained in your letter, I will lodge it in the patent office of the Secretary of state: or should you prefer a communication of it to the world, I would transmit it to the Philosophical society at Philadelphia. either the one or the other shall be done as you shall direct. in the mean time be pleased to accept my respects & best wishes.   TH: JEFFERSON

PrC (DLC); at foot of text: "Mr. Thomas Mc.lean at the foot of the North mountain Frederic county near Martinburg."

To Edward Savage

SIR   Washington June 9. 1802.

Having been absent during the month of May on a visit to Monticello, your letter of Apr. 29. has remained here unanswered. during my absence also the boxes containing the print frames arrived safe. mr John Barnes of Georgetown, who does business for me, will this day remit to his friend mr Ludlow of New York the sum of

61. D. 75 c. the amount of your bill the frames give perfect satisfaction. accept my best wishes & respects.   TH: JEFFERSON

PrC (DLC); at foot of text: "Mr. Edward Savage"; endorsed by TJ in ink on verso.

From William Thornton

Wednesday P.M.—[9 June 1802]

W: Thornton returns his respectful Compliments to the President of the United States.—He has perused, and returns Mr: Elgar's Letter; but is not acquainted with any Species of Serpentine Stone which he thinks can possibly possess the magnetic Power, as it is a species of Calcarious Stone, or Marble, denominated from its Spots and variegated appearance, not endued, to the best of his knowledge, with any peculiar quality. Indeed if any Stone exists subject to polar attraction, but not obedient to Iron, it might nevertheless be still subject to Loadstone, which no doubt abounds in various parts of our Country. The Inconveniences Mr: Elgar complains of are great, & the Correction would be of Consequence. The very Idea of a remedy may lead to Success.—

RC (DLC: Cass Gilbert Papers); partially dated; endorsed by TJ as received 9 June and so recorded in SJL.

MR. ELGAR'S LETTER: Joseph Elgar, Jr., to TJ, 24 Nov. 1801 (Vol. 35:715-17).

From DeWitt Clinton

SIR   Newtown 10 June 1802

As the politics of S. Carolina are very interesting, I enclose you a pamphlet ascribed to Mr. Marshall one of the Chancellors of that State, which will present them in a new point of view; as probably it has not reached you, you will excuse me for taking this liberty.—

Our political aspects here are very good: I have no doubt but that every thing will eventuate right.

I am with great respect & attachment Your most Obedt. Servt.

DEWITT CLINTON

RC (DLC); endorsed by TJ as received 14 June and so recorded in SJL. Enclosure: see below.

Perhaps Clinton enclosed the PAMPHLET published in Charleston in late

1801, entitled *Considerations on the Propriety of Adopting a General Ticket in South-Carolina, for the Election of Representatives in Congress and Electors of President and Vice-President of the United States. Addressed to the People of South*

Carolina by Crito (see Shaw-Shoemaker, No. 354). The essay was first published as a series in the Charleston *City Gazette and Daily Advertiser* between 3 Oct. and 13 Nov. 1801.

ASCRIBED TO MR. MARSHALL: Charleston attorney William Marshall,

a young Republican who served in the South Carolina General Assembly from 1791 to 1799 and then became chancellor of the court of equity (*S.C. Biographical Directory, House of Representatives*, 4:380-1).

From William Davidson

TO THE PRESIDENT OF THE UNITED STATES

With due deference the Subscriber prays leave respectfully to submit the following remarks on the Causes which most probably led to his recent arrest and detainer by General LeClerc in Hispaniola

As soon as General LeClerc got possession of Cape Francois, he laid an embargo on all American vessels, which continued for the space of fifteen days. By the expiration of this period several battles had been fought between the White and Black Troops, in which it was generally believed the former had been beaten. The Americans now wrote to their friends in the United States, and many of them blamed General LeClerc for the loss of the Town, alledging that had he came in the first day of the fleet's appearance off the harbour, it might have been preserved. Some of these called him—Coward! others a Fool,—many both, and imputed to his want of skill the many losses that had been sustained. These letters became subjects for publication in the Gazettes in the United States, which immediately finding their way out, were read by General LeClerc and his Officers. A coolness soon took place towards the Americans, which shortly ripened into enmity, and we were either insulted or treated with contempt whenever our business necessarily led us to appear before any of them. This to me obviously appeared the natural consequence resulting from the provocations given by my Countrymen as before mentioned, which had so often and so decidedly met my disapprobation, as can be testified by many of them.

At length an extract of a letter dated at Cape Francois the 20th February came out in one of the American Papers. This publication I heard read by its reputed author. I then reprobated it as highly improper and impolitic, and insisted that the Americans ought to observe a neutral conduct, and as I then expressed myself I trembled for the consequences. To this letter I beg leave to refer the President. Two or three days afterwards I was arrested as stated in my protest—

I now submit to the consideration of the President what I conceive to be the real causes of my imprisonment.

First, General LeClerc had been told by the Inhabitants of the Cape that the Americans had plundered the Town after the fire

Secondly The before mentioned publications which no doubt gave him offence, particularly the last and of which he had no other clue to discover the author than the mere circumstance of his mentioning the date of his arrival which would also apply to me as by a reference to the Custom House Books it appeared that the Ship Orion of Philadelphia, a Schooner of New York and myself in the Ship Saint Domingo Packet had all arrived on one and the same day; the two former vessels had sailed (tho' the Super Cargo of the Schooner was then in the town)—added to which the General by this time had received information that the head of my Ship was the Effigy of Toussaint and (as he has told an American in a private conversation since) that he had been informed that the Ship belonged to that Chief and had brought Powder and Arms for his use.

And in as much as General LeClerc had now become highly irritated by the conduct of the Americans as already mentioned, he thought it expedient to select me as the most proper object, on whom to manifest his displeasure.

Permit me here to subjoin a statement of the actual losses I have sustained in consequence of the arrest and detention of myself and property as beforementioned

My expences in prison	Dolls	81.–
Demurrage of the Ship 22 days @ $20		440.–
Commission on the Cargo consigned to myself which I was obliged to put in a Merchants hands in consequence of my being ordered away say $22000 @ 2½ pct		550.–
My passage home and stores		50.–
Master employed to conduct the Ship after I left her, his wages one month and a half		75.–
Dollars		1196.–

My expences to and from Washington not ascertained.

The loss of the above sum will be sensibly felt by me, particularly so as the Ship was built just before the close of the late European war, the one half cost me all the property I was worth, the other half I obtained on credit. The whole of the Ship will not at this day sell for more than will pay the residue of what I am indebted thereon. My personal suffering I shall set no value on, viewing it in the light of one of those misfortunes from which no man is exempt in perilous times.

Remuneration for my losses is in the present case only a secondary object—I have been interdicted from a personal intercourse with the Island of Hispaniola, and that under a severe penalty, no less than the pain of death! It is this trade to which I have been most accustomed and with which I am most intimately acquainted. From this source has been chiefly derived my living. And it is principally with a view to the establishment of my innocence, and of being released from an injurious proscription that the present representation is made, having for its aim a governmental interference in my behalf.

WM. DAVIDSON
Philadelphia 10th. June 1802

RC (DNA: RG 76, Claims against France); in an unidentified hand, signed and dated by Davidson.

The EXTRACT OF A LETTER from Cap-Français dated the 20TH OF FEBRUARY cited by Davidson was carried to Philadelphia by the schooner *Lydia*, appeared in the New York *Daily Advertiser* on 19 Mch., and was subsequently reprinted in other American newspapers. The unidentified author claimed to have arrived at Cap-Français six days after the city's destruction by rebel forces on 4 Feb. He accused Leclerc of "timidity" and condemned him for not using French forces to protect the city. "Had the troops boldly entered at first, lives and property would have been saved," the author claimed, "but instead of that, they kept aloof, and allowed the cosmopolites to do all the mischief that time would admit." The letter went on to deride Leclerc's promise to conquer the island in six weeks, asserting that Toussaint's forces would "baffle all his skill." Leclerc's assertions that American property and lives would be protected were also ridiculed by the author. "French gratitude is in every clime the same," he wrote, adding that he has been "perfectly satiated with complaints of French plunder, French oppression, and French cruelty." Leclerc's declared embargo was followed by the requisition of American vessels and crews, then by demands that American cargos be sold at prices fixed by Leclerc and payable in bills on France. Trade has ceased for lack of money and every cargo liable to seizure. "It would be madness to send further supplies to such a faithless people," the author concluded.

AS STATED IN MY PROTEST: Davidson refers to a "Public Instrument of Protest," dated Wilmington, Delaware, 2 June, in which he recorded a detailed narrative of his arrest, imprisonment, and release, which included sworn declarations that he abided by all known American and French regulations during his voyage and was not involved in any illicit trade (MS in DNA: RG 76, Claims against France; in a clerk's hand; attested by Edward Roche, notary public for the state of Delaware).

Davidson's memorial was evidently presented to TJ in person on 21 June, along with letters of recommendation from Caesar A. Rodney of 31 May (printed above) and another from William Jones of Philadelphia, dated 16 June, in which he describes Davidson as sustaining "a fair character" and as a man of "strict integrity and good conduct, and in all respects a very worthy citizen" (RC in DLC; at foot of text: "The President of the United States"; endorsed by TJ as received 21 June and "by Capt Davidson" and so recorded in SJL). Davidson's narrative, as well as one by fellow captive John Rodgers, were forwarded to Robert R. Livingston by James Madison on 6

July, with instructions "to press the subject on the French Government with the advantage to be derived from an accurate knowledge of its details" (Madison, *Papers, Sec. of State Ser.*, 3:372-5).

From Henry Dearborn

War Department
SIR,   10th. June 1802

I have the honor to propose for your approbation William King of the State of Pennsylvania and Joseph West of New Jersey to be Surgeons Mates, in the Army.

I have the honor &ca.   H. DEARBORN

FC (Lb in DNA: RG 107, LSP).

After being notified of their appointments, WILLIAM KING was assigned to Fort Massac, near the mouth of the Ohio River, while JOSEPH WEST was ordered to Fort Niagara in New York (Dearborn to King, 10 June 1802, Dearborn to West, 10 June 1802, both in DNA: RG 107, LSMA).

Memorandums to Albert Gallatin

	Nicholas Gilman	to be Commissioners of bankruptcy for New Hampshire.
	Henry S. Langdon	
	John Goddard	
	John Mc.Clintock	
N.York	John Broome.	to be do. for the State of New York.
	William Edgar	
	Jonathan Pearsee junr.	
	Daniel D. Tompkins	
	Nathan Sandford	
	James Fairlie	
Albany	Abraham G. Lansing	
	Nicholas N. Quackenbush	
	George Merchant.	
	Alexander J. Dallas.	to be do. for Pensylvania.
	Joseph Clay.	
	Mahlon Dickerson	
	John Serjeant	
	Thomas Cumpston	
	John W. Vancleve	

Richmond George Hay
William Duvall
George W. Smith
Benjamin Hatcher
Petersburg Archibald Thweatt
Thomas Bolling Robertson.
John Mc.rae
Thomas Burchett

} to be do. for Virginia.

TH: JEFFERSON
June 10. 1802

Frankfort. John Rowan
Daniel Weisger
John Inston
Lexington James Morrison
John A. Seitz
John Bradford

to be Commissioners of
bankruptcy for Kentucky

TH: JEFFERSON
June 10. 1802

Commissions to be made out.
John Rowan of N. Carolina to be surveyor of the port of Windsor in
N.C. vice   dead.
Alexander Scott of Maryland to be Collector of the port of Nanjemoy
vice John C. Jones dead
Richard Howard of Delaware to be Master of a revenue cutter.

Mr Gallatin will be pleased to examine whether the descriptions of
the commissions, as given above, be correct, and send the papers to
the Secretary of state's office. TH: JEFFERSON
June 10. 1802

PrC (DLC). Not recorded in SJL.

FOR PENSYLVANIA: when Gallatin returned to his office on 3 June after spending almost a month in New York, he probably gave TJ his recommendations for bankruptcy commissioners for Pennsylvania, as he had promised to do before he left. Gallatin wrote the names of five Philadelphians on a scrap of paper—the first five appointed by TJ as commissioners for Pennsylvania as indicated above—with "A. J. Dallas" heading the list. Five other recommendations were written on the same scrap of paper. These names are in a column to the left of those written by Gallatin and appear to be in the hand of Dallas, his longtime friend. Dickerson, Sergeant, and Cumpston appear on both lists. Dallas also proposed Tench Coxe and Hugh Moore (MS in DNA: RG 59, LAR, 7:0193, undated, unsigned; Raymond Walters, Jr., Albert Gallatin: Jeffersonian Financier and Diplomat [New York, 1957], 33, 159; National Intelligencer, 7 June 1802; first letter at Gallatin to TJ, 30 Apr.). For Dallas's recommendation of Moore, see also Appendix II, List 1.

Before Gallatin returned to his office in

early June, the Treasury Department sent TJ a letter from North Carolina Senator David Stone, dated 19 May, recommending JOHN ROWAN, a native of Ireland who had come to the U.S. in the 1770s and served in the Revolutionary War, for surveyor at Windsor. Stone described Rowan as an honest, intelligent man whose politics were "uniformly and decidedly republican" (RC in DLC, endorsed by TJ: "Stone David to mr Gallatin. John Rowan to be surveyor of the port of Windsor vice   dead"; TJ to Gallatin, 2 July 1802). On his list of appointments, TJ noted Rowan's selection as surveyor and inspector in place of William Benson at 21 June (see Appendix I).

The Treasury Department forwarded several letters of recommendation for ALEXANDER SCOTT to the president. In correspondence dated 14 May, former Maryland congressman George Dent, appointed U.S. marshal for the Maryland district by TJ, reported the death of the collector of customs at Nanjemoy and recommended Scott for the position. He described him as "liberally educated," "conveniently situated," and "uniformly attached to Republican principles." Scott lived on an estate along the Potomac River a few miles from the office kept by Jones (RC in DNA: RG 59, LAR, endorsed by TJ: "Dent G. to Mr. Gallatin} Alexr Scott to be Collector of Nanjemy vice J. C. Jones"; *Biog. Dir. Cong.*; Gallatin, *Papers*, 7:150). Scott had planned to deliver Dent's letter to Gallatin, but when he found the Treasury secretary was not in Washington, he left it with Daniel C. Brent, requesting him to leave it in Gallatin's office (RC in DNA: RG 59, LAR, endorsed by TJ: "Alexr Scott to D. C. Brent"). Scott also delivered a 14 May letter from his relative G. R. Brown addressed to Brent. Brown noted that Scott would be "a faithfull & very respectable officer" (RC in same; endorsed by TJ: "Brown G. R. to D. C. Brent} Alexr Scott to be Nanjemy"). Brent wrote Gallatin on Scott's behalf on 21 May. He described him as "of excellent character, well educated, & much respected" and "in the most trying times a *firm* & *decided* Republican." Brent went on to say that Scott was not a "violent" Republican who offended his political opponents by his conduct and concluded that TJ could not make an appointment that would give "more general satisfaction" (RC in same; endorsed by TJ: "D. C. Brent to Mr. Gallatin} Alexr Scott to be Collector Nanjomy vice John C. Jones. dead"). The final letter forwarded, dated 28 May, came from former Maryland congressman Richard Sprigg, Jr. He advised that the candidate was "a young Gentleman of good natural talents" who had given up his practice as an attorney and settled near Nanjemoy. A firm Jeffersonian Republican, Scott was very respected, although he lived "in the most federal & turbulent county" (RC in same; endorsed by TJ: "R. Sprig to mr Gallatin. Alexr. Scott to be Collector Nanjemy"). In a letter to Gallatin dated 25 May, William Wedderburn, who lived near Nanjemoy and had previously applied for a clerkship in the Treasury Department, also put his name forth as a candidate for the collectorship (RC in same, endorsed by TJ: "Wedderburne Wm. to Mr. Gallatin} to be collector Nanjemy"; Gallatin, *Papers*, 5:31, 338).

For the appointment of Captain RICHARD HOWARD, see TJ's List of Candidates for Appointments printed at 24 Apr. 1802.

From Samuel Miller

SIR,   New-York, June 10 1802.

I do myself the honor to transmit herewith a copy of the annual publication of our Missionary Society. The information which it contains respecting our exertions, & the result of them during the past year, may, perhaps, not be altogether uninteresting to you. Be pleased to accept of it, as a small testimony of that high respect with which I have the honor to be, your humble servant,

SAML: MILLER.

RC (DLC); at foot of text: "The President of the U. States"; endorsed by TJ as received 12 June and so recorded in SJL. Enclosure: *A Sermon, Delivered Before the New-York Missionary Society, at their Annual Meeting April 6th, 1802* (New York, 1802; Sowerby, No. 1658).

In addition to his sermon, Miller's PUB-LICATION also contained the annual report of the directors of the missionary society and reports of meetings with Indian councils. TJ replied to Miller on 13 June: "Th: Jefferson presents his salutations to the revd mr Millar, and his thanks for the copy of a sermon inclosed to him which he shall read with pleasure" (PrC in DLC; endorsed by TJ in ink on verso).

From Mitchell & Buel

SIR, Poughkeepsie (State N. York) June 10. 1802.

Among the many tributes of respect which you receive from the citizens of the United States, a country News-paper will, perhaps, be of but little consequence. We have, however, herewith, presented Your Excellency with the first No. of the *Political Barometer*, the succeeding Numbers of which we shall continue to send on, unless you should signify your wish to have them discontinued.

There are inauspicious circumstances which at present attend the establishment of a Republican paper in this part of the country. Some previous attempts have failed; but under the influence of the present general administration, we look, not only, for a more firm adherence among those of our own side, but also, for a renovation of principles, in some measure, as it respects the opposition.

We are, Sir, Your Excellency's most Obdt. Servts.

MITCHELL & BUEL

RC (DLC); endorsed by TJ as received 15 June and so recorded in SJL. Enclosure: *Political Barometer*, 8 June.

Isaac Mitchell (ca. 1759-1812), New York newspaper publisher and novelist, served as editor of the Poughkeepsie *American Farmer and Dutchess County Advertiser* in 1799. His novel, *Alonzo and Melissa*, printed as a newspaper serial in 1804, was later pirated and became a bestseller from 1811 to 1876 (DAB). Jesse Buel (1778-1839) was a Connecticut-born printer whose newspaper career started as an apprentice in New York City and progressed to editing partnerships in Poughkeepsie, Kingston, and Albany. He held the lucrative New York state printership from 1815 until his resignation in 1821, when he pursued his interests as an agricultural writer and reformer (ANB).

POLITICAL BAROMETER: the Republican weekly newspaper successor to the Poughkeepsie *Guardian* was established by Mitchell & Buel in June 1802 and continued until June 1805 when the partnership dissolved and Mitchell became sole publisher (Brigham, *American Newspapers*, 1:722, 726).

From Charles Willson Peale

The Bone from Mr Jno. Brown I have received to day, and great was my surprise to find it in form corrisponding to the ox, which the enclosed drawing will best explain. It is a proof that the Indian Tradition has a good foundation. It certainly must have been a Buffalo of vast size, for compairing this fragment with the same parts of a common Ox and its size may pretty nearly be computed to be at least 3 times as large: The width between the Horns of an ox (before me) is $3\frac{1}{2}$ Inches, and the Ohio Bone would measure[1] in width 14 Inches. The desparity would have been more apparent had the width of the head from the Horns forward been preserved. We have only the actual measurement of the hind & smallest part of a head, supposing it to be exactly formed like the ox. I have made a slight sketch to shew the direction of the horns viewing the Top of the head which shew them from their Base inclined back—and they have also about the same inclination downward.

The View of the Back part shews deeper furrows, lengthways of the horn, than is the other view—The whole appearance of this bone, is like that filling the horns of common cattle.

I cannot help saying that I am disappointed in not seeing a head to corrispond with my Skeleton of the Mammoth, yet pleased at the discovery of another Wonder. What are we to think of the former inhabitants of this Land[2] when we find Bones of such vast magnitude? A wonderful revolution is testified by these various relicks—I wish I could explore & put the Bones together of several of them! It is a vain wish—I am tyed at least for a[3] time to this spot.

The following is an extract of Mr. Browns letter, a part is evidently for my self alone—After naming the Captn. & Vessel he send it by, he says—

"I present to the Philosophical Society of America this Curiossity among the works of Nature as a mark of the High Oppinion I entertain of that Body of men & of their Usefullness to the Community their Liberal Persuits so nobly displayed & Promulgated for the satisfaction of men—

"I make you the Depot of this Extraordinary mass of Matter that you may have the opportunity to finish in some measure the great work of that enormous Skeleton which will always intitle you to the highest Respect among your fellow Citizens. In the course of a few months I may be in Philada. I will there do myself the pleasure to wait on you at the Museum &c"

I hope we shall soon see some other Bones—

with the highest respect your friend   C W PEALE

RC (DLC); endorsed by TJ as received 12 June and so recorded in SJL. Dft (Lb in PPAmP: Peale-Sellers Papers).

INDIAN TRADITION: several Native American groups in the Ohio Valley region had oral traditions that associated the bones of large prehistoric animals with an enormous form of bison. TJ included one such account, which had been told to him by Delaware Indians when he was governor of Virginia, in *Notes on the State of Virginia* (Stanley Hedeen, *Big Bone Lick: The Cradle of American Paleontology* [Lexington, Ky., 2008], 20-30; *Notes*, ed. Peden, 43-4).

BUFFALO OF VAST SIZE: the partial skull sent from Kentucky was the first specimen recorded by scientists of an Ice Age bison that was later named *Bison latifrons*. The American Philosophical Society formally received the fossil in a meeting held on 18 June 1802. In July, Peale put the piece on display in the "Mammoth Room" of his museum in Philadelphia, where visitors also saw Peale's new mastodon skeleton and casts of the megalonyx fossils that TJ conveyed to the APS in 1797. Rembrandt Peale obtained a cast of the bison skull, which he described and illustrated for the *Philosophical Magazine* while he was in London in 1803. He conjectured that the animal, "one of the ox or buffalo kind," must have stood at least ten feet high and that each of its horns was at least six feet long. He also referred to the Indians' stories about the "great Buffalo." Later that year, he included a brief de-

scription of the skull in his *Historical Disquisition on the Mammoth*. In that work the younger Peale gave a full text of one of the Native American traditions and mentioned the one recounted by TJ in the *Notes*. The extinct *Bison latifrons* is the largest species of bison discovered in North America. The Kentucky specimen became part of the collections of the Academy of Natural Sciences in Philadelphia (Rembrandt Peale, "Account of Some Remains of a Species of Gigantic Oxen Found in America and Other Parts of the World," *Philosophical Magazine*, 15 [1803], 325-7; Rembrandt Peale, *Historical Disquisition on the Mammoth, or, Great American Incognitum, an Extinct, Immense, Carnivorous Animal, Whose Fossil Remains Have Been Found in North America* [London, 1803], 84-9; Jerry N. McDonald, *North American Bison: Their Classification and Evolution* [Berkeley, Calif., 1981], 65-75, plate 2; Peale, *Papers*, v. 2, pt. 1:435n, 443n; v. 2, pt. 2:764; APS, *Proceedings*, 22, pt. 3 [1884], 325; *Philadelphia Gazette*, 24 July 1802; Richard Harlan, *Fauna Americana: Being a Description of the Mammiferous Animals Inhabiting North America* [Philadelphia, 1825], 273; Vol. 29:291-304).

[1] Word omitted in RC, supplied from Dft.

[2] Word written over "Country." Dft: "Land."

[3] Peale first wrote "the present." Dft: "a."

I
Diagrams: Top of Bison Skull

View of the Upper Part

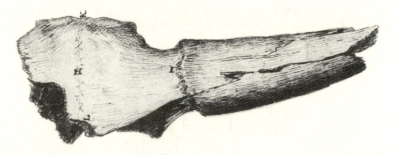

From the Suter H the center of the Head to root of the horn I 7 Inches
From the place of Insertion of the muscles of the Neck K to the fore part
of the upper head broke off at L 10 Inches.
The weight of this piece is 35 ℔

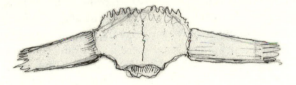

MS (DLC: TJ Papers, 124:21495); in Peale's hand.

II
Diagram: Back of Bison Skull

View of the Back part that Joins the neck

From A to B 2 feet 5 Inches.
Circumference at C 21 Inches.

{ The Hollow part above F I believe is part of the Cavity to receive the muscles that lift the under Jaw. at G is the inner surface corrisponding, measurement across 9 Inches. That part which should join the[1] hind part comprising the Ear is defficient.

ditto at D 17 Inches—
E hole for the spinal marrow 2 Inches wide & the debth in the recess for the Brains $8\frac{1}{2}$ Inches: the complete cavity for the brains
a, a, a, a, is the articulation for the Atlass

MS (DLC: TJ Papers, 124:21496); in Peale's hand.

[1] Peale here canceled "back."

From David Redick

SIR   Washington Penna June 10th 1802
about three weeks ago I received a letter from a Gentleman, residing amongst the Indians, concerned in the Missionary business of the United Brethern of Bethlehem.—In the letter he states as follows— Viz—"One Act however, if true may opperate in the decree of heaven, much against him in the long run. Viz that he should have told the Indian Chiefs who lately visited him: that they stood in no need of being taught in Christianity—that they were a seperate people and Nation from the Whites and their Mode of liveing (without the Religion of the Whites) was perfectly right, and conformable to the intention of their Creator, who had given them a different Skin—different Ideas, and a different way of Maintaining themselves and for that reason had placed them on a Seperate Island by themselves—this is reported here by Capt. George White Eyes, one of the Chiefs who Says he has it from the Mouth of those it was Spoken to by Mr. Jefferson *thro'* a french Interpreter at a private Conference however pleas mention not my name in relateing the Story"—
In my Answer to this letter I Just mentioned my disbelief of the truth of the Story, that I supposed it was no doubt propagated by political enemies to injure you; and thought[1] little about it for some days till I heard by accident of a letter from some person of the same purport having been read in a Presbytary in Kentucky, on which I began to fear that the story if uncontradicted might have Mischievous effects— The story after a continued Currency might gain Credit enough to be used by such of the Indians as may be most avers to Civilization as a peaceful mean of defeating the Missionaries and at the same time be

[584]

used by enemies amongst the pious Presbyterians and Moravians to banish Confidence in the Chief Magistrate—Under this impression I consulted some of my most Judicious friends on the subject Messrs: Edgard and McDowall especially advised that by any means you ought to be informed speedily that you might do with it as you might think it deserved.—you will observe I am not at liberty to Name the Gentleman who writes me. I may however Assure you that at a time Not long past he gave evidence of his high regard for your Character when Attacked by Mr. Martin. I am Sir with due respect your Obt Sert   DAVID REDICK

RC (ViW); at foot of text: "President of the United States"; endorsed by TJ as received 17 June and so recorded in SJL.

GENTLEMAN: Redick probably received his information from the Moravian missionary John Heckewelder. TJ corresponded with Heckewelder in 1798 and 1800 about the *Appendix to the Notes on Virginia*, and Redick was also in communication with Heckewelder in that period. Another Moravian who, like Heckewelder, lived near Native American communities in Ohio was David Zeisberger, but TJ was not as familiar with him (Paul A. W. Wallace, ed., *Thirty Thousand Miles with John Heckewelder* [Pittsburgh, 1958], 384; ANB; Vol. 30:264-5, 285, 288, 291, 305-10; Vol. 31:373n, 393, 552).

As a youth, GEORGE WHITE EYES received a grammar-school education in Princeton, including instruction in Latin and Greek, following the death of his father, the Delaware chief White Eyes, in 1778, when George was eight years old (C. A. Weslager, *The Delaware Indians: A History* [New Brunswick, N.J., 1972], 306, 309, 311; ANB).

DISBELIEF OF THE TRUTH OF THE STORY: Moravian missionaries on the White River in Indiana heard a different version of the story in June 1802. Among

rumors that "circulated among the young Indians, who are inimical to the gospel" was a report that "the Governor, in Philadelphia, had told them that the Word of God was only for white people, and not for the Indians, therefore they would drive us away pretty soon, etc." The missionaries learned from the chiefs at White River that the story was "the lie of bad Indians" (Lawrence Henry Gipson, ed., *The Moravian Indian Mission on White River: Diaries and Letters, May 5, 1799, to November 12, 1806*, trans. Harry E. Stocker, Herman T. Frueauff, and Samuel C. Zeller [Indianapolis, 1938], 473-4).

EDGARD AND MCDOWALL: James Edgar and John McDowell were long-time residents and political officeholders of Washington County, Pennsylvania (Boyd Crumrine, ed., *History of Washington County, Pennsylvania, with Biographical Sketches of Many of its Pioneers and Prominent Men* [Philadelphia, 1882], 238, 869-70).

TJ compiled the *Appendix to the Notes on Virginia* in response to a series of critical letters in Federalist newspapers that Luther MARTIN penned in 1797 and 1798 (Vol. 29:408-10, 452-5).

[1] MS: "though."

From Alexander White

Sir   Woodville 10th. June 1802

In the last conversation I had the honour to hold with you, you observed that you had not expected anything further would have been paid to the Commissioners on account of the square conveyed to the U. States for the site of Marine Barracks—This has occasioned me to reflect in what passed between us on that subject previous to the purchase; and if my memory does not fail me, the idea originated with you, having in view principally the putting the streets in a better state. Some doubt seemed to be entertained of the strict right thus to apply the money, and I was asked if I could not find an apology to excuse us to Congress. At our next meeting I stated that the Commissioners had expended much larger sums on objects authorised by the guarantee Law, than had been raised by the sale of property pledged and therefore I conceived the money proposed to be expended on the streets was entirely clear of the guarantee—It was then suggested as a doubt, whether money granted by the Proprietors of the soil for erecting the public buildings, could be applied to making streets— To which I answered, that the Land, being granted for the purpose of a City, and the President being authorised to lay it off in such streets &c. as he should deem necessary, it appeared to be a matter of course, that the streets should be opened and rendered passable; the President being Judge of the degree of repair into which they should be put; having regard to the means in his hands, and the various objects to which these means were applicable—On this explanation I thought all difficulties were removed, except that existing appropriations did not warrant the expenditure of a larger sum than $4000; the Comrs. certainly counted on the receipt of the balance whenever an appropriation could be made, and regulated their operations accordingly. The Secretary of the Navy recommended the appropriation which no doubt would have been made had his letter been laid before the Committee of Ways and Means; for want of this sum we found ourselves much embarrassed at the expiration of our office, and I consider it as the principal fund on which Mr. Munroe can rely to take up our note in Bank, and to pay other pressing demands

I would likewise observe that a purchase by the U. States of City property from the Comrs. is not unprecedented. During the former administration the secretary of the Navy, and my Colleague Scott were anxious to obtain a donation of City Land for the Navy Yard, but finding me inflexible (although a Majority of the Board would

have complied) the secretary thought proper to come forward with
$4000 and make a purchase

I have taken the liberty thus to recapitulate the circumstances attending this case, and to state the influence they had on the conduct of the
Board, in hopes, that you will be of opinion, that an appropriation
ought to be made, which I have no doubt will be done, unless it
should be known that the Presidents opinion is unfavourable to the
measure—With anxious wishes for the prosperity of our infant City,
I remain with sentiments of the highest respect

Sir Your most Ob Sevt   ALEXR. WHITE

RC (DLC); at foot of text: "President of the U.S"; endorsed by TJ as received 14 June and so recorded in SJL.

For TJ's earlier thoughts on applying funds for the MARINE BARRACKS toward the improvement of streets in Washington, see Vol. 35:167-8, 172-3.

From George Jefferson

DEAR SIR   Richmond 11th. June 1802

Your favor of the 8th. is duly received. The letter which it inclosed
for Mr. Craven Peyton, shall be held subject to his call.

I forwarded the day before yesterday 504 ℔. bacon to Mr. Lilly
agreeably to your direction, that having been the first opportunity
which has offered since the receipt of your letter on the subject. the
same boat brought down a Piano forte to go to Philadelphia, which
shall be forwarded by the first opportunity; and likewise a box for
Washington, which will go in a few days in a Vessel now loading
with Ammunition.

I suppose that you will before this, have heard that 12 Hhds only
of your Tobacco have yet come down—a part of which is stored in
our own lumberhouse, for want of room in the public Warehouses.
the current price for transient Tobacco is now only from 25 to 26/.
the post is closing.

Yr. Mt. humble Servt.   GEO. JEFFERSON

RC (MHi); endorsed by TJ as received 13 June and so recorded in SJL.

For the order of BACON, see TJ to George Jefferson, 27 May 1802.

TJ had arranged to have his PIANO

FORTE repaired by its Philadelphia-based maker, John Isaac Hawkins (TJ to Hawkins, 13 Apr. 1802, and Hawkins to TJ, 21 Apr.).

BOX FOR WASHINGTON: see enclosure listed at George Jefferson to TJ, 14 June.

From James Monroe

Dear Sir,   Richmond June 11th. 1802.

I find by your letter of the 3d., that you think Sierra Leone on the Coast of Affrica a suitable place for the establishment of our insurgent slaves, that it may also become so for those who are or may hereafter be emancipated, and that you are disposed to obtain the assent of the company to such a measure through our minister in London, while your attention will be directed in the interim to such other quarters, as may enable us to submit a more enlarged field to the option of our Assembly. By the information of mr. Thornton the British Chargé des affaires which you have been so kind as to communicate, it appears that Slavery is prohibited in that Settlement, hence it follows that we cannot expect permission to send any who are not free to it. In directing our attention to Africa for an assylum for insurgents, it is strongly implied that the legislature intended they should be free when landed there, as it is not known that there exists any market on that coast for the purchase of Slaves from other Countries. Still I am persuaded that such was not the intention of the legislature, as it would put culprits in a better condition than the deserving part of those people. This opinion is further supported by a law still in force, which authorizes the Executive to sell, subject to transportation, all Slaves who are guilty of that Crime. I submit this idea to your consideration, not with a view to prevent your application to the Company for its assent to the Settlement of insurgents within its limits, but as a motive, in case you concur with me in the above construction of the resolution, why you should more particularly seek an establishment for them in the Portuguese, Dutch or Spanish Settlements in America. In obtaining permission to send our Negroes to that Settlement we may avail ourselves of it, on the principles of the company, as far as it suits our interest and policy. If the legislature intends that insurgents shall enjoy their liberty on landing there, the accommodation would be general; but if they are excluded &[1] the door is opened on favorable conditions to such only as are or may hereafter become free, it will nevertheless[2] be important, as it will give the legislature an opportunity to deliberate on, and perhaps provide a remedy for an evil which has already become a serious one. I cannot otherwise than highly approve the idea of endeavoring to lighten the charge of transportation, to the publick, whither soever they be sent. A permission to send certain Articles of Merchandize, which would be sure to command a profit, if that could be relied on,

[588]

would contribute much to that end. Perhaps other means not incompatible with the Charter of the Company, might be devised. Do their regulations permit temporary servitude? If they do, might not those who are sent be bound to service for a few years, as the means of raising a fund to defray the Charge of transportation? The Ancestors of the present negroes were brought from Africa and sold here as slaves, they and their descendants forever. If we send back any of the race, subject to a temporary servitude, with liberty to their descendants, will not the policy be mild and benevolent? May not the same idea be held in view, in reference to any other place in which an establishment is sought for them? I do not know that Such an arrangement would be practicable in any country, but it would certainly be a very fortunate attainment, if we could make these people instrumental to their own emancipation, by a process gradual and certain, on principles consistent with humanity, without expence or inconvenience to ourselves. I am Dear Sir with great respect & esteem yr. friend & servt

JAS. MONROE

RC (DLC); in a clerk's hand, closing and signature by Monroe; at foot of first page: "The President of the United States"; endorsed by TJ as received 15 June and so recorded in SJL. FC (Vi: Executive Letterbook); in a clerk's hand; lacks complimentary closing.

LAW STILL IN FORCE: a Virginia act approved 15 Jan. 1801, in the aftermath of the aborted slave insurrection of the previous year, empowered the governor and council, "when it shall be deemed expedient, to contract and agree with any person, or persons, for the sale and purchase of all those slaves who now are or hereafter may be under sentence of death, for conspiracy, insurrection, or other crimes." The purchaser of a slave under the terms of the law was to give bond to guarantee that the slave would be transported out of the United States. Nothing in the act anticipated any change in the convicted person's status as a slave. If a person removed from Virginia under the act should ever return to the state, "he shall be apprehended and executed under the condemnation of the court, as if no reprieve had taken place" (*Acts Passed at a General Assembly of the Commonwealth of Virginia. Begun and Held at the Capitol, in the City of Richmond, on Monday the First Day of December One Thousand Eight Hundred* [Richmond, 1801], 24; Vol. 32:145n).

[1] Preceding three words and ampersand interlined by Monroe.
[2] Word interlined by Monroe.

To William Wardlaw

DEAR SIR   Washington June 11. 1802.

Mr. Barnes two days ago remitted to mrs Jackson 200 Dollars, which will of course get to her hands to-night. I think you mentioned that you should have further remittances to make her. I have to pay 30.

Dollars to John Perry, which if you will deliver to him, I will place the same sum for you in mrs Jackson's hands, it being easier to me to remit to Philadelphia than to Albemarle. I shall await your information on this subject. Accept my best wishes & friendly attachment.

TH: JEFFERSON

PrC (DLC); at foot of text: "Dr. William Wardlaw"; endorsed by TJ in ink on verso.

On 26 May, during his stay in Albemarle County, TJ received $100 from Wardlaw to be paid in Philadelphia to Susanna JACKSON, the widow of Dr. David Jackson. The following day TJ agreed to pay another $100 to Jackson for Wardlaw before 15 June, in exchange for which Wardlaw would pay some orders for TJ in Virginia. The same day that he and Wardlaw reached that agreement, TJ gave John PERRY an order on Wardlaw for $30 and gave William Maddox, who was a stonemason doing work at Monticello, an order on Wardlaw for $70 (MB, 2:1072n, 1073; Gallatin to TJ, 27 Dec. 1801).

From John Barnes

George Town 12th June 1802

Allow me Sir, to make my most grateful acknowledgemts. for your Acceptable communications last Evening—Under a pressure of disappointmt. and indisposition—they were indeed; very consoling.

in whatever situation it may be thought, necessary, for me to be employed in—suited—to my small Abilities, & time of Life—I shall most cheerfully, exert them, and hope to Merit the favr.

And if Sir, I can but pass, the remnant, of my Span, with decency & respect—and withal—enjoy a Continuance of your Friendship.—I am Content, and of course Happy.—

With unfeigned, Esteem & Respect—I am Sir, your most Obedt. H St.

JOHN BARNES

RC (ViU: Edgehill-Randolph Papers); at foot of text: "The President. UStates"; endorsed by TJ as received 12 June and so recorded in SJL.

TJ's ACCEPTABLE COMMUNICATIONS LAST EVENING have not been found, nor were they recorded in SJL.

To George Jefferson

DEAR SIR   Washington June 12. 1802.

Below is a list of my poor crop of tobo. made at Poplar forest the last year. how much can I get for it with you, in cash, and how much on 90. days credit? your answer will enable me to judge what to do with it. as I am informed it was sent off in April, I presume it is with you long before this date. accept my affectionate wishes.

TH: JEFFERSON

		Nett
TI.	No. 1152	1578.
PF.	1153	1686
	1154	1562
	1155	1569.
	1194.	1796.
	1195	1559
	1201.	1154
	1200.	1568
	945.	1551
	941.	1410
	359.	1515
	360	1631
		18,466

PrC (MHi); at foot of text: "Mr. George Jefferson"; endorsed by TJ in ink on verso. Recorded in SJL with notation "my tobo."

TJ had previously expressed frustration with his POOR CROP of 1801 (TJ to Thomas Leiper, 2 Dec. 1801). The calculation of 18,466 pounds included a deduction for the overseer's share (MB, 2:1075).

From Thomas McKean

DEAR SIR,   Philadelphia, June 12th. 1802.

Calling to recollection, that when in the city of Washington I named my son Robert as a suitable person for a Commissioner of Bankrupts in Pennsylvania, it appears to me proper to inform you that he died on Tuesday last, the 8th. instant: His brother-in-law, Andrew Pettit Esquire would, in my opinion, be well qualified to fill that office; he is a reputable Merchant and Alderman of this city, but tired with performing the duties of his office, and has refused the appointments of a Judge of the common pleas for the county of Philadelphia and Mayor of the city. Mr; Pettit is the only son of Charles Pettit Esquire, some years a member of Congress for this State and now President of the Insurance company of North America; he has a sister married to Mr; Ingersol, late Attorney General, who (I presume) is known to you. I have reason to believe, that the appointment of Mr; Pettit to this office would be not only unexceptionable, but agreeable to all parties, excepting the inveterate Tories, whom an Angel could not please.

Accept the best wishes for your health & happiness of, dear Sir, Your Excellency's Most obedient humble servant

THOS M:KEAN

RC (DLC); at foot of text: "His Excelly. Thomas Jefferson Esquire"; endorsed by TJ as received 13 June and so recorded in SJL.

HIS BROTHER-IN-LAW: Robert McKean's sister Elizabeth married Andrew Pettit in December 1791. A decade earlier, on 6 Dec. 1781, Andrew Pettit's sister Elizabeth married Jared Ingersoll (INGERSOL), Pennsylvania's attorney general from 1790 to 1799 and from 1811 to 1817. KNOWN TO YOU: Ingersoll served as a defense attorney in the 1799 impeachment trial of William Blount, over which TJ presided and took notes. As U.S. attorney from 1800 to 1801, Ingersoll also led prosecutions against William Duane (Rowe, McKean, 266, 321-2; DAB, 9:468-9; Vol. 30:614-16, 619n; Vol. 34:297, 300n).

From Joseph Priestley

DEAR SIR   Northumberland June 12. 1802

I hope you will excuse my request to dedicate to you one of the works of which you will find some account in the printed Prospectus, which I take the liberty to inclose, in order to shew you the extent of my views, and my wishes, in this world.

I have never gone beyond the bounds of what I thought the strict truth in any dedication that I have written, and I am confident I have not in this. This being the only opportunity that I shall probably ever have of giving my public testimony to your administration, I shall be exceedingly mortified if you forbid it.

I wish the state of my health may admit of my accepting your kind invitation to pay you a visit; and if towards the end of summer you should be at Washington, I may perhaps, with the assistance of my son, venture to take the journey.

In answer to your kind letter on my recovery from the illness at Philadelphia, I sent by the post an acknowledgment of the receipt of it, together with a 4to pamphlet, containing an account of experiments printed for the fifth volume of the Transactions of the Philosophical society at Philadelphia. These I hope you received. If you see the *Medical Repository* printed at New York, or *Nicholson's Journal*, you will see that I do not neglect philosophy.

With the greatest respect and gratitude I am Dear Sir, yours sincerely   J PRIESTLEY.

RC (NNPM); endorsed by TJ as received 17 June and so recorded in SJL. Enclosure: Untitled, undated, printed prospectus for Priestley's *A General History of the Christian Church, from the Fall of the Western Empire to the Present Time* and *Notes on all the Books of Scripture, for the Use of the Pulpit and Private Families* (DLC: TJ Papers, 128:22152; Shaw-Shoemaker, No. 2934).

In a letter of 19 June, TJ granted Priestley's REQUEST TO DEDICATE to him the second part of the *General History*, which was published in four volumes in 1802 and 1803. For the text of the dedication, see letter below.

YOUR KIND LETTER: TJ to Priestley, 21 Mch. 1801, to which Priestley responded on 10 Apr. 1801 (Vol. 33:393-5, 567-8).

I DO NOT NEGLECT PHILOSOPHY: that is, science. From 1798 to 1803, Priestley published articles and letters on a variety of subjects in *The Medical Repository of Original Essays and Intelligence, Relative to Physic, Surgery, Chemistry, and Natural History*, as well as in the London-based *Journal of Natural Philosophy, Chemistry, and the Arts*, which was edited by William Nicholson (Robert E. Schofield, *The Enlightened Joseph Priestley: A Study of His Life and Work from 1773 to 1804* [University Park, Pa., 2004], 415-18).

From Joseph Priestley

SIR, [on or before 12 June 1802]

My high respect for your character, as a politician, and a man, makes me desirous of connecting my name in some measure with yours while it is in my power, by means of some publication, to do it.

The first part of this work, which brought the history to the fall of the western empire, was dedicated to a zealous friend of civil and religious liberty, but in a private station. What he, or any other friend of liberty in Europe, could only do by their good wishes, by writing, or by patient suffering, you, Sir, are actually accomplishing, and upon a theatre of great and growing extent.

It is the boast of this country to have a constitution the most favourable to political liberty, and private happiness, of any in the world, and all say that it was yourself, more than any other individual, that planned and established it; and to this opinion your conduct in various public offices, and now in the highest, gives the clearest attestation.

Many have appeared the friends of the rights of man while they were subject to the power of others, and especially when they were sufferers by it; but I do not recollect one besides yourself who retained the same principles, and acted upon them, in a station of real power. You, Sir, have done more than this; having proposed to relinquish some part of the power which the constitution gave you; and instead of adding to the burdens of the people, it has been your endeavour to lighten those burdens tho the necessary consequence must be a diminution of your influence. May this great example, which I doubt not will demonstrate the practicability of truly republican principles, by the actual existence of a form of government calculated to answer all the useful purposes of government, (giving equal protection to all, and leaving every man in the possession of every power that he can exercise to his own advantage, without infringing on the equal liberty of others) be followed in other countries, and at length become universal

Another reason why I wish to prefix your name to this work, and more appropriate to the subject of it, is that you have ever been a strenuous and uniform advocate of religious no less than civil liberty, both in your own state of Virginia, and in the united states in general; seeing in the clearest light the various and great mischiefs that have arisen from any particular form of religion being favoured by the state more than any other; so that the profession and practice of religion is here as free as that of philosophy or medicine And now the experience of more than twenty years leaves little room to doubt but that it is a state of things the most favourable to mutual candour, which is of great importance to domestic peace and good neighbourhood, and to the cause of all truth, religious truth least of all excepted. When every question is thus left to free discussion, there cannot be a doubt but that truth will finally prevail, and establish itself by its own evidence; and he must know little of mankind, or of human nature, who can imagine that truth of any kind will be ultimately unfavourable to general happiness. That man must entertain a secret suspicion of his own principles who wishes for any exclusive advantage in the defence or profession of them.

Having fled from a state of persecution in England, and having been exposed to some degree of danger in the last administration here, I naturally feel the greater satisfaction in the prospect of passing the remainder of an active life (when I naturally wish for repose) under your protection. Tho arrived at the usual term of human life it is now only that I can say I see nothing to fear from the hand of power, the government under which I live being for the first time truly favourable to me. And tho it will be evident to all who know me that I have never been swayed by the mean principle of fear, it is certainly a happiness to be out of the possibility of its influence, and to end ones days in peace, enjoying some degree of rest before the state of more perfect rest in the grave, and with the hope of rising to a state of greater activity, security, and happiness beyond it. This is all that any man can wish for, or have; and this, Sir, under your administration I enjoy.

With the most perfect attachment, and every good wish, I subscribe myself not your subject, or humble servant, but your sincere admirer,   J. Priestley

RC (DLC); undated, but received by TJ on same date as preceding letter; at head of text: "To Thomas Jefferson, President of the united states of America"; endorsed by TJ as received 17 June and so recorded in SJL.

Priestley's ZEALOUS FRIEND, to whom he dedicated the General History of the Christian Church, to the Fall of the Western Empire published in Birmingham, England, in 1790, was Samuel Shore, a longtime associate who had contributed to Priestley's researches (Robert E. Schofield, The Enlightened Joseph Priestley: A Study of His Life and Work from 1773 to 1804 [University Park, Pa., 2004], 259-60).

Although Priestley altered the phrasing in a few places, the text here was largely the same as that which appeared in the first volume of his church history published in 1802 (Priestley, General History of the Christian Church, from the Fall of the Western Empire to the Present Time, 4 vols. [Northumberland, Pa., 1802-03], 1:iii-vii). In a letter of 19 June, TJ did, however, correct Priestley's contention that he had PLANNED AND ESTABLISHED the Constitution. Instead, Priestley wrote of TJ's "great merit with respect to several articles of the first importance to public liberty in the instrument itself," explaining in a footnote that TJ had urged the adoption of a bill of rights (same, iv).

HAVING BEEN EXPOSED TO SOME DEGREE OF DANGER: Priestley may have had an exaggerated sense of the dangers he faced in America, but his unconcealed

pro-French sympathies and willingness to associate with democratic societies had made him a frequent target of the pro-Federalist polemics of William Cobbett. Priestley, in turn, did not shy from political advocacy and published on 26 and 27 Feb. 1798 an anonymous essay entitled "Maxims of Political Arithmetic" in the Philadelphia Aurora, which later appeared in his Letters to the Inhabitants of Northumberland and its Neighborhood (Northumberland, Pa., 1799; Sowerby, No. 3217). The essay sharply criticized the commercial orientation of the Adams administration and predicted civil war as a possible consequence of the administration's pro-British sympathies. TJ praised the essay and sent it to political allies such as James Madison. After Priestley aided in the distribution of a similar collection of essays written by his close friend and associate Thomas Cooper, he drew the ire of Secretary of State Timothy Pickering, who urged President Adams to prosecute Priestley under the Alien Act. Adams, who had previously been on friendly terms with Priestley, declined, describing the minister as entirely under the influence of Cooper and "as weak as water, as unstable as Reuben, or the wind. His influence is not an atom in the world" (Jenny Graham, Revolutionary in Exile: The Emigration of Joseph Priestley to America, 1794-1804 [Philadelphia, 1995], 51-3, 119-26; Frederick S. Allis, ed., Timothy Pickering Papers, microfilm edition, 69 reels [Boston, 1966], 11:524-9; Charles Francis Adams, ed., The Works of John Adams, 10 vols. [Boston, 1850-56], 9:13-14; Vol. 31: 288-9, 319-23).

From Robert Smith

SIR; Nav: dep: 12. June—1802.—

I have the honor to enclose herewith a Warrant of Midshipman for William Sim. He is the son of a very meritorious officer in our revolutionary War.—

With much respect, I have the honor to be, Sir, Yr mo: ob: servt.—

RT SMITH

RC (DLC); in a clerk's hand, signed by Smith; at foot of text: "The President"; endorsed by TJ as received from the Navy Department on 12 June and "Midshipman" and so recorded in SJL. FC (Lb in DNA:RG 45, LSP).

After receiving his warrant, WILLIAM SIM was assigned to the frigate *John Adams*. He was probably the SON of Patrick Sim, a lieutenant colonel of Maryland troops during the Revolutionary War (NDBW, *Register*, 50; Heitman, *Register*, 497).

To Thomas Claxton

DEAR SIR Washington June 13. 1802.

I omitted to place in my memorandum 2. wire-screens for the windows of the Setting room, intended to exclude the candle flies and bugs in the evening, which abound here in most uncommon quantities. they should be 4 f. 9. I. square, & the meshes $\frac{1}{8}$ or $\frac{3}{16}$ of an inch wide & $\frac{1}{4}$ Inch. high. a single one does for each window. there is a mr Sellers 231. market street who works well in wire. I will trouble you to deliver the inclosed on the subject of the Quadrant to mr Whitney. Accept my friendly respects & good wishes.

TH: JEFFERSON

PrC (MHi); at foot of text: "Mr Thomas Claxton"; endorsed by TJ in ink on verso. Enclosure: TJ to Thomas Whitney, 13 June.

Nathan SELLERS, inventor of a method of drawing and annealing wire, had a shop at 231 High Street in Philadelphia. TJ had purchased wire netting from him for screen doors at Monticello and the

President's House. Sellers's younger brother David joined him in the business and his eldest son Coleman married a daughter of Charles Willson Peale (Joseph Jackson, *Market Street Philadelphia: The Most Historic Highway in America, Its Merchants and Its Story* [Philadelphia, 1918], 97-8; Robinson, *Philadelphia Directory for 1802*, 215; MB, 2:908).

From Thomas Claxton

HONORED SIR   Philaa. June 13. 1802

Before I left the City of Washington you mentioned a floor Cloth which you wished to have painted on Canvass—Since I have been here, I have seen a kind of grass matting which is used by the genteelest people,—it is, in my estimation very handsom and comes cheaper even than the common painted cloths of this country—Inclosed, Sir, you have a specimen of the stuff—it is a yard and a half wide and costs 7/6 pr. yard—I believe a square yard of canvass, that is good, will cost, before any paint is put on, nearly as much as a yard of this, which is yd & $\frac{1}{2}$ wide—If you should fancy it, I can procure that which is varigated in coulour white and red, and by forwarding to me the plan of your floor, Sir, I can have it made immediately— The making is an exclusive change—English painted cloth costs about 3 dollars pr. square yd and American I am told is scarsely ever used

I fully intended, Sir, before I left Washington, but forgot it, to propose to you the getting of a forte piano, which undoubtedly, is a piece of furniture, which will be pleaseing to every one—If you have no objection I shall imploy a skillful person to select one before I return

I am, Sir, with the most Sincere regard, Your Hble Svt.

                                                 THOS CLAXTON

P.S. When these cloths are made, they are strongly bound, and are said to weare well

RC (MHi); endorsed by TJ as received 17 June and so recorded in SJL.

Painted canvas FLOOR CLOTH was a popular and more expensive floor covering than straw or GRASS MATTING, a Chinese export item widely used in American homes after 1784 and obtainable in many shades and patterns. Made of heavy woven fabric known as canvas, the floor cloths were stitched together in strips and were adorned by freehand brush work, stenciled prints, or stamped block prints (Nina Fletcher Little, "Floor Coverings," *American Art Journal*, 7 [1975], 111-13).

To Roberts & Jones

GENTLEMEN   Washington June 13. 1802.

Having occasion to have a piece of work executed at Monticello which requires the very toughest iron it is possible to find, and some of the best German steel, I will pray you to send me a quarter ton of iron of the toughest quality you can procure, among which let there

[597]

be 2. bars from $1\frac{1}{2}$ I. to $1\frac{5}{8}$ I. square, the rest of smaller bars, some flat, some square; & also 100. ℔. best German steel.—the last supply of nailrod & hoop iron got safely to hand, and mr Barnes will remit for it at maturity. let the above articles be immediately shipped to Gibson & Jefferson to be forwarded to Monticello. accept my friendly respects & best wishes. TH: JEFFERSON

PrC (MHi); at foot of text: "Messrs. Roberts & Jones"; endorsed by TJ in ink on verso.

Joseph Roberts (ca. 1766-1802), a Philadelphia ironmonger, had been supplying TJ with nailrod since at least 1797. In 1800 he formed a partnership with Benjamin Jones to sell a variety of metal goods. After Roberts died in October 1802, Jones organized a new firm that subsequently filled TJ's iron orders. From 21 Apr. 1797 to 24 June 1802, TJ recorded in SJL almost 40 letters to or from Roberts or the firm of Roberts & Jones, but this is the only one that has been found (*Philadelphia Gazette & Daily Advertiser*, 14 Jan. 1800; *Gazette of the United States*, 2 Nov. 1802; MB, 2:964; TJ to Benjamin Jones, 6 Dec. 1802; TJ to Jones & Howell, 15 Dec. 1802).

For the LAST SUPPLY of iron for the Monticello nailery, see TJ to George Jefferson, 10 April 1802, and George Jefferson to TJ, 3 May 1802.

To Thomas Whitney

SIR   Washington June 13. 1802.

I observe in the European catalogues of Optical, Astronomical &c. Instruments, they advertize 'Artificial horizons by parallel glasses and quicksilver to take double altitudes by, £1–16. sterl.' I suppose it possible that this may be to supply the want of a good horizon at land and enable us to use Hadley's quadrant here as well as at sea. should this be the case, and you happen to have one, or if you can procure one I shall be glad to recieve it by mr Claxton, and will have the price remitted to you as soon as known. mr Claxton took charge of a limb of the fixed machinery of the Quadrant, which had got broke on it's passage, and which he was to desire you to repair. Accept my respects & best wishes. TH: JEFFERSON

RC (Herbert R. Strauss, Chicago, Illinois, 1953); addressed: "Mr. Thomas Whitney Mathematical instrumt maker Philadelphia"; endorsed by Whitney. PrC (MoSHi: Jefferson Papers); endorsed by TJ in ink on verso. Enclosed in TJ to Thomas Claxton, 13 June.

Thomas Whitney (d. 1823) manufactured, repaired, and imported astronomical, surveying, and optical instruments in Philadelphia beginning about 1797. He was an English immigrant who learned his craft in "the first manufactories in London." He also offered pilots' charts and navigation books for sale and gave instruction in the use of sextants and other instruments. Prior to the departure of the Corps of Discovery in 1803 in search of a route to the Pacific, Meriwether Lewis obtained several instruments for the expedition's use, including compasses of Whitney's manufacture, from Whitney's shop (*Philadelphia Gazette*, 12 May 1798, 29 Oct. 1801; Deborah Jean Warner, "Optics in Philadelphia during the Nineteenth Century," APS, *Proceedings*, 129 [1985], 292; Domenic Vitiello, "Reading the Corps of Discovery Backwards: The Metropolitan Context of Lewis and Clark's Expedition," in *The Shortest and Most Convenient Route: Lewis and Clark in Context*, ed. Robert S. Cox [Philadelphia, 2004], 26-7; Bedini, *Statesman of Science*, 347).

From George Jefferson

DEAR SIR   Richmond 14th. June 1802

As I suppose you will have to give Mr. Hawkins some instruction respecting the Piano, I think it unnecessary myself to write to him, and therefore inclose the bill of loading to you, which you will of course forward.

I likewise inclose you a bill of loading for the box mentioned in my last.

I am Dear Sir Your Very humble servt.   GEO. JEFFERSON

RC (MHi); at foot of text: "Thomas Jefferson esqr."; endorsed by TJ as received 16 June and so recorded in SJL. Enclosure: Bill of lading, Richmond, 11 June 1802, for one box of books shipped by Gibson & Jefferson to TJ on the *Welcome Return* bound for Washington, D.C., Charles Travers (Travis), master (MS in ViU: Edgehill-Randolph Papers; being a printed form with blanks filled by George Jefferson, signed by Travers; with receipt, in John Barnes's hand, on verso, for payment of £0.11.3 or $1.50 on 24 June 1802, signed by Travers, acknowledging payment; endorsed by Barnes as payment for freight from Richmond). Enclosed in TJ to Barnes, 17 June 1802. Bill of lading for piano not found.

MY LAST: George Jefferson to TJ, 11 June 1802.

To Tobias Lear

Monday June 14. 1802.

Will mr Lear do Th: Jefferson the favor of taking a family dinner with him to-day.

RC (InHi); addressed: "Colo. Lear"; endorsed by Lear.

To Thomas McKean

DEAR SIR   Washington June 14. 1802.

Your favor of the 12th. came to hand last night. while making out the commissions of bankruptcy the newspapers informed me of the death of your son, on which event I sincerely condole with you. his name was therefore omitted and another inserted so as to compleat the number before the reciept of your letter recommending mr Pettit.

Though I take for granted that the colonisation of Louisiana by France is a settled point, yet I suspect they must be much stronger in St. Domingo before they can spare troops to go there. what has been called a surrender of Toussaint to Le Clerc I suspect was in reality a surrender of Le Clerc to Toussaint: that Le Clerc was not in condition to hold his ports, and consented to any terms which would give the appearance of capitulation to his antagonist, who probably over-rated the number of French troops. a discovery of his error may very possibly lead to a correction of it. Accept assurances of my high respect and consideration.   TH: JEFFERSON

RC (PHi); addressed: "Governor Mc.kain Philadelphia"; franked and post-marked. PrC (DLC).

NEWSPAPERS INFORMED ME: a brief notice of the sudden death of Robert McKean appeared in *Poulson's American Daily Advertiser* on 10 June and in the *Philadelphia Gazette & Daily Advertiser* the next day. The *Aurora* carried a more extensive report on 12 June.

On 6 May, after brief negotiations, Toussaint-Louverture agreed to SUR-RENDER to the French forces of Victoire Emmanuel Leclerc. Toussaint was per-mitted to keep his rank and to retire to his plantation at Ennery. His officers were also allowed to retain their military ranks and were incorporated into the French army. The surrender of Toussaint and several of his generals, however, did not end black resistence on Saint-Domingue. By mid-May, yellow fever began to deci-mate French troops, while the remaining black forces on the island maintained a spirited and effective opposition. Believ-ing that Toussaint was behind this re-newed insurgency, Leclerc arrested him and his family on 7 June and immediately had them exiled to France, where Tous-saint died on 7 Apr. 1803 (Thomas O. Ott, *The Haitian Revolution, 1789-1804* [Knoxville, 1973], 159-61, 170-2; Lau-rent Dubois, *Avengers of the New World: The Story of the Haitian Revolution* [Cambridge, Mass., 2004], 275-9).

From David Mellinger

DEAR SIR/   June the 14th. 1802.

my Feather give me this Edvise, David when ever you have to send a Letter to a man who has a greath Burden on his bag make it as Short and so Sinseable as you can, whitch I would wish to follow here I send you one of my fourth hand Bills and Like wise a German one according to your desire please but that hand bill in print and let this other follow next, please to big out what you think Unsnassry of them Two English hand bills for my Share I can defant my selfe in all what is in it Because I hath Trails a nough before it was in print which I would Convince you in it if you hath been at home when I came in the Federal City, but I got quit uneasey about my famliy since I hath to wait Eleven days on you are alse I would made on anker of a fish hug Strong Enough to hold the bigest vessell that ever whent over the Salt water, if you hath given me a Text to Rone on (in them were afforsd.) Like wise I would get them hand Bills in German print according to your desire but I am unable to do it at present, I am one of you truest frinds that wishes to Live and die in your happey administration, please send me a Letter if you Reced. them or not,

DAVID MELLINGER

RC (DLC); endorsed by TJ as received 17 June and so recorded in SJL. Enclosures: Handbills not identified.

To Caesar A. Rodney

DEAR SIR   Washington June 14. 1802.

I am later in acknoleging the reciept of your favor of May 16. because it found me at Monticello just on my departure from that place. since my arrival here I have been in the constant hope of seeing mr Beckley & endeavoring to procure from his office a copy of the journals of the H. of Repr. for you. I do not know that they can be had any where else. his confinement by the remains of a fit of the gout has hitherto prevented my object, but I shall keep it in view.—I have recieved two addresses from meetings of democratic republicans at Dover, praying the removal of Allen Mc.Lane. one of them was forwarded by Govr. Hall. the grounds are stated so generally that I cannot judge from thence whether he has done any thing deserving removal since his former trial & acquittal. certainly nothing beyond that should be brought up a second time. I write this to you confidentially, and ask the favor of you to explain to me the real foundation of these applications. if he has been active in electioneering in favor of those who wish to subvert the present order of things, it would be a serious circumstance. I do not mean as to giving his personal vote in which he ought not to be controuled; but as to using his influence (which necessarily includes his official influence) to sway the votes of others. I withold answering these applications till I hear from you, and may do it on ground which will not fail me. I hope you are fixed on as the republican candidate at the ensuing election for Congress. Accept assurances of my great esteem & respect.

TH: JEFFERSON

P.S. will you also be so good as to recommend to me 4. Commissioners of bankruptcy for Wilmington & Newcastle. two should be lawyers & two merchants, all republicans. if one resided in New castle & three in Wilmington it would be desireable: but this circumstance must yield to respectability of character which is essential.

RC (DeHi); addressed: "Caesar Rodney esquire Wilmington"; franked and postmarked; endorsed by Rodney. PrC (DLC).

TWO ADDRESSES: see Delaware Democratic Republicans to TJ, 24 Mch. and 5

June. The first address was FORWARDED BY David Hall on 31 May 1802. TJ did not receive the subsequent address, which Hall enclosed in his letter of 9 June, until the 15th.

FORMER TRIAL & ACQUITTAL: see Vol. 36:182-3.

From Arthur Fenner and Theodore Foster

SIR,   Providence June 15th. 1802.

The Fourteenth Section of the Act of Congress of April 29th. 1802 entituled "*an Act to amend the Judiciary System of the United States*," devolves upon the President, the Appointment of "Commissioners of Bankruptcy"; and supposing that no Appointment has since been made, in this Town, We take the Liberty to recommend the following as suitable Characters, for discharging the Duties of Such an Appointment (Viz)

John S. Dexter,
Samuel Eddy,
Sylvanus Martin &
Seth Wheaton Esqrs.

Mr Dexter is the present Supervisor of the Revenue in this district; Mr. Eddy is the Secretary of the State;—both educated to the Profession of the Law. Mr. Martin has been heretofore a Representative of the Town, in the State Legislature and Mr Wheaton is now colonel of a Regiment of Militia—the two last named being mercantile Characters.—They are all respectable Citizens and Residents in this Town and are considered as possessing and disposed to support

[602]

genuine republican Principles. We think their Appointment will give general Satisfaction.—

We have the Honor to be, Sir, with Sentiments of much sincere Esteem and cordial Attachment very respectfully Your Obedient Servants

ARTHUR FENNER

THEODORE FOSTER

RC (DNA: RG 59, LAR); in Foster's hand, signed by Fenner and Foster; endorsed by TJ as received 22 June and "Commrs. bkrptcy" and so recorded in SJL.

FOURTEENTH SECTION OF THE ACT: see U.S. Statutes at Large, 2:164.

SUITABLE CHARACTERS: TJ entered the names of the four persons from Providence recommended by Governor Fenner and Senator Foster on his list of candidates for bankruptcy commissioners. The president appointed all four nominees on 23 June, the day after he received the recommendations (*Biog. Dir. Cong.*; Appendix II, Lists 1 and 2).

Memorandum from Thomas Munroe

[15 June 1802]

City of Washington Dr. to The State of Maryland

	to 1t. Apl 1802.	to 1. July 1802
Interest on $200,000 Loaned, from 1t. Jany. 1801.	$15,000.	$18,000
Ditto on $50,0000 from 1t. Octr. 1801.	$ 1,500.	2,250
	$16,500	$20,250
principal becoming due 1t. november 1802	$50,000	
Interest on Do. as above to 1 July 1802 $2,250		
Do. from 1 July to 1 novem " $ 1000	3,250	$53,250

The terms of the Loan of $200,000 are, Interest to be paid quarterly & principal Reimbursable at any time after the year 1803 by instalments not exceeding one fifth of the whole sum borrowed in any one year

RC (DLC: District of Columbia Papers); undated; endorsed by TJ as received from the Washington superintendent on 15 June and "state of debt to Maryland."

Thomas Munroe (1771-1852), son of Annapolis merchant William Munroe, settled in the District of Columbia around 1791. He held the office of postmaster for the city of Washington from 1799 to 1829. He served as clerk for the District of Columbia Commissioners, before the dissolution of the board. "Reposing special Trust and Confidence" in his "Integrity, Skill and Diligence," TJ signed a commission, dated 2 June 1802, appointing Munroe superintendent of the city of Washington, the new office created by Congress. The superintendent was to be appointed by and under the control of the president. Munroe remained in the position until 1815. He was also actively involved in the financial, business, and cultural affairs of the city. He became a founding trustee of the Washington public school system in 1805 and was one of the incorporators in 1808 of the Washington Bridge Company. He served as a director of the District of Columbia branch of the Bank of the United States and of several other local banks, becoming president of the National Bank of Washington in 1830 (Latrobe, *Correspondence*, 1:260-1; RCHS, 8 [1905], 28-9, 31, 38; 46-47 [1947], 282-3; *National Intelligencer*, 17 July, 7 Aug. 1805; Stets, *Postmasters*, 107; U.S. Statutes at Large, 2:175-6; FC of commission in Lb in DNA: RG 59, MPTPC).

On 11 June, TJ received an "Estimate of Debts Due to City of Washington" from Munroe, listing the names of those indebted to the city and the amounts of money owed. By Munroe's calculation, a total of $34,394 remained due to the city, including $18,500 for lots purchased by Uriah Forrest, Benjamin Stoddert, John Templeman, and Gustavus Scott, as well as $1,850 for lots from William Thornton. The estimate specifically excluded some $65,000 due from Robert Morris and John Nicholson and an additional $8,000 owed by the heirs of Walter Stewart. Regarding these latter debts, Munroe predicted that "there is no probability of collecting otherwise than by resale of the property purchased" (RC in DLC, undated, endorsed by TJ as received from the Washington superintendent on 11 June and "state of debts").

About the same time, Munroe prepared an "Estimate of Debts Due from the City of Washington," excluding the loans from the United States and the state of Maryland. The estimate totaled $4,882, including $2,500 due to the Bank of Columbia "early next month," $1,120 to Leonard Harbaugh "for building Executive Offices," $508 to James Hoban for the balance of his salary as superintendent of public buildings, $230 to John Thomson Mason in attorney fees, $160 to Robert King for wages as surveyor, $96 to Samuel Harrison Smith for advertising, and $45 to William Brent for his salary as "Assistant Clerk to December last." At the foot of the estimate, Munroe added a query "as to balance of about $2250 due for square purchased by U.S. for Marine barracks" (MS in same; undated).

Robert Smith's Observations on the Charges Against Arthur St. Clair

Observations upon the charges against Governor St. Clair—

1st. Charge is not established. It was not an usurpation, but an exercise of a legitimate power. The Ordinance of Congress has expressly given to the Governor the power of laying out the Territory into Counties and Townships subject only to this qualification—that the Legislature may thereafter make any alterations therein. The division is first to be made by the Governor. It is afterwards subject to the revision of the Legislature—The Legislature could not act in the first instance. If the Governor had abused this authority, such abuse might have been submitted to the Legislature. If the people had been aggreived by such abuse, they should have applied to the Legislature for redress. It does not appear that an application for such redress was ever made.

2nd. Charge is not established. A mere error of Judgment is not imputable to a Majistrate as a Crime. It must be such gross misconduct as induces a presumption of Corruption. No evidence of such corruption has been adduced. Of the Eleven Acts rejected by the Governor, Six were negatived under the impression that the Legislature had therein exceeded the limits of their authority. And this impression I cannot consider even erroneous. Other Objections, drawn from principles of expediency, as stated by the Governor, it may fairly be presumed had influence upon his mind in rejecting these Six Acts. The Governors Objections to the other five Acts are set forth in his Address to the Legislature. So far as these Objections may appear to have weight, they tend to remove the imputation of Corruption. They have, indeed, in my mind so much weight, that I am inclined to think that the Acts ought to have been negatived. I, however, cannot find any thing that creates even a suspicion of a wanton abuse of power.

3d. Charge, *as stated*, is not established. There is no evidence that the Governor in any instance refused to perform any of the duties of his Office because a fee was not paid to him—or that he ever demanded a fee of any kind as a Condition to his performing any Official duty. But altho the proof does not establish the charge *as exhibited*, it shews that the Governor has been in the practice of receiving certain fees for Official services. This practice with respect to Tavern Licences is warranted by an adopted Law page 97—with respect to Commissions to Prothonotaries Sheriffs &c by an adopted Law page 79. but with respect to the Cases of Marriage & Ferry Licenses I cannot find any authority of Law. And if there be not any such Law, the receipt of fees for such licences by the Governor without Law was a[1] misdemeanor. My mind is embarressed in ascertaining the degree of this Offence. The sum of money received for such licences is so trifling that I cannot allow myself to attribute the receiving of the fees to corruption. Admit him to be a man of *sense*, as he has ever been considered, it is difficult to believe that he would risk such disgrace for an Object so trivial.[2] But as we have not all the laws of the Territory here, it would be advisable to postpone the final decision on this charge until the whole Code be carefully examined.

4th. Charge is not established. The Act, which gave to the Governor the 500 Dollars, expressly states that that Sum of money was allowed him *"for his extraordinary services during the Session of the Legislature"* It was passed on the last day of the Session. The motive of the Legislature as set forth and declared in the Act must be considered the true one.

5th. Charge is not established. The Governors letter to the Delegate in Congress Mr Harrison recommends to his attention the petition of the people of St. Vincennes and at the same time expresses his approbation of its Object. He and those people urged the expediency of a Certain division of the Territory for the better government thereof.[3] I cannot understand how the petition or the Act of the Legislature[4] can affect the provision of the Original Ordinance which stipulates that whenever any of the said States (certain districts of the Territory) shall have 60000 free inhabitants, such state shall be upon the same footing with the Original States—i.e. shall be established one of the U. States. The petition above mentioned of part of the people of the Territory with the accompanying letter from the Governor to Mr Harrison could not indanger the boundaries of those States as described in the Original Ordinance, because Congress without[5] the concurrence of the whole Territory and perhaps of Virginia could not change this stipulation in the Original Compact. And his assent to the Act of the Legislature of the Territory proposing and submitting to Congress an alteration of the boundaries of any of those states cannot by the people of the Territory be deemed a Crime of the Governor, as it was only an assent to a legislative act of their Representatives. It cannot be deemed an Offence against the General Government. For as an Attempt to change the boundaries of those states could not be affected without the concurrence of Congress, he cannot reasonably be charged with a design of counteracting the wish of the general Government. It is not to be imagined that an agent has criminally intended to counteract the wish of the principal by an Act, which act could not be done without the formal expressed approbation of the principal.

6th. Charge is established. The explanation of the governor is not satisfactory. And viewing it in connection with the 3d. Charge I consider it sufficiently weighty to justify his removal from Office, provided that such 3d. Charge upon the proposed further examination of the Territorial Code be established and cannot be softened by extenuating circumstances.

7th. Charge is not established. Under an impression, it seems, that there was a defect in the Criminal Jurisprudence of the Territory, it became his duty to call the attention of the Legislature to the subject. The Judges it appears, had adopted the Common Law rule of

Evidence, which does not admit the party robbed to be a Competent witness. That, which the Governor did recommend as an amendment, does Obtain in some of the States to a Certain degree. He was only unfortunate in not using the correct technical language of the profession. He called it a Rule of Court instead of a Rule of Evidence. And this appears to have been his only error in this instance. With respect to his effecting the surrender of the Commission of a Justice I have not seen any evidence to this effect.

8th. Charge is not established by any Evidence that I have seen.

9th. Charge is not established. From the explicit declaration in the preamble of the Act passed in Decr. 1800 it appears that the delay is not attributable to the Governor; but to the Legislature.

10th. Charge is not established. The Evidence is ex parte Affidavits. Upon ex parte Affidavits interlocutory proceedings may and often are founded. But they should never be the foundation of an Ultimate decision. Upon such testimony a Sentence of disgrace ought not to be pronounced against any person. And deplorable indeed would be the situation of an Officer of Government, if he were to be deprived of Office and consigned to disgrace upon ex parte Affidavits and especially when made under circumstances which in no small degree affect their Credit. For it is to be remarked that these three Affidavits were taken on the same day and before the same Majistrate and about nine days after the transaction to which they alluded—and before a Majistrate who had on that day received a letter of Reprimand from the Governor for an alledged neglect of duty and who on that same day gave notice to the Governor that he would the next morning resign his Commission and that he would have done it that Evening "but for the Concurrence of Circumstances which prevented him" (meaning probably the taking of these three depositions). This Majistrate, altho he knew that the Governor was in the Town and altho he had that day written & sent two Letters to him, did not give him notice to attend the taking of the aforementioned three affidavits. Such Conduct evidently shews that this Majistrate was hostile to the Administration of the Governor and may throw some suspicion on his proceeding in the Case of the alledged Riots

RT SMITH
June 15. 1802.

MS (DLC); entirely in Smith's hand; endorsed by TJ: "St. Clair's case. Secy. of the Navy's opn."

For the ELEVEN ACTS REJECTED by St. Clair during the 1799 session of the territorial assembly, see Vol. 36:461-2, 467.

AN ADOPTED LAW: for the state laws adopted by the Northwest Territory,

Smith cites *Laws of the Territory of the United States North-West of the Ohio: Adopted and Made by the Governour and Judges, in Their Legislative Capacity, at a Session Begun on Friday, the XXIX Day of May, One Thousand, Seven Hundred, and Ninety-Five, and Ending on Tuesday the Twenty-Fifth Day of August Following* (Cincinnati, 1796). Page 97 refers to Section 4 of an act adopted from the Pennsylvania code, which granted the governor of the Northwest Territory four dollars for every license granted to sell wine and liquors. Page 79 refers to Section 23 of an act adopted from the New York and Pennsylvania codes, which gave the governor one dollar for commissions issued to the attorney general, treasurer, sheriffs, prothonotaries, and recorders of the territory. The governor also received one-third of the 50 cent fee on commissions issued to justices of the peace.

PETITION OF THE PEOPLE OF ST. VINCENNES: that is, the petition of George Tevebaugh and others from Knox County, dated 1 Jan. 1800, seeking a division of the Northwest Territory (see Notes on Charges Against Arthur St. Clair, at 29 Apr.).

ACT PASSED IN DECR. 1800: for the reorganization and derangement of the militia in the Northwest Territory, see Vol. 36:464-5n.

For the CASE OF THE ALLEDGED RIOTS at St. Clair's lodgings in Chillicothe on 26 Dec. 1801, see Vol. 36:464n. The correspondence between St. Clair and Justice of the Peace Samuel Finley regarding the event, as well as the affidavits of three witnesses gathered by Finley that denied the accusation of riotous activity, were printed in the 2 Jan. 1802 edition of the *Scioto Gazette*.

[1] Smith here canceled "high."
[2] Preceding three sentences written on a separate sheet of paper and keyed for insertion here in place of "and for such misconduct he ought to be removed from Office."
[3] Smith here canceled "I have not seen the petition nor the Act of the Territory proposing a division [...] not."
[4] Preceding eight words interlined in place of "they."
[5] Remainder of the 5th charge and all of the 6th charge rewritten on a separate sheet for insertion in place of heavily emended text.

From Andrew Jackson

SIR   Nashville June 16th. 1802

I have lately been informed that Mr. Anderson at present attorney for the united States in and for the District of West Tennessee, is about to resign that office—

Mr Thomas S[tuar]t of this District, has applied to me to make known to the President of the united States, his wish to fill that office, should it be vacated by the resignation of Mr. Anderson—

Mr S[tuart] is a man of respectability, and of considerable Standing at the Barr, he has been a practiseing lawyer in the Superior courts of this State for about four years with good Success—I have no doubt, if he is appointed, but he will descharge the duties of that office with credit to himself and satisfaction to the Publick—

I am Sir, with high consideration and respect, yr, Mo, ob, Serv,

ANDREW JACKSON

RC (DNA: RG 59, LAR); cut, with missing letters supplied in brackets (for similar instances involving letters of Aaron Burr, see Vol. 33:626-8; Vol. 34:178; Vol. 35:204, 337); at foot of text: "Citizen Thomas Jefferson President of the united States"; endorsement by TJ also almost entirely cut away. Recorded in SJL as received 4 July.

Andrew Jackson (1767-1845), at the time he wrote this letter to TJ, was a judge of the Superior Court of Tennessee and major general of the state's militia. He was also involved in land speculation and commerce. After reading law in North Carolina, Jackson had moved west in 1788 to become an attorney and prosecutor in Tennessee. He entered politics as a delegate to the constitutional convention for the new state in 1795. He sat in the House of Representatives in the second session of the Fourth Congress as Tennessee's first representative in the federal legislature. Jackson was a United States senator for a few months in 1797 and 1798 before resigning to seek the position on the Superior Court bench (ANB; *Biog. Dir. Cong.*; Harold D. Moser and others, eds., *The Papers of Andrew*

Jackson, 7 vols. [Knoxville, 1980-], 1:xxxvii-xxxviii).

William Preston ANDERSON did resign from his position. John Adams had appointed Anderson the U.S. attorney for Tennessee in 1798. When the Judiciary Act of February 1801 split the state into two districts, Anderson stayed in office as the attorney for the western district and a new appointment was made for the eastern district. In July 1802, following Anderson's resignation, TJ named Thomas Stuart as his replacement. Stuart had practiced in county courts since 1796. The Superior Court licensed him in December 1798 (JEP, 1:267, 268, 384; U.S. Statutes at Large, 2:90; James W. Ely, Jr., and Theodore Brown, Jr., eds., *Legal Papers of Andrew Jackson* [Knoxville, 1987], 355-6, 388; Madison, *Papers, Sec. of State Ser.*, 3:483; TJ to Gallatin, 6 July 1802).

On 4 July, the same day that he received Jackson's letter, TJ also got letters from Anderson, writing from Nashville; from William Dickson in that city; and from Daniel Smith of Sumner County, Tennessee. Those letters, all dated 18 June, are recorded in SJL but have not been found.

From George Jefferson

Dear Sir   Richmond 16th. June 1802.

In compliance with the desire expressed in your favor of the 12th., I have been endeavouring to get an offer for your Tobacco, but no one seems disposed to make a positive one, unless I were authorised to make sale of it.

Should I be authorised to sell it at such a price, a Mr. Rutherfoord tells me that he thinks it probable he will give 4.$\frac{3}{4}$ $ Cash, or 5$ at 90 days. this last price however I think may be had in Cash, but better than that I fear is not to be expected.

It is a rare thing now a days to meet with any one who will give an extra price on credit, who is with safety to be trusted.

No Earth-quake I suppose ever produced a greater crush, than Peace has amongst the Merchants. I have myself by fatal experience become a convert to your opinion—"that 500 acres of land is of more

value than the prospect of the fortune of any Merchant whatever."
Your goodness will, I trust, excuse these observations.

I am Dear Sir Your Very humble servt.   GEO. JEFFERSON

RC (MHi); at foot of text: "Thos. Jefferson esqr."; endorsed by TJ as received 18 June and so recorded in SJL.

From Lewis Littlepage

SIR,   Fredericksburg—16th. June 1802.

With many excuses for the liberty I took in importuning you with my private affairs, I have to entreat you to inclose to me the sealed paper which I left in your hands in December last. I hope shortly to see you on my way to the North, and in the mean time have the honor to be with the highest respect

Sir, your most obedient humble Servant

LEWIS LITTLEPAGE.

RC (MHi); at foot of text: "Thos. Jefferson—President of the United States"; endorsed by TJ as received 18 June and so recorded in SJL.

IN DECEMBER LAST: Littlepage to TJ, 23 Dec. 1801, to which TJ replied on the same day (Vol. 36:194).

From William Lovering

SIR   George Town June 16th 1802

Mr. Briesler the late Presidant's Steward, some time in October 1800 desired I would get a Mangle made for Callendering of Linen, the Smiths Work to complete it. I could not get done time enough, to deliver it before The Family left the City, Mr. Briesler desired me when it was done to apply to Mr Claxton, and that he would speak to Mr Claxton himself to receive it

I applied to Mr. Claxton some time since he told me he had nothing to do with it, under those Circumstances. I hope you will excuse me in taking the liberty of informing you, the Scetch of the apparatus is Anexed. It saves Labor and Tireing and makes Linen look considerable Better than Ironing, and is made Use of in General by Large Family's in Europe. If the Servants are unaquainted in Useing it, I Can instruct them, if you think proper to have it.

I am Sir your Obt. Hble Servt   WILLIAM LOVERING

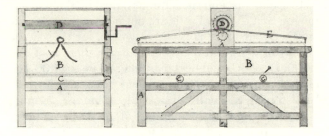

Scale of $\frac{1}{2}$ Inch to a foot.
A. The frame of the Mangle
B. A Loaded Box—
C. Roolers to rool the linen on
D. Rooler that works the loaded Box.
E. Rope that works the Box.

RC (ViW); with drawing and description of mangle on verso of address sheet; addressed: "His Excellency Thomas Jefferson Esqr. President of the United States"; endorsed by TJ as received 17 June and so recorded in SJL.

William Lovering, formerly of London, worked in Washington, Georgetown, and Alexandria as an architect, surveyor, and builder. In 1796 he supplied Robert Morris and John Nicholson with plans for the construction of 20 houses along the Square at South Capitol Street. By 1809, he relocated to Philadelphia, where he planned to teach architecture and carpentry (*Alexandria Advertiser*, 9 Oct. 1797; *Alexandria Daily Advertiser*, 11 Aug. 1804; *Poulson's American Daily Advertiser,* 26 Aug. 1809; Bryan, *National Capital*, 1:278-9).

John BRIESLER served as steward in the Adams family for nearly twenty years and managed their households in Massachusetts, England, and France, as well as the President's House in Washington (Seale, *The President's House*, 1:83).

MANGLE: a large box device filled with stones and attached to a wooden frame, this laundry invention was widely used in sixteenth-century Holland, Denmark, and Germany, and was later modified and adopted in the United States. A launderer wrapped clean, damp linen around wooden rollers placed under the box and used a crank handle or strap to move the box trundle forward and back over the rollers, producing a high standard of pressed linen (OED; Ian McNeil, ed., *An Encyclopaedia of the History of Technology* [New York, 2002], 932).

To Thomas Munroe

SIR   Washington June 16. 1802.

You will percieve by the inclosed letter from the Governor of Maryland that we are called on for the arrears of interest on the two loans of two hundred thousand and of fifty thousand dollars, the former guarantied by Congress, and the latter assumed by them in a specified mode. knowing that the city funds are not in cash to answer these demands, and that your office is constantly open for the sale of unsold lots, I request you to inform me what prospect there is of raising the sum of 18,000. D. which will be due in interest on the 200,000 on the 1st. day of the ensuing month, by sales at prices not unwarrantably low? and I also pray you with all possible diligence to compleat the statement you are engaged in making, of all the lots subject to be resold, that they may be advertised for sale at as short a day as the law will allow, in order to raise the principal of 50,000 D. and it's interest which will become payable on the 1st. day of November next.   Accept my respects & best wishes   Th: Jefferson

PrC (DLC); at foot of text: "Mr. Thomas Monroe, Superintendant of the City of Washington"; endorsed by TJ in ink on verso. Enclosure: John F. Mercer to TJ, 5 June 1802.

A list of LOTS SUBJECT TO BE RESOLD, attached to a letter from Munroe's office dated 19 June, appeared in the *Washington Federalist* and in the *National Intelligencer* on 23 June. Munroe noted in the advertisement that the lots, many of which were "amongst the best" in the city, were to be sold at public auction on 30 Aug. 1802.

To John Barnes

June 17. 1802

Th:J. incloses the within to mr Barnes because the captain will probably apply to him on his arrival.[1] a box for me is gone to Philadelphia. how shall I get the freight paid there?

RC (University Archives, Autographs and Historical Documents, Westport, Connecticut, 1996); addressed: "Mr. John Barnes George town"; endorsed by Barnes, in part: "for a Box expected from Richmond." Enclosure: see bill of lading for a box of books described as enclosure at George Jefferson to TJ, 14 June 1802.

For the box with the piano sent TO PHILADELPHIA, see George Jefferson to TJ, 11 and 14 June; and TJ to John Isaac Hawkins of this date.

[1] Remainder of text interlined by TJ.

From William Bentley

Sir,   Salem 17 June 1802

I take the liberty of inclosing the Letter of Mr Bowditch & the demonstrations of this ingenious young man, who has lately published an American Navigator, of deservedly high reputation. The

Letter will explain itself, & my apology must be, a desire to declare that with the highest respect for your public & private character,

  I am your most obedient, humble Sert   WILLIAM BENTLEY

RC (DLC); addressed: "Thomas Jefferson President of the United States of America President of the Phil: Academy of Arts & Sciences, Washington"; endorsed by TJ as received 24 June and so recorded in SJL. Enclosure: Nathaniel Bowditch to TJ, 11 June 1802, recorded in SJL as received from Salem on 24 June but not found. Other enclosure not found.

William Bentley (1759-1819), the minister of a Congregational church in Salem, Massachusetts, was interested in a wide range of scholarly subjects. A graduate of Harvard College, he assembled a large private library and mastered several languages. He also wrote regular news summaries and commentaries on intellectual developments for a Salem newspaper. Bentley's religious views were considered to be progressive, and in politics he was a dedicated supporter of TJ and Democratic Republicanism (ANB).

AMERICAN NAVIGATOR: Nathaniel Bowditch of Salem, who had limited formal schooling, had taught himself algebra, calculus, Latin, and French while working as a clerk for firms involved in overseas commerce. He prepared an American edition of a popular British manual, *The Practical Navigator* of John Hamilton Moore, calling it *The New Practical Navigator* (Newburyport, Mass., 1799). After making extensive revisions and corrections to the work, Bowditch brought it out under his own name with the title *The New American Practical Navigator* (Newburyport, Mass., 1802). Bowditch was 29 years old in 1802 (ANB).

To John Isaac Hawkins

SIR   Washington June 17. 1802

I have this moment recieved the inclosed bill of lading by which it appears that my Piano forte was shipped at Richmond on the 11th. inst. on board the Schooner Pearl capt. Nathaniel Thompson to your consignment. I have desired mr Barnes of this place, who acts for me in money matters, to give orders for the paiment of the freight. I see by the newspapers you have exhibited or were about exhibiting your Claviol. I shall be glad to learn it's success. perhaps, while my Piano forte is in your possession, you may be called on for a Piano forte for some one. in which case I should be willing you should dispose of mine, and consider me as free to ask a Claviole or another Piano forte: but perhaps also your departure for London may be too near to admit your executing a new order. of this you will be best judge. Accept my respects and best wishes.   TH: JEFFERSON

PrC (DLC); at foot of text: "Mr. John Hawkins"; endorsed by TJ in ink on verso. Enclosure not found, but see George Jefferson to TJ, 14 June.

Hawkins advertised his invention of the CLAVIOL and introduced it in a concert performance of vocal and instrumental music held in Philadelphia on 21 June

1802. The finger-keyed viol, which produced music from gut strings by rosined horse-hair bows, reputedly had "the sweet enchanting tones of the harmonica, the rich sounds of the Violin, and the full grand chords of the Organ" (*Gazette of the United States*, 11 and 21 June 1802). For the construction of the claviol, see Hawkins to TJ, 16 July 1802.

From Nathaniel Macon

SIR   Buck Spring 17 June 1802

Believing that it will not be disagreable to you to hear the sentiments of the people in the different parts of the Union and having since my return been in three of the adjoining Counties, I with real pleasure inform you, that all (except those who were not expected to be pleased) seem to be perfectly satisfied with the conduct of those, to whom they have entrusted the management of their public affairs, some who before the electoral election appeared to be almost indifferent as to the electn. have declared their sincere approbation of the choice and their Joy that the late election gave birth to an administration which deserves the support of every American

I was at Raleigh the first of June, Judge Hall of South Carolina not attending, there was no court for the trial of causes. Mr. Harris attended and done every thing which could be done by one Judge, I saw General Davie there, had some conversation with him, from which I hope he is inclined to give the present administration his support, I only mention this because very different reports were circulated at Washington last winter—The only hope of the dissatisfied is to produce a division among the Republicans, of which I hope there is no danger, I also hope none of them want offices, office hunters are never to be satisfied,

Every one pleased with the appointing Potter district Judge, and none that I know displeased with appointment of Harris

I am with respect Sir yr. most obt. Sevt   NATHL. MACON

RC (DLC); endorsed by TJ. Recorded in SJL as received 26 June.

TJ had appointed Dominick A. HALL chief judge of the U.S. Fifth Circuit Court in 1801 (Vol. 33:332n, 676). For the appointments of Edward HARRIS and Henry POTTER, see TJ to the Senate, 6 Apr., and TJ's List of Candidates for Appointments, printed at 24 Apr.

From Francis Peyton

D SIR   Alexandria 17. June 1802

Permit me to make you acquainted with Mr. Joseph Cowings a gentlemen just arrived here from England, who has solicited me to afford him this introduction

I am respectfully Yr Ob. Servt.   FRANCIS PEYTON

RC (DLC); endorsed by TJ as received 21 June "by mr Cowings" and so recorded in SJL.

Joseph Cowing settled in Alexandria, where he became a schoolmaster and filled leadership roles in several civic organizations (Miller, *Alexandria Artisans*, 1:7; 2:94, 197, 345; T. Michael Miller, *Portrait of a Town: Alexandria, District of Columbia* [*Virginia*], *1820-1830* [Bowie, Md., 1995], 187, 338).

To Thomas Claxton

DEAR SIR   Washington June 18. 1802.

Your favor of the 13th. is recieved. the samples of straw floor cloths are beautiful, especially the finest one; but would not answer for the purpose I have in view which is to lay down on the floor of a dining room when the table is set, & be taken up, when the table is removed, merely to save a very handsome floor from grease & the scouring which that necessitates. the straw would fur up with the grease itself, & would also wear with such repeated rolling & unrolling. but I thank you much for your information of the cost of English painted cloth. at 3. dollars a square yard, the floor cloth would cost me 100. D. which is far beyond the worth of the object.—

no doubt a Pianoforte would be a perfectly proper piece of furniture; but in the present state of our funds, they will be exhausted by articles more indispensable. before providing one also I should like to be still better assured by experience of the superiority of Hawkins's method indeed he has invented a new instrument called a Claviole of high expectations.—our workman on the blinds goes on well. he reforms a window a day. Accept my respects & best wishes

TH: JEFFERSON

PrC (MHi); at foot of text: "Mr. Claxton"; endorsed by TJ in ink on verso.

Sometime after TJ received Claxton's FAVOR OF THE 13TH, he made the following calculations under the heading "Prices":

"floor English painted canvas 3. D pr.
cloth.   sq. yard
          the canvas itself before painted
          costs 1. D pr. sq. yard
          Chinese straw floor cloth costs
          67. cents pr. sq. yard."

(MS in DLC; undated; entirely in TJ's hand; with TJ's note at foot of text: "see Claxton's lre from Phila June 13. 1802").

Memorandum from Albert Gallatin

[18 June 1802]

The Bank of Pennsylvania applies for relief—they fall regularly 100,000 drs. per week in debt to the Bank U. States, on account, as they say, of the deposits on account of Government made in the last. For a sketch of their situation compared with that of Bank of U. States, see the within paper—Their cashier is here come on purpose for assistance. In addition to the effect of Governmental deposits it is evident that they have extended their discounts too far. They say that these cannot at once be curtailed without ruining their customers who consist chiefly of retail shop-keepers. Those for whom the Bank U. States discounts are generally importers—There are but three means of affording them relief—1st Write to Bank United States to spare them—2dly Deposit 300,000 dollars with them, or direct collector Philada. to deposit part of his public monies with them—3dly Contract with them for part of Dutch debt, which, as we always pay considerably before hand, will have the effect of a deposit—I have proposed the last; but if we cannot agree on terms, should either of the two other modes be adopted? It is proper to prevent the exclusive monopoly in hands of Bank United States; but it is not proper to displease them, because they place instantly our money where we may want it from one end of the Union to the other, which is done on the tacit condition of our leaving our deposits with them, and because if we shall be hard run & want money, to them we must apply for a loan—   A.G.

MS (DLC); undated; entirely in Gallatin's hand; addressed: "The President of the United States"; endorsed by TJ as received from the Treasury Department on 18 June and "bank of Pensva" and so recorded in SJL. Enclosure not found.

The Pennsylvania legislature incorporated the BANK OF PENNSYLVANIA in 1793, thereby implementing a plan developed by Gallatin, as a member of the Ways and Means Committee in the state House of Representatives, to establish a bank with a relationship to the state government similar to that of the Bank of the United States and the federal government. The Bank of Pennsylvania was capitalized at $3,000,000, with one-third of the stock owned by the state. The state legislature appointed six of the twenty-five bank directors. Gallatin believed that the interest paid on the bank stock would provide the state with income to cover regular government expenses (Raymond Walters, Jr., *Albert Gallatin: Jeffersonian Financier and Diplomat* [New York, 1957], 43-4; *Acts of the General Assembly of the Commonwealth of Pennsylvania, Passed at a Session, which was Begun and Held at the City of Philadelphia on Tues-*

day, the Fourth Day of December, in the Year One Thousand Seven Hundred and Ninety-Two [Philadelphia, 1793], 323, 325-6).

CASHIER: Jonathan Smith. A 30 June letter from Samuel M. Fox, president of the Bank of Pennsylvania, convinced Gallatin that his fears regarding the bank were unfounded. Gallatin informed Fox on 6 July that his apprehensions were "owing to the erroneous impressions I had received from my verbal communica-tions with your Cashier.—The differences you state in the account of specie and in those for notes with other Banks affect materially the inferences I had drawn." Before the error was evident, Gallatin had advised Fox that if the bank needed to raise specie, the sale of some of its U.S. stock "was more eligible, and would be more effectual than a retrenchment of dis-counts" (*Gazette of the United States*, 19 Jan. 1802; Gallatin, *Papers*, 7:302; Vol. 35:705n).

To Lewis Littlepage

Washington June 18. 1802.

Th: Jefferson presents his friendly salutations to General Littlepage, and according to the desire expressed in his letter of the 16th. this moment recieved, he sends him the sealed paper deposited in his care. he shall be happy to see Genl. Littlepage here according to his intimation.

RC (ViHi); addressed: "General Lewis Littlepage Fredericksburg"; franked and postmarked. PrC (MHi); endorsed by TJ in ink on verso.

The contents of the SEALED PAPER that TJ had held for safekeeping since 23 Dec. are not known, but on 21 June, the day after Littlepage got the document back from TJ, Littlepage composed a new will. He was evidently suffering from some unidentified illness, from which he died on 19 July 1802, at the age of 40. Waller Holladay, his half-brother, attributed Littlepage's death to "exposure in Court and camp" during the time he spent in Europe (Nell Holladay Boand, *Lewis Littlepage* [Richmond, 1970], 288-9; Curtis Carroll Davis, *The King's Chevalier: A Biography of Lewis Littlepage* [Indianapolis, 1961], 386-9; Vol. 32:3-4; Vol. 36:194).

To William Lovering

Washington June 18. 1802

Th: Jefferson presents his compliments to mr Lovering and observes that the employment of the funds destined for furnishing the President's house, is confided by the legislature to mr Claxton solely. he knows however that those funds are all but exhausted, and thinks it probable mr Claxton can contract no new engagement on them.

PrC (ViW); endorsed by TJ in ink on verso.

PRESENTS HIS COMPLIMENTS: in answer to Lovering's letter of 16 June.

From Francis Peyton

DEAR SIR,   alexandria 18th. June 1802

Agreeably to my promise I now send you a list of the persons best qualified in my opinion for the office of Commissioners of Bankruptcy at this place, As you have been pleased to express a wish to include me in the commission, I do not feel disposed to disappoint your expectations, by declining to receive the appointment.

Accept Sir a tender of my warmest acknowledgments for the repeated testimonies afforded me of your esteem and confidence, and at the same time, permit me to assure you, that I shall always entertain a grateful sense, of the honor conferred on me, by your partiality and regard,

I am with great respect Yr. Obe. Servt.   FRANCIS PEYTON

Commissioners
George Gilpin
Jonah Thompson
Walter Jones Jr.

RC (DNA: RG 59, LAR); list of commissioners written in left margin; endorsed by TJ as received 20 June and so recorded in SJL with notation "Commrs. bkrptcy"; also endorsed by TJ: "George Gilpin Jonah Thompson Walter Jones junr. Francis Peyton to be commrs. bkrptcy."

COMMISSIONERS OF BANKRUPTCY: Gilpin, Thompson, Jones, and Peyton received commissions dated 22 June (list of commissions in Lb in DNA: RG 59, MPTPC). Shortly after he took office, TJ appointed Jones U.S. attorney for the Potomac district. The others served as justices of the peace for Alexandria County (Vol. 33:596, 674, 678; Vol. 36:314-17).

To Martha Jefferson Randolph

Washington June 18. 1802.

I recieved, my dear daughter, your's of the 13th. by post. I regret extremely the situation of your family, not only for my disappointment here, but for what they are to suffer. I acknolege that, knowing when I came away the measles were in the neighborhood, I saw it was but too possible your visit here would be delayed. as it is, we must agree to the fall visit, and as Maria will be at Monticello, I trust she will come on with you. I believe we shall conclude here to leave this place the last week of July; probably I shall be with you by the 24th. say 5. weeks from this time, and I shall endeavor that mr Eppes & Maria be there also by that time. I hope Peter Hemings will get the better of his complaint, or I know not what we should do, as it is next to impossible to send Ursula & her child home & bring them back again.—the servants here have felt great disappointment at your not coming. the coachman is particularly chagrined. I suppose he wishes to have an opportunity of shewing himself on his box; which with me he has never had. mr and mrs Trist are to set out in a very few days for Albemarle, and I believe the two young ladies go with them. he, I fancy will proceed immediately to the Missisipi.—present my best esteem to mr Randolph, abundance of soft things to the children, and warmest affections to yourself.

TH: JEFFERSON

RC (NNPM); at foot of text: "Mrs. Randolph." PrC (MHi); endorsed by TJ in ink on verso.

Randolph's letter of THE 13TH, recorded in SJL as received 16 June, has not been found.

PETER HEMINGS was at this point the chief cook at Monticello. Born in 1787, URSULA Hughes had been training in the kitchen at the President's House since the fall of 1801, but the birth of her child in March 1802 apparently disrupted her apprenticeship. After a year's service in Washington, she returned to Monticello, where she alternated between assisting in the kitchen and working in the fields. Her child, born in Washington, died young, but she and her husband Wormley Hughes had nine more children together (Stanton, *Free Some Day*, 45, 129-30; Annette Gordon-Reed, *The Hemingses of Monticello: An American Family* [New York, 2008], 563, 568-70; MB, 2:1069).

From William Bache

DEAR SIR.   Franklin June 19th. 1802.

As you requested me to be silent respecting New Orleans until the affair was in train, I have scrupulously kept the council, and should not now obtrude the remembrance of it upon you but for circumstances of some moment to me. By the last post my Brother informed me that my sister Harwood and family intended me a visit this summer, and would shortly make preparations for that purpose. Now if it will be necessary for me to leave Albemarle as soon as you stated, I think it will be but right to prevent an expensive Journey, which may end only in dissappointment to them. This cannot be so well done as by stating to them my intention & views, & indeed I owe this intelligence to my family, as soon as it can be communicated with propriety, as they may with justice be offended at my silence of a circumstance so nearly allied to my future destiny. Without permission from you, however, I do not feel my self at liberty to inform them. with sentiments of the higest respect I am yours.

WILLIAM BACHE

RC (DLC); endorsed by TJ as received 28 June and so recorded in SJL.

FRANKLIN was what Bache called his farm in Albemarle County (Vol. 33:241n).

Apparently during his stay in Albemarle County in May, TJ offered Bache the position of physician for the new marine hospital at NEW ORLEANS. As TJ explained to Caspar Wistar, he had determined to appoint William Barnwell as the hospital's surgeon before he learned of Bache's desire to move to the Mississippi Territory, as Bache's friend Hore Browse Trist was doing. Bache was "eminently qualified," TJ explained to Wistar, and "I could have no hesitation to offer the place to him." By the first of July, TJ arranged with Gallatin to appoint Bache to the post. The U.S. consul in New Orleans, Daniel Clark, would superintend the facility. Mindful that the annual season of severe illness in New Orleans was advancing and hopeful that the seamen's infirmary might be established while Louisiana was still administered by Spanish officials, with whom Clark had a relationship, rather than a new French regime, TJ urged Bache to go to New Orleans right away. The doctor did not reach the city until March 1803 (Jane Flaherty Wells, "Thomas Jefferson's Neighbors: Hore Browse Trist of 'Birdwood' and Dr. William Bache of 'Franklin,'" *Magazine of Albemarle County History*, 47 [1989], 8; Vol. 34:562n; TJ to Bache, 1 July, 11 Oct.; Gallatin to TJ, [1 July]; TJ to Wistar, 14 July; TJ to John Brown, 14 Aug.; Gallatin to TJ, 19 Aug. 1802; Bache to TJ, 29 Mch. 1803).

The BROTHER who had corresponded with Bache was probably Louis Bache. Born in 1779, he was six years younger than William. Another brother, Richard Bache, Jr., was 18 years old in 1802. One of their sisters, Elizabeth (or Eliza), had married John Edmund HARWOOD, a well-known comic stage actor, in January 1800 (Leonard W. Labaree and others, eds., *The Papers of Benjamin Franklin*, 39 vols. to date [1959-], 1:lxiii-lxv; Gerald Bordman and Thomas S. Hischak, eds., *The Oxford Companion to American Theatre*, 3d ed. [New York, 2004], 296; Don B. Wilmeth, ed., *The Cambridge Guide to American Theatre*, 2d hardcover ed. [Cambridge, 2007], 317-18).

To Albert Gallatin

TH:J. TO MR GALLATIN   June 19. 1802.

With respect to the bank of Pensva, their difficulties proceed from excessive discounts. the 3,000,000 D. due to them comprehend doubtless all the desperate debts accumulated since their institution. their buildings should only be counted at the value of the naked ground belonging to them; because if brought to market they are worth to private bidders no more than their materials, which are known by experience to be worth no more than the cost of pulling down and removing them. their situation then is

they owe		2,200,000
they have of good money	710,000	
	250,000	960,000
ground worth perhaps	5,000	965,000
		1,235,000

to pay which 1,235,000. They depend on 3,000,000. of[1] debts due to them, the amount of which shews they are of long standing, a part desperate, a part not commandable. in this situation it does not seem safe to deposit public money with them, and the effect would only be to enable them to nourish their disease by continuing their excessive discounts; the checking of which is the only means of saving themselves from bankruptcy. the getting them to pay the Dutch debt, is but a deposit in another, tho' a safer, form. if we can with propriety recommend indulgence to the bank of the US. it would be attended with the least danger to us, of any of the measures suggested, but it is in fact asking that bank to lend to the one of Pensylvania that they may be enabled to continue lending to others. the monopoly of a single bank is certainly an evil. the multiplication of them was intended to cure it: but it multiplied an influence of the same character with the first, and compleated the supplanting the precious metals by a paper circulation. between such parties the less we meddle the better.

Th:J.

RC (NHi: Gallatin Papers); endorsed. PrC (DLC).

THEIR BUILDINGS: Benjamin H. Latrobe designed and supervised the construction of the Bank of Pennsylvania in Philadelphia. Completed in 1801, the bank had a marble exterior and set a standard for civic buildings, becoming "one of the most influential prototypes for early nineteenth-century American architecture" (Latrobe, *Correspondence*, 1:128-9).

[1] Preceding word and number interlined in place of "the."

From John Langdon

DEAR PRESIDENT   Portsmo. June 19th. 1802

I wrote you the 14th. Ult. in answer to your's of the 5th. of the same month in which, Agreably to your Request, I named John Goddard Esqr. and John McClintock merchants, Henry S. Langdon, and Charles Cutts, Esqrs. Lawyers, all of this Town, for Commissioners of Bankruptcy, as there has no appointment yet taken place, I am fearful my letter, miscarried; have therefore taken the liberty to mention the names of those gentlemen again—we have some expectation of a failure or two, will soon take place, of course Commissioners will be Necessy. I have this moment return'd from our Legislature, have not time to copy my former letter—we have Obtain an Incorporation for our Republican Bank this Session, of course we are not looseing ground.—

Beleive me, ever, most sencerly yours   JOHN LANGDON

RC (DLC): at foot of text: "President Jefferson"; endorsed by TJ as received 28 June and so recorded in SJL.

OUR REPUBLICAN BANK: Langdon had been the primary organizer of the New Hampshire Union Bank in 1799. Only the second bank organized in the state, it was a direct challenge to the economic and political influence wielded by Federalists through their control of the rival New Hampshire Bank. Federalist legislators denied the Union Bank a charter, then passed an act prohibiting unincorporated banks and authorized the state to purchase additional stock in the New Hampshire Bank. Such actions proved highly unpopular with voters, however, and Republicans used the issue to their advantage. Efforts to incorporate the Union Bank in 1800 and 1801 were again defeated, but Republican gains in 1802 enabled them to secure incorporation during the June legislative session (Lynn Warren Turner, *The Ninth State: New Hampshire's Formative Years* [Chapel Hill, 1983], 178-88; Vol. 35:652-3).

James Madison's Opinions on the Charges Against Arthur St. Clair

The President having called on the heads of Departments for their opinion in writing whether certain charges made by Col. Worthington against Governor St. Clair be or be not established; and whether such as are established, be sufficiently weighty to render the removal of the Governor proper? the Secretary of State respectfully submits his opinion as follows;

Charge 1. Forming new Counties & fixing their seats of justice by his sole authority.

The fact is admitted and its legality contended for. The reasons given are unsatisfactory to the judgment of the Secretary of State; but he can not undertake to say that they have so little plausibility[1] as to preclude a difference of opinion

Ch. 2d. "Putting a negative on useful & necessary laws."

It appears that the Negative has been exercised in many cases, and in some probably, where the laws would have been salutary. The discretion however involved in the use of this power, requires stronger and clearer abuses of it, than are shewn, to justify a hasty or rigorous condemnation.

Ch. 3. "Taking illegal fees"

In the case of ferry licenses the charge seems undeniable. In that of tavern licenses, an act is found in the code of the Territory, authorizing the fees; but there is reason to believe that a latitude of construction or rather an abuse of power in which the Govr. himself participated, was employed in the adoption of the Act. With respect to the marriage fees, it is affirmed that a legal authority also exists. As the volume of laws however referred to on this point can not be consulted[2] no opinion will be given either on the tenor or the origin of the Act.

The taking of illegal fees is in itself an abuse of power, of so deep a die, as, unless mitigated by powerful circumstances, to justify a rigorous proceeding against the author of it[3] and as to be altogether excusable under no circumstances.

Ch. 4. "Negativing a bill for abolishing fees, and passing one giving the Govr. a sum meant by the Legislature as a substitute for them."

This charge involves questions which it would be difficult[4] to unravel, and perhaps improper to decide.

Ch. 5. "Concurring in the plan of changing the Constitutional boundaries of the proposed states N.W. of the Ohio."

The fact is certain, and the attempt of the Governor to explain obscure & unsatisfactory.

Ch. 6. "Appointing his son Attorney General, by an illegal commission during good behavior." The fact is admitted and without being palliated by the explanations given by the Governor.

Ch. 7. "Attempting to influence certain judiciary proceedings."

This charge as far as it can be judged of by what appears, can not be considered as established. In one at least of the transactions referred to the conduct of the Governor was justified by that of the Justices.

Ch. 8. "Appointing to offices requiring residence in one county, persons residing in another."

The fact here may be true, and conduct of the Govr. free from blame. If the offices were incompatible, the second appointment might be made on the presumption that the first would be relinquished. To judge fully of the case it ought also to be known what the law of the territory is with respect to the residence & deputyship of the different officers.

Ch. 9. "Neglecting to organize & discipline the Militia."

This charge is not established.

Ch. 10. "Hostility to republican form of Government."

The circumstances under which expressions to this effect are admitted to have been used, & under which the evidence of them appears to been collected, render it improper to lay stress on this charge.

Upon the whole, it appears that altho' the conduct of the Governor has been highly culpable in sundry instances, and sufficiently so in the particular cases of Commissioning his son during good behavior, and in what relates to fees, to plead, for a removal of him from his office, yet considering the revolutionary & other interesting relations in which he has stood to the public, with other grounds on which some indulgence may be felt for him, it is the opinion of the Secretary of State, that it will be proper to leave him in possession of his office under the influence of a salutary admonition

JAMES MADISON
June 19. 1802

MS (DLC); endorsed by TJ: "St. Clair's case. Secy. of state's opinion."

A SALUTARY ADMONITION: on 23 June, Madison wrote St. Clair to inform him that his defense against charges of misconduct "have been duly considered by the President." Despite St. Clair's many honorable past services to his country, the president "has judged it indispensible that his particular disapprobation should be expressed to you, of your conduct in granting your son an illegal tenure of office; and in accepting yourself illegal fees, an abuse which he expects will be immediately rectified by proper notice to the agents collecting them." The president also wishes it known that by continuing to lay out counties and fix seats of justice in the Northwest Territory by his sole authority, St. Clair has "not pursued the construction put by the Executive on the Ordinance constituting the Territorial Government." "From the regret which the President has felt at an occasion for the animadversions now conveyed," Madison concluded, "you will be sensible how much you will contribute to his satisfaction by such a line of official conduct as may best obviate discontents among the

people under your administration, foster their respect for the laws, and coincide with the benevolent policy of the federal Government towards their rights and interests." St. Clair replied to Madison on the same day, stating that it pained him to see that his conduct as governor "should have drawn forth the animadversions of the Presdt." He promised to cease the collection of fees and to "correct" his interpretation of the laws regarding the creation of new counties. He closed by asking Madison to convey his respect to the president, as well as his thanks "for the delicate manner in which you have been pleased to communicate the Animadversions . . . he has had occasion to make" (Madison, *Papers, Sec. of State Ser.*, 3:332, 335).

[1] Madison here canceled: "as to be <*incapable of [conferring]*> inconsistent with an honest excercise of those powers."
[2] Preceding three words interlined in place of "<*is not*> can not have been found."
[3] Madison here canceled: "The pleas need by this."
[4] Preceding five words interlined in place of "on which it is unnecessary."

From Thomas Munroe

Superintendants Office
SIR,   Washington 19th June 1802

In answer to your Letter of the 16th Instant I have the honor to inform you that, altho' I have attended the Office constantly, and used my utmost endeavors, since my appointment as Superintendant, to raise money by sales of the public Lots to discharge the claims against the City, I have not been able to sell but one Lot, for which I could not get more than $350, about one half the price similarly situated Lots have heretofore sold for.—

In addition to my own impressions of the necessity and propriety of offering and selling at reduced prices, I have considered the sentiments expressed by the President on the subject as not only warranting, but requiring it to be done—In consequence, however, of the number of Lots in the market being so much greater than the demand for them, and from the difficulty which I have experienced in selling, notwithstanding the low prices at which I have offered to sell, I think there is no probability of raising the sume of $18,000 which will be due to the State of Maryland on the 1st day of the ensuing month for Interest on the $200,000 by sales at prices not unwarrantably low.—

I have the honor to be with sentiments of the greatest respect, Sir, Yr mo Obt. Servt.   THOMAS MUNROE

RC (DLC); endorsed by TJ as received from "<*Munroe Thos.*> Washington Superintend's Office" on 19 June and so recorded in SJL.

To Joseph Priestley

DEAR SIR   Washington June 19. 1802.

Your favor of the 12th. has been duly recieved, and with that pleasure which the approbation of the good & the wise must ever give. the sentiments it expresses are far beyond my merits or pretensions: they are precious testimonies to me however that my sincere desire to do what is right & just is viewed with candour. that it should be handed to the world under the authority of your name is securing it's credit with posterity. in the great work which has been affected in America, no individual has a right to take any great share to himself. our people in a body are wise, because they are under the unrestrained and unperverted operation of their own understandings. those whom they have assigned to the direction of their affairs, have stood with a pretty even front. if any one of them was withdrawn, many others entirely equal, have been ready to fill his place with as[1] good abilities. a nation composed of such materials, and free in all it's members from distressing wants, furnishes hopeful implements for the interesting experiment of self-government: and we feel that we are acting under obligations not confined to the limits of our own society. it is impossible not to be sensible that we are acting for all mankind: that circumstances denied to others, but indulged to us, have imposed on us the duty of proving what is the degree of freedom and selfgovernment in which a society may venture to leave it's individual members.　　　one passage, in the paper you inclosed me, must be corrected. it is the following. 'and all say that it was yourself more than any other individual, that planned & established it.' i.e. the constitution. I was in Europe when the constitution was planned & established, and never saw it till after it was established. on receiving it I wrote strongly to mr Madison urging the want of provision for the freedom of religion, freedom of the press, trial by jury, habeas corpus, the substitution of militia for a standing army, and an express reservation to the states of all rights not specifically granted to the union. he accordingly moved in the first session of Congress for these Amendments which were agreed to & ratified by the states as they now stand. this is all the hand I had in what related to the Constitution. our predecessors made it doubtful how far even these were of any value. for the very law which endangered your personal safety, as well as that which restrained the freedom of the press, were gross violations of them. however it is still certain that tho' written constitutions may be violated in moments of passion or delusion, yet they furnish a text to which those who are watchful may again rally & recall the people: they fix too for the people principles for their political creed.—We shall all absent ourselves from this place during the sickly season; say from about the 22d of July to the last of September. should your curiosity lead you hither either before or after that interval, I shall be very happy to recieve you, and shall claim you as my guest. I wish the advantages of a mild over a winter climate had been tried for you before you were located where you are. I have ever considered this as a public as well as personal misfortune. the choice you made of our country for your asylum was honourable to it; and I lament that for the sake of your happiness and health it's most benign climates were not selected. certainly it is a truth that climate is one of the sources of the greatest sensual enjoiment. I recieved in due time the letter of Apr. 10. referred to in your last, with the pamphlet it inclosed, which I read with the pleasure I do every thing from you. Accept assurances of my highest veneration and respect.

TH: JEFFERSON

PrC (DLC); at foot of first page: "Doctr. Priestly." Priestley made a copy of this letter and enclosed it in one to John Wilkinson, his brother-in-law in England, on 31 July 1802 (RC and enclosure in Municipal Library, Warrington, England; with photostats of both in DLC).

After receiving an account of the Constitutional Convention in Dec. 1787, TJ did write STRONGLY TO MR MADISON, urging the inclusion of a bill of rights. He also enclosed an extract of his letter to Madison in a message to Uriah Forrest, apparently with the unrealized expecta-tion that Forrest would publish it anonymously (Vol. 12: 438-43, 475-9).

[1] MS: "as as."

To David Redick

SIR   Washington June 19. 1802.

Your letter of the 10th. has been received, and I am duly sensible of the favor of your attention to the calumny which was the subject of it. seeing the impossibility that special vindications should ever keep pace with the endless falshoods invented & disseminated against me, I came at once to a resolution to rest on the justice & good sense of my fellow citizens, to consider from my general character and conduct thro' life, not unknown to them, whether these [calumnies] were probable: and I have made it an invariable rule never to enter the lists of the public papers with the propagators of them. in private communications with my friends I have contradicted them without reserve. in this light you will be pleased to consider the present letter as meant for your own satisfaction, and to assure you that the falsehood may be contradicted with safety by yourself or any others, but not that this letter should get into the [public] papers, or itself or any copy of it [go out of your own hands]. I know not to what party of Indians the calumny is meant to allude, as there were several parties on visits here the last summer. but it is false as to every party. [I never] uttered the sentiments there stated, nor anything equivalent or like to them, to any Indian, or to any other person here or anywhere else. I had but one private conversation the last summer with any Indian. [that was] with the little Turtle in the presence of capt. Wells, his interpreter. I remember asking from him the opinions of the Indians with respect to a supreme being, the worship of him, and a future state. he answered me frankly. but I carefully avoided the impropriety of either controverting or concurring in those opinions, or of saying one syllable on the comparative merits of any religious opinions. the story therefore is a mere fabrication, false in it's substance & in all it's circumstances. I readily conjecture the Missionary who wrote to you on the subject, and know his worth & candour too well not to wish that his mind should be set to rights on this subject. I will ask, if you please, that addition to your favors, and pray you to accept my esteem & best wishes.   TH: JEFFERSON

PrC (ViW); faint; most text in brackets supplied from Alfred Creigh, *History of Washington County*, 2d ed. (Harrisburg, Pa., 1871), 371-2; at foot of text: "David Reddick esq."; endorsed by TJ in ink on verso.

For the public meetings between TJ and LITTLE TURTLE, which took place in January 1802, see Vol. 36:274-90. For official visits to Washington by other major Native American delegations since TJ's inauguration, see Vol. 34:505-11; Vol. 36:513-27; and Conference with Handsome Lake, Cornplanter, and Blue Eyes, 10 Mch. 1802.

From Caesar A. Rodney

HONORED & DEAR SIR,   Wilmington june: 19th. 1802.

On my return last evening from Philadelphia whither I had been for a few days I had the pleasure of receiving your confidential letter of the 14th inst.:—

On the subject of the memorials transmitted to you relative to our collector, I will candidly give you all the explanation in my power. The delicacy of my situation in this business absolutely requires that you should preserve it within your own bosom.

I have been one of those, as I frequently mentioned to you, whilst at Washington, who on all occasions reprobated the conduct of the late administration in excluding from all office those who differed from them in political sentiment. Such being my principles & avowed opinions, I determined when the cause of virtue triumphed in your election, not to be forward in getting those in office turned out. In this resolution my Republican friends acquiesced. But a neutrality was all I intended to preserve & at the same time that I assisted in turning no person *out*, I was not to be understood as interfering to keep any one in office. With a single exception I have rigidly adhered to this line of conduct & in that case the solicitations of many Republicans & the unfortunate situation of the officer compelled me to deviate from my usual practice. You my dear Sir, can bear me witness that whilst at Washington I strictly adhered to those principles. I neither solicited or opposed the change of the Collector here, but merely objected to the appointment of a character which our friends so generally thought unsuitable,[1] without attempting to recommend any other.

I have on the occasion of the late charges agt. Mr. M'Clane upon professional principles acted as his counsel, & in that capacity have conscienciously done my duty. These are the combined reasons which place me in a delicate situation. Could I, with propriety, have told Mr. M'Clane that I was about writing to you on this subject, I should not have hesitated to mention to him that placed in the situation I am—I was about to give you a candid explanation of the business.

I have ever had nerve enough hitherto to do any act for the benifit of the cause so near to my heart. And I should always prefer when doing any thing which might affect his tenure of office to go openly & tell him so. But I know well in your situation you often must call for confidential advice & I know also the importance at this moment that the communication to me should not on any account go further than myself nor shall it.

Perhaps I ought to add that as I have been selected by my fellow citizens as a candidate who will if elected, support you & your measures at every risk; that should Col. M'Clane who is perhaps the most indefatiguable man in the world,[2] thru' any channel know of this communication (& you cannot be to cautious of every one) that it might in a very considerable degree affect my election,[3] thwart the views of persons which I ought not to commit.

As I have touched on this subject, I must inform you, that the matter has been sometime in suspense, whether Bayard would stand or not. He seems to have halted between two opinions. I informed him immediately on his return, that I had come to a resolution, if taken up, to stand a poll & I transmit you a paper, containing the proceedings of the Democratic delegates chosen at a meeting of the people in the several Counties, in which they have fixed on me. Indeed my fellow citizens here would never have forgiven me had I refused. And when added to their solicitations, it was requested by you "whose situation commands a view of the whole ground" I at once yeilded to that request. What the event may be when parties are so equally ballanced is uncertain. I have only one wish, that delicacy did not forbid my making the tour of the state, & addressing the people at their various public meetings. Should the opposite candidate, adopt a course of this kind, I shall not hesitate to pursue him, and to meet him on every ground.

When the late charges were renewed agt. Mr. M'Clane, which had been made & abandoned under the former administration, those who were anxious for his removal on the manly ground of his public conduct, felt that they would only have the effect of embarrassing you. There is too much reason to believe that the real author of their renewal supposed you would at once remove him & that he had sufficient address to slip into his place however the step might affect the general cause. Your impartiality procured for Mr. M'Clane a just acquittal of those charges. Since that period the disinterested Republicans, who considered the real ground of objection, which ought to have been taken against him, & who awaited patiently the event of what has taken place, have manifested an extreme anxiety on the subject of his removal. Knowing my principles they have never called on me to act in this business. It is a service from which in obedience to my own wishes they have excused me. I have been a silent tho' not an inatentive observer of the proceedings which have been adopted, & of the spirit which has given birth to them. It is a spirit which the Federalists now blame, but which they first breathed into the people themselves. The current runs however so very strong in this State, that in my candid opinion it cannot without manifest hazzard be resisted. You can scarcely meet any of the principal Republicans who do not express the strongest anxiety that a removal should take place. The rest are more warm.[4] I wish it were not so. Personally I can have no desire to see any man loose his office, & particularly one who has been on intimate terms with me. But I am bound to be honest on all occasions. To you particularly Sir I owe it to be candid, on this. You ask me to inform you what his political conduct has been since the preferring of the late *personal*[5] charges for our Republicans do not consider that they included any thing *political*, which is the course they have taken at this time. *They* have been encited to those proceedings by his conduct both before & since your accession to office. I am bound to say he has pursued the same course since but has acted less openly

"Those secret enemies were worst of all
"We fearless brav'd the cannon's pointed ball."[6]

I am sensible it must be a painful task which the Republicans of this state have imposed on you. Could any conduct of mine have prevented it, & saved you the necessity of performing a reluctant duty, I would cheerfully have done it but from the temper which seems universally to pervade our friends, I should have fallen a victim in the unequal conflict of resistance to the general wishes & will of the Republicans. The county of Kent, & particularly the leading men will be paralized, unless their remonstrances succeed, it appears to me. I hope by your wise & prudent conduct we shall be[7] able in a little time by yeilding certain lenths to the strong impulse of the people to restrain it at a future period within due bounds. The *equality* of office is the just scale. Your address to the New-Haven *junto* precisely chalks out the true line. They ought to share no more of the *loaves & fishes* than their due proportion. I have on this subject published a piece in answer to the assertions of Messrs Bayard & Griswold. & we hope to give our Wilmington paper new life in the course of the summer.

In a few days, after collecting the sentiment on the subject, I will recommend agreeably to your wishes commissioners of Bankruptcy.

I shall not be able to get you two Republican lawyers. Except Mr. Read & Mr. McMullin who read with me, we have none beside myself. I will obtain you however one lawyer & three most respectable mercantile characters.

Your measures are daily producing new converts as The people are made better acquainted with them. Rely on it however this state or any other may veer a little, our cause is as fixed as the firmament.

Pray have you ever read "Logan's speech" printed in a small volume called "Love & Madness" founded on the tragic story of the murder of Miss Ray by Mr. Hackat in London. This book appeared before your notes. I find it is not noticed in your appendix, but you will upon reading it see that the speech agrees verbatim with the one you published.

With great esteem Yours Most Sincerely   C. A. RODNEY

Tuesday Mor. June 21st.
P.S. Having been frequently interrupted by professional intrusions, the mail passed thru' just as I was finishing the preceding letter on saturday morning. In the afternoon I went over to new-Castle to consult our friends about their Commissioners of Bankruptcy & have delayed sealing this letter under the expectation of hearing from them but have been disappointed. As soon as I do I will transmit you the names of all of them. I fear I shall not have the pleasure of seeing you until late in August tho' I want information on a number of points which will be important in the ensuing electioneering campaign.

C. A. RODNEY

RC (DLC); endorsed by TJ as received 23 June and so recorded in SJL. Enclosure not found, but see below.

SINGLE EXCEPTION: for Rodney's defense of John Stockton, see Rodney to TJ, 27 Dec. 1801.

TRANSMIT YOU A PAPER: on 9 June, the Wilmington *Mirror of the Times* printed an extract of the 5 June meeting at Dover (see Delaware Democratic Republicans to TJ, printed at 5 June).

In May 1801, Benjamin Reynolds RENEWED the charges against Allen McLane, which he had previously brought and ABANDONED during the Adams administration (see Vol. 34:170-1).

LOAVES & FISHES: Rodney wrote an anonymous piece to "correct" Federalist "errors," which appeared in the Wilmington *Mirror of the Times* on 29 May

and was reprinted in the Philadelphia *Aurora* on 28 June. Rodney reported James A. Bayard's opposition to the repeal of internal taxes, even though, the congressman contended, "*We participate not or expect to participate in the loaves and fishes!*" Connecticut Federalist Roger Griswold repeated the assertion in a debate three days later. Rodney proposed to look at Delaware to discover whether Federalists did not "really *share the loaves and fishes.*" Itemizing the salaries of several Federalists holding offices under the government of the United States, Rodney asserted that they received a combined compensation of almost $13,000. The salaries of the Republican district attorney, marshal, and a few postmasters had a combined compensation of no more than $1,000. Rodney concluded that because the Federalists "have not entire possession of the *whole loaf* and *all the fishes*, notwithstanding they have thirteen parts out of fourteen, they complain, forsooth, of having no share!" For both references to "loaves and fishes" in the congressional debates, see *Annals*, 11:1012-13, 1040.

LOGAN'S SPEECH: "*The Speech of a Shawanese Chief, to Lord Dunmore*" was reproduced as part of the thirteenth letter in *Love and Madness. A Story too True. In a Series of Letters between Parties, Whose Names Would Perhaps be Mentioned, Were They Less Known or Less Lamented.* First published anonymously in London in 1780, Sir Herbert Croft was recognized as the author of the volume based on the story of Martha Ray and James Hackman (see Sowerby, No. 4338). TJ first published his *Notes on the State of Virginia* in Paris in 1785 and in London in 1787

(same, No. 4167; *Notes*, ed., Peden, v). In 1797, TJ began compiling the APPENDIX, which was published in 1800 (see Vol. 29:409-10n).

[1] Rodney here altered the period to a comma and interlined the remainder of the sentence.

[2] Preceding two words interlined in place of "politics."

[3] Rodney originally ended the sentence here. He then altered the period to a comma and interlined the remainder of the sentence.

[4] Sentence interlined.

[5] Word interlined.

[6] Closing quotation mark supplied by Editors.

[7] Word supplied by Editors.

From Joseph Marie Lequinio de Kerblay

Newport le 20 Juin 1802—1er messidor

MONSIEUR LE PRÉSIDENT   an 10m de la R. fr.

j'ai l'honneur de vous adresser, Ci-incluses, deux lettres, l'une de mr. de la fayette, l'autre de mr. de liancourt; j'avais une grande ambition de vous les remettre moimême.—nommé par le premier Consul sous-commissaire des rélations Commerciales de france à Newport, mon projet était de vous aller offrir mon hommage et solliciter moimême Votre agrément. Vos vertus personnelles, Monsieur le président, et votre haute réputation me rendaient le Devoir bien Agréable À remplir; mais le citoyen pichon notre Commissaire général que j'ai trouvé À philadelphie, m'a dit que Cela n'était point l'uzage, qu'aucun Commissaire, ou sous-Commissaire des rélations Commerciales de france n'était encore allé directement solliciter lui-même son *admittatur*, qu'il fallait lui adresser ma Commission avec une lettre, qu'il se chargeait de m'obtenir cet admittatur et de me le faire passer, et que d'ailleurs vous étiez, en Ce moment, à votre Campagne à Cent lieues plus loin que Washington-city.

privé, par ces Contretems, de la jouissance Que je m'étais promise, je me suis rendu à mon poste où j'attendrai pour Entrer En éxersice, que Vous Veuilliez bien m'accorder mon admittatur.—je me regarderais bien heureux d'une occasion où je pusse vous aprocher et vous témoigner de vive voix Combien ardement je Desire obtenir votre estime. je vous prie de Croire, Monsieur le président, que je ferai tout pour la mériter et pour vous Convaincre de mon profond respect.   Lequinio Kerblay

I think, sir Président, it should Been much more Convenient to Write my letter in english, but I am yet so little acquainted With this language, that I Can not in it but Write very Badily, and perhaps in such rud a manner as to be not understood; from another Way taking right Consideration of your extensive skill, I don't doubt you are learned in french as Well as in english tongue; Both theze reasons, sir president, have produced my Determination, and I hope you be so good as to pardon it.

EDITORS' TRANSLATION

Newport, 20 June 1802—1 Messidor, Year
Mister President,   10 of the French Republic

I have the honor of sending you two letters, enclosed, one from Mr. Lafayette, the other from Mr. Liancourt, which I had high hopes of giving you in person. Having been named by the first consul vice commissary of French commercial relations in Newport, my plan was to pay my respects and solicit your approval. Your personal virtues, Mister President, and distinguished reputation rendered this duty very pleasant. But Citizen Pichon, our commissary general, whom I met in Philadelphia, told me that it was not customary: that no commissary or vice commissary of French commercial relations had ever gone directly to solicit his own admittatur. He said I should send him my appointment with a letter; he would be responsible for obtaining the admittatur and forwarding it to me. He said, further, that you were one hundred leagues from Washington right now, in your country home.

Since this disappointing turn of events prevents me from having the pleasure I had promised myself, I came directly to Newport, where I shall wait until you graciously grant my admittatur and I can take up my position. I would consider myself very fortunate to be able to meet you and tell you in person how ardently I wish to earn your esteem. I assure you, Mister President, that I will do everything to merit that esteem and to convince you of my deep respect.   Lequinio Kerblay

RC (MoSHi: Jefferson Papers); on printed letterhead stationery of the Republic of France including the heading "Relations commerciales de France" and "Lequinio Kerblay, Sous-commissaire des Relations commerciales de France à Newport, en Rhode-Island, États-unis d'Amérique" (identifying Lequinio de Kerblay as vice commissary for commercial relations of France at Newport); endorsed by TJ as received 2 July and so

recorded in SJL. Enclosures: (1) La Rochefoucauld-Liancourt to TJ, [11 Jan. 1802]. (2) Lafayette to TJ, 30 Jan. 1802.

Joseph Marie Lequinio de Kerblay (1740-1813), whose name also appears without "de Kerblay," was originally from near Vannes in western France. After engaging in the practice of law, he was an early and eager participant in the French Revolution, rising from local and regional offices to the national legislative assembly and the National Convention. He was denounced in 1795 for the brutality of his actions two years earlier, when he was the Convention's representative in the suppression of counterrevolutionary uprisings in the west of France. Those charges were later lifted by a blanket amnesty, and following Bonaparte's rise to power as first consul, Lequinio was named as a forest inspector and, subsequently, as commissary of commercial relations at Newport, Rhode Island. Some of his writings on agriculture and political economy were published but drew little attention. He sent one of his works, a description of a trip through the French department of Jura, to TJ in July (*Biographie universelle*, 24:243-4; J. C. F. Hoefer, *Nouvelle biographie générale depuis les temps les plus reculés jusqu'a nos jours*, 46 vols. [Paris, 1855-66], 30:860-2; Lequinio de Kerblay to TJ, 15 July 1802).

ADMITTATUR: Louis André Pichon wrote to Madison from Philadelphia on 29 May enclosing the commissions of Lequinio de Kerblay and Pierre Jean Marie Sotin de la Condière, who was to be the French commissary of commercial relations at Savannah, Georgia. TJ signed exequaturs officially recognizing Lequinio and Sotin on 15 June (FCs in Lb, DNA: RG 59, Exequaturs; Madison, *Papers, Sec. of State Ser.*, 3:269).

Memorandum from the Treasury Department

List of Collectors, who have not rendered accompts up to the 31. December 1801.

Joseph Hiller,	Coll: Salem	Accts. rendd. for 3d qr. 1801.	
Samuel R Gerry,	" Marblehead	"	" 1. do.
Joshua Head,	" Waldoboro'	"	" 3. do.
James Macconnell	" Louisville	"	" 3. do.

William Chribbs   " Massac   (He has rendd. a few very informal abstracts of tonnage and of duties on mdze for the 1. qr. 1802. and for the month of april following; but has rendd. no returns for 1801.)

David Duncan   " Michilimakinac   He has made no returns.

Note. This list embraces those Collectors only who are now in office.

Nn. Lufborough
Comptroller's Office,
20. June 1802.

S. R. Gerry, J. M'Connel, & W. Chribbs must be removed. On the subject of M'connel an official representation has already been made to the President. The continued neglect of Mr Gerry renders further indulgence improper. We were deceived in Chribbs by the recommendations; he is an infamous character. An official representation will in a few days be made in relation to both. D. Duncan cannot yet have made any reports. The annexed draft is intended for Hiller & Head—   A. G.

MS (DLC); in the hands of Lufborough and Gallatin; with note in TJ's hand below Gallatin's initials: "I am ready to appoint any person whom mr Gallatin shall approve in these cases. Th:J." (see TJ to Gallatin, 21 June); endorsed by TJ as received from the Treasury Department on 20 June and so recorded in SJL with notation "delinquent collectors." Enclosure: see below.

Nathan Lufborough, a clerk in the comptroller's office, prepared this list of delinquent collectors that Gallatin forwarded to the president. Lufborough began working in the Treasury Department before the federal government moved to Washington, D.C., in 1800. He remained in the comptroller's office throughout TJ's administration, becoming the chief clerk. William Duane characterized him as an "Aristocrat" (Gallatin, *Papers*, 6:334, 354, 936; Cunningham, *Process of Government*, 328, 332; ASP, *Finance*, 1:811).

OFFICIAL REPRESENTATION HAS ALREADY BEEN MADE: Gallatin sent TJ two letters on 8 Dec. 1801 (now missing), regarding the Louisville collector (see Vol. 36:681). For the Treasury secretary's recommendation that James McConnell be replaced, see also Gallatin to TJ, 24 Apr. 1802.

CONTINUED NEGLECT: for the earlier investigation of Samuel R. Gerry's accounts, see Gallatin to TJ, 24 Dec. 1801. William C. C. Claiborne and others supported William Chribbs (Vol. 35:392). Gallatin sent TJ more details on both collectors on 6 July.

The ANNEXED DRAFT has not been found, but Gallatin sent Joshua Head a letter dated 21 June. In that correspondence, the Treasury secretary drew attention to the 20 Aug. 1801 circular to collectors, which noted "that a rigid adherence to the regulation of rendering each quarterly account," prior to the expiration of the next quarter, was "indispensably necessary." The Treasury Department had not received Head's accounts for the last quarter of 1801, which were due 31 Mch. Gallatin requested notification on the reasons for the delay. A postscript indicated that no weekly returns had been received from the collector since 30 Sep. 1801 (Tr in DLC; in a clerk's hand, signed by Gallatin; at head of text: "Copy"). Gallatin enclosed the transcript of this letter to TJ on 19 Aug. 1802 (second letter).

From a "True Friend, Alltho a woman"

HONNORED SIR/   Lankester County June th20. 1802

Being at the City of Washington the latter end of the siting of Congress, & in the house whare Arthor St. Clare, as I understood, with a Major Zigler, & a Number of Men from the N. Western Country, whare St. Clare is govener, I apprehended that they ware treasenably inclined, from there discorse, in several evenings that I set in the next room, St. Clare said that Thomas Jefferson, the presidant was, A damed Villon & Albert Gallaten, was no better, & as he St. Clare as Govener, had very great influance in pittsburg, haveing two sons in that quarter, & one an Offiser in the garrison in fort pitt & a Son at Chilacothey, that was states atturney, & one at Cincinata & one at

Montgomary County whos Names I do not remember, but he said
that he was Collector of the tax's, on stills & Carrages, for that district, & that a Cornal Nicholas, at pootsgrove in the same County
with a Wm. Nicholas, who was if I under stood Marshall of that district that the above mentiond persons, had all sworn to do all in there
power, to turn you out of Offis, or sacrafise them selves in the attemt.
the reason I did not right before was I wanted to consult my husband,
who said it ought to be maid known to you whih I now do. I think it
my duty due to the president, in order that he may be apprised of it,
as I think it is a deep lad scame against you, you Honnored Sir, will
never know whom I am, but be asured your well wisher, & True
friend, alltho a woman.

RC (DLC); at foot of text: "Thos.
Jefferson Esqr."; endorsed by TJ as re-
ceived from "Anon." on 6 July and
"St. Clair" and so recorded in SJL.

MAJOR ZIGLER: David Zeigler, of Lancaster County, Pennsylvania, was a Revolutionary War veteran and former major
in the United States Army. As a witness
at the inquiry into Arthur St. Clair's disastrous Indian campaign of 1791, Zeigler
provided testimony that confirmed the
supply and logistical difficulties faced by
St. Clair's army. Resigning his commission in 1792, Zeigler settled in Cincinnati.
TJ appointed him marshal for Ohio in
1803 (Washington, *Papers, Rev. War
Ser.*, 13:216; *Pres. Ser.*, 10:15; William
Henry Engle, ed., *Notes and Queries Historical, Biographical and Genealogical Relating Chiefly to Interior Pennsylvania,
Annual Volume, 1897* [Harrisburg, 1898;

repr. Baltimore, 1970], 1-2; Smith,
St. Clair Papers, 2:290-2; JEP, 1:447).

St. Clair's SONS included Arthur
St. Clair, Jr., the attorney general for
the Northwest Territory, and Daniel
St. Clair, a veteran of the American Revolution and a collector of internal revenues
in Montgomery County, Pennsylvania.
St. Clair's son-in-law, Samuel Robb,
resided in Cincinnati (Engle, *Notes and
Queries*, 58-9, 62-3, 68-70; ASP, *Miscellaneous*, 1:282; Vol. 36:465).

CORNAL NICHOLAS: probably Colonel
Francis Nichols, a former officer in the
Continental army and resident of Potts-
grove, Pennsylvania. His brother, William Nichols, also a Revolutionary War
veteran, served as the U.S. marshal for
Pennsylvania from 1795 to 1799 (Syrett,
Hamilton, 16:484n; 18:233-4; PMHB, 20
[1896], 504; 24 [1900], 234-5; Heitman, *Register*, 413-14; JEP, 1:189, 325).

From Willem H. van Hasselt

MONSIEUR LE PRESIDENT   Hague le 20 Juin 1802

Il vous souviendra peut etre qu'il y a environ quatre ans, que je
prenais la liberté, de m'adresser a vous par lettre, souhaitant de trouver un emploi chez vous et sous votre toit que je pencais alors ne pouvoir trouver dans toute l'Amerique. Jetais alors dans l'idée que vous
avies une jeune famille Je m'offrais sous le titre de faire les fonctions
de Gouverneur aupres d'eux pour veiller a leur education. Je fus deçu
dans mon attente. Il est vrai vous m'honoriez d'une reponse polie,

come Jattendais d'une personne qui avait vu le monde; Mais Monsieur non obstant tous le menagement que vous gardies dans vos expressions, il y avait une Monosillabe de trop, qui ne laissait pas de me donner de la paine, Si je me souviens bien, de vos expressions car votre lettre il y a longtemps que je ne l'ai plus, vous disies *If I had those qualifications, it would not be difficult for me to find a place in Charleston.* Cet *if* Monsieur me Chifonait beaucoup. Je savais tres bien qú'un homme qui a vu son monde un Philosophe ne pouvait pas ignorer que ce monde fourmille d'escrocs, qu'il etait de sa prudence de s'en garder, en particulier a l'egard d'un inconnu, Mais alors je me souvenais aussi que je vous avais accusé des personnes qui me connaissaint, chez qui vous pouviez vous avoir informé quel etait mon caractere mes principes, avec les quels javais vecu comme de niveau, et qui n'etaient pas de la lie du peuple, il me vint bien dans l'esprit que peut etre la difference des principes politiques pouvait avoir rendu, particulierement dans ces temps cette discussion plus difficile, qu'elle ne valait et comme on dit que le jeu ne valait pas la chandelle. cependant tout cela ne Me Mettait pas a mon aise: Permettez-Moi d'avouer franchement que jy trouvais un espece de soupçon qui Me blessait cetait une nouvelle lecon a aprendre pour moi, a laquelle je n'etais pas trop accoutumé: Vous ne consideriez pas, qu aiant vecu avec ces personnes, sur un pied d'egalité, qúi ne me souffrait pas de pencer que je pourrais me produire sous les apparences d'un miserable pedagogue, et d'etre mesuré du haut en bas par des gens qui auparavant avaient recherche ma compagnie, l'idée de cet abaissement me paraissait insuportable; l'amour que je sens pour la liberté mon amour propre refuserent entierement de s'y soumettre, javais deja fait des efforts pour m'offrir a vous a un homme dont je respectais le caractere. que faire donc? Jetais venu en Amerique avec un honete capital forcé de quiter mon pais, a cause des Cabales, intrigues les usurpations du Stathouder, contre lesquelles je m'etais toujours oppose autant que javais pu, ici je ne connaissais ni etais connu de personne, je ne savais a qui me fier, tous les visages promettaient de la sincérite,—mais ce n'etaient que des visages. je resolus de me regler sur la conduite du publicq et celui qúi etait le mieux accueilli aurait la premiere place dans ma confidence. Je me trompais grossierement encore, j ai eté plumé derobé par des speculateurs, qui ne manquaient pas l'aveu du public, Vous devez avoir connu aumoins par reputation le fameux Commodore A Gillon lui seul m'enlevait une somme de 7000 Livres Sterlin, je souffrais des failllites, des banqueroutes dans les deux Carolines & en Virginie Meme tout cela me rendait incapable de vivre sur un pied de decence au quel j'etais acoutumé. Dans ces circonstances Votre lettre Monsieur me parvint a Statesburgh, elle me desarçonnait entierement, ne sachant ou donner de la tête. Tout d'un coup comme par inspiration, il me vient dans l'idee de m'enfoncer dans les bois de l'ouest. J'avais assez de Philosophie pour n'etre pas effraie de l'idee que je n'y trouverais que la nature brute des gens qui n'avaient aucune idee d'un commerce ou Societé rationale j'avais assez lu assez pensé pour me suffire a moi même: cette idee n'e-tait pas sitot née que mise en execution. Jarrivais donc ici. La pre-miere chose qúi m'occupait et qui occuperait tout homme d'un Sens commun etait d'examiner le local, l'air, le climat le Sol et puis le pro-gres de l'agriculture: Je trouvais l'air serein et pur, un climat moderé, un Sol assez fertile, ou au moins il ne s'y trouvait aucune terre en-tierement Sterile pareille a ces plages sabloneuses, qu'on rencontre a tout bout de champ dans ces plats pais voisins de l'ocean. l'eau de Source pure legere et delicieuse. En consequence des debris de ma fortune, je m'achetais une petite terre, je me batis un bicoque, que les gens du pais apellaient une jolie maison faute de Savoir mieux. Mon premier Soin fut de me faire et cultiver un jardin, autre Phenomene rare pour ces etres peu instruits. Mais lorsque Je considerais les pro-gres de l'agricultúre je les trouvais extremement negligés et mesquin. presque l'unique attention des agricoles etait tournée vers la culture du Mäis, et chacun plantait autant qu'il croiait suffire aux besoins de sa famille si l'annee etait mauvaise il se trouvait fort a l'etroit, faute de circulation d'especes, car tout echange presque se fait ici par troc: Si la Saison etait avantageuse le surplus etait porté au distilaleur pour le tourner en Whisky cela produsait deux effect extremement perni-cieux, encourageant la paresse et l'ivrognerie, l'on buvait sa liqueur au Cabaret, on jurait on se querellait on se battait, sans aucun regard pour la decence les bonnes Moeurs ou la situation de leurs familles qui tres souvent par la etaient destituées du necessaire. Si l'on avait besoin d'un peu de Monoie l'on plantait du tabac ou du coton. Mais toutes ces denrées etaient trop Volumineuses pour s'en promettre beaucoup d'avantage. les distances des marchés trop grandes fai-saient que tout le gain que le cultivateur s'en promettait s'absorbait dans les frais de transport, tout devant aller par terre les rivieres etant innavigables par des Cataractes ou bas fonds. il etait donc facile a voir qú'il leur falait une denrée si precieúse qúe les frais de chariage ne pouvait pas sensiblement empieter sur le revenant de la marchandise Je m'imaginais donc, que rien ne leur conviendrait Mieux qu'a elever des vers a Soie et consequement de planter et cultiver le Murier blanc comme le Seul capable de produire de tres bonne soie comme ce pais peut donner. Je sai quon l'a tenté a Purisburg Ebeneser et autres

places, avec peu de succes, mais ils n'avaient qu'a en accuser leur ignorance, n'ayant que decredite cette riche branche de commerce:
cependent comment persuader a des gens si simples si ignorants, que
cette ignorance parait Marqué au coin de l'idiotisme, d'entreprendre
un ouvrage dont jamais ils n'avaient entendu parler. Jaurais preche
cette doctrine ad Kalendas grecas Sans jamais avancer dune ligne. il
ne me restait donc rien a faire que de precher d'exemple. je me mis
donc en devoir de poursuivre mon plan, avec beaucoup de difficulté
Je me procurais quelques pieds de cet abre que jai triple depuis par
provignement et mes arbres plantés depuis trois ans viennent bien.
Peut etre Monsieur il vous surprendra qu'un Hollandais s'avise d'entreprendre de faire de la Soie ou la Hollande est un pais humide et
froid peu adaptée a cet espece de culture, et c'etait l'opinion generale
dans ce Pais, Mais comme je n'ai jamais fait beaucoup de fond sur les
opinions et prejugés du vulgaire, javais le courage etant en Hollande,
d'attaquer cette Hydre a cent têtes. en consequence J'etudiais cet object et malgré les obstacles d'un climat peu favorable, je reussissait
assez bien, & autant que la Societé de Savants de Harlem, dont je suis
Membre, m'invita de leur communiquer Mes observations: Je le fis
et vous trouverez mon Esquisse au volume 17, part 2 de leurs transactions. depuis mon arrivée dans ce pais, residant sur l'Ahslyrive jai
repeté mes recherches, et jai trouvé que ce pais est ún des Meilleurs
au monde pour produire des plus belles soies. dans l'année 1787 je
fis part du resultat de mes recherches à la Societé d'agricultúre a
Charleston. on a publié cette lettre avec une des votres, dans la quelle
vous tachiez a les persuade à encourager la propagation de l'olivier,
mais ma lettre à eté abregé de la sorte et mutilée autant qu'elle ne pro-
duisit aucun effect. Mais pour revenir a mon Sujet, pour la premiere
fois jai fait ún petit essai pour voir, si la grande idée que je metais for-
mée de la bonté du climat et du Sol, etait fondée sur dassez bonnes
raisons, et a ma satisfaction je trouve que je ne m'etais pas trompé;
pour cet effect je prens la liberté de vous presenter un echantillon du
premier essai. vous considerés s'il vous plait que cette Soie etant faite
a l'aide des mains rudes, qui n'avaient rien vu de pareil, que par con-
sequant le coup dessai ne saurait etre ún coup de Maitre et vous en
concluerez que le tirage de la Soie peut etre porté a une perfection in-
definitivement plus grande, et malgre cela je ne hesite pas a vous l'en-
voier comme le patron de tous ceux qui s'occupent du bien etre de la
Republique, vous priant de montrer ces Echevaux au Manufacturiers
en soie a Philadelphie pour avoir leur sentiment sur la bonte ou des
defauts de cette Soie. pourquoi jose vous prier de ne pas permettre
qu'elle passe trop les mains avant que les Manufacturiers l'ont vue,

afin qú'elle ne perde pas de son lustre et consequament de sa valeúr, Ma tache sera de multiplier mes arbres autant que je púis pour les distribuer gratis aux gens du pais qui paraissent en prendre du gout pour cette espece de Culture. Mais Monsieur une chose essencielle nous manque pour obtenir tout le succes que je desirerais. Tous les Muriers blancs en Ameriqúe sans exception sont des sauvageons, tout ce qui provient de la graine est de meme, et quoi que je conviens que le Sauvageon prodúit une belle soie, cependent elle est trop legere et ne profite pas le cultivateur, outre que cet arbre ne provient pas si bien, sa feuille est petite dechiquetée, et en cuillant année par année la feuille de cet arbre il devient buissonneux et de la plus difficile Cuillette. le Murier noir natif de ce pais ne vaut rien, sa feuille est rude Coriasse couverte d'un duvet et remplie d'un acide qui ne conviennent pas au ver qui la rejettent. Le Murier Espagnol a grande fúille ne vaut presque pas mieux mais en France on use la feuille du Murier qui est apellé le Murier d'italie: Dans le Lionois le haut Dauphiné Sevennes Provence il va sous le nom de Murier Rose, cet arbre croit rapidement fait des belles pousses, sa feuille est grande lisse d'un beau Vernis sans etre dechiquetée. Monsieur Thome un des meilleurs Autheurs que jai lu sur ce sujet, et j'en ai lu plusieurs, dans ses reponses sur les questions faites a lui par la Societe Roiale d'agriculture a Lions en parle avec enthousiasme "Le Murier Rose (dit il) est non seulement le plus convenable a la nouriture des vers a Soie mais il est encore celui, qui fournit la feuille en la plus grande abondance, nous avons comparé les depouilles de sa feuille a l'age de huit ans, contre un sauvageon de meme age, planté dans le meme champ: le premier nous a donné cinquante livres de feuilles; le second n'en pas eu dix livres, la depouille du premier a ete faite en moins de trente minutes, et celle du second a occupé le cuilleur une matinee entiere." je parle de cet arbre Monsieúr avec connaissance de Cause, je le possedais en Hollande javais meme embarqué avec moi une Douzaine. Mais les matelots les tuaient toús en les ecorchant a bord. Cest donc cet arbre qúil nous faut pour bien reusir dans cette entreprise, ma petite fortune ne me permet pas de pousser trop loin ma bonhomie, outre que je ne saurais comment m'y prendre: autrefois j'entretenais un commerce de lettres avec quelques Français, mais comme ils etaient toús de la noblesse, la derniere revolution les a tous dispersés ou detruits et je ne sai ce quils sont devenus. Mais Monsieur Vous qui etes a la tête de toute magistrature, vous pourries effectuer plus par un mot, que moi par des années de supplications. Si vous croiez que mon plan tend au bien de la Societé, car je ne dis-conviens pas que c'est ma marotte, et par la Capable de faire des chateaux en espagne quoi que cet un plaisir reël pour moi de pencer que je pourrais rendre quelque Service a ce pais avant ma mort car Je me fais vieux, et je dois pencer que mon tatoo bat deja quoi que encore assez robuste: ne me resentant pas beaucoup des infirmités de l'age, je considere pourtant cela comme un bien Ephemere qui peut s'echaper a tout moment, je voudrais vous prier de prendre cette tache sur vous, de faire venir quelques pieds de ce Murier Rose greffé, une douzaine suffirait, noús pourrions tres vite les multiplier par la greffe. toút ce qúi provient de sa graine est derechef sauvageon, quoi que d'une bonne espece. Si ma proposition vous plait, faites Moi l'honneur de me faire deux mots de reponce: et comme ma retraite est si hors de chemin ayez la bonté d'adresser votre lettre a Monsieur Florian Charles Mey commerçant et mon agent a Charleston, il sait ou m'adresser mes lettres. Excusez Monsieúr la longueur de cette lettre, qui vous a peut etre detenu des afaires plus importantes. La raison que je vous ecris celle ci en français etait, que ma lettre Anglaise n'ayant pas fait fortune, je voudrais essaier si ún autre dialecte vous plairait d'avantage, si encore celle ci ne me reusit pas, et je me trouverais dans la necessite de vous importuner une troisieme fois je vous ecrirai en Italien ma langue favorite, comme la plus harmonieuse, la plus sonore, et qui flatte le plus l'oreille, et si je súis bien informé vous la possedez γραφικως excusez ce petit mot grec il etait au bout de ma plume et je ne trouvais aucun Epethete français qui me revenait. Au reste je fais les veux les plus sinceres Monsieúr pour votre bien etre je sens fortement combien vous etes necessaire au bonheur des inhabitans de ce pais, je n'irai pas detailler ceci de peur d'etre cru un flatteur, mais cela jajouterai que jai cru que c'etait ún grand bonheur pour l'Amerique que dans la situation ou elle se trouvait, vous parvintes a la premiere Magistrature. je ne laisse pas d'inculquer cela a ceux qui avoisinent mon petit domaine, car je ne laisse pas d'avoir quelque influence sur leur façon de penser, qúi me croient quasi ún Demosthene un Ciceron puis que je sais lire et ecrire. je ne cesserai pas de faire des voeux pour votre prosperité et contentement etant avec un tres profond respect

Monsieur le President Votre tres Humble tres obeis: Serviteur

W H Van Hasselt

P.S. S'il vous ferait plaisir Monsieur d'avoir le desein de mon tour pour tirer la soie fait ici sous mes auspices qui est d'apres le celebre Vaucançon qúi file a deux echevaux a double croisiere et que jai la vanité de croire que jai corrigé de quelques defauts au moins qúi est superieur au toúr de Toscane dont on a fait tant de vacarme sans raison. vous n'avez qu'a le vouloir et je vous enverrai le plan.

excusez les fautes contre le francais que je puis avoir commises considerant quil y a pres de vingt ans que je n'ai presque pas parlé, ou ecrit dans, cette langue—

E D I T O R S '   T R A N S L A T I O N

Mister President Hague, [South Carolina], 20 June 1802

You may remember that about four years ago I took the liberty of writing to you, hoping to find a position which I did not believe I could find anywhere else in America, in your service and under your roof. Thinking at the time that you had a young family, I proposed my services to be their preceptor and to watch over their education. My hope was disappointed. It is true that you honored me with a courteous response, as I expected from someone who had travelled widely, but despite all the care you took in expressing yourself, Sir, there was one monosyllable too many, which has not stopped wounding me. If I remember the words accurately, since it has been a long time since I have had your letter in hand, you said that *if I had those qualifications, it would not be difficult for me to find a place in Charleston.* That *if,* Sir, irritated me greatly. I knew very well that a man who has seen the world as a philosophe could not be unaware that the world teems with swindlers and that it is prudent to protect oneself from them, especially in relation to an unknown person. But then I also remembered that I gave you references to people who knew me, from whom you could learn about my character and principles. Since I had lived with them as an equal and they were not the dregs of the population, it occurred to me that perhaps the difference in our political principles had made this discussion more difficult than necessary and, as they say, it was not worth the trouble. Nevertheless, this did not reassure me. Let me admit frankly that I felt a kind of suspicion that wounded me. It was a new lesson for me, to which I was not accustomed. You did not take into account that having lived with these people, on an equal footing, it pained me to think I could appear to them like a miserable pedagogue, and be measured from head to toe by those who had previously sought my company. I could not abide the idea of stooping to this. My pride, my love of liberty, totally refused to submit to this. I had already tried to offer my services to you, as a man whose character I respected. What more could I do? I came to America with an honest capital, forced to leave my country because of the plots, intrigues, and usurpations of the stadtholder, which I had always opposed as much as I could. I did not know anyone here, nor did anyone know me; I did not know whom to trust. All faces promised sincerity, but they were only faces. I resolved to align myself with public opinion; the person who was most favored would have first place in my trust. Once again, I was badly mistaken. I was fleeced and hoodwinked by speculators whom the public respected. You must have known, at least by reputation, the famous Commodore A. Gillon. He alone stole the sum of 7000 pounds Sterling. I endured bankruptcies in the two Carolinas and Virginia. All of that prevented me from living at the level of decency to which I was accustomed. Amid all these circumstances, Sir, your letter reached me in Statesburg; I was dumbfounded, reeling. All of a sudden, as if by inspiration, I had the idea of plunging into the western woods. I had had enough philosophy not to be terrified by the idea that I would find only the brute nature of people who had no idea of commerce or rational society. I had read enough and thought enough to be self-sufficient. This idea was no sooner hatched than enacted. I thus arrived here. The first thing that occupied me, and would occupy any sensible man, was to examine the area, climate, soil, and the state of agriculture. I found pure, calm air, a moderate climate, a relatively fertile soil, or at least an absence of totally barren soil like these sandy beaches one finds in every field in the plains near the ocean. The water came from a source that was pure, clear, and delicious. Given the paltry remains of my fortune, I bought a small plot of land and built myself a hut, which the locals called a pretty house, for want of knowing better. My first concern was to plant and tend a garden, another rare phenomenon for these uneducated people. But when I considered the state of agriculture, I found it extremely neglectful and paltry. The farmers devoted almost all their attention to raising corn, and each one planted what he thought would suffice for the needs of his family. If the year was bad, he found himself in dire straits, given the lack of circulating currency, since barter is the prevalent form of commerce here. If the season was bountiful, the surplus was taken to the distiller to turn into whisky. This produced two extremely pernicious effects: encouraging laziness and drunkenness. People drank liquor at the bar; they swore; they quarreled; they fought, with no regard for the decency of good society or their families, who were very often destitute. If they needed a little money, they planted tobacco or cotton, but these goods were too voluminous to offer much advantage. Because the markets were so far away, a farmer's profit was totally absorbed by transportation costs, since everything had to travel overland. The rivers were unnavigable because of waterfalls or shallowness. It was easy to see that they needed a crop valuable enough to compensate for the transportation costs. I decided what would suit them best was to raise silkworms and to plant and cultivate white mulberries, the only tree that can produce very good silk, which this country can. I know it was tried in Purysburg, Ebenezer, and elsewhere with little success, but they could only blame their ignorance, and simply brought discredit upon this rich branch of commerce. Yet how can one persuade such simple, ignorant people that it is sheer idiocy to undertake a project they had never heard of? I could have preached that doctrine *ad calendas grecas* without progressing one iota. My only choice therefore was to preach by example, so I set about pursuing my plan. With great difficulty I obtained a few mulberry cuttings which I have since trebled by grafting. My planted trees have been doing well for three years. You may be surprised, Sir, that a Dutchman should undertake to make silk, since Holland is a damp, cold country, unsuitable for this kind of cultivation. That was the general opinion in Europe. But since I have never given much credence to the opinions and prejudices of uneducated people, I had the courage, in Holland, to attack this hundred-headed hydra. As a consequence, I studied the topic and, despite the handicaps of a rather unfavorable climate, I succeeded enough to be invited to share my observations with the Haarlem society of savants, of which I am a member. I did so, and you will find my sketch in volume 17, part 2, of their proceedings. Since my arrival in this country, living on the banks of the Ashley River, I have gone through the same process and found that this is one of the best places in the world to produce beautiful silk. In 1787 I shared the results of my research with the Agricultural Society of South Carolina. They published this letter with one of yours, in which you sought to encourage the cultivation of olive trees. My letter was abridged and garbled so much, however, that it did not produce any effect. But to return to my subject: for the first time, I undertook a small experiment to see if the broad concept I had formed about the auspiciousness of the climate and soil was sufficiently well founded. To my satisfaction, I found that I was not mistaken. I am taking the liberty of giving you a sample of the first trial. If you take into account that this silk was made with the help of rough hands that had never seen anything like it, and therefore that the first attempt cannot be a masterpiece, you will conclude that silk production can be brought to immeasurably greater perfection. Nevertheless, I do not hesitate to send it to you as the patron of all those who watch over the well-being of the republic. I ask you to show these skeins to the silk manufacturers in Philadelphia to obtain their opinion on the quality or defects of this silk. Please take care that it isn't touched too much before the manufacturers see it, lest it lose its luster and hence its value. My goal is to multiply my trees as much as possible in order to give them out gratis to any local people who show an interest in this kind of cultivation. But one essential thing is lacking, Sir, to obtain the success I wish: all the white mulberry trees in America, without exception, are wild, as are all that come from seeds. And although I agree that wild stock produces beautiful silk, it is nevertheless too light and does not benefit the farmer; besides, this tree does not replicate very well; its leaves are small and jagged. Harvesting them year after year makes them tougher and harder to cut. The indigenous black mulberry is worthless; its leaves are rough, tough, covered with fuzz, and filled with an acid that does not suit silkworms, which reject it. Spanish mulberry, with its large leaves, is hardly better. In France they use the leaves of the Italian mulberry. In the regions of Lyons, Upper Dauphiné, the Cévennes, and Provence, it is called rose mulberry. This tree grows quickly and produces good shoots. Its leaves are large, smooth, and nicely shiny without being jagged. The Royal Society of Agriculture in Lyons addressed a series of questions to Mr. Thome, one of the best authors I have read on this subject (and I have read several). In his answers he spoke enthusiastically about it: "The rose mulberry is not only the most appropriate for nourishing silkworms but it is also the one that furnishes the most leaves. We compared the remains of eight-year-old leaves with those of a wild tree of the same age, planted in the same field. The first had produced fifty pounds of leaves; the second not even ten pounds. The first was harvested in less than thirty minutes; the second took all morning." I talk about this tree, Sir, with firsthand knowledge. I had one in Holland and even brought a dozen with me, but the sailors on the ship killed them all by removing the bark. That is the tree we need to succeed in this endeavor. My small fortune does not allow me to push my magnanimity too far, not to mention the fact that I do not know how to proceed. Previously, I was in correspondence with Frenchmen, but since they were all noblemen, the last revolution dispersed or destroyed them and I do not know what has become of them. But you, Sir, who oversee the entire government, you could accomplish more with one word that I could through years of supplication, if you believe my plan would enhance the well-being of society. I do not deny it is something of an obsession, and these might be pipe dreams, but it is a real pleasure for me to think that I might render service to this country before dying. For I am growing old and my tattoo is already beating. Although I am still relatively robust and do not feel many of the infirmities of old age, I nevertheless consider good health to be an ephemeral good which can vanish at any moment. I ask you to take this task upon yourself, to send for some shoots of this grafted rose mulberry. A dozen would suffice. We could multiply them quickly through grafting. If you find favor in my plan, do me the honor of a brief reply. Since my hideaway is off the road, be good enough to address your letter to a businessman, Mr. Florian Charles Mey, who is my agent in Charleston. He knows where to forward my letters. The reason I am writing this letter in French is because I did not achieve success with my English letter, so I am trying another dialect you might like more. If this one does not succeed, I will feel obliged to bother you a third time, writing in Italian, which is my favorite language, since it is the most harmonious, the most musical, the most flattering to the ear. I have it on good information that you have knowledge of its writing (γραφικως, *graphikôs*). Excuse this little word in Greek; it was on the tip of my pen and no French word came to mind. Finally, I send my sincerest wishes, Sir, for your well-being. I feel strongly how necessary you are to the happiness of the inhabitants of this country. I will not detail this, for fear of being taken as a flatterer, but I will add that I believed it was fortunate for America, in the situation in which it found itself, for you to become the chief executive. I do not cease inculcating this in those who surround my small domain, for I continue to have some influence on their thinking. They consider me a kind of Demosthenes or Cicero because I know how to read and write. I will not stop wishing for your prosperity and serenity, being, with a very deep respect, Mister President, your very humble and obedient Servant.

W H VAN HASSELT

P.S. My silk is made on a spindle, inspired by the famous Vaucanson, which is built here under my supervision. It spins two two-ply skeins. I flatter myself into thinking that I corrected some defects and that it is better than the Tuscan spindle which is so unjustly acclaimed. If you would like to have the design of my spindle, simply ask and I will send it to you.

Forgive the errors I may have made in French, considering that I have barely spoken or written the language for almost twenty years.

RC (DLC); blotted; endorsed by TJ as received from "Hague S.C." on 23 Aug. 1802 and so recorded in SJL.

LA LIBERTÉ DE M'ADRESSER A VOUS PAR LETTRE: van Hasselt wrote to TJ from Charleston, South Carolina, in June 1797 (Vol. 29:465-8).

VOUS DISIES IF I HAD THOSE QUALIFICATIONS: in his reply in August 1797, TJ explained that he did not need van Hasselt's offered services as a children's tutor. TJ then wrote: "I trust with confidence however that qualifications as good as yours, with views as moderate, cannot fail of meeting employment advantageous and agreeble to yourself" (Vol. 29:518).

Like van Hasselt, Alexander GILLON was a native of Holland. From the 1760s until his death in 1794, Gillon was a resident of South Carolina, where he was a merchant, politician, and real estate developer. In more than one instance, his handling of funds was controversial. He received the rank of commodore as the chief officer of South Carolina's naval forces during the American Revolution. Van Hasselt had first traveled to the United States aboard Gillon's ship (*S.C. Biographical Directory, House of Representatives*, 3:268-72; ANB; Vol. 29:466).

PURISBURG EBENESER ET AUTRES PLACES: Purysburg (or Purrysburg), South Carolina, and Ebenezer, Georgia, were both settled in the 1730s by European colonists—people from Switzerland, in the case of Purysburg, and from Salzburg in the case of Ebenezer. In both locales, silk production was an important economic activity during the colonial period, and the inhabitants planted white mulberry trees to supply food for the silkworms. The industry declined around the time of the American Revolution due to high labor costs, the loss of bounties and other incentives, and disruptions of war. Ebenezer was near the Savannah River, about 25 miles northwest of the city of Savannah. Purysburg was on the Savannah River a few miles downstream from Ebenezer (Joseph Ewan, "Silk Culture in the Colonies: With Particular Reference to the Ebenezer Colony and the First Local Flora of Georgia," *Agricultural History*, 43 [1969], 133-4, 137-8; James C. Bonner, "Silk Growing in the Georgia Colony," same, 146-7; George Fenwick Jones, *The Salzburger Saga: Religious Exiles and Other Germans Along the Savannah* [Athens, Ga., 1984], 14-15, 17, 66, 93, 104; Robert L. Meriwether, *The Expansion of South Carolina, 1729-1765* [Kingsport, Tenn., 1940], 34-7, 254; Jedidiah Morse, *The American Gazetteer*, 2d ed. [Charlestown, Mass., 1804]). Regarding silk production in the United States, see also Tench Coxe's letter to TJ of 22 Feb. 1802.

AD KALENDAS GRECAS: "never," or in the present context, "forever." The expression, recorded by Suetonius in his life of Augustus, refers to something that will occur on a nonexistent date (Evelyn S. Shuckburgh, ed., *C. Suetoni Tranquilli. Divus Augustus* [Cambridge, 1896], 155; F. P. Leverett, ed., *A New and Copious Lexicon of the Latin Language*, new ed. [Philadelphia, 1888], 113).

The Hollandsche Maatschappij der Wetenschappen, or Holland Society of Sciences, was founded at Haarlem (HARLEM) in 1752. Van Hasselt became a member in 1777 (Johan Abraham Bierens de Haan, *De Hollandsche Maatschappij der Wetenschappen, 1752-1952* [Haarlem, 1952], 273, 385).

PROPAGATION DE L'OLIVIER: writing from Paris on 30 July 1787, TJ addressed a long letter to William Drayton about rice and his observations of the cultivation of almonds, figs, capers, and other plants and trees in southern France and Genoa. TJ devoted a lengthy paragraph of that letter to the olive, "a tree the least known in America, and yet the most worthy of being known. Of all the gifts of heaven to man," TJ wrote, the olive, for its oil, "is next to the most precious, if it be not the most precious." Believing that South Carolina and Georgia offered good conditions for growing olives, TJ offered to aid the Agricultural Society of South Carolina in obtaining trees from France. An extract of that portion of TJ's letter was printed in newspapers in the United States and received wide circulation (Philadelphia *Federal Gazette*, 16 Oct. 1788; *Salem Mercury*, 4 Nov. 1788; Vol. 11:644-50; Vol. 32:123, 124).

MONSIEUR THOME: C. J. Thomé, *Mémoires sur la manière d'élever les Vers a soie, et sur la culture du Mûrier Blanc, Lus à la Société Royale d'Agriculture de Lyon, par M. T**** de la même Société* (Paris, 1767), took the form of answers to a set of questions about raising silkworms and cultivating mulberry trees. The passage that van Hasselt quoted about the rose (or Italian) mulberry was in response to a query about the best type of mulberry for the nourishment of silkworms (same, 277-8, 299-301).

The Charleston merchant FLORIAN CHARLES MEY was a well-established importer of goods from Amsterdam and other European ports (Charleston *South-Carolina Gazette and General Advertiser*, 26 Jan. 1785; Charleston *City Gazette and Daily Advertiser*, 18 Feb. 1800, 23 Sep. 1801, 10 Feb., 8 Oct. 1803, 23 Feb. 1804; *S.C. Biographical Directory, House of Representatives*, 3:268; Vol. 29:468).

LE CELEBRE VAUCANÇON: in the middle decades of the eighteenth century, French machinist and inventor Jacques de Vaucanson made innovations in machinery for spinning silk thread and weaving cloth. Among his developments was a reel that prevented the silk filament from sticking to itself as it was taken off the cocoon and wound onto a spool. Vaucanson was also known for creating automata, such as a robotic flute player and a mechanical duck that had a digestive system (Samuel Pullein, "A New Improved Silk-Reel," Royal Society of London, *Philosophical Transactions*, 51 [1759-60], 21-30; Silvio A. Bedini, "The Role of Automata in the History of Technology," *Technology and Culture*, 5 [1964], 36-8; Walter English, *The Textile Industry* [London, 1969], 29, 90, 109; *Biographie universelle*, 43:17-19).

From Mary Jefferson Eppes

Eppington June 21st [1802]

My little son & myself have both been very sick since I wrote to you last My Dear Papa. we are now however getting better tho' he is still very far from being well, his indisposition proceeded from mine I believe & cutting teeth together, which occasion'd constant fevers & have reduced him extremely, & perhaps nursing him in my weak state of health made me worse for I had only slight tho constant fevers on me & my stomack at last[1] so weak that nothing that I took remained on it. change of air & bark tho' have been allready of great service to me, for my dear mother hearing of my sickness went down, & continued with us, tho to her extremely inconvenient at that time,[2] till I was able to bear the journey up with her; I have kept Crity with me in consequence of it my Dear Papa she should have gone up otherwise in may but I was not well enough to undertake changeing his nurse, I am very much in hopes now that he will mend daily as we have procured a healthy nurse for him till I am stronger. I recieved a letter from my sister the other day mentioning they were all well & that she expected to go on to you in this month. I am afraid tho' she will put it off 'till the visit be hardly worth making.

I have been very uneasy about the measles as it is said to be in that neighbourhood & am very anxious to hear from there, I should dread it infinitely more than the whooping cough for Francis & the dear children, through you my dear Papa I hope to hear something of it for my sister writes so seldom that I should hardly hear from her again[3] if she was to remain there 'till I saw her. Mr Eppes will finish his harvest to morrow & after that is over there will be nothing to prevent our going up, should it be necessary sooner than we intended. Adieu my Dear Papa I recieved the books & am very much obliged to you for them believe me with the tenderest affection yours ever

M EPPES

RC (ViU); partially dated; endorsed by TJ as received 1 July and so recorded in SJL. Enclosed in John Wayles Eppes to TJ, 25 June.

SINCE I WROTE TO YOU LAST: Mary Jefferson Eppes to TJ, 21 April.

For the BOOKS TJ sent by George

Logan, see TJ to Mary Jefferson Eppes, 1 May.

[1] Preceding two words interlined.
[2] Eppes first wrote "tho extremely inconvenient" before revising the passage to read as above.
[3] Word interlined.

To Albert Gallatin

June 21. 1802.

I am ready to appoint any persons whom mr Gallatin shall approve in place of the delinquent Collectors. Th:J.

RC (NHi: Gallatin Papers); on verso of address sheet previously directed by Gallatin to the president; addressed by TJ: "The Secretary of the Treasury." Not recorded in SJL.

DELINQUENT COLLECTORS: see Memorandum from the Treasury Department, 20 June.

From Nathaniel Ingraham

HONOR,D SIR,   Bristol Rhode Island June 21st. 1802.

I now write from Prison where I think I am unjustly placed, I feel myself under no small degree of imbarrasment to apologize in this manner to address the Chief Magistrate of the U. States,—

But Sir permit me to address you with every sentiment of Esteem, and in that I presume I am Reciprocating with One, whose Soul is united to mine by the Indisoluble bonds of friendship, I shou'd be unworthy any of your favours shou'd I in this instance adopt the least disguise; I am here placed and have a Wife and a number of Children, and am the Only One ever yet confined for what is called the Illicit Trade,—

I submissively pray your Honor to answer this and inform me, whether you ever did recive the Petition from our Citizens for my Liberty.—

I am your most Obet. & very H,ble Servt.

NATHANIEL INGRAHAM

RC (DLC); endorsed by TJ as received 11 July and "let it proceed." Recorded in SJL as received 10 July with the notation "imprisd. slave trade."

PETITION: see Ingraham to TJ, 10 April 1802.

Memorandum to Albert Gallatin

[on or before 21 June 1802]

A Premium of 50. D. is offered for

The most approved plan of an Hospital of 4000. square feet area, two stories of 10 & 8. f. high with cellars below; the rooms for the sick to be well aired, & of varied sizes from 10. to 20. f. square. the appearance of the building, convenient distribution of the rooms, and economy of space & construction will be principally regarded in the decision. a ground plan, elevation & section will be expected to be delivered at the Treasury office on or before the   day of plans not approved shall be returned.

—————

Tʜ:J. proposes to mr Gallatin that some such advertisement as the above be published in Washington where there are many architects who will probably compete for the premium.

in the erection of public buildings, taste, convenience & economy should all be respected.

MS (NHi: Gallatin Papers); entirely in TJ's hand; undated. Not recorded in SJL.

PLAN OF AN HOSPITAL: the 3 May 1802 act for the relief of sick and disabled seamen included a $15,000 appropriation for the erection of a marine hospital in Massachusetts. On 21 June, Gallatin wrote Benjamin Lincoln, the customs collector at Boston, requesting that he advertise in one of the local newspapers to obtain an "eligible plan" for the hospital. Gallatin included the specifications provided by TJ above, noting that the designs were to be transmitted to the office of the secretary of the Treasury by 15 Aug. Lincoln sent an extract of Gallatin's letter to the Boston *Columbian Centinel*. On 30 June, the newspaper printed the extract and advertised a $50 premium for

the plan chosen. The *Independent Chronicle* and other New England newspapers also printed the notice (U.S. Statutes at Large, 2:192; Gallatin, *Papers*, 7:243; Boston *Independent Chronicle*, 1 July; *Newburyport Herald*, 2 July; *Salem Register*, 12 July; Burlington *Vermont Centinel*, 22 July; TJ to the Senate and the House of Representatives, 24 Feb. 1802).

VARIED SIZES: in his letter to Lincoln, Gallatin specified that the rooms should be 12 to 20 feet square and did not include APPEARANCE OF THE BUILDING as one of the deciding factors in the choice of a plan (Gallatin, *Papers*, 7:243).

Gallatin did not advertise in a WASHINGTON newspaper, explaining that it would please the people of Boston to have the hospital designed by "one of their own architects" (Gallatin to TJ, 7 Oct. 1802).

From Thomas Moore, with
Jefferson's Note

Retreat 6th. mo 21st. 1802

Thomas Moore respectfully invites the President of the United States to examine the condition of Butter in a newly invented Refrigiratory, put in the 21st Inst. at 6 OClock P.M. 20 miles distant from Washington—

[*Diagram and note by TJ:*] the oval was cooper's work the inner parallelogram was a box of tin turned down on the top and trimmed to the oval: a. and b. were 2 square holes at which ice was put into the vacuity between the tin & wood, the butter being in the tin.

RC (DLC); addressed: "The President U.S."; with diagram and note by TJ at foot of text; endorsed by TJ: "Cooler for butter."

Thomas Moore (1760-1822) was a cabinetmaker in Loudoun County, Virginia, before moving to Brookeville, in Montgomery County, Maryland, north of Washington. There he farmed, and, like his brother-in-law, Isaac Briggs, was part of a Quaker community. Moore made a study of agriculture, and Briggs, earlier in 1802, probably sent TJ Moore's pamphlet, *The Great Error of American Agriculture Exposed*. Moore sent a copy of that work to James Madison, hoping to promote sales of the publication to defray the printing costs. With Briggs and another brother-in-law, Moore established the Triadelphia cotton mills in Montgomery County in 1809. Working as an engineer beginning in 1805, he oversaw construction projects that included the James River and Kanawha Canal and a causeway near Washington. In 1806, TJ appointed Moore one of three commissioners to begin work on the Cumberland Road (later called the National Road). As the chief engineer for the Virginia Board of Public Works, Moore in 1820 reported on the feasibility of a canal along the Potomac River to Cumberland, Maryland,

that became the first segment of the Chesapeake and Ohio Canal (*Baltimore Patriot*, 11 Oct. 1822; Latrobe, *Correspondence*, 2:209n; T. H. S. Boyd, *The History of Montgomery County, Maryland, from its Earliest Settlement in 1650 to 1879* [Clarksburg, Md., 1879; repr. Baltimore, 1968], 90-2, 93; ASP, *Miscellaneous*, 1:474-7, 714-15; Ella Kent Barnard, "Isaac Briggs, A.M., F.A.P.S.," *Maryland Historical Magazine*, 7 [1912], 416; Julius Rubin, "Canal or Railroad? Imitation and Innovation in the Response to the Erie Canal in Philadelphia, Baltimore, and Boston," APS, *Transactions*, new ser., 51, pt. 7 [1961], 63; Madison, *Papers, Sec. of State Ser.*, 3:94-5; Vol. 36:458n; commission for Moore and others, 16 Apr. 1806, in DNA: RG 59, MPTPC).

REFRIGIRATORY: Moore soon decided that "the most appropriate term" for his invention was "refrigerator." The OVAL tub of the device was made of cedar, with a hinged lid, insulated on the outside with rabbit fur and coarse woolen cloth. The TIN chamber held 22 one-pound pieces of butter. Although Moore designed the prototype as a means of transporting butter to market, he anticipated modifications to the design that would make refrigerators for home use and for butchers, purveyors of fresh provisions, and carrying fish to market. After he received a patent for his "Refrigerator for domestic uses" in January 1803, he sought to implement a licensing system for rights to make and use refrigerators according to his specifications. He offered to allow free use of the technology for anyone carrying modest amounts of butter to market. Moore presented himself as a practical farmer with only a "small stock of philosophical knowledge," but his description of his invention discussed scientific principles concerning the conduction of heat and melting of ice. He calculated that the mean temperature inside a refrigerator of his design would be about 48° Fahrenheit. Because his device required the use of ice, Moore also recommended improvements in the design and insulation of icehouses (Thomas Moore, *An Essay on the Most Eligible Construction of Ice-Houses. Also, a Description of the Newly Invented Machine Called the Refrigerator* [Baltimore, 1803], preface, 5, 15-28; *Philadelphia Gazette*, 15 Sep. 1802; *List of Patents*, 31).

From Samuel Smith

SIR/   Baltimore 21. June 1802

I have recieved two letters from General Wilkinson. Since his Arrival in Georgia, he appears excessively mortified at the Conduct towards him of the Federal party & wounded at the Opposition of some of our friends to the Continuing of the Post of Brigadier—I pity him, he Knows no way of maintaining his family he wishes much to be appointed Surveyor General to the Missisippi territory, and will relinguish his Command for that Office—but he wishes even in that Case to hold his Commission & Grade, And to relinquish the Emoluments until Called into Service—It appears to me (as it does to him) that if the French should take possession of Louisiana that there ought to be a Military Commander at or near the Natchez as well to watch their Motion with the Indians as to be Capable of repelling any encroachments on their part—If he Can be indulged with the Appointment of Surveyor General under the Circumstance of holding his Grade, I would myself prefer it on the public Account—if he Cannot—I hope it may be agreeable to you to grant him the appointment without Such permission[1]—But permit me here to Say that I very much fear that Wilkinson's Services as a military Man Cannot be dispensed with, in Case the French should possess themselves of N. Orleans— It would be difficult to prevail on any other military Man equally Capable to Accept Command—I am Sir/

With unfeigned friendship your friend & servt   S. SMITH

RC (DLC): endorsed by TJ as received 23 June and so recorded in SJL.

James WILKINSON had arrived at Fort Wilkinson, Georgia, early in May. There he, Benjamin Hawkins, and Andrew Pickens negotiated a land purchase from the Creek Indians to clear the title to certain tracts of land under a provision of the "Articles of Agreement and Cession" between the United States and Georgia (Wilkinson to secretary of war, 8 May, and Wilkinson, Hawkins, and Pickens to same, 30 May, noted in DNA: RG 107, RLRMS; ASP, *Indian Affairs*, 1:668-9; ASP, *Public Lands*, 1:126).

[1] Smith first wrote "without permitting him to hold the Rank" before altering the clause to read as above.

John Barnes's Memorandum on William Short's Account

Memom. 22d June 1802. to shew the President US.

JB. wrote WShort 20th feby (tho not forwarded untill April—) this letter covered his a/c up to 18 feby. than Balance $3347 39/ in his favr—purporting JB intintions of purchasing $4000. 6 pCt deferred.—but owing to Various disappointmts. rise in Stock &c. &c. no purchase was affected—

on or abt. 15 May. JB. had drafted a letter which he proposed forwarding—but was not sent, expecting daily to effect a purchase—abt. this period JB. presume the President. wrote WShort. to same effect—

Now the purchase is compleated—altho at an advance price (unavoidable) owing to the unexpected continued Advance of the Market. and still rising—JB. flatters himself Mr Short will—notwithstandg. Approve—as well his a/c Annexed and therewith the Certificate No 1629. for the above $4000 6 pCt. deferred. which JB. hand to the President US.—and subjoins a draft of his intended letter to WShort—to accompany, his a/c up to 22d. June 1802.—present Also Genl Kosciusko a/c (Copy, 15 May—)

MS (DLC: William Short Papers); entirely in Barnes's hand; endorsed by Barnes; endorsed by TJ: "Short Wm. Barnes's statemt." Enclosures: (1) Barnes to William Short, 22 June 1802, informing Short that he has finally purchased $4,000 of United States stock for him; although the price was unfavorable, Barnes thought it best to purchase now rather than risk another advance in price; the purchase includes two months' interest on the shares, not payable until 1 Oct., which reduced the purchase price below par; Barnes also includes a statement of Short's account, with a balance in Short's favor of $154.94, and a letter for Short addressed to Barnes's care, which Barnes presumes to be a letter from his brother; Barnes assures Short that he will pay every attention toward increasing Short's public stock holdings "under the direction of the good President, to whom I yesterday presented said Certificate as well Copy of a/c &c."; Barnes also includes a list of stock prices at New York on the verso (Tr in same, endorsed by TJ: "Wm. Short. J. Barnes's lre & acct. June 22 1802"). (2) Copy of Tadeusz Kosciuszko's account with Barnes, 23 June 1800 to 15 May 1802 (Tr in MHi, endorsed by TJ: "Kosciuzko Genl. his acct with mr Barnes to May 15 1802"; see Barnes to TJ, 21 May 1802).

To James Dinsmore

SIR   Washington June 22. 1802

Yours of the 17th. is recieved. a very useful emploiment for mr. Fitch will be the partitioning the[1] side and end of the kitchen, and studding the 3. servants rooms. the kitchen partitions are to be of inch plank, planed on both sides, & square jointed. the front & partitions of the servants rooms and dairy[2] to be bricknogged, with good lime mortar: or perhaps the front of the dairy had better be of inch plank, as proposed for the kitchen, as it will be stronger.   I do not recollect whether I drew 2. doors or one to the North necessary. if two, and the wall is made accordingly, then the outer or Northwest door had better be pannelled, the two upper pannels to be of glass. but if the wall is not built up, we had better have no door to the Northwest, but have the earth flush on that side, and between the level of the ground & the under side of the plate (which I believe would not be more than a foot) have a sash window. still there must be a sink on that side of the N.W. necessary as there is to the S.E. one. the objection to a door on that side is on account of snow-storms from that quarter. the door in the counterpart of the outchamber, that is to say in the office under it, must be like the one intended to be in that under the Outchamber, to wit, in the N.E. side, near the outer corner, opening directly into the passage running along the front. thus it had better have a fire place and window as here stated. the intention of the framing over my bed in the chamber was to enable us to have a room above the chamber if it should ever be desired; the chamber itself would in that case be about 10. f. high & the room above it 8. f. the half way plates were inserted for this purpose. but I believe the framing above the half way plate next to the wall is useless. I mean that to which the shelves are fastened. I think the upper joisting is not supported by that plate, but runs parallel with it, to wit from S.W. to N.E. in that case I have no objections to cutting away what of it is above the halfway plate. I shall leave this on the 22d. of July and be at Monticello on the 25th. Accept my best wishes.   TH: JEFFERSON

P.S. it would be well to have stuff got for the ballusters of the parapet, as the turning them would be good employment for mr Fitch. chesnut, or heart of pine, or heart of poplar are equally good I believe.[3]

RC (ViU); addressed: "Mr. James Dinsmore Monticello near Milton"; franked and postmarked.

YOURS OF THE 17TH.: Dinsmore to TJ, 17 June, recorded in SJL as received from Monticello on 21 June, but not found.

Also recorded in SJL, but not found, are six other letters Dinsmore and TJ exchanged between 27 Mch. and 25 June 1802; see Appendix IV.

MR. FITCH: probably Gideon Fitz, a Virginia-born carpenter who worked at Monticello from 1802 to 1803 (MB, 2:1082; RS, 1:215).

A ROOM ABOVE THE CHAMBER: a small room above TJ's bed alcove with three oval windows. The space served as a clothes closet and was reached by a ladder. Inspired by the Hôtel de Salm in Paris, this design preserved the outward appearance of a single story but also provided for a mezzanine level that allowed six additional bedrooms (Jack McLaughlin, *Jefferson and Monticello: The Biography of a Builder* [New York, 1988], 20, 252; Stein, *Worlds*, 50-1).

¹ Canceled: "South East offices."
² Preceding two words interlined.
³ Postscript written in left margin perpendicular to text.

To Mitchell & Buel

GENTLEMEN   Washington June 22. 1802.

I become with pleasure a subscriber to your paper, the Political barometer. you will oblige me by information of the most convenient place where I can pay the subscription. this would be the most so; but I could have it done in Philadelphia. accept my wishes for it's success and my respects.   TH: JEFFERSON

PrC (DLC); at foot of text: "Messrs. Mitchell & Buel"; endorsed by TJ in ink on verso.

TJ received the POLITICAL BAROMETER gratis from its editors who wrote from Poughkeepsie on 2 July, "Your Excellency's acceptance of our paper is all the compensation we have ever contemplated" (RC in DLC; endorsed by TJ as received 9 July and so recorded in SJL).

To James Oldham

SIR   Washington June 22. 1802.

Yours of the 17th. is recieved. from my present view of the suit brought against the indorser of your note, I should think it better to let it go on, because if the law be here as it is in the other states (Pensylvania excepted) your account will be a set-off against it. it was so in Pensylvania till about 5. or 6. years ago when the banks had interest enough to get a law passed that when a note was expressed to be *without defalcation*, nothing should be good against it as a discount. however I will enquire of some of the lawyers here; and in the mean time if you will let me know who is your endorser against whom the action is brought, I will speak with him. as the suit is commenced, most of the costs are already incurred, so that it's going on till set for trial will add little to it.

I think the outer door of the South East necessary, must be a pan-elled door, hung flush with the inside of the wall, and the upper pan-nel (instead of being glass as I before proposed) had better be of Venetian blinds, as that will give air as well as light.   as soon as you have done the S.E. necessary, I would rather you should pro-ceed with the N.W. one. I shall be at home on the 25th. of July. Accept my best wishes.   TH: JEFFERSON

RC (MeB); addressed: "Mr. James Oldham Monticello near Milton"; franked and postmarked.

YOURS OF THE 17TH: neither Oldham's letter to TJ of 17 June, recorded in SJL as received on the 21st, nor one of 27 June, recorded in SJL as received on the 30th, has been found.

The SUIT may have been against Elisha Lanham on account of Oldham; see John Barnes to TJ, 28 Sep. 1802.

TJ enjoyed VENETIAN BLINDS or lou-vred shutters at both the President's House and Monticello (Jack McLaugh-lin, *Jefferson and Monticello: The Biogra-pher of a Builder*, [New York, 1988], 321-2, 327).

To Henry Sheaff

SIR   Washington June 22. 1802.

Your's of the 15th. has been duly recieved. before it would be pos-sible to get any of your Burgundy here I shall be about setting out for Monticello to pass the months of August & September there for the sake of health. but moreover I know that the fine Burgundy wines will not bear a single day's transportation either in very hot or very cold weather. they are brought to Paris only in Spring or autumn, & then if the weather be hot, they travel only in the night, and with all possible care often spoil on the road.   mr Barnes will in a few days remit you 87. Dollars now about becoming due for the Sherry and Sauterne sent to Monticello. about a month hence I shall write to you for a further supply of Sauterne to be forwarded to Richmond. accept my respects & best wishes.   TH: JEFFERSON

PrC (MHi); at foot of text: "Mr. Henry Sheaff"; endorsed by TJ in ink on verso.

YOUR'S OF THE 15TH.: Sheaff to TJ, 15 June, recorded in SJL as received from Philadelphia, 16 June, has not been found.

For TJ's order to Sheaff of SHERRY AND SAUTERNE SENT TO MONTICELLO, see TJ to George Jefferson, 10 Apr.

I SHALL WRITE TO YOU: TJ to Sheaff, 26 July 1802, not found but recorded in SJL with notation "6 dozen Sauterne."

To George Washington Varnum

SIR   Washington June 22. 1802.

Your favor of the 4th. inst. was recieved yesterday. Genl. Dearborne is absent for about a week; but on his return I will put your letter into his hands. I do not believe however there is a single Lieutenancy vacant, as a number of supernumerary lieutenants were lately dismissed on the reduction of the army. there are vacant ensigncies, because this office is newly created; there having been none on the former establishment. as you propose going by the stage to Massachusets, and this place is on your route, should you have set out before you hear any thing further on this subject, you will recieve your information as you pass here, by calling on General Dearborne. I shall be happy in every occasion of shewing my esteem for your father, Genl. Varnum. Accept my respects & best wishes.

TH: JEFFERSON

PrC (MoSHi: Jefferson Papers); at foot of text: "Mr. George Washington Varnum"; endorsed by TJ in ink on verso.

George Washington Varnum (1779-1812) was the eldest son of Republican congressman Joseph B. Varnum of Massachusetts. He settled in Amherst County, Virginia (later Nelson County), where he became a merchant, militia leader, and member of the state legislature. He wrote TJ at least once more, on 7 Apr. 1811 from Lovingston, Virginia, seeking information on public finance (John Marshall Varnum, *The Varnums of Dracutt (In Massachusetts)* [Boston, 1907], 183; Madison, *Papers, Pres. Ser.*, 2:401; Leonard, *General Assembly*, 267; *National Intelligencer*, 25 July 1812; RS, 3:543-4).

YOUR FAVOR OF THE 4TH. INST.: Varnum's letter of 4 June 1802, recorded in SJL as received 21 June from "Oakridge Amherst (Rives's)," has not been found. TJ's notation may indicate that the letter was written from the Oak Ridge estate of Amherst County merchant Robert Rives. A letter from Rives of 10 July 1802 from Warminster, recorded in SJL as received 25 July, has not been found (Alexander Brown, *The Cabells and Their Kin* [Richmond, 1939], 238; RS, 4:22).

On 8 July 1802, Henry Dearborn (DEARBORNE) informed Varnum that the president had appointed him a first lieutenant in the Corps of Engineers. If he accepted, Varnum was to repair immediately to West Point, New York, and report to Lieutenant Colonel Jonathan Williams (FC in Lb in DNA: RG 107, LSMA). Varnum replied to the secretary of war on 26 Aug., however, resigning the commission (Dearborn to Varnum, 3 Sep. 1802, in same).

To Albert Gallatin

June 23. 1802.

Mr Gallatin will be pleased to have this Maryland business finished in any form he pleases. I will desire mr Monroe to attend him for that purpose. it should be done without delay, as the Governor's letter has already been long unanswered. if an *account* is to be called for from Annapolis, it will have the appearance of an affected delay: for the guarantee having been a simple transaction appearing in the *laws of Congress* we can want no further evidence. if any alteration in my letter should be wanting in consequence of any change in form be so good as to sketch it on the face of the letter. TH:J.

RC (NHi: Gallatin Papers). Not recorded in SJL.

GOVERNOR'S LETTER: John F. Mercer

to TJ, 5 June. MY LETTER: on this day, TJ wrote a private letter to Mercer. TJ's official letter to the governor regarding the Maryland loan is dated 7 July.

From Thomas Leiper

DEAR SIR   Philada. June 23d. 1802

I suppose by this time your information respecting the quality of your Tobacco is correct—If it is of the first quality and for sale please to inform me of the quantity and Cash price delivered at Richmond—or if agreeable to you which will certainly be more agreeable to me your Credit price from one to six months for I am and have been these eighteen months very much a head of my money owing entirely to my not being able to collect my debts. If Mr. Randolphs Crop is not sold I should like to take it also indeed I would rather have his Tobacco than yours for I have always been of the opinion that the Albemarle Tobacco is the best in Virginia I am Dear Sir Your most Obedient Servant   THOMAS LEIPER

RC (MHi); endorsed by TJ as received 25 June and so recorded in SJL.

BY THIS TIME: for TJ's response to Leiper's previous inquiry about the tobacco crop, see Vol. 36:9-10.

From Thomas Leiper

DEAR SIR   Philada. June 23d. 1802

I am very much at a loss to know where to begin and perhaps I shall be at a greater loss to know where to end as I am going to write about myself—some time ago Mr. Duane wrote his son from Washington which letter was showen to me mentioning that Mr. Dickerson and myself were appointed Commissioners of Bankruptcy—Had this thing stopt here there would not have been much matter in it but Captain Patton of the Post Office informed Mr. Poyntell that the thing was absolutely so—I told Mr. Poyntell and every One else that

I thought I should be the first to know it but as I did not I did not believe it—From Patton's letter or some other it got into Rielfs paper and next day into the Aurora—now sir if you give it out the thing was to be so—figure to yourself the line of march you have placed me in—I know it will be a perfect part to a certain Class of men but I will grin a bear it as well as I can but of all things that of being laughed at setts the hardest on me—I never did place myself in the first second or third Rank with respect to abilities but with respect to Principle and Zeal I always placed myself in the first—I heard your secretary say there was nothing give you so much pain and trouble as the appointment to office this I believe—Captain Jones applied to me to sign a Petition to you in favor of Mr. Cumpson. I informed him it was improper in me as the Aurora had published me as one of them but I could have given another reason Cumpson most certainly belonged to the old order of things or he never would have obtained his former appointment or if he had been on our side I should have seen him some where with us—But his comming to Washington as I suppose so powerfully recommended I think it was impossible in the nature of thing you could do otherwise than appoint him[1]—I beg and Pray for our own sake you would not Trim—General Washington fell between two stools and it will be eternally the Case with every man who follows his example—Burr is Taking both sides with a view no doubt of getting upper most—he certainly will be disappointed—Callender is taking our first Characters one by one and believes he can put up and pul down at his pleasure—He says he will send me one of his papers till I desire him to stop—I think you have nothing to fear if you proceed in office as you have begun—Reduction of Taxes and the payment of our national Debt is certainly two of the first points in our goverment both of which you have begun—But I believe if you was to remove certain Characters from office I believe you would give satisfaction to some of your best friends—Pray tell me for I expect an answer how comes it to pass you have appointed six commissioners when Hopkinson Peters & Cumpson formerly did the business—I am certain Dallas has more industry & skill than all the three—If you mean to do as John Adams did multiply offices to strengthen goverment You will find yourself mistaken if you can make One man do the business of two and discharge one you may rely on it this is the Best way of strengthing Goverment.—I have been at my mills these two days—and have not seen a soul since my return and I beg you will consider this a work entirely my own and I mean it shall never come into the View of any person but your self—I am with esteem

Dear sir your most Obedt St.   THOMAS LEIPER

RC (DLC); endorsed by TJ as received 25 June and so recorded in SJL.

RIELFS PAPER: on 3 May, Samuel Relf's *Philadelphia Gazette* carried a notice that the president had appointed Mahlon Dickerson and Leiper commissioners of bankruptcy, being "substituted for gentlemen of known talents and unimpeached integrity." On 4 May, the *Aurora* noted the appointments without comment. On 22 June, the *Aurora* carried the official notice of those appointed, which included Dickerson but not Leiper.

Congressman William JONES and Joseph Clay recommended Thomas Cumpston (see Jones and Clay to TJ at 30 Apr.). Jones opposed the radical Philadelphia Republicans who made proscribing all Federalists a test of commitment to the Republican party (Andrew Shankman, *Crucible of American Democracy: The Struggle to Fuse Egalitarianism & Capitalism in Jeffersonian Pennsylvania* [Lawrence, Kans., 2004], 98-9).

ONE OF HIS PAPERS: James T. Callender was associated with the Richmond *Recorder* (see "A Lover of his Country" to TJ, 9 May).

For the SIX COMMISSIONERS of bankruptcy appointed by TJ to serve in Pennsylvania, see Memorandum to Gallatin, 10 June, and Appendix II, Lists 1 and 2.

[1] Preceding three words interlined.

To John F. Mercer

DEAR SIR   Washington June 23. 1802.

While we are fumbling about *forms* at the treasury, I am afraid you will think me long acknoleging your letter of the 5th. I therefore write you this *private* one, merely that you may acquit me of inattention. our treasury will pay yours in the first week of July all the interest which will be then due on the 200,000. D. to wit 18,000. D. as to the 50,000. D. lent to the Commrs. Congress have taken measures to have both principal and interest paid on the 1st. of Nov. without resorting to the Treasury of the Union, as will be explained in the *official* letter which will be written you as soon as some matters of form are settled at the Treasury.—the account of Toussaint's arrest seems authentic. it will need good evidence to clear Le Clerc of perfidiousness[1] in the eyes of the blacks. should he fail to establish some new crime on Toussaint, some other black leader will arise, and[2] a war of extermination ensue: for no second capitulation will ever be trusted by the blacks. Accept assurances of my affectionate esteem and high consideration.   TH: JEFFERSON

RC (J. Coleman Scal, New York City, 1948); addressed: "Governor Mercer Annapolis"; franked and postmarked. PrC (DLC).

OFFICIAL LETTER: TJ to Mercer, 7 July.

[1] Remainder of sentence interlined.
[2] TJ here canceled "there can never."

To Caesar A. Rodney

DEAR SIR   Washington June 24. 1802.

Your favor of the 19th. & 21st. was recieved last night. the contents of it shall be inviolably kept to myself. I shall advise with my constitutional counsellors on the application relative to mr Mc.lane. some considerations occur at once, that a trial & acquittal, where both parties are fully heard, should be deemed conclusive; that on any subsequent complaint it cannot be regular to look to any thing farther back than the trial; that to do this would expose us to a charge of inconsistency which would do great injury to the republican cause; that he could now be removed only on the principle of a general removal of all federalists, a principle never yet avowed by any one; that nothing short of this would reach him because his acquittal puts him on better ground than others. there may be considerations however, opposed to these; and they shall have their weight. I do not see any thing charged in the papers subsequent to his former trial. electioneering activity subsequent to that would be deemed serious. but I presume he is passive in that way. of those who may justly claim attention in the appointment to offices, could not the places of commissioners of bankruptcy be of some avail?—I have never seen, nor before heard of, the piece called Love & Madness in which you mention Logan's speech to be inserted, and should be glad to see it if you have the book. We shall leave this the 22d. of July to pass the two sickly months of Aug. & Sep.[1] somewhere off of the tide waters; myself at Monticello of course. I mention this because you speak of being here in August, and I should regret my absence. I wish your visit could rather be immediate: and with the present rapidity of the stage, a flying trip from Wilmington to this place is nothing. Accept assurances of my great esteem & respect.   TH: JEFFERSON

RC (Mrs. William S. Hilles, Wilmington, Delaware, 1946); at foot of text: "Caesar Rodney esq." PrC (DLC).

[1] TJ here canceled "in more healthy sur."

To Samuel Smith

DEAR SIR   Washington June 24. 1802.

Your favor of the 21st. was recieved last night. we had had letters from Genl. Wilkinson on the same subject of the office of Surveyor of the Missisipi territory. but there exists no such office: and the Executive cannot create such a one. this answer has been given to Wilkinson. when the Georgia convention shall be ratified by them, and a land office open a surveyor will be wanting. but candour obliges me to say that mr Dunbar a man of the first science in the US. without exception, an antient inhabitant there, has the first title to it, and that it would be a great abuse of the power of appointment not to give him the refusal. he is rich & probably would not accept of it. Genl. Wilkinson is so well apprized of mr Dunbar's superior qualification for it that he acknoleges it in his letter but says Dunbar is going to Europe in the Spring. we are throwing into Wilkinson's way every accidental emploiment that turns up in order to help him along. how far, in any case, it would be expedient, if the French come to New Orleans, for us to plant a person against them whose interest it would be to bring on a war, will deserve consideration. that war with France some day or other will ensue that measure, is probable. but that it is better it should be kept off till some demelé with England should give us the aid of her superiority on the ocean, seems certain. Accept assurances of my great esteem & respect.   TH: JEFFERSON

PrC (DLC); at foot of text: "Genl. Saml. Smith."

James Wilkinson wrote several LETTERS to Henry Dearborn during the spring. In one, on 30 May, he said that his position in the army "draws down on my best Friends much obloquy & abuse." Explaining his willingness to give up active military service if necessary to be the surveyor general of Mississippi Territory, Wilkinson noted "the privations of domestic Happiness" and his "solicitudes for an helpless Family." Dearborn's ANSWER was dated 2 June. "It is considered as doubtful whether we ought to preambulate the line between the Mississippi Territory and the Choctaw Nation," Dearborn informed the general, unless the Choctaws "will agree to the line formerly settled between them and the British Government." It was "the wish of the President" that Wilkinson should talk to the Choctaws and "endeavor by all the fair means in your power to induce them to consent to the establishing of the said line, on receiving from the Government of the U. States a reasonable consideration in money." If the Choctaws showed "a disposition to listen to any such propositions," Dearborn went on, Wilkinson should determine "the lowest sum they will consent to receive" and find out "the principal points of the line." Wilkinson was to inform the government of the results of those discussions but "consider the running and marking the line as suspended until the Government shall have decided on the subject, which cannot take place earlier than next winter" (*Terr. Papers*, 5:151-4).

GEORGIA CONVENTION: the "Articles of Agreement and Cession" signed by U.S. and Georgia commissioners in April was to go into effect once the Georgia legislature approved the boundaries of the state's cession of lands. The legislature RATIFIED the arrangement by an act passed on 16 June (ASP, *Public Lands*, 1:126; Madison, *Papers, Sec. of State Ser.*, 3:321; TJ to the Senate and the House of Representatives, 26 Apr.).

In his letter of 30 May, Wilkinson conceded that William DUNBAR was "doubtless the person best qualified" to be surveyor for the territory. According to Wilkinson, Dunbar, with the intention of going to Europe, had "refused any appointment from Govr Claiborne" (*Terr. Papers*, 5:152).

SOME DEMELÉ WITH ENGLAND: that is, a quarrel (*démêlé* in French) between France and Britain.

From John Wayles Eppes

DEAR SIR,   Bermuda-Hundred June 25.

I have just time while enclosing a Letter from Maria to acknowledge the reciept of your letter of the 13. of June. Maria has been very
unwell & is now at Eppington for change of air. As she is equally interested in the contents of your letter I shall postpone my answer
until we have an opportunity of perusing it together. In the mean
time I can only return my thanks for the offer you are kind enough to
make & repeat the assurance I have before made that I feel perfectly
satisfied with what you have already done for us & cannot easily reconcile to myself the idea of being a clog at a time when I apprehend
the expences of your present situation must require all your funds.
The residence you are kind enough to offer us at Monticello it will
not be in my power to accept as previous to receiving your letter I had
consented to be brought forward as a Representative for this District—This circumstance however need not retard the levelling as I
can employ a person to overlook the hands.

My crop here is all of the May Wheat—We have stacked up the
last of it today—I shall be able to get it in the House & finish my corn
in time to meet you at Monticello on the 24th. of July.

Accept for your health My best wishes. Yours sincerely

JNO: W: EPPES

RC (ViU); endorsed by TJ as received
1 July and so recorded in SJL. Enclosure:
Mary Jefferson Eppes to TJ, 21 June.

TJ's LETTER to Eppes of 13 June is
recorded in SJL but has not been found.

REPRESENTATIVE FOR THIS DIS-
TRICT: see Eppes to TJ, 2 Feb. 1802
(Vol. 36:490-1). Eppes was reelected
(Leonard, *General Assembly*, 227).

From Albert Gallatin

SIR,   Treasury Department June 25th. 1802.

I have the honor to enclose letters from the collectors of Charleston,
and Norfolk, in relation to the Marine Hospitals.

If the corporation of Charleston, will agree to the arrangement proposed by the collector, that is to say, consent to defray all the expenses
incident to the support of sick seamen, provided that they shall receive the monies collected in charleston, it will prove so economical
an arrangement for the United States, that I think it would be eligi-

ble on that condition, to agree that the building should be erected out of the general Fund. The result would be that we should have three hospitals, the property of the United States at Boston; Norfolk and charleston.

The Gosport Hospital is much too large, but it appears from the Collectors letter that some repairs are necessary in that part which is occupied. To what extent these should be carried, and whether a conditional engagement to erect the buildings at charleston should be entered into, it remains for the President to determine.

I have the honor to be, very respectfully, Sir, Your obdt. Servant:

ALBERT GALLATIN

RC (DLC); in a clerk's hand, signed by Gallatin; at foot of text: "The President of the United States"; endorsed by TJ as received from the Treasury Department on 26 June and "Marine hospitals at Charleston & Norfolk" and so recorded in SJL. Enclosures not found.

COLLECTORS OF CHARLESTON, AND NORFOLK: James Simons and William Davies, respectively. The seamen's act of 3 May 1802 directed that MONIES COL-LECTED for sick and disabled seamen at the ports be sent to the U.S. Treasury to be distributed, under the president's direction, from the GENERAL FUND established for the purpose (Gallatin, *Papers*, 7:276-7; Vol. 36:632n).

For Davies's earlier description of the repairs needed at GOSPORT HOSPITAL, see the enclosure described at Gallatin to TJ, 29 July 1801. See also Gallatin to TJ, 16 Feb. 1802.

From John Harshe

VERY HONOURABLE SIR   Cannsburgh June 25th. 1802

It will no doubt give you some surprize to receive a letter from a person entirely unknown to you, and much more when I tell you that it is from a person entirely in a private capacity. Sir to be short, the design I have in this letter is to pray for your patronage. And in order that you may have some idea of the person soliciting you, it may be proper to give you some account of my life hitherto. Before I enter upon this narration, I have one request to ask, that you would be pleased to grant me pardon for my presumption in addressing a person of your dignity! I was born of poor but honest parents, who being strongly attached to republican principles, initiated me to them in my younger years, which reason has since evinced me of. I had alway a strong inclination for learning, in the pursuit of which, my parents (according to their circumstances) asisted me, so that by the time I arrived at the age of fourteen, I had a tolerable knowledge of the mathemeticks—I afterwards was employed for some time in the practice of surveying,

untill about two and an half years ago, at which time I came to Cannsburgh academy (now Jefferson's college) in order to study the latin &
Greek languages, which I have effected now in such a manner that I
have obtained the public applause of the trustees of this college, at my
examination—It was my intention to teach the languages; but at present all offices of this kind are occupied in these parts—You will have
some idea of my present circumstances, when I inform you that I have
spent nearly all that I had in obtaining this degree. Now dear sir my
design by this is to solicit your patronage, if you would recommend
me to some employment by which I might mentain myself.—If you
would favour me with a letter informing me of your sentiments respecting it I would value it as the greatest favour.—Now sir having
wished for very great prosperity to attend you in the administration of
your office, I have only one request more to ask, that you would grant
me the privilege of subscribing my self sir, your humble and very obedient servant   JOHN HARSHE

RC (MHi); endorsed by TJ as received 8 July and so recorded in SJL.

Following his stint at Canonsburg Academy in Washington County, Pennsylvania, John Harshe taught school in neighboring Beaver County's Hanover township and engaged in politics. He represented Beaver County in the state House of Representatives for two terms during the 1830s (*Poulson's American Daily Advertiser*, 20 Aug. 1812; Harrisburg *Pennsylvania Reporter*, 15 Dec. 1835, 8 Dec. 1836, 8 Dec. 1837; Joseph H. Bausman, *History of Beaver County Pennsylvania and Its Centennial Celebration*, 2 vols. [New York, 1904], 1:408).

To George Jefferson

DEAR SIR   Washington June 25. 1802.
Roberts & Jones have just shipped by the schooner Nancy

	£
14. bars of bar iron	5—0— 8
11. bars German steel	1—0— 7
	6—0—15

which being of particular sizes and of particular quality, ordered for
a special peice of work, I will ask your attention to in forwarding to
Milton[1] that it may not get mixed with others. perhaps a mark of
chalk on each bar may be useful. accept my affectionate esteem.

TH: JEFFERSON

PrC (MHi); at foot of text: "Mr. George Jefferson"; endorsed by TJ in ink on verso. Recorded in SJL with notation "iron from Rob. & Jones."

For the order of IRON and STEEL, see TJ to Roberts & Jones, 13 June 1802. A reply from the firm, dated 22 June, has not been found but was recorded in SJL as received 24 June with the notation "iron & steel 52.73. D."

The SPECIAL PEICE OF WORK may have been for a carriage that TJ had his blacksmith William Stewart complete at Monticello. During a visit there in September 1802, Anna Thornton described in her diary TJ's enthusiasm for a "phaeton which he has had constructed after *eight years preparation*" and added "The mind of the P. of the U.S.—ought to have more important occupation" (MS in DLC: Anna Maria Brodeau Thornton Papers). A few years later, Augustus

John Foster, the secretary to the British legation to the United States, found that TJ retained his pride in the carriage, which he described as "a Sulky upon four wheels with the Spring in the Centre, a very rough sort of Carriage but which he preferred to any other as having been made by an Irish Mechanic at Monticello under his own Superintendence and to praise which was a sure way to prejudice him in your favour" (Margaret Bailey Tinkcom, "Caviar along the Potomac: Sir Augustus John Foster's 'Notes on the United States,' 1804-1812," WMQ, 3d ser., 8 [1951], 100).

[1] Preceding two words interlined.

To John Barnes

June 26. 1802.

Th: Jefferson being to go into the country tomorrow will thank mr Barnes for 25. D. in small bills.

RC (ViU: Edgehill-Randolph Papers); endorsed by Barnes; endorsed by TJ: "Barnes John."

GO INTO THE COUNTRY TOMORROW: in his financial records under 27 June, TJ recorded paying 68½ cents for ferriage "to & from the Carrs." It is not clear which members of the Carr family TJ met with that day, nor where or why the visit took place. It may have been at the residence of his nephew, Samuel Carr, or his in-law,

Overton Carr, both of whom resided near Washington. The visit probably related to the pending marriage of another nephew, Dabney Carr, who married Elizabeth Carr the following day, 28 June. Like his brother Samuel, Dabney married one of Overton Carr's daughters (MB, 2:1076; VMHB, 5 [1897-98], 441; DVB, 3:27; Vol. 34:5n; Overton Carr to TJ, 25 Dec. 1801; TJ to Mary Jefferson Eppes, 3 Mch. and 1 July 1802).

From Daniel Carroll Brent

SIR,   June 26th. 1802

Mr. Hadfield yesterday furnished me with the Plans and Specification, herewith sent, which are submitted for your inspection and directions. I think in some few instances he ought to have been more particular; this however can be easily rectified. The Jack Rafters are I think too far apart, they ought not to be more than nine Inches from center to center. From Blagden's note to me, you will see, nearly, the quantity of free stone necessary, as also the price—Mr. Hadfield having changed the plan of the steps a little and added some for the chimnies; the quantity is not accurately ascertained. There is no public Stone proper for the Stairs;—this can quickly be obtained from the quarries.

I have thought the Ground I pointed out to you, as laid down in the printed Plan of the City for the Court-House, Jail and Gardens, consisted of three distinct Squares & were intersected by the Streets E & F; but Mr. Munroe informs me that it is one entire Appropriation, and that no Street in the real Plan of the City passes through that or any other public appropriation: this I consider a lucky circumstance for upon examining the Ground on yesterday, I found by placing the Jail in the center of the supposed Square from east to west, and forty feet from E Street, that it will be thrown into low Ground, whereas, as no Street passes through the appropriation, by fixing the front upon a line with E Street, we shall have excellent Ground. At 12 OClock when I suppose you are about to ride out, I will call, and if convenient to you, will point out the Ground more correctly. With sentiments of high respect,

I am Sir, Yr. Mo: Obt Servt   DANIEL C. BRENT

RC (DLC); at foot of text: "President of the United States"; endorsed by TJ as received 26 June and so recorded in SJL. Enclosures not found.

BLAGDEN'S NOTE: George Blagden superintended the stonework and quarrying at the Capitol (MB, 2:1084).

AS LAID DOWN IN THE PRINTED PLAN OF THE CITY: early maps of Washington, D.C., had appropriated the area bound by 4th and 5th Streets and D through G Streets, N.W., for public use. This area was later designated "Judiciary Square" in the city maps prepared by surveyor Robert King, Jr. (RCHS, 51-52 [1951-52], 28; Bryan, *National Capital*, 1:544; Ralph E. Ehrenberg, "Mapping the Nation's Capital: The Surveyor's Office, 1791-1818," *Quarterly Journal of the Library of Congress*, 36 [1979], 287, 295, 314-15).

From Isaac Briggs

RESPECTED FRIEND,   Sharon, 26th. of the 6th. Month 1802

Wilt thou condescend to inform me, if a letter I wrote, dated 26th. of the 4th. Month 1802, ever reached thee? I meant it to be expressive of deference and respectful esteem; if I unfortunately used terms not adequate to that purpose, I have no other plea, in extenuation, than ignorance. I have not, nor have I had any views to office or emolument;—were I worthy, I think I know that I possess not the requisite qualifications to fill with dignity a political post: but some portion of thy esteem, as a lover of Science and of the useful and benevolent Arts, was indeed an object of my ambition. I have no claim upon thy attention which will bear the least competition with the momentous concerns of thy Country's good, I only hoped for a small share of thy *leisure*; and even this claim, I confess, is the creature of my own presumption. May I still hope for a line in reply to this? I am incapable of continuing my correspondence beyond the slightest intimation of a wish on thy part that it should cease. Feeling the irksomeness of suspense respecting the reception or miscarriage of my letter, and being unwilling to rest upon mere implication, I have ventured to make the enquiry.

With unabated respect, I am thy friend, ISAAC BRIGGS.

RC (DLC); at foot of text: "The President"; endorsed by TJ as received 28 June and so recorded in SJL.

Memorandum on Delaware River Piers

Congress having appropriated a sum of 30,000. D. for repairing and erecting public piers in the river Delaware we ought not so to employ the money as to oblige them to give double the sum, but to plan the works on the scale they have fixed. certainly a wharf is not a pier, and not authorised to be built with money appropriated to piers. I approve of the proposition to repair the decayed piers in the first place; to call for proposals for building those for fort Penn & Marcus hook; and in the mean time think we should enquire whether either or both of these be more important than those proposed at Newcastle, whether there be danger that any of them will obstruct the navigation, and ultimately decide to do what is most advantageous for the river on the whole, within the limits of the appropriation.

TH: JEFFERSON
June 26. 1802.

PrC (DLC).

The last section of the lighthouse bill, which TJ signed on 6 Apr. 1802, included an appropriation, "not exceeding" $30,000, for REPAIRING AND ERECTING PUBLIC PIERS in the Delaware River (U.S. Statutes at Large, 2:150-2). The Treasury secretary was to oversee the expenditures, "under the direction of the President," and TJ probably sent this memorandum to Gallatin. The PROPOSITION has not been found, but Gallatin applied to the customs offices at Philadelphia and Wilmington, Delaware, for information (see TJ to Gallatin, 13 July; Gallatin to TJ, 17 July 1802).

To James Monroe

Th:J. to J. Monroe.   Washington June 26. 1802.

We are waiting for your recommendation of Commissioners of bankruptcy for Norfolk. Moses Myers & Richd. Evers Lee have been proposed by some. mr Arthur Lee has been thought of. say frankly if any of them are proper or improper. Littleton W. Tazewell if he would accept would make an excellent one: but I believe he lives in or near Williamsburg.—I propose to be at Monticello during Aug. and September, & shall hope you will take the same recess. affectionate salutations.

Henry Hiort. Atty ⎫   ⎫ were the former commissioners. if
Thomas Willock ⎬ merchts. ⎬ republican & otherwise equal, pos-
John Dunn   ⎭   ⎭ session would add to their title. but hitherto it is has been so taken for granted that the former appointments were federal, that no enquiry has been made respecting them.

RC (Alfred M. Colby, Mansfield, Ohio, 1946). PrC (DNA: RG 59, LAR); endorsed by TJ in ink on verso; also endorsed by TJ: "Commrs. bkrptcy Norfolk."

In September 1801, Monroe had written TJ about ARTHUR LEE, the son of Richard Evers Lee, describing him as a republican and "a young man of merit" (Vol. 35:354-5).

Moses Myers, Richard Evers Lee, and Littleton W. Tazewell all received appointments as commissioners of bankruptcy for Norfolk. Myers and Tazewell declined their commissions, however, while Lee resigned his in October 1803 (Appendix II, List 2; Madison, *Papers, Sec. of State Ser.*, 3:417, 430; 5:587-8).

From John Ponsonby

Sir—   Sysonby near Petersburg June 26th: 1802

Messrs. Ackermann, Suardy & Co. of London having forwarded to me, some proofs of their Invention for making Woolen Cloth, Linen, Paper &c. Water proof, and lest you should not have recieved any account of the same thro' any other Channel, I have taken the liberty of transmitting to you their publication together with some proofs on the subject—

With much respect Sir Yr: mo: hble: St   JOHN PONSONBY

RC (ViW); at foot of text: "Thos. Jefferson Esqr"; endorsed by TJ as received 30 June and so recorded in SJL. Enclosures: (1) *Analytical Hints Relative* to the *Process of Ackermann, Suardy, & Co's. Manufactories for Waterproof Cloths, and Wearing Apparel* (London, 1801). (2) Declaration by the Prince of Wales, Carlton House, 24 Apr. 1801, that the experiments presented by Ackermann, Suardy & Co. on rendering cloth "Impenetrable to Water" receive his fullest approbation and, considering the general utility of the undertaking, they "shall receive his warmest support" (MS in ViW; in a clerk's hand, signed and sealed by Thomas Tyrwhitt).

John Ponsonby (d. 1805) also forwarded specimens of waterproof cotton and cloth (*Petersburg Intelligencer*, 3 Jan. 1806; TJ to Ponsonby, 14 July 1802). ACKERMANN, SUARDY & CO., patentees of a method for rendering materials inpenetrable to water, ran a waterproof manufactory at Belgrave Place in Chelsea. As of December 1801, TJ had already received a copy of their pamphlet and had forwarded it with a specimen of waterproof paper to Thomas Mann Randolph; see Vol. 36:20-1.

From John Condit

Essex County State New Jesey

SIR   June 28th 1802

Having been requested a short time before I left the City of Washington to consult my Colleagues and recommend some persons for General Commissioners of Bankruptcy in this State—But not being fully satisfied in our minds who to mention, We thought it best to Omit it, Untill we should return into the State, and consult our friends on the Subject—this having been done, it is thought it would be convenient for the State to have Six Commissioners Appointed—Three in the eastern part, and three in the western part of the State—In the Eastern part After Advising with Mr. Ketchell Mr. Southard and Others, as to the most proper Characters, I would Recommend Col. *Thomas Ward* of Essex County *Phineas Manning* Esqr. of Middlesex County And *John Cobb* Esqr. of Morris County—they Are all Men of Respectability, Integrity, and knowledge in Business—they are also well Disposed towards the present Administration—the other three in the Western part of the State Will be Named and Recommended by *Governor Bloomfield*—whose knowledge And Acquaintance in that part of the State, together with advice he has received from my Colleague Mr. Mott and others, will enable him to make a Nomination of the most Deserving and Suitable Characters—I have therefore no doubt but the Persons herein Named, and those that will be Named by the Governor will do Justice to the appointment and give as General Satisfaction as Possible—

This will be received Under Cover from the Governor to Whom I

shall enclose it, that the Whole recommendations may go Together—
Mr. Ketchells Letter to me on the Subject will be enclosed also—
I have the Honor to be Sir, with great Respect Your Obedt. Servt—

JOHN CONDIT

RC (DNA: RG 59, LAR); at head of text: "To the President of the United States"; endorsed by TJ as received 3 July and "Commrs. bkrptcy" and so recorded in SJL. Enclosure: Aaron Kitchell to Condit, 26 June 1802, recommending John Cobb of Morris County, a merchant who understands accounts and serves as a judge of the court of common pleas; he is a Republican in principles, but "by no means Violent" making him acceptable "even to the federal party" (RC in DNA: RG 59, LAR). Enclosed in Bloomfield to TJ, 30 June 1802.

Born in Orange, New Jersey, John Condit (1755-1834) studied medicine and served for a short time as a surgeon in the Revolutionary War. He returned to Essex County where he developed a medical practice, farmed, and in 1785 became a founder and trustee of the Orange Academy. He was a member of the New Jersey Assembly from 1788 to 1789 and of the Council from 1790 to 1798. Condit, Aaron Kitchell, and James Linn, three leaders of the Jeffersonian Republicans in the state, won election to Congress in 1798. In 1800, New Jersey Republicans swept the state's five congressional districts. Condit served in the House of Representatives from 1799 to 1803 and in the U.S. Senate from 1803 to 1817. Elected again to serve in the Sixteenth Congress, Condit resigned his House seat in November 1819 to accept an appointment as assistant collector of the port of New York in Jersey City, a position he held until 1830 when he was removed for criticism of President Jackson's policies (DAB; Biog. Dir. Cong.; Prince, New Jersey's Jeffersonian Republicans, 26-7, 31, 65; Walter R. Fee, The Transition from Aristocracy to Democracy in New Jersey, 1789-1829 [Somerville, N.J., 1933], 96-7).

CONSULT MY COLLEAGUES: the other members of the New Jersey delegation in the House of Representatives in 1802 were Ebenezer Elmer, William Helms, James Mott, and Henry Southard, all Republicans (Biog. Dir. Cong.; Prince, New Jersey's Jeffersonian Republicans, 63-8).

TJ appointed the three candidates recommended by Condit for the EASTERN PART of New Jersey (see Bloomfield to TJ, 30 June).

From Ebenezer Hazard

SIR,   Philadelphia June 28. 1802.

Some Years ago Edmund Randolph Esqr. lent me some volumes of public Records, with which I understood your Excellency had some Connection. I afterwards returned them; & as I thought, *the whole* of them; but, upon removing my Books into another Apartment lately, I have been surprized by finding myself still in possession of a volume of Records of Escheats. Major Rodgers has been so obliging as to undertake the Charge of delivering it safely, and I am happy in so good an Opportunity of Conveyance;—by him I send it, with many Thanks, & Assurances of the Consideration with which I remain

Your Excellency's most obedient Servt.   EBEN HAZARD

RC (MHi); at foot of text: "His Excy. Thomas Jefferson Esqr."; endorsed by TJ as received 4 July and so recorded in SJL.

Former postmaster general of the United States Ebenezer Hazard had collected PUBLIC RECORDS for his compilation, *Historical Collections: Consisting of State Papers . . . Intended as Materials for an History of the United States,* published in two volumes from 1792 to 1794 in Philadelphia (DAB; Sowerby, No. 3044; see also Vol. 1:144-9, Vol. 19:287-9).

From David Humphreys

DEAR SIR.   New Haven June 28th. 1802

I had fully determined, upon my arrival in the U.S., to have made a journey to the City of Washington, for the express & sole purpose of paying my respects to the President. But the fatigue & inconvenience which my wife suffered in our voyage from Europe prevented me from carrying that determination into effect; especially as She was unable to accompany me & unwilling to be left alone among Strangers in my absence. A few days ago I arrived in this place with the object of making provision for her residence. In the mean time the warm season having commenced & her health requiring a more cool position, I shall be under the necessity of attending her without delay to New Port. This state of facts I hope will be accepted as a sufficient apology for, as they are the real cause of, any seeming neglect of that homage which is due to the Chief Magistrate of the Union. If after our return from the eastward, which will of course be as soon as the principal heat of the summer shall be passed, you shall judge that any oral communication from me might be of any utility, I will with the highest satisfaction proceed directly to the Seat of Government.

Under these circumstances, I would not defer to have the honour of enclosing the answer of the Catholic King to the letter of Recall which you addressed to H.M., in my behalf. And I think it proper to mention at the same time, the measures which I took to avoid receiving the Royal Present usually offered on similar occasions. On the 24th of Janry last, I wrote to the first Secretary of State in the following terms. "It is not probably unknown to your Excy, that the Constitution of the U.S. prohibits every Person holding any Office of profit or trust under them from accepting any *Present* from any King, Prince or foreign State without the consent of Congress. Upon this principle, while I was Minister at the Court of Lisbon, I sent to my Government a Sabre & Belt richly mounted & ornamented in gold, which had been presented to me by the Dey of Algiers.

Notwithstanding I do not now hold any Office of profit or trust, or of any nature or kind whatsoever under the U.S., and therefore may not be prevented by a fair construction of that article from accepting a *Present* from a King, Prince or foreign State; yet from motives of personal delicacy & especially from respect to the opinions of some of my fellow Citizens, I should find it prudent to decline receiving the Present of H.C.M., in giving every proof in my power of my profound sensibility & thankfulness to the Royal Donor." On the 1st of Febry. he addressed to me the following reply. "Muy Sor: mio. Permitame V.S. le diga en contextacion al reparo que en oficio de 24 de Enero proximo pasado me expuso tenia, para reciber el regalo que el Rey mi Amo acostumbra á los Embaxadores y Ministros que han residido cerca de su Persona; que mas se funda en su escrupulosa delicadeza, que en lo que previene la Constitucion de los Estados Unidos sobre esta materia, y que habiéndole admitido los Predecésores de V.S. en la Legacion que acaba de servir; me parece no debe V.S. tener inconveniente en hazer lo mismo, mucho menos si le considera como una expresion honorosa y calificativa de un Soberano Amigo de su Gobierno.—Me répito con este motivo á los ordenes de V.S. y ruego a Dios gue su vida m. a. Aranjuez 1o. de Febrero de 1802. B.L.M. de V.S. su mas Ato. Servor. Pedro Cevallos."

Immediately on the receipt of this, I requested an interview with him, and went accordingly from Madrid to Aranjuez to confer on the subject. In this conversation, after repeating & enforcing the sentiments which I had already expressed verbally & in writing, I informed him, that, if after all I had said & done, it should still be the pleasure of His Majesty to send this token of the Royal favour, I could do no more than to hasten to lay it before the Supreme Executive of the U.S. to be disposed of in such manner as may be thought proper. This I shall perform, should the case however modified occur. For, notwithstanding all which has passed in the matter, I have reason to believe a Present will be sent in ornaments intended for my wife, who was so fortunate as to have obtained marks of the peculiar consideration & benevolence of the Queen.

I do not pretend to offer any informations or advices relative to the dispositions of the Court of Madrid or the subjects now in discussion with it, since my *Successor* will doubtless have superseded the necessity of my giving you that trouble. I flatter myself the reports made by me to the Department of State will have furnished the means of forming a pretty accurate opinion of the relations subsisting between the two Governments & Countries, during my Residence in Spain, in a Diplomatic Character. Yet I must claim indulgence for mentioning again the circumstances & merits of an Individual. Indeed I cannot

dispense with my consciencious obligation to renew my recommendation of Mr Moses Young, who has for so long a time, and with so
much fidelity & ability acted as Consul of the U.S. at Madrid, as
well as Secretary to me while Minister at that Court. From the former
Office, he has derived no emoluments in compensation for much
labour & an extensive correspondence, as troublesome to himself as
useful to others. The pay of the latter was sufficient merely to defray
his expences. This old & faithful Servant of the Public has been left
in a very disagreeable situation by the nomination of Mr Graham as
Secretary to the Legation. I shall only add, that I conceive Mr Young
merits well of the Republic on many accounts, & that few Persons are
. better calculated for executing the duties of a Commissioner for liq-
uidating & deciding the claims of Citizens of the U.S. on the Spanish
Government.

Three or four days previous to my departure from Lisbon, I had a
private Audience of considerable length of the Prince of Brazil. His
Royal[1] made many friendly observations, as they related to myself &
Country. He indicated some surprize at the suppression of the American Mission to Portugal, while such interesting connections exist
between the two Nations, in point of commerce, and just at the moment when a Minister Plenipotentiary named by him was on the eve
of sailing; expressed a desire to maintain the sincerest amity with
the U.S.; requested his best Compliments might be presented to the
President; and intimated his readiness to re-establish a Diplomatic intercourse by appointing a Minister whensoever it should be deemed
expedient.

I was sorry to learn from other sources, that there may soon be several unpleasant cases for official representation, respecting property
of Citizens of the U.S., detained in foreign Portuguese Possessions,
which, I presume, it will scarcely be supposed can be made with so
good a prospect of success by a Consul as by a proper Diplomatic
Agent.

I hope that a letter which I had the pleasure of writing to you, by
Duplicates, on the 8th of May 1801, was received: and I beg you will
be persuaded that

I have the honour to be, with perfect consideration & esteem, Your
mo: ob: & mo: hble Servt   D. HUMPHREYS

RC (DLC); at foot of text: "Thomas
Jefferson, President of the U.S. of America"; endorsed by TJ as received 2 July
and so recorded in SJL. Enclosure not
found, and no letter from King Carlos IV
to TJ in the appropriate time period is
recorded in SJL.

ARRIVAL IN THE U.S.: in March 1801,
in a letter signed by Levi Lincoln as

acting secretary of state, TJ notified Humphreys that he would be replaced as minister to Spain and should begin preparations to return to the United States. Humphreys's formal recall was written in June 1801, but he did not receive it until his successor, Charles Pinckney, arrived at the Spanish court in December. Humphreys then complained that his recall instructions allowed him only three months' salary to cover his return to America, but it was so late in the year that it would be longer than three months before he could make a safe ocean crossing. Pinckney, moreover, was ill and could not immediately assume the duties of minister. In March 1802, Humphreys traveled to Lisbon. He embarked from that port for New York, where he arrived late in May (New York *Commercial Advertiser*, 3, 29 May 1802; Madison, *Papers, Sec. of State Ser.*, 1:333-4; 2:321, 345-6; Vol. 33:321-3).

Humphreys's WIFE, Ann Frances Bulkeley Humphreys, was the daughter of Lisbon merchant John Bulkeley. Thomas Bulkeley, whom TJ had recently replaced as U.S. consul in that city, was her brother. In the early 1790s, when Humphreys was the U.S. minister to Portugal, John Bulkeley's firm acted as his bankers and, through him, handled payments for the subsistence and ransoming of American captives in Algiers. The firm also sold wine to TJ (ANB; Frank Landon Humphreys, *Life and Times of David Humphreys: Soldier—Statesman—Poet*, 2 vols. [New York, 1917], 2:253; Madison, *Papers, Sec. of State Ser.*, 3:112, 131; MB, 2:812, 829, 988; Vol. 22:170, 323; Vol. 24:4-5; Vol. 25:28-9, 88n, 160n, 235-6; Vol. 34:430n).

LETTER OF RECALL WHICH YOU ADDRESSED TO H.M.: regarding the letter that TJ wrote to the king in June 1801 to announce that Humphreys would be returning to the United States, see Vol. 33:323n.

Although he felt obliged to turn down the ROYAL PRESENT, Humphreys did receive something valuable from the Spanish government, in the form of permission to assemble and take with him a flock of 100 merino sheep. For centuries the

raising of that breed, prized for its wool, had been carefully controlled. When Humphreys's flock arrived in the United States in 1802, there may have been only one true Spanish merino in the country, a ram obtained by Étienne Delessert, a friend of Pierre Samuel Du Pont de Nemours. TJ had some sheep of Spanish origin at Monticello, the gift of Robert Morris, but they were evidently not pure merinos. Humphreys, who received special dispensation from the Portuguese government to export his herd through Lisbon, took the sheep with him across the Atlantic on the same ship on which he and his wife traveled. When the vessel arrived in New York, newspapers took note of the merinos and suggested that readers visit the docks to see the unusual cargo. Humphreys transported the sheep to his property at Derby, Connecticut, where he established a breeding flock and began to promote the qualities of merino wool. A couple of months after the arrival of Humphreys's sheep, a second, much smaller group of merinos appeared in the United States, sent from France by Robert R. Livingston. Those animals were from the breeding flock that had been established under royal patronage years earlier at Rambouillet, France, from Spanish stock (New Bedford, Mass., *Columbian Courier*, 18 June 1802; Boston *Mercury and New-England Palladium*, 7, 10 Sep. 1802; Humphreys, *Life and Times of David Humphreys*, 2:338-48; Carroll W. Pursell, Jr., "E. I. du Pont, Don Pedro, and the Introduction of Merino Sheep into the United States, 1801: A Document," *Agricultural History*, 33 [1959], 86-8; Carroll W. Pursell, Jr., "E. I. du Pont and the Merino Mania in Delaware, 1805-1815," *Agricultural History*, 36 [1962], 91-2; Frans A. Stafleu, "Benjamin Delessert and Antoine Lasègue," *Taxon*, 19 [1970], 923; *Antidote to the Merino-Mania Now Progressing through the United States, or, the Value of the Merino Breed, Placed by Observation and Experience, upon a Proper Basis* [Philadelphia, 1810], 7-8, 11; George Dangerfield, *Chancellor Robert R. Livingston of New York, 1746-1813* [New York, 1960], 428-9; Barbara McEwan,

Thomas Jefferson: Farmer [Jefferson, N.C., 1991], 123; Betts, *Farm Book*, 111-12; Vol. 28:267-8; TJ to James Ronaldson, 13 Feb. 1809, in DLC).

FIRST SECRETARY OF STATE: Pedro Cevallos Guerra, Spain's minister of state, was sometimes referred to as the first minister (Douglas Hilt, *The Troubled Trinity: Godoy and the Spanish Monarchs* [Tuscaloosa, Ala., 1987], 118; Vol. 33:295n).

SABRE & BELT RICHLY MOUNTED: although he remained in Portugal and delegated the negotiations to Joseph Donaldson, Humphreys oversaw the treaty with Algiers that was signed in 1795 and ratified by the Senate the following year. Following the conclusion of the pact, Ali Hassan, the DEY OF ALGIERS, sent a sword and sash to Humphreys. The United States gave the dey a golden tea set and other gifts worth about $300 (Louis B. Wright and Julia H. McLeod, *The First Americans in North Africa: William Eaton's Struggle for a Vigorous Policy against the Barbary Pirates, 1799-1805* [Princeton, 1945], 24-5; Miller, *Treaties*, 2:303-4).

MUY SOR: MIO: "My dear sir. Permit me, Your Excellency, to say in response to the misgiving that you explained you had in your communication of 24 Jan. last about receiving the present that the king my master is wont to make to the ambassadors and ministers who have resided near him, that that has more to do with your scrupulous discretion than with the prohibition of the Constitution of the United States on this matter, and given that Your Excellency's predecessors in

the legation you recently served accepted them, it appears to me that Your Excellency should have no objection to doing the same, especially when you consider it as a proper expression from a sovereign friend of your government. I am as ever on this occasion at Your Excellency's service and I pray that God preserve your life many years. Aranjuez, 1 Feb. 1802. Your most devoted servant kisses Your Excellency's hand. Pedro Cevallos."

John Adams appointed MOSES YOUNG as U.S. consul at Madrid in April 1798 (JEP, 1:268-9).

João, the prince regent of Portugal, had the title PRINCE OF BRAZIL. In an official letter in May 1801, acknowledged by João in September, TJ had announced the closure of the American diplomatic legation in Lisbon. The Portuguese government then canceled plans to send João Paulo Bezerra to the United States as resident minister (H. V. Livermore, *A History of Portugal* [Cambridge, 1947], 386; José Calvet de Magalhães, *História das Relações Diplomáticas entre Portugal e os Estados Unidos da América (1776-1911)* [Mem Martins, Portugal, 1991], 333; Vol. 34:209n; Vol. 35:507n).

A few American ships had been DETAINED for various reasons along the coast of Brazil. TJ and Madison expected consular officials to assist shipowners with any claims resulting from those detentions (Madison, *Papers, Sec. of State Ser.*, 2:437, 456; 3:131, 190, 398).

[1] Thus in MS; Humphreys evidently omitted a word.

From Henry Ingle

SIR/   Monday June 28th 1802

Agreeable to instructions from the House of Robt Sutcliff & Co of Sheffield, England; I have the pleasure of handing for your acceptance, A Small Mahy case contaning a Hand brace and bitts & a few other tools. I am sorry to find them a little damaged although they were very carefully put up.   Mr Hodgeson one of the firm being here on a visit last fall, I directed the bitts made as I judged most usefull but have omitted 2 lock picks of a Small Size, which if you think necessary can be made here.

I have the pleasure to be Sir Your obdt Sevt   HENRY INGLE

RC (MHi); at foot of text: "Mr Jefferson"; endorsed by TJ as received 28 June and so recorded in SJL.

On the same day, TJ purchased from Ingle a supply of screws of varying sizes and eight dozen small pullies (Invoice from Henry Ingle for 1 Oct. 1802, in MHi).

From Levi Lincoln

SIR   Washington June 28. 1802—

Deeming it of importance that you should know, as fully as possible, the state of the public mind; and the feelings, and opinions of the people, which you are obliged to meet, and to manage, especially, in that difficult part of the Country, of which I am an inhabitant, I have thought proper to submit to your inspection the inclosed letters— They prove, what I am sure has taken or will soon take, place, in that part of the Country. I trust wickedness & falshoods have had their time, or that their reign are drawing towards a close—Cutts writes me that republicans are highly pleased with the proceedings of the administration in his quarter, and not a doubt is entertained of the propriety or expediency of the measures adopted by the last Congress, and that federalism is certainly lossing ground in that part of the Country—

Genl. Dearborn & myself endeavoured to prepare a list of names this morning, for commissioners for Massachusetts, to submit to your consideration—As soon as we have done the best we can do, we will write on you with it—

With sentiments of the highest esteem I am Sir most respectfully your Obt Sevt   LEVI LINCOLN

RC (DLC); at head of text: "President of the United States"; endorsed by TJ as received 28 June and so recorded in SJL. Enclosures not found.

IN HIS QUARTER: Congressman Richard Cutts was from Maine (TJ to Cutts, 27 Jan. 1802).

For the LIST OF NAMES, see TJ's Memorandum on Appointments at 6 July 1802.

From Caesar A. Rodney

HONORED & DEAR SIR,   Wilmington June 28th. 1802.

I had the pleasure duly to receve your letter of the 24. inst: — In my last I gave you the information I possessed on the subject required. From an observation in your letter you may have misunderstood a part of mine. Indeed I write such a scrawl that it is scarcly legible. You observe, that "you presume Col. M'Clane has been passive in electioneering." In my letter I stated that his conduct continued the same, as before the honorable acquittal for which he was indebted to your justice & impartiality. I beleive neither his opinions or his exertions have been altered or relaxed. He is now less public but of course less liable to have his plans counteracted. In opposing the election of Col: Hall he on one occasion in this town went so far as to commit that of Genl. Mitchell's which he was with too much zeal supporting. On this point I presume you can have the most satisfactory proof that the nature of the case will admit. The system of neutrality on this subject which I had adopted (& which I do not concieve I am departing from when called on by you for my opinion, in performing what then becomes a duty, tho' a reluctant one) renders a remark necessary. Our friends will be apt to suppose I know, that it is because I have not interfered, that Col. M'Clane is not turned out. This will be most artfully managed by the Federalists, who are aware of it. They will pretend to speak of it in public as a *matter of credit* to me, knowing the injurious effect it will produce. Altho' Col. M'Clane's activity directed personally against me would affect the election in some degree, it would not be half as detrimental to me as the idea, I have suggested, being industriously spread abroad.

Our State requires some act of nerve & spirit at this moment. You saw published the infamous letter of the late Secy. of this State to the Committee of our House of Reps: & their disreputable conduct on the occasion. I was absent having been compelled by sickness to leave the house & as soon as I was out of it, the affair happened. We have never yet got the Executive papers. To the commissions granted by Col. Hall they refuse to give credence. Even a Recorder holds possession of an office & the seal after a new commission given to another. Backed by the Courts & a majority of the legislature this is the game *Federalism* is at this moment playing in this State, & the Collector undoubtedly classes himself with those people. It is important to furnish to those less informed, a strong evidence that power has changed hands. The consequences will be wonderful. In our State affairs I trust we shall not after this year be hampered. But to conclude this topic, Governor Hall will be here on the 4th. july & we will come on to see you immediately after. I will bring the book I mentioned to you in my former letter.

You will observe in the Fedl. papers an ext. of a letter from this state to New-bury Port. It is supposed to be written by a *Jos. Dana* a relation of the Congressman. Dana came to this State a Clergyman. Was afterwards employed at New-Castle as a teacher, & at the same time commenced reading law with our C. Justice Johns who was so active last year in harranguing the people at public meetings which in the reign of terror he had denounced in a charge from the bench. The conduct of C. Justice relative to the New-Castle Pier lottery which has since been exposed will silence his battery during the ensuing campaign. Such were Dana's principles in politics & so offensive to a majority of the trustees of the New-Castle school, that they were about to notify him that his services were no longer required when sensible of this he voluntarily relinquished his situation. Since that time, he has figured as *Chief* of a little gambling club there. The piece will be properly noticed in our paper, but I thought it proper to give the above information. It has already produced one good effect. A general meeting of our citizens for the County is to take place on saturday next. They will appoint a general committee of Correspondence, direct the hundreds to meet also & to choose hundred committees & will recommend the same proceedings to their brethren of Kent & Sussex.

I beg leave after due advice to recommend to you the following citizens as Commissioners of Bankruptcy agreeably to your request.

French Macmullen Esq. of New-Castle

James Brobson ⎫
John Warner ⎬ of Wilmington
& Isaac H. Starr ⎭

The first is a young gentleman who read law with me & was admitted about two years ago. The second is the present Chief Burgess of this place. The third is a member of the corporation & our most influential, active politician. The last is a man of uncommon talents education & sense. All those from this place of the society of friends but the last (Mr. Starr) is the only *full member* of the meeting. They are all honest disinterested[1] Republicans & men of respectability & well qualified for the duties they will have to perform. Messr. Warner & Brobson were selected by Judge Bedford in one of only two cases which have occurred under the Bankrupt law. They are both merchants & know nothing else. Mr. Starr is in the shipping line also but pursues the profitable profession of tanning also. We consider his name an acquisition as he has generally declined every thing of the sort. He will serve like the rest on the true & patriotic principles of supporting you & your administration.

I had a letter from my old friend A. H. Rowan the other day, dated at Altona, of which the following is an extract. "How I rejoice with you on the election of Mr. Jefferson. How my exultation is increased when I read his public addresses. Persevere in such principles & your nation will be invincible. If you have an opportunity tell Mr. Jefferson that I recollect the polite attention he was once pleased to shew me with honest pride."

I will thank you to preserve this & my preceding letter as I have not kept any copies of them.

With great esteem I remain Dr. Sir Yours Most Sincerely

C. A. RODNEY

RC (DLC); endorsed by TJ as received 30 June and so recorded in SJL.

For Federalist Nathaniel MITCHELL'S close run for governor against David Hall in 1801, see Vol. 35:427-9.

INFAMOUS LETTER: on 4 Feb., Governor Hall sent the Delaware house and senate a message, noting that Abraham Ridgely, the late secretary of state, had failed to turn over any official papers pertaining to the executive office dated after 20 May 1799, making it impracticable for him to perform his duties as governor. The House appointed a committee to determine why Ridgely had not delivered the papers. The next day, Outerbridge Horsey, from the committee, delivered a letter from Ridgely to the speaker of the House, Stephen Lewis. Ridgely explained that the delay was due to "his indisposition," which for some time preceding the governor's inauguration had kept him from carrying out the duties of his office. Philip Lewis, a House Republican, immediately moved that no notice be taken of the letter in the House journal and that it be "thrown under the table," because it included "a gross insult to the Chief Magistrate of the State." Later in the day, the Federalists introduced their own resolution, which admitted that Ridgely's letter contained "intemperate language," and argued that only the part stating the reasons why the papers were not delivered should be entered in the House journal. The Republicans failed in their effort to amend the resolution by adding that the "intemperate language" was insulting to the governor. The resolution passed (*Journal of the House of Representatives of the State of Delaware, at a Session of the General Assembly, Commenced and Held at Dover, on Tuesday the Fifth Day of January, and Ended on Friday the Fifth Day of February, in the Year of our Lord One Thousand Eight Hundred and Two* [Dover, Del., 1802], 4, 64-71).

On 1 Feb. 1802, the Delaware General Assembly passed legislation calling for Chief Justice Kensey JOHNS, treasurer of the NEW-CASTLE PIER LOTTERY, to turn over to newly appointed commissioners more than $3,000 in surplus monies and $653.45 in outstanding debts due to the lottery. The commissioners were charged with applying the monies to the "purposes intended by the original act," that is, erecting and repairing piers in the harbor of New Castle (*Laws of the State of Delaware; Passed at a Session of the General Assembly, Which was Begun and Held at Dover, on Tuesday, the 5th day of January, and Ended on Friday, the 5th Day of February, in the Year of our Lord One Thousand Eight Hundred and Two* [Dover, Del., 1802], 223-8).

LETTER FROM THIS STATE: on 19 June, the Boston *Columbian Centinel* printed an extract of a letter from Delaware dated 22 May, describing the large reception, a "genuine tribute of heartfelt gratitude and affection," Congressman James A. Bayard received at Christiana Bridge when he returned home from Washington on 17 May. Although Bayard had determined not to seek reelection, he felt obliged "to bend his will" to that of his constituents after their warm reception. Indeed, the writer asserted, the popularity of Bayard caused Rodney, the leader of the opposition, to decline to compete. On 30 June, the Wilmington *Mirror of the Times* printed the extract and a response. "Honestus" noted that the correspondent was a clergyman from New England who had resided in New Castle for several years and recently returned to Massachusetts. "Honestus" pointed out that Bayard's welcome at Christiana Bridge did not exceed 20 people and that he did not on the occasion consent to stand for reelection. Far from being popular in the state, "Honestus" contended, Bayard was "too lordly in his manners" and had never obtained a seat in the state legislature although he was several times a candidate. The great falsehood in the letter, "Honestus" noted, was that Rodney had declined to run against Bayard. "Honestus" predicted that Bayard would soon be retired from public service and that Rodney would be elected by a "considerable majority."

GENERAL MEETING: on 30 June the *Mirror of the Times* carried a notice for the 3 July meeting of the Democratic Republicans of New Castle at the Red Lion tavern. The results of the meeting were published in the Wilmington newspaper on 14 July.

TJ appointed Rodney's four candidates for COMMISSIONERS OF BANKRUPTCY on 1 July (list of commissions, FC in Lb in DNA: RG 59, MPTPC). On his personal list, TJ dated the Delaware appointments 2 July (see Appendix II, list 2).

The Irish nationalist Archibald Hamilton ROWAN resided in the U.S. from 1795 to 1800 (see Vol. 34:475n). An extract from Rowan's letter to Rodney of 3 Apr. 1802 appeared in the Wilmington *Mirror* on 16 June.

[1] Preceding two words interlined.

From John Steele

SIR,   Washington June 28th. 1802

About the 10th. of next month, I wish to be favored with your permission to visit my family in Carolina. Hitherto a variety of considerations have restrained me from removing them to this place. Among others, a desire not to do any thing which would render it inconvenient for me to conform to your views, whatever they might be, in relation to the disposition of my office. I thought it my duty also to postpone any communication of my sentiments to you on this delicate subject, until you should have had leisure to mature an opinion of my public conduct, and until Mr. Gallatin, with all the assistance which I could give him in the mean time, should have become sufficiently acquainted with the forms, and principles of business in the Department to experience no inconvenience from a New appointment if that should be your intention, or if circumstances on my part should render a resignation necessary. After leaving the seat of Government with the permission which I now solicit, I am not certain that it will suit me to return:—but if I should conclude to do so, my family will accompany me about the beginning of October, and in deliberating with them in the course of the summer on a step which must be attended with trouble, and the sacrifice of many domestic comforts, it will be extremely gratifying to me, to be certain that I understand your wishes. The politeness with which you have uniformly honored me since our first acquaintance, and a certain bias which is inseparable from the reflection, that we are Citizens of the same Geographical section of the United States cannot but increase my reluctance to withdraw my services, if they are considered of any importance to your administration. Salary altho necessary to me, in relation to my private circumstances is far from being my principal object in serving the public. In a country as free as this happily is, a man should have higher, and better views.—Mine are regulated by a desire, I trust an honest one,[1] to be useful and in that way to acquire reputation, by deserving it. I am sensible, however that in times like the present, it is not possible for any man to continue in such an office with satisfaction to himself, or advantage to the public unless he can have reason to be assured that your confidence in his fitness is entire.

I have the honor to be, Sir With sentiments of perfect respect Your most obt. servant　　　　　　　　　　　　　　　JNO. STEELE

RC (DLC); addressed: "Thomas Jefferson Esqr. President of the United States"; endorsed by TJ as received 28 June and so recorded in SJL. Dft (NcU: John Steele Papers); endorsed by Steele as a "Rough draft."

DISPOSITION OF MY OFFICE: as a Federalist and comptroller of the Treasury since 1796, Steele defended the practices of the previous administration. In a letter to Gallatin dated 4 June, Steele justified payments made by the Treasury Department to clerks and officers of the executive branch for expenses related to "the removal of themselves and families" to Washington, D.C. in 1800. In the 29 Apr. 1802 report issued by the congressional committee investigating government expenditures, doubt was cast on the legality of the payments. Steele presented evidence and argued that the expenses were "defensible as well in an equitable sense, as according to the strict letter of the law." On 21 June, Steele enclosed a copy of the letter to Madison for his perusal, with the request that he show it to the president, although he thought Gallatin might already have done so. When Madison returned the letter on 24 June, he noted that he "gave the President an opportunity of perusing it" (Biog. Dir. Cong.; ASP, Finance, 1:752, 811-16; Henry M. Wagstaff, ed., The Papers of John Steele, 2 vols. [Raleigh, N.C., 1924], 1:275-81, 283-4; Madison, Papers, Sec. of State Ser., 3:330, 337).

[1] Preceding five words canceled in Dft.

From Thomas Tingey

S<small>IR</small>   Navy Yard Washington 28th June 1802

I have the honor to enclose You, a memorandum of the particular dimensions, of the Frigate United States agreably to Your request of this morning.

Having it in contemplation to cover the Dock with a roof over the Ships—it would be adviseable to take out all the lower masts, before entering it—and for this purpose Sheers should be erected at the Dockhead—by which means the three Masts of each Ship may be taken out, in three hours or less, and with the most perfect safety—An excellent model of such a machine is now in the Navy office, brought from Toulon by Commodore Dale—This particular appendage to the *Navy Yard here*, is now much wanted: as there is always great risque in Sheers erected on Deck, for the purpose of taking in, and out Masts, of such dimensions as those of our Frigates—

The waste of time is also great, as is the danger of moving the Sheers *on deck*, and the labour too operose to be effected with a few people.—I dare affirm that the expence of taking out the Masts, which must necessarily be shifted, of the Ships now here, *ere they can proceed to Sea*; will by the last mentioned method, far exceed the cost of erecting the Machine I would advise: and which would last many, very many Years.

It is presumeable the Ships by being thus—and otherwise judiciously lightened, to come into Dock may be brought to 17 feet draft of water, or under. The *tight* work therefore of the entering bason, need not at the extreme, exceed in height 40 feet. Stopping at this height for the Ground or Solid work, the laves of the Roof need not exceed 15 feet more perpendicular height, to admit Line-of-Battle-Ships, of two-decks.

The depth of water, at the Bar in the Patowmac, near the mouth of Matawoming Creek (the shoalest I believe in the river) is at high water, *common tides* 23 ft 6 in to 23 ft 9 in—and I should feel no apprehension of danger, or doubt of success, in the attempt at a favorable time, of conducting any one of our largest Ships up—on a future occasion, without lightening in the smallest degree, in point of expence.

	Feet	in.
Extreme length of the Frigate United States from the 'aft'r-side of the Taffrel-rail, to the extent of the Figure-head	197.	4
Extension of the Bowsprit beyond the Figure	35.	8
ft	233.	

	ft.	in.
Perpendicular height of the Taffrel, above the waters edge	28.	6
Present draft of water abaft	20.	
Perpendicular height of the Taffrel, from the tread of the Keel }	48.	6

	ft.	in.
Perpendicular height of the Main-masthead, above the waters edge	92.	
Ship's present mean draft of water	18.	6
Extreme height of the surface of the Main-cap above the tread of the Keel a mid-ships }	110.	6
Extreme breadth of the Ship outside	45.	

Ever happy, with energy to execute your commands

I have the Honor to be with unfeigned respect Sir Your Obedt Servt

Thos: Tingey

RC (CSmH); addressed: "Thomas Jefferson Esquire President of the United States"; endorsed by TJ as received 28 June and so recorded in SJL.

Thomas Tingey (1750-1829) was born in London and held a warrant officer's commission in the Royal Navy before the American Revolution. Settling in Philadelphia, he spent many years as a merchant captain trading in the West and East Indies. In 1798, Tingey accepted a captain's commission in the U.S. Navy. He commanded the frigate *Ganges* in 1799, then was directed to oversee construction of a 74-gun ship at the nascent Washington Navy Yard in 1800. He was appointed superintendent of the navy yard the following year and remained in that post until his death (ANB; Michael A. Palmer, *Stoddert's War: Naval Operations During the Quasi-War with France, 1798-1801* [Columbia, S.C., 1987], 81; NDQW, Jan.-May 1800, 113-14; Dec. 1800-Dec. 1801, 293; Taylor Peck, *Round-Shot to Rockets: A History of the Washington Navy Yard and U.S. Naval Gun Factory* [Annapolis, 1949], 11-12, 91-3, 255).

YOUR REQUEST OF THIS MORNING: TJ's exchange with Tingey was the germination of a larger plan by the president to consolidate navy operations at Washington by constructing a massive covered dry dock, capable of holding up to 12 frigates. TJ argued such a facility would provide an effective and secure means to preserve supernumerary navy vessels laid up from active service. The scheme would occupy a considerable amount of TJ's attention during the latter half of 1802, which included commissioning plans from Benjamin Henry Latrobe and mentioning the proposed work in his annual message to Congress on 15 Dec. 1802. Ultimately, the dry dock plan failed to secure the support of Congress, whose members generally deemed it too costly and too visionary to succeed (Eugene S. Ferguson, "Mr. Jefferson's Dry Docks," *American Neptune*, 11 [1951], 108-14; Peck, *Round-Shot to Rockets*, 14-19; ASP, *Naval Affairs*, 1:104-8; TJ to Nathaniel Macon, 17 July 1802; TJ to Latrobe, 2 Nov. 1802; Robert Smith to TJ, 8 Dec. 1802).

From Anonymous

GREAT SIR, June 29th 1802

If you should chance to open this at a time which does not afford leisure to contemplate its contents, be pleased to lay it by, or at least reserve it for a second reading, until such time arives; for it is not a letter of business, which requires immediate attention—Neither, as the author supposes, does it contain a single idea which has not presented itself to you, at some time or other, with more or less force.

The importance of the subject, to every man in the united states of like sentiment with yourself (which importance can receive no real addition or diminution from the name of the writer) is the only apology Sir, for this tax upon your attention, by one who will not trust his name to a conveyance, from which, in his quarter, letters are, said to have been, taken out & coppied.

Among the many over whom you rightfully preside, there is, perhaps, not one who felt more rejoiced at your deserved elevation, & the resuscitation of those principles of sacred & eternal right, than the writer of this communication.

To give perpetuity to the operation of those principles, in the administration, is the wish of every genuine patriot.

When he contemplates the prospect of doing this, he confesses that he rejoices with trembleing. Perhaps it is his ignorance & weakness.

Be it so. Nevertheless Sir, though your superior comprehension may enable you to look through, or beyond the fancied mist which yet too much veils the prospect of those of less talents & erudition, you will yet, he presumes, have the complaisance to attend, for a moment, to the mention of some things which are supposed to be very formidable obstructions to the permanent establishment of a free & just government in North America, especially in the North Eastern quarter.

Those ideas, whether just or whimsical, have borne so hard on the mind of the writer, ever since your Election, that he has determined to make them the subject of a communication: And he does it with a view to suggest the query whether there cannot be some constitutional remedy.

Shall it be said "All bounteous Nature taught the fertile field, For each corporeal ill a balm to yield"—and yet confessed, by Philosophers, that the ills of the body politic admit no remedy?

Here, Sir, is his only hope, though he sees not, the remedy. He leaves this to greater physicians. But so strong are his hopes & wishes (he would that he could add faith) that he would go an hundred miles to have one hours conversation with you on the subject: For he cannot see how it is possible for an ecquitable government to exist long in New England, where he was born & bred up—where British literature is so predominant as to have poisoned the very sourse & fountain of almost every right idea, with regard either to religion or civil policy—where the principles of despotism (certainly such at bottom) have so long held the empire over the mind, by right of possession, that it is now very hard to eradicate them.

Though the people could be stirred up to oppose foreign despotism, it was *not* because they disliked civil or religious tyranny, provided they could excercise it themselves, & have a tyrant, or despot, of their own raising, or erecting—Mankind were always the slaves of form; & the worshipers of those idols which themselves had carved out & set up, whether of wood or whatsoever kind.

Hence some of those very men who, for a while, preached against the tyranny of George the 3d, do now virtually, & most faithfully, preach up, not only monarchy & priest craft, but also pope craft.

The regular clergy are foremost in this. They have, long since, assumed & held the direction of the education of youth. They not only direct the studies & teachings at all our schools & academies, but also the classics at the Colleges. Hence our Nothern members of Congress (being College learned Lawyers; educated in the above way, at school; in British classics, at College; & British practical law, when out of College; and thus accustomed, from their infancy, to authors who seldom, if ever, fail to hold up all the British systems as the most perfect standards of right on earth) are made what we see them to be.   Now Sir, if one of the antients was right, when he said he cared not who made the laws, provided he was allowed to write the fables & ballads, which should constitute the earliest reading of the youth; & give them their first ideas of right & wrong, as our political school masters do in New England; who being, generally, under the superintendance of the clergy, are actually obliged to teach their pupils what sentiments they ought to have, both in politics & religion, even before they can read: Obliged, because they else would not be allowed to teach by our wig-clad inspectors of schools, who likewise insist on their praying with their scholars, which affords a fine oppertunity to inculcate the anglo-federal creed of Church & State.

If man is thus, as appears to me to be generally the case, the mere creature of his oppertunity—the dupe of local prejudice, pious fraid,

& scientific deception, what wonder is it then that British sophisms have become as natural to most New England poeple as was ever their mother's milk?

This long established influence of British literature, in the hands of those who are coalesced to keep up British sophisms about liberty, & popish dogmas about faith—to read, & cause to be read, & mouth-plied, both at College & school, every book which has this tendency, appears to me to be most dangerous to truth & right.

Pardon me when I go so far as to say that in vain, I fear, will reason be left free to combat error, where the interest of a particular order is so great to support it, & while there is no law against it.

Being educated in the same manner, both at school & College, it was therefore owing to peculiar adventitious circumstances that the writer of this was not biggoted by such means—that he remained a monument of singularity—a mark for false wit & cold railery, during the late reign of terror—the only one out of eight or ten men of science in the same Town; & the almost only one in the County who has been openly & uniformly a decided republican—who still finds federal persecution to be almost intolerable; its malice rising, as its power decreases.

Another principal obstruction is the effect of the patronage system, which enabled your predecessor, particularly in the case of the direct tax, to bribe (if the expression is allowable, for it had this effect) to his interest & views, a vast number of the most distinguished & influencial Families in the country, by appointing individuals out of such Families to honourable, or lucrative, posts, or employments, under that & other acts.

This, however it may operate, for a while, to keep up party animosity & newspaper slander is, as I apprehend, by no means so deep rooted an evil as the before mentioned, which to remove requires both time & skill; and appears to depend almost entirely on the introduction & substitution of genuine American, or at least republican, literature into our Seminaries.

But how can this be done, unless made a general concern, & taken up by the general legislature, as such?

The literary Fair will not, I immagine, effect any change in our school books & College classics: And this not merely because there are few or no good substitutes extant; but because the authority which prescribes & proscribes, in this case, is the most bigoted, superstitious & obstinately incorrigible, to all rational improvements, of any authority on earth—It is also most arbitrary & extensively influential.

Neither, as I should guess, would any general encouragement given, by law, to American literature, & discouragement to foreign authors, effect the change so much to be desired.

Though the Chief Magistrate of the Nation, & the National Legislature should be ever so sensible that the late dereliction was greatly owing to the natural predomenance of British literature (from which contaminated sourse thousands of scholars, designed for future leaders in church & state, are daily dieted with principles & doctrines diametrically opposed to those of the present just administration) could the former recommend, & the latter enact, any thing which, in a constitutional way, would put a stop to that which is, in my opinion, more to be feared, as the enemy of rational liberty, than the invasion of foreign fleets & armies.

If such a thing can be done Sir, you may be sure of the hearty cooperation of one, so far as in his power, who now assures you of his highest respect & esteem, though he may, & probably will, remain forever unknown to one whom he thinks to be, according to history, the first man, properly qualified, who hath ever yet had the luck to be called to preside over so great a nation.

RC (DLC); addressed: "Thomas Jefferson Esqr. President of the United States of America. Washington City; or Monticello"; endorsed by TJ as received from "Anon. (Mass.)" on 12 Aug. and "influence of clergy in education" and so recorded in SJL.

FOR EACH CORPOREAL ILL: despite his stated distrust of the prominence of British literature in the United States, the author was quoting from "The Plaintive Shepherd: A Pastoral Elegy," by the eighteenth-century Scottish poet and critic Thomas Blacklock. He varied the phrasing of the original, which reads "All-bounteous nature taught the fertile field, For all our other ills a balm to yield" (*Poems by Mr. Thomas Blacklock*, 2d. ed. [London, 1756], 99). For the FABLES AND BALLADS, an allusion to a saying popularized by Scottish politician Andrew Fletcher, see Vol. 36:443-4.

Organized by Philadelphia bookseller Mathew Carey, the first American LITERARY FAIR took place in New York City during the first week of June 1802. Modeled after the long-standing book fairs of Frankfurt and Leipzig, the event sought to raise standards of publishing in the United States, discourage the unnecessary republication and importation of books, provide a venue where booksellers from around the country could conduct business, and promote cooperation in the book trade. The fair received positive attention from American newspapers and booksellers, but after a few years similar efforts foundered (New York *Commercial Advertiser*, 21 Dec. 1801, 1 June 1802; Philadelphia *Aurora*, 9 June 1802; Charles L. Nichols, "The Literary Fair in the United States," in *Bibliographical Essays: A Tribute to Wilberforce Eames* [Cambridge, Mass., 1924], 85-92).

To Isaac Briggs

Sir   Washington June 29. 1802.

Your favor of the 26th. came to hand last night. that of Jan. 30. had been recieved in due time. with more business than can be dispatched at once, I am often obliged to lay by to a more leisure moment that which will best bear delay. this lot falls often on my philosophical and literary correspondence. to this circumstance alone is owing the omission to answer that part of your letter which proposed to me the membership of your Agricultural society. notices of this kind cannot but be pleasing to me inasmuch as they are testimonies of the esteem of my fellow citizens: but it is so impossible for me at present to bestow attention or undertake correspondence on subjects out of the line of my immediate duties, these claiming the whole of my time, that I have been obliged to decline all new occasions of avocation from them. it is always painful too to reflect that one is of no use to the society of which he is a member. it is from this consideration alone that I would decline what you propose to me.

My proposition to the Agricultural society of New York had been made in the spring of the last year; but Chancellor Livingston their president had not brought it forward. I reminded Dr. Mitchel of it when he came to Congress in December, and thro' him the society has been led to put it into general motion. if the State societies come into it & select from among their members of Congress those who have zeal for Agriculture, it may effect the true object of such institutions which is that not an useful thought of any individual of the nation at large may be lost. Accept assurances of my esteem & good wishes.   Th: Jefferson

PrC (DLC); at foot of text: "Mr. Isaac Briggs."

TJ suggested to Robert R. Liv-ingston in February 1801 that the New York Society for the Promotion of Agri-culture, Arts, and Manufactures should take the initiative in building relationships among agricultural societies (Vol. 32:596-7). PUT IT INTO GENERAL MO-TION: see Ezra L'Hommedieu to TJ, 3 Apr.

To John Langdon

My Dear Sir   Washington June 29. 1802.

Your's of the 19th. was recieved last night. that of May 14. had arrived while I was on a short trip to Monticello from whence I returned on the 30th. Ult. commissioners of bankruptcy, made up from your's & some other recommendations were appointed[1] on the 14th. inst. and no doubt were recieved a few days after the date of your last. Nicholas Gilman, John Goddard, Henry S. Langdon & John Mc.Clintock were named. the three last were in your recommendation. although we have not yet got a majority into the fold of republicanism in your state, yet one long pull more will effect it. we can hardly doubt that one twelvemonth more will give an executive & legislature in that state whose opinions may harmonise with their sister states. unless it be true as is sometimes said that N.H. is but a satellite of Massachusets. in this last state the public sentiment seems to be under some influence additional to that of the clergy and lawyers. I suspect there must be a leven of state pride at seeing itself deserted by the publick opinion, and that their late popular song of 'Rule New England' betrays one principle of their present variance from the Union. but I am in hopes they will in time discover that the shortest road to rule is to join the Majority. Adieu and accept assurances of my sincere affection & respect.　　　　TH: JEFFERSON

RC (NhPoS: John Langdon Papers); addressed: "John Langdon esquire Portsmouth N.H"; franked; postmarked 30 June. PrC (DLC).

Former congressman NICHOLAS GILMAN of Exeter was a recent convert to the Republicans in New Hampshire, despite being the brother of Federalist governor John Taylor Gilman. He was recommended to TJ for a bankruptcy commission by Henry Dearborn and U.S. attorney John S. Sherburne (ANB; Appendix II, List 1).

RULE NEW ENGLAND was written by Federalist poet Robert Treat Paine, Jr., who, at the time, was still writing under his given name of Thomas Paine. The song was performed to much acclaim at the annual meeting of the Massachusetts Charitable Fire Society in Boston on 28 May 1802, with Federalist newspapers lauding the spirit and political sentiments of the piece, as manifested by its chorus: "Rule, New-England! New-England rules and saves! Columbians never, never shall be slaves." Complementing Paine's work, the *Boston Gazette* declared that while the "indivisibility of the states is a desirable object," New England was nevertheless "not to be nosed about, and subjected to the dominion of the visionary philosophists of bloated and besotted Virginia, and her sattelites." Republican newspapers were predictably less impressed by the piece. The *National Aegis* dismissed Paine's prose as pedantic and unoriginal, while the *Independent Chronicle* decried the "horrid political tenets" present in an ode composed for an allegedly charitable organization (ANB; *Boston Gazette*, 31 May 1802; Worcester *National Aegis*, 2 June 1802; Boston *Independent Chronicle*, 7 June 1802; Robert Treat Paine, Jr., *The Works, in Verse and Prose, of the Late Robert Treat Paine, Jr. Esq.* [Boston, 1812], 252-3).

[1] Word interlined in place of "signed."

From James Monroe

Dear Sir   Richmond June 29. 1802

Nothing is more difficult than to give you a suitable nomination for comrs. of bankry. at Norfolk. I relied on a gentn. who lately went there for information on that subject, and he declined writing me, preferring to communicate his ideas in person on his return, wh. was not till within a few days. Littleton W. Tazewell lives in Norfolk, but as he has taken a commn. of notary publick of the State wh. is worth four or five hundred pds pr annum it is presumable he wod. not resign it for the other office. Still it might be well to appoint him, as it wod be paying him a suitable attention & give time in case he resigned to find some person in his place. R. Evers Lee is a very fit person. The two first at present in the comn., are federalists, the third doubtful (according to my information), but moderate, if a federalist, & incling. to come over. Moses Myers is a federalist, but deservedly respected in the place, moderate, or rather liberal, whose appointmt., if a man of his politics is appointed, wod. give least offence to the republicans, & be conciliatory to the fedts. Colo. Newton has two sons in law, one named Thos. Blanchard, the other Jas. Taylor, both merchants, the first a man of abilities, (I am told) as a writer, active & enterprising, decidedly republican, but in embarrassed circumstances; the other well informd, respectable, rather heretofore of the federal party but not strongly marked, & now disposed to view things in a proper light. The appointment of either of these last wod. produce as little irritation in those who wod. be apt to take offence, at it, as the appointment of any person precisely in the situation of either cod. do. The circumstance of their being men of merit, well qualified for the office, nearly connected with the most respectable & wealthy man in the place, wod. tend to silence the objections of the fedts. to the appointment of the first, and of the republicans to that of the second, if the information wh. I have of his political character is correct. The persons above named have better pretentions to the office, according to the information I have recd., than any others at Norfolk, tho' there may be others of whom I have not heard, who ought to be preferr'd to any, Tazewell & R. E. Lee excepted. It will give me much pleasure to meet you in Albemarle in augt. or sepr., of wh. there can be no doubt, as the term of yr. visit there will certainly furnish a justifiable occasion for my absence from this place, more than once in the course of it. Sincerely I am yr. friend & servant

JAS. MONROE

Mr. Hay will not accept the appointment for this place He mentioned to me George Tucker—a nephew of the Judge, lately married to a daughter of Chs. Carter, (son of Edwd.) who is a Gt. niece of Geo. Washgtn. Little facts are important sometimes from the estimation in which they are held by others. I shod. certainly have as soon thought of tracing the genealogy of Mr. Tucker in the Island of Bermuda, as that of his wife under other circumstances. Mr. Tucker is a sensible man a lawyer & a republican, in the best society here. you will recollect what I said of the other gentn. in my former communication.

RC (DNA: RG 59, LAR); endorsed by TJ as received 3 July and "Commrs. bkrptcy Norfolk" and so recorded in SJL.

TWO FIRST AT PRESENT IN THE COMN.: Henry Hiort and Thomas Willock. THE THIRD: John Dunn. See TJ to Monroe, 26 June.

TJ included Thomas BLANCHARD among the bankruptcy commissioners appointed for Norfolk (Appendix II, List 2).

A native of Bermuda and a kinsman of St. George Tucker, GEORGE TUCKER was a fledgling Richmond attorney who went on to a distinguished career as a political economist and man of letters. In February 1802, he married Maria Ball Carter, a daughter of Charles Carter, a son of Edward Carter of Blenheim, and Betty Lewis, a niece of George Washington. After declining his bankruptcy appointment, George Hay recommended Tucker to James Madison, describing him as in "every way unexceptionable." TJ appointed Tucker in place of Hay as a bankruptcy commissioner at Richmond (George Hay to secretary of state, 23 June 1802, in DNA: RG 59, LAR, endorsed by TJ: "Hay George resigning as Commr. bkrptcy recommendg. George Tucker"; ANB; Robert Colin McLean, *George Tucker: Moral Philosopher and Man of Letters* [Chapel Hill, 1961], 12; Woods, *Albemarle*, 163-4; Washington, *Papers, Pres. Ser.*, 11:156; Madison, *Papers, Sec. of State Ser.*, 3:333-4; Appendix II, List 2).

From Joseph Bloomfield

Trenton, New-Jersey,
30th: June 1802.

SIR,

I do my Self the honor of transmitting the enclosed.

Mr. Mott who resides near Sandy Hook was lately in Trenton, and requested me whenever Dr. Condit & Mr. Southard should recommend Commissioners of Bankruptcy, for the Eastern part of New-Jersey; to mention his concurrence in their recommendation, and of the recommendation enclosed, of Isaiah Shinn, from Mr. Elmer's district, & that it is his wish and of those with whom he has advised; that Abraham Brown and Anthony F. Taylor, may be Appointed in the district, in which he resides.

The persons therefore recommended to be Commissioners of Bankruptcy in New-Jersey, are,—

Thomas Ward, of Newark, Essex-County.
Phineas Manning, of New-Brunswick, Middx. Co.
John Cobb, of Morris, Morris county.
Isaiah Shinn, of Woodstown, Salem county.
Abraham Brown, of Burlington, Burlington County.
Anthony F. Taylor, of Bordentown, Burlington county.

Thomas *Ward* & John *Cobb*, served in the Militia during the War—Cobb has been a Colonel of Militia & Thomas Ward, is now the senior Col. of Cavalry in New-Jersey.
Phineas Manning, served all the War in the American Cavalry & distinguished himself for his bravery. He follows merchandize.

Isaiah Shinn, is Major-General of the first Division of Militia, was brought up to Mercantile business & is universally esteemed.

Mr. *Brown*, is a Lawyer, & has been Secretary to the Commissioners of Bankruptcy in West-Jersey, is well acquainted with the duties & will, there is no doubt, give universal satisfaction.

A. F. *Taylor*, was brought up to Mercantile business, which he follows,—was on board the Alliance as a midshipman in the revolutionary War—& is well acquainted with business.

I beg leave to add, that all the persons recommended, are decided Republicans, and Attached to the present administration.

I had declined recommending any person, but the recommendations having been sent to me to forward, with a desire, that I would Concur, has induced me to trouble the Executive on this occasion.

I cannot add, to the high respect & Sincere esteem, with which I am, most truly, Your obedt. Servt.   JOSEPH BLOOMFIELD

RC (DNA: RG 59, LAR, 12:0098-0100); at foot of text: "The President"; endorsed by TJ as received 3 July and "commrs. bkrptcy" and so recorded in SJL. Enclosure: (1) John Condit to TJ, 28 June 1802, and enclosure. (2) Undated, unaddressed recommendation, perhaps to Ebenezer Elmer, signed by William Parret, Salem County representative in the state's legislative council, Artis Seagrave, Merriman Smith, and Edward Burroughs, representatives of Salem County in the New Jersey General Assembly, and Jacob Hufty, sheriff of Salem County, endorsing Isaiah Shinn, James Linn, and William Rossell as bankruptcy commissioners, "being Persons of Sound Minds and independent Republican Principals," who will discharge the "duty with Candour and In-

tegrity"; with a note adjacent to the signatures indicating that Linn and Rossell "decline" (RC in DNA: RG 59, LAR, 10:0250, with a note in TJ's hand at foot of text: "To Govr. Bloomfield"; *Votes and Proceedings of the Twenty-Seventh General Assembly of the State of New-Jersey* [Trenton, 1802], 3; Prince, *New Jersey's Jeffersonian Republicans*, 232-3; Trenton *True American*, 6 Oct. 1801).

Congressman Ebenezer ELMER'S DISTRICT included Cumberland, Salem, and Cape May counties, although the New Jersey congressional elections were held at large at the time. Elmer resided in Cumberland County (Prince, *New Jersey's Jeffersonian Republicans*, 2; Newark *Centinel of Freedom*, 16 Dec. 1800).

TJ appointed all six of the New Jersey

candidates recommended above as commissioners of bankruptcy. The commissions for the New Jersey appointees were dated 6 July. On his personal list, TJ dated the appointments 7 July (list of commissions in Lb in DNA: RG 59, MPTPC; Appendix II, List 2).

To John Steele

DEAR SIR   Washington June 30. 1802.

A press of business yesterday prevented my answering your letter recieved the evening before. I am happy in the occasion it presents of assuring you unequivocally that I have been entirely satisfied with your conduct in office; that I consider it for the public benefit that you should continue, & that I never have for one moment entertained a wish to the contrary. I will add, and with sincerity, that I should with great regret[1] see any circumstance arise which should render your continuance in office inconsistent with your domestic interests, or comfort; the possibility of which is intimated in your letter. your deliberations with your family therefore on their removal hither, may be safely bottomed on the sincerity of these dispositions on my part, & I shall be happy that they should have their just weight in[2] determining their & your resolutions in favor of[3] that measure.   with respect to your absence, I have too much confidence in your own sense of the public interest to imagine you would propose it, were any public inconvenience to ensue. on this subject yourself & mr Gallatin will make your own arrangements. it is expected there will be a general recess of the Executive about the last week of the[4] ensuing month, to seek situations in which we have more confidence to pass the months of August & September, so unfavorable[5] to health. I mention this merely for your information, and as it may enable you, with perhaps more satisfaction to yourself, to arrange your own movements. I pray you to[6] accept assurances of my esteem & high consideration.

TH: JEFFERSON

RC (Nc-Ar: John Steele Papers); addressed: "John Steele esquire Comptroller of the Treasury." FC (DLC); in TJ's hand. PrC (DLC).

[1] FC: "with reluctance."
[2] In FC, TJ wrote "if they should have the effect of" in place of the preceding eight words.
[3] FC lacks preceding three words, ending the sentence with "resolutions to that measure" and then beginning a new paragraph.
[4] In RC, TJ here canceled "next mon."
[5] FC: "trying."
[6] FC lacks preceding four words.

George Hadfield's Estimate of Cost for Building a Jail

[June 1802]

Summary Estimate of the expense necessary for building the Goal; by G. H.

275 Yards of digging for foundation at 20 Cents pr. yard	$ 55	
916 Perches of rough stone for walls, flues and floors @. $.1.25 pr. Perch.	1145	
1032 Bushels of Stone lime for mortar and grout @. 54 Cents pr. bushel.	557	28
206 Barrels of sand and gravel @. 20. Cents pr. Barrel	41	20
Mason's work and labour for 916 perch of stone @. $.1. Pr. Perch	916	
20,000 Bricks and tiles for paving and arching @. $.6. pr. Thousand	120	
Workmanship for Do. @ $.3. pr. Thousand	60	
Freestone windows, door casings and sills	1806	
Frestone steps for stairs and outside	204	
6,600. feet of Scantling for floors, partitions and roof @. $.4. pr. Hundred feet	264	
95 Squares of framing @. $.3 pr. Square	285	
14,600 weight of Iron for grates and cramps @. 6. Cents pr. ℔.	876	
Workmanship of Do. at 4. Cents Pr. ℔.	584	
1393 yards of plaistering @ 7. Cents pr. Yard	97	51
528 yards of Do. for outside @. 18. Cents pr. Yard	95	4
30 squars of plank for sheeting roof @. 3.$. pr. Square	90	
30 squares of slate @ $.10. pr. Square	300	
Workmanship of Do. @ $.2. pr. Square	60	
34 Strong Oak doors @. $.7. each	238	
Locks bolts & hinges.		
Contingent expencies.		

Dollars 7774. 03.

MS (DLC); undated; in Meriwether Lewis's hand; with TJ's 1804 notes on verso.

The SUMMARY ESTIMATE printed above is probably based on the plans and specifications for the Washington, D.C., jail prepared by George Hadfield and for-warded to TJ by Daniel C. Brent in his letter of 26 June. TJ's notation on the verso refers to excavating at the President's House conducted in 1804, about which time work commenced on extensive improvements to the grounds and the construction of wings for the building (Seale, *The President's House*, 1:109-18).

Notes on Building the Jail

[June 1802]

Notes for building the jail

Walls.   to be built of granite 2. f. thick

the mortar half of good lime in all the walls

half of clean gritty sand in all the inner walls

one fourth of clean gritty sand

one fourth of fine sifted gravel from ⎫ for the outer walls
    the beach of the Potomac   ⎬
                                ⎭

overcast on the outside with plaister of Paris

plaistered & white washed within.

Roof.   to have rafters 9. I. apart. raised $\frac{2}{9}$ of it's span hipped at the ends. covered with slate

entablature, a regular Tuscan from Palladio.

Floor.   of upper rooms. joists 9. I. apart 4. I. thick.

countersealed with brickbatts grouted.

paved with thin tile.

of Cells. a horizontal pavement first laid down on earth[1] of the largest peices of granite.

on this pieces of granite 2 f. wide, & of any thickness & length laid edge up & grouted, so that the upper edges shall form an even floor.

of the jailor's lower room to be filled with earth & paved with brick.

of the passages. to be arched with brick & paved with brick over that.[2]

the passages under the ground floor, being arched above, are to be left open, and a hole of 9. I. square communicating to every necessary, that they may be cleansed a semicircular aperture at the end of the passage through the underpinning large enough for a man to enter.

the necessary within each cell to be a circular hole in the floor 9 I. diameter, barred across thus ⊗ with a lid shutting smooth with the floor

Doors.   3 f. by 6 f[3] single iron grated doors for the 2. outer doors, the two passage doors below & 6. doors above   10

double grated doors for all the cells on the South side of the passage   16

a single grat[ed] [...] [for each] of the North cells   [...]

Windows. 3. f. square, double iron grated below (except in the
jailor's room, [single] [...]   [...]
                single grated above,   [...]
            window shutters to all strong   34
fireplaces. the cells adjoining the jailor's room to have fireplaces.
            the jailor's room below & all the ⎤
            rooms above to have them   ⎦ with grates for coal.
            all the flues to issue in 4 shafts on the ridge pole & to be
                barred in 2. places 2. f. one above the other
a right to be reserved to make changes at any time at the rates agreed
for similar work, and where none such is in the agreement, to be
arbitrated

PrC (DLC: TJ Papers, 124:41561); torn; faint; entirely in TJ's hand; endorsed by TJ in ink on verso: "Jail."

Daniel C. Brent began advertising for proposals for BUILDING THE JAIL in Washington on 30 June. Sealed proposals would be received until 7 July at Brent's office in Stelle's Hotel, where a plan of the jail, "the references thereto, and the manner in which the work is to be executed, may be seen there at any time" (*National Intelligencer*, 30 June 1802; Alexandria *Times; and District of Columbia Daily Advertiser*, 1 July 1802).

[1] Preceding two words interlined.
[2] TJ here canceled "[...] the [...] of the floor of the passage, to be open."
[3] Preceding dimensions interlined.

Appendix I

Jefferson kept an ongoing list of appointments and removals, which extended throughout his two terms as president, with entries extending from 5 Mch. 1801 to 23 Feb. 1809. For the first installment of this list, from 5 Mch. 1801 to 14 May 1802, see Vol. 33, Appendix I, List 4. This second installment continues at 3 June 1802, beginning shortly after the president's return to Washington following his short stay at Monticello, with Thomas Munroe's appointment, and includes the subsequent entries for the rest of this volume. This was a working list, which Jefferson updated, often partially canceling a name when he learned an appointee had declined the office or, as in the case of John W. Vancleve, had died. Jefferson usually entered the names on his list as he signed the commissions sent to him by the State Department. This explains why the date on the commission is often a few days before the entry date on Jefferson's list. Munroe's commission, for example, is dated 2 June. Robert Brent's commission as mayor of Washington is actually dated 1 June, but Jefferson did not offer him the position until 3 June. Brent accepted the same day. Commissions for bankruptcy commissioners for New Hampshire, New York, and Pennsylvania, all dated 10 June—a Thursday—are entered below at 14 June. The commissions for appointees at Richmond and Petersburg, Virginia, were also dated 10 June, but those for Charlottesville were made out six days later and the president entered all at the later date. All of the commissions dated 10 June were printed in the 18 June issue of the *National Intelligencer*. In the list below, the president entered two appointments twice, Rufus King at 11 and 16 June, and Isaac Cox Barnet at 19 and 23 June. The State Department issued the commission for King on 10 June and that for Barnet on 18 June. The president probably signed the commissions the next day and entered them on his list (list of commissions in Lb in DNA: RG 59, MPTPC; FC of commission for King in Lb in DNA: RG 59, Credences; FC of commission for Barnet in same, PTCC; William Irvine to TJ, 18 July 1802). It is not clear what prompted him to enter them a second time.

List of Appointments

[3-23 June 1802]

June 3. Thomas Munroe Superintendant of the city of Washington. new

4. Robert Brent. Mayor of the city of Washington. new
Oliver Barnett Marshal of N. Jersey vice Heard made Collector Perth Amboy

8. William Thornton
John Mc.kall Gant
<*Tristram*> Dalton.
   decld.
Saml. Hanson of Saml. } Commrs. of bkrptcy for the district of Columbia.

Constant Tabor.
Saml. Vernon
12   Thos. Peckham
Paul M. Munford[1] } do. R. I. (Newport)

11. Rufus King a commission to settle boundaries with Gr. Brit.

12. John Rowan
Daniel Weisgar } Frankfort
John Inston

James Morrison
John A. Seitz } Lexington
John Bradford

Commrs. bkrptcy Kentucky

14. Nicholas Gilman
John Goddard.
Henry S. Langdon } do. N. Hampshire
John Mc.lintock

John Broome
Wm. Edgar
Jonathan L. Pearsee. junr. } N. York
Daniel D. Tompkins
Nathan Sandford
James Fairlie

Abraham G. Lansing
Nicholas N. Quackenbush } Albany
George Merchant

to be do. of N. York

Alex. J. Dallas
Mahlone Dickerson
Joseph Clay } to be do. Pensylvania
Thomas Compston
John Sarjeant
<*John W.*> Vancleve } dead.

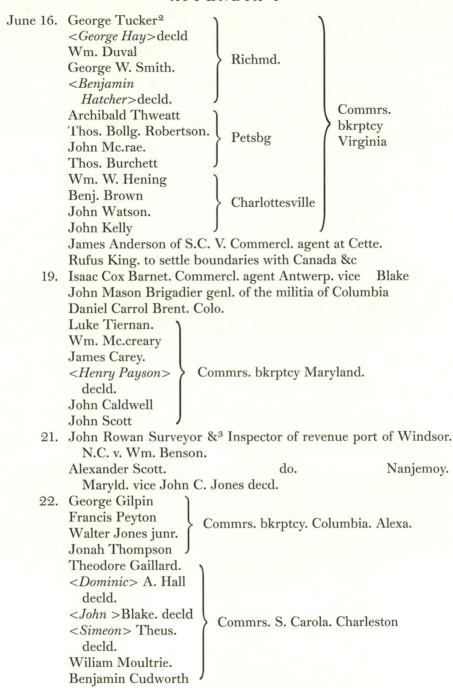

June 16. George Tucker[2]
<*George Hay*>decld
Wm. Duval
George W. Smith. } Richmd.
<*Benjamin
Hatcher*>decld.

Archibald Thweatt
Thos. Bollg. Robertson. } Petsbg
John Mc.rae.
Thos. Burchett

Wm. W. Hening
Benj. Brown } Charlottesville
John Watson.
John Kelly

} Commrs. bkrptcy Virginia

James Anderson of S.C. V. Commercl. agent at Cette.
Rufus King. to settle boundaries with Canada &c

19. Isaac Cox Barnet. Commercl. agent Antwerp. vice   Blake
John Mason Brigadier genl. of the militia of Columbia
Daniel Carrol Brent. Colo.
Luke Tiernan.
Wm. Mc.creary
James Carey.
<*Henry Payson*> } Commrs. bkrptcy Maryland.
decld.
John Caldwell
John Scott

21. John Rowan Surveyor &[3] Inspector of revenue port of Windsor.
N.C. v. Wm. Benson.
Alexander Scott.   do.   Nanjemoy.
Maryld. vice John C. Jones decd.

22. George Gilpin
Francis Peyton } Commrs. bkrptcy. Columbia. Alexa.
Walter Jones junr.
Jonah Thompson

Theodore Gaillard.
<*Dominic*> A. Hall
decld.
<*John* >Blake. decld } Commrs. S. Carola. Charleston
<*Simeon*> Theus.
decld.
Wiliam Moultrie.
Benjamin Cudworth

23. John S. Dexter
    Seth Wheaton
    Samuel Eddy   }   do. Rhode isld. Provdce.
    Sylvanus Martin
    Isaac Cox Barnet of N. Jersey. Comml. Agent Antwerp
       vice   Blake

MS (DLC: TJ Papers, 186:33096); entirely in TJ's hand, including cancellations and emendations made at later sittings; being the continuation of a list that extends from 5 Mch. 1801 to 23 Feb. 1809; for the first section of TJ's list with entries extending from 5 Mch. 1801 to 14 May 1802, see Vol. 33:674-9.

[1] This and preceding entry, including date, interlined.

[2] Interlined in place of George Hay.

[3] TJ interlined preceding word and ampersand.

Appendix II

Bankruptcy Commissions

I. LIST OF CANDIDATES FOR BANKRUPTCY COMMISSIONS,
[CA. 1 MAY-6 JULY 1802]

II. LIST OF NOMINATIONS FOR BANKRUPTCY COMMISSIONS,
[8 JUNE 1802-18 NOV. 1803]

E D I T O R I A L   N O T E

Section 14 of the 29 Apr. 1802 "Act to amend the Judicial System of the United States" gave the president the authority to appoint general commissioners of bankruptcy in each judicial district "as he may deem necessary." Before the modification, the Bankruptcy Act of 1800 called for the district judge in the case to appoint up to three "good and substantial" persons, who were U.S. citizens and residents of the district, to serve as commissioners. Jefferson believed that under the Act of 1800, Federalist judges usually appointed Federalists as bankruptcy commissioners and that the new legislation would allow the appointment of Republicans. During the weeks immediately following the passage of the act, Jefferson received many recommendations, solicited and unsolicited. Several Republican congressmen provided the names of candidates for their districts before they left Washington at the close of the session. Senator Christopher Ellery and Representative Joseph Stanton, Jr., on 30 Apr. submitted the candidates for Newport, Rhode Island, and on 3 May, Senators John Brown and John Breckenridge provided those for Kentucky. Others, including DeWitt Clinton and John Condit, left Washington promising to send the president their nominees after consulting with friends and obtaining accurate information (U.S. Statutes at Large, 2:21-2, 164; Bruce H. Mann, *Republic of Debtors: Bankruptcy in the Age of American Independence* [Cambridge, Mass., 2002], 225-6, 330n; Clinton to TJ, 3 May; TJ to Monroe, 26 June; Condit to TJ, 28 June). Jefferson solicited other nominations. He wrote John Langdon on 5 May, James Monroe and Thomas Sumter on 9 May, and Caesar A. Rodney on 14 June. He sought an equal number of merchants and lawyers, all Republicans, of respectable character, "which is essential." When Jefferson learned whether the candidate was a merchant or lawyer, he added the information to his list, sometimes with an "M." or "L." Finally, the president relied on members of his inner circle at Washington for nominations. Henry Dearborn and Levi Lincoln provided the candidates for Maine and Massachusetts, Gideon Granger for Connecticut, Gallatin for Pennsylvania, and Robert Smith for Maryland (see notes to Memorandums to Albert Gallatin, 10 June; Memorandum on Appointments, 6 July; and to List 1, below).

Jefferson probably began compiling List 1 in early May after he had received a number of recommendations, writing the name or abbreviation for each state in two major columns on a single sheet of paper, beginning with New Hampshire ("N.H.") and ending with Kentucky ("K."). It is clear he left insufficient space for all of the New Hampshire candidates as he was forced to interline a name and cancel and rewrite the designation for Maine after he received John Langdon's recommendations on 30 May. Jefferson kept adding names to the list as he received recommendations until early July. He entered the undated list of candidates provided by Dearborn and Lincoln sometime between 28 June and 6 July, when he sent the nominations for Maine and Massachusetts to the State Department. At the same time, Jefferson did not bother to enter the nominations for New Jersey, which were forwarded by Governor Joseph Bloomfield on 30 June and received by the president on 3 July. He entered the names immediately on List 2. The spaces Jefferson left for Vermont, North Carolina, and Tennessee nominees remained blank. He did not receive those nominations until later in 1802 and January 1803, when he added the names to List 2 as they were appointed (Madison, *Papers, Sec. of State Ser.*, 3:579; Langdon to TJ, 14 May; Stephen R. Bradley to TJ, 13 Sep.; Nathaniel Macon to TJ, 7 Nov.; Timothy Bloodworth to TJ, 30 Nov. 1802; Joseph Anderson, William Cocke, and William Dickson to TJ, 6 Jan. 1803).

Jefferson began compiling List 2 as he appointed the bankruptcy commissioners, the earliest being that of 8 June for Georgetown and Washington in the District of Columbia. His correspondence does not indicate who provided the recommendations. Jefferson dated the appointments not from the day he sent the nominations to the State Department, but on, or shortly after, he signed the commissions. For several weeks Jefferson was working on both lists. As he decided upon the appointments for New Hampshire, New York, Pennsylvania, Maryland, the District of Columbia, Richmond and Petersburg, Virginia, and Kentucky between 8 and 22 June, Jefferson drew a vertical stroke through the candidates names and wrote "done" vertically in the margin by the cities and states in List 1, presumably as he transferred the names of those appointed to List 2. The president drew a stroke through the Alexandria candidates, appointed 22 June, but he did not write "done" alongside the names. After the first week in July, List 2 became Jefferson's working list, on which he canceled the names of appointees as he received news of declinations and resignations and entered the names of new appointees. Commissions were issued on 18 Nov. 1803 for the last three entries on the president's list, appointments for the district of Williamsborough, North Carolina. The president signed the repeal of the Bankruptcy Act on 19 Dec. 1803 (list of commissions in Lb in DNA: RG 59, MPTPC; U.S. Statutes at Large, 2:248).

I. List of Candidates for Bankruptcy Commissions

[ca. 1 May-6 July 1802]

N.H.	*Timothy Walker. Concord.	by John S. Sherburne *Genl. Dearborne
	Jonathan Smith. Amherst.	J.S.S. <*Gen>
	*Nicholas Gilman.	J.S.S. * Genl. D.
	Jonathan Steele. Durham	J.S.S.
	John Goddard. mercht	J.S.S. * Genl. D. Langd.
	Jonathan Warner	J.S.S
	Samuel Sherburne	J.S.S
	<Joshua Bruckell>	J.S.S. * Genl. D.
	Edward Cutts	J.S.S.
	Charles Cutts. Langd. lawyer[1]	
	George Long	J.S.S.
	*Henry S. Langdon	J.S.S. Langd. Lawyer
<Maine>	*John Mc.clintock.	Langd. mercht.

	Joseph Mc.lellan		
	Joseph Boyd		
Maine	Salmon Chace	}	Portld.
	Wm. Widgery		

	Jonathan L. Austin		
	Thos. Dawes junr.		
	Saml. Brown		
Mass.	Otis. W.C.N.	}	Boston
	Joseph Blake		
	Thos. Edwards		

		Nathan Dana
		Isaac Story.
	Marblehead.	Jacob Crowninshield }
		Burley

	Josiah Smith	
	Ralph Cross	
	Joseph Markwan	} Newbury port.
	Joshua Carter	

R.I.			Constant Tabor
	Vernon,	} Ellery & Stanton	Samuel Vernon
	Tabor		Thomas Peckham
	Peckham	} for Newport	Paul M. Mumford
	Mumford		

John S. Dexter
Seth Wheaton
Saml Eddy   Provdce[2]
Sylvans. Martin

Conn.[3]

Hezekiah Huntington ⎫
Jonathan Bull   ⎪
Joseph Hart   ⎬ Hartford
John Dodd.   ⎭
Henry Waggaman Edwards. ⎫
Elihu Munson   ⎪
Jehosaphat Starr   ⎬ N. Haven & Middletn
John Nichols   ⎭
Elisha Hyde   ⎫
Jonathan Frisbie ⎪
Nichol Fosdick   ⎬ New London
Jacob Dewitt   ⎭

Verm.

N.Y.

Wm. Cutting. Brock. Livingston.   √ + M. John Broom
+ Bailey   √   M. Wm. Edgar
Van Ness   M. Solomon Townsend
+ Nathan Sandfort. Genl. Smith   √ + L. Jonathan Pearsee junr.
Pierre C. Van Wyck. N.Y.   √   L. Danl. D. Tompkins
  lawyer   √ + L. Nathan Sandford[4]
Saml. Hawkins lawyer.   ⎫
Jas. Talmadge junr.   ⎬ Bailey & V. Cortlandt
  Poughkeepsie lawyer   ⎭
√ Jas. Fairlie. Liv. & Mitchel

Albany.

Abraham G. Lansing
Nicholas N. Quackenbush
George Merchant.

N.J.   Linn
P.   Tenche Coxe.
√ Van cleve ⎫ Helms Condit.
Levy   ⎭ Leib.
√ Dickerson
Robert Mc.kean   ⎫
√ Al. J. Dalles   ⎬ Govr. Mc.kean.
Moore   Dallas
Lieper

	Robert Porter.	Genl Irwin
	John Read jr.	Meredith
	✓ Clay	
	✓ Compston.	Jones & Clay
	Hugh Ferguson.	J. Beckley
	✓ John Sergeant.	
D.	French Mc.Mullin	New castle
	James Brobson	
	John Warner	Wilmington
	Isaac H. Starr	
Mar.	John Scott	
	<Dr. Geo. Buchanan>	Mc.kean
	Wm. McCreery. mercht.	R.S.
	Henry Payson mercht	R.S.
	Luke Tiernan mercht.	R.S.
	James Carey	
	John Caldwell	
Col.	Hanson	
	<[Danl. Brent?]>	
	<Hewitt>	
	Dalton	
	Thornton	
	<Spriggs>	
	John Mackell Gant	
Alexa.	George Gilpin	
	Jonah Thompson	
	Walter Jones junr.	
	Francis Peyton	

V.
- Richmd.
  - ✓ Geo. Hay. L. see others also
  - ✓ Wm. Duvall L.
  - ✓ George W. Smith L.   } Monroe.
  - ✓ Benj. Hatcher M.
  - David Lambert
- Petsbg.
  - Archibald Thweatt. L.
  - Thos. Bolling Robertson. L.
  - John Mc.rae. M.   } Monroe.
  - Thos. Burchett. M.
- Norfolk
  - Littleton W. Tazewell.
  - Richd. Evers Lee
  - *<Meriwether Jones>*
  - Myers Moses.

N.C.

S.C.   *<Charleston. John Webb.>* qu. politics?
        √ + L. Mc.Intosh. Simon. L. repub.
        √   L. Moultrie Wm.
        √   L. Hall Dominic A.
        √   M. Cudworth Benj.
        √   L. Dickinson Francis
        √   M. Somarsall Thos.

G.   Robert Walker
        Richard Tubman
        Wm. H. Jack   } Augusta
        Joshua *<Meigs>* Meals
        Hugh Nesbit

T.

K.   Frankfort. John Rowan
                    Danl. Weisger
                    John Inston.   } Brown & Breckenridge
        Lexington. James Morrison
                    John A. Seitz.
                    John Bradford.

MS (DNA: RG 59, LAR, 6:0086-7); undated; entirely in TJ's hand; in two columns, arranged by states, with the candidates for Delaware, "D.," appearing at the head of the second column; TJ drew a vertical stroke through the names of candidates at New Hampshire, New York, Pennsylvania, Maryland, Columbia, Alexandria, Richmond, Petersburg, and Kentucky, presumably at the time he made the first appointments in June; TJ wrote "done" vertically in the margin beside the candidates names as organized by cities and states, except at Marblehead, Alexandria, Norfolk, and Georgia; at the foot of the second column TJ canceled "Richd. Howard of Pensylva to be."

w.c.n.: perhaps Wilson Cary Nicholas recommended Samuel A. Otis, but no direct evidence has been found.

conn.: Gideon Granger provided TJ with a list of 12 names for Connecticut, divided into three sets of four candidates each, exactly as entered by TJ above (MS in DNA: RG 59, LAR, 4:0086-7; undated; unsigned, in Granger's hand; endorsed by TJ: "Connecticut Commrs. Bkrptcy"). All were appointed (see List 2).

r.s.: that is, Robert Smith. The secretary of the navy provided TJ with all of the candidates for Maryland, except George Buchanan, who, as TJ indicates, was recommended by Thomas McKean (MS in DNA: RG 59, LAR, 10:0122-3; undated; in Robert Smith's hand; listing nine candidates, the six recorded by TJ for Maryland, above, and three whose names were canceled; endorsed by TJ: "Maryland Commrs. bankruptcy"). All six recommended by Smith received appointment (see List 2).

After conversing with Gallatin in New York, Peter Freneau, publisher of the *Carolina Gazette* at Charleston, sent the Treasury secretary his recommendations for South Carolina. He recommended William MOULTRIE and the following four candidates on the list above (Freneau to Gallatin, 19 May 1802, in DNA: RG 59, LAR; Brigham, *American Newspapers*, 2:1024). TJ did not make the

South Carolina appointments until he received Thomas Sumter's 30 May letter on 17 June, when he entered Sumter's recommendations directly on List 2.

Writing from Augusta to an unidentified recipient on 4 June 1802, John Milledge recommended ROBERT WALKER and the four other candidates from Augusta as "fit persons" for the positions. He requested that the names be given to the president (RC in DNA: RG 59, LAR, 12:0019-20; endorsed by TJ: "Commrs. bkrptcy. Augusta. Georgia"). TJ did not appoint commissioners for Augusta until 1 Mch. 1803. From the list above, Walker only was selected. Abraham Baldwin recommended him on the date of his appointment (list of commissions in Lb in DNA: RG 59, MPTPC; Baldwin to TJ, 1 Mch. 1803, in DNA: RG 59, LAR).

[1] Entry interlined.
[2] Written vertically alongside the four names. TJ entered the four candidates for Providence alongside those for Newport. He wrote "done" at each of the sets.
[3] Written over partially erased "Verm."
[4] TJ wrote "De W. Clinton" vertically in the inside margin alongside the preceding six names.

II. List of Nominations for Bankruptcy Commissions

[8 June 1802-18 Nov. 1803]

N. Hampshire.
June 14. Nicholas Gilman.
          <*John Goddard.*> resd. Richd. Cutts Shannon.
          Henry S. Langdon.
          John Mc.lintock.

Massachusets.
July 7.   Boston.   Jonathan Loring Austin
                       Thomas Dawes junr.
                       <*Samuel Brown*>. declined. Danl. Tilden
                       Joseph Blake.
                       <*Samuel Allen*> Otis decld. Edwd. Jones
                       Thos. Edwards.
          Newbury port Josiah Smith
                       Ralph Cross
                       Joseph Markwan.
                       Joshua Carter. declines.
          Portland.   <*Joseph Mc.lellen*>. declines
                       <*Joseph Boyd*>. nt qualifd. John Mussey
                       Salmon Chace
                       Wm. Widgery.
July 8.   Salem.   Jacob Crowninshield. declines.
Aug. 27.   Wm. Cleveland
                            Killam.

July 8.   Beverley.   Nathan Danna. declines
                                Wm. Burley. declines
             Marblehead.   Isaac Story. superseded.
Sep. 10.   Joseph Story
1803. June   Worcester.   Saml. Flagg
                                Abraham Lincoln
                                Francis Blake

Rhode island
June 8.   Newport.   Constant Tabor
                                Samuel Vernon.
    12.   Thomas Peckham
                                Paul M. Munford.
    23.   Providence.   John S. Dexter
                                Seth Wheaton
                                Samuel Eddy
                                Sylvanus Martin.

Connecticut.
July 2.   Hartford.   Hezekiah Huntington
                                Jonathan Bull   declined. Wm. Judd.
                                Joseph Hart
                                John Dodd. declines. Henry Seymour.
             N. Haven.   Henry Waggaman Edwards.
                                Elihu Monson
                                Jehosaphat Starr
                                John Nichols. declines. Obadiah Hodgkiss.
             N. London   Elisha Hyde. declined. Samuel Motte
                                Jonathan Frisbie
                                Nichol Fosdick
                                <*Jacob DeWitt*>. resd. Simeon Thomas.
Vermont.   Rutland.   Saml. Prentiss of Rutland
                                Darius Chipman declined. Horatio Seymour.
                                    Mid[. . .]
                                <*Richd. Skinner*> resd. Jonathan E. Robinson.
             Windsor.   Mark Richards of Westminster
                                Reuben Atwater. of do.
                                <*James Elliot of Brattleboro'*> resd.
                                Oliver Gallop. of Hartland.
New York.
June 14.   N. York.   John Broome
                                <*Wm. Edgar.*> resigns. Charles Ludlow.
                                Jonathan L. Pearsee junr.
                                Danl. D. Tompkins

		Nathan Sandford
		James Fairlee
	Albany.	Abraham G. Lansing.
		<Nichs N. Quackenbush>. resd. Abram Ten Wyck
		George Merchant.
	Willsboro'	Peter Sailly. Stephen Cuyler. Jas. Mc.rae.

New Jersey

July 7.	Newark.	Thos. Ward.
	N. Brunswick.	Phineas Manning
		John Cobb.
	Woodstown.	Isaiah Shinn.
	Burlington	Abraham Brown.
	Bordenton.	Anthony F. Taylor.

Pensylvania

June 14.	Philada.	A. J. Dallas
		Mahlone Dickerson
		<Joseph Clay>. resd. Blair Mc.lanahan.
		Thomas Compston
		John Sarjeant.
		John W. Vancleve. dead

Delaware.

July 2.	Wilmington.	James Brobson.
		John Warner.
		Isaac H. Starr.
	Newcastle.	French Mc.Mullin

Maryland.

June 19.	Baltimore.	Luke Tiernan
		Wm. Mc.Creary
		James Carey
		<Henry Payson>. declind. John Stephen
		John Caldwell
		<John Scott>.

Columbia.

June 8.	Washington.	Wm. Thornton
		<Tristram Dalton>. decld.
	George town.	*<John Mc.kall Gant>.* resd. Jas. S. Morsel
		Saml. Hanson.
		James S. Morsell
	Alexa.	George Gilpin
		Francis Peyton
		Walter Jones jr.
		Jonah Thompson.

Virginia.

June 16.	Richmd.	George Hay. declined. George Tucker
		<wm. Duval>. resd. Wm. Duval reappd.
		George W. Smith.
		<Benjamin Hutchins>. declind.
	Petersbg.	Archibald Thweatt.
		Thos. Bolling Robertson.
		John Mc.rae.
		Thos. Burchett.
July 7.	Norfolk	*<Lyttleton W. Tazewell. declind.>* — *<Nimmo>*.
		resd. Rd. H. Lee
		<Richd. Evers Lee>. resd. John E. Holt
		<Moses Myers>. declind.
		Thomas Blanchard.
	Fredsbg.	Francis Brooke, Stephen Winchester, Robert
		Patton.
June. 16.	Charlotvlle	Wm. W. Henning. resigned
		Benj. Brown
		John Watson
		John Kelly.

Kentucky.

June 12.	Frankfort	John Rowan.
		Danl. Weisgar.
		John Inston.
	Lexington	James Morrison.
		John A. Seitz.
		John Bradford.

N. Carolina.

[Nov]. 24.02.	Newbern.	Edward Harriss
		Wm. Blackledge
		<Thomas Webber>. declined
		Saml. Gerock.
	Wilmington	Joshua Potts.
		Christopher Dudley
		Caleb D. Howard
		James Walker
	Edenton	Nathanl. Allen. Edenton
		John Eaton ⎫
		Goodorum Davis ⎬ Halifx
		⎭
		Wm. Cherry junr. Bertie cy

Tennissee   *<Edward Scott>* } James Trimble
                          John Crozier } Knoxville
                          Moses Fish. } Nashville
                          George Mc.Deaderich }

S. Carolina.
June 22.   Charleston.   Theodore Gaillard.
                          <Dominic A. Hall>. declind. Simon Mc.Intosh
                          <John Blake>. declind. Wm. Lee jr.
                          <Simeon Theus>. declind. Guilliam Aertson
                          <William Moultrie>. resd. Francis Mulligan.
                          Benjamin Cudworth.

Georgia.   John Postel Williamson
            Edward Stebbins
            <Joseph Welscher> resd. } Savanna.
            Wm. B. Bullock
            Thomas Collier. Louisville
            Cowles Mead.
            Robert Walker } Augusta.
            George Watkins

N. Carolina additional
            James Lyne
            Wm. Roberts } Williamsboro'
            Wm. HuntMS

(DNA: RG 59, LAR, 6:0088-9); entirely in TJ's hand; partially dated; torn; at head of text: "Commrs. bankruptcy"; TJ continuously updated this list as he received news of changes, canceling the names of those who had declined or resigned their commissions and adding names as new commissions were issued.

ABRAM TEN WYCK: that is, Abraham Ten Eyck (Madison, *Papers, Sec. of State Ser.*, 5:101). WILLSBORO: TJ did not appoint these commissioners until 4 Mch. 1803 (list of commissions in Lb in DNA: RG 59, MPTPC).

FREDSBG.: the commissions for those at Fredericksburg were issued on 28 Feb. 1803 (same).

Appendix III

Letters Not Printed in Full

EDITORIAL NOTE

In keeping with the editorial method established for this edition, the chronological series includes "in one form or another every available letter known to have been written by or to Thomas Jefferson" (Vol. 1:xv). Most letters are printed in full. In some cases, the letter is not printed but a detailed summary appears at the document's date (for an example, see Joseph Yznardi, Sr., 16 Mch. 1802). Other letters have been described in annotation, which, for the period covered by this volume, are listed in this appendix. Arranged in chronological order, this list includes for each letter the correspondent, date, and location in the volumes where it is described. Among the letters included here are brief letters of transmittal, multiple testimonials recommending a particular candidate for office, repetitive letters from a candidate seeking a post, and official correspondence that the president saw in only a cursory way. In other instances, documents are described in annotation due to the near illegibility of the surviving text. Using the list in this appendix, the table of contents, and Appendix IV (correspondence not found but recorded in Jefferson's Summary Journal of Letters), readers will be able to reconstruct Jefferson's chronological epistolary record from 4 Mch. to 30 June 1802.

From Thomas Ballendine, received 4 Mch. 1802. Noted at Ballendine to TJ, 28 Feb. 1802.

Petition of John D. Thompson, 5 Mch. 1802. Noted at Joseph H. Nicholson to TJ, 8 Mch. 1802.

To the Senate, 11 Mch. 1802. Noted at TJ to the Senate, 10 Mch. 1802 (second letter).

From Joseph Stanton, 11 Mch. 1802. Noted at Christopher Ellery to TJ, 10 Mch. 1802.

From Gideon Granger, 17 Mch. 1802. Noted at Granger to TJ, 23 Mch. 1802.

From Joseph Anderson, 30 Mch. 1802. Noted at William Eustis to TJ, 30 Mch. 1802.

From Joseph Anderson, William Cocke, and William Dickson, received 30 Mch. 1802. Noted at David Campbell to TJ, 12 Feb. 1802.

From Robert Brown, Isaac Van Horne, and John Stewart, 30 Mch. 1802. Noted at John Beckley to TJ, 18 Mch. 1802.

From the Senate, 2 Apr. 1802. Noted at TJ to the Senate, 3 Apr. 1802.

To William C. C. Claiborne, 3 Apr. 1802. Noted at TJ to the Mississippi Territory House of Representatives, 3 Apr. 1802.

From the Senate, 6 Apr. 1802. Noted at TJ to the Senate, 8 Apr. 1802.

To the Senate, 7 Apr. 1802. Noted at Henry Dearborn to TJ, 6 Apr. 1802.

From Albert Gallatin, 8 Apr. 1802. Noted at TJ to Nicholas Reib, 9 Apr. 1802.

To the Senate, 17 Apr. 1802. Noted at James Madison to TJ, 16 Apr. 1802.

To the Senate and the House of Representatives, 20 Apr. 1802. Noted at Elias Boudinot to TJ, 17 Apr. 1802.

From Robert Smith, 20 Apr. 1802. Noted at Smith to TJ, 16 Apr. 1802.

To the Senate, 21 Apr. 1802. Noted at Robert Smith to TJ, 16 Apr. 1802.

From James Madison, Albert Gallatin, and Levi Lincoln, 26 Apr. 1802. Noted at TJ to the Senate and the House of Representatives, 26 Apr. 1802.

From Henry Dearborn, April 1802. Noted at Dearborn to TJ, 9 Apr. 1802.

From Thomas Newton, 1 June 1802. Noted at Newton to TJ, 1 June 1802.

From John Bird, 8 June 1802. Noted at Delaware Democratic Republicans to TJ, [5 June 1802].

To James Penn, 9 June 1802. Noted at Penn to TJ, 24 May 1802.

To Samuel Miller, 13 June 1802. Noted at Miller to TJ, 10 June 1802.

From William Jones, 16 June 1802. Noted at William Davidson to TJ, 10 June 1802.

Petition of David Jackson, undated. Noted at Daniel Brent to TJ, 21 May 1802.

Appendix IV

Letters Not Found

EDITORIAL NOTE

This appendix lists chronologically letters written by and to Jefferson during the period covered by this volume for which no text is known to survive. Jefferson's Summary Journal of Letters provides a record of the missing documents. For incoming letters, Jefferson typically recorded in SJL the date that the letter was sent and the date on which he received it. He sometimes included the location from which it was dispatched and an abbreviated notation indicating the government department to which it pertained: "N" for Navy, "P.M.G." for Postmaster General's Office, "S" for State, "T" for Treasury, and "W" for War.

From James Dinsmore, 6 Mch.; received 10 Mch. from Monticello.

To Benjamin Brown, 7 Mch.

From Oliver Ellsworth, received 8 Mch.; notation: "S."

To Henry Sheaff, 10 Mch.; notation: "220.50."

From Benjamin Brown, 11 Mch.; received 17 Mch.

From George R. Lawton, 11 Mch.; received 14 Mch. from Philadelphia; notation: "Rob. Lawton to be Navl. offic. Newp."

From Heath Norbury, 11 Mch.; received 14 Mch. from Philadelphia; notation: "to be public storekeeper Phila. W."

From Robert Patterson, 12 Mch.; received 14 Mch. from Philadelphia; notation: "Silas Engles to be pub. sto. keep. Phila."

From Samuel Carswell and others; received 14 Mch.; notation: "Jas. Mc.Glatheny to be keeper public stores Phila. W."

To James Dinsmore, 14 Mch.

From George Helmbold, 14 Mch.; received 17 Mch. from Philadelphia; notation: "to be public storekeeper W."

From Lewis D. Carpentier, 15 Mch.; received 18 Mch. from Philadelphia; notation: "S."

To John Thomson Mason, 16 Mch.

From Matthew Bunce, 17 Mch.; received 21 Mch. from New York; notation: "N."

From Thomas Martin, 17 Mch.; received 27 Apr. from Detroit.

From Thomas Procter, 18 Mch.; received 25 Mch. from Lancaster; notation: "to be public storekeeper Phila. W."

From Black Hoof, 19 Mch.; received 24 Mch. from Philadelphia; notation: "(Indian). W."

From William Jones, 19 Mch.; received 20 Mch. from Washington; notation: "Spencer to be Surgeon Marne. hosp. N.O."

From Gabriel Lilly, 19 Mch.; received 24 Mch. from Monticello.

To Benjamin Brown, 20 Mch.

From Henry Sheaff, 20 Mch.; received 24 Mch. from Philadelphia.

From Mordecai Yarnall, 21 Mch.; received 29 Mch. from Wheeling; notation: "T."

From Henry Sheaff, 22 Mch.; received 5 Apr. from Philadelphia.

From Richard Stanford, 22 Mch.; received 22 Mch. from Congress; notation: "Potter to be district judge."

From Philip Turner, 26 Mch.; received 31 Mch. from New York; notation: "to be in Medical line."

From Martin Dawson, 27 Mch.; received 31 Mch. from Milton.

From James Dinsmore, 27 Mch.; received 31 Mch. from Monticello.

From Anne Cary Randolph, 27 Mch.; received 31 Mch. from Edgehill.

From William Wedderburn, 27 Mch.; received 30 Mch. from Fredericksburg; notation: "to be P.M. Fredsbg., Alexa. P.M.G."

To Martin Dawson, 1 Apr.

To James Dinsmore, 1 Apr.

From Meriwether Jones, 1 Apr.; received 14 Apr. from Norfolk; notation: "Dr. John K. Read to be Superintendt. hospit. Norf."

To Roberts & Jones, 1 Apr.

From David Austin, 2 Apr.; received 1 Apr. from Washington; notation: "to be chapln. of the Presid's household."

From Watson & Higginbotham, 2 Apr.; received 6 Apr. from Milton.

From David Brown, 3 Apr.; received 3 Apr. from Washington.

To Gabriel Lilly, 3 Apr.; notation: "125."

From Warden and others, 3 Apr.; received 9 Apr.; notation: "marines. N."

From Joseph Leacock, 5 Apr.; received 9 Apr.; notation: "W."

From Roberts & Jones, 6 Apr.; received 9 Apr. from Philadelphia.

From Martin Dawson, 9 Apr.; received 13 Apr. from Milton.

To Robertson & Brown, 10 Apr.

From Philip Ludwell Grymes, 11 Apr.; received 15 Apr. from Brandon.

From Daniel Baldwin, 12 Apr.; received 14 Apr. from New York; notation: "lost leg at Germ.t. asks some employ. W."

From Benjamin Lincoln, 14 Apr.; received 26 Apr. from Boston; notation: "Cushing to be Consul at Marseilles."

From Joseph Stanton, 14 Apr.; received 14 Apr.; notation: "W. Nichols to be   ."

From James Dinsmore, 16 Apr.; received 19 Apr. from Monticello.

From James Oldham, 16 Apr.; received 19 Apr. from Monticello.

From Robertson & Brown, 17 Apr.; received 22 Apr. from Norfolk.

To James Dinsmore, 25 Apr.

From Gideon Granger, 26 Apr.; received 26 Apr.; notation: "post to Milton."

From John Archer, 1 May; received 2 May from Washington; notation: "Robt. Harris to be contd. Surgeon's mate. N."

From Goujon the younger ("Goujon jeune"), 1 May; received 22 Oct. from Poitiers.

From Joseph Monroe, 5 May; received 30 May from Northumberland; notation: "L. Edwards to be Suptdt. lighthouse."

From Miles King, 8 May; received 13 May from Norfolk; notation: "for office."

From Mann Page, 9 May; received 13 May from Mannsfield.

From Wilson Cary Nicholas, 11 May; received 18 May from Warren; notation: "C. Jouett to be Indn. Agent."

From Turner Anderson, 15 May; received 17 May from Green Springs.

From John F. Gaullier, 15 May; received 1 June from "Jefferson town Culpep."

To William Wirt, 15 May.

From Benoni Williams, 20 May; received 30 May from Providence; notation: "agt Loan officr. of Provdce."

From Ethan Curtis, received 23 May.

From Joseph Bloomfield, 24 May; received 30 May from Trenton; notation: "Dr. Olivr. Barnet to be Marsl."

From Reuben Broughton, 24 May; received 30 May from Fort Adams, Newport, Rhode Island; notation: "W."

From William Wardlaw, 26 May; received 26 May.

To Benjamin Brown, 27 May.

To Burgess Griffin, 27 May.

From Martin Huntur, 29 May; received 29 June from Port William, Kentucky.

From Richard Dinmore, received 30 May.

From John Perry, 2 June; received 8 June from Milton.

From Burgess Griffin, 3 June; received 11 June from Poplar Forest.

From George Frederick Stras, 3 June; received 6 June from Richmond.

To James Dinsmore, 4 June.

To William Maddox, 4 June.

From John F. Mercer, 4 June; received 12 June from Annapolis; notation: "Al. Scott to be Collectr. Nanjemy."

From George Washington Varnum, 4 June; received 21 June from "Oakridge Amherst (Rives's)."

From Mary Graham, 9 June; received 30 June from Mason County, Kentucky.

From Laurence Manning, 10 June; received 1 July from Jamesville, South Carolina; notation: "Adjt. Genl. S.C. 13,000 rifles, muskets, &c. 2073 cavalry 33712 infantry 35785 total."

From Thomas Mann Randolph, 10 June; received 20 June from Edgehill.

From Nathaniel Bowditch, 11 June; received 24 June from Salem.

From Martin Dawson, 11 June; received 16 June from Milton.

From Samuel Moody, 11 June; received 15 June from Richmond; notation: "his bror John to be Collector Petsbg."

To John Perry, 11 June.

From the Treasury Department, received 12 June; notation: "Mc.lane's case."

To John Wayles Eppes, 13 June.

From William Maddox, 13 June; received 16 June from Monticello.

From Martha Jefferson Randolph, 13 June; received 16 June from Edgehill.

From William Wirt, 14 June; received 17 June from Richmond.

From Henry Sheaff, 15 June; received 16 June from Philadelphia.

From James Dinsmore, 17 June; received 21 June from Monticello.

From James Oldham, 17 June; received 21 June from Monticello.

From William Wardlaw, 17 June; received 21 June from Charlottesville.

From William P. Anderson, 18 June; received 4 July from Nashville.

To Martin Dawson, 18 June.

From William Dickson, 18 June; received 4 July from Nashville.

From Daniel Smith, 18 June; received 4 July from Sumner County, Tennessee.

From the Treasury Department, 18 June; received 18 June; notation: "hospital ground at Boston."

From Martin Dawson, 21 June; received 24 June from Milton.

To William Maddox, 22 June.

From Roberts & Jones, 22 June; received 24 June from Philadelphia; notation: "iron & steel. 52.73 D."

From S. Foster, 24 June; received 10 July from Havana; notation: "imprisd. in Havanna. S."

From Francis Peyton, 24 June; received 25 June from Alexandria.

To James Dinsmore, 25 June.

From James Oldham, 27 June; received 30 June from Monticello.

From George Stevenson, 28 June; received 6 July from Pittsburgh; notation: "W."

From Amos and Ethan Stillman, 28 June; received 13 July from Farmington; notation: "W."

From Tuscarora Chiefs, 30 June; received 17 July from Fort Niagara; notation: "W."

From John Frederic Wrede, 30 June; received 31 Oct. from Oldenburg; notation: "S."

Appendix V

Financial Documents

E D I T O R I A L   N O T E

This appendix briefly describes, in chronological order, the orders and invoices pertaining to Jefferson's finances during the period covered by this volume that are not printed in full or accounted for elsewhere in this volume. The orders for payments to Étienne Lemaire and Joseph Dougherty pertain, for the most part, to expenses associated with running the President's House. The *Memorandum Books* are cited when they are relevant to a specific document and provide additional information.

Order on John Barnes for payment of $2.25 to Joseph Dougherty, Washington, 8 Mch. 1802 (MS in MHi; in TJ's hand and signed by him; signed by Dougherty acknowledging payment; endorsed by Barnes as paid on 8 Mch.). TJ recorded this transaction as payment for blacksmithing and "shavings for ice house" (MB, 2:1066).

Order on John Barnes for payment of $27.60 to Joseph Dougherty, Washington, 12 Mch. (MS in MHi; in TJ's hand and signed by him; signed by Dougherty acknowledging payment; endorsed by Barnes as paid on 12 Mch.). TJ recorded this transaction as payment for corn (MB, 2:1068).

Order on John Barnes for payment of $25 to the Reverend Thomas Lucas, Washington, 13 Mch. (MS in MHi; in TJ's hand and signed by him; signed by Lucas acknowledging payment; endorsed by Barnes as paid on 13 Mch.). TJ recorded this transaction as "charity for meetg. house for blacks" (MB, 2:1068).

Order on John Barnes for payment of $61.92 to Étienne Lemaire, Washington, 22 Mch. (MS in ICHi; in TJ's hand and signed by him; signed by Dougherty acknowledging payment). TJ recorded this transaction as payment of Lemaire's accounts from 14 to 20 Mch. for provisions, servants, contingencies, and "Stores for Montico." (MB, 2:1069).

Order on John Barnes for payment of $7.00 to Peter Lenox, 29 Mch. (MS in CSmH; in TJ's hand and signed by him; written on invoice from Lenox to TJ dated 20 Jan. for purchase of "a frame for the Cheese" at $4.50, hooks at $.50, and "board, 3 Rammers for ice house, & 2 ice hook—handle" at $2.00; signed by Lenox acknowledging payment; endorsed by Barnes as paid 29 Mch.). TJ recorded this transaction as payment for "carpenter's work for ice house & cheese" (MB, 2:1069).

Order on John Barnes for payment of $5 to William Duane for a one-year subscription to the *Aurora* for Thomas Mann Randolph, 2 Apr. (MS in MHi; in TJ's hand and signed by him; written on invoice from Duane to Randolph; signed by William Kean for Duane acknowledging payment on 6 Apr.; endorsed by Barnes). See MB, 2:1069.

Order on John Barnes for payment of $5 to William Duane for a one-year subscription to the *Aurora* for Reuben Lindsay, 2 Apr. (MS in MHi; in TJ's hand and signed by him; written on invoice from Duane to Lindsay; signed by William Kean for Duane acknowledging payment on 6 Apr.; endorsed by Barnes). See MB, 2:1069.

Order on John Barnes for payment of $50 to the Reverend William Parkinson, Washington, 7 Apr. (MS in ViU; in TJ's hand and signed by him; signed by Charles Peale Polk acknowledging payment on 13 Apr.; endorsed by Barnes). TJ recorded this transaction as charity "towards a Baptist meeting house" (MB, 2:1070).

Order on John Barnes for payment of $100 to the Reverend Samuel Stanhope Smith, Washington, 9 Apr. (MS in NjP; in TJ's hand and signed by him; signed by Smith acknowledging payment; endorsed by Barnes as paid on 9 Apr.). TJ recorded this transaction as charity "towards rebuilding Princeton college" (MB, 2:1070).

Order on John Barnes for payment of $10.80 to Henry Ingle, 17 Apr. (MS in CSmH; in TJ's hand and signed by him; written on invoice from Ingle to TJ dated 14 Apr. for purchase of a shingling hatchet at $1 on 20 Nov. 1801, a mahogany writing box at $9 on 19 Feb. 1802, two rulers at $.50 on 24 Feb., and five ounces of brass wire at $.30 on 14 Apr.; signed by William Huber for Ingle acknowledging payment; endorsed by Barnes as paid on 17 Apr.). TJ recorded this transaction as payment "for writing box & wire" (MB, 2:1070).

Order on John Barnes for payment of $113.70 to Étienne Lemaire, Washington, 19 Apr. (MS in InU; in TJ's hand and signed by him; signed by "C Julian" with his mark acknowledging payment; endorsed by Barnes as paid on 22 Apr.). TJ recorded this transaction as payment of Lemaire's accounts from 12 to 18 Apr. for provisions and stores (MB, 2:1071).

Order on John Barnes for payment of $12.29 to Joseph Dougherty, Washington, 26 Apr. (MS in MHi; in TJ's hand and signed by him; signed by Dougherty acknowledging payment on 26 Apr.; endorsed by Barnes). TJ recorded this transaction as payment of Dougherty's accounts for forage, a saddler and blacksmith, and servants (MB, 2:1071).

Order on John Barnes for payment of $140.97 to Étienne Lemaire, Washington, 26 Apr. (MS in PPAmP; in TJ's hand and signed by him; signed by Lemaire acknowledging payment; endorsed by Barnes as paid on 26 Apr.). TJ recorded this transaction as payment of Lemaire's accounts from 18 to 24 Apr. for provisions, an Alexandria butcher's account from 20 Feb. to 26 Mch., and servants (MB, 2:1071).

Order on John Barnes for payment of $27.50 to Joseph Dougherty, Washington, 29 Apr. (MS in MHi; in TJ's hand and signed by him; signed by Dougherty acknowledging payment; endorsed by Barnes as paid on 29 Apr.). TJ recorded this transaction as payment for forage (MB, 2:1071).

Order on John Barnes for payment of $30.30 to Joseph Dougherty, 1 May (MS in ICHi; in TJ's hand and signed by him; written on invoice from Captain Davidson to Dougherty dated 28 Apr. for purchase of 100 bushels of coal at $28 and hauling at $2.30; signed by Dougherty acknowledging payment; endorsed by Barnes as paid on 1 May). See MB, 2:1071.

Order on John Barnes for payment of $322.54 to Étienne Lemaire, Washington, 4 June (MS in TxU; in TJ's hand and signed by him; signed by Joseph Dougherty acknowledging payment on 7 June; endorsed by Barnes). TJ recorded this transaction as payment of Lemaire's accounts from 2 to 29 May for provisions, stores, servants, and contingencies, and for servants' wages through 4 June (MB, 2:1074).

Invoice submitted by Isaac Norris to TJ for "Different Repairs on Cheese Hoop" at £1.17.6 and blacksmithing at £0.11.3, totaling £2.8.9 or $6.50, 5 June (MS in CSmH; in Norris's hand and signed by him acknowledging payment on 7 June; endorsed by John Barnes). See MB, 2:1074.

Order on John Barnes for payment of $24 to Joseph Dougherty, Washington, 21 June (MS in MHi; in TJ's hand and signed by him; signed by Dougherty acknowledging payment 21 June; endorsed by Barnes). TJ recorded this transaction as payment for forage, servants, stable contingencies, and other contingencies (MB, 2:1075).

Order on John Barnes for payment of $23 to Peter Lenox, 22 June (MS in CSmH; in TJ's hand and signed by him; written on invoice from Lenox to TJ, dated 18 June, for labor and materials for "making floors in the stalls" at $22 and "a hoop for the use of the Cheese" at $1; signed by Lenox acknowledging payment on 22 June; endorsed by Barnes). See MB, 2:1076.

Order on John Barnes for payment of $6 to George Walker, Washington, 24 June (MS in MHi; in TJ's hand and signed by him; signed by Walker acknowledging payment on 30 June; endorsed by Barnes). TJ recorded this transaction as payment for a book. (MB, 2:1076).

Order on John Barnes for payment of $55.73½ to Joseph Dougherty, Washington, 28 June (MS in MHi; in TJ's hand and signed by him; signed by Dougherty acknowledging payment; endorsed by Barnes as paid on 28 June). TJ recorded this transaction as payment for 100 bushels of coal, forage, farrier work, and servants (MB, 2:1076).

INDEX

Abeel, John, 38n
abolition, 507n
Abrahams, Abraham David, 194-5, 325, 349
Abrégé chronologique de l'histoire ancienne des empires et des républiques (Jacques Lacombe), 232
Abrégé chronologique de l'histoire d'Angleterre (Thomas Salmon), 232
Abrégé chronologique de l'histoire de Pologne (Friedrich August von Schmidt), 232
Abrégé chronologique de l'histoire des Juifs (François Nicolas Charbuy), 232
Abrégé chronologique de l'histoire d'Espagne et de Portugal (Charles Jean François Henault), 232
Abrégé chronologique de l'histoire du Nord: ou des etats de Dannemarck, de Russie, de Suède, de Pologne, de Prusse, de Courlande, &c (Jacques Lacombe), 232
Abrégé chronologique de l'histoire universelle depuis les premiers empires du monde (Johannes Sleidanus, trans. Antoine Hornot), 232
Abridgment des plusieurs cases et resolutions del common ley (Henry Rolle), 230
Académie Française, 232
Academy of Natural Sciences (Philadelphia), 582n
Ackermann, Suardy, & Co., 668-9
Adams, Abigail, 84n
Adams, John: removals by, 27-8, 164n, 410n; late-term appointments, 53n, 89n, 99; makes appointments, 53n, 117, 135n, 136n, 253n, 356n, 363, 474, 609n, 658, 675n; family of, 84n; and the *Berceau,* 184, 185n; and V. du Pont, 223n; declarations of fast days, 294n; and President's House, 332n; administration praised, 436; and France, 436; and Saint-Domingue, 453, 456; and Priestley, 595n; steward of, 610, 611n; criticism of, 658; use of patronage by, 686
Adams, Samuel, 188, 189n
Adams, Fort, 52n, 129n
Adams (U.S. frigate), 71, 160n, 248
Adams's Mill (Orange Co., Va.), 534
Adet, Pierre Auguste, 564n
adultery, 392

Aertsen, Guilliam, 711
Africa: removal of condemned slaves to, 469, 531-3, 588-9
agriculture: viticulture, xi, 12n, 159, 185, 186; tenants, tenancy, 14-15, 289-90, 448, 472-4, 494, 503-4; scientific, 15; hoes, 40, 41n; plows, 95, 105n; crop rotation, 97, 289, 472-4, 503-4; fertilizer, 97, 194n; agricultural societies, 172-3, 177, 179, 217, 290, 339-40, 639, 643-4, 646n; promotion of, 172-3; recommendations for a national board or society, 172-3, 217, 227, 339-40, 537, 688; animal husbandry, 332n; publications on, 340; difficulty establishing farms, plantations, 448; superiority of, over commerce, 609-10; and self-sufficiency, 638, 643; and transportation costs, 638, 643; merino sheep, 674n. *See also* cotton; Indians: Economy; Jefferson, Thomas: Agriculture; tobacco
Ainsworth, Robert: *Latin and English Dictionary Abridged,* 232
Alabama River, 52n
Albany, Bank of, 538n
Albany Register, 312
Albemarle Co., Va.: courts, 15; T. M. Randolph's landholdings in, 15; migration from, 129n; parishes of, 247n; schools, 247n; land values in, 289-90; taverns, 384, 386n; roads, 386n; Franklin plantation, 619, 620n; quality of tobacco from, 657
alcoholism: among Indians, vii, 30, 32, 33-4; among judges, 463n; removals from office due to, 463n
Alembert, Jean Le Rond d': *Encyclopédie,* 232
Alexander I, Emperor of Russia, 202, 203, 204n
Alexander, Archibald, 78
Alexander, Charles, 154
Alexandria, D.C.: roads to, from, 134, 385; jail, 139n; warrant executions in, 142; Federalists in, 170; Republicans in, 170; mayors, 170n, 303n; merchants, 170n; capital punishment in, 208, 215; laws of Virginia adopted in, 212, 215; smallpox vaccination in, 291; collector at, 303n; physicians, 489n; booksellers, 537n; education in, 615; commissioners of bankruptcy,

CONGRESS, U.S. (*cont.*)
officers, 189-90, 429; capital punishment, 207-8, 215, 217n; and judiciary, 212, 214n, 215-17; Library of Congress, 228n, 233n; naturalization, 296, 297n; and Ga. land claims, 301n, 343-5; and British debt claims, 350n; marine hospitals, 377, 649, 663n; and Vincennes survey, 377; Ohio statehood, 380, 381n, 505n; establishment of revenue districts, 391n; militia laws, 399; Convention of 1800, 419n; publication of laws, 437, 477; reapportionment, 467; and state debts, 467; increase of government salaries, 467-8; and Northwest Terr., 606; Delaware River piers, 667n; lighthouses, 667n; and bankruptcy, 701. *See also* Judiciary Act (1801); Judiciary Act (1802); Military Peace Establishment Act (1802); taxes: repeal of

Public Opinion
party spirit undermines cooperation, 94

Senate
messages to, 23-4, 51-2, 52-3, 120-1, 136-8, 138-40, 149, 155-6, 176-7, 181, 187, 191-3, 343-5, 348-9, 349-50, 406; and Indian affairs, viii, 23-4, 51-2; and Washington jail, x, 138-40; Republican majority in, xi, 399-400; and TJ's nominations, 11n, 23-4, 44n, 52-3, 120-1, 144, 154-5, 155-6, 159-60, 176-7, 181, 182, 187, 195n, 249n, 348-9, 406, 465; and Ebenezer Stevens's claim, 133n; and British debt claims, 136-8, 218, 246n, 326, 349-50; and Jay Treaty, 136-8, 153-4, 191-3, 245-6; appropriations and expenditures, 149; military affairs, 149, 159-60; naturalization, 168n; and C. Lyman's nomination, 176-7; messages from cited, 176n, 192n, 713; messages to cited, 182n, 246n, 249n, 250n, 713, 714; sergeant at arms, 219; and the Mint, 249-50; and federal lands in Tenn., 251-2; committees, 251n; and Ga. land claims, 343-5; and Twelfth Amendment, 355; and Symmes purchase, 382-3; impeachment of J. Pickering, 463n; and Barbary states, 675n. *See also* Otis, Samuel A.

Connaissance des temps, 177
Connecticut: commissioners of bankruptcy, 210, 701, 704, 706n, 708; French prisoners in, 238n; newspapers, 312, 341-3; New London, 341-3, 704, 708; elections in, 400, 401n, 488; New London collectorship, 406-7; Norwich, 407n, 417; physicians, 407n; Hartford, 704, 708; Middletown, 704. *See also* Federalists; New Haven, Conn.; Republicans
Connecticut Courant (Hartford), 410n
Considerations on the Propriety of Adopting a General Ticket in South-Carolina ("Crito"), 573-4
Constantinople, 83, 91
Constellation (U.S. frigate), 140n, 160n
Constitution (U.S. frigate), 486n
Constitutional Telegraphe (Boston), 188, 189n, 312
Constitution and Laws of England Consider'd (William Pudsey), 231
Constitution de l'Angleterre (Jean Louis Delolme), 231
Constitution of Parliaments in England (Sir John Pettus), 231
Constitution of the United States: allegorical depictions of, l; Republicans threaten, 28; and District of Columbia, 72; and presidential pardons, 207; and executive powers, 212-14; and judiciary, 335; Twelfth Amendment, 355; and gifts, pensions, bounties, 366; praise for, 593; TJ's contributions to, 593, 595n, 625-7; and freedom of religion, 626; and freedom of the press, 626; and habeas corpus, 626; and standing armies, 626; and states' rights, 626; and trial by jury, 626; and bill of rights, 626-7; and gifts for officeholders, 671-2, 675n
Consuetudo, vel, Lex Mercatoria: or, the Ancient Law-Merchant (Gerard de Malynes), 230
Convention of 1800: and the *Berceau,* 183, 185n, 238-40n; return of captured vessels, 238-40n; French Council of Prizes, 238n, 240n, 419n, 527n; spoliation claims, 266n, 418-19, 452, 455, 482, 484n, 527n; funds to implement, 293n
Conway, Richard, 154, 170, 181
Cooke, Daniel, 118n, 543n
Cooper, Isaac, 134n
Cooper, Richard, 135-6, 150
Cooper, Thomas, 595n

Cooper, William, 136n

copper, 135-6, 150, 250-1n, 559

cork, 167, 172

corn: and self-sufficiency, 95, 97, 638, 643; yields, 95; and cotton, 97; and pinelands, 127; and crop rotation, 472-4, 503-4; in Jamaica, 479; distilled into whiskey, 638, 643; harvest of, 662; purchased by TJ, 719

Cornelius, William, 473

Cornplanter (Seneca Indian): conference with TJ and Dearborn, vii, 29-42; relationship with Handsome Lake, 30-1, 38n; address by, 38; identified, 38n

Cornwallis, Charles, Lord, 84n

Corny, Marguerite Victoire de Palerne de: letter to, 308-10; TJ sends news, advice to, 308-10; P. S. Du Pont carries letters to, 332, 334n; and A. Church, 347

Corps universel diplomatique du droit des gens (Jean Dumont), 229

Corpus juris civilis Romani (Denys Godefroy), 230

Corsica, 26

Cosway, Maria Hadfield, xlvii, 347, 485n

Cottom & Stewart (Alexandria, Va.), 537n

cotton: benefit of, to slaves, xii, 15; plantations, xii, 14-15, 65-7, 95-6, 97-8, 127-8, 133-4; profits from, xii, 15, 65, 67, 133; cultivation of, encouraged, 15, 92, 93n; trade in, 25-7; land values, 67, 95; manufacture of, 92, 93n, 650n; price of, 92, 95; varieties of, 95-6; and crop rotation, 472; as cash crop, 638, 643

Coughtry, Jay, 200n

Courts, U.S.

Circuit

and capital punishment, ix-x, 207-8, 215-16, 283-4; appointments to, 187, 325, 326n, 348, 614; District of Columbia, 195-6, 207-9, 212, 217n, 283-4, 522n; appointment powers of, 207, 208n; and suit against E. Randolph, 288-9; and case of the *Aurora*, 347n

District

appointments to, 19n, 187, 325, 348, 505n, 614; removals from, 462-3

Public Opinion

slowness of courts criticized, 6-7; compensation for jurors and witnesses,

7n; dominated by Federalists, 53n, 438, 462, 701; impeachment, removal of judges, 462-3; court costs and fees, 522n

Supreme Court

and Ga. land claims, 300n; meetings of, 335, 336-7n; and case of the *Aurora,* 347n; clerks, 389n

courts-martial, ix, 54-7, 176-7

Coward, Thomas, 388n

Cowing, Joseph, 615

Cowper, John, 336n

cowpox. *See* smallpox

Coxe, John Redman: letter to, 364-5; letter from, 310-11; and smallpox vaccination, 310-11, 364-5; *Practical Observations on Vaccination,* 311n

Coxe, Tench: letters from, 25-7, 92-3, 161-5, 260-3; advocates trade with China, 25-7; observations on Anglo-American commerce, 25; advocates trade with Turkey, 25-7; and privateering threat from Caribbean, 26-7; suggests acquisition of Cape Breton, 27; Reflections on Cotton, 92-3; and threat of slave insurrections, 92-3; seeks appointment, 161-5, 260-3; and A. Hamilton, 163, 165n; sends information for reports, 163, 164-5n; "American Merchant," 164, 165n; appointed supervisor, 164n; appointed commissioner of bankruptcy, 262, 704; as commissioner of the revenue, 404-5; as reference, 405; recommended for appointment, 578n

Coxe, William, Jr., 211n

Coyer, Gabriel François, 232

Craik, James, 488-9

Cranch, William: letter from, 195-6; and McGinnis's case, 195-6; and McGurk's case, 216, 284n

Crane, Silas, 325, 346, 348

Craven, John H., 66, 67n, 196n

Creek Indians. *See* Indians: Creeks (Muskogees, Muscogees)

"Crito" (pseudonym): *Considerations on the Propriety of Adopting a General Ticket in South-Carolina,* 573-4

Croft, Edward, 23, 53, 189

Croft, Sir Herbert: *Love and Madness,* 631, 632n, 660

Croke, Alexander: *Remarks on Mr. Schlegel's Work,* 230

Crooke, Robert, 325, 348

for TJ, 13; bookselling, stationery
business of, 182, 183, 197, 311; printing contracts, 228n; criticizes *New-
York Evening Post,* 241n; TJ orders
newspapers from, 311, 312, 719-20;
account with TJ, 312; as Republican
leader, 315-16; and M. Carey, 315-18;
sedition trial of, 592n; evaluates political sympathies of government clerks,
635n; and Leiper's appointment, 657.
See also *Aurora* (Philadelphia)
Duane, William J., 657
Dudley, Christopher, 710
duels, 241n, 393n
Dufief, Nicolas Gouin: letters to, 113-15,
156, 197-8; letters from, 5-6, 94, 182-
3, 233-4, 305-6, 352-3; TJ orders
books from, 5-6, 113-15, 156, 182-3,
197-8, 233-4, 305-6; catalogs, 94, 113;
account with TJ, 183n, 198n; forwards pamphlets to TJ, 352-3
Dufour, John James, 186n
Dumfries, Va., 134
Dumont, Jean, Baron de Carlscroon:
*Corps universel diplomatique du droit
des gens,* 229
Dunbar, William, 431, 434n, 563, 661
Duncan, David, 324, 325, 349, 634, 635
Duncan, William, 530
Dundas, John, 170, 181
Dungeness (Randolph estate), 329
Dunlap, Henry, 522n
Dunlavy, Francis, 360n
Dunn, John, 549, 668, 690, 691n
du Pont, Gabrielle Joséphine de la Fite
de Pelleport, 321, 322
du Pont, Victor Marie: returns to U.S.,
178; and U.S.-French relations, 222,
223; refused exequatur, 223n; and
family's business affairs, 321, 322,
458n; forwards letters, 362, 372, 375;
TJ's support for, 366; and Houdon,
454, 456
du Pont de Nemours, Éleuthère Irénée:
characterized, 321, 322; and gunpowder manufacturing, 321, 322, 454,
456, 457-8n; TJ's support for, 366
Du Pont de Nemours, Françoise Robin
Poivre, 334, 366
Du Pont de Nemours, Pierre Samuel:
letters to, 298, 332-4, 365-7, 403, 418-
19; letters from, 165-6, 170-1, 222-3,
320-2, 367-75, 451-8; carries letters
for TJ, ix, 263, 264, 287, 298, 332-4,
338, 362, 399, 403, 419, 422, 427,
428n; and Houdon's sculpture, 73,

321, 322, 366, 454, 456; seeks compensation for Lafayette, 93, 165-6,
170-1, 320-1, 322, 366, 453-4, 456;
returning to France, 222-3, 263, 298,
320-2, 332-4, 338, 365-7, 422; plan to
manufacture gunpowder, 321, 322,
454, 456-8; unofficial emissary to
France, 332-4, 367-75, 418-19, 451-2,
454-5, 493; TJ's opinion of, 421-2;
and Delessert, 674n
du Pont de Nemours, Sophie Madeleine
Dalmas, 321, 322
*Duty, Advantages, and Pleasure of Public
Worship* (John Smith), 424n
Duval (servant), 469-70, 471, 492
DuVal, William: recommended, appointed commissioner of bankruptcy,
510, 511n, 578, 699, 705, 710; and
R. Lawson, 520
Duvall, Gabriel, 303
D'Wolf (DeWolf), James, 200n, 376
D'Wolf (DeWolf) family, 200n

Eastern Branch. *See* Anacostia River
eastern states: given preference in mili-
tary appointments, 159-60
East India Company, 26
Easton, David, 17-18, 98-9
Easton, John, 10-11n, 325, 349
Eaton, John, 710
eclipses, 46
Eddy, Samuel, 602-3, 700, 704, 708
Edgar, James, 585
Edgar, William, 516, 577, 698, 704, 708
Edgehill (Randolph estate): Milledge
plans to visit, 96, 329, 384-6, 398,
405; TJ's directions to, from, 384-6,
534-5; tobacco crop at, 657
Edinburgh, 351n
Edinburgh, University of, 235n
education: of children, 15, 20-1, 49n, 71,
209, 246-7, 285, 506-7, 566-7, 585n;
of TJ's grandchildren, 15, 20-1, 71;
legal, 51n; academies, schools, 209,
541, 615n, 664, 670n; illiteracy, 475;
of blacks, 506-7; of women, 507n; foreign languages, 566-7; TJ's advice on,
566-7; of Indians, 585n; British influence in, 684-7. *See also* medicine
Edwards, Henry Waggaman, 210, 704,
708
Edwards, L., 716
Edwards, Pierpont: letter from, 210;
recommends aspirants for office, 210;
reports on elections, 488

from, 430, 431n; Nantucket, 539n; Plymouth collectorship, 555-6; attorneys, 555n; Newburyport, 555n, 678, 703, 707; Marblehead collectorship, 556n, 634; Congregationalists in, 613n; Salem, 613n, 707; Salem and Beverly collectorship, 634; influence of, in N.H., 689; Massachusetts Charitable Fire Society, 689n; Beverly, 708; Worcester, 708. *See also* Boston; Federalists; Maine; Republicans

Massachusetts Charitable Society, 189n

Masters, Josiah, 461n, 515n

mastodon: C. W. Peale displays skeleton of, 221n, 423, 550, 551-2, 566n, 581, 582n; remains discovered in Hudson Valley, 352n; and *Bison latifrons,* 489, 563, 581; writings on, 582n

mathematics: logarithms, 104; books on, 105n, 131-2, 241

Mathews (Matthews), George, 129n

Matthews Co., Va., 390

Maury, James, 247n

Maury, Matthew, 246, 247n

Mayer, Jacob, 235n

Mayo, John, 289, 291n

Mazzei, Antonia Antoni (second wife of Philip Mazzei), 202, 203, 204n

Mazzei, Elisabetta, 202, 203, 204n

Mazzei, Philip: letters from, 201-4, 252-3; correspondence with TJ lost, 201, 202; exchanges seeds, plants with TJ, 201, 203; finances of, 201, 203, 204n; printed Italian translation of inaugural address, 201, 203; journey to St. Petersburg, 202, 203, 204n; letter from cited, 204n; and Leghorn consulship, 252-3

Meade, Cowles, 711

Meals, Joshua, 706

Mease, James: letter from, 404-5; recommends father for appointment, 404-5

Mease, John, 404-5

medals: commemorative, xlvii, l, 318 (illus.), 134n; TJ's image on, l, 13, 134, 175, 196, 246, 299; from England, 49n

Medical Repository (New York), 592, 593n

medicine: medical schools, education, l, 18n, 69n, 70n, 112-13, 118n, 235n, 247-8, 249, 302n, 351n, 383n, 504n; physicians, l, 43n, 69-70, 112-13, 118n, 151-2, 205-6, 234-5, 239n, 247-8, 249, 302n, 350-1, 383, 407n, 489n,

504n, 670n; medical societies, 43n, 248n, 351n; teething, 61, 246, 299, 448, 647; insanity, mental illness, 68, 69n, 442n, 463n; surgeons, 69, 120n, 577, 670n; gout, 72, 235n, 601; tropical diseases, 75n, 205, 207n; exercise, 78; lancets, 151; measles, 151, 152n, 390n, 534, 618, 647; fractures, 174, 522; anatomy, 221-2n; medical devices, 234-5; rheumatism, 235n; bowels, 246; chicken pox, 246; fever, 246, 479, 647; shipborne diseases, 257; folk remedies, 284n; headaches, 284n, 383n; toothaches, 284n; eye injuries, disease, 470, 471, 536; flux, 520; longevity, 537; medicinal bark, 647. *See also* hospitals; smallpox; whooping cough; yellow fever

Mediterranean Sea. *See* Navy, U.S.

megalonyx, 489, 566n, 582n

megatherium, 565, 566n

Meigs, Return Jonathan, 132

Meigs, Return Jonathan, Jr., 359, 360n

Mellinger, David: letter from, 600-1; sends handbills to TJ, 600-1

Mémoires des commissaires du roi et de ceux de sa Majesté Britannique, sur les possessions & les droits respectifs des deux couronnes en Amérique (Étienne de Silhouette), 229

Memorials of the Method and Manner of Proceedings in Parliament (Henry Scobell), 231

Mendenhall, Thomas: letter from, 509-10; seeks appointment, 509-10

Mentges, Francis: letter from, 528-9; claim for compensation, 528-9

Mentor (ship), 226, 227n

Mercer, John F.: letter to, 659; letter from, 547-8; and repayment of Md. loans, 547-8, 611-12, 656-7, 659; advises on appointments, 717; letter from cited, 717

Merchant, George, 515n, 577, 698, 704, 709

Mercury and New-England Palladium (Boston), 189n

Meredith, Samuel: letter from, 357; advises on appointments, 357, 705

Meriwether family, 127, 129n

Mexico, 368-70, 372-4

Mey, Florian Charles (Charleston merchant), 641, 645, 646n

Michaux, André: *Histoire des chênes de l'Amerique,* 433, 435n

Michigan Territory, 517n

Munroe, Thomas (*cont.*)
  Washington, D.C., 604n; and sale of
    D.C. lots, 612, 624-5; and Washing-
    ton jail, 666
Munroe, William, 603n
Munson, Elihu, 704, 708
Muratori, Lodovico Antonio, 229
murder: of spouses, ix, 283-4; by, of In-
  dians, 7; imprisonment for, 139n; as
  capital offense, 214-15, 217n, 283-4
Murfree, Hardy, 314n
Murphy, Mary (Maria). *See* Dougherty,
  Mary Murphy
Murray, Alexander, 140n
Murray, William Vans, 80n
Muse, William T., 341, 343n
Mussey, John, 707
Myer, Philip: letter from, 88-9; asks TJ
  for assistance, 88-9
Myers, Moses: letter from, 523-4; intro-
  duces Hartsinck, 523-4; appointed
  commissioner of bankruptcy, 668,
  690, 705, 710
Myers, Robert, 24

nails, 490n. *See also* Jefferson, Thomas:
  Nailery
Nancy (schooner), 388n, 664
Nanny (b. ca. 1799, TJ's slave), 443
Nantes, France, 526-7, 538, 539
Naples, 500, 501n
Natchez, 15, 65, 425. *See also* Missis-
  sippi Territory
National Aegis (Worcester), 689n
National Bank of Washington, 604n
National Institute of Arts and Sciences.
  See France: National Institute of Arts
  and Sciences
National Intelligencer (Washington),
  312, 556n, 612n, 697. *See also* Smith,
  Samuel Harrison
Natural History (Pliny), 565n
naturalization. *See* immigrants
Naturalization Act (1798), vii, 168, 296,
  297n
"Nauticus" (pseudonym), 561, 563n
naval science, 226-7, 242, 482-3, 484-5n
navigation, 486-8, 612-13
Navy, U.S.: letter from, 115-16; provisions for, 16; officers' commissions and
  warrants, 24, 71, 140, 345, 416, 429-
  30, 485-6, 596; and S. Humphreys's
  contract, 115-16; timber for, 115-16,
  420; construction of 74-gun ships,
  116n, 683n; reinstatement of officers,

121, 150; reduction of, 151, 168, 296,
  458-9; sends squadrons to Mediterranean, 160-1, 296; ship plans, designs, 226-7; navy agents, 252-3,
  420; accountant of, 390n, 440; clerks,
  410n, 440n; salaries and compensation, 410n; appropriations and expenditures, 420, 440; naval stores, 420;
  and Saint-Domingue, 457n; fur-
  loughs, 464; dry docks, 682-3. *See
  also* Marines, U.S.; Peace Establishment Act (1801); Smith, Robert
Neal, Charles, 140n
Ned (slave, Norfolk), 336n
*Negotiations de monsieur le President
  Jeannin* (Pierre Jeannin), 229
Nellie (sloop), 428n
Nelson, Roger, 302
Nelson, Fort, 553n
Nero, 296
Nesbit, Hugh, 706
Netherlands: Batavian Republic, 84n,
  523-4; U.S. debt to, 158-9n, 187n,
  198n, 377, 616, 621; and France, 498,
  524n; U.S. relations with, 532; agri-
  culture in, 639, 643; Haarlem, 639,
  643-4, 646n. *See also* Amsterdam
Neue Philadelphische Correspondenz
  (Philadelphia), 318n
Neufforge, Jean-Françoise de, 64n
Neuilly, France, 485n
neutrality, league of armed, 84n
neutral rights, 8-9n
*Neutral Rights; or an Impartial Exami-
  nation of the Right of Search of Neutral
  Vessels Under Convoy* (Johan Frederik
  Wilhelm Schlegel), 230
New, Anthony, 150
New, Robert Anderson, 323, 324n, 325
New Abridgment of the Law (Matthew
  Bacon), 230
New American Practical Navigator
  (Nathaniel Bowditch), 612-13
*New and Complete Law-Dictionary, or,
  General Abridgment of the Law* (Tim-
  othy Cunningham), 230
New England: influence of British
  literature in, 684-7; hostility toward
  Va. in, 689n. *See also* Federalists;
  Republicans
New Hampshire: commissioners of
  bankruptcy, 210, 420-1, 462-3, 577,
  621, 688-9, 697, 698, 701-2, 703,
  707; marshal for, 324, 326n, 348;
  elections in, 400, 401n, 420-1, 462-3;
  governor, 400, 401n, 420-1, 462-3;

Edenton, 710; Halifax, 710. *See also* Federalists; Republicans

North West Company, 566n

Northwest Ordinance of 1784, 359-60

Northwest Ordinance of 1787: and slavery, 344n; and creation of counties, 357-8, 378, 569, 604, 624n; powers granted to governors by, 357-8, 568-9, 604; provisions for statehood in, 358, 380, 606; boundaries specified in, 380, 606

Northwest Territory: Indian affairs in, 29, 304; supervisor for, 211, 323, 325, 349; creation of counties in, 357-8, 569, 604-5, 622, 624n; location of county seats, 358, 378, 569, 622; redivision of, 358, 360n, 379, 380, 570, 606, 623; license fees in, 359, 378, 568, 605, 608n, 622-3; state laws adopted by, 359, 379, 605, 607-8n; militia in, 379, 571, 607, 623; salaries of public officers in, 379, 505; Symmes purchase, 382-3; commerce of, 419; secretary of, 505-6; party politics in, 505n; bounty lands in, 520n; delegate to Congress, 606. *See also* Ohio; St. Clair, Arthur

Notes and Observations on the Pine Lands of Georgia (George Sibbald), 66-7, 95, 98, 127

Notes on the State of Virginia: and Logan's speech, 631, 632n. *See also Appendix to the Notes on Virginia Relative to the Murder of Logan's Family*

Nourse, Joseph, 179n, 197n

Nouveau commentaire sur l'ordonnance de la marine (René Josué Valin), 230

Nouveau dictionnaire historique; ou histoire abrégée de tous les hommes qui se sont fait au nom par des talens, des vertus, des forfaits, des erreurs, &c. (Louis Mayeul Chaudon), 232

Nouvel abrégé chronologique de l'histoire de France (Charles Jean François Henault), 232

Nouvel abrégé chronologique de l'histoire des empereurs (Adrien Richer), 232

Nouvel abrégé chronologique de l'histoire et du droit public d'Allemagne (Chretien Frédéric Pfeffel), 232

Nova Scotia, 532

Oakley, John, 181

Oak Ridge (Rives estate, Amherst Co., Va.), 656n

oats, 472-3, 503-4

O'Bail (O'Beal), Charles, 31, 34, 35n, 36

O'Bail, Henry, 35n

Observationum Juris Romani libri quatuor (Cornelius van Bynkershoek), 229

observatories, 45

Ocmulgee River, 344n

Oconee River, 344n

Odes (Horace), 78

Odyssey (Homer), 5-6

Oeuvres complètes (Claude Adrien Helvétius), 113

Oeuvres de Sénèque le philosophe (Lucius Annaeus Seneca), 156, 183n, 197, 233, 234

Of the Judicature in Parliaments (John Selden), 231

Ogden, Aaron, 210-11

Ogeechee River (Ga.), 95

Ogilvie, James: letter from, 209; invites TJ to visit his academy, 209; *Cursory Reflections,* 209n; identified, 209n; resides along route to Monticello, 535

Ohio: Chillicothe, 77; immigrants to, 118n, 381n; marshal for, 118n, 636n; Clermont Co., 359, 379, 571, 572n; Hamilton Co., 359, 379, 381n, 571; Ross Co., 378, 381n; Adams Co., 379; statehood contest in, 380, 505n; Marietta collectorship, 391, 394, 395n; U.S. district court, 505n; Moravians in, 585n. *See also* Northwest Territory

Ohio River, 369, 373, 425

Oldham, James: letters to, 327, 654-5; works on privies at Monticello, 327, 655; account with TJ, 327n; and suit against E. Lanham, 654-5; letters from cited, 655n, 716, 717, 718

Opinions of Several Learned Antiquaries (Henry Elsynge), 231

Orange Court House, Va., 384, 385, 398, 464, 534

Order of Carlos III, 119n

Orders, Essentials, Fundamental, and Standing Orders of the House of Commons, 231

Original Institution, Power and Jurisdiction of Parliaments (Sir Matthew Hale), 231

Orion (ship), 575

Orleans Territory, 166n

orphans, 147-8

orreries, 108n, 193, 194n

Osgood, Samuel: letter from, 148-9;

plows, 95, 105n
Plutarch, 113, 114n
Pluto (Roman god), 499
Poland, 202, 203, 204n
Political Barometer (Poughkeepsie), 580-1, 654
Political Disquisitions: or, An Inquiry into Public Errors, Defects, and Abuses (James Burgh), 231
Political Intolerance, or The Violence of Party Spirit; Exemplified in a Recent Removal from Office (Winthrop Sargent), 19-20, 319
polygraphs, 224n
Ponsonby, John: letter from, 668-9; sends publications, samples of waterproofing, 668-9; identified, 669n
Pope, Alexander: *Essay on Man,* 49n
Poplar Forest (TJ's estate): travel to, from, 67; sale of tobacco from, 244, 441, 590-1, 657; land from, given to T. M. Randolph and J. W. Eppes, 448, 449n; lands adjacent to, 493
Portas, Louis: letter from, 185-6; recommends Raymond, 185-6; identified, 186n
Port-au-Prince (Port Républicain), Saint-Domingue, 130, 457n
Porter, John, 316
Porter, Moses, 159
Porter, Robert, 705
Port Royal, Va., 134
Portsmouth, N.H.: naval officer at, 23, 53; commissioners of bankruptcy, 420-1, 462-3, 621; attorneys, 462, 621; merchants, 462, 621; education in, 541; banks, 621-2
Portugal: vessels seized by, 346-7; threatened, attacked by France and Spain, 494; royal family of, 500; U.S. relations with, 532, 673, 675n; and export of Spanish merino sheep, 674n
postal service: schedules, efficiency of, 16-17, 66, 448, 459, 463, 493, 525, 534; and Federalists, 19; postmasters, 19, 77-8n, 115, 131, 219, 398, 399n, 421n, 603n, 657, 716; postal contracts, 50n; mail stages, 66; postage on newspapers, 308n; postmaster general, 671n; distrusted, 684. *See also* Granger, Gideon
Postlethwayt, Malachy: *Universal Dictionary of Trade and Commerce,* 230
potash, 194n
Potocki, Count Jan, 202, 203, 204n

Potomac Canal Company, 127n, 303n
Potomac District, 302, 303n, 618n
Potomac River, 126-7, 256, 682
Potter, Henry, 187, 325, 348, 614, 716
Potter, Samuel J., 44
Potts, Joseph, 194n
Potts, Joshua, 710
Poulson, Zachariah, Jr.: account with TJ, 64; identified, 64n; TJ orders newspapers from, 312
Poulson's American Daily Advertiser (Philadelphia), 64n, 312, 318n, 600n
Powell, Cuthbert, 154
Power, Jurisdiction and Priviledge of Parliament (Robert Atkyns), 231
Poyntell, William, 657
Practical Navigator (John Hamilton Moore), 613n
Practical Observations on Vaccination: Or Inoculation for the Cow-Pock (John Redman Coxe), 311n
Preble, Edward, 71
Preble, Henry, 99
Precedents of Proceedings in the House of Commons (John Hatsell), 231
Prentiss, Joshua, 430, 431n
Prentiss, Samuel, 708
Presbyterians, 119n, 338, 584-5
presents, 422
President (U.S. frigate), 429, 485-6
President's House: design of, criticized, 64n; furnishing of, 156, 508-9, 596, 597, 610-11, 615, 617; receptions, dinners at, 313n, 314; servants at, 331-2, 441-2, 443-4, 463, 469-72, 475, 492, 536, 618-19; staff of, accused of theft, 331-2; visitors to, 507n; screens for, 596; floor cloths for, 597, 615-16; piano for, 597, 615; mangle for, 610-11, 617; blinds for, 615; excavating at, 694n; ice house, 719; and Mammoth Cheese, 719, 721; stable and household accounts, 719-21. *See also* Jefferson, Thomas: Personal Affairs
press, freedom of, 296, 317, 407, 496, 626
Price, George, 111, 112n
Price, Isaac, 347-8, 394
Price, Joseph, 472, 504
Priestley, Joseph: letter to, 625-7; letters from, 592-3, 593-5; sends coins and medals to TJ, 49n; *Chart of Biography,* 232; *New Chart of History,* 232; health of, 592; asks to dedicate book to TJ, 592-3, 593-5; *General History*

A comprehensive index of Volumes 1-20 of the
First Series has been issued as Volume 21.
Each subsequent volume has its own index,
as does each volume or set of volumes
in the Second Series.

THE PAPERS OF THOMAS JEFFERSON are composed in Monticello, a font based on the "Pica No. 1" created in the early 1800s by Binny & Ronaldson, the first successful typefounding company in America. The face is considered historically appropriate for The Papers of Thomas Jefferson because it was used extensively in American printing during the last quarter-century of Jefferson's life, and because Jefferson himself expressed cordial approval of Binny & Ronaldson types. It was revived and rechristened Monticello in the late 1940s by the Mergenthaler Linotype Company, under the direction of C. H. Griffith and in close consultation with P. J. Conkwright, specifically for the publication of the Jefferson Papers. The font suffered some losses in its first translation to digital format in the 1980s to accommodate computerized typesetting. Matthew Carter's reinterpretation in 2002 restores the spirit and style of Binny & Ronaldson's original design of two centuries earlier.

✧